Microsoft® Windows® 2000 Server TCP/IP Core Networking Guide

IT Professional

PUBLISHED BY
Microsoft Press
A Division of Microsoft Corporation
One Microsoft Way
Redmond, Washington 98052-6399

Library of Congress Cataloging-in-Publication Data
Microsoft Windows 2000 Server Resource Kit / Microsoft Corporation.
p. cm.
Includes index.
ISBN 1-57231-805-8 (Resource Kit)
ISBN 0-7356-1798-8
1. Microsoft Windows 2000 Server. 2. Operating systems (Computers). I. Microsoft Corporation.
QA76.76.O63 M5241328 2000
005.4'4769--dc21 99-045616

Printed and bound in the United States of America.

1 2 3 4 5 6 7 8 9 QWT 7 6 5 4 3 2

Distributed in Canada by Penguin Books Canada Limited.

A CIP catalogue record for this book is available from the British Library.

Microsoft Press books are available through booksellers and distributors worldwide. For further information about international editions, contact your local Microsoft Corporation office or contact Microsoft Press International directly at fax (425) 936-7329. Visit our Web site at www.microsoft.com/mspress. Send comments to *rkinput@microsoft.com.*

Acquisitions Editor: Juliana Aldous Atkinson
Project Editor: Aileen Wrothwell

Body Part No. X08-78663

Thank you to those who contributed to this book:

Department Managers: Paul Goode, Ken Western
Documentation Managers: Laura Burris, Martin DelRe, Peggy Etchevers
Resource Kit Program Managers: Chris Hallum, Martin Holladay,
Louis Kahn, Ryan Marshall, Paul Sutton

TCP/IP Core Networking Guide

Technical Writing Lead: Martin DelRe
Writers: Wolfgang Baur, Joseph Davies, Glenn Geignetter,
Kristin King, Mario Matiev, Lauren Nelson

Editing Leads: Deborah Annan, Jennifer Hendrix, Kate O'Leary
Book Editing Lead: Scot Yonan
Developmental Editor: Gary W. Moore
Copy Editors: Kate McLaughlin, Mary Rose Sliwoski,
Scott Somohano, Debbie Uyeshiro
Glossary: Daniel Bell

Resource Kit Tools Software Developers: Dan Grube,
Michael Hawkins, Darryl Wood, Zeyong Xu
Documentation Tools Software Developers: Amy Buck, Tom Carey,
Ryan Farber, Mark Pengra, Fred Taub

Production Leads: Sandy Dean, Jane Dow, Keri Grassl, Jason Hershey
Production Specialists: Michael Faber, Dani McIntyre, Lori Robinson

Indexing Leads: Jane Dow, Veronica Maier
Indexers: Kumud Dwivedi, Cheryl Landes

Lead Graphic Designer: Flora Goldthwaite
Designers: Chris Blanton, Siamack Sahafi

Art Production: Blaine Dollard, Jenna Kiter, Amy Shear, Gabriel Varela

Test Lead: Jonathan Fricke
Testers: Brian Klauber, Jeremy Sullivan

Windows 2000 Lab Manager: Edward Lafferty
Administrators: Deborah Jay, Grant Mericle, Dave Meyer, Dean Prince,
Robert Thingwold, Luke Walker, Joel Wingert, Frank Zamarron
Lab Partners: Cisco Systems, Inc., Compaq, Inc.,
Hewlett-Packard Corporation, Intel Corporation

A special thanks to the following technical experts who contributed to and supported this effort:

Bernard Aboba, Mohammad Alam, Elena Apreutesei, Radu Bacioiu, Pradeep Bahl, Bill Bain, Drew Baron, Yoram Bernet, June Blender, Justin Bosanquet-Rossen, Chuck Chan, Frank Chidsey, Mike Cerceo, Glenn Curtis, Joseph Davies, Eric Davison, Ann Demirtjis, William Dixon, David Eitelbach, Levon Esibov, Cameron Etezadi, Ben Fathi, Eric Fitzgerald, Peter Ford, Tom Fout, Krishna Ganugapati, Lee Gibson, James Gilroy, Mario Goertzel, Gary Green, Ye Gu, Rich Hagemeyer, Tony Hain, Stephen Hui, Aamer Hydrie, Romano Jerez, Jawad Khaki, Shirish Koti, Sachin Kukreja, Stuart Kwan, Paul Leach, Brian Lieuallen, Mark Lloyd, Dave MacDonald, Sharon Maffett, Brad Mahugh, Randy McLaughlin, Wayne Melvin, Denise Miller, John Miller, Tim Moore, Vivek Nirkhe, Gurdeep Singh Pall, Balan Sethu Raman, Vamshidhar Reddy, Huiwen Ru, Brent Scallan, Walter Schmidt, Joseph Seifert, Mark Sestak, Vic Shahid, Art Shelest, Ron Sherrell, Anand Sivaramakichenane, David Smith, David Stern, Florin Teodorescu, Rob Trace, David Trulli, Ali Turkoglu, Luis Ulloa, Ruud van Velsen, Ramesh Vyaghrapuri, Glen Zorn

Contents

Part 2 Address Allocation and Name Resolution

Introduction

Welcome to the *Microsoft® Windows® 2000 Server Resource Kit TCP/IP Core Networking Guide*.

The *Microsoft® Windows® 2000 Server Resource Kit* consists of seven volumes and a single compact disc (CD) containing tools, additional reference materials, and an online version of the books. Supplements to the *Windows 2000 Server Resource Kit* will be released as new information becomes available, and updates and information will be available on the Web on an ongoing basis.

The *TCP/IP Core Networking Guide* provides you with in-depth technical information to help you understand, manage, and troubleshoot all facets of TCP/IP networking. This guide begins with a comprehensive analysis of the core Microsoft® Windows® 2000 TCP/IP protocols, continues with detailed information about TCP/IP addressing and name resolution services, and concludes with an analysis of advanced TCP/IP networking services. This information supplements the online documentation included with Microsoft® Windows® 2000 Server. Information about additional Windows 2000 networking protocols and services is contained in the *Internetworking Guide*.

Document Conventions

The following style conventions and terminology are used throughout this guide.

Element	Meaning
bold font	Characters that you type exactly as shown, including commands and switches. User interface elements are also bold.
Italic font	Variables for which you supply a specific value. For example, *Filename.ext* could refer to any valid file name for the case in question.
`Monospace font`	Code samples.
`%SystemRoot%`	The folder in which Windows 2000 is installed.

Reader Alert	Meaning
Tip	Alerts you to supplementary information that is not essential to the completion of the task at hand.
Note	Alerts you to supplementary information.
Important	Alerts you to supplementary information that is essential to the completion of a task.
Caution	Alerts you to possible data loss, breaches of security, or other more serious problems.
Warning	Alerts you that failure to take or avoid a specific action might result in physical harm to you or to the hardware.

Resource Kit Compact Disc

The *Windows 2000 Server Resource Kit* companion CD includes a wide variety of tools and resources to help you work more efficiently with Windows 2000.

Note The tools on the CD are designed and tested for the U.S. version of Windows 2000. Use of these programs on other versions of Windows 2000 or on versions of Microsoft® Windows NT® can cause unpredictable results.

The *Resource Kit* companion CD contains the following:

Windows 2000 Server Resource Kit Online Books An HTML Help version of the print books. Use these books to find the same detailed information about Windows 2000 as is found in the print versions. Search across all of the books to find the most pertinent information to complete the task at hand.

Windows 2000 Server Resource Kit Tools and Tools Help Over 200 software tools, tools documentation, and other resources that harness the power of Windows 2000. Use these tools to manage Active Directory™, administer security features, work with the registry, automate recurring jobs, and many other important tasks. Use Tools Help documentation to discover and learn how to use these administrative tools.

Windows 2000 Resource Kit References A set of HTML Help references:

- **Error and Event Messages Help** contains most of the error and event messages generated by Windows 2000. With each message comes a detailed explanation and a suggested user action.
- **Technical Reference to the Registry** provides detailed descriptions of Windows 2000 registry content, such as the subtrees, keys, subkeys, and entries that advanced users want to know about, including many entries that cannot be changed by using Windows 2000 tools or programming interfaces.
- **Performance Counter Reference** describes all performance objects and counters provided for use with tools in the Performance snap-in of Windows 2000. Use this reference to learn how monitoring counter values can assist you in diagnosing problems or detecting bottlenecks in your system.
- **Group Policy Reference** provides detailed descriptions of the Group Policy settings in Windows 2000. These descriptions explain the effect of enabling, disabling, or not configuring each policy, as well as explanations of how related policies interact.

Resource Kit Support Policy

The software supplied in the *Windows 2000 Server Resource Kit* is not supported. Microsoft does not guarantee the performance of the *Windows 2000 Server Resource Kit* tools, response times for answering questions, or bug fixes to the tools. However, we do provide a way for customers who purchase the *Windows 2000 Server Resource Kit* to report bugs and receive possible fixes for their issues. You can do this by sending e-mail to rkinput@microsoft.com. This e-mail address is only for *Windows 2000 Server Resource Kit* related issues. For issues relating to the Windows 2000 operating system, please refer to the support information included with your product.

PART 1

Windows 2000 TCP/IP

The TCP/IP protocol suite is the strategic internetworking technology of today and the future. This section examines the basics of TCP/IP and its implementation in Windows 2000.

In This Part

CHAPTER 1

Introduction to TCP/IP

Microsoft® Windows® 2000 has extensive support for the Transmission Control Protocol/Internet Protocol (TCP/IP) suite both as a protocol and a set of services for connectivity and management of IP internetworks. Knowledge of the basic concepts of TCP/IP is an absolute requirement for the proper understanding of the configuration, deployment, and troubleshooting of IP-based Windows 2000 and Microsoft® Windows NT® intranets.

In This Chapter

Related Information in the Resource Kit

- For more information about Windows 2000 network architecture, see "Windows 2000 Networking Architecture" in this book.
- For more information about the Windows 2000 implementation of TCP/IP, see "Windows 2000 TCP/IP" in this book.

TCP/IP Protocol Suite

TCP/IP is an industry-standard suite of protocols designed for large internetworks spanning wide area network (WAN) links. TCP/IP was developed in 1969 by the U.S. Department of Defense Advanced Research Projects Agency (DARPA), the result of a resource-sharing experiment called ARPANET (Advanced Research Projects Agency Network). The purpose of TCP/IP was to provide high-speed communication network links. Since 1969, ARPANET has grown into a worldwide community of networks known as the Internet.

Microsoft TCP/IP

Microsoft TCP/IP on Windows 2000 enables enterprise networking and connectivity on Windows 2000 and Windows NT–based computers. Adding TCP/IP to a Windows 2000 configuration offers the following advantages:

- A standard, routable enterprise networking protocol that is the most complete and accepted protocol available. All modern network operating systems offer TCP/IP support, and most large networks rely on TCP/IP for much of their network traffic.
- A technology for connecting dissimilar systems. Many standard connectivity utilities are available to access and transfer data between dissimilar systems, including File Transfer Protocol (FTP) and Telnet, a terminal emulation protocol. Several of these standard utilities are included with Windows 2000.
- A robust, scalable, cross-platform client/server framework. Microsoft TCP/IP offers the Windows Sockets interface, which is ideal for developing client/server applications that can run on Windows Sockets–compliant stacks from other vendors.
- A method of gaining access to the Internet. The Internet consists of thousands of networks worldwide, connecting research facilities, universities, libraries, and private companies.

Note The word *internet* (lowercase i) refers to multiple TCP/IP networks connected with routers. References to the *Internet* (uppercase I) refer to the worldwide public Internet. References to the *intranet* refer to a private internetwork.

TCP/IP Standards

The standards for TCP/IP are published in a series of documents called *Request for Comments* (RFCs). RFCs describe the internal workings of the Internet. Some RFCs describe network services or protocols and their implementations, whereas others summarize policies. TCP/IP standards are always published as RFCs, although not all RFCs specify standards.

TCP/IP standards are not developed by a committee, but rather by consensus. Anyone can submit a document for publication as an RFC. Documents are reviewed by a technical expert, a task force, or the RFC editor, and then assigned a status. The status specifies whether a document is being considered as a standard.

There are five status assignments of RFCs as described in Table 1.1.

Table 1.1 Status Assignments of RFCs

Status	Description
Required	Must be implemented on all TCP/IP-based hosts and gateways.
Recommended	Encouraged that all TCP/IP-based hosts and gateways implement the RFC specifications. Recommended RFCs are usually implemented.
Elective	Implementation is optional. Its application has been agreed to but is not a requirement.
Limited Use	Not intended for general use.
Not recommended	Not recommended for implementation.

If a document is being considered as a standard, it goes through stages of development, testing, and acceptance known as the Internet Standards Process. These stages are formally labeled maturity levels. Table 1.2 lists the three maturity levels for Internet Standards.

Table 1.2 Maturity Levels for Internet Standards

Maturity Level	Description
Proposed Standard	A Proposed Standard specification is generally stable, has resolved known design choices, is believed to be well understood, has received significant community review, and appears to enjoy enough community interest to be considered valuable.
Draft Standard	A Draft Standard must be well understood and known to be quite stable, both in its semantics and as a basis for developing an implementation.
Internet Standard	The Internet Standard specification (which might simply be referred to as a Standard) is characterized by a high degree of technical maturity and by a generally held belief that the specified protocol or service provides significant benefit to the Internet community.

When a document is published, it is assigned an RFC number. The original RFC is never updated. If changes are required, a new RFC is published with a new number. Therefore, it is important to verify that you have the most recent RFC on a particular topic.

RFCs can be obtained in several ways. To obtain any RFC or a full and current indexed listing of all RFCs published to date, see the Request For Comments link on the Web Resources page at http://windows.microsoft.com/windows2000/reskit/webresources.

TCP/IP Protocol Architecture

TCP/IP protocols map to a four-layer conceptual model known as the *DARPA model*, named after the U.S. government agency that initially developed TCP/IP. The four layers of the DARPA model are: Application, Transport, Internet, and Network Interface. Each layer in the DARPA model corresponds to one or more layers of the seven-layer Open Systems Interconnection (OSI) model.

Figure 1.1 shows the TCP/IP protocol architecture.

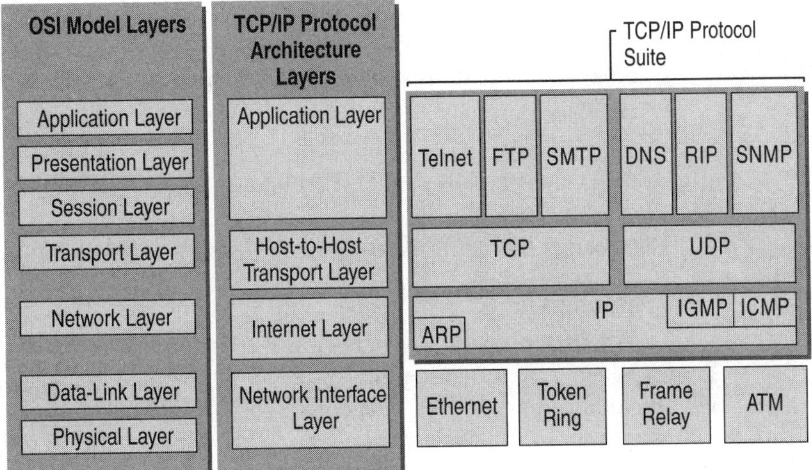

Figure 1.1 TCP/IP Protocol Architecture

Network Interface Layer

The *Network Interface layer* (also called the Network Access layer) is responsible for placing TCP/IP packets on the network medium and receiving TCP/IP packets off the network medium. TCP/IP was designed to be independent of the network access method, frame format, and medium. In this way, TCP/IP can be used to connect differing network types. These include LAN technologies such as Ethernet and Token Ring and WAN technologies such as X.25 and Frame Relay. Independence from any specific network technology gives TCP/IP the ability to be adapted to new technologies such as Asynchronous Transfer Mode (ATM).

The Network Interface layer encompasses the Data Link and Physical layers of the OSI model. Note that the Internet layer does not take advantage of sequencing and acknowledgment services that might be present in the Data-Link layer. An unreliable Network Interface layer is assumed, and reliable communications through session establishment and the sequencing and acknowledgment of packets is the responsibility of the Transport layer.

Internet Layer

The *Internet layer* is responsible for addressing, packaging, and routing functions. The core protocols of the Internet layer are IP, ARP, ICMP, and IGMP.

- The *Internet Protocol* (IP) is a routable protocol responsible for IP addressing, routing, and the fragmentation and reassembly of packets.
- The *Address Resolution Protocol* (ARP) is responsible for the resolution of the Internet layer address to the Network Interface layer address such as a hardware address.
- The *Internet Control Message Protocol* (ICMP) is responsible for providing diagnostic functions and reporting errors due to the unsuccessful delivery of IP packets.
- The *Internet Group Management Protocol* (IGMP) is responsible for the management of IP multicast groups.

The Internet layer is analogous to the Network layer of the OSI model.

Transport Layer

The *Transport layer* (also known as the Host-to-Host Transport layer) is responsible for providing the Application layer with session and datagram communication services. The core protocols of the Transport layer are *Transmission Control Protocol* (TCP) and the *User Datagram Protocol* (UDP).

- TCP provides a one-to-one, connection-oriented, reliable communications service. TCP is responsible for the establishment of a TCP connection, the sequencing and acknowledgment of packets sent, and the recovery of packets lost during transmission.
- UDP provides a one-to-one or one-to-many, connectionless, unreliable communications service. UDP is used when the amount of data to be transferred is small (such as the data that would fit into a single packet), when the overhead of establishing a TCP connection is not desired or when the applications or upper layer protocols provide reliable delivery.

The Transport layer encompasses the responsibilities of the OSI Transport layer and some of the responsibilities of the OSI Session layer.

Application Layer

The *Application layer* provides applications the ability to access the services of the other layers and defines the protocols that applications use to exchange data. There are many Application layer protocols and new protocols are always being developed.

The most widely-known Application layer protocols are those used for the exchange of user information:

- The Hypertext Transfer Protocol (HTTP) is used to transfer files that make up the Web pages of the World Wide Web.
- The File Transfer Protocol (FTP) is used for interactive file transfer.
- The Simple Mail Transfer Protocol (SMTP) is used for the transfer of mail messages and attachments.
- Telnet, a terminal emulation protocol, is used for logging on remotely to network hosts.

Additionally, the following Application layer protocols help facilitate the use and management of TCP/IP networks:

- The Domain Name System (DNS) is used to resolve a host name to an IP address.
- The Routing Information Protocol (RIP) is a routing protocol that routers use to exchange routing information on an IP internetwork.
- The Simple Network Management Protocol (SNMP) is used between a network management console and network devices (routers, bridges, intelligent hubs) to collect and exchange network management information.

Examples of Application layer interfaces for TCP/IP applications are Windows Sockets and NetBIOS. Windows Sockets provides a standard application programming interface (API) under Windows 2000. NetBIOS is an industry standard interface for accessing protocol services such as sessions, datagrams, and name resolution. More information on Windows Sockets and NetBIOS is provided later in this chapter.

TCP/IP Core Protocols

The TCP/IP protocol component that is installed in your network operating system is a series of interconnected protocols called the core protocols of TCP/IP. All other applications and other protocols in the TCP/IP protocol suite rely on the basic services provided by the following protocols: IP, ARP, ICMP, IGMP, TCP, and UDP.

IP

IP is a connectionless, unreliable datagram protocol primarily responsible for addressing and routing packets between hosts. Connectionless means that a session is not established before exchanging data. Unreliable means that delivery is not guaranteed. IP always makes a "best effort" attempt to deliver a packet. An IP packet might be lost, delivered out of sequence, duplicated, or delayed. IP does not attempt to recover from these types of errors. The acknowledgment of packets delivered and the recovery of lost packets is the responsibility of a higher-layer protocol, such as TCP. IP is defined in RFC 791.

An IP packet consists of an IP header and an IP payload. Table 1.3 describes the key fields in the IP header.

Table 1.3 Key Fields in the IP Header

IP Header Field	Function
Source IP Address	The IP address of the original source of the IP datagram.
Destination IP Address	The IP address of the final destination of the IP datagram.
Identification	Used to identify a specific IP datagram and to identify all fragments of a specific IP datagram if fragmentation occurs.
Protocol	Informs IP at the destination host whether to pass the packet up to TCP, UDP, ICMP, or other protocols.
Checksum	A simple mathematical computation used to verify the integrity of the IP header.
Time-to-Live (TTL)	Designates the number of networks on which the datagram is allowed to travel before being discarded by a router. The TTL is set by the sending host and is used to prevent packets from endlessly circulating on an IP internetwork. When forwarding an IP packet, routers are required to decrease the TTL by at least one.

Fragmentation and Reassembly

If a router receives an IP packet that is too large for the network to which the packet is being forwarded, IP fragments the original packet into smaller packets that fit on the downstream network. When the packets arrive at their final destination, IP on the destination host reassembles the fragments into the original payload. This process is referred to as *fragmentation and reassembly*. Fragmentation can occur in environments that have a mix of networking technologies, such as Ethernet or Token Ring.

The fragmentation and reassembly works as follows:

- When an IP packet is sent by the source, it places a unique value in the Identification field.
- The IP packet is received at the router. The IP router notes that the maximum transmission unit (MTU) of the network onto which the packet is to be forwarded is smaller than the size of the IP packet.
- IP divides the original IP payload into fragments that fit on the next network. Each fragment is sent with its own IP header that contains:
    - The original Identification field identifying all fragments that belong together.
    - The More Fragments Flag indicating that other fragments follow. The More Fragments Flag is not set on the last fragment, because no other fragments follow it.
    - The Fragment Offset field indicating the position of the fragment relative to the original IP payload.

When the fragments are received by IP at the remote host, they are identified by the Identification field as belonging together. The Fragment Offset field is then used to reassemble the fragments into the original IP payload.

ARP

When IP packets are sent on shared access, broadcast-based networking technologies such as Ethernet or Token Ring, the media access control (MAC) address corresponding to a forwarding IP address must be resolved. ARP uses MAC-level broadcasts to resolve a known forwarding IP address to its MAC address. ARP is defined in RFC 826.

For more information about ARP, see "Physical Address Resolution" later in this chapter.

ICMP

Internet Control Message Protocol (ICMP) provides troubleshooting facilities and error reporting for packets that are undeliverable. For example, if IP is unable to deliver a packet to the destination host, ICMP sends a Destination Unreachable message to the source host. Table 1.4 shows the most common ICMP messages.

Table 1.4 Common ICMP Messages

ICMP Message	Function
Echo Request	Troubleshooting message used to check IP connectivity to a desired host. The ping utility sends ICMP Echo Request messages.
Echo Reply	Response to an ICMP Echo Request.
Redirect	Sent by a router to inform a sending host of a better route to a destination IP address.
Source Quench	Sent by a router to inform a sending host that its IP datagrams are being dropped due to congestion at the router. The sending host then lowers its transmission rate. Source Quench is an elective ICMP message and is not commonly implemented.
Destination Unreachable	Sent by a router or the destination host to inform the sending host that the datagram cannot be delivered.

There are a series of defined Destination Unreachable ICMP messages. Table 1.5 describes the most common messages.

Table 1.5 Common ICMP Destination Unreachable Messages

Destination Unreachable Message	Description
Network Unreachable	Sent by an IP router when a route to the destination network can not be found. This message is obsolete.
Host Unreachable	Sent by an IP router when a route to the destination IP address can not be found.
Protocol Unreachable	Sent by the destination IP node when the Protocol field in the IP header cannot be matched with an IP client protocol currently loaded.
Port Unreachable	Sent by the destination IP node when the Destination Port in the UDP header cannot be matched with a process using that port.
Fragmentation Needed and DF Set	Sent by an IP router when fragmentation must occur but is not allowed due to the source node setting the Don't Fragment (DF) flag in the IP header.
Source Route Failed	Sent by an IP router when delivery of the IP packet using source route information (stored as source route option headers) fails.

ICMP does not make IP a reliable protocol. ICMP attempts to report errors and provide feedback on specific conditions. ICMP messages are carried as unacknowledged IP datagrams and are themselves unreliable. ICMP is defined in RFC 792.

IGMP

Internet Group Management Protocol (IGMP) is a protocol that manages host membership in IP multicast groups. An *IP multicast group*, also known as a *host group*, is a set of hosts that listen for IP traffic destined for a specific IP multicast address. IP multicast traffic is sent to a single MAC address but processed by multiple IP hosts. A specific host listens on a specific IP multicast address and receives all packets to that IP address. The following are some of the additional aspects of IP multicasting:

- Host group membership is dynamic, hosts can join and leave the group at any time.
- A host group can be of any size.
- Members of a host group can span IP routers across multiple networks. This situation requires IP multicast support on the IP routers and the ability for hosts to register their group membership with local routers. Host registration is accomplished using IGMP.
- A host can send traffic to an IP multicast address without belonging to the corresponding host group.

For a host to receive IP multicasts, an application must inform IP that it will receive multicasts at a specified IP multicast address. If the network technology supports hardware-based multicasting, the network interface is told to pass up packets for a specific IP multicast address. In the case of Ethernet, the network adapter is programmed to respond to a multicast MAC address corresponding the specified IP multicast address.

A host supports IP multicast at one of the following levels:

- Level 0: No support to send or receive IP multicast traffic.
- Level 1: Support exists to send but not receive IP multicast traffic.
- Level 2: Support exists to both send and receive IP multicast traffic. Windows 2000 and Windows NT 3.5 and later TCP/IP supports level 2 IP multicasting.

The protocol to register host group information is IGMP, which is required on all hosts that support level 2 IP multicasting. IGMP packets are sent using an IP header.

IGMP messages take two forms:

- When a host joins a host group, it sends an IGMP Host Membership Report message to the all-hosts IP multicast address (224.0.0.1) or to the specified IP multicast address declaring its membership in a specific host group by referencing the IP multicast address.
- When a router polls a network to ensure that there are members of a specific host group, it sends an IGMP Host Membership Query message to the all-hosts IP multicast address. If no responses to the poll are received after several polls, the router assumes no membership in that group for that network and stops advertising that group-network information to other routers.

For IP multicasting to span routers across an internetwork, multicast routing protocols are used by routers to communicate host group information so that each router supporting multicast forwarding is aware of which networks contain members of which host groups.

IGMP is defined in RFCs 1112 and 2236.

TCP

TCP is a reliable, connection-oriented delivery service. The data is transmitted in segments. *Connection-oriented* means that a connection must be established before hosts can exchange data. Reliability is achieved by assigning a sequence number to each segment transmitted. An acknowledgment is used to verify that the data was received by the other host. For each segment sent, the receiving host must return an acknowledgment (ACK) within a specified period for bytes received. If an ACK is not received, the data is retransmitted. TCP is defined in RFC 793.

TCP uses byte-stream communications, wherein data within the TCP segment is treated as a sequence of bytes with no record or field boundaries. Table 1.6 describes the key fields in the TCP header.

Table 1.6 Key Fields in the TCP Header

Field	Function
Source Port	TCP port of sending host.
Destination Port	TCP port of destination host.
Sequence Number	Sequence number of the first byte of data in the TCP segment.
Acknowledgment Number	Sequence number of the byte the sender expects to receive next from the other side of the connection.
Window	Current size of a TCP buffer on the host sending this TCP segment to store incoming segments.
TCP Checksum	Verifies the integrity of the TCP header and the TCP data.

TCP Ports

A TCP port provides a specific location for delivery of TCP segments. Port numbers below 1024 are well-known ports and are assigned by the Internet Assigned Numbers Authority (IANA). Table 1.7 lists a few well-known TCP ports.

Table 1.7 Well-Known TCP Ports

TCP Port Number	Description
20	FTP (Data Channel)
21	FTP (Control Channel)
23	Telnet
80	HTTP used for the World Wide Web
139	NetBIOS session service

For a complete list of assigned TCP ports, see the Internet Assigned Numbers Authority (IANA) Port Numbers link on the Web Resources page at http://windows.microsoft.com/windows2000/reskit/webresources.

TCP Three-Way Handshake

A TCP connection is initialized through a three-way handshake. The purpose of the three-way handshake is to synchronize the sequence number and acknowledgment numbers of both sides of the connection and exchange TCP Window sizes. The following steps outline the process:

1. The client sends a TCP segment to the server with an initial Sequence Number for the connection and a Window size indicating the size of a buffer on the client to store incoming segments from the server.
2. The server sends back a TCP segment containing its chosen initial Sequence Number, an acknowledgment of the client's Sequence Number, and a Window size indicating the size of a buffer on the server to store incoming segments from the client.
3. The client sends a TCP segment to the server containing an acknowledgment of the server's Sequence Number.

TCP uses a similar handshake process to end a connection. This guarantees that both hosts have finished transmitting and that all data was received.

UDP

UDP provides a connectionless datagram service that offers unreliable, best-effort delivery of data transmitted in messages. This means that neither the arrival of datagrams nor the correct sequencing of delivered packets is guaranteed. UDP does not recover from lost data through retransmission. UDP is defined in RFC 768.

UDP is used by applications that do not require an acknowledgment of receipt of data and that typically transmit small amounts of data at one time. NetBIOS name service, NetBIOS datagram service, and SNMP are examples of services and applications that use UDP. Table 1.8 describes the key fields in the UDP header.

Table 1.8 Key Fields in the UDP Header

Field	Function
Source Port	UDP port of sending host.
Destination Port	UDP port of destination host.
UDP Checksum	Verifies the integrity of the UDP header and the UDP data.

UDP Ports

To use UDP, an application must supply the IP address and UDP port number of the destination application. A port provides a location for sending messages. A port functions as a multiplexed message queue, meaning that it can receive multiple messages at a time. Each port is identified by a unique number. It is important to note that UDP ports are distinct and separate from TCP ports even though some of them use the same number. Table 1.9 lists well-known UDP ports.

Table 1.9 Well-Known UDP Ports

UDP Port Number	Description
53	Domain Name System (DNS) Name Queries
69	Trivial File Transfer Protocol (TFTP)
137	NetBIOS name service
138	NetBIOS datagram service
161	SNMP

For a complete list of assigned UDP ports, see the Internet Assigned Numbers Authority (IANA) Port Numbers link on the Web Resources page at http://windows.microsoft.com/windows2000/reskit/webresources.

TCP/IP Application Interfaces

For applications to access the services offered by the core TCP/IP protocols in a standard way, network operating systems like Windows 2000 make industry standard application programming interfaces (APIs) available. Application interfaces are sets of functions and commands that are programmatically called by application code to perform network functions. For example, a Web browser application connecting to a Web site needs access to TCP's connection establishment service.

Figure 1.2 shows two common TCP/IP network interfaces, Windows Sockets and NetBIOS, and their relation to the core protocols.

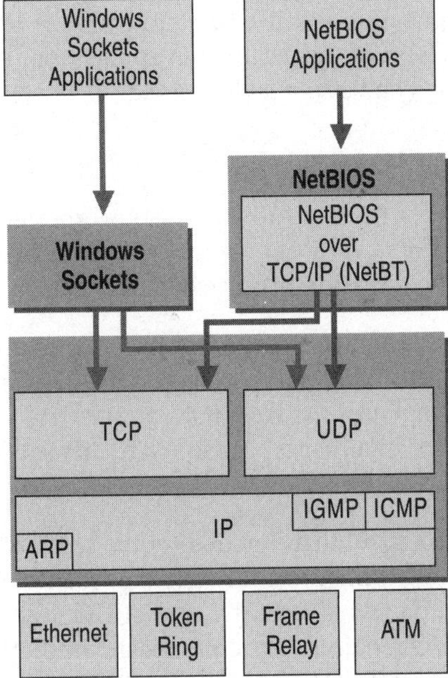

Figure 1.2 APIs for TCP/IP

Windows Sockets Interface

The *Windows Sockets* API is a standard API under Windows 2000 for applications that use TCP and UDP. Applications written to the Windows Sockets API run on many versions of TCP/IP. TCP/IP utilities and the SNMP service are examples of applications written to the Windows Sockets interface.

Windows Sockets provides services that allow applications to bind to a particular port and IP address on a host, initiate and accept a connection, send and receive data, and close a connection. There are two types of sockets:

1. A *stream socket* provides a two-way, reliable, sequenced, and unduplicated flow of data using TCP.
2. A *datagram socket* provides the bi-directional flow of data using UDP.

A socket is defined by a protocol and an address on the host. The format of the address is specific to each protocol. In TCP/IP, the address is the combination of the IP address and port. Two sockets, one for each end of the connection, form a bi-directional communications path.

To communicate, an application specifies the protocol, the IP address of the destination host, and the port of the destination application. After the application is connected, information can be sent and received.

NetBIOS Interface

NetBIOS was developed for IBM in 1983 by Sytek Corporation to allow applications to communicate over a network. NetBIOS defines two entities, a session level interface and a session management and data transport protocol.

The NetBIOS interface is a standard API for user applications to submit network input/output (I/O) and control directives to underlying network protocol software. An application program that uses the NetBIOS interface API for network communication can be run on any protocol software that supports the NetBIOS interface.

NetBIOS also defines a protocol that functions at the session/transport level. This is implemented by the underlying protocol software (such as the NetBIOS Frames Protocol (NBFP), a component of NetBEUI, or NetBIOS over TCP/IP (NetBT)) to perform the network I/O required to accommodate the NetBIOS interface command set. NetBIOS over TCP/IP is defined in RFCs 1001 and 1002.

NetBIOS provides commands and support for NetBIOS Name Management, NetBIOS Datagrams, and NetBIOS Sessions.

NetBIOS Name Management

NetBIOS name management services provide the following functions:

- Name Registration and Release

  When a TCP/IP host initializes, it registers its NetBIOS names by broadcasting or directing a NetBIOS name registration request to a NetBIOS Name Server such as a Windows Internet Name Service (WINS) server. If another host has registered the same NetBIOS name, either the host or a NetBIOS Name Server responds with a negative name registration response. The initiating host receives an initialization error as a result.

  When the workstation service on a host is stopped, the host discontinues broadcasting a negative name registration response when someone else tries to use the name and sends a name release to a NetBIOS Name Server. The NetBIOS name is said to be released and available for use by another host.

- Name Resolution

  When a NetBIOS application wants to communicate with another NetBIOS application, the IP address of the NetBIOS application must be resolved. NetBIOS over TCP/IP performs this function by either broadcasting a NetBIOS name query on the local network or sending a NetBIOS name query to a NetBIOS Name Server.

  For more information about NetBIOS name resolution, see "NetBIOS Name Resolution" later in this chapter.

The NetBIOS name service uses UDP port 137.

NetBIOS Datagrams

The NetBIOS datagram service provides delivery of datagrams that are connectionless, nonsequenced, and unreliable. Datagrams can be directed to a specific NetBIOS name or broadcast to a group of names. Delivery is unreliable in that only the users who are logged on to the network receive the message. The datagram service can initiate and receive both broadcast and directed messages. The NetBIOS datagram service uses UDP port 138.

NetBIOS Sessions

The NetBIOS session service provides delivery of NetBIOS messages that are connection-oriented, sequenced, and reliable. NetBIOS sessions use TCP connections and provide session establishment, keepalive, and termination. The NetBIOS session service allows concurrent data transfers in both directions using TCP port 139.

IP Addressing

Each TCP/IP host is identified by a logical *IP address*. The IP address is a network layer address and has no dependence on the Data-Link layer address (such as a MAC address of a network adapter). A unique IP address is required for each host and network component that communicates using TCP/IP.

The IP address identifies a system's location on the network in the same way a street address identifies a house on a city block. Just as a street address must identify a unique residence, an IP address must be globally unique and have a uniform format.

Each IP address includes a network ID and a host ID.

- The *network ID* (also known as a *network address*) identifies the systems that are located on the same physical network bounded by IP routers. All systems on the same physical network must have the same network ID. The network ID must be unique to the internetwork.
- The *host ID* (also known as a host address) identifies a workstation, server, router, or other TCP/IP host within a network. The address for each host must be unique to the network ID.

Note Network ID refers to any IP network ID, whether it is class-based, a subnet, or a supernet.

An IP address consists of 32 bits. Rather than working with 32 bits at a time, it is a common practice to segment the 32 bits of an IP address into four 8-bit fields called *octets*. Each octet is converted to a decimal number (the Base 10 numbering system) in the range 0-255 and separated by a period (a dot). This format is called dotted decimal notation. Table 1.10 provides an example of an IP address in binary and dotted decimal formats.

Table 1.10 An IP Address in Binary and Dotted Decimal Formats

Binary Format	Dotted Decimal Notation
11000000 10101000 00000011 00011000	192.168.3.24

The notation *w.x.y.z* is used when referring to a generalized IP address, and is shown in Figure 1.3.

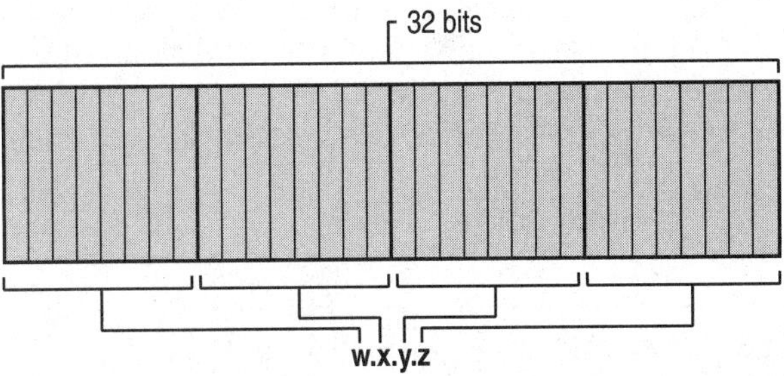

Figure 1.3 IP Address

Address Classes

The Internet community originally defined five *address classes* to accommodate networks of varying sizes. Microsoft TCP/IP supports class A, B, and C addresses assigned to hosts. The class of address defines which bits are used for the network ID and which bits are used for the host ID. It also defines the possible number of networks and the number of hosts per network.

Class A

Class A addresses are assigned to networks with a very large number of hosts. The high-order bit in a class A address is always set to zero. The next seven bits (completing the first octet) complete the network ID. The remaining 24 bits (the last three octets) represent the host ID. This allows for 126 networks and 16,777,214 hosts per network. Figure 1.4 illustrates the structure of class A addresses.

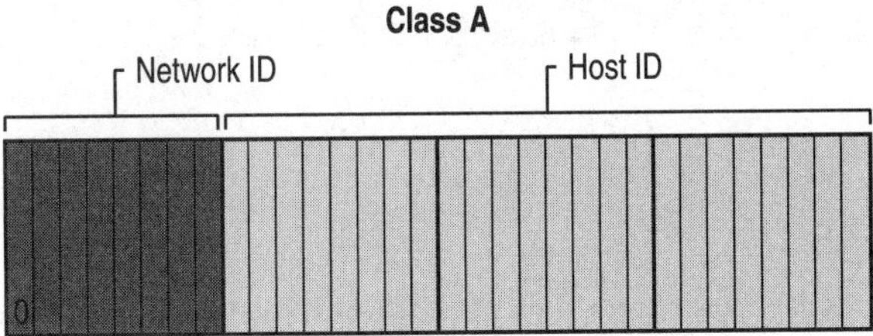

Figure 1.4 Class A IP Addresses

Class B

Class B addresses are assigned to medium-sized to large-sized networks. The two high-order bits in a class B address are always set to binary 1 0. The next 14 bits (completing the first two octets) complete the network ID. The remaining 16 bits (last two octets) represent the host ID. This allows for 16,384 networks and 65,534 hosts per network. Figure 1.5 illustrates the structure of class B addresses.

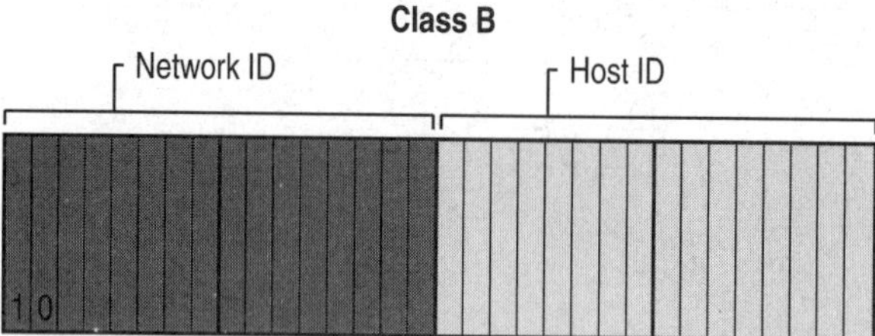

Figure 1.5 Class B IP Addresses

Class C

Class C addresses are used for small networks. The three high-order bits in a class C address are always set to binary 1 1 0. The next 21 bits (completing the first three octets) complete the network ID. The remaining 8 bits (last octet) represent the host ID. This allows for 2,097,152 networks and 254 hosts per network. Figure 1.6 illustrates the structure of class C addresses.

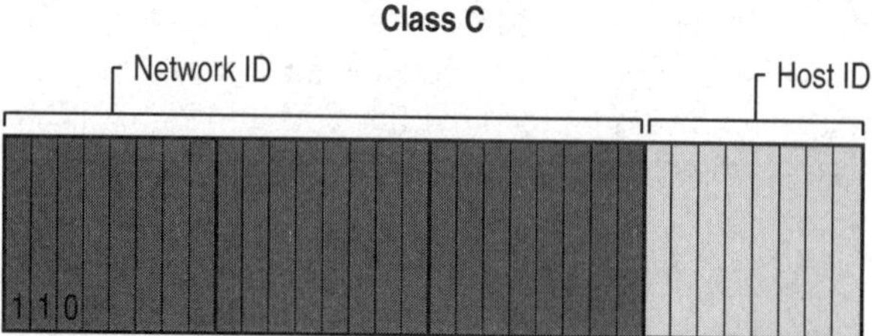

Figure 1.6 Class C IP Addresses

Class D

Class D addresses are reserved for IP multicast addresses. The four high-order bits in a class D address are always set to binary 1 1 1 0. The remaining bits are for the address that interested hosts recognize. Microsoft supports class D addresses for applications to multicast data to multicast-capable hosts on an internetwork.

Class E

Class E is an experimental address that is reserved for future use. The high-order bits in a class E address are set to 1111.

Table 1.11 is a summary of address classes A, B, and C that can be used for host IP addresses.

Table 1.11 IP Address Class Summary

Class	Value for w[1]	Network ID Portion	Host ID Portion	Available Networks	Hosts per Network
A	1–126	*w*	*x.y.z*	126	16,777,214
B	128–191	*w.x*	*y.z*	16,384	65,534
C	192–223	*w.x.y*	*z*	2,097,152	254

[1] The class A address 127.*x.y.z* is reserved for loopback testing and interprocess communication on the local computer.

Network ID Guidelines

The network ID identifies the TCP/IP hosts that are located on the same physical network. All hosts on the same physical network must be assigned the same network ID to communicate with each other.

Follow these guidelines when assigning a network ID:

- The network ID must be unique to the IP internetwork. If you plan on having a direct routed connection to the public Internet, the network ID must be unique to the Internet. If you do not plan on connecting to the public Internet, the local network ID must be unique to your private internetwork.
- The network ID cannot begin with the number 127. The number 127 in a class A address is reserved for internal loopback functions.
- All bits within the network ID cannot be set to 1. All 1's in the network ID are reserved for use as an IP broadcast address.
- All bits within the network ID cannot be set to 0. All 0's in the network ID are used to denote a specific host on the local network and are not routed.

Table 1.12 lists the valid ranges of network IDs based on the IP address classes. To denote IP network IDs, the host bits are all set to 0. Note that even though expressed in dotted decimal notation, the network ID is not an IP address.

Table 1.12 Class Ranges of Network IDs

Address Class	First Network ID	Last Network ID
Class A	1.0.0.0	126.0.0.0
Class B	128.0.0.0	191.255.0.0
Class C	192.0.0.0	223.255.255.0

Host ID Guidelines

The host ID identifies a TCP/IP host within a network. The combination of IP network ID and IP host ID is an IP address.

Follow these guidelines when assigning a host ID:

- The host ID must be unique to the network ID.
- All bits within the host ID cannot be set to 1 because this host ID is reserved as a broadcast address to send a packet to all hosts on a network.
- All bits in the host ID cannot be set to 0 because this host ID is reserved to denote the IP network ID.

Table 1.13 lists the valid ranges of host IDs based on the IP address classes.

Table 1.13 Class Ranges of Host IDs

Address Class	First Host ID	Last Host ID
Class A	*w*.0.0.1	*w*.255.255.254
Class B	*w.x*.0.1	*w.x*.255.254
Class C	*w.x.y*.1	*w.x.y*.254

Subnets and Subnet Masks

The Internet Address Classes accommodate three scales of IP internetworks, where the 32-bits of the IP address are apportioned between network IDs and host IDs depending on how many networks and hosts per network are needed. However, consider the class A network ID, which has the possibility of over 16 million hosts on the same network. All the hosts on the same physical network bounded by IP routers share the same broadcast traffic; they are in the same broadcast domain. It is not practical to have 16 million nodes in the same broadcast domain. The result is that most of the 16 million host addresses are unassignable and are wasted. Even a class B network with 65 thousand hosts is impractical.

In an effort to create smaller broadcast domains and to better utilize the bits in the host ID, an IP network can be subdivided into smaller networks, each bounded by an IP router and assigned a new subnetted network ID, which is a subset of the original class-based network ID.

This creates *subnets*, subdivisions of an IP network each with their own unique subnetted network ID. Subnetted network IDs are created by using bits from the host ID portion of the original class-based network ID.

Consider the example in Figure 1.7. The class B network of 139.12.0.0 can have up to 65,534 nodes. This is far too many nodes, and in fact the current network is becoming saturated with broadcast traffic. The subnetting of network 139.12.0.0 should be done in such a way so that it does not impact nor require the reconfiguration of the rest of the IP internetwork.

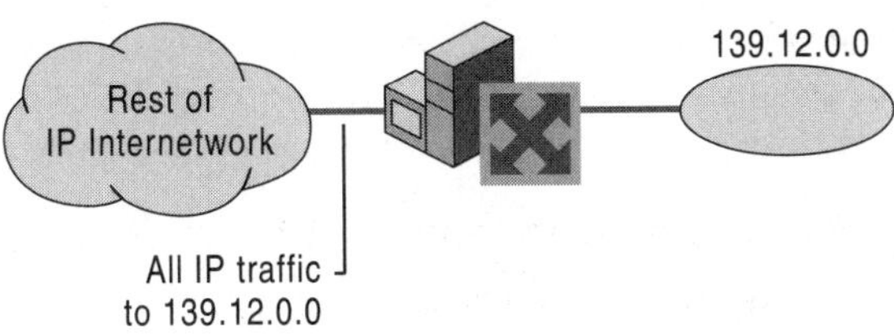

Figure 1.7 Network 139.12.0.0 Before Subnetting

Network 139.12.0.0 is subnetted by utilizing the first 8 host bits (the third octet) for the new subnetted network ID. When 139.12.0.0 is subnetted, as shown in Figure 1.8, separate networks with their own subnetted network IDs (139.12.1.0, 139.12.2.0, 139.12.3.0) are created. The router is aware of the separate subnetted networks IDs and routes IP packets to the appropriate subnet.

Note that the rest of the IP internetwork still regards all the nodes on the three subnets as being on network 139.12.0.0. The other routers in the IP internetwork are unaware of the subnetting being done on network 139.12.0.0 and therefore require no reconfiguration.

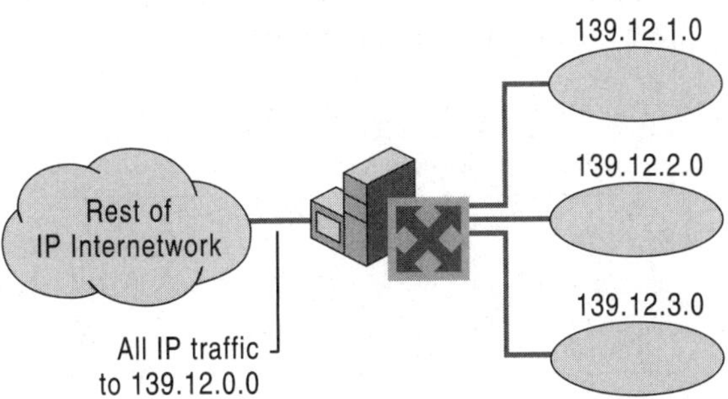

Figure 1.8 Network 139.12.0.0 After Subnetting

A key element of subnetting is still missing. How does the router who is subdividing network 139.12.0.0 know how the network is being subdivided and which subnets are available on which router interfaces? To give the IP nodes this new level of awareness, they must be told exactly how to discern the new subnetted network ID regardless of Internet Address Classes. A *subnet mask* is used to tell an IP node how to extract a class-based or subnetted network ID.

Subnet Masks

With the advent of subnetting, one can no longer rely on the definition of the IP address classes to determine the network ID in the IP address. A new value is needed to define which part of the IP address is the network ID and which part is the host ID regardless of whether class-based or subnetted network IDs are being used.

RFC 950 defines the use of a *subnet mask* (also referred to as an address mask) as a 32-bit value that is used to distinguish the network ID from the host ID in an arbitrary IP address. The bits of the subnet mask are defined as follows:

- All bits that correspond to the network ID are set to 1.
- All bits that correspond to the host ID are set to 0.

Each host on a TCP/IP network requires a subnet mask even on a single segment network. Either a default subnet mask, which is used when using class-based network IDs, or a custom subnet mask, which is used when subnetting or supernetting, is configured on each TCP/IP node.

Dotted Decimal Representation of Subnet Masks

Subnet masks are frequently expressed in dotted decimal notation. After the bits are set for the network ID and host ID portion, the resulting 32-bit number is converted to dotted decimal notation. Note that even though expressed in dotted decimal notation, a subnet mask is not an IP address.

A default subnet mask is based on the IP address classes and is used on TCP/IP networks that are not divided into subnets. Table 1.14 lists the default subnet masks using the dotted decimal notation for the subnet mask.

Table 1.14 Default Subnet Masks (Dotted Decimal Notation)

Address Class	Bits for Subnet Mask	Subnet Mask
Class A	11111111 00000000 00000000 00000000	255.0.0.0
Class B	11111111 11111111 00000000 00000000	255.255.0.0
Class C	11111111 11111111 11111111 00000000	255.255.255.0

Custom subnet masks are those that differ from these default subnet masks when you are doing subnetting or supernetting. For example, 138.96.58.0 is an 8-bit subnetted class B network ID. Eight bits of the class-based host ID are being used to express subnetted network IDs. The subnet mask uses a total of 24 bits (255.255.255.0) to define the subnetted network ID. The subnetted network ID and its corresponding subnet mask is then expressed in dotted decimal notation as:

```
138.96.58.0, 255.255.255.0
```

Network Prefix Length Representation of Subnet Masks

Because the network ID bits must always be chosen in a contiguous fashion from the high order bits, a shorthand way of expressing a subnet mask is to denote the number of bits that define the network ID as a network prefix using the network prefix notation: /<# of bits>. Table 1.15 lists the default subnet masks using the network prefix notation for the subnet mask.

Table 1.15 Default Subnet Masks (Network Prefix Notation)

Address Class	Bits for Subnet Mask	Network Prefix
Class A	11111111 00000000 00000000 00000000	/8
Class B	11111111 11111111 00000000 00000000	/16
Class C	11111111 11111111 11111111 00000000	/24

For example, the class B network ID 138.96.0.0 with the subnet mask of 255.255.0.0 would be expressed in network prefix notation as 138.96.0.0/16.

As an example of a custom subnet mask, 138.96.58.0 is an 8-bit subnetted class B network ID. The subnet mask uses a total of 24 bits to define the subnetted network ID. The subnetted network ID and its corresponding subnet mask is then expressed in network prefix notation as:

```
138.96.58.0/24
```

Network prefix notation is also known as *Classless Interdomain Routing* (CIDR) notation.

Note Because all hosts on the same network must use the same network ID, all hosts on the same network must use the same network ID as defined by the same subnet mask. For example, 138.23.0.0/16 is not the same network ID as 138.23.0.0/24. The network ID 138.23.0.0/16 implies a range of valid host IP addresses from 138.23.0.1 to 138.23.255.254. The network ID 138.23.0.0/24 implies a range of valid host IP addresses from 138.23.0.1 to 138.23.0.254. Clearly, these network IDs do not represent the same range of IP addresses.

Determining the Network ID

To extract the network ID from an arbitrary IP address using an arbitrary subnet mask, IP uses a mathematical operation called a logical AND comparison. In an AND comparison, the result of two items being compared is true only when both items being compared are true; otherwise, the result is false. Applying this principle to bits, the result is 1 when both bits being compared are 1, otherwise the result is 0.

IP performs a logical AND comparison with the 32-bit IP address and the 32-bit subnet mask. This operation is known as a bit-wise logical AND. The result of the bit-wise logical AND of the IP address and the subnet mask is the network ID.

For example, what is the network ID of the IP node 129.56.189.41 with a subnet mask of 255.255.240.0?

To obtain the result, turn both numbers into their binary equivalents and line them up. Then perform the AND operation on each bit and write down the result.

```
10000001 00111000 10111101 00101001  IP Address
11111111 11111111 11110000 00000000  Subnet Mask
10000001 00111000 10110000 00000000  Network ID
```

The result of the bit-wise logical AND of the 32 bits of the IP address and the subnet mask is the network ID 129.56.176.0.

Subnetting

Although the conceptual notion of subnetting by utilizing host bits is straightforward, the actual mechanics of subnetting are a bit more complicated. Subnetting requires a three step procedure:

1. Determine the number of host bits to be used for the subnetting.
2. Enumerate the new subnetted network IDs.
3. Enumerate the IP addresses for each new subnetted network ID.

Step 1: Determining the Number of Host Bits

The number of host bits being used for subnetting determines the possible number of subnets and hosts per subnet. Before you choose the number of host bits, you should have a good idea of the number of subnets and hosts you will have in the future. Using more bits for the subnet mask than required saves you the time of reassigning IP addresses in the future.

The more host bits that are used, the more subnets (subnetted network IDs) you can have—but with fewer hosts. Using too many host bits allows for growth in the number of subnets but limits the growth in the number of hosts. Using too few hosts allows for growth in the number of hosts but limits the growth in the number of subnets.

For example, Figure 1.9 illustrates the subnetting of up to the first 8 host bits of a class B network ID. If you choose one host bit for subnetting, you obtain 2 subnetted network IDs with 16,382 hosts per subnetted network ID. If you choose 8 host bits for subnetting, you obtain 256 subnetted network IDs with 254 hosts per subnetted network ID.

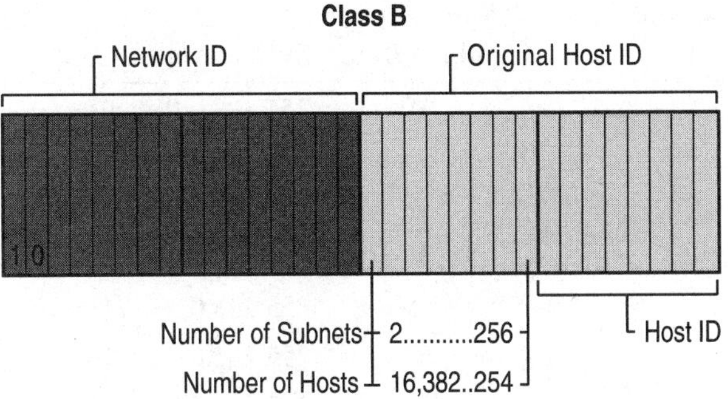

Figure 1.9 Subnetting a Class B Network ID

In practice, network administrators define a maximum number of nodes they want on a single network. Recall that all nodes on a single network share all the same broadcast traffic; they reside in the same broadcast domain. Therefore, growth in the number of subnets is favored over growth in the number of hosts per subnet.

Follow these guidelines to determine the number of host bits to use for subnetting.

1. Determine how many subnets you need now and will need in the future. Each physical network is a subnet. WAN connections can also count as subnets depending on whether your routers support unnumbered connections.
2. Use additional bits for the subnet mask if:
   - You will never require as many hosts per subnet as allowed by the remaining bits.
   - The number of subnets will increase in the future, requiring additional host bits.

To determine the desired subnetting scheme, start with an existing network ID to be subnetted. The network ID to be subnetted can be a class-based network ID, a subnetted network ID, or a supernet. The existing network ID contains a series of network ID bits that are fixed and a series of host ID bits that are variable. Based on your requirements for the number of subnets and the number of hosts per subnet, choose a specific number of host bits to be used for the subnetting.

Table 1.16 shows the subnetting of a class A network ID. Based on a required number of subnets, and a maximum number of hosts per subnet, a subnetting scheme can be chosen.

Table 1.16 Subnetting a Class A Network ID

Required Number of Subnets	Number of Subnet Bits	Subnet Mask	Number of Hosts per Subnet
1-2	1	255.128.0.0 or /9	8,388,606
3-4	2	255.192.0.0 or /10	4,194,302
5-8	3	255.224.0.0 or /11	2,097,150
9-16	4	255.240.0.0 or /12	1,048,574
17-32	5	255.248.0.0 or /13	524,286
33-64	6	255.252.0.0 or /14	262,142
65-128	7	255.254.0.0 or /15	131,070
129-256	8	255.255.0.0 or /16	65,534
257-512	9	255.255.128.0 or /17	32,766
513-1,024	10	255.255.192.0 or /18	16,382
1,025-2,048	11	255.255.224.0 or /19	8,190
2,049-4,096	12	255.255.240.0 or /20	4,094
4,097-8,192	13	255.255.248.0 or /21	2,046
8,193-16,384	14	255.255.252.0 or /22	1,022
16,385-32,768	15	255.255.254.0 or /23	510
32,769-65,536	16	255.255.255.0 or /24	254
65,537-131,072	17	255.255.255.128 or /25	126
131,073-262,144	18	255.255.255.192 or /26	62
262,145-524,288	19	255.255.255.224 or /27	30
524,289-1,048,576	20	255.255.255.240 or /28	14
1,048,577-2,097,152	21	255.255.255.248 or /29	6
2,097,153-4,194,304	22	255.255.255.252 or /30	2

Table 1.17 shows the subnetting of a class B network ID.

Table 1.17 Subnetting a Class B Network ID

Required Number of Subnets	Number of Subnet Bits	Subnet Mask	Number of Hosts per Subnet
1-2	1	255.255.128.0 or /17	32,766
3-4	2	255.255.192.0 or /18	16,382
5-8	3	255.255.224.0 or /19	8,190
9-16	4	255.255.240.0 or /20	4,094
17-32	5	255.255.248.0 or /21	2,046
33-64	6	255.255.252.0 or /22	1,022
65-128	7	255.255.254.0 or /23	510
129-256	8	255.255.255.0 or /24	254
257-512	9	255.255.255.128 or /25	126
513-1,024	10	255.255.255.192 or /26	62
1,025-2,048	11	255.255.255.224 or /27	30
2,049-4,096	12	255.255.255.240 or /28	14
4,097-8,192	13	255.255.255.248 or /29	6
8,193-16,384	14	255.255.255.252 or /30	2

Table 1.18 shows the subnetting of a class C network ID.

Table 1.18 Subnetting a Class C Network ID

Required Number of Subnets	Number of Subnet Bits	Subnet Mask	Number of Hosts per Subnet
1-2	1	255.255.255.128 or /25	126
3-4	2	255.255.255.192 or /26	62
5-8	3	255.255.255.224 or /27	30
9-16	4	255.255.255.240 or /28	14
17-32	5	255.255.255.248 or /29	6
33-64	6	255.255.255.252 or /30	2

Step 2: Enumerating Subnetted Network IDs

Based on the number of host bits you use for your subnetting, you must list the new subnetted network IDs. There are two main approaches:

- Binary—List all possible combinations of the host bits chosen for subnetting and convert each combination to dotted decimal notation.
- Decimal—Add a calculated increment value to each successive subnetted network ID and convert to dotted decimal notation.

Either method produces the same result: the enumerated list of subnetted network IDs.

Note There are a variety of documented shortcut techniques for subnetting. However, they only work under a specific set of constraints (for example, only up to 8 bits of a class-based network ID). The following methods described are designed to work for any subnetting situation (class-based, more than 8 bits, supernetting, variable length subnetting).

▶ **To create the enumerated list of subnetted network IDs using the binary method**

1. Based on *n*, the number of host bits chosen for subnetting, create a three-column table with 2^n entries. The first column is the subnet number (starting with 1), the second column is the binary representation of the subnetted network ID, and the third column is the dotted decimal representation of the subnetted network ID.

   For each binary representation, the bits of the network ID being subnetted are fixed to their appropriate values and the remaining host bits are set to all 0's. The host bits chosen for subnetting vary.
2. In the first table entry, set the subnet bits to all 0's and convert to dotted decimal notation. The original network ID is subnetted with its new subnet mask.
3. In the next table entry, increase the value within the subnet bits.
4. Convert the binary result to dotted decimal notation.
5. Repeat steps 3 and 4 until the table is complete.

For example, create a 3-bit subnet of the private network ID 192.168.0.0. The subnet mask for the new subnetted network IDs is 255.255.224.0 or /19. Based on $n = 3$, construct a table with 8 (= 2^3) entries. The entry for subnet 1 is the all 0's subnet. Additional entries in the table are successive increments of the subnet bits, as shown in Table 1.19. The host bits used for subnetting are underlined.

Table 1.19 Binary Subnetting Technique for Network ID 192.168.0.0

Subnet	Binary Representation	Subnetted Network ID
1	11000000.10101000.00000000.00000000	192.168.0.0/19
2	11000000.10101000.00100000.00000000	192.168.32.0/19
3	11000000.10101000.01000000.00000000	192.168.64.0/19
4	11000000.10101000.01100000.00000000	192.168.96.0/19
5	11000000.10101000.10000000.00000000	192.168.128.0/19
6	11000000.10101000.10100000.00000000	192.168.160.0/19
7	11000000.10101000.11000000.00000000	192.168.192.0/19
8	11000000.10101000.11100000.00000000	192.168.224.0/19

▶ To create the enumerated list of subnetted network IDs using the decimal method

1. Based on *n*, the number of host bits chosen for subnetting, create a three-column table with 2^n entries. The first column is the subnet number (starting with 1), the second column is the decimal (Base 10 numbering system) representation of the 32-bit subnetted network ID, and the third column is the dotted decimal representation of the subnetted network ID.
2. Convert the network ID (*w.x.y.z*) being subnetted from dotted decimal notation to *N*, a decimal representation of the 32-bit network ID:

   $N = w*16777216 + x*65536 + y*256 + z$
3. Compute the increment value *I* based on *h*, the number of host bits remaining:

   $I = 2^h$
4. In the first table entry, the decimal representation of the subnetted network ID is *N* and the subnetted network ID is *w.x.y.z* with its new subnet mask.
5. In the next table entry, add *I* to the previous table entry's decimal representation.
6. Convert the decimal representation of the subnetted network ID to dotted decimal notation (*W.X.Y.Z*) through the following formula (where *s* is the decimal representation of the subnetted network ID):

   $W = \text{INT}(s/16777216)$

   $X = \text{INT}((s \bmod(16777216))/65536)$

   $Y = \text{INT}((s \bmod(65536))/256)$

   $Z = s \bmod(256)$

   INT( ) denotes integer division, mod( ) denotes the modulus, the remainder upon division.
7. Repeat steps 5 and 6 until the table is complete.

For example, create a 3-bit subnet of the private network ID 192.168.0.0. Based on n = 3, construct a table with 8 entries. The entry for subnet 1 is the all 0's subnet. *N*, the decimal representation of 192.168.0.0, is 3232235520, the result of 192*16777216 + 168*65536. Because there are 13 host bits remaining, the increment *I* is 2^{13} = 8192. Additional entries in the table are successive increments of 8192 as shown in Table 1.20.

Table 1.20 Decimal Subnetting Technique for Network ID 192.168.0.0

Subnet	Decimal Representation	Subnetted Network ID
1	3232235520	192.168.0.0/19
2	3232243712	192.168.32.0/19
3	3232251904	192.168.64.0/19
4	3232260096	192.168.96.0/19
5	3232268288	192.168.128.0/19
6	3232276480	192.168.160.0/19
7	3232284672	192.168.192.0/19
8	3232292864	192.168.224.0/19

Note RFC 950 forbade the use of the subnetted network IDs where the bits being used for subnetting are set to all 0's (the *all-zeros subnet*) and all 1's (the *all-ones subnet*). The all-zeros subnet caused problems for early routing protocols and the all-ones subnet conflicts with a special broadcast address called the all-subnets directed broadcast address.

However, RFC 1812 now permits the use of the all-zeros and all-ones subnets in a CIDR-compliant environment. CIDR-compliant environments use modern routing protocols that do not have a problem with the all-zeros subnet and the all-subnets directed broadcast is no longer relevant.

The all-zeros and all-ones subnets may cause problems for hosts or routers operating in a classful mode. Before you use the all-zeros and all-ones subnets, verify that they are supported by your hosts and routers. Windows 2000 and Windows NT support the use of the all-zeros and all-ones subnets.

Step 3: Enumerating IP Addresses for Each Subnetted Network ID

Based on the enumeration of the subnetted network IDs, you must now list the valid IP addresses for new subnetted network IDs. To list each IP address individually would be too tedious. Instead, enumerate the IP addresses for each subnetted network ID by defining the range of IP addresses (the first and the last) for each subnetted network ID. There are two main approaches:

- Binary—Write down the first and last IP address for each subnetted network ID and convert to dotted decimal notation.
- Decimal—Add values incrementally, corresponding to the first and last IP addresses for each subnetted network ID and convert to dotted decimal notation.

Either method produces the same result: the range of IP addresses for each subnetted network ID.

▶ **To create the range of IP addresses using the binary method**

1. Based on *n*, the number of host bits chosen for subnetting, create a three-column table with 2^n entries. The first column is the subnet number (starting with 1), the second column is the binary representation of the first and last IP address for the subnetted network ID, and the third column is the dotted decimal representation of the first and last IP address of the subnetted network ID. Alternately, add two columns to the previous table used for enumerating the subnetted network IDs.
2. For each binary representation, the first IP address is the address in which all the host bits are set to 0 except for the last host bit. The last IP address is the address in which all the host bits are set to 1 except for the last host bit.
3. Convert the binary representation to dotted decimal notation.
4. Repeat steps 2 and 3 until the table is complete.

For example, the range of IP addresses for the 3 bit subnetting of 192.168.0.0 is shown in Table 1.21. The bits used for subnetting are underlined.

Table 1.21 Binary Enumeration of IP Addresses

Subnet	Binary Representation	Range of IP Addresses
1	11000000.10101000.00000000.00000001 - 11000000.10101000.00011111.11111110	192.168.0.1 - 192.168.31.254
2	11000000.10101000.00100000.00000001 - 11000000.10101000.00111111.11111110	192.168.32.1 - 192.168.63.254
3	11000000.10101000.01000000.00000001 - 11000000.10101000.01011111.11111110	192.168.64.1 - 192.168.95.254
4	11000000.10101000.01100000.00000001 - 11000000.10101000.01111111.11111110	192.168.96.1 - 192.168.127.254
5	11000000.10101000.10000000.00000001 - 11000000.10101000.10011111.11111110	192.168.128.1 - 192.168.159.254
6	11000000.10101000.10100000.00000001 - 11000000.10101000.10111111.11111110	192.168.160.1 - 192.168.191.254
7	11000000.10101000.11000000.00000001 - 11000000.10101000.11011111.11111110	192.168.192.1 - 192.168.223.254
8	11000000.10101000.11100000.00000001 - 11000000.10101000.11111111.11111110	192.168.224.1 - 192.168.255.254

▶ To create the range of IP addresses using the decimal method

1. Based on *n*, the number of host bits chosen for subnetting, create a three-column table with 2^n entries. The first column is the subnet number (starting with 1), the second column is the decimal representation of the first and last IP address for the subnetted network ID, and the third column is the dotted decimal representation of the first and last IP address of the subnetted network ID. Alternately, add two columns to the previous table used for enumerating the subnetted network IDs.
2. Compute the increment value *J* based on *h*, the number of host bits remaining:

   $J = 2^h - 2$
3. For each decimal representation, the first IP address is $N + 1$ where *N* is the decimal representation of the subnetted network ID. The last IP address is $N + J$.
4. Convert the decimal representation of the first and last IP addresses to dotted decimal notation (*W.X.Y.Z*) through the following formula (where *s* is the decimal representation of the first or last IP address):

   $W = \text{INT}(s/16777216)$

   $X = \text{INT}((s \text{ mod}(16777216))/65536)$

   $Y = \text{INT}((s \text{ mod}(65536))/256)$

$Z = s \bmod(256)$

INT( ) denotes integer division, mod( ) denotes the modulus, the remainder upon division.

5. Repeat steps 3 and 4 until the table is complete.

For example, the range of IP addresses for the 3-bit subnetting of 192.168.0.0 is shown in Table 1.22. The increment J is $2^{13} - 2 = 8190$.

Table 1.22 Decimal Enumeration of IP Addresses

Subnet	Decimal Representation	Range of IP Addresses
1	3232235521 - 3232243710	192.168.0.1 - 192.168.31.254
2	3232243713 - 3232251902	192.168.32.1 - 192.168.63.254
3	3232251905 - 3232260094	192.168.64.1 - 192.168.95.254
4	3232260097 - 3232268286	192.168.96.1 - 192.168.127.254
5	3232268289 - 3232276478	192.168.128.1 - 192.168.159.254
6	3232276481 - 3232284670	192.168.160.1 - 192.168.191.254
7	3232284673 - 3232292862	192.168.192.1 - 192.168.223.254
8	3232292865 - 3232301054	192.168.224.1 - 192.168.255.254

Variable Length Subnetting

One of the original uses for subnetting was to subdivide a class-based network ID into a series of equal-sized subnets. For example, a 4-bit subnetting of a class B network ID produced 16 equal-sized subnets (using the all-ones and all-zeros subnets). However, subnetting is a general method of utilizing host bits to express subnets and does not require equal-sized subnets.

Subnets of different size can exist within a class-based network ID. This is well-suited to real-world environments, where networks of an organization contain different numbers of hosts, and different-sized subnets are needed to minimize the wasting of IP addresses. The creation and deployment of various-sized subnets of a network ID is known as *variable length subnetting* and uses variable length subnet masks (VLSM).

Variable length subnetting is a technique of allocating subnetted network IDs that use subnet masks of different sizes. However, all subnetted network IDs are unique and can be distinguished from each other by their corresponding subnet mask.

The mechanics of variable length subnetting are essentially that of performing subnetting on a previously subnetted network ID. When subnetting, the network ID bits are fixed and a certain number of host bits are chosen to express subnets. With variable length subnetting, the network ID being subnetted has already been subnetted.

For example, given the class-based network ID of 135.41.0.0/16, a required configuration is one subnet with up to 32,000 hosts, 15 subnets with up to 2,000 hosts, and eight subnets with up to 250 hosts.

One Subnet with up to 32,000 Hosts

To achieve a requirement of one subnet with approximately 32,000 hosts, a 1-bit subnetting of the class-based network ID of 135.41.0.0 is done, producing 2 subnets, 135.41.0.0/17 and 135.41.128.0/17. This subnetting allows up to 32,766 hosts per subnet. 135.41.0.0/17 is chosen as the network ID, which fulfills the requirement.

Table 1.23 shows one subnet with up to 32,766 hosts per subnet.

Table 1.23 One Subnet with up to 32,766 Hosts

Subnet Number	Network ID (Dotted Decimal)	Network ID (Network Prefix)
1	135.41.0.0, 255.255.128.0	135.41.0.0/17

Fifteen Subnets with up to 2,000 Hosts

To achieve a requirement of 15 subnets with approximately 2,000 hosts, a 4-bit subnetting of the subnetted network ID of 135.41.128.0/17 is done. This produces 16 subnets (135.41.128.0/21, 135.41.136.0/21 . . . 135.41.240.0/21, 135.41.248.0/21), allowing up to 2,046 hosts per subnet. The first 15 subnetted network IDs (135.41.128.0/21 to 135.41.240.0/21) are chosen as the network IDs, which fulfills the requirement.

Table 1.24 illustrates 15 subnets with up to 2,046 hosts per subnet.

Table 1.24 Fifteen Subnets with up to 2,046 Hosts

Subnet Number	Network ID (Dotted Decimal)	Network ID (Network Prefix)
1	135.41.128.0, 255.255.248.0	135.41.128.0/21
2	135.41.136.0, 255.255.248.0	135.41.136.0/21
3	135.41.144.0, 255.255.248.0	135.41.144.0/21

(continued)

Table 1.24 Fifteen Subnets with up to 2,046 Hosts *(continued)*

Subnet Number	Network ID (Dotted Decimal)	Network ID (Network Prefix)
4	135.41.152.0, 255.255.248.0	135.41.152.0/21
5	135.41.160.0, 255.255.248.0	135.41.160.0/21
6	135.41.168.0, 255.255.248.0	135.41.168.0/21
7	135.41.176.0, 255.255.248.0	135.41.176.0/21
8	135.41.184.0, 255.255.248.0	135.41.184.0/21
9	135.41.192.0, 255.255.248.0	135.41.192.0/21
10	135.41.200.0, 255.255.248.0	135.41.200.0/21
11	135.41.208.0, 255.255.248.0	135.41.208.0/21
12	135.41.216.0, 255.255.248.0	135.41.216.0/21
13	135.41.224.0, 255.255.248.0	135.41.224.0/21
14	135.41.232.0, 255.255.248.0	135.41.232.0/21
15	135.41.240.0, 255.255.248.0	135.41.240.0/21

Eight Subnets with up to 250 Hosts

To achieve a requirement of eight subnets with up to 250 hosts, a 3-bit subnetting of subnetted network ID of 135.41.248.0/21 is done, producing eight subnets (135.41.248.0/24, 135.41.249.0/24 . . . 135.41.254.0/24, 135.41.255.0/24) and allowing up to 254 hosts per subnet. All 8 subnetted network IDs (135.41.248.0/24 to 135.41.255.0/24) are chosen as the network IDs, which fulfills the requirement.

Table 1.25 illustrates eight subnets with 254 hosts per subnet.

Table 1.25 Eight subnets with up to 254 Hosts

Subnet Number	Network ID (Dotted Decimal)	Network ID (Network Prefix)
1	135.41.248.0, 255.255.255.0	135.41.248.0/24
2	135.41.249.0, 255.255.255.0	135.41.249.0/24
3	135.41.250.0, 255.255.255.0	135.41.250.0/24
4	135.41.251.0, 255.255.255.0	135.41.251.0/24
5	135.41.252.0, 255.255.255.0	135.41.252.0/24
6	135.41.253.0, 255.255.255.0	135.41.253.0/24
7	135.41.254.0, 255.255.255.0	135.41.254.0/24
8	135.41.255.0, 255.255.255.0	135.41.255.0/24

The variable length subnetting of 135.41.0.0/16 is shown graphically in Figure 1.10.

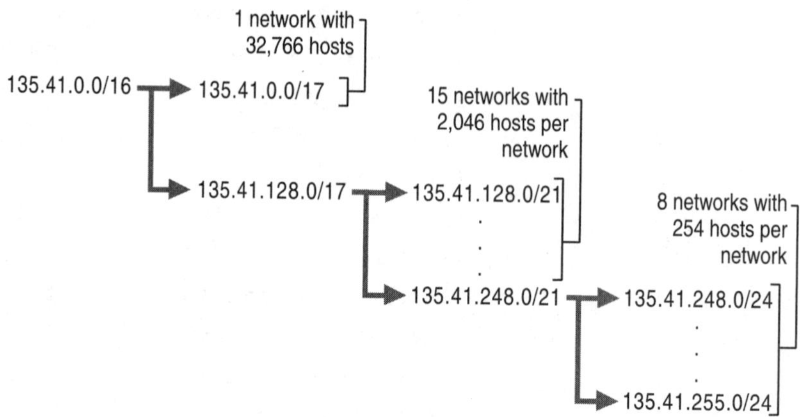

Figure 1.10 Variable Length Subnetting of 135.41.0.0/16

Note In dynamic routing environments, variable length subnetting can only be deployed where the subnet mask is advertised along with the network ID. Routing Information Protocol (RIP) for IP version 1 does not support variable length subnetting. RIP for IP version 2, Open Shortest Path First (OSPF), and Border Gateway Protocol version 4 (BGPv4) all support variable length subnetting.

Supernetting and Classless Interdomain Routing

With the recent growth of the Internet, it became clear to the Internet authorities that the class B network IDs would soon be depleted. For most organizations, a class C network ID does not contain enough host IDs and a class B network ID has enough bits to provide a flexible subnetting scheme within the organization.

The Internet authorities devised a new method of assigning network IDs to prevent the depletion of class B network IDs. Rather than assigning a class B network ID, InterNIC assigns a range of class C network IDs that contain enough network and host IDs for the organization's needs. This is known as *supernetting*. For example, rather than allocating a class B network ID to an organization that has up to 2,000 hosts, the InterNIC allocates a range of eight class C network IDs. Each class C network ID accommodates 254 hosts, for a total of 2,032 host IDs.

Although this technique helps conserve class B network IDs, it creates a new problem. Using conventional routing techniques, the routers on the Internet now must have eight class C network ID entries in their routing tables to route IP packets to the organization. To prevent Internet routers from becoming overwhelmed with routes, a technique called *Classless Interdomain Routing* (CIDR) is used to collapse multiple network ID entries into a single entry corresponding to all of the class C network IDs allocated to that organization.

Conceptually, CIDR creates the routing table entry: [Starting Network ID, count], where Starting Network ID is the first class C network ID and the count is the number of class C network IDs allocated. In practice, a supernetted subnet mask is used to convey the same information. To express the situation where eight class C network IDs are allocated starting with network ID 220.78.168.0:

Starting Network ID	220.78.168.0	11011100 01001110 10101000 00000000
Ending Network ID	220.78.175.0	11011100 01001110 10101111 00000000

Note that the first 21 bits (underlined) of all the above Class C network IDs are the same. The last three bits of the third octet vary from 000 to 111. The CIDR entry in the routing tables of the Internet routers becomes:

Network ID	Subnet Mask	Subnet Mask (binary)
220.78.168.0	255.255.248.0	11111111 11111111 11111000 0000000

In network prefix or CIDR notation, the CIDR entry is 220.78.168.0/21.

A block of addresses using CIDR is known as a *CIDR block.*

Note Because subnet masks are used to express the count, class-based network IDs must be allocated in groups corresponding to powers of 2.

In order to support CIDR, routers must be able to exchange routing information in the form of [Network ID, Network Mask] pairs. RIP for IP version 2, OSPF and BGPv4 are routing protocols that support CIDR. RIP for IP version 1 does not support CIDR.

Address Space Perspective

The use of CIDR to allocate addresses promotes a new perspective on IP network IDs. In the above example, the CIDR block [220.78.168.0, 255.255.248.0] can be thought of in two ways:

- A block of eight class C network IDs.
- An address space in which 21 bits are fixed and 11 bits are assignable.

In the latter perspective, IP network IDs lose their class-based heritage and become separate IP address spaces, subsets of the original IP address space defined by the 32-bit IP address. Each IP network ID (class-based, subnetted, CIDR block), is an address space in which certain bits are fixed (the network ID bits) and certain bits are variable (the host bits). The host bits are assignable as host IDs or, using subnetting techniques, can be used in whatever manner best suits the needs of the organization.

Public and Private Addresses

If your intranet is not connected to the Internet, any IP addressing can be deployed. If direct (routed) or indirect (proxy or translator) connectivity to the Internet is desired, there are two types of addresses employed on the Internet, *public addresses* and *private addresses*.

Public Addresses

Public addresses are assigned by InterNIC and consist of class-based network IDs or blocks of CIDR-based addresses (called CIDR blocks) that are guaranteed to be globally unique to the Internet.

When the public addresses are assigned, routes are programmed into the routers of the Internet so that traffic to the assigned public addresses can reach their locations. Traffic to destination public addresses are reachable on the Internet.

For example, when an organization is assigned a CIDR block in the form of a network ID and subnet mask, that [network ID, subnet mask] pair also exists as a route in the routers of the Internet. IP packets destined to an address within the CIDR block are routed to the proper destination.

Illegal Addresses

Private intranets that have no intent on connecting to the Internet can choose any addresses they want, even public addresses that have been assigned by the InterNIC. If an organization later decides to connect to the Internet, its current address scheme might include addresses already assigned by the InterNIC to other organizations. These addresses would be duplicate or conflicting addresses and are known as *illegal addresses*. Connectivity from illegal addresses to Internet locations is not possible.

For example, a private organization chooses to use 207.46.130.0/24 as its intranet address space. The public address 207.46.130.0/24 has been assigned to the Microsoft corporation and routes exist on the Internet routers to route all packets destined to IP addresses on 207.46.130.0/24 to Microsoft routers. As long as the private organization does not connect to the Internet, there is no problem because the two address spaces are on separate IP internetworks. If the private organization then connected directly to the Internet and continued to use 207.46.130.0/24 as its address space, then any Internet response traffic to locations on the 207.46.130.0/24 network would be routed to Microsoft routers, not to the routers of the private organization.

Private Addresses

Each IP node requires an IP address that is globally unique to the IP internetwork. In the case of the Internet, each IP node on a network connected to the Internet requires an IP address that is globally unique to the Internet. As the Internet grew, organizations connecting to the Internet required a public address for each node on their intranets. This requirement placed a huge demand on the pool of available public addresses.

When analyzing the addressing needs of organizations, the designers of the Internet noted that for many organizations, most of the hosts on the organization's intranet did not require direct connectivity to Internet hosts. Those hosts that did require a specific set of Internet services, such as the World Wide Web access and e-mail, typically access the Internet services through Application layer gateways such as proxy servers and e-mail servers. The result is that most organizations only required a small amount of public addresses for those nodes (such as proxies, routers, firewalls, and translators) that were directly connected to the Internet.

For the hosts within the organization that do not require direct access to the Internet, IP addresses that do not duplicate already-assigned public addresses are required. To solve this addressing problem, the Internet designers reserved a portion of the IP address space and named this space the *private address space*. An IP address in the private address space is never assigned as a public address. IP addresses within the private address space are known as *private addresses*. Because the public and private address spaces do not overlap, private addresses never duplicate public addresses.

The private address space specified in RFC 1918 is defined by the following three address blocks:

- 10.0.0.0/8

  The 10.0.0.0/8 private network is a class A network ID that allows the following range of valid IP addresses: 10.0.0.1 to 10.255.255.254. The 10.0.0.0/8 private network has 24 host bits that can be used for any subnetting scheme within the private organization.

- 172.16.0.0/12

  The 172.16.0.0/12 private network can be interpreted either as a block of 16 class B network IDs or as a 20-bit assignable address space (20 host bits) that can be used for any subnetting scheme within the private organization. The 172.16.0.0/12 private network allows the following range of valid IP addresses: 172.16.0.1 to 172.31.255.254.

- 192.168.0.0/16

  The 192.168.0.0/16 private network can be interpreted either as a block of 256 class C network IDs or as a 16-bit assignable address space (16 host bits) that can be used for any subnetting scheme within the private organization. The 192.168.0.0/16 private network allows the following range of valid IP addresses: 192.168.0.1 to 192.168.255.254.

The result of many organizations using private addresses is that the private address space is re-used, helping to prevent the depletion of public addresses.

Because the IP addresses in the private address space will never be assigned by the InterNIC as public addresses, there will never exist routes in the Internet routers for private addresses. Private addresses are not reachable on the Internet. Therefore, Internet traffic from a host that has a private address must either send its requests to an Application layer gateway (such as a proxy server), which has a valid public address, or have its private address translated into a valid public address by a network address translator (NAT) before it is sent on the Internet. For more information about NAT, see "Unicast IP Routing" in the *Microsoft® Windows® 2000 Server Resource Kit Internetworking Guide*.

Name Resolution

While IP is designed to work with the 32-bit IP addresses of the source and the destination hosts, computers users are much better at using and remembering names than IP addresses.

If a name is used as an alias for the IP address, a mechanism must exist for assigning that name to the appropriate IP node to ensure its uniqueness and resolving it to its IP address.

In this section, the mechanisms used for assigning and resolving host names (which are used by Windows Sockets applications), and NetBIOS names (which are used by NetBIOS applications) are discussed.

Host Name Resolution

A *host name* is an alias assigned to an IP node to identify it as a TCP/IP host. The host name can be up to 255 characters long and can contain alphabetic and numeric characters and the "-" and "." characters. Multiple host names can be assigned to the same host. For Windows 2000–based computers, the host name does not have to match the Windows 2000 computer name.

Windows Sockets applications, such as Microsoft® Internet Explorer and the FTP utility, can use one of two values for the destination to be connected: the IP address or a host name. When the IP address is specified, name resolution is not needed. When a host name is specified, the host name must be resolved to an IP address before IP-based communication with the desired resource can begin.

Host names can take various forms. The two most common forms are a nickname and a domain name. A nickname is an alias to an IP address that individual people can assign and use. A *domain name* is a structured name that follows Internet conventions.

Domain Names

To facilitate different organizations and their desires to have scaleable, customizable naming scheme in which to operate, the InterNIC has created and maintains a hierarchical namespace called the *Domain Name System* (DNS). DNS is a naming scheme that looks similar to the directory structure for files on a disk. However, instead of tracing a file from the root directory through subdirectories to its final location and its file name, a host name is traced from its final location through its parent domains back up to the root. The unique name of the host, representing its position in the hierarchy, is called its *Fully Qualified Domain Name* (FQDN). The top-level domain namespace is shown in Figure 1.11 with example second-level and subdomains.

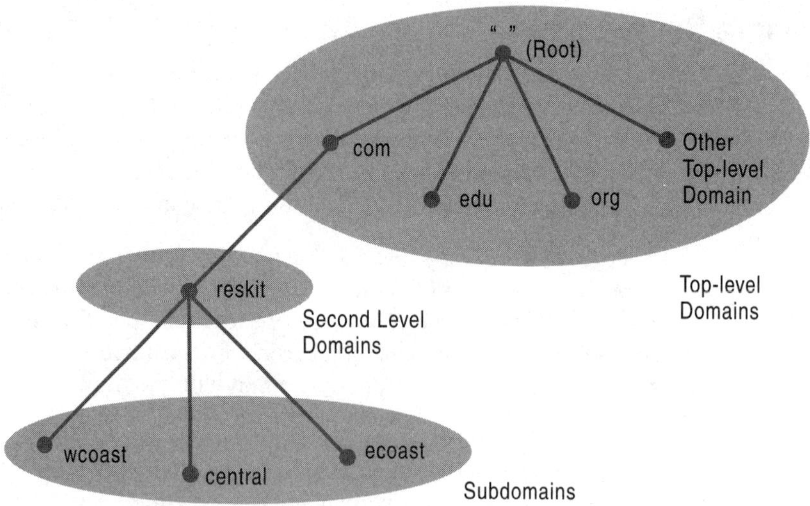

Figure 1.11 Domain Name System

The domain namespace consists of:

- The *root domain,* representing the root of the namespace and indicated with a "" (null).
- *Top-level domains*, those directly below the root, indicating a type of organization. On the Internet, the InterNIC is responsible for the maintenance of top-level domain names. Table 1.26 has a partial list of the Internet's top-level domain names.

Table 1.26 Internet Top-Level Domain Names

Domain Name	Meaning
COM	Commercial organization
EDU	Educational institution
GOV	Government institution
MIL	Military group
NET	Major network support center
ORG	Organization other than those above
INT	International organization
<country/region code>	Each country/region (geographic scheme)

- *Second-level domains*, below the top level domains, identifying a specific organization within its top-level domain. On the Internet, the InterNIC is responsible for the maintenance of second-level domain names and ensuring their uniqueness.
- *Subdomains* of the organization, below the second-level domain. The individual organization is responsible for the creation and maintenance of subdomains.

For example, for the FQDN **ftpsrv.wcoast.reskit.com**:

- The trailing period (.) denotes that this is an FQDN with the name relative to the root of the domain namespace. The trailing period is usually not required for FQDNs and if it is missing it is assumed to be present.
- **com** is the top-level domain, indicating a commercial organization.
- **reskit** is the second-level domain, indicating the Windows 2000 Resource Kit organization.
- **wcoast** is a subdomain of **reskit.com** indicating the West Coast division of the Windows 2000 Resource Kit organization.
- **ftpsrv** is the name of the FTP server in the West Coast division.

Domain names are not case sensitive.

Organizations not connected to the Internet can implement whatever top and second-level domain names they want. However, typical implementations do adhere to the InterNIC specification so that eventual participation in the Internet will not require a renaming process.

Host Name Resolution Using a Hosts File

One common way to resolve a host name to an IP address is to use a locally stored database file that contains IP-address-to-host-name mappings. On most UNIX systems, this file is /etc/hosts. On Windows 2000 systems, it is the Hosts file in the \\%*SystemRoot*%\\system32\\drivers\\etc directory.

Following is an example of the contents of the Hosts file:

```
#
# Table of IP addresses and host names
#
127.0.0.1       localhost
139.41.34.1     router
167.91.45.121   server1.central.slate.com s1
```

Within the Hosts file:

- Multiple host names can be assigned to the same IP address. Note that the server at the IP address 167.91.45.121 can be referred to by its FQDN (server1.central.slate.com) or a nickname (s1). This allows the user at this computer to refer to this server using the nickname **s1** rather than typing the entire FQDN.
- Entries can be case sensitive depending on the platform. Entries in the Hosts file for UNIX computers are case sensitive. Entries in the Hosts file for Windows 2000 and Windows NT–based computers are not case sensitive.

The advantage of using a Hosts file is that it is customizable for the user. Each user can create whatever entries they want, including easy-to-remember nicknames for frequently accessed resources. However, the individual maintenance of the Hosts file does not scale well to storing large numbers of FQDN mappings.

Host Name Resolution Using a DNS Server

To make host name resolution scalable and centrally manageable, IP address mappings for FQDNs are stored on *DNS servers*, computers that stores FQDN-to-IP-address mappings. To enable the querying of a DNS server by a host computer, a component called the *DNS resolver* is enabled and configured with the IP address of the DNS server. The DNS resolver is a built-in component of TCP/IP protocol stacks supplied with most network operating systems, including Windows 2000.

When a Windows Sockets application is given an FQDN as the destination location, the application calls a Windows Sockets function to resolve the name to an IP address. The request is passed to the DNS resolver component in the TCP/IP protocol. The DNS resolver packages the FQDN request as a DNS Name Query packet and sends it to the DNS server.

DNS is a distributed naming system. Rather than storing all the records for the entire namespace on each DNS server, each DNS server only stores the records for a specific portion of the namespace. The DNS server is authoritative for the portion of the namespace that corresponds to records stored on that DNS server. In the case of the Internet, hundreds of DNS servers store various portions of the Internet namespace. To facilitate the resolution of any valid domain name by any DNS server, DNS servers are also configured with pointer records to other DNS servers.

The following process outlines what happens when the DNS resolver component on a host sends a DNS query to a DNS server. This process is shown in Figure 1.12 and is simplified so that you can gain a basic understanding of the DNS resolution process.

1. The DNS resolver component of the DNS client formats a DNS Name Query containing the FQDN and sends it to the configured DNS server.
2. The DNS server checks the FQDN in the DNS Name Query against locally stored address records. If a record is found, the IP address corresponding to the requested FQDN is sent back to the client.
3. If the FQDN is not found, the DNS server forwards the request to a DNS server that is authoritative for the FQDN.
4. The authoritative DNS server returns the reply, containing the resolved IP address, back to the original DNS server.
5. The original DNS server sends the IP address mapping information to the client.

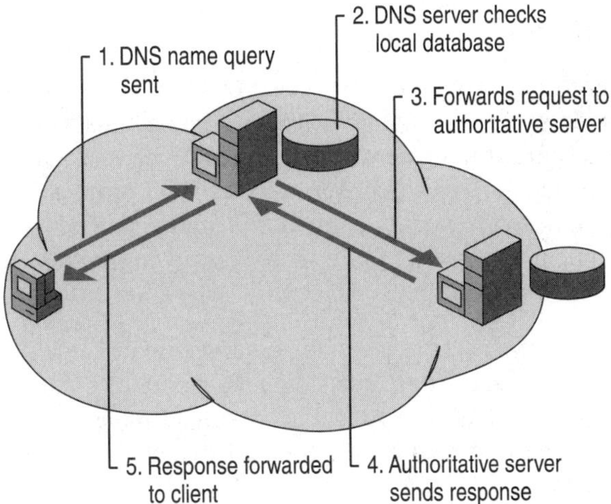

Figure 1.12 Resolving an FQDN Using DNS Servers

To obtain the IP address of a server that is authoritative for the FQDN, DNS servers on the Internet go through an iterative process of querying multiple DNS servers until the authoritative server is found. More details about this iterative process can be found in "Windows 2000 DNS" in this book.

Combining a Local Database File with DNS

TCP/IP implementations, including Windows 2000, allow the use of both a local database file and a DNS server to resolve host names. When a user specifies a host name in a TCP/IP command or utility:

1. TCP/IP checks the local database file (the Hosts file) for a matching name.
2. If a matching name is not found in the local database file, the host name is packaged as a DNS Name Query and sent to the configured DNS server.

Combining both methods gives the user the ability to have a local database file to resolve personalized nicknames and to use the globally distributed DNS database to resolve FQDNs.

NetBIOS Name Resolution

NetBIOS name resolution is the process of successfully mapping a NetBIOS name to an IP address. A *NetBIOS name* is a 16-byte address used to identify a NetBIOS resource on the network. A NetBIOS name is either a unique (exclusive) or group (nonexclusive) name. When a NetBIOS process communicates with a specific process on a specific computer, a unique name is used. When a NetBIOS process communicates with multiple processes on multiple computers, a group name is used.

The NetBIOS name acts as a session layer application identifier. For example, the NetBIOS Session service operates over TCP port 139. All NetBIOS over TCP/IP session requests are addressed to TCP destination port 139. When identifying a NetBIOS application with which to establish a NetBIOS session, the NetBIOS name is used.

An example of a process using a NetBIOS name is the file and print sharing server service on a Windows 2000–based computer. When your computer starts up, the server service registers a unique NetBIOS name based on your computer's name. The exact name used by the server service is the 15 character computer name plus a 16th character of 0x20. If the computer name is not 15 characters long, it is padded with spaces up to 15 characters long. Other network services also use the computer name to build their NetBIOS names so the 16th character is used to uniquely identify each service, such as the redirector, server, or messenger services. Figure 1.13 shows the NetBIOS names associated with the server, redirector, and messenger services.

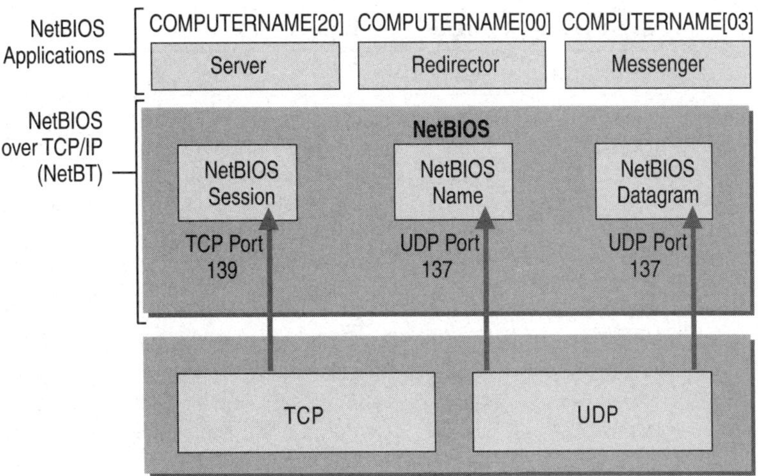

Figure 1.13 NetBIOS Names and Services

When you attempt to make a file-sharing connection to a Windows 2000–based computer by name, the server service on the file server you specify corresponds to a specific NetBIOS name. For example, when you attempt to connect to the computer called CORPSERVER, the NetBIOS name corresponding to the server service is "`CORPSERVER      <20>`" (note the padding using the space character). Before a file and print sharing connection can be established, a TCP connection must be created. In order for a TCP connection to be established, the NetBIOS name "`CORPSERVER      <20>`" must be resolved to an IP address.

To view the NetBIOS names registered by NetBIOS processes running on a Windows 2000 computer, type **nbtstat -n** at the Windows 2000 command prompt.

NetBIOS Node Types

The exact mechanism by which NetBIOS names are resolved to IP addresses depends on the node's configured *NetBIOS Node Type*. RFC 1001 define the NetBIOS Node Types, as listed in Table 1.27.

Table 1.27 NetBIOS Node Types

Node Type	Description
B-node (broadcast)	B-node uses broadcasted NetBIOS Name Queries for name registration and resolution. B-node has two major problems: (1) In a large internetwork, broadcasts can increase the network load, and (2) Routers typically do not forward broadcasts, so only *NetBIOS name* on the local network can be resolved.

(continued)

Table 1.27 NetBIOS Node Types *(continued)*

Node Type	Description
P-node (peer-peer)	P-node uses a *NetBIOS name server (NBNS)*, such as Windows Internet Name Service (WINS), to resolve *NetBIOS name*. P-node does not use broadcasts; instead, it queries the name server directly. The most significant problem with P-node is that all computers must be configured with the IP address of the NBNS, and if the NBNS is down, computers are not able to communicate even on the local network.
M-node (mixed)	M-node is a combination of B-node and P-node. By default, an M-node functions as a B-node. If it is unable to resolve a name by broadcast, it uses the NBNS of P-node.
H-node (hybrid)	H-node is a combination of P-node and B-node. By default, an H-node functions as a P-node. If it is unable to resolve a name through the *NetBIOS name* server, it uses a broadcast to resolve the name.

Windows 2000–based computers are B-node by default and become H-node when configured for a WINS server. Windows 2000 also uses a local database file called Lmhosts to resolve remote NetBIOS names.

For more information about WINS, see "Windows Internet Name Service" in this book. For more information about the Lmhosts file, see "LMHOSTS" in this book.

IP Routing

After the host name or NetBIOS name is resolved to an IP address, the IP packet must be sent by the sending host to the resolved IP address. *Routing* is the process of forwarding a packet based on the destination IP address. Routing occurs at a sending TCP/IP host and at an IP router. A *router* is a device that forwards the packets from one network to another. Routers are also commonly referred to as *gateways*. In both cases, sending host and router, a decision has to be made about where the packet is forwarded.

To make these decisions, the IP layer consults a routing table stored in memory. Routing table entries are created by default when TCP/IP initializes and additional entries are added either manually by a system administrator or automatically through communication with routers.

Direct and Indirect Delivery

Forwarded IP packets use at least one of two types of delivery based on whether the IP packet is forwarded to the final destination or whether it is forwarded to an IP router. These two types of delivery are known as direct and indirect delivery.

Direct delivery occurs when the IP node (either the sending node or an IP router) forwards a packet to the final destination on a directly attached network. The IP node encapsulates the IP datagram in a frame format for the Network Interface layer (such as Ethernet or Token Ring) addressed to the destination's physical address.

Indirect delivery occurs when the IP node (either the sending node or an IP router) forwards a packet to an intermediate node (an IP router) because the final destination is not on a directly attached network. The IP node encapsulates the IP datagram in a frame format, addressed to the IP router's physical address, for the Network Interface layer (such as Ethernet or Token Ring).

IP routing is a combination of direct and indirect deliveries.

In Figure 1.14, when sending packets to node B, node A performs a direct delivery. When sending packets to node C, node A performs an indirect delivery to Router 1. Router 1 performs an indirect delivery to Router 2. Router 2 performs a direct delivery to node C.

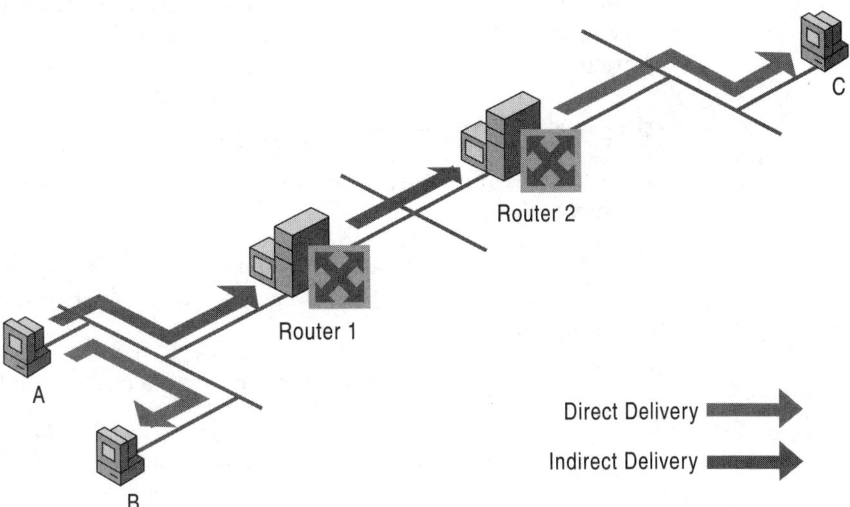

Figure 1.14 Direct and Indirect Deliveries

IP Routing Table

A routing table is present on all IP nodes. The routing table stores information about IP networks and how they can be reached (either directly or indirectly). Because all IP nodes perform some form of IP routing, routing tables are not exclusive to IP routers. Any node loading the TCP/IP protocol has a routing table. There are a series of default entries according to the configuration of the node and additional entries can be entered either manually through TCP/IP utilities or dynamically through interaction with routers.

When an IP packet is to be forwarded, the routing table is used to determine:

1. The forwarding or next-hop IP address:

   For a direct delivery, the forwarding IP address is the destination IP address in the IP packet. For an indirect delivery, the forwarding IP address is the IP address of a router.

2. The interface to be used for the forwarding:

   The interface identifies the physical or logical interface such as a network adapter that is used to forward the packet to either its destination or the next router.

IP Routing Table Entry Types

An entry in the IP routing table contains the following information in the order presented:

Network ID. The network ID or destination corresponding to the route. The network ID can be class-based, subnet, or supernet network ID, or an IP address for a host route.

Network Mask. The mask that is used to match a destination IP address to the network ID.

Next Hop. The IP address of the next hop.

Interface. An indication of which network interface is used to forward the IP packet.

Metric. A number used to indicate the cost of the route so the best route among possible multiple routes to the same destination can be selected. A common use of the metric is to indicate the number of hops (routers crossed) to the network ID.

Routing table entries can be used to store the following types of routes:

Directly Attached Network IDs. Routes for network IDs that are directly attached. For directly attached networks, the Next Hop field can be blank or contain the IP address of the interface on that network.

Remote Network IDs. Routes for network IDs that are not directly attached but are available across other routers. For remote networks, the Next Hop field is the IP address of a local router in between the forwarding node and the remote network.

Host Routes. A route to a specific IP address. Host routes allow routing to occur on a per-IP address basis. For host routes, the network ID is the IP address of the specified host and the network mask is 255.255.255.255.

Default Route. The default route is designed to be used when a more specific network ID or host route is not found. The default route network ID is 0.0.0.0 with the network mask of 0.0.0.0.

Route Determination Process

To determine which routing table entry is used for the forwarding decision, IP uses the following process:

- For each entry in a routing table, perform a bit-wise logical AND between the destination IP address and the network mask. Compare the result with the network ID of the entry for a match.
- The list of matching routes is compiled. The route that has the longest match (the route that matched the most amount of bits with the destination IP address) is chosen. The longest matching route is the most specific route to the destination IP address. If multiple entries with the longest match are found (multiple routes to the same network ID, for example), the router uses the lowest metric to select the best route. If multiple entries exist that are the longest match and the lowest metric, the router is free to choose which routing table entry to use.

The end result of the route determination process is the choice of a single route in the routing table. The route chosen yields a forwarding IP address (the next hop IP address) and an interface (the port). If the route determination process fails to find a route, IP declares a routing error. For the sending host, an IP routing error is internally indicated to the upper layer protocol such as TCP or UDP. For a router, an ICMP Destination Unreachable-Host Unreachable message is sent to the source host.

Example Routing Table for Windows 2000

Table 1.28 shows the default routing table for a Windows 2000–based host (not a router). The host has a single network adapter and has the IP address 157.55.27.90, subnet mask 255.255.240.0 (/20), and default gateway of 157.55.16.1.

Table 1.28 Windows 2000 Routing Table

Network Destination	Netmask	Gateway	Interface	Metric	Purpose
0.0.0.0	0.0.0.0	157.55.16.1	157.55.27.90	1	Default Route
127.0.0.0	255.0.0.0	127.0.0.1	127.0.0.1	1	Loopback Network
157.55.16.0	255.255.240.0	157.55.27.90	157.55.27.90	1	Directly Attached Network
157.55.27.90	255.255.255.255	127.0.0.1	127.0.0.1	1	Local Host
157.55.255.255	255.255.255.255	157.55.27.90	157.55.27.90	1	Network Broadcast
224.0.0.0	224.0.0.0	157.55.27.90	157.55.27.90	1	Multicast Address
255.255.255.255	255.255.255.255	157.55.27.90	157.55.27.90	1	Limited Broadcast

Default Route The entry corresponding to the default gateway configuration is a network destination of 0.0.0.0 with a network mask (netmask) of 0.0.0.0. Any destination IP address joined with 0.0.0.0 by a logical AND results in 0.0.0.0. Therefore, for any IP address, the default route produces a match. If the default route is chosen because no better routes were found, the IP packet is forwarded to the IP address in the Gateway column using the interface corresponding to the IP address in the Interface column.

Loopback Network The loopback network entry is designed to take any IP address of the form 127.x.y.z and forward it to the special loopback address of 127.0.0.1.

Directly Attached Network The local network entry corresponds to the directly attached network. IP packets destined for the directly attached network are not forwarded to a router but sent directly to the destination. Note that the Gateway and Interface columns match the IP address of the node. This indicates that the packet is sent from the network adapter corresponding to the node's IP address.

Local Host The local host entry is a host route (network mask of 255.255.255.255) corresponding to the IP address of the host. All IP datagrams to the IP address of the host are forwarded to the loopback address.

Network Broadcast The network broadcast entry is a host route (network mask of 255.255.255.255) corresponding to the all-subnets directed broadcast address (all subnets of class B network ID 157.55.0.0). Packets addressed to the all-subnets directed broadcast are sent from the network adapter corresponding to the node's IP address.

Multicast Address The multicast address, with its class D network mask, is used to route any multicast IP packets from the network adapter corresponding to the node's IP address.

Limited Broadcast The *limited broadcast address* is a host route (network mask of 255.255.255.255). Packets addressed to the limited broadcast are sent from the network adapter corresponding to the node's IP address.

To view the IP routing table on a Windows 2000-based computer, type **route print** at a Windows 2000 command prompt.

When determining the forwarding or next-hop IP address from a route in the routing table:

- If the gateway address is the same as the interface address, the forwarding IP address is set to the destination IP address of the IP packet.
- If the gateway address is not the same as the interface address, the forwarding IP address is set to the gateway address.

For example, when traffic is sent to 157.55.16.48, the most specific route is the route for the directly attached network (157.55.16.0/20). The forwarding IP address is set to destination IP address (157.55.16.48) and the interface is the network adapter, which has been assigned the IP address 157.55.27.90.

When sending traffic to 157.20.0.79, the most specific route is the default route (0.0.0.0/0). The forwarding IP address is set to the gateway address (157.20.16.1) and the interface is the network adapter, which has been assigned the IP address 157.55.27.90.

Routing Processes

The IP routing processes on all nodes involved in the delivery of an IP packet includes: the sending host, the intermediate routers, and the destination host.

IP on the Sending Host

When a packet is sent by a sending host, the packet is handed from an upper layer protocol (TCP, UDP, or ICMP) to IP. IP on the sending host does the following:

1. Sets the Time-to-Live (TTL) value to either a default or application-specified value.
2. IP checks its routing table for the best route to the destination IP address.

   If no route is found, IP indicates a routing error to the upper layer protocol (TCP, UDP, or ICMP).
3. Based on the most specific route, IP determines the forwarding IP address and the interface to be used for forwarding the packet.
4. IP hands the packet, the forwarding IP address, and the interface to Address Resolution Protocol (ARP), and then ARP resolves the forwarding IP address to its media access control (MAC) address and forwards the packet.

IP on the Router

When a packet is received at a router, the packet is passed to IP. IP on the router does the following:

1. IP verifies the IP header checksum.

   If the IP header checksum fails, the IP packet is discarded without notification to the user. This is known as a *silent discard*.

2. IP verifies whether the destination IP address in the IP datagram corresponds to an IP address assigned to a router interface.

   If so, the router processes the IP datagram as the destination host (see step 3 in the following "IP on the Destination Host" section).

3. If the destination IP address is not the router, IP decreases the time-to-live (TTL) by 1.

   If the TTL is 0, the router discards the packet and sends an ICMP Time Expired-TTL Expired message to the sender.

4. If the TTL is 1 or greater, IP updates the TTL field and calculates a new IP header checksum.
5. IP checks its routing table for the best route to the destination IP address in the IP datagram.

   If no route is found, the router discards the packet and sends an ICMP Destination Unreachable-Network Unreachable message to the sender.

6. Based on the best route found, IP determines the forwarding IP address and the interface to be used for forwarding the packet.
7. IP hands the packet, the forwarding IP address, and the interface to ARP, and then ARP forwards the packet to the appropriate MAC address.

This entire process is repeated at each router in the path between the source and destination host.

IP on the Destination Host

When a packet is received at the destination host, it is passed up to IP. IP on the destination host does the following:

1. IP verifies the IP header checksum.

   If the IP header checksum fails, the IP packet is silently discarded.

2. IP verifies that the destination IP address in the IP datagram corresponds to an IP address assigned to the host.

   If the destination IP address is not assigned to the host, the IP packet is silently discarded.

3. Based on the IP protocol field, IP passes the IP datagram without the IP header to the appropriate upper-level protocol.

   If the protocol does not exist, ICMP sends a Destination Unreachable-Protocol Unreachable message back to the sender.

4. For TCP and UDP packets, the destination port is checked and the TCP segment or UDP header is processed.

   If no application exists for the UDP port number, ICMP sends a Destination Unreachable-Port Unreachable message back to the sender. If no application exists for the TCP port number, TCP sends a Connection Reset segment back to the sender.

Static and Dynamic IP Routers

For IP routing between routers to occur efficiently in the IP internetwork, routers must have explicit knowledge of remote network IDs or be properly configured with a default route. On large IP internetworks, one of the challenges faced by network administrators is how to maintain the routing tables on their IP routers so that IP traffic flow is traveling the best path and is fault tolerant.

There are two ways of maintaining routing table entries on IP routers:

- Manually—Static IP routers have routing tables that do not change unless manually changed by a network administrator.

  Static routing relies on the manual administration of the routing table. Remote network IDs are not discovered by static routers and must be manually configured. Static routers are not fault tolerant. If a static router goes down, neighboring routers do not sense the fault and inform other routers.

- Automatically—Dynamic IP routers have routing tables that change automatically based on the communication of routing information with other routers.

  Dynamic routing employs the use of routing protocols, such as Routing Information Protocol (RIP) and Open Shortest Path First (OSPF), to dynamically update the routing table through the exchange of routing information between routers. Remote network IDs are discovered by dynamic routers and automatically entered into the routing table. Dynamic routers are fault tolerant. If a dynamic router goes down, the fault is sensed by neighboring routers who propagate the changed routing information to the other routers in the internetwork.

For more information about routing principles, see "Unicast Routing Overview" in the *Windows 2000 Internetworking Guide*. For more information about IP routing protocols, see "Unicast IP Routing" in the *Windows 2000 Internetworking Guide*.

Physical Address Resolution

Based on the destination IP address and the route determination process, IP determines the forwarding IP address and interface to be used to forward the packet. IP then hands the IP packet, the forwarding IP address, and the interface, to ARP.

If the forwarding IP address is the same as the destination IP address, then ARP performs a direct delivery. In a direct delivery, the MAC address corresponding to the destination IP address must be resolved.

If the forwarding IP address is not the same as the destination IP address, then ARP performs an indirect delivery. The forwarding IP address is the IP address of a router between the current IP node and the final destination. In an indirect delivery, the MAC address corresponding to the IP address of the router must be resolved.

To resolve a forwarding IP address to its MAC address, ARP uses the broadcasting facility on shared access networking technologies (such as Ethernet or Token Ring) to send out a broadcasted ARP Request frame. An ARP Reply, containing the MAC address corresponding to the requested forwarding IP address, is sent back to the sender of the ARP Request.

ARP Cache

To keep the number of broadcasted ARP Request frames to a minimum, many TCP/IP protocol stacks incorporate an *ARP cache*, a table of recently resolved IP addresses and their corresponding MAC addresses. The ARP cache is checked first before sending an ARP Request frame. Each interface has its own ARP cache.

Depending on the vendor implementation, the ARP cache can have the following qualities:

- ARP cache entries can be dynamic (based on ARP Replies) or static. Static ARP entries are permanent and are manually added using a TCP/IP utility such as the ARP utility provided with Windows 2000. Static ARP cache entries are used to prevent ARP Requests for commonly-used local IP addresses, such as routers and servers. The problem with static ARP entries is that they have to be manually updated when network interface equipment changes.
- Dynamic ARP cache entries have a time-out value associated with them to remove entries in the cache after a specified period of time. Dynamic ARP cache entries for Windows 2000 TCP/IP are given a maximum time of 10 minutes before being removed.

To view the ARP cache on a Windows 2000–based computer, type **arp -a** at a Windows 2000 command prompt.

ARP Process

IP sends information to ARP. ARP receives the IP packet, the forwarding IP address, and the interface to be used to forward the packet. Whether performing a direct or indirect delivery, ARP performs the following process, as displayed in Figure 1.15:

1. Based on the interface and the forwarding IP address, ARP consults the appropriate ARP cache for an entry for the forwarding IP address. If an entry is found, ARP skips to step 6.
2. If the entry is not found, ARP builds an ARP Request frame containing the MAC address of the interface sending the ARP Request, the IP address of the interface sending the ARP Request, and the forwarding IP address. ARP then broadcasts the ARP Request using the appropriate interface.
3. All hosts receive the broadcasted frame and the ARP Request is processed. If the receiving host's IP address matches the requested IP address (the forwarding IP address), its ARP cache is updated with the address mapping of the sender of the ARP Request.

   If the receiving host's IP address does not match the requested IP address, the ARP Request is silently discarded.
4. The receiving host formulates an ARP Reply containing the requested MAC address and sends it directly to the sender of the ARP Request.
5. When the ARP Reply is received by the sender of the ARP Request, it updates its ARP cache with the address mapping.

   Between the ARP Request and the ARP Reply, both hosts have each other's address mappings in their ARP caches.
6. The IP packet is sent to the forwarding host by addressing it to the resolved MAC address.

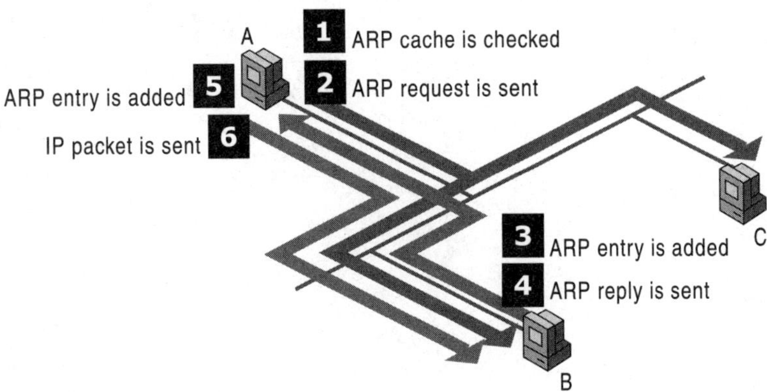

Figure 1.15 ARP Process

Additional Resources

For more information about TCP/IP, see:

- *Internetworking with TCP/IP, Vol. 1, 3rd Edition* by Douglas Comer, 1996, Englewood Cliffs, NJ: Prentice Hall.
- *Microsoft Windows 2000 TCP/IP Protocols and Services Technical Reference* by Thomas Lee and Joseph Davies, 1999, Redmond, WA: Microsoft Press.
- *TCP/IP Illustrated,* Volume *1, The Protocols* by Richard W. Stevens, 1994, Reading, MA: Addison-Wesley.

CHAPTER 2

Windows 2000 TCP/IP

Microsoft has adopted TCP/IP as the strategic enterprise network transport for its platforms. Microsoft 32-bit TCP/IP for Microsoft® Windows® 2000 is a high-performance, portable, 32-bit implementation of the industry-standard TCP/IP protocol. This chapter provides additional technical details about the Microsoft 32-bit TCP/IP protocol as implemented in Windows 2000. The Windows 2000 TCP/IP protocol driver described in this chapter is shared by all Microsoft 32-bit TCP/IP protocol stacks, including TCP/IP for Microsoft® Windows NT® Server, Microsoft® Windows NT® Workstation, Microsoft® Windows® 95, and Microsoft® Windows® 98. However, there are small differences in implementation, configuration methods, and available services.

This chapter is intended for network engineers and support professionals who are already familiar with TCP/IP or who have read the "Introduction to TCP/IP" in this book and the product documentation about TCP/IP supplied with Windows 2000.

In This Chapter

Related Information in the Resource Kit

- For more information about the Windows 2000 network architecture, see "Windows 2000 Network Architecture" in this book.
- For more information about the TCP/IP protocol, see "Introduction to TCP/IP" in this book.
- For more information about TCP/IP troubleshooting, see "TCP/IP Troubleshooting" in this book.

Note This chapter mentions many Windows 2000 registry entries for TCP/IP. For more information about these registry entries, see the *Technical Reference to the Windows 2000 Registry* (Regentry.chm) on the Windows 2000 Resource Kit CD-ROM.

Overview of Windows 2000 TCP/IP

The TCP/IP suite for Windows 2000 is designed to make it easy to integrate Microsoft systems into large-scale corporate, government, and public networks and to provide the ability to operate over those networks in a secure manner. With TCP/IP, Windows 2000 can immediately connect and operate on the Internet.

Standard Features and Performance Enhancements

Windows 2000 TCP/IP supports the following standard features:

- Ability to bind to multiple network adapters with different media types
- Logical and physical multihoming
- Internal IP routing capability
- Internet Group Management Protocol (IGMP) Version 2 (support for IP multicasting)
- Duplicate IP address detection
- Internet Control Message Protocol (ICMP) Router Discovery
- Multiple configurable default gateways
- Dead gateway detection for TCP traffic
- Automatic Path Maximum Transmission Unit (PMTU) discovery for TCP connections
- IP Security (IPSec)
- Quality of Service (QoS)
- TCP/IP over ATM services.
- Virtual Private Networks (VPNs)

In addition, Windows 2000 has the following new performance enhancements:

- Increased default window sizes
- TCP Scalable Window sizes
- Selective Acknowledgments (SACK)
- TCP Fast Retransmit
- RTT (Round Trip Time) and RTO (Retransmission Timeout) calculation improvements.

Services Available

Windows 2000 provides the following services:

- Dynamic Host Configuration Protocol (DHCP) client and server.
- Windows Internet Name Service (WINS), a network basic input/output system (NetBIOS) name client and server.
- Domain Name System (DNS) client and server.
- Dial-up (Point-to-Point Protocol/Serial Lines) support.
- Point-to-Point Tunneling Protocol (PPTP) and Layer Two Tunneling Protocol (L2TP) used for Virtual Private Networks.
- TCP/IP network printing (Lpr/Lpd).
- Simple Network Management Protocol (SNMP) agent.
- NetBIOS interface.
- Windows Sockets Version 2 (Winsock2) interface.
- Microsoft networking browsing support across IP routers.
- High-performance Microsoft® Internet Information Services.
- Basic TCP/IP connectivity tools, including: Finger, File Transfer Protocol (FTP), Rcp, Rexec, Rsh, Telnet, and Tftp.
- Client and server software for simple network protocols, including Character Generator, Daytime, Discard, Echo, and Quote of the Day.
- TCP/IP management and diagnostic tools, including: Arp, Hostname, Ipconfig, Lpq, Nbtstat, Netstat, Ping, Route, Nslookup, Tracert, and Pathping.

Internet RFCs Supported by Microsoft Windows 2000 TCP/IP

Requests for Comments (RFCs) are a continually evolving series of reports, proposals for protocols, and protocol standards used by the Internet community. RFCs supported by the Windows 2000 version of TCP/IP include those listed in Table 2.1.

Table 2.1 RFCs Supported by Windows 2000

RFC	Title
768	User Datagram Protocol (UDP)
783	Trivial File Transfer Protocol (TFTP)
791	Internet Protocol (IP)
792	Internet Control Message Protocol (ICMP)
793	Transmission Control Protocol (TCP)
816	Fault Isolation and Recovery
826	Address Resolution Protocol (ARP)
854	Telnet Protocol (Telnet)
862	Echo Protocol (ECHO)
863	Discard Protocol (DISCARD)
864	Character Generator Protocol (CHARGEN)
865	Quote of the Day Protocol (QUOTE)
867	Daytime Protocol (DAYTIME)
894	IP over Ethernet
919, 922	IP Broadcast Datagrams (broadcasting with subnets)
950	Internet Standard Subnetting Procedure
959	File Transfer Protocol (FTP)
1001, 1002	NetBIOS Service Protocols
1009	Requirements for Internet Gateways
1034, 1035	Domain Name System (DNS)
1042	A Standard for the Transmission of IP Datagrams over IEEE 802 Networks
1055	Transmission of IP over Serial Lines (IP-SLIP)
1112	Internet Group Management Protocol (IGMP)
1122, 1123	Host Requirements (communications and applications)
1144	Compressing TCP/IP Headers for Low-Speed Serial Links
1157	Simple Network Management Protocol (SNMP)
1179	Line Printer Daemon Protocol
1188	IP over FDDI
1191	Path Discovery
1201	IP over ARCNET
1256	ICMP Router Discovery Messages
1323	TCP Extensions for High Performance

(continued)

Table 2.1 RFCs Supported by Windows 2000 ***(continued)***

RFC	Title
1332	PPP Internet Protocol Control Protocol (IPCP)
1334	PPP Authentication Protocols
1518	An Architecture for IP Address Allocation with Classless Inter-Domain Routing (CIDR)
1519	CIDR: An Address Assignment and Aggregation Strategy
1533	DHCP Options and Bootstrap Protocol (BOOTP) Vendor Extensions
1534	Interoperation Between DHCP and BOOTP
1552	PPP Internetwork Packet Exchange Control Protocol (IPXCP)
1661	Point-to-Point Protocol (PPP)
1662	PPP in HDLC-like Framing
1748	IEEE 802.5 MIB using SMIv2
1749	IEEE 802.5 Station Source Routing MIB using SMIv2
1812	Requirements for IP Version 4 Routers
1828	IP Authentication using Keyed MD5
1829	ESP DES-CBC Transform
1851	ESP Triple DES-CBC Transform
1852	IP Authentication using Keyed SHA
1878	Variable Length Subnet Table For IPv4
1994	PPP Challenge Handshake Authentication Protocol (CHAP)
2018	TCP Selective Acknowledgment Options
2085	HMAC-MD5 IP Authentication with Replay Prevention
2104	HMAC: Keyed Hashing for Message Authentication
2131	Dynamic Host Configuration Protocol (DHCP)
2132	Clarifications and Extensions for the Bootstrap Protocol
2136	Dynamic Updates in the Domain Name System (DNS UPDATE)
2205	Resource Reservation Protocol (RSVP) – Version 1 Functional Specification
2236	Internet Group Management Protocol, Version 2
2401	Security Architecture for the Internet Protocol
2402	IP Authentication Header (AH)
2406	IP Encapsulating Security Payload (ESP)
2637	Point-to-Point Tunneling Protocol (PPTP)
2661	Layer Two Tunneling Protocol (L2TP)

Architecture of Microsoft TCP/IP for Windows 2000

The Microsoft TCP/IP core protocol elements, services, and the interfaces between them is shown in Figure 2.1. The Transport Driver Interface (TDI) and the Network Device Interface Specification (NDIS) are public, and their specifications are available from Microsoft. In addition, there are a number of higher level interfaces available to user-mode applications. The most commonly used are Windows Sockets, Remote Procedure Call (RPC), and NetBIOS. For more information about TDI, NDIS, Windows Sockets, RPC, and NetBIOS, see "Windows 2000 Networking Architecture" in this book. For more information about Windows Sockets support for Windows 2000 TCP/IP, see "Windows Sockets" in this chapter. For more information about NetBIOS support for Windows 2000 TCP/IP, see "NetBIOS over TCP/IP" in this chapter.

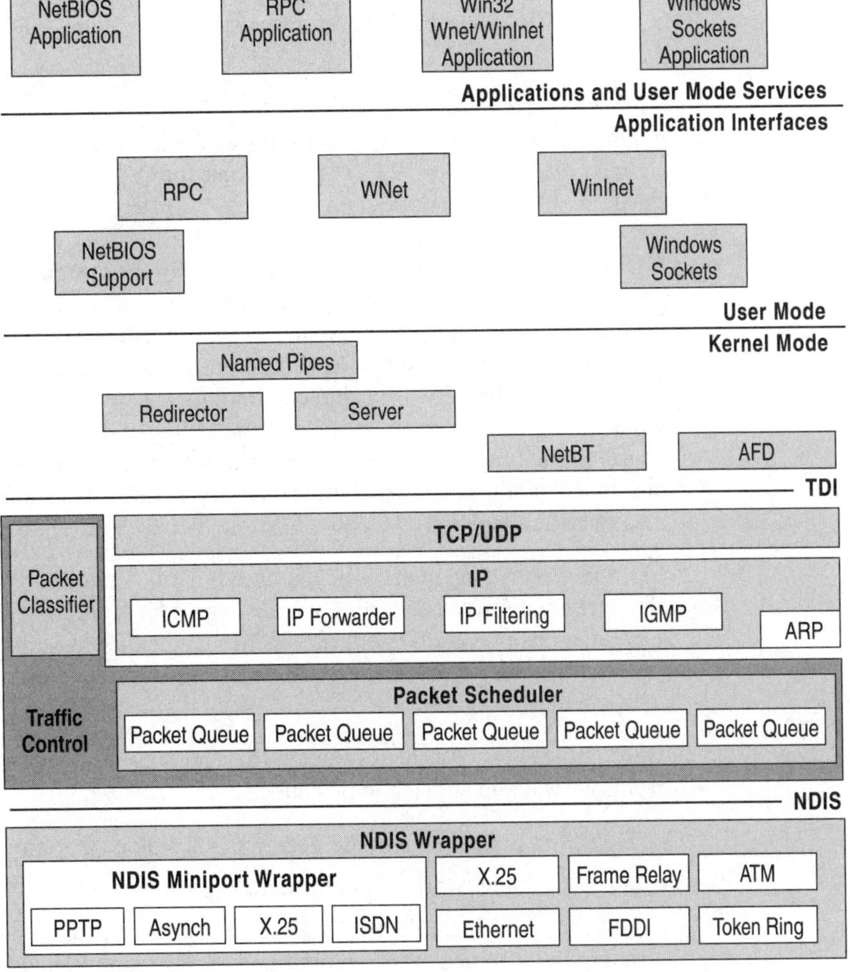

Figure 2.1 TCP/IP in the Windows 2000 Network Architecture

NDIS Interface and Below

Microsoft networking protocols use the Network Device Interface Specification (NDIS) to communicate with network card drivers. Much of the Open Systems Interconnection (OSI) model data-link layer functionality is implemented in the protocol stack. This makes development of network card drivers much simpler.

Network Driver Interface Specification and TCP/IP

NDIS 5.0 includes the following extensions:

- NDIS power management (required for Network Power Management and Network Wakeup).
- Plug-and-play.
- Task offload mechanisms for tasks such as TCP and UDP checksum, and fast packet forwarding.
- Support for QoS.
- Intermediate Driver Support (required for Broadcast PC, virtual local area networks (VLANs), Packet Scheduling for QoS, and for NDIS support of IEEE 1394 network devices).

NDIS can power down network adapters when the system requests a power level change. Either the user or the system can initiate this request. For example, the user might want to put the computer in sleep mode, or the system might request a power level change based on keyboard or mouse inactivity. In addition, disconnecting the network cable can initiate a power down request provided that the network adapter supports this functionality. In this case, the system waits a configurable time period before powering down the network adapter because the disconnect could be the result of temporary wiring changes on the network rather than the disconnection of a cable from the network device itself.

NDIS power management policy is based on no network activity. This means that all overlying network components must agree to the request before the network adaptercan be powered down. If there are any active sessions or open files over the network, the power down request can be refused by any or all of the components involved.

The computer can also be awakened from a lower power state based on network events. A wakeup signal can be caused by:

- Detection of a change in the network link state (for example, cable reconnect).
- Receipt of a network wakeup frame.
- Receipt of a Magic Packet. A Magic Packet is a packet that contains 16 contiguous copies of the receiving network adapter's media access control (MAC) address.

At driver initialization, NDIS queries the capabilities of the miniport driver to determine if it supports such things as Magic Packets, pattern match, or link change wakeups, and to determine the lowest required power state for each wakeup method. The network protocols then query the miniport capabilities. At run time, the protocol sets the wakeup policy using Object Identifiers, such as Enable Wakeup, Set Packet Pattern, and Remove Packet Pattern.

Currently, Microsoft TCP/IP is the only Microsoft protocol stack that supports network power management. It registers the following packet patterns at miniport initialization:

- Directed IP packet
- ARP broadcast for station IP address
- NetBIOS over TCP/IP broadcast for station's assigned computer name

NDIS-compliant drivers are available for a wide variety of network adapters from many vendors. The NDIS interface allows multiple protocol drivers of different types to bind to a single network adapter driver, and allows a single protocol to bind to multiple network adapter drivers. The NDIS specification describes the multiplexing mechanism used to accomplish this. Bindings can be viewed or changed from the Windows 2000 Network and Dial-up Connections folder.

Windows 2000 TCP/IP provides support for:

- Fiber Distributed Data Interface (FDDI).
- Token Ring (IEEE 802.5).
- Asynchronous Transfer Mode (ATM).

  Using LAN Emulation (LANE), ATM LAN cards appear to TCP/IP as an Ethernet card.
- Attached Resource Computer network (ARCnet).
- Dedicated wide area network (WAN) links such as Dataphone Digital Service (DDS) and T-carrier (Fractional T1, T1 and T3).
- Dial-up or permanent circuit switched WAN services such as analog phone, ISDN, and xDSL.
- Packet switched WAN services such as X.25, Frame Relay, and ATM.

- Ethernet.

  Ethernet II encapsulation is the default. You can select IEEE 802.3 SNAP encapsulation by changing the value of the **ArpUseEtherSNAP** registry entry (HKLM\SYSTEM\CurrentControlSet\Services\Tcpip\Parameters) to 1. Windows 2000 TCP/IP receives both frame types regardless of the value of **ArpUseEtherSNAP**.

Caution Do not use a registry editor to edit the registry directly unless you have no alternative. The registry editors bypass the standard safeguards provided by administrative tools. These safeguards prevent you from entering conflicting settings or settings that are likely to degrade performance or damage your system. Editing the registry directly can have serious, unexpected consequences that can prevent the system from starting and require that you reinstall Windows 2000. To configure or customize Windows 2000, use the programs in Control Panel or Microsoft Management Console (MMC) whenever possible.

▶ **To select IEEE 802.3 SNAP encapsulation**

1. On the taskbar, click the **Start** button, and then click **Run**.
2. In the **Open** box, type **regedt32.exe**, and then click **OK**.
3. In a registry editor, navigate to HKLM\SYSTEM\CurrentControlSet\Services\Tcpip\Parameters.
4. Select the **ArpUseEtherSNAP** entry, and change the value to 1.

Link Layer Functionality

Link layer functionality is divided between the network adapter/driver combination and the low-level protocol stack driver. For LAN media, the network adapter/driver combination filters are based on the destination MAC address of each frame.

Normally, the LAN hardware filters out all incoming frames except those containing one of the following destination addresses:

- The unicast MAC address of the adapter.
- The broadcast address (for Ethernet, the broadcast address is 0xFF-FF-FF-FF-FF-FF).
- Multicast addresses that are registered with the hardware by a protocol driver.

If the frame contains one of these addresses as the destination MAC address, the frame is checked for bit level integrity through a checksum calculation.

All frames that pass the destination address and checksum tests are then passed up to the network adapter driver through a hardware interrupt. The network adapter driver is software that runs on the computer, so any frames that make it this far require some CPU time to process. The network adapter driver brings the frame into system memory from the interface card. Then the frame is passed up to the appropriate bound transport drivers in the order that they are bound. The NDIS 5.0 specification provides more detail on this process.

As a packet traverses a network or series of networks, the source MAC address is always that of the network adapter that placed it on the media, and the destination MAC address is that of the network adapter that is intended to pull it off the media. This means that in a routed network, the source and destination MAC address change with each hop through a network-layer device (a router or layer 3 switch).

Maximum Transmission Unit

Each media type has a maximum frame size, called the *maximum transmission unit* (MTU), that cannot be exceeded. The link layer is responsible for discovering this MTU and reporting it to the protocols named earlier. NDIS drivers can be queried for the local MTU by the protocol stack. Knowledge of the MTU for an interface is used by upper layer protocols such as TCP, which optimizes packet sizes for each media automatically. For details, see the discussion of *Path Maximum Transmission Unit (PMTU) discovery* in "Internet Control Message Protocol" later in this chapter.

If a network adapter driver—such as an ATM driver—uses LAN emulation mode, it might report that it has an MTU that is higher than what is expected for that media type. For example, it might emulate Ethernet but report an MTU of 9180 bytes. Windows 2000 accepts and uses the MTU size reported by the adapter even when it exceeds the normal MTU for a particular media type.

Sometimes the MTU reported to the protocol stack may be less than what would be expected for a given media type. For instance, use of the 802.1p standard often reduces the MTU reported by 4 bytes due to larger data-link layer headers.

Core Protocol Stack Components

The core protocol stack components are those shown between the NDIS and TDI interfaces in Figure 2.1. They are implemented in the Windows 2000 Tcpip.sys driver and are accessible through the TDI and the NDIS interfaces. The Winsock2 interface also provides some support for "raw" access to the protocol stack.

Address Resolution Protocol

Address Resolution Protocol (ARP) performs IP address-to-media access control address resolution for outgoing packets. As each outgoing addressed IP datagram is encapsulated in a frame, source and destination MAC addresses must be added. Determining the destination MAC address for each frame is the responsibility of ARP.

As discussed in "Introduction to TCP/IP" in this book, the IP routing process for an outbound IP datagram results in the choice of an interface (a network adapter) and a forwarding IP address. ARP compares the forwarding IP address for every outbound IP datagram to the ARP cache for the network adapter over which the packet is sent. If there is a matching entry, then the MAC address retrieved from the cache is used. If not, ARP broadcasts an ARP Request frame on the local subnet, requesting that the owner of the IP address in question reply with its MAC address. When an ARP Reply is received, the ARP cache is updated with the new information, and it is used to address the packet at the data-link layer.

Note The ARP process and functionality described here only applies to unicast IP traffic. Multicast IP traffic is sent to a specific multicast MAC address that depends on the multicast IP address. For more details, see "Internet Group Management Protocol" later in this chapter.

Using the ARP Tool

You can use the ARP tool to view, add, or delete entries in the ARP cache. Examples follow. Note that entries added manually are static, and are not automatically removed through ARP cache entry aging.

The **arp -a** command can be used to view the ARP cache, as shown here:

```
C:\>arp -a

Interface: 192.168.40.123
  Internet Address      Physical Address      Type
  192.168.40.1          00-00-0c-1a-eb-c5     dynamic
  192.168.40.124        00-dd-01-07-57-15     dynamic
Interface: 10.57.8.190
  Internet Address      Physical Address      Type
  10.57.9.138           00-20-af-1d-2b-91     dynamic
```

The computer in this example is multihomed (has more than one network adapter), so there is a separate ARP cache for each interface.

In the following example, the **arp -s** command is used to add a static entry for the host whose IP address is 10.57.10.32 and whose MAC address is 00-60-8C-0E-6C-6A to the ARP cache for the second interface:

```
C:\>arp -s 10.57.10.32 00-60-8c-0e-6c-6a 10.57.8.190

C:\>arp -a

Interface: 192.168.40.123
  Internet Address      Physical Address      Type
  192.168.40.1          00-00-0c-1a-eb-c5     dynamic
  192.168.40.124        00-dd-01-07-57-15     dynamic

Interface: 10.57.8.190
  Internet Address      Physical Address      Type
  10.57.9.138           00-20-af-1d-2b-91     dynamic
  10.57.10.32           00-60-8c-0e-6c-6a     static
```

Use the command **arp -d** to delete entries from the cache. For example, to remove the ARP cache entry for 10.57.10.32 in the example:

```
C:\>arp -d 10.57.10.32

C:\>arp -a

Interface: 192.168.40.123
  Internet Address      Physical Address      Type
  192.168.40.1          00-00-0c-1a-eb-c5     dynamic
  192.168.40.124        00-dd-01-07-57-15     dynamic

Interface: 10.57.8.190
  Internet Address      Physical Address      Type
  10.57.9.138           00-20-af-1d-2b-91     dynamic
```

ARP Cache Aging

Windows 2000 adjusts the size of the ARP cache automatically to meet the needs of the system. If an entry is not used by any outgoing datagram for two minutes, the entry is removed from the ARP cache. Entries that are being referenced are given additional time, in two minute increments, up to a maximum lifetime of 10 minutes. After 10 minutes, the ARP cache entry is removed and must be rediscovered using an ARP Request frame. To adjust the time an unreferenced entry can remain in the ARP cache, change the value of the **ArpCacheLife** and **ArpCacheMinReferencedLife** registry entries (HKLM\SYSTEM\CurrentControlSet\Services\Tcpip\Parameters).

Static entries added with the **arp -s** command are not expired from the cache. The ARP cache is erased upon initialization of the TCP/IP protocol. To make static ARP cache entries persistent each time the computer is started, create a command file with the ARP commands and place a shortcut to the command file in the Startup folder.

Updating Entries in the ARP Cache

In addition to creating an ARP cache entry through the receipt of an ARP Reply, ARP cache entries are updated if the mapping is received through an ARP Request. In other words, if the IP address of the sender of an ARP Request is in the cache, update the entry with the sender's MAC address. This way, nodes that have static or dynamic ARP cache entries for the sender are updated with the ARP Request sender's current MAC address. A node whose interface and MAC address changes updates the ARP caches containing an entry for the node the next time the node sends an ARP Request.

ARP and UDP Messages

ARP queues only one outbound IP datagram for a given destination address while that IP address is being resolved to a MAC address. If a UDP-based application sends multiple IP datagrams to a single destination address without any pauses between them, some of the datagrams might be dropped if there is no ARP cache entry present. An application can compensate for this by calling the Iphlpapi.dll routine SendArp() to establish an arp cache entry, before sending the stream of packets. See the platform Software Development Kit (SDK) for additional information.

Internet Protocol

In the TCP/IP stack, IP is where packet sorting and delivery take place. At this layer, each incoming or outgoing packet is referred to as a datagram. Each IP datagram bears the source IP address of the sender and the destination IP address of the intended recipient. Unlike MAC addresses, the IP addresses in a datagram remain the same throughout a packet's journey across an internetwork unless altered by a network address translator (NAT). IP layer functions are described in the following sections.

Routing

Routing is a primary function of IP. Datagrams are handed to IP from the network adapters. Each datagram is labeled with a source and destination IP address. IP examines the destination address on each datagram, compares it to a locally maintained IP routing table, and decides what action to take. There are three possibilities for each datagram:

- It can be passed up to a protocol layer above IP on the local host.

- It can be forwarded using one of the locally attached network adapters.
- It can be discarded.

An entry in a Windows 2000 IP routing table contains the following information:

Network Destination The network ID corresponding to the route. The network destination can be class-based, subnet, or supernet, or an IP address for a host route.

Netmask The mask used to match a destination IP address to the network destination.

Gateway The forwarding or next-hop IP address for the network destination.

Interface The IP address corresponding to the network interface that is used to forward the IP datagram.

Metric A number used to indicate the cost of the route so the best route among possible multiple routes to the same destination can be selected. A common use of the metric is to indicate the number of hops (routers crossed) to the network destination. If two routes have the same Network Destination and Netmask, the route with the lowest metric is the best route.

Routing table entries can be used to store the following types of routes:

Directly Attached Network ID Routes These routes are for network IDs that are directly attached. For directly attached networks, the Gateway IP address is the IP address of the interface on that network.

Remote Network ID Routes These are for network IDs that are not directly attached but are available across other routers. For remote networks, the Gateway IP address is the IP address of a local router in between the forwarding node and the remote network.

Host Routes A route to a specific IP address. Host routes allow routing to occur on a per-IP address basis. For host routes, the Network Destination is the IP address of the specified host and the subnet mask is 255.255.255.255.

Default Route The default route is designed to be used when a more specific network ID or host route is not found. The default route Network Destination is 0.0.0.0 with the subnet mask of 0.0.0.0.

The Route Determination Process

To determine a single route to use to forward an IP datagram, IP uses the following process:

1. For each route in the routing table, IP performs a bit-wise logical AND between the Destination IP address and the netmask. IP compares the result with the network destination for a match. If they match, IP marks the route as one that matches the Destination IP address.
2. From the list of matching routes, IP determines the route that has the most bits in the netmask. This is the route that matched the most bits to the Destination IP address and is therefore the most specific route for the IP datagram. This is known as finding the longest or closest matching route.
3. If multiple closest matching routes are found, IP uses the route with the lowest metric.
4. If multiple closest matching routes with the lowest metric are found, IP randomly chooses the route to use.

When determining the forwarding or next-hop IP address from the chosen route, IP uses the following procedure:

- If the Gateway address is the same as the Interface address, the forwarding IP address is set to the destination IP address of the IP packet.
- If the Gateway address is not the same as the Interface address, the forwarding IP address is set to the Gateway address.

The end result of the *route determination process* is the choice of a single route in the routing table. The route chosen yields a forwarding IP address (the Gateway IP address or the Destination IP address of the IP datagram) and an interface (identified through the Interface IP address). If the route determination process fails to find a route, IP declares a routing error. For a sending host, an IP routing error is internally indicated to the upper layer protocol such as TCP or UDP. For a router, the IP datagram is discarded and an ICMP "Destination Unreachable-Host Unreachable" message is sent to the source host.

Using the Route Tool

You can use the Route tool to view, add, or delete routes in the IP routing table.

Viewing the IP Routing Table

You can use the **route print** command to view the route table from the command prompt. The following IP routing table is for a Windows 2000 computer with the IP address of 10.1.1.99, a subnet mask of 255.255.255.0, and a *default gateway* of 10.1.1.1:

```
C:\>route print
===========================================================================
Interface List
0x1 ........................... MS TCP Loopback interface
0x2 ...00 a0 24 e9 cf 45 ...... 3Com 3C90x Ethernet Adapter
===========================================================================
===========================================================================
Active Routes:
Network Destination        Netmask          Gateway       Interface  Metric
          0.0.0.0          0.0.0.0         10.1.1.1      10.1.1.99       1
         10.1.1.0    255.255.255.0        10.1.1.99      10.1.1.99       1
        10.1.1.99  255.255.255.255        127.0.0.1      127.0.0.1       1
   10.255.255.255  255.255.255.255        10.1.1.99      10.1.1.99       1
        127.0.0.0        255.0.0.0        127.0.0.1      127.0.0.1       1
        224.0.0.0        224.0.0.0        10.1.1.99      10.1.1.99       1
  255.255.255.255  255.255.255.255        10.1.1.99      10.1.1.99       1
===========================================================================
Persistent Routes:
  None
```

The default IP routing table for this Windows 2000 computer contains the following routes:

Default Route The route with the network destination of 0.0.0.0 and the netmask of 0.0.0.0 is the default route. Any destination IP address ANDed with 0.0.0.0 results in 0.0.0.0. Therefore, for any IP address, the default route produces a match. If the default route is chosen because no better routes are found, the IP datagram is forwarded to the IP address in the Gateway column using the interface corresponding to the IP address in the Interface column.

Directly Attached Network The route with the network destination of 10.1.1.0 and the netmask of 255.255.255.0 is a route for the directly attached network. IP packets destined for the directly attached network are not forwarded to a router but sent directly to the destination. Note that the Gateway Address and Interface are the IP address of the node. This indicates that the packet is sent from the network adapter corresponding to the node's IP address.

Local Host The route with the network destination of 10.1.1.99 and the netmask of 255.255.255.255 is a host route corresponding to the IP address of the host. All IP datagrams to the IP address of the host are forwarded to the loopback address.

All-Subnets Directed Broadcast The route with the network destination of 10.255.255.255 and the netmask of 255.255.255.255 is a host route for the all-subnets directed broadcast address for the class A network ID 10.0.0.0. The all-subnets directed broadcast address is designed to reach all subnets of class-based network ID. Packets addressed to the all-subnets directed broadcast will be sent out of the network adapter corresponding to the node's IP address. A host route for the all-subnets directed broadcast is only present for network IDs that are subnets of a class-based network ID.

Loopback Network The route with the network destination of 127.0.0.0 and the netmask of 255.0.0.0 is a route designed to take any IP address of the form 127.*x*.*y*.*z* and forward it to the special loopback address of 127.0.0.1.

Multicast Address The route with the network destination of 224.0.0.0 and the netmask of 224.0.0.0 is a route for all class D multicast addresses. An IP datagram matching this route is sent from the network adapter corresponding to the node's IP address.

Limited Broadcast The route with the network destination of 255.255.255.255 and the netmask of 255.255.255.255 is a host route for the limited broadcast address. Packets addressed to the limited broadcast are sent out of the network adapter corresponding to the node's IP address.

Note The order of routes in the display of the route print command does not affect the performance of the route determination process.

For example, when this host sends traffic to 10.1.1.72, the route determination process matches two routes; the default route and the directly attached network route. The directly attached network route is the closest matching route because there are 24 bits in the netmask as opposed to 0 bits in the default route. Because the Gateway address and the Interface address for the directly attached network route are the same, the forwarding IP address is set to the destination address 10.1.1.72. The interface on which to forward the IP datagram is identified by the IP address in the Interface column. In this case, the interface is the 3Com 3C90x Ethernet Adapter, which is assigned the IP address 10.1.1.99.

When this host sends traffic to 172.16.48.4, the route determination process matches the default route. Even though there are no bits in the subnet mask of the default route that matched 172.16.48.4, the default route is still a match with the Destination IP address. Because the Gateway address and the Interface address for the directly attached network route are different, the forwarding IP address is set to the IP address in the Gateway column, 10.1.1.1. The interface on which to forward the IP datagram is identified by the IP address in the Interface column. In this case, the interface is the 3Com 3C90x Ethernet Adapter, which is assigned the IP address 10.1.1.99.

The route table is maintained automatically in most cases. When a host initializes, routes for the local networks, loopback, multicast, and configured default gateway are added. More routes might appear in the table as the IP layer learns of them. For instance, the default gateway for a host might advise it (using ICMP) of a better route to a specific host. Routes also can be added manually using the route command, or by a routing protocol.

The **-p** (persistent) switch can be used with the **route** command to specify persistent routes. *Persistent routes* are stored in the PersistentRoutes registry subkey

HKEY_LOCAL_MACHINE\SYSTEM\CurrentControlSet\Services\Tcpip \Parameters\PersistentRoutes

Windows 2000 introduces a new configuration option for the metric of default gateways. This metric allows better control of which default gateway is active at any particular time. The default value for the metric is 1. A route with a lower metric value is preferred to a route with a higher metric. In the case of default gateways, the computer uses the default gateway with the lowest metric unless it appears to be inactive, in which case dead gateway detection may trigger a switch to the next lowest metric default gateway in the list. Default gateway metrics can be set through advanced TCP/IP configuration options. DHCP servers can provide a base metric and a list of default gateways. If a DHCP server provides a base metric of 100, and a list of three default gateways, the gateways will be configured with metrics of 100, 101, and 102 respectively. A DHCP-provided base metric does not apply to statically configured default gateways.

Most Autonomous System (AS) routers use a protocol such as Routing Information Protocol (RIP) or Open Shortest Path First (OSPF) to exchange routing tables with other routers. Windows 2000 Server includes support for these protocols with the Routing and Remote Access service. Windows 2000 also includes support for silent RIP using the RIP Listener, an optional networking service.

By default, Windows 2000–based systems do not act as routers and do not forward IP datagrams between interfaces. The Routing and Remote Access service is included in Windows 2000 Server and can be enabled and configured to provide full multi-protocol routing services. For more information, see “Routing and Remote Access Service,” in the *Microsoft® Windows® 2000 Server Resource Kit Internetworking Guide*.

Configuring Routing for Multinetted or Proxy ARP Environments

When using multiple logical subnets on the same physical network, known as *multinetting*, you need to add routes so that all IP addresses for the locally attached network segment are reachable through direct delivery. For example, if a network segment is using the class C network IDs 192.168.1.0/24 and 192.168.2.0/24 and a host is configured with the IP address of 192.168.2.31, the following route command adds an additional route so that all addresses on 192.168.1.0/24 are reachable:

```
route add 192.168.1.0 MASK 255.255.255.0 192.168.2.31
```

You can use the following command to tell IP to treat all subnets as local and to use ARP directly for the destination:

```
route add 0.0.0.0 MASK 0.0.0.0 <my local ip address>
```

Thus, packets destined for "non-local" subnets are transmitted directly onto the local media instead of being sent to a router. In other words, the local network adapter can be designated as the default gateway. This can be useful where several class C network IDs are used on one physical network with no router to the outside.

In a proxy ARP environment, a separate device forwards ARP Requests to other segments on behalf of hosts. Just as in a multinetted environment, multiple sets of addresses are directly reachable. Use the **route** command to add the appropriate routes to the host routing tables.

Duplicate IP Address Detection

Duplicate address detection ensures that an IP address being used by an IP node is unique to the attached network segment. When the stack is first initialized, Windows 2000 sends ARP Requests for the host's own IP address, known as *gratuitous ARPs*. The number of gratuitous ARPs to send is determined by the value of the **ArpRetryCount** registry entry (HKLM\SYSTEM\CurrentControlSet\Services\Tcpip\Parameters), which defaults to 3. If another host replies to any of these ARP Requests, the IP address is already in use. When this happens, the Windows 2000–based computer still boots. However, IP is disabled for the offending address, a system log entry is generated, and an error message is displayed.

If the host that is using the address is also a Windows 2000–based computer, a system log entry is generated and an error message is displayed on that computer, but its interface continues to operate. Recall that ARP cache entries are updated for ARP Requests received. Therefore, after transmitting the unicast ARP Reply to the offending system, the defending system broadcasts an additional gratuitous ARP Request so that other hosts on the network will maintain the correct mapping for the address in their ARP caches.

You can start a computer using a duplicate IP address while it is not attached to the network, in which case no conflict is detected. However, if you then plug it into the network, the first time it sends an ARP Request for another IP address, any Windows 2000–based computer with a conflicting address detects the conflict and remains operational. If both computers are running Windows 2000, IP remains operational for the duplicate address on both computers. The computer detecting the conflict displays an error message and logs a detailed event in the system log. A sample event log entry is shown as follows:

```
** The system detected an address conflict for IP address 199.199.40.123
with the system having network hardware address 00:DD:01:0F:7A:B5.
Network operations on this system may be disrupted as a result. **
```

Windows 2000 DHCP–enabled clients perform duplicate IP address detection when the client moves into the DHCP Selecting state. If a duplicate IP address is detected, the DHCP client sends a DHCPDecline message to the DHCP server, and move into the DHCP Initialization state. Upon receipt of the DHCPDecline message, the DHCP server marks the IP address as unusable.

For more information about DHCP messages and DHCP client states, see "Dynamic Host Configuration Protocol" in this book.

Multihoming

When a computer is configured with more than one IP address, it is referred to as a *multihomed* system. Multihoming is supported in three different ways:

- Multiple IP addresses per network adapter.

  NetBIOS over TCP/IP (NetBT) binds to only one IP address per network adapter. When a NetBIOS name registration is sent out, only one IP address will be registered per adapter. This registration will occur over the IP address that is listed first in the properties of the TCP/IP protocol for the adapter.
- Multiple network adapters per physical network.

  There are no restrictions other than hardware.
- Multiple networks and media types.

  There are no restrictions other than hardware and media support.

When an IP datagram is sent from a multihomed host, the IP route determination process determines the appropriate forwarding IP address and interface. Therefore, the datagram might contain the source IP address of one interface in the multihomed host, yet be placed on the media by a different interface. The source MAC address on the frame is that of the interface that actually transmitted the frame on the media, and the source IP address is the IP address from the sending application, not necessarily one of the IP addresses associated with the sending interface.

When a computer is multihomed with network adapters attached to disjoint network segments, network segments that are separated from each other by IP routers, there are additional routing considerations.

While it is possible to configure a default gateway IP address for each network interface, there is only a single active default route in the IP routing table. If there are multiple default routes in the IP routing table (assuming a metric of 1), then the specific default route to use is chosen randomly when TCP/IP is initialized. This behavior can lead to confusion and loss of connectivity. When you are configuring a computer to be multihomed on two disjoint networks, that you configure a default gateway IP on the interface that is attached to the portion of the IP internetwork that contains the most network segments. Then, either add static routes or use a routing protocol to provide connectivity to remote networks reachable through the other interfaces.

For more information about name registration and resolution and choice of network adapter on outbound datagrams with multihomed computers, see "Transmission Control Protocol," "NetBIOS Over TCP/IP," and "Windows Sockets" later in this chapter.

Classless Interdomain Routing

Windows 2000 provides full support for Classless Interdomain Routing (CIDR), also known as supernetting, described in RFCs 1518 and 1519. Windows 2000 also provides support for the use of the all-zeros and all-ones subnets in accordance with RFCs 1812 and 1878. Verify that other hosts and routers on your internetwork also support CIDR and the use of the all-ones and all-zeros subnets.

IP Multicasting

Windows 2000 provides full support for IP multicasting, including the ability to send and receive IP multicast traffic, and full support for the Internet Group Management Protocol (IGMP) version 2. For more information on support for IGMP, see "Internet Group Management Protocol" later in this chapter.

IP Over ATM

Windows 2000 introduces support for the sending of IP datagrams over an ATM network. IP over ATM, described in RFC 1577, is known as classical IP over ATM. Windows 2000 TCP/IP also supports IP over ATM LAN Emulation (LANE). For more information on IP over ATM support in Windows 2000, see "Asynchronous Transfer Mode," in the *Windows 2000 Internetworking Guide.*

Internet Control Message Protocol

ICMP is a maintenance protocol specified in RFC 792 and is normally considered to be part of the IP layer. ICMP messages are encapsulated within IP datagrams, so that they can be routed throughout an internetwork. ICMP is used by Windows 2000 to:

- Build and maintain route tables.
- Assist in PMTU discovery.
- Diagnose problems.
- Adjust flow control to prevent link or router saturation.
- Perform router discovery.

Maintaining Route Tables

A Windows 2000 host is normally configured with an IP address, subnet mask, and default gateway. When TCP/IP is initialized, a set of routes based on this configuration is created in the host's IP routing table as discussed in "Viewing the IP Routing Table" earlier in this chapter. If the host forwards an IP datagram to its default gateway and a better route exists through a router that has an interface on the same network segment as the sending host and the default gateway, the host's default gateway forwards the datagram and sends an ICMP Redirect message to the host informing it of the IP address of the better router to use to reach the destination IP address.

When a Windows 2000–based computer receives an ICMP Redirect message, IP verifies that it came from the first-hop gateway in the current route and that the gateway is on a directly connected network. If so, a host route with a 10-minute lifetime is added to the route table for that destination IP address. If the ICMP Redirect message did not come from the first-hop gateway in the current route, or if that gateway is not on a directly connected network, the ICMP Redirect message is ignored.

PMTU Discovery

Windows 2000 employs Path Maximum Transmission Unit (PMTU) discovery described in RFC 1191 for TCP connections.

When a connection is established, the two hosts involved exchange their TCP *maximum segment size* (MSS) values. The smaller of the two MSS values is used for the connection. Previously, the MSS for a host has been the MTU at the link layer minus 40 bytes for the IP and TCP headers. However, support for additional TCP options, such as timestamps, has increased the typical TCP and IP header to 52 or more bytes. The relationship between IP MTU and TCP MSS is shown in Figure 2.2

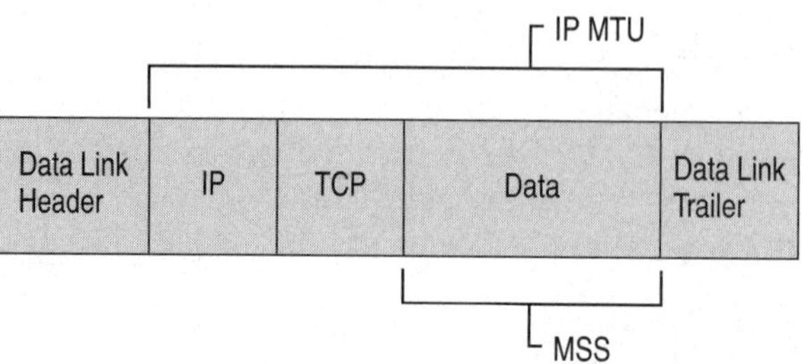

Figure 2.2 IP MTU and TCP MSS

By default, all Windows 2000 TCP segments are sent with the Don't Fragment flag set in the IP header. Routers that attempt to fragment the TCP segment discover the Don't Fragment flag. At this point, the router does one of the following:

- The router discards the IP datagram and sends an ICMP Destination Unreachable-Fragmentation Needed and DF Set message back to the sending host. This is the original purpose of these messages.
- The router discards the IP datagram and sends (to the sending host) an ICMP Destination Unreachable-Fragmentation Needed and DF Set message containing the MTU of the next hop. The MTU that is allowed for the next hop is stored in the low-order 16 bits of the ICMP header field that is labeled "unused" in RFC 792. See RFC 1191, section 4, for the format of this message. This is a PMTU-compliant router.
- The router discards the IP datagram without sending an ICMP Destination Unreachable-Fragmentation Needed and DF Set message. This type of router is known as a *PMTU black hole*.

Upon receipt of the ICMP Destination Unreachable-Fragmentation Needed and DF Set message containing the MTU of the next hop, the Windows 2000 implementation of TCP will adjust its MSS for the new MTU so that any further packets sent on the connection will be no larger than the maximum size that can traverse the path without fragmentation. The minimum MTU permitted by RFC 791 is 68 bytes, and Windows 2000 TCP/IP enforces this limit.

If there are non-PMTU-compliant routers or PMTU black hole routers on your IP internetwork, it might be necessary to change the configuration of PMTU Discovery behavior. You can reduce the problems caused by black hole routers by setting the values of the **EnablePMTUBHDetect** and **EnablePMTUDiscovery** registry entries (HKLM\SYSTEM\CurrentControlSet\Services\Tcpip\Parameters) to 1. Explanations of these registry entries are as follows:

EnablePMTUBHDetect Adjusts the PMTU discovery algorithm to attempt to detect PMTU black hole routers. PMTU Black Hole detection is disabled by default.

EnablePMTUDiscovery Enables or disables the PMTU discovery mechanism. When PMTU discovery is disabled, TCP connection traffic is sent without setting the Don't Fragment flag to 1. PMTU discovery is enabled by default.

▶ **To reduce problems caused by black hole routers**

1. In a registry editor, navigate to HKLM\SYSTEM\CurrentControlSet\Services\Tcpip\Parameters.
2. Select the **EnablePMTUBHDetect** entry, and change the value to 1.
3. Close the registry editor.

The PMTU between two hosts can be discovered manually using the **ping** command with the **-f** (don't fragment) switch, as follows:

```
ping -f -n <number of pings> -l <size> <destination IP address>
```

The size parameter can be varied until the MTU of the next hop is discovered. Note that the size parameter used by Ping is the size of the optional data in the ICMP Echo Request and does not include the ICMP Echo Request header (8 bytes long) and the IP header (normally 20 bytes long). Therefore, for Ethernet, the maximum ping buffer size is 1500–8–20 or 1472. The following example shows the results of pinging across a router on an Ethernet network with a buffer size of 1472 and then 1473:

```
C:\>ping -f -n 1 -l 1472 10.99.99.10
Pinging 10.99.99.10 with 1472 bytes of data:
Reply from 10.99.99.10: bytes=1472 time<10ms TTL=128
Ping statistics for 10.99.99.10:
    Packets: Sent = 1, Received = 1, Lost = 0 (0% loss),
Approximate round trip times in milli-seconds:
    Minimum = 0ms, Maximum = 0ms, Average = 0ms

C:\>ping -f -n 1 -l 1473 10.99.99.10
Pinging 10.99.99.10 with 1473 bytes of data:
Packet needs to be fragmented but DF set.
Ping statistics for 10.99.99.10:
    Packets: Sent = 1, Received = 0, Lost = 1 (100% loss),
Approximate round trip times in milli-seconds:
    Minimum = 0ms, Maximum =  0ms, Average =  0ms
```

In this example, the IP layer returned an ICMP error message that Ping interpreted. If the router is a PMTU black hole router, the ICMP Echo Reply sent by Ping cannot be answered once its size exceeded the MTU of the next hop. Ping can be used in this manner to detect a PMTU black hole router.

The following Network Monitor capture shows a sample PMTU-compliant ICMP Destination Unreachable-Fragmentation Needed and DF Set message:

```
+ FRAME: Base frame properties
+ ETHERNET: ETYPE = 0x0800 : Protocol = IP:  DOD Internet Protocol
+ IP: ID = 0x4401; Proto = ICMP; Len: 56
  ICMP: Destination Unreachable: 10.99.99.10   See frame 3
      ICMP: Packet Type = Destination Unreachable
      ICMP: Unreachable Code = Fragmentation Needed, DF Flag Set
      ICMP: Checksum = 0xA05B
      ICMP: Next Hop MTU = 576 (0x240)
      ICMP: Data: Number of data bytes remaining = 28 (0x001C)
    + ICMP: Description of original IP frame
```

This message was generated by using **ping -f -l 1000** on an Ethernet-based host to forward a 1028-byte datagram across a router interface that only supports an MTU of 576 bytes. When the router tried to place the large datagram onto the network with the smaller MTU, it found that fragmentation was not allowed. The router then discarded the IP datagram and sent back the ICMP message indicating that the largest datagram that could be forwarded was 0x240, or 576 bytes.

Use of ICMP to Diagnose Problems

The Ping tool is used to send ICMP Echo Requests to an IP address, and to wait for ICMP Echo Replies. Ping reports the number of responses received and the time interval between sending the request and receiving the response. There are many different options that can be used with the Ping tool. For more information about how Ping is used to troubleshoot, see "TCP/IP Troubleshooting" in this book.

Tracert is a route tracing tool that works by sending ICMP Echo Request messages to a specified IP address with increasing values of the Time To Live (TTL) field in the IP header. The first Echo Request message has a TTL of 1. The first router decreases the TTL to 0 and sends an ICMP Time Exceeded–TTL Expired in Transit message to the sender. From the Source IP Address field of the ICMP message, the sending host determines the IP address of the near-side router interface. Tracert then sends an ICMP Echo Request message with a TTL of 2, and so on. This process continues until the entire list of near-side router interfaces, from the sending host to the destination, is determined.

For more information about the Tracert command and how it is used to troubleshoot, see "TCP/IP Troubleshooting" in this book.

Flow Control Using ICMP

When a router becomes congested and begins to discard IP datagrams, it can send ICMP Source Quench messages to the sending host of the discarded datagrams. Windows 2000 TCP/IP honors an ICMP Source Quench message for TCP traffic provided that it contains the header fragment of one of its own datagrams from an active TCP connection. A Windows 2000–based router does not send ICMP Source Quench messages.

ICMP Router Discovery

As specified in RFC 1256, Windows 2000 TCP/IP provides host support for ICMP *router discovery*. Router discovery provides an improved method of detecting and configuring default gateways. Instead of configuring a default gateway manually or through DHCP, hosts can dynamically discover the best default gateway to use on their subnet and can automatically switch to another default gateway if the current default gateway fails or the network administrator changes router preferences.

When a host supporting router discovery initializes, it joins the all-hosts IP multicast group (224.0.0.1) and listens for ICMP Router Advertisement messages. ICMP router discovery–compatible routers periodically send ICMP Router Advertisements containing their IP address, a preference level, and a time after which they can be considered down. Hosts receive the ICMP Router Advertisements and select the router with the highest preference level as their default gateway.

Hosts can also send ICMP Router Solicitation messages to the all-routers IP multicast address (224.0.0.2) when an interface initializes or the host has not received a router advertisement from the router for the current default gateway within the router's advertised lifetime. Windows 2000 hosts send a maximum of three solicitations at intervals of approximately 600 milliseconds. The use of host router discovery is determined by the values of the **PerformRouterDiscovery** and **SolicitationAddressBCast** registry entries (HKLM\SYSTEM\CurrentControlSet\Services\Tcpip\Parameters\Interfaces*InterfaceName*).

The Windows 2000 Routing and Remote Access service supports ICMP router discovery as a router. For more information, see "Unicast IP Routing" in the *Internetworking Guide.*

Quality of Service and Resource Reservation Protocol

Another new feature in Windows 2000 is support for QoS and Resource Reservation Protocol (RSVP).

Generic QoS (GQoS) is an extension to the Winsock programming interface. It provides APIs and system components that are intended to provide network applications with a method of reserving network bandwidth between client and server. RSVP is an implementation of a bandwidth reservation protocol that is supported by Windows 2000. GQoS provides an application interface via Winsock2 to the RSVP protocol and components. The modular design of QoS and RSVP components allows other components to be added for increased functionality. For example, RSVP can be accessed by a control or management application if you want to provide some quality of service for non-QoS-enabled applications.

These concepts and protocols are discussed in more detail in "Quality of Service" in this book.

IP Security

IPSec is another new feature of Windows 2000. IPSec uses cryptography-based security to provide access control, connectionless integrity, data origin authentication, protection against replays, confidentiality, and limited traffic flow confidentiality. Because IPSec is provided at the IP layer, its services are available to the upper-layer protocols in the stack, and is transparently available to existing applications.

IPSec enables a system to select security protocols, decide which algorithms to use for the services, and to establish and maintain cryptographic keys for each security relationship. IPSec can protect paths between hosts, between security gateways, or between hosts and security gateways. The services available and required for traffic are configured using IPSec policy. IPSec policy can be configured locally on a computer, or can be assigned through Windows 2000 Group Policy mechanisms using Active Directory™. When using Active Directory, hosts detect policy assignment at startup, retrieve the policy, and periodically check for policy updates. The IPSec policy specifies how computers trust each other. The easiest trust to use is the Windows 2000 domain trust based on the Kerberos protocol. Predefined IPSec policies are configured to trust computers in the same or other trusted Windows 2000 domains.

Each IP datagram processed at the IP layer is compared against a set of filters that are provided by the security policy, which is maintained by an administrator for a computer, user, group, or a whole domain. IP can do one of three things with a datagram:

- Provide IPSec services to it
- Allow it to pass unmodified
- Discard it

Setting up IPSec involves describing the traffic characteristics on which to filter (such as source or destination IP address, protocol, and port) and then specifying what service characteristics to apply to traffic that matches the filters. For example, in a very simple case, two stand-alone computers can be configured to use IPSec between them by being members of the same Windows 2000 domain and activating the lockdown policy. If the two computers are not members of the same domain or a trusted domain, then trust must be configured using a password or "pre-shared" key in lockdown mode by:

- Setting up a filter that specifies all traffic between the two hosts.
- Choosing an authentication method. (Select pre-shared key, and enter a password.)
- Selecting a negotiation policy ("lockdown" in this case, indicating that all traffic matching the filters must use IPSec).
- Specifying a connection type (LAN, dial-up, or all).

Once the policy has been put in place, traffic matching the filters use the services provided by IPSec. When IP traffic (including something as simple as a ping in this case) is directed at one host by another, a Security Association (SA) is established via a short conversation over UDP port 500, (using the Internet Security Architecture Key Management Protocol, or ISAKMP), and then the traffic begins to flow.

Because IPSec typically encrypts the entire IP payload, capturing an IPSec datagram sent after the SA is established reveals very little of what is actually in the datagram. The only parts of the packet that can be parsed by Network Monitor are the Ethernet and IP headers.

IPSec features and implementation details are described in detail in "Internet Protocol Security" in this book.

Internet Group Management Protocol

Windows 2000 provides level 2 (full) support for IP multicasting and the Internet Group Management Protocol (IGMP) version 2 as described in RFC 1112 and RFC 2236. See "Introduction to TCP/IP" in this book for an overview of IP multicasting and IGMP.

Host group addresses are in the class D range 224.0.0.0 to 239.255.255.255 (as defined by setting the first four high order bits to 1110). Multicast addresses in the range 224.0.0.0 to 224.0.0.255 are reserved for local subnets and are not forwarded by IP routers regardless of the TTL in the IP header.

Multicast Route

To support IP multicasting, an additional route is defined on the host. The route specifies that if a datagram is being sent to a multicast host group, it should be sent to the IP address of the host group via the local interface card, and not forwarded to the default gateway. The following route illustrates this:

```
Network Destination        Netmask          Gateway       Interface  Metric
          224.0.0.0      224.0.0.0       10.1.1.99       10.1.1.99       1
```

Mapping Multicast IP Addresses to MAC Addresses

Multicast IP traffic does not use ARP to resolve the destination MAC address for the outbound IP datagram. To support IP multicasting, the Internet authorities have reserved the Ethernet multicast address range of 01-00-5E-00-00-00 to 01-00-5E-7F-FF-FF for IP multicast traffic. The high order 25 bits of the 48-bit Ethernet address are fixed and the low order 23 bits are variable, as shown in Figure 2.3.

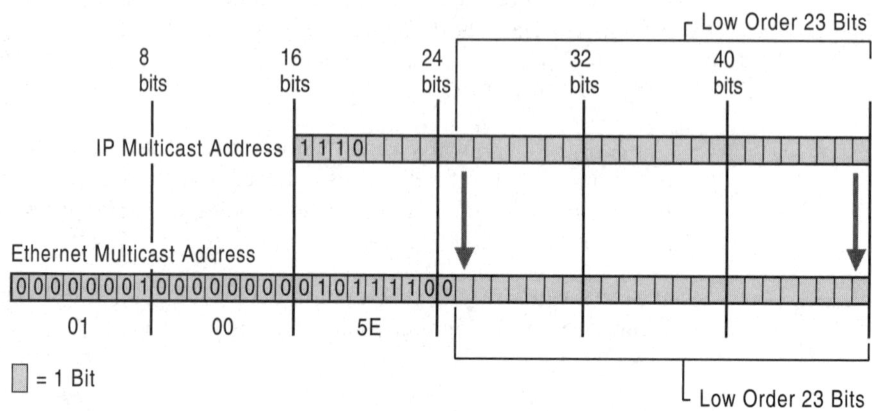

Figure 2.3 Mapping IP Multicast Addresses to Ethernet Media Access Control Addresses

To map an IP multicast address to an Ethernet multicast address, the low order 23 bits of the IP multicast address are mapped directly to the low order 23 bits in the Ethernet multicast address. Because the first 4 bits of an IP multicast address are fixed according to the Class D convention, there are 5 bits in the IP multicast address that do not map to the Ethernet multicast address. Therefore, it is possible for an Ethernet host to attempt to process IP multicast packets for groups to which it does not belong. These extra multicasts are silently discarded.

For example, a datagram addressed to the multicast address 225.0.0.5 would be sent to the Ethernet MAC address 0x01-00-5E-00-00-05. This MAC address is formed by the junction of 01-00-5E and the 23 low-order bits of 225.0.0.5 (0x00-00-05).

Fiber Data Distributed Interface (FDDI) also maps IP multicast addresses to MAC addresses.

Due to the nature of Token Ring MAC-level addressing and the limitation of Token Ring adapters, all IP multicast traffic is mapped to the Token Ring functional MAC address of 0xC0-00-00-04-00-00.

Multicast Extensions to Windows Sockets

IP multicasting is currently supported only on IP protocol family datagram and raw sockets. By default, IP multicast datagrams are sent with a TTL of 1. Applications can use the Windows Sockets **setsockopt( )** function to specify a TTL.

By convention, multicast routers use TTL thresholds to determine how far to forward datagrams. These TTL thresholds are defined as follows:

- Multicast datagrams with initial TTL 0 are restricted to the same host.
- Multicast datagrams with initial TTL 1 are restricted to the same subnet.
- Multicast datagrams with initial TTL 32 are restricted to the same site.
- Multicast datagrams with initial TTL 64 are restricted to the same region.
- Multicast datagrams with initial TTL 128 are restricted to the same continent.
- Multicast datagrams with initial TTL 255 are unrestricted in scope.

Use of IP Multicasting by Windows 2000 Components

The following Windows 2000 protocols and services use IP multicast traffic:

- ICMP Router Discovery (224.0.0.1, the all-hosts multicast address, and 224.0.0.2, the all-routers multicast address).
- RIP version 2 (224.0.0.9), used by Routing and Remote Access service.
- OSPF (224.0.0.5 and 224.0.0.6), used by Routing and Remote Access service.
- Site Server Lightweight Directory Access Protocol (LDAP) service is used to advertise IP multicast conferences on the network. You can also use it to publish user IP address mappings for H.323 IP telephony.
- WINS servers use multicasting (224.0.1.24) when attempting to locate replication partners. For more information about WINS, see "Windows Internet Name Service" in this book.

Transmission Control Protocol

Transmission Control Protocol (TCP) provides a connection-based, reliable byte-stream service to applications. Microsoft networking relies upon TCP for the logon process, file and print sharing, replication of information between domain controllers, transfer of browse lists, and other common functions. It can only be used for one-to-one communications. Windows 2000 TCP is compliant with RFC 793 and section 4.2 of RFC 1122.

TCP uses a checksum that checks for transmission errors on both the TCP header and payload of each segment to reduce the chance of network corruption going undetected. NDIS 5.0 provides support for task offloading, and Windows 2000 TCP takes advantage of this by allowing the network adapter to perform the TCP checksum calculations if the network adapter driver offers support for this function. Offloading the checksum calculations to hardware can result in performance improvements in very high throughput environments. The robustness of Windows 2000 TCP has also been improved and has been subject to an internal security review intended to reduce susceptibility to future hacker attacks.

TCP Receive Window Size Calculation and Window Scaling

The TCP receive window size is the amount of receive data (in bytes) that can be buffered at one time on a connection. The sending host can send only that amount of data before waiting for acknowledgments for data sent and window updates from the receiving host. Windows 2000 TCP/IP is designed to tune itself in most environments, and uses larger default window sizes than earlier versions.

Instead of using a hard-coded default receive window size, TCP adjusts to even increments of the maximum segment size (MSS) negotiated during connection setup. Matching the receive window to even increments of the MSS increases the percentage of full-sized TCP segments used during bulk data transmission.

The receive window size defaults to a value calculated as follows:

1. The first connection request sent to a remote host advertises a receive window size of 16 kilobytes (KB) or 16,384 bytes.
2. Upon establishing the connection, the receive window size is rounded up to an integral multiple of the TCP maximum segment size (MSS) that was negotiated during connection setup.
3. If the rounded-up value is not at least four times the MSS, then it is adjusted to 4 * MSS, with a maximum size of 64 KB, unless a window scaling option (RFC 1323) is in effect.

For Ethernet-based TCP connections, the window is normally set to 17,520 bytes, or 16 KB rounded up to twelve 1,460-byte segments. In previous versions of Microsoft® Windows NT® TCP/IP, the Ethernet window used was 8,760 bytes, or six MSS-sized segments.

There are two methods for setting the receive window size to specific values:

- The **TcpWindowSize** registry entry (HKLM\SYSTEM\CurrentControlSet\Services\Tcpip\Parameters\Interface\ <*interface*>).
- On a per-socket basis with the **setsockopt( )** Windows Sockets function.

To improve performance on high-bandwidth, high-delay networks, Windows 2000 TCP supports *TCP window scaling* described in RFC 1323. TCP window scaling supports TCP receive window sizes larger that 64 KB by negotiating a window scaling factor during the TCP three-way handshake. This allows for a receive window of up to 1 gigabyte (GB).

When you read captures of a connection that was established by two computers that support scalable windows, keep in mind that the window sizes advertised in the segment must be scaled by the negotiated scale factor. The window scale factor only appears in the first two segments of the TCP three-way handshake. The scale factor is 2^s, where s is the negotiated scale factor. For example, for an advertised window size of 65535 and a scale factor of 3, the actual receive window size is 524280, or $2^3 * 65535$.

The following Network Monitor capture shows the window scale option in the TCP SYN segment:

```
  Src Addr   Dst Addr  Protocol  Description
  HOST100   CORPSRVR   TCP       ....S., len:0, seq:725163-725163,
ack:0, win:65535, src:1217 dst:139

 + FRAME: Base frame properties
 + ETHERNET: ETYPE = 0x0800 : Protocol = IP:  DOD Internet Protocol
 + IP: ID = 0xB908; Proto = TCP; Len: 64
   TCP: ....S., len:0, seq:725163-725163, ack:0, win:65535, src:1217
dst:139 (NBT Session)
       TCP: Source Port = 0x04C1
       TCP: Destination Port = NETBIOS Session Service
       TCP: Sequence Number = 725163 (0xB10AB)
       TCP: Acknowledgement Number = 0 (0x0)
       TCP: Data Offset = 44 (0x2C)
       TCP: Reserved = 0 (0x0000)
     + TCP: Flags = 0x02 : ....S.
       TCP: Window = 65535 (0xFFFF)
       TCP: Checksum = 0x8565
       TCP: Urgent Pointer = 0 (0x0)
       TCP: Options
         + TCP: Maximum Segment Size Option
           TCP: Option Nop = 1 (0x1)
           TCP: Window Scale Option
               TCP: Option Type = Window Scale
               TCP: Option Length = 3 (0x3)
               TCP: Window Scale = 5 (0x5)
           TCP: Option Nop = 1 (0x1)
           TCP: Option Nop = 1 (0x1)
         + TCP: Timestamps Option
           TCP: Option Nop = 1 (0x1)
           TCP: Option Nop = 1 (0x1)
         + TCP: SACK Permitted Option
```

TCP window scaling is enabled by default and used automatically whenever the TCP window size for the connection is set to a value greater than 64 kilobytes (KB), either through the **TCPWindowSize** registry entry (HKLM\SYSTEM\CurrentControlSet\Services\Tcpip\Parameters\Interface \\<*interface*>) or through the **setsockopt( )** Windows Sockets function. TCP window scaling can be enabled through the **Tcp1323Opts** registry entry (HKLM\SYSTEM\CurrentControlSet\Services\Tcpip\Parameters).

Delayed Acknowledgments

As specified in RFC 1122, TCP uses delayed acknowledgments (ACKs) to reduce the number of packets sent on the media. Rather than sending an acknowledgment for each TCP segment received, Windows 2000 TCP takes a common approach to implementing delayed ACKs. As data is received by TCP on a given connection, it only sends an acknowledgment back if one of the following conditions is met:

- No ACK was sent for the previous segment received.
- A segment is received, but no other segment arrives within 200 milliseconds for that connection.

Normally an ACK is sent for every other TCP segment received on a connection, unless the delayed ACK timer (200 milliseconds) expires. The delayed ACK timer for each interface can be adjusted by setting the value of the **TCPDelAckTicks** registry entry (HKLM\SYSTEM\CurrentControlSet\Services\Tcpip\Parameters\Interfaces \<*interface*>), which was first introduced in Microsoft® Windows NT® version 4.0, Service Pack 4.

TCP Selective Acknowledgment

Windows 2000 introduces support for an important performance feature known as *Selective Acknowledgment* (SACK), described in RFC 2018. SACK is very important for connections using large TCP window sizes. Prior to SACK, a receiver could only acknowledge the latest sequence number of contiguous data that had been received, or the left edge of the receive window. With SACK enabled, the receiver continues to use the ACK number to acknowledge the left edge of the receive window, but the receiver can also individually acknowledge other non-contiguous blocks of received data.

SACK uses TCP header options to negotiate the use of SACK during the TCP connection establishment and to indicate the left edge and right edge of blocks of data received. Multiple blocks received can be indicated. For more details, see RFC 2018. By default, SACK is enabled.

When a segment or series of segments arrive in a non-contiguous fashion, the receiver is able to inform the sender of exactly which data has been received, implicitly indicating which data did not arrive. The sender can selectively retransmit the missing data without needing to retransmit blocks of data that have been successfully received. SACK is enabled by default through the value of the **SackOpts** registry entry (HKLM\SYSTEM\CurrentControlSet\Services\Tcpip\Parameters).

The following Network Monitor capture shows a host acknowledging all data up to sequence number 54857340, plus the data from sequence number 54858789-54861684.

```
 + FRAME: Base frame properties
 + ETHERNET: ETYPE = 0x0800 : Protocol = IP:  DOD Internet Protocol
 + IP: ID = 0x1A0D; Proto = TCP; Len: 64
   TCP: .A...., len:0, seq:925104-925104, ack:54857341, win:32722,
src:1242  dst:139
       TCP: Source Port = 0x04DA
       TCP: Destination Port = NETBIOS Session Service
       TCP: Sequence Number = 925104 (0xE1DB0)
       TCP: Acknowledgement Number = 54857341 (0x3450E7D)
       TCP: Data Offset = 44 (0x2C)
       TCP: Reserved = 0 (0x0000)
     + TCP: Flags = 0x10 : .A....
       TCP: Window = 32722 (0x7FD2)
       TCP: Checksum = 0x4A72
       TCP: Urgent Pointer = 0 (0x0)
       TCP: Options
           TCP: Option Nop = 1 (0x1)
           TCP: Option Nop = 1 (0x1)
         + TCP: Timestamps Option
           TCP: Option Nop = 1 (0x1)
           TCP: Option Nop = 1 (0x1)
           TCP: SACK Option
               TCP: Option Type = 0x05
               TCP: Option Length = 10 (0xA)
               TCP: Left Edge of Block  = 54858789 (0x3451425)
               TCP: Right Edge of Block = 54861685 (0x3451F75)
```

TCP Timestamps

In previous versions of Microsoft TCP/IP, TCP calculated the round trip time (RTT) for only one sample per window of data sent to adjust the retransmission time-out (RTO). To calculate the RTT, TCP recorded the time that the segment was sent and the time that an acknowledgement for the segment was received. For example, if the window size was 8760 (six full segments), a common value for Ethernet, one in six segments were used to recalculate the round trip time. This is an adequate sampling rate for such a small window size. However, with support for TCP window scaling, sampling one segment for the entire window size is not sufficient. For example, with the maximum window size using window scaling of 1 GB over an Ethernet network, there would only be one sample for every 735,440 segments.

TCP timestamps are implemented as TCP header options that record the time a segment was sent, The timestamp of the sent TCP segment is echoed in the acknowledgement. For more details, see RFC 1323.

The following Network Monitor capture shows the TCP timestamps option:

```
+ FRAME: Base frame properties
+ ETHERNET: ETYPE = 0x0800 : Protocol = IP:  DOD Internet Protocol
+ IP: ID = 0x1A0D; Proto = TCP; Len: 64
  TCP: .A...., len:0, seq:925104-925104, ack:54857341, win:32722,
src:1242  dst:139
      TCP: Source Port = 0x04DA
      TCP: Destination Port = NETBIOS Session Service
      TCP: Sequence Number = 925104 (0xE1DB0)
      TCP: Acknowledgement Number = 54857341 (0x3450E7D)
      TCP: Data Offset = 44 (0x2C)
      TCP: Reserved = 0 (0x0000)
    + TCP: Flags = 0x10 : .A....
      TCP: Window = 32722 (0x7FD2)
      TCP: Checksum = 0x4A72
      TCP: Urgent Pointer = 0 (0x0)
      TCP: Options
          TCP: Option Nop = 1 (0x1)
          TCP: Option Nop = 1 (0x1)
          TCP: Timestamps Option
            TCP: Option Type = Timestamps
            TCP: Option Length = 10 (0xA)
            TCP: Timestamp = 2525186 (0x268802)
            TCP: Reply Timestamp = 1823192 (0x1BD1D8)
          TCP: Option Nop = 1 (0x1)
          TCP: Option Nop = 1 (0x1)
        + TCP: SACK Option
```

TCP timestamps are disabled by default. You can enable TCP timestamps by changing the value of the **Tcp1323Opts** registry entry (HKLM\SYSTEM\CurrentControlSet\Services\Tcpip\Parameters).

Protection Against Wrapped Sequence Numbers

Using TCP timestamps provides *protection against wrapped sequence numbers* (PAWS). The TCP sequence number is a 32-bit value that indicates the first byte of data in the segment. With 32 bits in the sequence number, only 4 GB of data can be in transit between the sender and the receiver before the TCP sequence number begins to wrap around and become ambiguous. While this is not likely in typical Ethernet and Token Ring environments, high capacity networks using Gigabit per second (Gbps) or Terabit per second (Tbps) technologies can wrap the TCP sequence number in a matter of seconds. If a segment is dropped or delayed, a different segment could exist with the same sequence number. Corrupted data could result from the receiver misinterpreting the new sequence number with an old sequence number it is expecting to receive.

To avoid confusion in the event of duplicate sequence numbers, the TCP timestamp is used as an extension to the sequence number. Current packets have current and progressing timestamps. An old packet has an older timestamp and is discarded.

Dead Gateway Detection

Dead gateway detection is used by TCP traffic to detect the failure of the default gateway and to make an adjustment to the IP routing table to use another default gateway. Windows 2000 TCP/IP uses the triggered reselection method described in RFC 816, with slight modifications.

When any TCP connection that is routed through the default gateway has attempted to send a TCP packet to the destination a number of times equal to one-half of the value of the registry entry **TcpMaxDataRetransmissions** (default value of 5) without receiving a response, the forwarding IP address for the Destination IP Address is changed to use the next default gateway in the list. When 25 percent of the TCP connections have moved to the next default gateway, TCP informs IP to update the default route for the IP address of the next default gateway, the one that the changed connections are now using.

For example, assume that for a host:

- There are TCP connections to 11 different IP addresses that are routed through the default gateway.
- The host has multiple default gateways configured.
- **TcpMaxDataRetransmissions** is set at the default value of 5.

When the default gateway fails, the following process switches the default gateway to the next one in the list:

1. When the first TCP connection tries to send data, it does not receive any acknowledgments. After the third retransmission, the forwarding IP address for that remote IP address is switched to use the next default gateway in the list. At this point, any TCP connections to that remote IP address are switched over to the new default gateway, but the remaining connections will still try to use the original default gateway.
2. When the second TCP connection tries to send data, the same thing happens. Now, two of the 11 connections are using the new gateway.

3. When the third TCP connection tries to send data, its default gateway is changed to the next default gateway in the list. Three of 11 connections have been switched to the second default gateway. Because over 25 percent of the connections have been changed, the Gateway IP address for the default route in the routing table is updated with the IP address of the new gateway.
4. The new default gateway remains the primary one for the computer until it experiences problems, causing dead gateway detection to switch to the next gateway in the list again, or until the computer is restarted.

When the search reaches the last default gateway, it returns to the beginning of the list.

TCP Retransmission Behavior

TCP starts a retransmission timer when each outbound segment is handed down to IP. If no acknowledgment is received for the data in a given segment before the timer expires, then the segment is retransmitted. For new connection requests, the retransmission timer is initialized to three seconds, and the TCP connection request segment is resent up to the number of times specified by the value of **TcpMaxConnectRetransmissions** (2 by default) registry entry (HKLM\SYSTEM\CurrentControlSet\Services\Tcpip\Parameters). On existing connections, the number of retransmissions is controlled by the the value of the **TcpMaxDataRetransmissions** registry entry (5 by default) (HKLM\SYSTEM\CurrentControlSet\Services\Tcpip\Parameters).

The retransmission time-out (RTO) is adjusted on an ongoing basis to match the characteristics of the connection using Smoothed Round Trip Time (SRTT) calculations and Karn's algorithm. For more information about Karn's algorithm, see "Additional Resources" later in this chapter.

The timer for a given segment is doubled after each retransmission of that segment. Using this algorithm, TCP tunes itself to the "normal" delay of a connection. TCP connections over high-delay links take much longer to time out than those over low-delay links.

The following Network Monitor capture shows the retransmission algorithm for two hosts connected over Ethernet on the same subnet. An FTP file transfer was in progress when the receiving host was disconnected from the network. Because the SRTT for this connection was very small, the first retransmission was sent after about one-half second. The timer was then doubled for each of the retransmissions that followed. After the fifth retransmission, the timer was once again doubled, and since no acknowledgment was received before it expired, the connection was aborted.

```
 time  source ip    dest ip      pro flags description
 0.000  10.57.10.32  10.57.9.138  TCP .A.., len: 1460, seq: 8043781, ack:
8153124, win: 8760
 0.521  10.57.10.32  10.57.9.138  TCP .A.., len: 1460, seq: 8043781, ack:
8153124, win: 8760
 1.001  10.57.10.32  10.57.9.138  TCP .A.., len: 1460, seq: 8043781, ack:
8153124, win: 8760
 2.003  10.57.10.32  10.57.9.138  TCP .A.., len: 1460, seq: 8043781, ack:
8153124, win: 8760
 4.007  10.57.10.32  10.57.9.138  TCP .A.., len: 1460, seq: 8043781, ack:
8153124, win: 8760
 8.130  10.57.10.32  10.57.9.138  TCP .A.., len: 1460, seq: 8043781, ack:
8153124, win: 8760
```

Fast Retransmit

There are some circumstances under which TCP retransmits data prior to the retransmission timer expiring. The most common circumstance occurs due to a feature known as *fast retransmit*. When a receiver that supports fast retransmit receives data with a sequence number beyond the current expected one, then it is likely that some data was dropped. To help make the sender aware of this event, the receiver immediately sends an ACK with the acknowledgment number set to the sequence number that it was expecting. It continues to do this for each additional TCP segment that arrives containing data subsequent to the missing data in the incoming stream.

When the sender starts to receive a stream of ACKs that are acknowledging the same sequence number, and that sequence number is earlier than the current sequence number being sent, it can infer that a segment (or segments) has been dropped. Senders that support the fast retransmit algorithm immediately resend the segment that the receiver is expecting to fill in the gap in data, without waiting for the retransmission timer to expire for that segment. This optimization greatly improves performance in a high-loss network environment.

By default, Windows 2000 resends a segment if it receives three ACKs for the same sequence number, and that sequence number lags the current one. The maximum number of duplicate ACKs that triggers a resend is determined by the value of the **TcpMaxDupAcks** registry entry (HKLM\SYSTEM\CurrentControlSet\Services\Tcpip\Parameters).

TCP Keep-Alive Messages

A TCP keep-alive packet is simply an ACK with the sequence number set to one less than the current sequence number for the connection. A host receiving one of these ACKs will respond with an ACK for the current sequence number. Keep-alives can be used to verify that the computer at the remote end of a connection is still available. Windows 2000 TCP keep-alive behavior can be modified by changing the values of the **KeepAliveTime** and **KeepAliveInterval** registry entries (HKLM\SYSTEM\CurrentControlSet\Services\Tcpip\Parameters). TCP keep-alives can be sent once for every interval specified by the value of **KeepAliveTime** (defaults to 7,200,000 milliseconds, or two hours) if no other data or higher level keep-alives have been carried over the TCP connection. If there is no response to a keep-alive, it is repeated once every interval specified by the value of **KeepAliveInterval** in seconds. By default, the **KeepAliveInterval** entry is set to a value of one second.

NetBT connections, such as those used by many Microsoft networking components, send NetBIOS keep-alives more frequently, so normally no TCP keep-alives are sent on a NetBIOS connection. TCP keep-alives are disabled by default, but Windows Sockets applications can use the Windows Sockets **setsockopt( )** function to enable them.

Slow Start Algorithm and Congestion Avoidance

Windows 2000 TCP is compliant with the slow start and congestion avoidance algorithms. For more information about slow start and congestion avoidance algorithms, see "Additional Resources" later in this chapter.

When a connection is established, TCP sends data slowly at first to assess the bandwidth of the connection and to avoid overwhelming the receiving host or any other devices or links in the path. The send window is set to two TCP segments, and when both segments are acknowledged, the send window is increased to three segments. If those are acknowledged, then the send window is increased again, and so on until the amount of data being sent per burst reaches the size of the receive window advertised by the remote host. At that point, the slow start algorithm is no longer in use and flow control is governed by the advertised receive window.

At any time during transmission, congestion can occur. Congestion is detected when a retransmission timer expires, or when a host receives an ICMP Source Quench message for a TCP segment that was discarded by a router. If this happens, the TCP congestion avoidance algorithm is used to reduce the send window size and gradually grow it back to half the size of the send window when the congestion occurred. Then, the slow start algorithm is used to grow the send window up to the size of the receive window of the receiving host.

Silly Window Syndrome

Silly Window Syndrome (SWS) is the advertising of receive window sizes that are less than a full TCP segment. Silly Window Syndrome can cause very small TCP segments to be sent, resulting in an inefficient use of the network. Windows 2000 TCP/IP implements sender and receiver SWS avoidance as specified in RFC 1122. Receiver-side SWS avoidance is implemented by not opening the receive window in increments of less than a TCP segment. Sender-side SWS avoidance is implemented by not sending more data until there is a sufficient window size advertised by the receiving end to send a full TCP segment. There are exceptions to this rule for sender-side SWS avoidance, as described in RFC 1122.

Nagle Algorithm

Windows 2000 TCP/IP implements the Nagle algorithm, described in RFC 896. The purpose of this algorithm is to reduce the number of small segments sent, especially on high-delay (remote) links. A small segment is a segment that is smaller than the MSS. The Nagle algorithm allows only one small segment to be outstanding at a time without acknowledgment.

If more small segments are generated while awaiting the ACK for the first one, then these segments are accumulated into one larger segment. Any full-sized segment is transmitted immediately, assuming there is a sufficient receive window available. The Nagle algorithm is effective in reducing the number of packets sent by interactive applications, such as Telnet, especially over slow links.

The Nagle algorithm can be observed in the following Network Monitor capture. A Telnet (character mode) session was established, then the Y key was held down on the Windows 2000 workstation. At all times, one segment was sent, and further Y characters were held by the stack until an acknowledgment was received for the previous segment. In this example, three to four Y characters were buffered each time and sent together in one segment. Due to the Nagle algorithm, the number of segments sent was reduced by a factor of about three.

```
Time  Source IP     Dest IP       Prot   Description
0.644 204.182.66.83 199.181.164.4 TELNET To Server Port = 1901
0.144 199.181.164.4 204.182.66.83 TELNET To Client Port = 1901
0.000 204.182.66.83 199.181.164.4 TELNET To Server Port = 1901
0.145 199.181.164.4 204.182.66.83 TELNET To Client Port = 1901
0.000 204.182.66.83 199.181.164.4 TELNET To Server Port = 1901
0.144 199.181.164.4 204.182.66.83 TELNET To Client Port = 1901
. . .
```

Each segment contained several of the Y characters. The first segment is shown more fully parsed below, and the data portion is bolded in the hexadecimal display at the bottom.

```
Time  Source IP      Dest IP        Prot    Description
0.644 204.182.66.83  199.181.164.4  TELNET  To Server Port = 1901

+ FRAME: Base frame properties
+ ETHERNET: ETYPE = 0x0800 : Protocol = IP: DOD Internet Protocol
+ IP: ID = 0xEA83; Proto = TCP; Len: 43
+ TCP: .AP..., len: 3, seq:1032660278, ack: 353339017, win: 7766, src:
1901 dst: 23 (TELNET)
  TELNET: To Server From Port = 1901
    TELNET: Telnet Data

D2 41 53 48 00 00 52 41 53 48 00 00 08 00 45 00  .ASH..RASH....E.
00 2B EA 83 40 00 20 06 F5 85 CC B6 42 53 C7 B5  .+..@. .....BS..
A4 04 07 6D 00 17 3D 8D 25 36 15 0F 86 89 50 18  ...m..=.%6....P.
1E 56 1E 56 00 00 79 79 79                       .V.V..yyy
```

Windows Sockets applications can disable the Nagle algorithm for their connections by setting the **TCP_NODELAY** socket option. However, this practice should be avoided unless absolutely necessary as it increases network utilization. Some network applications might not perform well if their design does not take into account the effects of transmitting large numbers of small packets and the Nagle algorithm.

The Nagle algorithm is not applied to loopback TCP connections for performance reasons. Windows 2000 Netbt disables nagling for NetBIOS over TCP connections as well as NetBIOS-less redirector/server connections, which can improve performance for applications issuing numerous small file manipulation commands. An example is an application that uses file locking/unlocking frequently.

TCP TIME-WAIT Delay

When a TCP connection is closed, the socket pair is placed into a state known as TIME-WAIT so that a new connection does not use the same protocol, source IP address, destination IP address, source port, and destination port until enough time has passed to ensure that any segments that have been misrouted or delayed will not be delivered unexpectedly. The length of time that the socket-pair should not be reused is specified by RFC 793 as two maximum segment lifetimes (2MSL) or 240 seconds (four minutes). This is the default setting for Windows 2000. However, with this default setting, some network applications that perform many outbound connections in a short time might use up all available ports before the ports can be recycled.

Windows 2000 offers two methods of controlling this behavior. First, the **TcpTimedWaitDelay** registry entry (HKLM\SYSTEM\CurrentControlSet\Services\Tcpip\Parameters) can be used to alter this value. Windows 2000 allows this value to be set as low as 30 seconds, which should not cause problems in most environments. Second, the number of user-accessible ephemeral ports that can be used to source outbound connections is configurable with the **MaxUserPort** registry entry (HKLM\SYSTEM\CurrentControlSet\Services\Tcpip\Parameters). By default, when an application requests any socket from the system to use for an outbound call, a port between the values of 1024 and 5000 is supplied. You can use the **MaxUserPort** registry entry to set the value of the highest port number to be used for outbound connections. For example, setting this value to 10000 would make approximately 9000 user ports available for outbound connections. For more details, see RFC 793. See also the **MaxFreeTcbs** and **MaxHashTableSize** registry settings (HKLM\SYSTEM\CurrentControlSet\Services\Tcpip\Parameters).

TCP Connections To and From Multihomed Computers

When TCP connections are made to a multihomed host, both the WINS client and the Domain Name Resolver (DNR) attempt to determine whether any of the destination IP addresses provided by the name server are on the same subnet as any of the interfaces in the local computer. If so, these addresses are sorted to the top of the list so that the application can try them prior to trying addresses that are not on the same subnet. If none of the addresses are on a common subnet with the local computer, then behavior is different depending upon the namespace. The **PrioritizeRecordData** registry setting (HKLM\SYSTEM\CurrentControlSet\Services\Tcpip\Parameters) can be used to prevent the DNR component from sorting local subnet addresses to the top of the list.

In the WINS namespace, the client is responsible for choosing a random address among the provided addresses. The WINS server always returns the list of addresses in the same order, and the WINS client randomly picks one of them for each connection.

In the DNS namespace, the DNS server is usually configured to provide the addresses in round-robin order. The DNR does not choose a random address. In some situations, it is desirable to connect to a specific interface on a multihomed computer. The best way to accomplish this is to provide the interface with its own DNS entry. For example, a computer named Computer could have two separate DNS records with the same name, one for each IP address, and then records in the DNS for Computer1 and Computer2, each associated with just one of the IP addresses assigned to the computer.

For TCP connections made from a multihomed host, if the connection is a Winsock connection using the DNS namespace, once the target IP address for the connection is known, TCP attempts to connect from the best source IP address available. The IP routing table is used to make this determination, and if there is an interface in the local computer that is on the same subnet as the target IP address, its IP address is used as the source in the connection request. If there is no best source IP address to use, then the system chooses one randomly.

If the connection is a NetBIOS-based connection using the redirector, little routing information is available at the application level. The NetBIOS interface supports connections over various protocols and has no knowledge of IP. Instead, the redirector places calls on all of the logical networks that are bound to it. If there are two interfaces in the computer and one protocol installed, then there are two logical networks available to the redirector. Calls are placed on both, and NetBIOS over TCP/IP (NetBT) will submit connection requests to the stack using an IP addresses from each interface. It is possible that both calls will succeed. If so, then the redirector will cancel one of them. The choice of which one to cancel depends upon the value of the **ObeyBindingOrder** registry entry. If the value of this entry is 0, the default value, then the primary logical network determined by binding order is the preferred one, and the redirector waits for the primary transport to time out before accepting the connection on the secondary transport. If this value is 1, the binding order is ignored and the redirector accepts the first connection that succeeds and cancels any other connections.

Throughput Considerations

Windows 2000 TCP/IP can adapt to most network conditions, and can dynamically provide the best throughput and reliability possible on a per-connection basis. Attempts at manual tuning are often counter-productive unless a qualified network engineer first performs a careful study of data flow.

TCP is designed to provide optimum performance over varying link conditions, and Windows 2000 contains improvements, such as those supporting RFC 1323. Actual throughput for a link depends on a number of variables, but the most important factors are:

- Link speed (bits/second that can be transmitted).
- Propagation delay.
- Window size (amount of unacknowledged data that might be outstanding on a TCP connection).
- Link reliability.
- Network and intermediate device congestion.

Key considerations of throughput:

- The capacity of a communications channel, also known as a pipe, is known as the bandwidth-delay product and is the bandwidth (the bit rate) multiplied by round-trip time. If the link has a low number of bit level errors, the window size for best performance should be greater than or equal to the bandwidth-delay product so that the sender can fill the pipe. Without window scaling, 65,535 is the largest window size that can be specified due to the 16-bit Window field in the TCP header. Window scaling can be used for window sizes up to 1 GB.
- Throughput can never exceed the window size divided by round-trip time.
- If the link has a large number of bit-level errors or is badly congested and packets are being dropped, using a larger window size might not improve throughput. Windows 2000 supports SACK, for improved performance in high-loss environments, and TCP timestamps, for improved RTT estimation.
- Propagation delay is dependent upon the speed of transmission of electrical or optical signals in various media and latencies in transmission equipment and intermediate systems.
- Transmission delay depends on the speed of the media and the nature of the media access control scheme.
- For a particular path, propagation delay is fixed, but transmission delay depends upon the packet size and congestion.
- At low speeds, transmission delay is the limiting factor. At high speeds, propagation delay might become the limiting factor.

User Datagram Protocol

User Datagram Protocol (UDP) provides a connectionless, unreliable transport service. It is often used for one-to-many communications that use broadcast or multicast IP datagrams. As delivery of UDP datagrams is not guaranteed, applications using UDP must compensate for dropped UDP datagrams through simple retransmission or other reliable mechanisms. Microsoft networking uses UDP for logging on, browsing, and NetBIOS name resolution. UDP can also used to carry IP multicast streams for applications such as Microsoft® NetShow™.

UDP and Name Resolution

UDP is used for NetBIOS name resolution via unicast to a NetBIOS name server or via subnet broadcasts, and for Domain Name System (DNS) host name to IP address resolution. NetBIOS name resolution is accomplished over UDP port 137. DNS queries use UDP port 53. Because UDP itself does not guarantee delivery of datagrams, both of these services use their own retransmission schemes if they receive no answer to queries. Broadcast UDP datagrams are not usually forwarded over IP routers, so NetBIOS name resolution in a routed environment requires a name server such as a Windows Internet Name Service (WINS) server, or the use of a static database file such as the Lmhosts file.

Mailslots Over UDP

Many NetBIOS applications use mailslot messaging. A second-class mailslot is a simple mechanism for sending a message from one NetBIOS name to another over UDP. Mailslot messages can be broadcast on a subnet or directed to a specific host.

Network Application Interfaces

There are a number of ways that network applications can communicate using the TCP/IP protocol stack. Some of them, such as named pipes, go through the network redirector, which is part of the workstation service. Many older applications were written to the NetBIOS interface, which is supported by NetBIOS over TCP/IP. An overview of the Windows Sockets Interface and the NetBIOS Interface is presented in this section.

Windows Sockets

Windows Sockets specifies a programming interface based on the familiar socket interface from the University of California at Berkeley. It includes a set of extensions designed to take advantage of the message-driven nature of Microsoft Windows. Version 1.1 of the specification was released in January 1993, and version 2.2.0 was published in May of 1996. Windows 2000 supports version 2.2, commonly referred to as Winsock2.

Applications

There are many Windows Sockets applications available. A number of the tools that come with Windows 2000 are based on Windows Sockets, such as the Ping and Tracert tools, FTP and DHCP clients and servers, and Telnet client. There are also higher-level programming interfaces that rely on Winsock, such as the Windows Internet API (WININET) used by Microsoft® Internet Explorer.

Name and Address Resolution

Windows Sockets applications generally use the **gethostbyname( )** function to resolve a host name to an IP address. By default, the **gethostbyname( )** function uses the following name lookup sequence:

1. Check to see if the requested name matches the hosts host name.
2. Check the hosts file for a matching name entry.
3. If a DNS server is configured, query it.
4. If no match is found, try the NetBIOS name resolution sequence described in "NetBIOS Over TCP/IP" later in this chapter, up until the point at which DNS resolution is attempted.

Some applications use the **gethostbyaddr( )** function to resolve an IP address to a host name. The **gethostbyaddr( )** call uses the following (default) sequence:

1. Check the hosts file for a matching address entry.
2. If a DNS server is configured, query it.
3. Send a NetBIOS Adapter Status Request to the IP address being queried, and if it responds with a list of NetBIOS names registered for the adapter, parse it for the computer name.

Support for IP Multicasting

Winsock2 provides support for IP multicasting. Multicasting is described in the Windows Sockets 2.0 specification and in "Internet Group Management Protocol" earlier in this chapter. IP multicasting is currently supported only on IP family datagram and raw sockets.

Backlog Parameter

Windows Sockets server applications generally create a socket and then use the **listen()** function on the socket to receive connection requests. One of the parameters passed when using the **listen()** function is the backlog of connection requests that the application would like Windows Sockets to queue for the socket. The Windows Sockets 1.1 specification indicates that the maximum allowable value for backlog is 5; however, Microsoft® Windows NT® version 3.51 accepts a backlog of up to 100, Microsoft® Windows NT® 4.0 Server and Windows 2000 Server accepts a backlog of 200, and Microsoft® Windows NT® 4.0 Workstation and Windows 2000 Professional accepts a backlog of 5 (which reduces the memory footprint).

Push Bit Interpretation

By default, Windows 2000 TCP completes a Windows Sockets **recv( )** function when one of the following conditions is met:

- Data arrives with the push bit set. The push bit is used to indicate to TCP that the data in the TCP segment and all other data in the receive buffer (that is contiguous with this TCP segment) must be passed immediately to the application.
- The user **recv( )** buffer is full.
- 0.5 seconds have elapsed since any data has arrived.

If a client application is run on a computer with a TCP implementation that does not set the push bit on send operations, response delays might result. It is best to correct this on the client computer, however setting the the **IgnorePushBitOnReceives** registry entry (HKLM\SYSTEM\CurrentControlSet\Services\Afd\Parameters) to 1 can be used to treat all arriving packets as though the push bit were set.

NetBIOS Over TCP/IP

The Windows 2000 implementation of *NetBIOS over TCP/IP* is referred to as *NetBT*. NetBT uses the following TCP and UDP ports:

- UDP port 137 (name services)
- UDP port 138 (datagram services)
- TCP port 139 (session services)

NetBIOS over TCP/IP is specified by RFC 1001 and RFC 1002. The Netbt.sys driver is a kernel -mode component that supports the TDI interface. Services such as workstation and server use the TDI interface directly, while traditional NetBIOS applications have their calls mapped to TDI calls through the Netbios.sys driver. Using TDI to make calls to NetBT is a more difficult programming task, but can provide higher performance and freedom from historical NetBIOS limitations.

NetBIOS defines a software interface and a naming convention, not a protocol. NetBIOS over TCP/IP provides the NetBIOS programming interface over the TCP/IP protocol, extending the reach of NetBIOS client and server programs to the IP internetworks and providing interoperability with various other operating systems.

The Windows 2000 workstation service, server service, browser, messenger, and NetLogon services are all NetBT clients and use TDI to communicate with NetBT. Windows 2000 also includes a NetBIOS emulator. The emulator takes standard NetBIOS requests from NetBIOS applications and translates them to equivalent TDI functions.

Windows 2000 uses NetBIOS over TCP/IP to communicate with prior versions of Windows NT and other clients, such as Windows 95. However, the Windows 2000 redirector and server components now support direct hosting for communicating with other computers running Windows 2000. With direct hosting, NetBIOS is not used for name resolution. DNS is used for name resolution and the Microsoft networking communication is sent directly over TCP without a NetBIOS header. Direct hosting over TCP/IP uses TCP port 445 instead of the NetBIOS session TCP port 139.

By default, both NetBIOS and direct hosting are enabled, and both are tried in parallel when a new connection is established. The first to succeed in connecting is used for any given attempt. NetBIOS over TCP/IP support can be disabled to force all traffic to use TCP/IP direct hosting.

▶ **To disable NetBIOS over TCP/IP support**

1. From the **Network and Dial-up Connections** icon in **Control Panel**, select **Local Area Connection** and right-click **Properties**.
2. On the **General** tab, click **Internet Protocol (TCP/IP)** in the list of components, and click the **Properties** button.
3. Click the **Advanced** button.
4. Click the **WINS** tab. Click **Disable NetBIOS over TCP/IP**.

Applications and services that depend on NetBIOS over TCP/IP no longer function once NetBIOS over TCP/IP is disabled. Therefore, verify that any clients and applications no longer need NetBIOS over TCP/IP support before you disable it.

NetBIOS Names

The NetBIOS namespace is flat, meaning that all names within the namespace must be unique. NetBIOS names are 16 bytes long. Resources are identified by NetBIOS names, which are registered dynamically when services or applications start, or users log on. Names can be registered as unique names (one owner) or as group names (multiple owners). A NetBIOS Name Query is used to locate a resource by resolving the NetBIOS name to an IP address.

Microsoft networking components, such as the workstation and server services, allow the first 15 characters of a NetBIOS name to be specified by the user or administrator, but reserve the 16th character of the NetBIOS name to indicate a resource type (00-FF hex). Tables 2.2 and 2.3 have some example NetBIOS names used by Microsoft components:

Table 2.2 Unique NetBIOS Names Used by Microsoft Components

Unique Name	Service
<computer_name>[00] (space filled)[1]	Workstation Service
<computer_name>[03] (space filled)	Messenger Service
<computer_name>[06] (space filled)	RAS Server Service
<computer_name>[1F] (space filled)	NetDDE Service
<computer_name>[20] (space filled)	Server Service
<computer_name>[21] (space filled)	RAS Client Service
<computer_name>[BE] (0xBE filled)	Network Monitor Agent
<computer_name>[BF] (0xBF filled)	Network Monitor Application
<user_name>[03] (space filled)	Messenger Service
<domain_name>[1D] (space filled)	Master Browser
<domain_name>[1B] (space filled)	Domain Master Browser

1 The number in brackets is a hexadecimal number. (space filled) means that if the computer or domain name is not 15 characters long, the name is filled with spaces up to 15 characters.

Table 2.3 Group NetBIOS Names Used by Microsoft Components

Group Name	Service
<domain_name>[00] (space filled)	Domain Name
<domain_name>[1C] (space filled)	Domain Controllers
<domain_name>[1E] (space filled)	Browser Service Elections
[01h][01h]__MSBROWSE__[01h][01h]	Master Browser

NBTStat Tool

The NBTStat tool is used to view and register NetBIOS names on a Windows 2000 computer. To see which NetBIOS names a computer has registered over NetBT, type the following from a command prompt:

```
nbtstat -n
```

Windows 2000 allows you to reregister NetBIOS names with the name server after a computer has already been started. To reregister NetBIOS names, type the following from a command prompt:

```
nbtstat -RR
```

NetBIOS Name Registration and Resolution

Windows 2000 TCP/IP systems use several methods to locate NetBIOS resources:

- NetBIOS name cache.
- NetBIOS name server.
- IP subnet broadcasts.
- Static Lmhosts file.
- Static Hosts file (optional, depends on **EnableDns** registry entry (HKLM\SYSTEM\CurrentControlSet\Services\Netbt\Parameters)).
- DNS servers (optional, depends on **EnableDns** registry entry).

NetBIOS name resolution order depends upon the node type and system configuration. The following node types are supported:

- *B-node*—uses broadcasts for name registration and resolution.
- *P-node*—uses a NetBIOS Name Server for name registration and resolution.
- *M-node*—uses broadcasts for name registration. For name resolution, it tries broadcasts first, but switches to p-node if it receives no answer.
- *H-node*—uses NetBIOS name server for both registration and resolution. However, if no name server can be located, it switches to b-node. It continues to poll for name server and switches back to p-node when one becomes available.
- Microsoft-enhanced—uses the local Lmhosts file or WINS proxies plus Windows Sockets **gethostbyname( )** calls (using standard DNS and/or local Hosts files) in addition to standard node types.

Microsoft includes a NetBIOS name server known as the Windows Internet Name Service (WINS). Most WINS clients are set up as h-nodes; that is, they first attempt to register and resolve names using WINS, and if that fails, they try local subnet broadcasts. Using a name server to locate resources is generally preferable to broadcasting for two reasons:

- Broadcasts are not usually forwarded by routers.
- Broadcast frames are processed by all computers on a subnet.

Figures 2.4 through 2.5 illustrate the NetBIOS name resolution methods used by Windows 2000.

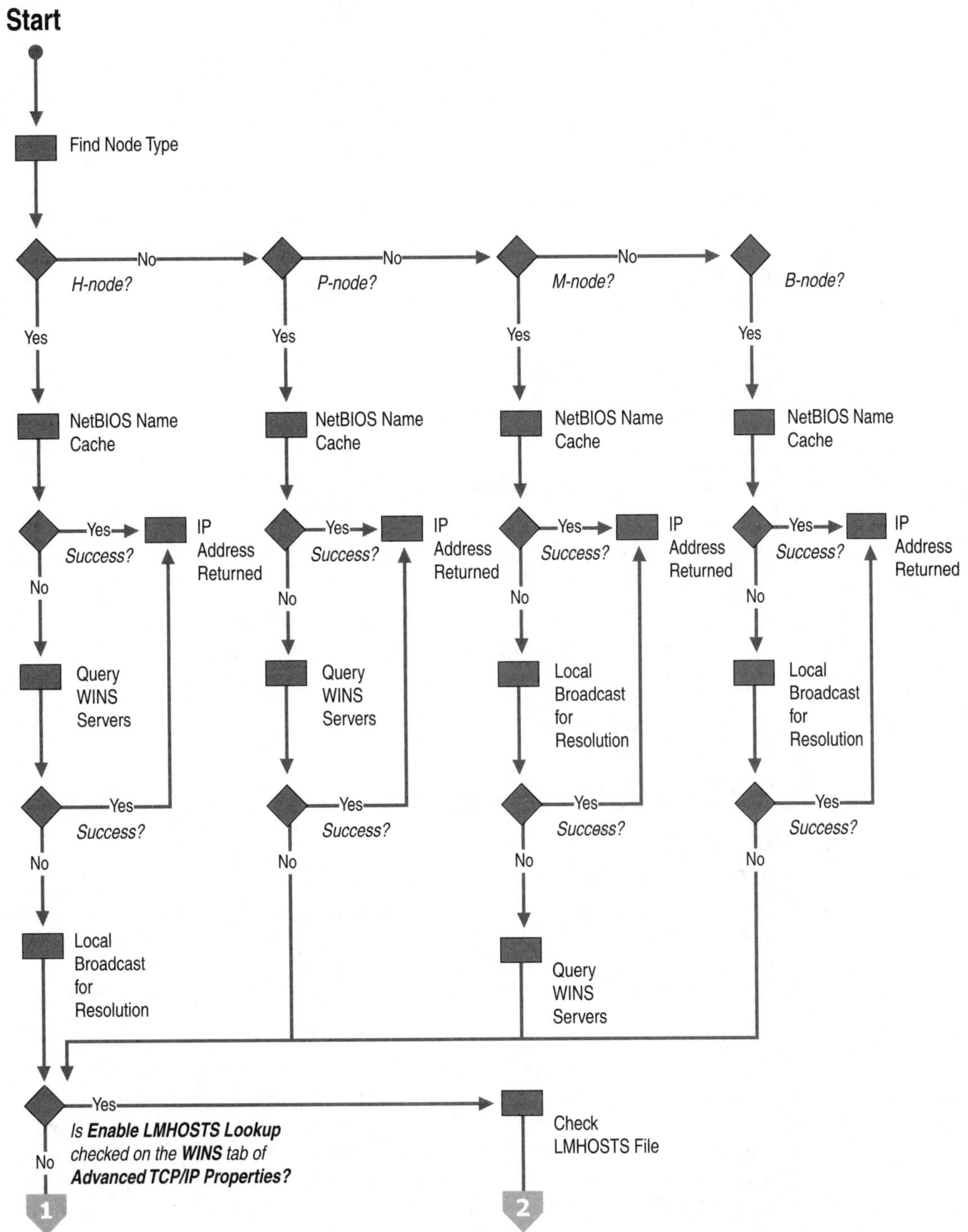

Figure 2.4 NetBIOS Name Resolution Flowchart (part 1 of 2)

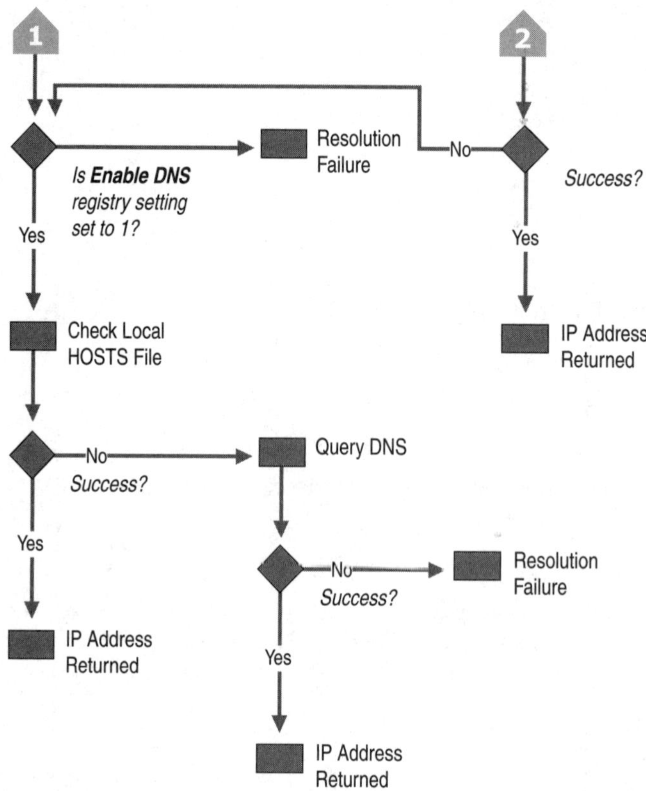

Figure 2.5 NetBIOS Name Resolution Flowchart (part 2 of 2)

NetBIOS Name Registration and Resolution for Multihomed Computers

NetBT binds to only one IP address per physical network interface. From the NetBT viewpoint, a computer is multihomed only if it has more than one network adapter installed. When a name registration packet is sent from a multihomed computer, it is flagged as a multihomed name registration so that it does not conflict with the same name being registered by another interface in the same computer.

If a multihomed computer receives a broadcast NetBIOS Name Query, all NetBT and interface bindings that receive the query respond with their addresses, and by default the client chooses the first response and connects to the address supplied by the responder. To have the responder randomly choose the IP address to put in the name query response, set the value of the **RandomAdapter** registry entry (HKLM\SYSTEM\CurrentControlSet\Services\Netbt\Parameters) to 1. This can be used by a server with two interfaces on the same network for load balancing.

When a directed name query is sent to a WINS server, the WINS server responds with a list of all IP addresses that are registered with WINS by the multihomed computer.

A Windows 2000 client uses the following process to choose the best IP address to connect to on a multihomed computer:

1. If one of the IP addresses in the name query response list is on the same logical subnet as the local computer, that address is selected. If more than one of the addresses meets the criteria, one is picked at random from those that match.
2. If one of the IP addresses in the list is on the same logical subnet as any binding of NetBT on the local computer, then that address is selected. If multiple addresses meet this criteria, one is picked at random.
3. If none of the IP addresses in the list is on the same subnet as any binding of NetBT on the local computer, then an address is selected at random from the list.
4. If none of the IP addresses in the list is on the same subnet as any binding of NetBT on the local computer, an address is selected at random from the list.

This algorithm provides a reasonable balancing of connections to a server across multiple network adapters, while still favoring local (same subnet) connections when they are available. To provide some fault tolerance, when there is a list of IP addresses returned, they are sorted into the best order, and NetBT attempts to ping each of the addresses in the list until one responds. NetBT then attempts a connection to that address. If no addresses respond, then a connection attempt is made to the first address in the list. This is tried in case there is a firewall or other device filtering ICMP traffic. Windows 2000 supports "per interface" NetBT name caching, and **nbtstat -c** displays the name cache on a per interface basis.

Windows 2000 NetBT Internet/DNS Enhancements

It is possible to connect from one Windows 2000–based computer to another using NetBT over the Internet. To do so, some means of name resolution has to be provided. Two common methods are the Lmhosts file or a WINS server. Several enhancements were introduced in Windows NT 4.0 and carried forward in Windows 2000 to eliminate these special configuration needs.

It is now possible to connect to a NetBIOS over TCP/IP resource in two new ways:

- Use the command **net use** \\\\<*ip address*>\\<*share_name*>. This eliminates the need for NetBIOS name resolution configuration.
- Use the command **net use** \\\\<*FQDN*>\\<*share_name*>. This allows the use of a DNS server to connect to a computer using its fully qualified domain name (FQDN).

Examples of using new functionality to map a drive to ftp.microsoft.com at the IP address of 198.105.232.1 are shown here.

- **net use f: \\ftp.microsoft.com\data**
- **net use \\198.105.232.1\data**
- **net view \\198.105.232.1**
- **dir \\ftp.microsoft.com\bussys\winnt**

In addition, various applications allow you to enter an FQDN or IP address in place of a computer name. This new behavior is illustrated in Figure 2.6.

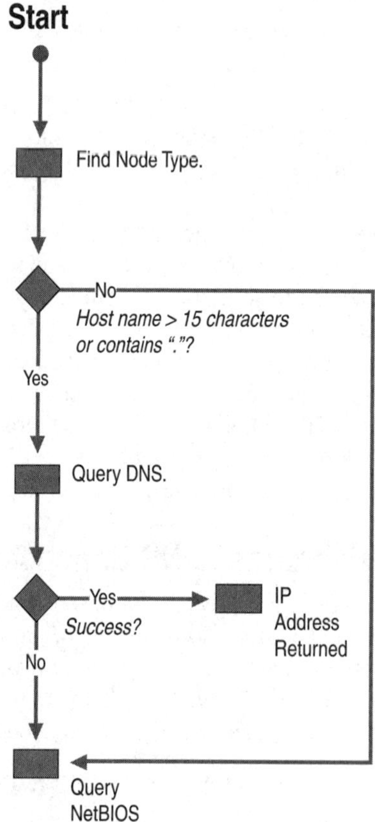

Figure 2.6 Behavior of NetBT Internet/DNS Enhancements

In Windows 2000, it is also possible to use direct hosting to establish redirector or server connections between Windows 2000 computers without the use of NetBIOS. By default, Windows 2000 attempts to make connections using both methods so that it can support connections to older versions of Windows computers. However, in Windows 2000–only environments, you can disable NetBIOS over TCP/IP as described in the "NetBIOS Over TCP/IP Sessions" following in this chapter.

The new interface in Windows 2000 that makes NetBIOS-less operation possible is called the Server Message Block (SMB) device. It appears to the redirector and server as another interface, much like an individual network adapter/protocol stack combination. However, at the TCP/IP stack, the SMB device is bound to ADDR_ANY, and uses the DNS namespace natively like a Windows Sockets application. Calls placed on the SMB device result in a standard DNS lookup to resolve the domain name to an IP address, followed by a single outbound connection request using the best source IP address and interface as determined by the route table.

Additionally, there is no "NetBIOS session setup" on top of the TCP connection, as there is with traditional NetBIOS over TCP/IP. By default, the redirector places calls on both the NetBIOS device(s) and the SMB device, and the file server receives calls on both. The file server SMB device listens on TCP port 445 instead of the NetBIOS over TCP port 139.

NetBIOS Over TCP/IP Sessions

NetBIOS sessions are established between two names. For example, when a Windows 2000 workstation service makes a file sharing connection to a Windows 2000 server service using NetBIOS over TCP/IP, the following sequence of events takes place:

1. The NetBIOS name for the server process is resolved to an IP address.
2. A TCP connection is established from the workstation to the server, using TCP port 139.
3. The workstation sends a NetBIOS Session Request to the server name over the TCP connection. Assuming the server is listening on that name, it will respond affirmatively and a session is established.

Once the NetBIOS session has been established, the client and server negotiate the file sharing connection with the Server Message Block (SMB) protocol. Microsoft networking uses only one NetBIOS session between two names at any point in time. Any additional file or print sharing connections made after the first one are multiplexed over the same NetBIOS session.

NetBIOS keep-alives are used on each connection to verify that the server and workstation are still both up and able to maintain their session. This way, if a workstation is shut down ungracefully, the server will eventually clean up the connection and associated resources, and vice versa. NetBIOS keep-alives are controlled by the **SessionKeepAlive** registry entry (HKLM\SYSTEM\CurrentControlSet\Services\Netbt\Parameters) and default to once per hour.

If Lmhosts files are used and an entry is misspelled, it is possible to attempt to connect to a server using the correct IP address but an incorrect name. In this case, a TCP connection is still established to the server. However, the NetBIOS session request using an invalid name will be rejected by the server. If attempting the connection with the **net use** command, "Error 51: Remote computer not listening" is returned.

NetBIOS Datagram Services

Datagrams are sent from one NetBIOS name to another over UDP port 138. The datagram service provides the ability to send a message to a unique name or to a group name. Group names can resolve to a list of IP addresses or a broadcast. For instance, the command **net send /d:mydomain test** sends a datagram containing the text "test" to the group name MYDOMAIN[03]. The MYDOMAIN[03] name resolves to an IP subnet broadcast, so the datagram is sent with the following characteristics:

- Destination MAC address: The MAC-level broadcast (0xFF-FF-FF-FF-FF-FF).
- Source MAC address: The MAC address of the local computer.
- Destination IP address: The local subnet broadcast address.
- Source IP address: The IP address of the local computer.
- Destination name: MYDOMAIN[03] (the messenger service on the remote computers).
- Source name: USERNAME[03] (the messenger service on the local computer).

All hosts on the subnet pick up the datagram and process it at least to the UDP protocol. On hosts running a NetBIOS datagram service, UDP hands the datagram to NetBT on port 138. NetBT checks the destination name to see if any application has registered that name, and if so, passes up the datagram. If no receive message was posted, the datagram is discarded.

Note that if support for NetBIOS is disabled in Windows 2000, then the NetBIOS datagram is discarded by UDP.

Client Services and Components

The focus of this chapter is on the Windows 2000 core TCP/IP stack components, not on the many available services provided by Windows 2000 that use them. However, the stack itself relies upon a few services for configuration information and for name and address resolution.

Automatic Client Configuration

One of the most important client services is the Dynamic Host Configuration Protocol (DHCP) client. The DHCP client has an expanded role in Windows 2000. The primary new feature is the ability to configure an IP address and subnet mask when the client is started on a network where no DHCP server is available to assign addresses. This feature allows autoconfiguration of an IP address and a subnet mask for small networks such as a home network.

If a Microsoft TCP/IP client is installed and set to dynamically obtain TCP/IP protocol configuration information from a DHCP server, then the DHCP client service is engaged each time the computer is restarted. The DHCP client service now uses a two-step process to configure the client with an IP address and other configuration information:

1. When the client is installed, it attempts to locate a DHCP server and obtain an IP address configuration. Most corporate and organizational TCP/IP networks use DHCP servers that are configured to hand out information to the clients on the network.
2. For a computer running Windows 2000, if this attempt to locate a DHCP server fails, the DHCP client autoconfigures the TCP/IP protocol with a selected IP address from the Internet Assigned Numbers Authority (IANA)-reserved class B network 169.254.0.0. with the subnet mask 255.255.0.0. The DHCP client performs duplicate address detection to ensure that the IP address it has chosen is not already in use. If the address is in use, it selects another IP address and reselects addresses up to 10 times. Once the DHCP client has selected an address that is verifiably not in use, it configures the interface with this address. The client continues to check for a DHCP server in the background every five minutes, and if a DHCP server is found, the autoconfiguration information is abandoned and the configuration offered by the DHCP server is used instead.

The autoconfiguration feature of Windows 2000 TCP/IP is known as *Automatic Private IP Addressing* (APIPA) and allows home users and small business users to create a functioning, single subnet TCP/IP network without having to manually configure the TCP/IP protocol or set up a DHCP server.

In case the DHCP client has previously obtained a lease from a DHCP server, the following modified sequence of events occurs:

1. If the client's lease is still valid at boot time (the lease has not expired), the client tries to renew its lease with the DHCP server. If the client fails to locate any DHCP server during the renewal attempt, it attempts to ping the default gateway that is listed in the lease. If pinging the default gateway succeeds, then the DHCP client assumes that it is still located on the same network where it obtained its current lease, and continues to use the lease. By default, the client attempts to renew its lease when 50 percent of its assigned lease time has expired.
2. If the attempt to ping the default gateway fails, the client assumes that it has been moved to a network that has no DHCP services currently available (such as a home network), and it auto-configures itself as described above. Once autoconfigured, it continues to try to locate a DHCP server every five minutes.

Media Sense

Windows 2000 TCP/IP supports Media Sense, which can improve the roaming experience for portable device users. Media Sense support, added in NDIS 5.0, provides a mechanism for the network adapter to notify the protocol stack of media connect and media disconnect events. Windows 2000 TCP/IP utilizes these notifications to assist in automatic configuration.

For instance, in Windows NT 4.0, when a portable computer was located and DHCP-configured on an Ethernet subnet, and then moved to another subnet without rebooting, the protocol stack received no indication of the move. This meant that the configuration parameters became stale, and not relevant to the new network segment. Additionally, if the computer was shut off, carried home, and rebooted, the protocol stack was not aware that the network adapter was no longer connected to a network, and again stale configuration parameters remained. This could produce problems, as subnet routes, default gateways, and other configuration parameters could conflict with dial-up parameters.

Media sense support allows the protocol stack to react to events and remove stale parameters. For example, if a Windows 2000 computer is unplugged from the network (assuming the network adapter supports Media Sense), after a damping period of 20 seconds, TCP/IP invalidates the parameters associated with the network that has been disconnected. The IP address(es) no longer allow sends, and any routes associated with the interface are invalidated.

If an application is bound to a socket that is using an address that is invalidated, it should handle the event and recover in a graceful way, such as attempting to use another IP address on the system or notifying the user of the disconnect.

Dynamic Update DNS Client

Windows 2000 includes support for dynamic updates to DNS as described in RFC 2136. Every time there is an address event such as a new address or renewal, the DHCP client sends option 81 and its fully qualified domain name to the DHCP server and requests the DHCP server to register a pointer resource record (PTR RR) on its behalf. The dynamic update client registers an address resource record (A RR). This is done because only the client knows which IP addresses on the host map to that name. The DHCP server might not be able to properly complete the A RR registration because it has incomplete knowledge. However, the DHCP server can be configured to instruct the client to allow the server to register both records with the DNS. Changing registry entries changes the behavior of the dynamic update DNS client.

The Windows 2000 DHCP server handles option 81 requests as specified in RFC 2136. If a Windows 2000 DHCP client talks to a DHCP server that does not handle option 81, it registers a PTR RR on its own. The Windows 2000 DNS server is capable of handling dynamic updates.

Statically configured (non-DHCP) clients register both the A RR and the PTR RR with the DNS server themselves.

If the remote access client connects to a Windows 2000 computer running the Routing and Remote Access service, the client must perform the DNS registrations itself, because the remote access server does not know the client name. If the line goes down, the address lease expires, or the client fails to unregister its records, the remote access server will unregister the PTR record on the client's behalf.

DNS Resolver Cache Service

Windows 2000 includes a caching DNS resolver service, which is enabled by default. For troubleshooting purposes this service can be viewed, stopped, and started like any other Windows 2000 service. The caching resolver reduces DNS network traffic and speeds name resolution by providing a local cache for DNS queries.

Name query responses are cached for the TTL specified in the response (not to exceed the value specified in the **MaxCacheEntryTtlLimit** registry entry (HKLM\SYSTEM\CurrentControlSet\Services\Dnscache\Parameters)), and future queries are answered from cache when possible. DNS Resolver Cache Service supports negative caching. For example, if a query is made to a DNS for a particular host name and the response is negative, succeeding queries for the same name will be answered (negatively) from the cache for an amount of time equal to the value in the **NegativeCacheTime** registry entry (HKLM\SYSTEM\CurrentControlSet\Services\Dnscache\Parameters) (the default value is 300 seconds). Another example of negative caching is that if all DNS servers are queried and none are available, for an amount of time equal to the value in the **NetFailureCacheTime** registry entry (HKLM\SYSTEM\CurrentControlSet\Services\Dnscache\Parameters) (the default value is 30 seconds), all succeeding name queries fail instantly instead of timing out. This feature saves time for services that query the DNS during the boot process, especially when the client is booted from the network.

TCP/IP Filtering

Windows 2000 includes support for TCP/IP filtering, a feature known as TCP/IP Security in Windows NT 4.0. TCP/IP filtering allows you to specify exactly which types of incoming IP traffic are processed for each IP interface. This feature is designed to isolate the traffic being processed by Internet and intranet servers in the absence of other TCP/IP filtering provided by Routing and Remote Access or other TCP/IP applications or services. TCP/IP filtering is disabled by default.

TCP/IP filtering can be enabled and disabled for all adapters through a single check box. This can help troubleshoot connectivity problems that might be related to filtering. Filters that are too restrictive might not allow expected kinds of connectivity. For example, if you specify a list of UDP ports and do not include UDP port 520, your computer will not receive Routing Information Protocol (RIP) announcements. This can impair the computer's ability to be a RIP router or a silent RIP host when using the RIP Listener service.

A packet is accepted for processing if it meets one of the following criteria:

- The destination TCP port matches the list of TCP ports. By default, all TCP ports are permitted.
- The destination UDP port matches the list of UDP ports. By default, all UDP ports are permitted.
- The IP protocol matches the list of IP protocols. By default, all IP protocols are permitted.
- It is an ICMP packet.

  You cannot filter ICMP traffic with TCP/IP filtering. If you need ICMP filtering, configure IP packet filters through Routing and Remote Access. For more information, see "Unicast IP Routing" in the *Internetworking Guide*.

Additional Resources

For more information about TCP/IP, see:

- *Internetworking with TCP/IP, Vol 1, 3rd Edition* by Douglas Comer, 1996, Englewood Cliffs, NJ: Prentice Hall.
- *Microsoft Windows 2000 TCP/IP Protocols and Services Technical Reference* by Thomas Lee and Joseph Davies, 1999, Redmond, WA: Microsoft Press.
- *TCP/IP Illustrated,* Volume *1, The Protocols* by Richard W. Stevens, 1994, Reading, MA: Addison-Wesley.
- "Improving Round Trip Time Estimates in Reliable Transport Protocols," by P. Karn & C. Partridge, Aug. 1987, ACM SIGCOMM-87.
- "Congestion Avoidance and Control," V. Jacobson, Aug. 1988, ACM SIGCOMM-88.

CHAPTER 3

TCP/IP Troubleshooting

Many network troubleshooting tools are available for Microsoft® Windows® 2000 Server and Microsoft® Windows® 2000 Professional. This chapter discusses the most common and most helpful tools included with the operating system or with the *Windows 2000 Resource Kit*.

Troubleshooting layer by layer is often a good way to quickly isolate problems; it allows you to discriminate between problems on the local host, a remote host, or a router. The troubleshooting tasks discussed here are organized using this layered approach.

In This Chapter

Related Information in the Resource Kit

- For more information about TCP/IP, see "Introduction to TCP/IP" and "Windows 2000 TCP/IP" in this book.

Overview of TCP/IP Troubleshooting Tools

Table 3.1 lists the diagnostic utilities included with Microsoft TCP/IP; they are described in more detail in the following pages. All are useful to identify and resolve TCP/IP networking problems.

Table 3.1 TCP/IP Diagnostic Utilities

Utility	Used to
Arp	View the ARP (Address Resolution Protocol) cache on the interface of the local computer to detect invalid entries.
Hostname	Display the host name of the computer.
Ipconfig	Display current TCP/IP network configuration values, and update or release Dynamic Host Configuration Protocol (DHCP) allocated leases, and display, register, or flush Domain Name System (DNS) names.
Nbtstat	Check the state of current NetBIOS over TCP/IP connections, update the NetBIOS name cache, and determine the registered names and scope ID.
Netstat	Display statistics for current TCP/IP connections.
Netdiag	Check all aspects of the network connection.
Nslookup	Check records, domain host aliases, domain host services, and operating system information by querying Internet domain name servers. Nslookup is discussed in detail in "Windows 2000 DNS" in this book.
Pathping	Trace a path to a remote system and report packet losses at each router along the way.
Ping	Send ICMP Echo Requests to verify that TCP/IP is configured correctly and that a remote TCP/IP system is available.
Route	Display the IP routing table, and add or delete IP routes.
Tracert	Trace a path to a remote system.

For a quick reference chart of these TCP/IP tools, as well as remote administration tools, see the appendix "TCP/IP Remote Utilities" in this book.

In addition to the TCP/IP-specific tools, the following Microsoft® Windows® 2000 tools can also make TCP/IP troubleshooting easier:

- Microsoft SNMP service—provides statistical information to SNMP management systems.
- Event Viewer—tracks errors and events.
- Microsoft Network Monitor—performs in-depth network traces. The full version is part of the Microsoft® Systems Management Server product, and a limited version is included with Windows 2000 Server.

- System Monitor—analyzes TCP/IP network performance.
- Registry editors—both Regedit.exe and Regedt32.exe allow viewing and editing of registry parameters.

These tools are discussed in their own chapters of the *Windows 2000 Resource Kit.*

Arp

Arp allows you to view and modify the ARP cache. If two hosts on the same subnet cannot ping each other successfully, try running the **arp -a** command on each computer to see whether the computers have the correct media access control (MAC) addresses listed for each other. You can use Ipconfig to determine a host's correct MAC address.

You can also use Arp to view the contents of the ARP cache by typing **arp -a** at a command prompt. This displays a list of the ARP cache entries, including their MAC addresses. Following is an example list of ARP cache entries.

```
C:\>arp -a

Interface: 172.16.0.142 on Interface 0x2
   Internet address      Physical AddressType
   172.16.0.1            00-e0-34-c0-a1-40    dynamic
   172.16.1.231          00-00-f8-03-6d-65    dynamic
   172.16.3.34           08-00-09-dc-82-4a    dynamic
   172.16.4.53           00-c0-4f-79-49-2b    dynamic
   172.16.5.102          00-00-f8-03-6c-30    dynamic
```

If another host with a duplicate IP address exists on the network, the ARP cache might have the MAC address for the other computer placed in it, and this can lead to intermittent problems with address resolution. When a computer on the local network sends an ARP Request to resolve the address, it forwards its data to the MAC address corresponding to the first ARP Reply it receives. **Arp** can help by listing, adding, and removing the relevant entries.

You can use **arp -d** *<IP address>* to delete incorrect entries. Use **arp -s** *<MAC address>* (where the MAC address is formatted as hexadecimal bytes separated by dashes) to add new static entries; these static entries do not expire from the ARP cache. However, static entries do not persist after a reboot. For persistent static ARP cache entries, you must create a batch file run from the Startup group.

Use **arp -N** *<IP address>* to list all the ARP entries for the network interface specified by *<IP address>*. Table 3.2 lists all Arp switches.

Table 3.2 Arp Switches

Switch	Name	Effect
-d *<IP address>*	Delete	Removes the listed entry from the ARP cache
-s *<MAC address>*	Static	Adds a static entry to the ARP cache
-N *<Interface IP address>*	Interface	Lists all ARP entries for the interface specified
-a	Display	Displays all the current ARP entries for all interfaces
-g	Display	Displays all the current ARP entries for all interfaces

Hostname

Hostname displays the name of the host on which the command is issued. The command has no other switches or parameters. The host name displayed matches the name configured on the Network Identification table in **Control Panel-System**.

Ipconfig

IPConfig is a command-line tool that displays the current configuration of the installed IP stack on a networked computer.

When used with the **/all** switch, it displays a detailed configuration report for all interfaces, including any configured WAN miniports (typically used for remote access or VPN connections). Output can be redirected to a file and pasted into other documents. A sample report is shown here:

```
C:>\ipconfig /all

Windows 2000 IP Configuration

        Host Name . . . . . . . . . . . . : TESTPC1
        Primary DNS Suffix . . . . . . .  : reskit.com
        Node Type . . . . . . . . . . . . : Hybrid
        IP Routing Enabled. . . . . . . . : No
        WINS Proxy Enabled. . . . . . . . : No
        DNS Suffix Search List. . . . . . : ntcorpdc1.reskit.com
                                            dns.reskit.com
                                            reskit.com
```

```
Ethernet adapter Local Area Connection:

      Connection-specific DNS Suffix  . : dns.reskit.com
      Description . . . . . . . . . . . : Acme XL 10/100Mb Ethernet NIC
      Physical Address. . . . . . . . . : 00-CC-44-79-C3-AA
      DHCP Enabled. . . . . . . . . . . : Yes
      IP Address. . . . . . . . . . . . : 172.16.245.111
      Subnet Mask . . . . . . . . . . . : 255.255.248.0
      Default Gateway . . . . . . . . . : 172.16.240.1
      DHCP Server . . . . . . . . . . . : 172.16.248.8
      DNS Servers . . . . . . . . . . . : 172.16.55.85
                                          172.16.55.134
                                          172.16.55.54

      Primary WINS Server . . . . . . . : 172.16.248.10
      Secondary WINS Server . . . . . . : 172.16.248.9

      Lease Obtained. . . . . . . . . . : Friday, May 05, 1999 2:21:40 PM
      Lease Expires . . . . . . . . . . : Monday, May 07, 1999 2:21:40 PM
```

A number of other useful parameters for Ipconfig include **/flushdns**, which deletes the DNS name cache; **/registerdns**, which refreshes all DHCP leases and re-registers DNS names; and **/displaydns** which displays the contents of the DNS resolver cache.

The **/release** *<adapter>* and **/renew** *<adapter>* options release and renew the DHCP-allocated IP address for a specified adapter. If no adapter name is specified, the DHCP leases for all adapters bound to TCP/IP are released or renewed.

For **/setclassid**, if no class ID is specified, then the Class ID is removed. Table 3.3 lists all Ipconfig switches.

Table 3.3 Ipconfig Switches

Switch	Effect
/all	Produces a detailed configuration report for all interfaces.
/flushdns	Removes all entries from the DNS name cache.
/registerdns	Refreshes all DHCP leases and reregisters DNS names
/displaydns	Displays the contents of the DNS resolver cache.
/release *<adapter>*	Releases the IP address for a specified interface.

(continued)

Table 3.3 Ipconfig Switches ***(continued)***

Switch	Effect
/renew *<adapter>*	Renews the IP address for a specified interface.
/showclassid *<adapter>*	Displays all the DHCP class IDs allowed for the adapter specified.
/setclassid *<adapter> <classID to set>*	Changes the DHCP class ID for the adapter specified.
/?	Displays this list.

The /showclassid and /setclassid options allow you to manipulate user class IDs from the command line. The user class IDs are options that a system administrator may set on the DHCP server to configure a client computer to identify itself with the server. Issuing the command **ipconfig /showclassid** *<adapter>* sends a query to the client's server; the server responds by providing the available classes. Once you know which classes are available, you can issue a command like **ipconfig /setdhcpclassid** *<adapter> <class ID to set on the server>* to set the class ID that the client will use from that point on. For more information about DHCP and class IDs, see "Dynamic Host Configuration Protocol" in this book.

Nbtstat

Nbtstat is designed to help troubleshoot NetBIOS name resolution problems. When a network is functioning normally, NetBIOS over TCP/IP (NetBT) resolves NetBIOS names to IP addresses. It does this through several options for NetBIOS name resolution, including local cache lookup, WINS server query, broadcast, LMHOSTS lookup, Hosts lookup, and DNS server query.

The **nbtstat** command removes and corrects preloaded entries using a number of case-sensitive switches. The **nbtstat -a <***name***>** command performs a NetBIOS adapter status command on the computer name specified by *<name>*. The adapter status command returns the local NetBIOS name table for that computer as well as the MAC address of the adapter card. The **nbtstat -A** *<IP address>* command performs the same function using a target IP address rather than a name.

The **nbtstat -c** option shows the contents of the NetBIOS name cache, which contains NetBIOS name-to-IP address mappings.

nbtstat -n displays the names that have been registered locally on the system by NetBIOS applications such as the server and redirector.

The **nbtstat -r** command displays the count of all NetBIOS names resolved by broadcast and by querying a WINS server. The **nbtstat -R** command purges the name cache and reloads all #PRE entries from the LMHOSTS file. #PRE entries are the LMHOSTS name entries that are preloaded into the cache. For more information about the LMHOSTS file, see the appendix "LMHOSTS" in this book.

Nbtstat -RR sends name release packets to the WINS server and starts a refresh, thus re-registering all names with the name server without having to reboot. This is a new option in Windows NT 4.0 with Service Pack 4 as well as in Windows 2000.

You can use **nbtstat -S** to list the current NetBIOS sessions and their status, including statistics. Sample output looks like this:

```
C:\>nbtstat -S

Local Area Connection:
Node IpAddress: [172.16.0.142]       Scope Id: []

              NetBIOS Connection Table

Local Name     State     In/Out Remote Host    Input   Output
--------------------------------------------------------------
TESTPC1 <00> Connected Out    172.16.210.25    6MB      5MB
TESTPC1 <00> Connected Out    172.16.3.1     108KB    116KB
TESTPC1 <00> Connected Out    172.16.3.20     299KB     19KB
TESTPC1 <00> Connected Out    172.16.3.4     324KB     19KB
TESTPC1 <03> Listening
```

Finally, **nbtstat -s** provides a similar set of session listings, but provides the remote computer names, rather than their IP addresses.

Note The options for the **Nbtstat** command are case sensitive.

The Nbtstat switches are listed in Table 3.4.

Table 3.4 Nbtstat Switches

Switch	Name	Function
-a *<name>*	adapter status	Returns the NetBIOS name table and MAC address of the address card for the computer name specified.
-A *<IP address>*	Adapter status	Lists the same information as -a when given the target's IP address.

(continued)

Table 3.4 Nbtstat Switches *(continued)*

Switch	Name	Function
-c	cache	Lists the contents of the NetBIOS name cache.
[*Number*]	Interval	Typing a numerical value tells Nbtstat to redisplay selected statistics each interval seconds, pausing between each display. Press Ctrl+C to stop redisplaying statistics.
-n	names	Displays the names registered locally by NetBIOS applications such as the server and redirector.
-r	resolved	Displays a count of all names resolved by broadcast or WINS server.
-R	Reload	Purges the name cache and reloads all #PRE entries from LMHOSTS.
-RR	ReleaseRefresh	Releases and reregisters all names with the name server.
-s	sessions	Lists the NetBIOS sessions table converting destination IP addresses to computer NetBIOS names.
-S	Sessions	Lists the current NetBIOS sessions and their status, with the IP address.
/?	Help	Displays this list.

Netdiag

Netdiag is a utility that helps isolate networking and connectivity problems by performing a series of tests to determine the state of your network client and whether it is functional. These tests and the key network status information they expose give network administrators and support personnel a more direct means of identifying and isolating network problems. Moreover, because this tool does not require parameters or switches to be specified, support personnel and network administrators can focus on analyzing the output, rather than training users about tool usage.

Netdiag diagnoses network problems by checking all aspects of a host computer's network configuration and connections. Beyond troubleshooting TCP/IP issues, it also examines a host computer's Internetwork Packet Exchange (IPX) and NetWare configurations.

Run Netdiag whenever a computer is having network problems. The utility tries to diagnose the problem and can even flag problem areas for closer inspection. It can fix simple DNS problems with the optional **/fix** switch.

For more information about Netdiag, see Windows 2000 Support Tools Help. For information about installing and using the Windows 2000 Support Tools and Support Tools Help, see the file Sreadme.doc in the \Support\Tools folder of the Windows 2000 operating system CD.

Netdiag performs its tests by examining .dll files, output from other tools, and the system registry to find potential problem spots. It checks to see which network services or functions are enabled and then runs the network configuration tests listed in Table 3.5, in the order presented. If a computer is not running one of the services listed, the test is skipped.

Table 3.5 Netdiag Tests

Test Name	Function	Details
NDIS	Network Adapter Status	Lists the network adapter configuration details, including the adapter name, configuration, media, globally unique identifier (GUID), and statistics. If this test shows an unresponsive network adapter, the remaining tests are aborted.
IPConfig	IP Configuration	This test provides most of the TCP/IP information normally obtained from **ipconfig /all**, pings the DHCP and WINS servers, and checks that the default gateway is on the same subnet as the IP address.
Member	Domain Membership	Checks to confirm details of the primary domain, including computer role, domain name, and domain GUID. Checks to see if NetLogon service is started, adds the primary domain to the domain list, and queries the primary domain security identifier (SID).
NetBTTransports	Transports Test	Lists NetBT transports managed by the redirector. Prints error information if no NetBT transports are found.
Automatic Private IP Addressing (APIPA)	APIPA Address	Checks if any interface is using Automatic Private IP Addressing (APIPA).
IPLoopBk	IP Loopback Ping	Pings the IP loopback address of 127.0.0.1.
DefGw	Default Gateway	Pings all the default gateways for each interface.
NbtNm	NetBT Name Test	Similar to the **nbtstat -n** command. It checks that the workstation service name <00> is equal to the computer name. It also checks that the messenger service name <03>, and server service name <20> are present on all interfaces and that none of these names are in conflict.
WINS	WINS Service Test	Sends NetBT name queries to all the configured WINS servers.

(continued)

Table 3.5 Netdiag Tests *(continued)*

Test Name	Function	Details
Winsock	Winsock Test	Uses Windows Sockets **WSAEnumProtocols** () function to retrieve available transport protocols.
DNS	DNS Test	Checks whether DNS cache service is running, and whether this computer is correctly registered on the configured DNS servers. If the computer is a domain controller, DNS Test checks to see whether all the DNS entries in Netlogon.dns are registered on the DNS server. If the entries are incorrect and the **/fix** option is on, try to re-register the domain controller record on a DNS server.
Browser	Redirector and Browser Test	Checks whether the workstation service is running. Retrieves the transport lists from the redirector and from the browser. Checks whether the NetBT transports are in the list of NetBT transports test. Checks whether the browser is bound to all the NetBT transports. Checks whether the computer can send mailslot messages. Tests both via browser and redirector.
DsGetDc	DC Discovery Test	First finds a generic domain controller from directory service, then finds the primary domain controller. Then, finds a Windows 2000 domain controller (DC). If the tested domain is the primary domain, checks whether the domain GUID stored in Local Security Authority (LSA) is the same as the domain GUID stored in the DC. If not, the test returns a fatal error; if the **/fix** option is on, DsGetDC tries to fix the GUID in LSA.
DcList	DC List Test	Gets a list of domain controllers in the domain from the directory services on an active domain controller (DC). If there is no DC info for this domain, tries to get a DC from DS (similar to the DsGetDc test). Tries to get an active DC as the target DC. Gets the DC list from the target DC. Checks the status of each DC. Adds all the DCs into the DC list of the tested domain. If the above sequence fails, uses the browser to obtain the DCs. Checks the status of all DCs and adds them to the DC list. If the **DcAccountEnum** registry entry option is enabled, Netdiag tries to get a DC list from the Security Accounts Manager (SAM) on the discovered DC.
Trust	Trust Relationship Test	Test trust relationships to the primary domain only if the computer is a member workstation, member server, or a Backup Domain Controller (BDC) domain controller that is not a PDC emulator Checks that the primary domain security identifier (SID) is correct. Contacts an active DC. Connects to the SAM server on the DC. Uses the domain SID to open the domain to verify whether the domain SID is correct Queries info of the secure channel for the primary domain. If the computer is a BDCDC, reconnects to the PDC emulator. If the computer is a member workstation or server, sets secure channel to each DC on the DC list for this domain.

(continued)

Table 3.5 Netdiag Tests ***(continued)***

Test Name	Function	Details
Kerberos	Kerberos Test	Tests Kerberos protocols only if the computer is a member computer or DC and the user is not logged onto a local account. Tests Kerberos protocols only when the user is logged onto a Windows 2000 domain account. Connects to LSA and looks up the Kerberos package. Gets the ticket cache of the Kerberos package. Checks if Kerberos package has a ticket for the primary domain and the local computer.
LDAP	Lightweight Directory Access (LDAP) Test	This per-domain test is run only if the DC is running DS. The computer must be a member computer or DC. NetDiag tests LDAP on all the active DCs found in the domain. It creates an LDAP connection block to the DC, then does a trivial search in the LDAP directory with three types of authentication: "unauthenticated", NTLM, and "Negotiate." If the **/v** (verbose) option is on, the LDAP test prints out the details of each entry retrieved.
Route	Route test	Displays the static and persistent entries in the routing table, including a destination address, subnet mask, gateway address, interface, and metric.
NetStat	NetStat test	Similar to Netstat tool. Displays statistics of protocols and current TCP/IP network connections.
Bindings	Bindings test	Lists all bindings, including interface name, lower module name, upper module name, whether the binding is currently enabled, and the owner of the binding.
WAN	WAN test	Displays the settings and status of current active remote access connections.
Modem	Modem test	Retrieves all the line devices that are available. Displays the configuration of each line device.
NetWare	NetWare test	Determines whether NetWare is using the directory tree or bindery logon process, determines the default context if Netware is using the directory tree logon process, and finds the server to which the host attaches itself at startup.
IPX	IPX test	Examines the network's IPX configuration, including Frame Type, Network ID, RouterMTU and whether packet burst or source routing are enabled.
IPSec	IP Security test	Tests whether IP security is enabled and displays a list of active IPSec policies.

Netdiag Syntax

The required syntax for Netdiag is simple. The tool can be configured to perform any subset of its exhaustive list of tests by careful use of the **/test** or **/skip** options.

Although no parameters or syntax need be specified, several options are available for Netdiag, primarily to increase or decrease the level of detail in its reports. These switches are shown in the Table 3.6. Complete details on the **/test** and **/skip** options can be found by typing **netdiag /?** at a command prompt; this returns a complete list of more than 20 tests that can be singled out or skipped.

Table 3.6 Netdiag Switches

Switch	Name	Function
/q	Quiet output	Lists only tests that return errors.
/v	Verbose output	More extensive listing of test data as tests are performed.
/l	Log output	Stores output in NetDiag.log, in the default directory.
/debug	Most verbose output	Complete list of test data with reasons for success or failure.
/d:<*DomainName*>	Find DC	Finds a domain controller in the specified domain.
/fix	Fix DNS problems	Compares DNS value to host file.
/DcAccountEnum	Enumerate DC	Enumerates Domain Controller computer accounts.
/test:<*test name*>	Single test	Runs only the test specified by <*test name*>. For a complete list, type **netdiag /?**.
/skip:<*test name*>	Skip test	Skips the named test.

In general, Netdiag calls Ipconfig and returns a structure that contains most of the general information that **ipconfig /all** prints. It takes that information from the registry and by calling the various drivers.

Netdiag prints the string [FATAL] when it detects a condition that needs to be fixed immediately. By contrast, the string [WARNING] signals a failure condition that can be put off for a while.

Netstat

Netstat displays protocol statistics and current TCP/IP connections. From a command prompt, type **Netstat -a** to display all connections and listening ports. Type **netstat -r** to display the contents of the IP routing table and any persistent routes. The **-n** switch tells Netstat not to convert addresses and port numbers to names, which speeds up execution. The **netstat -s** option shows all protocol statistics. The **netstat -p** *<protocol>* option can be used to show statistics for a specific protocol or together with the **-s** option to show connections only for the protocol specified. The **-e** switch displays interface statistics. Sample output for the **netstat -e** command is shown here:

```
C:\>netstat -e
Interface Statistics
                              Received            Sent

Bytes                        372959625       123567086
Unicast packets                 134302          145204
Non-unicast packets              55937             886
Discards                             0               0
Errors                               0               0
Unknown protocols              1757381
```

Discards are the packets received that contained errors or could not be processed. Errors indicate packets that are damaged, including packets sent by the local computer that were damaged while in the buffer.

Both of these types of errors should be at or near zero. If not, errors in the Sent column indicate that the local network might be overloaded or that there might be a bad physical connection between the local host and the network. High errors and discards in the Receive column indicate an overloaded local net, an overloaded local host, or a physical problem with the network.

The following output shows a sample report for the **netstat -a -n** command.

```
C:\>netstat -a -n

Active Connections
  Proto  Local Address          Foreign Address        State
  TCP    0.0.0.0:42             0.0.0.0:0              LISTENING
  TCP    0.0.0.0:88             0.0.0.0:0              LISTENING
  TCP    0.0.0.0:135            0.0.0.0:0              LISTENING
  TCP    0.0.0.0:389            0.0.0.0:0              LISTENING
  TCP    0.0.0.0:445            0.0.0.0:0              LISTENING
  TCP    0.0.0.0:593            0.0.0.0:0              LISTENING
  TCP    0.0.0.0:1038           0.0.0.0:0              LISTENING
  TCP    0.0.0.0:1041           0.0.0.0:0              LISTENING
  TCP    0.0.0.0:1048           0.0.0.0:0              LISTENING
```

```
TCP    0.0.0.0:1723         0.0.0.0:0              LISTENING
TCP    0.0.0.0:3268         0.0.0.0:0              LISTENING
TCP    10.99.99.1:53        0.0.0.0:0              LISTENING
TCP    10.99.99.1:139       0.0.0.0:0              LISTENING
TCP    10.99.99.1:389       10.99.99.1:1092        ESTABLISHED
TCP    10.99.99.1:1092      10.99.99.1:389         ESTABLISHED
TCP    10.99.99.1:3604      10.99.99.1:135         TIME_WAIT
TCP    10.99.99.1:3605      10.99.99.1:1077        TIME_WAIT
UDP    0.0.0.0:135          *:*
UDP    0.0.0.0:445          *:*
UDP    0.0.0.0:1087         *:*
UDP    10.99.99.1:53        *:*
UDP    10.99.99.1:137       *:*
UDP    10.99.99.1:138       *:*
```

The number after the colon indicates which port number each connection is using. For a complete port reference list, see the appendix "TCP and UDP Port Assignments" in this book.

The following output shows the TCP, IP, ICMP, and UDP statistics for the local host.

```
D:\>netstat -s

IP Statistics
  Packets Received                     = 3175996
  Received Header Errors               = 0
  Received Address Errors              = 38054
  Datagrams Forwarded                  = 0
  Unknown Protocols Received           = 0
  Received Packets Discarded           = 0
  Received Packets Delivered           = 3142564
  Output Requests                      = 3523906
  Routing Discards                     = 0
  Discarded Output Packets             = 0
  Output Packet No Route               = 0
  Reassembly Required                  = 0
  Reassembly Successful                = 0
  Reassembly Failures                  = 0
  Datagrams Successfully Fragmented    = 0
  Datagrams Failing Fragmentation      = 0
  Fragments Created                    = 0
```

```
ICMP Statistics
                              Received    Sent
  Messages                    462         33
  Errors                      0           0
  Destination Unreachable     392         4
  Time Exceeded               0           0
  Parameter Problems          0           0
  Source Quenchs              0           0
  Redirects                   0           0
  Echos                       1           22
  Echo Replies                12          1
  Timestamps                  0           0
  Timestamp Replies           0           0
  Address Masks               0           0
  Address Mask Replies        0           0

TCP Statistics
  Active Opens                          = 12164
  Passive Opens                         = 12
  Failed Connection Attempts            = 79
  Reset Connections                     = 11923
  Current Connections                   = 1
  Segments Received                     = 2970519
  Segments Sent                         = 3505992
  Segments Retransmitted                = 18

UDP Statistics
  Datagrams Received      = 155620
  No Ports                = 16578
  Receive Errors          = 0
  Datagrams Sent          = 17822
```

Table 3.7 summarizes the switches available for use with Netstat.

Table 3.7 Netstat Switches

Switch	Function
-a	Displays all connections and listening ports.
-r	Displays the contents of the routing table.
-n	Speeds execution by telling Netstat not to convert addresses and port numbers to names.
-s	Shows per-protocol statistics for IP, ICMP, TCP, and UDP.

(continued)

Table 3.7 Netstat Switches *(continued)*

Switch	Function
-p *<protocol>*	Shows connection information for the specified protocol. The protocol can be TCP, UDP, or IP. When used with the -s option, shows statistics for the specified protocol. In this case, the protocol can be TCP, UDP, IP, or ICMP.
-e	Shows Ethernet statistics, and can be combined with -s.
interval	Shows a new set of statistics each interval (in seconds). You can stop the redisplaying of Netstat statistics by typing CTRL-C. Without specifying an interval, Netstat shows the statistics once.

Nslookup

Nslookup is a useful tool for troubleshooting DNS problems, such as host name resolution. When you start Nslookup, it shows the host name and IP address of the DNS server that is configured for the local system, and then display a command prompt for further queries. If you type a question mark (**?**), Nslookup shows all available commands. You can exit the program by typing **exit**.

To look up a host's IP address using DNS, type the host name and press Enter. Nslookup defaults to using the DNS server configured for the computer on which it is running, but you can focus it on a different DNS server by typing **server** *<name>* (where *<name>* is the host name of the server you want to use for future lookups). Once another server is specified, anything entered after that point is interpreted as a host name.

Nslookup employs the domain name devolution method. If you type in a host name and press ENTER, Nslookup appends the domain suffix of the computer (such as cswatcp.reskit.com) to the host name before querying the DNS. If the name is not found, then the domain suffix is "devolved" by one level (in this case to reskit.com) and the query is repeated. Windows 2000 computers only devolve names to the second level domain (reskit.com in this example), so if this query fails, no further attempts are made to resolve the name. If a fully qualified domain name is typed in (as indicated by a trailing dot) then the DNS server is only queried for that name and no devolution is performed. To look up a host name that is completely outside your domain, you must type in a fully qualified domain name.

Nslookup's debug mode is a useful troubleshooting feature; you can set the local computer into this mode by typing **set debug**, or for even greater detail, **set d2**.

In debug mode, Nslookup lists the steps being taken to complete its commands, as shown in this example:

```
C:\>nslookup
(null)   testpc1.reskit.com
Address: 172.16.8.190

> set d2
> rain-city
(null) testpc1.reskit.com
Address: 172.16.8.190

------------
SendRequest(), len 49
    HEADER:
        opcode = QUERY, id = 2, rcode = NOERROR
        header flags: query, want recursion
        questions = 1,  answers = 0,  authority records = 0,  additional
= 0

    QUESTIONS:
        rain-city.reskit.com, type = A, class = IN

------------
------------
Got answer (108 bytes):
    HEADER:
        opcode = QUERY, id = 2, rcode = NOERROR
        header flags: response, auth. answer, want recursion, recursion
avail.
        questions = 1,  answers = 2,  authority records = 0,  additional
= 0

    QUESTIONS:
        rain-city.reskit.com, type = A, class = IN
    ANSWERS:
    ->  rain-city.reskit.com
        type = CNAME, class = IN, dlen = 31
        canonical name = seattle.reskit.com
        ttl = 86400 (1 day)
    ->  seattle.reskit.com
        type = A, class = IN, dlen = 4
        internet address = 172.16.2.3
        ttl = 86400 (1 day)

------------
(null)   seattle.reskit.com
Address: 172.16.2.3
Aliases: rain-city.reskit.com
```

In this example, the user issued the **set d2** command to set Nslookup to debug mode, then the user tried a simple address lookup for the host name "rain-city." The first two lines of output show the host name and IP address of the DNS server where the lookup was sent. As the next paragraph shows, the domain suffix of the local computer (reskit.com) was appended to the name "rain-city," and Nslookup submitted this question to the DNS server.

The next paragraph in the example indicates that Nslookup received an answer from the DNS server. The DNS server provided two answer records in response to one question. The question is repeated in the response, along with the two answer records. In this case, the first answer record indicates that the name "rain-city.reskit.com" is actually a *cname*, or *canonical name* (alias) for the host name "seattle.reskit.com." The second answer record lists the IP address for that host as 172.16.2.3.

Table 3.8 summarizes all Nslookup switches. Identifiers are shown in upper case, and optional commands are shown in brackets.

Table 3.8 Nslookup Switches

Switch	Function
nslookup	Launches the nslookup program.
set debug	Launches debug mode from within nslookup.
set d2	Launches verbose debug mode from within nslookup.
host name	Returns the IP address for the specified host name.
NAME	Displays information about the host/domain NAME using default server
NAME1 NAME2	As above, but uses NAME2 as server
help or ?	Displays information about common commands

(continued)

Table 3.8 Nslookup Switches *(continued)*

Switch	Function
set OPTION	Sets an option
All	Displays options, current server and host.
[no]debug	Displays debugging information.
[no]defname	Appends domain name to each query.
[no]recurse	Asks for recursive answer to query.
[no]search	Uses domain search list.
[no]vc	Always uses a virtual circuit.
domain=NAME	Sets default domain name to NAME.
srchlist=N1[/N2/.../N6]	Sets domain to N1 and search list to N1,N2, and so on.
root =NAME	Sets root server to NAME.
retry=X	Sets number of retries to X.
timeout=X	Sets initial timeout interval to X seconds.
type=X	Sets query type (such as A, ANY, CNAME, MX, NS, PTR, SOA, SRV).
querytype=X	Same as type.
class=X	Sets query class (ex. IN (Internet), ANY).
[no]msxfr	Uses MS fast zone transfer.
ixfrver=X	Current version to use in IXFR transfer request.
server NAME	Sets default server to NAME, using current default server.
lserver NAME	Sets default server to NAME, using initial server.
finger [USER	Fingers the optional NAME at the current default host.
root	Sets current default server to the root.
ls [opt] DOMAIN [> FILE]	Lists addresses in DOMAIN (optional: output to FILE).
-a	Lists canonical names and aliases.
-d	Lists all records.
-t TYPE	Lists records of the given type (For example, A, CNAME, MX, NS, PTR and so on).
view FILE	Sorts the output file from the 'ls' option described earlier and displays it page by page.
exit	Exits Nslookup and returns to the command prompt.

PathPing

The PathPing tool is a route tracing tool that combines features of Ping and Tracert with additional information that neither of those tools provides. PathPing sends packets to each router on the way to a final destination over a period of time, and then computes results based on the packets returned from each hop. Since PathPing shows the degree of packet loss at any given router or link, you can pinpoint which routers or links might be causing network problems. A number of switches are available, as shown in Table 3.9.

Table 3.9 PathPing Switches

Switch	Name	Function
-n	Host names	Does not resolve addresses to host names.
-h *<Max hops>*	Maximum hops	Maximum number of hops to search for target.
-g *<destination address> <router IP addresses or NetBIOS names>*	Router -list	Use a loose source route along host-list.
-p *<milliseconds>*	Period	Number of milliseconds to wait between pings.
-q *<Number queries>*	Num_queries	Number of queries per hop.
-R	RSVP test	Checks to see if each router in the path supports the Resource Reservation Protocol (RSVP), which allows the host computer to reserve a certain amount of bandwidth for a data stream. The -R switch is used to test for Quality of Service (QoS) connectivity.
-T	Layer 2 tag	Attaches a layer 2 priority tag (for example, for IEEE 802.1p) to the packets and sends it to each of the network devices in the path. This helps in identifying the network devices that do not have layer 2 priority configured properly. The -T switch is used to test for Quality of Service (QoS) connectivity.
-w *<milliseconds>*	Time-out	Waits this many milliseconds for each reply.

The default number of hops is 30, and the default wait time before a time-out is three seconds (3000 milliseconds). The default period is 250 milliseconds, and the default number of queries to each router along the path is 100.

Below is a typical PathPing report. Note that the compiled statistics that follow the hop list indicate packet loss at each individual router.

```
D:\>pathping -n testpc1

Tracing route to testpc1 [7.54.1.196]
over a maximum of 30 hops:
  0  172.16.87.35
  1  172.16.87.218
  2  192.168.52.1
  3  192.168.80.1
  4  7.54.247.14
  5  7.54.1.196

Computing statistics for 125 seconds...
            Source to Here   This Node/Link
Hop  RTT    Lost/Sent = Pct  Lost/Sent = Pct  Address
  0                                           172.16.87.35
                                0/ 100 =  0%   |
  1   41ms     0/ 100 =  0%     0/ 100 =  0%  172.16.87.218
                               13/ 100 = 13%   |
  2   22ms    16/ 100 = 16%     3/ 100 =  3%  192.168.52.1
                                0/ 100 =  0%   |
  3   24ms    13/ 100 = 13%     0/ 100 =  0%  192.168.80.1
                                0/ 100 =  0%   |
  4   21ms    14/ 100 = 14%     1/ 100 =  1%  7.54.247.14
                                0/ 100 =  0%   |
  5   24ms    13/ 100 = 13%     0/ 100 =  0%  7.54.1.196

Trace complete.
```

When PathPing is run, the first results you see list the route as it is tested for problems. This is the same path that is shown via Tracert. PathPing then displays a busy message for the next 125 seconds (this time varies by the hop count, requiring 25 seconds per hop). During this time PathPing gathers information from all the routers previously listed and from the links between them. At the end of this period, it displays the test results.

The two rightmost columns—"This Node/Link Lost/Sent=%" and "Address"—contain the most useful information. The link between 172.16.87.218 (hop 1), and 192.168.52.1 (hop 2) is dropping 13 percent of the packets. All other links are working normally. The routers at hops 2 and 4 also drop packets addressed to them (as shown in the "This Node/Link" column), but this loss does not affect their forwarding path.

The loss rates displayed for the links (marked as a "|" in the rightmost column) indicate losses of packets being forwarded along the path. This loss indicates link congestion. The loss rates displayed for routers (indicated by their IP addresses in the rightmost column) indicate that those routers' CPUs or packet buffers might be overloaded. These congested routers might also be a factor in end-to-end problems, especially if packets are forwarded by software routers.

Loss Calculation

The raw data that PathPing obtains describes how many ICMP Echo Requests are lost between the source and an intermediate router. Figure 3.1 shows how PathPing estimates the per-hop loss statistics. While at first this calculation might seem trivial, it is complicated by differences between the forwarding code path and the code path taken in responding to ping packets (ICMP Echo Requests/Replies).

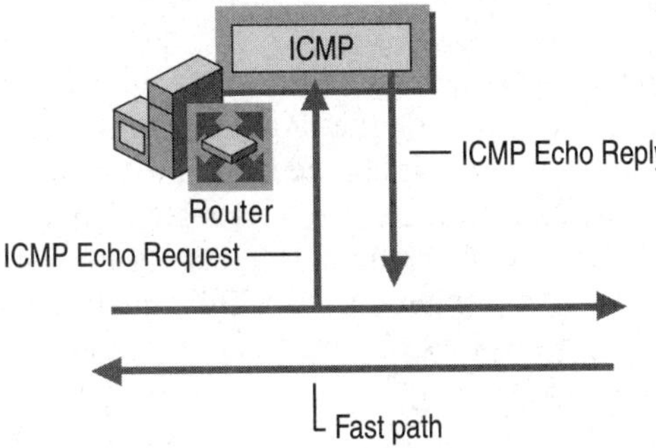

Figure 3.1 Packet Delivery Paths

The horizontal lines indicate the "fast path" of a router, which is taken by packets that are not sent to or from the local computer. That is, the fast path is the code path taken by transit packets that require no special processing other than forwarding, and is highly optimized for such packets.

In the diagram, the vertical lines indicate the extra processing taken when an ICMP Echo Request is sent to the local computer. This kicks it out of the fast path and delivers it to an ICMP module (often using separate queues and processors). Assuming no packets are dropped due to queue overflows, the ICMP module then generates an ICMP Echo Reply, which is forwarded back to the original sender.

Since packet loss can occur in the path indicated by the vertical lines (but such loss does not necessarily imply loss on the horizontal forwarding path itself), the raw numbers obtained from pings do not by themselves determine end-to-end packet loss. For example, pinging an intermediate router might create a 10 percent loss even though no end-to-end packet loss is occurring. PathPing's algorithm uses the change in values from hop-to-hop to estimate actual per hop loss rather than losses in the higher-level router components. This actual per hop loss is the result provided in the "This Node/Link" column of the final PathPing report.

Ping

Ping is the primary tool for troubleshooting IP-level connectivity. Type **ping -?** at a command prompt to see a complete list of available command-line options. Ping allows you to specify the size of packets to use (the default is 32 bytes), how many to send, whether to record the route used, what Time To Live (TTL) value to use, and whether to set the "don't fragment" flag.

When a **ping** command is issued, the utility sends an ICMP Echo Request to a destination IP address. Try pinging the IP address of the target host to see if it responds. If that succeeds, try pinging the target host using a host name. Ping first attempts to resolve the name to an address through a DNS server, then a WINS server (if one is configured), then attempts a local broadcast. When using DNS for name resolution, if the name entered is not a fully qualified domain name, the DNS name resolver appends the computer's domain name or names to generate a fully qualified domain name.

If pinging by address succeeds but pinging by name fails, the problem usually lies in name resolution, not network connectivity. Note that name resolution might fail if you do not use a fully qualified domain name for a remote name. These requests fail because the DNS name resolver is appending the local domain suffixes to a name that resides elsewhere in the domain hierarchy.

The following example illustrates how to send two pings, each 1450 bytes in size, to address 172.16.99.2:

```
C:\>ping -n 2 -l 1450 172.16.99.2

Pinging 172.16.99.2 with 1450 bytes of data:

Reply from 172.16.99.2: bytes=1450 time<10ms TTL=62
Reply from 172.16.99.2: bytes=1450 time<10ms TTL=62

Ping statistics for 172.16.99.2:
    Packets: Sent = 2, Received = 2, Lost = 0 (0% loss),
Approximate round trip times in milli-seconds:
    Minimum = 0ms, Maximum =  0ms, Average =  0ms
```

By default, Ping waits one second for each response to be returned before timing out. If the remote system being pinged is across a high-delay link such as a satellite link, responses might take longer to be returned. Use the -w (wait) switch to specify a longer time-out.

Note If Ping indicates a high packet loss or slow round-trip response on a LAN, your network might have a hardware problem. On a WAN, these results may be normal, and TCP/IP is designed to handle the variability. On a LAN, round-trip time is very low, and you see little or no packet loss. If this isn't the case, test your cables, cable terminations, hubs, switches, and transceivers.

Table 3.10 lists Ping switches.

Table 3.10 Ping Switches

Switch	Function
-t	Pings the specified host until stopped. To see statistics and continue type Control-Break. To stop type Control-C.
-a	Resolves addresses to host names.
-n <*count*>	Sets number of echo requests to send.
-l <*size*>	Sends packets of a particular size.
-f	Sets the "Don't Fragment" flag in outgoing packets.
-i <*TTL*>	Specifies a Time To Live for outgoing packets.
-v <*TOS*>	Specifies type of service.
-r <*count*>	Records the route for count hops.
-s <*count*>	Timestamp for count hops.
-j <*host-list*>	Loose source route along host-list.
-k <*host-list*>	Strict source route along host-list.
-w	Sets a long wait periods (in milliseconds) for a response.

Route

Route is used to view and modify the IP routing table. **Route Print** displays a list of current routes that the host knows. Sample output from the **route** command is shown in "Troubleshooting IP Routing" later in this chapter. **Route Add** adds routes to the table. **Route Delete** removes routes from the host's routing table.

Note Routes added to a routing table are not made persistent unless the **-p** switch is specified. Non-persistent routes only last until the computer is restarted or until the interface is deactivated. The interface can be deactivated when the plug-and-play interface is unplugged (such as for laptops and hot-swap PCs), when the wire is removed from the media card (if the adapter supports media fault sensing), or when the interface is manually disconnected from the adapter in the **Network and Dial-up Connections** folder.

For two hosts to exchange IP datagrams, they must both have a route to each other, or they must use a default gateway that knows a route between the two. Normally, routers exchange information using a protocol such as Routing Information Protocol (RIP) or Open Shortest Path First (OSPF). RIP Listening service is available for Microsoft® Windows® 2000 Professional, and full routing protocols are supported by Windows 2000 Server in the Routing and Remote Access service.

The usage for Route is **route** [**-f**] [**-p**] [*command* [*destination*]] [*MASK netmask*] [*gateway*] [**metric** *metric*] [**if** *interface*].

The commands usable in the syntax above are **Print**, **Add**, **Delete**, and **Change**. Table 3.11 lists these commands as well as the other Route switches and parameters.

Table 3.11 Route Switches

Switch	Function
-f	Clears the routing table of all gateway entries. If this is used in conjunction with one of the other commands, the tables are cleared prior to running the command.
-p	When used with the Add command, this switch adds the route to the routing table and to the Windows 2000 registry. The route is automatically added to the routing table each time the TCP/IP protocol is initialized. By default, routes added without the -p switch are only stored in the RAM-based IP routing table and are not preserved when the TCP/IP is restarted. This option is ignored for all other commands.
Print *<destination>*	Prints a route to the specified host. Optionally, prints the routes for the specified destination.

(continued)

Table 3.11 Route Switches *(continued)*

Switch	Function
Add *<destination>* Mask *<netmask>* *<gateway>* Metric *<metric>* if *<interface>*	Adds a route for the specified destination using the forwarding IP address of the gateway. The **metric** and **if** options are not required.
Delete *<destination>*	Deletes a route for the specified destination.
Change *<destination>* Mask *<netmask>* *<gateway>* Metric *<metric>* if *<interface>*	Modifies an existing route.
Mask *<netmask>*	Specifies that the next parameter is the network mask value. If a netmask value is not specified, it defaults to 255.255.255.255.
Metric *<metric>*	Specifies the cost to reach the destination. Routes with lower metrics are chosen over routes with higher metrics. A typical use of the metric value is to indicate the number of routers that must be crossed to reach the destination.
if *<interface>*	Specifies the IP address of the interface over which the destination is available.

All symbolic names used for the destination are looked up in the network database file NETWORKS. The symbolic names for the gateway are looked up in the host name database file HOSTS. If the command is **print** or **delete**, the destination value can be a wildcard value specified by an asterisk ("*"). If the destination specified contains a * or ?, it is treated as a shell pattern, and only matching destination routes are printed. The asterisk matches any string, and the question mark matches any one character. For example, 157.*.1, 157.*, 127.*, *224* are all valid uses of the wildcard asterisk.

Using an invalid combination of a destination and netmask value generates a "route: bad gateway address netmask" error. This sort of error message appears, for example, when a bitwise logical AND between the destination and mask does not equal the destination value.

Tracert

Tracert is a route tracing utility that display a list of near-side router interfaces of the routers along the path between a source host and a destination. Tracert uses the IP TTL field in ICMP Echo Requests and ICMP Time Exceeded messages to determine the path from a source to a destination through an IP internetwork.

Note that some routers silently drop packets with expired TTLs. These routers do not appear in the Tracert display.

How Tracert Works

Tracert works by incrementing the TTL value by one for each ICMP Echo Request it sends, then waiting for an ICMP Time Exceeded message. The TTL values of the Tracert packets start with an initial value of one; the TTL of each trace after the first is incremented by one. A packet sent out by Tracert travels one hop further on each successive trip.

Figure 3.2 shows how Tracert works. Tracert is being run on Host A, and is following the path to Host B. At Router 1 and Router 2, the TTL is decremented to 0, causing each router to send an ICMP Time Exceeded message. When the ICMP Echo Request is received at Host B, it sends back an ICMP Echo Reply.

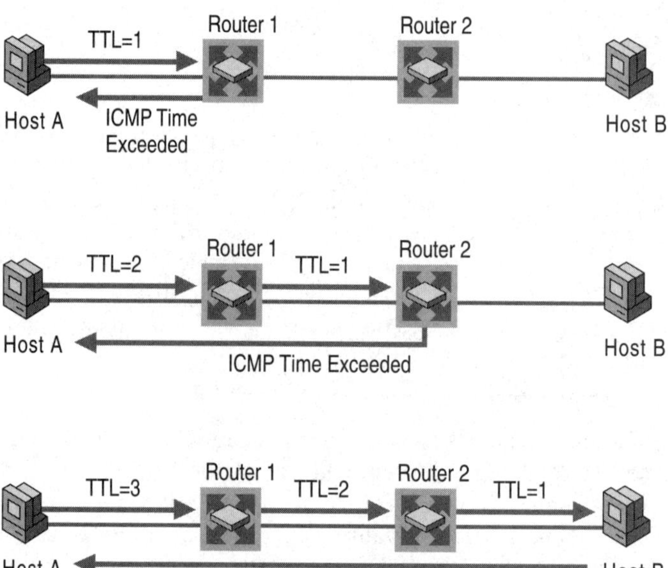

Figure 3.2 Step-by-Step Operation of the Tracert Tool

Note The UNIX version of Tracert performs the same function as the Windows version except that the IP payload is a UDP packet addressed to a (presumably) unknown destination UDP port. Intermediate routers send back ICMP Time Expired messages recording the route taken and the final destination sends back an ICMP Destination Unreachable-Port Unreachable message.

The UDP payload from the UNIX Tracert tool can cross routers and firewalls, whereas the ICMP Echo Request messages might not due to ICMP filtering. To avoid this problem in Windows 2000, turn off packet filtering as described in "Check Packet Filtering" later in this chapter, then try using Tracert again.

Interpreting Tracert Results

Following is an example of a **tracert** command output. Beginning with the first entry, it shows each router discovered on the way to the final destination in sequence; after the first two routers the trace reaches its destination. The lines of the tracert display have been indented for readability.

```
C:\tracert reskit
Tracing route to reskit.dns.microsoft.com [172.16.180.113] over a
maximum of 30 hops:
1      <10 ms    <10 ms     <10 ms
     ms28-rtr1-f10-00.network.microsoft.com [157.59.0.1]
2      <10 ms    <10 ms     <10 ms
     ms42-rtr1-a5-00-1.network.microsoft.com [157.54.247.98]
1      <10 ms    <10 ms     <10 ms
     RESKIT [172.16.180.113]
```

In cases where a trace either fails to reach its destination or no ICMP Time Exceeded messages are returned, the output shows an asterisk in each of the three time columns where the round-trip time is usually displayed, and shows a "Request timed out." or other error message in the right-hand column where a domain name or IP address is usually displayed.

Table 3.12 lists Tracert switches.

Table 3.12 Tracert Switches

Switch	Function
-d	Specifies to not resolve addresses of router interfaces to host names.
-h *<maximum_hops>*	Specifies a maximum number of hops to reach destination.
-j *<host_list>*	Specifies loose source routing along the host-list.
-w *<timeout>*	Indicates how many milliseconds to wait for each reply.

Troubleshooting Overview

When troubleshooting any problem, ask yourself the following questions:

- What application is failing? What works? What doesn't work?
- Is the problem basic IP connectivity or is it name resolution? If the problem is name resolution, does the failing application use NetBIOS names or DNS names and host names?
- How are the things that do and don't work related?
- Have the things that don't work ever worked on this computer or network?
- If so, what has changed since they last worked?

Ideally, a review of the location and timing of the problem helps narrow the problem's scope. In addition, you can examine TCP/IP failures systematically by referring to the steps needed for successful computer communications . These steps are described in the following sections; suggested methods for troubleshooting begin in the "Unable to Resolve a Host or NetBIOS Name" section of this chapter.

TCP/IP Communication

The TCP/IP process for two computers to communicate over a network breaks down into four distinct steps. The four steps the TCP/IP protocol takes on a sending host before sending out a packet are:

1. Resolves the host name or NetBIOS name to an IP address.
2. Using the destination IP address and the IP routing table, TCP/IP determines the interface to use and the forwarding IP address.
3. For unicast IP traffic on shared access technologies such as Ethernet, Token Ring, and Fiber Distributed Data Interface (FDDI), ARP resolves the forwarding IP address to a MAC address.

   For multicast IP traffic on Ethernet and FDDI, the destination multicast IP address is mapped to the appropriate multicast MAC address. For multicast IP traffic on Token Ring, the functional address of 0xC0-00-00-04-00-00 is used. For broadcast traffic on shared access technologies, the MAC address is mapped to OxFF-FF-FF-FF-FF-FF.
4. The IP datagram is sent to the MAC address resolved through ARP or through the multicast mapping.

The following sections describe each portion of this process. The TCP/IP stack always follows this sequence when determining how to get a packet from point to point. To skip directly to the standard troubleshooting sequence, see the "Unable to Resolve a Host or NetBIOS Name" section of this chapter.

Resolving a Name to an IP Address

If the destination to be reached by an application is in the format of a NetBIOS name or host name, then name resolution is required before IP can send the first packet. IP only understands IP addresses; host and NetBIOS names are each resolved to an IP address in different ways.

Resolving a NetBIOS Name to an IP Address

NetBIOS names can be directly resolved to an IP address through four mechanisms: consulting the cache, broadcasting, checking the LMHOSTS file or querying a WINS server. The order in which Windows 2000 uses these mechanisms depends upon the node type of the client.

Windows 2000 always begins by checking the host computer's internal NetBIOS name cache. If this fails to provide an IP address, the NetBIOS name can be resolved to an IP address using a broadcast, an LMHOST file, or a WINS servers. Which of these three is used first by any particular computer depends on its node type; the default node type is hybrid or H-node, which starts by querying a WINS server, then attempts a local broadcast to resolve the name. For a detailed discussion of node types, see "Windows 2000 TCP/IP" in this book. If these mechanisms are exhausted, a client queries its Host file, and failing that, queries its DNS server if it is configured to use one.

Note that if the only problem is NetBIOS name resolution, the computershould still be able to reach the remote resource by IP address. The tools used to diagnose NetBIOS name resolution problems are Nbtstat, Nslookup, and the **net use** command.

For more information about WINS, see "Windows Internet Name Service" in this book.

Resolving a Host or Domain Name to an IP Address

Host names can be directly resolved by the Hosts file or by a DNS server. Problems here usually involve a misconfigured Hosts file or DNS server, a misspelled Hosts file entry or IP address, or multiple entries for a single host in a Hosts file. The tools used to diagnose host or domain resolution problems are Nslookup or Netdiag.

For more information about DNS, see "Introduction to DNS" and "Windows 2000 DNS" in this book.

Determining Whether an Address Is Local or Remote

The subnet mask and the IP address are used together to determine whether a destination IP address is local or remote.

At this point, configuration mistakes, such as a misconfigured subnet mask, can lead to the host becoming unable to reach other hosts on other local subnets, though it can still communicate with remote hosts on distant networks and hosts on its own subnet.

If the Destination Address Is Local, IP Uses ARP to Identify the Destination MAC Address

If the address is local, delivery requires little additional effort. ARP resolves the IP address into a hardware address, typically a Media Access Control (MAC) address for the destination Ethernet card. The problems found here are typically problems with the ARP cache (such as duplicate addresses) or the subnet mask, and can be solved by using the Arp or Ipconfig tools.

If the Address Is Remote, Determine the Correct Gateway

If the address is remote, the next step is to determine which gateway to use to reach the remote address. In a network with only a single router acting as an external connection, the problem is relatively straightforward. However, in any network with more than one router attached, determining which gateway to use is more difficult.

IP solves the problem by consulting its routing table This routing table serves as a decision tree that enables IP to decide which interface and which gateway it should use to send the outgoing traffic. The routing table contains many individual routes; each route consists of a destination, net mask, gateway interface and metric.

If two routes are identical, the route with the lowest metric is chosen over the route with a higher metric. Note that the routing table is parsed from the most specific to the most general, so the packet is sent to the first gateway whose routing table entry matches the packet's destination. In the case of a tie, the choice is made in round-robin fashion. Problems found here are addressed with the Route tool or with network configuration changes.

ARP for Gateway Address

Once the correct gateway is determined, the ARP process is performed for the gateway address just as it is for any other local address. The ARP broadcast returns a hardware address, and the message is sent to the gateway to be routed further.

Unable to Reach a Host or NetBIOS Name

TCP/IP for Windows 2000 allows an application to communicate over a network with another computer by using three basic types of destination designations:

- IP address
- Host name
- NetBIOS name

This section describes how to troubleshoot either host name or NetBIOS name resolution problems. Problems with IP addressing are covered in "Unable to Reach an IP Address" later in this chapter. Both of these issues are outlined in Figures 3.3-3.5, which provide a simplified flowchart to guide troubleshooting.

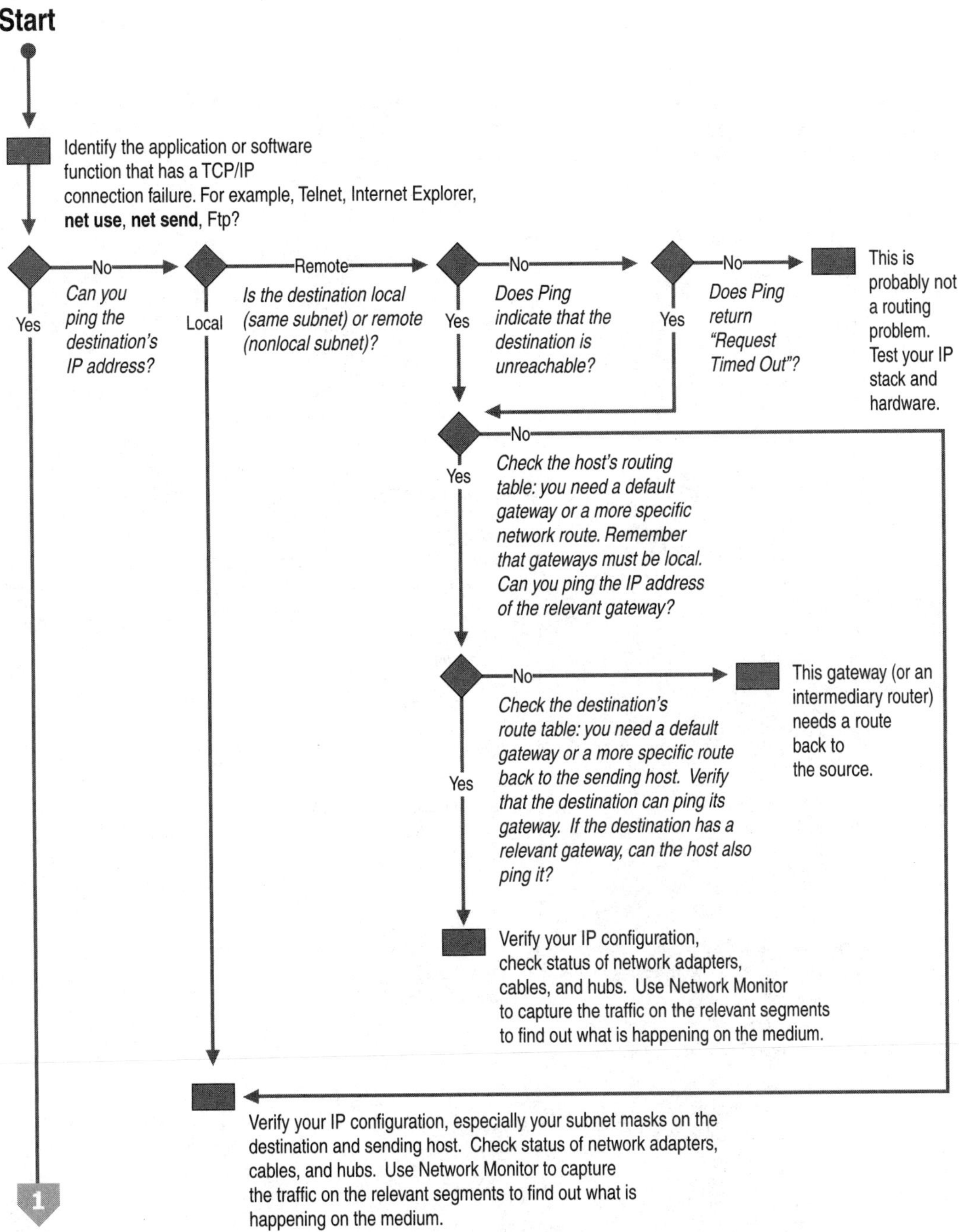
Start
Identify the application or software function that has a TCP/IP connection failure. For example, Telnet, Internet Explorer, net use, net send, Ftp?
No
Can you ping the destination's IP address?
Yes
Remote
Is the destination local (same subnet) or remote (nonlocal subnet)?
Local
No
Does Ping indicate that the destination is unreachable?
Yes
No
Does Ping return "Request Timed Out"?
Yes
No
This is probably not a routing problem. Test your IP stack and hardware.
No
Check the host's routing table: you need a default gateway or a more specific network route. Remember that gateways must be local. Can you ping the IP address of the relevant gateway?
Yes
No
Check the destination's route table: you need a default gateway or a more specific route back to the sending host. Verify that the destination can ping its gateway. If the destination has a relevant gateway, can the host also ping it?
Yes
This gateway (or an intermediary router) needs a route back to the source.
Verify your IP configuration, check status of network adapters, cables, and hubs. Use Network Monitor to capture the traffic on the relevant segments to find out what is happening on the medium.
Verify your IP configuration, especially your subnet masks on the destination and sending host. Check status of network adapters, cables, and hubs. Use Network Monitor to capture the traffic on the relevant segments to find out what is happening on the medium.
1

Figure 3.3 TCP/IP Troubleshooting Flowchart (Part 1 of 3)

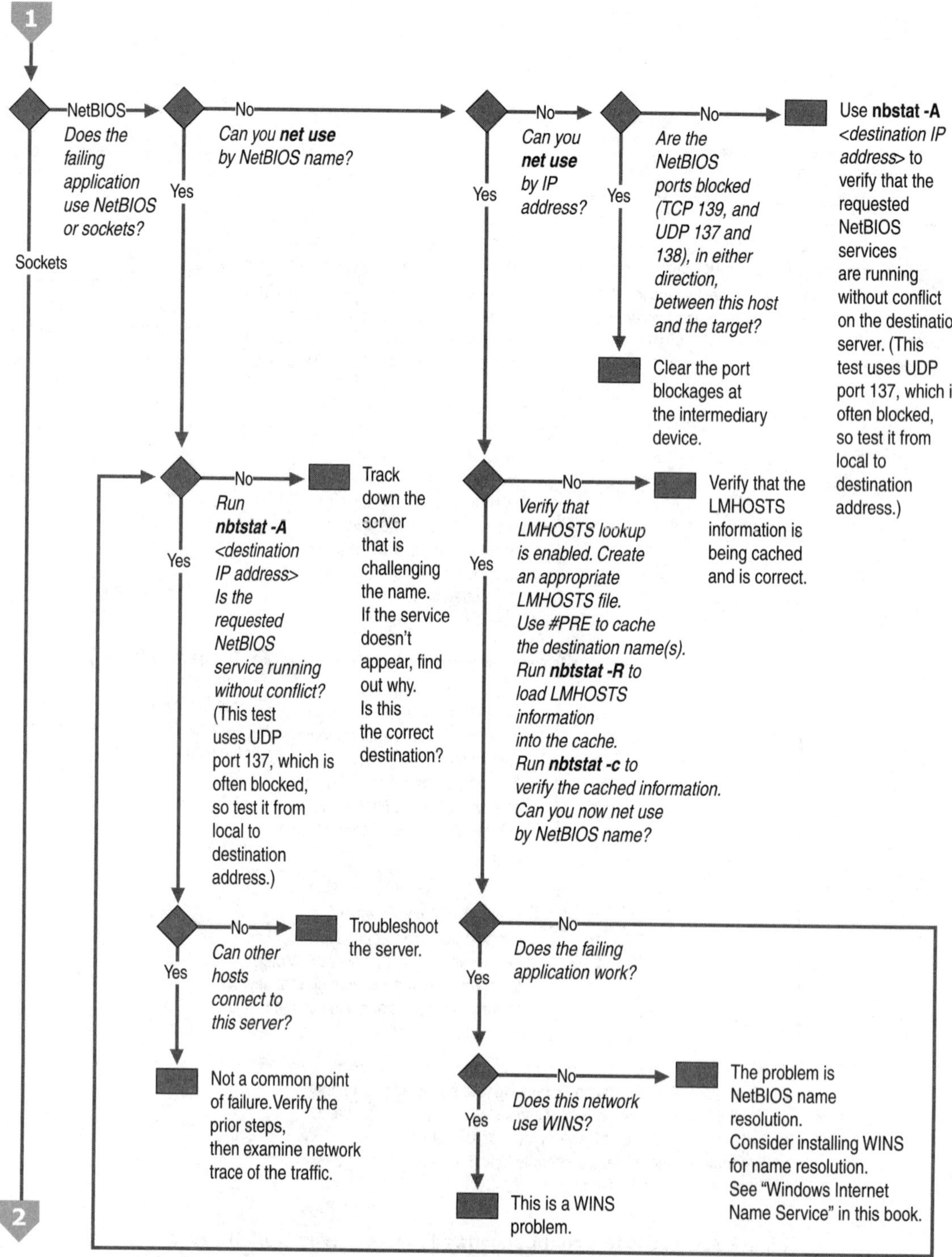

Figure 3.4 TCP/IP Troubleshooting Flowchart (Part 2 of 3)

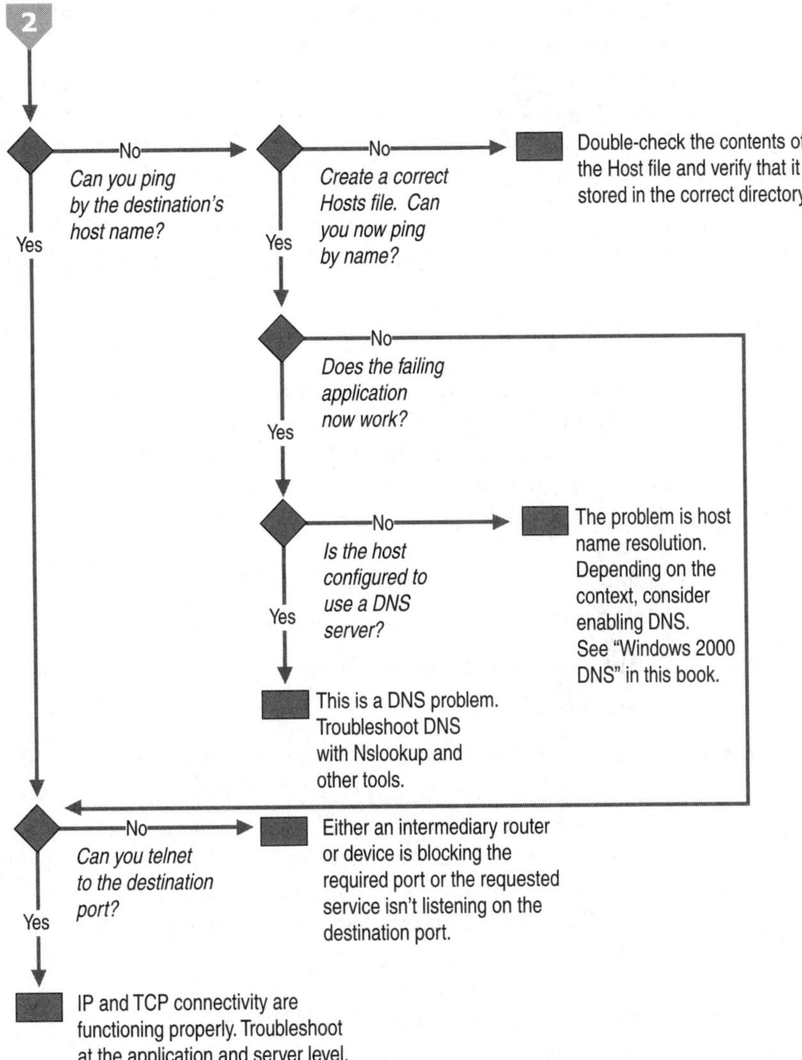

Figure 3.5 TCP/IP Troubleshooting Flowchart (Part 3 of 3)

The first step is to determine which application is failing. Typically, this is Telnet, Internet Explorer, **net use**, a server manager, or Ftp. Making this determination helps with the next step, which is to determine whether the problem is a host name or NetBIOS name resolution problem.

The easiest way to distinguish host name problems from NetBIOS name resolution problems is to find out whether the failing application uses NetBIOS or Sockets. If it uses Sockets, the problem lies with a DNS/host name resolution. Among the most common applications, the NetBIOS family includes the various NET commands or the Windows NT 4.0 administrator tools while Sockets and WinSockets applications include Telnet, Ftp, and web browsers.

The following sections describe the processes that occur when using a host name or a NetBIOS name to connect with hosts on a TCP/IP network.

Error 53

The most common symptom of a problem in NetBIOS name resolution is when the Ping utility returns an Error 53 message. The Error 53 message is generally returned when name resolution fails for a particular computer name. Error 53 can also occur when there is a problem establishing a NetBIOS session. To distinguish betweenthese two cases, use the following procedure:

▶ **To determine the cause of an Error 53 message**

1. From the **Start** menu, open a command prompt.
2. At the command prompt, type:

   net view \\<*hostname*>

   where <*hostname*> is a network resource you know is active.

   If this works, your name resolution is probably not the source of the problem. To confirm this, ping the host name, as name resolution can sometimes function properly and yet net use returns an Error 53 (such as when a DNS or WINS server has a bad entry). If Ping also shows that name resolution fails (by returning the "Unknown host" message), check the status of your NetBIOS session.

▶ **To check the status of your NetBIOS session**

1. From the **Start** menu, open a command prompt.
2. At the command prompt, type:

   net view \\<*IP address*>

   where <*IP address*> is the same network resource you used in the above procedure. If this also fails, the problem is in establishing a session.

If the computer is on the local subnet, confirm that the name is spelled correctly and that the target computer is running TCP/IP as well. If the computer is not on the local subnet, be sure that its name and IP address mapping are available in the DNS database, the Hosts or LMHOSTS file, or the WINS database.

If all TCP/IP elements appear to be installed properly, use Ping with the remote computer to be sure its TCP/IP protocol is working.

Cannot Connect to Remote Systems Using Host Name

If the problem is not NetBIOS but Sockets, the problem is related to either a Hosts file or a DNS configuration error. To determine why only IP addresses but not host names work for connections to remote computers, make sure that the appropriate Hosts file and DNS setup have been configured for the computer.

▶ **To check host name resolution configuration**

1. In Control Panel, click the **Network and Dialup Connection** icon.
2. Right-click **Local Area Connections,** and then select **Properties**.
3. Click on **Internet Protocol (TCP/IP)**, and then click **Properties**.
4. Click the **Advanced** tab in the **Microsoft TCP/IP Properties** dialog box.
5. Click the **DNS** tab.
6. Confirm that DNS is configured properly. If the DNS server IP address is missing, add it to the list of DNS server addresses.

Note that this procedure does not take DHCP clients into account; these clients do not have DNS server in the list.

Check the Hosts File

If you are having trouble connecting to a remote system using a host name and are using a Hosts file for name resolution, the problem may be with the contents of that file. Make sure the name of the remote computer is spelled correctly in the Hosts file and by the application using it.

The Hosts file or a DNS server is used to resolve host names to IP addresses whenever you use TCP/IP utilities such as Ping. You can find the Hosts file in *%SystemRoot%*\System32\Drivers\Etc.

This file is not dynamic; all entries are made manually. The file format is the following:

```
IP Address              Friendly Name
172.16.48.10            testpc1  # Remarks are denoted with a #.
```

The IP address and friendly host name are always separated by one or more space or tab characters.

Host Name Resolution Using a Hosts File

A computer using its Hosts file for name resolution performs the following steps.

1. Computer A enters a command using the host name of Computer B.
2. Computer A parses its Hosts file (in \%SystemRoot%\System32\Drivers\Etc), looking for the Computer B host name. When the host name of Computer B is found, it is resolved to an IP address.
3. The resolved IP address is passed to the IP routing component. The routing component returns either a routing error because a route was not found for the destination IP address or the forwarding IP address and interface over which the packet is to be forwarded cannot be found.
4. ARP resolves the forwarding IP address to a hardware address.

The following Hosts file problems can cause networking errors:

- The Hosts file does not contain the particular host name.
- The host name in the Hosts file or in the command is misspelled.
- The IP address for the host name in the Hosts file is invalid or incorrect.
- The Hosts file contains multiple entries for the same host on separate lines. Because the Hosts file is parsed from the top, the first entry found is used.

Check Your DNS Configuration

If you are using DNS, be sure that the IP addresses of the DNS servers are correct and in the proper order. Use Ping with the remote computer's host name and then with its IP address to determine whether the host address is being resolved properly. If the host name ping fails and the IP address ping succeeds, the problem is with name resolution. You can test whether the DNS servers are running by pinging their IP addresses or by opening a Telnet session to port 53 on the DNS server. If the connection is established successfully, the DNS service is working on the DNS server. Once you've verified that the DNS service is running, you can perform NSLookup queries to the DNS server to further verify the status of the records you are looking for.

If ping by IP address and by name fail, the problem is with network connectivity, such basic connectivity or routing. For more information about troubleshooting network connectivity, see "Troubleshooting IP Routing" later in this chapter.

A brief summary of how DNS resolves host names is provided in this section. For more information about DNS, see "Windows 2000 DNS" in this book.

Host Name Resolution Using a DNS Server

DNS is a distributed database that maps domain names to data. A user can query DNS using hierarchical, friendly names to locate computers and other resources on an IP network. This allows it to largely replace the function once performed by the Hosts file. To do so, it resolves friendly names to IP addresses as follows (in the worst-case scenario, an answer might be provided by any server along the line, preventing the need for further iterative queries):

1. The client contacts the DNS name server with a recursive query for name.reskit.com. The server must now return the answer or an error message.
2. The DNS name server checks its cache and zone files for the answer, but doesn't find it. It contacts a server at the root of the Internet (a root DNS server) with an iterative query for name.reskit.com.
3. The root server doesn't know the answer, so it responds with a referral to an authoritative server in the .com domain.
4. The DNS name server contacts a server in the .com domain with an iterative query for name.reskit.com.
5. The server in the .com domain does not know the exact answer, so it responds with a referral to an authoritative server in the reskit.com domain.
6. The DNS name server contacts the server in the reskit.com domain with an iterative query for name.reskit.com.
7. The server in the reskit.com domain does know the answer. It responds with the correct IP address.
8. The DNS name server responds to the client query with the IP address for name.reskit.com.

Note that this example is specific to the Internet. For more information about DNS host name resolution, recursive queries, and iterative queries, see "Introduction to DNS" in this book.

DNS Error Messages

Errors in name resolution can occur if the entries in a DNS server or client are not configured correctly, if the DNS server is not running, or if there is a problem with network connectivity. To determine the cause of any name resolution problem, you can use the Nslookup utility.

Failed queries will return a variety of messages, depending on the nature of the failure. For example, if the server cannot resolve the name, it returns a message in the following format:

```
C:\nslookup <Destination_host>
Server: <fully_qualified_domain_name>
Address: <server_IP_address>
***  <fully_qualified_domain_name> can't find <Destination_host>: Non-
existent domain
```

In other cases, the requests to the DNS service time out without a reply and returns a message in the following format:

```
C:\nslookup Valid_Host
Server: [IP_Address]
Address: w.x.y.z
DNS request timed out.
    timeout was 2 seconds.
```

If the server fails to answer the request, Nslookup returns an error message in the following format:

```
C:\nslookup
*** Can't find server name for address <IP_Address>: No response from
server
*** Default servers are not available.
```

This message indicates that the DNS server cannot be reached; it does not indicate why the server is unavailable. The server might be offline, the host computer might not have the DNS service enabled, or there might be a hardware or routing problem.

For more information about DNS troubleshooting, see "Introduction to DNS" in this book.

Check the LMHOSTS File

The name resolution problem might be in your LMHOSTS file, which looks for addresses sequentially from the top down. If more than one address is listed for the same host name, TCP/IP returns the first value it encounters, whether that value is accurate or not.

You can find the LMHOSTS file in \\%*SystemRoot*%\System32\Drivers\Etc. Note that this file does not exist by default; a sample file named LMHOSTS.SAM exists. This file must be renamed to LMHOSTS before it is used.

Note While \\%*SystemRoot*%\System32\Drivers\Etc is the default directory for this file, exactly which LMHOSTS file is consulted depends on the value of the HKEY_LOCAL_MACHINE\SYSTEM\CurrentControlSet\Services\Tcpip\Parameters**databasepath** registry entry. The database path tells the local computer where to look for the LMHOSTS file.

Long Connect Times Using LMHOSTS

To determine the cause of long connect times after adding an entry to LMHOSTS, take a look at the order of the entries in the LMHOSTS file.

Long connect times can occur when a large LMHOSTS file has the specified entry at the end of the file. To speed up resolution of the entry, mark the entry in LMHOSTS as a preloaded entry by following the mapping with the #PRE tag (see "Nbtstat" earlier in this chapter for an example). Then use the **nbtstat -R** command to update the local name cache immediately.

Alternately, you can place the mapping higher in the LMHOSTS file. As discussed in the appendix "LMHOSTS File" in this book, the LMHOSTS file is parsed sequentially from the top to locate entries without the #PRE keyword. Therefore, you should always place frequently used entries near the top of the file and place the #PRE entries near the bottom.

Check the WINS Configuration

Make sure your computer's WINS configuration is correct. In particular, check the address for the WINS server.

► **To examine your WINS configuration**

1. In **Control Panel**, click the **Network and Dial-up Connections** icon.
2. Right-click **Local Area Connection**, and then click **Properties**.
3. In the **Local Area Connection Properties** dialog box, select **Internet Protocol (TCP/IP)**, and then click **Properties**.
4. In the **Internet Protocol (TCP/IP) Properties** dialog box, click **Advanced**.
5. In the **Advanced TCP/IP Settings** dialog box, click the **WINS** tab.

In the **WINS Configuration** dialog box, add the server's IP address (if none is listed) and check to see whether LMHOSTS lookup is enabled. Also check to see whether NetBIOS over TCP/IP is taken from the DHCP server, enabled, or disabled. If you are using DHCP for this host computer, take the value from the DHCP server. Otherwise, enable NetBIOS over TCP/IP.

Unable to Reach an IP Address

If host name resolution occurs successfully, the problem might lie elsewhere. In this case, the problem might be simply a matter of correcting the IP configuration rather than examining the name resolution process.

TCP/IP troubleshooting generally follows a set pattern. In general, first verify that the problem computer's TCP/IP configuration is correct, and then verify that a connection and a route exist between the computer and destination host by using Ping, as described in "Testing Network Connection with Ping and PathPing" later in this chapter.

Compile a list of what works and what doesn't work, and then study the list to help isolate the failure. If link reliability is in question, try a large number of pings of various sizes at different times of the day, and plot the success rate or use the PathPing utility. When all else fails, use a protocol analyzer such as Microsoft Network Monitor.

Check Configuration with IPConfig

When troubleshooting a TCP/IP networking problem, begin by checking the TCP/IP configuration on the computer experiencing the problem. Use the **ipconfig** command to get the host computer configuration information, including the IP address, subnet mask, and default gateway.

When Ipconfig is used with the /all switch, it produces a detailed configuration report for all interfaces, including any configured remote access adapters. Ipconfig output may be redirected to a file and pasted into other documents. To do so, type **ipconfig** > *<directory\file name>*. The output is placed in the directory you specified with the file name you specified.

The output of Ipconfig can be reviewed to find any problems in the computer network configuration. For example, if a computer has been configured with an IP address that is a duplicate of an existing IP address that has already been detected, the subnet mask appears as 0.0.0.0.

The following example illustrates the results of an **ipconfig /all** command on a computer that is configured to use a DHCP server for automatic TCP/IP configuration, and WINS and DNS servers for name resolution:

```
Windows NT IP Configuration
    Host Name . . . . . . . . . : testpc1.reskit.com
    Node Type . . . . . . . . . : Hybrid
    IP Routing Enabled. . . . . : No
    WINS Proxy Enabled. . . . . : No
```

```
Ethernet adapter Local Area Connection:
    Adapter Domain Name . . . . : dns.reskit.com
    DNS Servers . . . . . . . . : 172.16.14.119
    Description . . . . . . . . : ELNK3 Ethernet Adapter.
    Physical Address. . . . . . : 00-20-AF-1D-2B-91
    DHCP Enabled. . . . . . . . : Yes
    IP Address. . . . . . . . . : 172.16.48.10
    Subnet Mask . . . . . . . . : 255.255.248.0
    Default Gateway . . . . . . : 172.16.48.03
    DHCP Server . . . . . . . . : 172.16.48.03
    Primary WINS Server . . . . : 172.16.48.04
    Secondary WINS Server . . . : 172.16.48.05
    Lease Obtained. . . . . . . : Sunday, May 2, 1999 11:43:01 PM
    Lease Expires . . . . . . . : Wednesday, May 5, 1999 11:43:01 PM
```

If no problems appear in the TCP/IP configuration, the next step is to test the ability to connect to other host computers on the TCP/IP network.

Test Network Connection with Ping and PathPing

Ping is a tool that helps to verify IP-level connectivity; PathPing is a tool that detects packet loss over multiple-hop trips. When troubleshooting, the **ping** command is used to send an ICMP Echo Request to a target host name or IP address. Use Ping whenever you want to verify that a host computer can send IP packets to a destination host. You can also use the Ping tool to isolate network hardware problems and incompatible configurations.

Note If you call **ipconfig /all** and receive a response, there is no need to ping the loopback address and your own IP address—Ipconfig has already done so in order to generate the report.

It is best to verify that a route exists between the local computer and a network host by first using ping and the IP address of the network host to which you want to connect. The command syntax is:

ping <*IP address*>

Perform the following steps when using Ping:

1. Ping the loopback address to verify that TCP/IP is installed and configured correctly on the local computer.

   ```
   ping 127.0.0.1
   ```

   If the loopback step fails, the IP stack is not responding. This might be because the TCP drivers are corrupted, the network adapter might not be working, or another service is interfering with IP.

2. Ping the IP address of the local computer to verify that it was added to the network correctly. Note that if the routing table is correct, this simply forwards the packet to the loopback address of 127.0.0.1.

   ```
   ping <IP address of local host>
   ```

3. Ping the IP address of the default gateway to verify that the default gateway is functioning and that you can communicate with a local host on the local network.

   ```
   ping <IP address of default gateway>
   ```

4. Ping the IP address of a remote host to verify that you can communicate through a router.

   ```
   ping <IP address of remote host>
   ```

5. Ping the host name of a remote host to verify that you can resolve a remote host name.

   ```
   ping <Host name of remote host>
   ```

6. Run a PathPing analysis to a remote host to verify that the routers on the way to the destination are operating correctly.

   ```
   pathping <IP address of remote host>
   ```

Note If your local address is returned as 169.254.y.z, you have been assigned an IP address by the Automatic Private IP Addressing (APIPA) feature of Windows 2000. This means that the local DHCP server is not configured properly or cannot be reached from your computer, and an IP address has been assigned automatically with a subnet mask of 255.255.0.0. Enable or correct the DHCP server, restart the local computer, and see if the networking problem persists.

If your local address is returned as 0.0.0.0, the Microsoft MediaSense software override started because the network adapter detects that it is not connected to a network. To correct this problem, turn off MediaSense by making sure that the network adapter and network cable are connected to a hub. If the connection is solid, reinstall the network adapter's drivers or a new network adapter.

Ping uses host name resolution to resolve a computer name to an IP address, so if pinging by address succeeds, but fails by name, then the problem lies in host name resolution, not network connectivity. For more information about troubleshooting host name resolution, see "Unable to Reach a Host or NetBIOS Name" earlier in this chapter.

If you cannot use Ping successfully at any point, check the following:

- The local computer's IP address is valid and appears correctly in the **IP Address** tab of the **Internet Protocol (TCP/IP) Properties** dialog box or when using the Ipconfig tool.
- A default gateway is configured and the link between the host and the default gateway is operational. For troubleshooting purposes, make sure that only one default gateway is configured. While it is possible to configure more than one default gateway, gateways beyond the first are only used if the IP stack determines that the original gateway is not functioning. Since the point of troubleshooting is to determine the status of the first configured gateway, delete all others to simplify your troubleshooting.

Important If the remote system being pinged is across a high-delay link such as a satellite link, responses might take longer to be returned. The **-w** (wait) switch can be used to specify a longer time-out. The following example shows a set of two pings, each 1450 bytes in size, that wait two seconds (2000 milliseconds) for a response before timing out.

```
C:\>ping -w 2000 -n 2 -l 1450 172.16.48.10
Pinging 172.16.48.10 with 1450 bytes of data:

Reply from 172.16.48.10: bytes=1450 time=1542ms TTL=32
Reply from 172.16.48.10: bytes=1450 time=1787ms TTL=32

Ping statistics for 172.16.48.10:
    Packets: Sent = 2, Received = 2, Lost = 0 (0% loss),
Approximate round trip times in milli-seconds:
    Minimum = 0ms, Maximum = 10ms, Average = 1664ms
```

Clear ARP Cache

If you can ping both the loopback address and your own IP address, the next step is to clear out the ARP cache and reload it. This can be done by using the Arp utility, first to display the cache entries with **arp -a** or **arp -g**. Delete the entries with **arp -d** *<IP address>*.

Verify Default Gateway

Next, look at the default gateway. The gateway address must be on the same network as the local host; if not, no messages from the host computer can be forwarded to any location outside the local network. Next, check to make sure that the default gateway address is correct as entered. Finally, check to see that the default gateway is a router, not just a host, and that it is enabled to forward IP datagrams.

Ping Remote Host

If the default gateway responds correctly, ping a remote host to ensure that network-to-network communications are operating as expected. If this fails, use Tracert to examine the path to the destination. For IP routers that are Windows NT or Windows 2000 computers, use the route utility or the Routing and Remote Access administrative tool on those computers to examine the IP routing table. For IP routers that are not Windows NT or Windows 2000 computers, use the appropriate utility or facility to examine the IP routing table.

Four error messages are commonly returned by Ping during troubleshooting. They are:

TTL Expired in Transit

The number of hops required to reach the destination exceeds the TTL set by the sending host to forward the packets. The default TTL value for ICMP Echo Requests sent by Ping is 32. In some cases, this is not enough to travel the required number of links to a destination. You can increase the TTL using the -i switch, up to a maximum of 255 links.

If increasing the TTL value fails to resolve the problem, the packets are being forwarded in a routing loop, a circular path among routers. Use Tracert to track down the source of the routing loop, which appears as a repeated series of the same IP addresses in the Tracert report. Next, make an appropriate change to the routing tables, or inform the administrator of a remote router of the problem.

Destination Host Unreachable

This message indicates one of two problems: either the local system has no route to the desired destination, or a remote router reports that it has no route to the destination. The two problems can be distinguished by the form of the message. If the message is simply "Destination Host Unreachable," then there is no route from the local system, and the packets to be sent were never put on the wire. Use the Route utility to check the local routing table.

If the message is "Reply From *<IP address>*: Destination Host Unreachable," then the routing problem occurred at a remote router, whose address is indicated by the "*<IP address>*" field. Use the appropriate utility or facility to check the IP routing table of the router assigned the IP address of *<IP address>*.

If you pinged using an IP address, retry it with a host name to ensure that the IP address you tried is correct.

Request Timed Out

This message indicates that no Echo Reply messages were received within the default time of 1 second. This can be due to many different causes; the most common include network congestion, failure of the ARP request, packet filtering, routing error, or a silent discard. Most often, it means that a route back to the sending host has failed. This might be because the destination host does not know the route back to the sending host, or one of the intermediary routers does not know the route back, or even that the destination host's default gateway does not know the route back. Check the routing table of the destination host to see whether it has a route to the sending host before checking tables at the routers.

If the remote routing tables are correct and contain a valid route back to the sending host, to see if the ARP cache lacks the proper address, use the **arp -a** command to print the contents of the ARP cache. Also, check the subnet mask to be sure that a remote address has not been interpreted as local.

Next, use Tracert to follow the route to the destination. While Tracert does not record the address of the last hop or the path that the packet followed on the return path, it might show that the packet made it to the destination. If this is the case, the problem is probably a routing issue on the return path. If the trace doesn't quite reach the destination, it might be because the target host is protected by a firewall. When a firewall protects the destination, ICMP packet filtering prevents the ping packets—or any other ICMP messages—from crossing the firewall and reaching their destination.

To check for network congestion, simply increase the allowed latency by setting a higher wait time with the **-w** switch, such as 5000 milliseconds. Try to ping the destination again. If the request still times out, congestion is not the problem; an address resolution problem or routing error is a more likely issue.

Unknown Host

This error message indicates that the requested host name cannot be resolved to its IP address; check that the name is entered correctly and that the DNS servers can resolve it.

Test IP-to-MAC Address Resolution with ARP

Windows 2000 TCP/IP allows an application to communicate over a network with another computer by using either an IP address, a host name, or a NetBIOS name. However, regardless of which naming convention is used, the destination must ultimately be resolved to a hardware address (media access control (MAC) address) for shared access media such as Ethernet and Token Ring.

The *Address Resolution Protocol (ARP)* allows a host to find the MAC address of a node with an IP address on the same physical network, when given the node's IP address. To make ARP efficient, each computer caches IP-to-MAC address mappings to eliminate repetitive ARP broadcast requests.

The Arp tool allows a user to view and modify ARP table entries on the local computer. The **arp** command is useful for viewing the ARP cache and resolving address resolution problems.

A static entry can be added to an ARP file by issuing the **arp -s** *<IP address> <MAC address>* command. However, adding such static ARP cache entries must be used with caution as it is easy to enter the wrong MAC address for an IP address.

Detecting Duplicate IP Addresses Using ARP

When starting up, Windows performs a gratuitous ARP to detect any duplication with its own IP address. While this detects most cases of duplicate IP addresses, in a few situations two TCP/IP hosts (either Microsoft or non-Microsoft) on the same network can be configured for the same IP address.

The MAC and IP address mapping is done by the ARP module, which uses the first ARP response it receives. Therefore, the impostor computer's reply sometimes comes back before the intended computer's reply.

These problems are difficult to isolate and track down. Use the **arp -a** command to display the mappings in the ARP cache. If you know the Ethernet address for the remote computer you wish to use, you can easily determine whether the two match. If not, use the **arp -d** command to delete the entry, then use Ping with the same address (forcing an ARP), and check the Ethernet address in the cache again by using **arp -a**.

If both computers are on the same network, you will eventually get a response from the imposter computer. If not, you might have to capture the traffic from the impostor host with Network Monitor to determine the owner or location of the system. For more information about Network Monitor, see "Monitoring Network Performance" in the *Microsoft® Windows® 2000 Professional Resource Kit.*

Detecting Invalid Entries in the ARP Cache

Troubleshooting the ARP cache can be one of the more difficult tasks in network administration because the problems associated with it are so often intermittent.

The exception to this rule is when you find that the wrong host responds to a command, perhaps a Netuse or Telnet command. The symptoms of invalid entries in the ARP cache are harder to reproduce and involve intermittent problems that only affect a few hosts. The underlying problem is that two computers are using the same IP address on the network. You only see the problems intermittently because the most recent ARP table entry is always the one from the host that responded more quickly to any particular ARP request.

To address the problem, display the ARP table using the **arp -a** command. Following is an example output of the **arp -a** command.

```
C:\>arp -a 172.16.0.142

Interface: 172.16.0.142
   Internet address      Physical AddressType
   172.16.0.1            00-e0-34-c0-a1-40    dynamic
   172.16.1.231          00-00-f8-03-6d-65    dynamic
   172.16.3.34           08-00-09-dc-82-4a    dynamic
   172.16.4.53           00-c0-4f-79-49-2b    dynamic
   157.59.5.102          00-00-f8-03-6c-30    dynamic
```

Since addresses assigned by DHCP do not cause address conflicts like those described here, the main source of these conflicts is likely to be static IP addresses. Maintaining a list of static addresses (and corresponding MAC addresses) as they are assigned can help you track down any address conflict just by examining the IP and MAC address pairs from the ARP table and comparing them to the recorded values.

If you do not have a record of all IP and MAC address pairs on your network, you might want to examine the manufacturer bytes of the MAC addresses for inconsistencies. These three-byte numbers are called Organizationally Unique Identifiers (OUIs) and are assigned by the Institute of Electrical and Electronics Engineers (IEEE); the first three bytes of each MAC address identify the card's manufacturer. Knowing what equipment you installed and comparing that with the values returned by **arp -a** might allow you to determine which static address was entered in error.

Finally, if neither an address pair record nor the manufacturer prefixes reveals the source of the problem, check the Event Viewer for additional clues to the problem. For instance, DHCP might have detected a duplicate card already on the network, and thus denied a computer's request to join. Other DHCP and related messages here can often quickly isolate and solve a problem.

Verify Persistent Routing Table Entries

The next area to examine are the persistent entries in your routing tables. You can view these using the Route utility. Persistent entries are added using the **route add -p** command. Use Arp to confirm that the IP address-to-hardware address mappings are correct. If you find an error, change the incorrect entry using the **route change** command. If you want to make the change permanent, use **route add -p**. For more information about the Route tool, see "Examine the Routing Table with Route" later in this chapter.

If the local routing table is correct, the problem might be at some point between the host computer and the destination computer. Use Tracert to search for the source of the problem at the router level.

Use Tracert and PathPing

If the routing table configuration is correct, the problem might be with a router or link at any point along the route. You can trace the path to the destination computer using Tracert and PathPing to pinpoint the problem. For more information about using the Tracert tool to examine routing paths, see "Examine Paths with Tracert" later in this chapter.

Use Tracert when you have no connectivity to a site under investigation, since it tells you where connectivity stops. PathPing is more useful when you have connectivity to a site but are experiencing some packet loss or high delay. In these cases, PathPing tells you exactly where packet loss is occurring.

Verify Server Services on the Remote Computer

Sometimes a system configured as a remote gateway or router is not functioning as a router. To confirm that the remote computer you wish to contact is set up to forward packets, you can either examine it with a remote administration tool (assuming that it is a computer you administer) or you can attempt to contact the person who maintains the computer.

You can contact the administrator responsible for a remote network using the databases maintained by InterNIC. The easiest way to do this is to use the Whois tool to find the appropriate person's name and contact information from the InterNIC database.

Windows 2000 does not have a local Whois tool. For more information about the local Whois tool, see the Whois link on the Web Resources page at http://windows.microsoft.com/windows2000/reskit/webresources. The Whois site provides the same functionality formerly provided by using Telnet.

Check IP Security on the Initiating Host

IPSec can increase the defenses of a network, but it can also make changing network configurations or troubleshooting problems more difficult. In some cases, IPSec running on the initiating host of a computer under investigation can create difficulties in connecting to a remote host. To determine if this is a source of problems, turn off IPSec and attempt to run the requested network service or function.

If the problem disappears when IPSec policies are turned off, you know that the additional IPSec processing burden or its packet filtering are responsible for the problem. To solve the problem, use the following procedure:

▶ **To stop IPSec policy agents from enforcing IPSec**

- From the **Group** or **Local Policy**, right-click the policy and click **Unassign**.

If you need to disable IP Security only for a specific computer, you can disable the IPSec Policy Agent Service on that computer.

▶ **To stop the IPSec Policy Agent**

1. Start the Services snap-in.
2. In the Services results pane, double-click **IPSec Policy Agent**.
3. Click **Stop** (or **Disable** if you do not want the Policy Agent to resume after the next system restart).

For more information about IPSec issues, see "Internet Protocol Security" in this book.

Check Packet Filtering

Any mistakes in packet filtering at the stack, router, proxy server, Routing and Remote Access service, or IPSec level can make address resolution or connectivity fail. To determine if packet filtering is the source of a network problem, you must disable the TCP/IP packet filtering.

▶ **To disable TCP/IP packet filtering**

1. Click Control Panel, and then double-click the **Network and Dial-up Connections** icon.
2. Right-click the **Local Area Connection**, and then click **Properties**.
3. Select **Internet Protocol (TCP/IP)**, and then click the **Properties** tab.
4. Click **Advanced**, and then click **Options**.

5. Click **TCP/IP Filtering** in the **Optional Settings** window, and then click the **Properties** tab.
6. Clear the **Enable TCP/IP Filtering (All Adapters)** check box, and then click **OK**.

Try pinging an address using its DNS name, its NetBIOS name, or its IP address. If the attempt succeeds, the packet filtering options might be misconfigured or might be too restrictive. For instance, the filtering might permit the computer to act as a web server, but might in the process disable tools like Ping or remote administration. Restore a wider range of permissible filtering options by changing the permitted TCP, UDP, and IP port values.

If the attempt still fails, another form of packet filtering might still be interfering with your networking. For more information about Routing and Remote Access filtering functions, see "Unicast IP Routing" in the *Microsoft® Windows® 2000 Server Resource Kit Internetworking Guide*. For more information about IPSec packet filtering, see "Internet Protocol Security" in this book.

Troubleshooting IP Routing

Windows 2000 supports routing on both single- and multi-homed computers with or without the Routing and Remote Access service. The Routing and Remote Access service includes the Routing Information Protocol (RIP) and the Open Shortest Path First (OSPF) routing protocols. Routers can use RIP or OSPF to dynamically exchange routing information.

This section provides information about the Windows 2000–based routing table as used on single- and multi-homed computers with or without the Routing and Remote Access service. This background information helps with TCP/IP troubleshooting. For more information about TCP/IP routing, see "Unicast IP Routing" in the *Windows 2000 Internetworking Guide*. For information about troubleshooting IP multicast routing, see "Multicast IP Support" in the *Windows 2000 Internetworking Guide*.

Cannot Connect to a Specific Server

To determine the cause of connection problems when trying to connect to a specific server using NetBIOS-based connections, use the **nbtstat -n** command to determine what name the server used to register on the network.

Nbtstat -n output lists several names that the computer has registered. A name resembling the computer's name as shown on the desktop should be present. If not, try one of the other unique names displayed by Nbtstat.

The Nbtstat tool can also display the cached entries for remote computers from either #PRE entries in the LMHOSTS file or from recently resolved names. If the name the remote computers are using for the server is the same, and the other computers are on a remote subnet, be sure that they have the computer's mapping in their LMHOSTS files or WINS servers.

Connection to Remote Host Hangs

To determine why a TCP/IP connection to a remote computer is not working properly, use the **netstat -a** command to show the status of all activity on TCP and UDP ports on the local computer.

A good TCP connection usually shows 0 bytes in the Sent and Received queues. If data is blocked in either queue or if the state is irregular, the connection is probably faulty. If not, you are probably experiencing network or application delay.

Examining the Routing Table with Route

In order for two hosts to exchange IP datagrams, they must both have a route to each other, or use default gateways that know of a route. Normally, routers exchange information with each other using a routing protocol such as RIP.

Enabling IP Routing

By default, IP routing is disabled. To enable IP routing, you must allow the computer to forward IP packets it receives. This requires a change to the Windows 2000 system registry. When you enable the Routing and Remote Access service for IP routing, this registry entry is made automatically.

▶ **To enable IP routing**

1. From the **Start** menu, click **Run**.
2. Type **regedt32.exe** or **regedit.exe**, and then click **OK**.
3. In a registry editor, navigate to HKEY_LOCAL_MACHINE\SYSTEM\CurrentControlSet\Services\Tcpip \Parameters
4. Select the **IPEnableRouter** entry.

5. To enable IP routing for all network connections installed and used by this computer, assign a value of **1**. To do this in regedit.exe, right-click the entry, and then click **Modify**. In regedt32.exe, click on the wanted entry, click on **Edit**, and then click on the appropriate menu choice.
6. Close the registry editor.

Caution Do not use a registry editor to edit the registry directly unless you have no alternative. The registry editors bypass the standard safeguards provided by administrative tools. These safeguards prevent you from entering conflicting settings or settings that are likely to degrade performance or damage your system. Editing the registry directly can have serious, unexpected consequences that can prevent the system from starting and require that you reinstall Windows 2000. To configure or customize Windows 2000, use the programs in Control Panel or Microsoft Management Console (MMC) whenever possible.

If the Windows 2000 router does not have an interface on a given subnet, it needs a route to get to that subnet. This can be handled using a default route or by adding static routes. For more information about dynamic routing environments, see "Unicast IP Routing" in the *Windows 2000 Internetworking Guide*.

To add a static route, use the Route utility as follows:

```
route add 172.16.41.0 mask 255.255.255.0 172.16.40.1 metric 2
```

In this example, the **route add** command states that to reach the 172.16.41.0 subnet with a mask of 255.255.255.0, use gateway 172.16.40.1. It also shows that the subnet is two hops away. You may need to add static routes on downstream routers telling packets there how to get back to the 172.16.40.0/24 subnet.

Examine Paths with Tracert

Tracert is a route tracing utility that uses incrementally higher values in the TTL field in the IP header to determine the route from one host to another through a network. It does this by sending ICMP echo request messages and analyzing ICMP error messages that return. Tracert allows you to track the path of a forwarded packet from router to router for up to 30 hops. If a router has failed or if the packet is routed into a loop, Tracert reveals the problem. Once the problem router is found, its administrator can be contacted if it is an offsite router, or the router can be restored to fully functional status if it is under your control.

Troubleshooting Gateways

If you see the message "Your default gateway does not belong to one of the configured interfaces..." during setup, find out whether the default gateway is located on the same logical network as the computer's network adapter. The easiest way to do this is to compare the network ID portion of the default gateway's IP address with the network IDs of the computer's network adapters. In other words, check that the bitwise logical AND of the IP address and the subnet mask equals the bitwise logical AND of the default gateway and the subnet mask.

For example, a computer with a single network adapter configured with an IP address of 172.16.27.139 and a subnet mask of 255.255.0.0 requires a default gateway of the form 172.16.*y*.*z*. The network ID of the IP interface is 172.16.0.0/16. Using the subnet mask, TCP/IP can determine that all traffic on this network is local; everything else must be sent to the gateway.

Troubleshooting ARP

Network traffic sometimes fails because a router's proxy ARP request returns the wrong address. A router makes this ARP request on behalf of an IP address on its intenal subnets (just as a remote access server makes a request on the LAN for its remote access clients). The problem is that the router's proxy ARP requests return the wrong MAC address to the sending host. As a result, the sending host sends its traffic to the wrong MAC address. In other words, the problem stems from proxy ARP replies.

To address this problem, use Network Monitor to capture a trace. If the trace reveals that when a sending host sends an ARP request for the MAC address of a destination IP address, a device (usually a router) replies with a MAC address other than the destination's correct MAC address.

To determine if this is the problem, check the ARP cache of the source host to make sure it is getting the correct IP address to MAC address resolution. Alternatively, you can capture all traffic with Network Monitor and later filter the captured traffic to display only the ARP and RARP protocols. The RARP protocol converts MAC addresses to IP addresses and is defined in RFC 903.

You can fix the ARP problem by disabling 'Proxy ARP' on the offending device. Exactly how this is done depends on the device's make and model; consult the manufacturer's documentation.

Troubleshooting Translational Bridging

Allowing nodes from Ethernet segments to communicate with nodes on Token rings presents a number of challenges. Following are the most common problems associated with translational bridging.

The primary factor responsible for problems in this situation are differing MTUs between segments. Token Ring MTUs range from 4,464 to 17,914 bytes, while the Ethernet MTU is 1,500. A FDDI segment has an MTU of 4,532 bytes. When a bridge or Layer 2 switch connects two of these differing networking technologies, packets can be dropped because the Layer 2 switch cannot fragment the data and cannot alert the sending node of the reduced MTU.

In the example shown in Figure 3.6, an Ethernet backbone connects two 16-MB token rings. Instead of a router, a translational bridge in the form of a Layer 2 switch connects the segments. In this case, local traffic on the Token Rings uses an MTU of 17,914 and is not affected by the bridge. However, when Computer A must communicate with Computer B, the bridge drops large packets without notifying Computer A of the need to fragment. In this situation, Computer A has no way to discover the MTU on the other side of the bridge.

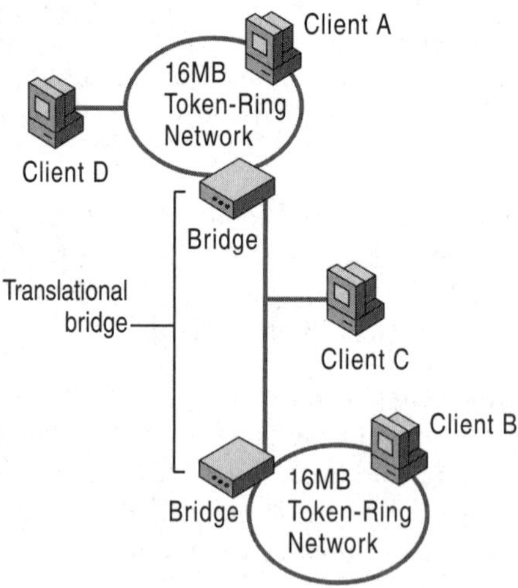

Figure 3.6 Connecting Two Token Ring Networks with an Ethernet Bridge

Other symptoms of translational bridging problems might include the ability to ping a computer on the far side of the bridge, being able to establish a connection, but not being able to send bulk data. This occurs because Echo Request messages and TCP connection establishment segments are small. When sending bulk data, however, large segments at the size of the MTU of the locally attached network are sent and dropped by the Layer 2 switch. Another example is when a computer is able to use FTP to establish a session, but is unable to use a **get** *<filename>* command, which requires sending a larger packet over the switch.

In Windows 2000, the **MTU** registry entry can be adjusted to meet the MTU requirement of the Ethernet segment connecting the two Token Ring segments, reducing all MTUs to the lowest common denominator. Each node's MTU is reduced to 1,500 to meet the requirements of the Ethernet backbone. However, this solution requires that all traffic (even traffic that is local on a Token Ring) is sent within the reduced MTU.

Using Ping to Determine Maximum Transmission Units

You can use the Windows 2000 **ping -l** command to send packets with a defined ICMP Echo Request data size. By sending packets of varying sizes, you can determine the MTU for any given bridge by noting which packet sizes cross the bridge successfully. For example, in Figure 3.6, a ping packet can be sent from Computer A to Computer C with a size of 1,472 bytes, which generates an Echo Reply packet from Computer C. However, if a size of 1,473 bytes or greater is used, the intermediate switch drops the packet. Computer C does not receive the Echo Request and no Echo Reply is generated.

The default ICMP Echo Request contains 32 bytes of data; you can use the **ping** *<IP address* or *Host Name>* **-l** *<data size>* command to specify a different data size. For example, you can ping with the maximum Ethernet data size by entering this command:

```
ping 134.56.78.1. -l 1472
```

The data size specified by the -l switch is 1,472 rather than the Ethernet IP MTU of 1,500 because 20 bytes are reserved to make room for the IP header and 8 bytes must be allocated for the ICMP Echo Request header.

When you have determined the MTU, you can set the packet size on either side of the bridge by changing the value in the registry entry. The **MTU** registry entry can be found at:

HKEY_LOCAL_MACHINE\SYSTEM\CurrentControlSet\Services\
Tcpip\Parameters\Interfaces*Adapter_GUID*

For more information about MTU, see "Windows 2000 TCP/IP" in this book.

Troubleshooting PMTU Black Hole Routers

Some routers do not send an "ICMP Destination Unreachable" message when they cannot forward an IP datagram. Instead, they ignore the datagram. Typically, an IP datagram cannot be forwarded because its maximum segment size is too large for the receiving server, and the Don't Fragment bit is set in the header of the datagram. Routers that ignore these datagrams and send no message are called PMTU black hole routers.

To respond effectively to black hole routers, you must enable the Path MTUBH Detect feature of TCP/IP. Path MTUBH Detect recognizes repeated unacknowledged transmissions and responds by turning off the Don't Fragment bit. After a datagram is transmitted successfully, it reduces the maximum segment size and turns the Don't Fragment bit on again.

The Path MTUBH Detect feature is disabled by default, but you can enable it by adding the **EnablePMTUBHDetect** entry to the registry and setting its value to **1**. **EnablePMTUBHDetect** is an optional entry that does not appear in the registry unless you add it. You must place it in:

HKEY_LOCAL_MACHINE\SYSTEM\CurrentControlSet\Services\Tcpip \Parameters.

You can disable Path MTUBH Detect by deleting **EnablePMTUBHDetect** from the registry or by setting the entry's value to **0**.

A second registry entry, **EnablePMTUDiscovery**, also helps address the PMTU black hole router problem. This key is enabled by default. **EnablePMTUDiscovery** completely enables or disables the PMTU discovery mechanism.When PMTU discovery is disabled, a TCP Maximum Segment Size (MSS)of 536 bytes is used for all non-local destination addresses.

Discovering PMTU with Ping

The PMTU between two hosts can be discovered manually using the **ping -f** command, as follows:

```
ping -f -n <number of pings> -l <size> <destination IP address>
```

The following example shows how Ping's size parameter can be varied until the MTU is found. Note that Ping's size parameter specifies just the size of the ICMP Echo Request data to send, not including the IP and ICMP Echo Request headers. The ICMP Echo Request header is 8 bytes, and the IP header is normally 20 bytes. In the Ethernet case shown here, the link layer MTU contains the maximum-sized Ping buffer plus 28, for a total of 1500 bytes on the first ping and 1501 on the second:

```
C:\>ping -f -n 1 -l 1472 10.99.99.10
Pinging 10.99.99.10 with 1472 bytes of data:
Reply from 10.99.99.10: bytes=1472 time<10ms TTL=128
Ping statistics for 10.99.99.10:
    Packets: Sent = 1, Received = 1, Lost = 0 (0% loss),
Approximate round trip times in milli-seconds:
    Minimum = 0ms, Maximum =  0ms, Average =  0ms

C:\>ping -f -n 1 -l 1473 10.99.99.10
Pinging 10.99.99.10 with 1473 bytes of data:
Packet needs to be fragmented but DF set.
Ping statistics for 10.99.99.10:
    Packets: Sent = 1, Received = 0, Lost = 1 (100% loss),
Approximate round trip times in milli-seconds:
    Minimum = 0ms, Maximum =  0ms, Average =  0ms
```

In the second ping, the IP layer returns an ICMP error message that Ping interprets. If the router had been a black hole router, Ping would not be answered once its size exceeded the MTU that the router could handle. Ping can be used in this manner to detect such a router.

Troubleshooting Services

In addition to its role in providing basic network communications, TCP/IP is the cornerstone of a number of network services such as Routing and remote Access, printing, IP Security, and the Browser Service. These services are discussed in more detail in other chapters, but a few examples of basic troubleshooting for these services are described below.

Cannot Ping Across a Router as a Remote Access Client

This problem occurs if you have selected **Use default gateway on remote network** under the **General** tab of the **Advanced Internet Protocol (TCP/IP) Properties** in the **Dial-Up Connections** page. This feature adds a default route to the routing table with a metric of 1 and changes the existing default route to a metric of 2. All non-local traffic is now forwarded to the gateway on the remote access link. However, to access the Internet, this feature must be enabled.

To ping or otherwise connect to computers in a remote subnet across a router while you are connected as a remote access client to a remote Windows remote access server, use the **route add** command to add the route of the subnet you want to use.

Troubleshooting TCP/IP Database Files

Table 3.13 lists the UNIX-style database files that are stored in the %SystemRoot%\System32\Drivers\Etc directory when you install Microsoft TCP/IP:

Table 3.13 TCP/IP Database Files

File Name	Use
Hosts	Provides host name-to-IP-address resolution for Windows Sockets applications
LMHOSTS	Provides remote NetBIOS name-to-IP-address resolution for NetBIOS applications such as Windows-based networking
Networks	Provides network name-to-network ID resolution for TCP/IP management
Protocols	Provides protocol name-to-protocol ID resolution for Windows Sockets applications
Services	Provides service name-to-port ID resolution for Windows Sockets applications

To troubleshoot any of these files on a local computer, make sure the entry format in each file matches the format defined in the sample file originally installed with Microsoft TCP/IP. Check for spelling errors, invalid IP addresses, and identifiers.

Removing and Reinstalling TCP/IP

When you attempt to reinstall a TCP/IP service, you might receive a "The registry subkey already exists" error message. To correct this problem, you should ensure that all the components of a given TCP/IP service are properly removed and then remove the appropriate registry subkeys.

Caution Do not use a registry editor to edit the registry directly unless you have no alternative. The registry editors bypass the standard safeguards provided by administrative tools. These safeguards prevent you from entering conflicting settings or settings that are likely to degrade performance or damage your system. Editing the registry directly can have serious, unexpected consequences that can prevent the system from starting and require that you reinstall Windows 2000. To configure or customize Windows 2000, use the programs in Control Panel or Microsoft Management Console (MMC) whenever possible.

If you removed TCP/IP and its related service components, you must also remove the following registry subkeys:

HKEY_LOCAL_MACHINE\SYSTEM\CurrentControlSet\Services\NetBT

HKEY_LOCAL_MACHINE\SYSTEM\CurrentControlSet\Services\Tcpip

HKEY_LOCAL_MACHINE\SYSTEM\CurrentControlSet\Services\TcpipCU

HKEY_LOCAL_MACHINE\SYSTEM\CurrentControlSet\Services\Dhcp

HKEY_LOCAL_MACHINE\SYSTEM\CurrentControlSet\Services\LmHosts

SNMP Registry Keys

If you removed the SNMP service components, you must also remove the following registry subkeys:

HKEY_LOCAL_MACHINE\SOFTWARE\Microsoft\RFC1156Agent

HKEY_LOCAL_MACHINE\SOFTWARE\Microsoft\Snmp

HKEY_LOCAL_MACHINE\SYSTEM\CurrentControlSet\Services\Snmp

TCP/IP Printing Registry Keys

If you removed the TCP/IP Printing service components, you must also remove the following registry subkeys:

HKEY_LOCAL_MACHINE\SOFTWARE\Microsoft\Lpdsvc

HKEY_LOCAL_MACHINE\SOFTWARE\Microsoft\TcpPrint

HKEY_LOCAL_MACHINE\SYSTEM\CurrentControlSet\Services\LpdsvcSimple TCP/IP Services

Simple TCP/IP Services Registry Keys

If you removed the Simple TCP/IP Services components, you must also remove the following registry subkeys:

HKEY_LOCAL_MACHINE\SOFTWARE\Microsoft\SimpTcp

HKEY_LOCAL_MACHINE\SYSTEM\CurrentControlSet\Services\SimpTcp

DHCP Registry Keys

If you removed the DHCP service components, you must also remove the following registry subkeys:

HKEY_LOCAL_MACHINE\SOFTWARE\Microsoft\DhcpMibAgent

HKEY_LOCAL_MACHINE\SOFTWARE\Microsoft\DhcpServer

HKEY_LOCAL_MACHINE\SYSTEM\CurrentControlSet\Services\DhcpServer

WINS Registry Keys

If you removed the WINS service components, you must also remove the following registry subkeys:

HKEY_LOCAL_MACHINE\SOFTWARE\Microsoft\Wins

HKEY_LOCAL_MACHINE\SOFTWARE\Microsoft\WinsMibAgent

HKEY_LOCAL_MACHINE\SYSTEM\CurrentControlSet\Services\Wins

DNS Registry Keys

If you have removed the DNS service components, you must also remove the following registry subkeys:

HKEY_LOCAL_MACHINE\SOFTWARE\Microsoft\Dns

HKEY_LOCAL_MACHINE\SOFTWARE\Microsoft\DnsMibAgent

HKEY_LOCAL_MACHINE\SYSTEM\CurrentControlSet\Services\Dns

Additional Resources

- For more information about TCP/IP, see *Internetworking with TCP/IP: Volume 1 Principles, Protocols, and Architectures* by Douglas E. Comer, 1995, Englewood Cliffs, New Jersey: Prentice Hall and *TCP/IP Illustrated, Vol. 1* by W. Richard Stevens, 1994, Reading, Massachusetts: Addison-Wesley.
- For more information about TCP/IP troubleshooting, see *Windows NT TCP/IP Network Administration* by Craig Hunt and Robert Bruce Thompson, 1998, Sebastopol, California: O'Reilly.

PART 2

Address Allocation and Name Resolution

Protocols that enable efficient management and automated configuration of network hosts are necessary tools for managers and administrators of large networks. This section examines the Windows 2000 features that provide these necessary functions.

In This Part:

C H A P T E R 4

Dynamic Host Configuration Protocol

Dynamic Host Configuration Protocol (DHCP) is a TCP/IP standard that reduces the complexity and administrative overhead of managing network client IP address configuration. Microsoft® Windows® 2000 Server provides the DHCP service, which enables a computer to function as a DHCP server and configure DHCP-enabled client computers on your network. DHCP runs on a server computer, enabling the automatic, centralized management of IP addresses and other TCP/IP configuration settings for your network's client computers. The Microsoft DHCP service also provides integration with the Active Directory™ directory service and Domain Name System (DNS) service, enhanced monitoring and statistical reporting for DHCP servers, vendor-specific options and user-class support, multicast address allocation, and rogue DHCP server detection.

In This Chapter

Related Information in the Resource Kit

- For information about deploying DHCP with IP Security, see "Internet Protocol Security" in the *Microsoft Windows 2000 Server Resource Kit TCP/IP Core Networking Guide.*
- For more information about DHCP options, see "DHCP Options" in this book.
- For more information about DHCP message formats, see "DHCP Message Formats" in this book.
- For more information about setting DHCP registry settings, see the "Technical Reference to the Windows 2000 Registry" (Regentry.chm) on the Windows 2000 Resource Kit CD.

What Is DHCP?

DHCP simplifies the administrative management of IP address configuration by automating address configuration for network clients. The DHCP standard provides for the use of DHCP servers, which are defined as any computer running the DHCP service. The DHCP server automatically allocates IP addresses and related TCP/IP configuration settings to DHCP-enabled clients on the network.

Every device on a TCP/IP-based network must have a unique IP address in order to access the network and its resources. Without DHCP, IP configuration must be done manually for new computers, computers moving from one subnet to another, and computers removed from the network.

By deploying DHCP in a network, this entire process is automated and centrally managed. The DHCP server maintains a pool of IP addresses and leases an address to any DHCP-enabled client when it logs on to the network. Because the IP addresses are dynamic (leased) rather than static (permanently assigned), addresses no longer in use are automatically returned to the pool for reallocation.

The DHCP service for Microsoft Windows 2000 Server is based on Internet Engineering Task Force (IETF) standards. DHCP specifications are defined in Requests for Comments (RFCs) published by the IETF and other working groups. RFCs are an evolving series of reports, proposals for protocols, and protocol standards used by the Internet community. The following RFCs specify the core DHCP standards that Microsoft supports with its DHCP service:

- RFC 2131: Dynamic Host Configuration Protocol (obsoletes RFC 1541)
- RFC 2132: DHCP Options and BOOTP Vendor Extensions

DHCP Terminology

Table 4.1 lists common DHCP terms that are used throughout this chapter.

Table 4.1 DHCP Terminology

Term	Description
DHCP server	Any computer running the Windows 2000 DHCP service.
DHCP client	Any computer that has DHCP settings enabled.
Scope	The full, consecutive range of possible IP addresses for a network. DHCP services can be offered to scopes, which typically define a single physical subnet on a network. DHCP servers primarily use scopes to manage network distribution and assignment of IP addresses and any related configuration parameters.

(continued)

Table 4.1 DHCP Terminology *(continued)*

Term	Description
Superscope	An administrative grouping of scopes that are used to support multiple, logical IP subnets on the same physical subnet. Superscopes contain a list of member scopes (or child scopes) that can be activated as a collection.
Exclusion range	Ensures that any IP address listed in that range is not offered by the DHCP server to any DHCP clients.
Address pool	Available IP addresses form an address pool within the scope. Pooled addresses are available for dynamic assignment by the DHCP server to DHCP clients.
Lease	The length of time, specified by the DHCP server, a client computer can use a dynamically assigned IP address. When a lease is made to a client, the lease is considered active. Before the lease expires, the client renews its lease with the DHCP server. A lease becomes inactive when it either expires or is deleted by the server. The lease duration determines when the lease expires and how often the client needs to renew its lease with the DHCP server.
Reservation	Creates a permanent address lease assignment from the DHCP server to the client. Reservations ensure that a specified hardware device on the subnet can always use the same IP address. This is useful for computers such as remote access gateways, WINS, or DNS servers that must have a static IP address.
Option types	Other client configuration parameters a DHCP server can assign when offering an IP address lease to a client. Typically, these option types are enabled and configured for each scope. Most options are predefined through RFC 2132, but you can use DHCP Manager to define and add custom option types as needed.
Option class	A way for the DHCP server to further submanage option types provided to clients. Option classes can be configured on your DHCP servers to offer specialized client support. When an option class is added to the server, clients of that class can be provided class-specific option types for their configuration.

How DHCP Works

DHCP is based on a client/server model, as illustrated in Figure 4.1.

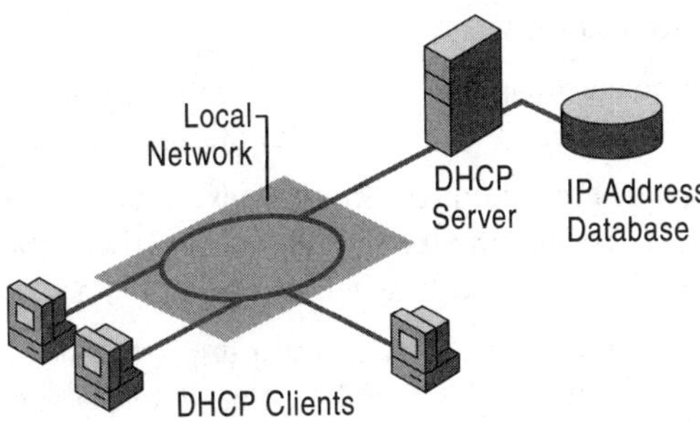

Figure 4.1 The Basic DHCP Model

The network administrator establishes one or more DHCP servers that maintain TCP/IP configuration information and provide address configuration to DHCP-enabled clients in the form of a lease offer. The DHCP server stores the configuration information in a database, which includes:

- Valid TCP/IP configuration parameters for all clients on the network.
- Valid IP addresses, maintained in a pool for assignment to clients, as well as reserved addresses for manual assignment.
- Duration of the lease offered by the server—the length of time for which the IP address can be used before a lease renewal is required.

A DHCP-enabled client, upon acceptance of a lease offer, receives:

- A valid IP address for the network it is joining.
- Additional TCP/IP configuration parameters, referred to as DHCP options.

Benefits of DHCP

Deploying DHCP on your enterprise network provides the following benefits:

- **Safe and reliable configuration.** DHCP minimizes configuration errors caused by manual IP address configuration, such as typographical errors, as well as address conflicts caused by a currently assigned IP address accidentally being reissued to another computer.

- **Reduced network administration.**
  - TCP/IP configuration is centralized and automated.
  - Network administrators can centrally define global and subnet-specific TCP/IP configurations.
  - Clients can be automatically assigned a full range of additional TCP/IP configuration values by using DHCP options.
  - Address changes for client configurations that must be updated frequently, such as remote access clients that move around constantly, can be made efficiently and automatically when the client restarts in its new location.
  - Most routers can forward DHCP configuration requests, eliminating the requirement of setting up a DHCP server on every subnet, unless there is another reason to do so.

New Features

The Windows 2000 DHCP service provides the following new features:

- Enhanced performance monitoring and server reporting capabilities

  New System Monitor counters have been added to Windows 2000 Server to specifically monitor DHCP server performance on your network. Additionally, DHCP Manager now provides enhanced server reporting through graphical display of current states for servers, scopes, and clients. For example, icons visually represent whether a server is disconnected, or if it has leased over 90 percent of its available addresses.
- Expanded support for multicast scopes and superscopes

  Multicast scopes now allow multicast-aware applications to lease Class D–type IP addresses (224.0.0.0 to 239.255.255.255) for participation in multicast groups.
- Support for user-specific and vendor-specific DHCP options

  This allows the separation and distribution of options for clients with similar or special configuration needs. For example, you might assign all DHCP-enabled clients on the same floor of your building to the same option class. You could use this class (configured with the same DHCP Class ID value) to distribute other option data during the lease process, overriding any scope or global default options.
- Integration of DHCP with DNS

  A DHCP server can enable dynamic updates in the DNS namespace for any DHCP clients that support these updates. Scope clients can then use DNS with dynamic updates to update their computer name–to–IP address mapping information whenever changes occur to their DHCP-assigned address.

- Rogue DHCP server detection

  This prevents rogue (unauthorized) DHCP servers from joining an existing DHCP network in which Windows 2000 Server and Active Directory are deployed. A DHCP server object is created in Active Directory, which lists the IP addresses of servers that are authorized to provide DHCP services to the network. When a DHCP server attempts to start on the network, Active Directory is queried and the server computer's IP address is compared to the list of authorized DHCP servers. If a match is found, the server computer is authorized as a DHCP server and is allowed to complete the system startup. If a match is not found, the server is identified as rogue, and the DHCP service is automatically shut down.

- Dynamic support for BOOTP clients

  Dynamic BOOTP is an extension of the BOOTP protocol, which permits the DHCP server to configure BOOTP clients without having to use explicit, fixed-address configuration. This feature reduces administration of large BOOTP networks by allowing automatic distribution of IP address much the same way that DHCP does.

- Read-only console access to DHCP Manager

  This feature provides a special-purpose local group, the DHCP Users group, which is automatically added when the DHCP service is installed. By adding members to this group, you can provide read-only access to information related to the DHCP service on the server computer. Using DHCP Manager, users in this group can view, but not modify, information and properties stored on the specified DHCP server.

DHCP Client Support

The term *client* is used to describe a networked computer that requests and uses the DHCP services offered by a DHCP server. Any Windows-based computer, or other network-enabled device that supports the ability to communicate with a DHCP server (in compliance with RFC 2132), can be configured as a DHCP client.

DHCP client support is provided for computers running under any of the following Microsoft operating systems:

- Microsoft® Windows NT® Workstation (all released versions)
- Microsoft® Windows NT® Server (all released versions)
- Microsoft® Windows® 98
- Microsoft® Windows® 95
- Microsoft® Windows® for Workgroups version 3.11 (with the Microsoft 32-bit TCP/IP VxD installed)

- Microsoft® Network Client version 3.0 for MS-DOS (with the real-mode TCP/IP driver installed)
- LAN Manager version 2.2c

IP Auto-Configuration

Windows 2000–based clients can automatically configure an IP address and subnet mask if a DHCP server is unavailable at system start time. This feature, Automatic Private IP Addressing (APIPA), is useful for clients on small private networks, such as a small-business office, a home office, or a remote access client.

The Windows 2000 DHCP client service goes through the following process to auto-configure the client:

1. The DHCP client attempts to locate a DHCP server and obtain an address and configuration.
2. If a DHCP server cannot be found or does not respond, the DHCP client auto-configures its IP address and subnet mask using a selected address from the Microsoft-reserved Class B network, 169.254.0.0, with the subnet mask 255.255.0.0. The DHCP client tests for an address conflict to make sure that the IP address it has chosen is not already in use on the network. If a conflict is found, the client selects another IP address. The client will retry auto-configuration for up to 10 addresses.
3. Once the DHCP client succeeds in self-selecting an address, it configures its network interface with the IP address. The client then continues, in the background, to check for a DHCP server every 5 minutes. If a DHCP server is found later, the client abandons its auto-configured information. The DHCP client then uses an address offered by the DHCP server (and any other provided DHCP option information) to update its IP configuration settings.

If the DHCP client had previously obtained a lease from a DHCP server:

1. If the client's lease is still valid (not expired) at system start time, the client will try to renew its lease.
2. If, during the renewal attempt, the client fails to locate any DHCP server, it will attempt to ping the default gateway listed in the lease, and proceed in one of the following ways:
   - If the ping is successful, the DHCP client assumes that it is still located on the same network where it obtained its current lease, and continue to use the lease. By default, the client will then attempt, in the background, to renew its lease when 50 percent of its assigned lease time has expired.

- If the ping fails, the DHCP client assumes that it has been moved to a network where DHCP services are not available. The client then auto-configures its IP address as described previously. Once the client is auto-configured, every 5 minutes it attempts to locate a DHCP server and obtain a lease.

Local Storage

Microsoft DHCP supports local storage, allowing clients to store DHCP information on their own hard disks. Local storage is useful because when the client system starts, it first attempts to renew the lease of the same IP address. Local storage also means that a client can be shut down and restarted using its previously leased address and configuration, even if the DHCP server is unreachable or offline at the time the client computer is restarted. Local storage also enables the ability to perform IP auto-configuration.

DHCP Lease Process

A DHCP-enabled client obtains a lease for an IP address from a DHCP server. Before the lease expires, the DHCP server must renew the lease for the client or the client must obtain a new lease. Leases are retained in the DHCP server database approximately one day after expiration. This grace period protects a client's lease in case the client and server are in different time zones, their internal clocks are not synchronized, or the client is off the network when the lease expires.

DHCP Messages

Table 4.2 describes the DHCP messages exchanged between client and server. This is necessary before proceeding with an explanation of how the DHCP lease process works. For more information about each message field, see "DHCP Message Formats" in this book.

Table 4.2 DHCP Messages

Message Type	Description
DHCPDiscover	The first time a DHCP client computer attempts to log on to the network, it requests IP address information from a DHCP server by broadcasting a DHCPDiscover packet. The source IP address in the packet is 0.0.0.0 because the client does not yet have an IP address. The message is either 342 or 576 bytes long—older versions of Windows use a longer message frame.
DHCPOffer	Each DHCP server that receives the client DHCPDiscover packet responds with a DHCPOffer packet containing an unleased IP address and additional TCP/IP configuration information, such as the subnet mask and default gateway. More than one DHCP server can respond with a DHCPOffer packet. The client will accept the first DHCPOffer packet it receives. The message is 342 bytes long.
DHCPRequest	When a DHCP client receives a DHCPOffer packet, it responds by broadcasting a DHCPRequest packet that contains the offered IP address, and shows acceptance of the offered IP address. The message is either 342 or 576 bytes long, depending on the length of the corresponding DHCPDiscover message.
DHCPAcknowledge (DHCPAck)	The selected DHCP server acknowledges the client DHCPRequest for the IP address by sending a DHCPAck packet. At this time the server also forwards any optional configuration parameters. Upon receipt of the DHCPAck, the client can participate on the TCP/IP network and complete its system startup. The message is 342 bytes long.
DHCPNak	If the IP address cannot be used by the client because it is no longer valid or is now used by another computer, the DHCP server responds with a DHCPNak packet, and the client must begin the lease process again. Whenever a DHCP server receives a request for an IP address that is invalid according to the scopes that it is configured with, it sends a DHCPNak message to the client.
DHCPDecline	If the DHCP client determines the offered configuration parameters are invalid, it sends a DHCPDecline packet to the server, and the client must begin the lease process again.
DHCPRelease	A DHCP client sends a DHCPRelease packet to the server to release the IP address and cancel any remaining lease.

(continued)

Table 4.2 DHCP Messages *(continued)*

Message Type	Description
DHCPInform	DHCPInform is a new DHCP message type, defined in RFC 2131, used by computers on the network to request and obtain information from a DHCP server for use in their local configuration. When this message type is used, the sender is already externally configured for its IP address on the network, which may or may not have been obtained using DHCP. This message type is not currently supported by the DHCP service provided in earlier versions of Windows NT Server and may not be recognized by third-party implementations of DHCP software.

How the Lease Process Works

The first time a DHCP-enabled client starts and attempts to join the network, it automatically follows an initialization process to obtain a lease from a DHCP server. Figure 4.2 shows the lease process.

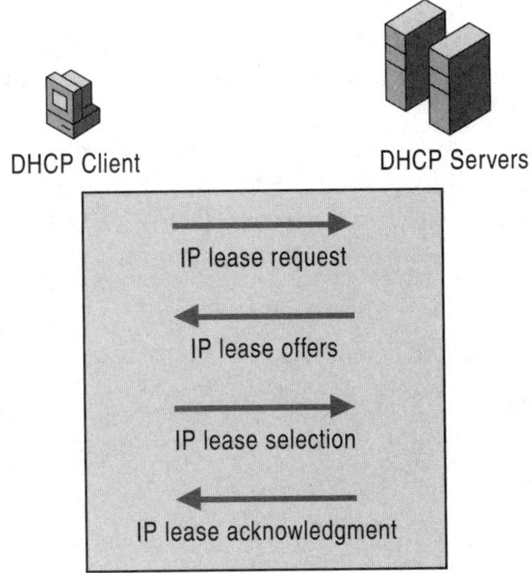

Figure 4.2 The DHCP Lease Process

1. The DHCP client requests an IP address by broadcasting a DHCPDiscover message to the local subnet.
2. The client is offered an address when a DHCP server responds with a DHCPOffer message containing an IP address and configuration information for lease to the client. If no DHCP server responds to the client request, the client can proceed in two ways:
   - If it is a Windows 2000–based client, and IP auto-configuration has not been disabled, the client self-configures an IP address for its interface.
   - If the client is not a Windows 2000–based client, or IP auto-configuration has been disabled, the client network initialization fails. The client continues to resend DHCPDiscover messages in the background (four times, every 5 minutes) until it receives a DHCPOffer message from a DHCP server.
3. The client indicates acceptance of the offer by selecting the offered address and replying to the server with a DHCPRequest message.
4. The client is assigned the address and the DHCP server sends a DHCPAck message, approving the lease. Other DHCP option information might be included in the message.
5. Once the client receives acknowledgment, it configures its TCP/IP properties using any DHCP option information in the reply, and joins the network.

In rare cases, a DHCP server might return a negative acknowledgment to the client. This can happen if a client requests an invalid or duplicate address. If a client receives a negative acknowledgment (DHCPNak), the client must begin the entire lease process again.

DHCP Client States in the Lease Process

DHCP clients cycle through six different states during the DHCP lease process, as illustrated in Figures 4.3 and 4.4. Figure 4.4 illustrates the DHCP lease process for clients that are renewing a lease.

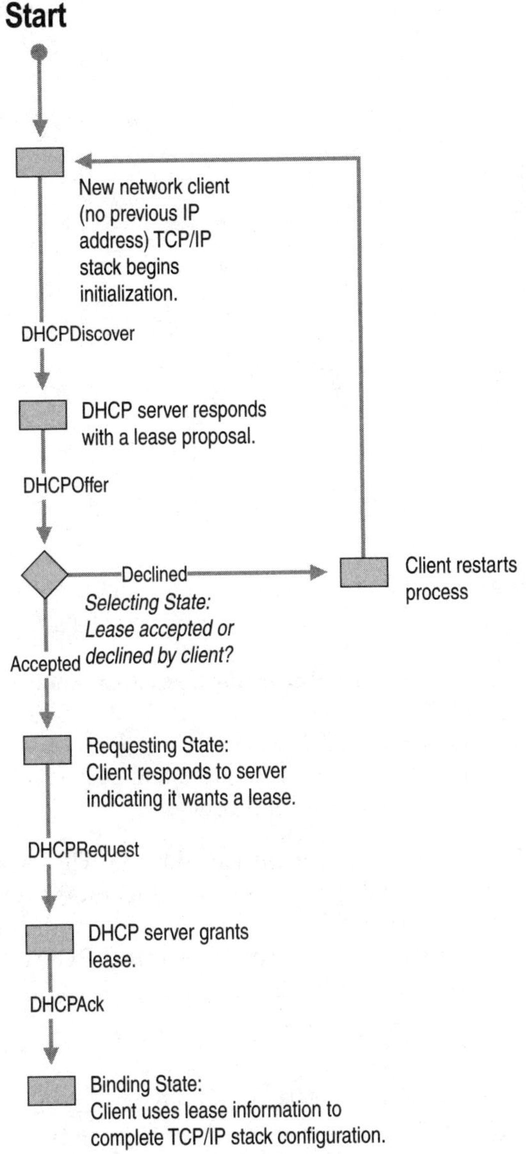
Start
New network client
(no previous IP
address) TCP/IP
stack begins
initialization.
DHCPDiscover
DHCP server responds
with a lease proposal.
DHCPOffer
Declined
Client restarts
process
Selecting State:
Lease accepted or
declined by client?
Accepted
Requesting State:
Client responds to server
indicating it wants a lease.
DHCPRequest
DHCP server grants
lease.
DHCPAck
Binding State:
Client uses lease information to
complete TCP/IP stack configuration.

Figure 4.3 DHCP Client States During the Lease Process

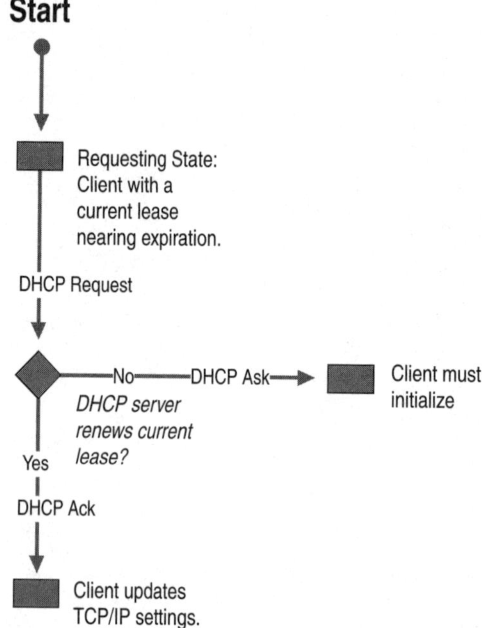
Start
Requesting State:
Client with a
current lease
nearing expiration.
DHCP Request
No
DHCP Ask
Client must
initialize
DHCP server
renews current
lease?
Yes
DHCP Ack
Client updates
TCP/IP settings.

Figure 4.4 DHCP Client States During the Lease Renewal Process

When the DHCP client and DHCP server are on the same subnet, the DHCPDiscover, DHCPOffer, DHCPRequest, and DHCPAck messages are sent via media access control and IP-level broadcasts.

In order for DHCP clients to communicate with a DHCP server on a remote network, the connecting router or routers must support the forwarding of DHCP messages between the DHCP client and the DHCP server using a BOOTP/DHCP Relay Agent. For more information, see "Supporting BOOTP Clients" and "Managing Relay Agents" later in this chapter.

Initializing

This state occurs the first time the TCP/IP protocol stack is initialized on the DHCP client computer. The client does not yet have an IP address to request from the DHCP servers. This state also occurs if the client is denied the IP address it is requesting or the IP address it previously had was released. Figure 4.5 shows the Initialization state.

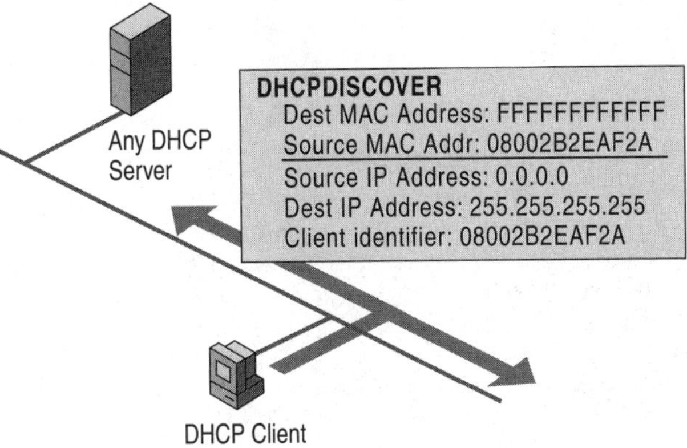

Figure 4.5 The Initialization State

When the DHCP client is in this state, its IP address is 0.0.0.0. To obtain a valid address, the client broadcasts a DHCPDiscover message from UDP port 68 to UDP port 67, with a source address of 0.0.0.0 and a destination of 255.255.255.255 (the client does not yet know the address of any DHCP servers). The DHCPDiscover message contains the DHCP client's media access control address and computer name.

Selecting

Next, the client moves into the Selecting state, where it chooses a DHCPOffer. All DHCP servers that receive a DHCPDiscover message and have a valid IP address to offer the DHCP client respond with a DHCPOffer message sent from UDP port 68 to UDP port 67. The DHCPOffer is sent via the media access control and IP broadcast because the DHCP client does not yet have a valid IP address that can be used as a destination. The DHCP server reserves the IP address to prevent it from being offered to another DHCP client.

The DHCPOffer message contains an IP address and matching subnet mask, a DHCP server identifier (the IP address of the offering DHCP server), and a lease duration. Figure 4.6 shows the Selecting state.

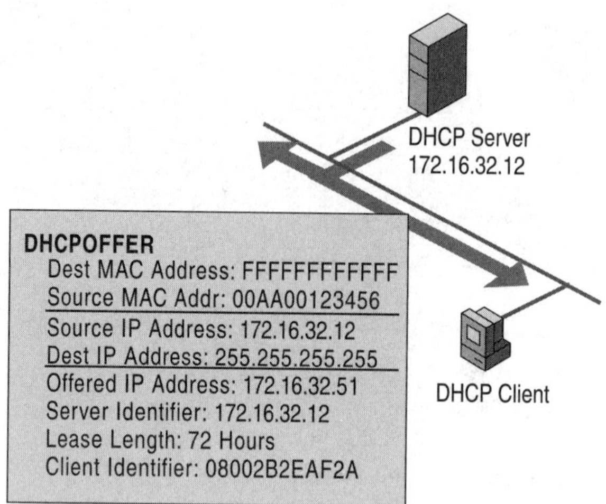

Figure 4.6 The Selecting State

The DHCP client waits for a DHCPOffer message. If a DHCP client does not receive a DHCPOffer message from a DHCP server on startup, it will retry four times (at intervals of 2, 4, 8, and 16 seconds, plus a random amount of time between 0 and 1,000 milliseconds). If a DHCP client does not receive a DHCPOffer after four attempts, it waits 5 minutes, then retries at 5-minute intervals.

Requesting

After a DHCP client has received a DHCPOffer message from a DHCP server, the client moves into the Requesting state. The DHCP client knows the IP address it wants to lease, so it broadcasts a DHCPRequest message to all DHCP servers. The client must use a broadcast because it still does not have an assigned IP address. Figure 4.7 shows the Requesting state.

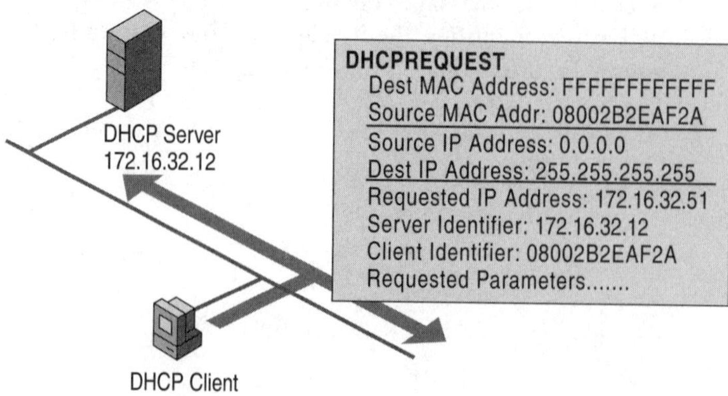

Figure 4.7 The Requesting State

If the IP address of the client was known (that is, the computer restarted and is trying to lease its previous address), the broadcast is looked at by all of the DHCP servers. The DHCP server that can lease the requested IP address responds with either a successful acknowledgment (DHCPAck) or an unsuccessful acknowledgment (DHCPNak). The DHCPNak message occurs when the IP address requested is not available or the client has been physically moved to a different subnet that requires a different IP address. After receiving a DHCPNak message, the client returns to the Initializing state and begins the lease process again.

If the IP address of the client was just obtained with a DHCPDiscover or DHCPOffer exchange with a DHCP server, the client puts the IP address of that DHCP server in the DHCPRequest. The specified DHCP server responds to the request, and any other DHCP servers retract their DHCPOffer. This ensures that the IP addresses that were offered by the other DHCP servers go back to an available state for another DHCP client.

Binding

The DHCP server responds to a DHCPRequest message with a DHCPAck message. This message contains a valid lease for the negotiated IP address, and any DHCP options configured by the DHCP administrator. Figure 4.8 shows the Binding state.

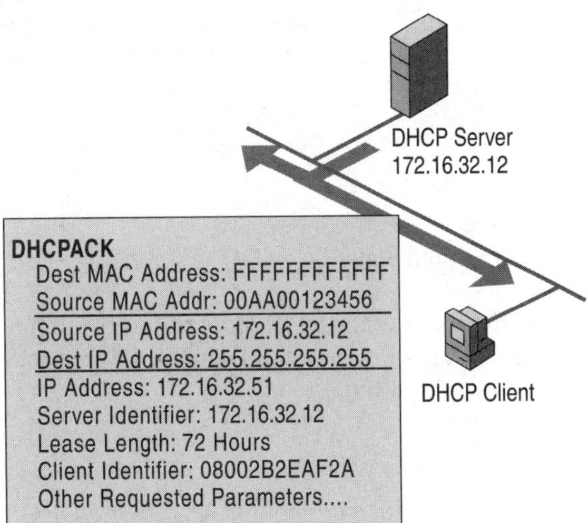

Figure 4.8 The Binding State

The DHCPAck message is sent by the DHCP server using an IP broadcast. When the DHCP client receives the DHCPAck message, it completes initialization of the TCP/IP stack. It is now considered a bound DHCP client that can use TCP/IP to communicate on the network.

The IP address remains allocated to the client until the client manually releases the address, or until the lease time expires and the DHCP server cancels the lease.

Renewing

IP addressing information is leased to a client, and the client is responsible for renewing the lease. By default, DHCP clients try to renew their lease when 50 percent of the lease time has expired. To renew its lease, a DHCP client sends a DHCPRequest message to the DHCP server from which it originally obtained the lease.

The DHCP server automatically renews the lease by responding with a DHCPAck message. This DHCPAck message contains the new lease as well as any DHCP option parameters. This ensures that the DHCP client can update its TCP/IP settings in case the network administrator has updated any settings on the DHCP server. Figure 4.9 illustrates the Renewing state.

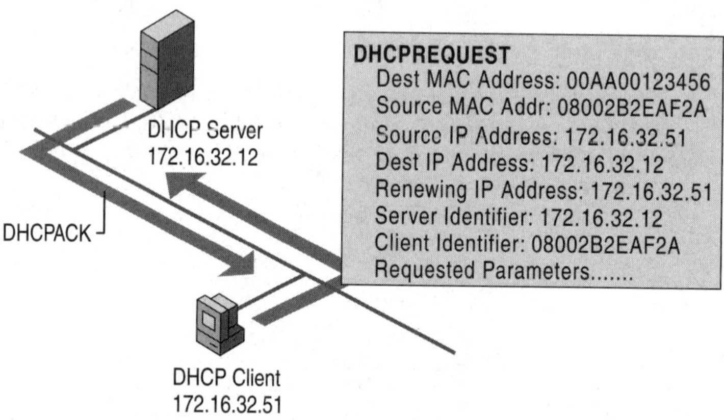

Figure 4.9 The Renewing State

Once the DHCP client has renewed its lease, it returns to the Bound state. Renewal messages (DHCPRequest and DHCPAck) are sent by media access control and IP-level unicast traffic.

Rebinding

If the DHCP client is unable to communicate with the DHCP server from which it obtained its lease, and 87.5 percent of its lease time has expired, it will attempt to contact any available DHCP server by broadcasting DHCPRequest messages. Any DHCP server can respond with a DHCPAck message, renewing the lease, or a DHCPNak message, forcing the DHCP client to initialize and restart the lease process. Figure 4.10 shows the Rebinding state.

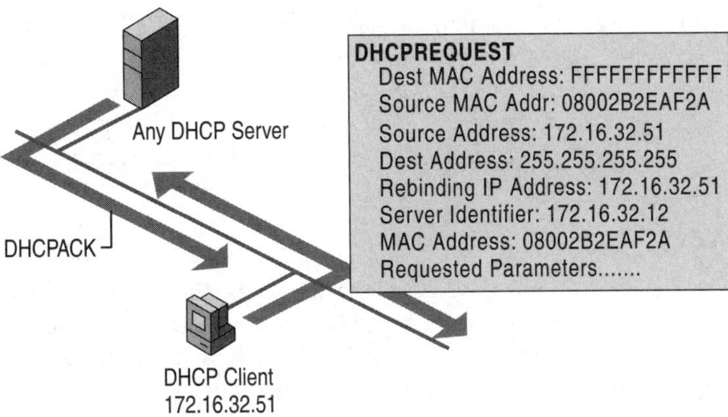

Figure 4.10 The Rebinding State

If the lease expires or a DHCPNak message is received, the DHCP client must immediately discontinue using its current IP address. If this occurs, communication over TCP/IP stops until a new IP address is obtained by the client.

Restarting a DHCP Client

When a client that previously leased an IP address restarts, it broadcasts a DHCPRequest message instead of a DHCPDiscover message. The DHCPRequest message contains a request for the previously assigned IP address.

If the requested IP address can be used by the client, the DHCP server responds with a DHCPAck message.

If the IP address cannot be used by the client because it is no longer valid, is now used by another client, or is invalid because the client has been physically moved to a different subnet, the DHCP server responds with a DHCPNak message. If this occurs, the client restarts the lease process.

If the client fails to locate a DHCP server during the renewal process, it attempts to ping the default gateway listed in the current lease, with the following results:

- If a ping of the default gateway succeeds, the DHCP client assumes it is still located on the same network where it obtained its current lease, and the client continues to use the current lease. By default, the client attempts, in the background, to renew its current lease when 50 percent of its assigned lease time has expired.

- If a ping of the default gateway fails, the DHCP client assumes that it has been moved to a different network, where DHCP services are not available (such as a home network). By default, the client auto-configures its IP address as described previously, and continues (every five minutes in the background) trying to locate a DHCP server and obtain a lease.

Lease Renewals

The renewal process occurs when a client already has a lease, and needs to renew that lease with the server. To ensure that addresses are not left in an assigned state when they are no longer needed, the DHCP server places an administrator-defined time limit, known as a lease duration, on the address assignment.

Halfway through the lease period, the DHCP client requests a lease renewal, and the DHCP server extends the lease. If a computer stops using its assigned IP address (for example, if a computer is moved to another network segment or is removed), the lease expires and the address becomes available for reassignment.

The renewal process occurs as follows:

1. The client sends a request to the DHCP server, asking for a renewal and extension of its current address lease. The client sends a directed request to the DHCP server, with a maximum of three retries at 4, 8, and 16 seconds.
   - If the DHCP server can be located, it typically sends a DHCP acknowledgment message to the client. This renews the lease.
   - If the client is unable to communicate with its original DHCP server, the client waits until 87.5 percent of its lease time elapses. Then the client enters a rebinding state, broadcasting (with a maximum of three retries at 4, 8, and 16 seconds) a DHCPDiscover message to any available DHCP server to update its current IP address lease.
2. If a server responds with a DHCPOffer message to update the client's current lease, the client renews its lease based on the offering server and continues operation.
3. If the lease expires and no server has been contacted, the client must immediately discontinue using its leased IP address. The client then proceeds to follow the same process used during its initial startup to obtain a new IP address lease.

Managing Lease Durations

When a scope is created, the default lease duration is set to eight days, which works well in most cases. However, because lease renewal is an ongoing process that can affect the performance of DHCP clients and your network, it might be useful to change the lease duration. Use the following guidelines to decide how best to modify lease duration settings for improving DHCP performance on your network:

- If you have a large number of IP addresses available and configurations that rarely change on your network, increase the lease duration to reduce the frequency of lease renewal queries between clients and the DHCP server. This reduces network traffic.
- If there are a limited number of IP addresses available and if client configurations change frequently or clients move often on the network, reduce the lease duration. This increases the rate at which addresses are returned to the available address pool for reassignment.
- Consider the ratio between connected computers and available IP addresses. For example, if there are 40 systems sharing a Class C address (with 254 available addresses), the demand for reusing addresses is low. A long lease time, such as two months, would be appropriate in such a situation. However, if 230 computers share the same address pool, demand for available addresses is greater, and a lease time of a few days or weeks is more appropriate.
- Use infinite lease durations with caution. Even in a relatively stable environment, there is a certain amount of turnover among clients. At a minimum, roving computers might be added and removed, desktop computers might be moved from one office to another, and network adapter cards might be replaced. If a client with an infinite lease is removed from the network, the DHCP server is not notified, and the IP address cannot be reused. A better option is a very long lease duration, such as six months. This ensures that addresses are ultimately recovered.

Managing Scopes

A scope must be defined and activated before DHCP clients can use the DHCP server for dynamic TCP/IP configuration. A DHCP scope is an administrative collection of IP addresses and TCP/IP configuration parameters that are available for lease to DHCP clients. The network administrator creates a scope for each logical or physical subnet.

A scope has the following properties:

- A scope name, assigned when the scope is created.
- A range of possible IP addresses from which to include or exclude addresses used in DHCP lease offers.

- A unique subnet mask, which determines the subnet for a given IP address.
- Lease duration values.

Each subnet can have a single DHCP scope with a single continuous range of IP addresses. To use several address ranges within a single scope or subnet, you must first define the scope and then set exclusion ranges.

Exclusion Ranges When you create a new scope, addresses of existing statically configured computers should be immediately excluded from the range. By using exclusion ranges, an administrator can exclude IP address ranges within a scope so those addresses are not offered to clients.

Because Windows 2000 Server requires that a computer running the DHCP service have its IP address statically configured, be sure that the server computer has its IP address either outside of, or excluded from, the range of the scope.

Excluded IP addresses can be active on your network, but only by manually configuring these addresses at computers that do not use DHCP to obtain an address. Exclusion ranges should be used for computers or devices that must have a static IP address, such as printer servers, firewalls, or routers.

Reservations An administrator can reserve IP addresses for permanent lease assignment to specified computers or devices on the network. Reservations ensure that a specified hardware device on a subnet can always use the same IP address. Reservations should be made for DHCP-enabled devices that must always have the same IP address on your network, such as print servers, firewalls, or routers. For more information, see "Managing Reservations" later in this chapter.

Deleting Entries There may be times when a scope needs to be modified in order to delete the lease of a DHCP client. The main reason for doing so is to remove a lease that conflicts with an IP address exclusion range or a reserved address that you want to specify. Deleting a lease has the same effect as if the client's lease expired—the next time the client system starts, it must go through the process of requesting a lease. There is nothing, however, to prevent the client from obtaining a new lease for the same IP address.

To prevent this, you must make the address unavailable before the client can request another lease by removing it from the scope and setting a reservation or exclusion. Delete scope entries only for clients that are no longer using the assigned DHCP lease or that are to be moved immediately to a new address. Deleting an active client could result in duplicate IP addresses on the network because deleted addresses are automatically reassigned to new clients.

After you delete a client's lease from the scope and set a reservation or exclusion, you should always run **ipconfig /release** at a command prompt on the client computer, to force the client to free its IP address with a DHCPRelease message.

80/20 Rule

You will probably install more than one DHCP server so that the failure of any individual server will not prevent DHCP clients from starting. However, DHCP does not provide a way for DHCP servers to cooperate in ensuring that assigned addresses are unique. Therefore, you must carefully divide the available address pool among the DHCP servers to prevent duplicate address assignment.

For balancing DHCP server usage, use the 80/20 rule to divide scope addresses between DHCP servers. Figure 4.11 is an example of the 80/20 rule.

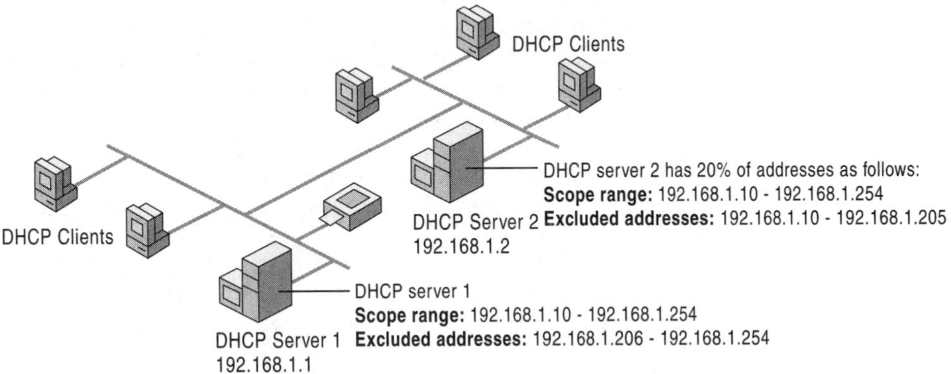

Figure 4.11 80/20 Rule Model

DHCP Server 1 is configured to lease most (about 80 percent) of the available addresses. DHCP Server 2 is configured to lease the remaining addresses (about 20 percent).

This scenario allows the local DHCP server (DHCP Server 1) to respond to requests from local DHCP clients most of the time. The remote or backup DHCP server (DHCP Server 2) assigns addresses to clients on the other subnet only when the local server is not available or is out of addresses. This same rule can be used in a multiple-subnet scenario to ensure the availability of a DHCP server when a client requests a lease.

Managing Reservations

By using reservations, you can reserve specific IP addresses for permanent use by a DHCP-enabled computer or device.

If multiple DHCP servers are each configured with scopes that cover a range of addresses that must be reserved, the reservation ranges must be specified on each DHCP server. Otherwise, those addresses could be given out by another DHCP server.

If you want to change a reserved address for a client, the client's existing address reservation must be removed before the new reservation can be added. DHCP option information can be changed while still keeping the reserved IP address.

Reserving a scope IP address does not automatically force a client currently using that address to stop using it. If you are reserving a new address for a client, or an address that is different from the client's current one, you should verify that the address has not already been leased. If the address is already in use, the client using the address must release it by issuing a DHCPRelease request. To achieve this, run **ipconfig /release** at a command prompt.

Reserving an address does not force the client for whom the reservation is made to immediately move to using the reserved address. The client must issue a renewal request to move to the newly reserved address. To achieve this, run **ipconfig /renew** at a command prompt.

For Windows 95 or Windows 98–based clients, use the Winipcfg.exe program to force the release or renewal of the reserved address. For clients using MS-DOS or other operating systems, restart the clients to force the change.

Once a release or renewal is complete, the reserved client is leased the newly reserved IP address for its permanent use.

Superscopes

A superscope allows a DHCP server to provide leases from more than one scope to clients on a single physical network. Before you can create a superscope, you must use DHCP Manager to define all scopes to be included in the superscope. Scopes added to a superscope are called member scopes. Superscopes can resolve DHCP service issues in several different ways; these issues include situations in which:

- Support is needed for DHCP clients on a single physical network segment—such as a single Ethernet LAN segment—where multiple logical IP networks are used. When more than one logical IP network is used on a physical network, these configurations are also known as multinets.
- The available address pool for a currently active scope is nearly depleted and more computers need to be added to the physical network segment.
- Clients need to be migrated to a new scope.
- Support is needed for DHCP clients on the other side of BOOTP relay agents, where the network on the other side of the relay agent has multiple logical subnets on one physical network. For more information, see "Supporting BOOTP Clients" later in this chapter.

> Versions of the DHCP service prior to Windows NT 4.0 with Service Pack 2 cannot create superscopes. One solution for this situation is to add additional network adapters to the server, and to address each of the network adapters to a given logical IP subnet. This involves additional and otherwise unnecessary hardware, and only works on segments local to the DHCP server.

A standard network with one DHCP server on a single physical subnet is limited to leasing addresses to clients on the physical subnet. Figure 4.12 shows Subnet A before a superscope is implemented.

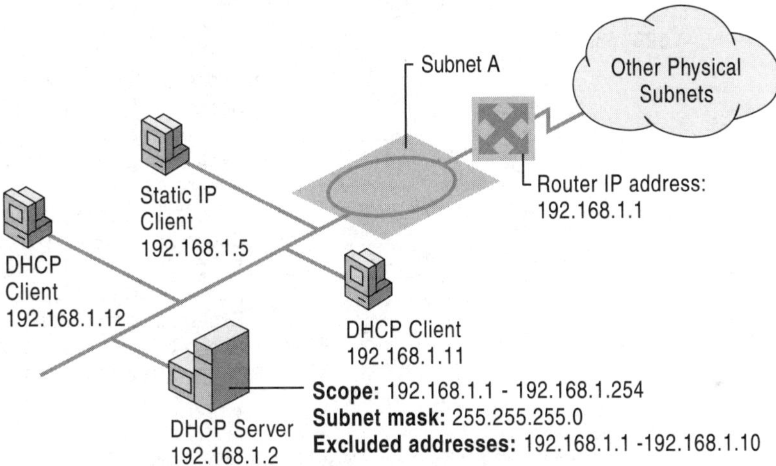

Figure 4.12 DHCP Servers Using Single Scopes

To include the multinets on Subnet B in the range of addresses leased by the DHCP server shown in Figure 4.13, you can create a superscope that includes member Scopes 2 and 3 for Subnet B in addition to the scope for Subnet A.

Figure 4.13 shows the superscope configuration.

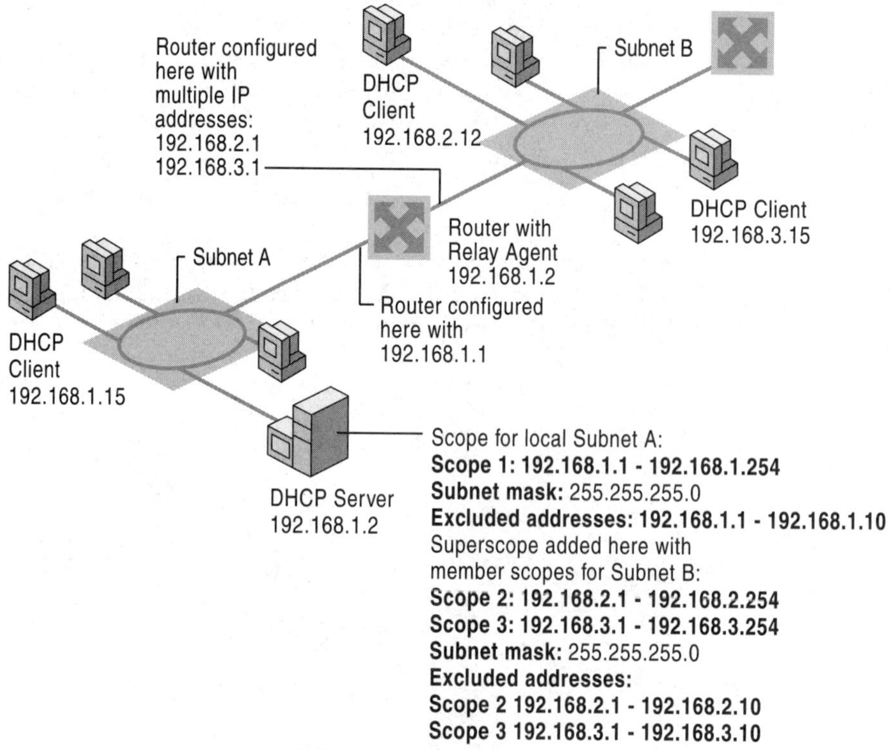

Router configured here with multiple IP addresses: 192.168.2.1 192.168.3.1

DHCP Client 192.168.2.12

Subnet B

DHCP Client 192.168.3.15

Router with Relay Agent 192.168.1.2

Subnet A

Router configured here with 192.168.1.1

DHCP Client 192.168.1.15

DHCP Server 192.168.1.2

Scope for local Subnet A:
Scope 1: 192.168.1.1 - 192.168.1.254
Subnet mask: 255.255.255.0
Excluded addresses: 192.168.1.1 - 192.168.1.10
Superscope added here with
member scopes for Subnet B:
Scope 2: 192.168.2.1 - 192.168.2.254
Scope 3: 192.168.3.1 - 192.168.3.254
Subnet mask: 255.255.255.0
Excluded addresses:
Scope 2 192.168.2.1 - 192.168.2.10
Scope 3 192.168.3.1 - 192.168.3.10

Figure 4.13 DHCP Servers Using Superscopes

To include multinets on remote networks in the range of addresses leased by the DHCP server, you can configure a superscope to include member Scope 1, Scope 2, and Scope 3.

Figure 4.14 shows the scope configuration that includes the multinets on remote networks.

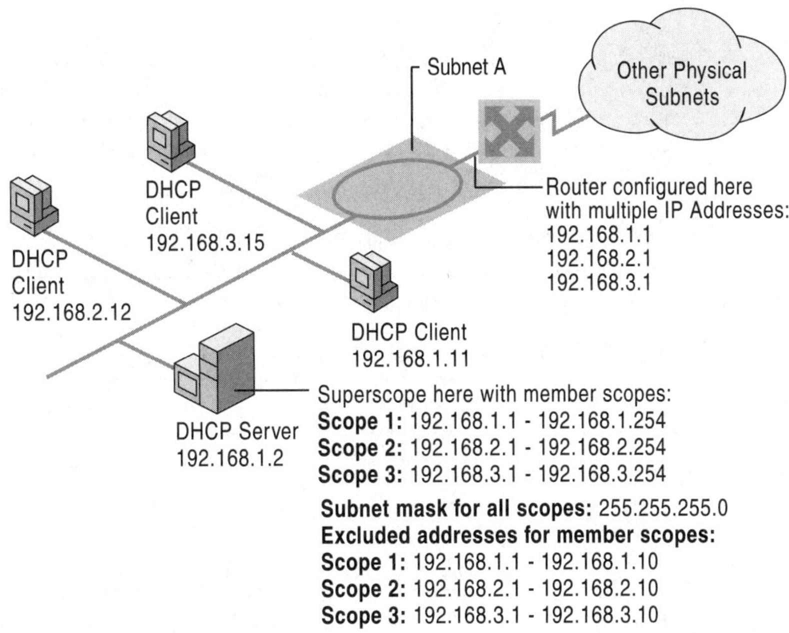

Figure 4.14 DHCP Servers Using Superscopes for Remote Networks

Table 4.3 shows how two DHCP servers, both located on the same physical subnet, are each configured with a single scope.

Table 4.3 DHCP Scope for Servers A and B

DHCP Server Name	Starting IP Scope Address	Ending IP Scope Address
DHCP Server A	211.111.111.1	211.111.111.255
DHCP Server B	222.222.222.1	222.222.222.255

If DHCP Server A manages a different scope of addresses from DHCP Server B, and neither has any information about addresses managed by the other, a problem arises if a client previously registered with Server A, for example, releases its name during a proper shutdown and later reconnects to the network after a restart and tries to lease an address from Server B.

If Server B receives a DHCPRequest packet from the client to renew use of an address before Server A does, Server B (which does not contain any of Server A's IP addresses) rejects the request and sends a DHCPNak packet to the client. The client must then renegotiate a DHCP lease by broadcasting a DHCPDiscover packet onto the local subnet. Server B can send a DHCPOffer packet offering the client an address, which it can accept by returning a DHCPRequest for that

Nothing in this example prevents a client from having its request to renew an address rejected every time it connects to the network. In the process of rejecting and obtaining an address lease, the client might be offered an address that places it on a different subnet for which the client is not configured. By using superscopes on both DHCP servers, you can avoid both of these problems, and addresses are managed predictably and effectively.

Table 4.4 describes the same situation, but using superscopes. Both servers are located on the same physical subnet, and each is configured to allow multiple servers to provide addresses for a multinet.

Table 4.4 Superscope: DHCP Servers A and B

DHCP Server	Starting IP Scope Address	Ending IP Acope Address	Exclusions in the Scope
DHCP-ServerA	211.111.111.1	211.111.111.254	
DHCP-ServerA	222.222.222.1	222.222.222.254	222.222.222.1 to 222.222.222.254
DHCP-ServerB	222.222.222.1	222.222.222.254	
DHCP-ServerB	211.111.111.1	211.111.111.254	211.111.111.1 to 211.111.111.254

By configuring superscopes as described in this table, DHCP Servers A and B each recognize IP addresses assigned by the other. This prevents either server from negatively acknowledging attempts by DHCP clients to renew their IP address or to obtain an address from the same logical range of addresses. This works because DHCP Server B has knowledge of the scope in DHCP Server A via the superscope defined in DHCP Server B. Thus, if a DHCP client attempts to renew and its address belongs to one of the member scopes in DHCP Server B's superscope, Server B ignores the request.

Warning When an IP address range that is too large for the subnet mask is specified, the administrator is given the option (by the DHCP Create Scope wizard) of creating a superscope. However, this might tax DHCP server resources. For example, if the new superscope includes more than 10,000 scopes, it might overload the server. In such cases, superscopes should be created manually with a smaller subset of scopes, or a smaller IP address range should be specified when using the wizard.

Removing Scopes

Scopes should be removed when a subnet is no longer in use or when you need to renumber your network to use a different IP address range.

You must deactivate a scope before removing it. This enables clients using the scope to renew their lease in a different scope. Otherwise, clients lose their leases and possibly network access (if they cannot auto-configure).

To ensure that all clients migrate smoothly to a new scope, you should deactivate the old scope for at least half of the lease time, or until you have manually renewed all clients, to remove them from the inactive scope. For more information about deactivating scopes, see Windows 2000 Server Help.

Preventing Address Conflicts

Windows 2000 has both server-side and client-side conflict detection to prevent duplicate IP addresses on your network.

Server Conflict Detection

The DHCP server detects conflicts by pinging an IP address before offering that address to clients. If the ping is successful (a response is received from a computer), a conflict is registered and that address is not offered to clients requesting a lease from the server. The DHCP server pings only addresses that have not been successfully and previously leased. If a client receives a lease on an IP address that it already had or is requesting a renewal, the DHCP server does not send a ping.

If conflict detection is enabled, an administrator-defined number of pings are sent. The server waits 1 second for a reply. Because the time required for a client to obtain a lease is equal to the number of pings selected, choose this value carefully as it directly impacts the overall performance of the server. In general, one ping should be sufficient.

A DHCP server receiving a reply to any of the pings (meaning there is a conflict) attaches a BAD_ADDRESS value to that IP address in the scope, and will try to lease the next available address. If the duplicate address is removed from the network, the BAD_ADDRESS value attached to the IP address can be deleted from the scope's list of active leases, and the address returned to the pool. Addresses are marked as BAD_ADDRESS for the length of the lease for which the scope is configured.

If your network includes legacy DHCP clients, enable conflict detection on the DHCP server. By default, the DHCP service does not perform any conflict detection. In general, conflict detection should be used only as a troubleshooting aid when you suspect there are duplicate IP addresses in use on your network. The reason for this is that, for each additional conflict detection attempt that the DHCP service performs, additional seconds are added to time needed to negotiate leases for DHCP clients.

Client Conflict Detection

Windows 2000 or 98-based client computers also check to determine if an address is already in use before completing address configuration with the DHCP server. If the client detects a conflict, it sends a DHCPDecline message to the DHCP server. The DHCP server attaches a BAD_ADDRESS value to the IP address in the scope, as detailed in "Server-Side Conflict Detection." The client begins the lease process again, and is offered the next available address in the scope.

For networks that include clients that are not running Windows 2000 or 98, server-side conflict detection should be enabled.

Managing DHCP Options

DHCP options can be configured for specific values and enabled for assignment and distribution to DHCP clients based on either server, scope, class or client-specific levels. The most specific take precedence over the least specific. In most cases, the client values provided are taken from the **DHCP Options Properties** dialog box on the DHCP server. These properties can be configured and set for an entire scope or for a single reserved scope client.

Although these options are not required for use by DHCP, assign and configure these options to automate client TCP/IP configuration when you have a sizable number of Microsoft-based DHCP client computers in active operation on your network. Options can also be used for DHCP communication between the server computer and client computers.

Options can be managed using different levels assigned for each managed DHCP server, including:

- Default global options

  These options are applied globally for all scopes and classes defined at each DHCP server and any clients that it services. Active global option types always apply unless they are overridden by other scope, class, or reserved client settings for the option type.

- Scope options

  These options are applied to any clients that obtain a lease within that particular scope. Active scope option types always apply to all computers obtaining a lease in a given scope unless they are overridden by class or reserved client settings for the option type.

- Class options

  These options are applied to any clients that specify that particular DHCP Class ID value when obtaining a scope lease. Active class option types always apply to all computers configured as members in a specified DHCP option class unless they are overridden by a reserved client setting for the option type.

- Reserved client options

  These options apply to any appropriate, reserved, client computer—any computer that has a reservation in the scope for its IP address. Where reserved client option types are active, settings for these option types override all other possible defaults (server, scope, or class assigned option settings for the option type).

In general, options are applied at each DHCP server at the server or scope level. To precisely manage or customize option settings, specify either a user or vendor class assignment that overrides the broader server or scope option defaults. For special requirements, such as clients with special functions, narrow the spectrum even further by assigning options for reserved clients.

Options can also be used to separate and distribute appropriate options for clients with similar or special configuration needs. For example, DHCP-enabled clients on the same floor can be assigned membership in the same option class (that is, configured with the same DHCP Class ID value). This class can then be used to distribute additional or varied option data during the lease process, overriding any scope or globally provided default options.

Many of these option types are predefined in Windows 2000 DHCP. Other standard DHCP option types can be added as needed to support any other DHCP client software that recognizes or requires the use of these additional option types. All DHCP options supported by the Windows 2000 DHCP service are defined in RFC 2132, although most DHCP clients use or support only a small subset of the available RFC-specified option types. This feature enables custom applications for enterprise networks to be introduced quickly. Equipment from multiple vendors on a network can also use different option numbers for different functions. The vendor class and vendor options are described in RFC 2132.

The Microsoft-based DHCP server usually allocates 312 bytes for DHCP options. That is more than enough for most option configurations. Some other DHCP servers and clients support option overlay, in which unused space in other standard DHCP message header fields within the DHCP packet can be overlaid to store and carry additional options. Microsoft DHCP service does not support this feature. If you attempt to use more than 312 bytes, some option settings will be lost. In that case, you should delete any unused or low-priority options. Table 4.5 contains a list of default DHCP options used by Microsoft Windows 2000 DHCP clients.

Table 4.5 Default DHCP Options

Code	Option name	Meaning
1	Subnet mask	Specifies the subnet mask of the client subnet. This option is defined in the DHCP Manager **Create Scope** or **Scope Properties** dialog box. It cannot be set directly in the **DHCP Options** dialog box.
3	Router	Specifies a list of IP addresses for routers on the client's subnet. Multihomed computers can have only one list per computer, not one per network adapter.
6	DNS servers	Specifies a list of IP addresses for DNS name servers available to the client.
15	Domain name	Specifies the DNS domain name that the client should use for DNS computer name resolution.
44	WINS/NBNS servers	Specifies a list of IP addresses for NetBIOS name servers (NBNS).
46	WINS/NBT node type	Allows configurable NetBIOS over TCP/IP (NetBT) clients to be configured as described in RFC 1001/1002, where 1 = b-node, 2 = p-node, 4 = m-node, and 8 = h-node. On multihomed computers, the node type is assigned to the entire computer, not to individual network adapters.
47	NetBIOS scope ID[1]	Specifies a text string that is the NetBIOS over TCP/IP scope ID for the client, as specified in RFC 1001/1002.
51	Lease time	Specifies the time, in seconds, from address assignment until the client's lease on the address expires. Lease time is specified in the DHCP Manager **Create Scope** or **Scope Properties** dialog box, and can be set directly in the **DHCP Options** dialog box.
58	Renewal (T1) time value	Specifies the time in seconds from address assignment until the client enters the Renewing state. Renewal time is a function of the lease time option, which is specified in the DHCP Manager **Create Scope** or **Scope Properties** dialog box and can be set directly in the **DHCP Options** dialog box.
59	Rebinding (T2) time value	Specifies the time, in seconds, from address assignment until the client enters the Rebinding state. Rebinding time is a function of the lease time option, which is specified in the DHCP Manager **Create Scope** or **Scope Properties** dialog box andcan be set directly in the **DHCP Options** dialog box.

[1] Option 47 (NetBIOS scope ID) is provided for backward compatibility. Don't use this option unless you already employ NetBIOS scope IDs in your environment.

Note If you are using Microsoft DHCP service to configure computers that should use the services of a WINS server for name resolution, be sure to use option 44, WINS Servers, and option 46, Node Type. These DHCP options automatically configure the DHCP client as an h-node computer that directly contacts WINS servers for NetBIOS name registration and name query instead of using only broadcasts.

DHCP Option Parameters

DHCP servers can be configured to provide optional data that fully configures TCP/IP on a client. Some of the most common DHCP option types configured and distributed by the DHCP server during leases include default gateway, router, DNS, and WINS parameters.

Clients can be configured with:

- Information options. You can explicitly configure these option types and any associated values provided to clients.
- Protocol options. You can implicitly configure these option types used by the DHCP service based on server and scope property settings.

You can use DHCP Manager to configure these properties and set them for an entire scope or for a single, reserved, client scope. The LAN Manager for OS/2 client does not support DHCP or WINS.

Information Options

Table 4.6 lists the most common types of DHCP information option types that can be configured for DHCP clients. Typically, these option types can be enabled and configured for each scope that you configure on a DHCP server.

Table 4.6 Common Information Option Types

Code	Description
3	Router
6	DNS server
15	DNS domain name
44	WINS server (NetBIOS name server)
45	NetBIOS datagram distribution server (NBDD)
46	WINS/NetBIOS node type
47	NetBIOS scope ID

Clients can receive these values to set their TCP/IP configurations, during the period of the lease.

Internal Protocol Options

Table 4.7 shows internal protocol option types that DHCP clients can be configured to use when communicating with a DHCP server to obtain or renew a lease.

Table 4.7 Common Internal Protocol Option Types

Code	Description
51	Lease time
53	DHCP message type
55	Special option type used to communicate a parameter request list to the DHCP server
58	Renewal time value (T1)
59	Rebind time value (T2)

In most cases, the actual values provided to clients with these option types are taken from the DHCP service property settings on the DHCP server.

Options for Remote Access Clients

When a remote access client obtains an IP address lease from a remote access server, run Winipcfg.exe (for Windows 95) or Ipconfig.exe (for Windows 2000 or Windows NT) to display information about the lease.

When a remote access server assigns an IP address to a remote access client, either from its own static address pool or from its cached DHCP address pool, there is no effective lease time for the IP address because it is released when the client disconnects.

However, remote access clients can still receive additional TCP/IP configuration information from the remote access server: WINS server assignments and DNS server assignments can be delegated to the client when it connects. These settings are delegated directly from the remote access server's settings. If a remote access server has WINS or DNS servers as configured entries in its dial-up connection properties, these settings are passed on to remote access clients that are DHCP-enabled.

Table 4.8 lists the DHCP option types that Windows-based clients support, which are assigned to the clients through a dial-up network connection with a remote access server.

Table 4.8 DHCP Options Used by Remote Access, Windows-Based, DHCP-Enabled Clients

Option	Description
IP Address	The remote access server proactively obtains an IP address from the DHCP server and builds a cached pool of DHCP leased addresses. The remote access server then distributes these cached IP addresses to the remote access client on demand and manages each lease. This is the only information from the DHCP server that the remote access client receives.
WINS server	Values provided with the option type are taken from the remote access server dial-up connection properties if the remote access server is configured with WINS server addresses. The client acquires the list of WINS servers that are configured on the remote access server.
DNS server	Values provided with the option type are taken from the remote access server dial-up connection properties if the remote access server is configured with DNS server addresses. The client acquires the first DNS server address listed in the remote access server's DNS server search list.
Subnet Mask	The subnet mask corresponds to the default subnet mask associated with the standard address class type (Class A, B, or C) of the given IP address.
NetBIOS Scope ID	NetBIOS scope ID information is not passed to the client. If you need to modify this setting, you must change it directly on the client.
Node Type	Node Type is not taken from the DHCP lease but can change on the remote access client, depending on WINS information. If the remote access server has no locally defined WINS servers, a b-node remote access client remains a b-node client. If the remote access server has locally defined WINS servers, a b-node remote access client switches to h-node for the duration of the connection. Windows 95 clients do not automatically switch between node types if the remote access server supplies WINS addresses. In these cases, you must manually switch the node type.

Option Classes

This feature allows quick introduction of custom applications for enterprise networks. DHCP option classes provide a way to easily configure network clients with the parameters necessary to meet the special requirements of custom applications. Equipment from multiple vendors on a network can also use different option numbers for different functions. The option types used to support vendor classes—the vendor class identifier and the vendor-specific option—are defined in the Internet DHCP options standard reference, RFC 2132.

For Windows 2000 Server, there are two types of option classes: vendor-defined and user-defined. These classes can be configured on your servers to offer specialized client support in the following ways:

- Add and configure vendor-defined classes for submanaging DHCP options assigned to clients identified by vendor type.
- Add and configure user-defined classes for submanaging DHCP options assigned to clients identified by a common need for a similar DHCP option configuration.

After options classes are defined on a DHCP server, scopes on the server must be configured to assign options for specific user-defined and vendor-defined option classes.

Vendor Classes

Vendor-defined option classes can be used by DHCP clients to identify the client's vendor type and configuration to the DHCP server when obtaining a lease. For a client to identify its vendor class during the lease process, the client needs to include the vendor class ID option (option code 60) when it requests or selects a lease from a DHCP server.

The vendor class identifier information is a string of character data interpreted by the DHCP servers. Vendors can choose to define specific vendor class identifiers to convey particular configuration or other identification information about a client. For example, the identifier might encode the client's hardware or software configuration. Most vendor types are derived from standard reserved hardware and operating system- type abbreviation codes listed in RFC 1700.

When vendor options are specified, the server performs the following additional steps to provide a lease to the client:

1. The server checks to see that the vendor class identified by the client request is a recognized class defined on the server.

   If the vendor class is recognized, the server checks to see if any additional DHCP options are configured for this class in the active scope.

   If the vendor class is not recognized, the server ignores the vendor class identified in the client request, and returns options allocated to the default vendor class (includes all DHCP Standard Options).

2. If the scope contains options configured specifically for use with clients in this vendor-defined class, the server returns those options using the vendor-specific option type (option code 43) as part of its acknowledgment message.

In most cases, the default vendor class—DHCP Standard Options—provides a default vendor class for grouping any Microsoft DHCP clients or other DHCP clients that do not specify a vendor class ID. In some cases, you might define additional vendor classes for other DHCP clients, such as printers or some types of UNIX clients. When you add other vendor classes for these purposes, be sure that the vendor class identifier you use to configure the class at the server matches the identifier used by clients for your third-party vendor.

User Classes

User classes allow DHCP clients to differentiate themselves by specifying what type of client they are, such as a remote access or desktop computer. For Windows 2000 computers, you can define specific user class identifiers to convey information about a client's software configuration, its physical location in a building, or about its user preferences. For example, an identifier can specify that DHCP clients are members of a user-defined class called "2nd floor, West," which has need for a special set of router, DNS, and WINS server settings. An administrator can then configure the DHCP server to configure different option types depending on the type of client receiving the lease.

Windows 2000 user classes can be used in the following ways:

- DHCP client computers can include the DHCP user class option when sending DHCP request messages to the DHCP server. This can specifically identify the client as part of a user class on the server.
- DHCP servers running the Microsoft DHCP service can recognize and interpret the DHCP user class option from clients and provide additional options (or a modified set of DHCP options) based on the client's user class identity.

For example, shorter leases should be assigned to remote access clients. Desktop clients on the same network might require special settings, such as CAD platforms. These variations could also include WINS and DNS server settings.

If user-defined option classes are not specified, default settings (such as server options or scope options) are assigned.

A user-defined class can be either a default or custom user class. Microsoft provides three default user classes, as described in Table 4.9.

Table 4.9 Default User Classes Provided by Microsoft DHCP

Class Type	Class ID String	Description
Default User Class	(Unspecified)	Used by the DHCP service to classify clients that do not further specify an identity or type. This class is typically used by most DHCP clients. Clients are assigned to this class under the following conditions: ▪ DHCP clients that have no concept of a user class or a user class ID. This is true for most DHCP clients prior to Windows 2000. ▪ Windows 2000 clients configured with a class ID unknown to the DHCP server (for example, the server has not defined this class).
Default Routing and Remote Access class	RRAS.Microsoft	Used by the Microsoft DHCP service to classify clients making a PPP-type connection through a remote access server. Typically, this class includes most dial-up networking clients that use DHCP to obtain a lease: ▪ remote access clients that have no concept of a Routing and Remote Access user class or a Routing and Remote Access user class ID. See the section titled "DHCP and Routing and Remote Access" later in this chapter for details on the interaction between server with the Routing and Remote Access feature and a DHCP server and how DHCP servers identify Routing and Remote Access clients.
Default BOOTP class	BOOTP	Used by the Microsoft DHCP service to classify any clients recognized as BOOTP clients.

Using the Microsoft default user classes can be useful for isolating configuration details specific for clients with special needs, such as older clients or clients that use BOOTP or Routing and Remote Access. For example, you might want to include and assign special BOOTP option types (such as option codes 66 and 67) for clients that are BOOTP type, or shorten the lease time for remote access clients.

You might also add and configure custom user classes for use by DHCP clients running Windows 2000. For custom user classes, you must specify a custom identifier that must correspond with a user class defined on the DHCP server computer.

Currently, the user class option field permits only one ASCII text string to be used for identifying clients. This means each client computer can only be identified as a member of a single user class by the DHCP server. If you need to, you can use additional user classes and make new hybrids from your other user classes. For example, if you have two user classes, one called "mobile" with short lease times assigned and another called "engineer" with an option assigned to configure a high-performance server for its clients, you could make a new hybrid class called "mobile-engineer" that would lease clients that have overlapping configuration needs specified in each class.

Configuring Options

The following steps can help you determine at what level to configure and assign DHCP options for clients on your network:

- Add or define new, custom option types only if you have new software or applications that requires a nonstandard DHCP option.
- If your network is large, be conservative and selective when assigning global options. These options apply to *all* clients of a DHCP server computer.
- Use scope-level options for most options that clients are assigned. In most networks, the scope level is typically the preferred level for assigning options.
- Use class options if you have a large network or groups of clients with diverse needs that are able to support membership in option classes (such as Windows 2000 clients).
- Use reserved client options only for clients that have special requirements—for example, if your intranet has a DNS server that performs forwarding for resolving Internet DNS names not authoritatively managed on your network. In this case, you need to add the IP address of an external DNS server on your DNS server computer. You can configure your DNS server as a reserved client in DHCP and set this address as another reserved client option.

Options Precedence

The DHCP service uses a bottom-up hierarchy in determining which option to enforce. This simplifies DHCP management and allows a flexible administration that can range from server-wide default settings to individualized client settings when needed for special circumstances.

Following are the basic rules of how options are used:

- Active global options always apply unless overridden by scope, class, or reserved options.
- Active scope options always apply to any computers obtaining a lease from that scope, unless overridden by class or reserved options.
- Active class options always apply to any computers configured as members of that class, unless overridden by a reserved option.
- Reserved options override all other possible options.
- Statically configured values on a client override any DHCP options of any type or level.

Multicast DHCP

Multicast DHCP, now referred to as MADCAP (Multicast Address Dynamic Client Allocation Protocol), is now included with the Windows 2000 DHCP service, and is used to support dynamic assignment and configuration of IP multicast addresses on TCP/IP-based networks.

Ordinarily, you use DHCP scopes to provide client configurations by allocating ranges of IP addresses from the Class A, B, or C address classes. By using these scopes and ranges of addresses, your clients are configured to use unicast for point-to-point communication between two networked computers.

With Windows 2000 Server, the DHCP service offers MADCAP support in the form of multicast scopes. You configure a multicast scope as you would a regular DHCP scope, but multicast scopes provide scope ranges of Class D multicast IP addresses. These addresses are reserved for multicast operation using directed transmission from one point to multiple points.

Background on Multicasting

A group of TCP/IP computers can use a multicast IP address to send directed communication to all computers with which they share the use of the group address. Multicast addresses are shared by many computers.

When the destination address for an IP datagram is a multicast address, the packet is forwarded to all members of that multicast group, which is a set of zero or more computers identified by that multicast address.

Dynamic Membership

Multicast addresses support dynamic membership, allowing individual computers to join or leave the multicast group at any time. Group membership is not limited by size, and computers are not restricted to membership in any single group. In addition, any computer that uses TCP/IP can send datagrams to any multicast group. A multicast group is similar to a group e-mail address in its usage. When an IP multicast address is used as the destination address for an IP datagram, the datagram is forwarded to all members of the multicast group identified by the address.

Multicast Address Ranges

You can permanently reserve multicast group addresses or temporarily assign and use them. A permanent group is made by permanently reserving a Class D IP address (224.0.0.0 to 239.255.255.255) with the Internet Assigned Numbers Authority (IANA). The reserved address then becomes a well-known address, indicating a specific multicast group that exists regardless of whether group member computers are present on the network. For multicast IP addresses not permanently reserved with the IANA, all Class D addresses that remain unreserved can then be used dynamically to assign and form temporary multicast groups. These temporary groups can exist as long as one or more computers on the network are configured with the group's address and actively share in its use.

Supporting MADCAP

Clients using MADCAP must be configured to use the MADCAP API. For more information on writing or programming applications that use this API, see the developer resources made available through the Microsoft Solution Developers Network (MSDN).

MADCAP assists in simplifying and automating configuration of multicast groups on your network, but it is not required for the operation of multicast groups or for the DHCP service. Multicast scopes provide only address configuration and do not support or use other DHCP-assignable options.

MADCAP address configuration for clients should be done independently of how the clients are configured to receive their primary IP address. Computers that use either static or dynamic configuration through a DHCP server can be MADCAP clients.

The Windows 2000 DHCP service supports both DHCP and MADCAP, although these services function separately. Clients of one are not dependent on the use or configuration of the other.

- Clients that are manually configured or use DHCP to obtain a unicast IP address lease can also use MADCAP to obtain multicast IP address configuration.

- Clients that do not support MADCAP service or are unable to contact and obtain multicast configuration from a MADCAP server can be configured in other ways so that they participate in either permanent or temporary multicast groups on the network.
- In all TCP/IP networks, each computer requires a unique primary computer IP address (that is not shared or duplicated) from one of the standard address classes used for building the network (Class A, B, or C range). You must assign this required primary computer IP address before you can configure a computer to support and use secondary IP addresses such as multicast IP addresses.
- When multicast address configuration is used, a MADCAP server can dynamically perform this configuration for clients that support the MADCAP protocol.

DHCP Database

Windows 2000 DHCP servers use the performance-enhanced Exchange Server Storage engine version 4.0.

The DHCP service database is a dynamic database that is updated as DHCP clients are assigned or as they release their TCP/IP configuration parameters. Because the DHCP database is not a distributed database like the WINS server database, maintaining the DHCP service database is less complex.

Database Management

The following describes the administrative tasks for managing your DHCP database. To avoid high cost of ownership, these are performed by Windows 2000 automatically, but can also be done manually by the network administrator.

Record Management

There is no built-in limit to the number of records that a DHCP server can store. The size of the database depends on the number of DHCP clients on the network. The DHCP database grows over time as a result of clients starting and stopping on the network. Over time, as some DHCP client entries become obsolete and are deleted, some unused space remains.

Storage Space Management

To recover unused space, the DHCP database must be compacted. Windows 2000 dynamically compacts the database in an automatic background process during idle time after a database update. Although dynamic compacting greatly reduces the need for performing offline compaction, it does not fully eliminate it. Offline compaction reclaims the space more efficiently and should be performed at least once a month for large, busy networks with 1,000 or more DHCP clients. For smaller networks, manual compaction might be required only every few months.

Because the dynamic database compaction occurs in the background while the database is in use, you do not need to stop the DHCP server. However, for manual compacting, the DHCP server must be taken offline.

Database Backup

The DHCP database and related registry entries are automatically backed up at a specific interval. You can modify the default interval by changing the value of the **BackupInterval** entry in the following registry subkey:

HKEY_LOCAL_COMPUTER\SYSTEM\CurrentControlSet

Caution Do not use a registry editor to edit the registry directly unless you have no alternative. The registry editors bypass the standard safeguards provided by administrative tools. These safeguards prevent you from entering conflicting settings or settings that are likely to degrade performance or damage your system. Editing the registry directly can have serious, unexpected consequences that can prevent the system from starting and require that you reinstall Windows 2000. To configure or customize Windows 2000, use the programs in Control Panel or Microsoft Management Console (MMC) whenever possible.

DHCP Service Database Files

When you install the DHCP service, the files shown in Table 4.10 are automatically created in the *%SystemRoot%*\System32\Dhcp directory.

Table 4.10 Database Files and Descriptions

File	Description
J50.log and J50*xxxx*.log	A log of all transactions done with the DHCP database. This file is used by DHCP to recover data if necessary. To increase speed and efficiency of data storage, the Jet database writes current transactions to log files rather than to the database directly. Therefore, the most current view of the data is the database plus any transactions in the log files. These files are also used for recovery if the DHCP service is stopped in an unexpected manner. If the service is stopped in an unexpected manner, the log files are automatically used to recreate the correct state of the DHCP database. Log files are always a certain size; however, they can grow quickly in number on a very busy DHCP server. It is inevitable that DHCP will write more transactions to a log than the size of the log can accommodate. When a log file becomes filled, it is renamed to indicate that it is an older log and not in use. A new transaction log is created with the J*n*.log filename (where *n* is a decimal number), such as J50.log. The naming format of the previous log file will be Jet*xxxxx*.log, where each *x* denotes a hexadecimal number from 0 to F. Previous log files are maintained in the same folder as the current log files. The log files are processed (all log entries written to the database) and deleted when a successful backup occurs or when the DHCP server is shut down gracefully. Therefore, if many J*n*.log files have accumulated, frequent backups should be scheduled to maintain the logs. After the entries have been processed, it is possible to manually delete the log files; however, this prevents a successful recovery of the database if it is needed. Because of this, it is important that the log files not be manually deleted or removed from the system until a backup has been performed.
J50.chk	A checkpoint file that indicates the location of the last information successfully written from the transaction logs to the database. It is also used for recovery purposes—that is, the checkpoint file indicates where the recovery or replaying of data should begin. This checkpoint file is updated every time data is written to the database file (DHCP.mdb).
Dhcp.mdb	The DHCP service database file that contains two tables: the IP-address-Owner-ID mapping table and the name–to–IP address mapping table.
Dhcptmp.mdb	A temporary file that is created by a DHCP server. This file is used by the database as a swap file during index maintenance operations and may remain in the *%SystemRoot%*\System32\DHCP directory after a crash.
Res*x*.log	These are reserved log files that are kept for emergency purposes. They are used if the server runs out of disk space. If a server attempts to create another transaction log file and there is insufficient disk space, the server flushes any outstanding transactions into these reserved log files. The service then shuts down and logs an event to the event log.

DHCP uses the Jet database format for storing its data. Jet produces J*n*.log and other files in the *%SystemRoot%*\System32\DHCP folder to increase the speed and efficiency of data storage.

Caution The J50.log, J50*xxxxx*.log, Dhcp.mdb, Dhcptmp.mdb, and Res*x*.log files should not be removed or tampered with in any manner.

Supporting BOOTP Clients

The Bootstrap Protocol (BOOTP) is a computer configuration protocol developed before DHCP. DHCP improves on BOOTP and resolves specific limitations BOOTP had as a computer configuration service. RFC 951 defines BOOTP.

BOOTP was intended to configure diskless workstations with limited boot capabilities, while DHCP was intended to configure frequently relocated networked computers (such as portables) that have local hard drives and full boot capabilities.

Because of the relationship between BOOTP and DHCP, both protocols share some defining characteristics. The common elements include:

- The format structure used to exchange client/server messages.

  BOOTP and DHCP use nearly identical request messages (sent by clients) and reply messages (sent by servers). Messages in either of these protocols use a single User Datagram Protocol (UDP) datagram of 576 bytes to enclose each protocol message. Message headers are the same for both BOOTP and DHCP with one exception: The final message header field used to carry optional data. For BOOTP, this optional field is called the vendor-specific area and is limited to 64 octets. For DHCP, this area is called the options field and can carry up to 312 octets of DHCP options information.

  Because DHCP and BOOTP messages use nearly identical format types and packet structures, and typically use the same well-known service ports, BOOTP or DHCP relay agent programs usually treat BOOTP and DHCP messages as essentially the same message type, without differentiating between them.

- Use of well-known UDP ports for client/server communication.

  Both BOOTP and DHCP use the same reserved protocol ports for sending and receiving messages between servers and clients. Both BOOTP and DHCP servers use UDP port 67 to listen for and receive client request messages. BOOTP and DHCP clients typically reserve UDP port 68 for accepting message replies from either a BOOTP server or DHCP server.

- IP address distribution as an integral part of configuration service.

  Although both BOOTP and DHCP allocate IP addresses to clients during startup, they use different methods of allocation. BOOTP typically provides fixed allocation of a single IP address for each client, permanently reserving this address in the BOOTP server database. DHCP typically provides dynamic, leased allocation of available IP addresses, reserving each DHCP client address temporarily in the DHCP service database.
- The downloading of the image file by the BOOTP client is performed using the Trivial File Transfer Protocol (TFTP).

  Clients contact TFTP servers to perform file transfer of their boot image. Because Windows 2000 does not provide a TFTP file service, you need a third-party TFTP server to support BOOTP clients that must boot from an image file (usually diskless workstations). You also need to configure your DHCP server to provide supported BOOTP/DHCP options.

The implementation of BOOTP support described in this section assumes that the DHCP service is already installed and correctly configured for DHCP clients.

For more information about BOOTP, see RFCs 1532, 2131, and 2132. Support for BOOTP is also available with Windows NT Server 4.0 with Service Pack 2 and later.

Differences Between BOOTP and DHCP

Despite these similarities, there are significant differences in the ways BOOTP and DHCP perform client configuration:

- BOOTP supports a limited number of client configuration parameters called vendor extensions, while DHCP supports a larger and extensible set of client configuration parameters called options.
- BOOTP uses a two-phase bootstrap configuration process in which clients contact BOOTP servers to perform address determination and boot file name selection, and clients contact Trivial File Transfer Protocol (TFTP) servers to perform file transfer of their boot image. DHCP uses a single-phase boot configuration process whereby a DHCP client negotiates with a DHCP server to determine its IP address and obtain any other initial configuration details it needs for network operation.
- BOOTP clients do not rebind or renew configuration with the BOOTP server except when the system restarts, while DHCP clients do not require a system restart to rebind or renew configuration with the DHCP server. Instead, clients automatically enter the Rebinding state at set timed intervals to renew their leased address allocation with the DHCP server. This process occurs in the background and is transparent to the user.

BOOTP Clients Requesting IP Address Information Only

Previously, BOOTP client support through the DHCP server required an explicit client reservation to be made for each BOOTP client.

With new support for dynamic BOOTP, a pool of addresses can be designated—similar to the way a scope is used for DHCP clients—to dynamically manage IP address assignment for BOOTP clients. The DHCP service can later reclaim addresses used in the dynamic BOOTP address pool, after first verifying that a specified lease time has elapsed and that each address is not still in use by the BOOTP client.

To configure your DHCP server to assign and distribute IP address information to BOOTP clients, you must configure a BOOTP address pool within a DHCP scope on the server.

Another option to the dynamic BOOTP address pool is to add a client reservation for each BOOTP client within your DHCP scopes. A reservation builds an association between the BOOTP client's media access control address (encoded in its physical hardware) and its leased IP address. When a reserved client requests the reservation of an IP address, the DHCP service returns the appropriate reserved IP address in the lease response based on the client's media access control address included in the BOOTP request message.

BOOTP Clients Requesting Boot File Information

To configure the DHCP service to provide boot file information to BOOTP clients, you must do the following:

1. Create a client address reservation for each BOOTP client within an active DHCP scope.

   BOOTP addresses must be reserved by an IP address reservation that you make for each BOOTP client. When you make client reservations, enter the BOOTP client's physical or media access control address, as assigned in LAN adapter hardware for the **Unique identifier** in the **Add Reservation** dialog box. BOOTP clients use this address when they start and send a BOOTP request. In the same dialog box, under **Allowed client types**, you should click either **BOOTP only** or **Both** when you create each BOOTP client reservation.
2. Create BOOTP entries for each client-specific platform in the BOOTP table on the DHCP server.

Information stored in the BOOTP table is returned to any requesting BOOTP clients on the network that broadcast a BOOTP request message. If at least one BOOTP entry has been added to the BOOTP table, the DHCP service replies to BOOTP client requests. If no BOOTP entries are configured, the DHCP service ignores BOOTP request messages.

The reply message returned by the DHCP service indicates the name and location of another server on the network (a TFTP server) that the client can then contact to retrieve its boot image file.

DHCP Options Supported for BOOTP Clients

BOOTP clients that do not specify the DHCP option code 55 (the Options Request List parameter) can still retrieve the following options from DHCP servers running Windows NT Server 4.0 or later. Table 4.11 lists the DHCP options available for BOOTP clients.

Table 4.11 DHCP Options for BOOTP Clients

Code	Description
1	Subnet Mask
3	Router
4	Time Server
5	Name Server
9	LPR Server
12	Computer Name
15	Domain Name
17	Root Path
42	NTP Servers
44	WINS Server
45	NetBIOS over TCP/IP Datagram Distribution Server
46	NetBIOS over TCP/IP Node Type
47	NetBIOS over TCP/IP Scope
48	X Window System Font Server
49	X Window System Display Manager
69	SMTP Server
70	POP3 Server

In order to obtain other options, the client must specify option 55 in the BOOTP request. Windows 2000 DHCP servers return the options in the order listed above and return as many options as can fit in a single datagram response.

Important When configuring client reservations for use with BOOTP clients, remember that DHCP options can apply equally to DHCP and BOOTP clients. Therefore, it is imperative that you correctly configure your scopes.

Configuring the BOOTP Table

Each record in the BOOTP table contains the three fields that contain information that is returned to the BOOTP client:

- **Boot Image.** Identifies the generic file name (such as "unix") of the requested boot file, based on the BOOTP client's hardware type.
- **File Name.** Identifies the full path of the boot file (such as "/etc/vmunix") returned to the client by the BOOTP server, using TFTP.
- **File Server.** Identifies the name of the TFTP server used to source the boot file.

To add entries in the BOOTP table, use DHCP Manager.

Planning for DHCP

DHCP implementation is so closely linked to the Windows Internet Name Service (WINS) and the Domain Name System (DNS) that network administrators will benefit from combining all three when planning deployment.

If you use DHCP servers for Microsoft network clients, you must use a name resolution service. Windows 2000 networks use the DNS service to support Active Directory (in addition to general name resolution). Networks supporting Windows NT 4.0 and earlier clients must use WINS servers. Networks supporting a combination of Windows 2000 and Windows NT 4.0 clients should implement both WINS and DNS.

Best Practices

Before you install Microsoft DHCP servers on your network, consider these best practices:

Use the 80/20 design rule Using more than one DHCP server on the same subnet provides increased fault tolerance for servicing DHCP clients located on the subnet. With two DHCP servers, if one server goes down, the other server can be made to take its place and continue to lease new addresses or renew existing clients. This also helps balance server usage.

Use superscopes for multiple DHCP server environments On each subnet in a LAN environment, with different scopes on each server, it is recommended that you use superscopes. Using superscopes as a way to share information about all scopes in the subnets on each of the DHCP servers resolves problems, such as a negative acknowledgment being sent to a client erroneously.

When started, each DHCP client sends a limited broadcast of the DHCPDiscover message to its local subnet to try to find a DHCP server. Because DHCP clients use broadcasts during their initial startup, you cannot predict which server will respond to a client's DHCP discover request if more than one DHCP server is active on the same subnet.

For example, if two DHCP servers—Server1 and Server2—are configured with different scope ranges of available addresses, a DHCP client can be leased by either server depending on which server responds first to the client's initial broadcast request to find a server at startup. Later, the DHCP server originally used by the client to obtain its lease may be temporarily unavailable during the client renewal state (by default, the client attempts renewal after 50 percent of its lease has elapsed).

If renewal fails, the client delays any attempt to renew its lease until it enters the Rebinding state (by default, the client enters the Rebinding state after 87.5 percent of its lease has elapsed). In the Rebinding state, the client broadcasts to the subnet to obtain a valid IP configuration for its continued use on the network. At this point, if a different DHCP server (that is, a DHCP server other than the one that first leased the client) responds to the client broadcast first, it sends a DHCPNak (a negative acknowledgment) message in reply. This happens because the client's current address is not known to the other server and recognized as a valid IP address for the subnet. This DHCPNak situation for the client can occur even if the original DHCP server that leased the client is available on the network.

To avoid these problems when using more than one DHCP server on the same subnet, use a new superscope configured similarly at all DHCP servers. The superscope should include all valid scopes for the subnet as member scopes. For configuring member scopes at each server, addresses must only be made available at a single DHCP server on the subnet. For all other DHCP servers on the subnet, use exclusion ranges when configuring the corresponding scope.

When a superscope is created, all DHCP servers are configured with member scopes that exclude addresses they do not service. When a server receives a renewal request, it checks to see if the client's IP address belongs to one of the scopes it is aware of:

- If it belongs to one of these scopes, and the address falls in a range that has been excluded on that server, the server ignores the renewal request.
- If the server cannot find any scopes that include this IP address, the server sends a DHCPNack in response to the request, indicating this address should not be used on that subnet.

- If the server is unavailable, the client times out and waits until the rebinding time (T2) interval occurs, usually when 87.5 percent of the lease time has expired. If the server is still unavailable at that time, the client keeps using its current IP address until the lease expires. The client then begins broadcasting a DHCPDiscover message to obtain a new lease. If the client's original DHCP server (the server from which it obtained its lease) is still unavailable, another DHCP server on the subnet handles the client request, and allocates an IP address and lease to the client.

Deactivate scopes only when removing a scope permanently from service.

Once you activate a scope and place it into service, it should not be deactivated until you are ready to retire the scope and its included range of addresses from use on your network. This is because once a scope is deactivated, the DHCP server no longer accepts those scope addresses as valid addresses. This can be useful when your intention is to permanently retire a scope from use. Otherwise, deactivating a scope can cause undesired DHCPNak messages to be sent to clients leased in the scope.

If your intent is only to effect temporary deactivation of scope addresses, edit or modify exclusion ranges in an active scope so you don't cause undesired DHCPNak problems that appear after a scope is deactivated.

Use conflict detection on DHCP servers only under unusual circumstances.

For Windows 2000, DHCP client computers that obtain an IP address use a gratuitous ARP request to perform client-based conflict detection before completing configuration and use of an offered IP address. If a client running Windows 2000 is configured to use DHCP and detects a conflict, it sends a DHCPDecline message to the DHCP server. Windows 95-based Microsoft TCP/IP clients typically do not perform conflict detection in this way.

If your network includes Windows 95-based DHCP clients, you should only use server-side conflict detection provided by the DHCP service. To enable conflict detection, increase the number of ping attempts that the DHCP service performs for each address before leasing that address to a client.

Note that for each additional conflict detection attempt the DHCP service performs, additional seconds are added to the time needed to negotiate leases for DHCP clients.

Reservations should be created on all DHCP servers that can potentially service the reserved client.

You can use a client reservation to assure that a DHCP client computer always receives lease of the same IP address at its startup. If you have more than one DHCP server reachable by a reserved client, add the reservation on each of your other DHCP servers. This allows other servers to honor the address reservation made for the client.

In this situation, all reachable DHCP servers for the reserved client should be configured as described earlier, using a superscope with similar scope ranges of addresses. Although the client reservation will be acted upon only by the DHCP server where the reserved address is available, you can create the same reservation on other DHCP servers that exclude this address.

For server performance, consider that DHCP is disk-intensive and purchase hardware with optimal disk performance characteristics.

DHCP causes frequent and intensive activity on server hard disks. To provide for the best performance, consider RAID solutions when purchasing hardware for your server computer to improve disk access time.

When evaluating performance of your DHCP servers, you should view DHCP as part of making a full performance evaluation of the server as a whole. By monitoring system hardware performance in the most demanding areas of utilization (that is, CPU, memory, disk input/output) you will obtain the best assessment of when a DHCP server is overloaded or in need of upgrades.

Note that for Windows 2000 Server, the DHCP service includes several new System Monitor counters that can be used to monitor service. For more information, see "Overview of Performance Monitoring" in the Microsoft Windows 2000 Server Resource Kit Server Operations Guide.

Keep audit logging enabled for use in troubleshooting. By default, the DHCP service enables audit logging of service-related events. With Windows 2000 Server, audit logging provides for a long-term service monitoring tool that makes limited and safe use of server disk resources.

Reduce lease times for DHCP clients that use Routing and Remote Access for dial-up networking.

If the Routing and Remote Access service is used on your network to support dial-up clients, you can adjust the lease time on scopes that service these clients to use a lease time reduced from the default for a scope of eight days. For Windows 2000, one recommended way to support remote access clients in your scopes is to add and configure the built-in Microsoft user class provided for identifying remote access clients.

Increase the lease duration of scope leases for large, stable, fixed networks if available address space is plentiful.

For small networks (for example, one physical LAN not using routers), the default lease duration of eight days is a typical period. For larger routed networks, consider increasing the length of scope leases to a longer period of time, such as 7 to 21 days. This can reduce DHCP-related network broadcast traffic, particularly if client computers generally remain in fixed locations and scope addresses are plentiful (at least 20 percent or more of the addresses are still available).

Integrate DHCP with other services, such as WINS and DNS. Either WINS or DNS (or possibly both) are used for registering dynamic name-to-address mappings on your network. To provide name resolution services, you must plan for interoperability of DHCP with these services. Most network administrators implementing DHCP also plan a strategy for implementing DNS and WINS servers.

Use either routers which are capable of relaying BOOTP and DHCP message traffic, or use relay agents and set appropriate timers to prevent undesired forwarding and relay of BOOTP and DHCP message traffic.

If you have multiple physical networks connected through routers, the routers must be capable of relaying BOOTP and DHCP traffic. In routed networks that use subnets to divide network segments, planning options for DHCP services must observe some specific requirements for a full implementation of DHCP services to function. These requirements include the following:

- One DHCP server must be located on at least one subnet in the routed network.
- For a DHCP server to support clients on other remote subnets separated by routers, a router or remote computer must be used as a DHCP and BOOTP relay agent to support forwarding of DHCP traffic between subnets.

If you do not have such routers, you can set up the DHCP Relay Agent component on at least one computer running Windows 2000 Server (or Windows NT Server) in each routed subnet. The relay agent relays DHCP- and BOOTP-type message traffic between the DHCP-enabled clients on a local physical network and a remote DHCP server located on another physical network. When using relay agents, be sure to set and increase the initial time that relay agents wait before relaying DHCP messages to servers. For more information, see the section titled "Relay Agent Deployment" later in this chapter.

For DNS with dynamic updates performed by the DHCP server, use the default client preference settings.

For Windows 2000 Server, the DHCP service performs dynamic updates for DHCP clients based on how clients request updates be done. This setting provides the best use of the DHCP service to perform dynamic updates on behalf of its clients as follows:

- Client computers running Windows 2000 explicitly request that the DHCP service only update pointer (PTR) resource records used in DNS for the reverse lookup and resolution of the client's IP address to its name. These clients update their address (A) resource records for themselves.
- Clients running earlier Windows versions cannot make an explicit request for dynamic update preference. For these clients, the DHCP service can be configured to update both the PTR and the A resource records for the client.

Follow the recommended process for moving a DHCP service database from old server computer hardware to new hardware.

For information on moving DHCP service data to another server computer, such as in the case of hardware failure or disaster recovery, see the Microsoft Knowledge Base.

DHCP Service Installation

Before you install a DHCP server, identify the following:

- The hardware and storage requirements for the DHCP server.
- Which computers you can immediately configure as DHCP clients for dynamic TCP/IP configuration and which computers you should manually configure with static TCP/IP configuration parameters.
- The DHCP option types and the option values that will be predefined for the DHCP clients.

DHCP Server Location Use the physical characteristics of your LAN or WAN infrastructure and not the logical groupings defined by Windows 2000 domains and your Active Directory structure. When subnets are connected by routers that support BOOTP relay agents, DHCP servers are not required on every subnet.

Also, DHCP servers can be administered remotely from a computer running Windows 2000 and DHCP Manager.

Resources Compile a list of requirements, including:

- The number and types of computers that need to be supported.
- Interoperability with existing systems, including your requirements for mission-critical accounting, personnel, and similar information systems.
- Hardware support and related software compatibility, including routers, switches, and other types of servers.
- Network monitoring software, such as Net Monitor (provided with Windows 2000).

Process Isolation Isolate the areas of the network where processes must continue uninterrupted, and then target these areas for the last stages of implementation.

Logical Subnet Planning Review the geographic and physical structure of the network to determine the best plan for defining logical subnets as segments of the intranet.

Test Phases Define the components in the new system that require testing, and then develop a phased plan for testing and adding components. For example, the plan could define the order of types of computers to be phased in, including Windows 2000 servers and workstations, Microsoft remote access servers and clients, Windows for Workgroups computers, and MS-DOS clients.

- Create a pilot and a second test phase, including tuning the DHCP and WINS server-client configuration for efficiency. This task includes determining strategies for backup servers and for partitioning the address pool at each server for local vs. remote clients.
- Document all architecture and administration issues for network administrators.
- Always run estimates of normal workloads during your testing scenarios, to gain accurate performance information and feedback.

Supporting Additional Subnets For the DHCP service to support additional subnets on your network, you must first determine if the routers used to connect adjoining subnets can support relaying of BOOTP and DHCP messages. If routers cannot be used for DHCP and BOOTP relay, you can set up either of the following for each subnet:

- A computer running either Windows 2000 Server or Windows NT Server 4.0 configured to use the DHCP Relay Agent component. This computer simply forwards messages back and forth between clients on the local subnet and a remote DHCP server, using the IP address of the remote server. The DHCP Relay Agent service is available only on computers running Windows 2000 Server or Windows NT Server 4.0.
- A computer running Windows 2000 Server configured as a DHCP server for the local subnet. This server computer must contain and manage scope and other address-configurable information for the local subnet it serves.

DHCP Traffic DHCP traffic does not use significant network bandwidth during normal periods of usage. Typical DHCP traffic does not exceed 1 percent of overall network traffic. However, there are two phases of DHCP client configuration that generate some network traffic load. These phases are IP address lease and IP address renewal.

When a client initializes TCP/IP for the first time (and is configured as a DHCP client), its first step is to acquire an IP address using DHCP. This process, as described earlier, results in a conversation between the DHCP client and server consisting of four packets, the first of which is the client computer broadcasting a DHCPDiscover packet in an attempt to locate a DHCP server.

As shown in the initial lease process earlier in this chapter, the entire process of acquiring an IP address lease through DHCP takes a total of four packets, each varying between 342 and 590 bytes in size. This process, on a clean network (when no other network traffic is using bandwidth), takes less than 1 second (about 300 milliseconds) on 10BaseT media. Results depend on media type in use.

DHCP conversations generally occur in the following instances:

- When a DHCP client initializes for the first time (all four frames are sent).
- When an automatic renewal occurs, which is done every one-half lease life (four days by default, or every 96 hours). This communication takes two packets (DHCPRequest and DHCPAck) and lasts approximately 200 milliseconds.
- When a client is moved to a new subnet (DHCPRequest, DHCPNak, then the four frames).
- When a DHCP client replaces its network adapter (all four frames are sent).
- Whenever a client manually refreshes or releases its address by using the Ipconfig utility.

If you want to reduce the amount of traffic generated by DHCP, it is possible to adjust the lease duration for IP address leases. This is done by using DHCP Manager, and adjusting **Lease Duration**.

Upgrading the DHCP Database for Windows 2000

When upgrading a Windows NT Server version 3.51 (or earlier) release for Windows 2000, the DHCP database must be converted to the new database format. The Windows 2000 database uses an improved database engine that is faster and compacts automatically to prevent fragmentation and consequent growth of the database. The database conversion procedure happens automatically as part of an upgrade installation.

When the DHCP service first starts after an upgrade to Windows 2000, it detects that the database needs to be converted. It then starts a conversion process by running a program called Jetconv.exe. The DHCP service stops and the conversion begins. Jetconv.exe finds and converts the databases for all of the installed services (DHCP and, if installed, WINS) to the new Windows 2000 database format.

After the DHCP database is converted successfully, the DHCP service is automatically restarted.

Note Prior to upgrading to Windows 2000, bring any Windows NT 3.51 or 4.0 databases for the DHCP server up to a consistent state. Do this by terminating the services, either by using the **Service** utility in Control Panel or by using the **net stop service** command. This is recommended because it prevents the Jetconv.exe conversion from failing due to an inconsistent Windows NT 3.51 or 4.0 database.

The conversion requires approximately the same amount of free disk space as the size of the original database and log files. You should have at least 5 MB free for the log files for each database.

The conversion process preserves the original database and log files in a subdirectory named 351db (if from Windows NT 3.51) or 40db (if from Windows NT 4.0) under the same directory where the original database and log files were located. On a DHCP server, this is the *%SystemRoot%*\System32\Dhcp*version*db directory. The administrator can later remove these files to reclaim the disk space.

The database conversion can take anywhere from a minute to an hour depending on the size of the database. The user must not restart the services while the databases are being converted. To check the status of the conversion, use Event Viewer to watch the application event log of the Jetconv.exe process.

In case this automatic procedure of converting databases fails for some reason (as can be determined from the event logs), the database that could not be converted can be converted manually using *%SystemRoot%*\System32*upgversiondb*.exe.

The new database engine uses log files named by using the prefix J50.

Warning You cannot convert the new database back to the previous database format. The converted database does not work with Windows NT 3.51 or earlier versions of DHCP services.

Configuring DHCP

The primary tool that you use to manage DHCP servers is DHCP Manager—a Microsoft Management Console (MMC) component that is added to the **Administrative Tools** menu when you install the DHCP service.

After you install a DHCP server, you can use DHCP Manager to:

- Define scopes, superscopes, and multicast scopes, including exclusion and reservation ranges.
- Activate scopes or superscopes.
- Monitor scope leasing activity.
- Define custom, default DHCP option types.
- Configure user-defined or vendor-defined option classes.
- Define other DHCP server properties, such as audit logging or BOOTP tables.

DHCP Manager also provides enhanced server performance monitoring, predefined DHCP option types, dynamic update support for clients using earlier versions of DHCP, and detection of unauthorized (rogue) DHCP servers on your network.

You can also define:

Enhanced Monitoring and Statistical Reporting Enhanced monitoring and statistical reporting provide notification when the number of IP addresses available for lease is below a user-defined threshold. For example, an alert can be triggered when 90 percent of IP addresses in a particular scope have been assigned. A second alert can be triggered when the pool of IP addresses is exhausted.

User-Specified and Vendor-Specified Option Classes The DHCP service for Windows 2000 allows user-specified and vendor-specified options to be defined as an alternative to the potentially lengthy process of obtaining IETF approval for a new standard option.

Integration of DHCP with DNS DHCP servers can enable dynamic updates in the DNS namespace for any of its clients that support these updates. This feature allows scope clients to use dynamic updates to update their computer name–to–address mapping information (which is stored in zones on the DNS server) when changes occur to their DHCP-assigned address.

Rogue DHCP Server Detection The DHCP service for Windows 2000 is designed to prevent rogue DHCP servers from creating address assignment conflicts. This solves problems that can occur because of unauthorized DHCP servers assigning improper or unintended IP addresses to clients elsewhere on the network.

Preventing Rogue DHCP Servers

The process of authorizing DHCP servers is useful or needed for DHCP servers running Windows 2000 Server. Where this scheme is used, authorization is neither used nor needed if the following conditions exist:

- If DHCP servers are running earlier versions of Windows NT Server, such as versions 3.51 or 4.0.
- If DHCP servers are running other DHCP server software.

For the directory authorization process to work properly, it is assumed and necessary that the first DHCP server introduced onto your network participate in the Active Directory service. This requires that the server be installed as either a domain controller or a member server. When you are either planning for or actively deploying Active Directory services, it is important that you do not elect to install your first DHCP server computer as a stand-alone server.

Most commonly, there will be only one enterprise root and therefore only a single point for directory authorization of the DHCP servers. However, there is no restriction on authorizing DHCP servers for more than one enterprise root.

When configured correctly and authorized for use on a network, DHCP servers provide a useful and intended administrative service. However, when a misconfigured or unauthorized DHCP server is introduced into a network, it can cause problems. For example, if a rogue DHCP server starts, it can begin leasing incorrect IP addresses to clients or negatively acknowledging DHCP clients attempting to renew their current address lease.

Either of these misconfiguration problems can produce further problems for DHCP-enabled clients. For example, clients that obtain a configuration lease from the unauthorized server can then fail to locate valid domain controllers, preventing clients from successfully logging on to the network.

Windows 2000 Server provides some integrated security support for networks that use Active Directory. This avoids most of the accidental damage caused by running DHCP servers with wrong configurations or on the wrong networks.

This support uses an additional object type (the DhcpServer object) to the base directory schema. This provides for the following enhancements:

- A list of IP addresses available for the computers that you authorize to operate as DHCP servers on your network.

- Detection of rogue DHCP servers and prevention of their starting or running on your network.

Note For the directory authorization process to work properly, it is necessary that the first Windows 2000 DHCP server introduced onto your network participate in the Active Directory service. This requires that the server be installed in a domain (as either a domain controller or a member server), and not in a workgroup. When you are either planning for or actively deploying Active Directory services, do not elect to install your first DHCP server as a workgroup server. You must have enterprise administrator rights to authorize a DHCP server in the Active Directory.

How DHCP Servers Are Authorized

The authorization process for DHCP server computers in Active Directory depends on the role of the server on your network. For Windows 2000 Server (as in earlier versions) there are three roles or server types for which each server computer can be installed:

- **Domain controller.** The computer keeps and maintains a copy of the Active Directory service database and provides secure account management for domain member users and computers.
- **Member server.** The computer is not operating as a domain controller but has joined a domain in which it has a membership account in the Active Directory database.
- **Stand-alone Server.** The computer is not operating as a domain controller or a members server in a domain. Instead, the server computer is made known to the network through a specified workgroup name, which can be shared by other computers, but is used only for browsing purposes and not to provide secured logon access to shared domain resources.

If you deploy Active Directory, all computers operating as DHCP servers must be either domain controllers or domain member servers before they can be authorized in the directory service or start providing DHCP service to clients. When a DHCP server is authorized, the server computer is added to the list of authorized DHCP servers maintained in the directory service database.

How Unauthorized Servers Are Detected

The DHCP implementation under Windows 2000 Server provides detection of both authorized and unauthorized DHCP servers in two ways:

- The use of information messaging between DHCP servers using the DHCPInform message.
- The addition of several new vendor-specific option types, used for communicating information about the directory service enterprise root.

The Windows 2000 DHCP service uses the following process to detect other DHCP servers currently running on the reachable network and determine if they are authorized to provide service.

When the DHCP service starts, it sends a DHCPInform request message to the reachable network, using the local limited broadcast address (255.255.255.255), to locate the directory service enterprise root on which other DHCP servers are installed and configured.

This message includes several vendor-specific option types that are known and supported by other DHCP servers running Windows 2000 Server. When received by other DHCP servers, these option types provide for the query and retrieval of information about the directory service enterprise root.

When queried, other DHCP servers reply with DHCPAck messages to acknowledge and answer with directory service enterprise root information. In this way, the initializing DHCP server collects and compiles a list of all currently active DHCP servers on the reachable network, along with the root of the directory service enterprise used by each server.

Typically, only one single enterprise root is detected: the same one for all DHCP servers that are reachable and that respond to acknowledge the initializing server. However, if additional enterprise roots are detected, each root is queried in turn to see if the computer is authorized for DHCP service for those other enterprises discovered during this phase.

After a list is built of all DHCP servers running on the network, the next step in the detection process depends on whether a directory service is available from the local computer.

If the directory service is not available (such as where the initializing DHCP server is installed in a confined network environment used for testing), the initializing server can start if no other DHCP servers are discovered on the network that are part of any enterprise. When this condition is met, the server successfully initializes and begins serving DHCP clients.

However, the server continues every 5 minutes to collect information about other DHCP servers running on the network, using DHCPInform as it did at startup. Each time, it checks to see whether the directory service is available. If a directory service is found, the server makes sure it is authorized by following the procedure, depending on whether the server is a member server or a stand-alone server.

- For member servers (a server joined to some domain that is part of the enterprise), the DHCP server queries the directory service for the DHCP server list of addresses that are authorized.
- If the server finds its IP address in the authorized list, it initializes and starts providing DHCP service to clients. If it does not find itself in the authorized list, it does not initialize, and stops providing DHCP services.
- For stand-alone servers (a server not joined to any domain or part of an existing enterprise), the DHCP server queries the directory service with the root of the enterprise returned by each of the other DHCP servers to see if it can find itself on the authorized list with any of the reported enterprises.

  The server initializes and starts providing DHCP services to clients only if the server finds its IP address in the authorized list for each of the enterprise roots reported by other DHCP servers. If it does not find itself in the authorized list for each of the reported enterprise roots, it does not initialize, and the DHCP service is stopped.

Clustering DHCP Servers

Windows Clustering allows two servers to be managed as a single system. The Windows 2000 (Advanced Server only) clustering service can be used for DHCP servers to provide higher availability, easier manageability, and greater scalability.

Windows Clustering can automatically detect the failure of an application or server and quickly restart it on a surviving server, with users only experiencing a momentary pause in service. With Windows Clustering, administrators can quickly inspect the status of all cluster resources and easily move workloads around onto different servers within the cluster. This is useful for manual load balancing and for performing rolling updates on the servers without taking important data and applications offline.

Windows Clustering allows DHCP servers to be virtualized so that if one of the clustered nodes crashes, the namespace and all the services are transparently reconstituted to the second node. This means no changes are visible to the client, which sees the same IP address for the clustered DHCP servers.

Without clustering, network administrators might split scopes between servers, so if one server goes down, at least half of the available addresses remain available. Clustering uses IP addresses efficiently by removing the need to split scopes. A database stored on a remote disk tracks address assignment and other activity so that if the active cluster node goes down, the second node becomes the DHCP server, with complete knowledge of what has been assigned and access to the complete scope of addresses. Only one node at a time runs as a DHCP server, with the Windows 2000 clustering database providing transparent transition when needed.

Example of Clustered DHCP Servers

Figure 4.15 is a generic example of clustered DHCP servers. DHCP Server 1 is the active DHCP server, and DHCP Server 2 is the backup DHCP server.

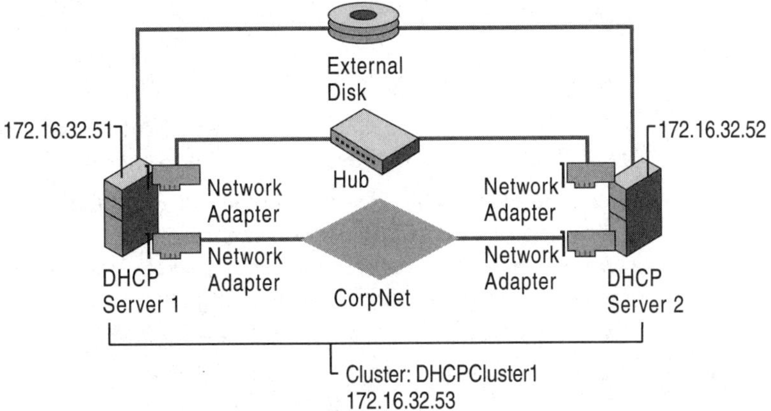

Figure 4.15 Clustered DHCP Servers

In Figure 4.15:

- DHCP Server 1 and DHCP Server 2 have Windows 2000 DHCP and Windows Clustering services installed.
- Each DHCP server has a unique server name and IP address.
- Each DHCP server has two network interfaces—one for the cluster identity and the connection to the enterprise network and the second for server-to-server communication. This is a private link only for cluster communication. The wire runs directly between the two servers.
- Both DHCP servers are configured with identical scopes. However, on Server 2, the scopes are not activated because Server 2 is not currently functioning as the active DHCP server. DHCP Server 2 can function as a hot spare, ready in the event of a shutdown of DHCP Server 1.

- To facilitate clustering and the sharing of resources, the DHCP servers are connected to an external disk system that holds the DHCP database and log files. This allows DHCP Server 2 to access the DHCP database files if it needs to take over as the active DHCP server. The clustering service installed on each DHCP server prevents one server from trying to exclusively claim the external disk and prevent sharing of the disk system between the DHCP servers.
- The cluster itself has a unique name and IP address, so that DHCP clients can use the cluster name and IP address to connect to the cluster and request DHCP services. This prevents rejected DHCP client requests if one of the DHCP servers is turned off. For example, if the client was configured with a specific DHCP server name and IP address instead of the cluster address, the client would not receive DHCP services. However, by configuring the DHCP clients with the cluster name and IP address, the client is able to communicate with the active DHCP server in the cluster.

Before implementing a similar scenario, consider the following recommendations:

- On each DHCP server in the cluster (whether backup or primary), install the DHCP service before you install the clustering service.
- Keep the second DHCP server turned off until the first server has the clustering service installed and is configured with a new cluster name and address. When the second server is turned on (and configured with DHCP and clustering services), it joins the existing cluster.
- The cluster name and IP address must be statically configured—they cannot be configured dynamically by another DHCP server.
- If a DHCP cluster is using an external disk system to store the DHCP database files, the DatabasePath and BackupDatabasePath registry entries must be configured on both DHCP servers in the cluster. The registry entries are located in

  HKLM\SYSTEM\CurrentControlSet\Services\DhcpServer\Parameters

  These registry entries must specify the path to the external disk system.
- Permissions: Any backup DHCP servers in the cluster will not be able to successfully take over DHCP tasks if the appropriate security permissions have not been enabled. Administrators must create a new domain security group to which the servers belong. This group must have permissions of Full Control for the DNS zone object in Active Directory where DHCP clients have their A and PTR records registered and updated. Alternatively, administrators can add the second server to the DNSUpdateProxyGroup for the domain. Otherwise, name resolution failures will result.

- Use the 80/20 rule when implementing clustered DHCP servers to provide additionally enhanced "failover" (hot-spare) services. The combination of clustering DHCP servers and using the 80/20 rule to manage scopes between the clustered server enables an enhanced failover solution. See the sections "80/20 Rule" and "Best Practices" for details in specifying scopes using the 80/20 rule.

For more information, see "Windows Clustering" in the *Microsoft® Windows® 2000 Distributed Systems Guide*.

DHCP Scenarios

The following sections discuss common DHCP deployment scenarios and issues.

DHCP in Small Networks

A single DHCP server can be used on a small LAN that does not include routers and subnetting. An example layout of a small network is shown in Figure 4.16.

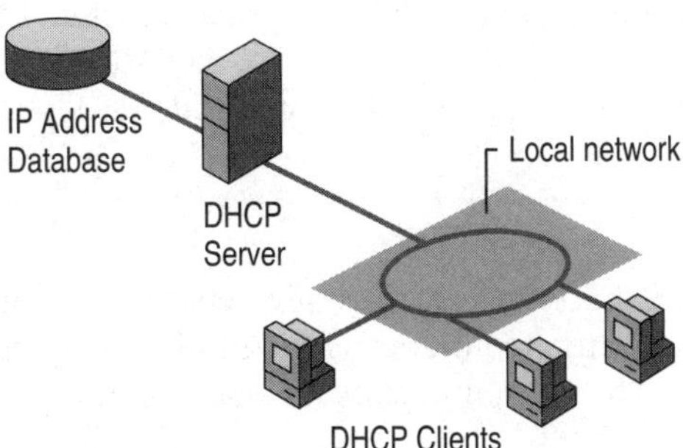

Figure 4.16 A Single Local Network Using Automatic TCP/IP Configuration with DHCP

Before installing a DHCP server computer on a small network, you need to identify:

- The hardware and storage requirements for the DHCP server.
- Which computers can be configured as DHCP clients for dynamic TCP/IP configuration and which computers should be manually configured with static TCP/IP configuration parameters, including static IP addresses.
- The predefined DHCP option types and their values.

DHCP in Large Networks

For an enterprise network, you should:

- Plan the physical subnets of the network and relative placement of DHCP servers. This includes planning for placement of DHCP (and WINS) servers among subnets in a way that reduces b-node broadcasts across routers.
- Specify the DHCP option types and their values to be predefined per scope for the DHCP clients. This can include planning for scopes based on the needs of particular groups of users. For example, for a unit that frequently moves computers to different locations, shorter lease durations can be defined for the related scopes. This approach collects IP addresses that are changed frequently and disposed of, and returns them to the pool of available addresses that can be used for new lease offerings.
- Recognize the impact that slower links have on your WAN environment. Place DHCP, WINS, and DNS servers to maximize response time and minimize low-speed traffic.

As one example of planning for a large enterprise network, the segmenting of the WAN into logical subnets can match the physical structure of the internetwork. Then one IP subnet can serve as the backbone, and off this backbone each physical subnet maintains a separate IP subnet address.

DHCP in Routed Networks

In routed networks that use subnets to divide network segments, administrators must observe some specific requirements for a full implementation of DHCP services to function. These requirements include one of the following:

- One DHCP server must be located on at least one subnet in the routed network.
- For a DHCP server to support clients on other remote subnets separated by routers, a router or remote computer must be used as a DHCP/BOOTP relay agent to support forwarding of DHCP traffic between subnets.

Figure 4.17 illustrates an example of a routed network with a DHCP server and DHCP clients.

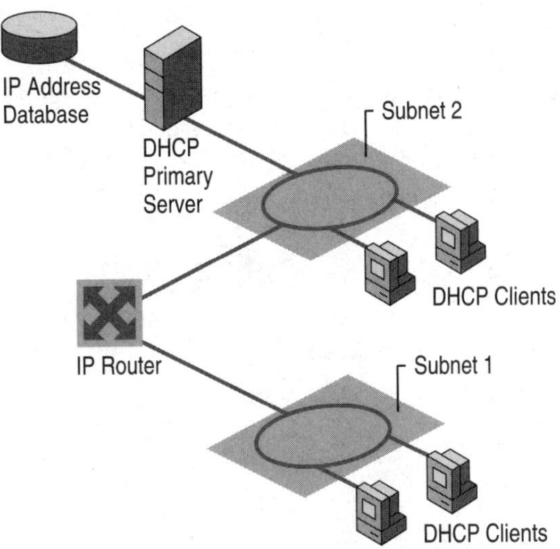

Figure 4.17 An Internetwork Using Automatic TCP/IP Configuration with DHCP

As explained earlier, routers that implement the DHCP/BOOTP relay agent can be used to route traffic between DHCP servers and clients located on different subnets. The relay agent on the router forwards requests from local DHCP clients to the remote DHCP server and subsequently relays the DHCP server responses back to the DHCP clients.

Relay Agent Deployment

When you have multiple DHCP servers, Microsoft recommends that you place your DHCP servers on different subnets to achieve a degree of fault tolerance, rather than having all the DHCP servers in one subnet. The servers should not have common IP addresses in their scopes (each server should have a unique pool of addresses).

If the DHCP server in the local subnet shuts down, requests are relayed to a remote subnet. The DHCP server at that location can respond to DHCP requests if it maintains a scope of IP addresses for the requesting subnet. If the remote server has no scope defined for the requesting subnet, it cannot provide IP addresses even if it has available addresses for other scopes. If each DHCP server has a pool of addresses for each subnet, it can provide IP addresses for remote clients whose own DHCP server is offline.

There are several relay agent configuration options available if you plan to incorporate a relay agent into your DHCP/BOOTP-enabled network. These include using third-party routers, Windows 2000 Routing and Remote Access, and the DHCP Relay Agent component provided in Windows NT Server 4.0. For more information about how relay agents work, see the section "Managing Relay Agents" later in this chapter.

Recommended General Configuration

Figure 4.18 shows a recommended relay agent implementation, which provides for the best network performance.

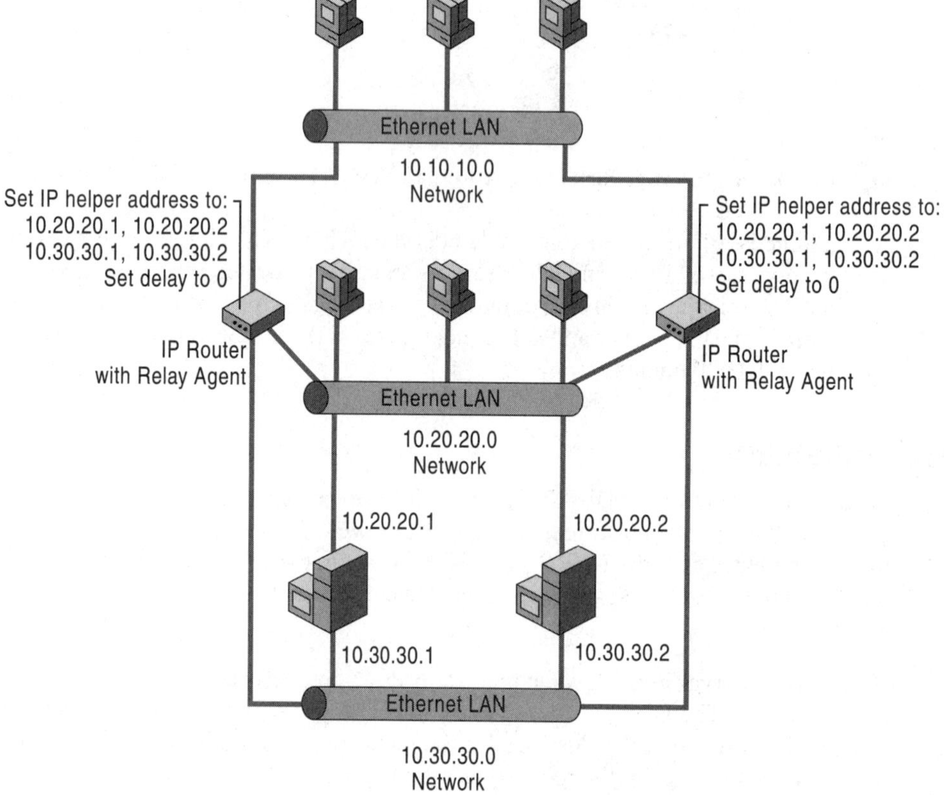

Figure 4.18 Windows 2000 Recommended Relay Agent Configuration

This figure illustrates a general configuration for relay agents. For specific scenarios, see the following sections and illustrations.

Windows 2000 Server Routing and Remote Access Relay Agents

Figure 4.19 shows the Windows 2000 Server Routing and Remote Access configuration. In this example, the Windows 2000 server is acting as an IP router between Subnet 1 and 2, as well as a relay agent between the DHCP server on Subnet 1 and the DHCP clients on Subnet 2.

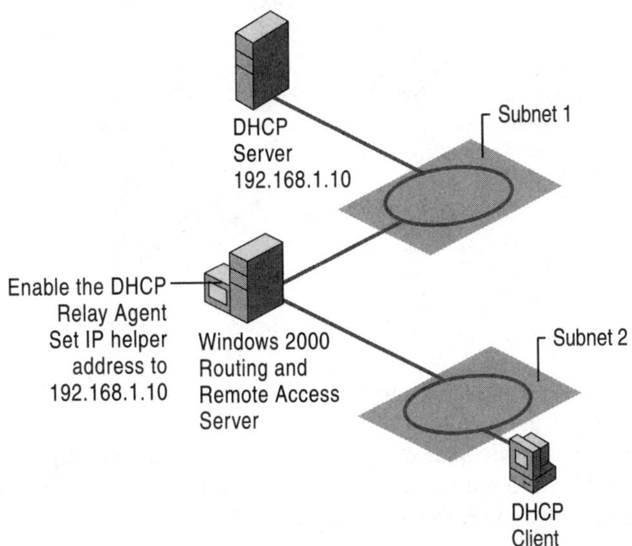

Figure 4.19 Windows 2000 Remote Access Server as a Relay Agent

The DHCP Relay Agent on the Windows 2000 server must be configured with the IP address of the DHCP server to relay DHCP requests between Subnet 1 and Subnet 2.

Windows NT Server 4.0 Relay Agents

Figure 4.20 shows a standard router configuration.

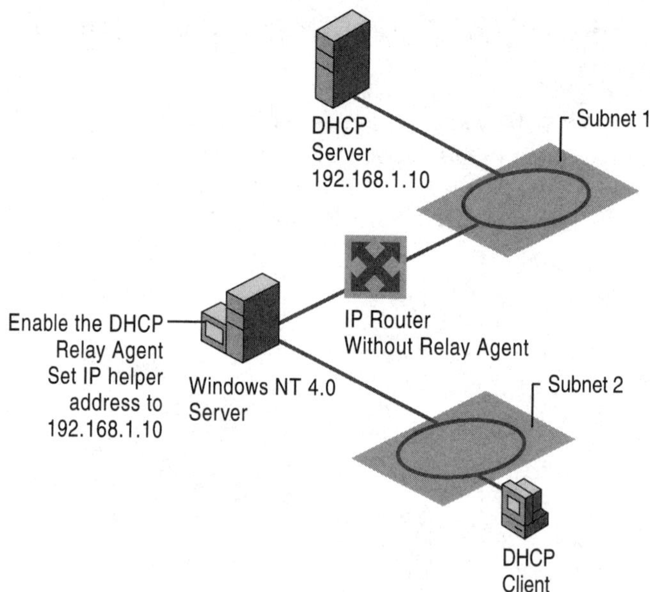

Figure 4.20 Standard Router as a Relay Agent

This example shows how a standard IP router can be implemented on a network, in combination with a Windows NT Server 4.0 relay agent relaying DHCP requests between Subnet 1 and Subnet 2.

DHCP and Routing and Remote Access

When the Routing and Remote Access service is configured to use DHCP to obtain IP addresses, the Routing and Remote Access service instructs the DHCP client component to obtain 10 IP addresses from a DHCP server. The Routing and Remote Access service uses the first IP address obtained from DHCP for the RAS server interface, and subsequent addresses are allocated to TCP/IP-based remote access clients as they connect. IP addresses freed due to remote access clients disconnecting are reused.

When all 10 IP addresses are used, the Routing and Remote Access service uses the DHCP client component to obtain 10 more. You can modify the number of IP addresses obtained at a time by changing the value of the **InitialAddressPoolSize** registry entry:

HKEY_LOCAL_MACHINE\System\CurrentControlSet\Services\RemoteAccess \Parameters\Ip

With the Windows NT 4.0 remote access server, the DHCP allocated addresses are recorded and reused when the remote access service is restarted. The Windows 2000 Routing and Remote Access service now releases all DHCP allocated IP addresses using DHCPRELEASE messages each time the service is stopped.

If the Routing and Remote Access service initially starts using DHCP-allocated addresses and the DHCP server becomes unavailable, then an IP address cannot be allocated to additional TCP/IP-based remote access clients.

If a DHCP server is not available when the Routing and Remote Access service is started, then the DHCP client returns 10 addresses in the range 169.254.0.1 to 169.254.255.254 to allocate to remote access clients. The address range 169.254.0.0/16 is used for Automatic Private IP Addressing (APIPA). APIPA addresses for point-to-LAN remote access connectivity work only if the network to which the Routing and Remote Access service computer is attached is also using APIPA addresses. If the local network is not using APIPA addresses, remote access clients are only able to obtain point-to-point remote access connectivity.

If a DHCP server does become available, the next time IP addresses are needed by the Routing and Remote Access service, DHCP-obtained addresses are then allocated to remote access clients that connect after the DHCP addresses were obtained.

The remote access server uses a specific LAN interface to obtain DHCP-allocated IP addresses for remote access clients. You can select which LAN interface to use from the **IP** tab on the properties of a server in the **Routing and Remote Access** snap-in.

DHCP and WINS

WINS is a naming service used to register and resolve name-to-address mappings for NetBIOS clients on TCP/IP-based networks.

Because NetBIOS naming is a required feature for networking that is supported in all previous versions of Windows, install and use WINS if you are operating the Windows 2000 DHCP service in a network environment that includes DHCP clients running under any of the following earlier Microsoft operating systems:

- Windows for Workgroups 3.11
- Windows 95
- Windows NT Advanced Server 3.1
- Windows NT 3.5*x*

- Windows NT 4.0
- MS-DOS client for Microsoft Networks

In many cases, it is not necessary to add WINS servers beyond the number of servers that are planned for DHCP server usage. In many cases, the same server computer can work effectively as both the WINS and DHCP server for a single internet on your network.

Where a single server is configured as both a WINS server and a DHCP server, it can:

- Administer a defined scope or superscope range of IP addresses for your network.
- Serve as the default gateway to provide IP forwarding between adjoining physical networks.

  To set the same default gateway for all DHCP clients located across subnets, assign DHCP option code 3 by using the server computer's IP address as the value in configuring the DHCP scope options.
- Serve as the primary WINS server for adjoining physical networks.

  To set the WINS server for all DHCP clients located across subnets, assign DHCP option code 44 (a list of IP addresses for WINS servers) and use the server computer's IP address as the value.

  To ensure that WINS is used first by all DHCP clients for NetBIOS name resolution (before broadcast name resolution is tried), assign option code 46 (WINS/NBT node type) to identify the WINS node type as h-node (hybrid node).

Adding Fault Tolerance to DHCP/WINS Service

To create a more fault-tolerant installation for DHCP and WINS, you can set up two server computers running Windows 2000 Server to act as backup service providers for each other. Table 4.12 shows the functions of each server (Server1 and Server2) when configured in this way.

Table 4.12 DHCP/WINS servers

Computer Name	WINS Server Status	DHCP Server Status
Server1	Primary WINS	Secondary DHCP
Server2	Secondary WINS	Primary DHCP

If you want to create a primary and backup relationship between DHCP servers, you can partition the address pool so that each server provides addresses to remote clients. One recommended practice is to allocate approximately 75 percent of the available IP address pool for your network to the primary DHCP server and the remaining 25 percent of your address pool to the backup DHCP server.

When defining a shared scope between two DHCP servers, you must ensure that the scope is configured to be disjointed (with no overlap) for each server, to avoid duplicating IP addresses in lease offerings for both servers.

Additional Recommendations

When using DHCP and WINS together on your network, consider the following options for interoperation:

Use additional DHCP scope options. Use DHCP options to assign WINS node types (option type 46) and to identify WINS servers for use by DHCP clients (option type 44). In some cases, this can involve adjusting these option types for each physical subnet where DHCP and WINS are implemented.

Assign a length of time for DHCP lease durations comparable to the time WINS uses for renew intervals.

By default, DHCP leases are eight days in length and the WINS renew interval is six days. If lease lengths for DHCP differ widely from WINS renew intervals, the effect on your network can be an increase in lease-management traffic and might cause a WINS registration for both services. If you shorten or lengthen the DHCP lease time for clients, modify the WINS renew interval accordingly.

Configure all installed connections as routable interfaces. Windows 2000 does not guarantee the binding order for NetBIOS when more than one connection is present and active. All multihomed WINS servers should have their primary IP addresses assigned to each network connection. When configuring a replication partner with the multihomed server as a push or pull partner, you can ensure that the partner always connects to the same adapter on the multihomed server by configuring the partner to refer to the multihomed server using the specific IP address to which you want the partner to connect. If the partner is configured to refer to the name of the multihomed server instead of a specific IP address, when the replication partner resolves the name to an IP address, it may end up sending WINS packets to the multihomed server using any of its IP addresses.

DHCP and DNS

Domain Name System (DNS) servers provide name resolution for network clients. DNS maintains (among other things) information that links a computer's fully qualified domain name (FQDN) to its assigned IP address(es).

While DHCP provides a powerful mechanism for automatically configuring client IP addresses, until recently DHCP did not notify the DNS service to update the DNS records on the client; specifically, updating the client name to an IP address, and IP address to name mappings maintained by a DNS server.

Without a way for DHCP to interact with DNS, the information maintained by DNS for a DHCP client may be incorrect. For example, a client may acquire its IP address from a DHCP server, but the DNS records would not reflect the IP address acquired nor provide a mapping from the new IP address to the computer name (FQDN).

In Windows 2000, DHCP servers and clients can register with DNS to provide this update service if the DNS server supports DNS with dynamic updates. The Windows 2000 DNS service supports dynamic updates. For more information, see the chapter "Windows 2000 DNS" in this book

A Windows 2000 DHCP server can register with a DNS server and update pointer (PTR) and address (A) resource records on behalf of its DHCP-enabled clients using the DNS dynamic update protocol.

The ability to register both A and PTR type records lets a DHCP server act as a proxy for clients using Microsoft Windows 95 and Windows NT 4.0 for the purpose of DNS registration. DHCP servers can differentiate between Windows 2000 and other clients. An additional DHCP option code (option code 81) enables the return of a client's FQDN to the DHCP server. If implemented, the DHCP server can dynamically update DNS to modify an individual computer's resource records with a DNS server using the dynamic update protocol. This DHCP option permits the DHCP server the following possible interactions for processing DNS information on behalf of DHCP clients that include Option Code 81 in the DHCPRequest message they send to the server:

- The DHCP server always registers the DHCP client for both the forward (A-type records) and reverse lookups (PTR-type records) with DNS.
- The DHCP server never registers the name-to-address (A-type records) mapping information for DHCP clients.
- The DHCP server registers the DHCP client for both forward (A-type records) and reverse lookups (PTR-type records) only when requested to by the client

DHCP and static DNS service are not compatible for keeping name-to-address mapping information synchronized. This might cause problems with using DHCP and DNS together on a network if you are using older, static DNS servers, which are incapable of interacting dynamically when DHCP client configurations change.

To avoid failed DNS lookups for DHCP-registered clients when static DNS service is in effect, do the following steps:

1. If WINS servers are used on the network, enable WINS lookup for DHCP clients that use NetBIOS.
2. Assign IP address reservations with an infinite lease duration for DHCP clients that use DNS only and do not support NetBIOS.

Wherever possible, upgrade or replace older, static-based DNS servers with DNS servers supporting updates. Dynamic updates are supported by the Microsoft DNS service, included in Windows 2000.

Additional Recommendations

When using DNS and WINS together, consider the following options for interoperation:

- If a large percentage of clients use NetBIOS and you are using DNS, consider using WINS lookup on your DNS servers. If WINS lookup is enabled on the Microsoft DNS service, WINS is used for final resolution of any names that are not found using DNS resolution. The WINS forward lookup and WINS-R reverse lookup records are supported only by DNS. If you use servers on your network that do not support DNS, use DNS Manager to ensure that these WINS records are not propagated to DNS servers that do not support WINS lookup.
- If you have a large percentage of computers running Windows 2000 on your network, consider creating a pure DNS environment. This involves developing a migration plan to upgrade older WINS clients to Windows 2000. Support issues involving network name service are simplified by using a single naming and resource locator service (such as WINS and DNS) on your network. For more information, see “Windows Internet Name Service” and “Windows 2000 DNS” in this book.

Windows-Based DHCP Clients and DNS with Dynamic Updates

Windows 2000 DHCP clients and earlier versions of Windows DHCP client interact with DNS in different ways. The DHCP server can be configured to always register the DHCP client for both the forward (A-type records) and reverse (PTR-type records) lookups with DNS. Windows 2000 DHCP clients update their own dynamic forward lookup names.

Figure 4.21 shows how Windows 2000 DHCP clients interact with dynamic updates:

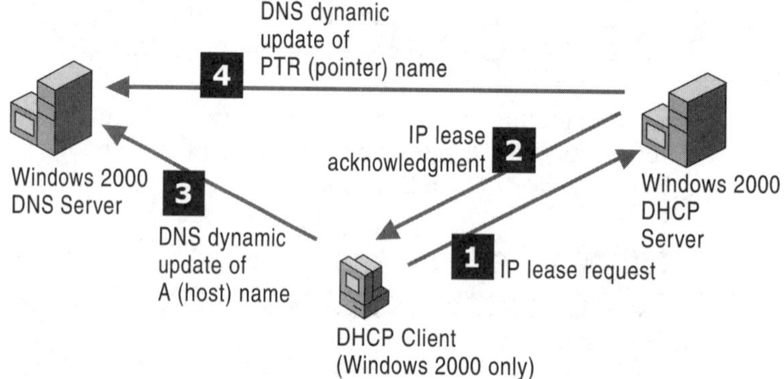

Figure 4.21 Windows 2000 DHCP Clients and Dynamic Updates

1. The Windows 2000 DHCP client makes an IP lease request.
2. The DHCP server grants an IP lease.
3. The Windows 2000 DHCP client updates its forward (A) name with the DNS server.
4. The DHCP server updates the DNS reverse (PTR) name for the client using the dynamic update protocol.

Earlier versions of Windows DHCP clients do not interact directly with DNS server that perform dynamic updates. Figure 4.22shows how the forward and reverse lookup names are updated by a DHCP server:

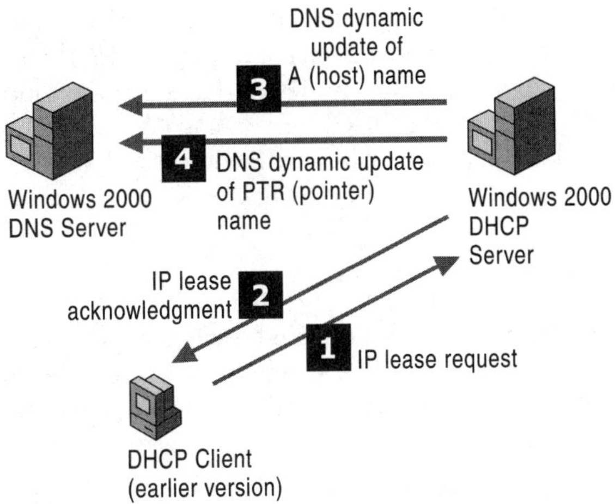

Figure 4.22 Older DHCP Clients and Dynamic Updates

1. The DHCP client makes an IP lease request.
2. The DHCP server grants an IP lease.
3. The DHCP server automatically generates the client's FQDN by appending the domain name defined for the scope to the client name obtained from the DHCPRequest message sent by the older client.
4. Using the dynamic update protocol, the DHCP server updates the DNS forward (A) name for the client.
5. Using the dynamic update protocol, the DHCP server updates the DNS reverse (PTR) name for the client.

DHCP and Automatic Private IP Addressing

Windows 2000 and Windows 98 provide Automatic Private IP Addressing (APIPA), a service for assigning unique IP addresses on small office/home office (SOHO) networks without deploying the DHCP service. Intended for use with small networks with fewer than 25 clients, APIPA enables Plug and Play networking by assigning unique IP addresses to computers on private local area networks.

APIPA uses a reserved range of IP addresses (169.254.*x.x*) and an algorithm to guarantee that each address used is unique to a single computer on the private network.

APIPA works seamlessly with the DHCP service. APIPA yields to the DHCP service when DHCP is deployed on a network. A DHCP server can be added to the network without requiring any APIPA-based configuration. APIPA regularly checks for the presence of a DHCP server, and upon detecting one replaces the private networking addresses with the IP addresses dynamically assigned by the DHCP server.

Multihomed DHCP Servers

For a server computer to be multihomed, each network connection must attach the computer to more than one physical network. This requires that additional hardware (in the form of multiple installed network adapters) be used on the computer.

A computer running Windows 2000 Server can function as a multihomed DHCP server. The DHCP server binds to the first IP address configured on each network connection (that is, each physical adapter interface) in use on the server. By default, the service binding depends on whether the connection is dynamically or statically configured for TCP/IP. If statically, the connection is enabled in the binding to listen to and provide service to DHCP clients. If dynamically, it is disabled in service bindings and does not provide service to DHCP clients. Dynamic configuration methods include the use of either another DHCP server to obtain a leased IP configuration or self-configuring an address through the use of the APIPA feature provided in Windows 2000. For more information, see "DHCP and Automatic Private IP Addressing" earlier in this chapter.

Server scopes use the primary IP address for each multihomed network connection to communicate with the DHCP clients. To verify the primary IP address for each of the connections used in a multihomed server configuration, you can review the Internet Protocol (TCP/IP) properties for each connection listed in the Network and Dial-up Connections folder on the server.

Configuring a Multihomed DHCP Server

Figure 4.23 is an example of a multihomed DHCP server with three network adapters installed. Each adapter is configured to lease addresses on separate physical subnets.

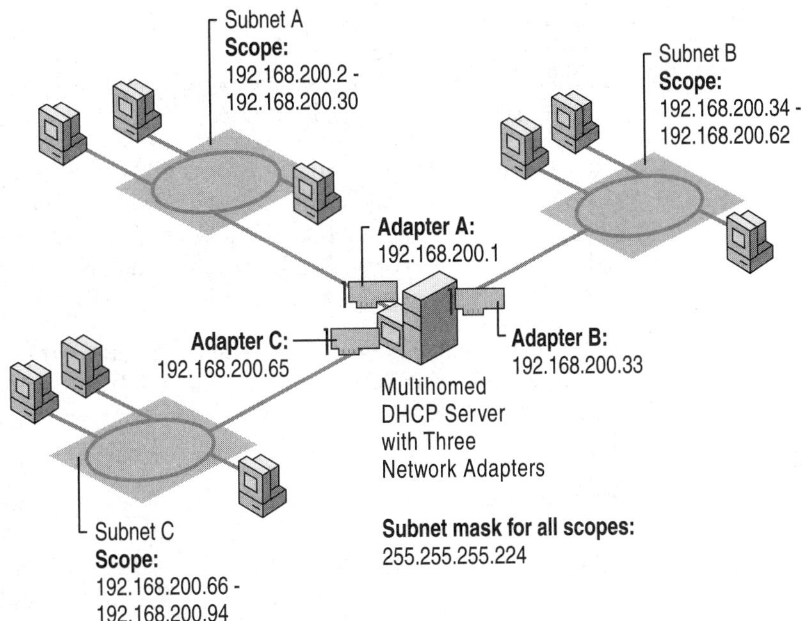

Figure 4.23 Multihomed DHCP Server Configuration

The multihomed DHCP server has three adapters installed and configured statically with a single IP address for each. Because the IP addressing for the DHCP server also uses an adjusted or custom subnet mask value (255.255.255.224), that value is applied for all the IP addresses that are configured at the server and for other computers in use on the same network. Here, a Class C range of IP addresses, 192.168.200.1 to 192.168.200.254, is used.

Each of the three adapters connects the server to three different physical subnets (Subnets A, B and C). To achieve the intended results of having the DHCP server provide leased configuration service to all clients in each of the respective subnets, two configuration details are essential and must be verified during deployment plans:

1. The server must use a statically configured IP address within the same range of valid IP addresses for the physical network on which it is servicing clients.
2. The server must have each of its valid subnet IP addresses excluded from the scope used to offer leases to clients.

For example, if no special subnetting was used in this environment, the selection of DHCP server IP addresses is not as critical because the IP network and IP subnet are the same. When the default subnet mask value (255.255.255.0) for this example network is applied and in use, all 254 possible computer IDs are considered part of one single unified subnet.

If, however, a custom subnet mask of 255.255.255.224 is applied, the network ID and subnet ID are not the same. When the subnet ID is not the same as the network ID, make sure the DHCP server is provided an IP address assignment within the same subnet it is meant to service.

For instance, with the mask set to 255.255.255.224 at all computers, the first 3 bit places of the last notated octet (224) are taken from the full 8 bit places that would normally comprise the full computer ID section. These bits are used by IP for physical subnet identification. This leaves the remaining 8 bit places to be used as the actual or reduced computer ID field.

In this way, the example network shown above requires of the three subnets in use that they have a maximum of eight (or 2^3) potentially different subnet IDs. Likewise, each of these subnets can, in turn, only support up to 32 (or 2^5) potential computer IDs.

Because of the use of subnetting, Subnet A in this example consists of the first 32 address values in the network, from 0 to 31. Because no computer IDs consisting of all 0s or all 1s in the computer ID field can be assigned for use to computers, the useful range of total available IP addresses for each subnet drops from 32 to 30.

Of the remaining 30 addresses, the DHCP server needs to use one. The remaining 29 can be configured in a regular DHCP scope and used for assigning leases to subnet clients. The choice of which address to use for the DHCP server is at the administrator's preference, as well as the decision to either include the DHCP server's statically assigned IP address within the scope defined for use in each subnet.

The multihomed server's IP addresses (192.169.200.1, 192.168.200.33, 192.168.200.65) are configured using the first IP address available for use in each of the three subnets. For the configuration shown, these addresses are excluded from the defined boundaries of each of the scopes created for use with these subnets.

Alternatively, you can set up your scopes to include these addresses within the defined boundaries of the scope. If you do, you need to create address exclusions to exclude these server IP addresses from each of the respective scopes.

If more than a single IP address is statically configured for a network connection, the Windows 2000 DHCP Server service permits only the first configured IP address to be used in the context of enabling or disabling service bindings.

Managing Relay Agents

A relay agent is a small program that relays a certain type of message to other hosts on a network. In TCP/IP networking, routers are used to interconnect hardware and software on different subnets and forward IP packets between the subnets.

To support and use the DHCP service across multiple subnets, routers connecting each subnet should comply with the DHCP/BOOTP relay agent capabilities described in RFC 1542. To comply with RFC 1542 and provide relay agent support, each router must be able to recognize BOOTP and DHCP protocol messages and process (relay) them appropriately. Because routers interpret DHCP messages as BOOTP messages (such as a UDP message sent through the same UDP port number and containing shared message structure), a router with BOOTP–relay agent capability typically relays DHCP packets and any BOOTP packets sent on the network.

In most cases, routers support DHCP/BOOTP relay. If your routers do not, contact your router manufacturer or supplier to find out if a software or firmware upgrade is available to support this feature.

Alternatively, if a router cannot function as a DHCP/BOOTP relay agent, each subnet must have either its own DHCP server or another computer that can function as a relay agent on that subnet.

In cases where it is impractical or impossible to configure routers to support DHCP/BOOTP relay, you can configure a computer running Windows 2000 or Windows NT Server 4.0 to act as a relay agent by installing the DHCP Relay Agent service. A DHCP relay agent is a hardware device or software program that can pass DHCP/BOOTP broadcast messages from one subnet to another subnet according to the RFC 2131 specification for DHCP. DHCP/BOOTP relay agents act as proxies, forwarding messages from one subnet to the next. By default, DHCP is a broadcast-based protocol, so without relay agents and the ability to pass DHCP and BOOTP messages across routers, every subnet on a network must have its own DHCP server.

How Relay Agents Work

Figure 4.24 shows how Client C on Subnet 2 obtains a DHCP address lease from DHCP Server 1 on Subnet 1.

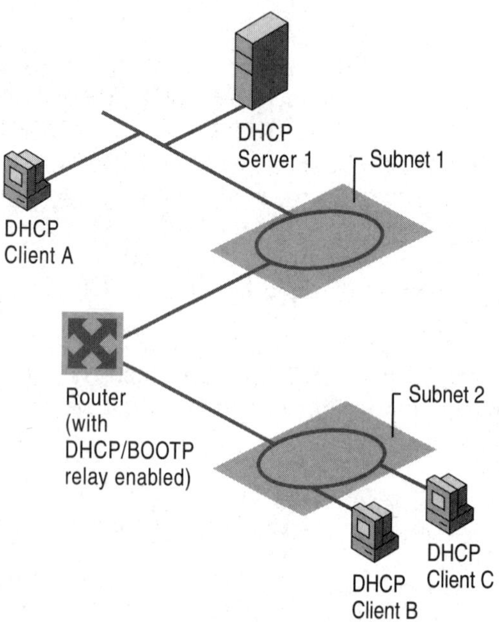

Figure 4.24 Using a Relay Agent

1. DHCP Client C broadcasts a DHCP/BOOTP discover message (DHCPDiscover) on Subnet 2, as a User Datagram Protocol (UDP) datagram using the well-known UDP server port of 67 (the port number reserved and shared for BOOTP and DHCP server communication).
2. The relay agent, in this case a DHCP/BOOTP relay-enabled router, examines the gateway IP address field in the DHCP/BOOTP message header. If the field has an IP address of 0.0.0.0, the agent fills it with the relay agent or router's IP address and forwards the message to the remote Subnet 1, where the DHCP server is located.
3. When DHCP Server 1 on remote Subnet 1 receives the message, it examines the gateway IP address field for a DHCP scope that can be used by the DHCP server to supply an IP address lease.
4. If DHCP Server 1 has multiple DHCP scopes, the address in the gateway IP address field (giaddr) identifies the DHCP scope from which to offer an IP address lease.

For example, if the giaddr field has an IP address of 201.2.45.2, the DHCP server checks its available set of address scopes for a scope range of addresses that matches the Class C IP network that includes the gateway address of the computer. In this case, the DHCP server checks to see which scope includes addresses between 201.2.45.1 and 201.2.45.254. If a scope exists that matches this criterion, the DHCP server selects an available address from the matched scope to use in an IP address lease offer response to the client.

5. When DHCP Server 1 receives the DHCPDiscover message, it processes the message and sends an IP address lease offer (DHCPOffer) directly to the relay agent identified in the gateway IP address field (giaddr).
6. The router relays the address lease offer (DHCPOffer) to the DHCP client.

   The client's IP address is still unknown, so it has to be a broadcast on the local subnet. Similarly, a DHCPRequest message is relayed from client to server, and a DHCPAck message is relayed from server to client, according to RFC 1542.

Troubleshooting

This section contains methods for determining the cause of DHCP-related communication problems, and tools that can verify DHCP statistics and operations.

Many DHCP problems involve incorrect or missing configuration details. To help prevent the most common types of problems, review "Best Practices" for deploying and managing your DHCP servers.

Most DHCP-related problems start as failed IP configuration at a client, so it is a good practice to start there.

After you have determined that a DHCP-related problem does not originate at the client, check the system event log and DHCP server audit logs for possible clues. When the DHCP service does not start, these logs generally explain the source of the service failure or shutdown.

Using Ipconfig and Winipcfg

Ipconfig is a TCP/IP utility that you can use at the command prompt. You can use the **ipconfig** command to get information about the configured TCP/IP parameters on local or remote computers on the network.

For more information on how to use the **ipconfig** command, type **ipconfig /?** at a command prompt.

Winipcfg is a similar utility for Windows 95 and Windows 98 clients.

Troubleshooting DHCP Clients

The most common DHCP client problem is a failure to obtain an IP address or other configuration parameters from the DHCP server during startup. When a client fails to obtain configuration, answer the following questions in order to quickly identify the source of the problem.

DHCP client does not have an IP address configured or has an IP address configured as 0.0.0.0.

The client was not able to contact a DHCP server and obtain an IP address lease, either because of a network hardware failure or because the DHCP server is unavailable.

Verify that the client computer has a valid, functioning network connection. First, check that related client hardware devices (cables and network adapters) are working properly at the client.

DHCP client has an auto-configured IP address that is incorrect for its current network.

The Windows 2000 or Windows 98 DHCP client could not find a DHCP server and has used the Automatic Private IP Addressing (APIPA) feature to configure its IP address. In some larger networks, disabling this feature might be desirable for network administration.

First, use the **ping** command to test connectivity from the client to the server. Next, verify or manually attempt to renew the client lease. Depending on your network requirements, it might be necessary to disable APIPA at the client.

Next, if the client hardware appears to be functioning properly, check that the DHCP server is available on the network by pinging it from another computer on the same network as the affected DHCP client.

Also, try releasing or renewing the client's address lease, and check the TCP/IP configuration settings on automatic addressing.

The DHCP client is missing configuration details.

The client might be missing DHCP options in its leased configuration, either because the DHCP server is not configured to distribute them or the client does not support the options distributed by the server.

For Microsoft DHCP clients, verify that the most commonly used and supported options have been configured at either the server, scope, client, or class level of option assignment. Check the DHCP option settings.

The client has the full and correct set of DHCP options assigned, but its network configuration does not appear to be working correctly. If the DHCP server is configured with an incorrect DHCP router option (option code 3) for the client's default gateway address, clients running Windows NT or Windows 2000 do not use the incorrect address. However, DHCP clients running Windows 95 use the incorrect address.

Change the IP address list for the router (default gateway) option at the applicable DHCP scope and server, and set the correct value in the **Scope Options** tab of the **Scope Properties** dialog box. In rare instances, you might have to configure the DHCP client to use a specialized list of routers different from other scope clients. In such cases, you can add a reservation and configure the router option list specifically for the reserved client.

DHCP clients are unable to get IP addresses from the server.

This problem can be caused the following:

- The IP address of the DHCP server was changed and now DHCP clients cannot get IP addresses.

  A DHCP server can only service requests for a scope that has a network ID that is the same as the network ID of its IP address. Make sure that the DHCP server IP address falls in the same network range as the scope it is servicing. For example, a server with an IP address in the 192.168.0.0 network cannot assign addresses from scope 10.0.0.0 unless superscopes are used.

- The DHCP clients are located across a router from the subnet where the DHCP server resides and are unable to receive an address from the server.

  A DHCP server can provide IP addresses to client computers on remote multiple subnets only if the router that separates them can act as a DHCP relay agent. Completing the following steps might correct this problem:

  1. Configure a BOOTP/DHCP relay agent on the client subnet (that is, the same physical network segment). The relay agent can be located on the router itself or on a Windows 2000 Server computer running the DHCP Relay service component.
  2. At the DHCP server, configure a scope to match the network address on the other side of the router where the affected clients are located.
  3. In the scope, make sure that the subnet mask is correct for the remote subnet.
  4. Use a default gateway on the network connection of the DHCP server in such a way that it is not using the same IP address as the router that supports the remote subnet where the clients are located.

5. Do not include this scope (that is, the one for the remote subnet) in superscopes configured for use on the same local subnet or segment where the DHCP server resides.
6. Make sure there is only one logical route between the DHCP server and the remote subnet clients.

- Multiple DHCP servers exist on the same local area network (LAN).

  Make sure that you do not configure multiple DHCP servers on the same LAN with overlapping scopes. You might want to rule out the possibility that one of the DHCP servers in question is a Small Business Server (SBS) computer. By design, the DHCP service, when running under SBS, automatically stops when it detects another DHCP server on the LAN.

Troubleshooting DHCP Servers

The most common DHCP server problems are the inability to start the server on the network in a Windows 2000 or Active Directory domain environment or the failure of clients to obtain configuration from a working server. When a server fails to provide leases to its clients, the failure most often is discovered by clients in one of three ways:

- The client might be configured to use an IP address not provided by the server.
- The server sends a negative response back to the client, and the client displays an error message or popup indicating that a DHCP server could not be found.
- The server leases the client an address but the client appears to have other network configuration–based problems, such as the inability to register or resolve DNS or NetBIOS names, or to perceive computers beyond its same subnet.

Common Problems

The following error conditions indicate potential problems with the DHCP server:

- The administrator can't connect to a DHCP server by using DHCP Manager. The message that appears might be "The RPC server is unavailable."
- DHCP clients cannot renew the leases for their IP addresses. The message that appears on the client computer is "The DHCP client could not renew the IP address lease."
- The DHCP client service or Microsoft DHCP service is stopped and cannot be restarted.

The first troubleshooting task is to make sure that the DHCP services are running. This can be verified by opening the DHCP service console to view service status, or by opening Services and Applications under Computer Manager. If the appropriate service is not started, start the service.

In rare circumstances, a DHCP server cannot start, or a Stop error might occur. If the DHCP server is stopped, complete the following procedure to restart it:

▶ **To restart a DHCP server that is stopped**

1. Start Windows 2000 Server, and log on under an account with Administrator rights.
2. At the command prompt, type **net start dhcpserver**, and then press ENTER.

Note Use Event Viewer in Administrative Tools to find the possible source of problems with DHCP services.

DHCP Relay Agent service is installed but not working

The DHCP Relay Agent service provided with Multi-Protocol Routing (MPR) does not provide a TCP/IP address from a remote DHCP server.

The DHCP Relay Agent service is running on the same computer as the DHCP service. Because both services listen for and respond to BOOTP and DHCP messages sent using UDP ports 67 and 68, neither service works reliably if both are installed on the same computer.

Install the DHCP service and the DHCP Relay Agent component on separate computers.

The DHCP console incorrectly reports lease expirations

When the DHCP console displays the lease expiration time for reserved clients for a scope, it indicates one of the following:

- If the scope lease time is set to an infinite lease time, the reserved client's lease is also shown as infinite.
- If the scope lease time is set to a finite length of time (such as eight days), the reserved client's lease uses this same lease time.

The lease term of a DHCP reserved client is determined by the lease assigned to the reservation.

To create reserved clients with unlimited lease durations, create a scope with an unlimited lease duration and add reservations to that scope.

DHCP server uses broadcast to respond to all client messages

The DHCP server uses broadcast to respond to all client configuration request messages, regardless of how each DHCP client has set the broadcast bit flag. DHCP clients can set the broadcast flag (the first bit in the 16-bit flags field in the DHCP message header) when sending DHCPDiscover messages to indicate to the DHCP server that broadcast to the limited broadcast address (255.255.255.255) should be used when replying to the client with a DHCPOffer response.

By default, the DHCP server in Windows NT Server 3.51 and earlier ignored the broadcast flag in DHCPDiscover messages and broadcasted only DHCPOffer replies. This behavior is implemented on the server to avoid problems that can result from clients not being able to receive or process a unicast response prior to being configured for TCP/IP.

Starting with Windows NT Server 4.0, the DHCP service still attempts to send all DHCP responses as IP broadcasts to the limited broadcast address unless support for unicast responses is enabled by setting the value of the **IgnoreBroadcastFlag** registry entry to **1**. The entry is located in:

HKEY_LOCAL_MACHINE\CurrentControlSet\Services\DHCPServer \Parameters**IgnoreBroadcastFlag**

When set to **1**, the broadcast flag in client requests is ignored, and all DHCPOffer responses are broadcast from the server. When it is set to **0**, the server transmission behavior (whether to broadcast or not) is determined by the setting of the broadcast bit flag in the client DHCPDiscover request. If this flag is set in the request, the server broadcasts its response to the limited local broadcast address. If this flag is not set in the request, the server unicasts its response directly to the client.

The DHCP server fails to issue address leases for a new scope

A new scope has been added at the DHCP server for the purposes of renumbering the existing network. However, DHCP clients do not obtain leases from the newly defined scope. This situation is most common when you are attempting to renumber an existing IP network.

For example, you might have obtained a registered class of IP addresses for your network or you might be changing the address class to accommodate more computers or networks. In these situations, you want clients to obtain leases in the new scope instead of using the old scope to obtain or renew their leases. Once all clients are actively obtaining lease in the new scope, you intend to remove the existing scope.

When superscopes are not available or used, only a single DHCP scope can be active on the network at one time. If more than one scope is defined and activated on the DHCP server, only one scope is used to provide leases to clients.

The active scope used for distributing leases is determined by whether the scope range of addresses contains the first IP address that is bound and assigned to the DHCP server's network adapter hardware. When additional secondary IP addresses are configured on a server using the **Advanced TCP/IP Properties** tab, these addresses have no effect on the DHCP server in determining scope selection or responding to configuration requests from DHCP clients on the network.

This problem can be solved in the following ways:

- Configure the DHCP server to use a superscope that includes the old scope and the new scope.

  If you cannot change the primary IP address assigned on the DHCP server's network adapter card, use superscopes to effect scope migration for DHCP clients on your network. Superscope support was added for Windows NT Server 4.0 with Service Pack 2 and is available for Windows 2000 Server. Superscopes provide ease and assistance in migrating DHCP scope clients. To effectively migrate clients from an old scope to a new scope using a superscope:

  1. Define the new scope.
  2. Assign and configure options for the new scope.
  3. Define a superscope and add the new scope and the old scope (that is, the scope that corresponds to the primary or first IP address assigned to the DHCP server on its **TCP/IP Properties** tab).
  4. Activate the superscope.
  5. Leave the original scope active and exclude all the addresses within that scope.

After renumbering in this manner using superscopes, the DHCP server, upon receiving a renewal request:

1. Checks to see if the client's IP address belongs to a scope it is aware of. Since the superscope includes the old scope, the server finds the scope and checks to see that this IP address has been marked as excluded.
2. The server checks if the client lease exists in its database. Since this server previously allocated the lease to this client, it sends a DHCPNack in response to the renewal request.
3. The client is forced to request a new address (the client broadcasts a DHCPDiscover message).
4. The server responds to the DHCPDiscover with a lease from the new scope.

The second step in this process (when the server checks the existence of the lease in its database), is what differentiates a renumbering scenario from a using multiple servers on the same subnet:

- If the server finds the lease in its database, it sends a DHCPNack to the renewal request.
- If the server does not find the lease, it ignores the renewal request.

For more information about using superscopes, see the section "Superscopes."

Note To migrate to the new scope, you can either deactivate the old scope or exclude all the addresses in the old scope. The server interprets both methods identically.

- Change the primary IP address (the address assigned in the **TCP/IP Properties** tab) on the DHCP server's network adapter to an IP address that is a part of the same network as the new scope.

  For Windows NT Server 3.51, support for superscopes is not available. In this case, you must change the first IP address configured for the DHCP server's network adapter to an address in the new scope range of addresses. If necessary, you can still maintain the prior address that was first assigned as an active IP address for the server computer by moving it to the list of multiple IP addresses maintained on the **Advanced TCP/IP Properties** tab.

Monitoring Server Performance

Because DHCP servers are of critical importance in most environments, monitoring the performance of servers can help in troubleshooting cases where server performance degradation occurs.

For Windows 2000 Server, the DHCP service includes a set of performance counters that can be used to monitor various types of server activity. By default, these counters are available after the DHCP service is installed. To access these counters, you must use System Monitor (formerly Performance Monitor). The DHCP server counters can monitor:

- All types of DHCP messages sent and received by the DHCP service.
- The average amount of processing time spent by the DHCP server per message packet sent and received.
- The number of message packets dropped because of internal delays on the DHCP server computer.

DHCP System Monitor Counters

Table 4.13 provides a list of the DHCP system monitor counters and their meaning:

Table 4.13 DHCP System Monitor Counters

Name	Description
Packets Received/sec	The number of message packets received per second by the DHCP server. A large number indicates heavy DHCP-related message traffic to the server.
Duplicates Dropped/sec	The number of duplicated packets per second dropped by the DHCP server. A large number indicates clients are probably timing out too fast or the server is not responding very fast.
Packets Expired/sec	The number of packets per second that expire and are dropped by the DHCP server. Packets expire because they are in the server's internal message queue for too long. A large number here indicates that the server is either taking too long to process some packets while other packets are queued, or traffic on the network is too high for the DHCP server to handle.
Milliseconds per packet (Avg.)	The average time, in milliseconds, used by the DHCP server to process each packet it receives. This number can vary depending on the server hardware and its I/O subsystem. A sudden or unreasonable increase may indicate trouble, possibly with the I/O subsystem getting slower or because of some intrinsic processing overhead on the server computer.
Active Queue Length	The current length of the internal message queue of the DHCP server. This number equals the number of unprocessed messages received by the server. A large number may indicate heavy server traffic.
Conflict Check Queue Length	The current length of the conflict check queue for the DHCP server. This queue holds messages not responded to while the DHCP server performs address conflict detection. A large value here may indicate heavy lease traffic at the server or that **Conflict Detection Attempts** has been set too high.
Discovers/sec	The number of DHCPDiscover messages received per second by the server. A sudden or abnormal increase indicates that a large number of clients are probably attempting to initialize and obtain an IP address lease from the server, such as when a number of client computers are started at one time.
Offers/sec	The number of DHCPOffer messages sent per second by the DHCP server to clients. A sudden or abnormal increase in this number indicates heavy traffic on the server.
Requests/sec	The number of DHCPRequest messages received per second by the DHCP server from clients. A sudden or abnormal increase in this number indicates that a large number of clients are probably trying to renew their leases with the DHCP server. This may indicate scope lease times are too short.

(continued)

Table 4.13 DHCP System Monitor Counters *(continued)*

Name	Description
Informs/sec	The number of DHCPInform messages received per second by the DHCP server. DHCPInform messages are used when the DHCP server queries the directory service for the enterprise root and when dynamic updates are being done on behalf of clients by the DNS server.
Acks/sec	The number of DHCPAck messages sent per second by the DHCP server to clients. A sudden or abnormal increase in this number indicates that a large number of clients are being renewed by the DHCP server. This may indicate scope lease times are too short.
Nacks/sec	The number of DHCP negative acknowledgment messages sent per second by the DHCP server to clients. A very high value might indicate potential network trouble, either misconfiguration of clients or the server. Where servers can be misconfigured, one possible cause is a deactivated scope. For clients, a very high value could be caused by computers (such as laptop portables or other mobile devices) moving between subnets.
Declines/sec	The number of DHCPDecline messages received per second by the DHCP server from clients. A high value indicates that several clients have found their address to be in conflict, possibly indicating network trouble. In this situation, it may help to enable conflict detection on the DHCP server. If used on the server, conflict detection should only be used temporarily. Once the situation returns to normal, it should be turned off.
Releases/sec	The number of DHCPRelease messages received per second by the DHCP server from clients. This number is only generated when clients manually release their address, such as when the **ipconfig /release** command is used at the client computer. Because clients rarely release their address, this counter should not be high for most networks and configurations.

DHCP Manager Statistical Data

The DHCP service, which supports Simple Network Management Protocol (SNMP) and Management Information Base (MIBs) object types, provides a graphical display of statistical data. This helps administrators monitor system status, such as the number of available versus depleted addresses, or the number of leases processed per second. Additional statistical information includes the number of messages and offers processed, as well as the number of requests, acknowledgments, declines, NACKS, and releases received.

Also viewable by DHCP Manager is the total number of scopes and addresses on the server, the number used, and the number available. These statistics can be provided for a particular scope, or at the server level, which shows the aggregate of all scopes managed by that server.

DHCP Audit Logging

The Windows 2000 DHCP service includes several new logging features and server parameters that provide enhanced auditing capabilities.

The audit logging behavior discussed in this section applies only to the DHCP service provided with Windows 2000 Server. It replaces the previous DHCP logging behavior used in earlier versions of Windows NT Server, which do not perform audit checks and use only a single log file named Dhcpsrv.log for logging service events.

The formatted structure of DHCP service logs and the level of reporting maintained for audited logging are the same as in earlier versions of the Windows DHCP service. For more information on the structure of the logs, you can review the header section of each log in a text-editing program such as Notepad.

You can now specify the following features:

- The directory path in which the DHCP service stores audit log files.
- A maximum size restriction (in MB) for the total amount of disk space available for all the audit log files created and stored by the DHCP service.
- An interval for disk checking that is used to determine how many times the DHCP server writes audit log events to the log file before checking for available disk space on the server.
- A minimum size requirement (in MB) for server disk space that is used during disk checking to determine if sufficient space exists for the server to continue audit logging.

Through the **DHCP Properties** dialog boxes, you can specify:

- The directory path in which the DHCP server stores audit log files.
- A maximum size restriction (in megabytes) for the total amount of disk space available for all audit log files created and stored by the DHCP service.
- An interval for disk checking that is used to determine how many times the DHCP server writes audit log events to the log file before checking for available disk space on the server.
- A minimum size requirement (in megabytes) for server disk space that is used during disk checking to determine if sufficient space exists for the server to continue audit logging.

See the online documentation for procedural information about specifying these parameters.

Naming Audit Log Files

The name of the audit log file is based on the current day of the week, as determined by the server's current date and time.

For example, when the DHCP server starts, if the current date and time is Saturday, January 1, 1900, at 12:00:00 A.M. then the server's audit log file is named DhcpSrvLog.Sat.

Starting a Daily Audit Log

When the DHCP server starts or whenever a new day of the week occurs (when local time on the computer is 12:00 A.M.), the server writes a header message in the audit log file, indicating that logging started. Depending on whether the audit log file is a new or existing file, the following actions occur next:

- If the audit log file has existed without modification for more than 24 hours, it is overwritten.
- If the file has existed but was modified within the previous 24 hours, the file is not overwritten. New logging activity is appended to the existing file.

Disk Checks

After audit logging starts, the DHCP server performs disk checks at regular intervals to ensure the ongoing availability of server disk space and that the current audit log file does not become too large or that log-file growth is not occurring too rapidly.

The DHCP server performs a full disk check whenever either of the following conditions occurs:

- A set number of events are logged.
- The date changes on the server computer.

The interval that is used to determine the frequency of periodic disk checks is set for *n* number of logged events, where *n* is specified by the value of the registry entry **DhcpLogDiskSpaceCheckInterval**.

Each time a disk check is completed, the DHCP service checks to see if the server disk space is full. The disk is considered full if either of the following conditions is true:

- Disk space on the server computer is lower than the required minimum amount for DHCP audit logging. This is determined by the configured value of the **DhcpLogMinSpaceOnDisk** entry. The default is **20 MB**.
- The current audit log file is larger than one-seventh (1/7) of the maximum allotted space or size for the combined total of all audit logs currently stored on the server. This is determined by a value obtained by dividing the value of the **DhcpLogFilesMaxSize** entry by 7—the maximum number of potential audit log files that can be stored on the server computer. For example, if the **DhcpLogFilesMaxSize** entry is set to its default value of **7**, the largest size that the current audit file could reach is 1 MB.

If the disk is full, the DHCP server closes the current file and ignores further requests to log audit events until either 12:00 A.M. or until disk status is improved and the disk is no longer full.

Even if audit log events are ignored because of a full-disk condition, the DHCP server continues checking every *n* number of attempted log events to see if disk conditions on the server computer have improved. The number is set in the **DhcpLogDiskSpaceCheckInterval** entry. If subsequent disk checks determine that the required amount of server disk space is available, the DHCP service reopens the current day's log file and resumes logging.

Ending a Daily Audit Log

At 12:00 A.M. local time on the server computer, the DHCP server closes the existing log and moves to the log file for the next day of the week. For example, if the day of the week changes at 12:00 A.M. from Wednesday to Thursday, the log file named DhcpSrvLog.wed is closed and the file named DhcpSrvLog.thu is opened and used for logging events.

Restoring Server Data

Restoring the DHCP server database can be useful if the database either becomes corrupted or lost. When this happens, Windows 2000 Server provides a progressive set of recovery and repair options for restoration of DHCP data on the server computer.

In troubleshooting data corruption problems, use the following steps to detect corruption and restore DHCP service.

- First, confirm that the source of data loss or corruption is with the DHCP server and perform preliminary diagnosis or repairs, such as compaction of the DHCP server database. Also, it is a good idea to verify that corruption is not related to other problems or conditions with hardware or software changes. Where data loss occurs, verify the server computer disk drives are operating properly. In most cases, database corruption first appears in the form of Jet database error messages in the System event log.
- Second, where repair fails, you can use simple recovery of the DHCP server from your available options for server backup. DHCP Manager provides a simple backup option to effectively back up the DHCP server database. You can also have other options for obtaining a backup copy of the database for use during restoration, such as from a recent tape backup of the server computer disk drives.
- Third, when simple data recovery options are not available or are tried but unsuccessful, you can also try advanced data recovery methods provided with the DHCP console and Windows 2000 Server to recover specific information related to individual scopes stored in the DHCP server database.

If you determine that the DHCP services are running on both the client and server computers but the error conditions described earlier under "Troubleshooting DHCP Servers" persist, then the DHCP database is not available or has become corrupted. If a DHCP server fails for any reason, you can restore the database from a backup copy.

▶ **To restore a DHCP database**

1. Before starting, make a copy of the DHCP server database files.
2. In the *%SystemRoot%*\System32\Dhcp directory, delete the J50.log, J50*xxxxx*.log, and Dhcp.tmp files.
3. Copy an uncorrupted backup version of the Dhcp.mdb (from your manual or automatic database backup media) to the *%SystemRoot%*\System32\Dhcp directory.
4. Restart the Microsoft DHCP server.

Detecting DHCP Jet Data Corruption

Table 4.14 lists the possible DHCP service messages that might appear in the System event log when the DHCP server database becomes corrupted:

Table 4.14 Corrupt Jet Database Messages

Event ID	Source	Description
1014	DhcpServer	The Jet database returned the following Error: –510.
1014	DhcpServer	The Jet database returned the following Error: –1022.
1014	DhcpServer	The Jet database returned the following Error: –1850.

Typically, Jet errors can be resolved by manual offline compaction of the database using the Jetpack utility. In cases where Jetpack.exe fails to repair the database, restoration of the DHCP server database as described in the following sections can be used to recover the server database and restore DHCP service at the server computer.

To recover a corrupted DHCP database, you can use the following options for restoring the database:

- **Simple recovery.** Restore the database from a backup copy of the database file, Dhcp.mdb.

  This method is recommended as the preferred method of recovery because it involves less risk of losing information previously configured and stored by the DHCP server and is much simpler to perform.

- **Advanced recovery.** The registry can be modified to force creation of a new database file. This method can be useful as an additional method for data recovery when simple restoration of the database is not possible. However, this should be done with extreme caution. For more information about restoring a corrupted DHCP database, see the Microsoft Knowledge Base link on the Web Resources page at http://windows.microsoft.com/windows2000/reskit/webresources. Search the Knowledge Base using the keywords *DHCP*, database, and recovery.

Simple Recovery: Restoring from Backup

If the DHCP server database becomes corrupted or is lost, simple recovery is possible by replacing the server database file (Dhcp.mdb), located in the *%SystemRoot%*\System32\Dhcp folder, with a backup copy of the same file. You can then perform a simple file copy to overwrite the current corrupted database with a backup copy of the same file.

If DHCP Manager has been used previously to enable backup, you can obtain the backup copy of the server database file located in the *%SystemRoot%*\System32\Dhcp\Backup folder. As an option, you can also choose to restore the Dhcp.mdb file from a tape backup or other backup media.

Before restoring the database file from backup, the DHCP service must first be stopped. Once you have copied the backup file to the *%SystemRoot%*\System32\Dhcp folder from your preferred backup source, you can restart the DHCP service.

To stop the DHCP server service, type the following at a command prompt:

net stop dhcpserver

Once the DHCP service has been stopped, the following procedure can be used to safely restore a backup copy of the database from either backup media or the DHCP service backup folder.

First, move the files from your existing DHCP folder to a different folder location, such as \Olddhcp. Be careful to keep the DHCP folder structure intact. For example, type the following set of commands at a command prompt to perform this step:

md c:\Olddhcp

move *%SystemRoot%*\system32\DHCP*.* C:\Olddhcp

Next, remove the corrupted server database file. This can also be done at the command prompt:

del *%SystemRoot%*\system32\DHCP\Dhcp.mdb

You can then copy the backup database file into the DHCP service folder. The path to be used when performing the actual copy operation varies (as shown in Table 4.15), depending on the specific server version of Windows running on the computer where the DHCP database file is being restored.

Table 4.15 Location of DHCP Database Files

Server version	Copy command usage
Windows NT Server 3.51	**copy *%SystemRoot%*\system32\dhcp\backup\jet\dhcp.mdb *%SystemRoot%*\system32\dhcp\dhcp.mdb**
Windows NT Server 4.0	**copy *%SystemRoot%*\system32\dhcp\backup\jet\new\dhcp.mdb *%SystemRoot%*\system32\dhcp\dhcp.mdb**
Windows 2000 Server	**copy *%SystemRoot%*\system32\dhcp\backup\jet\new\dhcp.mdb *%SystemRoot%*\system32\dhcp\dhcp.mdb**

Once the backup database file has been copied to the correct DHCP folder location for your server computer, you can restart the DHCP service.

To restart the service, type the following at the command prompt:

net start dhcpserver

The previous procedure should allow the DHCP service to start, but if scope information is missing, it might be necessary to use a backup copy of your registry to reconfigure the values necessary for restoring your scope and client reservation information.

Rebuilding a Stopped DHCP Server

If the hardware for the DHCP server is malfunctioning or other problems prevent you from running Windows 2000, you must rebuild the DHCP database on another computer.

▶ **To rebuild a DHCP server**

1. If you can start the original DHCP server by using the **net start DHCP** command, use the **copy** command to make backup copies of the files in the *%SystemRoot%*\System32\Dhcp directory. If you cannot start the computer at all, you must use the last backup version of the DHCP database files.
2. Install Windows 2000 Server to create a new DHCP server using the same hard drive location and *%SystemRoot%* directory. That is, if the original server stored the DHCP files on *%SystemRoot%* \System32\Dhcp, then the new DHCP server must use this same path to the DHCP files.
3. Make sure the Microsoft DHCP service on the new server is stopped, and then use a registry editor to restore the DHCP keys from backup files.
4. Copy the DHCP backup files to the *%SystemRoot%*\System32\Dhcp directory.
5. Restart the new, rebuilt DHCP server.

Moving the DHCP Server Database

You may need to move a DHCP database to another computer. To do this, use the following procedure.

▶ **To move a DHCP database**

1. Stop the Microsoft DHCP service on the current computer.
2. Copy the \System32\Dhcp directory to the new computer that has been configured as a DHCP server. Make sure the new directory is under exactly the same drive letter and path as on the old computer. If you must copy the files to a different directory, copy Dhcp.mdb, but do not copy the .log or.chk files.
3. Start the Microsoft DHCP service on the new computer. The service automatically starts using the .mdb and .log files copied from the old computer.

When you check DHCP Manager, the scope still exists because the registry holds the information on the address range of the scope, including a bitmap of the addresses in use. You need to reconcile the DHCP database to add database entries for the existing leases in the address bitmask. As clients renew, they are matched with these leases, and eventually the database is again complete.

▶ **To reconcile the DHCP database**

1. In DHCP Manager, on the **Scope** menu, click **Active Leases**.
2. In the **Active Leases** dialog box, click **Reconcile**.

Although it is not required, you can force DHCP clients to renew their leases in order to update the DHCP database as quickly as possible. To do so, type **ipconfig/renew** at the command prompt.

Compacting the DHCP Server Database

Windows 2000 and Windows NT Server 4.0 are designed to automatically compact the DHCP server database. However, if you are using Windows NT Server version 3.51 or earlier, the database might need to be compacted after DHCP has been running for awhile to improve performance. You should compact the DHCP database whenever it approaches 30 MB.

You can use the Jetpack.exe utility provided with Windows NT Server 3.5 and 3.51 to compact a DHCP database. Jetpack.exe is a command-line utility that is run in the Windows NT Server command window. The utility is found in the *%SystemRoot%*\System32 directory.

The Jetpack.exe syntax is:

Jetpack.exe *database_name temp_database_name*

For example:

```
CD %SystemRoot%\SYSTEM32\DHCP
JETPACK DHCP.MDB TMP.MDB
```

In the preceding example, Tmp.mdb is a temporary database that is used by Jetpack.exe. Dhcp.mdb is the DHCP server database file.

When Jetpack.exe is started, it performs the following tasks:

1. Copies database information to a temporary database file called Tmp.mdb.
2. Deletes the original database file, Dhcp.mdb.
3. Renames the temporary database file to the original file name.

▶ **To compact the DHCP database**

1. Open the DHCP Manager console.
2. Select the applicable DHCP server.
3. Click **Action**, point to **All Tasks**, and click **Stop**. (Alternatively, you can type **net stop DHCP** at the command prompt.)
4. At the command prompt, type **jetpack** to run the Jetpack program.
5. Restart the DHCP service by using the **Services** dialog box.

Using Reconcile to Salvage Scopes

Before using the Reconcile feature to fully recover DHCP scope client information from the registry, the server computer needs the following:

- All DHCP server registry keys must be either restored or exist and remain intact from previous service operation on the server computer.
- A fresh version of the DHCP server database file must be regenerated in the *%SystemRoot%*\System32\Dhcp folder on the server computer.

When the registry and database meet these criteria, you can restart the DHCP service. At this point, you might notice that, upon opening the DHCP console, scope information is present but there are no active leases displayed. To regain your active leases for each scope, you use the Reconcile feature to recover each scope. Use the following steps for Windows 2000 Server to perform reconciliation and recovery of scope data.

1. In DHCP Manager, click a scope to select and expand it.
2. Click the Active Leases folder.
3. Right-click and select **Task**, and then click **Reconcile**.
4. When the **Reconciling Database** dialog window appears, click **OK**.

This process can be repeated for each scope to add client lease and reservation information from the registry back into the list of active leases for each scope previously configured for the DHCP server.

After using the Reconcile feature, you might notice that, when viewing properties for individual clients shown in the list of active leases, client information is displayed incorrectly. This information is corrected and updated in DHCP Manager as scope clients renew their leases.

If your DHCP server is running under Windows NT Server 4.0, Service Pack 2 or later, enable address conflict detection after using this recovery method. This is recommended since the backup may have been performed on an older database or from a slightly out-of-date system registry. For more information about when to use and how to enable conflict detection, see the "Server Conflict Detection" section in this chapter and the Microsoft Knowledge Base.

Although the Reconcile feature can be used to recover scope information in the event of disaster recovery for a DHCP server, it is not intended as a replacement for other traditional backup measures. Implement other methods (such as backing up to a tape drive) to provide further safe offline storage and duplicate archives of your DHCP database.

Analyzing Server Log Files

Because Windows 2000 Server uses audit logging when writing DHCP server log files, DHCP server logging is not resource-intensive. It can be left enabled because it uses a limited amount of disk space on server hard drives.

DHCP Server Log File Format

DHCP server logs are comma-delimited text files with each log entry representing a single line of text. The fields and their order as they appear in each log file entry are:

ID Date, Time, Description, IP Address, Computer Name, MAC Address

Each of these fields is described in further detail in Table 4.16.

Table 4.16 Log File Fields

Field	Description
ID	A DHCP server event ID code.
Date	The date at which this entry was logged on the DHCP server.
Time	The time at which this entry was logged on the DHCP server.
Description	A description of this DHCP server event.
IP Address	The IP address of the DHCP client.
Computer Name	The computer name of the DHCP client.
MAC Address	The media access control address used by the client's network adapter hardware.

DHCP Server Log Event Codes

The DHCP server log also uses special event ID codes to specifically indicate information about the type of service event logged.

Table 4.17 describes these event ID codes.

Table 4.17 Event ID Codes

Event ID	Description
00	The log was started.
01	The log was stopped.
02	The log was temporarily paused due to low disk space.
10	A new IP address was leased to a client.
11	A lease was renewed by a client.
12	A lease was released by a client.
13	An IP address was found in use on the network.
14	A lease request could not be satisfied because the scope's address pool was exhausted.
15	A lease was denied.
20	A BOOTP address was leased to a client.

Additional Resources

For more information about using DHCP, refer to the following books:

- *Internetworking with TCP/IP, Volume I: Principles, Protocols, and Architecture* Third Edition by Douglas Comer, 1995, Englewood Cliffs, NJ: Prentice Hall.
- *Managing a Microsoft Windows NT Network* by Microsoft Corporation, 1999, Redmond, WA: Microsoft Press.
- *Mastering TCP/IP For NT Server* by M. Minasi, T. Lammle, and M. Lammle, 1997, Alameda, CA: Sybex.
- *Optimizing Network Traffic* by Microsoft Corporation, 1999, Redmond, WA: Microsoft Press.
- *TCP/IP Unleashed* by T. Parker, 1996, Indianapolis, IN: Sams Publishing.
- *TCP/IP Illustrated, Volume 1: The Protocol* by W.R. Stevens, 1994, Reading, MA: Addison-Wesley.
- *Windows NT TCP/IP Network Administration* by C. Hunt, and R.B. Thompson, 1998, Sebastopol, CA: O'Reilly and Associates.

CHAPTER 5

Introduction to DNS

Domain Name System (DNS) enables you to use hierarchical, friendly names to easily locate computers and other resources on an IP network. The following sections describe the basic DNS concepts, including features explained in newer Requests for Comments (RFCs), such as dynamic update, from the Internet Engineering Task Force (IETF). The Microsoft® Windows® 2000–specific implementation of DNS is not covered within this chapter, except where indicated.

For information about the Windows 2000 implementation of DNS, see "Windows 2000 DNS" in this book.

DNS is a distributed database that contains mappings of DNS domain names to data. It is also a protocol for Transmission Control Protocol/Internet Protocol (TCP/IP) networks, defined by the Requests for Comments (RFCs) that pertain to DNS. DNS defines the following:

- Mechanism for querying and updating the database.
- Mechanism for replicating the information in the database among servers.
- Schema for the database.

In This Chapter

Related Information in the Resource Kit

- For more information about TCP/IP protocols, see "Introduction to TCP/IP" in this book.
- For information about the Windows 2000 implementation of DNS, see "Windows 2000 DNS" in this book.

Introduction to the Domain Name System

Although TCP/IP uses IP addresses to locate and connect to hosts (computers and other TCP/IP network devices), users typically prefer to use friendly names. For example, users prefer the friendly name ftp.reskit.com, instead of its IP address, 172.16.23.55. The Domain Name System (DNS), defined in RFCs 1034 and 1035, is used on the Internet to provide a standard naming convention for locating IP-based computers.

On the Internet, before the implementation of DNS, the use of names to locate resources on TCP/IP networks was supported by a file called Hosts. Network administrators entered names and IP addresses into Hosts, and computers used the file for name resolution.

Both the Hosts file and DNS use a namespace. A *namespace* is a grouping in which names can be used to symbolically represent another type of information, such as an IP address, and in which specific rules are established that determine how names can be created and used. Some namespaces, such as DNS, are hierarchically structured and provide rules that allow for the namespace to be divided into subsets of names for distributing and delegating parts of the namespace. Other namespaces, such as the Hosts namespace cannot be divided and must be distributed in their entirety. Because of this, using the Hosts file posed a problem for network administrators. As the number of computers and users on the Internet grew, the task of updating and distributing the Hosts file became unmanageable.

DNS replaces the Hosts file with a distributed database that implements a hierarchical naming system. This naming system allows for growth on the Internet and the creation of names that are unique throughout the Internet and private TCP/IP-based intranets.

Domain Namespace

The naming system on which DNS is based is a hierarchical and logical tree structure called the *domain namespace*. Organizations can also create private networks that are not visible on the Internet, using their own domain namespaces. Figure 5.1 shows part of the Internet domain namespace, from the root domain and top-level Internet DNS domains, to the fictional DNS domain named reskit.com that contains a host (computer) named Mfgserver.

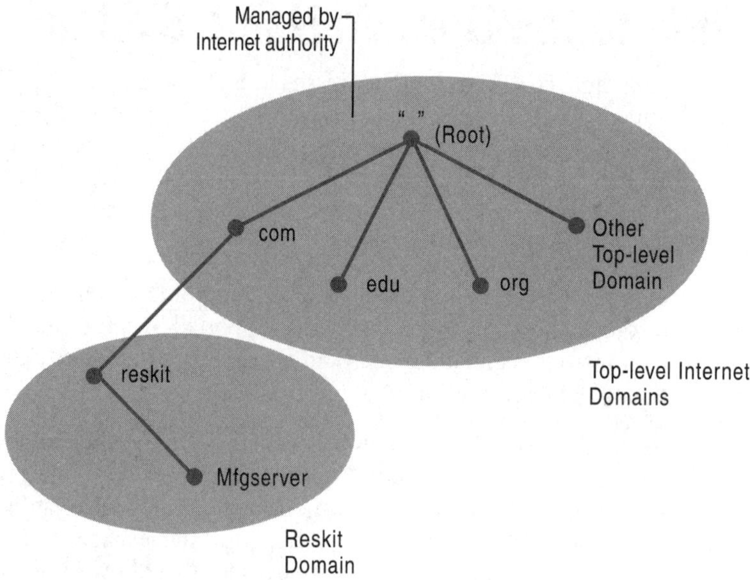

Figure 5.1 Domain Name System

Each node in the DNS tree represents a DNS name. Some examples of DNS names are DNS domains, computers, and services. A DNS domain is a branch under the node. For example, in Figure 5.1, reskit.com is a DNS domain. DNS domains can contain both hosts (computers or services) and other domains (referred to as *subdomains*). Each organization is assigned authority for a portion of the domain namespace and is responsible for administering, subdividing, and naming the DNS domains and computers within that portion of the namespace.

Subdividing is an important concept in DNS. Creating subdivisions of the domain namespace and private TCP/IP network DNS domains supports new growth on the Internet and the ability to continually expand name and administrative groupings. Subdivisions are generally based on departmental or geographic divisions.

For example, the reskit.com DNS domain might include sites in North America and Europe. A DNS administrator of the DNS domain reskit.com can subdivide the domain to create two subdomains that reflect these groupings: noam.reskit.com. and eu.reskit.com. Figure 5.2 shows an example of these subdomains.

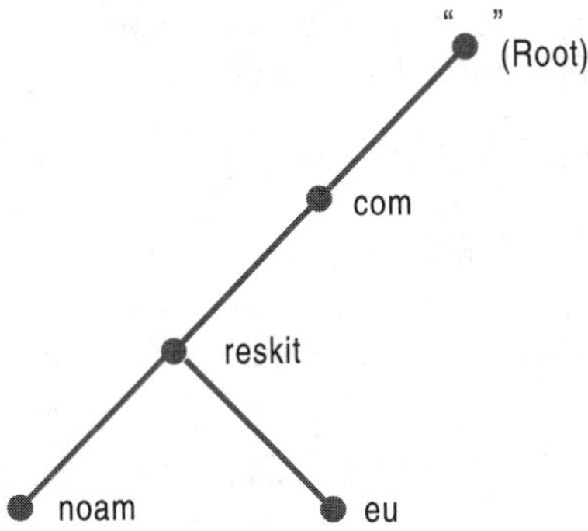

Figure 5.2 Subdomains

Domain Name

Computers and DNS domains are named based on their position in the domain tree. For example, because reskit is a subdomain of the .com domain, the domain name for reskit is reskit.com.

Every node in the DNS domain tree can be identified by a *fully qualified domain name* (FQDN). The FQDN is a DNS domain name that has been stated unambiguously so as to indicate with absolute certainty its location relative to the root of the DNS domain tree. This contrasts with a relative name, which is a name relative to some DNS domain other than the root.

For example, the FQDN for the server in the reskit.com DNS domain is constructed as Mfgserver.reskit.com., which is the concatenation of the host name (Mfgserver) with the primary DNS suffix (reskit.com), and the trailing dot (.). The trailing dot is a standard separator between the top-level domain label and the empty string label corresponding to the root.

Note In general, FQDNs have naming restrictions that allow only the use of characters a-z, A-Z, 0-9, and the dash or minus sign (-). The use of the period (.) is allowed only between domain name labels (for example, "reskit.com") or at the end of a FQDN. Domain names are not case-sensitive.

You can configure the Windows 2000 DNS server to enforce some or all RFC character restrictions or to ignore all character restrictions. For more information, see "Windows 2000 DNS" in this book.

Internet Domain Namespace

The root (the top-most level) of the Internet domain namespace is managed by an Internet name registration authority, which delegates administrative responsibility for portions of the domain namespace to organizations that connect to the Internet.

Beneath the root DNS domain lie the top-level domains, also managed by the Internet name registration authority. There are three types of top-level domains:

- Organizational domains. These are named by using a 3-character code that indicates the primary function or activity of the organizations contained within the DNS domain. Organizational domains are generally only for organizations within the United States, and most organizations located in the United States are contained within one of these organizational domains.
- Geographical domains. These are named by using the 2-character country/region codes established by the International Standards Organization (ISO) 3166.
- Reverse domains. This is a special domain, named in-addr.arpa, that is used for IP address-to-name mappings (referred to as *reverse lookup*). For more information, see "Name Resolution" later in this chapter. There is also a special domain, named IP6.INT, used for IP version 6 reverse lookups. For information, see RFC 1886.

The most commonly used top-level DNS name components for organizations in the United States are described in the Table 5.1.

Table 5.1 Top-Level Name Component of the DNS Hierarchy

Top-Level Name Component	Description	Example DNS Domain Name
.com	An Internet name authority delegates portions of the domain namespace under this level to commercial organizations, such as the Microsoft Corporation.	microsoft.com
.edu	An Internet name authority delegates portions of this domain namespace to educational organizations, such as the Massachusetts Institute of Technology (MIT).	mit.edu
.gov	An Internet name authority delegates portions of this domain namespace to governmental organizations, such as the White House in Washington, D.C.	whitehouse.gov
.int	An Internet name authority delegates portions of this domain namespace to international organizations, such as the North Atlantic Treaty Organization (NATO).	nato.int
.mil	An Internet name authority delegates portions of this domain namespace to military operations, such as the Defense Date Network (DDN).	ddn.mil

(continued)

Table 5.1 Top-Level Name Component of the DNS Hierarchy *(continued)*

Top-Level Name Component	Description	Example DNS Domain Name
.net	An Internet name authority delegates portions of this domain namespace to networking organizations, such as the National Science Foundation (NSF).	nsf.net
.org	An Internet name authority delegates portions of this domain namespace to noncommercial organizations, such as the Center for Networked Information Discovery and Retrieval (CNIDR).	cnidr.org

In addition to the top-level domains listed above, individual countries have their own top-level domains. For example, .ca is the top-level domain for Canada.

Beneath the top-level domains, an Internet name authority delegates domains to organizations that connect to the Internet. The organizations to which an Internet name authority delegates a portion of the domain namespace are then responsible for naming the computers and network devices within their assigned domain and its subdivisions. These organizations use DNS servers to manage the name-to-IP address and IP address-to-name mappings for host devices contained within their portion of the namespace.

Basic DNS Concepts

This section provides brief definitions of additional DNS concepts, which are described in more detail in the following sections of this chapter.

DNS servers. Computers that run DNS server programs containing DNS database information about the DNS domain tree structure. DNS servers also attempt to resolve client queries. When queried, DNS servers can provide the requested information, provide a pointer to another server that can help resolve the query, or respond that it does not have the information or that the information does not exist.

DNS resolvers. Programs that use DNS queries to query for information from servers. Resolvers can communicate with either remote DNS servers or the DNS server program running on the local computer. Resolvers are usually built into utility programs or are accessible through library functions. A resolver can run on any computer, including a DNS server.

Resource records. Sets of information in the DNS database that can be used to process client queries. Each DNS server contains the resource records it needs to answer queries for the portion of the DNS namespace for which it is authoritative. (A DNS server is authoritative for a contiguous portion of the DNS namespace if it contains information about that portion of the namespace.)

Zones. Contiguous portions of the DNS namespace for which the server is authoritative. A server can be authoritative for one or more zones.

Zone files. Files that contain resource records for the zones for which the server is authoritative. In most DNS implementations, zones are implemented as text files.

Zones

A zone is a contiguous portion of the DNS namespace. It contains a series of records stored on a DNS server. Each zone is anchored at a specific domain node. However, zones are not domains. A *DNS domain* is a branch of the namespace, whereas a zone is a portion of the DNS namespace generally stored in a file, and can contain multiple domains. A domain can be subdivided into several partitions, and each partition, or zone, can be controlled by a separate DNS server. Using the zone, the DNS server answers queries about hosts in its zone, and is authoritative for that zone. Zones can be primary or secondary. A *primary zone* is the copy of the zone to which the updates are made, whereas a *secondary zone* is a copy of the zone that is replicated from a master server.

Zones can be stored in different ways. For example, they can be stored as zone files. On Windows 2000 servers, they can also be stored in the Active Directory™ directory service. Some secondary servers store them in memory and perform a zone transfer whenever they are restarted.

Figure 5.3 shows an example of a DNS domain that contains two primary zones. In this example, the domain reskit.com contains two subdomains: noam.reskit.com. and eu.reskit.com. Authority for the noam.reskit.com. subdomain has been delegated to the server noamdc1.noam.reskit.com. Thus, as Figure 5.3 shows, one server, noamdc1.noam.reskit.com, hosts the noam.reskit.com zone, and a second server, reskitdc1.reskit.com, hosts the reskit.com zone that includes the eu.reskit.com subdomain.

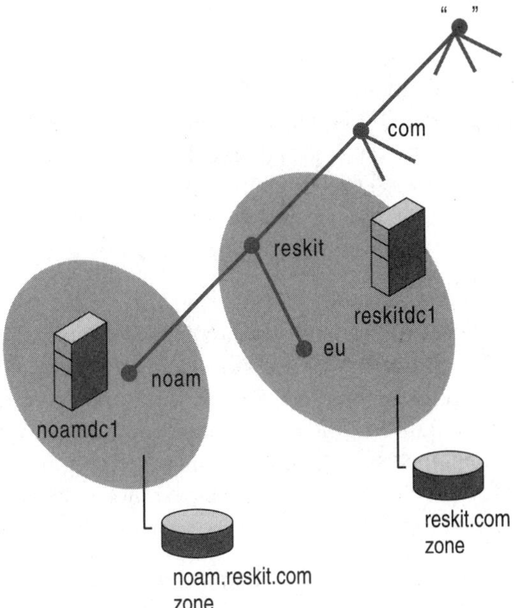

Figure 5.3 Domains and Zones

Rather than delegating the noam.reskit.com zone to noamdc1.noam.reskit.com, the administrator can also configure reskitdc1 to host the zone for noam.reskit.com.

Also, you cannot configure two different servers to manage the same primary zones; only one server can manage the primary zone for each DNS domain. There is one exception: multiple computers can manage Windows 2000 Active Directory–integrated zones. For more information, see "Windows 2000 DNS" in this book.

You can configure a single DNS server to manage one zone or multiple zones, depending on your needs. You can create multiple zones to distribute administrative tasks to different groups and to provide efficient data distribution. You can also store the same zone on multiple servers to provide load balancing and fault tolerance.

For information about what zones contain, see "Resource Records and Zones" later in this chapter.

DNS Servers

DNS servers store information about no zones, one zone, or multiple zones. When a DNS server receives a DNS query, it attempts to locate the requested information by retrieving data from its local zones. If this fails because the server is not authoritative for the DNS domain requested and thus does not have the data for the requested domain, the server can check its cache, communicate with other DNS servers to resolve the request, or refer the client to another DNS server that might know the answer.

DNS servers can host primary and secondary zones. You can configure servers to host as many different primary or secondary zones as is practical, which means that a server might host the primary copy of one zone and the secondary copy of another zone, or it might host only the primary or only the secondary copy for a zone. For each zone, the server that hosts the primary zones is considered the *primary server* for that zone, and the server that hosts the secondary zones is considered the *secondary server* for that zone.

Primary zones are locally updated. When a change is made to the zone data, such as delegating a portion of the zone to another DNS server or adding resource records in the zone, these changes must be made on the primary DNS server for that zone, so that the new information can be entered in the local zone.

In contrast, secondary zones are replicated from another server. When a zone is defined on a secondary server for that zone, the zone is configured with the IP address of the server from which the zone is to be replicated. The server from which the zone file replicates can either be a primary or secondary server for the zone, and is sometimes called a *master server* for the secondary zone.

When a secondary server for the zone starts up, it contacts the master server for the zone and initiates a zone transfer. The secondary server for the zone also periodically contacts the master server for the zone to see whether the zone data has changed. If so, it can initiate a transfer of the zones, referred to as a *zone transfer*. For more information about zone transfers, see "Zone Transfer" later in this chapter.

You must have a primary server for each zone. Additionally, you should have at least one secondary server for each zone. Otherwise, if the primary server for the zone goes down, no one will be able to resolve the names in that zone.

Secondary servers provide the following benefits:

Fault tolerance When a secondary server is configured for a zone, clients can still resolve names for that zone even if the primary server for the zone goes down. Generally, plan to install the primary and secondary servers for the zone on different subnets. Therefore, if connectivity to one subnet is lost, DNS clients can still direct queries to the name server on the other subnet.

Reduction of traffic on wide area links You can add a secondary server for the zone in a remote location that has a large number of clients, and then configure the client to try those servers first. This can prevent clients from communicating across slow links for DNS queries.

Reduction of load on the primary server for the zone The secondary server can answer queries for the zone, reducing the number of queries the primary server for the zone must answer.

The following sections describe servers that act as caching-only servers, forwarders, and slaves.

Caching-Only Servers

All DNS servers perform *caching*; whenever they receive information from other servers, they store the information for a certain amount of time. This speeds the performance of DNS resolution, reduces DNS-related query traffic, and improves reliability. For more information, see "Caching and Time to Live" later in this chapter.

Certain DNS servers, known as *caching-only servers,* simply perform queries, cache the answers, and return the results. They are not authoritative for any DNS domains and do not host any zones. They only store data that they have cached while resolving queries.

The benefit provided by caching-only servers is that they do not generate zone transfer network traffic because they do not contain any zones. However, there is one disadvantage: when the server is initially started, it has no cached information and must build up this information over time as it services requests.

Forwarders and Slaves

When a DNS server receives a query, it attempts to locate the requested information within its local zones and from the cache. If it cannot locate the requested information and is not authoritative for the requested information, it must communicate with other servers to resolve the request. However, in some cases network administrators might not want the server to communicate directly with other servers. For example, if your organization were connected to the Internet by means of a slow wide area link, you might not want every DNS server in your organization to connect directly to DNS servers on the Internet.

To solve this problem, DNS allows for the use of *forwarders*. Forwarders are DNS servers that are designated to provide forwarding of off-site queries for other DNS servers. For example, you could designate one DNS server as a forwarder for names of computers on the Internet, and then configure your other servers to use that forwarder to resolve names for which they are not authoritative.

You do not need to perform any special configuration on the computer designated as a forwarder. You must configure the DNS server that needs to forward queries by providing the IP address of the forwarders.

A server can use a forwarder in a nonexclusive or exclusive mode. In a nonexclusive mode, when a server receives a DNS query for which it is not authoritative and cannot resolve through its own zones or cache, it passes the query to one of the designated forwarders. The forwarder then carries out whatever communication is necessary to resolve the query and returns the results to the requesting server, which returns the results to the original requester. If the forwarder cannot resolve the query, the server that received the original query attempts to resolve the query on its own.

In an exclusive mode, servers rely completely on the name-resolving ability of the forwarders. Servers using forwarders in an exclusive mode are known as *slaves*. When a slave receives a DNS query that it cannot resolve through its own zones, it passes the query to one of the designated forwarders. The forwarder then carries out whatever communication is necessary to resolve the query and returns the results to the slave, which returns the results to the original requester. If the forwarder cannot resolve the request, the slave returns a query failure to the original requestor. Slaves make no attempt to resolve the query on their own if the forwarder cannot satisfy the request.

Load Sharing

DNS servers use a mechanism called round-robin or *load sharing*, explained in RFC 1794, to share and distribute loads for network resources. Round-robin rotates the order of resource record data returned in a query answer in which multiple RRs exist of the same RR type for a queried DNS domain name.

For example, suppose you have three World Wide Web servers with the same domain name, WWWServer, that all display the Web page for www.reskit.com, and you want to share the load between them. On the name server, you would create the following resource records:

```
www.reskit.com.      IN  A       172.16.64.11
www.reskit.com.      IN  A       172.17.64.22
www.reskit.com.      IN  A       172.18.64.33
```

A name server configured to perform round-robin rotates the order of the A resource records when answering client requests. In this example, the name server would reply to the first client request by ordering the addresses as 172.16.64.11, 172.17.64.22, and 172.18.64.33. It would reply to the second client response by ordering the addresses as 172.17.64.22, 172.18.64.33, and 172.16.64.11. The rotation process continues until data from all of the same type of resource records associated with a name have been rotated to the top of the list returned in answering client queries. The client is required to try the first IP address listed.

By default, a Windows 2000 DNS server uses a different method to order the records returned to a client. It attempts to find the resource record containing the IP address closest to the client, then returns this resource record first in the list of records. However, you can modify the default so it performs traditional round-robin. For information, see "Windows 2000 DNS" in this book. Versions of BIND 4.9.3 and later perform this type of load sharing. Earlier versions of BIND performed a different type of load sharing; for more information, see RFC 1794.

Name Resolution

DNS clients use libraries called *resolvers* that perform DNS queries to servers on behalf of the client. Keep in mind throughout this discussion that a DNS server can also be a client to another server.

Note Computers running under Microsoft® Windows NT® Workstation or Microsoft® Windows NT®Server version 4.0 use DNS name resolution when a name query contains a name that contains a period or is greater than 15 bytes in length. Computers running Windows 2000 always try DNS name resolution. For more information about DNS and NetBIOS name resolution, see "TCP/IP Troubleshooting" and "Windows 2000 DNS" in this book.

DNS clients can make two types of queries: recursive and iterative.

Recursive and Iterative Queries

With a *recursive name query*, the DNS client requires that the DNS server respond to the client with either the requested resource record or an error message stating that the record or domain name does not exist. The DNS server cannot just refer the DNS client to a different DNS server.

Thus, if a DNS server does not have the requested information when it receives a recursive query, it queries other servers until it gets the information, or until the name query fails.

Recursive name queries are generally made by a DNS client to a DNS server, or by a DNS server that is configured to pass unresolved name queries to another DNS server, in the case of a DNS server configured to use a forwarder.

An *iterative name query* is one in which a DNS client allows the DNS server to return the best answer it can give based on its cache or zone data. If the queried DNS server does not have an exact match for the queried name, the best possible information it can return is a *referral* (that is, a pointer to a DNS server authoritative for a lower level of the domain namespace). The DNS client can then query the DNS server for which it obtained a referral. It continues this process until it locates a DNS server that is authoritative for the queried name, or until an error or time-out condition is met.

This process is sometimes referred to as "walking the tree," and this type of query is typically initiated by a DNS server that attempts to resolve a recursive name query for a DNS client.

Figure 5.4 shows an example of iterative and recursive queries. This example assumes that none of the servers have the requested information in their caches.

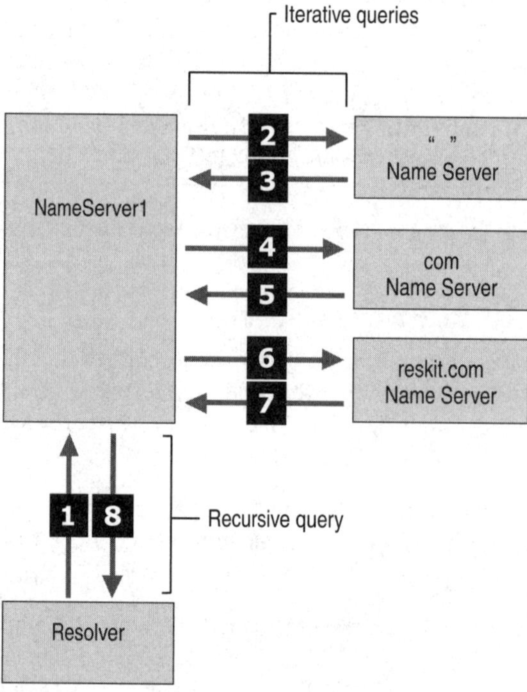

Figure 5.4 Iterative and Recursive Queries

In the example shown in Figure 5.4, a client somewhere on the Internet needs the IP address of noam.reskit.com. The following events take place:

1. The client contacts NameServer1 with a recursive query for noam.reskit.com. The server must now return either the answer or an error message.
2. NameServer1 checks its cache and zones for the answer, but does not find it, so it contacts a server authoritative for the Internet (that is, a *root server*) with an iterative query for noam.reskit.com.
3. The server at the root of the Internet does not know the answer, so it responds with a referral to a server authoritative for the .com domain.
4. NameServer1 contacts a server authoritative for the .com domain with an iterative query for noam.reskit.com.
5. The server authoritative for the .com domain does not know the exact answer, so it responds with a referral to a server authoritative for the reskit.com domain.
6. NameServer1 contacts the server authoritative for the reskit.com domain with an iterative query for noam.reskit.com.
7. The server authoritative for the reskit.com domain does know the answer. It responds with the requested IP address.
8. NameServer1 responds to the client query with the IP address for noam.reskit.com.

Caching and Time to Live

When a server is processing a recursive query, it might be required to send out several queries to find the definitive answer. The server caches all of the information that it receives during this process for a time that is specified in the returned data. This amount of time is referred to as the *time to live (TTL)* and is specified in seconds. The server administrator of the primary zone that contains the data decides on the TTL for the data. Smaller TTL values help ensure that information about the domain is more consistent across the network, in the event that this data changes often. However, this also increases the load on the name servers that contain the name, and it also increases Internet traffic. Because data is cached, changes made in resource records might not be immediately available to the entire Internet.

Once data is cached by a DNS server, the DNS server must start decreasing the TTL from its original value so that it will know when to flush the data from its cache. When the DNS server answers a query with its cached data, it includes the remaining TTL for the data. The resolver can then cache this data, using the TTL sent by the server.

Negative Caching

In addition to caching resolved queries, resolvers and servers can also cache negative responses, that is, the information that a specific resource record set (RRset) or DNS domain name does not exist. Negative caching can reduce the response time for negative answers. It can also reduce network traffic by reducing the number of messages that must be sent between resolvers and name servers or between name servers.

Negative caching is specified in RFCs 1034 and 2308. RFC 1034 describes how to cache negative responses and makes negative caching optional. RFC 2308 requires resolvers to cache negative responses if they cache any responses. It also describes a way for name servers to forward cached negative responses to resolvers. Just as with ordinary caching, they must also start decreasing the TTL.

For more information about negative caching with Windows 2000 DNS, see "Windows 2000 DNS" in this book.

Resource Records and Zones

To resolve names, servers consult their zones (also called DNS database files or simply db files). The zones contain resource records (RRs) that make up the resource information associated with the DNS domain. For example, some resource records map friendly names to IP addresses, and others map IP addresses to friendly names.

Certain resource records not only include information about servers in the DNS domain, but also serve to define the domain by specifying which servers are authoritative for which zones. These resource records, the SOA and NS resource records, are described in more detail later in this section.

Resource Record Format

Resource records have the following syntax:

```
Owner   TTL     Class   Type    RDATA
```

Table 5.2 describes each of these fields.

Table 5.2 Typical Resource Record Fields

Name	Description
Owner	The name of the host or the DNS domain to which this resource record belongs.
Time to Live	A 32-bit integer that represents, in seconds, the length of time that a DNS server or resolver should cache this entry before it is discarded. This field is optional, and if it is not specified, the client uses the Minimum TTL in the SOA record.
Class	Defines the protocol family in use. It is almost always IN for the Internet system. The other value defined in RFC 1034 is CH for the Chaos system, which was used experimentally at the Massachusetts Institute of Technology.
Type	Identifies the type of resource record.
RDATA	The resource record data. It is a variable type that represents the information being described by the type. For example, in an A record, this is the 32-bit IP address that represents the host defined by the resource record.

Resource records are represented in binary form in packets when lookups and responses are made using DNS. In the database files, however, resource records are represented as text entries. Most resource records are represented as single-line text entries. If an entry is going to span more than one line, you can use parentheses to encapsulate the information. In many implementations of DNS, only the Start of Authority (SOA) record can be multiple lines. For readability, blank lines and comments are often inserted in the zone files, and are ignored by the DNS server. Comments always start with a semicolon (;) and end with a carriage return.

Resource Record Types

Different types of resource records can be used to provide DNS-based data about computers on a TCP/IP network. This section describes the following resource records:

- SOA
- NS
- A
- PTR
- CNAME
- MX
- SRV

Next, it lists some of the other resource records specified by RFC standards. Finally, it lists resource records that are specific to the Windows 2000 implementation and one resource record specified by the ATM Forum.

SOA Resource Records

Every zone contains a Start of Authority (SOA) resource record at the beginning of the zone. SOA resource records include the following fields:

- The **Owner**, **TTL**, **Class**, and **Type** fields, as described in "Resource Record Format" earlier in this chapter.
- The **authoritative server** field shows the primary DNS server authoritative for the zone.
- The **responsible person** field shows the e-mail address of the administrator responsible for the zone. It uses a period (.) instead of an at symbol (@).
- The **serial number** field shows how many times the zone has been updated. When a zone's secondary server contacts the master server for that zone to determine whether it needs to initiate a zone transfer, the zone's secondary server compares its own serial number with that of the master. If the serial number of the master is higher, the secondary server initiates a zone transfer.
- The **refresh** field shows how often the secondary server for the zone checks to see whether the zone has been changed.
- The **retry** field shows how long after sending a zone transfer request the secondary server for the zone waits for a response from the master server before retrying.
- The **expire** field shows how long after the previous zone transfer the secondary server for the zone continues to respond to queries for the zone before discarding its own zone as invalid.
- The **minimum TTL** field applies to all the resource records in the zone whenever a time to live value is not specified in a resource record. Whenever a resolver queries the server, the server sends back resource records along with the minimum time to live. Negative responses are cached for the minimum TTL of the SOA resource record of the authoritative zone.

The following example shows the SOA resource record:

```
noam.reskit.com.  IN  SOA (
                 noamdc1.noam.reskit.com.      ; authoritative  server
                                                    for the zone
                 administrator.noam.reskit.com.    ; zone admin e-mail
                                                   ; (responsible person)
                 5099                              ; serial number
                 3600                              ; refresh (1 hour)
                 600                               ; retry (10 mins)
                 86400                             ; expire (1 day)
                 60        )                       ; minimum TTL (1 min)
```

NS Resource Records

The name server (NS) resource record indicates the servers authoritative for the zone. They indicate primary and secondary servers for the zone specified in the SOA resource record, and they indicate the servers for any delegated zones. Every zone must contain at least one NS record at the zone root.

For example, when the administrator on reskit.com delegated authority for the noam.reskit.com subdomain to noamdc1.noam.reskit.com., the following line was added to the zones reskit.com and noam.reskit.com:

```
noam.reskit.com.     IN     NS        noamdc1.noam.reskit.com.
```

A Resource Records

The address (A) resource record maps an FQDN to an IP address, so the resolvers can request the corresponding IP address for an FQDN. For example, the following A resource record, located in the zone noam.reskit.com, maps the FQDN of the server to its IP address:

```
noamdc1          IN        A      172.16.48.1
```

PTR Records

The *pointer (PTR) resource record*, in contrast to the A resource record, maps an IP address to an FQDN. For example, the following PTR resource record maps the IP address of noamdc1.noam.reskit.com to its FQDN:

```
1.48.16.172.in-addr.arpa.        IN       PTR
    noamdc1.noam.reskit.com.
```

CNAME Resource Records

The canonical name (CNAME) resource record creates an alias (synonymous name) for the specified FQDN. You can use CNAME records to hide the implementation details of your network from the clients that connect to it. For example, suppose you want to put an FTP server named ftp1.noam.reskit.com on your noam.reskit.com subdomain, but you know that in six months you will move it to a computer named ftp2.noam.reskit.com, and you do not want your users to have to know about the change. You can just create an alias called ftp.noam.reskit.com that points to ftp1.noam.reskit.com, and then when you move your computer, you need only change the CNAME record to point to ftp2.noam.reskit.com. For example, the following CNAME resource record creates an alias for ftp1.noam.reskit.com:

```
ftp.noam.reskit.com.     IN       CNAME        ftp1.noam.reskit.com.
```

Once a DNS client queries for the A resource record for ftp.noam.reskit.com, the DNS server finds the CNAME resource record, resolves the query for the A resource record for ftp1.noam.reskit.com, and returns both the A and CNAME resource records to the client.

Note According to RFC 2181, there must be only one canonical name per alias.

MX Resource Records

The mail exchange (MX) resource record specifies a mail exchange server for a DNS domain name. A mail exchange server is a host that will either process or forward mail for the DNS domain name. Processing the mail means either delivering it to the addressee or passing it to a different type of mail transport. Forwarding the mail means sending it to its final destination server, sending it using Simple Mail Transfer Protocol (SMTP) to another mail exchange server that is closer to the final destination, or queuing it for a specified amount of time.

Note Only mail exchange servers use MX records.

If you want to use multiple mail exchange servers in one DNS domain, you can have multiple MX resource records for that domain. The following example shows MX resource records for the mail servers for the domain noam.reskit.com.:

```
*.noam.reskit.com.   IN      MX      0    mailserver1.noam.reskit.com.
*.noam.reskit.com.   IN      MX      10   mailserver2.noam.reskit.com.
*.noam.reskit.com.   IN      MX      10   mailserver3.noam.reskit.com.
```

The first three fields in this resource record are the standard owner, class, and type fields. The fourth field is the mail server priority, or preference value. The preference value specifies the preference given to the MX record among MX records. Lower priority records are preferred. Thus, when a mailer needs to send mail to a certain DNS domain, it first contacts a DNS server for that domain and retrieves all the MX records. It then contacts the mailer with the lowest preference value.

For example, suppose Jane Doe sends an e-mail message to JohnDoe@noam.reskit.com on a day that mailserver1 is down, but mailserver2 is working. Her mailer tries to deliver the message to mailserver1, because it has the lowest preference value, but it fails because mailserver1 is down. This time, Jane's mailer can choose either mailserver2 or mailserver3, because their preference values are equal. It successfully delivers the message to mailserver2.

To prevent mail loops, if the mailer is on a host that is listed as an MX for the destination host, the mailer can deliver only to an MX with a lower preference value than its own host.

Note The **sendmail** program requires special configuration if a CNAME is not referenced in the MX record.

SRV Records

With MX records, you can have multiple mail servers in a DNS domain, and when a mailer needs to send mail to a host in the domain, it can find the location of a mail exchange server. But what about other applications, such as the World Wide Web or telnet?

Service (SRV) resource records enable you to specify the location of the servers for a specific service, protocol, and DNS domain. Thus, if you have two Web servers in your domain, you can create SRV resource records specifying which hosts serve as Web servers, and resolvers can then retrieve all the SRV resource records for the Web servers.

The format of an SRV record is as follows:

_Service._Proto.Name TTL Class SRV Priority Weight Port Target

- The **_Service** field specifies the name of the service, such as http or telnet. Some services are defined in the standards, and others can be defined locally.
- The **_Proto** field specifies the protocol, such as TCP or UDP.
- The **Name** field specifies the domain name to which the resource record refers.
- The **TTL** and **Class** fields are the same as the fields defined earlier in this chapter.
- The **Priority** field specifies the priority of the host. Clients attempt to contact the host with the lowest priority.
- The **Weight** field is a load balancing mechanism. When the priority field is the same for two or more records in the same domain, clients should try records with higher weights more often, unless the clients support some other load balancing mechanism.
- The **Port** field shows the port of the service on this host.
- The **Target** field shows the fully qualified domain name for the host supporting the service.

The following example shows SRV records for Web servers:

```
_http._tcp.reskit.com. IN  SRV 0  0  80      webserver1.noam.reskit.com.
_http._tcp.reskit.com. IN  SRV 10 0  80      webserver2.noam.reskit.com.
```

Note This example does not specify a TTL. Therefore, the resolver uses the minimum TTL specified in the SOA resource record.

If a computer needs to locate a Web server in the reskit.com DNS domain, the resolver sends the following query:

```
_http._tcp.www.reskit.com.
```

The DNS server replies with the SRV records listed above. The resolver then chooses between WebServer1 and WebServer2 by looking at their priority values. Because WebServer1 has the *lowest* priority value, the DNS server chooses WebServer1.

Note If the priority values had been the same, but the weight values had been different, the client would have chosen a Web server randomly, except that the server with the *highest* weight value would have had a higher probability of being chosen.

Next, the resolver requests the A record for webserver1.reskit.com, and the DNS server sends the A record. Finally, the client attempts to contact the Web server.

For more information about SRV records, see the link to the Internet Engineering Task Force (IETF) on the Web Resources page at http://windows.microsoft.com/windows2000/reskit/webresources. Windows 2000 supports the Internet Draft titled "A DNS RR for specifying the location of services (DNS SRV)."

Less Common Resource Records

Table 5.3 shows some other resource records and the RFCs that define them. Many of these resource records are considered experimental.

Table 5.3 Less Common Resource Record Types

Record Type	RFC	Description
AAAA	1886	Special address record that maps a host (computer or other network device) name to an IPv6 address.
AFSDB	1183	Gives the location of either an Andrew File System (AFS) cell database server, or a Distributed Computing Environment (DCE) cell's authenticated server. The AFS system uses DNS to map a DNS domain name to the name of an AFS cell database server. The Open Software Foundation's DCE Naming Service uses DNS for a similar function.
HINFO	1035	The host information resource record identifies a host's hardware type and operating system. The CPU Type and Operating System identifiers come from the computer names and system names listed in RFC 1700.
ISDN	1183	The Integrated Services Digital Network (ISDN) resource record is a variation of the A (address) resource record. Rather than mapping an FQDN to an IP address, the ISDN record maps the name to an ISDN address. An ISDN address is a phone number that consists of a country/region code, an area code or country/region code, a local phone number, and optionally, a subaddress. The ISDN resource record is designed to be used in conjunction with the route through (RT) resource record.
MB	1035	The mailbox (MB) resource record is an experimental record that specifies a DNS host with the specified mailbox. Other related experimental records are the mail group (MG) resource record, the mailbox rename (MR) resource record, and the mailbox information (MINFO) resource record.
MG	1035	The mail group (MG) resource record is an experimental record that specifies a mailbox that is a member of the mail group (mailing list) specified by the DNS domain name. Other related experimental records are the MB resource record, the MR resource record, and the MINFO resource record.
MINFO	1035	The MINFO resource record is an experimental record that specifies a mailbox that is responsible for the specified mailing list or mailbox. Other related experimental records are the MB resource record, the MG resource record, and the MR resource record.

(continued)

Table 5.3 Less Common Resource Record Types ***(continued)***

Record Type	RFC	Description
MR	1035	The MR resource record is an experimental record that specifies a mailbox that is the proper rename of another specified mailbox. Other related experimental records are the MB resource record, the MG resource record, and the MINFO resource record.
RP	1183	Identifies the responsible person (RP) for the specified DNS domain or host.
RT	1183	The route through (RT) resource record specifies an intermediate host that routes packets to a destination host. The RT record is used in conjunction with the ISDN and X25 resource records. It is syntactically and semantically similar to the MX record type and is used in much the same way.
TXT	1035	The text resource (TXT) record associates general textual information with an item in the DNS database. A typical use is for identifying a host's location (for example, Location: Building 26S, Room 2499). A single TXT record can contain multiple strings, up to 64 kilobytes (KB).
WKS	1035	The well-known service (WKS) resource record describes the services provided by a particular protocol on a particular interface. The protocol is usually UDP or TCP, but can be any of the entries listed in the Windows 2000 Protocols file located in *%SystemRoot%*\System32\Drivers\Etc\Protocol. The services are the services below port number 256 from the Windows 2000 Services file located in *%SystemRoot%*\System32\Drivers\Etc\Services.
X.25	1183	The X.25 resource record is a variation of the A (address) resource record. Rather than mapping a FQDN to an IP address, the X.25 record maps the name to an X.121 address. X.121 is the International Standards Organization (ISO) standard that specifies the format of addresses used in X.25 networks. The X.25 resource record is designed to be used in conjunction with the route through (RT) resource record.

Resource Records Not Defined in RFCs

In addition to the resource record types listed in the RFCs, Windows 2000 uses the following resource record types, shown in Table 5.4.

Table 5.4 Resource Record Types Not Defined in the RFCs

Name	Description
WINS	The Windows 2000 DNS server can use a WINS server for looking up the host portion of a DNS name that does not exist in the DNS zone authoritative for the name.
WINS reverse lookup (WINS-R)	This entry is used in a reverse lookup zone for finding the host portion of the DNS name if given its IP address. A DNS server issues a NetBIOS adapter status query if the zone authoritative for the queried IP address does not contain the record and does contain the WINS-R resource record.
ATMA	The ATMA resource record, defined by the ATM Forum, is used to map DNS domain names to ATM addresses. For more information, contact the ATM Forum for the ATM Name System Specification Version 1.0.

Delegation and Glue Records

Delegation and glue records are records that you add to a zone in order to delegate a subdomain into a separate zone. A *delegation* is an NS record in the parent zone that lists the name server authoritative for the delegated zone. A *glue record* is an A record for the name server authoritative for the delegated zone.

For example, suppose the name server for the DNS domain reskit.com, delegated authority for the noam.reskit.com zone to the name server noamNS.noam.reskit.com. You add the following records to the reskit.com zone:

```
noam.reskit.com.             IN      NS  noamNS.noam.reskit.com
noamNS.noam.reskit.com.           IN      A   172.16.54.1
```

Delegations are necessary for name resolution. Glue records are also necessary if the name server authoritative for the delegated zone is also a member of that domain. A glue record is necessary in the example above because noamNS.noam.reskit.com. is a member of the delegated domain noam.reskit.com. However, if it was a member of a different domain, the resolver can perform standard name resolution to resolve the name of the authoritative name server to an IP address.

When a resolver submits a query for a name in the child zone to the name server that is authoritative for the parent zone, the server authoritative for the parent zone checks its zone. The delegation tells it which name server is authoritative for the child zone. The server authoritative for the parent zone can then return a referral to the resolver.

Zones

The DNS standards do not specify the internal data structure that stores resource records, and various implementations differ. Generally, servers use zones stored on that server in plain text, but it is not required. With Windows 2000, you can integrate your DNS database with the Active Directory database, in which case the zones are stored in the Active Directory database.

One common implementation of DNS, the Berkeley Internet Name Domain (BIND) implementation, generally uses the file names shown in Table 5.5.

Table 5.5 Zone Names Used in BIND

Name	Description
db.*domain*	Forward lookup zone. For example, if your DNS domain is reskit.com, then this file is called db.reskit.com.
db.*addr*	Reverse lookup zone. For example, if your network is the class C network address 172.16.32 then this file is called db.172.16.32.
db.cache	Also known as the *root hints file*, this file contains the names and IP addresses for the name servers that maintain the root DNS domain. This file is essentially the same on all servers that use Internet root DNS servers, but must be modified for servers that use private root DNS servers. (A *root DNS server* is a DNS server that is authoritative for the root of the namespace.)
db.127.0.0.1	Used to resolve queries to the loopback address. It is essentially the same on all name servers.

The names of the database files are arbitrary and are specified in the configuration of the DNS server. By default, the Microsoft Windows 2000 DNS server does not use the same file names as a typical BIND DNS server but instead uses *zone_name*.dns. However, if you are porting DNS db files from another DNS server, you can configure the Microsoft Windows 2000 DNS server to use the BIND file names.

The following sections explain the contents of the zones and describe one additional file, the BOOT file, which is used by BIND servers, though not specified in the DNS standards.

Forward Lookup Zone

Forward lookup zones contain information needed to resolve names within the DNS domain. They must include SOA and NS records and can include any type of resource record except the PTR resource record.

Reverse Lookup Zone

Reverse lookup zones contain information needed to perform reverse lookups. They usually include SOA, NS, PTR, and CNAME records.

With most queries, the client supplies a name and requests the IP address that corresponds to that name. This type of query is typically described as a *forward lookup*.

But what if a client already has a computer's IP address and wants to determine the DNS name for the computer? This is important for programs that implement security based on the connecting FQDN, and is also used for TCP/IP network troubleshooting. The DNS standard provides for this possibility through *reverse lookups*.

If the only means to answer a reverse lookup were to conduct a thorough search of all DNS domains in the DNS namespace, the reverse query search would be too exhaustive to perform in any practical way.

To solve this problem, a special DNS domain called in-addr.arpa was created. This domain uses a reverse ordering of the numbers in the dotted-decimal notation of IP addresses. With this arrangement, administration of lower limbs of the in-addr.arpa domain can be delegated to organizations as they are assigned their class A, B, or C IP network IDs. For more information about creating classless reverse lookup zones, see "Windows 2000 DNS" in this chapter. See also RFC 2317, "Classless IN-ADDR.ARPA delegation."

Figure 5.5 shows a branch of the in-addr.arpa namespace.

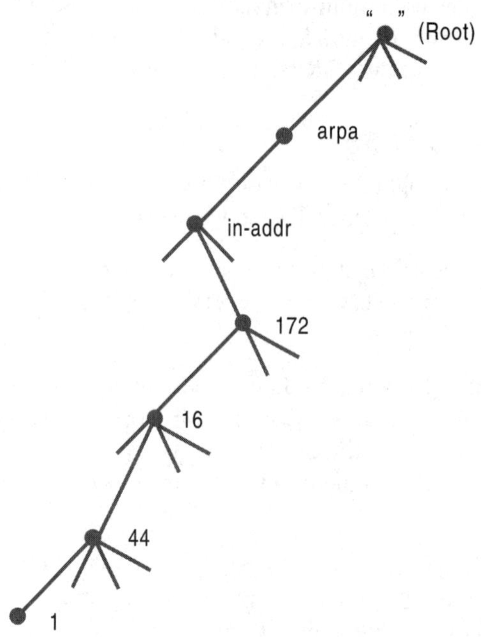

Figure 5.5 In-addr.arpa Namespace

The in-addr.arpa domain tree requires PTR resource records to store and provide reverse mappings for IP addresses of their corresponding FQDNs.

If a client needs to find the FQDN associated with the IP address 172.16.44.1, the client queries for the PTR record of the 1.44.16.172.in-addr.arpa domain name.

Inverse Queries

In addition to reverse lookups, some DNS servers support what is known as an inverse query. Just as with a reverse lookup, a client making an inverse query provides the IP address and requests the FQDN. However, the server does not use the in-addr.arpa domain to find the answer, and it does not query any other servers. Instead, it simply checks its own zones for the answer, and if it does not find the answer, it returns an error message. There is no way for either the server or the client to know whether the IP address is simply missing from the zones of that server, or whether the IP address does not exist.

Because support for inverse queries is optional and because servers often cannot provide a definitive answer, inverse queries are of limited use. Only certain applications use inverse queries, such as earlier versions of **nslookup**.

The Windows 2000 server responds to inverse query requests by replying with the IP address specified in the query enclosed in square brackets. For example, if it receives an inverse query for 172.16.72.1, it responds with [172.16.72.1].

For more information about inverse queries, see RFC 1035.

Root Hints Files

The *root hints file*, also called the *cache hints file*, contains host information that is needed to resolve names outside of the authoritative DNS domains. It contains the names and addresses of root DNS servers.

If your network is connected to the Internet, the root hints file should contain records for the root DNS servers on the Internet. In Windows 2000, a root hints file with current Internet root DNS mappings is installed as the file Cache.dns in the directory *%SystemRoot%*\System32\Dns.

If your network is not connected to the Internet, you must replace the NS and A records in the cache file with NS and A records for the DNS servers that are authoritative for the root of your private TCP/IP network.

For example, suppose you have created two internal root DNS servers (InternalRoot1.reskit.com. and InternalRoot2.reskit.com.). You then create a root hints file on other DNS servers in your network, pointing to the internal root DNS servers. That way, if other name servers receive a query they cannot resolve, they can simply query the internal root servers specified in the file.

The following reskit root hints file provides NS resource records and name-to-IP address mappings for name servers in the reskit.com domain.

```
; Internal root hints file for reskit.com, which is not connected to
; the Internet
.    86400        IN      NS       InternalRoot1.reskit.com.
.    86400        IN      NS       InternalRoot2.reskit.com.

InternalRoot1.reskit.com.    86400    IN  NS      172.16.64.1
InternalRoot2.reskit.com.    86400    IN  NS      172.16.64.2
```

Note The Windows 2000 Configure DNS Server wizard makes a best effort to determine whether the network is connected to the Internet and, if not, creates its own cache file.

Boot Files

Although the boot file is not actually defined in the RFCs and is not needed for a server to be RFC compliant, it is described here for completeness. This file is part of the BIND-specific implementation of DNS.

It is not used by default in the Microsoft implementation of DNS. If advantageous, you can port an existing BIND boot file to a Microsoft DNS server. The Windows 2000 DNS server supports only a subset of the BIND boot file directives, and only for the file type used by BIND 4.*x*.*x* servers.

The BIND Boot file controls the startup behavior of the DNS server. Commands must start at the beginning of a line and no spaces can precede commands. Table 5.6 shows descriptions of some of the boot file commands supported by Windows 2000.

Table 5.6 Descriptions of Boot File Commands

Command	Description
Directory command	Specifies a directory where other files referred to in the boot file can be found.
Cache command	Specifies a file used to help the DNS server contact name servers for the root domain. This command and the file it refers to must be present.

(continued)

Table 5.6 Descriptions of Boot File Commands *(continued)*

Command	Description
Primary command	Specifies a primary zone for which this name server is authoritative and a zone file that contains the resource records for that zone. Multiple primary command records can exist in the boot file.
Secondary command	Specifies a secondary zone for which this name server is authoritative and a list of IP addresses of master servers from which to attempt zone transfer. It also defines the name of the local file for saving this zone. Multiple secondary command records can exist in the boot file.

Table 5.7 shows the syntax of some of the boot file commands supported by Windows 2000.

Table 5.7 Syntax of Boot File Commands Supported by Windows 2000

Syntax	Example
directory *<directory>*	directory c:\winnts\system32\dns
cache *<file name>*	cache cache
primary *<domain> <file name>*	primary reskit.com reskit.com.dns primary dev.reskit.com dev.reskit.com.dns
secondary *<domain> <hostlist> <local file name>*	secondary test.reskit.com 157.55.200.100 test.reskit.com.dns
forwarders *<hostlist>*	forwarders 172.16.64.4 172.16.64.8
slave (follows the forwarders parameter)	forwarders 172.16.64.4 172.16.64.8 slave

For more information about the BIND boot file, see the link to the Microsoft TechNet Web site on the Web Resources page at http://windows.microsoft.com/windows2000/reskit/webresources. On the TechNet Web site, search for the keywords "structure" and "domain name system" and "boot file."

Zone Transfer

When changes are made to the zone on a master server, these changes must be replicated to all the secondary servers for that zone, using a mechanism called *zone transfer*. In the original DNS specifications, only one form of zone transfer was available, known as full zone transfer. New RFCs discuss an additional type of zone transfer: incremental zone transfer. This section describes both types. It also describes DNS Notify, a mechanism by which the master server for a zone can notify the secondary servers of zone changes.

Full Zone Transfer

In a *full zone transfer*, defined in the original DNS specifications, the master server for a zone transmits the entire zone database to the secondary server for that zone. Secondary servers initiate full zone transfers using the following process:

1. The secondary server for the zone waits a certain amount of time (specified in the **Refresh** field of the SOA resource record), and then polls the master server for its SOA.
2. The master server for the zone responds with the SOA resource record.
3. The secondary server for the zone compares the returned serial number to its own serial number. If the serial number sent by the master server for the zone is higher than its own serial number, that means its zone database is out of date, and it sends an AXFR request (a request for a full zone transfer).
4. The master server for the zone sends the full zone database to the secondary server.

If the master server for the zone does not respond to polling by the secondary server, the secondary server continues to retry after the interval specified in the **Retry** field of the SOA resource record. If there is still no answer after the interval specified in the **Expire** field since the last successful zone transfer, it discards its zone.

Note Name servers running versions of BIND earlier than 4.9.4 can send and receive only one resource record per message during a full zone transfer. Name servers running versions of BIND 4.9.4 and later, and Windows 2000, can send and receive multiple resource records per message. This improves the performance of full zone transfers.

However, to provide backward compatibility, name servers running Windows 2000 default to sending only one resource record per message if any secondary servers that are not running Windows are configured for the zone. If you have secondary name servers running versions of BIND 4.9.4 and later, configuring Windows 2000 to send multiple resource records per message improves performance. For more information, see the link to the Microsoft TechNet Web site on the Web Resources page at http://windows.microsoft.com/windows2000/reskit/webresources. On the TechNet Web site, search for "DNS Compatibility," "BIND," and "4.9.4."

Incremental Transfer

Full zone transfers can consume a great deal of network bandwidth, especially for complex DNS configurations. To solve this problem, RFC 1995 specifies an additional standard, *incremental zone transfer*. With incremental zone transfer, only the modified part of the zone must be transferred.

Incremental zone transfer works much the same as full zone transfer. The secondary server for the zone still uses the SOA resource record to determine when to poll the master server for the zone, when to retry, and so on. However, if it needs to perform a zone transfer, it sends an incremental zone transfer (IXFR) query instead of an AXFR query, requesting that the master server for the zone perform an incremental zone transfer.

The master server for the zone, meanwhile, maintains a recent version history of the zone, which observes any record changes that occurred in the most recent version updates of the zone. Then, if the master server for the zone has a newer version of the zone, it can forward only those record changes that have occurred between the two different versions of the zone (the current versions on the master and secondary servers) to the secondary server for the zone. The master server sends the oldest updates first and the newest updates last.

When the secondary server receives an incremental zone transfer, it creates a new version of the zone and begins replacing its resource records with the updated resource records, starting with the oldest updates and ending with the newest updates. When all of the updates have been made, the secondary server replaces its old version of the zone with the new version of the zone.

The master server for the zone is not required to perform an incremental transfer. It can perform a full zone transfer if it does not support incremental zone transfer, if it does not have all the necessary data for performing an incremental zone transfer, or if an incremental zone transfer takes more bandwidth than a full zone transfer.

Even though incremental zone transfer saves network bandwidth, it uses space on the server to record the version history. To conserve space, servers can purge the version history.

DNS Notify

DNS Notify is a revision to the DNS standard (RFC 1996) that proposes that the master server for a zone notify certain secondary servers in that zone of changes, and the secondary servers can then check to see whether they need to initiate a zone transfer. This process can help improve consistency of zone data among secondary servers.

To determine which secondary servers in a zone to send the changes to, the master server for the zone contains a *notify list*, which is a list of the IP addresses for those secondary servers. The master server for the zone notifies only listed servers when zone updates occur.

When the local zone on a master server for the zone is updated, the following events take place:

1. The **Serial Number** field in the SOA record is updated to indicate that a new version of the zone has been written to a disk.
2. The master server then sends a notify message to other servers that are part of its notify list.
3. All secondary servers for the zone that receive the notify message respond by initiating an SOA-type query back to the notifying master server to determine if the zone of the notifying server is a later version than the currently stored copy of the zone.

4. If a notified server determines that the serial number used in the SOA record of the zone of the notifying server is higher (more recent) than the serial number used in the SOA record for its current zone copy, the notified server requests an AXFR or IXFR zone transfer.

Note On servers running Windows 2000, you can configure the Notify set.

Dynamic Update

Dynamic update is a new standard, specified in RFC 2136, that provides a means of dynamically updating zone data on a zone's primary server.

Originally, DNS was designed to support only static changes to a zone database. Because of the design limitations of static DNS, the ability to add, remove, or modify resource records could only be performed manually by a DNS system administrator.

For example, a DNS system administrator would edit records on a zone's primary server and the revised zone database is then propagated to secondary servers during zone transfer. This design is workable when the number of changes is small and updates occur infrequently, but can otherwise become unmanageable.

With dynamic update, on the other hand, the primary server for the zone can also be configured to support updates that are initiated by another computer or device that supports dynamic update. For example, it can receive updates from workstations registering A and PTR resource records, or from DHCP servers. Updates are sent using a standard UPDATE message format and can include the addition or deletion of individual resource records (RRs) or sets of resource records (RRsets). For information about the UPDATE message format, see RFC 2136.

In order for a request for a dynamic update to be performed, several prerequisite conditions can also be identified. Where prerequisites are set, all such conditions must be met before an update is allowed. Some examples of prerequisites that can be set are:

- A required RR or RRset already exists or is in use prior to an update.
- A required RR or RRset does not exist or is not in use prior to an update.
- A requester is permitted to initiate an update of a specified RR or RRset.

Each prerequisite must be satisfied in order for an update to occur. After all prerequisites are met, the zone's primary server can then proceed with an update of its local zones. Multiple updates can be processed concurrently only if one update does not depend on the final result of another update.

DNS Standards

Although the core DNS standards (as set forth in RFCs 1034 and 1035) have been well-established since their acceptance as standards in 1987, numerous revisions to DNS have been made in the intervening years. These revisions have been brought about by additional RFCs and Internet drafts, which are independently authored and submitted to the IETF for further circulation and review before being accepted as standards throughout the Internet.

Table 5.8 lists the accepted and proposed RFC standards that Windows 2000 supports.

Table 5.8 DNS-related RFC Standards Supported by Windows 2000

Number	Status	Title
1034	Standard	Domain Names - Concepts and Facilities
1035	Standard	Domain Names - Implementation and Specification
1123	Standard	Requirements for Internet Hosts - Application and Support
1886	Proposed	DNS Extensions to Support IP Version 6
1995	Proposed	Incremental Zone Transfer in DNS
1996	Proposed	A Mechanism for Prompt DNS Notification of Zone Changes
2136	Proposed	Dynamic Updates in the Domain Name System (DNS UPDATE)
2181	Standards Track	Clarifications to the DNS Specification
2308	Standards Track	Negative Caching of DNS Queries (DNS NCACHE)

Additional Resources

- For more information about conceptual information about DNS, see *DNS and BIND, 3rd Edition* by Paul Albitz and Cricket Liu, 1998, O'Reilley & Associates, Inc..
- For more information about Requests for Comments (RFCs) and Internet drafts, see the link to the IETF on the Web Resources page at http://windows.microsoft.com/windows2000/reskit/webresources.

CHAPTER 6

Windows 2000 DNS

Microsoft® Windows® 2000 DNS is compliant with the standard Domain Name System (DNS) as described in the Request for Comments (RFC) documents of the Internet Engineering Task Force (IETF). DNS is the de facto naming system for Internet Protocol (IP)–based networks and the naming service that is used to locate computers on the Internet. Because Windows 2000 DNS is RFC-compliant, it interoperates with most of the other DNS server implementations, such as those DNS servers that use the Berkeley Internet Name Domain (BIND) software. This chapter describes the new features and enhancements of Windows 2000 DNS and explains how to set up and configure some of the features. For more information about DNS-related RFC standards that are supported by Windows 2000, see "Introduction to DNS" in this book.

In This Chapter

Related Information in the Resource Kit

- For more information about TCP/IP, see "Introduction to TCP/IP" in this book.
- For more information about the Windows Internet Name Service, see "Windows Internet Name Service" in this book.
- For information about Domain Name System concepts, see "Introduction to DNS" in this book.
- For more information about Active Directory, see "Active Directory Logical Structure" in *Microsoft® Windows® 2000 Server Resource Kit Distributed Systems Guide*.

Introduction to the Windows 2000 Implementation of DNS

The Windows 2000 DNS server and resolver have several new features and improvements over those of Microsoft® Windows NT® version 4.0. This chapter describes the following features:

Support for Active Directory as a Locator Service for Domain Controllers

DNS is required for support of Active Directory. You can also use another DNS server implementation solution to support Active Directory deployment.

Integration with Active Directory

You can integrate DNS zones into Active Directory, providing increased fault tolerance and security. Every Active Directory-integrated zone is replicated among all domain controllers within the Active Directory domain. All DNS servers running on these domain controllers can act as primary servers for the zone, accepting dynamic updates. Also, Active Directory replicates on a per-property basis, propagating only relevant changes.

Support for Dynamic Updates

The DNS service allows client computers to dynamically update their resource records in DNS. This improves DNS administration by reducing the time needed to manually manage zone records. The dynamic update feature can be used in conjunction with Dynamic Host Configuration Protocol (DHCP) to dynamically update resource records when a computer's IP address is released and renewed. Computers that run Windows 2000 can send dynamic updates.

Support for Aging and Scavenging of Records

The DNS service is capable of aging and scavenging records. When enabled, this feature can prevent stale records from remaining in DNS.

Support for Secure Dynamic Updates in Active Directory–Integrated Zones

You can configure Active Directory–integrated zones for secure dynamic update. With secure dynamic update, only authorized users can make changes to a zone or record.

Improved Ease of Administration

The DNS console offers an improved graphical user interface (GUI) for managing the DNS service. Also, Windows 2000 Server provides several new configuration wizards and other tools to help you manage and support DNS servers and clients on your network.

Administration from the Command Prompt

You can use the command-line tool Dnscmd.exe to perform most of the tasks that you can perform from the DNS console. For example, you can create, delete, and view zones and records; reset server and zone properties; and perform routine administration operations such as updating the zone, reloading the zone, refreshing the zone, writing the zone back to a file or Active Directory, pausing and resuming the zone, clearing the cache, stopping and starting the DNS service, and viewing statistics.

You can also use Dnscmd.exe to write scripts and for remote administration. For more information about Dnscmd.exe, see Windows 2000 Support Tools Help. For information about installing and using the Windows 2000 Support Tools and Support Tools Help, see the file Sreadme.doc in the directory \Support\Tools on the Windows 2000 operating system CD.

Enhanced Name Resolution

The Windows 2000 resolver generally tries to resolve names with DNS before trying to do so with Network Basic Input/Output System (NetBIOS). Also, it can query different servers based on the adapters to which they are assigned.

Enhanced Caching and Negative Caching

You can now view and flush the resolver cache by using the command-line tool Ipconfig, and you can flush the server cache from within the DNS console. Also, the resolver performs *negative caching*, which stores the information that a name or type of record does not exist. Negative caching reduces lookup time when the user queries for a name that the resolver has already determined does not exist. For more information about caching, see "Windows 2000 Resolver" later in this chapter.

Additional Client Enhancements

The cache can be preloaded with Hosts file entries. Also, the resolver server list can be dynamically reordered to prioritize responsive DNS servers.

Support for a Pure DNS Environment

If all of the computers on your network are running Windows 2000, you do not need any WINS servers. Even in a mixed environment, you do not need to configure WINS on your Windows 2000–based clients if you have configured WINS lookup. By using WINS lookup, you can direct DNS to query WINS for name resolution, so that DNS clients can look up the names and IP addresses of WINS clients.

Interoperability with Other DNS Server Implementations

Because the Windows 2000 DNS server is RFC-compliant, it interoperates with other DNS server implementations, such as BIND.

Integration with Other Network Services

The Windows 2000 DNS server is integrated with DHCP and WINS.

Incremental Zone Transfer

In addition to performing full zone transfers (sending a copy of the entire zone), the DNS server can now send and receive incremental zone transfers, in which only changes to the zone are transferred. This can reduce the amount of time and bandwidth required for zone transfers.

Support for New Resource Record Types

Windows 2000 includes support for two new record types: the SRV resource record, which is used by computers to locate domain controllers, and the ATMA resource record.

Naming Hosts and Domains

In Windows NT 4.0 and earlier, a computer is identified primarily by a NetBIOS name—it is by this name that the computer is known on the network. In Windows 2000, a computer is identified primarily by its full computer name, which is a DNS fully qualified domain name (FQDN). The same computer could be identified by more than one FQDN. However, only the FQDN that is a concatenation of the host name and the primary DNS suffix is the full computer name. In this chapter, the first label of the full computer name is known as the *host name*, and the remaining labels form a primary DNS suffix.

By default, the *primary DNS suffix* of a computer that is running Windows 2000 is set to the DNS name of the Active Directory domain to which the computer is joined. The primary DNS suffix can also be specified by Group Policy, discussed later in this section.

Note You can set and view the FQDN from the **Network Identification** tab of the **System Properties** dialog box, which you can go to by right-clicking **My Computer**, and then clicking **Properties**. To change the host name, click **Properties** and then to change the primary DNS suffix, click **More**.

Suppose that you have a WINS client named Client1. The name "Client1" will be the computer's NetBIOS name. Next, suppose that you replace WINS with DNS on your network and make Client1 a DNS client in the domain eu.reskit.com. The name Client1 is now also the computer's host name, and it is by default concatenated with the primary DNS suffix eu.reskit.com to make the FQDN Client1.eu.reskit.com.

The NetBIOS name is derived from the host name, but the two names might not be identical. The NetBIOS name is a 16-byte string that uniquely identifies a computer or service for network communication. It is used by all the Windows 2000 network services to uniquely identify themselves. If the DNS host name is 15 or fewer bytes, the NetBIOS name is the host name plus enough spaces to form a 15-byte name, followed by a unique identifier, the sixteenth byte, that specifies the network service. If the DNS host name is longer than 15 bytes, then by default, the NetBIOS name is the host name, truncated to 15 bytes, plus the service identifier. If you try to create two DNS host names and the first 15 bytes are the same, you are prompted to enter a new name for NetBIOS.

Note Because host names are encoded in UTF-8 format, they do not necessarily have only 1 byte per character. ASCII characters are 1 byte each, but the size of extended characters is more than 1 byte.

Windows 2000 also allows each adapter to have its own DNS suffix, which is known as a connection-specific DNS suffix. The connection-specific DNS suffix is usually assigned by a DHCP server that leases an IP address to the adapter. On computers that are running Windows 2000, in addition, an administrator can assign a connection-specific DNS suffix to statically configured adapters.

Depending on the configuration, the connection-specific DNS suffix can be appended to the host name to create an FQDN that is registered in DNS. For example, suppose that the computer Client1 has the primary DNS suffix reskit.com, and Client1 is connected to both the Internet and the corporate intranet. For each connection, you can specify a connection-specific DNS suffix. For the connection to the corporate intranet, you specify the name reskit.com, and the FQDN is then Client1.reskit.com. For the connection to the Internet, you specify the name isp01-ext.com, and the FQDN is then Client1.isp01-ext.com. Figure 6.1 shows this configuration.

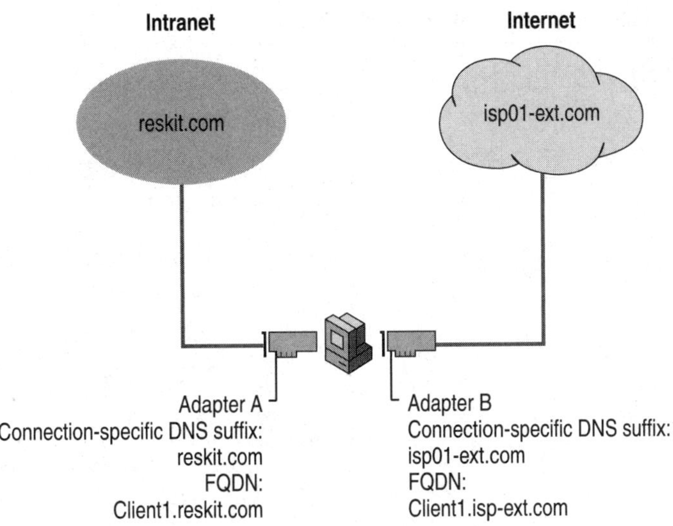

Figure 6.1 Connection-Specific Domain Names

You can specify connection-specific DNS suffixes for statically configured adapters and adapters configured by DHCP on the **DNS** tab in the **Advanced TCP/IP Settings** dialog box. In that dialog box, you can also specify whether the client uses its connection-specific DNS suffix in addition to its primary DNS suffix when it registers its FQDN. For more information about configuring DHCP clients for DNS, see "Dynamic Update" later in this chapter.

Caution If you have any multihomed dynamic update clients and at least one adapter is using DHCP, configure the DHCP server to update resource records according to the request of the client. For more information about how to configure DHCP servers to update resource records, see "Dynamic Update" later in this chapter. If the DHCP server is configured to register both A and PTR resource records, the DHCP server replaces all A resource records for the name it attempts to register. As a result, A resource records that correspond to the IP addresses for the computer's other addresses might be deleted.

Table 6.1 summarizes the differences between each kind of name using the example FQDN client1.reskit.com.

Table 6.1 DNS and NetBIOS Names

Name Type	Description
NetBIOS name	The NetBIOS name is used to uniquely identify the NetBIOS services listening on the first IP address that is bound to an adapter. This unique NetBIOS name is resolved to the IP address of the server through broadcast, WINS, or the LMHosts file. By default, it is the same as the host name up to 15 bytes, plus any spaces necessary to make the name 15 bytes long, plus the service identifier. The NetBIOS name is also known as a *NetBIOS* computer name. For example, a NetBIOS name might be Client1.
Host name	The term *host name* can mean either the FQDN or the first label of an FQDN. In this chapter, *host name* refers to the first label of an FQDN. For example, the first label of the FQDN client1.reskit.com is client1.
Primary DNS suffix	Every Windows 2000–based computer can be assigned a primary DNS suffix to be used in name resolution and name registration. The primary DNS suffix is specified on the **Network Identification** tab of the properties page for **My Computer**. The primary DNS suffix is also known as the primary domain name and the domain name. For example, the FQDN client1.reskit.com has the primary DNS suffix reskit.com.
Connection-specific DNS suffix	The connection-specific DNS suffix is a DNS suffix that is assigned to an adapter. The connection-specific DNS suffix is also known as an *adapter-specific DNS suffix.* For example, a connection-specific DNS suffix might be acquired01-ext.com.
Full computer name	The full computer name is a type of FQDN. The same computer could be identified by more than one FQDN. However, only the FQDN that is a concatenation of the host name and the primary DNS suffix is the full computer name.
Fully qualified domain name	The FQDN is a DNS name that uniquely identifies the computer on the network. By default, it is a concatenation of the host name, the primary DNS suffix, and a period. For example, an FQDN might be client1.reskit.com.

Complying With Name Restrictions for Hosts and Domains

Different DNS implementations impose different character and length restrictions. Table 6.2 shows the restrictions for each implementation.

Table 6.2 Name Restrictions

Restriction	Standard DNS (Including Windows NT 4.0)	DNS in Windows 2000	NetBIOS
Characters	Supports RFC 1123, which permits "A" to "Z", "a" to "z", "0" to "9", and the hyphen (-).	Several different configurations are possible, as described at the end of this section.	Unicode characters, numbers, white space, symbols: ! @ # $ % ^ & ') (. - _ { } ~
Fully qualified domain name length	63 bytes per label and 255 bytes for an FQDN	63 bytes per label and 255 bytes for an FQDN; the FQDN for an Active Directory domain name is limited to 64 bytes.	15 bytes

Note Although you can create long, complex DNS names, it is recommended that you create shorter, user-friendly names.

According to RFC 1123, the only characters that can be used in DNS labels are "A" to "Z", "a" to "z", "0" to "9", and the hyphen ("-"). (The period [.] is also used in DNS names, but only between DNS labels and at the end of an FQDN.) Many DNS servers, including Windows NT 4.0–based DNS servers, follow RFC 1123.

However, adherence to RFC 1123 can present a problem on Windows 2000 networks that still use NetBIOS names. NetBIOS names can use additional characters, and it can be time consuming to convert all the NetBIOS names to standard DNS names.

To simplify the migration process to Windows 2000 from Windows NT 4.0, Windows 2000 supports a wider character set. RFC 2181, "Clarifications to the DNS Specification," enlarges the character set allowed in DNS names. It states that a DNS label can be any binary string, and it does not necessarily need to be interpreted as ASCII. Based on this definition, Microsoft has proposed that the DNS name specification be readjusted to accommodate a larger character set: UTF-8 character encoding, as described in RFC 2044. UTF-8 character encoding is a superset of ASCII and a translation of the UCS-2 (also known as Unicode) character encoding. The UTF-8 character set includes characters from most of the world's written languages; this enables a far greater range of possible names. The Windows 2000 DNS service includes support for UTF-8 character encoding.

However, before using additional characters, consider the following issues:

- Some third-party resolver software supports only the characters listed in RFC 1123. If you have any third-party resolver software, that software is probably not able to look up computers with names that have non-standard characters.
- A DNS server that does not support UTF-8 encoding might accept a zone transfer of a zone containing UTF-8 names, but it cannot write back those names to a zone file or reload those names from a zone file. Therefore, you must not transfer a zone that contains UTF-8 characters to a DNS server that does not support them.

You can configure the Windows 2000 DNS server to allow or disallow the use of UTF-8 characters on your Windows 2000 server. You can do so on a per-server basis from within the DNS console. From the **Advanced** tab of the server properties page, set **Name checking** to one of the following:

- *Strict RFC (ANSI).* Allows "A" to "Z", "a" to "z", the hyphen (-), the asterisk (*) as a first label; and the underscore (_) as the first character in a label.
- *Non RFC (ANSI).* Allows all characters allowed when you select **Strict RFC (ANSI)**, and allows the underscore (_) anywhere in a name.
- *Multibyte (UTF-8).* Allows all characters allowed when you select **Non RFC (ANSI)**, and allows UTF-8 characters.
- *Any character.* Allows any character, including UTF-8 characters.

Note If you enter a DNS name that includes UTF-8 or underscore characters that are not listed in RFC 1123 when you are modifying a host name or DNS suffix or creating an Active Directory domain, a warning message appears explaining that some DNS server implementations might not support these characters.

Using Group Policy to Specify a DNS Suffix

When a Group Policy exists, the suffix set in the Group Policy supersedes the local primary DNS suffix, which by default is the same as the Active Directory domain name. Users can still enter a suffix in the **System Properties** dialog box, but the suffix is not used unless the Group Policy is disabled or unspecified.

If you make the primary DNS suffix of the computer different from the Active Directory domain name, however, you must perform additional configuration in order to enable the modified full computer name to be registered in the DNS host name attribute and the Service Principal Name attribute for the computer object in Active Directory.

By default, the name registered in those attributes must have the following syntax:

<NetBIOS name>.<Active Directory domain name>

where *NetBIOS name* is the NetBIOS name of the computer and *Active Directory domain name* is the DNS name of the Active Directory domain. To enable registration of the modified full computer name, you must modify the access control list (ACL) for the appropriate domain by following the steps in the following procedure. You must also perform this procedure if any computers joined to the domain have host names of more than 15 bytes.

▶ **To modify the ACL to enable registration of the full computer name**

1. Click **Start**, highlight **Programs**, highlight **Administrative Tools**, and then click **Active Directory Users and Computers**.
2. In the **View** menu, click **Advanced Features**.
3. Right-click the domain you want to modify, and then click **Properties**.
4. Click the **Security** tab.
5. Click **Add**, click **SELF**, click **ADD**, and then click **OK**. This adds the SELF group to the ACL.
6. Click the **Advanced** button.
7. Click **SELF** and then click **View/Edit**.
8. Click the **Properties** tab.
9. In the **Apply onto** box, click **Computer objects**.

10. In the **Permissions** box, check **Allow** next to **Write dNSHostName**, and then click **OK** until you have closed the **Active Directory Users and Computers** dialog box.

Caution If you modify the ACL to enable registration of the modified full computer name, any computer in the domain can register itself under a different name.

Windows 2000 Resolver

Windows 2000 DNS includes a *caching resolver* service. The caching resolver reduces DNS network traffic and speeds name resolution by providing a local cache for DNS queries. For troubleshooting purposes, this service can be viewed, stopped, and started like any other Windows 2000 service by using the **Component Services** console; but the caching resolver is enabled by default.

The Windows 2000 resolver performs the following tasks:

- Name resolution.
- General caching of queries.
- Negative caching.
- Keeps track of transient (Plug and Play) network adapters and their IP configurations.
- Keeps track of connection-specific domain names.
- When a server fails to respond to a query, the resolver ceases to query that server for a certain amount of time.
- When the resolver receives multiple A resource records from a DNS server, it prioritizes them based on their IP address.

Name Resolution

Name resolution in Windows 2000 differs significantly from name resolution in Windows NT 4.0. In Windows NT 4.0, the resolver generally tried NetBIOS name resolution first and then DNS name resolution. In Windows 2000, however, the resolver generally tries DNS name resolution first, and then it tries NetBIOS name resolution. Windows 2000 also includes improvements for multihomed computers.

When the GetHostByName API is used, the Windows 2000 resolver first submits the name query to DNS. If DNS name resolution fails, the resolver checks whether the name is longer than 15 bytes. If it is longer, resolution fails. If not, the resolver then checks whether NetBIOS is running. If it is not running, resolution fails. If it is running, the resolver then tries NetBIOS name resolution. For information about NetBIOS name resolution and flowcharts for NetBIOS name resolution, see "Windows 2000 TCP/IP" in this book.

Figure 6.2 shows an overview of the process.

Note The flowchart in Figure 6.2 directs you to other flowcharts in other figures. To locate the correct flow chart, see the figure captions.

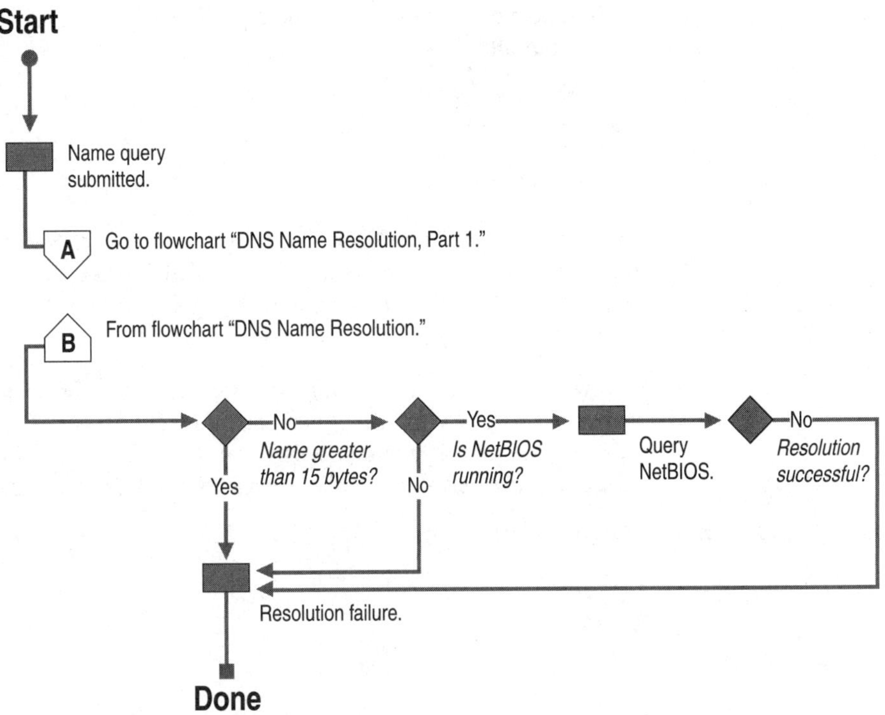

Figure 6.2 Overview of Name Resolution

DNS Name Resolution

When DNS name resolution begins, the resolver first checks what kind of name was submitted. Three types of names can be submitted:

- Fully qualified domain names

  These names are terminated with a period. For example:

  host.reskit.com.

- Single-label, unqualified domain names

  These names contain no periods. For example:

  host

- Multiple-label, unqualified domain names

  These names contain one or more periods but are not terminated with a period. For example:

  host.reskit.com

  –Or–

  host.reskit

When a user enters an FQDN, the resolver queries DNS using that name. Likewise, when a user enters a multiple-label, unqualified (not terminated with a period) name, the DNS resolver adds a terminating period and queries DNS using that name.

However, if the user enters a multiple-label, unqualified name and it fails to resolve as an FQDN, or if the user enters a single-label, unqualified name, the resolver systematically appends different DNS suffixes to the name that the user entered, adding periods to make them FQDNs, and resubmitting them to DNS.

If the user has not entered a domain suffix search list, the resolver appends the following names:

1. The primary DNS suffix, which is specified on the **Network Identification** tab of the **System Properties** dialog box in the properties for **My Computer**. Click the **Properties** button, and then click **More**.
2. If resolution is not successful, the resolver appends each connection-specific DNS suffix. This suffix can be dynamically assigned by the DHCP server. You can also specify suffixes on the **DNS** tab in the **Advanced TCP/IP Settings** dialog box for each connection. You open the **Advanced TCP/IP Settings** dialog box by right-clicking the connection and then clicking **Properties** to reach the properties from the connection, then double-clicking **Internet Protocol (TCP/IP)** to reach the **Internet Protocol (TCP/IP) Properties** dialog box, and then clicking **Advanced**.

If resolution is still not successful, the resolver devolves the FQDN by appending the parent suffix of the primary DNS suffix name, and the parent of that suffix, and so on, until only two labels are left. For example, if the user enters the name **client** and the primary DNS suffix is eu.reskit.com, the resolver will try client.eu.reskit.com and then client.reskit.com.

On the other hand, if the user has entered a domain suffix search list on the **DNS** tab in the **Advanced TCP/IP Settings** dialog box in the properties for the network connection, both the primary DNS suffix and the connection-specific domain name are ignored, and neither is appended to the host name before the FQDN is submitted to DNS. Instead, the resolver appends each suffix from the search list in order and submits it to the DNS server until it finds a match or reaches the end of the list.

Figures 6.3 and 6.4 show how FQDNs are formed. Figure 6.5 shows what happens when a name is submitted to DNS.

Note The flowcharts in Figures 6.3 and 6.4 direct you to other flowcharts in other figures. To locate the correct flow chart, see the figure captions.

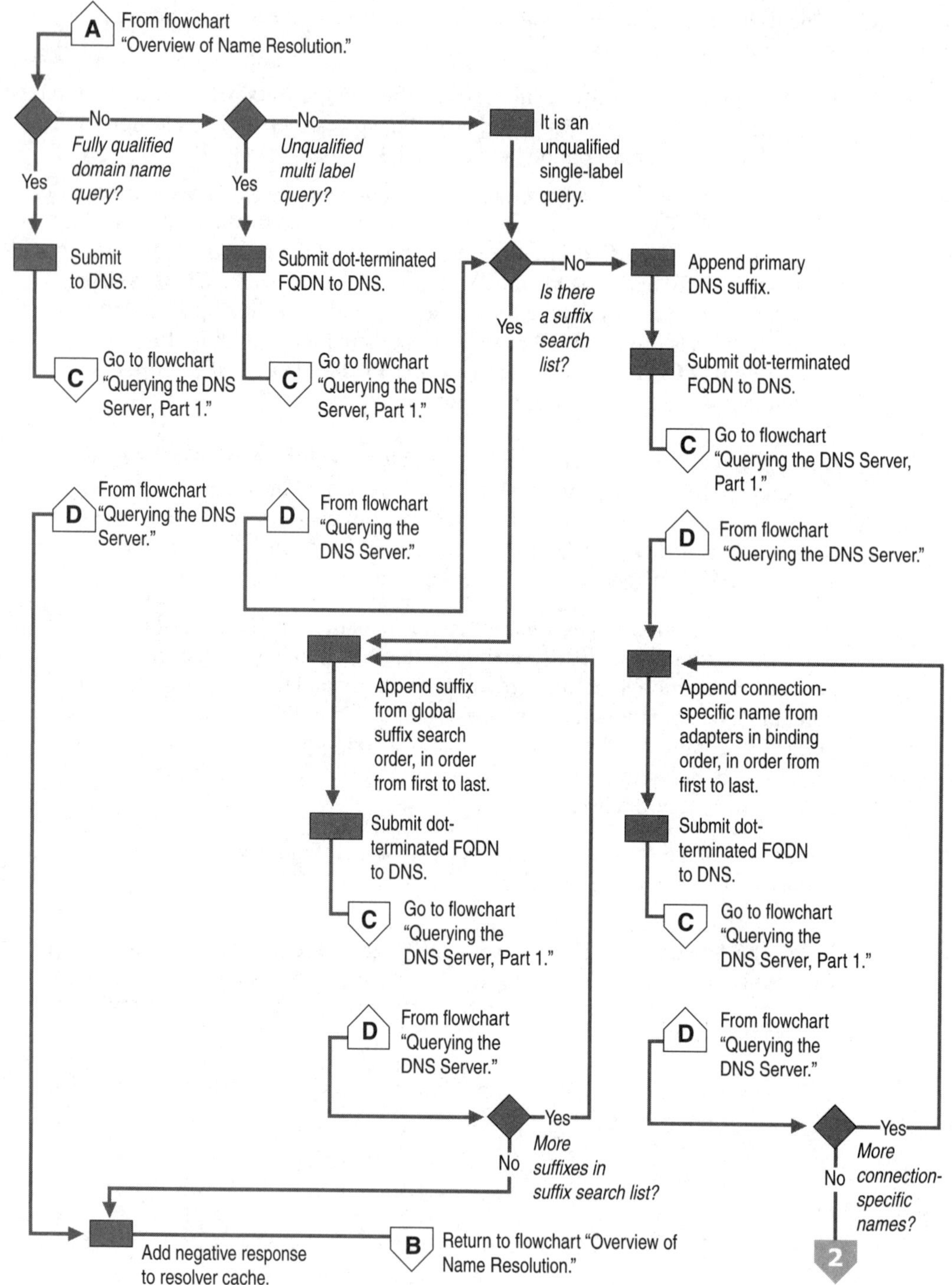

Figure 6.3 DNS Name Resolution, Part 1

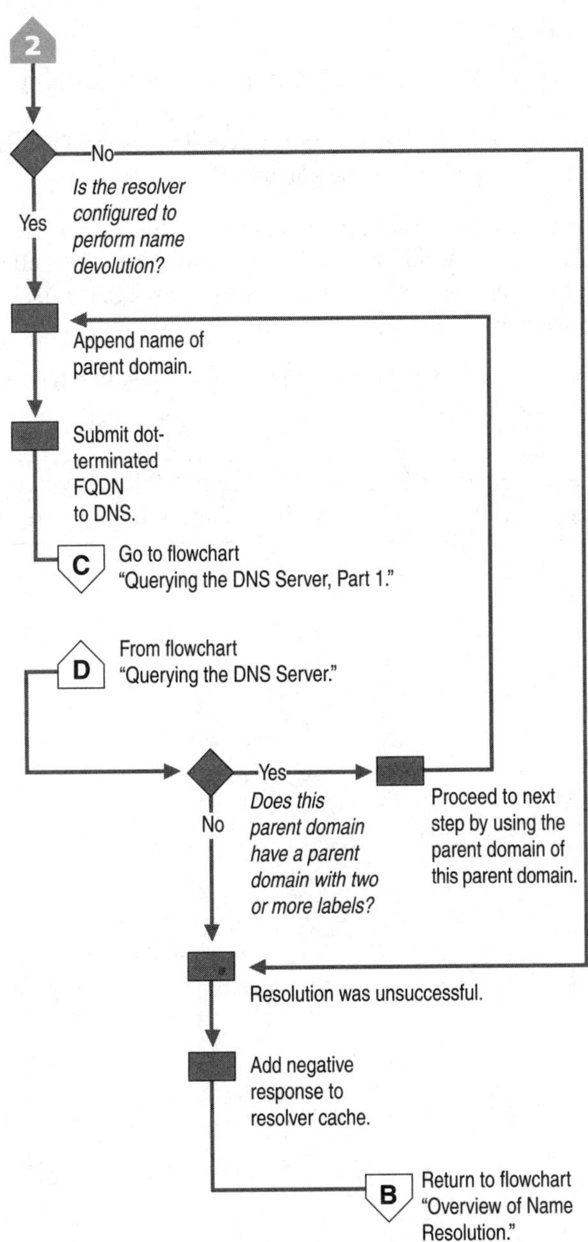

Figure 6.4 DNS Name Resolution, Part 2

DNS Queries

When a name is submitted to DNS, if the resolver is caching names, the resolver first checks the cache. If the name is in the cache, the data is returned to the user. If the name is not in the cache, the resolver queries the DNS servers that are listed in the TCP/IP properties for each adapter.

The resolver can query through all adapters in the computer, including remote access adapters. In Windows NT 4.0, the resolver queried all servers through all adapters. In Windows 2000, however, you can specify a list of DNS servers to query for each adapter.

Figures 6.5, 6.6, and 6.7 illustrate the process by which the resolver queries the servers on each adapter.

Note The flowcharts in Figures 6.5, 6.6, and 6.7 direct you to other flowcharts in other figures. To locate the correct flow chart, see the figure captions.

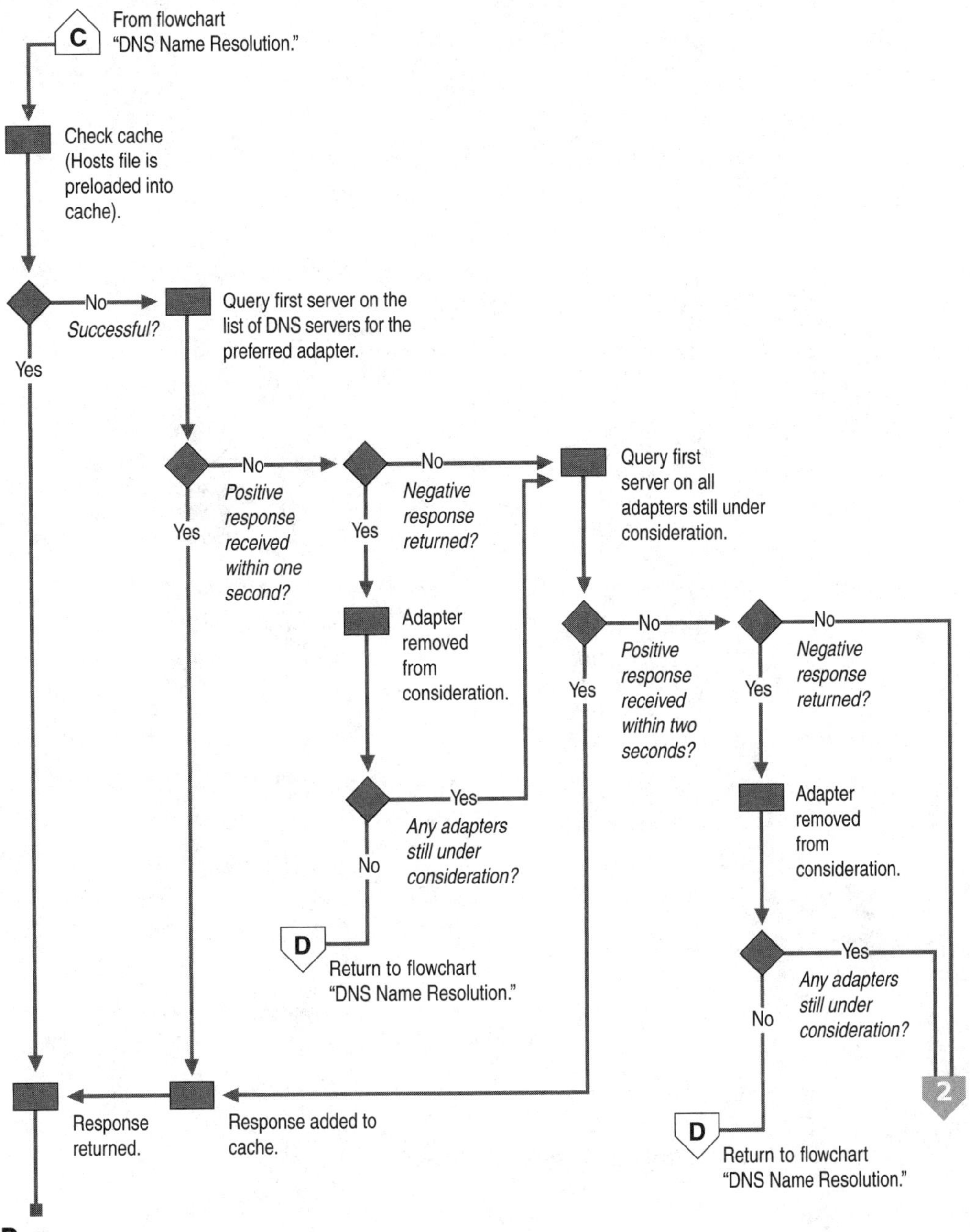

Figure 6.5 Querying the DNS Server, Part 1

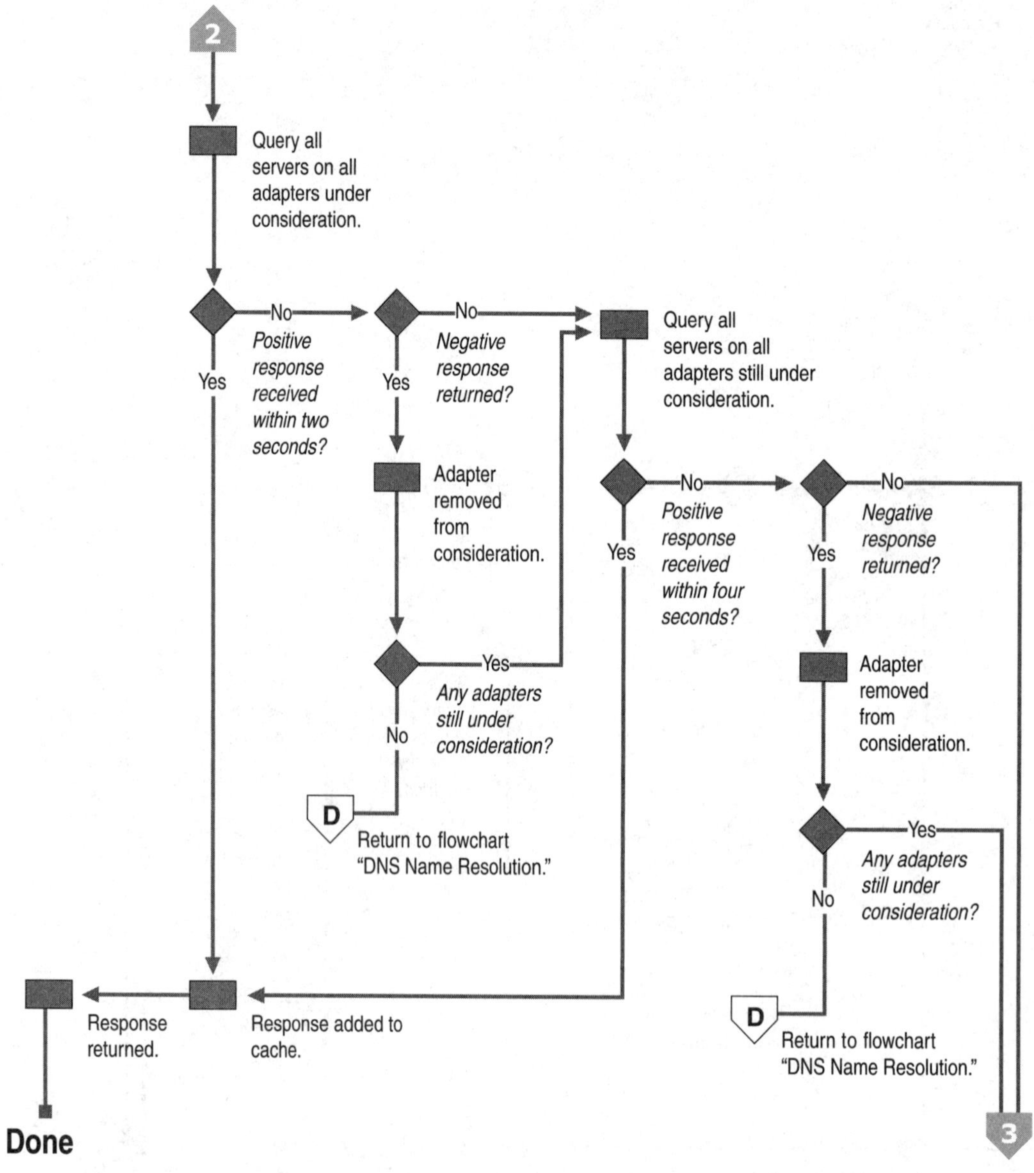

Figure 6.6 Querying the DNS Server, Part 2

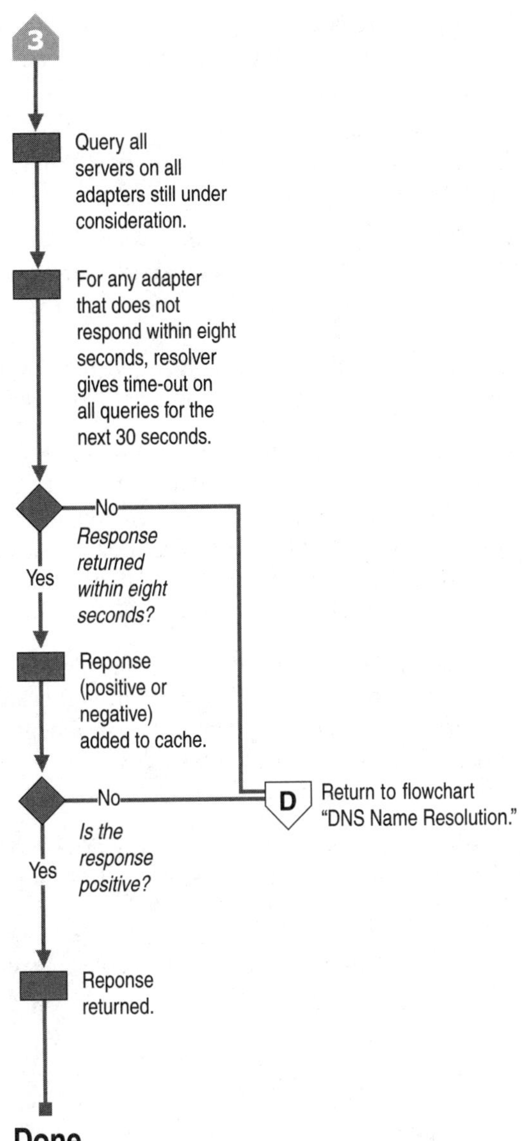

Figure 6.7 Querying the DNS Server, Part 3

The resolver queries the DNS servers in the following order:

1. The resolver sends the query to the first server on the preferred adapter's list of DNS servers and waits for one second for a response.
2. If the resolver does not receive a response from the first server within one second, it sends the query to the first DNS servers on all adapters that are still under consideration and waits two seconds for a response.

3. If the resolver does not receive a response from any server within two seconds, the resolver sends the query to all DNS servers on all adapters that are still under consideration and waits another two seconds for a response.
4. If the resolver still does not receive a response from any server, it sends the query to all DNS servers on all adapters that are still under consideration and waits four seconds for a response.
5. If it still does not receive a response from any server, the resolver sends the query to all DNS servers on all adapters that are still under consideration and waits eight seconds for a response.

If the resolver receives a positive response, it stops querying for the name, adds the response to the cache and returns the response to the client.

If the resolver has not received a response from any server by the end of the eight-second time period, the resolver responds with a time-out. Also, if it has not received a response from any server on a specified adapter, then for the next 30 seconds, the resolver responds to all queries destined for servers on that adapter with a time-out and does not query those servers. This time-out is sent only by computers running Windows 2000 Professional.

If at any point the resolver receives a negative response from a server, it removes every server on that adapter from consideration during this search. For example, if in step 2, the first server on Alternate Adapter A gave a negative response, the resolver would not send the query to any other server on the list for Alternate Adapter A.

The resolver keeps track of which servers answer queries more quickly, and it might move servers up or down on the list based on how quickly they reply to queries.

Figure 6.8 shows how the resolver queries each server on each adapter.

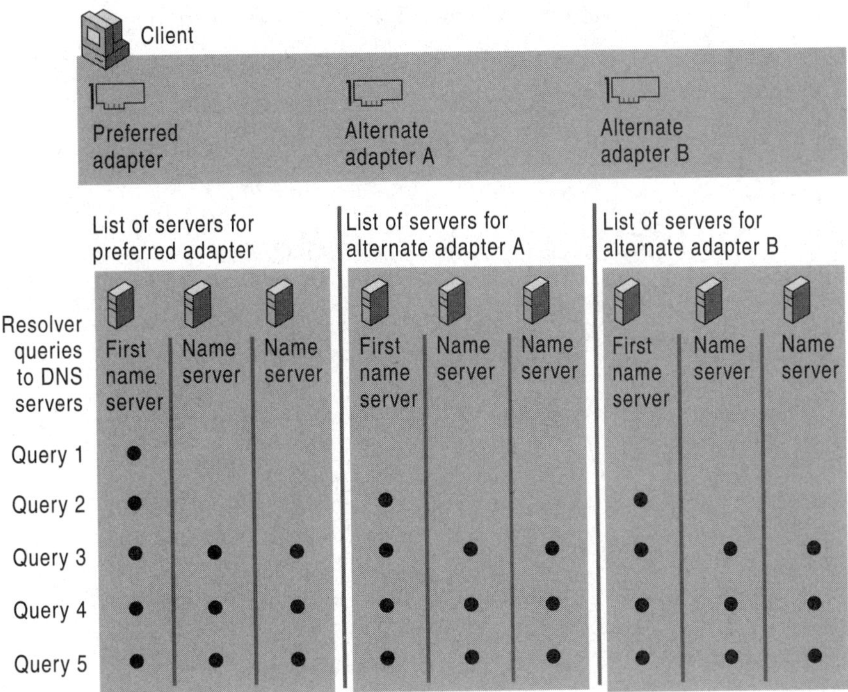

Figure 6.8 Multihomed Name Resolution

Configuring Query Settings

The resolver attaches DNS suffixes to a name that you enter in a query if either of the following conditions is true:

- Name is a single-label unqualified name.
- Name is a multiple-label unqualified name, and the resolver did not resolve it as an FQDN.

Note For information about what happens when FQDNs and multiple-label domain names are submitted to DNS, see "DNS Name Resolution" earlier in this chapter.

You can configure which suffixes are added to queries from within the **Advanced TCP/IP Settings** dialog box.

▶ **To view the Advanced TCP/IP Settings dialog box**

1. Right-click **My Network Places**, and then click **Properties**.
2. Right-click the connection that you want to view, and then click **Properties**.
3. Click **Internet Protocol (TCP/IP)**, and then click **Properties**.
4. Click **Advanced**, and then click the **DNS** tab.

Figure 6.9 shows the **Advanced TCP/IP Settings** dialog box.

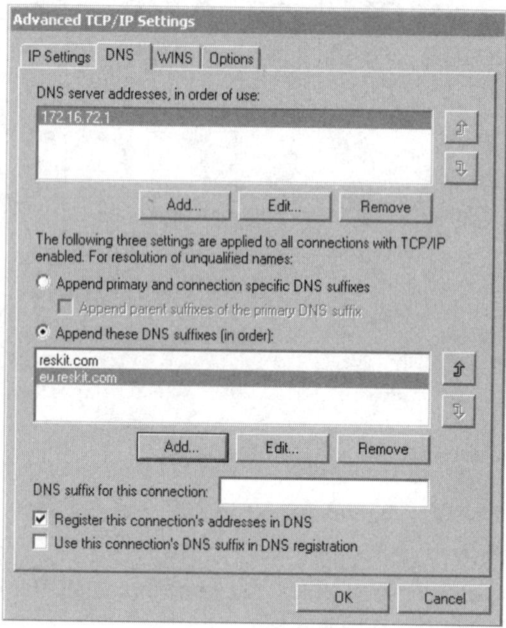

Figure 6.9 DNS Tab in the Advanced TCP/IP Settings Dialog Box

The box labeled **Append these DNS suffixes (in order)** lets you specify a list of DNS suffixes to try, called a DNS suffix search list. If you enter a DNS suffix search list, the resolver adds those DNS suffixes in order and does not try any other domain names. For example, if the **Append these DNS suffixes (in order)** box includes the names listed in Figure 6.9 and you submit the unqualified, single-label query "coffee," the resolver queries in order for the following FQDNs:

coffee.reskit.com.

coffee.eu.reskit.com.

If you do not enter a DNS suffix search list, the resolver first appends the primary DNS suffix, which you specify on the **Network Identification** tab of the **System Properties** dialog box. For example, if your primary DNS suffix is fareast.isp01-ext.com, the resolver queries for the following FQDN:

coffee.fareast.isp01-ext.com.

Next, if that query fails and if a connection-specific DNS suffix is specified in the **DNS suffix for this connection** box or assigned by the DHCP server, the resolver appends that suffix. For example, if you entered the name noam.reskit.com in the **DNS suffix for this connection** box and then queried for the unqualified, single-label name "coffee," the resolver queries for the following FQDN:

coffee.noam.reskit.com.

Next, if you select the check box **Append parent suffixes of the primary DNS suffix**, the resolver performs name devolution on the primary DNS suffix. It strips off the leftmost label and tries the resulting domain name until only two labels remain. For example, if your primary DNS suffix is mfg.fareast.isp01-ext.com, and you selected the check box **Append parent suffixes of the primary DNS suffix** and then queried for the unqualified, single-label name "coffee," the resolver queries in order the following FQDNs:

coffee.fareast.isp01-ext.com.

coffee.isp01-ext.com.

You can disable name devolution by clearing the check box **Append parent suffixes of the primary DNS suffix**.

Configuring Caching and Negative Caching

When the Windows 2000 resolver receives a positive or negative response to a query, it adds that positive or negative response to its cache. The resolver always checks the cache before querying any DNS servers, so if a name is in the cache, the resolver uses the name from the cache rather than querying a server. This expedites queries and decreases network traffic for DNS queries.

You can use the command-line tool Ipconfig to view and flush the cache.

▶ **To view the resolver cache**

- At the command prompt, type the following and then press ENTER:

  ipconfig /displaydns

Ipconfig displays the contents of the DNS resolver cache, including names that are preloaded from the Hosts file and any recently queried names resolved by the system.

After a certain amount of time, specified by the time to live (TTL) associated with the name, the resolver discards the name from the cache. You can view and change the TTL associated with the record from within the DNS console.

▶ **To view the TTL for a record**

1. In the DNS console, point to **View** and click **Advanced** to select Advanced View.

   This step is not necessary to view the TTL for a start of authority (SOA) record.

2. Right-click the record, and click **Properties**.

You can also flush the cache manually. After you flush the cache, the computer needs to query DNS servers.

▶ **To flush the cache manually by using Ipconfig**

- At the command prompt, type the following and then press ENTER:

  ipconfig /flushdns

The local Hosts file is preloaded into the resolver's cache and reloaded into the cache whenever the local Hosts file is updated.

Note The resolver cache and server cache are maintained separately. For information about the server cache, see Windows 2000 Server Help.

The length of time for which a positive or negative response is cached on a DNS client depends on the values in the following registry key:

HKEY_LOCAL_MACHINE\SYSTEM\CurrentControlSet\Services\DNSCache\Parameters

---

Caution Do not use a registry editor to edit the registry directly unless you have no alternative. The registry editors bypass the standard safeguards provided by administrative tools. These safeguards prevent you from entering conflicting settings or settings that are likely to degrade performance or damage your system. Editing the registry directly can have serious, unexpected consequences that can prevent the system from starting and require that you reinstall Windows 2000. To configure or customize Windows 2000, use the programs in Control Panel or Microsoft Management Console (MMC) whenever possible.

Positive responses are cached for the number of seconds specified in the query response that the resolver received, but never for longer than the value of the **MaxCacheEntryTtlLimit** (DWORD) registry entry. The default value is 86,400 seconds.

Windows 2000 supports negative caching, as specified in RFC 2308 with some modifications in the resolver cache. In the resolver cache, negative responses are cached for the number of seconds specified in the **NegativeCacheTime** value (DWORD). The default data is 300 seconds. If you do not want negative responses to be cached at all, set the value of **NegativeCacheTime** to 0.

Note The Windows 2000 DNS server caches negative responses according to the minimum TTL in the SOA record. However, it cannot be less than one minute or greater than 15 minutes. Thus, if the minimum TTL in the SOA record is 20 minutes, the negative response is cached for only 15 minutes. You can use the DNS console or Dnscmd.exe to change the minimum TTL.

If all DNS servers on an adapter are queried and none of them reply, either positively or negatively, all subsequent name queries to any server listed on that adapter fail instantly and continue to fail for a default of 30 seconds. This feature decreases network traffic. It is available only on Windows 2000 Professional.

Configuring Subnet Prioritization

If the resolver receives multiple A resource records from a DNS server, and some have IP addresses from networks to which the computer is directly connected to, the resolver orders those resource records first. This reduces network traffic across subnets by forcing computers to connect to network resources that are closer to them.

For example, suppose that you have three Web servers that all host the Web page for www.reskit.com, and they are all located on different subnets. On the name server, you can create the following resource records:

```
www.reskit.com.      IN  A        172.16.64.11
www.reskit.com.      IN  A        172.17.64.22
www.reskit.com.      IN  A        172.18.64.33
```

When users query for www.reskit.com, the resolver puts first in the list IP addresses from networks to which the computer is directly connected. For example, if a user with the IP address 172.17.64.93 queries for www.reskit.com, the resolver returns the resource records in the following order:

```
www.reskit.com.      IN  A        172.17.64.11
www.reskit.com.      IN  A        172.16.64.22
www.reskit.com.      IN  A        172.18.64.33
```

Subnet prioritization prevents the resolver from using the round robin feature, defined in RFC 1794. Using the round robin feature, the server rotates the order of resource record data returned in a query answer in which multiple resource records of the same type exist for a queried DNS domain name. Thus, in the example described earlier, if a user queries for www.reskit.com, the name server replies to the first client request by ordering the addresses as the following:

```
172.16.64.11
172.17.64.22
172.18.64.33
```

The name server replies to the second client response with the addresses ordered as follows:

```
172.17.64.22
172.18.64.33
172.16.64.11
```

If clients are configured to use the first IP address in the list that they receive, different clients use different IP addresses; so the load is balanced among multiple network resources that have the same name. However, if the resolvers are configured for subnet prioritization, the resolvers reorder the list to favor IP addresses from networks to which they were directly connected; so the effectiveness of the round robin feature is reduced.

Although subnet prioritization does reduce network traffic across subnets, in some cases you might prefer to have the round robin feature work as described in RFC 1794. If so, you can disable the subnet prioritization feature on your clients by adding the **PrioritizeRecordData** registry entry with a value of 0 (REG_DWORD) to the following registry subkey:

HKEY_LOCAL_MACHINE\SYSTEM\CurrentControlSet\Services
\DnsCache\Parameters

Caution Do not use a registry editor to edit the registry directly unless you have no alternative. The registry editors bypass the standard safeguards provided by administrative tools. These safeguards prevent you from entering conflicting settings or settings that are likely to degrade performance or damage your system. Editing the registry directly can have serious, unexpected consequences that can prevent the system from starting and require that you reinstall Windows 2000. To configure or customize Windows 2000, use the programs in Control Panel or Microsoft Management Console (MMC) whenever possible.

Configuring Subnet Prioritization on the Server

In addition to configuring the resolver to perform subnet prioritization for records that it receives, you can configure the server to do the same for records that it sends. How the server behaves depends on the setting of the **Enable round robin** option on the **Advanced** tab of the server **Properties** dialog box in the DNS snap-in, and the value of the **LocalNetPriority** (REG_DWORD) registry entry in the following registry subkey:

HKEY_LOCAL_MACHINE\SYSTEM\CurrentControlSet
\Services\DNS\Parameters\

You can also change the round robin setting from the registry; however, do so from the DNS snap-in instead.

If **Enable round robin** is selected (the default) and the value of **LocalNetPriority** is 1, the server rotates among the A resource records that it returns in the order of their similarity to the IP address of the querying client.If **Enable round robin** is deselected and the value of **LocalNetPriority** is 1, the server returns the records in local net priority order. It does not rotate among available addresses.

If **Enable round robin** is selected and the value of **LocalNetPriority** is 0 (the default), the server rotates among the available records in the order in which the records were added to the database.If **Enable round robin** is deselected and the value of **LocalNetPriority** is 0 (the default), the server returns the records in the order in which they were added to the database. The server does not attempt to sort them or rotate the records it returns.

Caution Do not use a registry editor to edit the registry directly unless you have no alternative. The registry editors bypass the standard safeguards provided by administrative tools. These safeguards prevent you from entering conflicting settings or settings that are likely to degrade performance or damage your system. Editing the registry directly can have serious, unexpected consequences that can prevent the system from starting and require that you reinstall Windows 2000. To configure or customize Windows 2000, use the programs in Control Panel or Microsoft Management Console (MMC) whenever possible.

Preventing the Resolver from Accepting Responses from Non-Queried Servers

By default, the resolver accepts responses from the servers that it did not query. This feature speeds performance but can be a security risk. If you want to disable this feature, add the registry entry **QueryIpMatching** with the value 1 (REG_DWORD) to the following registry subkey:

HKEY_LOCAL_MACHINE\SYSTEM\CurrentControlSet\Services
\DnsCache\Parameters

Caution Do not use a registry editor to edit the registry directly unless you have no alternative. The registry editors bypass the standard safeguards provided by administrative tools. These safeguards prevent you from entering conflicting settings or settings that are likely to degrade performance or damage your system. Editing the registry directly can have serious, unexpected consequences that can prevent the system from starting and require that you reinstall Windows 2000. To configure or customize Windows 2000, use the programs in Control Panel or Microsoft Management Console (MMC) whenever possible.

Setting Up DNS for Active Directory

Basic Concepts of DNS and Active Directory

Active Directory is the Windows 2000 directory service. A directory service consists of the following components:

- An information repository used to store information about objects
- The services that make that information available to users and applications

Like DNS, Active Directory is a distributed database that can be partitioned and replicated. Active Directory domains are identified with DNS names. Active Directory uses DNS as its *location service*, enabling computers to find the location of domain controllers. To find a domain controller in a particular domain, a client queries DNS for SRV and address (A) resource records that provide the names and IP addresses of the Lightweight Directory Access Protocol (LDAP) servers for the domain. LDAP is the protocol used to query and update Active Directory, and all domain controllers run an LDAP server. For more information about A and SRV resource records, see "Introduction to DNS" in this book. For more information about the domain locator service, see "Active Directory Logical Structure" in the *Microsoft® Windows® 2000 Server Resource Kit Distributed Systems Guide*.

For information about how to set up DNS to support Active Directory, see "Setting Up DNS for Active Directory" later in this chapter.

You cannot install Active Directory without having DNS on your network, because Active Directory uses DNS as its location service. However, you can install DNS separately, without Active Directory. If you install DNS on a domain controller, you can also choose whether or not to use Active Directory to provide storage and replication for DNS. Using Active Directory for storage and replication provides the following benefits:

- Increased fault tolerance
- Security
- Easier management
- More efficient replication of large zones

For DNS to function as a location service for Active Directory, you must have a DNS server to host the locator records (A, SRV, and CNAME). For more information about the locator, see "Active Directory Logical Structure" in the *Microsoft® Windows® 2000 Server Resource Kit Distributed Systems Guide*.

You can configure your Windows 2000 DNS server automatically by using the Active Directory Installation wizard, which is a wizard provided in Windows 2000 that installs and configures Active Directory. The Active Directory Installation wizard can perform all the installation and configuration necessary for DNS, and the Netlogon service adds the necessary locator records. For more information about the Active Directory Installation wizard, see "Using the Active Directory Installation Wizard" later in this chapter.

Unless you are using a DNS server other than Windows 2000 or you want to perform special configuration, you do not need to manually configure DNS to support Active Directory. However, if you want to set up a configuration other than the default configuration that the Active Directory Installation wizard sets up, you can manually configure DNS. In Windows 2000, you can configure DNS by using the DNS console. For information about the DNS console and when you might want or need to use it, see "Using the Configure DNS Server Wizard" later in this chapter.

If you are using a third-party DNS server, you must also perform manual configuration. For information about issues related to configuring DNS when you are using a third-party DNS server, see "Configuring Non-Windows 2000 DNS Servers to Support Active Directory" later in this chapter.

Using the Active Directory Installation Wizard

The Active Directory Installation wizard promotes the computer to the role of domain controller, installs Active Directory, and can install and configure the DNS server. For more information about the Active Directory Installation wizard, see "Active Directory Data Storage" in the *Microsoft® Windows® 2000 Server Resource Kit Distributed Systems Guide*.

When you start the Active Directory Installation wizard and choose to create a new domain, the wizard finds the DNS server that is authoritative for the name of the new Active Directory domain and then checks whether that server is going to accept dynamic updates. If the test is positive, the wizard does not install and configure a local DNS server.

If the Active Directory Installation wizard cannot find the DNS server that is authoritative for the name, or if the server it finds does not support dynamic updates or is not configured to accept dynamic updates, the Active Directory Installation wizard asks you whether you want the wizard to automatically install and configure a local DNS server. If you answer yes, the wizard automatically installs and configures the DNS Server service.

During automatic configuration, the Active Directory Installation wizard adds to the DNS server the forward lookup zone that will host the locator records and configures the DNS server to accept dynamic updates. (A *forward lookup zone* is a zone that contains information needed to resolve names within the DNS domain.) In some cases, it also primes the root hints with the names of the root servers. The wizard uses the following process to determine whether to prime the root hints:

The Active Directory Installation wizard examines the TCP/IP configuration of the computer and checks whether the computer is configured to use any DNS servers. If so, the Active Directory Installation wizard queries for the root servers. If it finds root DNS servers, it primes the root hints with the names of the root DNS servers.

If the resolver is not configured to use any DNS servers, the Active Directory Installation wizard queries for the root DNS servers specified in the file Cache.dns. By default, these are the Internet root servers. If it finds root DNS servers, it primes the root hints with the names of the root DNS servers. If it does not find any root servers, it creates a root zone on the DNS server, making it a root server.

After the Active Directory Installation wizard finishes, you are prompted to restart the computer. After the computer restarts, Netlogon attempts to add locator resource records to the DNS server by sending a dynamic update request to the authoritative DNS server. Locator resource records are necessary for other computers to locate this domain controller.

Note You can also invoke the Active Directory Installation wizard by executing an answer file that contains all of the settings that you need to configure. An *answer file* is a file that a wizard uses to provide answers to questions. For more information about the answer file for the Active Directory Installation wizard, see "Active Directory Data Storage" in the *Microsoft® Windows® 2000 Server Resource Kit Distributed Systems Guide.*

Follow the steps below to install and configure DNS and Active Directory. For more information about installing and configuring Active Directory, see "Active Directory Data Storage" in the *Microsoft® Windows® 2000 Server Resource Kit Distributed Systems Guide.*

▶ To configure DNS and Active Directory

1. Log on as Administrator.
2. Check the TCP/IP settings of your computer to make sure it is configured to use a DNS server. If your computer is the first DNS server on the network, you can configure your computer to use itself as a DNS server.

3. If the Windows 2000 Configure Your Server wizard is not already open on your computer, click **Start**, point to **Programs** and **Administrative Tools**, and then click **Configure Your Server**.
4. Use the Windows 2000 Configure Your Server wizard to install and configure Active Directory. The Windows 2000 Configure Your Server wizard asks you questions about your configuration and then starts the Active Directory Installation wizard, which installs and configures Active Directory. If it's necessary, the Active Directory Installation wizard also guides you through the installation and configuration of the DNS server component.
5. When directed to do so, restart your computer.

After you have run the Active Directory Installation wizard, you might need to add a delegation in the parent zone of the zone you created. If this server is a root DNS server, there is no parent zone; therefore, you do not need to add a delegation. However, if there are other DNS servers that are running on the network, you must add a delegation.

▶ **To add a delegation**

1. Locate the zone that the Active Directory Installation wizard created. The Active Directory Installation wizard automatically creates a zone with the same name as the Active Directory domain you created.
2. Locate the parent zone for this zone.
3. On the parent zone, add the delegation.

Using the Configure DNS Server Wizard

In most cases, you do not need to manually configure DNS to support Active Directory; you can let the Active Directory Installation wizard automatically configure DNS. However, you can use the Configure DNS Server wizard to configure DNS if you want a DNS configuration other than the default configuration that the Active Directory Installation wizard sets up. For example, you might want your DNS server to be different from your domain controller.

If you plan to use the Configure DNS Server wizard to configure your DNS server, perform the following tasks before running the wizard:

- If the DNS server is not already installed, install it.
- If this server will not be the root DNS server, configure its network connections to point to one or more DNS servers in your network.

While you are running the wizard or after you have completed the wizard, you must create a forward lookup zone that is authoritative for the locator records that Netlogon will add.

After you have completed configuration of your DNS server by using the wizard, you must perform the following tasks:

- Enable dynamic updates on that zone.
- Unless this is a root zone, add a delegation to the new forward lookup zone in its parent zone.
- Make sure that the server that will be a domain controller has network connectivity to this server.

To configure a DNS server that is not running on a domain controller, you must be a member of the Administrators group for that computer.

To configure a DNS server that is running on a domain controller, you must be a member of at least one of the groups listed in the access control list (ACL) of the MicrosoftDNS container in Active Directory. The group must also have Full Control permissions. By default, the following groups are listed in the ACL:

- DNS Administrators
- Domain Administrators
- Enterprise Administrators

Before configuring DNS, verify that your DNS client settings are correct.

▶ **To verify DNS client settings**

1. Right-click **My Network Places**, and then click **Properties**.
2. Right-click the connection for which you want to configure the DNS server, and then click **Properties**.
3. Click **Internet Protocol (TCP/IP)** and then click **Properties**.
4. On the **Internet Protocol (TCP/IP) Properties** page, enter the IP address of the existing DNS server in the **Preferred DNS server** field. You can also add the IP address of an alternate DNS server in the **Alternate DNS server** field.
5. If you need to specify more than one alternate DNS server, click **Advanced**, click the **DNS** tab, and then enter the servers in the **DNS server addresses** box.

The Configure DNS Server wizard uses the DNS client information to determine whether there are any root DNS servers on the network. For more information about setting the DNS server IP address, see Windows 2000 Server Help.

Also, you must install the DNS server before configuring the server. To install and configure the DNS server, perform the following procedures:

▶ To install the DNS server

1. In Control Panel, double-click **Add/Remove Programs**, and then click **Add/Remove Windows Components**.
2. Click **Components**, and then click **Next**.
3. Click **Networking Services**, and then click **Details**.
4. If it is not already selected, select the check box next to **Domain Name System (DNS)**, and then click **OK**.
5. Click **Next**. Windows 2000 installs DNS.
6. Click **Finish**.

▶ To configure the DNS server

1. In Control Panel, double-click **Administrative Tools** and then double-click **DNS**.
2. Click the DNS server to expand it.
3. Right-click the name of the server, and select **Configure the server** from the context menu. The Configure DNS Server wizard starts and guides you through the process of setting up DNS. In some cases, this includes creating a reverse lookup zone. For more information about creating a reverse lookup zone, see "Adding a Reverse Lookup Zone" later in this chapter.
4. Optionally, if Active Directory has already been installed, integrate the zone with Active Directory. For information about integrating the zone with Active Directory, see "Active Directory Integration and Multimaster Replication" later in this chapter.

The Configure DNS Server wizard prompts you for all the information needed to create the appropriate forward and reverse lookup zones.

The Configure DNS Server wizard also primes the root hints and creates a root zone, if necessary, exactly as the Active Directory Installation wizard does. However, it does not create a reverse lookup zone, so you must do that later. For more information about creating reverse lookup zones, see "Adding a Reverse Lookup Zone" later in this chapter.

If you are creating an Active Directory domain, you must perform some additional configuration.

▶ To configure the DNS server to support Active Directory

1. Make sure that you have a forward lookup zone that is authoritative for the resource records registered by Netlogon.
2. Configure the forward lookup zone to enable dynamic update.
3. Unless this DNS server is a root DNS server, from the parent server, delegate the forward lookup zone to this server.

Adding a Reverse Lookup Zone

The Active Directory Installation wizard does not automatically add a reverse lookup zone and PTR resource records, because it is possible that another server, such as the parent server, controls the reverse lookup zone. You might want to add a reverse lookup zone to your server if no other server controls the reverse lookup zone for the hosts listed in your forward lookup zone. Reverse lookup zones and PTR resource records are not necessary for Active Directory to work, but you need them if you want clients to be able to resolve FQDNs from IP addresses. Also, PTR resource records are commonly used by some applications to verify the identities of clients.

The following sections explain where to put reverse lookup zones and how to create, configure, and delegate them. For information about any of the IP addressing concepts discussed in the following sections, see "Introduction to TCP/IP" in this book.

Planning for Reverse Lookup Zones

To determine where to place your reverse lookup zones, first gather a list of all the subnets in your network, and then examine the class (A, B, or C) and type (class-based or subnetted) of each subnet.

To simplify administration, create as few reverse lookup zones as possible. For example, if you have only one class C network identifier (even if you have subnetted your network), it is simplest to organize your reverse lookup zones along class C boundaries. You can add the reverse lookup zone and all the PTR resource records on an existing DNS server on your network.

Subdomains do not need to have their own reverse lookup zones. If you have multiple class C network identifiers, for each one you can configure a reverse lookup zone and PTR resource records on the primary name server closest to the subnet with that network identifier.

However, organizing your reverse lookup zones along class C boundaries might not always be possible. For example, if your organization has a small network, you might have received only a portion of a class C address from your ISP. Table 6.3 shows how to configure your network with each type of subnet.

Table 6.3 Planning Reverse Lookup Zones

Network Type	Recommended Action	See Section in This Chapter
Class A network	Configure your reverse lookup zone on the primary name server for the top-level domain.	"Configuring a Standard Reverse Lookup Zone"
Class B network	Configure your reverse lookup zone on the primary name server for the top-level domain.	"Configuring a Standard Reverse Lookup Zone"
Class C network	Configure your reverse lookup zone on the primary name server for the top-level domain.	"Configuring a Standard Reverse Lookup Zone"
Subnetted class A network	Divide your network into class B or C networks.	"Configuring a Standard Reverse Lookup Zone"
Subnetted class B network	Divide your network into class C networks.	"Configuring a Standard Reverse Lookup Zone"
Subnetted class C network, owner of class C network manages the reverse lookup zone	Rely on the owner of the class C network to manage the reverse lookup zone.	Not applicable.
Subnetted class C network, owner of class C network has delegated the reverse lookup zone for your network to you	Configure a classless In-addr.arpa reverse lookup zone.	"Configuring and Delegating a Classless In-addr.arpa Reverse Lookup Zone"

Configuring a Standard Reverse Lookup Zone

The following procedures describe how to add a reverse lookup zone for a class C network ID.

▶ **To add a reverse lookup zone**

1. In Control Panel, double-click **Administrative Tools** and then double-click **DNS**.
2. Optionally, if the server to which you want to add a reverse lookup zone does not appear in the list, right-click **DNS**, click **Connect to Computer**, and then follow the instructions to add the desired server.
3. To display the zones, click the server name.
4. Right-click the **Reverse Lookup Zones** folder, and click **New Zone**. A zone configuration wizard appears.

Windows 2000-based clients and Windows 2000 DHCP servers can automatically add PTR resource records, or you can configure PTR resource records at the same time as when you create A resource records; otherwise, you might want to add PTR resource records manually.

▶ **To add PTR resource records**

1. In Control Panel, double-click **Administrative Tools** and then double-click **DNS**.
2. To display the zones, click the server name.
3. Right-click the zone in the **Reverse Lookup Zones** folder, point to **New**, and then point to **Pointer**.
4. To create the PTR resource record, follow the instructions in the dialog box.

Note If you can't select the **Pointer** field because it is shaded, double-click the zone.

Configuring and Delegating a Classless In-addr.arpa Reverse Lookup Zone

Many organizations divide class C networks into smaller portions. This process is referred to as "subnetting a network." If you have subnetted a network, you can create corresponding subnetted reverse lookup zones, as specified in RFC 2317. Although your network has been subnetted, you do not need to create corresponding subnetted reverse lookup zones. It is an administrative choice. DNS servers and zones are independent of the underlying subnetted infrastructure.

However, in certain situations, you might want to create and delegate classless reverse lookup zones. If you own one class C address, and you want to distribute the addresses in the range to several different groups (for example, branch offices), but you do not want to manage the reverse lookup zones for those addresses, you would create classless reverse lookup zones and delegate them to those groups. For example, suppose that an ISP has a class C address and has given the first 624 addresses to Reskit. The ISP can include records in its zone indicating that the name server on Reskit has information about that portion of the namespace. Reskit can then manage that portion of the namespace by including resource records with the IP address–to–host mappings, also known as a *classless in-addr.arpa reverse lookup zone.*

The following sections, explain the syntax of classless reverse lookup zones and describe how to delegate and configure reverse lookup zones by using the preceding example. For more information about delegating reverse lookup zones, see the Request for Comments link on the Web Resources page at http://windows.microsoft.com/windows2000/reskit/webresources. Search for RFC 2317, "Classless in-addr.arpa delegation."

Note Dynamic update does not work with classless in-addr.arpa zones. If you need to dynamically update PTR resource records, do not use classless zones.

Syntax of a Classless In-addr.arpa Reverse Lookup Zone

You can use the following notation to specify the name of the classless in-addr.arpa reverse lookup zone:

*<subnet-specific label>.<octet>.<octet>.<octet>***.in-addr.arpa**

where *octet* specifies an octet of the IP address range. The octets are specified in reverse order of the order in which they appear in the IP address.

Although *subnet-specific label* could be comprised of any characters allowed by the authoritative DNS server, the most commonly used formats include the following:

- *<minimum value of the subnet range>-<maximum value of the subnet range>*
- *<subnet>/<subnet mask bit count>*
- *<subnet ID>*

Subnet specifies which segment of the class C IP address this network is using. *Subnet mask bit count* specifies how many bits the network is using for its subnet mask. *Subnet ID* specifies a name the administrator has chosen for the subnet.

For example, suppose that an ISP has a class C address 192.168.100.0 and has divided that address into four subnets of 624 hosts per network, with a subnet mask of 255.255.255.192, and given the first 624 host addresses to a company with the DNS name Reskit.com. The name of the classless reverse lookup zone can use any of the following syntax lines:

- 0-26.100.168.192.in-addr.arpa
- 0/26.100.168.192.in-addr.arpa
- Subnet1.100.168.192.in-addr.arpa

You can use any of this syntax in Windows 2000 DNS by entering the zones into a text file. For more information about creating and delegating subnetted reverse lookup zones through text files, see the Microsoft TechNet link on the Web Resources page at http://windows.microsoft.com/windows2000/reskit/webresources. Search Microsoft TechNet using the phrases "subnetted reverse lookup zone" and "Windows NT."

Delegating a Classless Reverse Lookup Zone

You never need to delegate a classless reverse lookup zone, even if your network is subnetted. However, there are a few cases in which you might want to delegate a classless reverse lookup zone. For example, you might want to do so if you gave a merged organization a portion of your class C address, or if you had a remote subnetted network and wanted to avoid sending replication or zone transfer traffic across a wide area link.

Figure 6.10 shows how an administrator for a class C reverse lookup zone would then configure its DNS server.

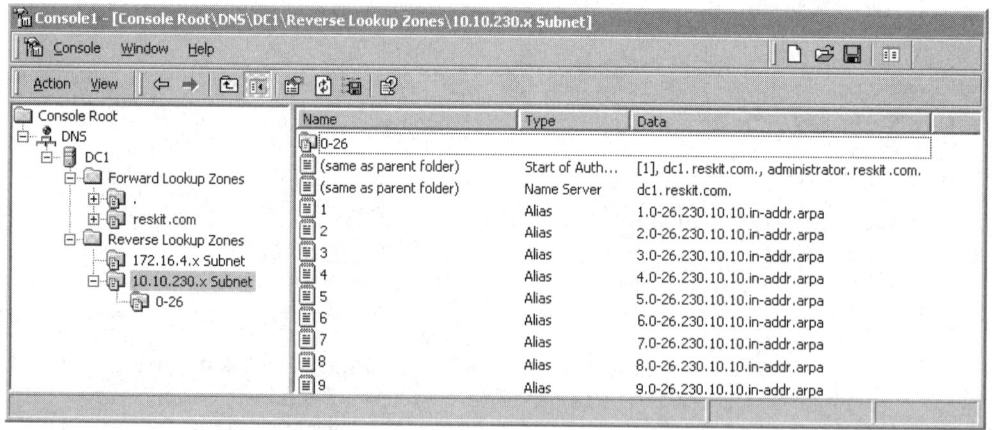

Figure 6.10 Reverse Lookup Delegations

You can delegate and create classless reverse lookup zones from within the DNS console.

▶ **To delegate a classless reverse lookup zone**

1. On the DNS server for your domain, create a reverse lookup zone.

   For the preceding example, create the reverse lookup zone 100.168.192.in-addr.arpa. The reverse lookup zone is added on the server for ISP.com, not Reskit.com.

2. Right-click the reverse lookup zone that you created, point to **New Delegation**.
3. In the New Delegation wizard, enter the name of the delegated domain and the name and IP address of the delegated name server. In the preceding example, the delegated domain is 0-26.
4. Right-click the reverse lookup zone and click **New alias**.
5. Add CNAME records for all the delegated addresses.

   For example, for the IP address 192.168.100.5, create a CNAME record of 5 that points to 5.0-26.100.168.192.in-addr.arpa.

6. Create the classless reverse lookup zone in the subdomain, by following the procedure in the following section.

Configuring a Classless In-addr.arpa Reverse Lookup Zone

You must configure a classless reverse lookup zone if one has been delegated to you. In the preceding example, an administrator for an ISP delegated a reverse lookup zone to Reskit.com, and an administrator for Reskit.com must therefore configure a classless reverse lookup zone. Figure 6.11 shows how Reskit.com would configure its classless reverse lookup zone.

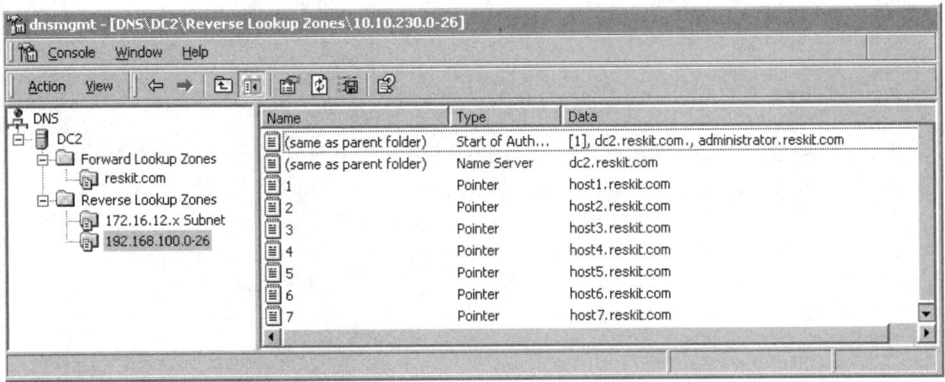

Figure 6.11 Classless Reverse Lookup Zone

▶ **To create a classless reverse lookup zone**

1. In the DNS console, click the server name to display configuration detail it, right-click the **Reverse Lookup Zones** folder, and then click **Create a New Zone**. The Add New Zone wizard appears.
2. When you reach the **Network ID** page, in the field named **Enter the name of the zone directly**, enter the name of the classless reverse lookup zone.

   For example, type **0-26.100.168.192.in-addr.arpa**.

Then add any necessary PTR resource records in that zone.

Active Directory Integration and Multimaster Replication

In addition to storing zone files on DNS servers, you can store a primary zone in Active Directory. When you store a zone in Active Directory, zone data is stored as Active Directory objects and replicated as part of Active Directory replication.

Active Directory replication provides an advantage over standard DNS alone. With standard DNS, only the primary server for a zone can modify the zone. With Active Directory replication, all domain controllers for the domain can modify the zone and then replicate the changes to other domain controllers. This replication process is called *multimaster replication* because multiple domain controllers, or *masters*, can update the zone.

Although Active Directory–integrated zones are transferred by using Active Directory replication, you can also perform standard zone transfers to secondary servers as you can with standard DNS zones.

Active Directory–integrated storage provides the following benefits:

Fault Tolerance Although you can still perform standard zone transfers with Active Directory–integrated zones, Active Directory multimaster replication provides greater fault tolerance than using standard zone transfers alone. Standard zone transfers and updates rely on a single primary DNS server to update all the secondary servers. With Active Directory replication, however, there is no single point of failure for zone updates.

Security You can limit access to updates for any zone or record, preventing insecure dynamic updates. For more information about configuring secure dynamic update, see "Dynamic Update and Secure Dynamic Update" later in this chapter.

Simpler Management Because Active Directory performs replication, you do not need to set up and maintain a separate replication topology (that is, zone transfers) for DNS servers.

More Efficient Replication of Large Zones Active Directory replicates on a per-property basis, propagating only relevant changes. This is more efficient than full zone transfers.

Integrated Storage

When you configure a primary zone to be Active Directory–integrated, the zone is stored in Active Directory.

Figure 6.12 shows this configuration.

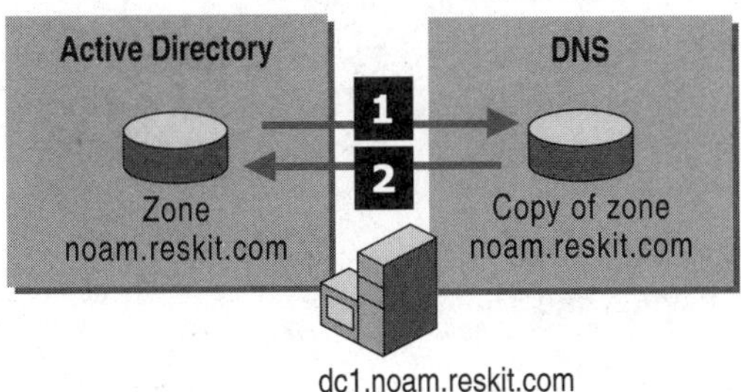

Figure 6.12 Active Directory–Integrated Zone

The DNS server component contains only a copy of the zone. When it starts up, it reads a copy of the zone from Active Directory (step 1). Then, when the DNS server receives a change, it writes the change to Active Directory (step 2).

Through Active Directory replication, the zone is replicated to other domain controllers. Also, through standard zone transfer, the DNS server can send its copy of the zone to any secondary DNS servers that request it. The DNS server can perform both incremental and full zone transfers. Figure 6.13 shows how the same zone can be replicated by using both Active Directory replication and standard zone transfer.

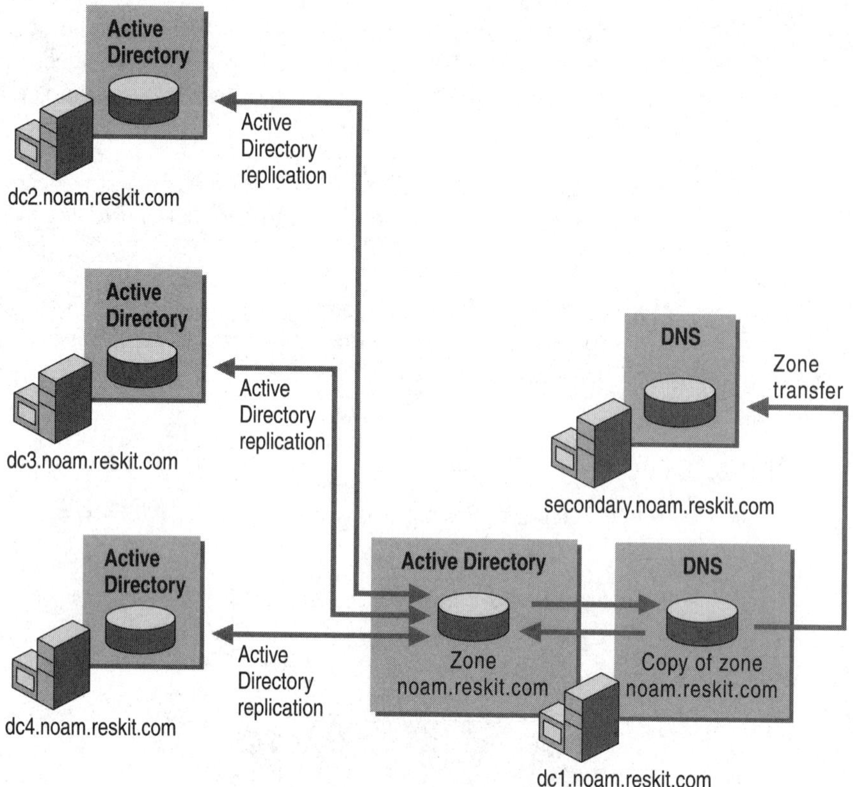

Figure 6.13 Replication and Zone Transfer

By default, when an Active Directory–integrated DNS server starts up, it checks whether Active Directory is available and if it contains any DNS zones. If Active Directory does have zones, the DNS server loads zones from a location specified by the setting of **Load data on startup** in the properties page for the server within the DNS console. The DNS server can load zones from the following locations:

- If **Load data on startup** is set to **From registry**, the DNS server loads all local standard zone files and Active Directory–integrated zones specified in the following registry subkey:

  HKEY_LOCAL_MACHINE\SYSTEM\CurrentControlSet \Services\DNS\Zones

- If **Load data on startup** is set to **Boot From File**, the DNS server uses a BIND-style boot file to determine the location of the zone files.

Note The DNS server automatically writes back to the boot file at regular intervals. You can also update the boot file by clicking on the server from within the DNS console and then by clicking the **Action** menu and selecting **Update Server Data Files**. Alternatively, you can stop and restart the server to update the boot file by right-clicking on the server from within the DNS console, pointing to **All Tasks** in the context-sensitive menu, and then clicking **Restart**.

- If **Load data on startup** is set to **From Active Directory and registry** (the default), the DNS server loads all Active Directory–integrated zones in the directoryand all local standard zone files specified in the registry. (The DNS server must load *all* the files in the directory; you cannot configure the DNS server to load only some of the zones.)

The DNS server also loads the root hints and server and zone parameters from different locations depending on the **Load data on startup** setting. Table 6.4 shows the locations from which the DNS server loads and to which it writes zones, root hints, and server and zone parameters depending on the setting of **Load data on startup**.

Table 6.4 How the DNS Server Loads Zones, Root Hints, and Parameters

	Load Data on Startup: Boot from File	**Load Data on Startup: Boot from Registry**	**Load Data on Startup: Boot from Active Directory and Registry**
Read root hints from:	Root hints file	If available, the root hints file. Otherwise, if the Directory is available and contains root hints, the Directory.	If the Directory is available and contains root hints, from the Directory. Otherwise, the root hints file.
Write root hints to:	Root hints file	Root hints file.	If the Directory is available, the Directory.
Read zones from:	Boot file	Registry.	The Directory (for Active Directory–integrated zones) and the registry.
Write zones to:	Boot file and the registry	Registry and, if the zone is Active Directory–integrated, the Directory.	Registry and, if the zone is Active Directory–integrated, the Directory.

(continued)

Table 6.4 How the DNS Server Loads Zones, Root Hints, and Parameters *(continued)*

	Load Data on Startup: Boot from File	Load Data on Startup: Boot from Registry	Load Data on Startup: Boot from Active Directory and Registry
Read server and zones parameters from:	Boot file and the registry	Registry and (for Active Directory–integrated zones) the Directory.	The Directory (for Active Directory–integrated zones) and the registry.
Write server and zones parameters to:	Boot file and the registry	Registry (for all zones) and (for Active Directory–integrated zones) the Directory.	The Directory (for Active Directory–integrated zones) and the registry.

If you change the setting of **Load data on startup**, the DNS server first writes the root hints file, zones, and parameters to the locations specified in the original setting of **Load data on startup** and then reads them from the new setting.

If the server has loaded Active Directory–integrated zones, it periodically polls Active Directory for changes to those zones. The server also checks for the addition of new zones or the deletion of existing zones.

The DNS server can modify Active Directory if an administrator makes a change to the zone, or if the server is configured to accept dynamic updates and a dynamic update occurs. (Dynamic Update is described in "Dynamic Update and Secure Dynamic Update" later in this chapter.)

DNS servers update Active Directory by using the following procedure:

1. When an update occurs, the DNS server polls Active Directory to make sure that the copy of the zone in the memory of the DNS server is up to date. If not, the DNS server polls for any changes and incorporates those changes in the in-memory copy.
2. Next, the server verifies that all prerequisites are satisfied. Prerequisites are conditions that must be satisfied before records can be updated.
3. Finally, to accept the change, it updates the primary zone data in Active Directory.

Storage Location

The Active Directory directory service is an object-oriented database that organizes network resources in a hierarchical structure. Every resource is represented by an object.

Each object has attributes that define its characteristics.

The classes of objects and the attributes of each object are defined in the Active Directory schema.

Table 6.5 shows the DNS objects in Active Directory.

Table 6.5 DNS Objects in Active Directory

Object	Description
dnsZone	Container created when a zone is stored in Active Directory
dnsNode	Leaf object used to map and associate a name in the zone to resource data
dnsRecord	Multivalued attribute of a dnsNode object used to store the resource records associated with the named node object
dnsProperty	Multivalued attribute of a dnsZone object used to store zone configuration information.

Figure 6.14 shows how DNS objects are represented in Active Directory.

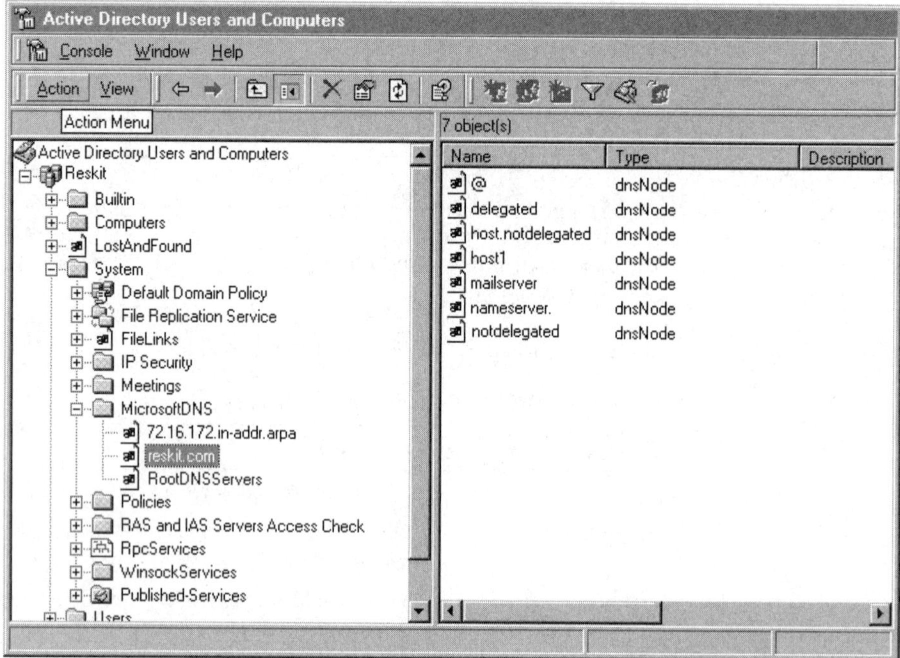

Figure 6.14 DNS Objects in Active Directory

Within the MicrosoftDNS container object are the dnsZone container objects. In Figure 6.14, MicrosoftDNS contains the following dnsZone objects:

- The reverse lookup zone, 72.16.172.in-addr.arpa
- The forward lookup zone, reskit.com
- The root hints, RootDNSServers

The dnsZone container object contains a dnsNode leaf object for every unique name within that zone. Figure 6.14 shows the following dnsNode objects within the dnsZone container object for reskit.com:

- @, which signifies that the node has the same name as the dnsZone object.
- **delegated**, a delegated subdomain.
- **host.notdelegated**, a host in the domain notdelegated.reskit.com, a domain that is controlled by the zone on reskit.com.
- **host1**, a host in the domain reskit.com.
- **mailserver**, the mail server in the domain reskit.com.
- **nameserver**, the name server in reskit.com.
- **notdelegated**, the domain notdelegated.reskit.com, which is controlled by the zone on reskit.com.

The dnsNode leaf object has a multivalued attribute called dnsRecord with an instance of a value for every record associated with the object's name. In this example, the dnsNode leaf object mailserver.reskit.com has an "A" attribute containing the IP address.

You can view the DNS objects from within the Active Directory Users and Computers console.

▶ **To view zones stored in Active Directory**

1. Click **Start**, point to **Programs** and **Administrative Tools**, and then click **Active Directory Users and Computers**.
2. In the **View** menu, click **Advanced Features**.
3. Double-click the Domain object, the System object, and then the MicrosoftDNS object to display the dnsZone objects.
4. Double-click the zone that you want to view.

Although you can see the zone objects from within the Active Directory Users and Computers component, the Active Directory Users and Computers component cannot interpret the values of the dnsRecord attribute. If you want to view the DNS domain hierarchy and associated records, you do so from within the DNS console. For information about the DNS console, see "Setting Up DNS for Active Directory" earlier in this chapter. Alternatively, if you want to view the zones, you can retrieve them by using Nslookup. For more information about Nslookup, see "Troubleshooting" later in this chapter.

Creating, Converting, and Deleting Zones

You can store any number of zones in Active Directory. Zones stored in Active Directory act like primary zones: Any DNS server running on a domain controller in the domain can modify the zone.

To store a zone in Active Directory, you can either create an Active Directory–integrated zone or convert a primary or secondary zone to be Active Directory–integrated. You can also convert Active Directory–integrated zones back to standard primary or secondary zones. This section explains issues you need to consider when you create, convert, and delete zones. For information about how to create, convert, and delete zones, see Windows 2000 Server Help.

Creating an Active Directory–Integrated Zone

Any zone you create is automatically replicated to all domain controllers in the zone. Therefore, do not create the same zone on more than one domain controller.

Caution If you create a zone on one domain controller, and then create the same zone on a second domain controller before Active Directory has replicated the zone, Active Directory deletes the zone on the first domain controller. As a result, you lose any changes that you made to the version of the zone that you created on the first domain controller.

Converting a Standard Zone to an Active Directory–Integrated Zone

You can convert either a standard primary or secondary zone to an Active Directory–integrated zone. When you integrate a zone with Active Directory, consider the following issues:

- For a DNS server to use an Active Directory–integrated zone, that server must be running on a domain controller.
- You cannot load Active Directory–integrated zones from other domains. If you want your DNS server to be authoritative for an Active Directory–integrated zone from another domain, the server can only be a secondary server for that zone.
- There is no such thing as an Active Directory–integrated secondary zone. When you store a zone in Active Directory, all domain controllers can update the zone.
- You cannot have at the same time both an Active Directory–integrated zone and a standard primary copy of the same zone.

Converting an Active Directory–Integrated Zone to a Standard Zone

You can convert an Active Directory–integrated zone to either a standard primary or standard secondary zone.

If you convert an Active Directory–integrated zone to a standard *secondary* zone, the zone is copied to the name server on which you converted the zone. That server no longer loads the zone from Active Directory, but it has its own secondary copy of the zone. It requests zone transfers from whatever server you specified as the primary server for the zone.

If you convert an Active Directory–integrated zone to a standard *primary* zone, the zone is copied to a standard file on that server and is deleted from Active Directory. The zone no longer appears on other Active Directory–integrated DNS servers.

Deleting Zones

If you delete an Active Directory–integrated zone from a domain controller and **Load data on startup** is set to **Registry**, the DNS console asks you whether you also want to delete the zone from Active Directory. If you click **Yes**, the zone is completely deleted from Active Directory and is no longer available to be loaded onto any domain controllers. If you click **No**, the zone is removed from the registry but remains in Active Directory. The next time that the DNS server polls the directory for changes, if **Load data on startup**, on the **Advanced** tab of the DNS server properties page in the DNS console, is set to **From Active Directory and registry**, the zone reappears. If **Load data on startup** is set to **Registry**, on the other hand, the zone does not reappear.

If you delete a standard secondary zone from a domain controller, it is generally deleted from that domain controller. However, if a corresponding Active Directory–integrated zone exists, and you have configured the DNS server to load data on startup from Active Directory and the registry, the zone reappears as an Active Directory–integrated primary zone. You can then delete the Active Directory–integrated zone from the computer or from Active Directory.

Creating a Secondary Copy of an Active Directory–Integrated Zone

It is possible to integrate a zone in Active Directory and then add a secondary copy of the zone on another DNS server. You might want to create a secondary copy of an Active Directory–integrated zone; for example, if you have a remote site from which your users need to be able to resolve names, but you do not want to increase your network traffic by adding a domain controller, you might want to create a secondary copy of the zone.

Preventing Problems When Converting or Deleting Zones

When you delete a zone, or convert an Active Directory–integrated zone to a standard secondary zone, you can cause configuration errors. For example, if you delete a copy of the zone from a server and a secondary server is configured to pull zone transfers from that server, the secondary server is no longer able to pull zone transfers.

In another example, if you convert an Active Directory–integrated zone to a standard *primary* zone, the DNS server loading the new primary zone becomes the single master of the zone. Therefore, Active Directory removes the converted zone from Active Directory, which means that the zone is deleted from all domain controllers.

This can cause problems for secondary servers in some configurations. For example, suppose domain the noam.reskit.com has two Active Directory–integrated name servers, DC1.noam.reskit.com and DC2.noam.reskit.com; the domain has one secondary name server, SecondaryNS.noam.reskit.com, that has a secondary copy of the zone for noam.reskit.com and that points to DC2.noam.reskit.com as the master server for the zone. Figure 6.15 shows this configuration.

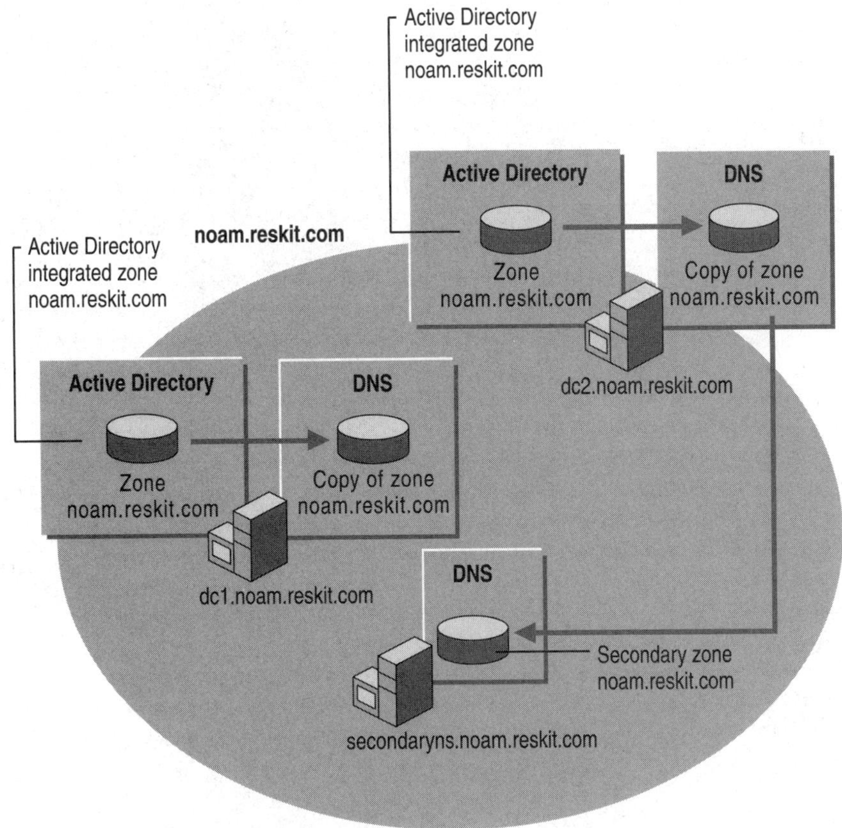

Figure 6.15 Sample Domain Structure

Now, suppose that a user with the proper permissions logs on to DC1.noam.reskit.com and converts the zone from an Active Directory–integrated zone to a standard primary zone. As Figure 6.16 shows, DC1.noam.reskit.com will have a standard primary zone, and DC2.noam.reskit.com will not have a copy of the zone. Even though the zone is deleted from DC2.noam.reskit.com, SecondaryNS.noam.reskit.com still points to DC2.noam.reskit.com as the master server from the zone, and SecondaryNS.noam.reskit.com has no way to get a copy of the zone by using zone transfers.

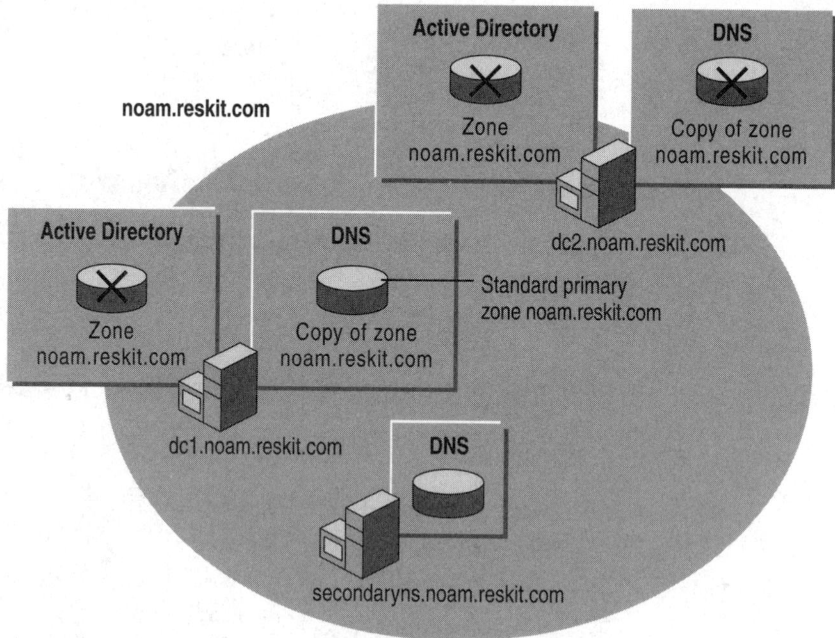

Figure 6.16 Orphaned Secondary Server

To prevent this problem, be sure to update all secondary servers for the zone that you are converting from an Active Directory–integrated zone to a standard primary zone.

This problem occurs only if you delete a zone from a server or you are converting an Active Directory–integrated zone to a standard primary zone, and a secondary server is pointing at a server from which the zone was deleted. The problem will not occur if you are converting an Active Directory–integrated zone to a standard secondary zone, because converting an Active Directory–integrated zone to a standard secondary does not cause the zone to be deleted from any server.

Multimaster Replication

Active Directory supports *multimaster replication*, which is replication in which any domain controller can send or receive updates of information stored in Active Directory. Replication processing is performed on a per-property basis, which means that only relevant changes are propagated. Replication processing differs from DNS full zone transfers, in which the entire zone is propagated. Replication processing also differs from incremental zone transfers, in which the server transfers all changes made since the last change. With Active Directory replication, however, only the final result of all changes to a record is sent.

When you store a primary zone in Active Directory, the zone information is replicated to all domain controllers within the Active Directory domain. Every DNS server running on a domain controller is then authoritative for that zone and can update it.

Name Collisions

Because all domain controllers in the domain can make changes to the same zone, it is possible for someone to update a property of an Active Directory object on one domain controller and someone else to update the same property on another domain controller simultaneously (or nearly simultaneously), thus making the information about the property on one domain controller inconsistent with that on the other domain controller. When a property changes in a second domain controller before a change from the first server replica has been propagated, a *replication collision* occurs.

Replication collisions can affect Active Directory–integrated DNS zones. Suppose that the same name is simultaneously created within the same domain and on two different domain controllers. The changes replicate, and Active Directory determines that there are two different dnsNode objects that have the same name. To solve the problem, the replication subsystem of Active Directory changes the name of the object that was created first by adding to the name a special character and a globally unique identifier (GUID), which is a unique 128-bit number that Active Directory associates with an object to make the object unique. This "disambiguates" the name of the object so that the two objects have different names. The next time that the DNS server pulls changes from Active Directory, the DNS server deletes the copy of the host object with the GUID. Thus, DNS accepts the last name to be created.

If you simultaneously modify a name object on two different server replicas, Active Directory must decide which change (attribute value) will be accepted and which will be discarded. To do so, Active Directory selects the attribute value that has the highest version number. If the version numbers are the same, Active Directory selects the attribute value that has the latest timestamp. Thus, DNS accepts the second change. For more information about replication collisions, see "Active Directory Replication" in the *Microsoft® Windows® 2000 Server Resource Kit Distributed Systems Guide*.

Causing Immediate Replication

When setting up DNS or troubleshooting replicas, you might not want to wait for the normal replication cycle. If so, you can cause replication to take place immediately. Keep in mind that your network performance affects how long it takes to update the target domain controller.

▶ **To cause immediate replication**

1. Click **Start**, point to **Programs**, point to **Administrative Tools**, and then click **Active Directory Sites and Services**.
2. Double-click the **Sites** icon to expand it.

   All sites are displayed—including the first site, labeled **Default-First-Site-Name**—and any other site that has been manually configured.
3. Double-click the site that you want to expand.
4. Under the site you want, double-click the **Servers** icon to expand it, and then expand the icon for the computer. The **NTDS Settings** icon is displayed.
5. Click the **NTDS Settings** icon.

   One or more objects are listed in the right pane. One of those objects is a link to the domain controller on which you want to cause immediate replication.
6. Right-click the object that links to the domain controller on which you want to cause immediate replication, and then click **Replicate Now**.

Dynamic Update and Secure Dynamic Update

Windows 2000 supports both dynamic update, defined in RFC 2136, and secure dynamic update, defined in the IETF Internet-Draft "GSS Algorithm for TSIG (GSS-TSIG)."

With dynamic update, clients can automatically send updates to the name server that is authoritative for the record they want to change. The authoritative name server then checks to make sure that certain prerequisites have been met. *Prerequisites* are resource records that must be present or absent before records can be updated. For more information about prerequisites, see "Introduction to DNS" in this book. If the prerequisites have been met, the authoritative name server makes the change. The change can be adding records, deleting records, or modifying records.

Note Both clients and servers can send dynamic updates.

Dynamic update provides the following benefits:

- Enables clients, including DHCP clients, to dynamically register A and PTR resource records with a primary server. This reduces the administrative resources needed to manually manage those records.
- Enables DHCP servers to register A and PTR resource records on behalf of DHCP clients. This reduces the time needed to manually manage those records and provides support for DHCP clients that cannot perform dynamic updates.
- Simplifies the setup of Active Directory by allowing domain controllers to be dynamically registered by using SRV records.

Secure dynamic update works like dynamic update, with the following exception: the authoritative name server accepts updates only from clients and servers that are authorized to make dynamic updates to the dnsZone and dnsNode objects.

Secure dynamic update provides the following benefits:

- Protects zones and resource records from being modified by users without authorization.
- Enables you to specify exactly which users and groups can modify zones and resource records.

Note Any primary zone can be configured for dynamic update. However, only Active Directory–integrated zones can be configured for secure dynamic update.

By default, the dynamic update client attempts a dynamic update first, and if it fails, negotiates a secure dynamic update. However, you can also configure it to always attempt insecure dynamic update or to always attempt secure dynamic update by adding the **UpdateSecurityLevel** registry entry to the following subkey:

HKEY_LOCAL_MACHINE\SYSTEM\CurrentControlSet
\Services\Tcpip\Parameters

The value of **UpdateSecurityLevel** can be set to the decimal values 0, 16, or 256, which configure security as follows:

- *256*. Specifies the use of secure dynamic update only.
- *16*. Specifies the use of insecure dynamic update only.
- *0*. Specifies the use of secure dynamic update when an insecure dynamic update is refused. This is the default value.

Caution If you disable secure dynamic update, the client is not able to perform updates on zones that have been configured for secure dynamic update.

Also, if you configure a zone to use only secure dynamic update, make sure that the DHCP servers that update records in the zone are not installed on domain controllers. Otherwise, the DHCP server that performs registration of A resource records on behalf of any of its clients can take ownership of names that belong to computers that register their own records.

Dynamic Update

This section describes the Windows 2000 implementation of dynamic update. For information about the dynamic update standard specified in RFC 2136, see "Introduction to DNS" in this book.

Note Dynamic updates can be sent on behalf of different services such as the DHCP client, the DHCP server, Netlogon, and cluster services. The following sections describe only dynamic updates performed by the DHCP client and server.

In Windows 2000, clients can send dynamic updates for three different types of network adapters: DHCP adapters, statically configured adapters, and remote access adapters. Regardless of which adapter is used, the DHCP client service sends dynamic updates to the authoritative DNS server. The DHCP client service runs on all computers regardless of whether they are configured as DHCP clients.

By default, the dynamic update client dynamically registers its A resource records and possibly all of its PTR resource records every 24 hours or whenever any of the following events occur:

- The TCP/IP configuration is changed.
- The DHCP address is renewed or a new lease is obtained.
- A Plug and Play event occurs.
- An IP address is added or removed from the computer when the user changes or adds an IP address for a static adapter. (The user does not need to restart the computer for the dynamic update client to register the name–to–IP address mappings.)

By default, the dynamic update client automatically deregisters name–to–IP address mappings whenever the DHCP lease expires. You can configure the client not to register its name and IP address in DNS. If you configure the client not to automatically register name–to–IP address mappings and the DHCP server is running Windows 2000, and it is configured to register DNS resource records on behalf on clients that are running versions of Windows earlier than Windows 2000, the DHCP server attempts to update the mappings instead.

▶ **To prevent the client from registering name–to–IP address mappings**

1. Double-click the **Network** icon in Control Panel.
2. Right-click the icon for the connection on which you want to disable registration of name–to–IP address mappings, and then click **Properties**.
3. Click **Internet Protocol (TCP/IP)**, and then click **Properties**.
4. Click **Advanced**, and then click the **DNS** tab.
5. Clear the check box **Register this connection's address in DNS**.

You can force a re-registration by using the command-line tool Ipconfig. For Windows 2000–based clients, type the following at the command prompt:

ipconfig /registerdns

For Windows NT 4.0–based clients, type the following:

ipconfig /release
ipconfig /renew

For Microsoft® Windows® 98–based and Microsoft® Windows® 95–based clients, type the following:

winipcfg /renew

Dynamic Update Process

In a dynamic update, the following events occur:

1. The client queries its local name server (using the process described in "DNS Queries," earlier in this chapter) to find the primary name server and the zone that is authoritative for the name it is updating. The local name server then performs the standard name resolution process to discover the primary name server that is authoritative for the name. (The local name server can also be the server that is authoritative for the name.) Then it responds with the name of the authoritative server and zone.
2. The client sends a dynamic update request to the primary server that is authoritative for the zone. The dynamic update request can include a list of prerequisites that must be fulfilled before the update can be made. The authoritative server then begins the dynamic update process. (For information about what happens if the zone has been configured for secure dynamic update, see "Secure Dynamic Update" later in this chapter.) The authoritative server then checks whether the prerequisites have been fulfilled. If they have, the server performs the update, then replies to the client.

Figure 6.17 shows a typical dynamic update process.

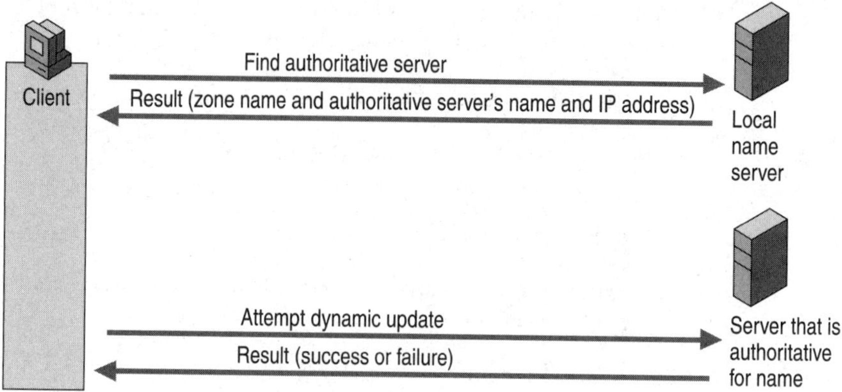

Figure 6.17 Dynamic Update Process

Updates can fail for the following reasons:

- The primary server that is authoritative for the name does not respond.

  The primary server might not respond if it is down or if the local name server has an incorrect or outdated name server listed in its SOA resource record. DNS servers with standard zones (including secondary servers for Active Directory–integrated zones) can cause problems by sending incorrect or outdated SOA records when dynamic update clients request them. However, DNS servers with Active Directory–integrated zones always include their name in the SOA records, so DNS servers with Active Directory–integrated zones do not send incorrect or outdated SOA records.

  If the primary server does not respond but the zone is replicated through multimaster replication, the client attempts to register the name with the other primary DNS servers that are authoritative for the name.

  If the update fails because the server is not available, the client logs a message in the event log, which you can view by using Event Viewer. You can also configure the server log, Dns.log, to show a failure. For more information about Event Viewer, see "Troubleshooting" later in this chapter.

- The server is not accepting dynamic updates because the zone is being transferred.
- The server accepts only secure dynamic updates, and the insecure dynamic update operation failed.

  For more information about secure dynamic update, see "Secure Dynamic Update" later in this chapter.

- The prerequisites have not been met. For example, the dynamic update client might be trying to update a name for which no records currently exist.

The following sections describe the dynamic update process for adapters configured by DHCP, statically configured adapters (adapters for which a user or administrator has manually entered the IP address), and remote access adapters.

DHCP Clients and Servers

Windows 2000 DHCP clients are dynamic update–aware and can initiate the dynamic update process. A DHCP client negotiates the process of dynamic update with the DHCP server when the client leases an IP address or renews the lease, determining which computer will update the A and PTR resource records of the client for the FQDN (which can contain a connection-specific DNS suffix). Depending on the negotiation process, the DHCP client, the DHCP server, or both, update the records by sending a dynamic update request to a primary DNS server that is authoritative for the name that is to be updated.

Clients and servers that are running versions of Windows earlier than Windows 2000 do not support dynamic update. However, Windows 2000 DHCP servers can perform dynamic updates on behalf of clients that do not support the FQDN option (which is described in the following section). For example, clients that are running Windows 95, Windows 98, and Windows NT do not support the FQDN option. To enable this functionality, in the **DNS** tab of the server properties for the DHCP console, select the option **Enable updates for DNS clients that do not support dynamic updates**. The DHCP server first obtains the name of legacy clients from the DHCP REQUEST packet. It then appends the domain name given for that scope and registers the A and PTR resource records.

For information about how security for clients that do not support the FQDN option is implemented through secure dynamic update, see "Secure Dynamic Update" later in this chapter.

In some cases, stale PTR or A resource records can appear on DNS servers when the lease of a DHCP client expires. For example, when a Windows 2000 DHCP client tries to negotiate a dynamic update procedure with a Windows NT 4.0 DHCP server, the Windows 2000 DHCP client must register both A and PTR resource records itself. Later, if the Windows 2000 DHCP client is improperly removed from the network, the client cannot deregister its A and PTR resource records; thus, they become stale.

If a stale A resource record appears in a zone that allows only secure dynamic updates, no person or computer is able to use the name in that A resource record.

To prevent problems with stale PTR and A resource records, you can enable the aging and scavenging feature. For more information about the aging and scavenging feature, see "Aging and Scavenging" later in this chapter.

To provide fault tolerance, consider integrating with Active Directory those zones that accept dynamic updates from Windows 2000–based clients. If you want to speed up the discovery of authoritative servers, you can configure each client with a list of preferred and alternate DNS servers that are authoritative for that directory-integrated zone. If a client fails to update with its preferred server because the server is unavailable, the client can try an alternate server. When the preferred server becomes available, it loads the updated, directory-integrated zone that includes the update from the client.

Dynamic Update Process for Adapters Configured by DHCP

To negotiate the dynamic update process, the DHCP client sends its FQDN to the DHCP server in the DHCPREQUEST packet by using the FQDN option. The server then replies to the DHCP client by sending a DHCP acknowledgment (DHCPACK) message by using the FQDN option.

Table 6.6 lists the fields of the FQDN option of the DHCPREQUEST packet.

Table 6.6 Fields in the FQDN Option of the DHCPREQUEST Packet

Field	Explanation
Code	Specifies the code for this option (81).
Len	Specifies the length of this option (minimum of 4).
Flags	Can be one of the following values:: *0*. Client wants to register the A resource record and requests that the server update the PTR resource record. *1*. Client wants server to register the A and PTR resource records. *3*. DHCP server registers the A and PTR resource records regardless of the request of the client.
RCODE1 and RCODE 2	The DHCP server uses these fields to specify the response code from an A resource record registration performed on the client's behalf and to indicate whether it attempted the update before sending DHCPACK.
Domain Name	Specifies the FQDN of the client.

As Figures 6.18 and 6.19 show, the conditions under which DHCP clients send the FQDN option and the action taken by DHCP servers depend on the operating system that the client and server are running and how the client and server are configured.

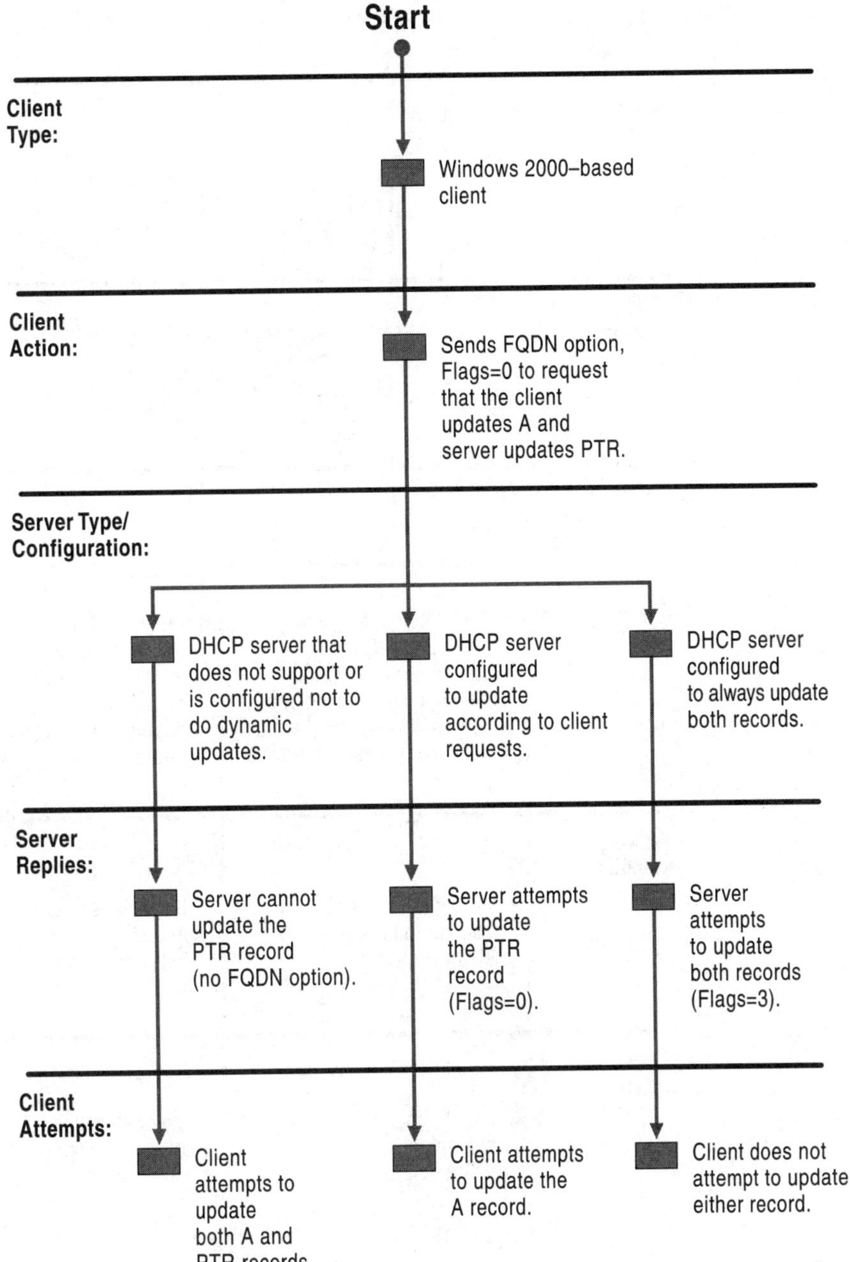

Figure 6.18 Windows 2000–based Client

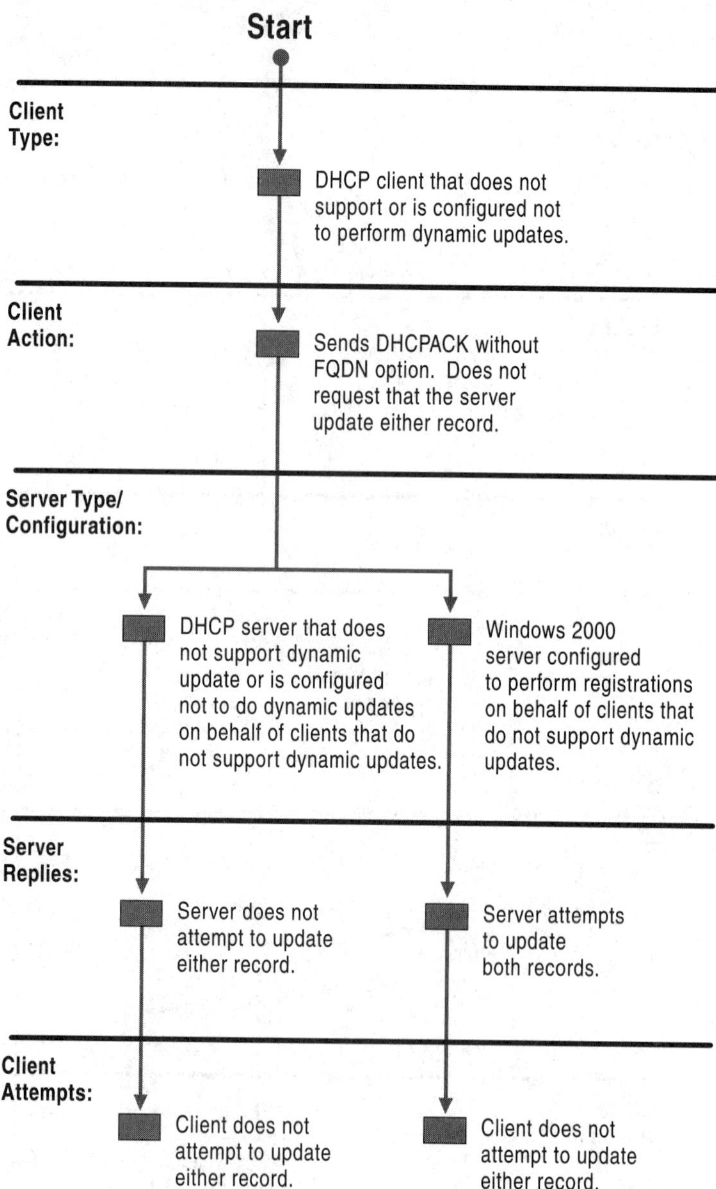

Figure 6.19 Client That Does Not Perform Dynamic Updates

Whether the client requests dynamic update depends on whether the client is running Windows 2000 or another version of Windows. It also depends on and how the client is configured. Clients can take any of the following actions:

1. By default, the Windows 2000 DHCP client sends the FQDN option with the Flags field set to 0 to request that the client update the A resource record, and the DHCP server updates the PTR resource record. After the client requests the update, it waits for a response from the DHCP server. Unless the DHCP server sets the Flags field to 3, the client then initiates an update for the A resource record. If the DHCP server does not support or is not configured to perform registration of the DNS record, the client attempts registration of the A and PTR resource records.
2. DHCP clients that are running Windows operating systems of a version earlier than Windows 2000 and Windows 2000 DHCP clients configured not to register DNS resource records do not send the FQDN option. In this case, the client does not try to update either record.

Depending on what the client requests, the server can take different actions. If the DHCP client sends a DHCPREQUEST message without the FQDN option, what happens depends on the type of server and how the server is configured. The server can update both records anyway. The server does so if it is configured to update records on behalf of clients that do not support the FQDN option.

Alternatively, the server might do nothing. In the following cases, the server does nothing:

1. The server does not support dynamic update (for example, a Windows NT 4.0 server).
2. The server is running Windows 2000 and is configured not to do dynamic updates for clients that do not support the FQDN option.
3. The server is running Windows 2000 and configured not to register DNS resource records.

If the Windows 2000–based DHCP client requests that the server updates the PTR resource record but not the A resource record, what happens depends on the type of server and how it is configured. The server can perform any of the following actions:

1. If the server is running either Windows NT 4.0 or Windows 2000 and is configured not to perform dynamic updates, the server does not reply using the FQDN option and does not update either record. If this happens, the DHCP client attempts to update both the A and PTR resource records.
2. If the server is running Windows 2000 and is configured to update according to the request of the client, the server attempts to update the PTR resource record. The server sends a DHCPACK message to the client. The client then attempts to update the A resource record.

3. If the server is running Windows 2000 and is configured to always update both records, the server attempts to update both resource records. It sends a DHCPACK message to the client. If the client requested that the server update the PTR resource record but not the A resource record, the server also sets the Flags field to 3. In this case, the client does not attempt to update either resource record.

Configuring Dynamic Update for DHCP Clients and Servers

By default, Windows 2000 DHCP clients are configured to send the FQDN option with the Flags field set to 0, to request that the client register the A resource record and the server register the PTR resource record. The name used in the DNS registration is a concatenation of the host name and the primary DNS suffix of the computer. You can change this default from within the TCP/IP properties of your network connection.

Note From this page, you can specify whether to use the connection-specific DNS suffix in DNS registration and whether to register the connection's IP address at all.

▶ **To change the dynamic update defaults on the dynamic update client**

1. Right-click **My Network Places**, and then click **Properties**.
2. Right-click the connection you want to configure, and then click **Properties**.
3. Select **Internet Protocol (TCP/IP)**, click **Properties**, and click **Advanced**, and select the **DNS** tab.
4. By default, **Register this connection's address in DNS** is selected and **Use this connection's DNS suffix in DNS registration** is not selected, causing the client to request that the server update the PTR resource record and the client updates the A resource record using the primary DNS suffix.

   To configure the client to register the connection-specific DNS suffix as well as the primary DNS suffix, select **Use this connection's DNS suffix in DNS registration**.

   To configure the client not to register its IP address in DNS, deselect **Register this connection's addresses in DNS**.

You can configure the Windows 2000 DHCP server to do one of the following: update whichever records the client requests that it update; always update both A and PTR resource records, regardless of the request of the client; or to not update any DNS records.

▶ **To configure dynamic update for the Windows 2000 DHCP server**

1. Click **Start**, point to **Programs** and **Administrative Tools**, and then click **DHCP**.
2. Expand the tree next to the name of the server.
3. Right-click the scope you're configuring, and then click **Properties**.
4. Click the **DNS** tab.
5. If it is not already selected, select **Automatically update DHCP client information in DNS**.
6. If you want the server to register whichever records the client requested that it register, select the option **Update DNS only if DNS client requests**.
7. If you want the server to always register both A and PTR resource records, select the option **Always update DNS**.
8. If you want the server to always register both A and PTR resource records on behalf of clients that do not support the FQDN option, select **Enable updates for DNS clients that do not support dynamic update**.

Caution If you have any multihomed dynamic update clients and at least one adapter is using DHCP, select the option **Update according to client request** (the default). If the DHCP server is configured to register both A and PTR resource records, the DHCP server replaces all A resource records for the name it attempts to register.

To update A or PTR resource records, the DHCP server sends a dynamic update request to the DNS server. If the DHCP server updated an A or PTR resource record, it removes that record when the lease of the client expires. You can also configure the server to remove the A resource record of the client when the lease of the client expires, even if the DHCP client and not the server registered the A resource record. When the DHCP lease is renewed, DHCP clients re-register their resource records.

▶ **To configure the Windows 2000 DHCP server to remove A resource records when the lease expires**

1. Click **Start**, point to **Programs** and **Administrative Tools**, and then click **DHCP**.
2. Expand the tree next to the name of the server.
3. Right-click the scope you're configuring, and then click **Properties**.
4. Click the **DNS** tab.
5. Select the option **Discard forward (name-to-address) lookups when leases expire**.

For more information about the FQDN option and integration between DNS and DHCP, see the Internet Engineering Task Force (IETF) link on the Web Resources page at http://windows.microsoft.com/windows2000/reskit/webresources. Search for the IETF Internet-Draft "Interaction Between DHCP and DNS."

Statically Configured and Remote Access Clients

Statically configured clients and remote access clients do not rely on the DHCP server for DNS registration. Statically configured clients dynamically update their A and PTR resource records every time they start, or every 24 hours if the computer stays up longer than a day, in case the records become corrupted or need to be refreshed in the DNS database. Remote access clients dynamically update A and PTR resource records when a dial-up connection is made. They also attempt to deregister the A and PTR resource records when the user closes down the connection. However, if a remote access client fails to deregister a resource record within four seconds, it closes the connection, and the DNS database will contain a stale record. If the remote access client fails to deregister a resource record, it adds a message to the event log, which you can view by using Event Viewer. The remote access client never deletes stale records. However, the RRAS server attempts to deregister the PTR resource record when the client is disconnected.

Multihomed Clients

If a dynamic update client is multihomed (has more than one adapter and associated IP address), by default it registers the first IP address for each adapter. If you do not want it to register these IP addresses, you can configure it to not register IP addresses for one or more adapters from the properties page for the network connection.

▶ **To prevent the computer from registering an IP address for an adapter**

1. Right-click **My Network Places**, and then click **Properties**.
2. Select the connection you want to configure, and then click **Properties**.
3. Select **Internet Protocol (TCP/IP)**, click **Properties**, click **Advanced**, and then select the **DNS** tab.
4. Clear the check box **Register this connection's address in DNS**.

The dynamic update client does not register all IP addresses with all DNS servers. For example, Figure 6.20 shows a multihomed computer, client1.noam.reskit.com, that is connected to both the Internet and the corporate intranet. Client1 is connected to the intranet by adapter A, a DHCP adapter with the IP address 172.16.8.7. Client1 is also connected to the Internet by adapter B, a remote access adapter with the IP address 10.3.3.9. Client1 resolves intranet names by using a name server on the intranet, NoamDC1, and resolves Internet names by using a name server on the Internet, ISPNameServer.

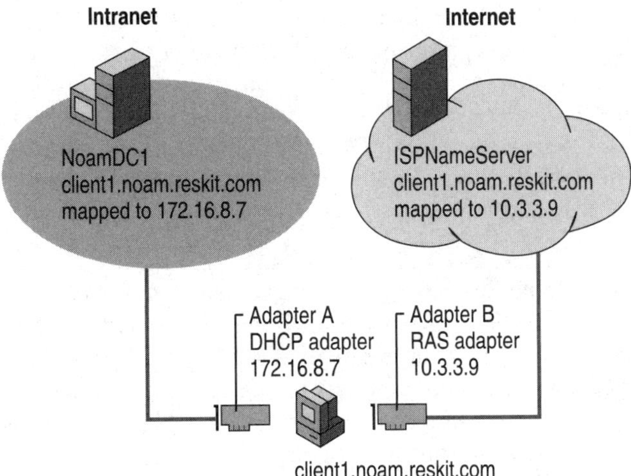

Figure 6.20 Dynamic Update for Multihomed Clients

Notice that although Client1 is connected to both networks, the IP address 172.16.8.7 is reachable only through adapter A, and the IP address 10.3.3.9 is reachable only through adapter B. Therefore, when the dynamic update client registers the IP addresses for Client1, it does not register both IP addresses with both name servers. Instead, it registers the name–to–IP address mapping for adapter A with NoamDC1 and the name–to–IP address mapping for adapter B with ISPNameServer.

By default, the computer registers a concatenation of the host name and primary DNS suffix. You can also configure the computer to register the domain name that is a concatenation of the host name and the connection-specific DNS suffix. For example, if you have a client that is connected to two different networks, and you want it to have a different domain name on each network, you can configure it to do so. For more information about configuring multiple domain names, see "Connection-Specific Domain Names" earlier in this chapter.

Time to Live

Whenever a dynamic update client registers in DNS, the associated A and PTR resource records include the TTL, which by default is set to 20 minutes. You can change the default setting by modifying the **DefaultRegistrationTTL** entry in the following registry subkey:

HKEY_LOCAL_MACHINE\SYSTEM\CurrentControlSet\Services
\Tcpip\Parameters

The entry has a DWORD value and lists the TTL in seconds. A small value causes cached entries to expire sooner, which increases DNS traffic but decreases the risk of entries becoming stale. Expiring entries quickly is useful for computers that frequently renew their DHCP leases. A large value causes cached entries to be retained longer, decreasing DNS traffic but increasing the risk of entries becoming stale. Long retention times are useful for computers that renew their DHCP leases infrequently.

Caution Do not use a registry editor to edit the registry directly unless you have no alternative. The registry editors bypass the standard safeguards provided by administrative tools. These safeguards prevent you from entering conflicting settings or settings that are likely to degrade performance or damage your system. Editing the registry directly can have serious, unexpected consequences that can prevent the system from starting and require that you reinstall Windows 2000. To configure or customize Windows 2000, use the programs in Control Panel or Microsoft Management Console (MMC) whenever possible.

Resolving Name Conflicts

If during dynamic update registration a client determines that its name is already registered in DNS with an IP address that belongs to another computer, by default the client attempts to replace the registration of the other computer's IP address with the new IP address. This means that for zones that are not configured for secure dynamic update, any user on the network can modify the IP address registration of any client computer. For zones that are configured for secure dynamic update, however, only authorized users are able to modify the resource record.

You can change the default setting so that instead of replacing the IP address, the client backs out of the registration process and logs the error in Event Viewer. To do so, add the **DisableReplaceAddressesInConflicts** entry with a value of 1 (DWORD) to the following registry subkey:

HKEY_LOCAL_MACHINE\SYSTEM\CurrentControlSet\Services
\Tcpip\Parameters

The entry can be 1 or 0, which specify one of the following:

- *1.* If the name that the client is trying to create already exists, the client does not try to overwrite it.

- *0*. If the name that the client is trying to create already exists, the client tries to overwrite it. This is the default value.

Caution Do not use a registry editor to edit the registry directly unless you have no alternative. The registry editors bypass the standard safeguards provided by administrative tools. These safeguards prevent you from entering conflicting settings or settings that are likely to degrade performance or damage your system. Editing the registry directly can have serious, unexpected consequences that can prevent the system from starting and require that you reinstall Windows 2000. To configure or customize Windows 2000, use the programs in Control Panel or Microsoft Management Console (MMC) whenever possible.

Secure Dynamic Update

You can configure any Active Directory–integrated zone for secure dynamic update, and then use the ACL to specify which users and groups have authority to modify the zone and records in the zone. The following sections describe the standards that comprise secure dynamic update, describe the secure dynamic update process, and explain how to configure secure dynamic update.

Note Secure dynamic update is available only on Active Directory–integrated zones.

Configuring Secure Dynamic Update

When you create an Active Directory–integrated zone, it is configured by default to allow only secure dynamic updates. If you created the zone as a standard primary zone and then converted it to an Active Directory–integrated zone, it is configured for non-secure dynamic updates or for no dynamic updates, depending on how the primary zone was previously configured.

▶ **To configure secure dynamic update**

1. In the DNS console, right-click the zone for which you want to configure dynamic update, and then click **Properties**.
2. In the **Allow dynamic updates?** box, select **Only secure updates**.

Controlling Update Access to Zones

With secure dynamic update, only the computers and users you specify in an ACL can create or modify dnsNode objects within the zone. By default, the ACL gives Create permission to all members of the Authenticated User group, the group of all authenticated computers and users in an Active Directory forest. This means that any authenticated user or computer can create a new object in the zone. Also by default, the creator owns the new object and is given full control of it.

You can view and change the permissions for all DNS objects on the **Security** tab for the object, from within the Active Directory Users and Computers console or through the properties of zone and resource record in the DNS console.

▶ **To view the ACL for a dnsZone or dnsNode object**

1. In the DNS console, right-click the zone or record you want to view, and then click **Properties**.
2. Click the **Security** tab.

Note ACLs are assigned on a per-name basis. Therefore, if you had two different records for the same FQDN, they map to the same object in Active Directory and have the same ACLs. For example, the following records have the same ACLs:

host1.reskit.com A 172.16.15.9

host1.reskit.com MX mailer.reskit.com

Reserving Names

You can reserve FQDNs so that only certain users can use them. To do so, create the FQDN in the DNS console, then modify its ACL so that only particular computer, user, or users can change the set of records associated with the FQDN.

DNS Standards for Secure Dynamic Update

Windows 2000 supports secure dynamic updates through the Generic Security Service Application Program Interface (GSS-API, specified in RFC 2078) rather than Domain Name System Security Extensions (RFC 2535) or Secure Domain Name System Dynamic Update (RFC 2137). The GSS-API provides security services independently of the underlying security mechanism.

The GSS-API specifies a way to establish a security context by passing security tokens. The client generates the initial token and sends it to the server. The server processes the token and, if it is necessary, returns a subsequent token to the client. The process repeats until negotiation is complete and a security context has been established. After the security context has been established, it has a finite lifetime during which it can be used to create and verify the transaction signature on messages between the two parties.

Windows 2000 implements the GSS-API using an algorithm specified in the IETF Internet-Draft "GSS Algorithm for TSIG (GSS-TSIG)." This algorithm uses Kerberos v5 authentication protocol as its underlying security mechanism. Other security providers such as smart cards or certificates have not been tested. The algorithm uses the following resource records to provide security services:

TKEY. A resource record specified in the IETF Internet-Draft "Secret Key Establishment for DNS (TKEY RR)," as the vehicle to transfer security tokens between the client and the server and to establish secret keys to use with the TSIG resource record.

TSIG. A resource record specified in the IETF Internet-Draft "Secret Key Transaction Signatures for DNS (TSIG)," to send and verify signature-protected messages.

To see the TKEY and TSIG records being passed across the network, you can use Network Monitor. Versions 6.12 and later decode the resource records.

TKEY Resource Record

Table 6.7 describes the structure of the TKEY resource record, as described in the IETF Internet-Draft "Secret Key Establishment for DNS (TKEY RR)."

Table 6.7 TKEY Resource Record

Field	Data Type	Comment
NAME	domain name	Differs with mode and context
TTYPE	u_int16_t	TKEY
CLASS	u_int16_t	Ignored; should be zero
TTL	u_int32_t	Should be zero
RDLEN	u_int16_t	Length of **RDATA** field
RDATA		
Algorithm	domain name	Determines how the secret keying material exchanged by using the TKEY resource record is used to derive the algorithm-specific key
Inception	u_int	In number of seconds since January 1, 1970 GMT
Expiration	u_int32_t	In number of seconds since January 1, 1970 GMT
Mode	u_int16_t	Scheme for key agreement
Error	u_int16_t	Error code
Key size	u_int16_t	Size of **Key data** field in octets
Key data	octet stream	Differs with mode
Other size	u_int16_t	Not used
Other data	octet stream	Not used

TSIG Resource Record

Table 6.8 describes the structure of the TSIG resource record, as described in the IETF Internet-Draft "Secret Key Transaction Signatures for DNS (TSIG)," to send and verify signature-protected messages.

Table 6.8 Structure of TSIG Resource Record

Field	Data Type	Comment
Algorithm name	domain name	Name of the algorithm, expressed as a domain name
Time signed	u_int48_t	Seconds since 1-Jan-70 UTC
Fudge	u_int16_t	Seconds of error permitted in **Time signed** field
Signature size	u_int16_t	Number of octets in **Signature** field
Signature	octet stream	Defined by **Algorithm name** field
Error	u_int16_t	Expanded RCODE covering signature processing
Other len	u_int16_t	Length, in octets, of **Other data** field
Other data	octet stream	Undefined

Secure Dynamic Update Process

To initiate a secure dynamic update, the client first initiates the TKEY negotiation process, to determine the underlying security mechanism and to exchange keys. Next, the client sends the dynamic update request containing resource records to add, delete, or modify to the server, signed with the TSIG resource record, and the server sends an acknowledgment. Finally, the server attempts to update Active Directory on behalf of the client.

Figure 6.21 shows the dynamic update process that takes place between a Windows 2000–based client and server, if both are configured with the default settings.

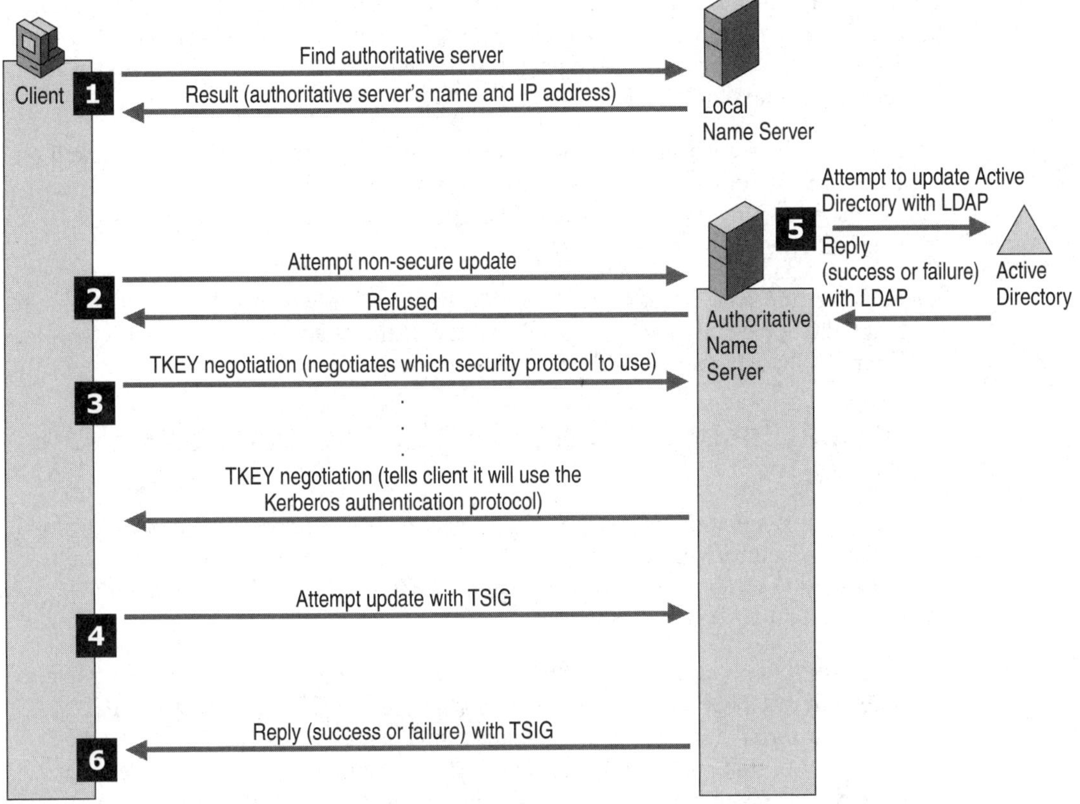

Figure 6.21 Secure Dynamic Update Process

In step 1, the client queries the local name server to determine which server is authoritative for the name it is attempting to update (using the process described in "DNS Queries," found earlier in this chapter). The local name server responds with the name of the zone and the primary server that is authoritative for the zone.

In step 2, the client attempts a non-secure update, and the server refuses the non-secure update. Had the zone been configured for non-secure dynamic update rather than secure dynamic update, the server would have instead attempted to add, delete, or modify resource records in Active Directory.

In step 3, the client and server begin TKEY negotiation. First, the client and server negotiate an underlying security mechanism. Windows 2000 dynamic update clients and servers both propose the Kerberos protocol, so they decide to use it. Next, by using the security mechanism, they verify one another's identity and establish security context.

In step 4, the client sends the dynamic update request to the server, signed with the TSIG key that was generated by using the security context established in step 3. The DNS server verifies the origin of the dynamic update packet by using the security context and the TSIG key.

In step 5, the server attempts to add, delete, or modify resource records in Active Directory. Whether or not it can make the update depends on whether the client has the proper permissions to make the update and whether the prerequisites have been satisfied.

In step 6, the server sends a reply to the client stating whether or not it was able to make the update, signed with the TSIG key. If the client receives a spoofed reply, it throws it away and waits for a signed response.

Security for DHCP Clients That Do Not Support the FQDN Option

DHCP clients that do not support the FQDN option are not capable of dynamic updates. Therefore, if you want their A and PTR resource records dynamically registered in DNS, you must configure the DHCP server to perform dynamic updates on their behalf.

However, you do not want the DHCP server to perform *secure* dynamic updates on behalf of DHCP clients that do not support the FQDN option. If a DHCP server performs a secure dynamic update on a name, the DHCP server becomes the owner of that name, and only that DHCP server can update the name. This can cause problems in a few different circumstances. For example, suppose that the DHCP server DHCP1 created an object for the name nt4host1.reskit.com and then stopped responding, and that the backup DHCP server, DHCP2, tried to update the name; DHCP2 is not able to update the name because it does not own the name. In another example, suppose DHCP1 added an object for the name nt4host1.reskit.com, and then the administrator upgraded nt4host1.reskit.com to a Windows 2000–based computer. Because the Windows 2000–based computer did not own the name, it would not be able to update its own name.

Therefore, if you have enabled secure dynamic update, you might want to perform a special configuration for any DHCP server that will perform dynamic updates. Place the server in a special security group called DNSUpdateProxy. Objects created by members of the DNSUpdateProxy group have no security; therefore, any authenticated user can take ownership of the objects.

▶ **To add a DHCP Server to the DNSUpdateProxy group**

1. Click **Start**, point to **Programs**, point to **Administrative Tools**, and then click **Active Directory Users and Computers**.
2. In the console tree, double-click the domain node.
3. Double-click the **Users** folder.

4. In the details pane, right-click the group and click **Properties**.
5. Click the **Members** tab, then click **Add**.
6. Click **Look in** to display a list of domains from which users and computers can be added to the group and click the domain containing the server you want to add.
7. Click the server to be added and then click **Add**.

Caution If you have installed the DHCP service on a domain controller, be absolutely certain not to make that server a member of the DNS Update Proxy group. Doing so would give any user or computer full control of the DNS records corresponding to the domain controllers, unless you manually modified the corresponding ACL. Moreover, if a DHCP server that is running on a domain controller is configured to perform dynamic updates on behalf of its clients, that DHCP server is able to take ownership of any record, even in the zones that are configured to allow only secure dynamic update. This is because a DHCP server runs under the computer account, so if it is installed on a domain controller it has full control over DNS objects stored in the Active Directory.

Windows 2000 DHCP clients register their own A resource records; therefore, putting a DHCP server in the DNSUpdateProxy group does not affect the security of the A resource records for Windows 2000 DHCP clients.

Note The A resource record corresponding to the DHCP server has no security if the server is placed in the DNSUpdateProxy group. However, you can manually modify the ACL through the DNS console.

For more information about interaction between DNS and DHCP, see the Windows 2000 Server Help.

Aging and Scavenging of Stale Records

With dynamic update, records are automatically added to the zone when computers and domain controllers are added. However, in some cases, they are not automatically deleted. For example, if a computer registers its own A resource record and is improperly disconnected from the network, the A resource record might not be deleted. If your network has many mobile users, this can happen frequently.

Having many stale resource records presents a few different problems. Stale resource records take up space on the server, and a server might use a stale resource record to answer a query. As a result, DNS server performance suffers.

To solve these problems, the Windows 2000 DNS server can "scavenge" stale records; that is, it can search the database for records that have aged and delete them. Administrators can control aging and scavenging by specifying the following:

- Which servers can scavenge zones
- Which zones can be scavenged
- Which records must be scavenged if they become stale

The DNS server uses an algorithm that ensures that it does not accidentally scavenge a record that must remain, provided that you configure all the parameters correctly. By default, the scavenging feature is off.

Caution By default, the scavenging mechanism is disabled. Do not enable it unless you are absolutely certain that you understand all the parameters. Otherwise, you might accidentally configure the server to delete records that it should retain. If a name is accidentally deleted, not only do users fail to resolve queries for that name, but also, any user can create that name and then take ownership of it, even on zones configured for secure dynamic update.

You can manually enable or disable aging and scavenging on a per-server, per-zone, or per-record basis. You can also enable aging for sets of records by using the command line tool Dnscmd.exe. (For information about Dnscmd.exe, see Windows 2000 Support Tools Help. For information about installing and using the Windows 2000 Support Tools and Support Tools Help, see the file Sreadme.doc in the directory \Support\Tools on the Windows 2000 operating system CD.) Keep in mind that if you enable scavenging on a record that is not a dynamic update record, the record will be deleted if it is not periodically refreshed, and you must recreate the record if it is still needed.

If scavenging is disabled on a standard zone and you enable scavenging, the server does not scavenge records that existed before you enabled scavenging. The server does not scavenge those records even if you convert the zone to an Active Directory–integrated zone first. To enable scavenging of such records, use the AgeAllRecords in Dnscmd.exe.

Aging and Scavenging Parameters

The Windows 2000 DNS server uses the timestamp that it gives each record, along with parameters that you configure, to determine when to scavenge records.

Table 6.9 lists the zone parameters that affect when records are scavenged. You configure these properties on the zone.

Table 6.9 Aging and Scavenging Parameters for Zones

Zone Parameter	Description	Configuration Tool	Notes
No-refresh interval	Time during which the server does not accept refreshes for the record. (The server still accepts updates.) This value is the interval between the last time a record was refreshed and the earliest moment it can be refreshed again.	DNS console and Dnscmd.exe	When an Active Directory–integrated zone is created, this parameter is set to the DNS server parameter **Default no-refresh interval**. This parameter replicates through Active Directory replication.
Refresh interval	The refresh interval comes after the no-refresh interval. At the beginning of the refresh interval, the server begins accepting refreshes. After the refresh interval expires, the DNS server can scavenge records that have not been refreshed during or after the refresh interval.	DNS console and Dnscmd.exe	When an Active Directory–integrated zone is created, this parameter is set to the DNS server parameter **Default refresh interval**. This parameter is replicated by Active Directory.
Enable Scavenging	This flag indicates whether aging and scavenging is enabled for the records in the zone.	DNS console and Dnscmd.exe	When an Active Directory–integrated zone is created, this parameter is set to the DNS server parameter **Default enable scavenging**. This parameter is replicated by Active Directory.
ScavengingServers	This parameter determines which servers can scavenge records in this zone.	Only Dnscmd.exe	This parameter is replicated by Active Directory.
Start scavenging	This parameter determines when a server can start scavenging of this zone.	Not configurable	This parameter is not replicated by Active Directory.

Table 6.10 lists the server parameters that affect when records are scavenged. You set these parameters on the server.

Table 6.10 Aging and Scavenging Parameters for Servers

Server Parameter	Description	Configuration Tool	Notes
Default no-refresh interval	This value specifies the no-refresh interval that is used by default for the Active Directory–integrated zone.	DNS console (shown as **No-refresh interval**) and Dnscmd.exe	By default, this is 7 days.
Default refresh interval	This value specifies the refresh interval that is used by default for the Active Directory–integrated zone.	DNS console (shown as **Refresh interval**) and Dnscmd.exe	By default, this is 7 days.
Default Enable Scavenging	This value specifies the Enable Scavenging parameter that is used by default for the Active Directory–integrated zone.	DNS console (shown as **Enable scavenging**)and Dnscmd.exe	By default, scavenging is disabled.
Enable scavenging	This flag specifies whether the DNS server can perform scavenging of stale records. If scavenging is enabled on a server, it automatically repeats scavenging as often as specified in the **Scavenging Period** parameter.	DNS console, Advanced View (shown as **Enable automatic scavenging of stale records**) and Dnscmd.exe	By default, scavenging is disabled.
Scavenging Period	This period specifies how often a DNS server enabled for scavenging can remove stale records.	DNS console, Advanced View (shown as **Scavenging Period**) and Dnscmd.exe	By default, this is 7 days.

Record Life Span

You can also invoke the Active Directory Installation wizard by executing an answer file that contains all of the settings that you need to configure. An *answer file* is a file that a wizard uses to provide answers to questions. For more information about the answer file for the Active Directory Installation wizard, see "Active Directory Data Storage" in the *Microsoft® Windows® 2000 Server Resource Kit Distributed Systems Guide*.

Figure 6.22 shows the life span of a scavengeable record.

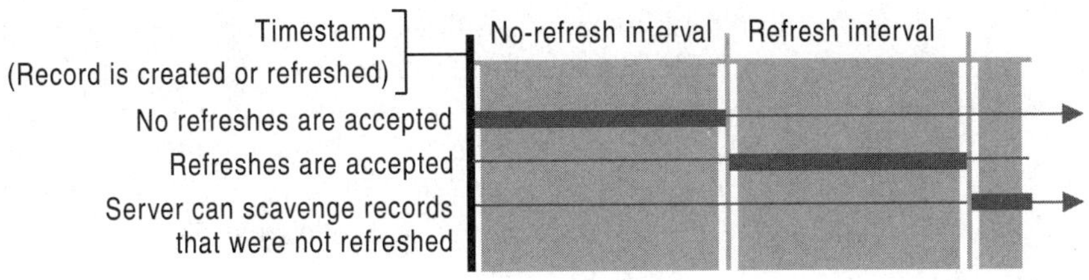

Figure 6.22 Life Span of a Scavengeable Record

When a record is created or refreshed on an Active Directory–integrated zone or on a standard primary zone for which scavenging is enabled, a timestamp is written.

Caution Because of the addition of the timestamp, a standard primary zone file for which scavenging is enabled is has a slightly different file format than a standard DNS zone. This does not cause any problems with standard zone transfer. However, you cannot copy a standard zone file for which scavenging is enabled to a non-Windows 2000 DNS server.

The value of the timestamp is the time the record was created or the record was last refreshed. By default, if the record is not dynamically updated, the timestamp equals zero, and the record is not scavengeable. Also, the timestamp is never changed if it contains a zero value. If the record belongs to an Active Directory–integrated zone, then every time the timestamp is refreshed, the record is replicated to the other domain controllers in the domain.

By default, the timestamps of records that are created by any method other than dynamic update are set to zero. A zero value indicates that the timestamp must not be refreshed and the record must not be scavenged.

After the record is refreshed, it cannot be refreshed again for the interval specified by the no-refresh interval. The no-refresh interval, a zone parameter, prevents unnecessary Active Directory replication traffic.

However, the record can still be updated during the no-refresh interval. If a dynamic update request requires modification to a record, the request is considered an update. If the request requires no modifications, it is considered a refresh. Therefore, prerequisite-only updates, updates that include a list of prerequisites but no zone changes, are also considered refreshes.

The no-refresh interval is followed by the refresh interval. After the expiration of the no-refresh interval, the server begins to accept refreshes, and the server continues to accept refreshes for the life span of the record. The record can be refreshed as long as the current time is greater than the value of the timestamp plus the no-refresh interval. When the server accepts a refresh or an update, the value of the timestamp changes to the current time.

Next, after the expiration of the refresh interval, the server can scavenge the record if it has not been refreshed. The record can be scavenged if the current time is greater than the value of the timestamp plus the value of the no-refresh interval plus the value of the refresh interval. However, the server does not necessarily scavenge the record at that time. The time at which records are scavenged depends on several server parameters.

Server Behavior

You can configure the server to perform scavenging automatically, using a fixed frequency. In addition, you can manually trigger scavenging on a server to perform immediate scavenging. When scavenging starts, the server attempts to scavenge all primary zones and succeeds if all the following conditions are met:

- The **EnableScavenging** parameter is set to **1** on the server.
- The **EnableScavenging** parameter is set to **1** on the zone.
- Dynamic update is enabled on the zone.
- The zone parameter **ScavengingServers** is not specified or contains the IP address of this server.
- The current time is greater than the value of the zone parameter **StartScavenging**.

Note The zone parameter ScavengingServers is configurable only by using Dnscmd.exe. For more information about Dnscmd.exe, see Windows 2000 Support Tools Help.

The server sets **StartScavenging** whenever any of the following events occur:

- Dynamic update is turned on.
- **EnableScavenging** is set from **0** to **1** on the zone.
- The zone is loaded.
- The zone is resumed.

StartScavenging is equal to the time that one of the preceding events occur plus the amount of time specified in the refresh interval for the zone. This prevents a problem that can occur if the client is unable to refresh records because the zone isn't available—for example, if the zone is paused or the server is not working. If that happens and the server does not use **StartScavenging**, the server could scavenge the zone before the client has a chance to update the record.

When the server is ready to scavenge records, it examines all the records in the zone one by one. If the timestamp is not zero and the current time is later than the time specified in the timestamp for the record plus the no-refresh interval plus the refresh interval for the zone, it deletes the record.

Configuring Scavenging Parameters

This section discusses issues you must consider when configuring scavenging parameters.

To ensure that no records are deleted before the dynamic update client has time to refresh them, make certain that the refresh interval is greater than the refresh period for each record within a zone. Many different services might refresh records at different intervals; for example, Netlogon refreshes records once an hour, cluster servers generally refresh records every 15 to 20 minutes, DHCP servers refresh records at renewal of IP address leases, and Windows 2000–based computers refresh their A and PTR resource records every 24 hours.

Usually, the DHCP service requires the longest refresh interval of all services. If you are using the Windows 2000 DHCP service, you can use the default scavenging and aging values. If you are using another DHCP server, you might need to modify the defaults.

The longer you make the no-refresh and refresh intervals, the longer stale records remain. Therefore, you might want to make those intervals as short as is reasonable. However, if you make the no-refresh interval too short, you might cause unnecessary replication by Active Directory.

Integration with WINS

Windows Internet Name Service (WINS) provides dynamic name resolution for the NetBIOS namespace. Before Windows 2000, WINS was required on all clients and servers. The Windows NT 4.0 DNS server provided a feature called WINS lookup. With *WINS lookup*, you can direct DNS to query WINS for name resolution, so that DNS clients can look up the names and IP addresses of WINS clients. Windows 2000 still supports WINS lookup, although for DHCP clients, you can use dynamic update instead, provided that the DHCP server is running Windows 2000.

For more information about dynamic update, see "Dynamic Update and Secure Dynamic Update" earlier in this chapter. For more information about WINS, see "Windows Internet Name Service" in this book.

Note WINS is not required in a purely Windows 2000 environment.

To use WINS lookup integration, you add two special resource records—the WINS and WINS-R resource records—to your forward and reverse lookup zones, respectively. When a DNS server that is authoritative for that zone is queried for a name that it does not find in the authoritative zone, and the zone is configured to use WINS resolution, the DNS server queries the WINS server. If the name is registered with WINS, the WINS server returns the associated record to the DNS server.

Reverse lookups work slightly differently. When an authoritative DNS server is queried for a nonexistent PTR record, and the authoritative zone contains the WINS-R record, the DNS server uses a NetBIOS node adapter status lookup.

Finally, the DNS server returns the name or IP address in response to the original DNS request. Thus, DNS clients do not need to know whether a client is registered with WINS or DNS, nor do they need to query the WINS server.

Note For fault tolerance, you can specify multiple WINS servers. The server that is running the Windows 2000 Server DNS service tries to locate the name by searching the WINS servers in the order specified by the list.

Format of WINS and WINS-R Resource Records

The WINS resource record is used for forward lookups. When a resolver sends a query to the DNS server, requesting the corresponding A resource record, and the DNS server does not find the name in the forward lookup zone, it uses the WINS record to locate a WINS server that might be authoritative for the leftmost label of the FQDN. If present, the WINS record only applies for the topmost level within a zone and not for subdomains used in the zone. A WINS resource record has the following syntax:

<domain> *<class>* WINS [*<TTL>*] *<Local>* *<LookupTimeout>* *<CacheTimeout>* *<IP address of WINS server>*

where the placeholders have the following meanings:

domain. Domain name where the WINS record is found. It is always @.

class. Class is always IN for WINS records.

TTL. Time that a WINS record can be cached before it must be discarded.

Local. Specifies whether the record must be included in zone replication.

LookupTimeout. Time in seconds that a DNS server that uses WINS lookup waits before it gives up.

CacheTimeout. Time in seconds that a DNS server that uses WINS lookup can cache the response from the WINS server.

WINSServers. List of IP addresses of the WINS servers to be used.

The following is an example of a WINS resource record:

```
@       IN  WINS LOCAL 5 3600 172.16.72.3
```

The WINS-R resource record is used for reverse lookups. When a resolver sends a query to the DNS server, requesting the corresponding PTR resource record, and the DNS server does not find the name in the authoritative reverse lookup zone, it uses a NetBIOS adapter node status query for the queried IP addresses. A WINS-R resource record has the following syntax:

<domain> <class> WINSR [*<TTL>*] *<Local> <LookupTimeout>*
<CacheTimeout> <NameResultDomain>

where the placeholders have the following meanings:

domain. Domain name where the WINS record is found. It is always @.

class. Class the field is IN.

TTL. Time that a WINS record can be cached before it must be discarded.

Local. Specifies whether the record must be included into zone replication.

LookupTimeout. Time in seconds that a DNS server that uses WINS lookup waits before it gives up.

CacheTimeout. Time in seconds that a DNS server that uses WINS lookup can cache the response from the WINS server.

NameResultDomain. Domain to append to returned NetBIOS names.

The following is an example of a WINS-R resource record::

```
@       IN  WINS-R LOCAL 5 3600 reskit.com.
```

Example of WINS Lookup

Suppose a user at a client workstation issues the following command:

net use \\host-a.noam.reskit.com.\public

This command establishes a connection between the client workstation and the Public folder on the computer host-a.noam.reskit.com, which is a client that is running Windows NT 4.0. However, before the connection can be established, the FQDN host-a.noam.reskit.com must be resolved by DNS—or, in this case, WINS—to an IP address. Figure 6.23 shows how this name is resolved, assuming that no server has cached the data and that no server is forwarding queries.

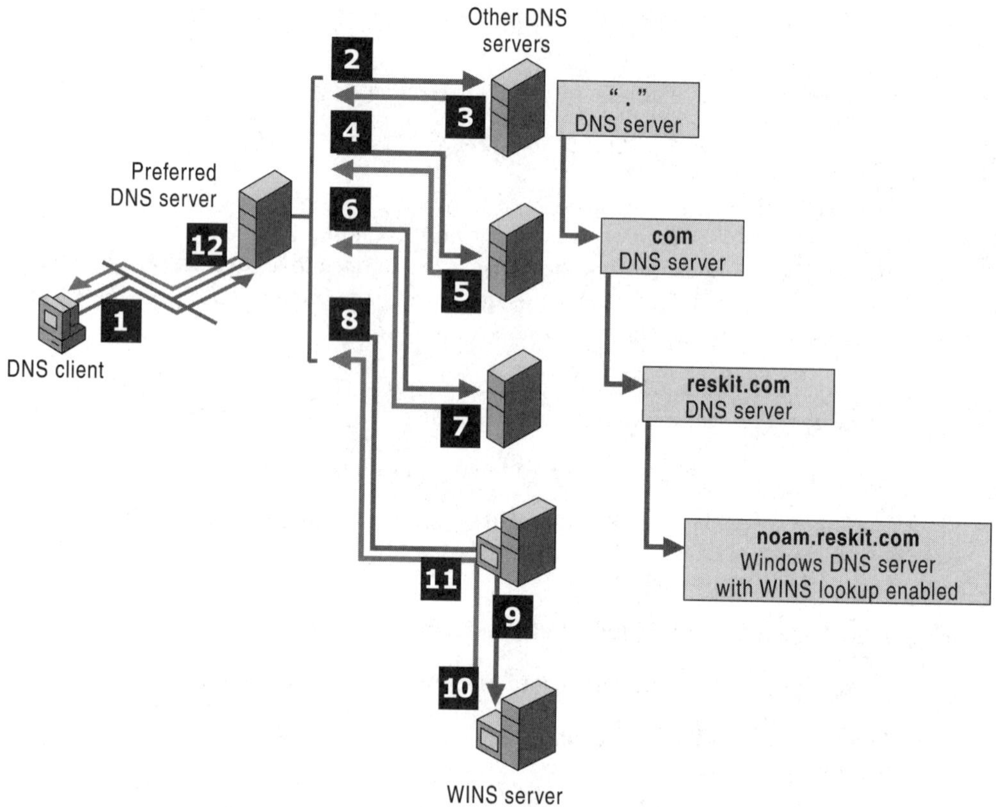

Figure 6.23 Example of WINS Lookup

1. The client queries its preferred DNS server.
2. DNS servers carry out the normal process of recursion as the preferred DNS server queries other DNS servers in succession on behalf of the client. This process concludes at Step 8, when the DNS server for the noam.reskit.com zone is located through the previous chain of referral answers. At this point in the process, the server that is contacted is a Windows DNS server that is running either Windows NT Server 4.0 or Windows 2000 Server.

When the Windows DNS server authoritative for the noam.reskit.com zone receives the query for "host-a," it looks in its configured zone to see whether a matching A resource record can be found. If no A resource record is found and the zone is configured to use WINS lookup, the server does the following:

3. The DNS server separates the host part of the name (host-a) from the FQDN contained in the DNS query.

   The host part of the name is the first label.
4. The server then sends a NetBIOS name request to the WINS server using the host name host-a.
5. If the WINS server can resolve the name, it returns the IP address to the DNS server.
6. The Windows DNS server then returns this IP address information to the original preferred DNS server that was queried by the requesting client.
7. The preferred DNS server then passes the query answer back to the requesting client.

The client workstation establishes the session with host-a.noam.reskit.com and connects to the public folder.

In this example, only the last name server in the referral chain had knowledge of WINS. To the client resolver and all other name servers, it appears that DNS was responsible for the entire name resolution process. Furthermore, if the IP address changes for host-a.noam.reskit.com, WINS automatically handles it. Nothing needs to change with DNS.

A reverse lookup with WINS integration works a little differently than the previous example. Because the WINS database is not indexed by IP address, the DNS server cannot send a reverse name lookup to a WINS server to get the name of a computer given its IP address. The DNS server instead sends a node adapter status request directly to the IP address implied in the DNS reverse query. When the DNS server gets the NetBIOS name from the node status response, it appends the DNS domain name specified in the WINS-R record to the NetBIOS name provided in the node status response and forwards the result to the requesting client.

Configuring WINS Lookup

You can configure WINS lookup on both primary and secondary servers. To configure WINS lookup on a DNS server, perform the following steps:

▶ **To configure WINS lookup**

1. In the DNS console, right-click the zone for which you are enabling WINS lookup, and then click **Properties**.
2. In the **Properties** dialog box for the zone, click the **WINS** tab.

3. Select the **Use WINS forward lookup** check box.
4. Under **IP address**, type the WINS Server IP address that will be used for resolution, and then click **Add**.

Repeat the procedure to add any other desired WINS servers. You can configure WINS lookup on both primary and secondary servers. You might want to configure WINS lookup on a secondary server, for example, if your primary and secondary servers are located at different sites and you want the secondary server to use local WINS servers. If you do so, however, you must disable replication from the primary server by clicking the check box **Do not replicate this record** on the **WINS** tab of the properties page for the zone.

Caution The WINS and WINS-R resource records are proprietary to the DNS service provided by Windows 2000 Server and earlier versions of Windows NT Server. It is best to make sure that all DNS servers that are authoritative for a zone are running Windows 2000 or any version of Windows NT; otherwise, resolvers can only look up WINS and WINS-R records intermittently. If you do make a server that is running another implementation of DNS authoritative for the zone, you must prevent these resource records from being included in zone transfers to other DNS server implementations by clicking the check box **Do not replicate this record** on the **WINS** tab of the zone properties. For more information about disabling WINS replication, see "WINS Lookup Interoperability Considerations" later in this chapter.

Advanced Parameters for WINS Lookups

You can use the following advanced timing parameters with the WINS and WINS-R records:

Cache Time-out Indicates to a DNS server how long to cache any of the information returned in a WINS lookup. By default, this value is set to 15 minutes.

Lookup Time-out Specifies how long to wait for a response from a WINS server before timing out and querying the next WINS server specified in a WINS record. By default, this value is 2 seconds.

You configure these parameters by using the Advanced button in the **Properties** dialog box for the zone. This button appears on either the WINS or WINS-R tabbed sheet, depending on whether the zone you are configuring is being used for forward lookup or reverse lookup.

Interoperability with Other DNS Servers

Windows 2000 DNS is RFC-compliant and interoperates with other DNS implementations. It has been tested to work with Windows NT 4.0, BIND 8.2, BIND 8.1.2, and BIND 4.9.7. However, Windows 2000 supports some features that other implementations of DNS do not support. Table 6.11 compares Windows 2000 to Windows NT 4.0, BIND 8.2, BIND 8.1.2, and BIND 4.9.7.

Table 6.11 Comparison of Features

Feature	Windows 2000	Windows NT 4.0	BIND 8.2	BIND 8.1.2	BIND 4.9.7
Support for the IETF Internet-Draft "A DNS RR for specifying the location of services (DNS SRV)." (SRV records)	Yes	Yes (with Service Pack 4)	Yes	Yes	Yes
Support for dynamic update	Yes	No	Yes	Yes	No
Support for secure dynamic update based on the GSS-TSIG algorithm	Yes	No	No	No	No
Support for WINS and WINS-R records	Yes	Yes	No	No	No
Support for fast zone transfer	Yes	Yes	Yes	Yes	Yes
Support for incremental zone transfer	Yes	No	Yes	No	No
Support for UTF-8 character encoding	Yes	No	No	No	No

The following sections describe issues to consider when implementing features that other DNS servers do not support, and describes how to set up DNS to support Active Directory when you are using third-party DNS servers.

Dynamic Update and Secure Dynamic Update Considerations

Clients and servers that are running versions of Windows earlier than Windows 2000 do not support dynamic update. However, Windows 2000 DHCP servers can perform dynamic updates on behalf of clients that do not support the FQDN option. If a Windows 2000 DHCP server must perform a secure dynamic update on behalf of clients that are running a version of Windows earlier than Windows 2000, you can place that DHCP server in a special security group called DNS Update Proxy. Objects created by the DNS Update Proxy group have no security, so they can be updated by any computer on the network.

For more information about these issues, see "Dynamic Update and Secure Dynamic Update" earlier in this chapter.

WINS Lookup Interoperability Considerations

For a zone that is configured for WINS lookup, WINS lookup works best if all authoritative servers are running Windows 2000 or Windows NT 4.0. WINS lookup requires the use of WINS and/or WINS-R resource records, two special, Windows-specific resource records. Computers that are running third-party implementations of DNS do not support WINS and WINS-R records. If you attempt to use a mixture of Microsoft and third-party DNS servers to host a zone, the mixture might cause data errors or failed zone transfers at the third-party DNS servers unless you configure the Windows 2000 server to disable replication of WINS and WINS-R records.

▶ **To disable replication of WINS and WINS-R records**

1. In the DNS console, double-click your server to view its zones.
2. If you want to disable replication in a forward lookup zone, double-click the **Forward Lookup Zone** folder.

   -Or-

   If you want to disable replication in a reverse lookup zone, double-click the **Reverse Lookup Zone** folder.
3. Right-click the zone for which you want to disable replication of WINS and WINS-R records, and then click **Properties**.
4. Click the WINS tab.
5. Select the **Do not replicate this record** check box.

However, if you do disable replication of WINS and WINS-R records, queries directed at the primary and secondary servers return different results. When the authoritative primary server is queried for the name of a WINS client, it queries WINS, then returns the result to the client. However, when an authoritative secondary server is queried, it replies that the name was not be found.

The best way to prevent this problem is to configure your DNS servers to use WINS referral, described in the next section.

Using WINS Referral

If you have a domain that needs to contain WINS lookup resource records, but some of the authoritative name servers for that domain are running third-party DNS implementations, you can prevent interoperability problems by disabling WINS replication. Alternately, you can prevent interoperability problems by creating and delegating a WINS referral *zone*. This zone does not perform any registrations or updates, but only refers DNS lookups to WINS.

After you have created your WINS referral zone, you configure your DNS clients to append the WINS referral zone name to unqualified queries. The easiest way is to configure the DHCP server to assign a connection-specific DNS suffix to all DHCP adapters on all computers in your network. That suffix is appended to unqualified queries.

Alternatively, you can specify a domain suffix search list on each computer, as described in "Configuring the Resolver," earlier in this chapter. Keep in mind that when you specify a domain suffix search list, your primary DNS suffix and connection-specific DNS suffix are not used unless you specifically add them to the domain suffix search list.

Figure 6.24 shows an example of WINS referral in a network that includes servers that are running third-party implementations of DNS and that includes clients that are running both Windows 2000 and Windows NT 4.0.

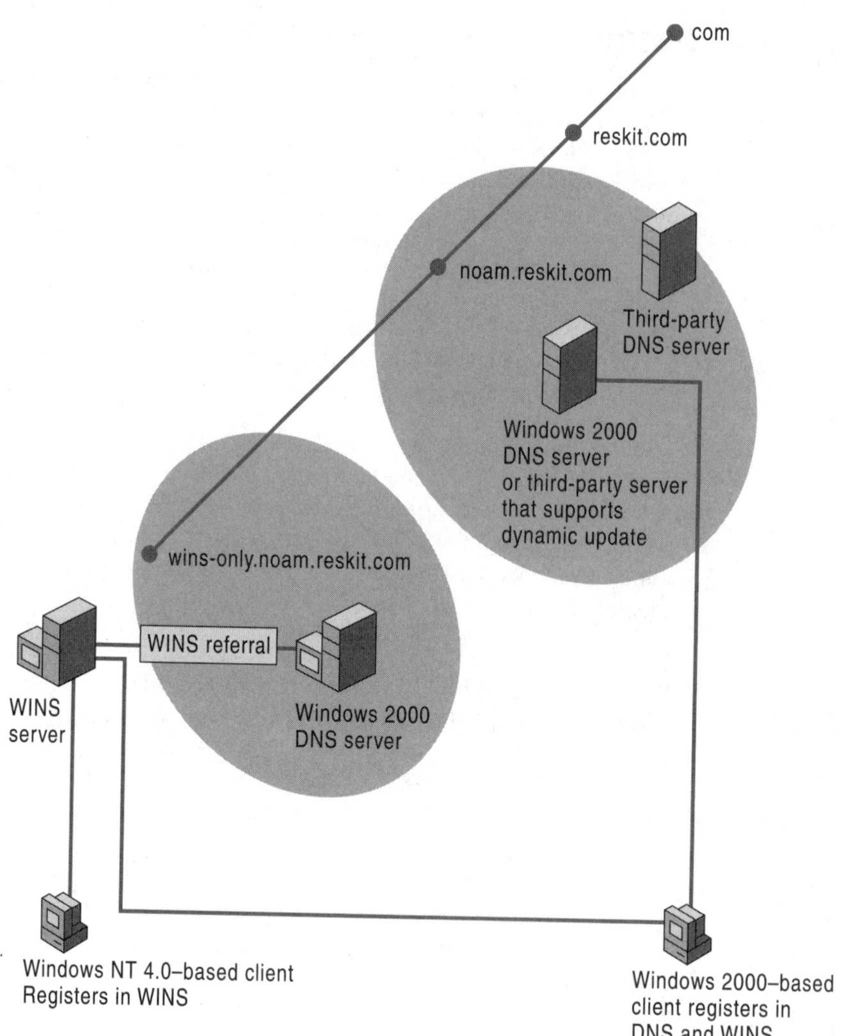

Figure 6.24 WINS Referral

In this example, the noam.reskit.com zone is stored and replicated between Windows 2000 servers and servers that are running other DNS implementations. To support WINS lookup, the network administrator created a new zone called wins-only.noam.reskit.com that is devoted to providing DNS-WINS integrated lookups for WINS clients. The network administrator enabled WINS lookup only on this zone, and did not add any resource records other than WINS resource records.

To register in DNS, Windows 2000–based clients send dynamic update requests to a DNS server that is authoritative for the domain noam.reskit.com. Both Windows 2000 and Windows NT 4.0–based clients register in WINS as well.

In this example, when a Windows 2000–based DNS client looks up a computer by its short name, it appends all the domain suffixes that it is configured to append, including the domain suffix wins-only.noam.reskit.com to produce the FQDN. For example, if the WINS host queried for is host-a, the client would use a DNS query for host-a.wins-only.noam.reskit.com.

Having only one WINS-integrated zone provides other advantages as well. When a DNS forward lookup for the host name of a computer uses WINS lookup, the DNS name specified and used in the query explicitly indicates that the source used to resolve the name was a DNS server that uses WINS lookup integration. This integrated solution can also prevent the confusing situation in which DNS queries for different FQDNs resolve to the same WINS client name and IP address. This result can easily occur if you add and configure multiple zones and enable each of them to use WINS lookup integration.

For example, suppose you have two zones, both configured to use WINS lookup. The zones are rooted and originate at the following DNS domain names:

- noam.reskit.com.
- eu.reskit.com.

With this configuration, a query for a WINS client named host-a can be resolved by using either of the following FQDNs:

- host-a.noam.reskit.com.
- host-a.eu.reskit.com.

Zone Transfer Considerations

Windows 2000 supports a method of zone transfer called fast zone transfer. With *fast zone transfer*, the Windows 2000 DNS server can send more than one resource record per message. This is more efficient than sending only one. However, some third-party DNS servers, including servers that are running versions of BIND earlier than 4.9.5 do not support fast zone transfer. If you use a secondary server that does not support fast zone transfer, disable fast zone transfers on the master server by selecting the check box **Bind secondaries** on the Advanced tab of the properties for your server, from within the DNS console.

Many DNS servers, including servers that are running versions of BIND earlier than 8.2, do not support *incremental zone transfer*, another method of zone transfer. With incremental zone transfer, instead of transferring a whole zone, a DNS server can transfer only those portions of the zone that changed since the last time the secondary server queried. However, this does not cause interoperability problems, because Windows 2000 can still use full zone transfer if any of the secondary servers do not support incremental zone transfer.

Windows 2000 also supports resource record types that other servers might not support, such as the WINS record and the WINS-R record. If you have a primary copy of a zone on a Windows 2000 DNS server and a secondary copy of a zone on a third-party DNS server, and the primary zone includes resource records the third-party server does not support, the secondary server might drop those resource records, or it might not be able to transfer the zone. For information about WINS records, see "WINS Considerations" earlier in this chapter.

It is also possible that a third-party DNS server might support a resource record type that Windows 2000 does not support, such as resource records not listed in the RFCs. If you have a primary copy of the zone on a third-party DNS server and a secondary copy on a Windows 2000 server, and the primary zone includes resource records that the Windows 2000 DNS server does not support, the Windows 2000 DNS server drops those resource records. If it receives any circular CNAME records, it drops those as well. You can also configure your DNS server to halt a zone transfer when it receives a resource record it does not support.

For information about problems with zone transfer, see "Diagnosing Name Resolution Problems" later in this chapter.

Unicode Character Set Considerations

Windows 2000 supports RFC 2044, which enlarges the character set allowed in DNS names to include UTF-8 character encoding. However, many DNS servers, including Windows NT 4.0 DNS servers, follow RFC 1123, which permits a smaller character set. If you perform a zone transfer from a zone containing UTF-8 encoded characters to a third-party secondary server that does not support UTF-8 encoded characters, the secondary server might drop resource records, or the zone transfer might fail. Therefore, if you plan to use any characters from the UTF-8 character set, consider the issues described in "Naming Restrictions for Hosts and Domains," earlier in this chapter.

Configuring Non-Windows 2000 DNS Servers to Support Active Directory

For the domain controller locator to work properly, the primary DNS server that is authoritative for the names that are to be registered by the Netlogon service on the domain controller, must support the service location resource record (SRV RR). The SRV resource record is specified in the IETF Internet-Draft "A DNS RR for specifying the location of services (DNS SRV)." Other DNS servers that are authoritative for the domain must also support SRV records.

In addition, you can simplify administration by making sure that the DNS servers that are authoritative for the names that Netlogon registers support the dynamic update protocol, as described in RFC 2136. You can use as the primary master for the domain name a DNS server that does not support dynamic update. However, this is not recommended, because you will need to manually update the primary zone when you configure Active Directory. For information about how to configure and verify the DNS records that are used to support Active Directory, see "Verifying Your Basic DNS Configuration" later in this chapter.

If you are using a DNS server that does not support the IETF Internet-Draft "A DNS RR for specifying the location of services (DNS SRV)," you must upgrade your DNS server or add a DNS server that does supports those standards. The server supporting those standards must be the primary DNS server that is authoritative for the DNS names that will be registered by the Netlogon service on the domain controller. You must then perform special configuration on both DNS servers.

This section explains which DNS servers can be used to support Active Directory and how to configure DNS and Active Directory when you are using servers that cannot support Active Directory.

If you are using a DNS service other than the Windows 2000 DNS service, it is a good idea to test it for compatibility with Active Directory and DHCP.

Using Non-Microsoft DNS Servers to Support Active Directory

The following servers support SRV records:

- Windows 2000
- Windows NT 4.0 Service Pack 4 and later
- BIND 4.9.6 and later

The following servers support dynamic update:

- Windows 2000
- BIND 8

If you use a third-party server, however, you cannot use the DNS console or Dnscmd.exe, Active Directory integration, secure dynamic update, aging and scavenging of stale records, or remote administration.

Also, it is a good idea to verify your DNS configuration after you install Active Directory.

The DNS database must include locator resource records (SRV, CNAME, and A) to support each domain controller.

Using the Name of a Delegated Zone as an Active Directory Domain Name

If your organization already has a DNS domain (for example, reskit.com), and the primary DNS server that is authoritative for that domain does not support RFC 2136 and the IETF Internet-Draft "A DNS RR for specifying the location of services (DNS SRV)"—and you cannot upgrade the server to a server that does—you can still create an Active Directory domain. To provide DNS support for an Active Directory domain in such a situation, delegate a subdomain (for example, child.reskit.com) from your first DNS server to a second DNS server that does support these standards. Next, make that second DNS server authoritative for the subdomain, and create an Active Directory domain that has the same name as the DNS subdomain. Figure 6.25 shows an example of implementing the Windows 2000 DNS server and making it authoritative for a delegated subdomain.

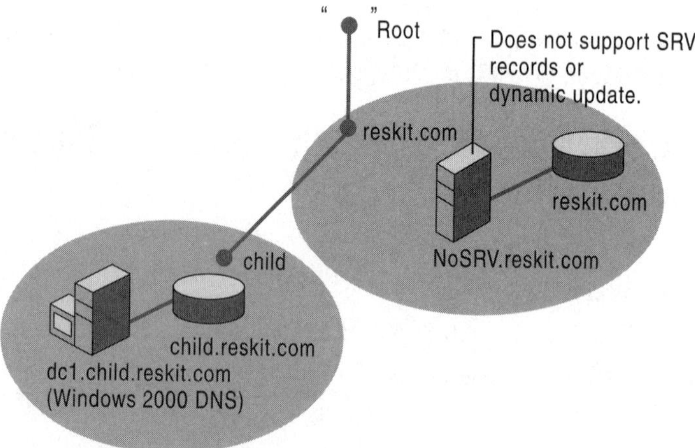

Figure 6.25 Implementing a Windows 2000 DNS Server to Support a Delegated Subdomain

In this example, the primary name server for reskit.com, NoSRV.reskit.com, does not support SRV records and, therefore, cannot be used to support Active Directory. Because of this, the administrator of NoSRV.reskit.com delegated the subdomain **child.reskit.com** to a Windows 2000 DNS server. The Windows 2000 DNS server provides the same capabilities for this zone as for any other zone. For example, it can be stored in Active Directory, as described in "Active Directory Integration and Multimaster Replication" earlier in this chapter.

Using the Existing Zone Name as the Active Directory Domain Name

If your organization already has a DNS domain (for example, reskit.com), and the DNS server that is authoritative for that domain does not support RFC 2136 and the IETF Internet-Draft "A DNS RR for specifying the location of services (DNS SRV)," and you cannot upgrade the server, you can still implement Active Directory with the name of the existing DNS zone. To implement Active Directory, add another DNS server that does support those standards and delegate certain zones to this server.

On the DNS server that does not support SRV records and dynamic update, delegate the following zones to the DNS server that does:

- _tcp.*<Active Directory domain name>*
- _udp.*<Active Directory domain name>*
- _msdcs.*<Active Directory domain name>*
- _sites. *<Active Directory domain name>*

On the DNS server that does support these features, create and then enable dynamic update on each of the zones in the preceding list. The domain controllers dynamically update the appropriate records in these zones.

Figure 6.26 illustrates this configuration for the example domain reskit.com:

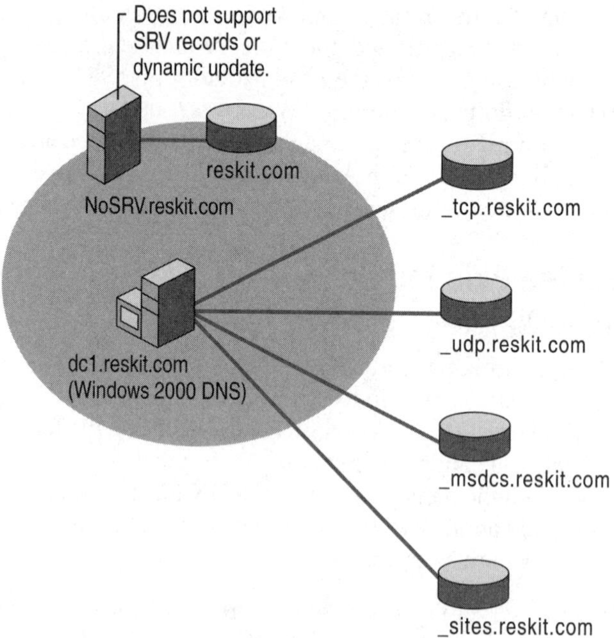

Figure 6.26 Delegating Zones to a DNS Server That Can Support Active Directory

The Netlogon service sends dynamic updates to the delegated zones. By default, the Netlogon service attempts a dynamic update of an A resource record that contains an *owner name* that is the same name as the Active Directory domain name. An owner name is the name of the node to which the resource record pertains. In this example, Netlogon fails the dynamic update; this causes an error message to appear in Event Viewer that says a dynamic update failed. To prevent Netlogon from registering A resource records, add the entry **RegisterDnsARecords** to the registry in the following registry subkey:

HKEY_LOCAL_MACHINE\SYSTEM\CurrentControlSet\Services
\NetLogon\Parameters

Set the value of **RegisterDnsARecords** to 0x0 (DWORD).

Caution Do not use a registry editor to edit the registry directly unless you have no alternative. The registry editors bypass the standard safeguards provided by administrative tools. These safeguards prevent you from entering conflicting settings or settings that are likely to degrade performance or damage your system. Editing the registry directly can have serious, unexpected consequences that can prevent the system from starting and require that you reinstall Windows 2000. To configure or customize Windows 2000, use the programs in Control Panel or Microsoft Management Console (MMC) whenever possible.

Internet Access Considerations

For your organization to be visible on the Internet, you must have an external namespace, a public namespace that anyone on the Internet can access. An Internet name authority must assign to you a DNS domain and make sure that a parent DNS zone includes a delegation to the DNS server that is authoritative for the DNS domain. However, to help prevent malicious access of your network, you can use an internal namespace, a private namespace that only users within your organization can see, preventing unauthorized people from learning the names and IP addresses of the computers on your network.

If you plan to have both an internal and external namespace, you must configure your DNS servers to enable internal clients to resolve names in both namespaces. How you plan your namespace depends on the type of clients that you have.

Planning Your Namespace

When planning your namespace, you must decide whether to use a private root and whether you want your internal and external namespaces to have the same domain name.

Whether you can use a private root depends on the type of clients you have. You can use a private root only if each of your clients has one of the following:

- *name exclusion list.* A list of DNS suffixes that are internal.
- *proxy autoconfiguration (PAC) file.* A list of DNS suffixes and exact names that are internal or external.

If you have clients lacking both of these, the DNS server hosting your organization's top-level internal domain must forward queries to the Internet.

Table 6.12 shows, based on the proxy capability of your client, whether you can use a private root. (Note that a *local address table* is a list of IP addresses that are internal and external.)

Table 6.12 Configuring Internal and External Namespaces Based on Proxy Capability

	No Proxy	Local Address Table (LAT)	Name Exclusion List	Proxy Auto-configuration (PAC) File
Microsoft software with corresponding proxy capability	Generic Telnet	Windows Sockets Proxy (WSP) 1.*x*, WSP 2.*x*	WSP 1.*x*, WSP 2.*x*, and all versions of Microsoft® Internet Explorer.	WSP 2.*x*, Internet Explorer 3.01 and later.
Can you forward queries?	Must forward queries.	Must forward queries.	Possible.	Possible.
Can you use a private root?	Not possible.	Not possible.	Possible.	Possible.

To simplify name resolution for internal clients, use a different domain name for your internal and external namespaces. For example, you can use the name reskit01-ext.com for your external namespace and reskit.com for your internal namespace. You can also use the name reskit.com for your external namespace and noam.reskit.com for your internal namespace. However, do not make your external domain a subdomain of your internal domain; that is, in the context of this example, do not use reskit.com for your internal namespace and noam.reskit.com for your external namespace.

You can use the same name internally and externally, but doing so causes configuration problems and generally increases administrative overhead. If you want to use the same domain name internally and externally, you need to perform one of the following actions:

- Duplicate internally the public DNS zone of your organization.
- Duplicate internally the public DNS zone and all public servers (such as Web servers) that belong to your organization.
- In the PAC file on each of your clients, maintain a list of the public servers that belong to your organization.

Caution Make sure that the domain name for your internal namespace is not used anywhere on the Internet. Otherwise, you might have problems with ambiguity in the name resolution process.

Which action you need to perform to use the same domain name internally and externally varies. Table 6.13 shows whether you can use the same domain name for your internal and external namespaces, and if so, which method you must use, based on your client software proxy capability.

Table 6.13 Using the Same Name for Internal and External Namespaces Based on Proxy Capability

	No Proxy	Local Address Table (LAT)	Name Exclusion List	Proxy Auto-configuration (PAC) File
Use different domain names.	Possible.	Possible.	Possible.	Possible (using simple exclusion)
Use the same domain name; internally duplicating organization's public DNS namespace (records).	Possible.	Possible (by populating LAT).	Not possible.	Possible. When a PAC file is used, duplicated external records are not used.
Use the same domain name; internally duplicating organization's public DNS namespace and public servers.	Possible.	Possible.	Possible.	Possible.
Use the same domain name; maintaining list of public servers in the PAC files.	Not possible.	Not possible.	Not possible.	Possible.

Namespace Planning Example

The following sections explain some of the issues you must consider when planning your namespace by describing the configuration of two fictitious organizations. The first organization, which has reserved the DNS domain names reskit.com and reskit01-ext.com, has only proxy clients that support either exclusion lists or PACs. In contrast, the second organization, which has reserved the DNS domain names acquired01-int.com and acquired01-ext.com, has no such proxy clients. Both organizations use a different domain name for their internal and external namespaces.

Reskit.com and acquired01-int.com both need a configuration that does the following:

- Exposes only the public part of the organization's namespace to the Internet.
- Enables any computer within the organization to resolve any internal or external name.
- Enables any computer within the organization to resolve any name from the Internet.

Moreover, both organizations have merged, and every computer from within each private namespace must be able to resolve any name from the other namespace.

The following sections describe how both organizations have configured their external and internal namespaces to satisfy these requirements. Figure 6.27 shows this configuration.

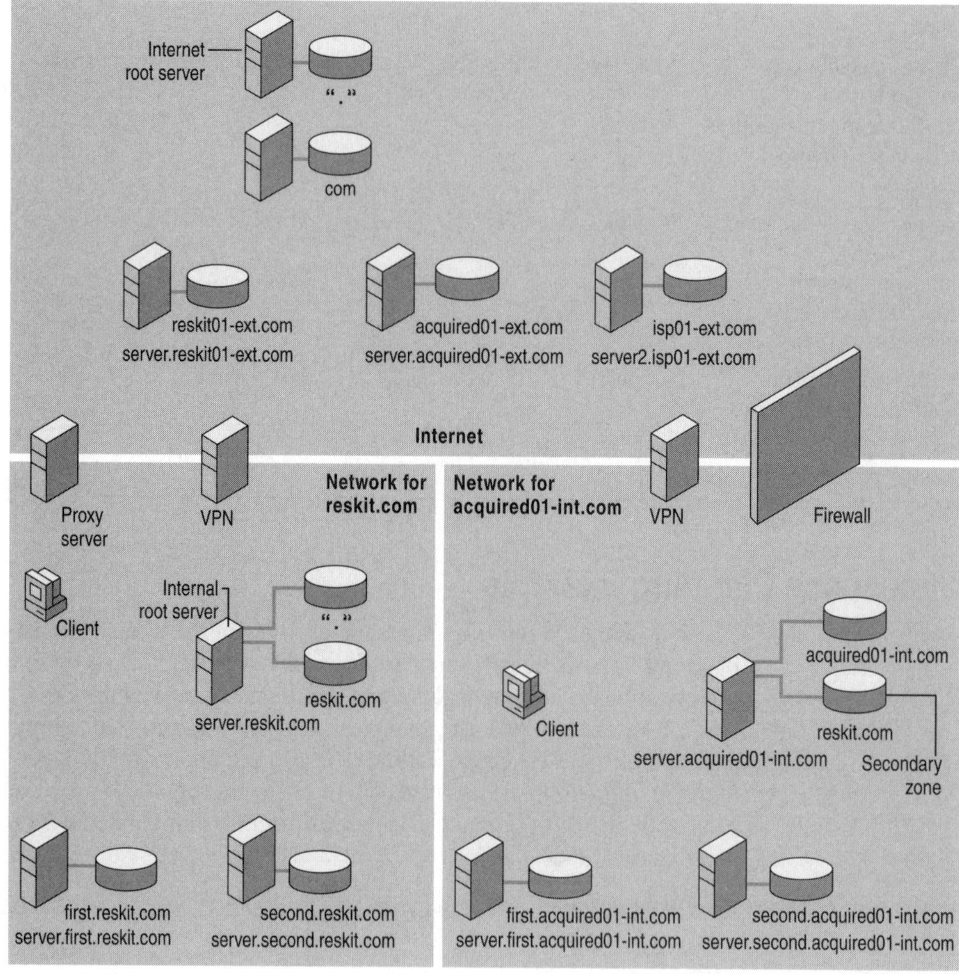

Figure 6.27 Example Configuration of the DNS Domains Reskit.com and Acquired01-int.com

Configuring the External Namespace

In the external namespace, two zones exist: reskit01-ext.com and acquired01-ext.com. The zones contain only the records (the names and delegations) that the companies want to expose to the outside world. The server server.reskit01-ext.com. hosts the zone reskit01-ext.com, and the server server.acquired01-ext.com hosts the zone acquired01-ext.com. The names reskit01-ext.com and acquired01-ext.com must be registered with an Internet name authority.

Configuring the Internal Namespace

The internal namespace for the organization that hosts reskit01-ext.com externally is reskit.com. Similarly, the internal namespace for the organization that hosts acquired01-ext.com externally is acquired01-int.com. The server server.reskit.com hosts the zone reskit.com, and the server server.acquired01-int.com hosts the zone acquired01-int.com. The names reskit.com and acquired01-int.com must be registered with an Internet name authority.

All the computers in reskit.com support either exclusion lists or PACs, and none of the computers in acquired01-int.com support either exclusion lists or PACs.

Namespace Without Proxy Clients That Support Exclusion Lists or PACs

For a namespace in which none of the computers are proxy clients that support either exclusion lists or PACs (in this example, the namespace of acquired01-int.com), an organization must devote one or more DNS servers to maintain zones that contain all names from the internal namespace. Every DNS client must send DNS queries to one or more of these DNS servers. If a DNS server contains the zone for the top level of the organization's namespace (for example, acquired01-int.com), then it must forward those queries through a firewall to one or more DNS servers in the Internet namespace. All other DNS servers must forward queries to one or more DNS servers that contain the zone for the top level of the organization's namespace.

To make sure that any client within the organization can resolve any name from the merged organization, every DNS server containing the zone for the top level of the organization's namespace must also contain the zones that include all the internal and external names of the merged organization.

This solution places a significant load on the internal DNS servers that contain the organization's internal top-level zones. Most of the queries generated within the organization are forwarded to these servers, including queries for computers in the external namespace and in the merged organization's private namespace. Also, the servers must contain secondary copies of the merged organization's zones.

Namespace with Proxy Clients That Support Exclusion Lists or PACs

For a namespace in which all of the computers are proxy clients that support either exclusion lists or PACs (for example, the namespace of reskit.com), the private namespace can include a private root. In the internal namespace, there can be one or more root servers, and all other DNS servers must include the name and IP address of a root server in their root hints files.

To resolve internal and external names, every DNS client must submit all queries to either the internal DNS servers or to a proxy server, based on an exclusion list or PAC file.

To make sure that every client within the organization can resolve every name from the merged organization, the private root zone must contain a delegation to the zone for the top level of the merged organization.

Using proxy clients and a private root simplifies DNS configuration because none of the DNS servers need to include a secondary copy of the zone. However, this configuration requires you to create and manage exclusion lists or PAC files, which must be added to every proxy client in the network.

Examples of Queries

The following examples show how queries for the following names are resolved:

- Internal name
- Name on the Internet
- Name in the external namespace of an organization
- Name in the internal namespace of a merged organization

Note In all of these examples, no DNS server has cached the name for which the client is querying. An actual query might progress differently, because the name might be cached.

Query for a Name in the Internal Namespace

Suppose that a computer in reskit.com needs to resolve a DNS query for host.second.reskit.com. First, the computer consults its exclusion list or its PAC file and discovers that host.second.reskit.com is in the internal namespace. Therefore, the computer submits the query to a local DNS server. Figure 6.28 shows how the query proceeds.

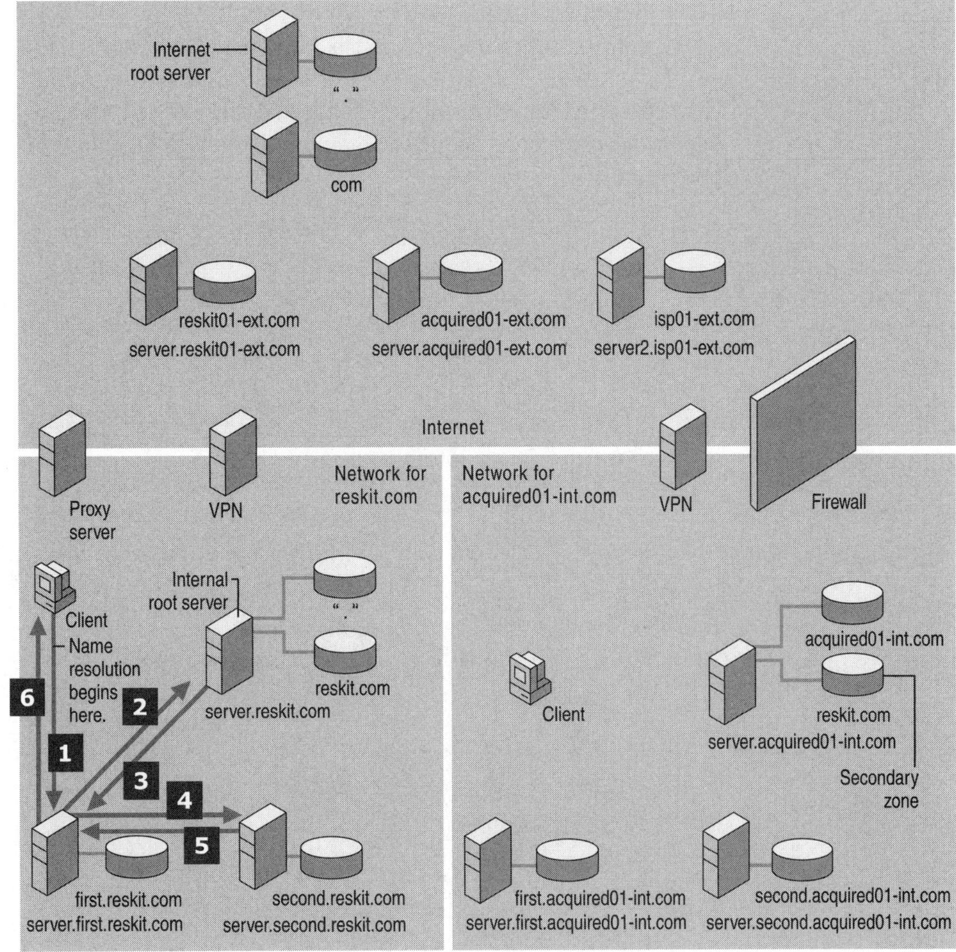

Figure 6.28 Query for an Internal Name in the Domain Reskit.com

The query proceeds as follows:

1. The computer submits a query to its local DNS server, server.first.reskit.com.
2. If the local server is not authoritative for host.second.reskit.com, the local DNS server queries a root server.
3. The root server returns a reference to the authoritative server, server.second.reskit.com.
4. The local server, server first.reskit.com, queries server.second.reskit.com.

5. Server.second.reskit.com resolves the query and returns the response to the local server.
6. Server.first.reskit.com passes the response to the client.

Now suppose that a computer in acquired01-int.com needs to resolve a DNS query for host.second.acquired01-int.com. Figure 6.29 shows how the query proceeds.

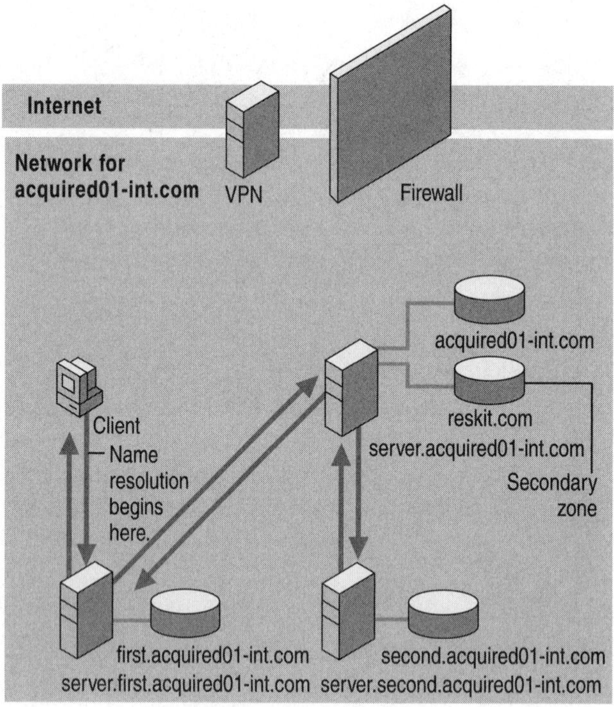

Figure 6.29 Query for an Internal Name in the Domain Acquired01-int.com

The query proceeds as follows:

1. The computer submits the query to its local DNS server, server.first.acquired01-int.com.
2. If the local server is not authoritative for host.second.acquired01-int.com, the local DNS server forwards the query to the DNS server that is authoritative for the acquired01-int.com zone.
3. The DNS server that is authoritative for the acquired01-int.com zone finds a delegation to the server server.second.acquired01-int.com and queries that server.
4. Server.second.acquired01-int.com resolves the query and returns the name to the DNS server authoritative for the acquired01-int.com zone.

5. The DNS server that is authoritative for the acquired01-int.com zone returns the name to the local DNS server.
6. Server.first.acquired01-int.com returns the name to the client.

Query for a Name in the External Namespace

Suppose that a computer in reskit.com needs to access a Web page on the computer host.isp01-ext.com. Figure 6.30 shows how the query proceeds.

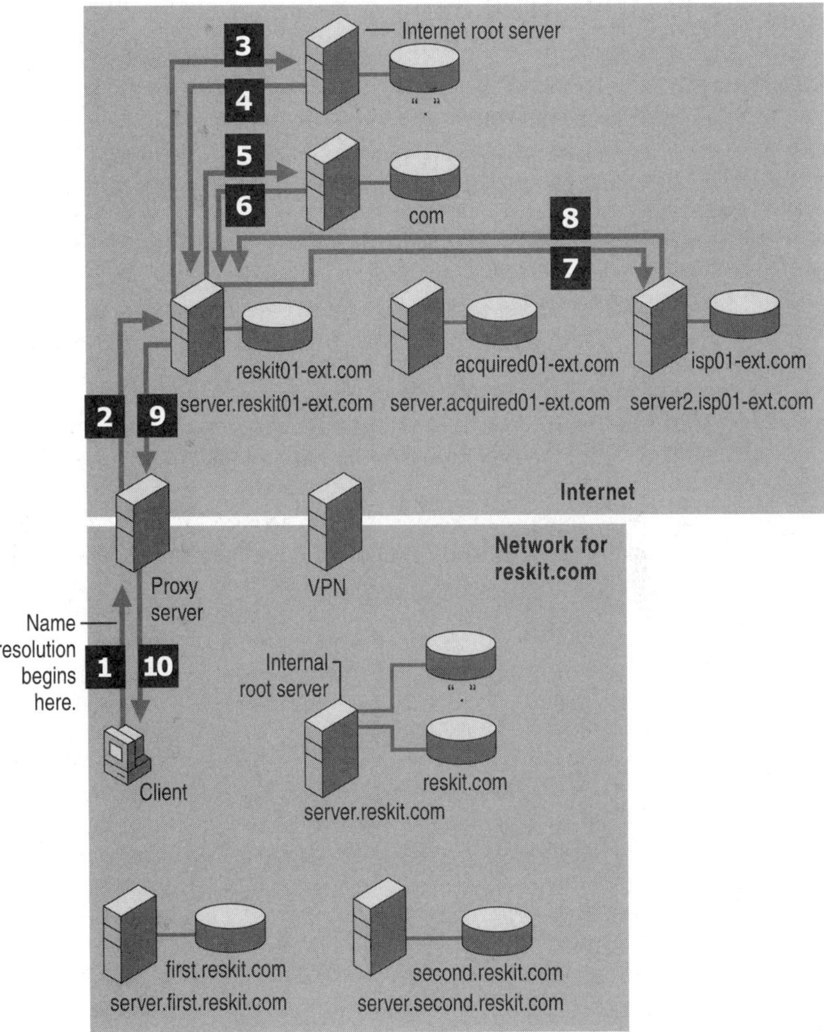

Figure 6.30 Query in the Domain Reskit.com for a Name on the Internet

The query proceeds as follows:

1. Because the client is a proxy client, it consults its exclusion list or its PAC file and determines that the name is not in the internal namespace. Therefore, the client sends the request to the proxy server.
2. The proxy server sends a query to the DNS server to which it is configured to send queries. In this case, the server is server.reskit01-ext.com.
3. The server server.reskit01-ext.com sends a query to the Internet root server.
4. The Internet root server returns a referral to a server that is authoritative for the Internet zone com.
5. The server server.reskit01-ext.com queries the server that is authoritative for the com zone.
6. The server that is authoritative for the zone com returns a referral to the server that is authoritative for the zone isp01-ext.com.
7. The server server.reskit01-ext.com queries the server that is authoritative for the zone isp01-ext.com.
8. The server that is authoritative for the zone isp01-ext.com returns the IP address that corresponds to the name host.isp01-ext.com.
9. The server server.reskit01-ext.com returns the response to the proxy server.
10. The proxy server uses the IP address to contact host.isp01-ext.com and provides necessary information to the client.

Now suppose that a computer in acquired01-int.com needs to resolve a DNS query for host.isp01-ext.com. Figure 6.31 shows how the query proceeds.

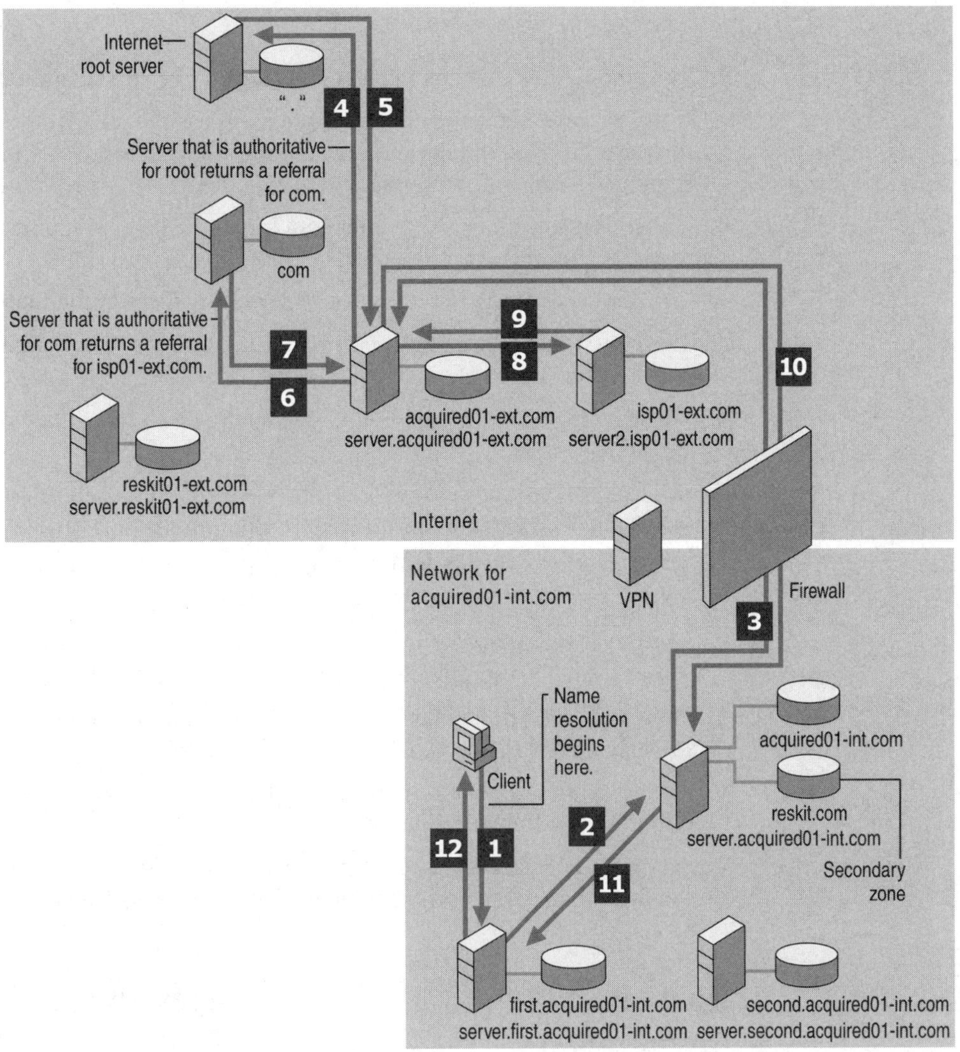

Figure 6.31 Query in the Domain Acquired01-int.com for a Name on the Internet

The query proceeds as follows:

1. The computer queries its local DNS server, server.first.acquired01-int.com.
2. If the server cache does not contain the requested data, the local DNS server forwards the query to the DNS server that is authoritative for the zone acquired01-int.com, server.acquired01-int.com.
3. The server server.acquired01-int.com forwards the query to the external server, server.acquired01-ext.com, through the firewall.
4. The server server.acquired01-ext.com sends a query to the Internet root server.
5. The Internet root server returns a referral to a server that is authoritative for the Internet zone com.
6. The server server.acquired01-ext.com queries the server that is authoritative for the zone com.
7. The server that is authoritative for the zone com returns a referral to the server that is authoritative for the zone isp01-ext.com.
8. The server server.acquired01-ext.com queries the server that is authoritative for the zone isp01-ext.com.
9. The server that is authoritative for the zone isp01-ext.com returns the IP address that corresponds to the name host.isp01-ext.com.
10. The server server.acquired01-ext.com returns the IP address to server.acquired01-int.com through the firewall.
11. Server.acquired01-int.com returns the IP address to the local DNS server, server.first.acquired01-int.com.
12. Server.first.acquired01-int.com returns the IP address to the client. The client can then contact the host through the firewall and download the desired Web page.

Query for a Name in the External Namespace of an Organization

Suppose that a computer in reskit.com needs to access a Web page in the external zone www.reskit01-ext.com. Figure 6.32 shows how the query proceeds.

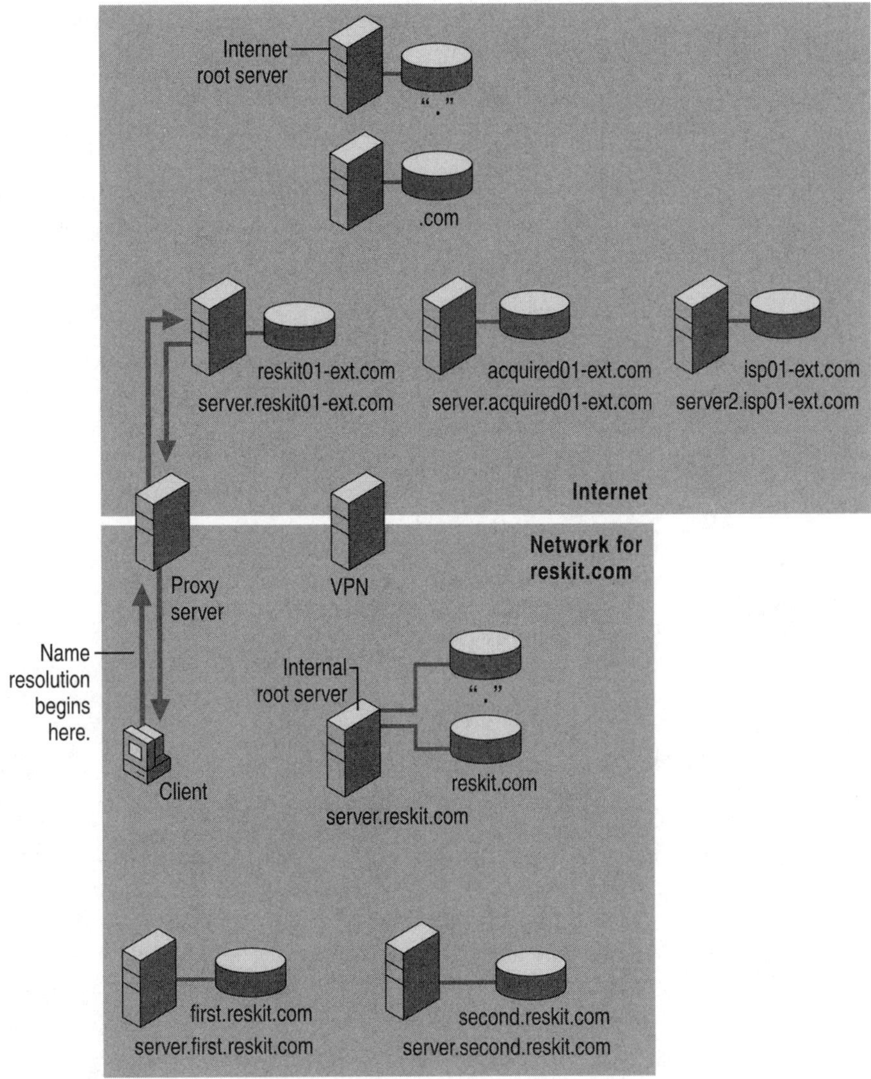

Figure 6.32 Query for a Name in the External Zone Reskit01-ext.com

The query proceeds as follows:

1. Because the computer is a proxy client, it consults its exclusion list or its PAC file. After finding that the name is not in the exclusion list, it sends a request to the proxy server.
2. The proxy server submits the query to the DNS server that the proxy server is configured to use, server.reskit01-ext.com. In this example, server.reskit01-ext.com also happens to be authoritative for www.reskit.com.

3. The server server.reskit01-ext.com resolves the query and returns the response to the proxy server.
4. The proxy server uses the resulting IP address to contact server.reskit.com and provides the necessary information to the client.

Now suppose that a computer in the zone acquired01-int.com needs to open a Web page in the external zone www.acquired01-ext.com. Figure 6.33 shows how the query proceeds.

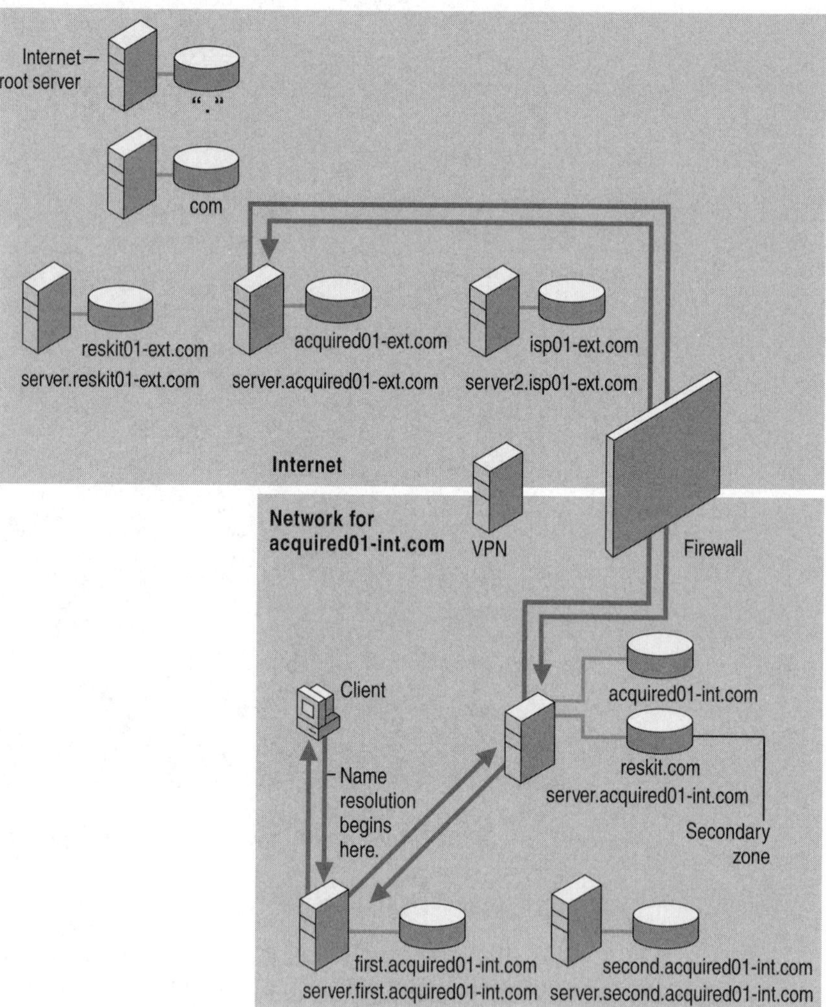

Figure 6.33 Query for a Name in the External Zone Acquired01-ext.com

The query proceeds as follows:

1. The computer submits the query to its local DNS server, server.first.acquired01-int.com.
2. If the cache does not contain the necessary data, server.first.acquired01-int.com forwards the query to the DNS server that is authoritative for the zone acquired01-int.com.
3. The server that is authoritative for the zone acquired01-int.com forwards the request through the firewall to server.acquired01-ext.com.
4. Server.acquired01-ext.com resolves the name and returns the response through the firewall to server.acquired01-int.com.
5. Server.acquired01-int.com returns the response to server.first.acquired01-int.com.
6. Server.first.acquired01-int.com returns the response to the client, and the client then uses the IP address to connect through the firewall to the Web server, which is located on the Internet.

Query for a Name in the Namespace of the Merged Organization

Suppose that a computer in reskit.com needs to contact the computer host.acquired01-int.com. Figure 6.34 shows how the query proceeds.

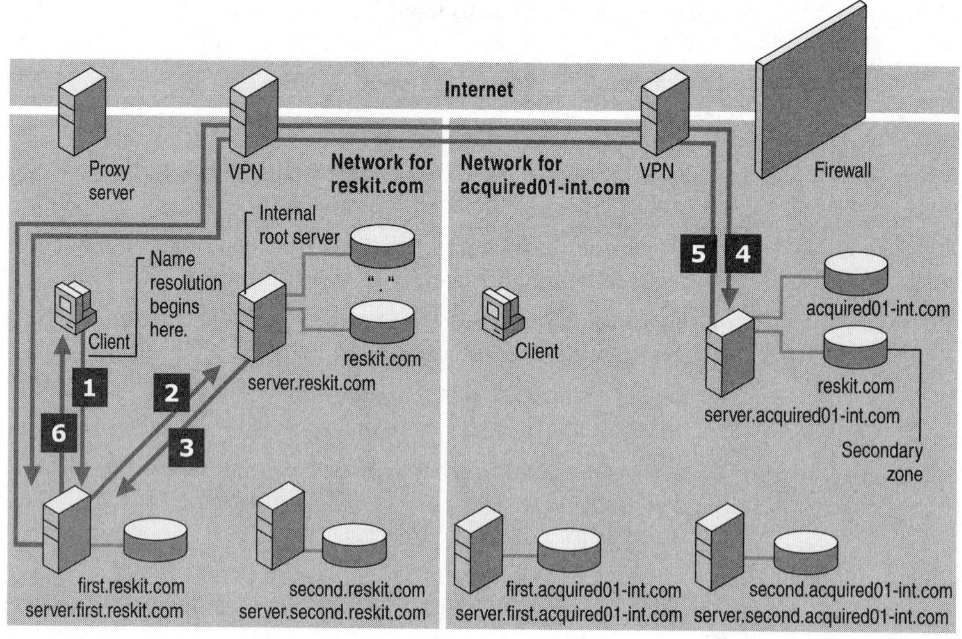

Figure 6.34 Query for a Name in the Acquired01-int.com Namespace

The query proceeds as follows:

1. Because the computer is a proxy client, it consults its exclusion list or its PAC file and submits a query for the name host.acquired01-int.com to the local DNS server, server.first.reskit.com.
2. If the cache does not contain the necessary data, the server queries the internal root server.
3. The root server finds a delegation to the zone acquired01-int.com and returns the IP address of the server that is authoritative for acquired01-int.com to the local DNS server.
4. The local DNS server submits the query to the server that is authoritative for acquired01-int.com.
5. Because that server is authoritative for host.acquired01-int.com, the server resolves the query and returns the answer to the local DNS server.
6. Server.first.reskit.com returns the response to the client.

Now suppose that a computer in acquired01-int.com needs to contact the computer host.reskit.com. Figure 6.35 shows how the query proceeds.

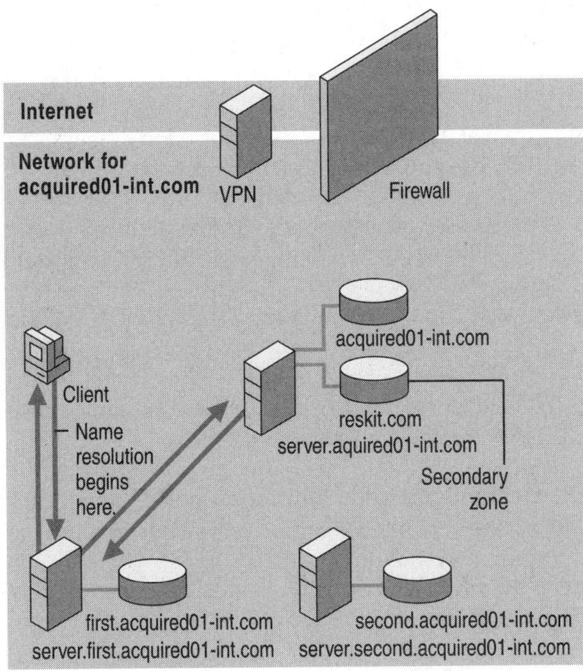

Figure 6.35 Query for a Name in the Reskit.com Namespace

The query proceeds as follows:

1. The computer submits a query to its local DNS server, server.first.acquired01-int.com.
2. If the cache does not contain the necessary data, the server forwards the query to the DNS server that is authoritative for the zone acquired01-int.com.
3. Because the DNS server that is authoritative for the zone acquired01-int.com contains a secondary copy of the zone reskit.com, it resolves the query and returns the response to server.first.acquired01-int.com.
4. Server.first.acquired01-int.com returns the response to the client.

Troubleshooting

The following sections describe useful troubleshooting tools, provides best practices to help you avoid common errors, lists procedures to help you verify that you have correctly configured your name servers, and explains how to diagnose and solve common DNS problems.

Troubleshooting Tools

Windows 2000 provides many tools that can help you diagnose and solve problems with DNS. This section discusses the following tools:

Nslookup You can use Nslookup to perform DNS queries and to examine the contents of zone files on local and remote servers.

Ipconfig You can use Ipconfig to view DNS client settings, display and flush the resolver cache, and force a dynamic update client to register its DNS records.

Event Viewer You can use Event Viewer to view DNS client and server error messages.

DNS Log You can configure the DNS server to monitor certain events and log them in the DNS log for your examination.

Network Redirector Command You can stop DNS client caching and flush the cache by using the network redirector commands **net start** and **net stop**.

Monitoring in the DNS Console You can perform test queries by using options on the **Monitoring** tab in the DNS console.

You can examine the packets that the DNS servers on your network send and receive by using Network Monitor. For more information about Network Monitor, see "Monitoring Network Performance" in the *Microsoft® Windows® 2000 Server Resource Kit Server Operations Guide*.

You can also use the Netdiag tool to quickly identify problems with your DNS configuration. For more information about Netdiag, see "TCP/IP Troubleshooting" in this book.

Nslookup

Nslookup is a standard command-line tool provided in most DNS server implementations, including Windows 2000. Nslookup offers the ability to perform query testing of DNS servers and obtain detailed responses at the command prompt. This information can be useful for diagnosing and solving name resolution problems, for verifying that resource records are added or updated correctly in a zone, and for debugging other server-related problems. This section describes how to perform troubleshooting tasks and lists and explains Nslookup error messages.

For information about the exact syntax of Nslookup, see Windows 2000 Server Help, or in Nslookup, type **help** at the command prompt.

Performing Simple Tasks with Nslookup

This section describes how to perform the following simple troubleshooting tasks:

- Use Nslookup in non-interactive mode to look up a single piece of data
- Enter interactive mode and use the debug feature
- Perform the following tasks from within interactive mode:
  - Set options for your query
  - Look up a name
  - Look up records in a zone
  - Perform zone transfers
  - Exit Nslookup

Note When you are entering queries, it is generally a good idea to enter FQDNs, so you can control what name is submitted to the server. However, if you want to know which suffixes are added to unqualified names before they are submitted to the server, you can enter Nslookup in debug mode and then enter an unqualified name.

▶ **To use Nslookup in non-interactive mode**

- Type the following and then press ENTER:

  nslookup *<name> <server>*

  where *name* is the owner of the record you are looking for, and *server* is the server you want to query.

With interactive mode, you can look up more than one piece of data. Starting Nslookup with the command-line parameter **-d2** puts Nslookup in interactive mode with verbose debugging enabled. Verbose debugging enables you to examine the query and response packets between the resolver and the server.

▶ **To start Nslookup in interactive mode**

- Type the following and then press ENTER:

  nslookup [**-d2**]

▶ **To exit interactive mode**

- At the Nslookup prompt, type:

  exit

In interactive mode, you can use the **set** command to configure how the resolver will carry out queries. Table 6.14 shows a few of the options available with **set**:

Table 6.14 Command-Line Options Available With Set

Option	Purpose
set all	Shows all the options available with the **set** option.
set d2	Puts Nslookup in debug mode, so you can examine the query and response packets between the resolver and the sever.
set domain=<*domain name*>	Tells the resolver what domain name to append for unqualified queries.
set timeout=<*time-out*>	Tells the resolver what time-out to use. This option is useful for slow links where queries frequently time-out and the wait time must be lengthened.
set type=<*record type*> –Or– **set querytype=**<*record type*> –Or– **set q=**<*record type*>	Tells the resolver what type of resource records to search for (for example, A, PTR, or SRV). If you want the resolver to query for all types of resource records, type **set type=all**.

You can look up a single name.

▶ To look up names from interactive mode

- Type the following:

  <*name*> [*server*]

  where *name* is the owner name for the record you are looking for, and *server* is the server that you want to query.

  You can use the wildcard character (*) in your query. For example, if you want to look for all resource records that have "K" as the first letter, you can type the following:

  K*

You can view the contents of a domain.

▶ To view the contents of a domain

- Type the following:

  set type=<*record type*>

  ls -t <*domain name*>

  where *record type* is the type of record (use **any** to view all resource records) and *domain name* is the name of the domain you want to view.

By adding the **-d** switch, you can simulate and test a zone transfer. This can help you determine whether or not the server you are querying allows zone transfers to your computer.

▶ **To simulate a zone transfer**

- Type the following:

  ls -d *<domain name>*

Nslookup provides help from the Nslookup prompt.

▶ **To get help from interactive mode**

- At the Nslookup command prompt, type **help** or **?**.

Nslookup Errors

A successful Nslookup response looks like this:

Server: *<Name of DNS server>*

Address: *<IP address of DNS server>*

<Response data>

Nslookup might also return one of several errors. The following message means that the resolver did not locate a PTR resource record (containing the host name) for the server IP address. Nslookup can still query the DNS server, and the DNS server can still answer queries. For more information about using Nslookup to verify your DNS configuration, see "Verifying Your Basic DNS Configuration" later in this chapter.

DNS request timed out.

Timeout was *<x>* seconds.

*** Can't find server name for address *<IP Address>*: Timed out

*** Default servers are not available

Default Server: Unknown

Address: *<IP address of DNS server>*

The following message means that a request timed out. This might happen, for example, if the DNS service was not running on the DNS server that is authoritative for the name.

*** Request to <*Server*> timed-out

The following message means that the server is not receiving requests on UDP port 53. For more information about troubleshooting server problems, see "Checking the DNS Server for Problems" later in this chapter.

*** <*Server*> can't find <*Name or IP address queried for*>: No response from server

The following message means that this DNS server was not able to find the name or IP address in the authoritative domain. The authoritative domain might be on that DNS server or on another DNS server that this DNS server is able to reach.

*** <*Server*> can't find <*Name or IP address queried for*>: Non-existent domain

The following message generally means that the DNS server is running, but is not working properly. For example, it might include a corrupted packet, or the zone in which you are querying for a record might be paused. However, this message can also be returned if the client queries for a host in a domain for which the DNS server is not authoritative and the DNS server cannot contact its root servers, or is not connected to the Internet, or has no root hints.

*** <*Server*> can't find <*Name or IP address queried for*>: Server failed.

Using IPConfig

You can use the command-line tool Ipconfig to view your DNS client settings, to view and reset cached information used locally for resolving DNS name queries, and to register the resource records for a dynamic update client.

If you use Ipconfig with no parameters, it displays DNS information for each adapter, including the domain name and DNS servers used for that adapter.

Table 6.15 shows some command-line options available with Ipconfig.

Table 6.15 Ipconfig Command-Line Examples

Command	Action
ipconfig /all	Displays additional information about DNS, including the FQDN and the DNS suffix search list.
ipconfig /flushdns	Flushes and resets the DNS resolver cache. For more information about this option, see "Viewing and Displaying the Cache" earlier in this chapter.
ipconfig /displaydns	Displays the contents of the DNS resolver cache. For more information about this option, see "Viewing and Displaying the Cache" earlier in this chapter.
ipconfig /registerdns	Refreshes all DHCP leases and registers any related DNS names. This option is available only on Windows 2000–based computers that run the DHCP Client service. For more information about this option, see "Dynamic Update and Secure Dynamic Update" earlier in this chapter.
ipconfig /release [*adapter*]	Releases all DHCP leases.
ipconfig /renew [*adapter*]	Refreshes all DHCP leases and dynamically updates DNS names. This option is available only on systems that are running the DHCP Client service.

Event Viewer

The Event Viewer logs errors with the Windows 2000 operating system and services such as the DNS server. If you are having problems with DNS, you can check Event Viewer for DNS-related events.

▶ **To open the event viewer**

- Click Start, point to **Programs**, point to **Administrative Tools**, and then click **Event Viewer.**

  To view messages about the DNS server, click **DNS Server**.

  –Or–

  To view messages about the DNS client, click **System Log**.

For more information about Event Viewer, see Windows 2000 Help.

DNS Log

You can configure the DNS server to create a log file that records the following types of events:

- Queries
- Notification messages from other servers
- Dynamic updates
- Content of the question section for DNS query message
- Content of the answer section for DNS query messages
- Number of queries this server sends
- Number of queries this server has received
- Number of DNS requests received over a UDP port
- Number of DNS requests received over a TCP port
- Number of full packets sent by the server
- Number of packets written through by the server and back to the zone

The DNS log appears in *% Systemroot%*\System32\dns\Dns.log. Because the log is in RTF format, you must use WordPad to view it.

You can change the directory and file name in which the DNS log appears by adding the following entry to the registry with the REG_SZ data type:

> HKEY_LOCAL_MACHINE\SYSTEM\CurrentControlSet\Services\DNS \Parameters**LogFilePath**

Set the value of **LogFilePath** equal to the file path and file name where you want to locate the DNS log.

By default, the maximum file size of Dns.log is 4 MB. If you want to change the size, add the following entry to the registry with the REG_DWORD data type:

> HKEY_LOCAL_MACHINE\SYSTEM\CurrentControlSet\Services\DNS \Parameters**LogFileMaxSize**

Set the value of **LogFileMaxSize** equal to the desired file size in bytes. The minimum size is 64 Kb.

Once the log file reaches the maximum size, Windows 2000 writes over the beginning of the file. If you make the value higher, data persists for a longer time, but the log file consumes more disk space. If you make the value smaller, the log file uses less disk space, but the data persists for a shorter time.

Caution Do not leave DNS logging during normal operation because it consumes both processing and hard disk resources. Enable it only when diagnosing and solving DNS problems.

▶ **To configure the server to log DNS events**

1. In the DNS console, click the box next to the server, right-click the server, and then click Properties.
2. Click the **Logging** tab, and then select the options you want to log.

Stopping and Flushing the Cache

In addition to flushing the cache by using Ipconfig, you can stop and flush the cache by stopping and starting the client.

▶ **To stop the client**

- At the command prompt, type the following:

  net stop "dns client"

▶ **To start the client**

- At the command prompt, type the following:

  net start "dns client"

Monitoring in the DNS Console

You can use the DNS console to perform a test query to determine whether or not your server is working properly.

▶ **To perform test queries from within the DNS console**

1. In the DNS console, double-click the server name to expand the server information.
2. Right-click the server, and then click **Properties**.
3. Click the **Monitoring** tab.
4. Select the tests you want to perform, and then click **Test Now**.

If the simple query fails, check whether the local server contains the zone 1.0.0.127.in-addr.arpa. If the recursive query fails, check whether your root hints are correct and whether your root servers are running. For more information about simple queries and recursive queries, see "Introduction to DNS" in this book.

For more information about troubleshooting recursion problems, see "Checking for Recursion Problems" later in this chapter.

Best Practices for Configuring and Administering DNS

Observe the following suggestions to prevent common configuration errors:

- Enter the correct e-mail address of the responsible person for each zone you add to or manage on a DNS server.

  This field is used by applications to notify DNS administrators for a variety of reasons. For example, this field can be used to report query errors, incorrect data returned in a query, and security problems. Although most Internet e-mail addresses contain the at sign (@) when used in e-mail applications, you must replace this symbol with a period (.) when typing an e-mail address for this field. For example, instead of administrator@reskit.com, you would use administrator.reskit.com.
- When designing your DNS network, use standard guidelines and wherever possible, follow preferred practices for managing your DNS infrastructure.
- Make sure that you have at least two servers hosting each zone. They can host either primary and secondary copies of the zone, or two directory-integrated copies of each zone.
- If you are using Active Directory, use directory-integrated storage for your zones.

  In an integrated zone, domain controllers for each of your Active Directory domains correspond in a direct one-to-one mapping to DNS servers. When you troubleshoot DNS and Active Directory replication problems, the same server computers are used in both topologies, which simplifies planning, deployment, and troubleshooting.

  Using directory-integrated storage also simplifies dynamic updates for DNS clients that are running Windows 2000. When you configure a list of preferred and alternate DNS servers for each client, you can specify servers corresponding to domain controllers located near each client. If a client fails to update with its preferred server because the server is unavailable, the client can try an alternate server. When the preferred server becomes available, it loads the updated, directory-integrated zone that includes the updates that the client made.

- If you are not using Active Directory integration, correctly configure your clients and understand that a standard primary zone becomes a single point of failure for dynamic updates and for zone replication.

  Standard primary zones are required to create and manage zones in your DNS namespace if you are not using Active Directory. In this case, a single-master update model applies, with one DNS server designated as the primary server for a zone. Only the primary server, as determined in the SOA record properties for the zone, can process an update to the zone.

  For this reason, make sure that this DNS server is reliable and available. Otherwise, clients cannot update their A or PTR resource records.

- Consider using secondary or caching-only servers for your zones to offload DNS query traffic.

  Secondary servers can be used as backups for DNS clients, but they can also be used as the preferred DNS servers for legacy DNS clients. For mixed-mode environments, this enables you to balance the load of DNS query traffic on your network and, thus, reserve your DNS-enabled primary servers for Windows 2000–based clients that need primary servers to perform dynamic registration and updates of their A and PTR resource records.

The IETF has published several Requests for Comment (RFCs) that cover best practices for DNS, as recommended by DNS architects and planners for the Internet. You might find the following RFCs useful, especially if you are planning a large DNS design:

- RFC 1912, "Common DNS Operational and Configuration Errors"
- RFC 2182, "Selection and Operation of Secondary DNS Servers"
- RFC 2219, "Use of DNS Aliases for Network Services"

Verifying Your Basic DNS Configuration

If you use a third-party DNS server to support Active Directory, you must perform configuration tasks manually, and doing so, you might cause common configuration errors that prevent DNS and Active Directory from working properly. The following sections describe tests that you can perform to verify that your DNS server is working properly, that the forward and reverse lookup zones are properly configured, and that DNS can support Active Directory.

If you use either the Configure DNS Server wizard or the Active Directory Installation wizard to install your Windows 2000 DNS server, most configuration tasks are performed automatically and you can avoid many common configuration errors, but you might still want to perform the tests in this section.

Before checking anything else, check the event log for errors. For more information about Event Viewer, see "Troubleshooting Tools" earlier in this chapter.

Verifying That Your DNS Server Can Answer Queries

Use the following process to verify that your DNS server is started and can answer queries.

- Make sure that your server has basic network connectivity. For more information about verifying basic network connectivity, see "Checking the DNS Server for Problems" later in this chapter.
- Make sure that the server can answer both simple and recursive queries from the Monitoring tab in the DNS console. For more information about the Monitoring tab, see "Troubleshooting Tools" earlier in this chapter.
- From a client, use Nslookup to look up a domain name and the name of a host in the domain. For more information about using Nslookup, see "Troubleshooting Tools" earlier in this chapter.
- On the server, run **netdiag** to make sure the server is working properly and that the resource records Netlogon needs are registered on a DNS server. For more information about Netdiag, see "Troubleshooting Tools" earlier in this chapter.
- Make sure that the server can reach a root server by typing the following:

  nslookup

  server *<IP address of server>*

  set querytype=NS

  .

- Make sure that there is an A and PTR resource record configured for the server. For information about PTR resource records, see "Testing for Reverse Lookup Zones and PTR Records" later in this chapter.

Verifying That the Forward Lookup Zone Is Properly Configured

After you create a forward lookup zone, you can use Nslookup to make sure it is properly configured and to test its integrity to host Active Directory. To start Nslookup, type the following

Nslookup
server *<IP address of server on which you created zone>*
set querytype=any

Nslookup starts. If the resolver cannot locate a PTR resource record for the server, you see an error message, but you are still able to perform the tests in this section.

To verify the zone is responding correctly, simulate a zone transfer by typing the following:

ls -d *<domain name>*

If the server is configured to restrict zone transfers, you might see an error message in Event Viewer. (For more information about Event Viewer, see "Troubleshooting Tools" earlier in this chapter.) Otherwise, you see a list of all the records in the domain.

Next, query for the SOA record by typing the following and pressing ENTER:

<domain name>

If your server is configured correctly, you see an SOA record. The SOA record includes a "primary name server" field. To verify that the primary name server has registered an NS record, type the following:

set type=ns
<domain name>

If your server is configured correctly, you see an NS record for the name server.

Make sure that the authoritative name server listed in the NS record can be contacted to request queries by typing the following:

server *<server name or IP address>*

Next, query the server for any name for which it is authoritative.

If these tests are successful, the NS record points to the correct hostname, and the hostname has the correct IP address associated with it.

Testing for Reverse Lookup Zones and PTR Resource Records

You do not need reverse lookup zones and PTR resource records for Active Directory to function. However, you need them if you want clients to be able to resolve FQDNs from IP addresses. Also, PTR resource records are commonly used by some applications for security purposes, to verify the identity of the client.

You do not need to have the reverse lookup zones and PTR resource records on your own servers; instead, another DNS server can contain these zones.

After you have configured your reverse lookup zones and PTR resource records, manually examine them in the DNS console. A reverse lookup zone must exist for each subnet, and the parent reverse lookup zone must have a delegation to your reverse lookup zone. For example, if you have a private root and the subnets 172.32.16.x and 172.32.17.x, the private root can host all reverse lookup zones, or it can contain the reverse lookup zone 172.32.x and delegate the reverse lookup zones 172.32.16.x and 172.32.17.x to other servers. Also, PTR resource records must exist for all the computers in your network. For more information about adding a reverse lookup zone, see "Adding a Reverse Lookup Zone" earlier in this chapter.

You can also use Nslookup to verify that the reverse lookup zones and PTR resource records are configured correctly.

▶ **To make sure your reverse lookup zones and PTR resource records are configured correctly**

1. Start Nslookup by typing **Nslookup** at the command prompt and then pressing ENTER.
2. Switch to the server you want to query by typing the following:

   server *<Server IP Address>*
3. Enter the IP address of the computer whose PTR resource record you want to verify, and then press ENTER.

   If the reverse lookup zone and PTR resource record are configured correctly, Nslookup returns the name of the computer.
4. To quit Nslookup, type **exit** and then press ENTER.

Verifying Your DNS Configuration After Installing Active Directory

When you use third-party DNS servers to support Active Directory, you can verify the registration of domain controller locator resource records. If the server does not support dynamic update, you need to add these records manually.

The Netlogon service creates a log file that contains all the locator resource records and places the log file in the following location:

%SystemRoot%\System32\Config\Netlogon.dns

You can check this file to find out which locator resource records are created for the domain controller.

The locator resource records are stored in a text file, compliant with RFC specifications. If your server is configured correctly, you see the LDAP SRV record for the domain controller:

```
_ldap._tcp.<Active Directory domain name>    IN  SRV <priority>
<weight> 389 <domain controller name>
```

For example:

```
_ldap._tcp.reskit.com.  IN  SRV 0   0   389 dc1.reskit.com
```

Next, use the Nslookup command-line tool to verify that the domain controller registered the SRV resource records that were listed in Netlogon.dns.

Note During the following test, if you have not configured a reverse lookup zone and PTR resource record for the DNS server you are querying, you might see several time-outs. This is not a problem.

▶ **To verify that SRV resource records are registered for the domain controller**

1. At the command prompt, type **nslookup** and then press ENTER.
2. To set the DNS query type to filter for SRV records only, type **set type=SRV** and then press ENTER.
3. To send a query for the registered SRV record for a domain controller in your Active Directory domain, type **_ldap._tcp.**<*Active Directory domain name*> and then press ENTER.
4. You should see the SRV records listed in Netlogon.dns. If you do not, SRV resource records might not be registered for the domain controller.

The following example shows a full Nslookup session, used to verify SRV resource records that are registered for locating two domain controllers on a network. In this example, the two domain controllers (DC1 and DC2) are registered for the domain noam.reskit.com.

```
C:\>nslookup
Default Server:  dc1.noam.reskit.com
Address:  10.0.0.14
> set type=SRV
> _ldap._tcp.noam.reskit.com
Server:  dc1.noam.reskit.com
Address:  10.0.0.14
_ldap._tcp.noam.reskit.com   SRV service location:
          priority       = 0
          weight         = 0
          port           = 389
          svr hostname   = dc1.noam.reskit.com
_ldap._tcp.noam.reskit.com   SRV service location:
          priority       = 0
          weight         = 0
          port           = 389
          svr hostname   = dc2.noam.reskit.com
dc1.noam.reskit.com     internet address = 10.0.0.14
dc2.noam.reskit.com     internet address = 10.0.0.15
```

Diagnosing Name Resolution Problems

Most failed name resolution attempts fail in one of two general ways:

- A user receives a negative response when attempting to resolve a name, such as an error message indicating "name not found."
- A user receives a positive response when attempting to resolve a name, but the information returned is incorrect.

Important Whenever you are trying to troubleshoot problems with name resolution, always submit an FQDN. In that way, you can make sure that your problem is not caused by an incorrect domain suffix appended to the queried name.

The following flowcharts and associated text in Figures 6.36–6.41 explain how to diagnose each of these problems. For another good source of information for diagnosing common problems, see RFC 1912, "Common DNS Operational and Configuration Errors."

Note The flowcharts in Figures 6.36–6.41 direct you to other flowcharts in other figures. To locate the correct flow chart, see the figure captions.

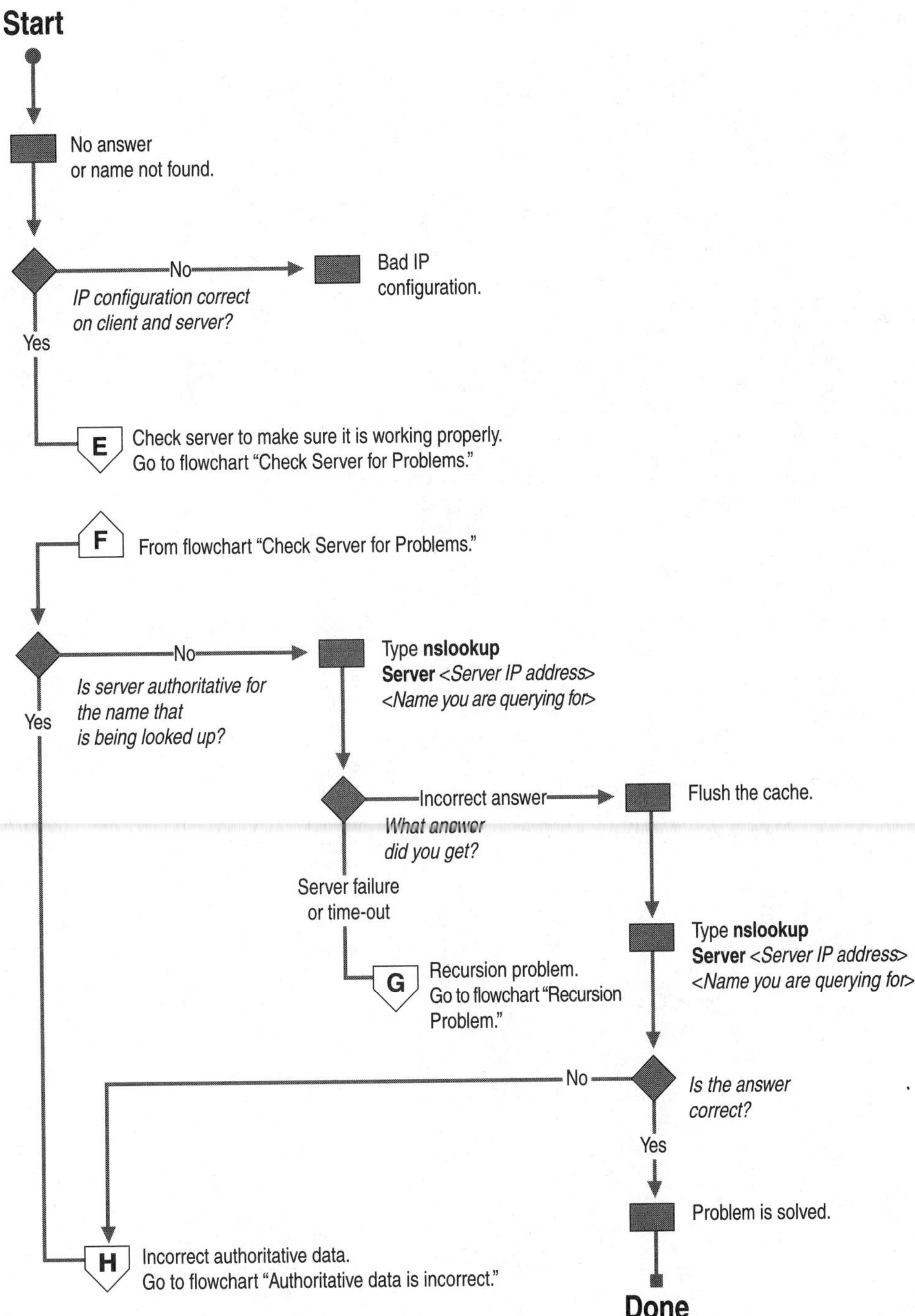
Start
No answer
or name not found.
No
IP configuration correct
on client and server?
Bad IP
configuration.
Yes
E
Check server to make sure it is working properly.
Go to flowchart "Check Server for Problems."
F
From flowchart "Check Server for Problems."
No
Is server authoritative for
the name that
is being looked up?
Yes
Type nslookup
Server <Server IP address>
<Name you are querying for>
Incorrect answer
What answer
did you get?
Flush the cache.
Server failure
or time-out
G
Recursion problem.
Go to flowchart "Recursion
Problem."
Type nslookup
Server <Server IP address>
<Name you are querying for>
No
Is the answer
correct?
Yes
Problem is solved.
H
Incorrect authoritative data.
Go to flowchart "Authoritative data is incorrect."
Done

Figure 6.36 No Answer or Name Not Found

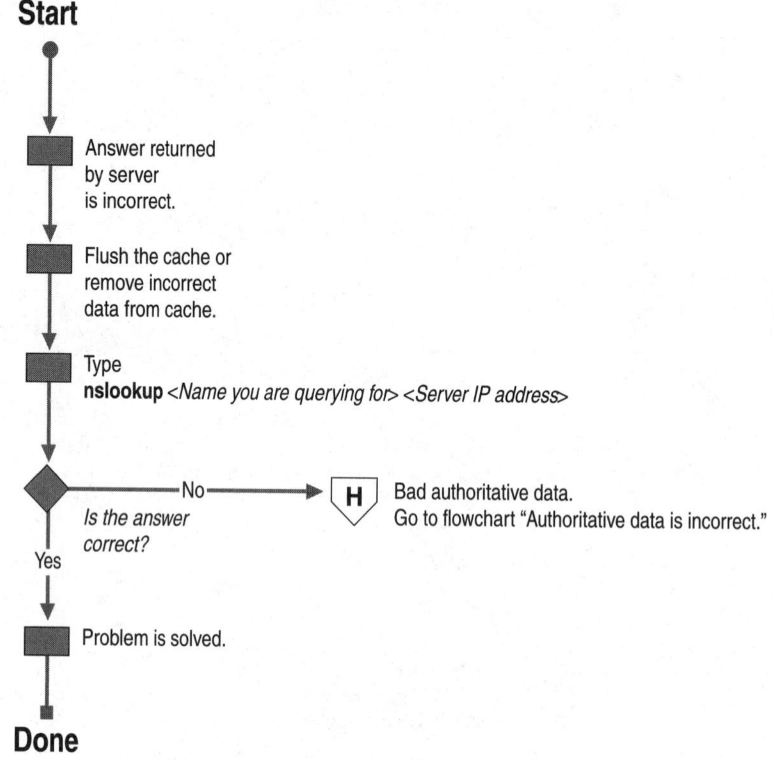

Figure 6.37 Answer Is Incorrect

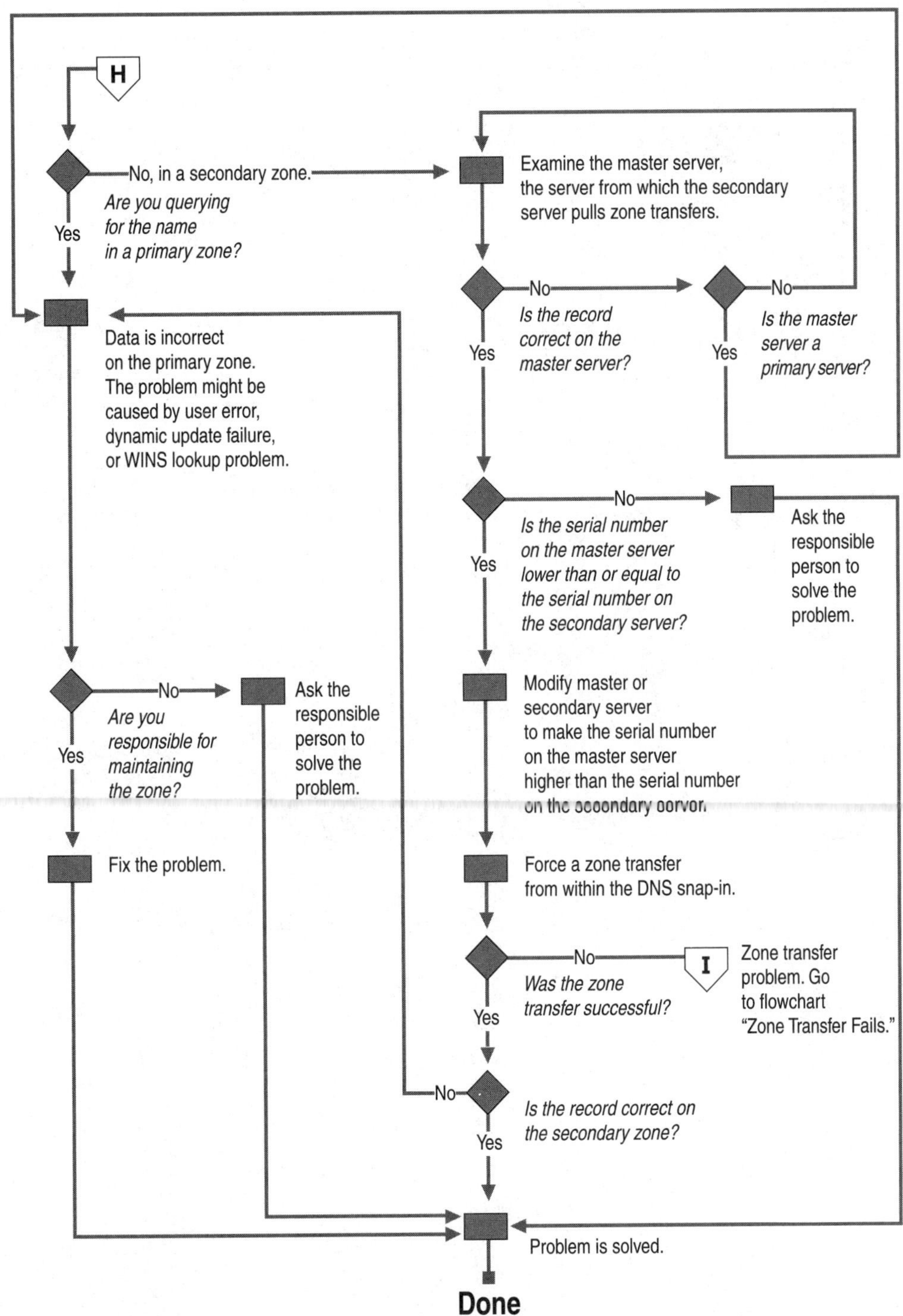

Figure 6.38 Authoritative Data Is Incorrect

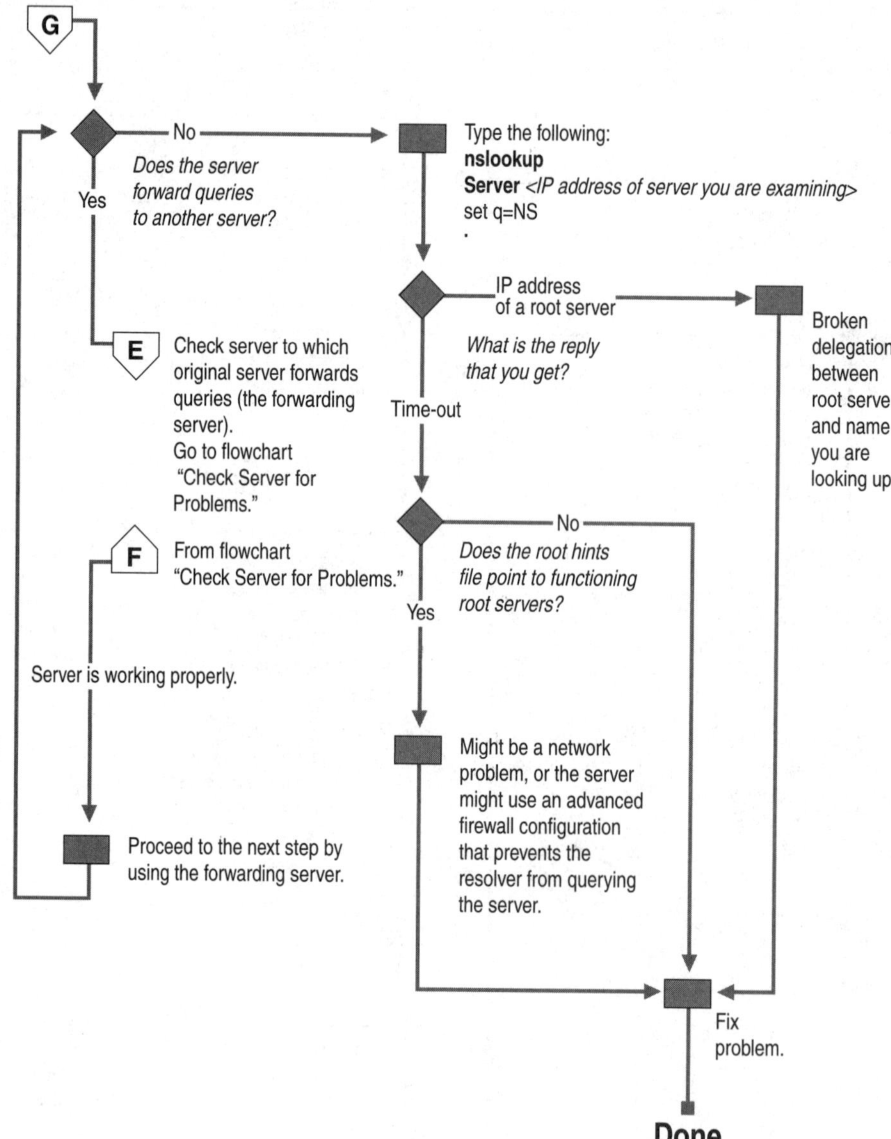

Figure 6.39 Recursion Problem

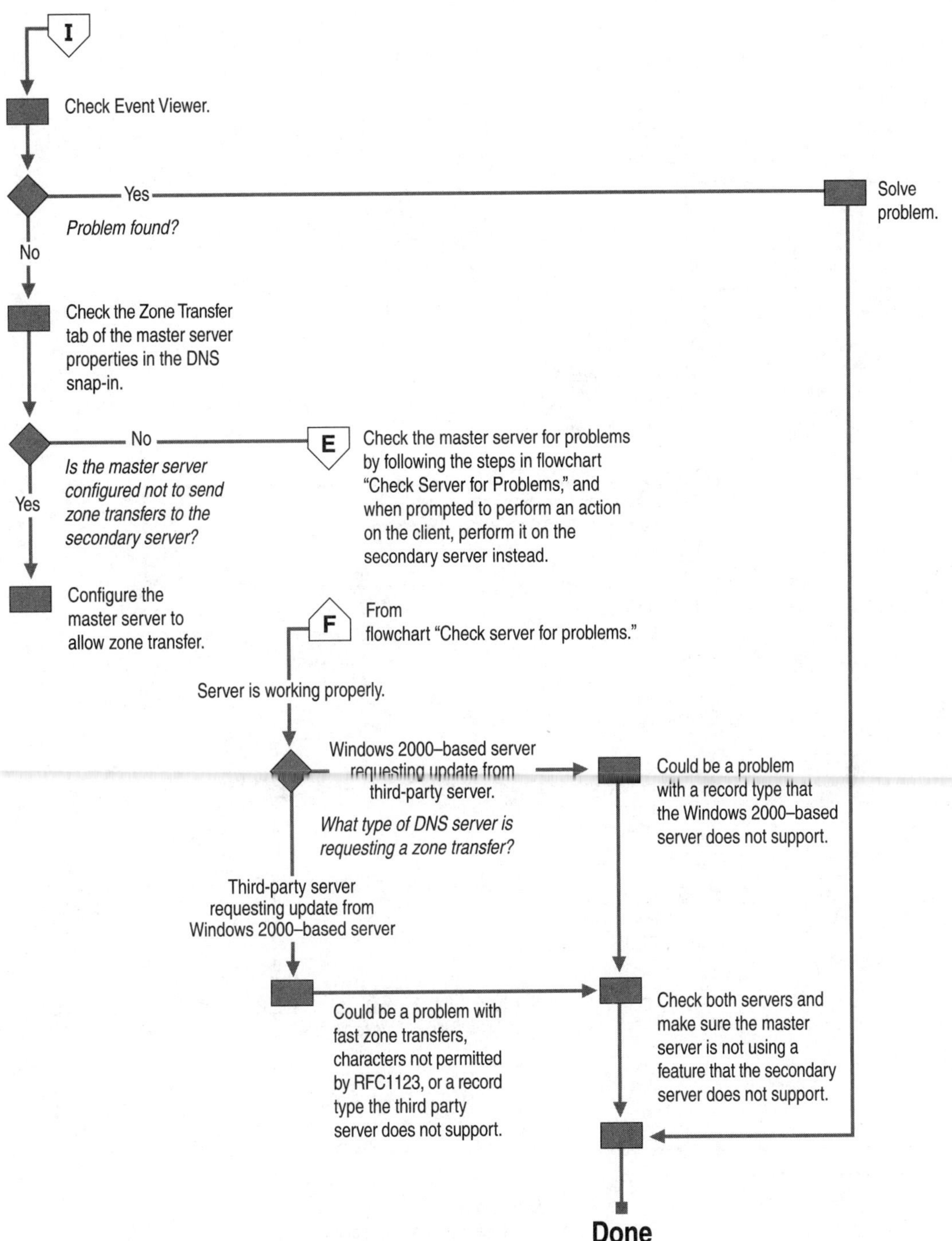
I
Check Event Viewer.
Yes
Problem found?
No
Solve problem.
Check the Zone Transfer tab of the master server properties in the DNS snap-in.
No
Is the master server configured not to send zone transfers to the secondary server?
Yes
E
Check the master server for problems by following the steps in flowchart "Check Server for Problems," and when prompted to perform an action on the client, perform it on the secondary server instead.
Configure the master server to allow zone transfer.
F
From flowchart "Check server for problems."
Server is working properly.
Windows 2000–based server requesting update from third-party server.
What type of DNS server is requesting a zone transfer?
Could be a problem with a record type that the Windows 2000–based server does not support.
Third-party server requesting update from Windows 2000–based server
Could be a problem with fast zone transfers, characters not permitted by RFC1123, or a record type the third party server does not support.
Check both servers and make sure the master server is not using a feature that the secondary server does not support.
Done

Figure 6.40 Zone Transfer Fails

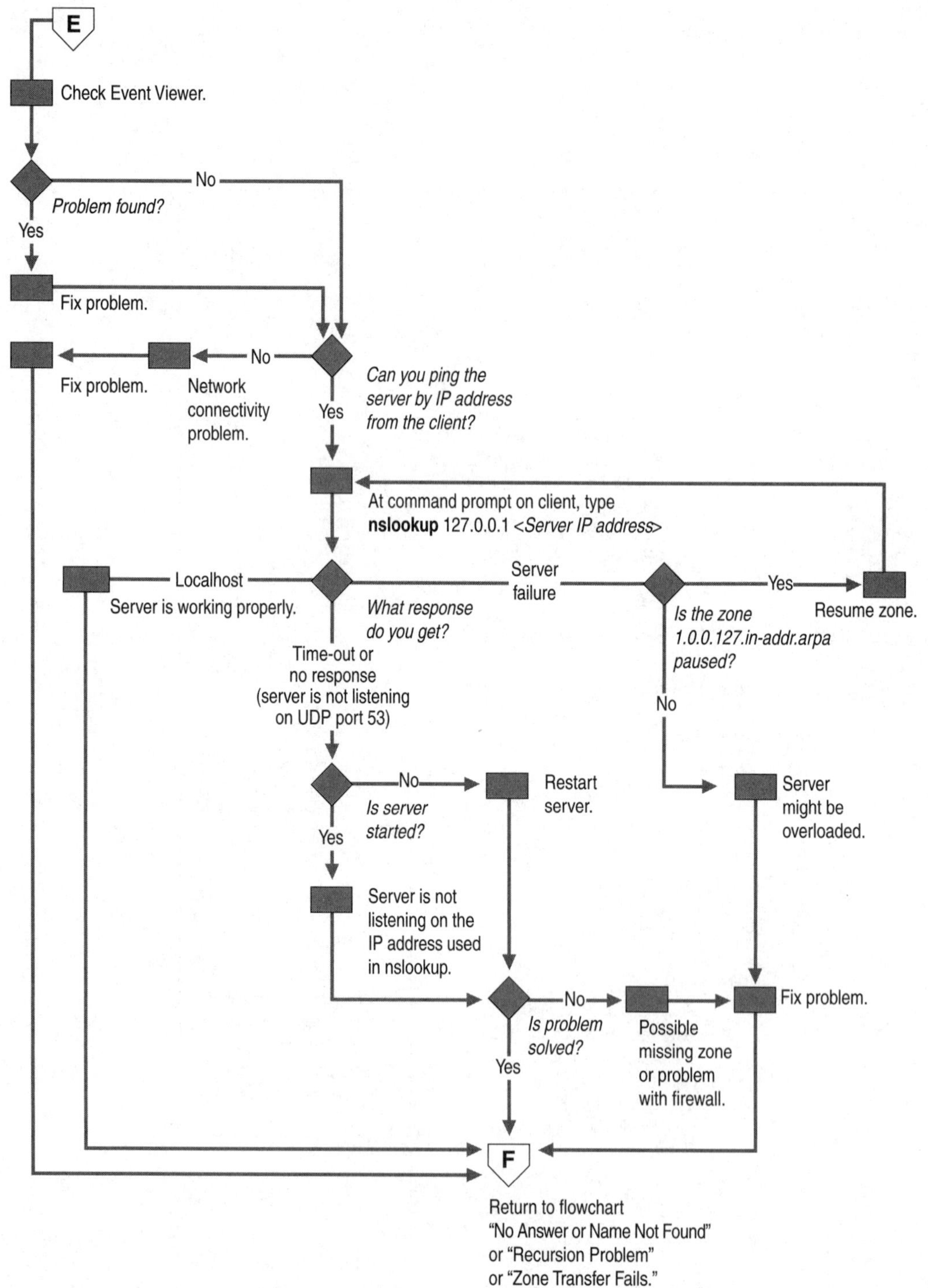

Figure 6.41 Check Server for Problems

Cannot Find Name or IP Address

If a query fails because you get the response **Non-existent domain** from Nslookup or the response **Unknown host** from Ping, the DNS server did not find the name or IP address that you are looking up. Use the following process, shown in Figure 6.36, to help troubleshoot the problem:

1. Check that the client and server computers have a valid IP configuration.

   To check IP configuration, type **ipconfig /all** at the command prompt. In the command-line output, verify the IP address, subnet mask, and default gateway.

2. Check that the server is working properly. For more information about verifying that the server is working properly, see "Checking the DNS Server for Problems" later in this chapter.

3. Check whether the DNS server is authoritative for the name that is being looked up.

   If the DNS server is authoritative for the name that is being looked up, you probably have a problem with authoritative data. For more information about checking for problems with authoritative data, see "Checking for Problems with Authoritative Data" later in this chapter.

   –Or–

   If the DNS server is not authoritative for the name that is being looked up, proceed to the next step.

4. Query for the name by using Nslookup. At the command prompt, type the following:

   Nslookup *<query address>* *<IP address of server>*

   where *IP address of server* is the IP address of the server that you queried originally, and *query address* is the name or IP address you are attempting to resolve. If you get the message "Server failed" or "Request to *server* timed out," you probably have a problem involving a broken delegation. For more information about problems with broken delegations, see "Checking for Recursion Problems" later in this chapter.

   –Or–

   If you get an incorrect answer or the message "Non-existent domain," proceed to the next step.

5. Flush the resolver cache. At the command prompt, type the following:

   Nslookup *<query address>* *<IP address of server>*

where *IP address of server* is the IP address of the server that you queried originally, and *query address* is the name or IP address you are attempting to resolve. If the answer is correct, the problem was a stale cache entry, and your problem is solved.

–Or–

If the answer is still not correct, you probably have a problem with authoritative data. For more information about problems with authoritative data, see "Checking for Problems with Authoritative Data" later in this chapter.

Incorrect Answer

If you query a DNS server and it responds with incorrect information, use the following process, shown in Figure 6.37, to solve the problem.

1. Flush the resolver cache.
2. At the command prompt, type the following:

   Nslookup *<query address> <IP address of server>*

   where *IP address of server* is the IP address of the server that you queried originally, and *query address* is the name or IP address you are attempting to resolve. If the answer is correct, the problem was a stale cache entry, and your problem is solved.

   –Or–

   If the answer is still not correct, you probably have a problem with authoritative data. For more information about how to diagnose problems with authoritative data, see "Checking for Problems with Authoritative Data" later in this chapter.

Checking the DNS Server for Problems

Use the following process, shown in Figure 6.41, to check the DNS server for problems.

1. Check Event Viewer for error messages. For information about Event Viewer, see "Troubleshooting Tools" earlier in this chapter.
2. Check for basic connectivity between the client computer and the DNS server that you used for your original query by pinging the DNS server by its IP address.

   If the DNS server does not respond to a direct ping of its IP address, you probably have a network connectivity problem between the client and the DNS server.

3. At the command prompt on the client computer, type the following:

   nslookup 127.0.0.1 *<IP address of server>*

   If the resolver returns the name of the local host, the server does not have any problems.

   –Or–

   If the resolver returns the response "Server failure," proceed to step 4.

   –Or–

   If the resolver returns the response "Request to *server* timed out" or "No response from server," proceed to step 5.

4. If the resolver returns the response "Server failure," the zone 1.0.0.127.in-addr.arpa is probably paused, or the server is possibly overloaded. You can find out whether it is paused by checking the **General** tab of the zone properties, from within the DNS console.

5. If the resolver returns the response "Request to *server* timed out" or "No response from server," the DNS server probably is not running. Try to restart the server by typing the following at the command prompt on the server:

   net start DNS

   –Or–

   If it is running, the server might not be listening on the IP address that you used in your Nslookup query. From the **Interfaces** tab of the server properties page in the DNS console, administrators can restrict a DNS server to listen only on selected addresses. If the DNS server has been configured to limit service to a specific list of its configured IP addresses, it is possible that the IP address used to contact the DNS server is not in the list. You can try a different IP address in the list or add the IP address to the list. For more information about restricting a DNS server to listen only on selected addresses, see Windows 2000 Help.

   –Or–

   In rare cases, the DNS server might be configured to disable the use of its automatically created default zones. By default, the DNS service automatically creates the following standard reverse lookup zones based on RFC recommendations:

   - 0.in-addr.arpa
   - 127.in-addr.arpa
   - 255.in-addr.arpa

   The automatic creation of these zones can only be disabled through the registry, so it is unlikely that this has happened. However, if you think automatic creation has been disabled, you can use the DNS console to make sure that the zones exist.

   –Or–

In rare cases, the DNS server might have an advanced security or firewall configuration. If the server is located on another network that is reachable only through an intermediate host (such as a packet filtering router or proxy server), the DNS server might use a non-standard port to listen for and receive client requests. By default, Nslookup sends queries to DNS servers on UDP port 53, so if the DNS server uses any other port, Nslookup queries fail. If you think this might be the problem, check whether an intermediate filter is intentionally used to block traffic on well-known DNS ports. If not, try to modify the packet filters or port rules on the firewall to allow traffic on UDP/TCP port 53.

Diagnosing Problems with Incorrect Authoritative Data

If you have determined that the server contains incorrect authoritative (non-cached) data, use the following process to help troubleshoot the problem:

1. Determine whether the server that is returning the incorrect response is either a primary or secondary server for the zone.

   If the server is a primary server for the zone—either the standard primary server for the zone or a server that uses Active Directory integration to load the zone—the data is incorrect on the primary zone. Go to step 5.

   –Or–

   If the server is hosting a secondary copy of the zone, proceed to the next step.

2. Examine the zone on the master server (the server from which this server pulls zone transfers). You can determine which server is the master server by examining the properties of the secondary zone in the DNS console. Is the name correct on the master server?

   If the name is not correct on the master server, go to step 1. When prompted to examine a server, examine the server from which this server pulls zone transfers.

   –Or–

   If the name was correct on the master server, proceed to the next step.

3. Check whether the serial number on the master server is lower than or equal to the serial number on the secondary server. If not, proceed to the next step.

   –Or–

   If the serial number on the master server is lower than or equal to the serial number on the secondary server, modify either the master server or the secondary server so that the serial number on the master server is higher than the serial number on the secondary server. Then, proceed to the next step.

4. Force a zone transfer from within the DNS console. (For information about how to force a zone transfer, see Windows 2000 Server Help.) Next, examine the secondary server again to see whether the zone was transferred correctly. If not, you probably have a zone transfer problem; see "Zone Transfer Problems" later in this chapter.

   –Or–

   If the zone was transferred correctly, check whether the data is now correct. If not, the data is incorrect on the primary zone. Proceed to the next step.

5. If the data is incorrect on the primary zone, the problem might be caused by user error when entering data into the zone, a problem with Active Directory replication, a problem with dynamic update, or a WINS lookup problem. For information about problems with user error and Active Directory replication, see "Troubleshooting DNS Problems" later in this chapter. For information about problems with dynamic update, see "Troubleshooting Dynamic Update." For information about WINS lookup problems, see "Solving Common DNS Problems" later in this chapter.

   If you are responsible for maintaining the zone, you can solve the problem. Otherwise, ask the person who is responsible for maintaining the zone to solve the problem.

Diagnosing Problems with Recursion

For recursion to work successfully, all DNS servers that are used in the path of a recursive query must be able to respond and forward correct data. If they cannot, a recursive query can fail for any of the following reasons:

- The query times out before it can be completed.
- A server used during the query fails to respond.
- A server used during the query provides incorrect data.

If you have determined that you have a problem with recursion, use the following process, shown in Figure 6.39, to help troubleshoot the problem. Start with the server used in your original query:

1. Check whether this server forwards queries to another server by examining the **Forwarders** tab in the server properties in the DNS console. If the check box **Enable forwarders** is selected and one or more servers are listed, this server forwards queries.

   If this server does forward queries to another server, check for problems with the server to which this server forwards queries. To check for problems, follow the troubleshooting steps in "Checking the DNS Server for Problems." When that section instructs you to perform a task on the client, perform it on the server instead.

If the server is healthy and can forward queries, repeat this step, examining the server to which this server forwards queries.

–Or–

If this server does not forward queries to another server, proceed to the next step.

2. Test whether this server can query a root server by typing the following:

   nslookup
   server ***<IP address of the server you are examining>***
   set querytype=NS
   .

If the resolver returns the IP address of a root server, you probably have a broken delegation between the root server and the name or IP address that you are attempting to resolve. Follow the procedure "To test for a broken delegation" to determine where you have a broken delegation.

–Or–

If the resolver returns the response "Request to *server* timed out," check whether the root hints points to functioning root servers by following the procedure "To view the current root hints." If the root hints does point to functioning root servers, you might have a network problem, or the server might use an advanced firewall configuration that prevents the resolver from querying the server, as described in "Checking the Server for Problems," earlier in this chapter. It is also possible that the recursive time-out default (15 seconds) is too short. For information about how to change this time-out, see the Windows 2000 Server Help. Search for "tuning advanced parameters."

Note Begin the tests in the following procedure by querying a valid root server. The test takes you through a process of querying all the DNS servers from the root down to the server that you are testing for a broken delegation.

► To test for a broken delegation

1. At the command prompt on the server that you are testing, type the following:

   nslookup

   server *<server IP address>*
   set norecursion
   set querytype=*<resource record type>*

   <FQDN >

   where *resource record type* is the type of resource record that you were querying for in your original query, and *FQDN* is the FQDN for which you were querying (terminated by a period).

2. If the response includes a list of NS and A resource records for delegated servers, repeat step 1 for each server and use the IP address from the A resource records as the server IP address.

   –Or–

   If the response does not contain an NS resource record, you have a broken delegation.

   –Or–

   If the response contains NS resource records, but no A resource records, type **set recursion** and query individually for A resource records of servers listed in the NS records. If for each NS resource record in a zone, you do not find at least one valid IP address of an A resource record for each NS resource record, you have a broken delegation.

If you determine that you have a broken delegation, fix it by adding or updating an A resource record in the parent zone with a valid IP address for a correct DNS server for the delegated zone.

▶ **To view the current root hints**

1. Start the DNS console.
2. Add or connect to the DNS server that failed a recursive query.
3. Right-click the server and select **Properties**.
4. Click **Root Hints**.
5. Check for basic connectivity to the root servers.
6. If root hints appear to be configured correctly, verify that the DNS server used in a failed name resolution can ping the root servers by IP address.

   If the root servers do not respond to pinging by IP address, the IP addresses for the root servers might have changed. However, reconfiguration of root servers, is uncommon.

Diagnosing Zone Transfer Problems

If you have determined that a secondary server cannot pull a zone transfer from a master server, use the following process, shown in Figure 6.40, to diagnose and solve your zone transfer problems.

1. Check Event Viewer for both the primary and secondary DNS server. For information about Event Viewer, see "Troubleshooting Tools" earlier in this chapter.

2. Check the master server to see whether it is refusing to send the transfer for security reasons. Check the **Zone Transfers** tab of the zone properties in the DNS console. If the server restricts zone transfers to a list of servers, such as those listed on the **Name Servers** tab of the zone properties, make sure that the secondary server is on that list. Make sure that the server is configured to send zone transfers.
3. Check the master server for problems by following the steps in "Checking the DNS Server for Problems" earlier in this chapter. When prompted to perform a task on the client, perform the task on the secondary server instead.
4. Check whether the secondary server is running another DNS server implementation, such as BIND. If so, the problem might have one of several causes:
   - The Windows 2000 master server might be configured to send fast zone transfers, but the third-party secondary server might not support fast zone transfers. If so, disable fast zone transfers on the master server by selecting the check box **Bind secondaries** on the **Advanced** tab of the properties for your server, from within the DNS console.
   - If a forward lookup zone on the Windows 2000 server contains a WINS lookup record or the reverse lookup zone contains a WINS-R record, the BIND server might not be able to transfer the zone. For information about diagnosing problems in which a BIND server cannot transfer a zone, see "Solving Common DNS Problems" later in this chapter.
   - If a forward lookup zone on the Windows 2000 server contains a record type (for example, an SRV record) the secondary server does not support, the secondary server might have problems pulling the zone.
5. Check whether the master server is running another DNS server implementation, such as BIND.

   If so, it is possible that the zone on the master server includes incompatible resource records that Windows 2000 does not recognize. For a complete list of all RFC-compliant resource record types that are supported by DNS servers that are running under Windows 2000 Server, see Windows 2000 Server Help.
6. If either the master or secondary server is running another DNS server implementation, check both servers to make sure that they support the same features. You can check the Windows 2000 server from the **Advanced** tab of the properties page for the server from within the DNS console. In addition to the **Bind secondaries** box, this page includes the **Name checking** drop down list, which enables you to select enforcement of strict RFC compliance for characters in DNS names.

Solving Other Common DNS Problems

This section lists several common DNS problems and explains how to solve them.

Event ID 7062 appears in the event log.

If you see event ID 7062 in the event log, the DNS server has sent a packet to itself. This is usually caused by a configuration error. Check the following:

- Make sure that there is no lame delegation for this server. A *lame delegation* occurs when one server delegates a zone to a server that is not authoritative for the zone.
- Check the forwarders list to make sure that it does not list itself as a forwarder.
- If this server includes secondary zones, make sure that it does not list itself as a master server for those zones.
- If this server includes primary zones, make sure that it does not list itself in the notify list.

Zone transfers to secondary servers that are running BIND are slow.

By default, the Windows 2000 DNS server always uses a fast method of zone transfer. This method uses compression and includes multiple resource records in each message, substantially increasing the speed of zone transfers. Most DNS servers support fast zone transfer. However, BIND 4.9.4 and earlier does not support fast zone transfer. This is unlikely to be a problem, because when the Windows 2000 DNS Server service is installed, fast zone transfer is disabled by default. However, if you are using BIND 4.9.4 or earlier, and you have enabled fast zone transfer, you need to disable fast zone transfer.

▶ **To disable fast zone transfer**

1. In the DNS console, right-click the DNS server, and then click **Properties**.
2. Click the **Advanced** tab.
3. In the **Server options** list, select the **Bind secondaries** check box, and then click **OK**.

You see the error message "Default servers are not available."

When you start Nslookup, you might see the following error message:

*** Can't find server name for address <*address*>: Non-existent domain

*** Default servers are not available

Default Server: Unknown

Address: 127.0.0.1

If you see this message, your DNS server is still able to answer queries and host Active Directory. The resolver cannot locate the PTR resource record for the name server that it is configured to use. The properties for your network connection must specify the IP address of at least one name server, and when you start Nslookup, the resolver uses that IP address to look up the name of the server. If the resolver cannot find the name of the server, it displays that error message. However, you can still use Nslookup to query the server.

To solve this problem, check the following:

- Make sure that a reverse lookup zone that is authoritative for the PTR resource record exists. For more information about adding a reverse lookup zone, see "Adding a Reverse Lookup Zone" earlier in this chapter.
- Make sure that the reverse lookup zone includes a PTR resource record for the name server.
- Make sure that the name server you are using for your lookup can query the server that contains the PTR resource record and the reverse lookup zone either iteratively or recursively.

User entered incorrect data in zone.

For information about how to add or update records by using the DNS console, see Windows 2000 Server Help. For more information about using resource records in zones, search for the keywords "managing" and "resource records" in Windows 2000 Server Help.

Active Directory-integrated zones contain inconsistent data.

For Active Directory–integrated zones, it is also possible that the affected records for the query have been updated in Active Directory but not replicated to all DNS servers that are loading the zone. By default, all DNS servers that load zones from Active Directory poll Active Directory at a set interval—typically, every 15 minutes—and update the zone for any incremental changes to the zone. In most cases, a DNS update takes no more than 20 minutes to replicate to all DNS servers that are used in an Active Directory domain environment that uses default replication settings and reliable high-speed links.

User cannot resolve name that exists on a correctly configured DNS server.

First, confirm that the name was not entered in error by the user. Confirm the exact set of characters entered by the user when the original DNS query was made. Also, if the name used in the initial query was unqualified and was not the FQDN, try the FQDN instead in the client application and repeat the query. Be sure to include the period at the end of the name to indicate the name entered is an exact FQDN.

If the FQDN query succeeds and returns correct data in the response, the most likely cause of the problem is a misconfigured domain suffix search list that is used in the client resolver settings.

Name resolution to Internet is slow, intermittent, or fails.

If queries destined for the Internet are slow or intermittent, or you cannot resolve names on the Internet, but local Intranet name resolution operates successfully, the cache file on your Windows 2000–based server might be corrupt, missing, or out of date. You can either replace the cache file with an original version of the cache file or manually enter the correct root hints into the cache file from the DNS console. If the DNS server is configured to load data on startup from Active Directory and the registry, you must use the DNS console to enter the root hints.

▶ **To enter root hints in the DNS console**

1. In the DNS console, double-click the server to expand it.
2. Right-click the server, and then click **Properties**.
3. Click the **Root Hints** tab.
4. Enter your root hints, and then click **OK**.

▶ **To replace your cache file**

1. Stop the DNS service by typing the following at the command prompt:

   net stop dns
2. Type the following:

   cd %Systemroot%\System32\DNS
3. Rename your cache file by typing the following:

   ren cache.dns cache.old
4. Copy the original version of the cache file, which might be found in one of two places, by typing either of the following:

   copy backup\cache.dns

   –Or–

   copy samples\cache.dns
5. Start the DNS service by typing the following:

   net start dns

If name resolution to the Internet still fails, repeat the procedure, copying the cache file from your Windows 2000 source media.

▶ **To copy the cache file from your Windows 2000 source media**

- At the command prompt, type the following:

  expand <*drive*>:\i386\cache.dn_ *%Systemroot%*\system32\dns\cache.dns

  where *drive* is the drive that contains your Windows 2000 source media.

Resolver does not take advantage of round robin feature.

Windows 2000 includes subnet prioritization, a new feature, which reduces network traffic across subnets. However, it prevents the resolver from using the round robin feature as defined in RFC 1794. By using the round robin feature, the server rotates the order of A resource record data returned in a query answer in which multiple resource records of the same type exist for a queried DNS domain name. However, if the resolver is configured for subnet prioritization, the resolver reorders the list to favor IP addresses from networks to which they are directly connected.

If you would prefer to use the round robin feature rather than the subnet prioritization feature, you can do so by changing the value of a registry entry. For more information about configuring the subnet prioritization feature, see "Configuring Subnet Prioritization" earlier in this chapter.

WINS Lookup record causes zone transfer to a third-party DNS server to fail.

If a zone transfer from a Windows 2000 server to a third-party DNS server fails, check whether the zone includes any WINS or WINS-R records. If it does, you can prevent these records from being propagated to a secondary DNS server.

▶ **To prevent propagation of WINS lookup records to a secondary DNS server**

1. In the DNS console, double-click your DNS server, right-click the zone name that contains the WINS record, and then click **Properties**.
2. In the **Properties** dialog box for the zone, click the **WINS** tab and select the check box **Do not replicate this record.**

▶ **To prevent propagation of WINS-R records to a secondary DNS server**

1. In the DNS console, double-click your DNS server, right-click the reverse lookup zone that contains the WINS-R record, and then click **Properties**.
2. In the properties page for the zone, click the **WINS-R** tab and select the check box **Do not replicate this record**.

WINS lookup record causes a problem with authoritative data.

If you have a problem with incorrect authoritative data in a zone for which WINS lookup integration is enabled, the erroneous data might be caused by WINS returning incorrect data. You can tell whether WINS is the source of the incorrect data by checking the TTL of the data in an Nslookup query. Normally, the DNS service answers with names stored in authoritative zone data by using the set zone or resource record TTL value. It generally answers only with decreased TTLs when providing answers based on non-authoritative, cached data obtained from other DNS servers during recursive lookups.

However, WINS lookups are an exception. The DNS server represents data from a WINS server as authoritative but stores the data in the server cache only, rather than in zones, and decreases the TTL of the data.

▶ To determine whether data comes from a WINS server

1. At the command prompt, type the following:

   nslookup -d2

   server *<server>*

   where *<server>* is a server that is authoritative for the name that you want to test.

   This starts nslookup in user-interactive, debug mode and makes sure that you are querying the correct server. If you query a server that is not authoritative for the name that you test, you are not able to tell whether the data comes from a WINS server.

2. To test for a WINS forward lookup, type the following:

   set querytype=a

   –Or–

   To test for a WINS reverse lookup, type the following:

   set querytype=ptr

3. Enter the forward or reverse DNS domain name that you want to test.
4. In the response, note whether the server answered authoritatively or non-authoritatively, and note the TTL value.
5. If the server does not answer authoritatively, the source of the data is not a WINS server. However, if the server answered authoritatively, repeat a second query for the name.
6. In the response, note whether the TTL value decreased. If it did, the source of the data is a WINS server.

If you have determined that the data comes from a WINS server, check the WINS server for problems. For more information about checking the WINS server for problems, see "Windows Internet Name Service" in this book.

A zone reappears after you delete it.

In some cases, when you delete a secondary copy of the zone, it might reappear. If you delete a secondary copy of the zone when an Active Directory-integrated copy of the zone exists in Active Directory, and the DNS server from which you delete the secondary copy is configured to load data on startup from Active Directory and the registry, the zone reappears.

If you want to delete a secondary copy of a zone that exists in Active Directory, configure the DNS server to load data on startup from the registry, and then delete the zone from the DNS server that is hosting the secondary copy of the zone. Alternatively, you can completely delete the zone from Active Directory when you are logged into a domain controller that has a copy of the zone.

You see error messages stating that PTR records could not be registered

When the DNS server that is authoritative for the reverse lookup zone cannot or is configured not to perform dynamic updates, the system records errors in the event log stating that PTR records could not be registered. You can eliminate the event log errors by disabling dynamic update registration of PTR records on the DNS client. To disable dynamic update registration, add the **DisableReverseAddressRegistrations** entry, with a value of 1 and a data type of REG_DWORD, to the following registry subkey:

HKEY_LOCAL_MACHINE\SYSTEM\CurrentControlSet\Services \Tcpip\Parameters\Interfaces\<*name of the interface*>

where *name of the interface* is the GUID of a network adapter.

Solving Dynamic Update and Secure Dynamic Update Problems

If you have problems with dynamic update, use the following steps to diagnose and solve your problem.

Troubleshooting Dynamic Update

If dynamic update does not register a name or IP address properly, use the following process to diagnose and solve your problem.

- Force the client to renew its registration by typing **ipconfig /registerdns**.
- Check whether dynamic update is enabled for the zone that is authoritative for the name that the client is trying to update.

  For more information about dynamic update and secure dynamic update, see "Dynamic Update and Secure Dynamic Update" earlier in this chapter.
- To rule out other problems, check whether the dynamic update client lists the primary DNS server for the zone as its preferred DNS server.

  This is not necessary for dynamic update to work; however, if the client lists a preferred server other than the primary DNS server for the zone, many other problems might cause the failure, such as a network connectivity problem between the two servers or a prolonged recursive lookup for the primary server of the zone. To ascertain the preferred DNS server for the client, check the IP address configured in the TCP/IP properties of the network connection for the client, or at the command prompt type **ipconfig /all**.

  If the zone is Active Directory-integrated, any DNS server that hosts an Active Directory-integrated copy of the zone can process the updates.
- Check whether the zone is configured for secure dynamic update.

  If the zone is configured for secure dynamic update, the update can fail if zone or record security does not permit this client to make changes to the zone or record, or the update can fail if this client does not have ownership of the name that it is trying to update. To see whether the update failed for one of these reasons, check Event Viewer on the client. For more information about Event Viewer, see "Troubleshooting Tools" earlier in this chapter.

For information about what to do if the update failed because the zone is configured for secure dynamic update, see "Troubleshooting Secure Dynamic Update" later in this chapter.

Troubleshooting Secure Dynamic Update

Secure dynamic update can prevent a client from creating, modifying, or deleting records, depending on the ACL for the zone and the name. By default, secure dynamic update prevents a client from creating, deleting, or modifying a record if the client is not the original creator of the record. For example, if two computers have the same name and both try to register their names in DNS, dynamic update fails for the client that registers second.

If a client failed to update a name in a zone that is configured for secure dynamic update, the failure could be caused by one of the following conditions:

- *The system time on the client and the system time on the DNS server are not in sync.*
- *You have modified the* **UpdateSecurityLevel** *registry entry to disallow the use of secure dynamic update on the client.* For more information about dynamic update and secure dynamic update, see "Dynamic Update and Secure Dynamic Update" earlier in this chapter.
- *The client does not have the appropriate rights to update the resource record.* You can confirm this by checking the ACL associated with the name to be updated.

  If the client does not have the appropriate rights to update the resource record, check whether the DHCP server registered the name of the client and that the DHCP server is the owner of the corresponding dnsNode object. If so, you might consider placing the DHCP server in the DNSUpdateProxy security group. Any object created by a member of the DNSUpdateProxy security group has no security.

  For more information about the DNSUpdateProxy security group, see "Dynamic Update and Secure Dynamic Update Interoperability Considerations" earlier in this chapter.

Additional Resources

- For more information about DNS, see *DNS and BIND*, 3d ed., by Paul Albitz and Cricket Liu, 1998, Sebastopol, CA: O'Reilly & Associates.
- For more information about Request for Comments (RFC) documents and IETF Internet-Drafts, see the Internet Engineering Task Force (IETF) link on the Web Resources page at http://windows.microsoft.com/windows2000/reskit/webresources.

CHAPTER 7

Windows Internet Name Service

While Windows 2000 uses Domain Name System (DNS) as its primary method for matching a host name to its IP address, Windows 2000 also supports Windows Internet Name Service (WINS) for the same purpose. WINS is the name resolution system used for Windows NT Server 4.0 and earlier operating systems.

Windows 2000 DNS uses hierarchical fully qualified domain names (FQDNs) rather than the flat NetBIOS naming conventions supported by WINS. However, WINS provides an important service for network administrators with heterogeneous systems supporting clients running older operating systems, such as Windows 95 and Windows NT 4.0. These older systems do support DNS name resolution but do not support dynamic updates to DNS records.

In This Chapter

Related Information in the Resource Kit

- For more information about DNS, see “Introduction to DNS” in this book.
- For information about the Windows 2000 implementation of DNS, see “Windows 2000 DNS” in this book.

WINS Overview

While WINS servers are not needed in a network consisting entirely of Windows 2000–based computers, they are crucial for any network containing computers based on the older architectures of Windows NT 4.0, Windows 98, or Windows 95. This section describes the high-level architecture as well as the new features offered in this latest version of WINS. It also briefly covers the basic background of how WINS developed from the NetBIOS naming conventions of the 1980s.

New for Windows 2000

The new implementation of WINS for Windows 2000 provides the following enhancements:

Persistent Connections Now you can configure each WINS server to maintain a persistent connection with one or more replication partners. This increases the speed of replication and eliminates the overhead of opening and terminating connections.

Manual Tombstoning You can manually mark a record for eventual deletion, called tombstoning. The tombstone state of the record then replicates across all WINS servers, preventing an active copy on a different server database from propagating the record.

Improved Management Utility The WINS management console is fully integrated with the Microsoft Management Console (MMC), a user-friendly and powerful environment you can customize for efficiency. Because all server administrative utilities included with Windows 2000 Server are part of MMC, new MMC-based utilities are easier to use and faster to learn. MMC-based utilities operate more predictably and follow a common design.

Enhanced Filtering and Record Searching Improved filtering and new search functions help you locate records by showing only those records that fit the criteria you specify. These functions are particularly useful for analyzing very large WINS databases.

Dynamic Record Deletion and Multi-Select Dynamic record deletion and multi-select help you manage the WINS database. With the WINS management console, you can point, click, and delete one or more WINS static or dynamic entries. This function was not available in earlier command-based utilities for WINS administration (such as Winscl). You can also now delete records that use names containing non-alphanumeric characters.

Record Verification and Version Number Validation Record verification compares the IP addresses returned by a NetBIOS name query of different WINS servers. Version number validation examines the owner address–to–version number mapping tables. These features quickly check the consistency of names stored and replicated on your WINS servers.

Export Function You can export WINS data to a comma-delimited text file, which you can import or process with Microsoft Excel, reporting tools, scripting programs, or other programs for analysis and reporting.

Increased Fault Tolerance for Clients Clients running Windows 2000 or Windows 98 can specify a maximum of 12 WINS servers per interface (up from the earlier limit of two). The extra WINS server addresses are used only if the primary and secondary WINS servers fail to respond.

Dynamic Renewal of Clients A WINS client does not need to restart after it renews its registration of local NetBIOS names. Nbtstat includes a new option, **–RR**, which provides the ability to release and then renew a NetBIOS name registration. This feature of Nbtstat can also be used on WINS client computers running under Windows NT 4.0 that have been updated to Service Pack 4 or later.

Read-Only Console Access to the WINS Management Console WINS Setup automatically adds a special-purpose local users group, the WINS Users group, when WINS is installed. By adding members to this group, you can provide read-only access via the WINS management console to WINS-related information on this server computer for non-administrators. Membership allows a user to view—but not to modify—information and properties stored at a specific WINS server.

All of these features make Windows 2000 WINS the ideal choice for NetBIOS name resolution. WINS makes life easier for managers of routed networks, and solves the problems of internetwork name resolution in complex wide area networks (WANs).

Origins of WINS

Whether your network uses DNS or WINS, name resolution is an essential part of network administration. Name resolution allows you to search your network and connect to resources using names such as "myprinter" or "ourfileserver" rather than memorizing a host's Internet Protocol (IP) address. Remembering IP addresses would be even more impractical when using Dynamic Host Configuration Protocol (DHCP) for address assignment because the assignments may change overtime.

WINS is supported by DHCP services. Whenever the computer you named "fileserver01" is dynamically assigned a new IP address, the change is transparent. When you connect to fileserver01 from another node, you can use the name fileserver01 rather than the new IP address because WINS keeps track of the changing IP addresses associated with that name.

WINS was created to solve the problems of broadcast-based name resolution and the burden of maintaining LMHOSTS files. With LMHOSTS files, name resolution information is stored in a static format, making it a management-intensive chore to maintain. With broadcast-based name resolution systems such as NetBIOS, larger networks became more congested as hosts come online and broadcast messages to all other nodes to resolve IP addresses. In addition to the congestion, these broadcasts cannot cross routers, meaning that names can only be resolved locally.

WINS is built on a protocol, defined by an Internet Engineering Task Force (IETF) Request for Comments (RFC) that performs name registration, resolution, and deregistration using unicast datagrams to NetBIOS name servers. This allows the system to work across routers and eliminates the need for an LMHOSTS file, restoring the dynamic nature of NetBIOS name resolution and allowing the system to work seamlessly with DHCP. For example, when dynamic addressing through DHCP creates new IP addresses for computers that move between subnets, the WINS database tracks the changes automatically.

The complete Windows 2000 WINS system includes a WINS server, clients, proxy agents, a WINS database, and a WINS management console. Each of these is described in this chapter.

WINS is compatible with the protocols defined for NetBIOS name servers (NBNS) in RFCs 1001 and 1002, so it is interoperable with other implementations of these RFCs. Another RFC-compliant implementation of the client can talk to the WINS server and, similarly, a Microsoft TCP/IP client can talk to other implementations of the NBNS. However, because the WINS server-to-server replication protocol is not specified in the standard, the WINS server does not interoperate with other implementations of NBNS. Data cannot be replicated between the WINS server and the non-WINS NBNS. Without replication, name resolution cannot be guaranteed.

NetBIOS Legacy of WINS

To understand the need for WINS, you must understand the history of NetBIOS, which started more than 10 years ago as a high-level programming language interface to IBM PC-Network broadband LANs for PC-DOS applications. Microsoft used this NetBIOS interface for designing its networking components. NetBIOS is a session-level interface that applications use to communicate over NetBIOS-compatible transports. It establishes logical names on the network, establishes sessions between two logical names on the network, and supports reliable data transfer between computers that have established a session. Protocols implemented under Microsoft networking components, including TCP/IP, include a NetBIOS interface or a mapping layer. This layer allows nonnative NetBIOS components to fit into a NetBIOS environment. NetBIOS-based communications use NetBIOS names to uniquely identify resources and other nodes on the network.

NetBIOS names are 16 bytes in length. The NetBIOS name space is flat, meaning that names can be used only once within a network. (DNS, in contrast, uses a fully qualified domain name (FQDN), which combines the host name with the name of its domain. A NetBIOS name such as "WINserver01" might be "WINserver01.itreskit.com" as an FQDN.) For more information about NetBIOS names, see "NetBIOS Names" later in this chapter.

NetBIOS names are registered dynamically when computers and services start and when users log on. A NetBIOS name can be registered as a unique name, which maps to a single address, or as a group name, which maps to multiple addresses. Each of these name types is discussed in "Microsoft WINS Servers" later in this chapter.

NetBIOS Name Resolution

NetBIOS name resolution is the process of successfully converting a NetBIOS name to an IP address. A NetBIOS name is a 16-byte address used to identify a NetBIOS resource on the network. A NetBIOS name is either a unique name, exclusive to a single process on a single computer, or a group name, which might address multiple processes on multiple computers.

An example of a process that uses a NetBIOS name is the File and Printer Sharing for Microsoft Networks service on a computer running Windows 2000. When your computer starts, File and Printer Sharing for Microsoft Networks registers a unique NetBIOS name based on the name of your computer. The name registered by the service is the 15-character computer name plus a 16th character of 0x20. If the computer name is not 15 characters long, it is padded with spaces to make it 15 characters long.

When you initiate a file-sharing connection by name to a computer running Windows 2000, that connection uses File and Printer Sharing for Microsoft Networks on the file server you specify. File and printer sharing always corresponds to a specific NetBIOS name. For example, when you attempt to connect to a computer called CORPSERVER, the NetBIOS name corresponding to File and Printer Sharing for Microsoft Networks on that computer is:

```
CORPSERVER      [20]
```

Note the use of spaces to pad the computer name. Before you can establish a file and print sharing connection, a TCP connection must be created. To establish that TCP connection, the NetBIOS name CORPSERVER [20] must be resolved to an IP address.

The exact mechanism by which NetBIOS names are resolved to IP addresses depends on which NetBIOS node type is configured for the computer seeking to resolve a name. RFC 1001 defines the NetBIOS node types; they are also listed in Table 7.1.

Table 7.1 NetBIOS Node Types

NetBIOS name resolution mode	Description
B-node	Uses IP broadcast messages to register and resolve NetBIOS names to IP addresses. Windows 2000–based computers can use modified B-node name resolution.
P-node	Uses point-to-point communication with a NetBIOS name server (in Windows 2000–based networks, this is the WINS server) to register and resolve computer names to IP addresses.
M-node	Uses a mix of B-node and P-node communication to register and resolve NetBIOS names. M-node first uses broadcast resolution; then, if necessary, it uses a server query.
H-node	Uses a hybrid of B-node and P-node. An H-node computer always tries a server query first and uses broadcasts only if direct queries fail.

Computers running Windows 2000 use B-node name resolution by default and use H-node when configured with a WINS server.

In order for remote NetBIOS names to be resolved, you must configure your computers running Windows 2000 with the IP address of a WINS server. You must configure Active Directory–enabled computers running Windows 2000 with the IP address of a WINS server if they are to communicate with computers running Windows NT, Windows 2000, Windows 95, or Windows 98 that are not Active Directory enabled.

Broadcasts in NetBIOS Name Resolution

Name resolution in a NetBIOS network in a small and self-contained network is broadcast-based. A name registration request can be broadcast and heard by all B-, H-, and M-nodes on the local network. If no objections are received, the application broadcasting the request assumes that it has permission to use the name and issues a name overwrite demand. If the name is already in use, a negative name registration response is sent by the node using the name. In this case, the requesting application does not have permission to use the name.

In a larger, interconnected series of subnets, broadcast-based name resolution creates certain problems. First, nodes may interact with one another within a broadcast area, but they cannot interact across routers in a routed network. Second, broadcasts for name resolution generate significant network traffic. Third, every node within the broadcast area must examine each broadcast datagram, consuming resources on every node. Broadcast-based name resolution works fine within a small LAN, but as the LAN grows and merges into a WAN, this method is not effective. Large LANs experience bandwidth problems, and once routers are introduced, the broadcast-based name resolution becomes inoperable.

WINS avoids the problems of NetBIOS name resolution by providing dynamic database maintenance for name registration and resolution. WINS reduces broadcast traffic while allowing the clients to locate remote systems easily across local or wide-area networks.

LMHOSTS Files

The LMHOSTS file was introduced to assist with remote NetBIOS name resolution. The LMHOSTS file is a static, local database file that maps NetBIOS names to IP addresses. This is similar in functionality to the Hosts file in DNS, but the Hosts file is used for mapping IP addresses for host names in the hierarchical DNS namespace, rather than NetBIOS names. Recording a NetBIOS name and its IP address in the LMHOSTS file enables a node that cannot respond to name query broadcasts to resolve an IP address for that NetBIOS name.

When Windows 2000 uses an LMHOSTS file to resolve remote NetBIOS names, it examines the LMHOSTS file that is stored in the directory *%SystemRoot%*\System32\Drivers\Etc.

As noted earlier, a computer in a Microsoft-based network can resolve NetBIOS names in several different ways. If one method of resolution fails, the computer tries the next method in a fixed order. In a broadcast-based network, the node first checks its remote name cache before broadcasting a name query (the name will be in the cache if it has been used recently or loaded from LMHOSTS). As a last resort, the computer uses the LMHOSTS file to obtain the IP address assigned to the NetBIOS name it is trying to resolve (for example, to obtain the IP address for the name of a computer across a router in a broadcast-based network).

For more information about LMHOSTS files, see "LMHOSTS File" in this book.

Despite the many uses of the LMHOSTS file, its design imposes some limitations. Its greatest limitation is that it is a static file, which means that entries must be updated by hand if the name or the IP address of the computer changes (such as when a computer is moved to a new subnet, or when a remote user dials in and connects via Routing and Remote Access). This limitation of the LMHOSTS file is exacerbated by the introduction of DHCP. A DHCP server assigns IP addresses to nodes dynamically, making it nearly impossible to keep the LMHOSTS file updated.

Continuing Need for WINS

If your network contains only computers running Windows 2000 or other TCP/IP-based systems that do not require the use of NetBIOS names (such as most versions of UNIX), your network no longer needs to use WINS. Instead, you should use Microsoft DNS service to resolve IP addresses.

However, many networks still include computers running Windows NT, Windows 98, and Windows 95. For these networks, WINS is needed to support earlier Windows and Microsoft TCP/IP clients. These networks will need WINS until all clients are migrated to Windows 2000.

Microsoft WINS Clients

To configure WINS clients with the IP address of one or more WINS servers, open **Network and Dial-up Connections** and click **Local Area Connections**. Click the **Properties** button, select the **Internet Protocol (TCP/IP) Properties** entry in the list, and click **Properties**, then click **Advanced** and select the **WINS Address** tab. Figure 7.1 illustrates this configuration page.

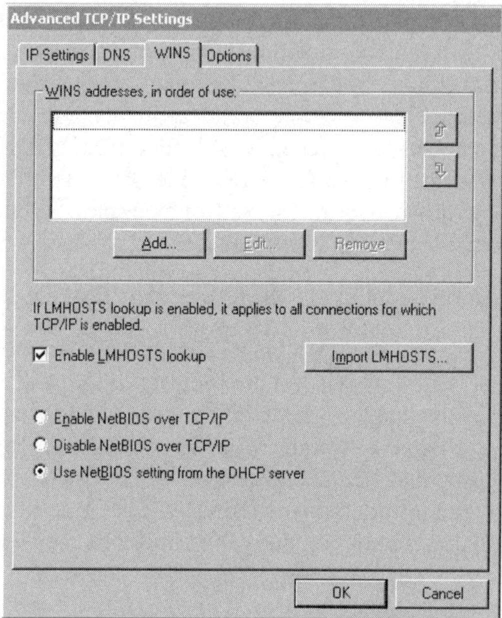

Figure 7.1 WINS Service on a Windows 2000 Client

NetBIOS names are linked to the various network services that each client computer can use with other computers on the network.

Microsoft supports WINS clients on the following platforms:

- Windows 2000
- Windows NT Server
- Windows NT Workstation
- Windows 98
- Windows 95
- Windows for Workgroups
- LAN Manager 2.*x*

A WINS-enabled client communicates with the WINS server to:

- Register in the WINS database NetBIOS names of processes running on the client.
- Release from the WINS database the NetBIOS names of processes that are no longer running on the client.
- Renew client names in the WINS database.
- Resolve names by obtaining mappings for user names, NetBIOS names, DNS names, and IP addresses from the WINS database.

Clients that are not configured to use WINS can participate in these processes to a limited extent, but they must use WINS proxy agents to do so. For more information about proxy agents, see "Microsoft WINS Proxy" in this chapter. Each of the other tasks performed by a WINS client is described in this section.

How WINS Clients Register Their Names

When a WINS-enabled computer starts, it attempts to register its NetBIOS names and corresponding IP address directly with the WINS server. If the registration fails, the WINS client tries again every 10 minutes until it is successful. The message the client sends is referred to as a name registration request. The WINS client sends one name registration request (which includes the computer IP address) for each NetBIOS-based networking service running on the computer.

Note that the IP address is dynamically assigned by a DHCP server if the client is DHCP-enabled. If DHCP is not used, the IP address is a statically assigned number which you must get from a network administrator and manually configure on the computer.

▶ **To create a static mapping with WINS**

1. In the WINS management console, click **Active Registrations** in the console tree for the appropriate active WINS server.
2. On the **Action** menu, click **New Static**.
3. In the **Create Static Mapping** dialog box, type the static address in the **IP address** box.

Figure 7.2 shows the **Create Static Mapping** dialog box.

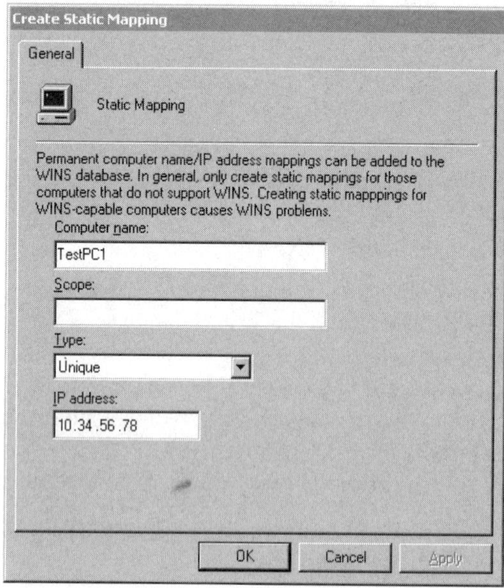

Figure 7.2 Static Mapping in WINS

When the WINS server receives a name registration request for a unique NetBIOS name, it checks whether the name already exists in its WINS database. The WINS server responds with either a positive or negative name registration response. Table 7.2 describes each type of WINS server name registration response.

Table 7.2 WINS Server Responses

Server response	Explanation
No response	The WINS client sends another name registration request for the same name.
Positive	The WINS server does not find a duplicate name in the WINS database, and sends a positive response to the registering client. The response includes a Time-To-Live (TTL) value, which sets the time the server the name registration will be active in the database. The client must renew the registration before the TTL expires.

(continued)

Table 7.2 WINS Server Responses *(continued)*

Server response	Explanation
Negative	The WINS server finds an existing registration for the requested name in the database. The server sends a wait for acknowledgment (WACK) packet to the client and then sends a challenge, referred to the registered owner of the name. Having received a response from the registered owner, the server sends a negative name registration response to the WINS client attempting to register the name.

When a WINS server receives a name registration request for a name already in its database, the server sends a challenge, known as a name query request, to the owner of the registered name. The server waits 500 milliseconds between challenges, and if the client is multihomed, the WINS server tries each IP address it has for the computer until the WINS server receives a response or until it has tried all of the IP addresses.

Figure 7.3 illustrates the flow of messages between client, server, and challenged client. The first message is the name registration request; the last is the name response.

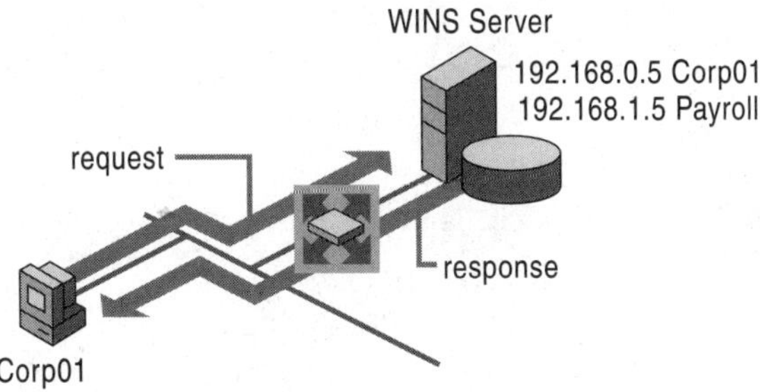

Figure 7.3 WINS Client Name Registration

In the first step in Figure 7.3, the Corp01 computer sends a message to its WINS server to register its address using a NetBIOS name registration message. The server replies with an acknowledgment of the address with a NetBIOS name registration response. Note that there is a second WINS server on the far side of the router; this server learns about the Corp01 address when the WINS server database replicates itself.

How WINS Clients Renew Their Names

WINS clients must renew their name registrations before the renewal interval expires. The renewal interval determines how long the server stores the name registration as an active record in the WINS database.

When a WINS client renews its name registration, it sends a name refresh request to the WINS server. The name refresh request includes the IP address and the NetBIOS name that the client seeks to refresh. The WINS server responds to the name refresh request with a name refresh response that includes a new renewal interval for the name.

When a WINS client refreshes its name, it performs the following steps:

1. When a client has consumed ½ of its renewal interval, it sends a name refresh request to the primary WINS server.
2. If its name is not refreshed by the primary WINS server, the WINS client tries to refresh again in 10 minutes and continues to try the primary WINS server repeatedly every 10 minutes for a total of 1 hour.
3. The WINS client, after trying to refresh its name registration with the primary WINS server for one hour, stops trying and attempts to refresh its name with the secondary WINS server.
4. If it is not refreshed by the secondary WINS server, the WINS client tries to refresh its name again using the secondary WINS server in 10 minutes and continues to try every 10 minutes for a total of 1 hour.
5. The WINS client after trying to refresh on the secondary WINS server for one hour, stops trying and tries to refresh using the primary WINS server.
6. This process of trying the primary WINS server and then the secondary WINS server continues until the renewal interval is consumed or the WINS client has its name refreshed.
7. If the WINS client succeeds in refreshing its name, the renewal interval is reset on the WINS server.
8. If the WINS client fails to register during the renewal interval on either the primary or secondary WINS server the name is released.

How WINS Clients Release Their Names

NetBIOS names can be released either explicitly or silently. They are explicitly released when a client shuts down gracefully. A silent release occurs when an client fails or is powered off. The silent release is noted at the WINS server when a name is not refreshed within the renewal interval.

When a name is released, the database entry is marked as released and given a time stamp with the current time plus the *extinction interval*. The extinction interval is the interval between when an entry is marked as released and when it is marked as extinct. The extinction timeout specifies the interval between when an entry is marked extinct and when the entry is finally scavenged from the database. This information is not propagated to partner WINS servers. If the release is explicit, the WINS server makes itself the owner of the record if it is not already.

In Windows 2000, the release of a WINS database entry is handled differently if the owner ID of the entry is different from the owner ID of the server that registered the name. If this is the case, the entry is marked as extinct and given a time stamp that is the current time plus the sum of the extinction interval and the extinction timeout. This is done to avoid windows of inconsistency between secondary and primary WINS servers. Because a released record is not replicated again, having already been replicated once, its name remains released on one WINS server and active on another for undesirably long periods.

Changing the released record to the extinct state results in its replication and enables rapid synchronization of WINS databases. Without extinction, inconsistencies might linger. For example, if the primary WINS server of a client is unavailable when the client shuts down, the name release would be directed to the secondary WINS server. If the primary WINS server is available again when the client restarts, the client would register and continue to refresh with the primary WINS server, which has not recorded any change in the status of the client, while the secondary WINS server would still reflect the released state of the client record.

How WINS Clients Resolve Names

WINS clients perform NetBIOS name–to–IP address mapping resolution by using the NetBIOS over TCP/IP (NetBT) component. A Windows NT–based computer is automatically configured to use one of four different NetBT name resolution modes (that is, methods for resolving names), based on how TCP/IP is configured on the computer. Table 7.1 describes the NetBIOS modes and how they resolve IP addresses from NetBIOS names.

To display a computer's TCP/IP configuration, including its node type, type **ipconfig /all** at the command prompt. For example, on a computer that is configured as a WINS client, the node type "Hybrid" appears when you type **ipconfig /all**.

The name resolution process between an H-node WINS client and a WINS server follows this sequence:

1. When a user types a network-related command at the command prompt, such as **net use**, the client computer checks its NetBIOS name cache for the NetBIOS name and IP address of the destination host. If the client finds a mapping, the name is resolved without generating network activity.
2. If the client computer does not find the name in the NetBIOS name cache, the client makes three attempts to contact the first WINS server (if one is configured). If the first WINS server does not respond, the client attempts to contact the next WINS server until it has attempted to contact all configured WINS servers. If the name is resolved, the IP address is returned to the client.

3. If the name is not resolved by any WINS server, the client generates three B-node broadcasts on the local network. If the NetBIOS name is found on the local network, the name is resolved to an IP address.
4. If the NetBIOS name cannot be resolved using B-node broadcasts and LMHOSTS lookup is enabled, the client parses the local LMHOSTS file. If the NetBIOS name is in the LMHOSTS file, the name is resolved to an IP address.
5. If the NetBIOS name is not resolved from the LMHOSTS file, the client computer attempts to resolve the name through other host name resolution techniques. If the **Enable DNS for Windows Resolution** box is checked in the **WINS Address** property page of the **Internet Protocol (TCP/IP)** dialog box, it attempts to resolve the name using a local Hosts file or a DNS server.

   To resolve a host name, WINS checks the local Hosts file for a match against the local host name first. If the host name is found in the Hosts file, it is resolved to an IP address. The Hosts file must reside on the local computer.
6. If the name is not resolved from the Hosts file, the client sends a request to its configured DNS server. If the host name is found by a DNS server, it is resolved to an IP address.

   If none of these methods resolve the NetBIOS name, the **net use** command returns an error, indicating that the computer could not be found.

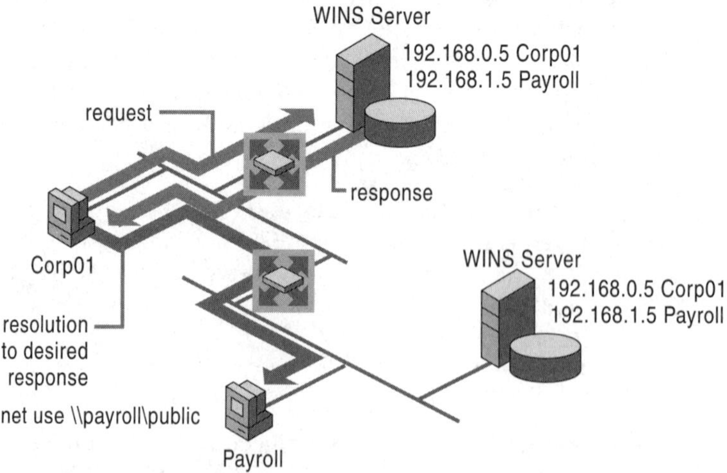

Figure 7.4 Name Resolution via WINS

In Figure 7.4, the initial message is the name request from the client to its primary WINS server. This is followed by the response from the WINS server, returning the desired IP address. Once the response is received, the client uses this address to establish a connection to the desired resource.

Client Conflicts Detected During Registration

When a client node registers or refreshes a name, the name might already exist in the WINS database. The action taken by the WINS server depends on the state of the registered name. It might be active, released, or extinct. (An extinct name is referred to as a tombstone.) The name might be a unique name or a group name, owned by the server or a replica, a database entry copied from another WINS server, with a statically or dynamically assigned IP address. The IP address might be the same as or different from that specified in the registration request of the client.

Two cases are always handled the same way: Normal group entries and static entries are never overwritten. The WINS server always returns a negative name registration response to registration requests for a name that is already in the database as a group or static name. Internet groups get additional members through the use of Internet group registration. Internet groups, or "special groups" as they are sometimes called, are used for special, user-defined administrative groups. These internet groups are sometimes used to group resources such as, file servers and printers. In this case, if the record in conflict has been released or tombstoned, the name registration request is treated as the registration of a new name.

With unique, dynamic names, if the IP addresses are the same, the WINS server returns a positive name registration response and acts as described in Table 7.3.

Table 7.3 Name Registration Responses

State of Name	Server Action
Owned and active	Update time stamp
Replica and active	Update time stamp, take ownership, increment version ID
Released	Update time stamp, make active, increment version ID
Owned tombstone	Update time stamp, make active, increment version ID
Replica tombstone	Update time stamp, take ownership, make active, increment version ID

If the IP address of the registration request is different from the IP address of the database record, and the existing database record is already released or tombstoned, then the name registration is treated as new. The server sends a positive name registration response and updates the entry to reflect the new time, ownership, version ID, and active state.

If the existing database entry is active and has an IP address that is different from the IP address of the registration request, the WINS server must determine whether the name and IP address in the database entry are still in use. The WINS server does this by sending a name query request to the client computer with the IP address in question. Figure 7.5 shows the initial step of a registration request sent from the client to the server, followed by a challenge sent by the server to the old IP address.

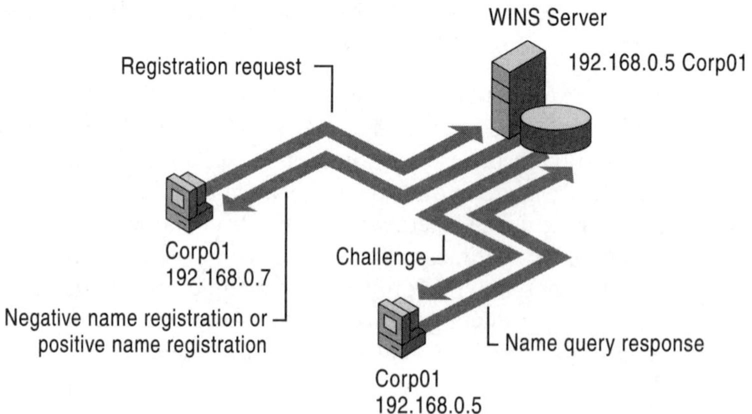

Figure 7.5 A WINS Server Challenges an Old Address

If the server receives a positive name query response from the old IP address, it rejects the new registration by sending a negative name registration response to the client that originally requested the name registration. If the old address does not respond to the name query request, the server assumes there is no computer with that name and IP address and accepts the new name registration. In this case, the last arrow indicates a positive name registration response.

WINS Client Behavior

This section looks at how WINS clients react to various basic scenarios, including:

- Daily startup of the WINS client.
- Plugging into a different subnet.
- Prolonged shutdowns.
- Joining two WINS systems.

Daily Startup

An active WINS client name registration in a WINS server database is replicated to all of the *push partners* of that server. A push partner is a WINS server that sends data to other servers to start replication. After some time, the active name registration is replicated to all WINS servers on the network.

When the WINS client is turned off at the end of the day, it releases the name. With the default extinction interval, it does not enter the extinct state during the night, and therefore it is not replicated again that night. When the computer is started the next morning, the WINS client registers the name again with the WINS server and receives a new version ID. This new, active name registration entry is replicated to the pull partners of the WINS server as on the previous day. A pull partner is a WINS server that requests data to be sent to it from other servers.

The number of name registration entries replicated each day is roughly equivalent to the number of computers started each day multiplied by the number of NetBIOS names registered by each computer.

On large networks (50,000 or more computers), the biggest traffic load may be the name registration requests generated when WINS clients start on the network. Fortunately, the difference in time zones in large enterprise networks provides some distribution of this WINS client startup load.

Plugging Into a Different Subnet

A roaming user who powers down a computer and then moves it to a different subnet with another primary WINS server generates name challenge traffic. Typically the name registration request is answered with the wait for acknowledgment message. Then, assuming the active entry was replicated, the new WINS server generates a name query packet to challenge the IP address currently in its database for the name. Because the computer that registered that address is no longer active on that subnet and no longer using that IP address, it makes no reply. Just to be sure that the lack of response is not a fluke, the WINS server repeats the query three times.

Usually the name challenge never travels over the subnet that the computer has left because the ARP request fails. However, the challenge message does travel on the subnet of the new WINS server and the links between the routers. The WINS server assigns a new version ID to the new entry so that it will replicate from its new owner to other WINS servers.

Prolonged Shutdowns

Some computers do not start up for a period longer than the *verification interval.* The verification interval is the interval after which the WINS server must verify that any old names that it does not own that are in its database are still active. The WINS server does not delete replica entries for these computers because the owned entries never become extinct, remaining active in the database. A computer that occasionally starts up refreshes all of its replica entries by giving each of them a new version ID. This new version ID prompts replication of the replicas to other WINS databases on the network.

Sometimes the computer stays shut down for an extended period, and therefore its replicas are not refreshed for a period longer than the verification interval. When a WINS server has such an old replica, it tries to verify this entry with the owning WINS server. If the owning server does not find this entry, it is removed from the database of the verifying server. If the entry is verified, its new state is recorded.

Joining Two WINS Systems

When two organizations merge, their computer systems must merge as well, including their WINS systems. When merging two WINS systems, the initial replication load and the potential for conflicting NetBIOS names might present problems. After a WINS server from one system is connected to a WINS server from the other, they eventually replicate their records with each other; because they have no shared records, the whole database from each system must be replicated. Then their replication partners copy the new entries, until all the databases have converged.

To avoid making this process any more difficult, merge the systems and force replication at a time when the connecting WAN links are more or less idle. When the databases contain conflicting names, the conflicts are resolved, which may result in other traffic. This process is described in "Client Conflicts Detected During Registration" earlier in this chapter.

Note The users of computers with conflicting names will probably call the help desk when they get the "duplicate name" messages and their computers refuse to open new sessions.

Best Practices for WINS Clients

To configure and manage clients properly requires some attention. The best options for WINS clients are outlined here.

Configure Clients with a Full List of WINS Servers

In previous versions of Windows NT, clients were only able to use a primary and secondary WINS server. For Windows 2000, WINS clients can be configured with up to 12 WINS servers. These servers can be configured either statically at the **Internet Protocol (TCP/IP)** properties dialog box or dynamically through DHCP (using option 44). By configuring additional WINS servers, clients gain additional fault tolerance.

Use Nbtstat –RR to Manage Client Connectivity

The Nbtstat command-line tool—new in Windows 2000—allows you to purge the local NetBIOS names cache of remote names and force immediate renewal and re-registration of the local names of the client. This is useful as a first recourse for troubleshooting WINS client connectivity problems; in particular, you can use this tool to repopulate the client entries and replicate them to the partner WINS server without rebooting the clients.

Client Configuration Practices

WINS is a client/server system requiring software on both the client and the server in order for the NetBIOS computer name–to–IP address resolution to occur. Getting the client configuration right can head off many problems.

Windows NT clients that participate in the WINS process register NetBIOS names. These names are configured through the **System** utility in Control Panel and can be altered at any time. Problems might arise if a user changes his or her computer's NetBIOS name to the same name as that of a Windows 2000 computer, or to the name of an existing Windows NT domain. This client impersonates the server and essentially is registered with the WINS service as a Windows 2000 computer. This problem only happens when the server or domain controller is not available to defend the name in a WINS challenge. To avoid this problem:

- The first, but least desirable, method of dealing with impersonation in Windows 2000 is to place static entries in the WINS database, ensuring that no user can configure his or her computer to dynamically impersonate a server. This method, as with any static process, is more administratively intensive than the use of dynamic registration of the computer NetBIOS name.
- The second method is to set the client computers' configurations so that users cannot alter the NetBIOS names of their computers. This method allows for minimal administrative overhead for WINS NetBIOS name registrations and provides a controlled client environment. You can control Windows 95 and Windows NT Workstation clients through system policies that determine what access a user can or cannot have to altering features on their own computers.

All clients should be upgraded to the newest client platform to control access to desktop configuration parameters. Use system policies in the Computer Management console to prevent users from changing their computers' NetBIOS names. To access the Computer Management console, right-click **My Computer** and choose **Manage** on the drop-down menu.

Microsoft WINS Servers

The WINS system for name resolution can be viewed as a set of tightly integrated components:

- **WINS server.** A computer that provides the WINS service and replicates the WINS database with other WINS servers so that complete name-to-address resolution information is available regardless of which WINS server a WINS client uses.
- **WINS client.** Any WINS-enabled computer that uses the WINS service to register or refresh its NetBIOS name and IP address.
- **WINS proxy.** A WINS-enabled computer that helps resolve name queries in routed TCP/IP intranets for computers that are not WINS-enabled.
- **WINS database.** Dynamically updated list of NetBIOS names and their associated IP addresses, including IP addresses assigned by DHCP. In networks with multiple WINS servers, the servers exchange database updates through replication.
- **WINS Management Console.** A plug-in to the Microsoft Management Console that provides a range of management tools.

The next sections take a closer look at each of these components, beginning with the WINS servers and proxies that form the backbone of the entire system.

Overview of WINS Servers

WINS servers prevent the administrative difficulties inherent in the use of both NetBIOS name query broadcasts and static mapping files such as LMHOSTS files. Microsoft WINS eliminates the need for NetBIOS name query broadcasts, saving valuable network bandwidth while maintaining a dynamic database of NetBIOS name–to–IP address mappings.

The databases replicated between WINS servers contain NetBIOS names and their associated IP addresses. When Windows-based computers log on to the network, their NetBIOS names and IP addresses are registered and added to the WINS server database, providing support for dynamic updates. The WINS server database is replicated among multiple WINS servers in a LAN or WAN. This database replication prevents users from registering duplicate NetBIOS names for different computers on the network.

A Microsoft WINS server solves the problems inherent in resolving names through IP broadcasts and frees network administrators from the demands of updating static mapping files. WINS automatically updates the WINS database when dynamic addressing through DHCP assigns new IP addresses—for instance, when computers move between subnets.

WINS servers also provide the following benefits:

- Dynamic database that supports NetBIOS name registration and resolution in an environment where DHCP-enabled clients are configured for dynamic TCP/IP address allocation.
- Centralized management of the NetBIOS name database and replication to other WINS servers.
- Reduction of NetBIOS name query broadcast traffic.
- Support for client computers running Windows NT Server, Windows NT Workstation, Windows 95, Windows 98, Windows for Workgroups, and LAN Manager 2.*x*.
- Support for transparent browsing across routers for client computers running Windows NT Server, Windows NT Workstation, Windows 95, Windows 98, and Windows for Workgroups.

Microsoft WINS servers communicate with other Microsoft WINS servers to fully replicate their databases with each other. This ensures that a name registered with one WINS server is replicated to all other Microsoft WINS servers within the intranet, providing a consistent enterprise-wide database. When a network uses multiple WINS servers, every WINS server is configured as a pull partner or a push partner of at least one other WINS server.

A pull partner is a WINS server that requests new WINS database entries, called replicas, from its partner. The pull occurs at set intervals, defined by the replication interval, or in response to an update notification from a push partner.

A push partner is a WINS server that sends update notification messages after the database receives the number of updates that exceed the update count threshold or sends them immediately if the server is configured to send updates when an address changes (by selecting the **On Address Change** check box in the **Replication Partners** window of the WINS console). If you have configured the WINS server this way, it propagates the triggers received from a partner to all other partners when its WINS database changes. The partners of the WINS server then pull these changed entries from the WINS server with the updated database.

Registration of Group Names

In addition to registration of unique names, mentioned in the preceding description of NetBIOS, WINS allows registration of group names. WINS recognizes two types of groups: normal groups and special groups.

Normal Group Names

A normal group name has several key differences compared to a normal unique name. Most important, it does not actually have an address associated with it. It is assumed to be valid on any subnet. The same group can be registered at more than one WINS server. The whole group has a single time associated with it that indicates the last time a node on any subnet registered or refreshed the name. When it receives a name query for the group, WINS returns the limited broadcast address (255.255.255.255). The WINS client then issues a broadcast to its subnet to resolve the name.

As the group names replicate from one WINS server to another, the name is added to the database of servers that do not already have it. However, since there is no address to propagate with the name, the entry for the group is just a name, without an associated address. When a group name is not refreshed, it is released and eventually becomes a tombstone.

The released and tombstoned states, however, have a slightly different meaning for group names than for unique entries. The WINS server answers name queries for released and tombstone groups. Unique name registrations that clash generate a negative response. For group entries, you can think of released and tombstoned states as pseudo states (pseudo-released and pseudo-tombstoned). These two states change at the end of the extinction interval, a configured value that establishes how long entries linger in the released and tombstoned states. After that interval, the version ID is incremented; this change means that the state information is then replicated to other WINS servers.

Special Group Names

When a name registration is received for a special group, WINS stores the actual address, rather than the limited broadcast address. A time stamp, reflecting the last registration or refresh received for that entry, and an owner ID are stored with each address entry in the group. When the WINS server receives a name query for such a group, it returns the IP addresses that have not expired. These groups, like normal groups, are replicated from the WINS server where they first registered to replication partners of that server.

Static NetBIOS name mappings can be any of the types listed in Table 7.4.

Table 7.4 Static NetBIOS Name Mappings

Type Option	Description
Unique	A unique name that maps to a single IP address.
Group	Also referred to as a "Normal" Group. When adding an entry to Group by using the WINS snap-in, you must enter the computer name and IP address. The IP addresses of individual members of Group are not stored in the WINS database. Because the member addresses are not stored, there is no limit to the number of members that can be added to a Group. Broadcast name packets are used to communicate with Group members.
Domain	A NetBIOS name–to–IP address mapping that has 0x1C as the 16th byte. A domain group stores up to 25 addresses for members. For registrations after the 25th address, WINS overwrites a replica address, or if none is present, it overwrites the oldest registration. Domain names are used to add a static entry for the computer, specified by name in a static mapping to a list of domain controllers used on the network.
Internet group	Internet groups are user-defined groups that allow you to access group resources, such as printers, for easy reference and browsing. The default 16th byte of an Internet group name is set to 0x20. An Internet group can store a maximum of 25 addresses for members. When you add an Internet group three unique records are added: InternetGroupName<0x20> is used for file registration. InternetGroupName<0x0> is used for workgroup registration, and InternetGroupName<0x3> is used by messenger service. (The messenger service is used for pop-up messages on the screen. For example the printer messages that tell you that printing is complete.) This is similar to the domain group. Internet group members can be added via dynamic group registrations. A dynamic member, however, does not replace a static member added by using the WINS management console or importing the LMHOSTS file.
Multihomed	A unique name that can have more than one address, used for multihomed computers. No more than 25 addresses can be registered as multihomed. For registrations after the 25th address, WINS overwrites a replica address, or if none is present, it overwrites the oldest registration.

Secondary WINS Servers

Client computers should be configured with both a primary and secondary WINS server. If the primary WINS server cannot be reached for a WINS function (such as registration, refresh, release, query), the client requests that function from its secondary WINS server. The client periodically retries its primary WINS server.

Note While Windows 2000 Advanced Server supports the use of clustering for WINS servers, in almost all cases this service is unnecessary. Configuring secondary WINS servers provides the same function. In addition, maintaining secondary WINS servers is easier, and secondary WINS servers can be at a different location For more information about clustering WINS servers, see "Burst Handling" later in this chapter and "Windows Clustering" in the Microsoft® *Windows® 2000 Server Resource Kit Distributed Systems Guide*.

In networks with both a primary and secondary WINS server, it is best to configure half the clients with one server as the primary and the other server as secondary, and configure the other half of the clients with the opposite selections for primary and secondary servers. This cuts the burden on each server in half, while ensuring that a secondary server does not sit idle until the primary server fails.

Microsoft WINS Proxy

RFC 1001 recommends against using the B-node name resolution in a routed network—that is, relying on broadcasts for name queries. However, in practice, B-nodes are sometimes useful in routed networks, and sometimes B-nodes cannot be removed or updated. For this reason, Microsoft introduced WINS proxies. A WINS proxy is a WINS-enabled computer that helps resolve name queries for computers that are not WINS-enabled in routed TCP/IP networks.

By default, computers that are not WINS-enabled use B-node name resolution. The WINS proxy listens on the local subnet for B-node name service broadcasts (such as registration, refresh, release, query) and responds for those names that are not on the local network. A WINS proxy communicates with the WINS server with directed datagrams to retrieve the information necessary to respond to these broadcasts.

The WINS proxy resolves names for non-WINS clients in this way:

1. When a non-WINS client sends a name query broadcast, the WINS proxy accepts the broadcast and checks its cache for an IP address associated with the NetBIOS name.
2. If the WINS proxy has the IP address in its cache, the WINS proxy sends this information to the non-WINS computer as a NetBIOS name response.

3. If the IP address is not in cache, the WINS proxy queries a WINS server for the IP address associated with the requested name.
4. If a WINS server is not available on the local subnet, the WINS proxy can query a WINS server across a router, caching the NetBIOS names and IP addresses for subsequent queries.

The role of the WINS proxy is similar to that of the DHCP and BOOTP relay agents, which forward DHCP client requests across routers. Because the WINS server does not respond to broadcasts, a computer configured as a WINS proxy should always be installed on subnets containing computers that are not WINS-enabled.

The WINS proxy checks broadcast name registrations against the WINS database by sending name query requests to ensure that the names do not conflict with other names in the database. If a name exists in the WINS database, by default the WINS proxy might send a negative name registration response to the computer trying to register the name. In response to a name release request, the WINS proxy simply deletes the name from its cache of remote names.

When the WINS proxy server receives a name query, it checks its remote name table. The WINS proxy always differentiates name queries for names on the local subnet from remote names elsewhere in the network. It compares the address of names it resolves to its own address using the subnet mask, and if the two match, the WINS proxy does not respond to the name query.

If the WINS proxy does not find the name in the remote name table, it queries the WINS server, and then enters the name into the remote name table in a "resolving" state. If the WINS proxy receives a query for the same name before the WINS server has responded, the WINS proxy does not query the WINS server again. When the WINS proxy receives the response from the WINS server, the WINS proxy updates the remote table entry with the correct address and changes the state to "resolved." The WINS proxy only sends a reply message to the client if the WINS proxy has the response already in its cache.

The behavior of a B-node client does not change when a WINS proxy is added to the local subnet. If the first name resolution query times out, the client tries again. If the WINS proxy has the answer cached by the time it intercepts the new query, the WINS proxy answers the client.

Note Only one computer should be configured as a WINS proxy on each subnet. Because each WINS proxy on a network relays every broadcast it hears, configuring more than one WINS proxy per subnet can overload the WINS servers.

When the WINS proxy receives the next name query for that name, it again sends a response to the client. NetBIOS contains no provision for a name server to "deliver" a name resolution to a client; a name is always resolved in response to a query. Therefore, computers using the WINS proxy for B-node name resolution must be configured to retry the name query. To reduce duplicate traffic, only one WINS proxy should be active on any given subnet.

The name–to–IP address mappings that the WINS proxy receives from the WINS proxy are stored in the WINS proxy server cache for a limited time. By default, this value is 10 minutes; the minimum value is 1 minute.

To configure a computer as a WINS proxy server, you must edit the registry of that computer. The value of the **EnableProxy** registry entry must be set to 1 (REG_DWORD). This entry is located in the following registry subkey:

HKEY_LOCAL_MACHINE\SYSTEM\CurrentControlSet\Services\
Netbt\Parameters

Caution Do not use a registry editor to edit the registry directly unless you have no alternative. The registry editors bypass the standard safeguards provided by administrative tools. These safeguards prevent you from entering conflicting settings or settings that are likely to degrade performance or damage your system. Editing the registry directly can have serious, unexpected consequences that can prevent the system from starting and require that you reinstall Windows 2000. To configure or customize Windows 2000, use the programs in Microsoft Management Console (MMC) or Control Panel whenever possible.

Querying with a WINS Proxy

In Figure 7.6, a small broadcast-based LAN consisting of two clients (A and B) is connected to a larger network through a router. A NetBIOS application on client B wants to communicate with client C. Normally, this would not be possible because client C is on the other side of the router from client B. However, by configuring a computer running Windows 2000 Professional to act as a WINS proxy on the LAN, clients B and C can communicate.

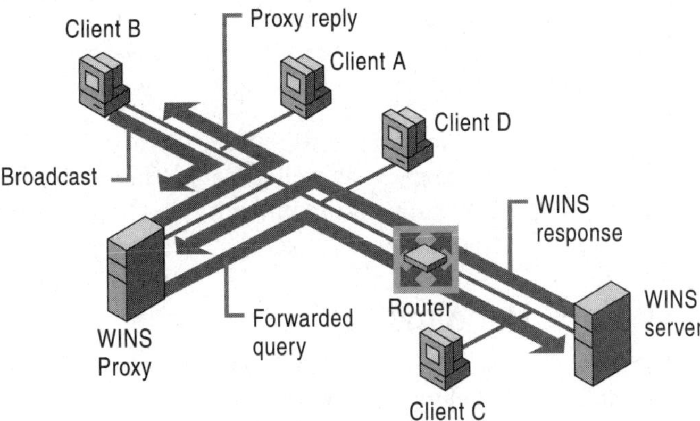

Figure 7.6 Operation of a WINS Proxy Server

Client B broadcasts a name query request to obtain the IP address of client C. Client C does not receive the request because the router does not pass along the broadcast. The WINS proxy sees a name query request broadcast for a node on a different subnet and sends a name query request, a directed datagram, to the WINS server. The WINS server returns a positive name query response containing the IP address for client C to the WINS proxy, where it is cached for future queries. The WINS proxy also passes this information to client B.

Burst Handling

With the addition of burst handling features in Windows 2000, WINS servers can now support high-volume—or "burst"—server loads. In these situations, many WINS clients actively seek to register their names with their local WINS server at the same time. In burst mode, the WINS server responds positively to clients that submit registration requests before the WINS server has processed and physically entered these updates in the WINS server database.

Burst mode uses a burst queue size as a threshold value to determine how many requests to process normally before enabling burst mode handling. By default, the burst queue allows 500 requests before a WINS server engages burst handling. For more information about changing the burst queue size, see "Configuring Burst Mode Support" in this chapter.

The burst queue allows WINS to handle intermittent periods of heavy registration and refresh traffic, such as when the WINS server is either started with a clean database or when many WINS clients come online for the first time. Either situation creates a large number of requests for registration and refreshment of names.

The function of burst handling is to answer requests superficially (with a positive response), therefore decreasing the load on the network. Burst handling also extends and varies the delay interval to distribute the load over time.

Burst handling is enabled for any WINS server running Windows NT Server 4.0 with the current service pack, as well as with Windows 2000 Server. A WINS server that supports burst handling initiates burst handling once the number of WINS client registration requests exceeds the burst queue size.

How Burst Handling Works

With burst handling, additional client requests beyond the burst queue size are immediately answered with a positive response from the WINS server. The response also includes a varying delay interval or a Time to Live (TTL) interval to help regulate the client registration load and handling of requests received in a single burst period.

Including a delay interval in the success responses lowers the rate at which new WINS clients attempt to refresh and retry name registration, and it regulates the burst of WINS client traffic.

For each additional round of 100 client requests, the delay interval is incremented by the WINS server by an additional 5 minutes until the delay interval reaches a maximum of 50 total minutes. If WINS client traffic is still arriving at burst levels once the delay interval reaches its maximum, the WINS server answers the next round of 100 client requests with the initial delay interval value of 5 minutes, and the incrementing process begins again.

For example, if the default burst queue size of 500 entries is used, the WINS server replies normally to the first 500 requests. It replies immediately to the next 100 WINS client registration requests by sending early success responses. Those early success responses use a starting delay interval value of 5 minutes.

The WINS server continues to handle burst-level request traffic in this manner until the server reaches its maximum intake level of 25,000 name registration and refresh queries. At this point, the WINS server begins dropping queries.

Configuring Burst Mode Support

You can change the level of burst mode support or disable it by using the **WINS Services Properties** dialog box from the WINS server. To reach this interface, open Control Panel, double-click **Administrative Tools**, then choose **Computer Management** and open the **Services and Applications** section. In this section, click **WINS**, and then, on the **Action** menu, click **Properties**. To further configure or disable burst mode support where desired, click **Advanced**.

Four buttons are available for configuring burst mode: **Low**, **Medium**, **High**, and **Custom**. **Custom** allows you to enter a number of queries from 50 to 5,000. **Low**, **Medium**, and **High** configure burst queue sizes of 300, 500, and 1,000, respectively.

By default, burst handling is enabled, and the burst queue is sized to Medium.

▶ **To modify burst handling**

1. In the console tree in MMC, click the name of the WINS server for which you want to modify burst handling properties.
2. On the **Action** menu, click **Properties**.
3. Click the **Advanced** tab.
4. In **Enable burst handling**, modify default settings as needed.
5. To view a description of a dialog box item, right-click the item, and then click **What's This?**

Clustering

Windows 2000 supports clustering of WINS servers. However, before simply adding WINS service to a set of clustered servers, be sure to consider both the advantages and disadvantages of doing so. In many cases, where the overall number of WINS servers is small, clustering WINS is simply not necessary—replication makes WINS fault tolerant. Instead, configure your WINS clients with the address of a secondary WINS server to ensure uninterrupted service.

▶ **To add WINS to a cluster**

1. Be sure the WINS service is installed and started on both servers.
2. Right-click in the resources dialog box and, on the menu that appears, click **New Resource**.
3. Click **Next**, and choose the group you want to add.
4. Choose the possible owners—that is, the other members of the cluster.
5. Set the dependencies for the resource: the disk, the IP address, and the network name.
6. Type the path to the backup database, and click **Finish**.

Be sure that the owner to which you add WINS service has a disk, an IP address, and a name resource. Also, the database path must end with a backslash (\)and specify a location on the dependent disk that you select. For example, if the dependent disk is drive G, you must choose a database path on drive G.

To test that the clustering is working correctly, bring the dependent disk online (it begins offline), then right-click on the window and move the group to the other node. Groups will show the drive as a resource that can be moved; the drive is moved from one node to the next with the group to which it belongs. You should see the entry in the Owner category change as the resource moves.

For more information about clustering WINS servers, see "Windows Clustering" in the *Windows 2000 Resource Kit Distributed Systems Guide*.

Note If you choose to cluster your WINS servers, be sure to equip those servers with a hard disk with high-speed I/O that is dedicated to WINS service. This helps speed up the database response, and ensures that clustering efficiency is high.

Best Practices for WINS Servers

Keeping WINS servers up and functioning prevents WINS clients from reverting to B-node name resolution and flooding a network with broadcast requests. Here are a few suggestions for keeping servers operating efficiently.

Use the Default Configuration

The default settings of WINS, set when the service is first installed, provide the optimal configuration for most conditions and should be used in most WINS network installations. If you modify the default settings, be sure that the need to do so is clear and necessary, and that you understand all the implications.

Minimize the Number of WINS Servers

Using too many WINS servers can complicate network problems, so be conservative when adding WINS servers to your network. Use the minimum number of WINS servers to support all your clients while maintaining acceptable performance.

When planning your servers, remember that each WINS server can simultaneously handle hundreds of registrations and queries per second. In part, this is because the data exchanged between WINS servers and WINS clients is typically small. The average WINS record is about 40 bytes.

WINS network traffic during client registration can be much less than that of DHCP, which uses client broadcasts to discover servers. By default, most WINS clients first send directed point-to-point datagrams to the primary WINS servers.

In general, avoid deploying large numbers of WINS servers unless they are strictly necessary. Limiting the number of WINS servers minimizes WAN traffic related to WINS replication, provides good NetBIOS name resolution, and reduces administrative problems without sacrificing functionality. To design a WINS installation that includes more than 20 WINS servers, seek assistance from Microsoft Product Support Services.

Requests to WINS servers are directed datagrams, meaning that WINS requests are routed. Therefore, one WINS server is adequate for a network of 10,000 nodes, although to provide fault tolerance, at least two WINS servers are recommended. Because the data exchange between WINS servers and clients is typically about 40 bytes in size, and WINS communicates using directed datagrams, a single WINS server may be enough for very small networks.

Based on the number of CPUs in the computer, WINS determines how many threads to create to handle client queries; it creates one thread per CPU. Each name registration takes about 40 milliseconds with logging enabled. If logging is disabled, registrations are much faster, but this configuration introduces the risk of losing the last few updates to the WINS database when a failure occurs.

Use High-Performance Disk Hardware

WINS causes frequent and intense activity on server hard disks. To provide the best performance, consider RAID-based solutions that improve disk access time when you purchase hardware for a WINS server. You should include WINS when evaluating the performance of a server. By monitoring system hardware performance in the most demanding areas of utilization (CPU, memory, and disk I/O), you make the best assessments of when a WINS server is overloaded and should be upgraded.

Add Network Interface Hardware Carefully

Be careful when adding more network adapters to a computer running Windows 2000. You can increase the reliability of mission-critical systems while adding the hardware simply by reducing the number of services running on the computer. Many of the services running on a mission-critical computer (such as a primary domain controller) can be offloaded to other computers and then returned to the upgraded original computer once the change is complete.

Configure Each Server to Point to Itself

Each WINS server you install on your network must register in WINS its own set of unique and group NetBIOS names. WINS service problems can occur when registration and ownership of a WINS record become split—that is, when names registered for a particular WINS server are owned by different WINS servers. To prevent these problems, configure each WINS server as its own primary and secondary WINS servers.

WINS Server Fault Tolerance

To prevent a WINS failure from affecting server communications, you may want to consider using an LMHOSTS file to provide secondary name resolution in the event of a WINS failure. While these files are not a recommended solution, in rare circumstances they may provide an effective stopgap measure. LMHOSTS files must be tightly managed because changes in the NetBIOS environment will not automatically update static name files.

To use LMHOSTS for name resolution, you must make a correctly configured LMHOSTS file available for locating Windows 2000 computers when WINS servers fail. A master LMHOSTS file should contain static IP address mappings for Windows 2000 computers. This file should be distributed to each Windows domain using one of the following three options:

- The typical Windows 2000 LMHOSTS file contains a universal naming convention (UNC) path to a central file. By pointing to a single file, you need only maintain one copy of the LMHOSTS file.
- For computers without Windows 2000, you can schedule a job using the scheduler service to distribute the master LMHOSTS file to the required servers automatically. The **winat** command from the *Windows 2000 Resource Kit* may make this task easier. Send the file to the primary domain controller (PDC) and one backup domain controller (BDC) on each domain.
- The least efficient option is to manually copy the file to each server and client that needs it, or to update each LMHOSTS file locally. This may be still be worthwhile for a network with a single WINS server.

Once the LMHOSTS file is prepared and distributed, if a server fails, the local LMHOSTS file of each server references the master LMHOSTS file on the PDC sharepoint. If you use an #INCLUDE statement, the central LMHOSTS file is also available from alternate servers.

Do Not Use Extended Characters

Do not use extended characters in NetBIOS names, especially the underscore (_) and the period (.). The underscore character is converted to a dash in DNS host names. For example, NTServer_1 becomes NTServer-1, leading to failure of name resolution of a name that may, in fact, be recorded in the DNS files.

Align the Lease and Refresh Periods for DHCP and WINS

When you configure a network to use both DHCP and WINS, set the DHCP lease period to be roughly equal to or greater than the WINS renewal period. This prevents a situation in which the WINS server fails to notice that a DHCP client releases a DHCP-assigned IP address; the client cannot send a WINS renewal request if the client fails to renew its IP address. If another computer is assigned that IP address before the WINS server notes the change, the WINS server mistakenly directs requests for the address to the new client.

WINS Database

When a client needs to contact another host on the network, it first contacts the WINS server to resolve the query using mapping information from the database of the server. The relational database engine of the WINS server accesses an indexed sequential access method (ISAM) database. The ISAM database is a replicated database that contains NetBIOS computer names and IP address mappings.

For a WINS client to log on to the network, it must register its computer name and IP address with the WINS server. This creates a single mapped entry in the WINS database for the client. Because these entries are updated each time a WINS-enabled client logs on to the network, information stored in the WINS server database remains accurate.

Managing the WINS Server Database

The Windows 2000 WINS database uses the performance-enhanced Extensible Storage Engine, an updated version of the generic storage engine that serves both Microsoft Exchange 5.5 servers and Windows 2000 servers. This database imposes no limit to the number of records that a WINS server can replicate or store. The size of the database depends on the number of WINS clients on the network, but it is not directly proportional to the number of active client entries. As inactive entries proliferate, the WINS database grows, and many WINS client entries become obsolete. Eventually, these entries clutter the database.

To recover the unused space, the WINS database is compacted. In Windows 2000, WINS server database compaction occurs as an automatic background process during idle time after a database update. Because the database compaction is also dynamic, you do not need to stop the WINS server to compact the database; this is also known as online compaction. However, while WINS performs regular online compaction, this reduces but does not eliminate the need for offline compaction. The WINS service will still need to be stopped periodically for offline compaction. For more information, see "Managing the WINS Server Database" later in this chapter.

The database files, stored in the directory *%SystemRoot%*\System32\Wins, are described in Table 7.5.

Table 7.5 WINS Server Database Files

File	Description
J50.log and J50*xxxxx*.log	A log of all transactions done with the database. This file is used by WINS to recover data if necessary.
J50.chk	A checkpoint file, used when the WINS database starts up to determine whether the last shutdown was clean and all databases are consistent. If not, the checkpoint file helps determine from what log file to begin recovery.
Wins.mdb	The WINS server database file, which contains two tables, an IP address–to–owner ID mapping table, and a name–to–IP address mapping table.
Winstmp.mdb	A temporary file created by the WINS service. The database uses it as a swap file during index maintenance operations. It might remain in the directory *%SystemRoot%*\System32\Wins after a crash.

Caution The files J50.log, J50*xxxxx*.log, Wins.mdb, and Winstmp.mdb should not be removed or tampered with in any manner.

The WINS management console provides the tools you need to maintain, view, back up, and restore the WINS server database. For example, you use the WINS management console to back up the WINS server database files.

Backing Up the WINS Database

The WINS management console provides backup tools so that you can back up the WINS database. After you specify a backup directory for the database, WINS performs complete database backups every three hours, by installation default. For specific instructions on how to back up and restore the WINS database, see the Windows 2000 Server Help. You should also periodically back up the registry entries for the WINS server.

Repairing a WINS Database

If your WINS database becomes corrupted, you can use various options to renew its integrity. In cases in which the corruption is limited to a specific set of records, you can repair them by selectively increasing or decreasing the starting version number used by the WINS server that owns the affected records. If you choose this method, you can adjust the starting version used by the server to force replication of uncorrupted WINS records, which removes the affected records from other WINS servers.

If the corruption can't be repaired, you can delete the WINS database and entirely restore it from a backup (assuming that one exists). You can use the WINS backup feature in the WINS management console to make backup copies of the WINS database.

Sometimes you can repair WINS database corruption by increasing the highest version number of the local WINS server database; to do this, you must increase the value specified in the **Starting Version Count** box in the WINS server preferences. Then, the next time WINS restarts, the specified WINS server updates its local version number for any records it owns.

Increasing the value of the starting version number on the owning WINS server forces replication for all records owned by the specified WINS server to other remote partner WINS servers during the next replication cycle.

Note that you can set the value of the starting version number only to a value higher than the existing highest version number used by any locally owned records on the selected server. If there are no locally owned WINS records for the server, you can only set the starting version number to a higher number than the current starting version number count. Once a higher value is set, you cannot lower the value without first deleting the local WINS database and reinstalling WINS on the server computer.

Also, values entered and used for **Starting Version Count** are interpreted as hexadecimal numbers. WINS might adjust the value you specify to a higher value to ensure that database records are quickly replicated to other WINS servers. The maximum value that the WINS management console accepts as a valid starting number is a hexadecimal value of **FFFFFFFF**.

Using Replication to Restore Data

If the time to WINS convergence is low (that is, changes are replicated among the WINS servers quickly), the preferred method of restoring a local WINS server database is to use a replication partner to restore data after corruption. This method is most effective if the WINS data is mostly up to date on the replication partner.

The easiest way to restore a local server database is to replicate data back from a replication partner. Two registry entries control this feature: **InitTimeReplication** and **InitTimePause**. **InitTimeReplication** is an entry in the following subkey:

```
HKEY_LOCAL_MACHINE\System\CurrentControlSet\Services
\Wins\Partners\Pull
```

The value of this entry is 1 by default and causes WINS to replicate with the partner at initialization time. **InitTimePause** is an entry in the WINS Parameters subkey that tells WINS to pause while the replication takes place. These entries are discussed in this section.

Name: InitTimeReplication

Data Type: REG_DWORD

Description: If the value of **InitTimeReplication** is set to 1, the default value, the WINS server pulls replicas of new database entries from its partners when the system is initialized or when a replication-related parameter changes; if the value is 0, replication occurs only as often as specified by the value set for **Replication interval** in the Replication Partner Properties dialog box (shown in Figure 7.10).

Name: InitTimePause

Data Type: REG_DWORD

Description: The value set here determines whether WINS starts in a paused state and remains in that state until its first replication is complete. If the value of **InitTimePause** is 1, WINS starts in a paused state; if the value is 0, the default value, WINS does not start in a paused state. In the paused state, WINS does not accept any name registrations, releases, or queries. WINS remains in the paused state until it has replicated with its partners or until its first replication attempt has failed. Note that if the value of **InitTimePause** is set to **1**, then **InitTimeReplication** (in the Pull partners subkey) should be set to **1** or be deleted from the registry.

Compacting the WINS Database

In Windows 2000 Server, the WINS service performs dynamic Jet compaction of the WINS database while the server is online. This reduces the need to use Jetpack.exe for offline compaction. Therefore, this procedure might not be as critical now as it was in the past for WINS and DHCP servers running earlier versions of Windows NT Server.

Windows 2000 Server includes the Jetpack.exe utility so that it can be used to compact the WINS and other Jet databases (such as DHCP) when those databases are offline. Microsoft recommends you use Jetpack.exe to compact a Jet database periodically whenever the database grows beyond 30 megabytes or more in size.

Use the Jetpack.exe command-line tool to perform offline compaction. The correct syntax for Jetpack.exe is:

jetpack *<database name>* *<name of the temporary database>*

Suppose that you have a temporary database with the file name Tmp.mdb, and the WINS database has the file name Wins.mdb. To compact the database in this example, you enter the following commands:

cd *%SystemRoot%***System32\Wins**

net stop wins

jetpack wins.mdb tmp.mdb

net start wins

Jetpack compacts the WINS database; first it copies database information to the temporary database file, Tmp.mdb, then it deletes the original WINS database file, Wins.mdb. Finally, it renames the temporary database file to the original file name, Wins.mdb.

Scavenging the Database

Like any database, the WINS server database becomes littered with junk entries over time and must periodically be cleaned and backed up. Scavenging the WINS server database takes care of this. It is usually performed at the same time as regular backups.

Scavenging updates the name state of WINS database entries, clearing the local WINS server database of released entries. It also clears away entries replicated from a remote WINS server that were not removed from the local WINS database when they were removed from the remote database. This scavenging process occurs automatically over intervals defined by the relationship between the renewal and extinction intervals defined in the **Configuration** dialog box. You can also find this dialog box on the **Name Record** tab of the **Server Properties** page, and the configuration page is shown in Figure 7.8.

Table 7.6 describes the effects of scavenging on WINS database entries.

Table 7.6 State of WINS Database Entries Before and After Scavenging

State before scavenging	State after scavenging
Owned active name for which the renewal interval has not expired	Unchanged
Owned active name for which the renewal interval has expired	Marked released

(continued)

Table 7.6 State of WINS Database Entries Before and After Scavenging *(continued)*

State before scavenging	State after scavenging
Owned release name for which the extinction interval has not expired	Unchanged
Owned released name for which the extinction interval has expired	Marked extinct
Owned extinct name for which the extinction timeout has not expired	Unchanged
Owned extinct name for which the extinction timeout has expired	Deleted
Replica of extinct name for which the extinction timeout has expired	Deleted
Replica of active name for which the verification interval has not expired	Unchanged
Replica of active name for which the verification interval has expired	Revalidated
Replica of extinct or deleted name	Deleted

Scavenging maintains the correct state information in the database by examining each record the WINS server owns, comparing its time stamp to the current time, then changing the state of those records whose state has expired (changing a record's state from active to released, for example).

Scavenging occurs on a preset schedule. The scavenging timer starts when the server starts up and is equal to half the renewal interval. Because of this, the WINS service should not be stopped or restarted before half the renewal interval has passed, or scavenging will not occur. Scavenging first occurs after half of the renewal interval has elapsed. During the first scavenging, all scavenging actions are performed except one: the deletion of the tombstones. Tombstones are not deleted until at least three days have elapsed since startup of the server, to allow sufficient time for their replication. Scavenging recurs at one-half the renewal interval (or can be initiated manually).

Scavenging follows the algorithm shown in Figure 7.7.

```
Get records owned by self
If Current Time > Time Stamp
    Change State
        Active -> Released
        Released -> Tombstone
        Tombstone -> Delete from database
Get replica Tombstones
If Current Time > Time Stamp
    Delete record from database
Get Active replicas
If Current Time > Time Stamp
    Verify with owner that record still exists
        If exists
            Time Stamp = Current Time + Verification Interval
        Else
            Delete record from database
```

Figure 7.7 WINS Scavenging Algorithm

The results of this scavenging algorithm are also detailed in Table 7.6.

Consistency Checking

Consistency checking helps maintain database integrity among WINS servers in a large network. When consistency checking is initiated using the WINS management console, WINS pulls all of the records directly from each owning server in its database, including any servers for which it has stored local records that are not among its replication partners.

All records pulled from remote databases are compared to records in the local database using the following checks for consistency:

- If the record in the local database is identical to the record pulled from the owner database, its time stamp is updated.
- If the record in the local database has a lower version ID than the record pulled from the owner database, the pulled record is added to the local database and the original local record is marked for deletion.
- If the records have the same version ID but a different name, the local record will be marked deleted and the pulled record will replace it.

Note that if a WINS database is extremely large, the consistency checking process might be network-intensive. In Windows 2000, consistency checking can be performed using the WINS management console, by checking the **Enable Periodic Database Consistency Checking** box on the **Name Record** tab of the server properties page.

WINS Database Files

The format of the WINS database increases the speed and efficiency of data storage by writing current transactions to log files rather than to the database directly. Therefore, the most current view of the state of the WINS database requires examination of the database plus any transactions in the log files. These files are also used for recovery; if the service fails (for example, due to a power failure), the log files can recreate the correct state of the WINS database.

Log files are always about 1 megabyte in size; however, they can grow quickly on a very busy WINS server. When a WINS server reaches the maximum size of its current log file, it creates another log file.

The effective size of the database of each connected WINS server is roughly identical. Each database has the same number of entries, neglecting latencies, and the size of the database is proportional to the number of entries. Unique entries typically occupy 42 bytes (they require no scope ID). Internet Group entries might occupy as many as 25 addresses and, therefore, more bytes. The real size might be much larger because unused space is only reclaimed efficiently by compacting.

The name–to–IP address mapping table stores NetBIOS names and the IP addresses currently assigned to them. The entries in this table are created from NetBIOS name registration requests received over TCP/IP nodes and from replicas received from other WINS servers. A *clustered index* on the name field enables quick retrieval of records required for name queries. A clustered index is an index in which the logical or indexed order of the key values is the same as the physical stored order of the corresponding rows that exist in a table. A primary index is built from the concatenation of the owner ID and version ID fields, and stored in ascending order. This allows quick access to records falling within ranges of version IDs for a particular owner.

The IP address–to–owner ID mapping table contains a row for each WINS server that has entries in the name–to–IP address mapping table. Rows contain the IP address of WINS servers and their identifier as stored in the owner ID field of the entries that this server owns.

Timers

The WINS database records are governed by four configurable timer values:

- Renewal interval
- Extinction interval
- Extinction timeout
- Verification interval

Microsoft has chosen the defaults for these four values with care and, in general, they should not be modified. They keep the level of network traffic and the load on WINS servers at a minimum. They represent the best tradeoff, considering the various configurations in which WINS servers might be deployed, between these goals and minimizing the window during which the databases remain out of sync. Considerations such as long weekends, avoidance of unnecessary replication traffic, ability to handle a large number of clients quickly under worst-case scenarios—as well as tradeoffs between removing clutter quickly and retaining entries to ensure replication—have been factored into the determination of these intervals.

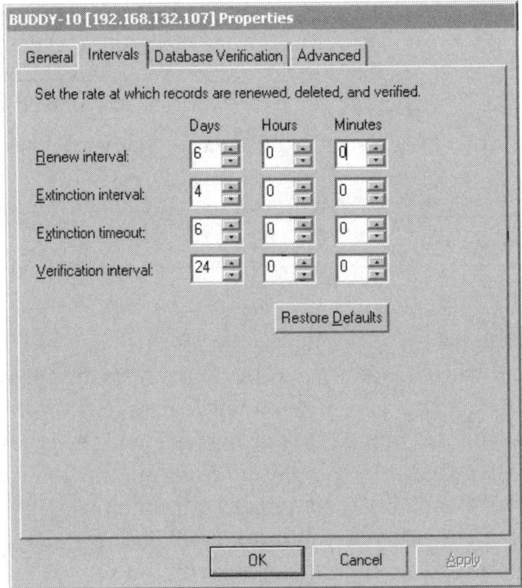

Figure 7.8 Name Record Configuration Dialog Box

These four values are listed in Table 7.7, and are described in more detail in this section. They are configured in the dialog box shown in Figure 7.8.

Table 7.7 WINS Server Timers

Configuration option	Description
Renewal Interval	Specifies how often a client reregisters its name. The default is six days.
Extinction Interval	Specifies the interval between when an entry is marked as released and when it is marked as extinct. The default depends on the renewal interval and, if the WINS server has replication partners, on the maximum replication time interval. Maximum allowable value is six days.
Extinction Timeout	Specifies the interval between when an entry is marked extinct and when the entry is finally scavenged from the database. The default depends on the renewal interval and, if the WINS server has replication partners, on the maximum replication time interval. The default is six days.
Verification Interval	Specifies the interval after which the WINS server must verify that old names it does not own are still active. The default depends on the extinction interval. The maximum allowable value is 24 days.

Renewal Interval

The renewal interval is also known as the name refresh timeout, or the Time To Live (TTL). When a name is registered with the WINS server, the database entry is time stamped with the sum of the current time and the renewal interval. A client must refresh its name with the WINS server within this interval or the name is released. When a name is released, either by timing out or by the explicit release of the name by the client, no action is taken other than changing the entry to the released state and time stamping the entry with the sum of the current time and the extinction interval. This change is not replicated to other WINS servers. When a name is in the released state and a new registration comes in with a different address, the name can be immediately given to the new client without challenge because it is known that the old client is no longer using the name. The default renewal interval is six days.

Extinction Interval

The extinction interval is also known as the name age timeout and the tombstone interval. This is the interval at which released names enter the tombstone state. At this time, the entry is time stamped with the sum of the current time and the extinction timeout; and the entry's version ID is updated, ensuring that this information is propagated to all WINS servers at the next replication.

When tombstone entries are created, they are time stamped with the sum of the current time and the extinction timeout at the pulling WINS server. The default extinction interval is based on renewal and replication times. This is typically six days in Windows 2000.

Extinction Timeout

The extinction timeout is also known as the tombstone timeout. Tombstone records older than the extinction timeout are removed from the database. As noted earlier, manual extinction is available in Windows 2000 from the WINS console. The default extinction timeout is six days.

Verification Interval

Replication should ensure that the databases stay synchronized. However, under certain abnormal conditions, names no longer in use could remain in the database, creating database clutter. For example, if a tombstone record is removed before being replicated, the active state of the record in the replica databases never changes. This could happen if the replication partner was not reachable during the extinction timeout period.

When an active entry is replicated, it is time stamped with the sum of the current time and the verification interval on the pulling WINS server. If, at scavenge time, WINS finds records older than the verification interval, WINS sends a query to the WINS server that owns that name, asking if the version ID is still valid. If the owning WINS server responds negatively (invalid record), the record is removed. If the owning WINS server sends a positive response (valid record), the time stamp is updated. If the WINS server cannot be contacted, the entries are left until the next verification interval or until the administrator triggers scavenging. No records are removed if the owning WINS server cannot be contacted. The default verification interval is 24 days.

Server Clocks

The replication and scavenging algorithms rely on a reasonably consistent system clock. Of course, setting the system clock forward or backward affects these algorithms. However, because the time stamps are always entered locally, the WINS servers do not need to be time-synchronized. As long as the time is consistent on each server, the intervals and timers function correctly.

Deletion of WINS Database Records

The WINS management console provides improved database management by supporting the following deletion operations:

- Simple deletion of WINS database records stored on a single-server database.
- Tombstoned deletion of WINS database records replicated to databases on other WINS servers.
- The ability to select multiple groups of displayed database records when performing either simple or tombstoned deletion.

In addition, the WINS management console allows you a simpler and more convenient tool for administratively removing dynamically registered records. In previous releases of WINS, the WINS management console utilities only removed static mappings.

WINS records can be removed in one of two ways: either through simple deletion or by using tombstoned deletion. The rest of this section discusses how to use both to manage your WINS database.

When simple deletion is used, records selected using the WINS console are removed from the current local WINS server that you are managing.

If WINS records deleted this way have been replicated to other WINS servers, these additional records will not be removed fully. The records on other WINS servers remain in those databases unless you specifically use the WINS console to remove them from each server, one at a time. In addition, records deleted on just one server might reappear when replication next occurs between WINS servers configured as replication partners.

When you use tombstoned deletion to remove a record owned by your selected server, the selected records are removed from all WINS servers that replicate the records as described in this section.

The owning WINS server changes the status of selected WINS records from active to tombstoned in its database. WINS then treats the records as inactive and released from use. Once these records are tombstoned locally, the owning WINS server neither responds to nor resolves NetBIOS name queries for these names from other WINS clients and WINS servers unless the records are registered again by the WINS client. The owning WINS server replicates the selected records as "tombstoned" to other WINS servers during subsequent replication cycles.

The records are not forcibly and immediately removed from WINS; instead, they are flagged for eventual deletion. The exact replication cycle interval is configured based on the Name Record properties of the server set in the WINS console. Records are not removed from WINS databases until their extinction interval has actually expired. This allows other WINS servers to learn that these records are no longer in use, update their replicated record mappings, and further replicate this updated WINS data to other servers. The records are marked extinct on all replicated WINS servers.

Once all WINS servers have completed a full replication cycle, the tombstoned records expire and are removed from the database on each WINS server during the next database scavenging operation. Once scavenging occurs on all servers, the records no longer appear in the WINS management console and are no longer physically stored in the WINS database.

Note that even if records are manually tombstoned (or otherwise marked as released by WINS), released records remain in the WINS database briefly before being removed during subsequent scavenging operations. Exactly how long they remain depends on the length of time required by the WINS server to determine extinction. Typically, the time to extinction for records is equal to the sum of the extinction interval, the extinction timeout, and the verification interval.

Example of Record Registration and Extinction

As an example, a WINS client registers the name TESTPC1 with the WINS server WINS1, and the server provides a refresh interval of three days. Once the name is registered, WINS1 replicates this record to its replication partners, such as WINS server WINS2. When the verification interval has expired, WINS2 verifies the record with WINS1. WINS1 takes no further action with this record; it simply waits until the client refreshes its name or reregisters it.

If the client does not refresh its name within the refresh interval, WINS1 sets the state for the name TESTPC1 to "released." If the client does not refresh the name within the extinction interval, the name is tombstoned; at that point, it is again replicated to WINS2 (because the version ID of the record for TESTPC1 is increased).

When the record is replicated, WINS2 copies the tombstoned entry from WINS1 and stamps it with the current time plus the verification interval. WINS2 does not query WINS1 until after the verification interval elapses. On the other hand, WINS1 waits for the duration of the extinction interval for the client to refresh or reregister its name. If the client does not do so, WINS1 removes the name from the database. WINS2 then queries WINS1 when the verification interval expires; if the record is not present at WINS1, then WINS2 removes the record from its database.

If WINS2 queries WINS1, and WINS1 does not respond (due to failure, maintenance, or simply a slow link), then the record is not removed. In this case, the entry's verification interval is reset, and WINS2 queries WINS1 after the verification interval has again expired.

Manual Tombstoning

With earlier versions of WINS, records were not deleted on multiple servers simultaneously. A window existed during which replication could occur between servers whose records were inconsistent. In other words, deleted records could return to a server from which they were just deleted.

The manual tombstoning option of Windows 2000 WINS prevents this problem. The length of the tombstoned state is greater than the propagation delay incurred with replication across the network. When the time limit is reached, tombstoned records are deleted by normal scavenging.

Manual tombstoning provides an excellent way of dealing with static records, too.

When the tombstoned records are replicated, the tombstone status is updated and applied by other WINS servers that store replicated copies of these records. Each replicating WINS server updates and individually tombstones these records. Once all WINS servers have replicated these records, the records are automatically removed from WINS after the period set by the verification interval of each server.

Manual tombstoning is available from both the WINS graphical user interface and the WINS command-line interface. To access this feature, open the **WINS** dialog box, select the owning server, then view all the records of that server. Highlight the record you want to delete, and delete it from the **Action** menu. At this point, you can either delete or tombstone the record. While the ability to manually tombstone records requires Windows 2000 WINS servers, tombstoned records replicate normally to Windows NT 3.51 and Windows NT 4.0 servers.

Best Practices for WINS Databases

With dynamic compaction and the WINS management console, WINS databases are much easier to maintain in Windows 2000, but they still require certain administrative practices and regular upkeep.

Perform Periodic Consistency Checking For Windows 2000, WINS consistency checking is available from the WINS management console. Use this feature periodically to check the WINS database for consistency.

Consistency checking consumes a great deal of network and computer system resources because the WINS server must replicate itself for each owner whose records are being checked for consistency. For this reason, check the consistency of WINS database records during times of low network traffic, such as at night or on weekends.

Perform Regular Offline Compaction Dynamic database compaction occurs on WINS servers as an automatic background process during idle time after a database update. This dynamic database compaction occurs while the database is in use; you do not need to stop the WINS server for dynamic compacting.

Although dynamic compacting greatly reduces the need for offline compaction, it does not fully eliminate the need for it. Offline compaction using the JETPACK utility reclaims more space than dynamic compaction and should be performed once a month for networks with 1,000 or more WINS clients. For smaller networks, manual compaction may be useful if only performed every few months.

Although manual compaction of the WINS server database is not as important for Windows 2000 Server as it was for earlier versions, it is still useful. You should perform monthly or weekly offline compaction for disk defragmentation and improved disk performance. Monitor any changes to the size of the server database file, Wins.mdb, which is located in the directory *%SystemRoot%*\System32\Wins.

Checking the file size of Wins.mdb both before and after compaction allows you to measure growth and reduction. This information helps you determine the actual benefits to using offline compaction. Based on this information, you can gauge how often to repeat offline compaction for measurable gains.

Perform Regular Backups to Ease Restoration In addition to tape backups of the WINS server computer, the WINS management console offers a backup option that allows you to restore a WINS database after the database file has been corrupted. For more information on restoring data after corruption or loss of the WINS server database, see "Restoring Data" in the "Troubleshooting" section of this chapter.

You can also restore the database through a replication partner. If the WINS data is current on the replication partner, you can use this data to update the failed server. Two registry entries control this feature, **InitTimeReplication** and **InitTimePause**. **InitTimeReplication** is in the following subkey:

HKEY_LOCAL_MACHINE\SYSTEM\CurrentControlSet\Services
\Wins\Partners\Pull

The value of this entry is 1 by default, which causes WINS to replicate with the partner at the time specified in the key. The **InitTimePause** entry is stored in the following subkey:

HKEY_LOCAL_MACHINE\SYSTEM\CurrentControlSet\Services
\Wins\Parameters

It tells WINS to pause while the replication takes place.

Use the Scavenge Function The **scavenge** function is an automatic function of Windows 2000 WINS. It releases records old enough to be released, removes extinct records, and verifies records after the verification interval passes.

Using the default WINS configuration in Windows 2000, **scavenge** runs after WINS has been running for 72 hours, or half the renewal interval. If WINS is stopped and restarted before 72 hours have elapsed, the 72-hour window to the next scheduled scavenge is reset. If the WINS service is stopped on a daily basis, scavenging cannot take place.

To verify that scavenging is occurring, on the WINS server properties page, on the **Advanced** tab, select the **Log Detailed Events to Event Log** check box. This feature adds overhead processing, and should be used only when verifying the scavenging process. If scavenging is not taking place, establish a scavenge policy as part of your WINS database maintenance.

Avoid Using Static WINS Entries Static WINS entries require administrative action to assure their successful and intended use. However, static entries can be useful for specific purposes, such as protecting registration of names used by critically important servers.

For example, you can add a static entry to the WINS database to prevent other computers from registering the name of a critical server while that server is down. Reserving names in this manner prevents anyone from hijacking the server name (via DHCP) by registering another computer with the same name on the network. If the server is not responding at the time, a WINS server issuing a name challenge does not receive a response indicating that the name is in use, and the address is taken over by the new computer.

The biggest disadvantage of using static WINS entries is that it complicates administration of name and address changes in your network. For example, if either the IP address or the computer name of a static WINS entry changes, you might need to update other configurations, such as DHCP servers, DNS servers, end systems, LMHOSTS files, and so forth.

If you do use static WINS entries, use reservations to minimize the impact on DHCP. For each IP address used in static WINS mapping, use a corresponding client address reservation to reserve the IP address at the DHCP server. Also, if you do use static entries, carefully monitor and track the servers where these entries are added (the owning servers). Ideally, all static entries should only be entered on a single server. This makes later removal of these entries easier. For more information about address reservations, see "Dynamic Host Configuration Protocol" in this book.

WINS Replication

You can configure all WINS servers on a network to fully replicate their database entries to other WINS servers. This replication ensures that a name registered with one WINS server is eventually registered to all other WINS servers. This section examines the replication process in detail.

Overview of the Replication Process

Replicating databases between WINS servers maintains a consistent set of WINS information throughout a network. An example of WINS database replication is shown in Figure 7.9. Two WINS servers, WINS-A and WINS-B, are both configured to fully replicate their records with each other.

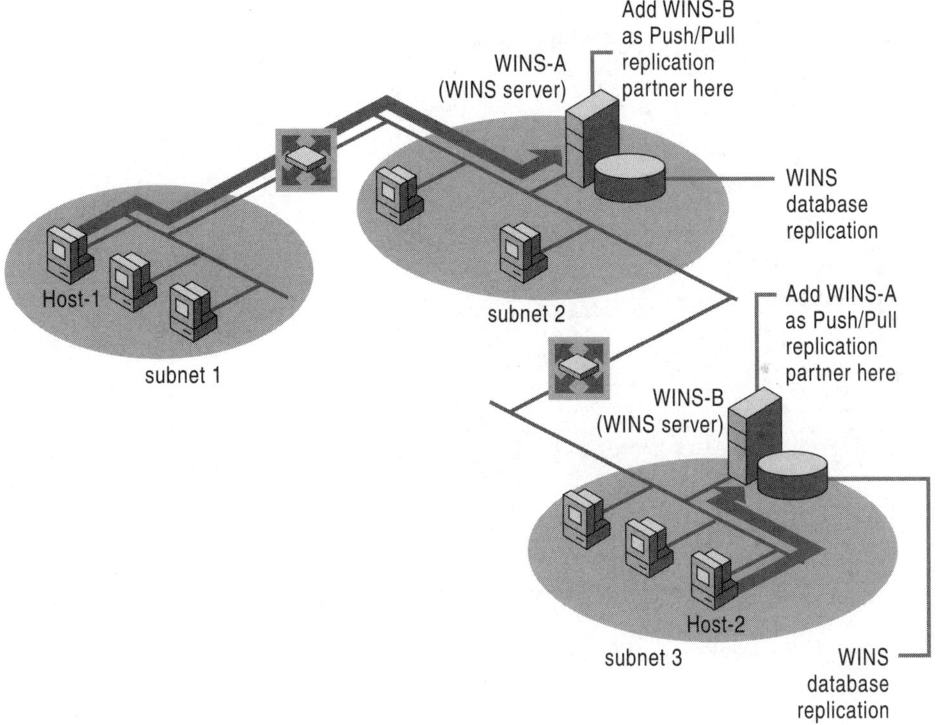

Figure 7.9 WINS Replication Overview

In Figure 7.9, a WINS client, HOST-1 on subnet 1, registers its name with its primary WINS server, WINS-A. Another WINS client, HOST-2 on Subnet 3, registers its name with its primary WINS server, WINS-B. If either of these hosts later attempts to locate the other host using WINS—for example, HOST-1 queries to find an IP address for HOST-2—replication of WINS registration information between the WINS servers makes it possible to resolve this query.

Note WINS replication is always incremental, meaning that only changes in the database are replicated each time replication occurs, not the entire database.

For replication to work, each WINS server must be configured with at least one other WINS server as its replication partner. This ensures that a name registered with one WINS server is eventually replicated to all other WINS servers in the network. A replication partner can be added and configured as either a push partner, a pull partner, or a push/pull partner, which uses both methods of replication. The push/pull partner is the default configuration and is the type recommended for use in most cases.

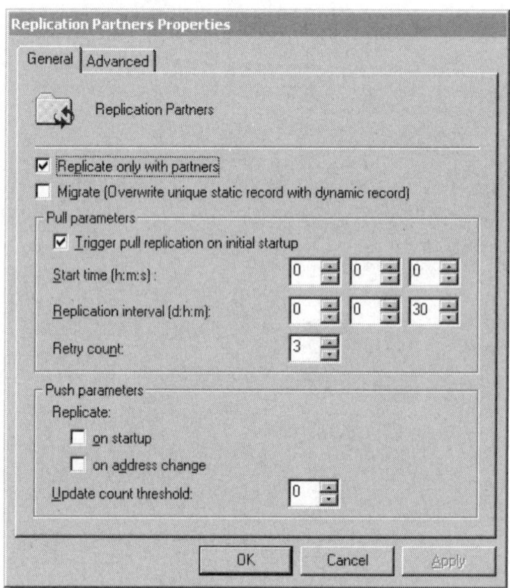

Figure 7.10 Replication Partners Properties Dialog Box

When WINS servers replicate, a latency period exists before the name-to-address mapping of a client from any given server is propagated to all other WINS servers in the network. This latency is known as the convergence time for the entire WINS system. For example, a name release request by a client does not propagate as quickly as a name registration request. This is because names are commonly released and then reused with the same mapping, such as when computers are restarted or when they are turned off for the evening and restarted in the morning. Replicating each of these name releases would unnecessarily increase the network load of replication.

Also, when a WINS client computer is shut off improperly, such as during an unexpected power outage, the computer's registered names are not released normally with a request to the server. Therefore, the presence of a record in the WINS database does not necessarily mean that a client computer is still using the name or its associated IP address. It only means that a computer recently registered that name and its associated IP address.

Note The primary and secondary WINS servers assigned to any client must have push and pull relationships with each other. You might want to keep a list of pairs of push/pull WINS servers for use when assigning servers to clients.

To replicate database entries, each WINS server in a network must be configured as either a pull partner or a push partner with at least one other WINS server.

WINS Server Push and Pull Partners

The WINS database is collectively managed by the WINS servers, each of which has a copy of the WINS database. To keep these copies consistent, servers replicate their records among themselves. Each WINS server is configured with a set of one or more replication partners. When new computers are added or substituted on the network, they register their name and IP address with another server, which in turn propagates the new record to all other WINS servers in the enterprise. The result is that every server has the record pertaining to that new computer.

Detailed Replication Example

The figure below shows an extremely large WINS implementation, serving more than 100,000 nodes. In a configuration with so many WINS servers, it is tempting to create many push/pull relationships for redundancy. This can lead to a system that, while functional, is overly complex and difficult to understand and troubleshoot.

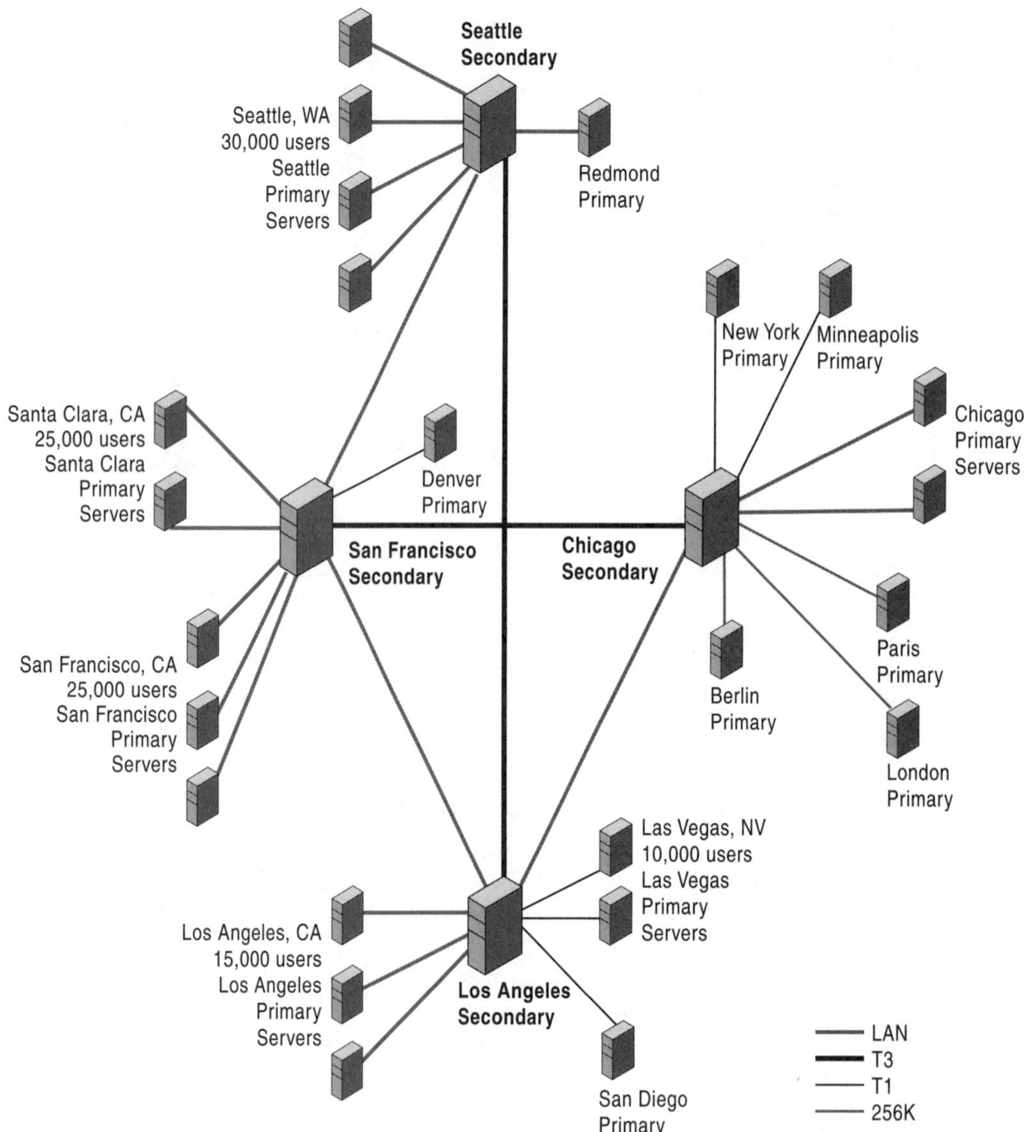

Figure 7.11 Large-Scale WINS Deployment Using Hub Topology

The hub structure imposes order on the sample configuration shown in Figure 7.11. Four major hubs are located in Seattle, San Francisco, Chicago, and Los Angeles. These hubs serve as secondary WINS servers for their regions while connecting the four geographic locations. All primary WINS servers are configured as push/pull partners with the hubs, and the hubs are configured as push/pull partners with other hubs.

For example, assume the primary WINS servers in Figure 7.11 replicate with the hubs every 15 minutes, and the hub-to-hub replication interval is 30 minutes. The convergence time of the WINS system is the time it takes for a node registration to be replicated to all WINS servers. In this case the longest time would be from a Seattle primary server to a Chicago primary server. The convergence time can be calculated by adding up the maximum time between replication from the Seattle primary to Seattle secondary, Seattle secondary to San Francisco secondary, San Francisco secondary to Chicago secondary, and finally Chicago secondary to Chicago primary. This yields a total convergence time of 15 + 30 + 30 + 15 minutes, or 1.5 hours.

However, the convergence could be longer if some of these WINS servers are connected across slow links. It is probably not necessary for the servers in Paris or Berlin to replicate every 15 minutes. You might configure them to replicate every two hours or even every 24 hours, depending on the volatility of names in the WINS system.

This example network contains some redundancy, but not much. If the link between Seattle and Los Angeles is down, replication still occurs through San Francisco, but what happens if the Seattle hub itself goes down? In this case, the Seattle area can no longer replicate with the rest of the WINS system. Network connectivity, however, is still functional—all WINS servers contain the entire WINS database, and name resolution functions normally. All that is lost are changes to the WINS system that occurred since the Seattle hub went down. A Seattle user cannot resolve the name of a file server in Chicago that comes online after the Seattle hub does down. Once the hub returns to service, all changes to the WINS database are replicated normally.

Small-Scale Replication Example

While the large-scale deployment shown in the four-hub diagram of Figure 7.11 is possible, it is also valuable to examine a much smaller example of replication. The simplest case involves just two servers, as shown in Figure 7.12.

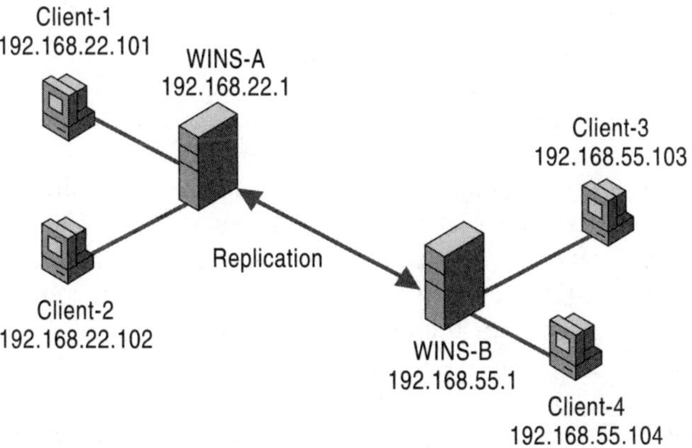

Figure 7.12 Database Replication Between Two WINS Servers

Tables 7.8 and 7.9 are the database tables for WINS-A and WINS-B on January 1, 2000. All four clients are powered on in the morning between 8:00 A.M. and 8:15 A.M. Client2 has just been shut down. WINS-A and WINS-B have the following parameters:

- WINS-A and WINS-B are push/pull partners to each other.
- The replication interval is 30 minutes.
- The renewal interval is 4 days.
- The extinction interval is 4 days.
- The extinction timeout is 1 day.
- The verification interval is 24 days.

Before replication, WINS-A has two entries in its database. These entries are for Client1 and Client2, as shown in Table 7.8.

Table 7.8 WINS-A Database Before Replication

Name	Address	Flags	Owner	Version ID	Time stamp
Client1	192.168. 22.101	Unique, active, H-node, dynamic	WINS-A	4B3	1/5/00 8:05:32 AM
Client2	192.168. 22.102	Unique, released, H-node, dynamic	WINS-A	4C2	1/5/00 8:23:43 AM

Before replications, WINSB has the two entries shown in Table 7.9, one each for Client3 and Client4.

Table 7.9 WINS-B Database Before Replication

Name	Address	Flags	Owner	Version ID	Time stamp
Client3	192.168. 55.103	Unique, active, H-node, dynamic	WINS-B	78F	1/5/00 8:11:12 AM
Client4	192.168. 55.104	Unique, active, H-node, dynamic	WINS-B	79C	1/5/00 8:12:21 AM

Client1, Client3, and Client4 were time stamped with the sum of the current time and the renewal interval at the time they booted, and Client2 was time stamped with the sum of the current time and the extinction interval when it was released. The version IDs indicate the value of the registration counter at the time of registration. The registration counter is incremented by 1 (hexadecimal) each time it generates a new version ID in the database. Each WINS server has its own registration counter. The version ID jumps from 4B3 for Client1 to 4C2 for Client2. This indicates that 14 registrations (or extinctions or releases to active transition) took place between the registration of Client1 and Client2.

Replication takes place at 8:30:45 by WINS-A's clock. WINS-B's clock is 8:31:15 at this time. Of course replications will not all take place in the same second, but the servers use these times to generate the time stamps. Note that replication does not mean both pull at the same time—each pulls according to its own schedule. After replication, WINS-A's database contains the entries shown in Table 7.10.

Table 7.10 WINS-A Database After Replication

Name	Address	Flags	Owner	Version ID	Time stamp
Client1	192.168.22.101	Unique, active, H-node, dynamic	WINS-A	4B3	1/5/00 8:05:32 AM
Client2	192.168.22.102	Unique, released, H-node, dynamic	WINS-A	4C2	1/5/00 8:23:43 AM
Client3	192.168.55.103	Unique, active, H-node, dynamic	WINS-B	78F	1/25/00 8:30:45 AM
Client4	192.168.55.104	Unique, active, H-node, dynamic	WINS-B	79C	1/25/00 8:30:45 AM

After replication, WINS-B's database contains the entries shown in Table 7.11.

Table 7.11 WINS-B Database Before Replication

Name	Address	Flags	Owner	Version ID	Time stamp
Client1	192.168.22.101	Unique, active, H-node, dynamic	WINS-A	4B3	1/25/00 8:31:15 AM
Client3	192.168.55.103	Unique, active, H-node, dynamic	WINS-B	78F	1/5/00 8:11:12 AM
Client4	192.168.55.104	Unique, active, H-node, dynamic	WINS-B	79C	1/5/00 8:12:21 AM

Client1 has been replicated to WINS-B, and Client3 and Client4 have been replicated to WINS-A. The replicas have all kept their original owner and version ID and have been time stamped with the sum of the current time and the verification interval. Client2 has not been replicated, because it is in the released state. This is a little unusual (but possible) because Client2 shut down before its first replication. If Client2 had not been shut down until after the replication, WINS-B would have a replica of Client2 in the active state. This replica would remain in the active state even after Client2 released, because the change in state would not be replicated.

Assuming Client2 remains shut down for the duration of the extinction interval, it is placed in the tombstone state. At the first scavenging after 8:23:43 AM on January 5, 2000 (assuming an extinction interval of four days), the database on WINS-A contains the entries shown in Table 7.12.

Table 7.12 WINS-A Database After Scavenging

Name	Address	Flags	Owner	Version ID	Time stamp
Client1	192.168.22.101	Unique, active, H-node, dynamic	WINS-A	4B3	1/9/00 6:35:26 AM
Client2	192.168.22.102	Unique, tombstone, H-node, dynamic	WINS-A	657	1/6/00 9:50:53 AM
Client3	192.168.55.103	Unique, active, H-node, dynamic	WINS-B	78F	1/25/00 8:30:45 AM
Client4	192.168.55.104	Unique, active, H-node, dynamic	WINS-B	79C	1/25/00 8:30:45 AM

Note that Client2 has entered the tombstone state and that both its time stamp and its version ID have changed. The time stamp is now the sum of the current time and the extinction timeout, and the new version ID means that this entry is replicated at the next replication. Note also that Client1 has a new time stamp while retaining its version ID. It has been renewed throughout the last four days. The renewal rate depends the client stack.

After replication at 10:00:23 A.M., the database on WINS-B contains the entries shown (note that Client3 and 4 were renewed) as shown in Table 7.13.

Table 7.13 WINS-B Database After Replication

Name	Address	Flags	Owner	Version ID	Time stamp
Client1	192.168.22.101	Unique, active, H-node, dynamic	WINS-A	4B3	1/25/00 8:31:15 AM
Client2	192.168.22.102	Unique, tombstone, H-node, dynamic	WINS-A	657	1/6/00 10:00:23 AM
Client3	192.168.55.103	Unique, active, H-node, dynamic	WINS-B	78F	1/9/00 8:11:12 AM
Client4	192.168.55.104	Unique, active, H-node, dynamic	WINS-B	79C	1/9/00 8:12:21 AM

If Client2 remains down for one more day, exceeding the extinction timeout, it will be removed from the databases when it is next scavenged.

Once Client2 is removed, the database on WINS-A contains the entries shown in Table 7.14.

Table 7.14 WINS-A Database After Client 2 Is Removed

Name	Address	Flags	Owner	Version ID	Time stamp
Client1	192.168.22.101	Unique, active, H-node, dynamic	WINS-A	4B3	1/11/00 9:45:56 AM
Client3	192.168.55.103	Unique, active, H-node, dynamic	WINS-B	78F	1/25/00 8:30:45 AM
Client4	192.168.55.104	Unique, active, H-node, dynamic	WINS-B	79C	1/25/00 8:30:45 AM

After Client2 is removed, the database on WINS-B contains the entries shown in Table 7.15.

Table 7.15 WINS-B Database After Client 2 Is Removed

Name	Address	Flags	Owner	Version ID	Time stamp
Client1	192.168.22.101	Unique, active, H-node, dynamic	WINS-A	4B3	1/25/00 8:31:15 AM
Client3	192.168.55.103	Unique, active, H-node, dynamic	WINS-B	78F	1/11/00 9:44:27 AM
Client4	192.168.55.104	Unique, active, H-node, dynamic	WINS-B	79C	1/11/00 9:46:44 AM

During the first scavenging after 8:30 A.M. on January 25, 2000, WINS-A verifies with WINS-B that Client3 and Client4 are still valid active names. WINS-B does the same for Client1 with WINS-A.

Pulling WINS Database Entries by Version Number

The WINS server database maintains a table that stores the IP addresses and owner IDs of remote WINS servers that own entries in the local database.

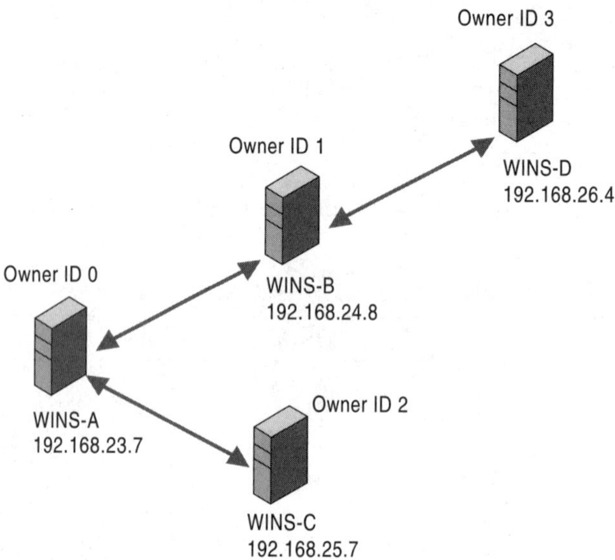

Figure 7.13 A Sample Replication Pattern

Based on an example replication pattern like that shown in Figure 7.13, a table mapping IP addresses to owner IDs for a sample server—again called WINS-A—would contain entries like those shown in Table 7.16.

Table 7.16 Example Remote WINS Server IP Addresses and Owner IDs

IP address	Owner ID
192.168.23.7	0
192.168.24.8	1
192.168.25.7	2
192.168.26.4	3

During WINS initialization, the WINS server scans the NetBIOS name–to–IP address mapping table to determine the maximum version number corresponding to each owner registered in its database. Initializing it with the information retrieved, the WINS server creates a table in memory that maps push partner IDs to version numbers. This table is never committed to the database. Example WINS server WINS-A creates a table like that shown in Table 7.16; other servers will have different tables.

As you might expect, the push partner–to–version number table contains an entry for each push partner, and each entry contains the maximum version ID found for all owners in the local database of the push partner. For example, if the local WINS server has an owner ID of 0, then given the preceding example IP address–to–owner ID mapping table, the push partner–to–version number mapping table might look like that shown in Figure 7.14.

	0	1	2
0	100	900	630
1			
2			

Figure 7.14 Example Push Partner–to–Version Number Table

Figure 7.14 shows that the local database of the WINS server, identified by owner ID 0, contains entries owned by three WINS servers with owner IDs of 0, 1, 2. The highest version numbers for the entries are 100, 900, and 630, respectively.

WINS server WINS-A is now ready to determine whether it needs to update its database. It sends a message to each of its push partners, asking it to respond with the highest version numbers pertaining to IP addresses in its local database. As push partners respond, the WINS server fills and expands its own table. The table might expand to fill more columns, each corresponding to another server.

For example, if WINS server WINS-B at IP address 192.168.24.8 (owner ID 1) responds with a record for WINS server WINS-D at IP address 192.168.26.4, WINS-A adds a column to the local push partner–version number mapping table for indirect push partner WINS-D with an owner ID 3. At the same time, IP address and owner ID WINS-D are stored in the IP address–to–owner ID mapping table. The relevant cells in the new table are initialized. After WINS-B, at 192.168.24.8, responds with the following three records:

```
192.168.24.8999
192.168.26.4700
192.168.23.789
```

the WINS server adds a record containing IP address 192.168.26.4 and owner ID 3 to the IP address–to–owner ID mapping table and updates the local push partner–to–version number mapping table to resemble that shown in Figure 7.15.

	0	1	2	3
0	100	900	630	0
1	89	999	0	700
2				

Figure 7.15 Example Push Partner–to–Version Number Table After Response from WINS-B

After all push partners have responded, the IP address–to–version number mapping table contains the information shown in Figure 7.16.

	0	1	2	3
0	100	900	630	0
1	89	999	0	700
2	93	879	820	0

Figure 7.16 Example Push Partner–to–Version Number Table After All Responses

The WINS server examines this table to determine which push partner has the latest data for each owner. A WINS server always has the highest version ID for entries it owns. For example, in Figure 7.16, the entry with the ID 0 is recorded in three databases: 0, 1, and 2. Because the entry is owned by WINS-A, the entry for 0,0 has the highest version ID number (100) for that entry.

However, some WINS servers might not be partners of the requesting pull partner. The WINS server determines the starting version ID required to synchronize the local database, and requests that the push partner send the database records with version IDs that are equal or greater. If a push partner has the latest data for more than one owner, a single request can be sent to retrieve the records for all. Of course, in this simple example, the WINS server that has the most current data for a database never changes. When WINS-A pulls data, WINS-B has the latest data for itself and WINS-D; WINS-C has the latest data for itself. In a more complex model, the replication paths might form loops, and replication takes place at differing intervals.

When the push partner receives a request from another WINS server—a pull partner—it retrieves the required records from its local database and sends them to the requesting server. The push partner retrieves records by seeking the record that starts the range and moving sequentially over the records, retrieving them, until the push partner retrieves the last record in the range. When the pull partner receives the data from the push partners, the pull partner updates its database.

All entries with version IDs greater than those in the pulling database are replicated. However, not every change to a database increments a record's version ID.

How Records Change and Update

A WINS server always enters name registrations in its database in an active state and time stamped with the sum of the current time and the renewal interval. The version ID is taken from the version ID counter, and the counter is then incremented.

If a name is explicitly released or not refreshed during the renewal interval, the name enters the released state. The WINS server gives the database entry a time stamp using the sum of the current time and the extinction interval, and leaves the version ID unchanged. Thus, released records are not replicated. If a record remains released past the extinction interval, the WINS server changes the state of the record to tombstone, gives the record a time stamp using the sum of the current time and the extinction timeout, and increments the version ID of the record so that the record will be replicated. If a record remains in the tombstone state for a period longer than the extinction timeout, it is deleted from the database.

WINS replicates only records in the active and tombstone states. In the WINS database, WINS enters these replica records with the fields received from the owner database, with the exception of owner ID and time stamp. (The owner ID comes from the local IP address–to–owner ID mapping table because the value used locally to represent a particular WINS server differs from server to server. For example, WINS-D might be represented by a 2 on WINS-B and by a 3 on WINS-A.) WINS gives an active record a time stamp that is the sum of the local current time and the verification interval. WINS gives a tombstone record a time stamp that is the sum of the local current time and the extinction timeout.

Conflicts Detected During Replication

Although name conflicts are normally handled at the time of name registration (see "Client Conflicts Detected During Registration" earlier in this chapter), it is possible for the same name to be registered at two different WINS servers. This would happen if a WINS client registered the same name at a second WINS server before the database from the first WINS server replicated to the second. In this case, WINS resolves the conflict at replication time.

Conflict at replication can be between two unique entries, between a unique entry and a group entry, or between two group entries.

Conflict Between Unique Entries WINS resolves conflicting unique entries according to three factors:

- **State of the entries.** The database entry can be in the active, released, or tombstone state; the replica can be either in the active or tombstone state.
- **Ownership of entries.** The WINS server might or might not own the database entry.
- **Addresses of the entries.** The addresses of the entries might or might not be the same.

Conflict Between Two Replicas When two replicas conflict, the new replica overwrites the replica in the database, regardless of whether the addresses match or not. The only exception to this rule is if the replica in the database is active and the new replica is a tombstone. If the new replica is a tombstone, the replica in the database does not overwrite the new replica, unless they are both owned by the same WINS server.

Conflict Between an Owned Entry and a Replica with the Same IP Address The replica replaces the database record, unless the database record is active and the replica is a tombstone. In that case, WINS increments the version ID of the database record so that the record is propagated at replication time.

Conflict Between an Owned Entry and a Replica with Different IP Addresses The replica replaces the database record unless the database record is active. If the record is active and the replica is a tombstone, WINS increments the version ID of the database record so that the record can be propagated by replication. If the replica is also active, the server receiving the replica challenges the client that owns the name in the local database to determine whether the client still uses the name. If it does, WINS sends the client node designated in the replica record a *name conflict demand*, a message that puts the client in a conflict state. This forces the node to place the name in the conflict state. A name in the conflict state is marked and the name is no longer used.

Conflict Between a Unique Entry and a Group Entry When a unique entry and a group entry conflict, WINS keeps the group entry. If the WINS server owns the unique entry and the entry is not in the released or tombstone state, the WINS server asks the client named in the unique entry to release the name.

Conflict Between Two Special Group Entries The replica replaces the database record unless the database record is active. If the record is active, WINS increments its version ID so that the record is propagated at replication time. If the replica is also active, the WINS server updates the member list of the database record with any new members from the replica. If the list of active members grows to more than 25, the extra members are not added but are dropped silently.

Conflict Involving a Multihomed Record If a multihomed replica conflicts with a tombstone or released entry in the database, WINS replaces the entry in the database with the replica, unless the entry is a normal group and is in the released state. This is no different from the other scenarios in which a single-address entry conflicts with a released normal group entry.

If a multihomed replica in the tombstone state conflicts with an active database entry owned by the same server as that of the multihomed replica, the database entry is replaced. If the active database entry is a replica owned by a different owner, WINS does not replace the database entry. If the active database entry is owned by the local WINS server and is a unique entry, the WINS server increments the version ID of the database record to prompt propagation.

If an active multihomed replica conflicts with an active, unique, multihomed replica in the local database with the same owner, the database entry is replaced. If the owner is different, it is not replaced. If the entry in the database is owned by the local WINS server, and if the members of the record (a single member in the case of a unique record) is a subset of the members in the replica, WINS changes the time stamp of the database record and increments its version ID to force propagation. If the members of the replica are not a subset, the addresses in the database record are challenged. If all challenges succeed—that is, the clients challenged do not respond to any challenge—the database record is replaced. If at least one challenge fails, WINS tells the client to release the name from all addresses prior to replacing the database record with the replica.

If a multihomed replica conflicts with an active group entry in the database, WINS increments the version ID of the entry in the database to cause propagation.

If a single-address replica conflicts with an inactive multihomed record in the database, WINS replaces the database record with the replica. If the replica conflicts with an active multihomed entry in the database owned by the same owner, WINS replaces the database record with the replica. If the multihomed entry in the database is a replica owned by a different server, WINS does not replace it. If, however, the multihomed entry is owned by the local WINS server, and the pulled replica is a unique record, then WINS issues a challenge to the clients using the addresses in the multihomed record. If all challenges succeed, WINS replaces the database record. If at least one challenge fails, WINS sends the addresses in the database record requests for the name, and then the database record is updated. Note that the address in the unique replica, if present in the member list, is ignored in the above situation.

Persistent Connections

Windows 2000 WINS introduces persistent connections between WINS server replication partners. Earlier versions of WINS required servers to establish a new connection whenever they replicated databases. Because establishing and terminating each connection required a modest number of CPU cycles and the sending of network packets, network managers set their systems to accumulate a configurable number of records before establishing connections with replication partners. Waiting for records to accumulate introduces a delay to the updating of the entire database—perhaps as long as several minutes—which can cause windows of inconsistency with replication partners.

A Windows 2000 WINS server can be configured in the WINS management console to request a persistent connection with one or more replication partners; this eliminates the overhead of opening and terminating connections. Persistent connections increase the speed of replication because a server sends records to its partners immediately, without establishing temporary connections each time. This immediately updates every record across the network, making records more consistent. The bandwidth required is minimal because the connection is usually idle.

It is also possible to configure a persistent connection to replicate only when it reaches a certain update count threshold. Normally the minimum update count threshold is 20 records. However, when persistent connections are employed, that minimum is waived.

Autodiscovery of WINS Partners

The autodiscovery feature enables a WINS server to discover its replication partners automatically, rather than being manually configured with a predetermined set of replication partners. To turn this feature on from the Microsoft Management Console, on the **Replication Partners Properties** page, check the **Enable automatic partner configuration** check box.

Periodically, WINS servers announce their presence on the network. The WINS announcements are sent on a multicast address reserved for WINS (224.0.1.24). WINS servers with autodiscovery enabled listen for these announcements and learn about other WINS servers on the network. Any WINS servers discovered this way are automatically added to the partners list as both a push and pull partner. This feature should be used only when you are sure that no unauthorized WINS servers will be placed on the network. Otherwise, the unauthorized servers are picked up as partners.

Best Practices for WINS Replication

Configuring replication correctly can avert many problems, and doing so enables a group of WINS servers to function more effectively.

Configure Push/Pull Replication Partners

In general, push/pull replication is the simplest and most effective way to ensure full WINS replication between partners. This also ensures that the primary and secondary WINS servers for any particular WINS client are push and pull partners of each other, a requirement for proper WINS functioning in the event of a failure of the primary server of the client.

For most WINS installations, avoid the use of limited replication partnerships (push only or pull only) between WINS servers. In some large enterprise WINS networks, limited replication partnering can effectively support replication over slow network links. However, when you plan limited WINS replication, pay attention to the design and configuration. Each server must still have at least one replication partner, and each slow link that employs a unidirectional link should be balanced by a unidirectional link elsewhere in the network that carries updated entries in the opposite direction.

Use a Hub-and-Spoke Design for WINS Replication and Convergence

Convergence is a critical part of WINS planning. The central question of convergence time for a WINS network design is "How long does it take for a change in WINS data at one WINS server to replicate and appear at other WINS servers on the network?" The answer is the sum of the replication periods from one server to the next over the path containing the longest replication periods. For more information on convergence, see "Detailed Replication Example" in this chapter.

In most cases, the hub-and-spoke model provides a simple and effective planning method for organizations that require full and speedy convergence with minimal administrative intervention. For example, this model works well for organizations with centralized headquarters or a corporate data center (the hub) and several branch offices (the spokes). Also, a second or redundant hub (that is, a second WINS server in the central location) can increase the fault tolerance for WINS.

For an example of a simple hub-and-spoke configuration, see Figure 7.17.

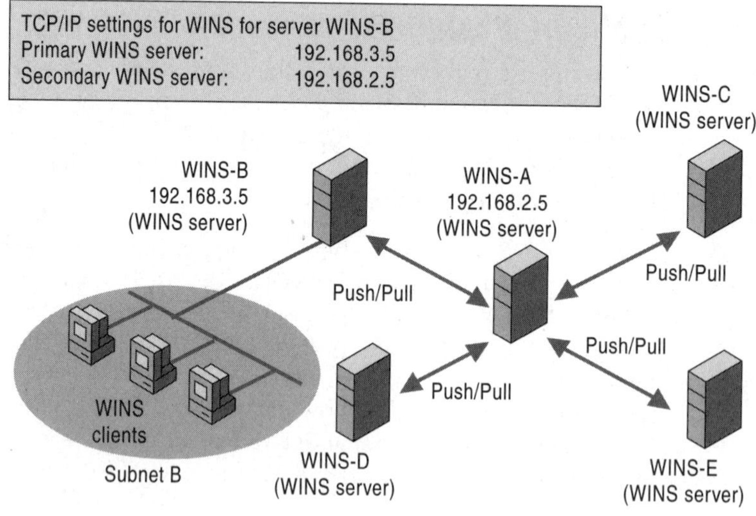

Figure 7.17 A Hub-and-Spoke Deployment of WINS Servers

The convergence time for the system shown in Figure 7.17 is the sum of the two longest convergence times to the hub. For instance, if WINS-B and WINS-D replicate with WINS-A every 30 minutes, and WINS-C and WINS-E are configured to replicate every 4 hours, the convergence time is 8 hours.

Replication Across a Firewall

In some large networks, WINS replication is desirable across a firewall. WINS replication occurs over TCP port 42, so this port must not be blocked on any intervening network device between two WINS replication partners when configuring replication across network firewalls.

Managing WINS Servers

Windows 2000 provides an updated version of WINS Manager, a graphical administrative utility that you can use to manage WINS on your network. The updated version of WINS Manager is a Microsoft Management Console snap-in, giving you the ability to further integrate and customize WINS administration to your network management needs.

The WINS management console contains significant enhancements, as compared to earlier versions, many of which were suggested by network managers. These new features include:

- Persistent connections
- Manual tombstoning
- Improved management utilities
- Enhanced filtering and record searching
- Dynamic record deletion and multiple selection
- Record verification and version number validation
- Export function
- Increased fault tolerance
- Dynamic renewal of clients

The WINS management console provides the utilities you need to maintain, view, back up, and restore the WINS server database. To view and change parameters for WINS servers, use the WINS management console. For more information about specific administration and configuration tasks, see WINS management console Help.

System Monitor and SNMP agent service are also valuable tools for managing a WINS server. You can use System Monitor to monitor WINS server performance.

You can use the SNMP service to monitor and configure WINS servers by using third-party SNMP manager utilities. When using a third-party SNMP manager utility, some WINS queries may time out; if so, you should increase the timeout on the SNMP utility you are using. Microsoft Information Base objects are supported by Windows 2000 SNMP Service. MIB objects are formally described objects that provide support for SNMP to allow the monitoring of processes, such as error counts, status records, and the contents of the IP routing table of a computer. For more information about MIB object types see "MIB Object Types" in this book. For more information about System Monitor and SNMP agent service, see "Simple Network Management Protocol" in this book and "Monitoring Network Performance" in the *Microsoft® Windows® 2000 Server Resource Kit Server Operations Guide*.

Viewing WINS Server Operational Status

The WINS management console displays administrative and operational information about WINS servers. To display basic statistics about a specific WINS server, open the WINS management console, highlight that server, on the pull-down menu, select **Action**, and then click **Show Server Statistics**. This provides WINS server information similar to that shown in Figure 7.18.

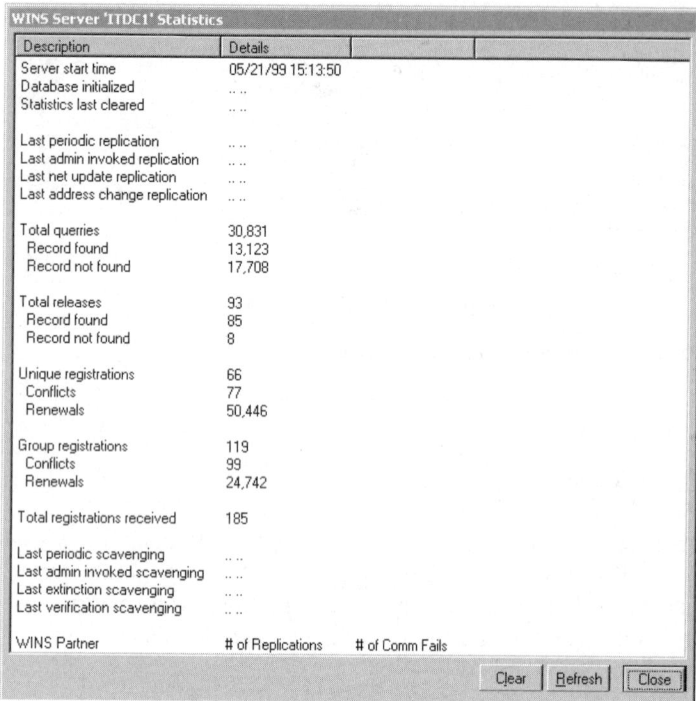

Figure 7.18 WINS Server Statistics

Table 7.17 describes the basic WINS server statistics shown in Figure 7.18. These include both the basic and detailed statistics from Windows NT 4.0.

Table 7.17 WINS Server Statistics

Statistic	Description
Database initialized	The last time static mappings were imported into the WINS database.
Statistics last cleared	The last time the administrator cleared statistics for the WINS server with the **Clear Statistics** command on the **View** menu.
Last replication times	The times at which the WINS database was last replicated.
Periodic	The last time the WINS database was replicated based on the replication interval specified in the **Preferences** dialog box.
Admin trigger	The last time the WINS database was replicated because the administrator clicked the **Replicate Now** button in the **Replication Partners** dialog box.
Net update	The last time the WINS database was replicated as a result of a network request, which is a push notification message that requests propagation.
Total queries	The number of name query request messages received by this WINS server. "Record found" indicates the number of names that were successfully matched in the database, and "Record not found" indicates the number of names the server could not resolve.
Total releases	The number of messages received that indicate a NetBIOS program has stopped. "Record found" indicates how many names were successfully released, and "Record not found" indicates how many names this WINS server could not release.
Total registrations	The number of name registration messages received from clients.
Last address change replication	Indicates when the last WINS database change was replicated.
Last scavenging times	Indicates the last times the database was cleaned for specific types of entries.
Periodic	Indicates when the database was cleaned based on the renewal interval specified in the **WINS Server Properties** dialog box on the **Name Record** tab.
Admin trigger	Indicates when the database was last cleaned because the administrator chose **Initiate Scavenging**.
Extinction	Indicates when the database was last cleaned based on the extinction interval.
Verification	Indicates when the database was last cleaned based on the verification interval

(continued)

Table 7.17 WINS Server Statistics *(continued)*

Statistic	Description
Unique registrations	Indicates the number of name registration requests accepted by this WINS server.
Unique conflicts	The number of conflicts encountered during registration of unique names owned by this WINS server.
Unique renewals	The number of renewals received for unique names.
Group registrations	The number of registration requests for groups that have been accepted by this WINS server.
Group conflicts	The number of conflicts encountered during registration of group names.

Configuring Server and Client Behavior

You can use the configuration options of the WINS management console to change how a WINS server manages its WINS client mappings.

The timer options are found on the **Name Record** tab of the **WINS Server Properties** dialog box shown in Figure 7.8 in the "WINS Replication" section of this chapter. Using these options, you can specify the various timers that govern WINS client behavior: the renewal interval, the extinction interval, the extinction timeout, and the verification interval. All of these are described in "Timers" in this chapter.

In addition, you can change the frequency with which the statistics are updated, and change the backup path for the database, under the **General** tab of the WINS server **Properties** page. Finally, you can change the advanced properties of the server, as shown in Figure 7.19.

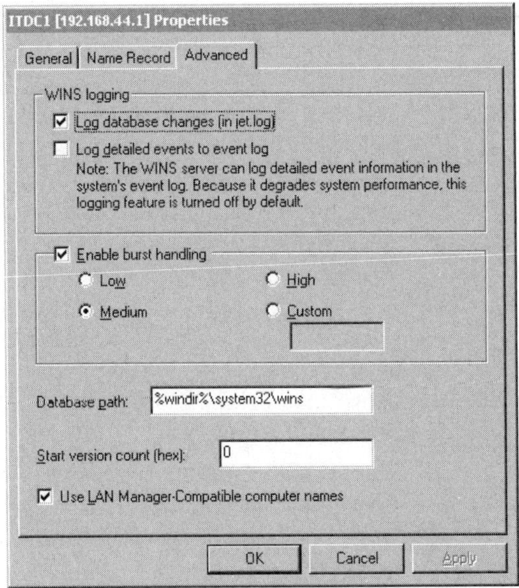

Figure 7.19 Advanced Configuration Options for WINS Server

To more finely tune a WINS server, configure the options shown in Figure 7.19, which shows the advanced logging and burst handling dialog box. Changing the values of the parameters described in Table 7.18 allows you to alter the most advanced features of your WINS server.

Table 7.18 Advanced WINS Server Configuration Options

Configuration Option	Description
Log database changes	Specifies whether logging of database changes to J50.log files should be turned on.
Log detailed events to event log	Specifies whether events are logged using verbose mode, typically used when troubleshooting. This requires considerable computer resources and should be turned off if you are tuning for performance.
Replicate only with partners	Specifies that replication occur only with configured WINS pull or push partners. If this option is not selected, an administrator can ask a WINS server to pull from or push to an unlisted WINS server partner. By default, this option is selected.
Backup on termination	Automatically backs up the database when the WINS management console stops, except when the computer is shut down.
Migrate	Static unique and multihomed records in the database are treated as dynamic when they conflict with a new registration or replica. If they are no longer valid, they are overwritten by the new registration or replica. Check this option if you are migrating non-Windows NT-based computers to Windows NT. By default, this option is not checked.
Start version count	Specifies the highest version ID number for the database. Usually, you do not need to change this value unless the database becomes corrupted. In this case, set this value to a number higher than the version number counter for this WINS server on all the remote partners that earlier replicated the records to the local WINS server. WINS might increase the value you specify to ensure that database records are quickly replicated to other WINS servers. The maximum allowable value is $2^{31}-1$. This value can be seen in the **View Database** dialog box in the WINS management console.
Database backup path	Specifies the directory that stores the WINS database backup. If you specify a backup path, WINS automatically performs a full backup of its database to this directory every 24 hours. WINS uses this directory to perform an automatic restoration of the database if the database is found to be corrupted when WINS is started. Do not specify a network directory.

Managing Static Address Mappings

Static mappings are non-dynamic database entries of NetBIOS computer names and IP addresses for computers on the network that are not WINS-enabled or for special groups of network devices.

To view, add, edit, import, or delete static mappings in the WINS management console, on the **Mappings** menu, click **Static Mappings**.

Once entered to the WINS server database, static name–to–IP address mappings cannot be challenged or removed, except by an administrator who removes the specific mapping using the WINS management console. All changes made to the WINS server database with the WINS management console take effect immediately. Note that a DHCP reserved (or a static) IP address for a unique name in a multihomed computer overrides an obsolete WINS static mapping if the WINS server advanced configuration option **Migration On/Off** is checked.

Managing Multihomed Servers

For all computers that use WINS and/or NetBIOS over TCP/IP (NetBT), a single IP address is bound and used. In default configurations, the IP address used to bind NetBT is the primary IP address configured for the first network adapter installed and recognized by Windows 2000.

The order of binding of the adapters can be changed. To do so, open **Network and Dial-up Connections** in **Control Panel**, and then select **Advanced** on the menu bar. Next, select the **Advanced Settings...** command, and then choose the **Adapters and Bindings** tab.

However, you can modify the order of adapter bindings from the **Adapter and Bindings** tab of the **Advanced Settings** screen in the **Network and Dial-up Connections** folder. This dialog screen is located off of the **Advanced** menu. To modify bindings order, use the up and down arrows to re-order the list present in the **Connections list box.**

Because of the reliance of NetBIOS on the first adapter installed and bound in the system, you must verify the IP address of the adapter when using a multihomed WINS server. Once this address is known, assign only this IP address to WINS clients (either dynamically using a DHCP server or by manually configuring clients).

In addition, all WINS push and pull replication partners should be configured through this bound IP address and its physical network adapter. You may need to verify that the bound IP address is also configured at other partner WINS servers.

Administering WINS Through a Firewall

When you administer WINS remotely, an initial session is established to TCP port 135. This is followed by another session to a random TCP port above 1024. These two sessions to specific ports are established because the WINS Administrator uses dynamic endpoints in the remote procedure call (RPC) protocol. Internet firewalls cannot be configured to pass WINS remote administration traffic when the port is not consistent. To solve this problem, in Windows 2000, the default system settings for dynamic port allocation can be changed, in the registry, to a fixed port assignment.

Caution Do not use a registry editor to edit the registry directly unless you have no alternative. The registry editors bypass the standard safeguards provided by administrative tools. These safeguards prevent you from entering conflicting settings or settings that are likely to degrade performance or damage your system. Editing the registry directly can have serious, unexpected consequences that can prevent the system from starting and require that you reinstall Windows 2000. To configure or customize Windows 2000, use the programs in Control Panel or Microsoft Management Console (MMC) whenever possible.

To allow remote administration of WINS through a firewall, you must define a list of all ports available (or not available) from the Internet in the registry in the following entries. These entries are located in the following registry path:

HKEY_LOCAL_MACHINE\SOFTWARE\Microsoft\Rpc\Internet

In particular, the three entries are Ports, PortsInternetAvailable, and UseInternetPorts. Each of these is described in more detail here.

Name: Ports

Data Type: REG_MULTI_SZ — Set of IP port ranges

Description: Specifies a set of IP port ranges consisting of either all of the ports available from the Internet or all of the ports not available from the Internet. Each string represents a single port or an inclusive set of ports (for example, "1000-1050" or "1984"). If any entries are outside the range of zero to 65,535, or if any string cannot be interpreted, the RPC run time will treat the entire configuration as invalid.

Name: PortsInternetAvailable

Data Type: REG_SZ — Y or N (not case sensitive)

Description: If Y, the ports listed in the Ports key are all the Internet-available ports on that computer. If N, the ports listed in the Ports key are all those ports that are not Internet-available.

Name: UseInternetPorts

Data Type: REG_SZ — Y or N (not case sensitive)

Description: Specifies the system default policy. If Y, processes using the default are assigned ports from the set of Internet-available ports, as defined above. If N, processes using the default are assigned ports from the intranet-only ports.

Best Practices for WINS Management Console

The WINS management console provides flexibility and control over your WINS network, but in many cases the default settings are appropriate. Logging and migration are two of the most common trouble spots.

Use Default Configuration Settings The WINS default settings provide the optimal configuration for most conditions and can be used without modification in the majority of WINS network installations. When you modify default settings, be sure that the need to modify is clear and necessary and that you understand the implications.

Do Not Modify the Migrate Setting If you use static WINS entries only to support temporary changes on your network, keep the default **Migrate (Overwrite unique static record with dynamic record)** setting selected in the WINS management console.

When **Migrate (Overwrite unique static record with dynamic record)** is checked, any temporary static entries that are unique or multihomed can be challenged and dynamically updated by clients. Any later attempt by a WINS client to register a dynamic name that is unique or multihomed over an existing static entry of the same name results in a challenge.

In the challenge, the WINS server compares the IP address in the static mapping to any IP address that the named client attempts to dynamically register in WINS. If the two addresses are different and the static IP address is no longer active, the IP mapping can be changed from static to dynamic and the IP address updated in WINS.

If you use static WINS entries on a permanent basis, you should disable **Migrate (Overwrite unique static entry with dynamic entry).** This prevents a dynamic WINS entry from overriding a static WINS entry that maps to the name and address of a critical server on your network. This is primarily necessary in environments that include many UNIX systems, which do not register with WINS.

Leave WINS Database Logging Enabled When logging is enabled, WINS logs database update activity temporarily to a log file before writing changes back to the server database file. By enabling logging, WINS can process a bulk set of updates that are logged, and then write back the updates to the server database file at periodic intervals. If logging is not enabled, the WINS server database file is written back to disk every time an individual record is changed or updated.

If logging is disabled, registrations are much faster, but this configuration introduces the risk of losing the last few updates to the WINS database when a failure occurs.

Checking the **Log detailed events to event log** box provides a verbose mode with even more detail, and is typically used when troubleshooting. It requires considerable computer resources and should be turned off if you are tuning for performance.

Deploying Microsoft WINS Service

Before you install WINS servers on your network, you must consider the following issues. Each issue is described in more detail later in this section.

Determine the Number of WINS Servers Needed One WINS server can handle NetBIOS name resolution requests for 10,000 computers. However, when deciding how many WINS servers you need, you must consider the location of routers on your network and the distribution of clients in each subnet. For more information, see "How Many Servers to Use" in this section.

Design the WINS Replication Partners Planning WINS replication involves determining whether WINS servers are configured as pull or push partners and setting partner preferences for each server. For more information about how to decide between push or pull replication, see "Configuring WINS Replication" in this section.

Assess the Impact of WINS Traffic on Slow Links Although WINS helps reduce broadcast traffic within and between local subnets, it does create some traffic between servers and clients. Estimate this traffic, particularly on routed TCP/IP networks. In addition to routing traffic, consider the effects of low-speed links (such as those typically used for wide area networking) upon replication traffic between WINS servers and WINS clients registering and renewing NetBIOS names. For more information, see "Network Performance" later in this section.

Assess the WINS Fault Tolerance Within a Network To plan a successful WINS installation, you must consider the effect of a WINS server being shut down or temporarily disconnected from the network. Use additional WINS servers for disaster recovery, backup, and redundancy. For more information on planning a fault-tolerant WINS installation, see "Fault Tolerance" later in this section.

Test and Revise Your Planned WINS Installation By testing the performance of your installation of WINS, you can better identify the source of potential problems before they occur.

WINS Configuration Examples

In the example illustrated in Figure 7.20, a medium-sized company has two main sites (labeled Site 1 and Site 3) with 500 computers each, all connected through relatively high-speed links. The company also has more than 160 small branches. To save on the costs of the links, some branches act as concentrators for a region (such as Site 2).

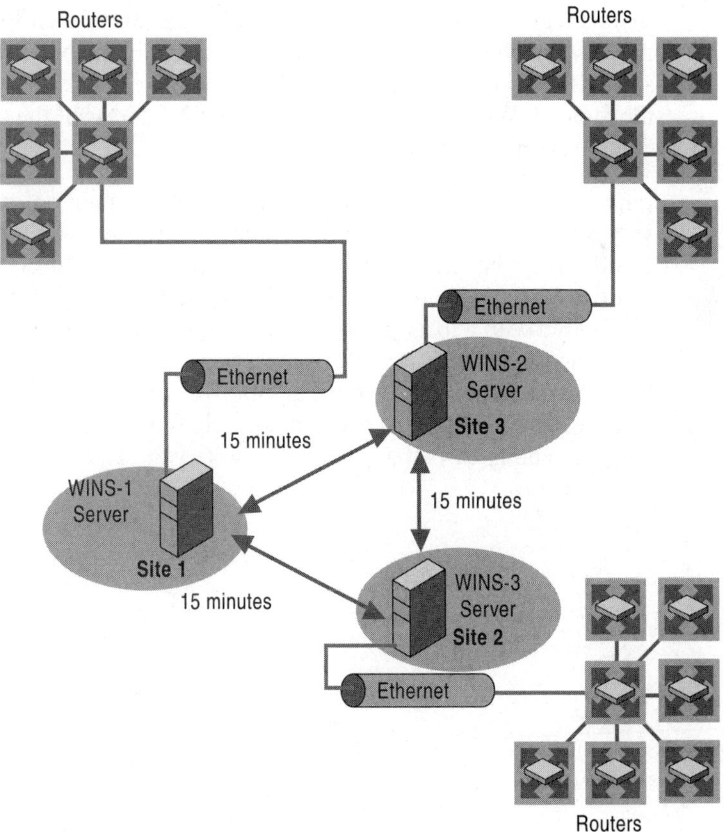

Figure 7.20 A Typical WINS Deployment

The branches might have local WINS servers, but in most cases, they do not—there is simply no need for a separate server for each branch. Instead, the company adds regional WINS servers when the costs of registration and query traffic increase above the cost of deploying the additional server. When the link to a regional WINS server fails, local names can still be resolved by the broadcast mechanism.

The regional WINS servers are not required for this configuration to function correctly, but they do provide a cost optimization. From a network efficiency point of view, the company's system administrators should avoid deploying the regional servers whenever possible because they increase the convergence time. Administrators configure regional WINS servers (such as the one at site 2) as replication partners of the WINS servers in the main sites (sites 1 and 3). Clients in the main site are configured with the IP address of their local WINS server as primary and the IP address of the WINS server in the other main site as secondary. Clients in the regional branches are configured with the IP address of the regional WINS server as primary and the address of the closest main site WINS server as secondary.

Figure 7.21 shows the network configuration of another example company that is very different. The network serves a larger company with three sites, each with 5,000 users. The sites are connected with multiple T1 links. The number of users justifies a primary and a secondary WINS server at each site. The clients are configured with a local primary and secondary WINS server. Half of the clients have one local WINS server as primary and the other as secondary. The other half have exactly the opposite configuration. This balances the registration and query load over both WINS servers, and it provides a hot backup for maintenance purposes and in case of a calamity.

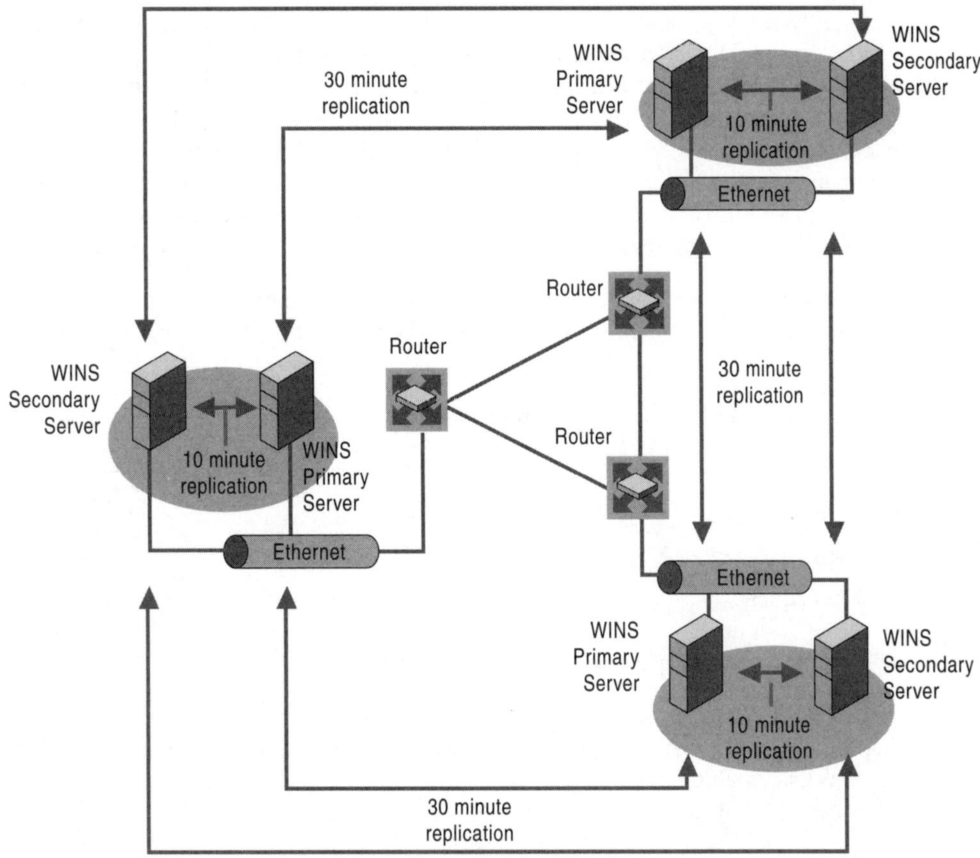

Figure 7.21 A Triangular WINS Deployment

The local WINS servers use a very short pull replication interval of 10 minutes, so all computers within the same building are reachable within 10 minutes of an address registration or change. The replication interval between the sites can be longer—about 30 minutes—because most users work with resources on their local servers.

Assessing Network Traffic

The performance of a WINS system depends on other traffic in the network. When the WINS server is not on the local subnet but is somewhere on the WAN, server requests and responses must go through router queues, causing delays at peak times. Even during replication, bulk transport gets its fair share of the network bandwidth.

The messages described later in this section are UDP/TCP messages. Before they can be sent, the physical address, or *media access control (MAC) address* must be known. If the IP address is already in the ARP cache, the WINS message generates no new ARP message. Otherwise, the client machine will send an ARP packet to resolve the MAC address from the destination IP address, if the destination is on the same local subnet, or from the IP address of the gateway, if the destination is on a remote subnet. Registrations are usually done in groups. Only one ARP message is required per group; this message is not WAN traffic.

All message sizes given in this section are for the messages without a scope ID. The message sizes described here are for Ethernet. On token ring, FDDI, WAN, and so on, the headers (and therefore the total length) vary.

WINS clients generate the following four basic messages:

- Name registration
- Name refresh
- Name release
- Name query

These four messages are discussed in more detail in "WINS Clients" in this chapter.

A Windows 2000–based WINS client usually registers more NetBIOS names than other WINS-enabled clients. The name registration requests generated by a Windows 2000–based computer include the following:

- Workstation component
- Server component
- Messenger service name
- Domain name or names
- Replicator service name
- Browser service name
- Additional network program and service names

When a WINS-enabled client starts on the network, it sends a name registration request for the Workstation service, the Server service, the Messenger service, and any additional Microsoft network services running on the computer. In other words, when a WINS client starts on the network, it generates a minimum of three name registration requests and three entries in the WINS database.

Typical Network Traffic

A name registration request is sent for every NetBIOS name that an application uses. The application makes the request when it (often implemented as a service) starts, which is usually when the computer starts. For a client, the minimum number of names is the two computer names (one for the workstation component with a last byte of <00> and one for the messenger with a last byte of <03>); the domain name; and the user name (messenger name, last byte <03>).

A server usually has additional names, including server name (the same as the computer name but with a last byte of <20>); more variants of the domain name (<1B> and <1D> for browsing, and <1C>for the domain controllers); a replicator account; a Systems Management Server account; and so forth. The name registration request packet is 110 bytes. A positive name registration response is 104 bytes.

A name release request is sent for a name when its service stops, typically when the system shuts down. The name release request is 110 bytes and the name release response is 104 bytes.

A name refresh request (also called a renewal) is sent regularly while the name is registered. The request is 110 bytes, the response is 104 bytes. The time between renewals depends on the client implementation and the renewal interval. The implementation of WINS in Windows 2000 sends name refresh requests after half the renewal interval to the primary WINS server. When the primary goes down, the renewals are sent at the rate as specified by the renewal interval of the secondary. Only half the renewal attempts are actually done at the secondary; the other attempts are sent to the primary. If the WINS service at the primary WINS server is stopped, then the renewal attempt fails. However, the attempt still generates three packets.

Name query traffic depends on the application and the server. The application might disconnect from the server regularly to release the NetBIOS session. The file server might disconnect idle sessions. Different applications might connect to different servers. This all results in name query traffic; the name query request is 92 bytes, the response is 104 bytes.

Replication and Verification Traffic

Replication and verification traffic is slightly more complicated than typical network traffic because WINS servers perform replication and verification in batches to reduce traffic. In addition, replication and verification sometimes trigger challenge traffic when entries are verified at their owner.

Implementing replication and verification also requires the basic load of connecting and disconnecting with TCP. Each unique name entry requires WINS servers to exchange between 12 and 50 bytes; other types of name entries, such as a group name, which creates a load that depends on the number of clients in the group, might require servers to exchange more data. You can configure the replication interval to reduce the connection overhead, and configuring a persistent connection reduces the overhead to zero.

WINS Client Traffic on Routed Networks

When planning for WINS client traffic on large routed networks, consider the effect of name query, registration, and response traffic routed between subnets. Name requests and responses that occur at the daily startup of computers must pass through the traffic queues on the routers and might cause delays at peak times.

Traffic and Topology

You can estimate WINS client traffic based on the behavior of the WINS clients as described in the preceding sections. However, when estimating WINS client traffic, you must also consider the network topology and the design or configuration of the routers in the network—it might not be possible to predict the traffic load on a specific network router because the routers might be designed or configured to autonomously route traffic based on factors other than traffic load.

How Many Servers To Use

The number of Windows NT–based WINS servers an enterprise requires depends on two factors: the number of WINS clients per server and the network topology. The number of users each server can support depends on usage patterns, data storage, and the processing capabilities of the server. You might need to upgrade your server hardware to handle WINS service.

Clients Per Server

A single WINS server can adequately service up to 10,000 clients for NetBIOS name resolution requests and for WINS service, which is enough for a small network. To provide additional fault tolerance, you should configure a second computer running Windows 2000 and use it as a secondary (or backup) WINS server for clients.

If your network uses only two WINS servers, they should be configured as each other's replication partners. For simple replication between two servers, you should configure one server as a pull partner and the other server as a push partner. You can configure replication manually, or you can set it to be performed automatically by selecting the **Enable Automatic Partner Configuration** check box, which is on the **Advanced** property tab under **Replication Partner** properties.

WINS Server Performance

A WINS server should always be a dedicated device; it should not also be a domain controller, a mail server, or anything else. It should also have a high-performance disk subsystem, such as a RAID array. In general, avoid deploying WINS on domain controllers or on servers that perform other tasks unless absolutely necessary.

A WINS server can typically register 1,500 names per minute or answer 4,500 queries per minute. A conservative recommendation is to install one WINS server and a backup server for every 10,000 computers on the network, which is based on these query response rates. You should plan for the worst cases, such as large-scale power outages that force many computers to restart simultaneously.

Two factors enhance WINS server performance:

1. A dual-processor WINS server increases performance almost 25 percent.
2. A dedicated disk drive measurably improves WINS server name replication response time.

After you establish WINS servers on an intranet, you can also adjust the renewal interval. Setting this interval to reduce the numbers of registrations can improve server response time. You can set the renewal interval when you configure the server, and you can change the interval later in the **WINS Replication Partner** property sheet.

Configuring Replication

Configuring WINS replication correctly is essential to an efficient WINS-capable network. The most important features of a proper WINS configuration are described below.

Automatic Partner Configuration

A WINS server can be configured to automatically accept other WINS servers as its replication partners. When a server uses automatic partner configuration, it finds other WINS servers as they join the network and adds them to its list of replication partners.

Automatic configuration is possible because each WINS server announces its presence on the network through periodic multicast announcements. These announcements are sent as IGMP messages for the multicast group address of 224.0.1.24 (the well-known multicast IP address reserved for use by WINS servers).

When WINS uses automatic replication configuration, it monitors the traffic for these multicast announcements. When it detects a new server, it automatically:

- Adds IP addresses for discovered servers to its list of replication partners.
- Configures any discovered servers to be both push and pull partners.
- Configures pull replication with discovered servers to occur every two hours.

If a remote server is discovered and added as a partner through multicasting, it is removed as a replication partner when WINS is shut down properly. To allow automatic partner information to persist when WINS is restarted, you must use manual partner configuration instead.

To manually configure replication with other WINS servers, configure each partner server using the WINS management console.

Automatic partner configuration is most useful in single-subnet environments. It can also be useful for situations in which the reachable network for WINS multicast traffic is extended by configuring routers between subnets to forward WINS multicast traffic between routed subnets.

Because periodic multicast announcements between WINS servers add traffic to your network, automatic partner configuration is only recommended for use if you have three or fewer installed WINS servers on the reachable network.

Replication Between Untrusted Domains

WINS replication can be set up between WINS servers in untrusting domains without requiring a valid user account in the untrusting domain. To configure replication, administrators for each WINS server must use the WINS management console to configure their respective server to allow replication with the WINS server in the remote domain.

Replication Across Wide Area Networks

Selecting the right replication interval requires careful consideration. The WINS server database should be replicated frequently enough that the down time of a single WINS server does not affect the reliability of the mapping information in the database of other WINS servers. However, you do not want the frequency of database replication to interfere with network throughput, which can occur if the replication interval is short.

You also need to consider the topology of your network . If your network has multiple hubs connected by relatively slow WAN links, configure replication between WINS servers on the slow links to occur less frequently than replication between WINS servers on fast links. This reduces traffic across the slow links and reduces contention between replication traffic and client name queries.

Consider an example network in which WINS servers at a central LAN site replicate every 15 minutes, while WINS servers in different WAN hubs replicate every 30 minutes, and WINS servers on different continents replicate just twice each day. Figure 7.22 illustrates this variation in replication frequency.

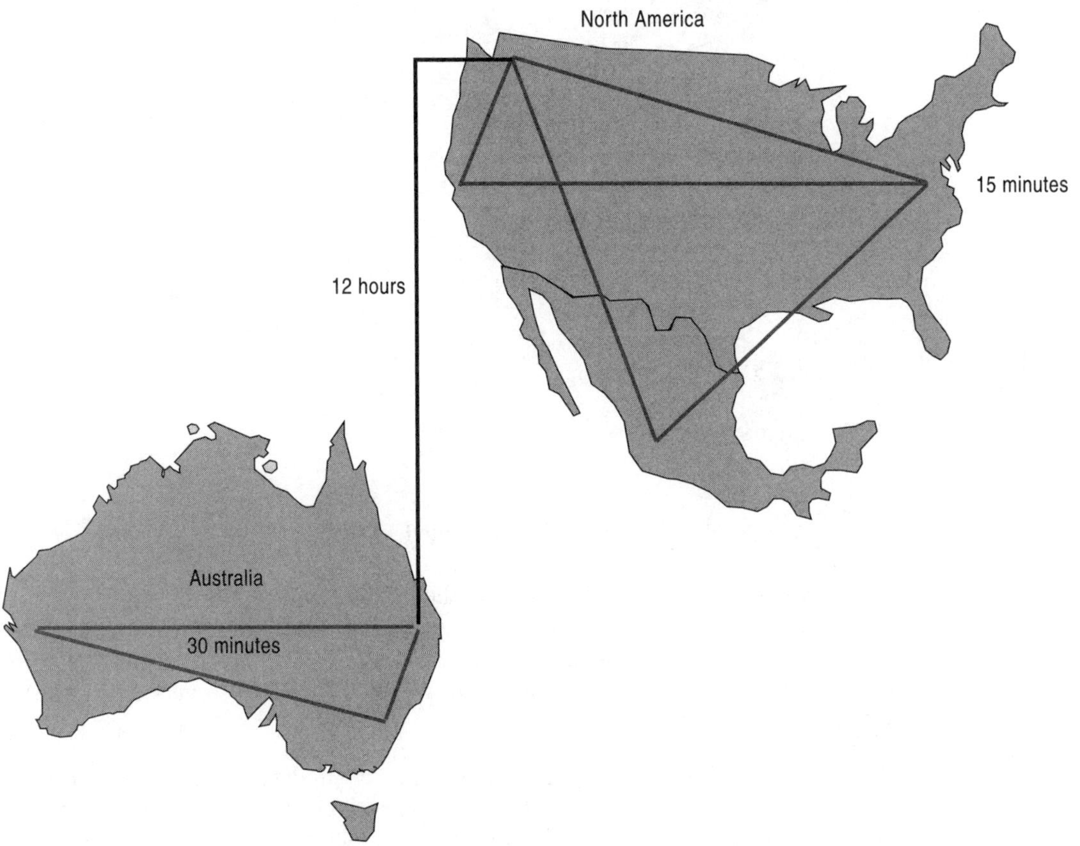

Figure 7.22 Replication over Enterprise Network Configuration

Configurations of other enterprise networks might involve even more zones, each replicating internally on a constant basis with persistent connections, or replicating in short cycles (every 10–30 minutes) to keep the time to convergence short. The servers connecting any two of these zones might replicate daily or hourly.

Replication Convergence Time

When deploying WINS servers, you must choose an acceptable convergence time for your network. Figure 7.23 illustrates a network with WINS servers and the database replication interval between them. This sample network configuration shows how the replication interval between WINS servers affects the convergence time.

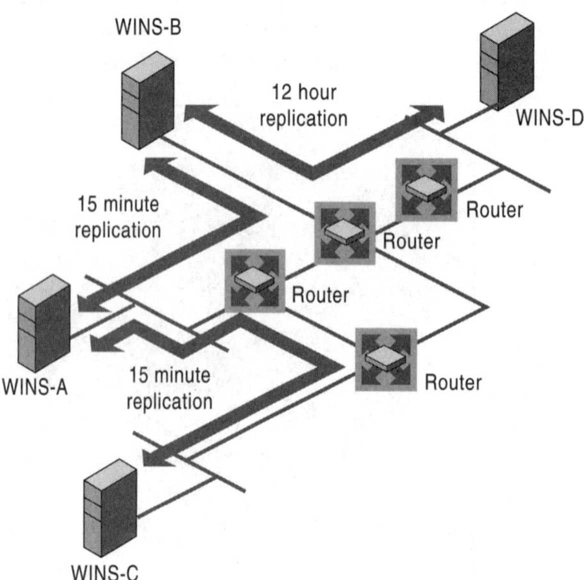

Figure 7.23 Replication Intervals in a Routed TCP/IP Network

If a WINS client registers its name with the WINS server WINS-C, other WINS clients can query WINS-C for this name and get the name–to–IP address mapping. WINS clients that query any of the other WINS servers do not get a positive response until the entry is replicated from WINS-C to WINS servers to WINS-A, WINS-B, and WINS-D.

WINS-C is configured to start replication when the update count exceeds the push threshold or when the pull replication interval expires on its WINS pull partner, WINS-A. The update count is the number of changes to database entries required to trigger push replication. (In this example, WINS-A is configured with a pull replication interval of 15 minutes, rather than an update count threshold.)

In this example, the entry is replicated only when the pull replication interval expires, but queries for the new name to WINS servers WINS-B and WINS-D might still fail. The interval for replication to WINS-B is 15 minutes; to WINS-D, it is 12 hours. Calculate the convergence time as follows:

```
12 hours + ( 2 x 15 minutes ) = 12.5 hours
```

However, name query requests sometimes succeed before the convergence time has passed. For example, this happens when the entries are replicated over a shorter path than the worst-case path. It also happens when an update count threshold is passed before the replication interval expires; this results in earlier replication of the new entry. The longer the replication path, the longer the convergence time.

Example of WINS Server Fault Tolerance

The WINS server database inherently provides fault-tolerant service because it is replicated among multiple WINS servers in a LAN or WAN. This replicated database design prevents users from registering duplicate NetBIOS computer names on the network. In general, even small networks should have more than one WINS server to distribute the load of processing NetBIOS name queries and registration, and to provide WINS database redundancy, backup, and disaster recovery.

WINS server failures come in two basic types:

- **Server failure.** A WINS server might crash, or it might be stopped for maintenance.
- **Network failure.** Routers or link stations might fail.

The failure of an individual WINS server within a network affects multiple WINS servers. An example routed network, shown in Figure 7.23, contains four separate physical segments separated by routers and four WINS servers. Each segment has a single WINS server to provide primary service to local clients on its own segment. Three of the servers (WINS-A, WINS-B, and WINS-C) are linked by routers contained within a single high-speed LAN link topology. The fourth server, WINS-D, is located on a remote segment that uses a low-speed WAN link.

In this example, a failure of WINS-A or WINS-B would segment the distribution of NetBIOS names. Entries would no longer be replicated from WINS-C to WINS-D, and vice versa. Because the IP address and name would no longer match for updated clients, other clients would not be able to connect to the updated computers. Adding replication between WINS-B and WINS-C would improve the configuration for cases in which WINS-A fails. Adding replication between WINS-D and WINS-C would improve fault tolerance in a case where the WINS-B server fails.

Failures of a single link between A, B, and C would not disable the WINS configuration because the underlying router network would reroute the traffic. Although this is not very efficient compared with a fully operational network, WINS replication does continue relatively undisturbed. Failure of the link between WINS-B and WINS-D, however, segments the WINS configuration. Because this makes other network traffic impossible, the network needs an on-demand backup link between WINS-D and WINS-C. This link would allow the underlying router infrastructure to reroute the WINS replication traffic.

In Figure 7.23, the routers are all single points of failure. When one of them fails, it segments the WINS configuration.

Segmented Configurations

When a link or router between two subnets fails, replication between two WINS servers may well be interrupted or prevented by the link failure. However, a segmented WINS configuration can provide many of the services of a fully functional system. Clients can usually resolve addresses from names. Local WINS servers and/or broadcasts resolve most name queries. The only names that cannot be resolved are new entries that were registered remotely, or those that have been updated since the network was segmented. Entries are not dropped at scavenging time when the owning WINS server cannot be reached. To restore the segmented network to full function, install WINS service on another computer when the hardware of the regular WINS server fails, and restore the database by forcing replication from a replication partner.

Improving Fault Tolerance

Windows 2000 and Windows 98 provide an extra measure of fault tolerance by allowing a client to specify more than two WINS servers (up to a maximum of 12) per interface through either the **DHCP** or the **WINS** option under Administrative Tools. The additional WINS servers resolve names only if the primary and secondary WINS servers fail to respond. If one of the additional WINS servers answers a query, the client caches the address of the WINS server that responded and uses it the next time the primary and secondary WINS servers fail to resolve the name. This feature is enabled by default in NetBT. However, if this feature is activated for too many computers, the result is excessive duplication of name queries, resulting in performance degradation.

To plan for fault tolerance, determine the maximum period you ever expect any given WINS server to be out of service. Remember to factor into your assessment the length of both planned and unplanned outages. Also, consider the effect on your WINS clients when their primary WINS server is shut down. By maintaining and assigning secondary WINS servers for clients, the effects of a single WINS server being offline can often be reduced, if not fully eliminated. In addition, clustering can provide further fault tolerance. For more information, see "WINS Clustering" in this chapter.

Duplicate Replication Traffic

Finely tuning your replication intervals might conserve some bandwidth on WAN links. Improving the example network in Figure 7.23 results in a network like that shown in Figure 7.24. This new configuration is not only more fault tolerant, but it also has a shorter convergence time. In Figure 7.23, the longest path was from WINS-C over WINS-A and WINS-B to WINS-D. Now the longest path is from WINS-A or WINS-C over WINS-B to WINS-D, with a convergence time of 12 hours and 15 minutes.

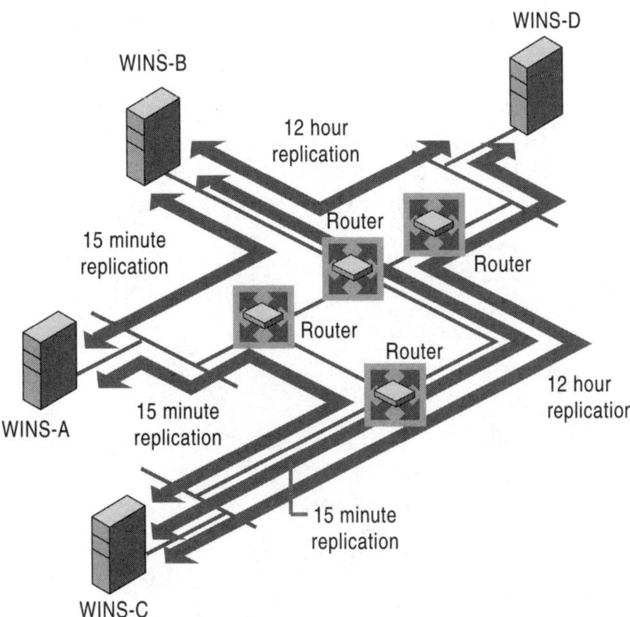

Figure 7.24 An Improved Replication Configuration

By keeping the pull replication intervals between WINS-C and WINS-B short (15 minutes), WINS servers WINS-A, WINS-B, and WINS-C are always reasonably well synchronized. Replicas are never pulled more than once, and only replicas with higher version IDs are copied. When WINS-B pulls an entry directly from WINS-C, it does not pull that replica again from WINS-A.

WINS-D and WINS-B might pull replicas from WINS-C over the link between WINS-B and WINS-C, if WINS-B pulls the replicas from WINS-C, and WINS-D then pulls replicas from WINS-C. This increases the load on the link between WINS-B and WINS-C. To avoid this problem, configure WINS-D to pull from WINS-B first and then check WINS-C. The pull replication interval between servers WINS-D and WINS-C remains 12 hours.

To ensure that the replication is triggered by the pull replication interval and not the update count threshold, you must configure push update counts on WINS servers WINS-D and WINS-C that are high enough to exceed the 12 hours pull replication interval. If these counts are too low, the update count threshold triggers unexpected replication.

Replication Partners and Network Configuration

Choosing whether to configure another WINS server as a push partner or pull partner depends on several considerations, including the specific configuration of servers at your site, whether the partner is across a wide area network (WAN), and how important it is to distribute changes throughout the network immediately.

In the hub-and-spoke configuration, you can configure one WINS server as the central server and all other WINS servers as both push partners and pull partners of this central server. Such a configuration ensures that the WINS database on each server contains addresses for every node on the WAN.

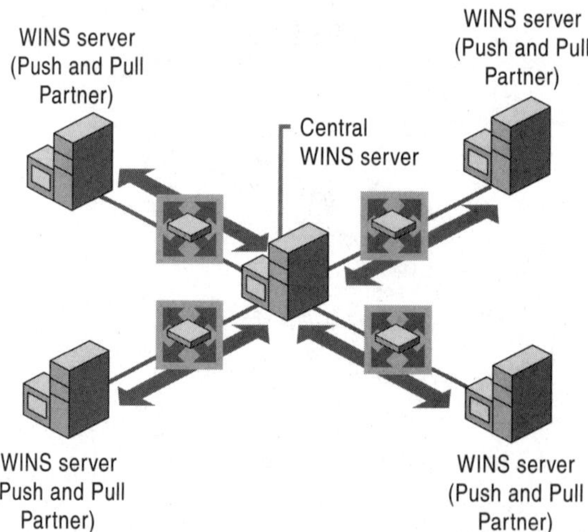

Figure 7.25 Replication using a Central WINS Server

You can select other configurations for replication partner configurations to meet the particular needs of your site. For example, in Figure 7.26, Server1 has only Server2 as a partner, but Server2 has three partners. So Server1 gets all the replicated information from Server2, but Server2 gets information from Server1, Server3, and Server4.

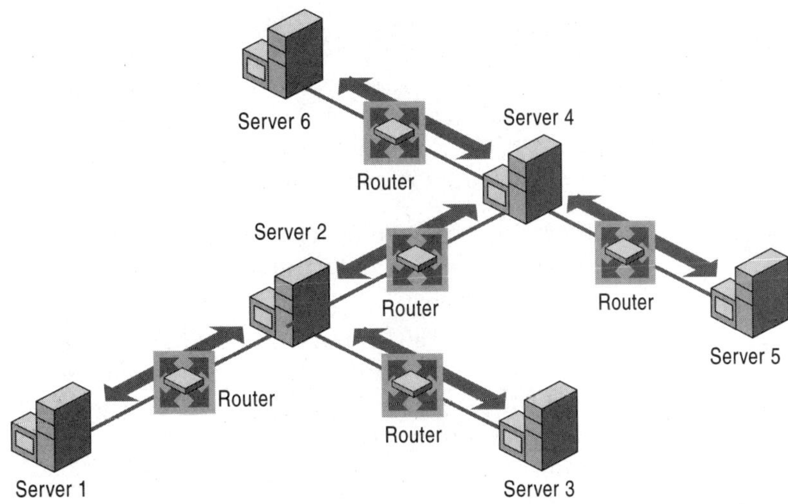

Figure 7.26 Replication in a T Network Configuration

If, for example, Server2 needs to perform pull replications with Server3, make sure it is a push partner of Server3. If Server2 needs to push replications to Server3, it should be a pull partner of Server3.

Decommissioning WINS

For Windows 2000 environments, you might want to reduce or eliminate the need to use WINS on your network. The process of removing installed WINS servers from your network is referred to as decommissioning. For this process to succeed, first consider the following:

- Are any Windows-based computers on your network running earlier versions of Windows or Windows NT?
- Do any client computers in your enterprise still use older Windows-based or MS-DOS-based applications, such as NET command-line utilities, that still require NetBIOS name service?

If the answer to either question is "yes," you still need WINS servers on your network to provide compatibility with older clients and applications. If the answer is "no," you can proceed with designing and implementing a process for removing WINS from your network.

To decommission WINS, you must also implement DNS as your primary naming service for all Windows-based computers active on your network. For more information about implementing DNS on your network, see "Windows 2000 DNS" in this guide. Once DNS is implemented, you can decommission WINS as described in the following sections.

Reconfigure Client Computers' Use of WINS

When you want to remove servers from your network, you must first reconfigure their clients to stop registering and renewing their names with WINS servers. Clients register in WINS on the basis of their being configured for TCP/IP. This reconfiguration is done in one of two ways:

- For clients manually configured to use TCP/IP, remove IP addresses for any WINS servers from the TCP/IP properties for each network connection used by the client computer.
- For clients dynamically configured by DHCP, reconfigure options at your DHCP server (including any options configured by server, scope, or client) not to distribute option code 44 to clients. This option provides a list of WINS server IP addresses to clients.

Verify DNS Configuration

While reconfiguring WINS clients to stop registering of their names and using WINS servers, verify that DNS is fully configured for all clients. Once you are sure that DNS is active for all your clients, you can remove WINS servers from your network.

Clients register in DNS on the basis of their TCP/IP configuration. You can ensure this configuration in two ways:

- For clients that are manually configured to use TCP/IP, add IP addresses for either primary or secondary DNS servers in the TCP/IP properties for each network connection used by the client computer.
- For clients that are dynamically configured by DHCP, reconfigure options at your DHCP server (including any options configured by server, scope, or client) to distribute option code 6 to clients. This option provides to clients a list of IP addresses of DNS servers.

Decommission WINS Servers

Once clients are configured to use DNS rather than WINS for name service, you can decommission individual WINS servers.

Use the WINS management console to mark all records as released for the owner server that you are decommissioning. This tombstone status information is then passed to other WINS servers on your network during the next replication, when they update their local database copies of these records.

Once the records for this server are tombstoned on the other WINS servers on your network, they are automatically removed from other WINS server databases when they have aged to the point of extinction.

To decommission the server, click **Start**, point to **Programs** and then to **Administrative Tools**, and then click **WINS**. If the WINS server you want to decommission does not appear in the console tree, you can add it.

In the console tree, click the WINS server you want to decommission, and then click **Active Registrations**. On the **Action** menu, click **Delete Owner**. In **Delete Owner**, for **Delete this owner**, click the IP address for the WINS server you want to decommission. If the WINS server is not running locally on this computer, it might take a while to load the records for the selected server.

For **Use this operation to delete the selected owner and its records**, click **Replicate deletion to other WINS servers (tombstone)**, and then click **OK**. When prompted to confirm tombstoning, click **Yes**.

In the console tree, click **Replication Partners**. On the **Action** menu, click **Replicate Now**. Once you have verified that records tombstoned in the previous step have been replicated to other partner servers, stop and remove WINS on the decommissioned server.

Important Before decommissioning a WINS server, make sure that any computers previously configured as WINS clients of this server are reconfigured to use other servers as their primary or secondary WINS servers. Reconfiguration is necessary only if these clients will use WINS to register and resolve network names.

Tombstoning ensures that the WINS servers that are replication partners with the decommissioned WINS server are updated properly so that they release the records. If tombstone status is not properly replicated, you can manually delete the records at each WINS server on which tombstone replication failed.

WINS supports remote record deletion for servers running Windows NT Server 4.0, if updated to Service Pack 4 (SP4) or later.

Reducing and Redirecting WINS Traffic

Even after deploying a majority of Windows 2000 computers, most networks must continue using WINS for some time. Once you have begun decommissioning servers, several additional reconfiguration options can reduce both the number of WINS servers on your network and the amount of WINS traffic.

One recommended server-side option is to enable WINS lookup for each of your DNS zones where you are using Microsoft DNS servers. This allows the DNS servers to use WINS to look up names for clients and also to cache frequently requested WINS names. For more information about how to configure WINS lookup for DNS zones, see "WINS Lookup" in this chapter.

As a final step in decommissioning WINS, Windows 2000–based computers allow you to perform client-side configuration changes to disable NetBIOS over TCP/IP. You only need do this where you want to prevent NetBIOS name query and registration traffic from being sent on the network at its source—that is, at each client computer. However, in most networks some limited use of WINS will remain necessary for the foreseeable future. Therefore, disabling NetBIOS over TCP/IP is not recommended for most installations.

Interoperability

The WINS service can share information and functions with DHCP and DNS. The most important interoperability issues are described in this section.

Using DHCP with WINS

When using DHCP and WINS together on your network, consider using additional DHCP scope options to assign WINS node types and to identify WINS primary and secondary servers for DHCP clients. Adjust the options for each physical subnet where DHCP and WINS are implemented on your network.

Assign lease durations of comparable length for both DHCP and WINS. If lease lengths for WINS and DHCP differ widely, the effect on network service is an overall increase in lease management traffic for both services. This is significant only if you do not use the default lease lengths for both services, and lease durations have been changed for either DHCP or WINS individually.

Create DHCP Reservations for Windows 2000 Hosts

Statically mapped Windows 2000–based computers can be problematic when these computers are not periodically stopped and restarted and their initial registration record in WINS becomes damaged. You can have a more reliable and more manageable network by creating DHCP reservations for Windows 2000–based computers. Configure Windows 2000–based domain controllers and domain member servers as DHCP clients with reserved TCP/IP addresses.

You can enter a DHCP reservation at the DHCP server using the media access control address of the network adapter installed in the computer. This reservation ensures that the Windows 2000–based computer gets the same IP address from the DHCP server each time it starts on the network. You can renew WINS registrations for a DHCP client by typing **ipconfig /renew** at a command prompt or by restarting the computer; either procedure corrects the offending WINS registration record.

Configure WINS-Reliant Computers for Fault Tolerance

For fault tolerance in the case of link failure, configure computers that depend on the WINS service located on other subnets as follows. For their primary WINS server, these clients should point to a local WINS server. For their secondary WINS server, these clients should point to the secondary WINS hub. Computers running Windows 95 or Windows NT Workstation send a directed message to the secondary WINS server when the primary WINS server does not contain the requested NetBIOS name. Ideally, this secondary WINS server is located in a separate building and on a separate power grid from the primary WINS server.

Using DNS with WINS

WINS works with the Windows 2000 implementation of Domain Name System (DNS), which is an Internet and TCP/IP networking protocol that provides a scalable and dynamic database service. DNS in Windows 2000 registers and resolves DNS domain names used on private networks and on the Internet. It can provide DNS name service for networked clients, as described in the DNS standard. For more information about DNS, see "Introduction to DNS" and "Windows 2000 DNS" in this book.

In Windows 2000, as with Windows NT 4.0, implementation of DNS is tightly integrated with WINS. This allows non-WINS clients to resolve NetBIOS names by querying a DNS server. Administrators can now remove static entries for Microsoft-based clients in older DNS server zone files in favor of the dynamic integration of WINS and DNS. For example, if a third-party client wants to access a Web page on a WWW server that is enabled for DHCP and WINS, the client can query the DNS server, the DNS server queries WINS, and the name is resolved and returned to the client. Before the integration of WINS and DNS, dynamic IP addressing would have made it impossible to reliably resolve the name in such a situation.

WINS Interoperability Options for DNS

If most of your clients use NetBIOS and you are using Windows 2000 DNS, consider enabling WINS lookup on your DNS servers. When WINS lookup is enabled on DNS servers, WINS resolves any names that DNS resolution does not find. The WINS forward lookup and WINS-R reverse lookup records are supported by Windows 2000 DNS only. If you use third-party DNS servers, use DNS Manager to prevent these WINS records from propagating to the third-party DNS servers that do not support WINS lookup.

If most of your networked computers run Windows 2000, consider upgrading older WINS clients to Windows 2000 and establishing DNS as your only method of name resolution. Support issues involving network name service are simplified if you use a single naming and resource locator service on your network. For more information on moving from an environment combining WINS and DNS to an environment using only Windows 2000 DNS, see "Decommissioning WINS" in this chapter.

Best Practices

Keeping various services working well together is often a matter of dealing with their internal problems rather than their shared elements. This section provides basic practices to help interoperability.

Consolidate Subnets

When you have multiple subnets in a small remote office, consider consolidating the office to one subnet address. You can do this using asynchronous transfer mode (ATM) switching or a virtual private network (VPN) configuration. By consolidating to one subnet address, a local broadcast can be used to resolve names before a request must traverse the WAN to contact a WINS server.

Changing the client to M-node allows it to broadcast locally for resources before contacting a WINS server for NetBIOS name resolution. This can help to reduce the overall amount of WINS-associated traffic, especially WAN traffic.

Update Older Clients

Update client computers running Windows for Workgroups that use the Microsoft TCP/IP-32 protocol stack to the latest Vredir and Vserver files. These files are located on the Windows NT Server 4.0 compact disc (revision 3.11b).

Troubleshooting WINS

This section describes some basic troubleshooting steps for common problems. It also describes how to restore or rebuild the WINS database.

The following conditions can indicate basic problems with WINS:

- Administrator cannot connect to a WINS server using the WINS console. A message appears stating "The RPC server is unavailable."
- TCP/IP NetBIOS Helper service on the WINS client is down and cannot be restarted.
- WINS service is down and cannot be restarted.

First, make sure the appropriate services are running. To do so, complete the following steps at both the WINS server and WINS client:

1. Verify that the WINS services are running.
2. If a necessary service is not started on either computer, start the service.

If services do not start properly, you can use **Computer Management,** available in **Administrative Tools** in Control Panel, to check the status column of the services and try to start them manually. If the service cannot be started, use Event Viewer to check the system event log and determine the cause of failure.

For WINS clients, "Started" should appear in the status column for **TCP/IP NetBIOS Helper Service**. For WINS servers, "Started" should appear in the status column for **Windows Internet Name Service (WINS)**.

Common problems

Following are common WINS problems and steps to solve them.

How can I locate the cause of "duplicate name" error messages?

Check the WINS database for the name. If you find a static record, remove it from the database of the primary WINS server for the client where the duplicate name was detected.

Alternatively, select the **Migrate (Overwrite unique static record with dynamic record)** check box in **Replication Partners Properties** for the WINS server. Now the static mappings in the database can be updated by dynamic registrations (after WINS successfully challenges the old address).

How can I locate the cause of "Network path not found" error messages on a WINS client?

Check the WINS database for the name. If the name is not present in the database, check whether the computer uses B-node name resolution. If so, add a static mapping for it in the WINS database.

If the computer is configured as a P-node, M-node, or H-node, and if its IP address is different from the one in the WINS database, then its address might have changed recently, and the new address has not yet replicated to the local WINS server. To get the latest records, you can start replication at the WINS server that registered the record with the changed address to perform a push replication with propagation to the local WINS server.

Why can't the WINS server pull or push replications to another WINS server?

If the servers are located across routers, confirm that the problem is not a loss of network connectivity or router failure on an intermediate link.

Ensure that each server is correctly configured as either a pull or push partner.

For example, suppose the two WINS servers are named WINS-A and WINS-B. If WINS-A needs to perform pull replications with WINS-B, make sure it is a push partner of WINS-B. Likewise, if WINS-A needs to push replications to WINS-B, it should be a pull partner of WINS-B.

To determine the current configuration of a replication partner, using the WINS console, check the **Type** column for the list of replication partners at each WINS server. If necessary, you can change the replication partner type. Also, make sure that TCP port 42 is not blocked on an intervening network device, such as a router or firewall.

Why are WINS backups failing consistently?

Make sure the path for the WINS backup directory is on a local disk on the WINS server. WINS cannot back up its database files to a remote drive.

Troubleshooting WINS Clients

The most common WINS client problem is failed name resolution. When name resolution fails at a client, answer the following questions to identify the source of the problem.

Was the name that failed to resolve a NetBIOS or DNS name?

NetBIOS names are 15 characters or less and not structured like DNS names, which are generally longer and use periods to delimit each domain level within a name. For example, the short NetBIOS name "PRINT-SRV1" and the longer DNS name "print-srv1.example.microsoft.com" might both refer to the same Windows 2000 resource computer—a network print server—configured to use either name.

In the previous example, if the short name was used at the client, Windows 2000 would first involve NetBIOS name services, such as WINS or NetBT broadcasts, in its initial attempts to resolve the name. If a longer DNS name (or a name that uses dots) was involved in the failure, DNS is more likely the cause of the failed name resolution.

Is the client using an application or version of Windows that requires WINS to resolve names?

Not all Windows computers or applications require WINS or NetBIOS over TCP/IP (NetBT). For example, if the failed name resolution was a URL entered in a Web browser or FTP program, or if it was part of an address entered in an Internet e-mail program, a more likely explanation for the problem is a DNS failure.

In pure Windows 2000 environments, DNS can replace WINS as a naming service. For a pure environment to exist, both the client and the resource server (the computer the client has targeted for locating by name) must both be running Windows 2000; Active Directory must be in use as well. For all other cases involving either the client or resource server running an earlier version of Windows or MS-DOS, a mixed environment exists.

In mixed environments, name resolution could fail when any clients need access to shared resources not published via Active Directory, such as older file and print servers, or to complete logon or browsing of Windows NT domains. Some examples of applications that a client might use and need WINS to assist in name resolution include My Network Places, the **Map Network Drive** feature in Windows Explorer, or the **net** command (Net.exe) and any of its supported options, such as **net use** or **net view**.

Is the client computer able to use WINS, and is it correctly configured?

First, check that the client is configured to use both TCP/IP and WINS. Client configuration of WINS-related settings can be done manually by an administrator setting the TCP/IP configuration of the client, or it can be done dynamically by a DHCP server providing the client its TCP/IP configuration.

In most cases, computers running earlier versions of Microsoft operating systems are already able to use WINS once TCP/IP is installed and configured at the client. For Windows 2000, administrators can optionally disable NetBIOS over TCP/IP (NetBT) for each client. If you disable NetBT, WINS cannot be used at the client.

Also, check that the client computer has valid IP addresses. To check the IP configuration of a client computer, use the **ipconfig /all** command. (To slow or pause the output, use **ipconfig /all | more** for screen-by-screen review.)

In the command output, verify that the client computer has a valid IP address, a valid subnet mask, a default gateway, and both a primary and secondary WINS server.

If the client has an invalid configuration, you can either use the **ipconfig /renew** command to force the client to renew its IP configuration with the DHCP server or you can update the TCP/IP configuration for the client manually.

Does the client have basic connectivity with its configured WINS servers?

To verify that a client has basic TCP/IP access to the WINS server, first try pinging the IP address of the WINS server.

For example, if the client uses a primary WINS server at IP address 10.0.0.1, type **ping 10.0.0.1** at the command prompt on the client computer. If you are not sure of the IP address of the WINS server, you can usually learn it typing **ipconfig /all | more** at the command prompt.

If the WINS server responds to a direct ping of the IP address, use the **nbtstat –RR** command at both the client and the resource server that the client seeks to locate by name. This command forces the WINS client services on each computer to send name release and refresh requests to the WINS server and reregister their names.

If the WINS server does not respond to a direct ping, the source of the problem is likely to be a network connectivity problem between the client and the WINS server. Follow basic TCP/IP network troubleshooting steps to fix the problem. For more information, see "TCP/IP Troubleshooting" in this book.

Is the primary or secondary WINS server able to service the client?

At the primary or secondary WINS server for the client, use Event Viewer or the WINS management console to see if WINS is currently running. If WINS is running on the server, search for the name previously requested by the client to see if it is in the WINS server database.

If the name does not appear in the server database, check that replication is configured correctly and is operational between your WINS servers. For more information, see "Troubleshooting WINS Replication" in this chapter.

Troubleshooting WINS Servers

The most common WINS server problem is the inability to resolve names for clients. When a server fails to resolve a name for its clients, the failure most often is discovered by clients in one of two ways:

- The server sends a negative query response back to the client, such as an error message indicating "Name not found."
- The server sends a positive response back to the client, but the information contained in the response is incorrect.

Many WINS problems involve incorrect or missing configuration details. To help prevent the most common types of problems, review WINS best practices for deploying and managing your WINS servers.

Success in fixing WINS problems nearly always follows if you use an orderly approach to troubleshooting. Most WINS-related problems start as failed queries at a client, so it is a good practice to start with examination of the client. For more information, see "Troubleshooting WINS Clients" in this section.

If you determine that a WINS-related problem does not originate at the client, answer the following questions to further troubleshoot the source of the problem at the WINS server of the client.

Is the WINS server able to service the client?

At the primary or secondary WINS server for the client that cannot locate a name, use Event Viewer or the WINS management console to see if WINS is currently running. If WINS is running on the server, search for the name previously requested by the client to see if it is in the WINS server database.

If the WINS server is failing or registering database corruption errors, you can use WINS database recovery techniques to help restore WINS operations. For more information, see the "Troubleshooting WINS databases" section of this chapter.

If the name does not appear in the server database, verify that replication is configured correctly and is operational between your WINS servers. For more information, see "Troubleshooting WINS replication" in this section.

Is the name entry affected by a static mapping issue?

In general, static mappings are not recommended for clients that can use WINS to dynamically update their name and address information. If the information returned to a client during name resolution is incorrect or stale, check to see if the name entry in the WINS servers database is a static entry. If it is, you can update WINS by performing the following steps:

1. In **Replication Partners Properties,** check the **Enable Migrate box** (shown in Figure 7.10).This enables WINS to overwrite static records with dynamic records.
2. Edit the static mapping to update the mapped address information.
3. Delete the static entry from WINS.

Is replication occurring between all WINS servers?

In some WINS deployments, the use of one-way replication partnerships, such as push-only or pull-only partners, can create situations where names are not regularly replicated to all servers in the network. For more information, see "Troubleshooting WINS Replication" in this chapter.

The following error conditions can indicate problems with the WINS server:

- Administrator cannot connect to a WINS server with the WINS management console and receives an error message when attempting to do so.
- WINS client service or Windows Internet Name Service is down and cannot be restarted.

Troubleshooting WINS Replication

Many WINS problems can be corrected by troubleshooting WINS replication when a client and servers are involved in a failed name resolution. In some cases, such as for large networks with complex replication designs and a large number of WINS servers in use, problems with the accuracy or availability of names data are related to timely replication of the WINS database throughout the network.

After you have first investigated common problems related to WINS clients and servers, answering the following questions can help to further troubleshoot the source of the problem in a replicated WINS network.

Is the replication pattern of your network correct and appropriate?

In general, deployment of more than 20 WINS servers is strongly discouraged. Also, for best results and simpler administration, follow a hub-and-spoke replication topology when designing a replicated WINS network that uses push/pull partnerships between each WINS hub server and its member spoke servers.

If a single hub-and-spoke design exceeds the recommended maximum of 20 WINS servers, you should consult with Microsoft Consulting Services or Microsoft Product Support Services about how to revise or reduce your current WINS installation. For larger or enterprise installations, multiple hub-and-spoke designs are effective solutions.

In rare cases, you might need to use push-only and pull-only partner relationships. You should, however, carefully review added WINS administration issues where these configurations are deployed. At a minimum, establish reliable support procedures for occasions when you might need to manually trigger replication between WINS servers configured to operate using these types of limited replication partnering.

Is the version ID incrementing for WINS entries when replicating on all servers?

The version ID is incremented in the WINS database by each server that owns and registers a name record. The version ID is a hexadecimal value stored with each name record in the database, and WINS uses it for version tracking when a record is replicated to other servers.

Version IDs are incremented only for certain types of record changes. For example, when a name is refreshed, WINS typically does not increment the version ID. For other changes, such as a change in IP address, WINS increments the version ID in most cases.

When the version ID is not consistently incrementing for a name record at all servers in the replicated WINS network, you can use either the WINS management console or command-line options to increase the starting version count for the server and correct the problem.

Server Troubleshooting Utilities

Two utilities are useful when troubleshooting server problems: Hotfix.exe and Srvinfo.exe. Hotfix.exe provides specific information on which current hotfixes are installed on a server. This program is on the Microsoft FTP server and is included with posted hotfixes. Srvinfo.exe gives details on a particular server, such as which services or drivers are present; it can also give disk information for a remote server. This utility is found in the *Windows 2000 Resource Kit*. Information on running the utility can be found in online Help.

Other recommendations when preparing for troubleshooting include the following:

- Ensure server partitions have adequate space for Dumpfile.
- Configure critical servers for use of symbols for debug and dumpfile troubleshooting procedures.

Troubleshooting the WINS Server

The WINS database is essential for name resolution with WINS. When a WINS database server suffers a failure, consult "Restoring a WINS Database" earlier in this chapter.

Resources

This section provides reference material for NetBIOS names, including specifics on all unique and group name suffixes, as well as Netshell commands, RFCs, and other WINS documentation.

NetBIOS Names

Microsoft networking components, such as the Workstation service and Server service, allow the first 15 characters of a NetBIOS name to be specified by the user or administrator, but reserve the 16th character of the NetBIOS name (00–FF hex) to indicate a resource type. Following are some examples of NetBIOS names used by Microsoft components.

NetBIOS Names Reference

A user can specify the first 15 characters of a name in all Microsoft operating systems that support and use NetBIOS names. However, the 16th character of the name (00–FF hex) is always reserved to indicate a resource type.

Tables 7.20 and 7.21 contain additional details of the NetBIOS names used by Microsoft networking components when registering unique and group names.

Table 7.19 NetBIOS Unique Names

Format	Description
computer_name[00h]	Registered by the Workstation service on the WINS client. In general, this name is called the NetBIOS computer name.
computer_name[03h]	Registered by the Messenger service on the WINS client. The client uses this service when sending and receiving messages. This name is usually appended to the NetBIOS computer name for the WINS client computer and to the name of the user logged on to that computer when sending messages on the network.
computer_name[06h]	Registered by Routing and Remote Access on the WINS client (when the Routing and Remote Access service is started).
domain_name[1Bh]	Registered by each Windows 2000 Server domain controller running as the domain master browser. This name record is used to allow remote browsing of domains. When a WINS server is queried for this name, a WINS server returns the IP address of the computer that registered this name.
computer_name[1Fh]	Registered by the Network Dynamic Data Exchange (NetDDE) services; appears only if the NetDDE services are started on the computer.
computer_name[20h]	Registered by the Server service on the WINS client. This service is used to provide points of service for the WINS client to share its files on the network.
computer_name[21h]	Registered by the Routing and Remote Access Client service on the WINS client (when the Routing and Remote Access Client is started).
computer_name[BEh]	Registered by the Network Monitoring Agent Service and appears only if the service is started on the WINS client computer. If the computer name has fewer than 15 characters, plus symbols (+) are added to expand the name to 15 characters.
computer_name[BFh]	Registered by the Network Monitoring Utility (included with Microsoft® Systems Management Server). If the computer name has fewer than 15 characters, plus symbols (+) are added to expand the name to 15 characters.
user_name[03h]	User names for the currently logged-on users are registered in the WINS database. Each user name is registered by the Server service component so that the user can receive any **net send** commands sent to that user name. If more than one user logs on with the same user name, only the first computer logged on with that user name registers the name.

Table 7.20 NetBIOS Group Names

Format	Description
domain_name[00h]	Registered by the Workstation service so that it can receive browser broadcasts from LAN Manager–based computers.
domain_name[1Ch]	Registered for use by the domain controllers within the domain, and can contain up to 25 IP addresses.
domain_name[1Dh]	The name *domain_name*[1Dh] is registered for use by a master browser; there is only one master browser per subnet. Backup browsers use this name to communicate with the master browser to retrieve the list of available servers from the master browser. WINS servers always return a positive registration response for *domain_name*[1D], even though the WINS server does not register this name in its database. Therefore, when a WINS server is queried for *domain_name*[1D], the server always responds with a broadcast address, which forces the client to broadcast to resolve the name.
group_name[1Eh]	A normal group name. Any computers configured to be network browsers can broadcast to this name and listen for broadcasts to this name to elect a master browser. A statically mapped group name uses this name to register itself on the network. When a WINS server receives a name query for a name ending with [1E], the WINS server always returns the network broadcast address for the local network of the requesting client. The client can then use this address to broadcast to the group members. These broadcasts are for the local subnet and should not cross routers.
group_name[20h]	A special group name called the Internet Group is registered with WINS servers to identify groups of computers for administrative purposes. For example, "printersg" could be a registered group name used to identify an administrative group of print servers.
[01h][01h] __MSBROWSE__ [01h][01h]	Registered by the master browser for each subnet. When a WINS server receives a name query for this name, the WINS server always returns the network broadcast address for the local network of the requesting client.

NetShell Commands

The NetShell commands for WINS are an alternative to console-based management, and they are especially useful in certain special situations. They offer a fully equivalent command-line utility for administrating WINS servers.

For instance, when managing WINS servers in wide area networks (WANs), you can use NetShell commands in interactive mode at the NetShell command prompt to better manage WINS servers across slow-speed network links.

You can also issue commands as batch processes to script and automate administrative tasks that must be routinely performed for all WINS servers. This is especially useful when you manage a large number of WINS servers.

Table 7.21 lists commands that you can use at the NetShell command prompt—which is not the same as the Windows 2000 command prompt—to manage WINS servers. Each of these commands has additional notes on switches and usage, which can be obtained by typing the command name followed by **/?** At the command prompt.

Table 7.21 Netshell Commands

Command	Description
list	Lists all the available WINS commands.
dump	Dumps WINS server configuration to command output.
add name	Registers a name to the server.
add partner	Adds a replication partner to the server.
add pngserver	Adds a list of persona non grata servers for the current server.
check database	Checks the consistency of the database.
check name	Checks a list of name records against a set of WINS servers.
check version	Checks the consistency of the version number.
delete name	Deletes a registered name from the server database.
delete partner	Deletes a replication partner from the list of replication partners.
delete records	Deletes or tombstones all or a set of records from the server.
delete owner	Deletes a list of owners and their records.
delete pngserver	Deletes all or selected persona non grata (PNG) servers from the list. Replicas from PNG servers are not accepted during replication.
init backup	Initiates backup of WINS database.
init import	Initiates import from an LMHOSTS file.
init pull	Initiates replication and sends a pull trigger to another WINS server.
init pullrange	Initiates replication and pulls a range of records from another WINS server.
init push	Initiates replication and sends a push trigger to another WINS server.

(continued)

Table 7.21 Netshell Commands *(continued)*

Command	Description
init replicate	Initiates replication of database with replication partners.
init restore	Initiates restoring of database from a file.
init scavenge	Initiates scavenging of WINS database for the server.
init search	Initiates search on the WINS database for the server.
reset counter	Resets the server statistics.
set autopartnerconfig	Sets the automatic replication partner configuration info for the server.
set backuppath	Sets the backup parameters for the server.
set burstparam	Sets the burst handling parameters for the server.
set logparam	Sets the database and event logging options.
set migrateflag	Sets the migration flag for the server.
set namerecord	Sets registration interval and timeout values for the server, determining the rate at which registration records are renewed, deleted, and verified.
set periodicdbchecking	Sets periodic database checking parameters for the server.
set pullpartnerconfig	Sets the configuration parameters for the specified pull partner.
set pushpartnerconfig	Sets the configuration parameter for the specified push partner.
set pullparam	Sets the default pull parameters for the server.
set pushparam	Sets the default push parameters for the server.
set replicateflag	Sets the replication flag for the server.
set startversion	Sets the start version ID for the database.
show browser	Displays all active domain master browser [1Bh] records.
show database	Displays the database records for the specified server.
show info	Displays configuration information.
show name	Displays the detail information for a particular record in the server.
show partner	Displays all or pull or push partners for the server.
show partnerproperties	Displays default partner configuration.
show pullpartnerconfig	Displays configuration information for a pull partner.
show pushpartnerconfig	Displays configuration information for a push partner.
show reccount	Displays the number of records owned by a specific owner server.

(continued)

Table 7.21 Netshell Commands *(continued)*

Command	Description
show recbyversion	Displays records owned by a specific server.
show server	Displays the currently selected server.
show statistics	Displays the statistics for the WINS server.
show version	Displays the current version counter value for the WINS server.
show versionmap	Displays the mapping of owner IDs to maximum version numbers.

WINS Specifications (RFCs)

Requests for Comments (RFCs) are an evolving series of reports, proposals for protocols, and protocol standards used by the Internet community. Windows Internet Name Service (WINS) specifications are based on approved RFCs published by the Internet Engineering Task Force (IETF) and other working groups.

The following RFCs contain the core specifications used to design WINS:

RFC 1001: Protocol Standard for a NetBIOS Service on a TCP/UDP Transport: Concepts and Methods

RFC 1002: Protocol Standard for a NetBIOS Service on a TCP/UDP Transport: Detailed Specifications

Note RFCs 1001 and 1002 define a standard protocol to support NetBIOS services in a TCP/IP environment. These RFCs describe NetBIOS-over-TCP/IP (NetBT) protocols in a general manner, emphasizing the underlying ideas and techniques used by all NetBT implementations.

WINS complies with these RFCs and provides open, standards-based interoperability as a NetBIOS name service. However, because Microsoft has added significant enhancements beyond the protocol specified in the RFCs, WINS servers are more accurately described as enhanced NetBIOS name servers.

PART 3

Network Security and Management

Security and automated network management are necessary features for managers and administrators of large networks. This section examines additional Windows 2000 features that provide network security, bandwidth management, and automated client management.

In This Part

CHAPTER 8

Internet Protocol Security

Internet Protocol security (IPSec) is a framework of open standards for ensuring private, secure communications over Internet Protocol (IP) networks, through the use of cryptographic security services. The Microsoft® Windows® 2000 implementation of IPSec is based on standards developed by the Internet Engineering Task Force (IETF) IPSec working group.

In This Chapter

Related Information in the Resource Kit

- For general information about the Internet Protocol (IP), "Introduction to TCP/IP in this book.
- For additional information about VPN concepts, see "Virtual Private Networking" in the *Windows 2000 Internetworking Guide*.
- For general security information, see the chapters under "Distributed Security" in the *Microsoft® Windows® 2000 Server Resource Kit Distributed Systems Guide*.

Security Issues with IP

Without security, both public and private networks are susceptible to unauthorized monitoring and access. Internal attacks might be a result of minimal or nonexistent intranet security; while risks from outside the private network stem from connections to the Internet and extranets. Password-based user access controls alone do not protect data transmitted across a network.

Common Types of Network Attacks

Without security measures and controls in place, your data might be subjected to an attack. Some attacks are passive, meaning information is monitored; others are active, meaning the information is altered with intent to corrupt or destroy the data or the network itself.

Your networks and data are vulnerable to any of the following types of attacks if you do not have a security plan in place.

Eavesdropping

In general, the majority of network communications occur in an unsecured or "cleartext" format, which allows an attacker who has gained access to data paths in your network to "listen in" or interpret (read) the traffic. When an attacker is eavesdropping on your communications, it is referred to as sniffing or snooping. The ability of an eavesdropper to monitor the network is generally the biggest security problem that administrators face in an enterprise. Without strong encryption services that are based on cryptography, your data can be read by others as it traverses the network.

Data Modification

After an attacker has read your data, the next logical step is to alter it. An attacker can modify the data in the packet without the knowledge of the sender or receiver. Even if you do not require confidentiality for all communications, you do not want any of your messages to be modified in transit. For example, if you are exchanging purchase requisitions, you do not want the items, amounts, or billing information to be modified.

Identity Spoofing (IP Address Spoofing)

Most networks and operating systems use the IP address of a computer to identify a valid entity. In certain cases, it is possible for an IP address to be falsely assumed— identity spoofing. An attacker might also use special programs to construct IP packets that appear to originate from valid addresses inside the corporate intranet.

After gaining access to the network with a valid IP address, the attacker can modify, reroute, or delete your data. The attacker can also conduct other types of attacks, as described in the following sections.

Password-Based Attacks

A common denominator of most operating system and network security plans is password-based access control. This means your access rights to a computer and network resources are determined by who you are, that is, your user name and your password.

Older applications do not always protect identity information as it is passed through the network for validation. This might allow an eavesdropper to gain access to the network by posing as a valid user.

When an attacker finds a valid user account, the attacker has the same rights as the real user. Therefore, if the user has administrator-level rights, the attacker also can create accounts for subsequent access at a later time.

After gaining access to your network with a valid account, an attacker can do any of the following:

- Obtain lists of valid user and computer names and network information.
- Modify server and network configurations, including access controls and routing tables.
- Modify, reroute, or delete your data.

Denial-of-Service Attack

Unlike a password-based attack, the denial-of-service attack prevents normal use of your computer or network by valid users.

After gaining access to your network, the attacker can do any of the following:

- Randomize the attention of your internal Information Systems staff so that they do not see the intrusion immediately, which allows the attacker to make more attacks during the diversion.
- Send invalid data to applications or network services, which causes abnormal termination or behavior of the applications or services.
- Flood a computer or the entire network with traffic until a shutdown occurs because of the overload.
- Block traffic, which results in a loss of access to network resources by authorized users.

Man-in-the-Middle Attack

As the name indicates, a man-in-the-middle attack occurs when someone between you and the person with whom you are communicating is actively monitoring, capturing, and controlling your communication transparently. For example, the attacker can re-route a data exchange. When computers are communicating at low levels of the network layer, the computers might not be able to determine with whom they are exchanging data.

Man-in-the-middle attacks are like someone assuming your identity in order to read your message. The person on the other end might believe it is you because the attacker might be actively replying *as you* to keep the exchange going and gain more information. This attack is capable of the same damage as an application-layer attack, described later in this section.

Compromised-Key Attack

A key is a secret code or number necessary to interpret secured information. Although obtaining a key is a difficult and resource-intensive process for an attacker, it is possible. After an attacker obtains a key, that key is referred to as a compromised key.

An attacker uses the compromised key to gain access to a secured communication without the sender or receiver being aware of the attack.With the compromised key, the attacker can decrypt or modify data, and try to use the compromised key to compute additional keys, which might allow the attacker access to other secured communications.

Sniffer Attack

A *sniffer* is an application or device that can read, monitor, and capture network data exchanges and read network packets. If the packets are not encrypted, a sniffer provides a full view of the data inside the packet. Even encapsulated (tunneled) packets can be broken open and read unless they are encrypted *and* the attacker does not have access to the key.

Using a sniffer, an attacker can do any of the following:

- Analyze your network and gain information to eventually cause your network to crash or to become corrupted.
- Read your communications.

Application-Layer Attack

An application-layer attack targets application servers by deliberately causing a fault in a server's operating system or applications. This results in the attacker gaining the ability to bypass normal access controls. The attacker takes advantage of this situation, gaining control of your application, system, or network, and can do any of the following:

- Read, add, delete, or modify your data or operating system.
- Introduce a virus program that uses your computers and software applications to copy viruses throughout your network.
- Introduce a sniffer program to analyze your network and gain information that can eventually be used to crash or to corrupt your systems and network.
- Abnormally terminate your data applications or operating systems.
- Disable other security controls to enable future attacks.

Introducing IPSec

IPSec is the long-term direction for secure networking. It provides a key line of defense against private network and Internet attacks, balancing ease of use with security.

IPSec has two goals:

- To protect IP packets.
- To provide a defense against network attacks.

Both goals are met through the use of cryptography-based protection services, security protocols, and dynamic key management. This foundation provides both the strength and flexibility to protect communications between private network computers, domains, sites, remote sites, extranets, and dial-up clients. It can even be used to block receipt or transmission of specific traffic types.

IPSec is based on an end-to-end security model, meaning that the only computers that must know about the traffic being secured are the sending and receiving computers. Each handles security at its respective end, with the assumption that the medium over which the communication takes place is not secure. Any computers that only route data from source to destination are not required to support IPSec. This model allows IPSec to be successfully deployed for your existing enterprise scenarios:

- Local area network (LAN): client/server, peer to peer.
- Wide area network (WAN): router to router, gateway to gateway.
- Remote access: dial-up clients; Internet access from private networks.

The Windows 2000 implementation of IPSec is based on industry standards currently in development by the Internet Engineering Task Force (IETF) IPSec working group. IPSec and its related services in Windows 2000 have been jointly developed by Microsoft and Cisco Systems, Inc.

In-Depth Defense

Data must be protected from interception, modification, or access by unauthorized parties. Network attacks can result in system downtime and public exposure of sensitive information.

Network protection strategies generally focus only on preventing attacks from outside the private network by using firewalls, secure routers (security gateways), and user authentication of dial-up access. This is referred to as perimeter security, and it does not protect against attacks from within the network.

User access control security methods (smart cards; Kerberos v5 authentication), are not adequate to protect against most network-level attacks, because they rely solely on user names and passwords. Many computers are shared by multiple users. As a result, the computer is often left in a logged-on state, making it unsecured. If a user name and password have been hijacked, user access control security cannot stop the attacker's access to network resources.

Physical-level protection strategies, which are not commonly used, protect the actual network wires from being accessed and the network access points from being used. However, this rarely guarantees protection of the entire path the data must travel through the network from source to destination.

The best level of protection is provided with IPSec's end-to-end model: the sending computer secures the data prior to transmission (before it ever reaches the network wires), and the receiving computer unsecures the data only after it has been received. For this reason, IPSec should be one of the components in a layered enterprise security plan. It protects your private data in a public environment by providing a strong, cryptography-based defense against attacks. All network traffic is secured packet by packet rather than for a whole communication (that is, a flow of packets). Used in combination with strong user access control, perimeter, and possibly physical level security, IPSec ensures an in-depth defense for your data.

Aggressive Protection Against Attacks

IPSec protects the data so that an attacker finds it extremely difficult or impossible to interpret. The level of protection provided is determined by the strength of the security levels specified in your IPSec policy structure.

IPSec has a number of features that significantly reduce or prevent the attacks discussed previously:

Sniffers, Lack of Privacy IPSec's Encapsulating Security Payload (ESP) protocol provides data privacy by encrypting the IP packets.

Data Modification IPSec uses cryptography-based keys, shared only by the sending and receiving computers, to create a digital checksum for each IP packet. Any modifications to the packet data alter the checksum, which indicates to the receiving computer that the packet was modified in transit.

Identity Spoofing, Password-Based, Application-Layer, and Denial-of-Service IPSec allows the exchange and verification of identities without exposing that information to interpretation by an attacker. Mutual verification (authentication) is used to establish trust between the communicating systems; only trusted systems can communicate with each other.

Man-in-the-Middle IPSec combines mutual authentication with shared, cryptography-based keys.

Denial-of-Service IPSec uses IP packet filtering methodology as the basis for determining whether communication is allowed, secured, or blocked, according to the IP address ranges, protocols, or even specific protocol ports.

Layer 3 Protection

Usually the level of protection that IPSec provides requires system modification. However, IPSec's strategic implementation at the IP transport level (network Layer 3) enables a high level of protection transparently for most all applications, services and upper layer protocols, with little overhead: deploying IPSec requires no changes to existing applications or operating systems, and policies can be centrally defined in Active Directory™ or managed locally on a computer.

The implementation of security at Layer 3 provides protection for all IP and upper layer protocols in the TCP/IP protocol suite, such as TCP, UDP, ICMP, Raw (protocol 255), and even custom protocols that send traffic at the IP layer. (See "Introduction to TCP/IP" in this book for more information about the network layer model.) The primary benefit of securing information at a lower layer is that all applications and services using IP for transport of data can be protected with IPSec without any modification to those applications or services.

Other security mechanisms that operate above Layer 3, such as Secure Sockets Layer (SSL), only provide security to applications that know how to use SSL (such as Web browsers). To protect communications for all your applications on your computer with SSL requires modifications to each application. Security mechanisms that operate below layer 3, such as link layer encryption, are only protecting the link, not necessarily all links along the data path. This makes link layer encryption unsuitable for end-to-end data protection on Internet or routed intranet scenarios.

Policy-Based Security

Although stronger security methods based on cryptography have become necessary to fully protect communication, it can often greatly increase administrative overhead. IPSec avoids this with its use of policy-based administration.

IPSec policies, rather than applications programming interfaces (APIs) or operations systems, are used to configure IPSec security services. The policies provide variable levels of protection for most traffic types in most existing networks.

IPSec provides access control by enabling an administrator to designate specific filters and filter actions in an IPSec policy. Two types of access control are provided: simple IP packet filtering and successful authentication. Additionally, permit and block actions (see "Filter Actions" later in this chapter), allow control over the *type* of IP packets a computer may send or receive, or the addresses with which a computer may communicate.

Your network security administrator can configure IPSec policies to meet the security requirements of a user, group, application, domain, site, or global enterprise. Windows 2000 provides an administrative interface, called IPSec Policy Management, to define IPSec policies for computers at the Active Directory level for any domain members, or on the local computer for non-domain members.

Simplified Deployment

To achieve secure communications with a low cost of ownership, Windows 2000 simplifies the deployment of IPSec with the following features:

Integration with the Windows 2000 Security Framework IPSec uses the Windows 2000 secure domain as a trust model. By default, IPSec policies use the Windows 2000 default authentication method (Kerberos v5 authentication) to identify and trust communicating computers. Computers that are members of a Windows 2000 domain and in trusted domain can easily establish IPSec secured communications.

Centralized IPSec Policy Administration at the Active Directory Level
IPSec policies can be assigned through the Group Policy features of Active Directory. This allows the IPSec policy to be assigned at the domain or organizational unit level, which eliminates the administrative overhead of configuring each computer individually.

Transparency of IPSec to Users and Applications Tight integration at the IP layer (Layer 3) provides security for any protocol in the TCP/IP suite. You do not need separate security packages for each protocol in the TCP/IP suite, because applications using TCP/IP pass the data to the IP protocol layer, where it is secured.

Flexible Security Configuration The security services within each policy can be customized to meet the majority of security requirements for the network and data traffic.

Automatic Key Management Internet Key Exchange (IKE) services dynamically exchange and manage cryptography-based keys between communicating computers.

Automatic Security Negotiation Internet Key Exchange (IKE) services dynamically negotiate a mutual set of security requirements between communicating computers, eliminating the need for both computers to have identical policies.

Public Key Infrastructure Support Using public key certificates for authentication is supported, to allow trust and secure communication with computers that do not belong to a Windows 2000 trusted domain, with non-Windows 2000-based systems, between computers which have membership in untrusted domains, or where computer access must be restricted to a smaller group than what domain authentication allows.

Pre-Shared Key Support If authentication using the Kerberos v5 protocol or public key certificates is not possible, a pre-shared authentication key can be configured. For more information, see the sections titled "Authentication" and "Best Practices" later in this chapter.

Services

IPSec provides a high level of security by using cryptography-based mechanisms. Cryptography allows information to be transmitted securely by hashing (integrity) and encrypting (confidentiality) the information.

A combination of an algorithm and a key is used to secure information:

- The *algorithm* is the mathematical process by which the information is secured.
- A *key* is the secret code or number required to read, modify, or verify secured data.

Windows 2000 IPSec supports the following services.

Security Properties

IPSec provides the following properties for secured communications:

Non-Repudiation Verifies that the sender of the message is the only person who could have sent it. The sender cannot deny having sent the message. Non-repudiation is a property of messages containing digital signatures when using public key technology. With public key technology, the sender's private key is used to create a digital signature that is sent with the message. The receiver uses the sender's public key to verify the digital signature. Because only the sender has possession of the private key, only the sender could have generated the digital signature. Non-repudiation is not a property of message authentication codes and hashes on messages using secret key technologies, because both the sender and the receiver have the secret key.

Anti-Replay Also called *replay prevention*, it ensures the uniqueness of each IP packet. Anti-replay ensures that data captured by an attacker cannot be re-used or "re-played" to establish a session or gain information illegally. This protects against attempts to intercept a message and then use the identical message to illegally gain access to resources, possibly even months later.

Integrity Protects data from unauthorized modification in transit, ensuring that the data received is exactly the same as the data sent. Hash functions sign each packet with a cryptographic checksum using one of the shared keys, which the receiving computer checks before opening the packet. Only the sender and receiver have the key used to calculate the checksum. If the packet—and therefore signature—has changed, the packet is discarded.

Confidentiality (Encryption) Ensures that data is only disclosed to intended recipients. This is achieved by encrypting the data before transmission. This ensures that the data cannot be read during transmission, even if the packet is monitored or intercepted. Only the party with the shared, secret key is able to read the data (after decryption). This property is optional and is dependent on IPSec policy settings.

Authentication Verifies the origin of a message through the process of one side sending a credential and the receiver verifying the legitimacy of the credential. Windows 2000 IPSec provides multiple methods of authentication, to ensure compatibility with legacy systems, non-Windows-based systems, and remote computers. For more information on authentication, see the chapters under "Distributed Security" in the *Microsoft® Windows® 2000 Server Resource Kit Distributed Systems Guide.*

Public Key Certificate–Based Authentication

A well-implemented public key infrastructure, in which security credentials can be presented without compromising those credentials in the process, resolves many security problems. IPSec works with your public key infrastructure to allow certificate-based authentication of computers.

A public key certificate (PKC) ensures that who you *say you are* and who you *really are* do not differ. A PKC is one type of authentication that reliably provides this verification.

PKCs are like digital passports. They are used to verify the identities of non-Windows 2000 computers, stand-alone computers, clients that are not members of a trusted domain, or computers that are not running the Kerberos v5 authentication protocol (the default Windows 2000 authentication method.)

For information about implementing a public key infrastructure, see "Choosing Security Solutions That Use Public Key Technology" in the *Windows 2000 Server Resource Kit Distributed Systems Guide.*

Pre-Shared Key Authentication

IPSec can also use pre-shared keys for authentication. Pre-shared means the parties must agree on a shared, secret key that becomes part of the IPSec policy. During security negotiation, information is encrypted before transmission using the shared key, and decrypted on the receiving end using the same key. If the receiver can decrypt the information, identities are considered authenticated.

Microsoft does not recommend frequent use of pre-shared key authentication, because the authentication key is stored, unprotected, in the IPSec policy. Pre-shared key methodology is provided *only* for interoperability purposes and to adhere to the IPSec standards set forth by the IETF. To safely use this authentication method, the policy must be restricted to administrator-only read and write access, encrypted for privacy when communicated between the domain controller and domain member computers, and restricted to system-only read access on each computer.

Public Key Cryptography

IPSec implements public key cryptography methods for authentication (certificate signing), and key exchange (the Diffie-Hellman algorithm). Public key cryptography has all the capabilities of secret key cryptography, but is generally more secure because it requires two keys—one for signing and encrypting the data, and one for verifying the signature and decrypting the data. This is often referred to as asymmetric cryptography, which simply means that two keys are required for the process.

Each user has a private key that is known only to that person, and a public key that is widely distributed. For example, if Alice wants to send a secured message to Bob, she uses Bob's public key to encrypt the message. Only Bob can decrypt the message because that requires his private key. Although the keys in the pair are related, it is mathematically infeasible to generate one key using the other key. This is why the public key can be widely distributed. The private key, often referred to as the secret key, must remain closely guarded.

Integrity with Hash Functions

Hash message authentication codes (HMAC) "sign" packets to verify that information received is exactly the same as the information sent (integrity). This is critical when data is exchanged over unsecured media.

HMACs provide integrity by means of a hash function (algorithm), combined with a shared, secret key. A hash is more commonly described as a signature on the packet. This is somewhat inaccurate, because a hash differs from a digital signature: a hash uses a secret, shared key; a digital signature uses public key technology and the sending computer's key. Hash functions are also sometimes referred to as message digests or one-way transforms. One-way transforms or functions are so named for two reasons: each party must perform the computation on their respective end, and because it is easy to go from message to digest but mathematically infeasible to go from digest to message. Conversely, two-way functions can go either way; encryption schemes are examples of two-way functions.

The hash signature itself is actually a cryptographic checksum or Message Integrity Code (MIC) that each party must compute to verify the message. For example, the sending computer uses an HMAC algorithm and shared key to compute the checksum for the message and includes it with the packet. The receiving computer must perform an HMAC computation on the received message, and compare it to the original (included in the packet from the sender). If the message has changed in transit, the hash values are different and the packet is rejected.

For integrity, you can choose between two hash functions when setting policy:

- *HMAC-MD5*

  Message Digest 5 (MD5) is based on RFC 1321. It was a response to a weakness found in MD4, the previous incarnation of the original MD. MD5 is a little slower, but stronger.

  MD5 makes four passes over the data blocks (whereas MD4 made three passes), using a different number constant for each message word on every pass. This equates to 64, 32-bit constants used during the MD5 computation.

  Ultimately, this produces a 128-bit key used for integrity check.

- *HMAC-SHA*

  Secure Hash Algorithm (SHA) was developed by the National Institute of Standards and Technology as described in *FIPS PUB 180-1*. The SHA process is closely modeled after MD5.

  SHA uses 79, 32-bit constants during the computation, which results in a 160-bit key that is used for integrity check. Longer key lengths provide greater security, so SHA is considered the stronger of the two.

For clarity and brevity, "sign" or "signature" is used for the remainder of this chapter when discussing how the hash function provides integrity.

Data Encryption: Confidentiality

Windows 2000 IPSec uses the US Data Encryption Standard (DES) to provide confidentiality (data encryption).

DES

The DES algorithm was published in 1977 by the US National Bureau of Standards. IPSec enables the ability to frequently regenerate keys during a communication. This prevents the entire data set from being compromised if one DES key is broken. For more information, see "Key Lifetimes" later in this chapter.

DES uses a 56-bit key, and maps a 64-bit input block into a 64-bit output block. The key appears to be a 64-bit key, but one bit in each of the 8 bytes is used for odd parity, resulting in 56 bits of usable key.

The input block is initially put through rounds to produce a 64-bit output block. A round is like shuffling a deck of cards—it is a randomization process to ensure that different values are produced each time. This key is used to generate 16, 48-bit, per-round keys. Each round takes as its input the outcome (key) of the previous round, plus the 48-bit key, and produces the next 56-bit key. After the sixteenth round, the key is permutated with the inverse of the initial permutation.

Cipher Block Chaining (CBC) is also used to hide patterns of identical blocks of data within a packet. An Initialization Vector (an initial random number) is used as the first random block to encrypt and decrypt a block of data. Different random blocks are used in conjunction with the secret key to encrypt each block. This ensures that identical cleartext data (unsecured data) results in unique, encrypted data blocks. Repeats can compromise the security of the key by providing a pattern with which an attacker can crack your encryption. Lack of repeats also prevents data expansion during encryption.

Windows 2000 IPSec supports the use of:

- **3DES:** It is highly secure, and therefore slower in performance. 3DES processes each block three times, using a unique key each time:
  1. Encryption on the block with key 1
  2. Decryption on the block with key 2
  3. Encryption on the block with key 3

  This process is reversed if the computer is decrypting a packet. Windows 2000 IPSec uses 3DES for confidentiality.
- **DES:** This is provided when the high security and overhead of 3DES is not necessary.

Key Management

A key is a secret code or number required to read, modify, or verify secured data. Keys are used in conjunction with algorithms (a mathematical process) to secure data. Windows 2000 automatically handles key generation and implements the following keying properties that maximize protection:

Dynamic Re-Keying

IPSec policy controls how often a new key is generated during the communication, using a method called *dynamic re-keying*. The communication is sent in blocks, and each block of data is secured with a different key. This prevents an attacker who has obtained part of a communication, and the corresponding session keys, from obtaining the rest of the communication. This on-demand security negotiation and automatic key management service is provided using the IETF-defined Internet Key Exchange (IKE), RFC 2409.

IPSec policy allows expert users to control how often a new key is generated. If no values are configured, keys are regenerated automatically at default intervals.

Key Lengths

Every time the length of a key is increased by one bit, the number of possible keys doubles, making it exponentially more difficult to break the key. IPSec policy provides multiple algorithms to allow for short or long key lengths.

Key Material Generation: The Diffie-Hellman Algorithm

To enable secure communication, two computers must be able to gain the same, shared key (session key), without sending the key across a network because that would severely compromise the secret.

The *Diffie-Hellman algorithm* (DH) predates Rivest-Shamir-Adleman (RSA) encryption and offers better performance. It is one of the oldest and most secure algorithms used for key exchange.

The two parties publicly exchange some keying information, which Windows 2000 additionally protects with a hash function signature. Neither party ever exchanges the actual key; however, after their exchange of keying material, each is able to generate the identical shared key. At no time is the actual key ever exchanged.

DH keying material exchanged by the two parties can be based on 96 or 128 bytes of keying material, known as *DH groups*. The strength of the DH group is directly related to the strength of the key. Strong DH groups combined with longer key lengths increase the degree of computational difficulty in trying to break the key.

IPSec uses the DH algorithm to provide the keying material for all other encryption keys. DH on its own provides no authentication; in the Windows 2000 IPSec implementation, identities are authenticated after the DH exchange takes place.

For more detailed information on the key generation process, see the "Internet Key Exchange" section of this chapter.

IPSec Protocol Types

IPSec protocols provide data and identity protection services for each IP packet by adding their own security protocol header to each IP packet.

Authentication Header

Authentication Header (AH) provides authentication, integrity, and anti-replay for the entire packet (both the IP header and the data payload carried in the packet). It does not provide confidentiality, which means it does not encrypt the data. The data is readable, but protected from modification. AH uses the HMAC algorithms described earlier to sign the packet for integrity.

For example, Alice on Computer A sends data to Bob on Computer B. The IP header, the AH header, and the data are protected with integrity. This means Alice can be certain it was really Bob who sent the data and that the data was unmodified.

Integrity and authentication are provided by the placement of the AH header between the IP header and the transport (layer 4) protocol header, which is shown as TCP/UDP in the Figure 8.1. AH uses an IP protocol ID of 51 to identify itself in the IP header.

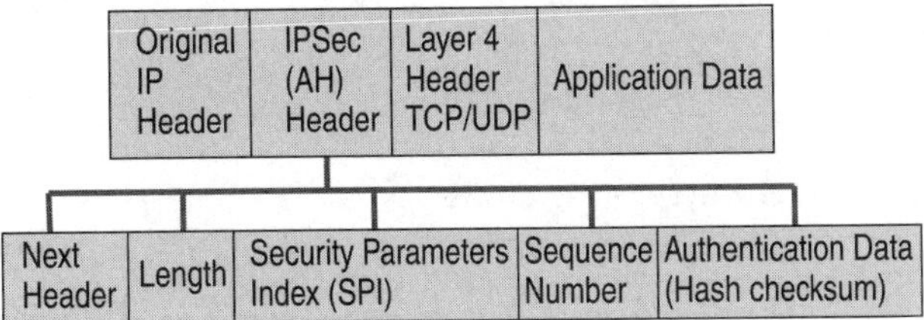

Figure 8.1 Authentication Header

AH can be used alone or in combination with the Encapsulating Security Payload (ESP) protocol.

The AH header contains the following fields:

Next Header Identifies the next header that uses the IP protocol ID. For example, the value might be "6" to indicate TCP.

Length Indicates the length of the AH header.

Security Parameters Index (SPI) Used in combination with the destination address and the security protocol (AH or ESP) to identify the correct security association for the communication. (For more information, see the "Internet Key Exchange" section later in this chapter.) The receiver uses this value to determine with which security association this packet is identified.

Sequence Number Provides anti-replay protection for the SA. It is 32-bit, incrementally increasing number (starting from 1) that is never allowed to cycle and that indicates the packet number sent over the security association for the communication. The receiver checks this field to verify that a packet for a security association with this number has not been received already. If one has been received, the packet is rejected.

Authentication Data Contains the Integrity Check Value (ICV) that is used to verify the integrity of the message. The receiver calculates the hash value and checks it against this value (calculated by the sender) to verify integrity.

Packet Signature

AH is inserted after the IP header and before an upper layer protocol such as TCP, UDP, or ICMP. If another security protocol is being used in addition to AH, the AH header is inserted before any other IPSec headers. The packet signature is shown graphically in Figure 8.2.

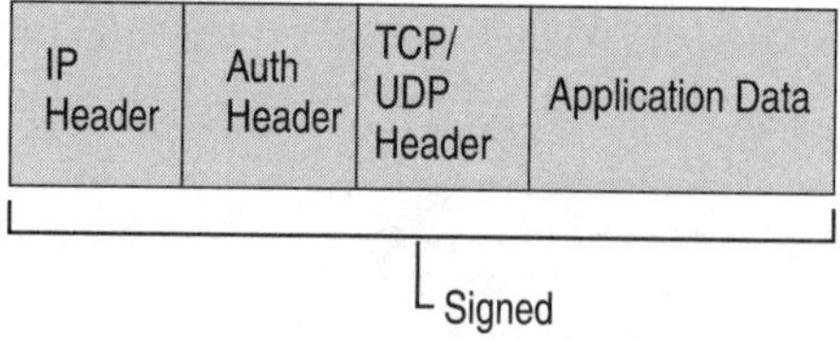

Figure 8.2 AH Integrity Signature

AH signs the entire packet for integrity, except certain fields in the IP header which may change such as the Time To Live and Type of Service fields.

Encapsulating Security Payload

Encapsulating Security Payload (ESP) provides confidentiality, in addition to authentication, integrity, and anti-replay. ESP can be used alone, or in combination with AH.

ESP does not normally sign the entire packet unless it is being tunneled—ordinarily, just the IP data payload is protected, not the IP header.

For example, Alice on Computer A sends data to Bob on Computer B. The data payload is encrypted and signed for integrity. Upon receipt, after the integrity verification process is complete, the data payload in the packet is decrypted. Bob can be certain it was really Alice who sent the data, that the data is unmodified, and that no one else was able to read it.

ESP indicates itself in the IP header using the IP protocol ID of 50. As shown in the Figure 8.3, the ESP header is placed prior to the transport layer header (TCP or UDP) or the IP payload data for other IP protocol types.

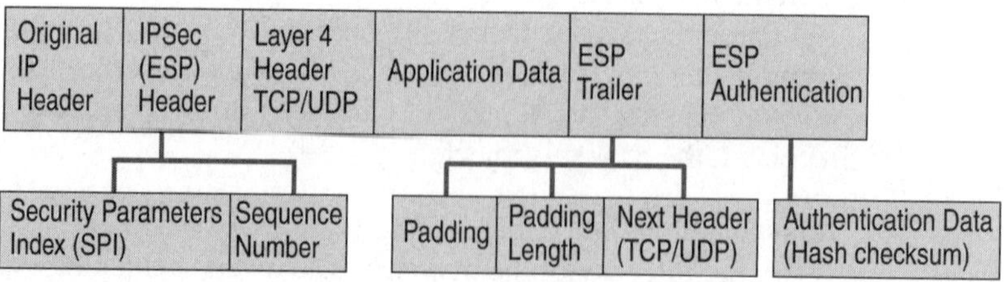

Figure 8.3 ESP

The ESP header contains the following fields:

Security Parameters Index Identifies, when used in combination with the destination address and the security protocol (AH or ESP), the correct security association for the communication. The receiver uses this value to determine the security association with which this packet should be identified.

Sequence Number Provides anti-replay protection for the SA. It is 32-bit, incrementally increasing number (starting from 1) that indicates the packet number sent over the security association for the communication. The sequence number is never allowed to cycle. The receiver checks this field to verify that a packet for a security association with this number has not been received already. If one has been received, the packet is rejected.

The ESP trailer contains the following fields:

Padding 0 to 255 bytes is used for 32-bit alignment and with the block size of the block cipher.

Padding Length Indicates the length of the Padding field in bytes. This field is used by the receiver to discard the Padding field.

Next Header Identifies the nature of the payload, such as TCP or UDP.

The ESP Authentication Trailer contains the following field:

Authentication Data Contains the Integrity Check Value (ICV), and a message authentication code that is used to verify the sender's identity and message integrity. The ICV is calculated over the ESP header, the payload data and the ESP trailer.

Packet Signature and Encryption

As shown in Figure 8.4, ESP provides protection for upper layer protocols. The Signed area indicates where the packet has been signed for integrity. The Encrypted area indicates what information is protected with confidentiality.

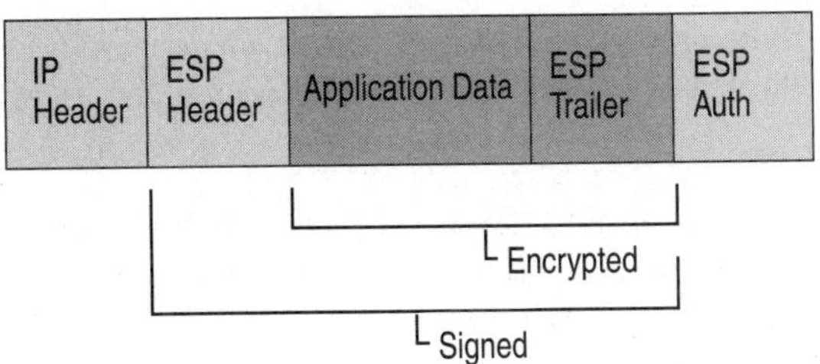

Figure 8.4 ESP: Signature and Encryption

ESP is inserted after the IP header and before an upper layer protocol, such as TCP, UDP, or ICMP, or before any other IPSec headers that have already been inserted. Everything following ESP (the upper layer protocol, the data, and the ESP trailer) is signed. The IP header is not signed, and therefore not necessarily protected from modification. The upper layer protocol information, the data, and the ESP trailer are encrypted.

IPSec Components

The following sections describe IPSec components that are installed with Windows 2000.

IPSec Policy Agent Service

The purpose of the policy agent is to retrieve IPSec policy information and pass it to the other IPSec mechanisms that require that information to perform security services, as shown in Figure 8.5.

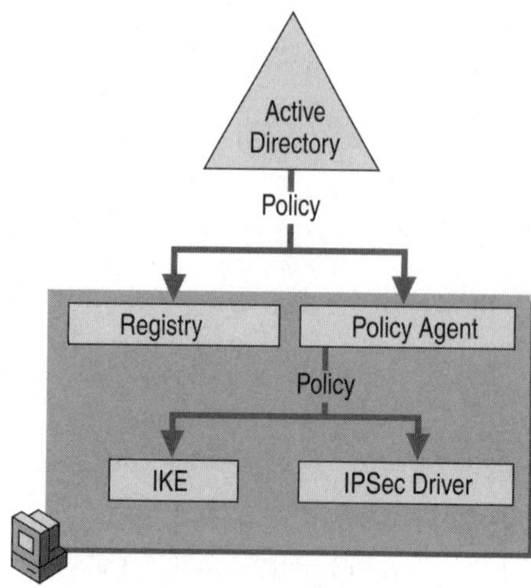

Figure 8.5 IPSec Policy Agent

The policy agent is an IPSec service residing on each Windows 2000 computer, appearing in the list of system services. The policy agent performs the following tasks:

- Retrieves the appropriate IPSec policy (if one has been assigned) from Active Directory if the computer is a domain member or from the local registry if the computer is not joined to a domain.
- Sends the active IPSec policy information to the IPSec driver.

Retrieval of the policy occurs both at system start time, at the interval specified in the IPSec policy (if the computer is joined to a domain), and at the default Winlogon polling interval (if a joined to a domain):

- If IPSec policy information is centrally configured for computers which are domain members, the IPSec policy information is stored in Active Directory and cached in local registry of the computer to which it applies.
- If the computer is temporarily not connected to the domain and is cached policy, when the computer reconnects to the domain any new policy information for that computer overrides the old, cached policy information.
- If a computer is a stand-alone computer, or is a member of a domain that is not using Active Directory for policy storage, IPSec policy is stored in the local registry.

The policy agent starts automatically at system start time. If there are no IPSec policies in the directory service or registry, or if the policy agent cannot connect to the directory service, the policy agent waits for policy to be assigned or activated.

Internet Key Exchange

Before secured data can be exchanged, a contract between the two computers must be established. In this contract, called a *security association* (SA), both agree on how to exchange and protect information, as shown in Figure 8.6.

Figure 8.6 Internet Key Exchange

To build this contract between the two computers, the IETF has established a standard method of security association and key exchange resolution, called Internet Key Exchange which:

- Centralizes security association management, reducing connection time.
- Generates and manages the authenticated keys used to secure the information.

This process protects not only computer to computer communications, but also protects remote computers that are requesting secure access to a corporate network; or any situation in which the negotiation for the final destination computer (endpoint) is actually performed by a security router or other proxy server.

What Is an SA?

A *security association* (SA) is a combination of a mutually agreed-upon key, security protocol, and SPI which together define the security that will be used to protect the communication from sender to receiver. The *security parameters index* (SPI) is a unique, identifying value in the SA used to distinguish among multiple security associations existing at the receiving computer. For example, multiple associations might exist if a computer is securely communicating with multiple computers simultaneously. This situation occurs mostly when the computer is a file server or a remote access server that serves multiple clients. In these situations, the receiving computer uses the SPI to determine which SA is used to process the incoming packets.

Phase I SA

To ensure successful, secure communication, IKE performs a two-phase operation. Confidentiality and authentication during each phase is ensured by the use of encryption and authentication algorithms agreed on by the two computers during security negotiations. With the duties split between two phases, keying can be accomplished with great speed.

During the first phase, the two computers establish a secure, authenticated channel—the Phase I SA. It is so named in order to differentiate between the SAs established in each of the two phases. IKE automatically provides the necessary identity protection during this exchange. This ensures no identity information is sent without encryption between the communicating computers, thus enabling total privacy.

Phase I Negotiation

Following are the steps in a Phase I negotiation.

1. Policy Negotiation

   The following four mandatory parameters are negotiated as part of the Phase I SA:

   - The encryption algorithm (DES, 3DES).
   - The hash algorithm (MD5 or SHA).
   - The authentication method (Certificate, pre-shared key, Kerberos v5 authentication).
   - The Diffie-Hellman (DH) group to be used for the base keying material.

   If certificates or pre-shared keys are used for authentication, the computer identity is protected. However, if Kerberos v5 authentication is used, the computer identity is unencrypted until encryption of the entire identity payload takes place during authentication.

2. DH Exchange (of public values)

   At no time are actual keys exchanged; only the base information needed by DH to generate the shared, secret key is exchanged. After this exchange, the IKE service on each computer generates the master key used to protect the final round: authentication.

3. Authentication

   The computers attempt to authenticate the DH exchange. Without successful authentication, communication cannot proceed. The master key is used, in conjunction with the negotiation algorithms and methods, to authenticate identities. The entire identity payload—including the identity type, port, and protocol—is hashed and encrypted using the keys generated from the DH exchange in the second round. The identity payload, regardless of which authentication method is used, is protected from both modification and interpretation.

The sender presents an offer for a potential security association to the receiver. The responder cannot modify the offer. Should the offer be modified, the initiator rejects the responder's message. The responder sends either a reply accepting the offer or a reply with alternatives.

Messages during this phase have an automatic retry cycle which repeats five times. After a brief interval, fall back to clear is established (if IPSec policy allows). Should a response be received before the cycle times out, standard SA negotiation begins.

There is no limit to the number of exchanges that can take place. At a given time, the number of SAs formed are only limited by system resources.

Phase II SA

In this phase, SAs are negotiated on behalf of the IPSec service.

Phase II Negotiation

The following are the steps in Phase II negotiation.

1. Policy negotiation

   The IPSec computers exchange their requirements for securing the data transfer:

   - The IPSec protocol (AH or ESP)
   - The hash algorithm for integrity and authentication (MD5 or SHA)
   - The algorithm for encryption, if requested: 3DES, DES

   A common agreement is reached, and two SAs are established: one for inbound and one for outbound communication.

2. Session key material refresh or exchange

   IKE refreshes the keying material and new, shared, or secret keys are generated for authentication, and encryption (if negotiated), of the packets. If a re-key is required, a second DH exchange (as described in "Phase I Negotiation") takes place prior to this, or a refresh of the original DH is used for the re-key.

3. The SAs and keys are passed to the IPSec driver, along with the SPI.

During this second negotiation of shared policy and keying material—this time to protect the data transfer—the information is protected by the Phase I SA.

As the first phase provided identity protection, the second phase provides protection by refreshing the keying material to prevent bogus SAs. IKE can accommodate a key exchange payload for an additional DH exchange, should a re-key be necessary (master key PFS is enabled). Otherwise, IKE refreshes the keying material from the DH exchange in the first phase.

Phase II results in a pair of security associations: one SA for inbound communication and one SA for outbound; each with its own SPI and key.

The retry algorithm for a message here is almost identical to the process discussed in "Phase I Negotiation," with only one difference: If this process reaches a time-out for any reason during the second or greater negotiation off the same Phase I SA, a re-negotiation of the Phase I SA is attempted. If a message for this phase is ever received with no Phase I SA established, it is rejected.

Using a single Phase I SA for multiple Phase II SA negotiations makes the process extremely fast. As long as the Phase I SA does not expire, re-negotiation and re-authentication are not necessary. The number of Phase II SA negotiations that can be performed is determined by IPSec policy attributes. Note that excessive re-keying off the same Phase I SA could compromise the shared, secret key.

SA Lifetimes

The Phase I SA is cached to allow multiple Phase II SA negotiations (unless PFS is enabled for the master key, or the session key policy lifetimes have been reached). When a key lifetime is reached for the master or session key, the SA is renegotiated, in addition to the key refresh or regeneration.

When the default time-out period is reached for the Phase I SA, or the master or session key lifetime is reached, a delete message is sent to the responder. The IKE delete message tells the responder to expire the Phase I SA. This prevents bogus Phase II SAs from being formed because Phase II SAs are valid until their lifetime is expired by the IPSec driver, independently of the Phase I SA lifetime. IKE does not expire the Phase II SA, because only the IPSec driver knows the number of seconds or bytes that have passed to reach the key lifetime.

Use caution when setting very disparate key lifetimes, which also determine the lifetime of the SA. For example, setting a master key lifetime of eight hours and a session key lifetime of two hours can mean that you have an Phase II SA in place for almost two hours after the Phase I SA expired. This can occur if the Phase II SA is generated immediately before the Phase I SA expires.

Key Protection

The base prime numbers (keying material) and the strength of the keys for the master and session keys are enhanced by the following features. The features discussed here apply to one or both keys, as stated.

Key Lifetimes

Key lifetimes determine when a new key is generated, rather than how it is generated. Also called dynamic re-keying or key regeneration, a key lifetime allows you to force a key regeneration after a specific interval. For example, if the communication takes 10,000 seconds and you specify the key lifetime as 1,000 seconds, 10 keys are generated to complete the transfer. This ensures that even if attackers gain part of a communication, they are not able to gain the entire communication. Automatic key regeneration is provided; configuration is optional. Key lifetimes can be specified for both the master and session keys. Any time a key lifetime is reached, the SA is also renegotiated in addition to the key refresh or regeneration. The amount of data processed by a single key should not exceed 100 megabytes. Administrators should check current security and encryption guidelines to be sure of providing adequate protection for the type of data being communicated.

Session Key Refresh Limit

Repeated re-keying off a session key can compromise the Diffie-Hellman shared secret. Thus, a session key refresh limit is implemented to avoid a security compromise.

For example, Alice on Computer A sends a message to Bob on Computer B, and then sends another message to Bob a few minutes later. The same session key material might be reused because an SA was recently established with that computer. If you want to limit the number of times this occurs, set the session key refresh limit to a low number.

If you have enabled Perfect Forward Secrecy (PFS) for the master key, the session key refresh limit is ignored because PFS forces key regeneration. Setting a session key refresh limit to 1 is identical to enabling master key PFS. If both a master key lifetime and a session key refresh limit is specified, whichever limit is hit first causes the subsequent re-key. By default, IPSec policy does not specify a session key refresh limit.

Diffie-Hellman Groups

Diffie-Hellman (DH) groupsare used to determine the length of the base prime numbers (key material) for the DH exchange. The strength of any key derived from a DH exchange depends in part on the strength of the DH group on which the primes are based.

Each DH group defines the length of the key material to be used. Group 2 (medium) is stronger than Group 1 (low). Group 1 protects 768 bits of keying material; Group 2 protects 1024 bits. A larger group means the resulting DH has more entropy and, therefore, is harder to break.

IKE takes care of negotiating which group to use, ensuring that there are not any negotiation failures as a result of a mismatched DH group between the two peers.

If PFS for the session is enabled, the DH is passed in the SA with the key information during the first message of the Phase II SA negotiation. This forces a new DH permutation which removes the session keying material from the initial DH exchange.

If the sender is using PFS for the session key, the responder is not required to use it as well. However, if the initiator is not using PFS for the session and the responder is using PFS, negotiation fails.

The DH group is the same for both the Phase I and Phase II SA negotiations. This means that when session key PFS is enabled, even though the DH group is set as part of the Phase I SA negotiation, it affects any re-keys during session key establishment.

Perfect Forward Secrecy

Unlike key lifetimes, *Perfect Forward Secrecy (PFS)* determines how a new key is generated, rather than when it is generated. Specifically, PFS ensures that compromise of a single key permits access only to data protected by that single key—not necessarily to the entire communication. To achieve this, PFS ensures that a key used to protect a transmission, in whichever phase, cannot be used to generate any additional keys. In addition, if the key used was derived from specific keying material, that material cannot be used to generate any other keys.

Master key PFS requires a re-authentication, so use it with caution. When it is enabled, the IKE service must re-authenticate identities, causing additional overhead for any domain controllers. It requires a new Phase I negotiation for every Phase II negotiation that will take place.

However, session key PFS can be done without the re-authentication and is therefore less resource-intensive. Session key PFS results in a DH exchange to generate new key material. It requires only four messages and no authentication.

PFS is not required to be enabled on both peers because it is not a negotiable property. If the responder requires PFS and the sender's Phase II SA expires, it simply rejects the sender's message and requires a new negotiation. The sender expires the Phase I SA and renegotiates. PFS can be individually set for both the master and session keys.

IPSec Driver

The IPSec driver, using the IP Filter List from the active IPSec policy, watches for outbound IP packets that must be secured and inbound IP packets that need to be verified and decrypted.

As shown in Figure 8.7, the IPSec driver receives the IP filter list from the IPSec policy agent. The IPSec driver watches all outgoing IP packets on the computer for a match with the stored IP filter list. Outbound packets initiate the negotiation for security when a match occurs. The IPSec driver notifies IKE to begin security negotiations.

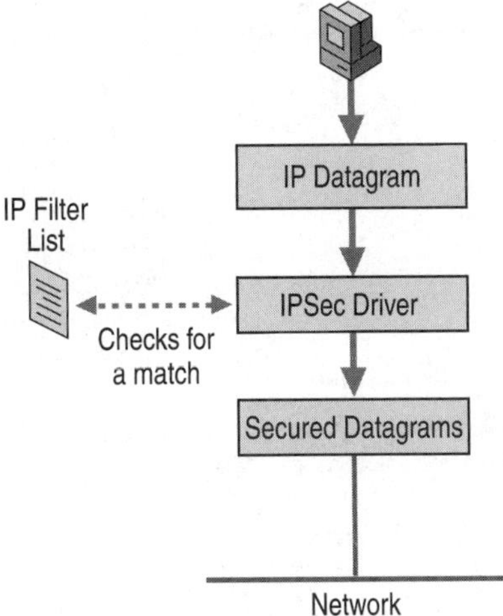

Figure 8.7 IPSec Driver Services

After a successful negotiation is complete, the IPSec driver on the sending computer:

1. Receives the SA containing the session key from IKE.
2. Looks up the outbound SA in its database, and inserts the SPI from the SA into the IPSec header.
3. Signs, and if confidentiality is required, encrypts the packets.
4. Sends packets with SPI to the IP layer to be forwarded to the destination computer.

The IPSec driver on the receiving computer:

1. Receives the session key, SA and SPI from IKE.
2. Looks up the inbound SA in its database by destination address and SPI.
3. Checks the signature and decrypts the packets (if required).
4. Sends packets to the TCP/IP driver for passage to the receiving application.

The IPSec driver stores all current SAs in a database. If multiple SAs are present, the driver uses the SPI as needed to determine which SA goes with which packet.

IPSec Model

Now that the function of each component has been explained individually, a comprehensive picture is necessary to complete an understanding of the architecture, as shown in Figure 8.8.

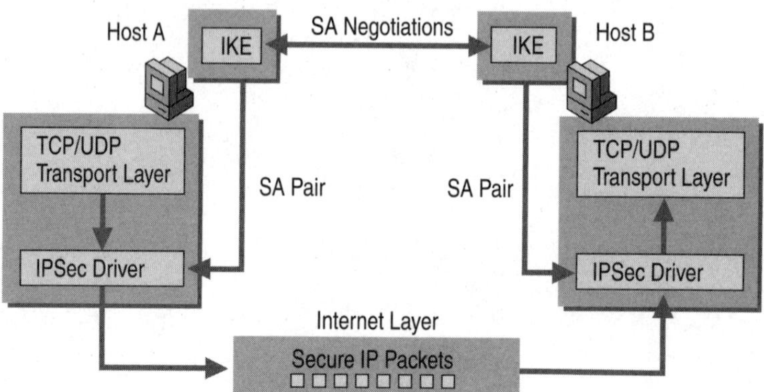

Figure 8.8 Overview: the IPSec Process

For simplicity, this is an intranet computer example. Each computer has an active IPSec policy.

1. Alice, using a data application on Host A, sends a message to Bob on Host B.
2. The IPSec driver on Host A checks its stored IP Filter Lists to see whether the packets should be secured.
3. The driver notifies IKE to begin negotiations.

4. The IKE service on Host B receives a message requesting secure negotiation.
5. The two computers establish a Phase I SA and shared master key.

Note If Host A and Computer B already have an Phase I SA in place from a previous communication (and Phase I PFS is not enabled nor have key lifetimes expired), the two computers can go directly to establishing the Phase II SA.

---

6. A pair of Phase II SAs are negotiated: one inbound SA, and one outbound SA. The SAs include the keys used to secure the information, and the SPI.
7. The IPSec driver on Host A uses the outbound SA to sign and/or encrypt the packets.
8. The driver passes the packets to the IP layer, which routes the packets toward Host B.
9. Host B's network adapter driver receives the encrypted packets and passes them up to the IPSec driver.
10. The IPSec driver on Host B uses the inbound SA to check the integrity signature and/or decrypt the packets.
11. The driver passes the decrypted packets up to the TCP/IP driver, which passes them to the receiving application on Host B.

Although this appears to be a long series of time-consuming and complicated steps, it actually all happens quickly and transparently to each user.

Any routers or switches in the data path between the communicating computers simply forward the encrypted IP packets to their destination. However, if there is a firewall, security router, or proxy server, it must have IP forwarding enabled, so that IPSec and IKE protocol traffic will pass through and not be rejected. Security negotiations are not able to pass through a network address translator (NAT). The IKE negotiation contains IP addresses in the encrypted messages which can not be changed by a NAT because the integrity hash will be broken, or because the packets are encrypted.

Tunneling

Tunneling is also referred to as encapsulation because the original packet is hidden or encapsulated inside of a new packet. A tunnel is the logical data path through which the encapsulated packets travel to their destination. For additional information about tunneling concepts or L2TP integration with IPSec, see "Virtual Private Networking" in the *Windows 2000 Internetworking Guide*. The following sections are related to IPSec tunneling only.

ESP Tunnel Mode

As shown in Figure 8.10, when in tunnel mode the inner IP header (the original packet header) carries the ultimate source and destination addresses, and the outer IP header might contain addresses of security gateways.

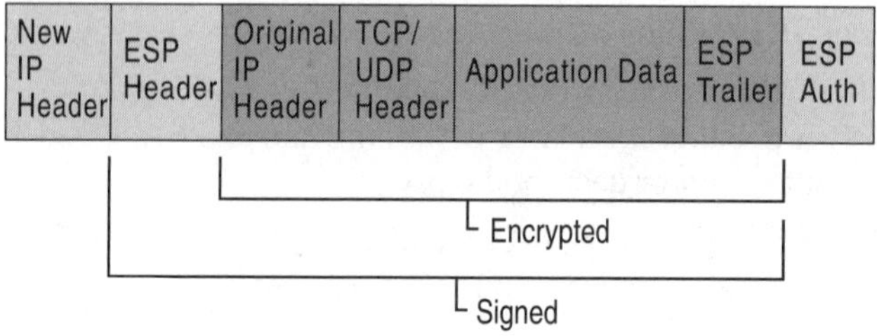

Figure 8.10 ESP Tunnel Mode

The Signed area indicates where the packet has been signed for integrity and authentication. The Encrypted area indicates what information is protected with confidentiality.

Because a new header for tunneling is placed on the packet, everything following the ESP header is signed (except for the ESP authentication trailer), as it is now encapsulated in the tunneled packet. The original header is placed after the ESP header.

The entire packet is appended with an ESP trailer prior to encryption. Everything following the ESP header, except for the ESP authentication trailer, is encrypted, including the original header because it is now considered to be part of the data portion.

The entire ESP payload is then encapsulated within the new tunnel header, which is not encrypted. Thc information in the new tunnel header is only used to route the packet from origin to destination.

If the packet is being sent across a public network, the packet is routed to the IP address of the tunnel server for the receiving intranet. The packet itself is most likely destined for an intranet computer. The tunnel server decrypts the packet, throws away the ESP header, and uses the original IP header to route the packet to the intranet computer.

AH Tunnel Mode

The only difference between AH tunnel mode and ESP tunnel mode is how the packet is handled. As shown in Figure 8.11, AH signs the entire packet for integrity, including the new Tunnel Header (ESP does not sign the tunnel header), and encryption is not provided by AH.

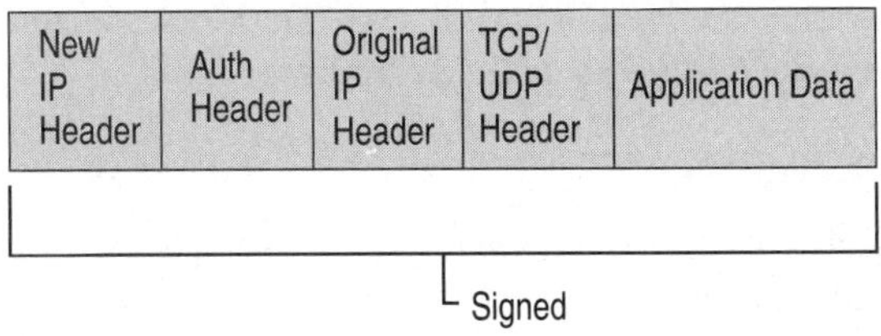

Figure 8.11 AH Tunnel Mode

ESP and AH can be combined to provide tunneling which includes both integrity for the entire packet, and confidentiality for the original IP packet, which contains the data being sent.

IPSec Policy Structure

IPSec policies can be applied to computers, sites, domains, or any organizational units (OUs) you create in the Active Directory.

Your IPSec policies should be based on your organization's written (and unwritten) guidelines for secure operations. Through the use of security actions, called *rules*, one policy can be applied to heterogeneous security groups of computers or organizational units. For more information about choosing guidelines for secure operations, see "Best Practices" later in this chapter.

There are two storage locations for IPSec policies:

1. Active Directory
2. Locally defined in the registry for stand-alone computers and computers which are not joined to the domain (when the computer is temporarily not joined to a trusted Windows 2000 domain, the policy information is cached in the local registry). For more information, see the section titled "Policy Agent" previously in this chapter.

Each policy you create should apply to a scenario you listed when you established a security plan. Special configuration settings might apply if you are assigning policies to a DHCP server, Domain Name System (DNS), Windows Internet Name Service (WINS), Simple Network Management Protocol (SNMP), or remote access server. For more information, see "Special IPSec Considerations" later in this chapter.

Policy Inheritance

Policy precedence follows the Group Policy model. Group policy is applied hierarchically from the least restrictive object (site) to the most restrictive object (OU). For more information about Active Directory and Group Policy, see chapters under the "Active Directory" and "Desktop Configuration Management" parts in the *Windows 2000 Distributed Systems Guide*.

Things to keep in mind when assigning an IPSec policy:

- IPSec policies assigned to domain policy override any local IPSec policy when that computer account is a domain member.
- Precedence of Group Policy. An IPSec policy assigned to an OU overrides domain IPSec policy for that computer account. IPSec policy assigned to a child OU might override the IPSec policy assigned at the parent OU, depending on how Group Policy security permissions are configured.

Rules

Rules govern how and when an IPSec policy protects communication. A rule provides the ability to trigger and control secure communication based on the source, destination, and type of IP traffic.

Each rule contains a list of IP filters and a collection of security actions that take place upon a match with that filter list:

- Filter Actions
- Authentication methods
- IP tunnel settings
- Connection types

Each policy can contain one or multiple rules; one or all of which can be active simultaneously. For example, you might want to have one policy for a site router, but you require different security actions for intranet and Internet communications. One policy can be used for the router by creating multiple rules: one for each possible communication scenario.

Default rules are provided with IPSec, and encompass a variety of client and server based communications. These can be used as is, or modified to your requirements.

IP Packet Filtering

An IP address identifies a computer system's location on the network. Each IP address is separated internally into two parts, a network ID and a computer ID:

- The network ID identifies a single network within a larger TCP/IP network (that is, a network of networks). This ID is also used to identify each network uniquely within the larger network.
- The computer ID for each device (such as a workstation or router) identifies a system within its own network.

Multihomed computers have multiple IP addresses: one for each network adapter.

Filters

A rule provides the ability to trigger security negotiations for a communication based on the source, destination, and type of IP traffic, a process called IP packet filtering. This provides a way for the network administrator to define precisely what IP traffic triggers are secured, blocked, or passed through (unsecured).

Each IP Filter List contains a list of filters. Each filter within an IP Filter List describes a particular subset of network traffic to be secured, both for inbound and outbound traffic:

- Inbound filters. Apply to traffic received, allow the receiving computer to match the traffic with the IP Filter List. Inbound filters respond to requests for secure communication or match the traffic with an existing SA and process the secured packets.
- Outbound filters. Apply to traffic leaving a computer toward a destination, trigger a security negotiation that must take place before traffic is sent.

You must have a filter to cover any traffic for which the associated rule applies. For example, if Computer A always wants to exchange data securely with Computer B:

- In order to send secured data to Computer B, Computer A's IPSec policy must have a filter for any outbound packets going to Computer B.
- In order to receive secured data from Computer A, Computer B's IPSec policy must have a filter for any inbound packets from Computer A.

A filter contains the following parameters:

- The source and destination address of the IP packet. These can be configured from a very granular level, such as a single IP address, to a global level that encompasses an entire subnet, or network.
- The protocol over which the packet is being transferred. This defaults to cover all protocols in the TCP/IP protocol suite. However, it can be configured to an individual protocol level to meet special requirements, including custom protocol numbers.
- The source and destination port of the protocol for TCP and UDP. This also defaults to cover all ports, but can be configured to apply to only packets sent or received on a specific protocol port.

Filter Actions

The *filter action* sets the security requirements for the communication. These requirements are specified in a list of security methods contained in the filter action, including which algorithms, security protocols, and key properties are to be used.

A filter action can also be configured as:

- A pass-through policy: one that does not allow secure communication. IPSec simply ignores traffic in this case. This is appropriate for traffic that cannot be secured because the remote computer is not IPSec-enabled, traffic that is not sensitive enough to require protection, or traffic that provides its own security (for example, Kerberos, SSL, PPTP protocols).
- A blocking policy: to stop communication from a rogue computer.
- A policy that negotiates for security but still enables communication with non-IPSec-enabled computers. A filter action can be configured to use fall back to clear. If you need to configure a filter action like this, limit the IP Filter List to a minimal scope. However, it should be used with extreme caution: any communications affected by that policy could result in data being sent without protection if negotiation fails for any reason. If the initiator of an IKE negotiation receives a reply from the responder, then the negotiation does not allow fallback to clear.

Connection Types

Connections refers to anything you create in your Windows 2000 **Network Connections** console on the computer.

Designating a connection type for each rule allows you to determine what computer connections (interfaces) are affected by your IPSec policy—dial-up adapters or network cards. Each rule has a connection property that designates whether the rule applies to multiple connections or just one connection. For example, you might want rules that require extremely high security to only apply to dial-up connections, not to local area network (LAN) connections.

Authentication

A rule can specify multiple authentication methods to ensure a common method is found when negotiating with a peer.

IPSec supports all of the following authentication methods:

- The Kerberos v5 authentication protocol is the default authentication technology in Windows 2000. This authentication method can be used for any clients running the Kerberos v5 protocol (whether or not they are Windows-based clients) that are members of a trusted domain. For more information about the Windows 2000-based Kerberos v5 authentication protocol, see "Authentication" in the *Windows 2000 Distributed Systems Guide*.
- Use a public key certificate in situations that include Internet access, remote access to corporate resources, external business partner communications, any L2TP-based communications, or computers that do not run the Kerberos v5 authentication protocol. This requires that at least one trusted Certificate Authority (CA) has been configured. For information about the Windows 2000 public key infrastructure and certificates, see the *Windows 2000 Distributed Systems Guide*.

  Windows 2000 IKE has basic compatibility with several certificate systems, including those offered by Microsoft, Entrust, VeriSign, and Netscape. IKE uses the Cryptographic API version 2.0 (CAPIv2) functionality of Windows 2000 for processing certificates. IKE does not require a specific type of certificate, only that it be resident in the computer account, have a valid signature, a valid trust chain, and is used within the period of validity.

  Certificates obtained from the Microsoft Certificate Services with the advanced option set for **strong private key protection** will not work for IKE authentication. You must select the certificate authority that issued your computer a certificate, or its issuing root certificate authority (CA).

Coordination with the administrator of the remote computer is required to agree on certificate configuration. Otherwise, IKE negotiation may fail. For detailed information about certificates, CA configuration, and certificate revocation see the chapters under "Distributed Security" in the *Distributed Systems Guide*.

- A *pre-shared key* can be specified. This is a shared, secret key that is previously agreed upon by two users. It is quick to use and does not require the client to run the Kerberos v5 protocol or have a public key certificate. Both parties must manually configure their IPSec policies to use this pre-shared key. This can be used on a limited basis when Kerberos- or certificate-based authentication is not available. Note that this key is for authentication protection only; it is not used to encrypt the data. See the section titled "Best Practices" later in this chapter.

  Microsoft does not recommend frequent use of pre-shared key authentication, because the authentication key is stored, unprotected, in the IPSec policy. Pre-shared key methodology is provided only for interoperability purposes and to adhere to the IPSec standards set forth by the IETF. To safely use this authentication method, the policy must be restricted to administrator-only read and write access, encrypted for privacy when communicated between the domain controller and domain member computers, and restricted to system-only read access on each computer.

  Using Kerberos or certificate-based authentication is recommended, to avoid security risks associated with pre-shared key authentication.

IPSec Planning

The following sections can be used as general guidelines or examples when planning your IPSec deployment.

Best Practices

The Windows 2000 IP Security Policy Management snap-in greatly simplifies deployment. To take advantage of this and to avoid problematic implementations, you should:

- Evaluate the type of information being sent over your network: is it sensitive financial data, proprietary information, or electronic mail? Some departments might require a higher level of security than the majority of the enterprise because of the nature of their function.
- Determine where your information is stored, how it routes through the network, and from what computers access can be gained. This provides information about the speed, capacity, and utilization of the network prior to IPSec implementation, which is helpful for performance optimization.

- Evaluate your vulnerability to the network attacks discussed at the beginning of this chapter.
- Design and document an enterprise-wide network security plan. Take into account the following:
  - The general security framework of Windows 2000, including the Active Directory model and how security is applied to Group Policy objects.
  - Your likely communication scenarios: intranet, remote access, extranets for business partners, communication between sites (router to router).
  - The level of security necessary for each scenario. For example, you might decide only Internet communications require confidentiality.
- Design, create, and test the IPSec policies for each scenario in your plan. This allows you to clarify and refine what policies and policy structures are necessary.

Establishing an IPSec Security Plan

Implementing IPSec, whether for a large domain or a small workgroup, means finding a balance between making information easily available to the largest number of users, and protecting sensitive information from unauthorized access.

Finding the proper balance requires:

- Assessing the risk and determining the appropriate level of security for your organization.
- Identifying valuable information.
- Defining security policies that use your risk management criteria and protect the identified information.
- Determining how the policies can best be implemented within the existing organization.
- Ensuring that management and technology requirements are in place.
- Providing all users with both secure and efficient access to the appropriate resources, according to their needs.

Security considerations are also influenced by the operational context of the computer to which they apply. For example, the security required may differ depending on whether the computer is a domain controller, Web server, remote access server, file server, database server, intranet or remote client.

The Windows 2000 security framework is designed to fulfill the most stringent security requirements. However, software alone is less effective without careful planning and assessment, effective security guidelines, enforcement, auditing, and sensible security policy design and assignment.

There is no exact definition of the measures that define standard security. These can vary widely, depending on an organization's policies and infrastructures. The following security levels can be considered as a general basis for planning your IPSec deployment.

Minimal Security

Computers do not exchange sensitive data. IPSec is not active by default. No administrative action to disable IPSec is required.

Standard Security

Computers, especially file servers, are used to store valuable data. Security must be balanced so it does not become a barrier to legitimate users trying to perform their tasks. Windows 2000 provides predefined IPSec policies that secure data, but do not necessarily require the highest level of security: Client (Respond Only) and Server (Request Security). These, or similar custom policies, optimize efficiency without compromising security.

High Security

Computers that contain highly sensitive data are at risk for data theft, or accidental or malicious disruption of the system; especially in remote dial-up scenarios, or any public network communications. The predefined policy, Secure Server (Require Security), requires IPSec protection for all traffic sent or received with the exception of the initial unsecured connection request. Secure Server (Require Security) includes strong confidentiality and integrity algorithms, Perfect Forward Secrecy, key lifetimes and limits, and strong Diffie-Hellman Groups. Unsecured communication, due to non-IPSec-aware computers or failed security negotiation, is blocked.

Special IPSec Considerations

The following considerations help simplify administration of IPSec policies:

IP Filter Lists

Some recommendations for IP Filter Lists:

- Try to use general filters if you want to cover a group of computers with only one filter. For example, in the Filter Properties dialog box, use **Any IP Address** or an IP subnet address rather than specifying a specific computer's source and destination IP address.
- Define filters that allow you to group and secure traffic from logically associated segments of your network.

- The order in which the filters apply is not related to the ordering displayed when viewing the IPSec policy. All filters are simultaneously retrieved by the IPSec Policy Agent during system startup, and are processed and sorted from most specific to least specific. There is no guarantee that a specific filter will be applied before a general filter until all the filters have been processed, and that may affect some communications behavior during system startup.

Filter Actions

Some recommendations for Filter Actions:

- If you need to prevent communication with rogue computers, ensure that security is not negotiated for non-essential data or when peers are not IPSec-enabled, make use of Filter Actions such as blocking or pass-through policies.
- When configuring custom security methods, only set the ESP confidentiality selection to **None** when a higher layer protocol will provide data encryption.
- For remote communication scenarios (including IPSec tunneling), consider a list of security methods that specifies high levels of security, such as 3DES only, short key lifetimes (less than 50 MB), and Perfect Forward Secrecy for the master and session keys. This helps protect against known-key attacks.

Remote Access Communications

Some recommendations for remote access communications:

- The list of authentication methods must include certificates, and at least one computer-level public key certificate must be configured on each peer (remote client or remote access server). Windows 2000 domain controllers can be configured to auto-enroll domain members in a certificate authority.
- If you require the ability to remotely administer computers in your enterprise, you must add a rule to your active IPSec policy to prevent RPC TCP traffic from being blocked when it comes from the internal network. (This type of traffic is used by the remote access configuration tools in Windows 2000). For example:
  - The IP Filter List in the rule should specify an outgoing address of the corporate subnet (the location of your administrative console), and an incoming address of the managed computer's internal IP address. The protocol type should be set to TCP.
  - The Filter Action in the rule should have **Accept unsecured communication** and **Allow communication with non-IPSec-enabled computers** enabled.

SNMP

If a computer is running an SNMP service, you must add a rule to prevent SNMP messages from being blocked:

- The IP Filter List should specify the source and destination addresses of the SNMP management systems and agents. The Protocol type should be set to UDP, to and from ports 161 and 162. This requires two filters: one for UDP, to and from port 161, and the other for UDP, to and from port 162.
- Set the Filter Action to **Permit**, which blocks negotiation for security and passes through any traffic that matches the IP Filter List.

Security Gateways

For a security gateway, firewall, proxy server, router or any server that is an access point from the intranet to the outside world, special filtering must be enabled on that computer to ensure that packets secured with IPSec are not rejected. At a minimum, the following input and output filters must be defined for the Internet interface on the computer:

Input Filters

- IP Protocol ID of 51 (0x33) for inbound IPSec Authentication Header traffic.
- IP Protocol ID of 50 (0x32) for inbound IPSec Encapsulating Security Protocol traffic.
- UDP port 500 (0x1F4) for inbound IKE negotiation traffic.

Output Filters

- IP Protocol ID of 51 (0x33) for outbound IPSec Authentication Header traffic.
- IP Protocol ID of 50 (0x32) for outbound IPSec Encapsulating Security Protocol traffic.
- UDP port 500 (0x1F4) for outbound IKE negotiation traffic.

DHCP, DNS, and WINS Services; Domain Controllers

Before enabling IPSec for computers functioning as a DHCP, DNS, WINS server, or domain controller, determine if all the clients are also IPSec-capable. Otherwise, if IPSec policy is not configured to allow fall back to clear or to permit unsecured traffic to accommodate older clients, secure negotiation might erroneously fail, and access to these network services might be blocked.

Predefined Configurations

Windows 2000 provides a set of predefined IPSec configurations. By default, all predefined policies are designed for computers that are members of a Windows 2000 domain. The predefined policies, filter lists, and filter actions provided are not intended for immediate use. Rather, they are intended to indicate, for deployment testing purposes, the different behaviors that are possible with different policy settings.

Following are descriptions of Windows 2000 predefined policies.

Client (Respond Only)

This policy is for computers that (for the majority of the time) do not secure communications. For example, intranet clients may not require IPSec except when requested by another computer. This policy enables the computer on which it is active to appropriately respond to requests for secured communications. It contains a Default Response rule, which enables negotiation with computers requesting IPSec. Only the requested protocol and port traffic for the communication is secured.

Server (Request Security)

This policy is for computers that (for the majority of the time) secure communications, such as servers that transmit sensitive data. This policy enables the computer to accept unsecured traffic, but always attempt to secure additional communications by requesting security from the original sender. This policy allows the entire communication to be unsecured if the other computer is not IPSec-enabled.

Secure Server (Require Security)

This policy is for computers that always require secure communications, such as a server that transmits highly sensitive data. This policy allows unsecured, incoming communication requests, but always responds with secured communications. Unsecured communications beyond the intial incoming connection request is not permitted.

Predefined Rules

Like the predefined policies, the Default Response rule is provided for activation without further action, modification, or as a template for defining custom rules. It is added to each new policy you create, but not automatically activated. It is for any computer that does not require security, but must be able to appropriately respond when another computer requests secured communications.

Predefined Filter Actions

Like the predefined rules, these are provided for activation without further action, modification, or as a template for defining custom Filter Actions. They are available for activation in any new or existing rule:

- Require Security

  High security. Unsecured communication is not allowed except initial incoming communication requests.

- Request Security (Optional)

  Medium to low security. Unsecured communication is allowed, to enable communication with computers that do not or cannot negotiate IPSec.

Common IPSec Example

This describes a deployment example for a common IPSec configuration. While your network configuration might be different than what is discussed here, the basic concepts apply.

Providing security for groups that normally exchange highly sensitive information often required segmenting the intranet. Groups of computers on different, physical segments prevents security violations. IPSec provides protection while still allowing groups of secure computers to reside within the same physical intranet.

Figure 8.14 represents a domain comprised of computers in a financial department. Most intranet clients do not need to communicate securely. However, a group of servers in the network store highly sensitive information that some intranet clients need to access. All computers have computer accounts in the Active Directory.

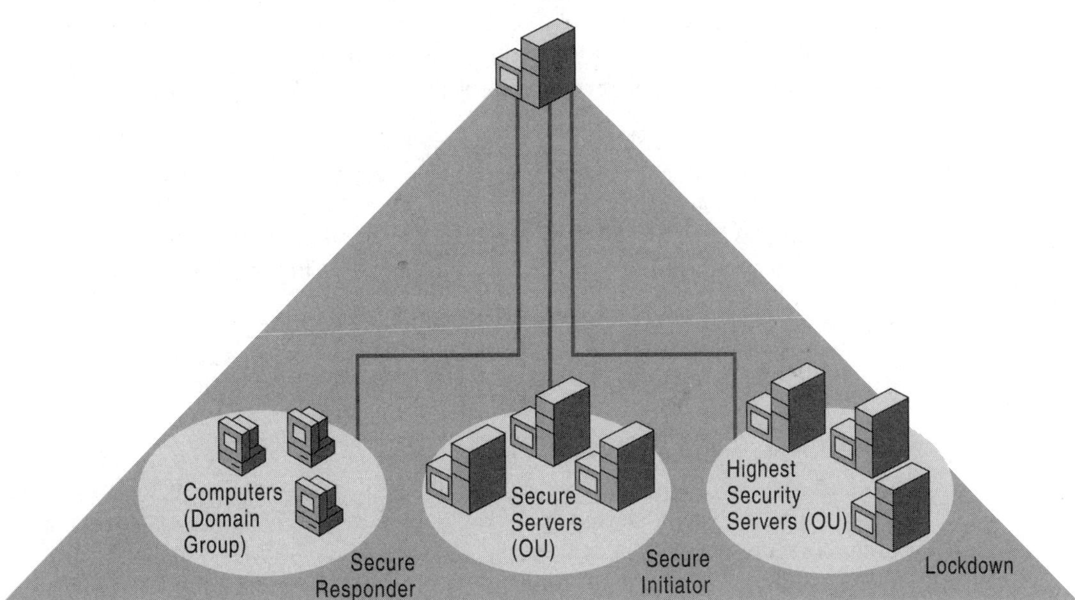

Figure 8.14 An Intranet Domain with End-to-End Communications

The computers accounts are grouped into Active Directory Organizational Units (OU) for security reasons. This enables the appropriate assignment of IPSec policies, based on the function of the computers:

- Servers that store and exchange highly sensitive information belong to the Highest Security Servers OU.
- Servers that might use unsecured communication to enable data exchange with non-Windows 2000 computers in the domain belong to the Secure Servers OU.
- Clients that require the ability to appropriately respond when secure communications are required. These are in the default Computers group.

Grouping computers into OUs enables the assignment of IPSec policies to only those that require IPSec. It also allows the appropriate level of security to be assigned, avoiding excessive security overhead. In this scenario, the Active Directory stores the IPSec policies for all computers.

High security between the clients and the domain controller is unnecessary: Kerberos-related exchanges between the clients and the domain controller are already encrypted, and the IPSec policy transmission from the Active Directory to the member computers is protected by Windows 2000 LDAP security.

In this example, IPSec should be combined with access control security. User permissions are still a necessary part of using security to protect access to the file shares available on any of the Highest Security or Secure Servers. IPSec secures the network level traffic, so that attackers can not interpret or modify the data. For information about setting user permissions, see the Windows 2000 Help.

Policies Required

The following are the types of required IPSec policies to consider.

Computers: Client (Respond Only)

Domain member computers receive the IPSec policy assigned to the domain security policy. The predefined policy, Client (Respond Only), is assigned to the domain group security policy to ensure these computers can respond as needed to requests for secure communications.

Secure Servers: Server (Request Security)

Computer accounts in this OU generally communicate securely, but also might need to communicate with computers that cannot respond to secure requests. Assigning the predefined policy, Server (Request Security), enables initiation of secure communications when necessary, but also initiates communication with non-Windows 2000 legacy systems that might be part of the domain.

Highest Security Servers: Secure Server (Require Security)

Computer accounts in this OU do not communicate with any computers that do not or cannot initiate and successfully negotiate security. These servers store and transmit highly sensitive data. The predefined policy, Secure Server (Require Security), is assigned to ensure that outgoing communication never falls back to unsecured if negotiations fail or the other computer is not IPSec-capable. Even communication with the domain controller is negotiated and secured. Due to the strictness of this policy, you might have to add exemptions for special traffic types such as SNMP traffic. For information about altering IPSec policy, see "Special IPSec Considerations" earlier in this chapter.

Troubleshooting

This section contains methods for determining the cause of IPSec-secured communication problems, and tools that can verify IPSec-secured communications.

Note Failure in core networking services, such as DHCP, DNS, and WINS, can cause unpredictable IPSec failures.

General Troubleshooting

The following are possible reasons for secured communication failures and suggested resolutions for these failures.

Remote Communications Fail

If you are a remote client, and only secured communication attempts are failing, review "Best Practices" earlier in this chapter and its remote communications scenarios to verify that your authentication method is correct, and you have compatible security methods with the remote access server.

Intranet Communications Fail

If two computers have been communicating successfully and secured communication between them suddenly fails, do the following:

1. Ping the other computer to verify the computer is still on the network. You should receive a message indicated IPSec is being negotiated. If you do not, check to see if the list of acceptable security methods in your Filter Action has changed since the last communication with that computer. The old security associations that are based on previous security methods might still be in effect. If so, try the next step. Note that if you are using default policies, unmodified, ping will not be blocked by IPSec. However, if you have created custom policies and have not exempted the ICMP protocol used by the Ping tool, it may erroneously fail.
2. Restart the policy agent. This clears up any old security associations. For information about how to restart the policy agent, see "Only IPSec-Secured Communication Fails" later in this chapter.

Other Causes of Failure

- Try a policy integrity check to verify that changes made to any policy settings have been updated in Active Directory or the registry. See the Windows 2000 Online Help for more information about testing policy integrity.
- If you have removed an existing computer from a domain or have changed to using local policy instead of Active Directory policy, you might have to restart the policy agent. Otherwise, the policy agent continues to attempt to reach Active Directory and does not use registry policy.
- Multihomed computers have multiple default routes, which might cause problems.

▶ **To specify a default route**

1. At a command prompt, type:

   ```
   route print
   ```

   and press ENTER.
2. Verify whether more than one route line has a destination of 0.0.0.0 and whether there is more than one route line with the lowest metric (generally 1).
3. If either is true, delete one of the default routes or verify that one of the default routes has a metric value that is lower than all the others.

Solving Basic IPSec Problems

These are some methods for resolving basic IPSec-related problems.

IPSec Policy Mismatch Error

If negotiations are failing, it might be due to incompatible IPSec policy settings. Follow these steps to correct the problem:

1. Run Event Viewer and examine the Security Log. Recent events include attempts at IKE negotiation with a description of their success or failure.
2. Check the security log on the computer specified by the IP address in the log message.
3. Determine the cause of policy mismatch and fix:
   - Verify that authentication methods are compatible.
   - Verify that there is at least one compatible security method.

"Bad SPI" Messages in Event Viewer

This error might occur if a key lifetime value is set too low, or the SA has expired but the sender continues to transmit data to the receiver. It is a benign error, and only if a large amount of these messages are being logged should notice be taken. To determine and correct the problem:

1. Run IPSecMon.
2. Examine the number of re-keys.

If the number of re-keys is very large compared to the amount of time the connections have been active, set the key lifetimes in the policy to be longer. Good values for high-traffic Ethernet connections are greater than 50 MB and greater than five minutes.

This might not entirely eliminate bad SPIs, but should significantly reduce the occurrences.

Verifying IPSec Secured Communications

This section covers tools and procedures that can be used to determine if IPSec is active and to make sure IPSec-secured communication is successful.

Using Ping to Verify a Valid Network Connection

This procedure determines if standard, unsecured communication can take place. This allows you to separate network problems from IPSec issues.

1. Open a command prompt window.
2. Type

   ```
   ping <IP address>
   ```

   where *<IP address>* is the IP address of the computer with which you are trying to communicate.

You should receive four replies to the ping. This verifies that you can communicate with your partner. Note that if you are using the default policies, unmodified, ping will not be blocked by IPSec. However, if you have created custom policies and have not exempted the ICMP protocol used by Ping, it may erroneously fail.

If you do not receive a response from the **ping** command, see "TCP/IP Troubleshooting" in this book for more information about determining the problem.

Verifying Policy Has Been Assigned

You can use the following procedures to verify that the assigned policy is active.

IPSec Monitor

1. Click **Start**, then **Run**.
2. Type:

```
ipsecmon <computername>
```

When IPSec Monitor opens, you will see a message in the lower-right corner indicating whether IPSec is enabled on the computer. For IPSec to be enabled, a policy must be assigned. However, no policies are listed in the IPSec Monitor Security Association list unless an SA with another computer is currently active.

Event Viewer

The IPSec Policy Agent makes entries to the System Log to indicate the source of its policy. It also indicates the polling interval as specified by the active policy for checking for policy changes in the Active Directory. Administrators who edit the active IPSec policy on the local computer cause the changes to take effect immediately.

You can also see whether the computer is using local policy or policy from the Active Directory by viewing the Event Log. Specifically, examine the System Log informational entry by the IPSec Policy Agent.

TCP/IP Properties

By displaying the properties for Internet Protocol (TCP/IP), you can see the active IPSec policy. If the computer is running local IPSec policy, the name is displayed in an editable form. If the computer is running policy assigned through the Active Directory Group Policy, the name and dialog is displayed as grayed out, and is not editable. See Windows 2000 Help for instructions on displaying TCP/IP properties.

IPSec Monitoring Tool

The IPSec monitor can confirm whether your secured communications are successful, by displaying the active security associations on local or remote computers.

For example, you can use IPSec Monitor to determine whether there has been a pattern of authentication or security association failures, possibly indicating incompatible security policy settings.

The IPSec monitor can be run on the local computer or it can be run remotely if you have a network connection to the remote computer.

▶ **To start the IPSec monitor**

1. Click **Start**, and then click **Run**.
2. Type:

   ipsecmon *<computername>*

3. Use the **Options** button to set the refresh rate.

An entry is displayed for each active security association. The information contained in each entry includes the name of the active IPSec policy, the active Filter Action and IP Filter List (including details of the active filter), and the tunnel endpoint (if one was specified).

It can also provide statistics to aid in performance tuning and troubleshooting, including the following statistics:

- The number and type of active security associations.
- The total number of master and session keys. Successful IPSec security associations initially cause one master key and one session key. Subsequent key regenerations are shown as additional session keys.
- The total number of confidential (ESP) or authenticated (ESP or AH) bytes sent or received.

  Note Because ESP provides authenticity and confidentiality, both counters are incremented.

- The total number of soft associations.

The refresh rate is the only configurable option. By default, the statistics update every 15 seconds. The statistics are accumulated with each communication that uses IPSec.

Only IPSec-Secured Communication Fails

This section contains procedures for determining and correcting possible reasons for IPSec-secured communications.

Broken Links in Policy Components

Because Active Directory treats the last information saved as current, if multiple administrators are editing a policy it is possible to break the links between policy components. For example:

- Policy A uses Filter A.

- Policy B uses Filter B.

  This means that Filter A has a link to Policy A, and Filter B links to Policy B.
- Bob edits Policy A, and adds a rule that uses Filter C.
- At the same time, Alice edits Policy B from a different location, and adds a rule that also uses Filter C.

  If both save the changes simultaneously, it is possible for Filter C to link to both Policy A and Policy B. Because that is unlikely, if Policy A is saved last, it overwrites the link from Filter C to Policy B. Filter C only links to Policy A. This causes problems when Filter C is modified. Only Policy A picks up the new changes; Policy B does not.

The policy integrity check eliminates this problem by verifying the links in all IPSec policies. It is a good idea to run the integrity check after making modifications to a policy.

▶ **To check policy integrity**

1. Start the **IP Security Management snap-in**.
2. Click **Action**.
3. Point to **Task**, and click **Policy integrity check**.

All the IPSec policies listed in the console are checked. If any filters or settings are invalid, an error message is displayed.

Restarting the Policy Agent

Restarting the policy agent might be necessary to clear up old SAs, or to force a policy download from the Active Directory to domain clients. The computer must be restarted in order to properly restart the policy agent.

The restart of the policy agent also forces the restart of the IPSec driver.

Use Event Viewer to determine possible causes of failure if the policy agent does not start.

Reinstalling IPSec Components

If the files necessary for IPSec components, such as IKE, the IPSec policy agent, or the IPSec Driver have been removed or deleted, you can reinstall the IPSec components by removing and reinstalling TCP/IP. The IPSec components are reinstalled as part of the Internet Protocol installation. For procedural information on how to remove and reinstall the Internet Protocol, see the Windows 2000 Help.

Additional Resources

- For more information about IPSec RFCs, Internet Drafts, and other IPSec-related links, see the International Engineering Task Force (IETF) link on the Web Resources page at http://windows.microsoft.com/windows2000/reskit/webresources.

  Refer to the following IPSec RFCs:

  - RFC 2085: *HMAC-MD5 IP Authentication with Replay Prevention*
  - RFC 2104: *HMAC: Keyed Hashing for Message Authentication*
  - RFC 2401: *Security Architecture for the Internet Protocol*
  - RFC 2402: *IP Authentication Header (AH)*
  - RFC 2403: *The Use of HMAC-MD5-96 within ESP and AH*
  - RFC 2404: *The Use of HMAC-SHA-1-96 within ESP and AH*
  - RFC 2405: *The ESP DES-CBC Cipher Algorithm with Explicit IV*
  - RFC 2406: *IP Encapsulating Security Payload (ESP)*
  - RFC 2407: *The Internet IP Security Domain of Interpretation for IKE*
  - RFC 2410: *The NULL Encryption Algorithm and Its Use with IPSec*
  - RFC 2411: *IP Security Document Roadmap*
  - RFC 2451: *The ESP CBC-Mode Cipher Algorithms*

  RFCs are a continually evolving group of documents. Refer to the IETF web page to obtain the most current RFCs and Internet Drafts.

- For more information about Windows 2000 security deployment, see the Microsoft Security Advisor link on the Web Resources page at http://windows.microsoft.com/windows2000/reskit/webresources.
- For more information about Windows 2000 networking and communications, see the Microsoft Networking and Communication link on the Web Resources page at http://windows.microsoft.com/windows2000/reskit/webresources.
- For more information about the standards and technology for IPSec, as well as export regulations, see the National Institute of Standards and Technology Computer Security Resource Clearinghouse link on the Web Resources page at http://windows.microsoft.com/windows2000/reskit/webresources.

CHAPTER 9

Quality of Service

Quality of Service (QoS) facilitates the deployment of media-rich applications, such as video conferencing and Internet Protocol (IP) telephony, without adversely affecting network throughput. Microsoft® Windows® 2000 QoS also improves the performance of mission-critical software such as Enterprise Resource Planning (ERP) applications. Windows 2000 supports the QoS Admission Control Service, a policy mechanism that offers the ability to centrally designate how, when, and by whom network resources are used on a per-subnet basis. QoS is an emerging technology, with standards that are being developed and revised based on customer feedback and industry-wide cooperation.

This chapter focuses on the Windows 2000 deployment of QoS and the QoS Admission Control Service. These technologies are based on standards created by the Internet Engineering Task Force (IETF).

In This Chapter

Related Information in the Resource Kit

- For more information about Kerberos, see the *Microsoft Windows 2000 Server Resource Kit Distributed Systems Guide*.
- For more information about Active Directory policy, see the *Microsoft Windows 2000 Server Resource Kit Distributed Systems Guide.*
- For more information about general networking concepts, see "Introduction to TCP/IP" and "Windows 2000 TCP/IP" in this book.

What is QoS?

In a general context, quality of service is a set of methods and processes a service-based organization implements to maintain a specific level of quality. In the context of networking, Quality of Service (QoS) refers to a combination of mechanisms that cooperatively provide a specific quality level to application traffic crossing a network or multiple, disparate networks. Implementing QoS means combining a set of IETF-defined technologies designed to alleviate the problems caused by shared network resources and finite bandwidth.

QoS provides two distinct benefits:

- A mechanism for applications to request service quality parameters, such as low network delay.
- Higher levels of administrative control over congested subnet bandwidth resources.

Implementing QoS enables administrators to make the most efficient use of subnet bandwidth when deploying resource-intensive applications. A QoS-enabled network provides guarantees for sufficient resources, giving a congested, shared network segment the level of service approaching that of a private network. Different classes of applications have varying degrees of tolerance for delay in network throughput. A QoS guarantee ensures the ability of an application to transmit data in an acceptable way, in an acceptable time frame so that the transmission is not delayed, distorted, or lost.

To uphold such guarantees, QoS requires cooperation from the sending and receiving hosts (end nodes), the link layer (OSI model layer 2) devices (switches), the network layer (OSI model layer 3) devices (routers), and any wide area network (WAN) links in between. Without QoS, each of these network devices treat all data equally and provide service on a first-come, first-served basis. In addition, for an application to make use of QoS it must have some level of QoS awareness, so that it can request bandwidth and other resources from the network.

The efficient use and allocation of bandwidth is critical for productivity. Real-time applications, media-rich applications, and Enterprise Resource Planning applications require a large amount of uninterrupted bandwidth for transmission to be successful, and therefore can strain existing network resources. When traffic is heavy, overall performance degrades and results in traffic delay (such as latency and jitter) and packet loss. This degradation causes problems with video conferencing, real-time audio, and interactive communication, causing distortion of voices and images. Because media-rich applications use large quantities of bandwidth, traditional mission-critical applications suffer from the lack of available resources. QoS provides a delivery system for network traffic that guarantees limited delays and data loss.

It is important to realize that QoS cannot create bandwidth; it can only efficiently partition bandwidth based on different parameters.

Windows 2000 QoS Components

The Windows 2000 QoS architecture is built upon a tightly-integrated set of industry standard protocols, services and mechanisms that control access to network resources, classify and schedule network traffic, and protocols that signal network devices to apply QoS by handling specific traffic flows with priority. Figure 9.1 illustrates the Windows 2000 QoS architecture.

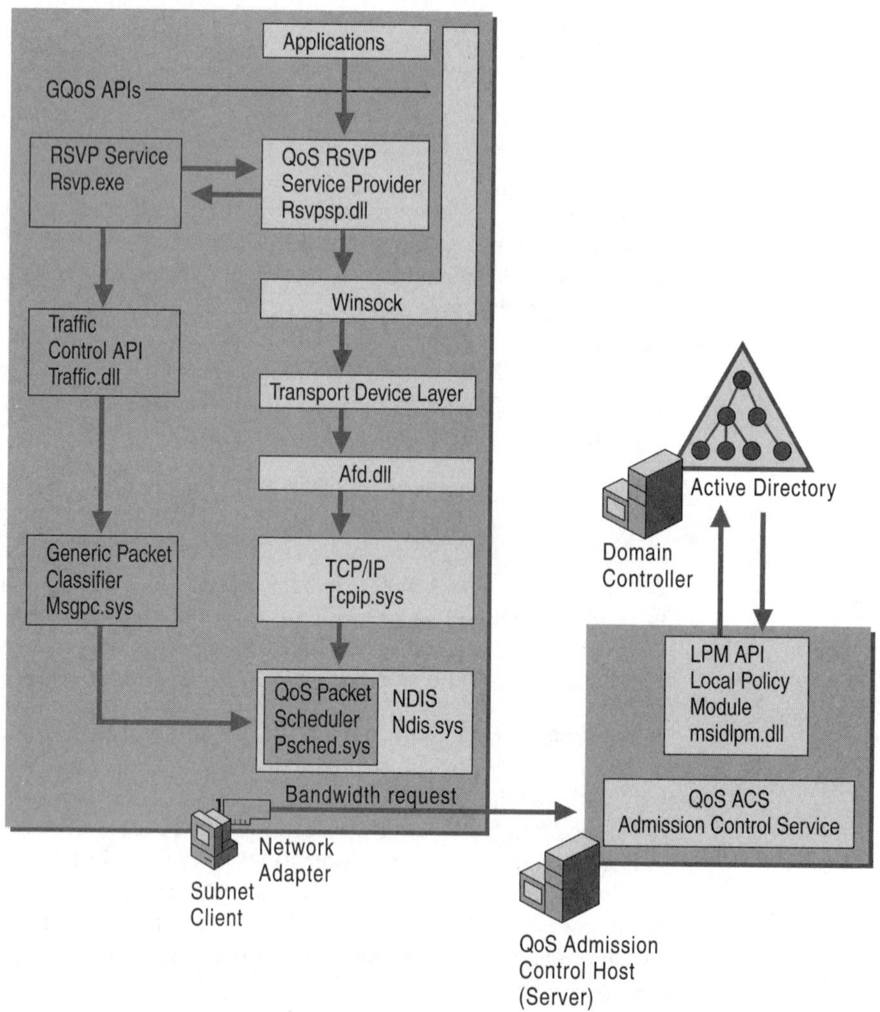

Figure 9.1 Windows 2000 QoS Components

All of these components work together seamlessly to provide QoS on a network. Appearing as shaded boxes in this Figure are the Windows 2000 QoS components. Not pictured in Figure 9.1 are the elements in the network infrastructure required to fully guarantee QoS end-to-end. The OSI model layer 2 and layer 3 devices in between the end nodes (that is, sender and receiver) must also support QoS. Otherwise, traffic receives standard network treatment (best-effort delivery) on that segment.

Generic QoS (GQoS) API (part of Winsock 2.0) Windows 2000 QoS is designed with a Generic QoS API, an abstract interface to the QoS technologies in Windows 2000. Application programmers can use GQoS to specify or request bandwidth requirements particular to their application for diverse media such as Ethernet or IP over Asynchronous Transfer Mode (ATM).

RSVP SP (Rsvpsp.dll) When QoS is requested, GQoS calls upon the services of the underlying QoS service provider, Resource Reservation Protocol Service Provider (RSVP SP). The RSVP SP invokes RSVP to signal all network devices along the data path of the bandwidth requirements, traffic control, and QoS Admission Control support.

RSVP Service (Rsvp.exe) Resource Reservation Protocol (RSVP) is an IETF-defined signaling protocol that carries QoS requests for priority bandwidth through the network. RSVP bridges the gap between the application, the operating system, and the media-specific QoS mechanisms. RSVP sends messages in a format that is media-independent, so that end-to-end QoS is possible over networks that combine different types of low-layer network devices.

Traffic Control (Traffic.dll) Traffic control creates and regulates data flows by using defined QoS parameters. It also facilitates the creation of filters to direct selected packets through a data flow. The capabilities of traffic control are accessed via the Traffic Control API. Traffic control is called upon by the GQoS API.

Generic Packet Classifier (Msgpc.sys) The Generic Packet Classifier determines the service class to which an individual packet belongs. Packets are then queued by service level. The queues are managed by the QoS Packet Scheduler.

QoS Packet Scheduler (Psched.sys) The QoS Packet Scheduler enforces QoS parameters for a particular data flow. Traffic is marked with a particular priority by the QoS Packet Scheduler. The QoS Packet Scheduler then determines the delivery schedule of each packet queue and handles competition between queued packets that need simultaneous access to the network. Packets are marked with an 802.1p priority for prioritization in layer 2 devices, and a Differentiated Class of Service for prioritization in layer 3 devices.

QoS Admission Control Service (QoS ACS) QoS ACS manages network resources on congested, shared network segments (subnets). It is not required to implement the QoS ACS on every subnet; the highest benefit is realized from implementing the QoS ACS on congested segments. The QoS ACS provides a control point for bandwidth requests, determining if the necessary network resources are currently available, and whether or not the user has the necessary permissions to request that amount of bandwidth and service.

Local Policy Module (Msidlpm.dll) The Local Policy Module (LPM) is a component of the QoS ACS that provides a policy enforcement point (PEP) and policy decision point (PDP). The LPM included in Windows 2000 provides the QoS ACS with a means of retrieving policy information from the Active Directory™ directory service. The QoS ACS invokes the LPM DLL Msidlpm.dll when a RSVP message with a Windows 2000 Kerberos ticket is detected. The LPM extracts the user name from the RSVP message and looks up the user's admission control policy in Active Directory. An LPM API is also included.

How QoS Works

This section describes how these components work together in a common QoS scenario. Figure 9.2 illustrates a common QoS deployment.

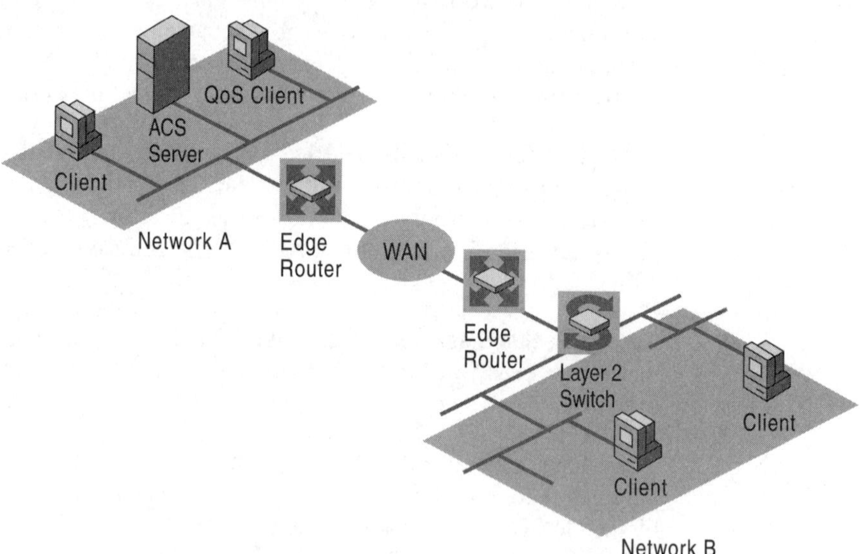

Figure 9.2 How QoS Works

1. A client on Network A requests QoS. The application used to transmit data is QoS-enabled. The application requests QoS from the RSVP SP.
2. The RSVP SP requests the RSVP service to signal the necessary bandwidth requirements, and notifies traffic control that QoS has been requested for this flow. Traffic is currently sent at a best-effort delivery level.
3. An RSVP message is sent to the QoS ACS server, requesting a reservation. Note that it is RSVP messages that are passed to the QoS ACS, not the data packets which are ultimately transmitted from sender to receiver.
4. The QoS ACS server verifies that enough network resources are available to meet the QoS level requested, and that the user has the policy rights to request that amount of bandwidth. The Local Policy Module uses the Kerberos ticket in the RSVP request to authenticate the user identity and look up the user policy in Active Directory. Note that the QoS ACS can verify resources for the sender, receiver, or both.
5. After verification is complete, the QoS ACS server approves the request and logically allocates bandwidth. The QoS ACS server forwards the request toward the receiver (client) on Network B.
6. When the RSVP request passes the edge router on Network A, the router keeps track of the resources (bandwidth) that are requested. The bandwidth is not yet physically allocated (RSVP is a receiver-initiated protocol and bandwidth can only be reserved by the receiver). The same process is repeated on the edge router for Network B.
7. The request is passed through each network device in the data path before it arrives at the receiver. The receiving client indicates it wants to receive the data and returns an RSVP message requesting a reservation.
8. When the receiver's request for bandwidth passes through the edge router on Network B, it already has cached the information about the requested bandwidth (from the sender's request). The router matches the receiver request with the sender's request, and installs the reservation by physically granting the bandwidth. The same process is repeated on the edge router for Network A.
9. The reservation is sent back to the sender. The layer 3 network devices (the edge routers) are capable of approving and allocating the physical bandwidth. The reservation simply passes through the layer 2 switch.
10. During this process, the traffic is sent by traffic control on the sender as best-effort. Upon receiving the reservation message, the traffic control on the sending host begins the process of classifying, marking, and scheduling the packets to accommodate the QoS level requested. The QoS Packet Scheduler performs the priority marking for RSVP, 802.1p for prioritization on layer 2 devices (illustrated here as the switch), and for Differentiated Class of Service for layer 3 devices (illustrated here as edge routers).

11. The QoS Packet Scheduler begins sending the prioritized traffic. The data is handled as priority by all devices along the data path, providing greater speed of throughput and a more successful transmission to the client on Network B.

Note that this example is a general description. Variations are possible depending on network topology as well as the presence of different network devices.

Invoking QoS

The Generic QoS API (GQoS) and the QoS service provider simplify the deployment of QoS by providing an application interface and support for applications that request QoS from the network.

Generic QoS API

The Generic QoS API provides a standard interface for developers and a mechanism for adding new QoS components without completely redesigning existing QoS-enabled applications. GQoS is part of the Windows Sockets 2.0 (Winsock2) API. This enables applications to invoke QoS without needing a full knowledge of the QoS mechanisms available or the specific underlying network media.

Application programmers can use the GQoS API to specify or request bandwidth requirements particular to their application, such as preventing latency when streaming audio. They can also use the GQoS API to prioritize traffic generated by mission-critical applications. GQoS is abstract and requires only very simple directives from the application. Extensions to the API provide additional control. Applications requesting QoS should utilize the GQoS API.

The Windows 2000 Software Development Kit provides the necessary conceptual and reference materials for using the GQoS API.

QoS Service Provider (RSVP SP, RSVP Service)

When QoS is requested, GQoS invokes the services of the underlying QoS service provider (RSVP SP). The RSVP SP provides the following services:

- RSVP (signaling)

  The RSVP SP initiates and terminates all RSVP signaling on behalf of applications by communicating with the RSVP service (Rsvp.exe). It provides status regarding the QoS reservation to applications that are interested, and minimizes the need for applications to understand RSVP signaling.

- Policy Support

  The RSVP service communicates with the Kerberos Domain Controller to generate policy elements that are included in RSVP signaling messages. These identify the user so that per-user or per-subnet admission control policies can be applied to network resources.

- Traffic Control

  The RSVP service uses the Traffic Control API to invoke traffic control on behalf of QoS-aware applications in response to GQoS calls or RSVP signaling messages. The RSVP service hides the complexity of the Traffic Control API from applications using the GQoS API, so that applications do not need to be redesigned to make use of traffic control.

- QoS Admission Control Support

  The RSVP service communicates with an admission control server, like the Windows 2000 QoS ACS server, to prevent over-commitment of bandwidth on shared segments.

Traffic Control

The RSVP service invokes traffic control on behalf of an application when QoS is requested. Traffic control refers to a collection of mechanisms that control and police a specific data flow once a QoS reservation has been established. Traffic control is used to segregate the traffic into the appropriate service classes, and regulate its delivery to the network. Figure 9.3 illustrates the traffic control components.

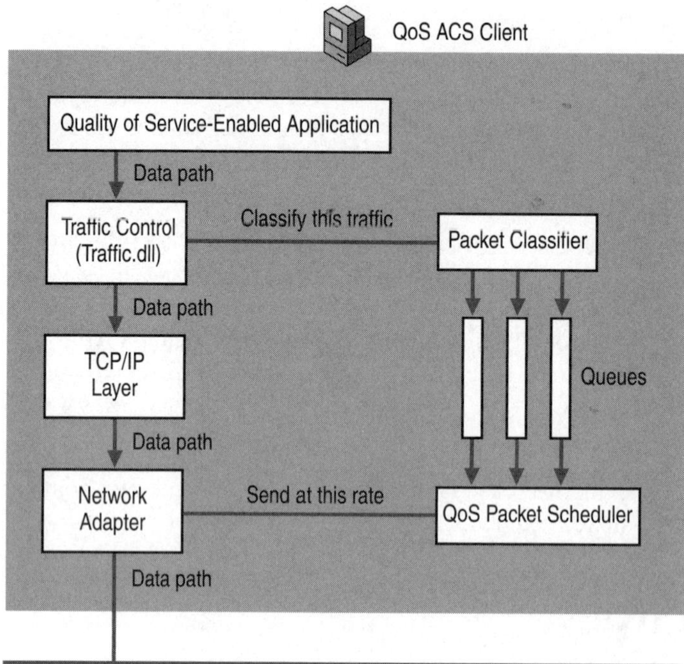

Figure 9.3 Traffic Control Components

A key element of traffic control is establishing the service parameters for a sequence of packets (known as flowspec) and then treating all member packets as a single flow. Traffic control uses information from the flowspec to create a flow with defined QoS parameters, and then creates filters to direct selected packets into this flow (known as filterspec).

Traffic control works with the QoS Admission Control Service and RSVP to meet the service level and priority required by the bandwidth request. Traffic control is also available in certain cases by using certain tools for subnet clients that are not QoS-aware, and controls data flow through network devices that are not RSVP-compliant by marking packets for 802.1p (layer 2 devices) or Differentiated Class of Service (layer 3 devices).

Traffic Control API (TC API) The TC API is a programmatic interface to the traffic control components that regulate network traffic on a host. The TC API allows the aggregation of traffic from a number of sources (on the same sending host) into a single traffic control flow. For example, all traffic to destination net 1.2.3.0 can be placed on the same flow, regardless of source address port and destination port. By comparison, the Generic QoS API limits the use of a traffic control flow to traffic from a single "conversation" only (a conversation is defined by source and destination address and port).

The TC API also works with GQoS to enable third-party traffic management applications that might request QoS on behalf of applications that are unable to do so on their own, or in situations where a system administrator wants to better control the QoS provided to applications. For more information about using the Traffic Control API, see the Software Development Kit link on the Web Resources page at http://windows.microsoft.com/windows2000/reskit/webresources.

Traffic Control Components

On each host, traffic is marked and transmitted as priority QoS traffic by the process of packet classification and scheduling.

Generic Packet Classifier (Msgpc.sys)

Packet classification provides a means by which packets generated by an application can be classified and subsequently prioritized before being sent across a network. The Generic Packet Classifier is the mechanism by which traffic control determines the flow for any packet, and therefore, the treatment that the packet receives. Once a packet has been classified as belonging to a particular flow, the QoS Packet Scheduler is able to give it treatment in accordance with that flow's parameters.

QoS Packet Scheduler (Psched.sys)

Packet scheduling is the means by which data (packet) transmission management (a key function of Quality of Service) is achieved. The QoS Packet Scheduler enforces QoS parameters for a particular flow. Traffic shaping (smoothing bursts and peaks in traffic to an even flow) relies on the packet classifier to assign packets into queues based upon their QoS parameters. The QoS Packet Scheduler retrieves the packets from the queues and transmits them according to the QoS parameters, which generally include a scheduled rate and some indication of priority. The scheduled rate is used to pace the transmission of packets to the network. The priority is used to determine the order in which packets need to be submitted to the network when congestion occurs. This smoothes bursts or peaks of traffic over a period of time, thereby effecting a steadier use of the network and maintaining resource integrity.

The QoS Packet Scheduler can be installed on any computer on which you want to have traffic control services. The QoS Packet Scheduler must be installed on all end-systems that make reservations on subnets where you are running an QoS Admission Control Service, such as any host that sends data to other hosts (for example, a multimedia server or inventory control server).

Packet Marking

To ensure quality of service, packets must be marked in such a way that network devices along the data path can properly provide the required QoS, or at least attempt to if they are not RSVP-enabled. The QoS Packet Scheduler provides 802.1p marking while Differentiated Class of Service marking is done by TCP/IP. The QoS Packet Scheduler cannot be installed on Microsoft® Windows® 98–based computers; therefore, 802.1p functionality is not available on them. Diff-serv Code Point (DSCP) marking is available on Windows 98–based computers using the RSVP SP. Windows 2000 defines a default mapping to 802.1p and Differentiated Class of Services in the registry. This is discussed in more detail later in this chapter. Network devices can override this default mapping by inserting a special object into RSVP signaling messages. This is done at the determination of a QoS policy server that might map a user's traffic to a lower or higher priority than the default mapping. A policy server may insert a traffic class (T class) object to override the 802.1p class and a D class object to override the Diff-serv class.

Traffic Service Levels

Traffic patterns fall into two primary groups:

- Elastic traffic

  Elastic traffic adapts easily to change. When little bandwidth is available, elastic traffic delivery is slow. Delivery is faster when bandwidth is abundant. The data sender is automatically tuned to the rate of the network. Elastic traffic is usually generated by transaction-oriented applications, such as bulk data transfers.

- Real-time traffic

  Real-time traffic is generated primarily by real-time applications that require dedicated bandwidth, such as video conferencing. Real-time traffic is limited in its ability to adapt to changing network conditions, and delays can significantly reduce intelligibility and usefulness.

Traffic control supports four service levels to meet the needs of the two primary traffic pattern groups:

- Best-effort

  Best-effort is the standard service level of many IP-based networks. It is a connectionless model of delivery that is suitable for elastic traffic. Packets are sent with no guarantees for low delay or adequate bandwidth.

The next two levels are suitable for real-time applications, giving them preferential service:

- Controlled load

  Controlled load approximates the behavior of best-effort service in unloaded (not heavily loaded or congested) conditions. A flow receiving controlled load service at a network device can experience little or no delay or congestion loss. Any unreserved bandwidth or reserved bandwidth not currently in use remains available for other traffic. See the Internet Engineering Task Force (IETF)–defined Request for Comment (RFC) 2211 for detailed information about this service level.

- Guaranteed service

  Guaranteed service guarantees the maximum limit on delay. This is most useful if every host on the data path provides this level of service, including routers or switches that are compliant with QoS and RSVP. However, the impact of guaranteed traffic on the network is heavy, so it is not desirable for applications that generate elastic or best-effort traffic. Any unreserved or reserved bandwidth not currently in use remains available for other traffic. See the IETF-defined RFC 2212 for more information about this service level.

- Qualitative service

  Qualitative service is designed for applications that require prioritized traffic handling but cannot quantify their QoS requirements in terms of a concrete flow specification. These applications typically send out traffic that is intermittent or burst-like in nature. In the case of qualitative service, it is the network that determines the treatment of qualitative flows. Mission-critical ERP applications generate this kind of traffic. For more information about this service level, see the IETF link on the Web Resources page at http://windows.microsoft.com/windows2000/reskit/webresources. See the IETF-defined Internet Draft titled "Specification of the Qualitative Service Type" for detailed information about this service level.

The QoS Admission Control policy determines which service level a user receives.

Resource Reservation Protocol

Resource Reservation Protocol (RSVP) is an IETF-defined (RFC 2205) signaling protocol that uses Integrated Services (Intserv) to convey QoS requests to the network. The Intserv architecture specifies extensions to the best-effort traffic model – the standard delivery model used in most IP networks and the Internet. Intserv provides for special handling of priority-marked traffic, and a mechanism by which QoS-aware applications can choose service levels for traffic delivery: controlled load or guaranteed service. Windows 2000 supports an extension of the standard Intserv service types in the form of the qualitative service type. The qualitative service type is designed for applications that require QoS but cannot quantify their QoS requirements due to the intermittent or burst-like nature of their traffic. Integrated Services also defines QoS signaling (RSVP) for the purpose of making resource reservations across a network.

RSVP is a layer 3 protocol, making it independent of the underlying network media. Customer networks generally include heterogeneous media, including Ethernet or token ring local area network (LAN) media, WANs made up of low and high-speed leased lines, modem links, and ATM technology. RSVP bridges the gap between applications, the operating system, and media-specific QoS mechanisms. This enables RSVP to send QoS messages structured in media-independent terms, making it an effective signaling protocol for end-to-end QoS over networks that combine different types of low-layer media. For example, end nodes can exchange RSVP messages across a network comprised of 802-type LANs, routers, ATM and WAN regions, with each making the appropriate admission control decisions and providing QoS if approved.

RSVP is well-suited to both mission-critical applications, such as Enterprise Resource Planning software, and session-oriented applications, such as IP telephony and video conferencing. Both applications exchange QoS data between fixed end nodes for some degree of persistence. These types of applications tend to stream data. QoS-enabled connections are unidirectional. To enable a connection with service guarantees for both sending and receiving from a host, two individual QoS-enabled connections are required.

RSVP is primarily for use with IP traffic, operating on top of IPv4 or IPv6, whereas a transport protocol resides in the protocol stack. However, it is a signaling protocol, not a routing protocol. Routing protocols determine where packets get forwarded; RSVP configures reservations for data flows along a data path predetermined by the network routing protocol.

The RSVP protocol is installed as part of the Windows 2000 installation of Windows Sockets 2.0. The RSVP protocol does the following:

- Works with any current-generation network routing protocol and supports a number of network layer protocols, including TCP/IP.
- Supports multicast and unicast transmissions.
- Carries the bandwidth reservation request to each network device or hop (routers, switches, or proxies) responsible for managing resources in the data path between the sender and receiver (end nodes).
- Maintains the reservation at each hop by caching that information in the hop, creating a reservation soft-state or *state*.
- Passes transparently through devices that do not support RSVP.

If a network device does not support RSVP, QoS is not truly guaranteed along that particular network segment. The messages simply pass through each hop, and since they are not recognized, no priority bandwidth or handling is allocated. Throughout that segment, traffic is handled best-effort, meaning that end-to-end and low-delay guarantees for the requested service level are not available. This situation can arise in areas of the network where there is an abundance of bandwidth or where the network elements themselves are the resource constraint. Currently, some high-end routers and switches are RSVP-compliant.

The RSVP Service Provider (RSVP SP), which invokes and facilitates QoS and RSVP signaling, enables application developers to directly interact with RSVP. For additional information about the RSVP Service Provider, see the Software Development Kit link on the Web Resources page at http://windows.microsoft.com/windows2000/reskit/webresources.

Direct interaction with RSVP by an application or service enables fine-tuning or special service requests. However, most application programmers find that enabling an application or service to use the RSVP SP, which initiates and maintains RSVP signaling on behalf of applications or services, is sufficient to enable their application or service to take advantage of QoS capabilities.

The QoS API is the programmatic interface to the RSVP SP. Under most circumstances, the QoS API is the only interface that programmers require to create QoS-aware or QoS-enabled applications.

RSVP Messages

RSVP messages identify what application and user is requesting QoS, the service level requested from the network, the quantity of bandwidth requested, and the end nodes (source and destination addresses). Based on administrator-defined admission control policies and network resource availability, the QoS request is either approved or denied by the host performing admission control duties. If the request is approved, QoS mechanisms are invoked to classify and schedule the traffic flow, logically allocate bandwidth, and notify the requesting host of the approval so that it might begin sending priority traffic. Until this occurs, the transmission is treated as standard traffic by the network.

Information encased in RSVP messages is per data flow (a flow is a data stream between two end nodes). RSVP messages carry the following information:

- *Traffic classification information*. The source and destination IP addresses and ports identify the traffic flow (filterspec).
- *Traffic parameters*. Expressed using Intserv's token-bucket model, these identify the data rate of the flow (flowspec).
- *Service level information*. From the Intserv-defined service types, conveys the flow requirements for the RSVP request.
- *Policy information*: Allows the system to verify that the requester is entitled to the resources and to the amount of resources being requested.

RSVP uses the message types listed in Table 9.1 to establish and maintain reserved bandwidth on a subnet.

Table 9.1 RSVP Message Types

Message Type	Function
PATH	Carries the data flow information from the sender to the receiver. The PATH message marks out the path that requested data must take when returning to the receiver. PATH messages contain bandwidth requirements, traffic characteristics, and addressing information, such as the source and destination IP addresses. PATH messages are issued for a particular session, which is determined by the destination address and port of the data flow. It is necessary to have a unique session identifier, since a sender can offer multiple traffic flows and receive RESV messages from multiple receivers. The unique session identifier enables the ability to associate the correct PATH messages with the correct RESV messages.
RESV	Carries the reservation request from the receiver. RESV messages contain the actual bandwidth reservation, the service level requested, and the source IP address. This is the message that causes the reservation to become active.
PATH-ERR	Indicates an error in response to the PATH message.
RESV-ERR	Indicates an error in response to the RESV message.

(continued)

Table 9.1 RSVP Message Types *(continued)*

Message Type	Function
PATH-TEAR	Removes the PATH state along the route.
RESV-TEAR	Removes the reservation along the route.
RESV -CONF	Optional. If a receiver requests a confirmation, the sender transmits this message to the receiver.

When an application on an end node requests QoS, RSVP constructs PATH messages that express the QoS requirements of the sending application, in abstract, Layer 3 terms that each network device can interpret. The receiving-end node sends back an RESV message that establishes the reservation along the data path. For the reservation to be truly guaranteed, each hop must grant the reservation and physically allocate the requested bandwidth. By granting the reservation, the hop commits to providing adequate resources. Devices might reject resource requests based on lack of policy rights by the requesting user or lack of network resources at the time of the request.

If the reservation is rejected, the application receives an immediate response that the subnet cannot currently support the amount or type of bandwidth, or the requested service level. It is up to the application to determine whether to resend the data and accept a best-effort service level or wait and repeat the bandwidth request at a later time. Note that the end nodes must periodically refresh the reservation by sending PATH and RESV messages every few seconds (generally this is set to 30 second intervals).

Flowspecs and Filterspecs

RSVP messages carry very specific classification information that enable RSVP-aware devices to separate traffic into flows associated with individual conversations and to ensure that each flow gets the treatment determined under the RSVP request. Fine-grain classification provides a better guarantee of service.

RESV messages contain a flow specification (flowspec) and a filter specification (filterspec) to provide information about the data flow. The combined flowspec and filterspec are referred to as the *flow descriptor*.

Filterspec

Traffic is classified based on the source and destination IP address and port specified in the packet. This group of parameters is referred to as the filter specification or *filterspec*. QoS-aware devices base the handling of the packet on a match with the filterspec.

The filterspec, together with a session specification, defines the set of data packets to be included in the flow. The filterspec is used to set parameters in the Packet Classifier. Data packets that are addressed to a particular session but do not match any of the filterspecs for that session are handled as best-effort traffic.

Filter Styles

A reservation includes options, referred to as the reservation style. This style determines how the reservation is treated from the sender's perspective.

A reservation can either be distinct for each sender or it can be shared by a set of specified senders. It can also be an explicit list of all selected senders, or a wildcard specification that implicitly selects all senders for the session.

Wildcard Filter Style

The Wildcard Filter (WF) reservation style contains a sender selection specified in wildcard format and a shared reservation. A WF style reservation creates one reservation for all sender flows. The amount of resources reserved by shared reservation is determined by the largest of the resource requests that were merged. A WF reservation is automatically offered to new senders. No filter spec is needed.

Fixed-Filter Style

In contrast, the Fixed Filter (FF) style reservation contains an explicit sender selection format and unique reservation parameters (as opposed to merged). The FF style reservation is a distinct reservation for packets from a single sender. Multiple FF reservations can be requested at the same time, using a list of flow descriptors. The filter spec must match exactly one sender.

Shared Explicit Style

The Shared Explicit (SE) style reservation involves a single reservation that is shared among an explicit list of senders. The SE style reservation is specified by one flowspec and a list of filterspecs.

Flowspec

Through RSVP and Intserv semantics, GQoS enables applications to describe the quality of service they require for transmitting a data flow. The QoS parameters are carried in a generic Intserv flowspec.

The flowspec specifies the type of QoS requested, and is used to set parameters in the QoS Packet Scheduler. It is included in reservation requests and includes:

- *Rspec*. Defines the level of QoS requested.
- *Tspec*. Describes the data flow.

The flowspec structure provides the following QoS parameters to RSVP. This allows QoS-aware applications to invoke, modify, or remove QoS settings for a particular flow.

TokenRate Specifies the permitted rate at which data can be transmitted over the network for the duration of the flow. TokenRate is similar to other token-bucket models seen in WAN technologies such as Frame Relay, in which the token is analogous to a credit. If such tokens are not used immediately, they accrue to allow data transmission up to a specified amount (the token bucket size). Flows are also limited to a burst rate (the peak bandwidth specified). This avoids situations where flows that are inactive for some time suddenly flood the available bandwidth with accrued tokens. Traffic control is maintained because flows cannot send too much data at once, and network resource integrity is maintained because such devices are spared from high traffic bursts.

TokenRate is expressed in bytes per second. It is important that applications base their TokenRate requests on reasonable expectations for transmission requirements. For example, in video applications, the TokenRate is typically set to the average bit rate, peak to peak. If the TokenRate member is set to –1, limits on the transmission rate will not be in effect.

TokenBucketSize The maximum amount of credits a particular direction of a flow can accrue, regardless of time. In video applications, TokenBucketSize is likely the largest average frame size. In constant rate applications, TokenBucketSize needs to be set to allow for small variations. TokenBucketSize is expressed in bytes.

PeakBandwidth The upper limit on time-based transmit permissions for a given flow, sometimes called a *burst limit*. PeakBandwidth restricts flows from overburdening network resources with one-time or cyclical data bursts by enforcing a per-second data transmission ceiling. Some intermediate systems can take advantage of this information, resulting in more efficient resource allocation. PeakBandwidth is expressed in bytes per second.

Latency Maximum acceptable delay between transmission of a bit by the sender and its receipt by one or more intended receivers. The precise interpretation of this number depends on the level of guarantee specified in the QoS request. Latency is expressed in microseconds.

DelayVariation Difference between the maximum and minimum delay a packet can experience. Applications use DelayVariation to determine the amount of buffer space needed at the receiving end of the flow, in order to restore the original data transmission pattern. DelayVariation is expressed in microseconds.

ServiceType Specifies the level of service for the flow:

- *NoTraffic*. Indicates that no traffic is transmitted in the specified direction. On duplex-capable media, this value signals underlying software to set up unidirectional connections only.
- *BestEffort*. Specifies that the network devices must make a reasonable effort to maintain the level of service requested, without making any guarantees on delivery. This is the standard level of network service.
- *ControlledLoad*. Provides end-to-end QoS that closely approximates a level of transmission quality that mirrors unloaded network conditions (light traffic) from the associated network devices along the data path. The packet loss closely approximates the basic packet error rate of the transmission medium. The transmission delay for a very high percentage of the delivered packets will not greatly exceed the minimum transit delay experienced by any successfully delivered packet.
- *Guaranteed*. Initiates a queuing algorithm within the QoS service provider that isolates a particular flow as much as possible from the effects of other flows. This guarantees the ability to transmit data at the TokenRate for the duration of the connection. However, if the corresponding end node transmits data faster than the TokenRate, the network might delay or discard the excess traffic. If TokenRate is not exceeded over time, latency is also guaranteed.
- *Qualitative*. Qualitative service is meant for applications that cannot quantify their QoS requirements. An application that requests qualitative service is in effect asking the network to figure out how to treat its traffic. A request for qualitative service is usually accompanied with an application ID so that a policy server on the network can figure out how to treat the traffic for that application. The policy server can then instruct Windows 2000 to mark traffic for the qualitative flow with a particular Differentiated Services Code Point (DSCP).

How RSVP Works

RSVP is based on signaling messages that traverse the network, allocating resources along the way. RSVP is receiver-initiated, because sender initiation does not scale well to large, multicast scenarios in which there are heterogeneous receivers. In multicast scenarios, the application server sends out only one PATH message to multiple receiving computers, thus conserving network bandwidth. In the case of multicast traffic flows, RESV messages from multiple receivers are merged by taking the maximum values requested.

RSVP is a soft-state protocol, meaning that the reservation must be periodically refreshed or it expires. The reservation information, or *state*, is cached in each hop tasked with managing resources. If the network's routing protocol alters the data path, RSVP attempts to reinstall the reservation state along the new route. When refresh messages are not received, reservations time out and are dropped, releasing bandwidth. The sender refreshes PATH messages, and the receiver refreshes RESV messages. Because RSVP sends its messages as best-effort IP datagrams with no reliability enhancement, some messages might be lost, but the periodic transmission of refresh messages by hosts and routers compensates for the occasional loss of an RSVP message. To ensure receipt of refresh messages, the network traffic control mechanism must be statically configured to grant some minimal bandwidth for RSVP messages to protect them from congestion losses. At any time, the sender, receiver, or other network device providing QoS, can terminate the session by sending a PATH-TEAR or RESV-TEAR message.

Policy is checked by the RSVP-aware routers and switches along the path. Devices might reject resource requests based on the results of these policy checks. If the reservation is rejected due to lack of resources, the requested application is immediately informed that the network cannot currently support that amount and type of bandwidth or the requested service level. The application determines whether to wait and repeat the request later or to send the data immediately using best-effort delivery. QoS-aware applications, such as those controlling multicast transmissions, generally begin sending immediately on a best-effort basis, which is then upgraded to QoS when the reservation is accepted.

Figure 9.4 is a basic example of how RSVP messages flow between a sender and receiver, through the admission control host and intermediary hops.

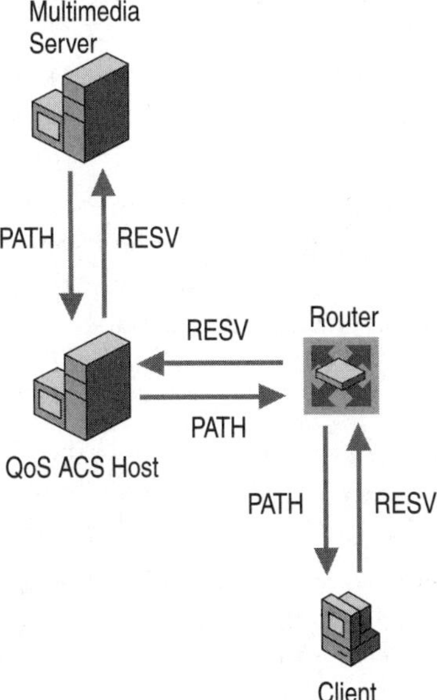

Figure 9.4 How RSVP Works

1. The multimedia server sends a PATH message requesting priority bandwidth to the QoS ACS host (a Windows 2000 server running the QoS Admission Control Service). The message is ultimately headed to the receiver of the data. In the case of multicast (multiple receivers), the PATH message is sent to the multicast address and received by all hosts that are members of the multicast group. Note that it is RSVP messages that are passed to the QoS ACS, not the data packets ultimately transmitted from sender to receiver.

   Until confirmation of a reservation is received with a RESV message, data for the connection is sent at a best-effort service level from the sending host. The best-effort service type instructs the RSVP SP to use the application or service's QoS parameters as guidelines for service quality requests, and makes reasonable effort to maintain the requested level of service. It does not make any guarantees that requested QoS parameters are implemented or enforced.

2. If a QoS ACS server is present in the local subnet, the PATH message is routed via the QoS ACS server. In this example, a QoS ACS host approves the request and forwards it to the receiver (client). The PATH message travels through the network to the receiver, along the data path determined by the network routing protocol.
3. A PATH state is maintained at each hop. Each PATH state contains a copy of the PATH message and the IP address of the previous hop.
4. When a PATH message arrives at the intended receiver, the receiving host (if interested in receiving the data) responds by sending a RESV message that reserves the resources along the same network path traveled by the PATH message.

   Here, the receiver creates a RESV message, indicating that it wants to receive the data from the multimedia server.

5. The RESV message follows the reverse data path back to the multimedia server, using the addressing information stored in the PATH state at each hop, to determine the route.
6. As the RESV message propagates back toward the sender, each hop determines whether or not to accept the proposed reservation and commit resources. If an affirmative decision is made, physical bandwidth is allocated and RESV messages are propagated to the next hop on the path from source to destination. If a hop is unable to commit, it sends a RESV-ERR message to the receiving host.

   When the RESV message arrives at the router hop, the reservation is granted and physical bandwidth is allocated. The hop maintains the reservation (RESV) state and notifies the traffic control service that data is to be sent.

   The reservation is considered to be installed when the first RESV message arrives at the sender in response to the PATH message for the corresponding session. The reservation remains until the session is terminated by either host or a network device. As long as the reservation is in place, the sender is able to transmit prioritized data.

7. The multimedia server and the client periodically send PATH and RESV messages during the data transmission, to keep the reservation state in place.

Every hop might not be RSVP-capable, especially when data crosses the Internet. Both RSVP and non-RSVP routers forward PATH messages towards the destination address using their local unicast or multicast routing table. This means that the routing of PATH messages is unaffected by non-RSVP routers in the path. Although a group of non-RSVP routers cannot perform a resource analysis and grant a reservation, if such a cloud has sufficient bandwidth capacity, it may still provide some level of useful real-time service.

RSVP dynamically adapts to new routes during the flow of a data stream. When a route changes (for example, when a router or switch can no longer commit to the requested resources), the next PATH message initializes the path state on the new route, and future RESV messages establish a reservation state for the new route.

You might need to enable special filtering for the RSVP messages to pass through security gateways, firewalls, or proxy servers without generating a PATH-ERR message. Windows 2000 IP Security (IPSec) does not interfere with the interpretation of RSVP messages.

RSVP Message Structures

Each RSVP message consists of a common header. The fields of the common header are listed in Table 9.2.

Table 9.2 Fields of the Common Header

Field	Size	Description
Vers	4 bits	RSVP version number (this implementation is version 1.)
Flags	4 bits	Reserved. As of this implementation, no flag bits have been defined.
Message Type	8 bits	1 = PATH 2 = RESV 3 = PATH-ERR 4 = RESV-ERR 5 = PATH-TEAR 6 = RESV-TEAR 7 = RESV-CONF

(continued)

Table 9.2 Fields of the Common Header ***(continued)***

Field	Size	Description
RSVP Checksum	16 bits	A checksum to provide message integrity. An all-zero value means that no checksum was transmitted.
Send TTL	8 bits	Provides the IP Time to Live (TTL) value contained in the message. With normal IP forwarding, RSVP can detect a non-RSVP hop by comparing the IP TTL when the PATH message is sent to the TTL when it is received; for this purpose, the transmission TTL is placed in the common header.
RSVP Length	16 bits	The total length of the RSVP message in bytes, including the common header and the variable length objects that follow.

Every object consists of one or more 32-bit words with a one-word header. Table 9.3 lists the fields in the object header.

Table 9.3 Object Formats

Field	Size	Description
Length	16 bits	Contains the total object length in bytes. It must be a multiple of 4, and a minimum of 4.
Class-Num		The object class. Implementations of RSVP must recognize certain classes. For a list of classes implementations of RSVP must recognize, see Table 9.3a.
C-Type		The object type. Unique within Class-Num. The Class-Num and C-Type fields can be used together as a 16-bit number to define a unique type for each object. C-Types are defined for the two Internet address families IPv4 and IPv6 (only IPv4 is shown here). All unused fields must be sent as zero and ignored on receipt. For a list of C-Type field values, see Table 9.3b.

Table 9.3a Class-Num Fields

Field	Description
Null	Length must be at least 4, or any multiple of 4. Can appear anywhere within a sequence of objects; contents are ignored by the receiver.
Session	The destination IP address, protocol ID, and destination port. Defines a specific session for the other objects that follow. Required field.
RSVP_Hop	IP address of the RSVP-capable node that sent the message, and a logical outgoing interface handle.
Time_Values	Refresh period. Required for PATH and RESV messages.
Style	The reservation style, and style-specific information not already contained in the FLOWSPEC or FILTER_SPEC. Required for RESV messages.
Flowspec	The requested QoS parameters. Part of a RESV message.
Filter_Spec	Defines which session data packets must receive the requested QoS. Part of a RESV message.
Sender_Template	The sender's IP address and possibly de-multiplexing information to identify the sender. Required for PATH messages.
Sender_Tspec	The traffic characteristics of a sender's data flow. Required for PATH messages.
Adspec	Carries OPWA data, in PATH messages. OPWA is the abbreviation for "One Pass With Advertising," and identifies a reservation setup model in which PATH messages gather information (the advertisement) that the receivers can use to estimate the end-to-end service.
Error_Spec	The actual error in a PATH-ERR, RESV-ERR or the confirmation in a RESV-CONF message.
Policy_Data	Carries the information that the local policy module uses to determine if the reservation is administratively permitted. In PATH, RESV, PATH-ERR, or RESV-ERR messages. This object is not fully specified at this time.
Integrity	Contains cryptographic data that authenticates the sender node and verifies the contents of the RSVP message.
Scope	An explicit list of sender nodes towards which the information in the message must be forwarded. In a RESV, ResvErr, or ResvTear message.
RESV_Confirm	The IP address of the receiver node that requested confirmation. In RESV or ResvConf messages.

Table 9.3b C-Type Fields

Object Name	C-Type	Class	Contains	Additional Information
IPv4/UDP SESSION object	1	1	IPv4 DestAddress (4 bytes), Protocol ID, Flags, DestPort	Used in PATH messages to determine the network boundary, to control traffic policing. If the sender is not capable of policing, it sets this bit On in all PATH messages it sends, indicating to the first RSVP-capable hop to perform policing (and turn the flag off).
IPv4 RSVP_HOP object	1	3	IPv4 Next/Previous Hop Address, Logical Interface Handle (LIH)	LIH distinguishes logical outgoing interfaces. The LIH must be zero if there is no logical interface handle.
Time_Values	1	5	Refresh Period R	The refresh time-out period R used to generate this RSVP message, in milliseconds.
IPv4 Error_Spec	1	6	IPv4 Error Node Address (4 bytes), Flags, Error Code, Error Value, Error Node Address	Error Node Address is the IP address of the node in which the error was detected. **Flags:** 0x01 = InPlace. This flag is used only for an ERROR_SPEC object in a RESV-ERR message. If On, this flag indicates that there was, and still is, a reservation in place at the failure point. 0x02 = NotGuilty. This flag is used only for an ERROR_SPEC object in a RESV-ERRmessage, and it is only set in the interface for the receiver application. If On, this flag indicates that the FLOWSPEC that failed was strictly greater than the FLOWSPEC requested by this receiver. Error Code is a one-octet error description. Error Value is a two-octet field containing additional information about the error. Its contents depend upon the Error Type. See Table 9.12 for more information.
Scope		7	This object contains a list of IP addresses used for routing messages by using a wildcard scope without loops.	The addresses must be listed in ascending numerical order.

(continued)

Table 9.3b C-Type Fields ***(continued)***

Object Name	C-Type	Class	Contains	Additional Information
IPv4 Scope_List	1	7	IPv4 Source Address (4 bytes)	
Style	1	8	Flags (8 bits), Option Vector (24 bits)	A set of bit fields giving values for the reservation options. If new options are added in the future, corresponding fields in the option vector are assigned from the least-significant end. If a node does not recognize a style ID, it can interpret as much of the option vector as it can, ignoring new fields that might have been defined. **Flags**: None yet assigned. **Option Vector**, assigned (from the left): 19 bits: Reserved 2 bits: Sharing control 00b: Reserved 01b: Distinct reservations 10b: Shared reservations 11b: Reserved 3 bits: Sender selection control 000b: Reserved 001b: Wildcard 010b: Explicit 011b - 111b: Reserved The low order bits of the option vector are determined by the Style: WF 10001b FF 01010b SE 10010b
Flowspec	1	9	Reserved (obsolete), Flowspec object	

(continued)

Table 9.3b C-Type Fields *(continued*

Object Name	C-Type	Class	Contains	Additional Information
Intserv Flowspec	2	9	The contents and encoding rules for this object are specified in documents prepared by the Intserv working group (as described in RFC 2210).	
IPv4 Filter_Spec	1	10	IPv4 SourceAddress (4 bytes), SourcePort	
IPv4 Sender_Templat e	1	11	IPv4 SourceAddress (4 bytes), SourcePort	
Intserv Sender_Tspec	2	12	The contents and encoding rules for this object are specified in documents prepared by the Intserv working group.	
Intserv Adspec	2	13	The contents and encoding rules for this object are specified in documents prepared by the Intserv working group.	
Type 1 Policy_Data	1	14	The contents of this object are set aside for further study.	
IPv4 RESV_Confirm	1	15	IPv4 Receiver Address (4bytes)	

Windows 2000 QoS Support

The following section describe the standards and technologies supported by Windows 2000 QoS.

Signaled QoS Architecture

Signaled QoS uses signaling protocols, such as RSVP, to alert the network to dynamically adapt traffic handling when priority treatment is required. This is in contrast to configured QoS in which the network is hardwired for QoS.

Windows 2000 deploys a signaled QoS architecture to provide QoS on an as-needed basis and to clear bandwidth for any other type of traffic when QoS is not in use for priority transmission. In this way, different types of network traffic can coexist. Configured QoS reserves bandwidth, whether needed or not, and wastes network resources that otherwise might be available to other types of traffic.

The use of a signaled QoS architecture also provides real-time feedback based on current network conditions, support for admission control, and topology awareness by using RSVP messages that flow from device to device, coordinating the allocation of resources and establishing a QoS reservation along the data path.

Qualitative Applications

Enterprise network administrators might be primarily concerned with providing QoS for mission-critical applications, such as Enterprise Resource Planning (ERP) applications, and secondarily concerned with providing QoS for multimedia applications.

As a result, Microsoft supports both quantitative and qualitative QoS in order to support ERP and other mission-critical applications that are qualitative in nature. Traditional RSVP signaling uses the IETF-defined Integrated Services (Intserv) model for expressing network resource requirements in a quantitative form. While this is suitable for multimedia applications such as IP telephony or video conferencing, it is not suitable for qualitative applications that cannot easily express resources required in the quantitative form required by Intserv.

Through extensions to RSVP signaling, Microsoft provides the necessary support for qualitative applications by enabling a new service type called the Qualitative Service Type (see "Traffic Control" in this chapter). Applications must be designed to include the requested service type in the basic QoS parameters. Applications must also be designed to create a policy element that includes the application and subapplication names. This policy element is compared against the policy database to determine which policy must be applied to that application traffic. All other QoS functionality is handled by the operating system. See the IETF-defined Internet Draft titled "Specification of the Qualitative Service Type" for detailed information about this service level.

The application and subapplication names are included in the signaling message with the service type. When this service type is requested, network devices interpret the request as a data flow that requires some special treatment, although the network devices do not know exactly what that treatment is. The network devices look up this application, the type of application subflow, and the requesting user in the policy database, and determine the best prioritization policy for this traffic. Therefore, the network devices do not actually allocate a specific quantity of resources to the application's traffic, but rather assign it to a particular Differentiated Class of Service. In addition, the network administrator must specify (using policy or registry settings) how to map data flows from different applications into a smaller set of aggregate service classes. This enables the prioritization of traffic from specific qualitative applications.

Layer 2 Integration

Windows 2000 QoS supports mapping of RSVP signals to layer 2 signals using IEEE 802.1p priority markings to enable the prioritization of traffic across layer 2 devices, such as switches, on a network segment. IEEE 802 refers to the layer 2 technology, including the Data Link layer and the Media Access Control (MAC) layer. The IEEE 802.1p standard defines how layer 2 devices handle traffic marked with 802.1p priority. The QoS Packet Scheduler performs 802.1p marking for any application that requests QoS using GQoS or the Traffic Control API.

On Ethernet, 802.1p priority is carried in Virtual Local Area Network (VLAN) tags defined in IEEE 802.1q/p (802.1p). A field in the 802.1q tag carries one of eight priority values (3 bits in length), recognizable by layer 2 devices on a network segment. This marking determines the service level the packet receives when crossing an 802.1p-enabled network segment. Figure 9.5 shows the location of the 802.1p priority bits within the 802.1q tag.

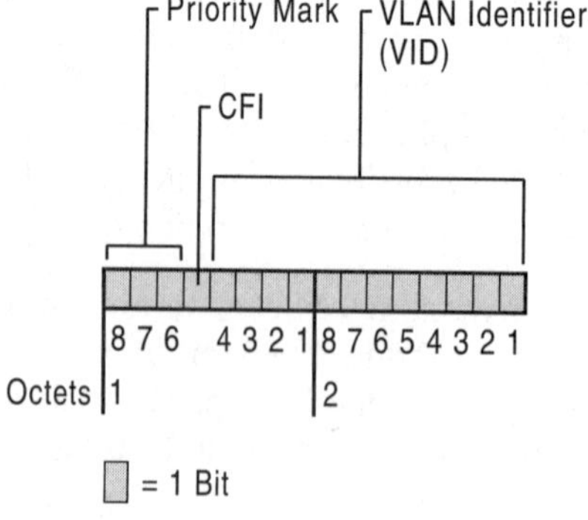

Figure 9.5 802.1p Tag

The 802.1p tag is placed inside the Ethernet header, between the MAC header and the data payload. A mapping from the service-type used by RSVP is made to one of these 802.1p priority values. A default mapping is defined on the hosts, however, sophisticated switches might direct hosts or routers to use mappings other than the default. The default markings for 802.1p priority service levels listed in Table 9.4 are hard-coded into the Windows 2000 QoS Packet Scheduler and can only be modified via the host registry.

Table 9.4 Windows 2000 Default 802.1p Priority Levels

Priority Marking	Service Level
0	Best-effort
1	< Best-effort
2	Reserved
3	Reserved
4	Controlled load
5	Guaranteed service 100ms bound
6	Guaranteed service 10ms bound
7	Reserved

The QoS Packet Scheduler must be installed on any host that performs 802.1p marking. If the layer 2 devices between the end nodes are not 802.1p-capable or enabled, layer 2 prioritization cannot be guaranteed across that segment.

Differentiated Class of Service

Windows 2000 QoS supports layer 3 Differentiated Services (Diff-serv), also called Class of Service (CoS). Diff-serv extends QoS across networks that are not RSVP-enabled, such as large transit networks that make up the core of the Internet.

The QoS Packet Scheduler performs Diff-serv marking for any application that requests marking from the GQoS API or the Traffic Control API. The IP header of the packet is marked with a priority value in the Type of Service (ToS) fields, also referred to as the Diff-serv Code Point (DSCP). This marking determines the service level the packet receives when crossing a Diff-serv network segment.

Type of Service Field and DSCP The DSCP value is established by setting the first six bits of the ToS field. Figure 9.6 illustrates the IP header with the ToS field enclosed.

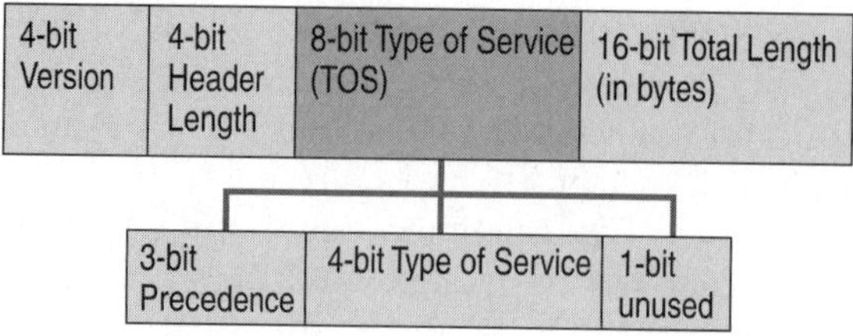

Figure 9.6 IP Header with TOS Field

The default mappings for DSCP, in decimal, are listed in Table 9.5. These 6-bit DSCP values show up in the upper 6 bits of the ToS field as specified in RFC 2474.

Table 9.5 DSCP Default Priority Markings

Priority Marking	Service Level
0	Best-effort
24	Controlled load
40	Guaranteed
48	Network control
0	Qualitative

The DSCP value has subsumed IP Precedence and is therefore backward compatible with IP Precedence. The IP Precedence contains the upper 3 bits of the DSCP field. These values are listed in Table 9.6:

Table 9.6 IP Precedence Markings

Priority Marking	Service Level
0	Best-effort
3	Controlled load
5	Guaranteed
6	Network control
0	Qualitative

The QoS Packet Scheduler must be installed on any host that performs or interprets Diff-serv markings. If the layer 3 devices between the end nodes are not Diff-serv–capable or enabled, QoS cannot be guaranteed across that segment.

Integrated Services over Slow Links

Special mechanisms are provided to perform traffic shaping on slow links, such as 28.8-kilobyte per second (KBps) modem links. On such links, large packets can occupy the link long enough to delay small audio packets that must be sent on the same link. This can cause problems with audio quality. To avoid this problem, traffic control fragments large packets at the link layer, sending only one fragment at a time. Latency-sensitive audio packets can then be inserted in between the larger packet's fragments, thus reducing audio latency and improving audio quality.

ISSLOW, Integrated Services over Slow links, is a queuing mechanism that is used to optimize slow (low-capacity) network interfaces by reducing latency. In particular, it is designed for interfaces that forward traffic to modem links, ISDN B- channels, and sub-T1 links.

A typical packet occupies a modem link for up to half a second. Other packets queued behind it can experience significant delays. Packets that are long enough in length to exceed the maximum tolerable delay for their QoS flow are fragmented before transmission through the link, so that high-priority packets can be inserted between the fragments of the larger packet, and meet the required QoS parameters for speedy transmission. Figure 9.7 illustrates a Point-to-Point Protocol (PPP) link using ISSLOW.

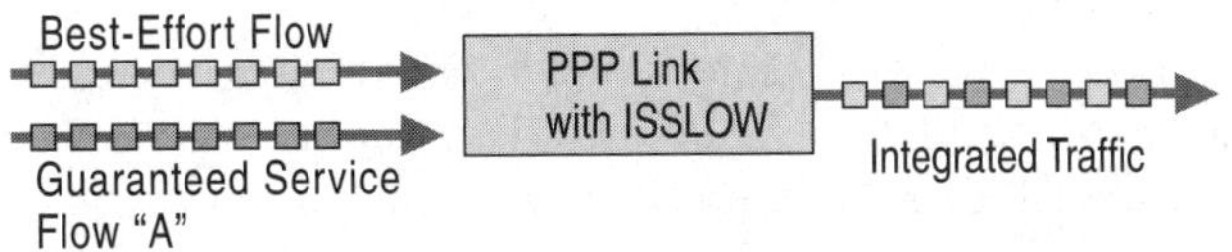

Figure 9.7 PPP Link with ISSLOW

For example, a PPP link is carrying best-effort traffic in addition to guaranteed service level flow "A." The PPP link capacity is 100 KBps and the average latency is 100 milliseconds (ms). The best-effort traffic is consuming the majority of the bandwidth on the link, which is starving flow A of the resources it requires to provide guaranteed service levels. In this example, flow A cannot tolerate a delay of more than 145 ms. As the best-effort traffic fills the queue, packets from flow A arrive. The first best-effort packet (10 kilobits) is fragmented into 2-kilobit packets. The 8-kilobit packet from flow A is fragmented into 2-kilobit packets as well, and the flow A fragments are inserted between the best-effort fragments in order to meet the required latency guarantees of flow A.

ATM

ATM is a flexible protocol that transmits packets in 53-byte cells. ATM has emerged as a popular backbone technology because of its scalability and ability to integrate different types of network traffic. ATM-capable interfaces do not require ISSLOW because ATM already fragments packets into small cells to reduce latency and precisely schedule traffic as opposed to sending it best-effort. ATM negotiates a traffic contract between the end system and the ingress ATM switch prior to connection establishment, which includes a set of QoS parameters. Signaling includes a traffic contract that specifies an ATM service class. Table 9.7 describes the ATM-to-QoS Mappings.

Table 9.7 ATM-to-QoS Service Mappings

Intserv Service Class	ATM Service Class
Guaranteed Service	Constant Bit Rate (CBR) or Real-Time Variable Bit Rate (rtVBR).
Controlled Load	Non-Real-Time Variable Bit Rate (nrtVBR) or Available Bit Rate (ABR) with a minimum cell rate.
Best-Effort	Unspecified Bit Rate (UBR) or Available Bit Rate (ABR).

Service Level Agreements

It becomes difficult to guarantee QoS when data crosses a WAN. When traffic is carried end-to-end, for example, between remote offices, it traverses multiple domains, including the Internet. At the boundary of each domain, traffic is passed from one service provider to the other to cross the Internet. The different providers must negotiate agreements on how they must carry and handle each other's traffic in order to ensure QoS. These negotiated contracts are called service level agreements (SLAs).

SLAs specify the rate at which traffic from one provider (the customer) must be carried by the other provider–usually the ISP. The administrator for each domain must ensure adequate network resources are available to support SLAs offered by their domain. The SLA might specify classes and marking rules. In addition, when providers agree to carry a customer's traffic, they are agreeing to consume resources in their own network that might otherwise be sold to another customer. For example, some traffic flows consume more resources, making that flow expensive to carry. As a result, most providers limit the amount of traffic that they agree to designate as priority. This limitation is referred to as policing, and these limits are negotiated in the SLA. If packets arrive that exceed the agreed-upon SLA, the provider discards the flow or demotes the priority of the flow to one that meets the terms of the SLA.

In general, the source domain marks the priority of the packets before they leave the source network boundary, because it is easier to determine the appropriate marking closer to the sending application before the packets have been aggregated with other flows by another provider. However, sometimes another provider is requested to mark packets on behalf of the customer, such as when the customer is a legacy network. In such a case, the provider marks the packets only to the extent that the priority rate specified does not exceed what has been negotiated in the SLA.

Windows 2000 QoS Admission Control Service

IP telephony provides an excellent example of the need for QoS admission control. When a user makes an IP telephone call to another user, the success of the communication relies on available priority bandwidth. Any new IP telephony sessions have the potential to degrade the quality of the first call that is still in progress, since these calls must share the same bandwidth. To guarantee QoS and successful throughput of the original call, admission control is needed to protect network resources.

When admission control is implemented, new calls are not permitted unless there is bandwidth available in the appropriate service class, and policy checking is used to verify who has access to high-priority bandwidth and on what subnet. For example, a user can have rights to request video from a local multimedia server, but might be restricted from requesting any video if the traffic must traverse a backbone network and exceed the limits for that backbone.

QoS Admission Control Service (QoS ACS) is a Windows 2000 component for managing network resources on a shared network segment (subnet). The QoS ACS provides a control point for bandwidth requests from the servers so that requests do not flood the subnet simultaneously. It is not required to implement the QoS ACS on every subnet; the highest benefit is realized from implementing the QoS ACS on congested segments.

As shown in Figure 9.8, the QoS ACS exerts its authority by placing itself within the RSVP message path, intercepting PATH and RESV messages, and passing the user information to the Local Policy Module (LPM) for authentication and policy lookup.

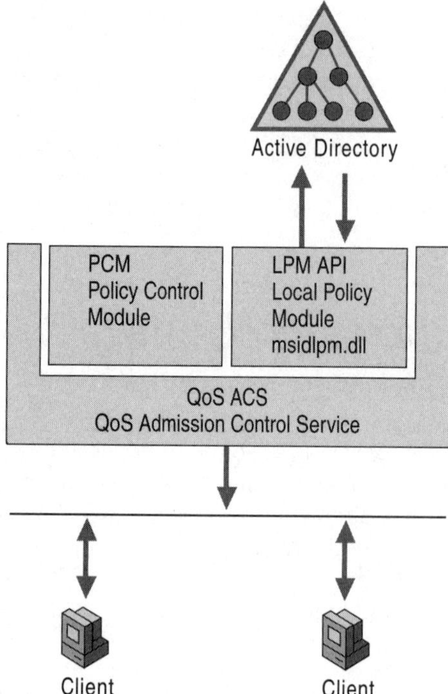

Figure 9.8 QoS Admission Control Service

The QoS ACS simplifies subnet administration by implementing:

- Centralized subnet bandwidth policy configuration on a per-user or per-subnet or subnet basis, via the QoS Admission Control Service snap-in.
- Transparency to users.
- The ability to partition subnet resources between low-priority and high-priority traffic.
- End-to-end network service with low delay guarantees.
- Interoperability with LAN, WAN, ATM, Ethernet, and Token Ring configurations.
- Support for multicast transmission of bandwidth reservation messages.

How QoS ACS Works

To deploy real-time multimedia or other mission-critical applications with an acceptable traffic rate, a network must commit to some level of guaranteed resource availability. In addition, the subnet management service must find some way for this priority traffic to coexist with traditional traffic. The alternative is a different physical network for each type of traffic: a very costly, high-administration solution.

The QoS ACS solves this problem by allowing the network administrator to centrally designate how, by whom, and when shared network resources are used. An QoS ACS performs logical allocation of network resources by participating in the signaling protocol, but does not allocate physical network resources such as network bandwidth or network queues. Note that it is RSVP messages that are passed to the QoS ACS, not the data packets which are ultimately transmitted from sender to receiver.

A host application can still send traffic not associated with a RSVP request and potentially overcommit the network. However, QoS ACS deployed with other traffic separation mechanisms can prevent network overcommitment. For example, on an Ethernet switch supporting IEEE 802.1p priority management, an QoS ACS can perform admission control to the high-priority band of traffic, and the 802.1p priority mechanism prevents the best-effort traffic from starving the high-priority traffic.

The QoS ACS server controls bandwidth for the subnet to which it is connected. Any devices on the same subnet (subnet clients) submit their priority bandwidth requests to that QoS ACS server.

Figure 9.9 shows an QoS ACS server configured to allow a maximum bandwidth reservation of 20 megabytes (MB). Each client represents a device on the managed subnet.

As each request is received by the QoS ACS server:

- The QoS ACS verifies whether network resource levels are adequate. The ACS can verify for the sender, receiver, or both.
- The requesting user identity is verified using the Kerberos protocol (the default Windows 2000 authentication service).
- The QoS ACS policy for that user is retrieved from Active Directory (it might already be cached on the QoS ACS server).
- The QoS ACS server checks the policy to see if the user has adequate rights for the request.
- The QoS ACS approves or rejects the request.

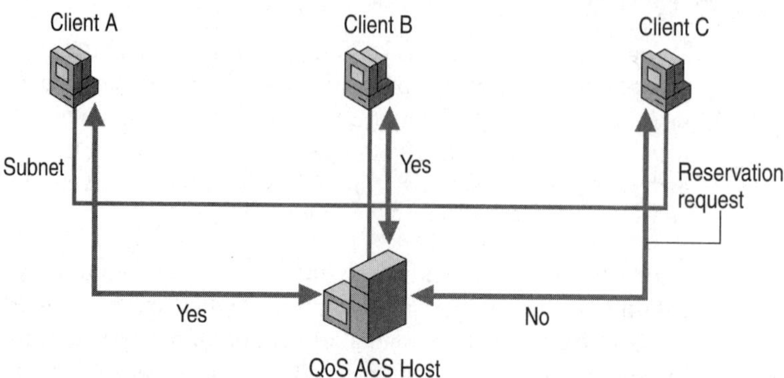

Figure 9.9 How QoS ACS Works

1. A video-conferencing application on Client A requests 10 MB of reserved bandwidth. The QoS ACS server determines that there is available bandwidth and logically grants the reservation. This leaves 10 MB of available bandwidth out of the possible 20 MB.
2. A video-conferencing application on Client B requests 10 MB of reserved bandwidth. Because there is still bandwidth available, the QoS ACS server logically grants the reservation. No additional bandwidth is available.
3. A video-conferencing application on Client C requests 10 MB of reserved bandwidth. Because no priority bandwidth is available at this time, the QoS ACS server rejects the reservation. The application on Client C can then determine whether to send the data now at a best-effort service level or wait until priority bandwidth becomes available.

Clients and servers running Microsoft® Windows® 98 or Windows 2000 or subnet bandwidth management client software are automatically configured to use an available QoS ACS server to request priority bandwidth. The QoS ACS server sends IP multicast beacons, messages that notify subnet clients that the QoS ACS server is ready to receive bandwidth reservation requests. A client does not attempt to send a request to an QoS ACS server that is not currently beaconing on the subnet. The beacon protocol is documented in the IETF RSVP working group draft on Subnet Bandwidth Manager (SBM). A client connected to the shared media subnet listens for an QoS ACS beacon, and if it hears the beacon it sends its RSVP and PATH messages to the QoS ACS. If the client is not on an QoS ACS-managed subnet, or there is not currently an QoS ACS server operating on the subnet, RSVP messages are forwarded following standard IP routing methodology. Routers and bridges supporting the Subnet Bandwidth Manager client, that are connected to shared media such as Ethernet must also detect the QoS ACS on the segment and forward RSVP messages to the QoS ACS for that subnet.

The QoS ACS server grants or rejects bandwidth requests based on the QoS ACS policy rights of the requesting user. When the request is granted, priority bandwidth is logically (each hop must physically allocate bandwidth when it grants the request) allocated by the QoS ACS server, and the request is forwarded to the receiving client. The QoS ACS server rejects a request if the user does not have the right to reserve priority bandwidth on that subnet, to reserve the requested amount of bandwidth, or if the subnet itself is not capable of making the guarantee at the time of the request.

Traffic is never blocked if a request cannot be granted. Instead, the sending application is immediately notified and it determines whether to continue sending the data at a best-effort service level or wait and request priority bandwidth later. If the application chooses to send the data anyway, the traffic is carried by the network as best-effort traffic with no reservation.

Note that the QoS ACS performs admission control for both PATH (sender) and RESV (receiver) RSVP messages.

Implementing the QoS ACS

The QoS ACS is a Microsoft implementation. Subnet Bandwidth Manager (SBM), which defines using a standardized signaling protocol to enable 802 type LAN-based admission control for RSVP flows, is an IETF standard technology the Microsoft QoS ACS implements. The Windows 2000 QoS ACS incorporates SBM technology in order to perform admission control duties.

In heterogeneous networks, there can be several potential SBMs on a subnet. Eligible devices are (in ascending order of precedence):

- SBM-capable switches that comprise the shared network
- Attached SBM-capable routers
- Attached SBM-capable hosts (includes any Windows 2000 QoS ACS servers)

These devices participate in an IP multicast–based election to determine the Designated SBM (DSBM) for that subnet. Any QoS ACS (SBM) clients on a subnet forward all RSVP messages to the DSBM. The remaining potential SBMs act as backups in the event that the DSBM stops functioning.

To maintain the integrity of RSVP reservations on a shared subnet, it is important that any router or host sending messages onto the subnet (and thereby consuming its resources) is an QoS ACS (SBM) client. On a managed subnet, network clients running Windows 2000 or Subnet Bandwidth Manager client software can use the QoS ACS to request bandwidth. The applications must also be QoS-enabled.

The QoS ACS can be deployed on any host running Windows 2000 Server. The QoS ACS operates at the IP network layer, servicing the most common application protocols, including all transport protocols in the TCP/IP protocol suite (TCP, UDP, and RTP). Applications that are not QoS-aware do not interact with the QoS ACS server, and receive best-effort service traffic levels from the network.

One QoS ACS server can be configured to manage multiple subnets or nonshared media such as demand-dial connections (for example, those found in Routing and Remote Access service configurations). The only restriction is that the QoS ACS cannot manage two different types of media at the same time. That is, it cannot manage a shared Ethernet segment and a demand-dial connection at the same time.

Before setting up admission control servers on your subnet, make sure your hardware, Windows configuration, and QoS ACS policies meet the necessary requirements outlined in this section.

Hardware Network adapters must be compatible with the IEEE 802.1p standard. This standard provides the mechanism necessary for traffic control.

Windows Configuration The QoS Admission Control Service must be installed on a Windows 2000 server that is a member of the domain that contains the subnets you intend to manage. A QoS ACS server must not also be an RSVP (QoS-aware) application server. However, it can be a file or print server.

QoS Packet Scheduler This must be installed on every client in the subnet that makes reservations by using the QoS ACS server. In addition, it is always a good practice to install the QoS Packet Scheduler on the QoS ACS server. Otherwise, heavy network traffic might cause RSVP messages sent by QoS ACS to be dropped.

Admission Control Logs Administrators can choose to enable the QoS ACS logging when needed as an aid to troubleshooting by using the logs to verify that RSVP messages are sent and received. Circular log files are created and are subject to administrative control in terms of their size, location, and total number. See "Troubleshooting" later in this chapter for more information.

QoS Admission Control Policies

A policy is a specification of resource limits. Policy is central to any implementation of QoS. Policy must be applied when deciding which traffic is eligible for preferential treatment. As a result, QoS deployment must include the following policy components:

- *Data-store*. Contains the policy parameters, such as user names, and the network resources to which these are entitled. For the Windows 2000 QoS ACS, the policy store is Active Directory.
- *Policy Decision Points (PDPs)*. Inspects resource requests and accepts or rejects them based on the applicable policy. In Windows 2000 QoS ACS, this is the Local Policy Module (LPM).
- *Policy Enforcement Points (PEPs)*. Acts on PDP decisions. Network devices that physically or logically grant resources to flows. For the Windows 2000 QoS ACS, PEPs are routers, switches, or DSBMs.

Local Policy Module

The Local Policy Module (LPM) is the component on the QoS ACS server that retrieves and returns policy information from Active Directory. LPM is a generic term used to denote the implementation of a courier service used to provide the QoS ACS with a means of retrieving policy information from a particular policy store. LPMs are an integral part of the QoS ACS. The default Windows 2000 LPM, Msidlpm.dll, handles authentication by comparing the user information within the Kerberos ticket contained in the RSVP message with Active Directory policy information.

QoS ACS policy decisions to logically allocate bandwidth are enabled through the LPM's access to the Windows 2000 Active Directory policy store. The QoS ACS server invokes the LPM when a policy object with a Windows 2000 Kerberos ticket is detected. The LPM takes the user name from the RSVP message policy object and looks up the applicable policy in the Active Directory. The LPM then:

- Vetoes (rejects based on policy).
- Accepts (note that the request can still be rejected by a third-party LPM).
- Snubs (ignores; this allows acceptance).

The request is granted when at least one LPM accepts and no LPMs veto. The QoS ACS server can then decide to logically allocate bandwidth.

The LPM resides on the admission control server and provides authentication services. The QoS ACS also exposes an LPM API that allows independent software vendors to write customized LPMs. Third-party development of LPMs and policy elements (PEs) are possible in the future.

Security

There must be a secure way to prove to a QoS ACS server that an RSVP message is from a valid user in a trusted Windows 2000 domain. The message must contain the name of the user and the information must be cryptographically hashed by an entity that the QoS ACS trusts. Kerberos tickets are inserted into RSVP messages for this purpose.

The RSVP SP on a host, using the Kerberos Key Distribution Center (KDC) in the domain, can construct a one-way Kerberos ticket containing the identity of the user, a session key for the QoS ACS and a lifetime for the ticket. The ticket is encrypted with a shared key known by the KDC and the QoS ACS. The QoS ACS server uses the shared key to decrypt the ticket and get the session key, subsequently checking the cryptographic hash to make sure the RSVP policy object is genuine and has not been modified. This method also protects against ticket reuse via the cut-and-paste method.

An invalid Kerberos ticket causes an error log entry and a PATH-ERR or RESV-ERR message to be sent back to the originator. QoS ACS servers can be configured to generate network management alerts (SNMP traps) in such an event. For more information about SNMP, see "Simple Network Management Protocol" in this book.

Policy Store

The policy store for QoS ACS policy is Windows 2000 Active Directory. This provides a secure, replicated, persistent store of QoS ACS policy information. The information for the QoS ACS is owned by the QoS ACS and can only be changed by programs that run with QoS ACS administration privileges. QoS ACS objects in Active Directory are protected by security settings, so a QoS ACS server needs at least read-access to those objects. Creating and manipulating these objects requires administrative privileges.

The QoS ACS can access the policy data once it knows the name of the subnet for which it is the QoS ACS. The name of the subnet is configured when the QoS ACS service is installed on a Windows 2000-based server. Each subnet must be named so that configuration and policy information can be stored in the Active Directory. For a single LAN Ethernet configuration, the name of the subnet can be the IP prefix, for example, 192.1.1.0/24. Alternately, the network administrator can select names other than IP prefix names if there is more than one shared subnet per logical IP subnet.

Each QoS ACS locates its configuration using its subnet name to navigate to the correct container in Active Directory and read and cache the policy data at startup. Within Active Directory there is a QoS ACS service node that is the container for all information pertaining to QoS ACS policies and configurations. A QoS ACS server pulls its configuration information from Active Directory and the configuration information can be cached if it is sufficiently small.

Defining QoS ACS Policies

The following sections provide helpful considerations when defining QoS ACS policy. For procedural information on configuring individual policy parameters, see Windows 2000 Server Help.

Policy Hierarchy

QoS ACS policies are hierarchical, from most specific (a particular user on a specific subnet) to least specific (a user policy for all QoS Admission Control Service–managed subnets).

When a user requests priority bandwidth, the QoS ACS searches Active Directory for policy values in the following order:

- A subnet-level user policy for the subnet on which the user is requesting priority bandwidth.
- An enterprise-level user policy.

When a user has a group profile defined in addition to a user policy, precedence is applied in the following priority:

- User policy on the current subnet
- Group policy on the current subnet
- Authenticated user on the current subnet
- User in the Enterprise container
- Authenticated user in the Enterprise container

Higher priority policy values always override lower priority policy values if the user has policies in both locations, and the same values are configured in both policies.

Enterprise-Level Policies

Enterprise-level policies are network-wide policies, and apply to traffic sent across any QoS ACS-managed subnet. This container holds two predefined policies:

1. *Any Authenticated User*: This policy is applied to all authenticated users in the domain. An authenticated user is any user logged on to a domain account with a valid user identity and password for that domain. It is recommended that this policy be customized with your common enterprise QoS parameters, and that it only define additional Enterprise policies if particular users have special requirements. These exception policies need only specify attributes that must be different from the default policy. The exception policy and default policy are aggregated when a user makes a bandwidth request.
2. *Unauthenticated User*: This policy is applied when an unauthenticated user makes a priority bandwidth request. This is useful for controlling the traffic of users who access the network but are not authenticated by a trusted Windows 2000 domain. An unauthenticated user is any user who is not logged on under a domain account but is connected to the network. For example, if you log on to a computer as a local user, the QoS ACS considers you unauthenticated because you are not logged on to a domain.

The values in the predefined Enterprise policies are listed in Table 9.8.

Table 9.8 Default Enterprise-Level Policy Values

Traffic Property	Any Authenticated User	Unauthenticated User
Data Rate	500 kilobits per second	64 kilobits per second
Peak Data Rate	500 kilobits per second	64 kilobits per second
Number of Flows	Two (2)	One (1)

Enterprise policies apply to all subnets unless the user also has a subnet-level policy. For example, if User A has a policy in the Enterprise container and a policy in the Subnet container for traffic on Subnet A, the Enterprise policy applies unless User A sends or receives data on Subnet A—then the Subnet policy applies.

Subnet-Level Policies

Under a subnet object, you can create subnet-level user policies. A particular user may have special requirements for specific subnets. To meet these requirements, you can create a user policy under that subnet object. Only those attributes that are different from the Enterprise policies must be configured.

It is recommended that first the default Unauthenticated and Authenticated user policies in the subnet container are modified to meet the needs of most users sending data on the subnet. If a user still has special resource requirements for that subnet, exception policies can be created. For example, to override the aggregate bandwidth for a particular user, you can create a subnet policy for the user with only the aggregate bandwidth value configured. All other values necessary for the bandwidth reservation come from one of the default enterprise policies.

Subnet Objects in the QoS ACS Console

For each managed subnet, you must create a subnet object. The properties in this object are used to configure all QoS ACS server properties on that subnet. This ensures that all QoS ACS servers (whether primary or backup) on the subnet handle client requests in the same way.

A subnet object is linked to the physical subnet and the QoS ACS server by the subnet IP address. The subnet object properties determine:

- The traffic limits and service levels for the subnet
- The logging and accounting properties for the QoS ACS servers
- QoS ACS properties on each QoS ACS server

You must first create a subnet object before you can add subnet-level user policies.

Subnet properties are not to be confused with subnet-level user policies. You create a subnet object to set the traffic limits for the subnet and the QoS ACS server properties for the QoS ACS servers managing the subnet. Subnet-level policies, held in the Subnet container in the QoS ACS snap-in, specify user policies for requesting bandwidth on that subnet.

Troubleshooting

This section contains methods for determining the cause of QoS ACS- or QoS-related communication problems, and tools that can verify statistics and operations.

Basic Troubleshooting

Table 9.9 is a quick reference guide to basic troubleshooting steps to try in the event of unsuccessful QoS deployment:

Table 9.9 Basic QoS Troubleshooting

Symptom	Suggested Remedy/Investigation
No connectivity	▪ 802.1p enabled on sender but not on receiver. ▪ Non-802.1p—capable device between sender and receiver. ▪ Failed traffic control installation; remove and reinstall QoS Packet Scheduler Service. ▪ Registry entry ***MaxOutstandingSends*** in \Psched\Parameters set too low.
No discernible effect of QoS	▪ End-to-end QoS signaling failure or traffic control failure. See "Troubleshooting Methodology" later in this chapter for assistance with tracing the source of the failure. ▪ Network not congested. ▪ No active QoS elements in those parts of the network that are congested. ▪ Packets not tagged correctly with 802.1p. ▪ Packets not marked correctly with DSCP.
QoS ACS policy ineffective	▪ Policy configured in QoS ACS that is not the DSBM on the relevant segment (use the tool Wdsbm to find out which QoS ACS is the DSBM). ▪ Verify that the QoS ACS is running under the account name of *QoS ACSService*. See Windows 2000 Server Help for procedural information.
RSVP messages dropped in the network	▪ Router in path dropping RSVP messages. Use Rsping to verify integrity of RSVP path. ▪ RSVP messages dropped due to congestion; verify 802.1p and DSCP marking for RSVP network control flow.
RSVP reservation requests rejected	▪ Insufficient resources provisioned in intervening routers or QoS ACS. ▪ Policy denial by QoS ACS.
Packets not tagged 802.1p	▪ Traffic control not installed. ▪ 802.1p not enabled on interface. ▪ QoS request denied for traffic flow. ▪ Non-802.1p-capable interface.
Packets tagged with unexpected 802.1p tag	▪ This is being overridden by a registry setting by the administrator. ▪ TCLASS override in effect. ▪ Packets nonconforming.
Packets marked with unexpected DSCP	▪ Registry override in effect. ▪ DCLASS override in effect.

Troubleshooting Methodology

A key to troubleshooting QoS is to verify that the signaling messages are traversing the network as expected and are not dropped or blocked for any reason. Once this is verified, the next step is to verify that traffic control is being effectively and correctly invoked for controlled load and guaranteed service levels.

The practical first step is mapping out the network topology to identify all the network devices in the path from sender to receiver, and identify which devices participate in the RSVP signaling. It is important to identify these devices as they intercept RSVP messages that transit the shared segments. Tracert and Wdsbm are useful tools for determining network topology.

Tracking RSVP Messages from Source to Destination Figure 9.10 describes the process of how to verify end-to-end signaling. Figure 9.11 describes the process of how to track the passage of RSVP messages.

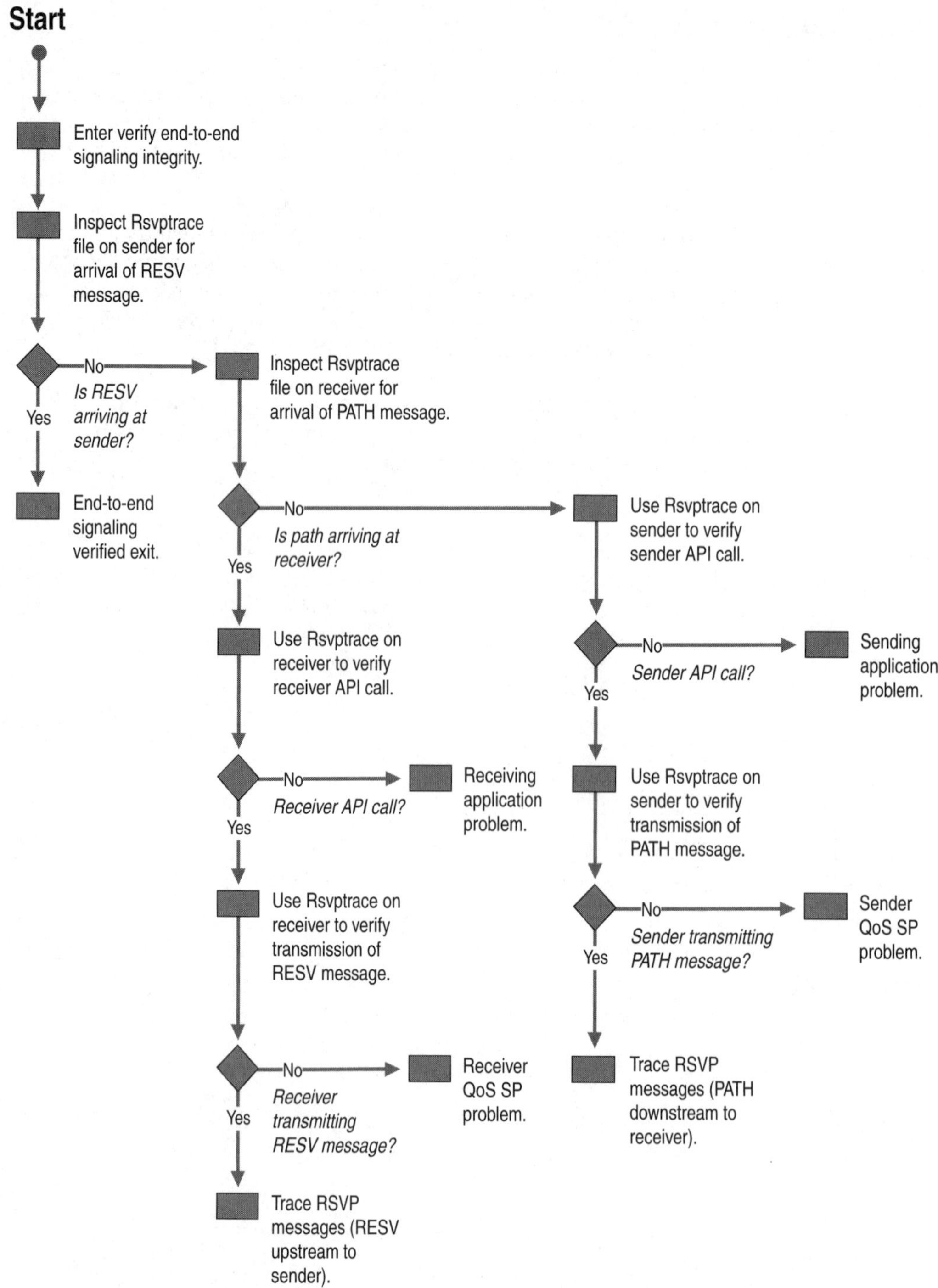

Figure 9.10 Verifying of End-to-end Signaling

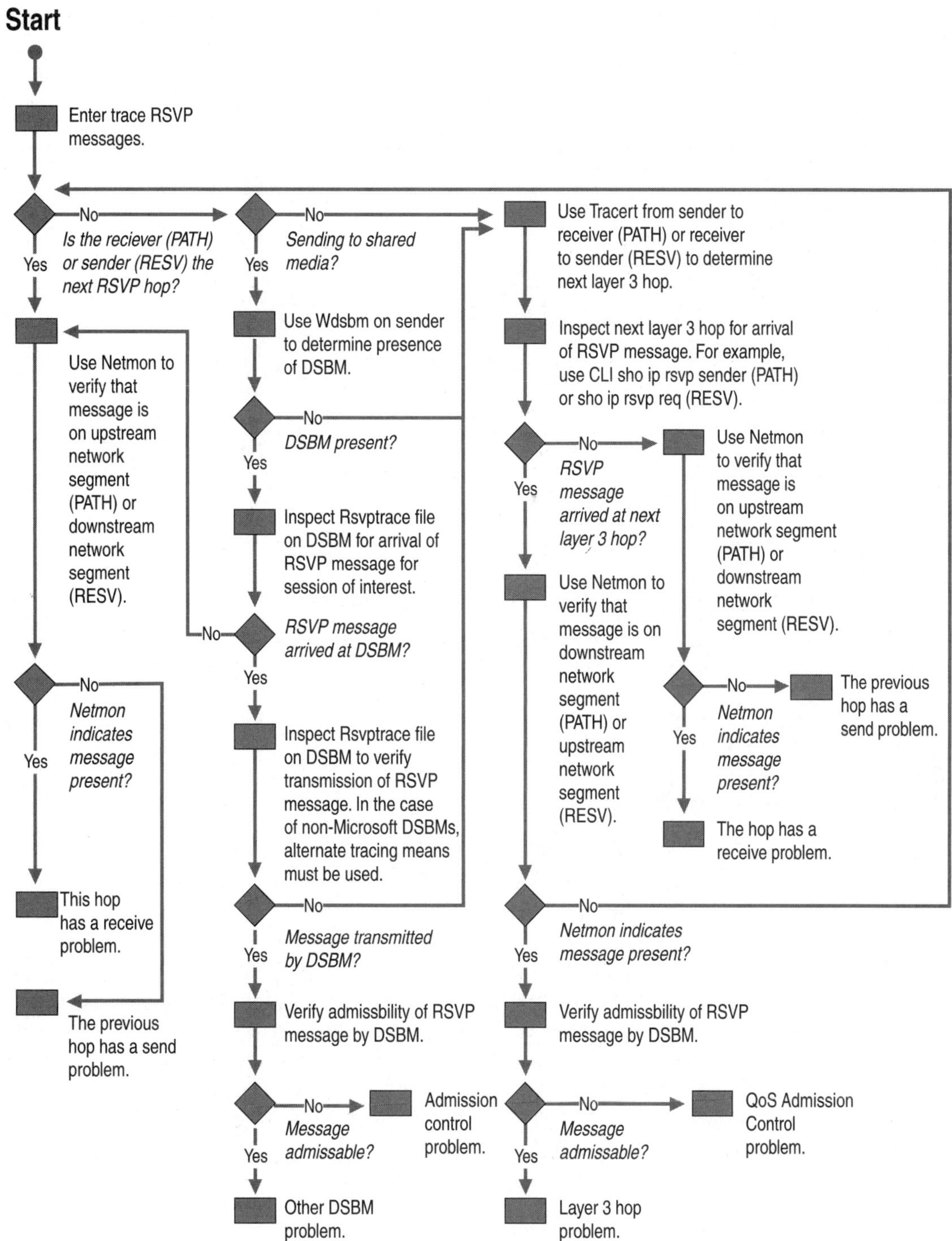

Figure 9.11 Tracing RSVP Messages

Figure 9.12 describes how to verify the functionality of traffic control.

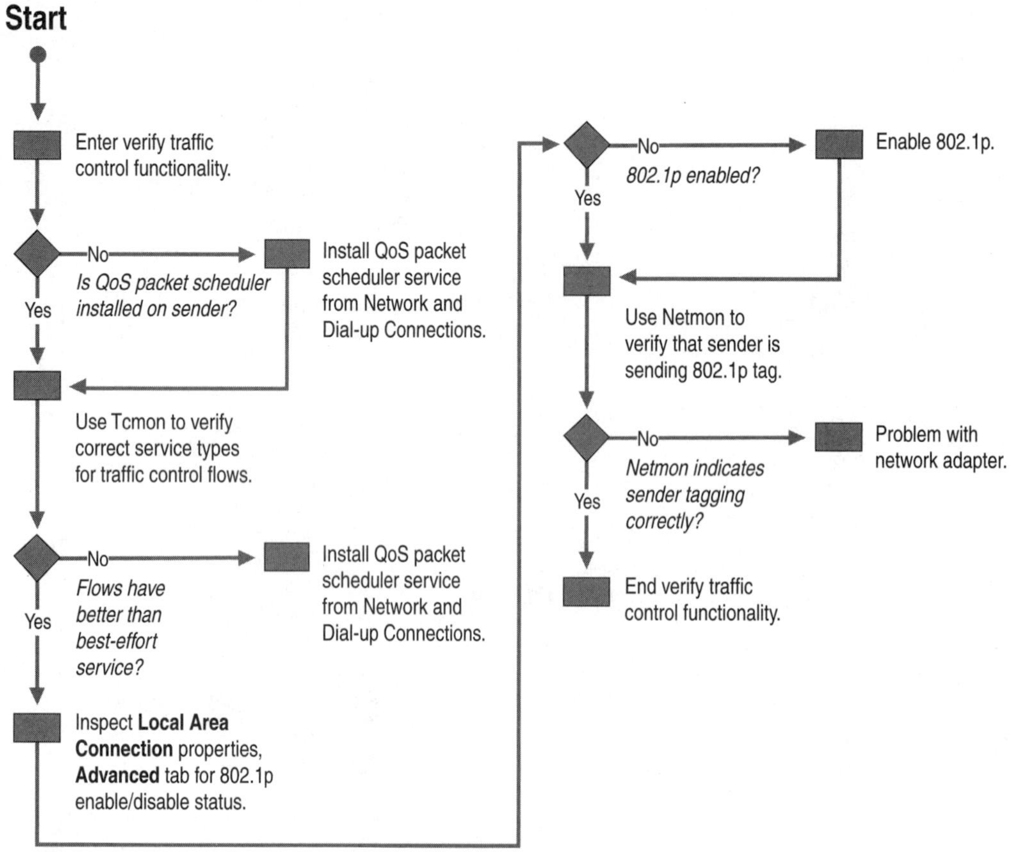

Figure 9.12 Verifying Traffic Control Functionality (802.1p)

QoS ACS Logs

QoS ACS transactions (RSVP messages) can be collected by configuring the QoS ACS service logs. The QoS Admission Control accounting service and RSVP logging service log messages can be viewed in the Windows 2000 Server Event Viewer. These logs are more detailed and are recorded as fixed (not customizable) ASCII-format files that can be viewed with a text editor or converted to an open database connectivity (ODBC) database. Do not confuse QoS ACS logs with the default logging carried out by Windows 2000 Server (viewed by using the Event Viewer).

You can control a number of options for the creation of each type of log, including the directory in which the files are created, and whether to create single or multiple files. The log files are circular. When you specify a maximum file size, one of two things occur when that limit is reached:

- Another log file is created, until the maximum number of log files you specified is also reached. This is useful for viewing a history of transactions for a pattern versus viewing only the latest information.

  –Or–

- The first file is simply overwritten each time the maximum file size is reached. This prevents the ability to look at historical data.

You do not have to stop QoS ACS services to view log files. New log entries are generated whenever bandwidth is requested. This causes a progressive increase in log file size or in the number of log files. Therefore, you might need to balance the gathering of detailed data against the need to limit files to a manageable size and number. Extremely large log files can compromise performance because each file contains approximately 500 messages per megabyte. Additionally, smaller log files are easier for the administrator to search for specific events. Consider available disk space when setting log file sizes and monitor the storage space in use whenever using any logging features.

Accounting Logs

The accounting log information is useful for:

- Planning for the number of users who regularly reserve resources on the network.
- Assessing current and future network bandwidth needs.
- Troubleshooting QoS Admission Control Service–related network communication errors.

Accounting log information includes:

- Who is using network resources.
- The date and time of individual sessions.
- Addressing information for individual sessions.

All fields in the log are terminated with a semicolon (;). Following is an example of an accounting log record:

1998/11/18 13:58:00:0578;192.168.3.5:4000[17];Start Sender;ENGR\Vincent;192.168.3.4:4000;New; 250000,1500,300000,10,1500

For accounting purposes, the most significant values in the entry show that the QoS Admission Control host approved a bandwidth request on November 18, 1998 (1998/11/18), at 1:58 P.M. (13:58:00:0578), which initiated a session (StartSender) with ID 192.168.3.4 and began sending data from a host in the Engineering (ENGR) domain for user Vincent.

Table 9.10 describes each field in the log.

Table 9.10 Log File Fields

Field	Description
Date/time	Date and time of the record, in Greenwich Mean Time (GMT).
Session IP addressing information	The receiver's IP address, the port number on which the data is sent (following the colon), and the decimal protocol ID of the protocol used, enclosed in brackets ([ ]). To match protocol IDs with protocol names, see RFC 1700.
Record type	One of the following: Start Sender, Start Receiver, Stop Sender, Stop Receiver, Reject Sender, or Reject Receiver.
User ID	The domain and user name, preceded by a backslash (\), of the sender or receiver.
IP addressing information for the last hop	The IP address of the last hop and either the port number on which the data is sent (following the colon) or the hexadecimal address of the network adapter (if the host relaying the message is a multihomed device). For example, 192.168.2-2.106:0x00000000.
Message status	One of the following: New, Modify, Stop Sender reason, Reject Sender, or source IP address of the data flow.
Message detail	Sender's traffic information, receiver's traffic information, Stop Receiver reason, and Reject Receiver reason.

Accounting and Billing

You can use information generated by the QoS ACS for accounting and billing. From the standpoint of network management, the accounting functions give you an overview of the ways in which your QoS resources are used. QoS ACS accounting shows you exactly who is using a resource, and for how long. Failed requests are also recorded, providing a record of who is trying to use QoS services without permission.

This information is available because QoS ACS servers log RSVP messages recording start and ending times of the flow, the resource requested and the user who is making the request. These records can be collected from the QoS ACS server and used to generate utilization reports for network managers. Alternately, these records can be processed to generate network usage billing.

RSVP Logs

You can configure the logging of RSVP messages. The RSVP log provides information similar to that of Network Monitor (NetMon). Using the log, you can trace who sends and receives RSVP messages and whether RSVP messages are accepted or rejected. This information is useful whenever QoS Admission Control Service–related network communication errors occur.

RSVP log information can help you troubleshoot by identifying:

- The date and time of the RSVP message.
- Addressing information of the message sender and receiver.

In the RSVP log file, each field is terminated with a comma (**,**). A vertical bar (|) indicates the end of a group of traffic information. Following is an example of an RSVP log record:

1998/02/06 15:35:05, PATH ,192.168.3.6,4000,17,|,
192.168.3.5,0x00000000,|,30000,|,
192.168.3.4,4000,|,3.000E+004,1.50E+003,3.300E+004,10,1500,|,
0,0.000E+000,1500,1.#IOE+000

The most significant values in the entry show that on February 6, 1998, at 3:35 P.M., a PATH message originating on host 192.168.3.4 was sent to receiver 192.168.3.6.

Table 9.11 describes each item in the log in detail, showing the parameters that each message in the RSVP log contains.

Table 9.11 RSVP Log File Fields

Field	Description
Date/time	Date and time of the message, in Greenwich Mean Time (GMT)
Type of message	PATH, RESV, PATH-ERR, RESV-ERR, PATH-TEAR, or RESV-TEAR, with additional parameters: *Confirmation request*: RESV-CONF or No RESV-CONF, indicating whether the receiver wants a reservation confirmation. *Scope*: An explicit list of sender hosts (in wildcard reservation-style format) toward which the information in the message is forwarded. *Reservation style*: Determining whether resources are reserved by fixed filter, share explicit, or wildcard. For more information about these styles, see RFCs 2205, 2210, 2215, and 2216. For detailed information about these parameters, see RFC 2205.

(continued)

Table 9.11 RSVP Log File Fields *(continued)*

Field	Description
Session IP addressing information	The receiver's IP address, the port number on which the data is sent, and the decimal protocol ID of the protocol used, followed by a vertical bar (|). For a list matching protocol IDs with protocol names, see RFC 1700.
IP addressing information for the last hop	Either the IP address of the last hop and the port number on which the data is sent (following the colon), or the hex address of the network adapter if the host relaying the message is a multihomed device, followed by a vertical bar (|).
Refresh interval	The frequency at which, in milliseconds, this message is sent.
Sender IP addressing information	The sender's IP address, the port number on which the data is sent, and the decimal protocol ID of the protocol used, followed by a vertical bar (|).
Bucket rate	The bucket data rate.
Bucket size	The size of the bucket in which packets are grouped for transmission. For more information on packet buckets, see RFCs 2210, 2215, and 2216.
Peak rate	The burst rate of the packets.
Packet size	The minimum packet size for transmission.
MTU size	The maximum packet size for transmission, followed by a vertical bar (|). This field, plus the previous four fields, make up the Tspec (traffic parameters for the flow). For more information on the Tspec, see RFCs 2205, 2210, 2215, and 2216.
Adspec	The remaining fields in the record indicate the traffic parameters for the receiver.

RSVP Error Codes

Table 9.12 lists the error codes that appear in RESV-ERR messages.

Table 9.12 Error Codes and Values

Error Code	Description
00	Confirmation. Reserved for use in the ERROR_SPEC object of a RESV-CONF message. The Error Value will also be zero.

(continued)

Table 9.12 Error Codes and Values *(continued)*

Error Code	Description
01	Admission control failure. Reservation request was rejected by admission control due to unavailable resources. The 16 bits of the Error Value field are ssur, cccc cccc, and cccc, where the bits are: ss = 00: Low-order 12 bits contain a globally-defined sub-code (values listed below). ss = 10: Low-order 12 bits contain a organization-specific sub-code. RSVP is not expected to be able to interpret this except as a numeric value. ss = 11: Low-order 12 bits contain a service-specific sub-code. RSVP is not expected to be able to interpret this except as a numeric value. Since the traffic control mechanism might substitute a different service, this encoding might include some representation of the service in use. u = 0: RSVP rejects the message without updating local state. u = 1: RSVP may use the message to update local state and then forward the message. This means that the message is informational. r: Reserved bit, must be zero. cccc cccc cccc: 12-bit code. The following globally-defined sub-codes can appear in the low-order 12 bits when ssur = 0000: Sub-code = 1: Delay bound cannot be met. Sub-code = 2: Requested bandwidth unavailable Sub-code = 3: MTU in flowspec larger than interface MTU.
02	Policy Control failure. Reservation or path message has been rejected for administrative reasons (for example, required credentials not submitted, insufficient quota or balance, or administrative preemption). This Error Code can appear in a PATH-ERR or RESV-ERR message. Contents of the Error Value field are to be determined in the future.
03	No path information for this RESV message. No path state for this session. RESV message cannot be forwarded.
04	No sender information for this RESV message. There is path state for this session, but it does not include the sender matching some flow descriptor contained in the RESV message. RESV message cannot be forwarded.
05	Conflicting reservation style. Reservation style conflicts with styles of existing reservation state. The Error Value field contains the low-order 16 bits of the Option Vector of the existing style with which the conflict occurred. This RESV message cannot be forwarded.
06	Unknown reservation style. Reservation style is unknown. This RESV message cannot be forwarded.
07	Conflicting destination ports. Sessions for same destination address and protocol have appeared with both zero and non-zero destination port fields. This Error Code can appear in a PATH-ERR or RESV-ERR message.

(continued)

Table 9.12 Error Codes and Values *(continued)*

Error Code	Description
08	Conflicting sender ports Sender port is both zero and non-zero in PATH messages for the same session. This Error Code can appear only in a PATH-ERR message.
09, 10, 11	(reserved)
12	Service preempted. The service request defined by the STYLE object and the flow descriptor has been administratively preempted. For this Error Code, the 16 bits of the Error Value field are: ssur cccc cccc cccc The high-order bits ssur are as defined under Error Code 01. The globally-defined sub-codes that can appear in the low-order 12 bits when ssur = 0000 are to be defined in the future.
13	Unknown object class. Error Value contains 16-bit value composed of (Class-Num, C-Type) of unknown object. This error must be sent only if RSVP is going to reject the message, as determined by the high-order bits of the Class-Num. This Error Code can appear in a PathErr or ResvErr message.
14	Unknown object C-Type. Error Value contains 16-bit value composed of Class-Num or C-Type of object.
15-19	(reserved)
20	Reserved for API. Error Value field contains an API error code, for an API error that was detected asynchronously and must be reported via an upcall.
21	Traffic Control Error. Traffic Control call failed due to the format or contents of the parameters to the request. The RESV or PATH message that caused the call cannot be forwarded, and repeating the call is futile. For this Error Code, the 16 bits of the Error Value field are: ss00 cccc cccc cccc The high-order bits ss are as defined under Error Code 01. The following globally-defined sub-codes can appear in the low order 12 bits (cccc cccc cccc) when ss = 00: Sub-code = 01: Service conflict. Trying to merge two incompatible service requests. Sub-code = 02: Service unsupported. Traffic control can provide neither the requested service nor an acceptable replacement. Sub-code = 03: Bad Flowspec value. Malformed or unreasonable request. Sub-code = 04: Bad Tspec value. Malformed or unreasonable request. Sub-code = 05: Bad Adspec value. Malformed or unreasonable request.
22	Traffic Control System error. A system error was detected and reported by the traffic control modules. The Error Value contains a system-specific value giving more information about the error. RSVP is not expected to be able to interpret this value.
23	RSVP System error. The Error Value field provides implementation-dependent information on the error. RSVP is not expected to be able to interpret this value.

In general, every RSVP message is rebuilt at each hop, and the node that creates an RSVP message is responsible for its correct construction. Similarly, each node is required to verify the correct construction of each RSVP message that it receives. If a programming error allows an RSVP to create a malformed message, the error is not generally reported to end systems in an ERROR_SPEC object; instead, the error is simply logged locally, and perhaps reported through network management mechanisms.

The only message formatting errors that are reported to end systems are those that can reflect version mismatches, and which the end system might be able to circumvent (for example, by falling back to a previous C-Type for an object; see code 13 and 14 above).

The choice of message formatting errors that an RSVP may detect and log locally is implementation-specific, but it typically includes the following:

- Wrong-length message: RSVP Length field does not match message length.
- Unknown or unsupported RSVP version.
- Bad RSVP checksum.
- INTEGRITY failure.
- Illegal RSVP message type.
- Illegal object length: not a multiple of 4, or less than 4.
- Next hop/Previous hop address in HOP object is illegal.
- Bad source port: Source port is non-zero in a filterspec or sender template for a session with destination port zero.
- Required object class (specify) missing.
- Illegal object class (specify) in this message type
- Violation of required object order.
- Flow descriptor count wrong for style or message type.
- Logical Interface Handle invalid.
- Unknown object Class-Num.
- Destination address of RESV-CONF message does not match Receiver Address in the RESV_CONFIRM object it contains.

Tools

This section describes various tools and their roles in troubleshooting QoS implementations. Certain tools are described only briefly; for further details, see the *Microsoft® Windows® 2000 Resource Kit* Tools Help.

PathPing

This TCP/IP utility has new functional parameters related to QoS:

-t

If packets are sent with an 802.1p tag, during the transition between a 802.1p aware network and network that is not 802.1p–aware, the switch connecting these two networks may be configured to strip out the tag before forwarding the packets onto the non-802.1p–aware network. Otherwise, non-802.1p–aware devices which cannot recognize the tag may discard the packet, wrongly assuming that it was a corrupted. Enabling this parameter sends the packets with a tag that identifies the network element that is tossing the tagged packet.

-r

This switch tests whether each node in the path is RSVP-aware. A node is considered RSVP-aware if it responds to a protocol 46 message (or times out). It is considered non-RSVP–aware if it sends an ICMP protocol unreachable error message. Note that if the RSVP service is not running on the node, it will return an ICMP Protocol unreachable error message.

For more information about PathPing, see "TCP/IP Troubleshooting" in this book.

Wdsbm

This tool identifies the QoS ACS that manages the segment to which a specific host is attached.

```
wdsbm -i <local interface IP address>
```

Wdsbm prints information (including the IP address) that pertains to the QoS ACS that is intercepting RSVP messages to and from the specified interface. Since the QoS ACS can block RSVP messages, it is useful to know the IP address of the QoS ACS when attempting to isolate the location at which RSVP messages are blocked.

Rsvptrace

Rsvptrace generates a log of RSVP messages that are sent and received by the RSVP SP on a host. The tool also shows API calls from sending and receiving applications to the RSVP SP. By running Rsvptrace on the sender and receiver, it is easy to verify that applications are making the required calls to the API, the RSVP SP is generating RSVP messages, and the messages are arriving from the network. Rsvptrace can be run on the QoS ACS to inspect received and transmitted RSVP messages. However, since QoS ACS servers do not run multimedia applications, no API entries will appear in the trace.

To enable RSVP tracing on a host, add the entry **EnableTracing** to the following registry subkey:

HKEY_LOCAL_MACHINE\System\CurrentControlSet\Services\RSVP \Parameters

with a data type of REG_DWORD. Set the value of the entry to 0x1.

The RSVP service must be restarted after this entry is added to the registry. Use Computer Management to restart the RSVP service.

Caution Do not use a registry editor to edit the registry directly unless you have no alternative. The registry editors bypass the standard safeguards provided by administrative tools. These safeguards prevent you from entering conflicting settings or settings that are likely to degrade performance or damage your system. Editing the registry directly can have serious, unexpected consequences that can prevent the system from starting and require that you reinstall Windows 2000. To configure or customize Windows 2000, use the programs in Control Panel or Microsoft Management Console (MMC) whenever possible.

The RSVP service must be restarted after this value is added to the registry. Use the Computer Management interface to restart the RSVP service.

The RSVP SP begins generating the Rsvptrace log in the directory *%windir%\system32\logfiles*.

Log files are named RsvpTrace*XX*.txt, where "*XX*" is a number from 00 to 09. Each log file is limited in size. When a log file fills up, another one is created using the next sequence number for the "*XX*" part of the log file name. Once the last log file sequence number is used and the last log file is filled, the first log file is overwritten. The user should inspect the list of log files and their creation dates to see which log file is currently being written.

The user can monitor data being written to the log file in real time by typing:

```
tail -f RsvpTraceXX.TXT
```

where "*XX*" is the trace-file number.

Following is a sample from a sender's Rsvptrace log:

```
1999/04/20 17:53:42:0679; From API; PATH
;172.31.8.159,5003,17;0.0.0.0,0x00000000;30000;172.31.3.21,3128;1.028E+0
1999/04/20 17:53:42:0679; 172.31.8.159 <= 172.31.3.21; PATH
;172.31.8.159,5003,17;172.31.3.21,0x00000000;1500;172
1999/04/20 17:53:44:0679; 172.31.8.159 <= 172.31.3.21; PATH
;172.31.8.159,5003,17;172.31.3.21,0x00000000;3000;172
1999/04/20 17:53:46:0773; 172.31.8.159 <= 172.31.3.21; PATH
;172.31.8.159,5003,17;172.31.3.21,0x00000000;6000;172
1999/04/20 17:53:54:0617; 172.31.8.159 <= 172.31.3.21; PATH
;172.31.8.159,5003,17;172.31.3.21,0x00000000;12000;17
1999/04/20 17:54:07:0664; 172.31.8.159 <= 172.31.3.21; PATH
;172.31.8.159,5003,17;172.31.3.21,0x00000000;24000;17
1999/04/20 17:54:12:0601; 172.31.3.1 => 172.31.3.21; RESV
;172.31.8.159,5003,17;172.31.3.1,0x00000000;30000;No Re
1999/04/20 17:54:12:0679; From API; PATH
;172.31.8.159,5003,17;0.0.0.0,0x00000000;30000;172.31.3.21,3128;1.028E+0
```

1. The first entry shows that at 17:53:42:0679, the sending application invokes the QoS API, which transmits a PATH message.
2. The next entry shows the PATH message transmitted to the network. There is no guarantee that it is actually sent to the network, but it does verify that the RSVP SP has passed the message to the TCP/IP stack for transmission to the network.
3. Additional PATH messages are sent to the network. Messages are refreshed at 30-second intervals.
4. At 17:54:12:0601, a RESV message arrives at the sender for the session, completing the reservation process. This indicates that the PATH message arrived at the end node (receiver) and the receiver responded with a RESV message.
5. At 17:54:12:0679, another API PATH is logged. This indicates that a proxy for the application (in the RSVP SP) is refreshing the RSVP state on behalf of the application.

The IP addresses in the PATH message log entries show that the RSVP session is 172.31.8.159 and the sender is 172.31.3.21. The session address is equivalent to the receiver address in the case of unicast, and to the multicast session address in the case of multicast.

The IP addresses in the RESV message entry show that the RESV message is sent to the sender at IP address 172.31.3.21. However, it shows that the RESV message arrives from the previous hop—172.31.3.1—which is the IP address for the router that sent the RESV message to the sender.

Netmon

Network Monitor (Netmon) monitors traffic on a network. Versions of Netmon later than version 2 include RSVP-parsing functionality. Netmon can also monitor 802.1p tagging.

Netmon can be run on the sending host, the receiving host, QoS ACS servers and on intermediary hops. Netmon requires installation. For information about installing Netmon, see the Windows 2000 Server Help.

Running Netmon on a Host

Generally, Netmon needs to be run on a computer that is used strictly as a traffic monitor, as opposed to end nodes or QoS ACS servers (any hosts that generate RSVP messages). It is also important that the monitoring computer is not attached to the network by use of a dedicated port on a learning bridge type switch (most modern chassis-based switches). Otherwise, the switch can prevent the monitoring computer from seeing traffic that is not addressed to it specifically. Generally, smaller, cheaper hubs do not act as learning bridges and flood traffic from each port to all other ports. Use this type of hub to attach the monitoring computer to the same switch port as the next or previous hop.

Installing and using Netmon on both the sender and receiver is recommended.

Capture and Display Filters

Set a capture filter for all messages to and from the end node. The capture needs to be started on each node before the sending application is started. RSVP messages are typically refreshed every 30 seconds; take this into account when deciding how long to let the capture run.

Once the capture is complete, use the display filter to extract RSVP messages only from the captured data. Traces of RSVP messages should indicate a PATH message sent by the sender, arriving some time later at the receiver. The receiver responds with a RESV message, which arrives at the sender. If the traces do not confirm this behavior, one or both of the message types might have been dropped in transit or were not generated by the end node. As long as the application is running, no PATH-TEAR or RESV-TEAR messages display in the trace. PATH-TEAR or RESV-TEAR messages might indicate that one of the application peers has terminated, or that a RSVP-aware network node has rejected a request.

Monitoring 802.1p

Netmon only reveals 802.1p tags if it is run on a host that does not have 802.1p-capable drivers (or on which 802.1p functionality has been disabled). Drivers that are 802.1p-capable strip off the 802.1p tags before handing the packets to Netmon.

Rsping

Rsping determines whether a specific network path is blocking RSVP signaling messages. If you suspect that certain RSVP messages are not arriving at their intended destination, Rsping can detect if the network is at fault. Unlike Rsvptrace, which allows the user to observe RSVP messages arriving at or generated from a specific node, Rsping enables the user to generate specific styles of RSVP messages for transmission to an RSVP peer.

Both PATH and RESV messages are generated when Rsping is run. It is also possible to specify:

- If these messages are multicast or unicast.
- Intserv service type.
- Flow rate.

With Rsping, multicast RESV messages use the wildcard filter (WF) style, while unicast messages use the fixed filter (FF) style. In addition, the peak rate requested is always twice the flow rate specified.

Invoke Rsping using the parameters that most closely emulate the RSVP messages generated by the real application. These messages can be observed by inspecting the Rsvptrace file on the transmitting host.

Tcmon

Tcmon is a traffic control monitor that can be used to:

- Verify the creation of kernel traffic flows.
- Identify characteristics and statistics associated with interfaces (such as whether or not 802.1p is enabled).
- Identify characteristics and statistics associated with each flow (such as service type, tagging or marking in effect, bytes transmitted on the flow, and so on).

For example, the Microsoft® NetMeeting® video conferencing application creates a single flow for audio traffic and another flow for video traffic. These should both be visible by using Tcmon (invoke Tcmon for the appropriate transmit interface and to set it to Auto Refresh mode). In addition, Tcmon indicates a third flow for the Network Control service type. This flow is for RSVP signaling traffic and remains active as long as RSVP is active.

Initially, Tcmon reports that the two traffic flows created on behalf of the application are the best-effort service type. The service type remains best-effort until the network approves the sender's RSVP request. At that time, traffic control is invoked and the flow's service types change to controlled load or guaranteed. If this does not happen, then either the network has not confirmed the QoS request, or a problem exists with local traffic control or the RSVP SP.

To install Tcmon, run Setup.exe from the Tcmon Install directory on the *Resource Kit* Tools Help.

To run Tcmon, at a command line type:

```
tcmon
```

The Tcmon dialog box appears. Select the appropriate interface for which traffic control is to be monitored. When looking for changes in flow parameters (such as changes in service type), it is helpful to enable the Auto Refresh mode (on the Refresh menu of the Tcmon dialog box).

System Monitor

System Monitor (Sysmon) monitors traffic control, RSVP, and QoS ACS components. It is a standard component of Windows 2000. See the Windows 2000 Server Help for instruction on running System Monitor.

Once System Monitor is active, from the Add Counters dialog box:

- Select **Psched Pipe** to monitor traffic control parameters such as number of flows installed and number of packets queued in various QoS Packet Scheduler components.
- Select **QoS ACS/RSVP Service** to monitor parameters such as API calls and RSVP messages.

Qtcp

Qtcp measures end-to-end network integrity and service quality for QoS verification. Qtcp sends a sequence of test packets through a network and reports on the queuing delay experienced by each packet. Packets that do not arrive at the destination are recorded as dropped packets.

Qtcp performs the following:

1. Reports precise microsecond delay variations.
2. Invokes network QoS by default, and is useful for evaluating QoS mechanisms.
3. Can simulate traffic flows for a range of user-selected packet sizes.
4. Can simulate traffic flows shaped to a specific range of token bucket parameters.
5. Can be used on an isolated, controlled network, or on a production network.
6. Generates detailed result logs.

A Qtcp session is invoked on both sending and receiving hosts. Qtcp uses the GQoS API to invoke QoS from local traffic control and from the network. The Qtcp sender causes an RSVP PATH message to be sent towards the receiver and waits until a response is received. The Qtcp receiver waits for an RSVP PATH message from the sender and responds by transmitting an RSVP RESV message.

Receipt of the RESV message at the sender initiates the *measurement* phase. At this time, the sender submits buffers to the kernel for transmission. The kernel paces the transmission of traffic according to the token bucket parameters and service type selected by the user. As packets are transmitted, the sequence number and the local time (to a precision of 100 nanoseconds) is recorded on each packet.

When packets arrive at the receiver's traffic control, the local time of the receiving host is recorded in each packet, and traffic control passes the packets to the receiving Qtcp peer. The receiving Qtcp peer process maintains a list of all received packets, including the packet sequence number, the time sent, and the time received.

The sending portion of the test terminates on the sending side when the transmitter has sent the required number of packets (the default of 2,048 packets can be overridden). Following the transmission of the last packet, the sender sends a terminating sequence of 10 termination packets. The test terminates on the receiving side upon receipt of a termination packet, or upon receipt of the required number of packets. On particularly congested links, the receiver might never receive the required number of packets, because the termination packets can be dropped. In this case, the Qtcp receiver can be manually terminated by typing:

q

Upon termination, the receiver Qtcp parses and processes the log of received packets. Three logs are generated:

- *<File_name>*.sta contains summary statistics. It reports the total number of packets received and specifies the sequence number of each dropped packet.
- *<File_name>*.raw contains a detailed log showing normalized send time and receive time for each packet, the latency (difference between sent and received time), packet size and sequence number.
- *<File_name>*.log is a result of normalizing the results of the second file to account for any clock discrepancies between the two hosts. Normally, this is negligible, but on lightly loaded, high-speed LANs it can be significant.

To run Qtcp on the sender, at a command line type:

```
qtcp -l 64 -t <IP Address>
```

where 64 is the buffer size in bytes, and *<IP Address>* is the IP address of the receiver. The following is displayed:

```
Initiated QoS connection. Waiting for receiver.
```

To run Qtcp on the receiver, at a command line type:

```
qtcp -f <filename> -r
```

The following is displayed:

```
Waiting for QoS sender to initiate QoS connection.
```

The receiver and the sender await the required exchange of RSVP messages before starting the data transfer. By default, kernel traffic control paces transmitted packets at a rate of 100 KBps (kilobytes per second).

Qtcp displays a series of dots on the node consoles. Each dot corresponds to 100 packets sent or received. The first dot is printed on the receiver prior to the actual receipt of the first 100 packets. The dots indicate that Qtcp is functional.

Upon transmission of the specified number of packets, the sender terminates with a message regarding the transmission rate. Next, upon receipt of the required number of packets (or termination packets), the receiver terminates with the message

```
Received 2048 buffers.
```

followed by statistics. However, these statistics might not be accurate. Use the *File_name*.sta, *File_name*.raw and *File_name*.log files to view the session statistics.

To generate the Qtcp log files, press the ENTER key on the receiver console after the session terminates.

Readpol

Readpol displays the QoS ACS policies that are in effect within a particular domain. Readpol provides a method of identifying the policies that apply to a particular user without using the QoS ACS console or having administrator privileges. Readpol is particularly useful in tracking the propagation of PATH or RESV messages when the QoS ACS is suspected of blocking these due to restrictive policies.

Rsvpsm

Rsvpsm is an interactive tool that allows the user to query the status of RSVP sessions on a remote computer. Information available by use of Rsvpsm includes all PATH state blocks, RESV state blocks, and Traffic Control state blocks maintained by a remote host.

This tool can be used to track complex RSVP problems spanning multiple hosts.

Qossp.aid, Rapilib.aid

Qossp.aid and Rapilib.aid generate diagnostic output from the RSVP SP. These tools are particularly useful for tracking problems with an application's use of the QoS API, or with the RSVP SP itself.

To enable RSVP SP logging, add the registry entry **EnableDebugAid** to the following subkey:

HKEY_LOCAL_MACHINE\System\CurrentControlSet\Services\RSVP \Parameters

with a data type of REG_DWORD.

To enable RSVP SP debugging related to an application's use of the API, set the least significant bit of the value (bit 0) to **1**.

To enable diagnostic output regarding the internal functioning of the RSVP SP, set the 2nd least significant bit of the value (bit 1) to **1**.

Use Computer Management to restart the RSVP service in order to initiate RSVP SP logging.

The RSVP SP logs are stored in the directory *%windir%*\system32\logfiles. Files are generated for each application that makes use of the RSVP SP. Log files named QoSSP.aid.<*XXXX*> are generated when bit 0 of the registry value is set to 1 Log files named rapilib.aid.<*XXXX*> are generated when bit 1 is set to 1. In each case, <*XXXX*> is the process ID of the application.

Ttcp

Ttcp is a noise generation tool. The effects of QoS are very noticeable when resources are scarce (some part of the network is congested). To test QoS deployments, it is helpful to artificially congest a network in a controlled manner by generating multiple simultaneous conversations, and generating traffic with a packet size distribution that mimics the traffic pattern in your production network.

Ttcp generates a single UDP or TCP session between two hosts. Buffer size, number of buffers, ports used, and other miscellaneous parameters can be set and controlled. It is not possible to control the rate at which the transmitter sends (other than by using the QoS Packet Scheduler and Tcmon to create a shaped flow for the Ttcp traffic). A single conversation is generated for each instance of Ttcp. Multiple conversations can be established by invoking multiple instances of Ttcp.

To induce Ttcp to drive the network more aggressively, invoke it by use of the ***-a*** and ***-c*** options.

Tracert

Tracert determines the route to a destination by sending Internet Control Message Protocol (ICMP) echo packets with varying Time to Live (TTL) values. Each router along the path is required to decrement the TTL on a packet by at least 1 before forwarding it. When the TTL on a packet reaches 0, the router is supposed to send back an ICMP Time Exceeded message to the source system. The Tracert usage is:

tracert [**-d**] [**-h** *<maximum_hops>*] [**-j** *<computer-list>*] [**-w** *<time-out>*] *<target_name>* *<receiver IP address>*

Tracert Parameters

-d

Specifies not to resolve addresses to computer names.

-h *<maximum_hops>*

Specifies maximum number of hops to search for target.

-j *<computer-list>*

Specifies loose source route along *<computer-list>*.

-w *<time-out>*

Waits the number of milliseconds specified by *<time-out>* for each reply.

<target_name>

Name of the target computer.

<receiver IP address>

Causes the sending host to print the IP addresses for a single interface on each router that exists along the path from sender to receiver. This list is helpful in identifying nodes that might be dropping or blocking RSVP messages or data.

Additional Resources

For more information about QoS RFCs, Internet Drafts, and other QoS-related links, see the International Engineering Task Force (IETF) link on the Web Resources page at http://windows.microsoft.com/windows2000/reskit/webresources.

The following Internet Drafts relate to QoS:

- *Providing Integrated Services Over Low-Bit-Rate Links*
- *SBM (Subnet Bandwidth Manager): A Proposal for Admission Control Over IEEE 802-Style Networks*
- *A Framework for Providing Integrated Services Over Shared and Switched IEEE 802 LAN Technologies*
- *Integrated Services over IEEE 802.1D/802.1p Networks*
- *Integrated Service Mappings on IEEE 802 Networks*
- *RSVP Cryptographic Authentication*
- *RSVP Extensions for Policy Control*
- *Partial Service Deployment in the Integrated Services Architecture*

The following RFCs relate to QoS:

- RFC 2205: *Resource Reservation Protocol (RSVP) Version 1 Functional Specification*
- RFC 2207: *RSVP Extensions for IPSEC Data Flows*
- RFC 2208: *Resource Reservation Protocol (RSVP) Version 1: Applicability Statement: Some Guidelines on Deployment*
- RFC 2209: *Resource Reservation Protocol (RSVP) Version 1: Message Processing Rules*
- RFC 2210: *The Use of RSVP with IETF Integrated Services*
- RFC 2211: *Specification of the Controlled-Load Network Element Service*
- RFC 2212: *Specification of Guaranteed Quality of Service*

CHAPTER 10

Simple Network Management Protocol

To answer the challenges of designing an effective network management platform for heterogeneous Transmission Control Protocol/Internet Protocol (TCP/IP)–based networks, the Simple Network Management Protocol (SNMP) was defined in 1988 and approved as an Internet standard in 1990 by the Internet Activities Board (IAB). SNMP service provides the ability to monitor and communicate status information between a variety of hosts. This chapter provides an administrator with the background and conceptual material necessary to understand and implement SNMP within the context of Microsoft® Windows® 2000.

In This Chapter

Related Information in the Resource Kit

- For information about securing SNMP messages, see "Internet Protocol Security" in this book.
- For more information about MIB object types, see "MIB Object Types" in this book
- For more information about installing and configuring Microsoft SNMP service, see Windows 2000 Server Help.

What is SNMP?

SNMP is a network management standard widely used with TCP/IP networks and, more recently, with Internetwork Packet Exchange (IPX) networks. The SNMP standard includes the following Request for Comment (RFC)–compliant constructs:

- The Management Information II (MIB II), RFC 1213. A set of manageable objects that represent various types of information about the network configuration, such as the list of network interfaces, the routing table, the ARP table, the list of opened TCP connections, or ICMP statistics.
- The Structure for Management Information (SMI), RFC 1902. A separate Internet RFC that describes the object syntax for specifying how MIB data can be referenced and stored.
- Simple Network Management Protocol (SNMP), RFC 1157. A standard that defines how communication occurs between SNMP-capable devices and the types of messages that are allowed.

SNMP provides a method of managing network nodes (servers, workstations, routers, bridges, and hubs) from a centrally located host. SNMP performs its management services by using a distributed architecture of management systems and agents. As shown in Figure 10.1, the centrally located host, which is running network management software, is referred to as an SNMP management system or SNMP manager. Managed network nodes are referred to as SNMP *agents*.

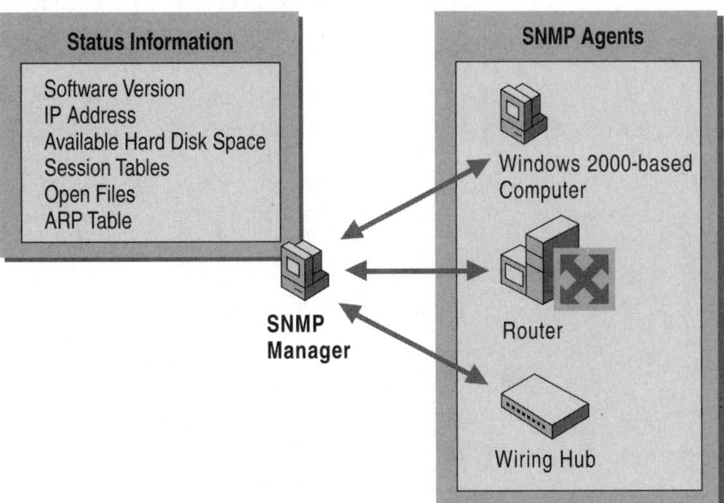

Figure 10.1 Distributed Architecture of SNMP

Network management is critical for resource management and auditing. SNMP can be used in several ways:

Configure remote devices You can configure information so that it can be sent to each networked host from the management system.

Monitor network performance You can track the speed of processing and network throughput and collect information about the success of data transmissions.

Detect network faults or inappropriate access You can configure trigger alarms on network devices that alert you to the occurrence of specific events. When an alarm is triggered, the device forwards an event message to the management system. Common types of events for which an alarm can be configured include:

- The shutdown or restart of a device.
- The detection of a link failure on a router.
- Inappropriate access.

Audit network usage You can monitor overall network usage to identify user or group access or types of usage for network devices or services. This information can be used to generate direct billing of individual or group accounts or to justify current network costs or planned expenditures.

The Windows 2000 implementation of SNMP is a 32-bit service that supports computers that are running TCP/IP and IPX protocols. It is an optional service on Microsoft® Windows® 2000 Professional, and can be installed after TCP/IP and IPX have been successfully configured. Windows 2000 implements SNMP versions 1 and 2C. These versions are based on industry standards that define how network management information is structured, stored, and communicated between agents and management systems for TCP/IP-based networks.

The Windows 2000 SNMP service provides an agent that allows centralized, remote management of computers that are running the following software:

- Microsoft® Windows® 2000 Server.
- Microsoft® Windows® 2000 Professional.
- Windows 2000 and Microsoft® Windows NT®–based Windows Internet Name Service (WINS).
- Windows 2000 and Windows NT–based Dynamic Host Configuration Protocol (DHCP).
- Windows 2000 and Windows NT–based Microsoft® Internet Information Service (IIS).

- Microsoft® LAN Manager.
- Windows 2000 Quality of Service Admission Control Service.
- Windows 2000 Routing and Remote Access service.
- Windows 2000 Internet Authentication Service.

To use the information that Windows 2000 SNMP service provides, you must have at least one centrally located host that is running an SNMP management software application. The Windows 2000 SNMP service provides only the SNMP agent; it does not include SNMP management software. You can use some third-party SNMP management software application on the host to act as the management system. Alternatively, you can develop your own SNMP management software application by using the two application programming interfaces (APIs) that are provided with Windows 2000:

- WinSNMP API (WinSNMP.dll), which provides a set of functions for encoding, decoding, sending, and receiving SNMP messages.
- Management API (Mgmtapi.dll), which provides a basic set of functions that can be used to develop fast and simple SNMP management systems.

The SNMPUtil.exe tool, which is provided on the *Microsoft® Windows® 2000* operating system CD, is meant to be used as an example of a management software application built on top of the Management API. For more information about the Management API, see "Architecture of Windows 2000 SNMP" later in this chapter. The Windows 2000 SNMP service also supports network management programs provided by third-party vendors.

Overview of SNMP

SNMP uses a distributed architecture of management systems and agents. The following sections discuss the role of each component, including the objects and messages used to store and retrieve managed information.

Management Systems and Agents

Utilizing SNMP services requires two components, as shown in Figure 10.2:

- An SNMP management system.
- An SNMP agent.

The SNMP management software application does not have to run on the same computer as the SNMP agents.

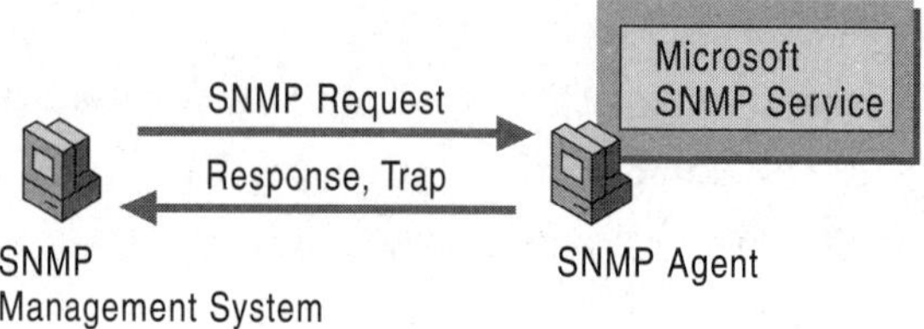

Figure 10.2 SNMP Management System and Agent

The SNMP management system, also known as the *SNMP Management console*, can request the following information from managed computers (SNMP agents):

- Network protocol identification and statistics.
- Dynamic identification of devices attached to the network (a process referred to as *discovery*).
- Hardware and software configuration data.
- Device performance and usage statistics.
- Device error and event messages.
- Program and application usage statistics.

The management system can also send a configuration request to the agent that requests the agent to change a local parameter; however, this is a rare occurrence because most client parameters have read-only access.

Several SNMP management tools are provided on the *Windows 2000 Resource Kit* companion CD. For more information about management tools, see "Architecture of Windows 2000 SNMP" in this chapter.

SNMP agents provide SNMP management systems with information about activities that occur at the Internet Protocol (IP) network layer and respond to management system requests for information. Any computer that is running SNMP agent software, such as the Windows 2000 SNMP Service, is an SNMP agent. The agent service can be configured to determine what statistics are to be tracked and what management systems are authorized to request information.

In general, agents do not originate messages—they only respond to messages. The exception is an alarm message triggered by a specific event. An alarm message is known as a *trap message*. A *trap* is an alarm-triggering event on an agent computer, such as a system reboot or illegal access. Traps and trap messages provide a rudimentary form of security by notifying the management system any time such an event occurs.

For more information about SNMP requests and trap messages, see "SNMP Messages" in this chapter.

Management Information Base

A *Management Information Base (MIB)* is a container of objects, each of which represents a particular type of information. This collection of objects contains information required by a management system. For example, one MIB object represents the number of active sessions on an agent; another represents the amount of available hard drive space on the agent. All of the information that a management system might request from an agent is stored in various MIBs.

A MIB defines the following values for each object it contains:

- Name and identifier.
- Defined data type.
- A textual description of the object.
- An index method used for complex data type objects (usually described as a multidimensional array or as tabular data).

  Examples of complex data are a list of all the network interfaces configured into the system, a routing table, or the Address Resolution Protocol (ARP) table.
- Read/write permissions.

Each object in a MIB has a unique identifier that includes the following information:

- Type (counter, string, gauge, or address).
- Access level (read or read/write).
- Size restriction.
- Range information.

The Windows 2000 SNMP service supports the Internet MIB II, LAN Manager MIB II, Host Resources MIB, and Microsoft proprietary MIBs.

For more information about the Windows 2000–based MIBs and descriptions of MIB objects, see "MIB Object Types" in this book.

SNMP Messages

Both agents and management systems use SNMP messages to inspect and communicate information about managed objects. SNMP messages are sent via the User Datagram Protocol (UDP). IP is used to route messages between the management system and host.

When SNMP management programs send requests to a network device, the agent program on the device receives the requests and retrieves the requested information from the MIBs. The agent sends the requested information back to the initiating SNMP manager program. An SNMP agent sends information:

- When it responds to a request for information from a management system.
- When a trap event occurs.

To perform these tasks, the management system and agent programs use the following messages:

- GET

  The basic SNMP request message. Sent by a management system, it requests information about a single MIB entry on an agent—for example, the amount of free drive space.
- GET-NEXT

  An extended type of request message that can be used to browse the entire hierarchy of management objects. When it processes a GET-NEXT request for a particular object, the agent returns the identity and value of the object that logically follows the previous information that was sent. The GET-NEXT request is useful mostly for dynamic tables, such as an internal IP route table.
- SET

  A message that can be used to send and assign an updated MIB value to the agent when write access is permitted.
- GET-BULK

  A request that the data transferred by the agent be as large as possible within the given restraints of message size. This minimizes the number of protocol exchanges required to retrieve a large amount of management information.
- NOTIFY

  Also called a trap message, NOTIFY is an unsolicited message that is sent by an agent to a management system when the agent detects a certain type of event. For example, a trap message might be sent when a system restart occurs. The management system that receives the trap message is referred to as the *trap destination*.

By default, UDP port 161 is used to listen for SNMP messages and port 162 is used to listen for SNMP traps. You can change these port settings by configuring the local Services file. For more information about how to do this, see "Changing SNMP Port Settings" in this chapter.

The example illustrated in Figure 10.3 shows how management systems and agents communicate information.

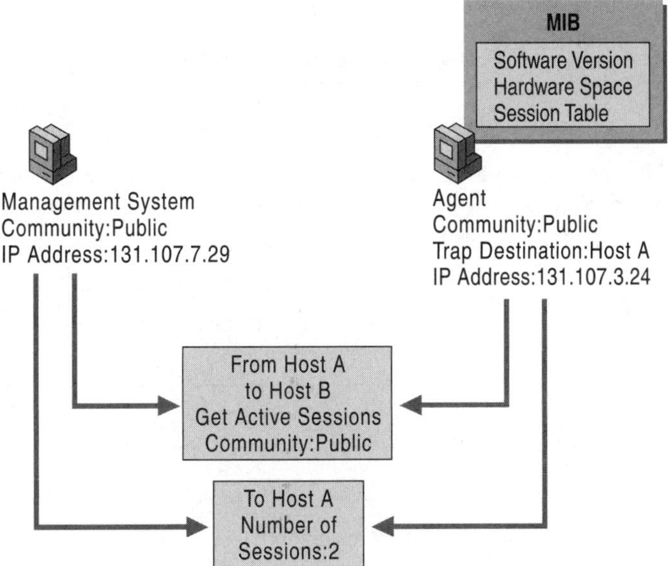

Figure 10.3 SNMP Manager and Agent Interaction

The communication process is as follows:

1. A management system forms an SNMP message that contains an information request (GET), the name of the community to which the management system belongs, and the destination of the message—the agent's IP address (131.107.3.24).
2. The SNMP message is sent to the agent.
3. The agent receives the packet and decodes it. The community name (Public) is verified as acceptable.
4. The SNMP service calls the appropriate subagent to retrieve the session information requested from the MIB.
5. The SNMP takes the session information from the subagent and forms a return SNMP message that contains the number of active sessions and the destination —the management system's IP address (131.107.7.29).
6. The SNMP message is sent to the management system.

Windows 2000 SNMP Agent Properties

Table 10.1 lists the types of services that can be configured for the management of computers on your system.

Table 10.1 SNMP Agent Services

Type of Agent Service	Conditions for Selecting the Type of Service
Physical	The computer manages physical devices, such as a hard disk partition.
Management of logical devices	The computer uses applications that send data using the TCP/IP protocol suite. This service should always be enabled.
Datalink/Subnetwork	The computer manages a bridge.
Internet	The computer functions as an IP gateway (router).
End-to-end	The computer functions as an IP host. This service should always be enabled.

The configuration of the SNMP service contains information about the following:

- The name of the person to contact, such as the network administrator.
- The location of the contact person.

You can configure these agent properties by using the **Agent** tab in the **Microsoft SNMP Properties** dialog box. This information can also be retrieved remotely by means of SNMP requests. For more information about configuring agent properties, see Windows 2000 Help.

Security

The SNMP service provides a rudimentary form of security through the use of community names and authentication traps. You can restrict SNMP communications for the agent and allow it to communicate with only a set list of SNMP management systems.

Traps

Traps can be used for limited security checking. When traps are configured for an agent, the SNMP service generates trap messages when specific events occur. For example, an agent can be configured to initiate an authentication trap if a request for information is sent by a management system the agent doesn't recognize. A message from such a management system is sent to a trap destination, which is specified explicitly in the SNMP service configuration. Trap messages can also be generated for events such as host system startup, shutdown, or password violation.

Trap destinations consist of the host name, the IP address or IPX address of the management system. The trap destination must be a network-enabled host that is running SNMP management software. Although trap destinations are configured by the administrator, the events (such as a system reboot) that generate a trap message are internally defined by the agent.

You can configure trap destinations by using the **Traps** tab in the **Microsoft SNMP Properties** dialog box. For more information about configuring trap destinations, see Windows 2000 Help.

Communities

Each SNMP management host and agent belongs to an SNMP community. An SNMP community is a collection of hosts grouped together for administrative purposes. Deciding what computers should belong to the same community is generally, but not always, determined by the physical proximity of the computers. Communities are identified by the names you assign to them.

Community names can be used to authenticate SNMP messages and thus provide a rudimentary security scheme for the SNMP service. Although a host can belong to several communities at the same time, an SNMP agent does not accept requests from a management system in a community that is not on its list of acceptable community names.

There is no relationship between community names and domain names or workgroup names. A community name can be thought of as a password shared by SNMP management consoles and managed computers. It is your responsibility as a system administrator to set hard-to-guess community names when you install the SNMP service.

In the example illustrated in Figure 10.4, there are two communities—Public and Public2. Agent1 can respond to SNMP requests from and can send traps to Manager2 because they are both members of the Public2 community. Agent2, Agent3, and Agent4 can respond to SNMP requests from and can send traps to Manager1 because they are all members of the (default) Public community.

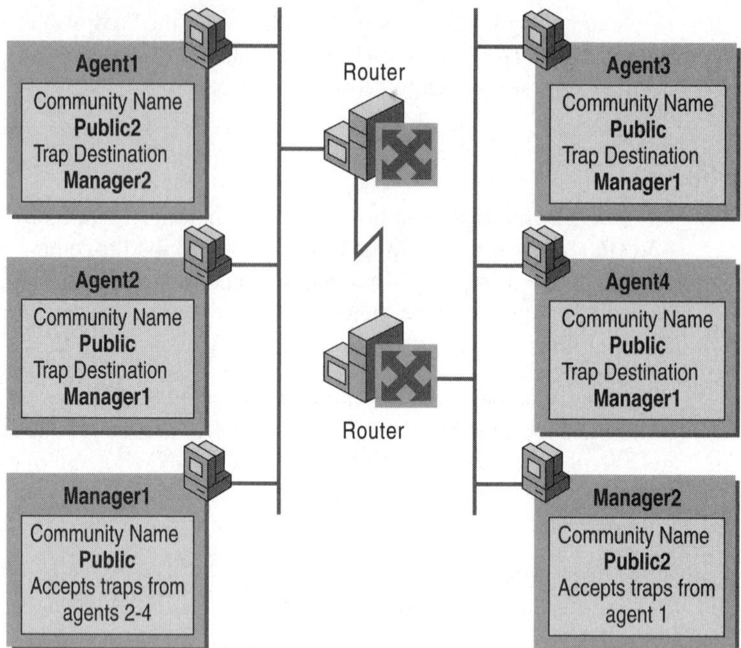

Figure 10.4 Example of SNMP Communities

Community names are managed by configuring the SNMP security properties. For more information about configuring security properties, see Windows 2000 Server Help.

When an SNMP agent receives a message, the community name contained in the packet is verified against the agent's list of acceptable community names. After the name is determined to be acceptable, the request is evaluated against the agent's list of access permissions for that community. The types of permissions that can be granted to a community include the following:

- None

  The SNMP agent does not process the request. When the agent receives an SNMP message from a management system in this community, it discards the request and generates an authentication trap.

- Notify

  This is currently identical to the permission of None.

- Read Only

  The agent does not process SET requests from this community. It processes only GET, GET-NEXT, and GET-BULK requests. The agent discards SET requests from manager systems in this community and generates an authentication trap.

- Read Create

  The SNMP agent processes or creates all requests from this community. It processes SET, GET, GET-NEXT, and GET-BULK requests, including SET requests that require the addition of a new object to a MIB table.

- Read Write

  Currently identical to Read Create.

Community permissions are configured by using the SNMP **Security** tab of the **Microsoft SNMP Properties** dialog box.

Community names are transmitted as *cleartext*, that is, without encryption. Because unencrypted transmissions are vulnerable to attacks by hackers with network analysis software, the use of SNMP community names represents a potential security risk. However, Windows 2000 IP Security can be configured to help protect SNMP messages from these attacks. For more information about configuring for IP security, see "Securing SNMP Messages with IP Security" in this chapter.

Configuring SNMP Security Options

The following options can be configured to enable SNMP security:

- **Accepted Community Names**. The SNMP service requires the configuration of at least one default community name. The name Public is generally used as the community name because it is the common name that is universally accepted in all SNMP implementations. You can delete or change the default community name or add multiple community names. If the SNMP agent receives a request from a community that is not on this list, it generates an authentication trap. If no community names are defined, the SNMP agent will deny all incoming SNMP requests.
- **Permissions**. You can select permission levels that determine how an agent processes SNMP requests from the various communities. For example, you can configure the permission level to block the SNMP agent from processing any request from a specific community.
- **Accept SNMP Packets from Any Host**. In this context, the source host and list of acceptable hosts refer to the source SNMP management system and the list of other acceptable management systems. When this option is enabled, no SNMP packets are rejected on the basis of the name or address of the source host or on the basis of the list of acceptable hosts. This option is enabled by default.

- **Only Accept SNMP Packets from These Hosts**. Selecting this option provides limited security. When the option is enabled, only SNMP packets received from the hosts on a list of acceptable hosts are accepted. The SNMP agent rejects messages from other hosts and sends an authentication trap. Limiting access to only hosts on a list provides a higher level of security than limiting access to specific communities because a community name can encompass a large group of hosts.
- **Send Authentication Traps**. When an SNMP agent receives a request that does not contain a valid community name or the host that is sending the message is not on the list of acceptable hosts, the agent can send an authentication trap message to one or more trap destinations (management systems). The trap message indicates that the SNMP request failed authentication. This is a default setting.

SNMP security is configured by using the **Security** tab in the **Microsoft SNMP Properties** dialog box. For more information about configuring SNMP security, see Windows 2000 Server Help.

SNMP Event Translator

This new feature allows an administrator to specify SNMP events to be translated as SNMP traps. The frequency of event translation can also be specified, along with log file options.

A command line tool, Evntcmd.exe, or a user interface, Evntwin.exe, can be used for configuration. Both files, along with the event translator Evntagnt.dll, are created in the *%SystemRoot%*\system32 directory when the SNMP service is installed, and can be launched through a Windows 2000 command window.

The event translator uses the SNMP service to generate the trap. By default, no events are translated. For information about how to use and configure this utility, see the SNMP online documentation.

Architecture of Windows 2000 SNMP

The internal architecture of the Windows 2000 implementation of SNMP is divided into management and agent functions; in some cases, these functions overlap, as illustrated in Figure 10.5.

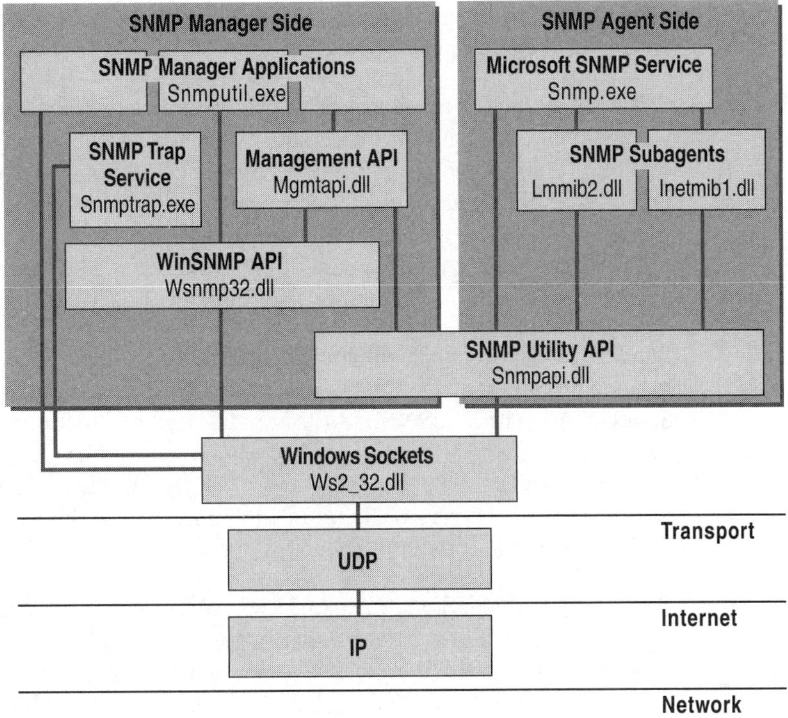

Figure 10.5 Windows 2000 SNMP Architecture

The internal components directly involved in carrying out SNMP functions are the following:

Microsoft SNMP Service (Snmp.exe) The SNMP service receives the SNMP packets from the network, decodes them, and then dispatches them to the appropriate SNMP subagents. The SNMP service is also called the SNMP Master Agent or the SNMP Extendible Agent. The service is also responsible for intercepting events (traps) from the SNMP subagents and forwarding trap messages to the appropriate management systems.

SNMP Subagents Also known as SNMP Extension Agents (such as Inetmib1.dll, Hostmib.dll, Lmmib2.dll), subagents are dynamic-link libraries that export a set of entry points. When an SNMP message is received, the SNMP service decodes the content and passes it to the appropriate subagent by calling one of these entry points. After it processes the message, the subagent passes the information back to the SNMP service. In turn, the service forms the data into an SNMP message and sends it back to the management system. The SNMP service and all SNMP subagents depend on the SNMP Utility API.

SNMP Utility API (Snmpapi.dll) This API provides the functions required by both the agent and manager for processing SNMP messages. The SNMP service uses this library for memory management operations, address-decoding routines, Object Identifier handling routines, and so forth. A set of routines is also provided that helps the SNMP subagents handle and order the SNMP objects. Although it is not necessary to use the Snmpapi.dll, the development of additional SNMP subagents is greatly facilitated by the framework defined by this tool.

WinSNMP API (Wsnmp32.dll) and Management API (Mgmtapi.dll) These APIs are provided to facilitate the development of SNMP management software applications. The WinSNMP API provides a set of functions for encoding, decoding, sending, and receiving SNMP messages. The Management API is a simple, limited API that is written on top of the WinSNMP and SNMP Utility APIs. It provides a very basic set of functions that can be used to quickly develop basic SNMP management software applications.

SNMP Trap Service (Snmptrap.exe) The trap service is a separate SNMP component that allows management software applications to receive trap messages sent by SNMP agents. The service receives incoming trap messages from the network and forwards them through the WinSNMP API (Wsnmp32.dll) to the appropriate management system.

SNMP Manager Applications (Snmputil.exe) This tool, which is provided on the *Windows 2000* operating system CD, is meant to be used as an example of a management software application that is built on top of the Management API. You can develop applications by using either the Management API or the WinSNMP API, or both. Alternatively, you can develop a management application directly on top of the Microsoft Windows Sockets API and not use either the Management API or the WinSNMP API. For more information about developing an SNMP management application, see the *Microsoft® Windows® 2000 Platform SDK* documentation.

Special Considerations in Implementing SNMP

To take advantage of the SNMP service, review the following sections to avoid problematic implementations.

Changing SNMP Port Settings

SNMP uses the default UDP port 161 for general SNMP messages and UDP port 162 for SNMP trap messages. If these ports are being used by another protocol or service, you can change the settings by modifying the local Services file on the agent. The Services file is located in \%*SystemRoot*%\System32\Drivers\Etc

There is no file name extension. You can use any text-based editor to modify the file. The management system must also be configured to listen and send on the new ports.

Caution If you have previously configured IP security to encrypt SNMP messages on the default ports, you must also update the IP security policy with the new port settings. Otherwise, communication can be erroneously blocked or SNMP communications might not be secured.

Securing SNMP Messages with IP Security

If you want to use IPSec to protect SNMP messages, you must configure all SNMP-enabled systems to use IPSec, or the communications will fail. If you can't configure all SNMP-enabled systems to use IPSec, at a minimum, you must configure the IPSec policies of the systems that are SNMP-enabled so that they can send cleartext (unencrypted) information. However, this somewhat defeats the idea of trying to secure messages because all communications will be unsecured.

IP Security does not automatically encrypt the SNMP protocol. You must create filter specifications in the appropriate IP filter list for traffic between the management systems and SNMP agents. The filter specification must include two sets of settings.

The first set of filter specifications are for typical SNMP traffic (SNMP messages) between the management system and the SNMP agents:

- Mirrored: enabled
- Protocol Type: TCP
- Source and Destination Ports: 161
- Mirrored: enabled
- Protocol Type: UDP
- Source and Destination Ports: 161

The second set of filter specifications are for SNMP trap messages sent to the management system from the SNMP agents:

- Mirrored: enabled
- Protocol Type: TCP
- Source and Destination Ports: 162
- Mirrored: enabled
- Protocol Type: UDP
- Source and Destination Ports: 162

For additional information about creating filter specifications, see Windows 2000 Help.

Managing DHCP, Windows Internet Name Service, and Internet Authentication Service

A network administrator might use SNMP to assist in the following duties:

- Viewing and changing parameters in the LAN Manager and MIB-II MIBs.
- Monitoring and configuring parameters for any WINS servers on the network.
- Monitoring DHCP servers.
- Using System Monitor to monitor TCP/IP-related performance counters (Internet Control Message Protocol (ICMP), IP, Network Interface, TCP, UDP, DHCP, FTP, WINS, and IIS performance counters).

For more information about System Monitor, see the Microsoft® Windows® 2000 Professional Resource Kit.

Use the tools on the *Windows 2000 Resource Kit* companion CD to perform simple SNMP management functions.

System Monitor Counters

All System Monitor counters installed on a computer can be viewed with SNMP.

Managing DHCP

The Windows 2000–based DHCP server objects and IIS objects can be monitored but not configured by using SNMP.

Managing WINS

All but a few of the WINS server objects can be monitored and configured by using SNMP. For information about what WINS parameters can be configured using SNMP, see "MIB Object Types" in this book. Any WINS objects defined with read/write permissions can be configured.

Managing IAS

Internet Authentication Server (IAS) implements the RADIUS authentication and accounting MIBs, which permit IAS objects to be monitored and configured using SNMP. Any IAS objects defined with read/write permissions can be configured.

SNMP Tools

Table 10.2 contains descriptions of SNMP-related tools and files that are provided on the *Windows 2000 Resource Kit* companion CD. For additional information about using these tools, see Tools Help on the companion CD.

For more information about Snmputil.exe, see Windows 2000 Support Tools Help. For information about installing and using the Windows 2000 Support Tools and Support Tools Help, see the file Sreadme.doc in the \Support\Tools folder of the Windows 2000 operating system CD.

Table 10.2 SNMP Tools

File Name	Description
Mibcc.exe	Converts the ASN.1 MIB description into the binary Mib.bin file.
Snmputil.exe	An example of a management software application that is built on top of the Management API. For more information about the Management API, see "Architecture of Windows 2000 SNMP" in this chapter.

Registry Settings

The SNMP service converts the information in the registry into a format that can be used by third-party SNMP network management programs. Whenever possible, use the Windows 2000 SNMP service user interface to alter service settings. When changes are made to SNMP service properties through the user interface, the corresponding SNMP registry settings are modified, with the exception of the following registry setting, which defines the list of extension agents (subagents) that are configured:

```
HKEY_LOCAL_MACHINE\System\CurrentControlSet\Services\SNMP\Parameters\
ExtensionAgents
```

The SNMP service detects any registry changes while running. SNMP parameter changes are activated without the need to restart the SNMP service.

Caution Do not use a registry editor to edit the registry directly unless you have no alternative. The registry editors bypass the standard safeguards provided by administrative tools. These safeguards prevent you from entering conflicting settings or settings that are likely to degrade performance or damage your system. Editing the registry directly can have serious, unexpected consequences that can prevent the system from starting and require that you reinstall Windows 2000. To configure or customize Windows 2000, use the programs in Control Panel or Microsoft Management Console (MMC) whenever possible.

Troubleshooting SNMP

This section contains methods for determining the cause of SNMP-related communication problems. Run normal workloads during your testing to gain realistic feedback.

Event Viewer

SNMP error handling has been improved in Windows 2000 Server and Windows 2000 Professional. Manual configuration of SNMP error-logging parameters has been replaced with improved error handling that is integrated with Event Viewer. Use Event Viewer if you suspect a problem with the SNMP service. For troubleshooting procedures, see Windows 2000 Help.

▶ **To use Event Viewer**

1. Click **Start**, point to **Settings**, click **Control Panel**, double-click **Administrative Tools**, and then double-click **Event Viewer**.
2. Select **System Log**.
3. Double-click an SNMP event in the **Scope** pane to display event details.

You can configure a **View** filter to display only SNMP messages. For more information about using Event Viewer, refer to Windows 2000 Help.

WINS Service

When querying a WINS server, you might need to increase the SNMP time-out period on the SNMP management system. If some WINS queries work and others time out, increase the time-out period.

IPX Addresses

If you enter an IPX address as a trap destination when installing SNMP service, the following error message might appear when you restart your computer:

```
Error 3
```

This occurs when the IPX address has been entered incorrectly, using a comma or hyphen to separate a network number from a Media Access Control (MAC) address. For example, SNMP management software might normally accept an address like: 00008022,0002C0-F7AABD. However, the Windows 2000 SNMP service does not recognize an address with a comma or hyphen between the network number and MAC address.

The address used for an IPX trap destination must follow the IETF defined 8.12 format for the network number and MAC address. For example, the following format is valid, where *xxxxxxxx* is the network number and *yyyyyyyyyyyy* is the MAC address:

xxxxxxxx.yyyyyyyyyyyy

SNMP Service Files

For your convenience and as a possible aid in troubleshooting, Table 10.3 contains a list of the SNMP-associated files provided as part of the Microsoft Windows 2000 SNMP service.

Table 10.3 SNMP Service Files

File Name	Description
Wsnmp32.dll, Mgmtapi.dll	Windows 2000–based SNMP manager APIs. Listen for manager requests and send the requests to and receive responses from SNMP agents.
Mib.bin	Installed with the SNMP service and used by the Management API (Mgmtapi.dll). Maps text-based object names to numerical object identifiers.
Snmp.exe	SNMP agent service. A master (proxy) agent. Accepts manager program requests and forwards the requests to the appropriate extension-subagent DLL for processing.
Snmptrap.exe	A background process. Receives SNMP traps from the SNMP agent and forwards them to the SNMP Management API on the management console. Starts only when the SNMP manager API receives a manager request for traps.

Additional Resources

For more information about SNMP, see the following books:

- *Windows NT SNMP* by J. D. Murray, 1998, Sebastopol: O'Reilly & Associates.
- *Understanding SNMP MIBs* by D. Perkins and E. McGinnis, 1997, New York: Prentice Hall PTR.
- *The Simple Book: An Introduction to Management of TCP/IP-based Internets* by M. T. Rose, 1994, New York: Prentice-Hall, Inc.
- *SNMP Versions 1 & 2: Simple Network Management Protocol Theory and Practice* by M. Hein and D. Griffiths, 1995, New York: International Thomson Computer Press.
- *SNMP, SNMPv2 and CMIP: The Practical Guide to Network-Management Standards* by W. Stallings, 1993, Addison-Wesley Publishing Company.
- For additional information about the Windows 2000 implementation of SNMP, see the Microsoft TechNet link on the Web Resources page at http://windows.microsoft.com/windows2000/reskit/webresources.

The following RFCs relate to SNMP version 1:

- RFC 1155: *Structure and Identification of Management Information for TCP/IP-based Internets.*
- RFC 1157: *Simple Network Management Protocol (SNMP).*
- RFC 1213: *Management Information Base for Network Management of TCP/IP-based Internets. MIB-II.*
- RFC 1573: *Evolution of the Interfaces Group of MIB-II.*

The following RFCs relate to SNMP version 2:

- RFC 1902: *Structure of Management Information for Version 2 of the Simple Network Management Protocol (SNMPv2).*
- RFC 1904: *Conformance Statements for Version 2 of the Simple Network Management Protocol (SNMPv2).*
- RFC 1905: *Protocol Operations for Version 2 of the Simple Network Management Protocol (SNMPv2).*
- RFC 1906: *Transport Mappings for Version 2 of the Simple Network Management Protocol (SNMPv2).*
- RFC 1907: *Management Information Base for Version 2 of the Simple Network Management Protocol (SNMPv2).*
- RFC 1908: *Coexistence between Version 1 and Version 2 of the Internet-standard Network Management Framework.*

PART 4

Appendixes

The appendixes provide additional information on core protocols. The detailed, technical information in this section is useful for network administrators when implementing or troubleshooting network issues.

In This Part

APPENDIX A

OSI Model

In the early years of networking, sending and receiving data across a network was confusing, because large companies such as IBM, Honeywell, and Digital Equipment Corporation had individual standards for connecting computers. It was unlikely that applications operating on different equipment from different vendors could communicate. Vendors, users, and standards bodies needed to agree upon and implement a standard architecture that would allow computer systems to exchange information even though they were using software and equipment from different vendors.

In 1978, the International Standards Organization (ISO) introduced a networking model, called the Open Systems Interconnection (OSI) model, as a first step toward standardizing data communications standards to promote multi-vendor network interoperability.

The OSI model consists of layers, each with a specific set of network functions. The model specifies the set of protocols and interfaces to implement at each layer and provides guidelines for implementation of the interfaces between layers.

In This Appendix

Related Information in the Resource Kit

- For more information about the Windows 2000 networking architecture, see "Windows 2000 Networking Architecture" in this book.

OSI Layers

Each layer of the OSI model exists as an independent module. In theory, you can substitute one protocol for another at any given layer without affecting the operation of layers above or below.

The design of the OSI model is based on the following principles:

- A layer should be created only when an additional level of abstraction is required.
- Each layer should perform a well-defined function.
- The function of each layer should be chosen with the goal of defining internationally standardized protocols.
- The layer boundaries should be chosen to minimize the information flow across the interfaces.
- The number of layers should be large enough to enable distinct functions to be separated, but few enough to keep the architecture from becoming unwieldy.

Figure A.1 shows the layers in the OSI model, beginning with the physical layer, which is closest to the network media.

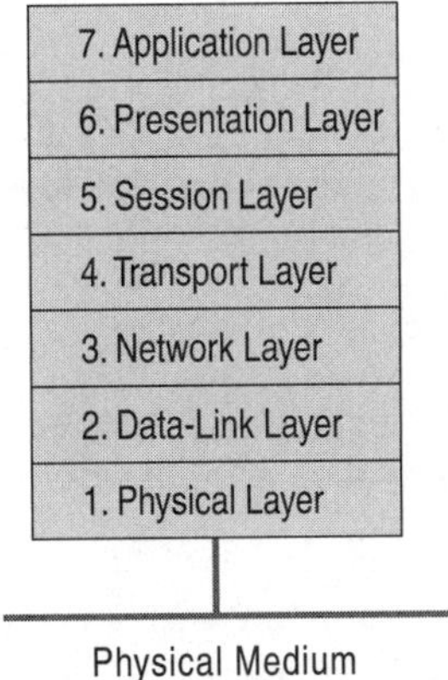

Figure A.1 Layers of the OSI Model

Physical Layer

The physical layer is the lowest layer of the OSI model. This layer controls the way unstructured, raw, bit -stream data is sent and received over a physical medium. This layer is composed of the electrical, optical, and physical components of the network. The physical layer carries the signals for all of the higher layers.

To better accommodate the characteristics of the physical medium and to assist in bit and frame synchronization, data encoding modifies the simple, digital signal pattern (1s and 0s) used by the computer.

Data encoding determines:

- Which signal pattern represents a binary 0 and a binary 1.
- How the receiving station recognizes when an encoded bit starts.
- How the receiving station delimits a frame.

The physical components (such as wiring, connectors, and pin-outs) determine:

- Whether an external transceiver is used to connect to the medium.
- How many pins the connectors have and what role each pin performs.

The transmission technique determines whether the encoded bits are transmitted by means of baseband (digital) signaling or broadband (analog) signaling.

The physical means of transmission,such as a network adapter or fiber optic adapter, determines whether it is appropriate to transmit bits as electrical or optical signals.

Data-Link Layer

The data-link layer provides error-free transfer of data frames from one computer to another over the physical layer. The layers above this layer can assume virtually error-free transmission over the network.

The data-link layer provides the following functions:

- Establishment and termination of logical links (virtual-circuit connection) between two computers identified by their unique network adapter addresses.
- Control of frame flow by instructing the transmitting computer not to transmit frame buffers.
- Sequential transmission and reception of frames.
- Providing and listening for frame acknowledgment, and detecting and recovering from errors that occur in the physical layer by retransmitting non-acknowledged frames and handling duplicate frame receipts.
- Management of media access to determine when the computer is permitted to use the physical medium.
- Delimiting of frames to create and recognize frame boundaries.

- Error-checking of frames to confirm the integrity of the received frame.
- Inspection of the destination address of each received frame and determination of whether the frame should be directed to the layer above.

Note While the services of the data-link layer provide for reliable delivery of data, many routable protocol suites such as TCP/IP and IPX/SPX do not provide for, nor utilize reliable data-link layer delivery services. Instead, reliable data delivery is provided by protocols operating at the transport layer.

Network Layer

The network layer controls the operation of the subnet. It determines what physical path the data takes based on the network conditions, the priority of service, and other factors.

The network layer provides the following functions:

- Transfer of frames to a router if the network address of the destination does not indicate the network to which the computer is attached.
- Control of subnet traffic to allow an intermediate system to instruct a sending station not to transmit its frames when the router's buffer fills up. If the router is busy, the network layer can instruct the sending station to use an alternate router.
- Fragmentation of frames by a router when the size of a link to a downstream router's maximum transmission unit (MTU) is smaller than the frame size. The frame fragments are reassembled by the destination station.
- Resolution of the logical computer address (on the network layer) with the physical network adapter address (on the data-link layer), if necessary.

The network layer at the transmitting computer must build its header in such a way that the network layers of the subnet's intermediate systems can recognize the header and use it to route the data to the destination address.

In the network layer and the layers below it, the peer protocols are between each computer and its immediate neighbor, which is often not the ultimate destination. The source and destination computers may be separated by many intermediate systems.

The network layer eliminates the need for higher layers to know anything about the data transmission or intermediate switching technologies used to connect systems. The network layer is responsible for establishing, maintaining, and terminating the connection to intermediate systems in the communication subnet.

Transport Layer

The transport layer ensures that messages are delivered in the order in which they are sent and that there is no loss or duplication.

The size and complexity of a transport protocol depends on the type of service available from the network and data-link layers. For a reliable network layer or data-link layer with virtual-circuit capability, such as the LLC layer of NetBEUI, the transport layer is required only to pass the data through to the next layer. If the network layer or data-link layer is unreliable or supports only datagrams, like the IP layer of TCP/IP and the IPX layer of IPX/SPX do, the transport layer includes sequencing and acknowledgment, and associated error detection and recovery.

Functions of the transport layer include the following:

- Accepting messages from the layer above and, if necessary, splitting them into segments.
- Providing reliable, end-to-end message delivery with acknowledgments.
- Instructing the transmitting computer not to transmit when no reception buffers are available.
- Multiplexing several process-to-process message streams or sessions onto one logical link and tracking which messages belong to which sessions.

The transport layer can accept large messages, but there are strict size limits imposed by the layers at the network level and lower. Consequently, the transport layer must break up the messages into smaller units, called segments, and attach a header to each frame.

If the lower layers do not maintain sequence, the transport header must contain sequence information, which enables the transport layer on the receiving end to present data in the correct sequence to the next higher layer.

Unlike the lower layers that have protocols that are concerned with connecting to immediately adjacent nodes or computers, the transport layer and the layers above it are true source-to-destination layers, also known as end-to-end layers. These upper layers are not concerned with the details of the underlying communications facility. Software for these layers communicates with similar software on the destination computer by using message headers and control messages.

Session Layer

The session layer establishes a communications session between processes running on different computers and can support message-mode data transfer.

Functions of the session layer include the following tasks:

- Permits application processes to register unique process addresses, such as NetBIOS names. The session layer uses these stored addresses to help resolve the addresses of network adapters from process addresses.
- Establishing, monitoring, and terminating a virtual-circuit session between two processes identified by their unique process addresses. A virtual-circuit session is a direct link that exists between the sender and receiver.
- Delimiting messages to add header information that indicates where a message starts and ends. The receiving session layer can then refrain from indicating the presence of any message data to the overlying application until the entire message is received.
- Performing message synchronization. Message synchronization is the coordination of the data transfer between the sending session layer and the receiving session layer. Synchronization prevents the receiving session layer from being overrun with data. This transfer is coordinated with acknowledgement messages (ACKs). ACKs are sent back and forth between both ends of the transfer and notify of the state of the receiving buffer to accept additional data.
- Performing other support functions that allow processes to communicate over the network, such as user authentication and resource-access security.

Presentation Layer

The presentation layer serves as the data translator for the network. This layer on the sending computer translates the data sent by the application layer into a common format. At the receiving computer, the presentation layer translates the common format to a format known to the application layer.

The presentation layer provides the following functions:

- Character-code translation, such as from ASCII to EBCDIC.
- Data conversion, such as bit order reversal, CR to CR/LF, and integer to floating point.
- Data compression, which reduces the number of bits that need to be transmitted.
- Data encryption and decryption, which secures data for transmission across a potentially insecure network. One use of encryption is for transmission of a password to a receiving computer.

Application Layer

The application layer serves as the window for users and application processes to access network services. The application layer provides the following functions:

- Resource sharing and device redirection
- Remote file access
- Remote printer access
- Interprocess communication support
- Remote procedure call support
- Network management
- Directory services
- Electronic messaging, including e-mail messaging
- Simulation of virtual terminals

Data Flow in the OSI Model

The OSI model presents a standard data flow architecture, with protocols specified in such a way that the receiving layer at the destination computer receives exactly the same object as sent by the matching layer at the source computer. Figure A.2 shows the OSI model data flow.

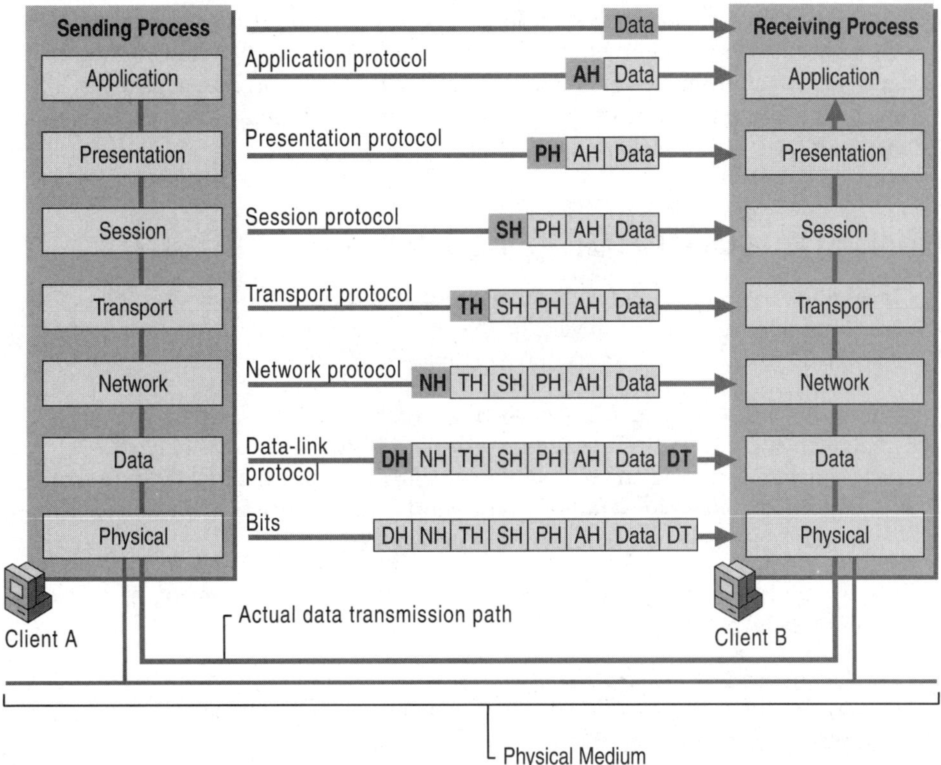

Figure A.2 OSI Model Data Flow

The sending process passes data to the application layer. The application layer attaches an application header and then passes the frame to the presentation layer.

The presentation layer can transform data in various ways, if necessary, such as by translating it and adding a header. It gives the result to the session layer. The presentation layer is not aware of which portion (if any) of the data received from the application layer is the application header and which portion is actually user data, because that information is irrelevant to the presentation layer's role.

The process of adding headers is repeated from layer to layer until the frame reaches the data link layer. There, in addition to a data-link header, a data-link trailer is added. The data-link trailer contains a checksum and padding if needed. This aids in frame synchronization. The frame is passed down to the physical layer, where it is transmitted to the receiving computer.

On the receiving computer, the various headers and the data trailer are stripped off one by one as the frame ascends the layers and finally reaches the receiving process.

Although the actual data transmission is vertical, each layer is programmed as if the transmission were horizontal. For example, when a sending transport layer gets a message from the session layer, it attaches a transport header and sends it to the receiving transport layer. The fact that the message actually passes through the network layer on its own computer is unimportant.

Vertical Interface Terminology in the OSI Model

In addition to defining an idealized network architecture and the network functions allocated to each layer, the OSI model also defines a standard set of rules that govern the interfaces between layers.

The active protocol elements in each layer are called entities, typically implemented by means of a software process. Entities in the same layer on different computers are called *peer entities*. For example, the TCP/IP protocol suite contains two entities within its transport layer: Transmission Control Protocol (TCP) and User Datagram Protocol (UDP).

Layer *n-1*, the layer directly below the entities of layer *n*, implements services that are used by layer *n*.

For data transfer services, OSI defines the terminology for the discrete data components passed across the interface and between peer entities. Figure A.3 illustrates vertical interface entities.

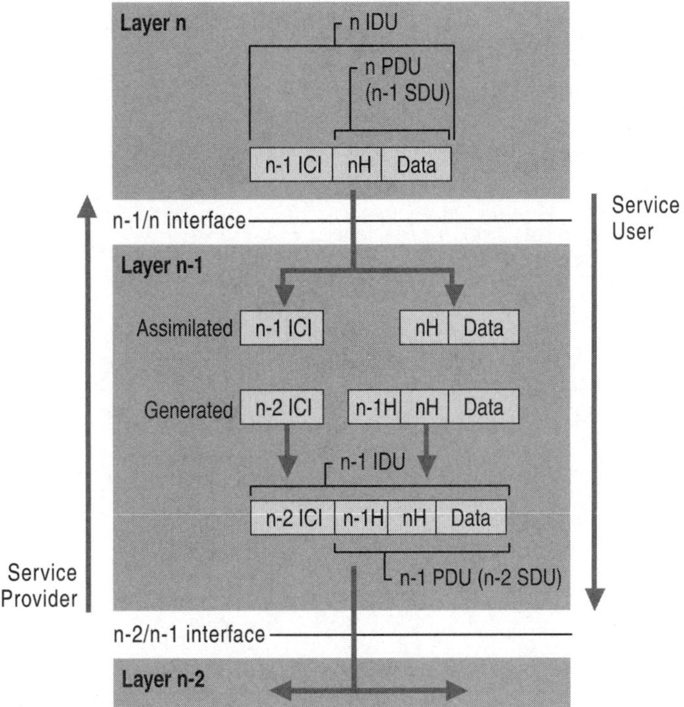

Figure A.3 Vertical interface entities

- The layer-*n* entity passes an *interface data unit* (IDU) to the layer-(*n–1*) entity.
- The IDU consists of a *protocol data unit* (PDU) and some *interface control information* (ICI). The ICI is information, such as the length of the SDU, and the addressing information that the layer below needs to perform its function.
- The PDU is the data that the layer-*n* entity wishes to pass across the network to its peer entity. It consists of the layer-*n* header and the data that layer *n* received from layer *(n+1)*.
- The layer-*n* PDU becomes the layer-(*n–1*) service data unit (SDU), because it is the data unit that will be serviced by layer *n*.
- When layer *n–1* receives the layer-*n* IDU, it strips off and "considers" the ICI, adds the header information for its peer entity across the network, adds ICI for the layer below, and passes the resulting IDU to the layer *n–2* entity.

Problems can occur in the data path between two network stations, including errant, restricted, or even halted communication.

APPENDIX B

Windows 2000 Network Architecture

Microsoft® Windows® 2000 network architecture is composed of software components that provide networking abilities to the Windows 2000 operating system. This appendix describes the components, protocols, and interfaces within Windows 2000. In addition, it introduces the networking concepts that provide a foundation for the other chapters in this book to build upon.

In This Appendix

Related Information in the Resource Kit

- For more information about SNA protocols, see "Interoperability with IBM Host Systems" in the *Microsoft® Windows® 2000 Server Resource Kit Internetworking Guide*.

Overview of Windows 2000 Network Architecture

This chapter describes software and hardware components and the connections between them that allow computers to function as a network. Windows 2000 network components are arranged in layers. Each layer has specific tasks to perform and within each layer more than one component can perform a similar task.

The Windows 2000 network layers are described in the following sections from the bottom of the network architecture model up to the top. The layers are:

Network Driver Interface Specification (NDIS) Layer NDIS is the layer that provides a communication path from a network transport to a physical device, such as a network adapter. NDIS acts as a boundary layer between network adapters and network protocols and manages the binding between these components. NDIS adds support for connection-oriented network media such as ATM and Integrated Services Digital Network (ISDN) and continues to support traditional connectionless network media such as Ethernet, Token Ring, and Fiber Distributed Data Interface (FDDI). This layer contains the miniport drivers that interface directly with the network adapter.

Network Protocol Layer The network protocols provide services for clients. These services allow applications or clients to send data over a network. Network protocols include TCP/IP, ATM, NWLink Internetwork Packet Exchange/Sequenced Packet Exchange (IPX/SPX), NetBEUI, Infrared Data Association (IrDA), AppleTalk and Data Link Control (DLC). Systems Network Architecture (SNA) protocols are available with the addition of Microsoft® SNA Server.

Transport Driver Interface Layer The transport driver interface (TDI) provides a standard interface between network protocols and clients of these protocols (such as applications, network redirectors or networking Application Programming Interfaces (APIs)).

Network Application Programming Interface Layer The network application programming interface (API) provides standard programming interfaces for network applications and services. They support Winsock, NetBIOS, Telephony API (TAPI), Messaging API (MAPI), WNet API and other services.

Interprocess Communications Layer Interprocess communications (IPC) support client/server computing and distributed processing. Some of the services that they support are remote procedure calls (RPC), Distributed Component Object Model (DCOM), named pipes, mailslots, and Common Internet File System (CIFS).

Basic Network Services Layer Basic network services support network user applications by providing services. These include network address management, name services, file services and advanced network services such as Internet Protocol Security (IPSec) and Quality of Service (QoS).

The International Organization for Standardization has a model for computer networking, also called the Open Systems Interconnection (OSI) Reference Model. This model is useful to describe network layers. The OSI model defines a modular approach to networking, with each layer responsible for some discrete aspect of the networking process. The OSI model does not correspond exactly to most existing network architectures. However, models assist in understanding how networks function by providing a structure to use as a comparison. For more information about the OSI model, see "OSI Model" in this book.

Network communication begins when an application program attempts to access resources on another computer. Data and requests move from layer to layer within a computer. Each layer is able to communicate with the layer immediately above it and the layer immediately below it. If the packet is not meant for use by the current layer, it passes the packet to an adjacent layer. Packets travel down the network protocol stack of the first computer. If the destination is on another networked computer, the packets of data are sent across the physical media (such as wiring, fiber optic cable or satellite). The data is passed upward through the lower layers of the second computer up to the same layer that started the exchange of data.

Figure B.1 represents a model of Windows 2000 network architecture.

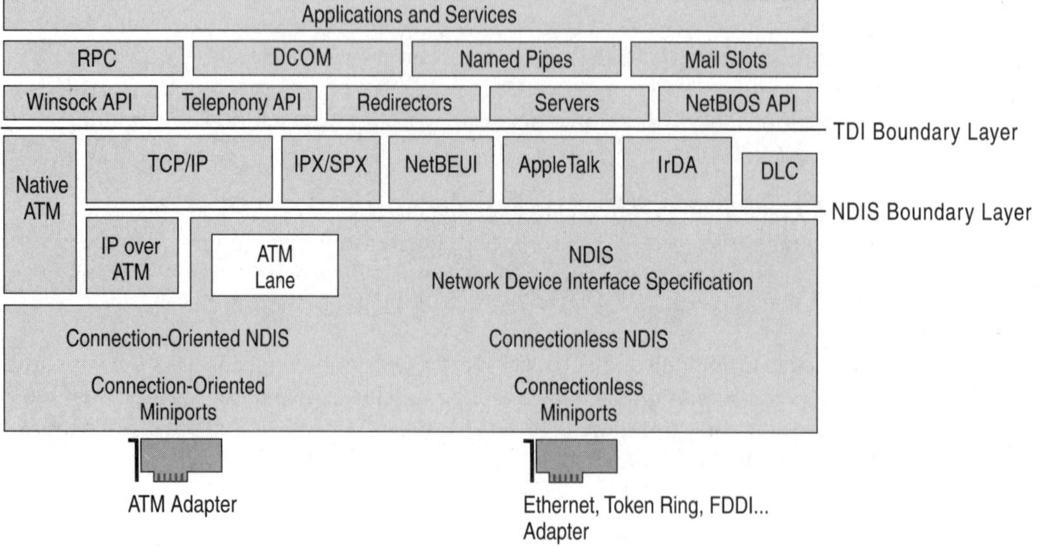

Figure B.1 Windows 2000 Network Architecture

Software components are represented by rectangles. These components are in horizontal layers. Components that are on the same horizontal level provide similar functionality. The top layer of the diagram is where user applications reside. In order to communicate with other networked computers, additional software and hardware support is needed. Each layer below the applications and services layer provides services that are necessary to create packets of data, arrange for their delivery and send them across the physical media to another computer.

Boundary layers are interfaces between functional layers in the Windows 2000 network architecture model. Creating boundaries as breakpoints in the network layers helps standardize programming for developers. Because the functionality between the layers is well-defined, developers need to program only to a boundary layer instead of having to code from the top (an application program) to the bottom of the protocol stack (network adapter). If software is correctly written to a boundary layer, then support on the other side of that layer already exists and does not need to be written. Both the transport device interface (TDI) and Network Driver Interface Specification (NDIS) are boundary layers. In the diagram, DLC and Native ATM both have a gap between the top edge of DLC, Native Asynchronous Transfer Mode (ATM) and the TDI layer because they do not interface through the TDI layer.

Binding is the linking of network components on adjacent layers of the protocol stack. Binding occurs at boundary layers and other adjacent layers. Binding enables communication between the various layers.

Components are portions of software that perform specific tasks. A network component can bind to one or more network components above or below it. When adding network software, Windows 2000 binds all needed and associated components together. During binding, an information file (.inf) contains the instructions necessary to establish the required binding relationships.

Figure B.2 shows two protocols binding to two network adapters inside the same computer.

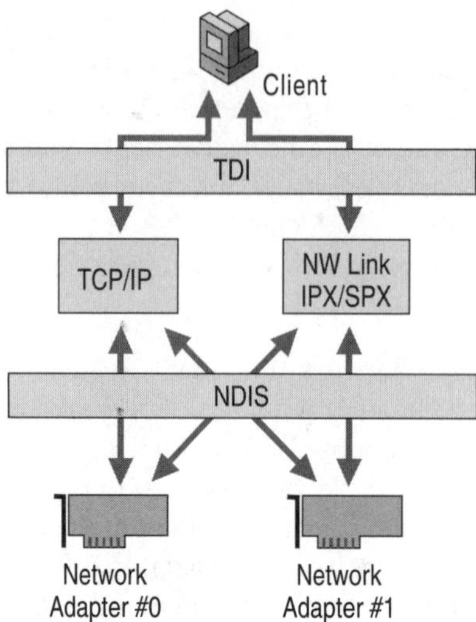

Figure B.2 Binding

Network Driver Interface Specification

The Network Driver Interface Specification (NDIS) is a specification for network driver architecture that allows transport protocols such as TCP/IP, Native ATM, IPX, and NetBEUI to communicate with an underlying network adapter or other hardware device. The network adapter can then send or receive data over the network. NDIS permits the high-level protocol components to be independent of the network adapter by providing a standard interface to the network protocols. Because Windows 2000 network architecture supports NDIS, it requires that network adapter drivers be written to the NDIS specification.

Windows 2000 NDIS provides both a standard connectionless interface and also defines a connection-oriented interface. Microsoft® Windows NT® version 4.0 network architecture supported traditional connectionless network standards such as Ethernet, Token Ring, and FDDI. Connectionless networking does not negotiate, manage, and maintain a connection before transmitting data. Connectionless networking, also known as a datagram service, is a "best-effort" delivery service. There is no guarantee that messages won't be lost, duplicated or delivered out of order. These services are usually provided by the network protocols if required.

Windows 2000 continues to support traditional connectionless networking, but adds support for connection-oriented mediums, such as Asynchronous Transfer Mode (ATM) and Integrated Services Digital Network (ISDN). In connection-oriented networking, a connection is created and all data is sent in sequence over a virtual circuit. Windows 2000 negotiates connections using a call manager. A call manager is a portion of software that can initiate and maintain connections, creating virtual circuits (VCs) between two network endpoints. Virtual circuits act as conduits for the transmission of data, allowing greater control of bandwidth, latency, delay variation, and sequencing. These services provide greater support for distributed voice, data, and video applications.

Windows 2000 NDIS is implemented by a file called Ndis.sys, referred to as the "NDIS wrapper." The NDIS wrapper is code that surrounds all NDIS device drivers. The NDIS wrapper provides a uniform interface between protocol drivers and NDIS device drivers, and contains supporting routines that make it easier to develop NDIS drivers. NDIS allows an unlimited number of network adapters in a computer and an unlimited number of protocols bound to one or more network adapters.

Figure B.3 shows the NDIS wrapper architecture.

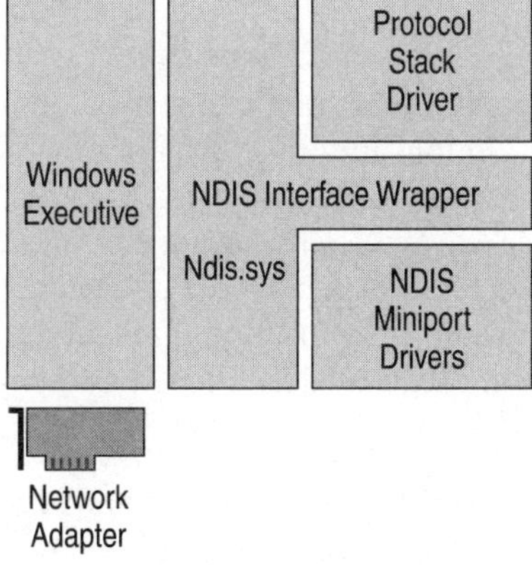

Figure B.3 NDIS Wrapper (Ndis.sys)

The NDIS wrapper defines the way protocols communicate with network adapters. The protocols communicate with the NDIS wrapper rather than the network adapter. This is an example of the modular structure of a layered network model. The network adapter is independent from the transport protocols.

NDIS New Features

Windows 2000 NDIS includes many new features, such as connection-oriented NDIS and new intermediate and miniport driver support. Other Windows 2000 NDIS features include:

- Connection-Oriented NDIS
- Wake-On-LAN
- Media-Sense
- Network Plug and Play
- TCP/IP Task Offload

Connection-Oriented NDIS

Connection-oriented NDIS (CoNDIS) is the portion of NDIS that supports connection-oriented media. CoNDIS supports connection-oriented media such as dial-up networking, ATM and network streaming over connection-oriented media. Connection-oriented NDIS provides the support to establish, maintain, and close connections.

Wake-On-LAN

Wake-On-LAN controls the wake-up of computers based on network events. It is a subset of the OnNow Power Options initiative. In order for Wake-On-LAN to function, the network adapter must be Wake-On-LAN–capable and the device driver must support Wake-On-LAN. A network adapter may be put into a low power mode when the system requests a power level change. The user or system can initiate the request. For example, the user might want to put the system into sleep mode, or the system might request sleep mode based on keyboard or mouse inactivity.

Unless initiated by a user, all overlying network components must agree to the request before the network adapter can be turned off. If there are any active sessions or open files over the network, the turn-off request can be refused by any or all of the components involved.

Many events enable a system to wake up without user intervention. The system may be able to wake up from a lower power state based on network events specified by the networking software. This capability means that any standard Windows network access (such as connections to shared folders, Winsock connections, and service and management applications) can wake the system from lower power states. This is done by:

- Receipt of a previously registered packet.

- Receipt of a magic packet. A magic packet is a packet that contains 16 contiguous copies of the receiving network adapter's Ethernet address.
- A connection event, such as plugging in a network cable.

Network drivers and hardware that do not support Wake-On-LAN can still be used on Windows 2000. Systems having network adapters with no Wake-On-LAN capabilities can be suspended and resumed based on user activity, but not resumed based on network events.

Media Sense

Media Sense is the capability of a network adapter to indicate when it does or does not have a connection to the physical network medium. Most Windows 2000 network technologies support Media Sense. Protocols and applications can receive these notifications and act accordingly. For example, an icon can be displayed indicating the media is disconnected, an event can be logged, and TCP/IP can manage addresses with the knowledge of the state of the network.

Network Plug and Play

Network Plug and Play is a combination of hardware and software support that enables a computer system to recognize and adapt to hardware configuration changes with little or no user intervention. A user can add or remove Plug and Play devices dynamically. No intricate knowledge of computer hardware is necessary. For example, a user can dock a portable computer and use the docking station's Ethernet card to connect to the network without changing the configuration. Later, the user can undock that same computer and use a modem to connect to the network, again without making any manual configuration changes.

TCP/IP Task Offload

TCP/IP *Task offload* allows tasks normally performed by the transport layer to be processed by the network adapter. This reduces the overhead required of the system CPU for these tasks. This allows the system CPU to do more work, possibly increasing the throughput to the network. A special query is made by the transport driver to find out if the network adapter supports the offload of the computation of TCP/IP checksums, TCP/IP segmentation (large send), Fast Packet Forwarding and IPSec Offload. If one or more of these conditions is detected, the transport can request that the network adapter furnish these services.

TCP/IP Checksum Task Offload Capability

TCP/IP checksums verify the integrity of the data packet. TCP/IP queries the miniport to determine its ability to perform checksum calculations. If the miniport is capable of handling offloads, then it performs these calculations. These computations can consume many CPU cycles. This can include send and receive checksum calculations for TCP, User Datagram Protocol (UDP), and IP. The miniport driver requests that the network adapter perform the calculations rather than requiring the CPU to process this request. This can result in enhanced performance.

TCP/IP Segmentation Offload

TCP/IP segmentation (large send) is the creation of TCP packets from data that is too large for transmission over network media. TCP/IP splits data into small segments, adds IP and TCP headers, and creates TCP packets. TCP/IP segmentation can now be performed by NDIS miniports and a capable network adapter. The adapter must be able to calculate IP and TCP checksums for send packets and have an appropriate miniport driver. Offloading these calculations from the CPU results in greater performance for the system.

Fast Packet Forwarding

Fast Packet Forwarding allows multiport network adapters (FastEthernet, FDDI, or similar single-port network adapters) to use Windows 2000 to route packets from one port to another port without passing the packet to the host processor. This increases throughput to the network and reduces work for the CPU.

IPSec Offload Capability

Internet Protocol Security (IPSec) is an Internet Engineering Task Force (IETF) standard for security at the packet processing layer of IP networks. IPSec provides two security services:

- Authentication Header. Allows sender authentication.
- Encapsulating Security Payload. Supports both sender authentication and payload encryption.

The IPSec protocol information associated with each of these services is inserted into the packet in a header that follows the regular IP header. Included in this information is the Security Parameter Index, which is a 32-bit value used to distinguish between different Security Associations (SAs) terminating at the same destination and using the same IPSec protocol.

The work of encrypting and decrypting each packet can be assigned to the network adapter through the use of NDIS and the associated miniport drivers. With proper configuration of security policy in Windows 2000, outgoing IP packets are authenticated and encrypted before transmission to the network, and incoming IP packets are validated and decrypted.

For more information about new features in NDIS, see the Platform Software Development Kit (SDK). For more information about IPSec, see "Internet Protocol Security" in this book.

NDIS Driver Types

NDIS drivers allow the transport protocols to communicate with the hardware layer. These drivers can be implemented in different configurations, described in the following sections.

Intermediate Drivers

The *intermediate driver* are found just below the transport protocols and above the miniport drivers in the network protocol stack. There are two types of intermediate drivers that are used: the LAN Emulation Intermediate driver and the Filter driver.

LAN Emulation Intermediate Driver

The LAN Emulation Intermediate Driver translates packets from the overlying connectionless transport's local area network (LAN) format to the connection-oriented format (such as ATM) below. Therefore, the transport protocols appear to communicate with a LAN network adapter (Ethernet) but in reality they are communicating with a different hardware device. The LAN Emulation Intermediate driver translates the packets coming and going to the protocol layer above. It converts these packets into packets that can be sent over a different medium. Figure B.4 illustrates the LAN Emulation Intermediate driver architecture.

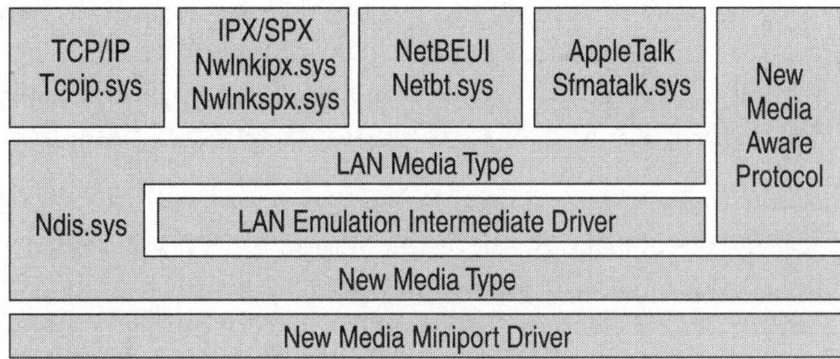

Figure B.4 LAN Emulation Intermediate Driver

Currently, the only supported application for this driver is LAN Emulation for ATM. However, this driver configuration can be used for other types of "new media" in future configurations.

For more information about NDIS, see the Platform Software Development Kit (SDK).

Filter Driver

Filter drivers perform special operations (such as compression, encryption and tracing) on packets being transported through them. Figure B.5 shows the filter driver architecture.

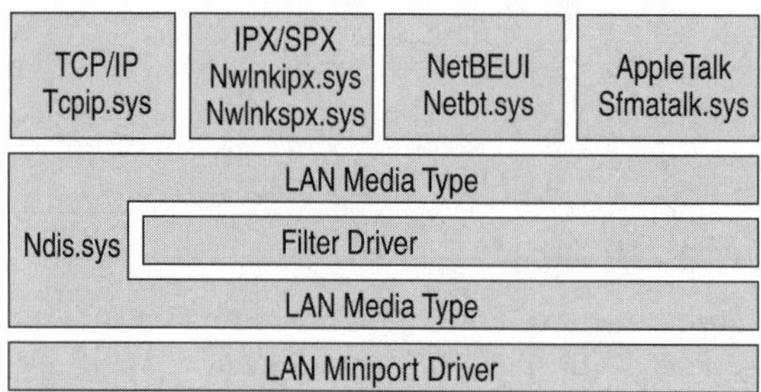

Figure B.5 The Filter Driver

As packets are transported through the filter driver, compression and encryption can be performed. Several services utilize this type of intermediate driver, such as the packet scheduler in *Quality of Service* (QoS) and *Network Load Balancing*.

Miniport Drivers

A *miniport driver* is a driver that connects hardware devices to the protocol stack. The miniport driver is connected to an intermediate or protocol driver and a hardware device. A miniport driver handles the hardware-specific operations necessary to manage a network adapter or other hardware device. They implement sending and receiving data on the network adapter. Microsoft produces some intermediate drivers for Windows 2000. This is helpful to hardware manufacturers because it is not necessary for them to implement added functionality. To add additional functionality, hardware vendors can also create intermediate drivers. In this chapter, miniport drivers are also referred to as miniports.

Windows Driver Model (WDM) is a specification for device drivers. WDM makes device drivers compatible between Windows 2000 and Microsoft® Windows® 98. To help reduce the effort necessary for hardware vendors to support all Windows platforms, WDM enables devices designed for either Windows 2000 or Windows 98 to be installed and used with computers running under either operating system. WDM developers write smaller code pieces (miniports) that talk to their hardware directly and call the appropriate class driver to do the bulk of the common tasks.

Miniport drivers can be serialized or deserialized. Serialized drivers rely on NDIS to sequence calls to miniport functions and to manage send queues. Deserialized miniport drivers on multiprocessor systems can perform faster by serializing access to their internal data structures rather than by allowing NDIS to perform this function. They also queue all incoming send packets rather than using NDIS. This can result in a better full duplex performance. However, deserialized miniport drivers are more difficult to design and require more testing and debugging.

Common Miniport Drivers

The most common miniport drivers are:

- Connectionless miniport drivers
- NDISWAN miniport drivers
- Non-NDIS Lower Interface miniport drivers
- Connection-oriented miniport drivers

Connectionless Miniport Drivers

Connectionless miniport drivers control network adapters for connectionless network media such as Ethernet, FDDI, and Token Ring.

Figure B.6 shows the architecture of connectionless miniport drivers.

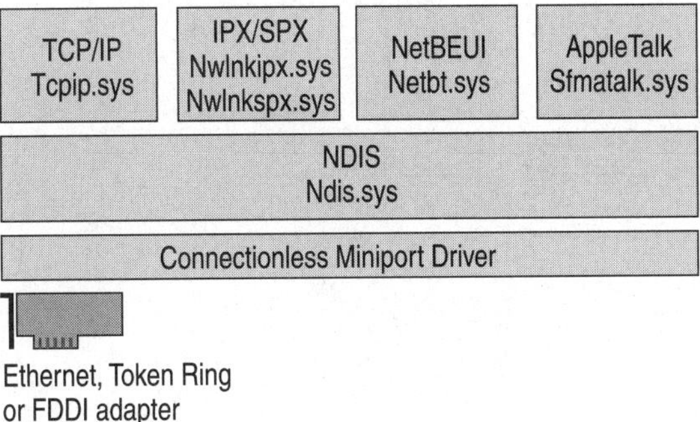

Figure B.6 Connectionless Miniport Driver Architecture

The most common use of connectionless miniports is for LAN-based network adapters. Network mediums such as Ethernet, Token Ring and FDDI do not support connection-oriented communications. Packets are sent to or received from a destination without any existing connection.

NDISWAN Miniport Drivers

There are many types of NDISWAN miniports. NDISWAN miniports are used with ISDN, Frame Relay and X.25 to provide dial-up networking. Ndiswan.sys is a Microsoft driver that provides Point-to-Point Protocol (PPP encapsulation), compression, and encryption. Ndiswan.sys communicates with the Routing and Remote Access service.

Figure B.7 illustrates the NDISWAN miniport driver architecture and usage.

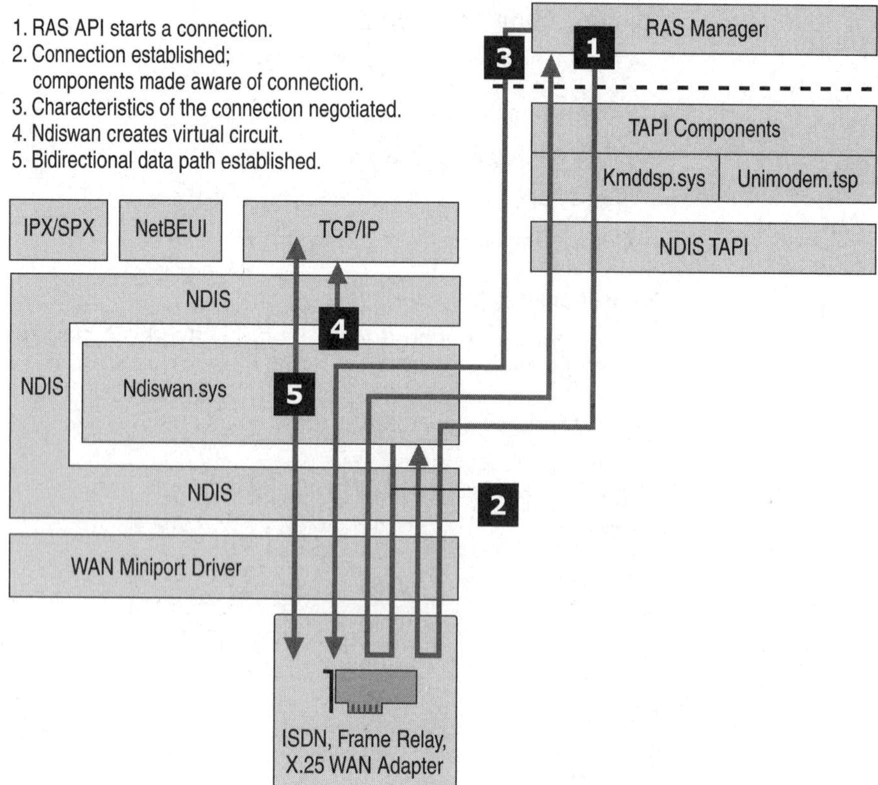

Figure B.7 NDISWAN Miniport Driver Architecture and Usage

Figure B.7 shows an example of NDISWAN usage. The numbered arrows show the steps for the Routing and Remote Access service to set up a PPP session using an NDISWAN miniport driver.

1. The Routing and Remote Access service initiates a connection by passing information down through the TAPI components, (kmddsp.tsp, NDIS TAPI) to the WAN miniport driver (NDISWAN).
2. A reply is passed back to the Routing and Remote Access service to inform it that a connection is established by the same path. All components are made aware that the call attempt was completed.
3. The RAS Manager negotiates the characteristics of the PPP connection. This includes compression protocols and frame types.
4. Ndiswan.sys creates a virtual circuit for the appropriate protocol.
5. Data is both sent and received through the connection that has been established by Ndiswan.sys.

Non-NDIS Lower Interface Miniport Driver

A Non-NDIS lower interface driver is a connection-oriented miniport driver that interfaces to network protocols on the top, but on the bottom can interface to devices, such as Universal Serial Bus (USB) and Institute of Electrical and Electronics Engineers (IEEE) 1394 devices. Figure B.8 shows the Non-NDIS miniport driver architecture.

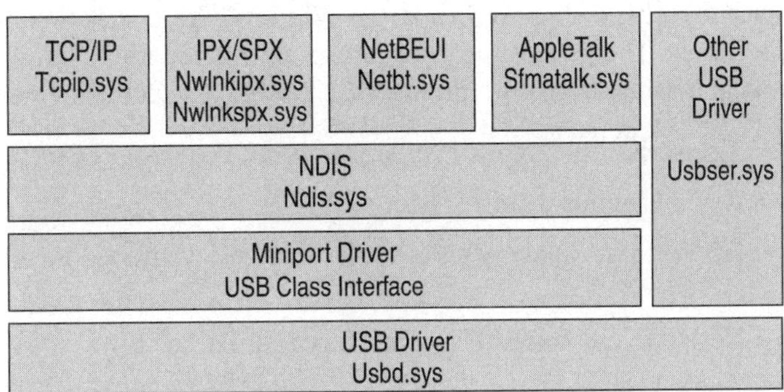

Figure B.8 Non-NDIS Miniport Driver Architecture

Connection-Oriented Miniports

The connection-oriented miniport transports data on a particular connection rather than to a particular destination. It is a new NDIS driver architecture. Connection-oriented miniports differ from connectionless miniports because a connection must be established between two points before data can be exchanged. Connection-oriented miniports support media such as ATM.

Certain applications rely on connection-oriented communication. Since data is sent over a connection, it remains in sequence and all data follows the same path. Because all data follows the same path, QoS parameters can be controlled more easily than connectionless data transfer. QoS requirements for the connection are negotiated by a call manager if the medium supports QoS. Call managers create and maintain connections. There are two types of call managers:

- A stand-alone call manager is a discrete software entity separate from the miniport driver.
- An integrated call manager has code that is an integral part of the connection-oriented miniport driver.

Connection-oriented miniports support many types of data transmission. Data, voice and videoconferencing using data streaming are made possible with connection-oriented miniport drivers. NDIS can offload synchronization and queue management details to the miniport driver. NDIS connection-oriented miniport drivers can expose a connection to the network protocols. For a diagram and additional information about connection-oriented miniport drivers supporting ATM, see "ATM" later in this chapter.

Network Protocols

Protocols are specifications for standardized packets of data that make it possible for networks to share information. Windows 2000 supports many different protocols. The packets of information are moved up and down the protocol stack, and across the transmission media. Network protocols include:

- Transmission Control Protocol/Internet Protocol (TCP/IP)
- Asynchronous Transfer Mode (ATM)
- NetWare Internetwork Packet Exchange/Sequenced Packet Exchange (IPX/SPX)
- NetBIOS Enhanced User Interface (NetBEUI)
- AppleTalk
- Data Link Control (DLC)
- Infrared Data Association (IrDA)

Note The Systems Network Architecture (SNA) protocols are not included in Windows 2000. SNA protocols are available with the addition of Microsoft SNA Server. SNA Server is a separate product that supports interoperability with IBM midrange and mainframe computers. For more information about SNA protocols, see "Interoperability with IBM Host Systems" in the *Windows 2000 Internetworking Guide*.

TCP/IP

Transmission Control Protocol/Internet Protocol (TCP/IP) has been adopted by Microsoft as the strategic enterprise transport protocol for Windows 2000. The Windows 2000 TCP/IP suite is designed to make it easy to integrate Microsoft enterprise networks into large scale corporate, government, and public networks, and to provide the ability to operate over those networks in a secure manner.

Several factors have lead to the success of TCP/IP. The protocol is routable, which means that data packets can be switched (routed to a different subnet) by use of the packet's destination address. TCP/IP's ability to be routed allows greater fault tolerance. If a network failure occurs, packets are transported by a different route. Another factor contributing to the success of TCP/IP is the massive interest in the Internet. TCP/IP is the standard for computer interconnectivity.

Windows 2000 TCP/IP includes several performance improvements for networking within high-bandwidth LAN and wide area network (WAN) environments. These features include the following:

Large Window Support

Large window support improves performance of TCP/IP when there are large amounts of data in transit or unacknowledged between two connected. In TCP-based communication, the window size is the maximum number of packets that can be sent in a streamed sequence before the first packet must be acknowledged. Large window support allows for more data packets to be in transit on the network at one time and increases effective bandwidth.

Selective Acknowledgments

Selective acknowledgments is a TCP option that allows the receiver to selectively notify and request from the sender only those packets that were missing or corrupted during initial delivery. Selective acknowledgments allow networks to recover quickly from a state of congestion or temporary interference by requiring only lost packets to be resent. In previous TCP/IP implementations, if a receiving host failed to receive a single TCP packet, the sender might retransmit not just the corrupted or missing packet, but all subsequent packets. With selective acknowledgments, fewer packets are sent so better utilization of the network results.

RTT Estimation

Round Trip Time Estimation (RTT) is a technique of estimating packet transit times and adjusting for the optimum retransmission time for packets. Round Trip Time is the amount of time it takes for a round-trip communication between a sender and receiver on a TCP-based connection. Because performance depends on knowing how long to wait for a missing packet, improving the accuracy of RTT estimation results in better retransmission time-out values being set on each host. Better timing particularly improves performance over long round-trip network links, such as WANs that span large distances (continent-to-continent) or use either wireless or satellite links.

IP Security

Internet Protocol Security (IPSec) is an encryption process that allows data to be scrambled to make it virtually impossible to view its contents. IPSec uses cryptography-based security to provide integrity, data origin authentication, protection against replays, confidentiality, and limited traffic flow confidentiality. Because IPSec is provided at the IP layer, its services are available to the upper-layer protocols in the stack, and are transparently available to existing applications.

IPSec enables a system to select security protocols, decide which algorithm to use for the service, and establish and maintain cryptographic keys for each security relationship. IPSec can protect paths between hosts, between security gateways, or between hosts and security gateways. IPSec policy can be configured locally on a computer, or can be assigned through Windows 2000 Group Policy mechanisms using the Active Directory™ directory service.

When IPSec is used to encrypt data, network performance is generally reduced due to the processing overhead of encryption. One method of reducing the processing overhead is to offload the processing to a hardware device. Since NDIS supports task offloading, it is feasible to include encryption hardware on network adapters.

For more information about IPSec, see "Internet Protocol Security" in this book.

For more information about TCP/IP, see "Introduction to TCP/IP" and "Windows 2000 TCP/IP" in this book.

Generic Quality of Service

Generic Quality of Service (GQoS) is implemented in Winsock, so Windows 2000 GQoS can run on any network that supports TCP/IP. GQoS ensures the quality of a connection. QoS allows developers to deploy real-time applications over IP networks while providing acceptable levels of bandwidth, latency, and jitter. GQoS allows TCP/IP to provide the benefits of ATM in a TCP/IP environment.

For more information about QoS, see "Quality of Service" in this book.

ATM

The Asynchronous Transfer Mode (ATM) protocol is a connection-oriented protocol that is ideal for voice, video and data communications. ATM is a high-speed networking technology that transmits data in cells of a fixed length. ATM is a native connection-oriented transport protocol. It is composed of a number of related technologies including software, hardware, and connection-oriented media. A cell is a fixed-length packet containing 53 bytes of information. Since the number of bytes—and consequently the transit time—of the cell is constant, the cells can be switched at a constant interval.

An ATM endpoint establishes a connection or virtual circuit prior to sending any data on the network. It then sends cells along this path toward the destination. This virtual circuit is a direct path from one endpoint to another. While establishing the connection, the ATM endpoint also negotiates a Quality of Service contract for the transmission. This contract spells out the bandwidth, maximum delay, acceptable variance, and other parameters the virtual circuit (VC) provides, and this contract extends from one endpoint to the other. Since the virtual circuit is connection-oriented, the data arrives at the receiving end in proper order and with the specified service levels. ATM is an excellent compromise for the transmission of both voice and data on a network. ATM provides a guaranteed Quality of Service on a LAN, a WAN, and a public internetwork.

Figure B.9 illustrates the connection-oriented miniport driver architecture as implemented in ATM.

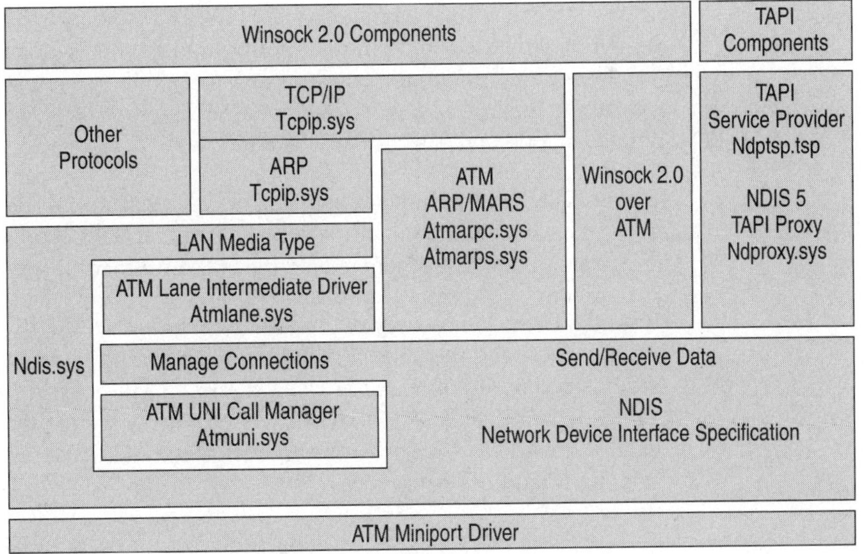

Figure B.9 ATM Using Connection-Oriented Miniports

ATM is supported by Windows 2000 architecture with the following components. This diagram is used for:

- LANE (LAN Emulation)
- IP over ATM
- PPP over ATM
- Native ATM through Winsock 2.0

For more information about ATM, see "Asynchronous Transfer Mode" in the *Windows 2000 Internetworking Guide*.

LANE LAN Emulation (LANE) is a method by which other protocols (not just TCP/IP) that only understand connectionless media can communicate over ATM. It allows ATM to utilize both legacy networks and applications. Traditional LAN-aware applications and protocols can communicate over an ATM network without modification.

LANE consists of two primary components: the LANE client (Atmlane.sys) and the LANE services. The LANE client allows LAN protocols and LAN-aware applications to function as if they were communicating with a traditional LAN. The LANE client communicates LAN commands to the network protocols and native ATM commands to the ATM protocol layer. The LANE services are a group of ATM components, usually on a switch that supports LAN emulation.

IP Over ATM IP over ATM is a means of carrying IP packets over an ATM network. IP over ATM uses the connection-oriented properties of ATM to overcome the connectionless nature of IP. It functions in a manner similar to LANE. A central IP server (called an ATMARP server) maintains a database of IP and ATM addresses, and provides configuration and broadcast services. IP over ATM is a group of components that doesn't reside in one place. The services are not usually on an ATM switch. IP over ATM server services are provided with Windows 2000 and can reside on a Windows 2000 server.

IP over ATM is a small layer between the ATM protocol and the TCP/IP protocols. The client emulates standard IP to the TCP/IP protocol at its top edge and uses native ATM commands to the ATM protocol layers underneath.

IP over ATM is handled by two primary components: the IP over ATM server (Atmarps.sys) and the IP over ATM client (Atmarpc.sys). The IP over ATM server is composed of an ATMARP server and Multicast Address Resolution Service (MARS). The ATMARP server provides services that emulate standard IP functions, while MARS provides broadcast and multicast services. Both services maintain IP address databases.

ATM Over xDSL Digital Subscriber Line (xDSL) technology is a means by which plain old telephone service (POTS) can be used to send ATM cells over a pair of copper wires to the central station of a phone company. ATM over xDSL offers high-speed network access from the home and small office environment. Several standards are being developed in these areas, including asymmetric digital subscriber line (ADSL) and universal ADSL (UADSL). These technologies use the local loop, the copper wires that connect the local central office in a user's neighborhood to the customer's phone jack. In many areas, this local loop connects directly to an ATM core network run by a telephone company.

ATM over xDSL service preserves the high-speed characteristics and QoS guarantees available in the core ATM network without changing protocols. This creates the potential for an end-to-end ATM network to the residence or small office.

Point-to-Point Protocol (PPP) over this end-to-end architecture adds functionality and usefulness. PPP allows necessary features such as authentication, encryption and compression. To support these architectures (such as residential broadband, PPP over ATM), Windows 2000 has additional components. Ndttsp.tsp is a TAPI service provider that allows NDIS proxy to interface with call control through TAPI. Ndproxy.sys provides call control over connection-oriented media.

Native ATM Access Through Winsock 2.0 Applications can directly use Winsock 2.0 to gain access the ATM protocols natively. Applications that using native ATM can access QoS guarantees such as bandwidth, and latency.

For more information about ATM, see "Asynchronous Transfer Mode" in the *Windows 2000 Internetworking Guide*.

NWLink

NWLink is a Microsoft-compatible IPX/SPX protocol for Windows 2000. NWLink does not allow a computer running Windows 2000 to access files or printers shared on a NetWare server, or to act as a file or print server to a NetWare client. To access files or printers on a NetWare server, a redirector must be used, such as the Client Service for NetWare on Microsoft® Windows® 2000 Professional, or the Gateway Service for NetWare on Microsoft® Windows® 2000 Server.

NWLink is useful if there are NetWare client/server applications running that use Winsock or NetBIOS over IPX/SPX protocols. A Microsoft-compatible NetWare client, NWLink can be run on a Windows 2000 Server or Windows 2000 Professional computer to access the server portion on a NetWare server.

NetWare NetBIOS Link (NWNBLink) contains Microsoft enhancements to NetBIOS. The NWNBLink component is used to format NetBIOS-level requests and pass them to the NWLink component for transmission on the network.

For more information about NetWare IPX/SPX, see "Interoperability with NetWare" in the *Windows 2000 Internetworking Guide.*

NetBEUI

NetBEUI (NetBIOS Extended User Interface) was originally developed as a protocol for small departmental LANs of 20 to 200 computers. NetBEUI is not routable since it doesn't have a network layer. NetBEUI is included with Windows 2000 Server and Windows 2000 Professional. It is primarily a legacy protocol to support existing workstations that have not been upgraded to Windows 2000.

For more information about NetBEUI, see "NetBEUI" in the *Windows 2000 Internetworking Guide.*

AppleTalk

AppleTalk is a protocol suite developed by Apple Computer Corporation for communication between Macintosh computers. Windows 2000 includes support for AppleTalk which allows Windows 2000 to be a router and a dial-up server. Support is natively provided as a service for file sharing and printer sharing.

For more information about AppleTalk, see "Services for Macintosh" in the *Windows 2000 Internetworking Guide.*

DLC

Data Link Control (DLC) was originally developed for IBM mainframe communications. The protocol was not designed to be a primary protocol for network use between personal computers. The other use of DLC is to print to Hewlett-Packard printers connected directly to networks. Network-attached printers use the DLC protocol because the received frames are easy to disassemble and because DLC functionality can easily be coded into read-only memory (ROM). DLC's usefulness is limited because it doesn't directly interface with the Transport Driver Interface layer. DLC needs to be installed only on those network machines that perform these two tasks, such as a print server sending data to a network Hewlett Packard printer. Clients sending print jobs to a network printer do not need the DLC protocol. Only the print server communicating directly with the printer needs the DLC protocol installed.

For more information about DLC, see "Data Link Control" in the *Windows 2000 Internetworking Guide.*

IrDA

Infrared Data Association (IrDA) has defined a group of short-range, high speed, bidirectional wireless infrared protocols, generically referred to as IrDA. IrDA allows a variety of devices to communicate with each other. Cameras, printers, portable computers, desktop computers, and personal digital assistants (PDAs) can communicate with compatible devices using this technology. The IrDA protocol stack is accessed using NDIS connectionless drivers. Figure B.10 illustrates the IrDA protocol architecture.

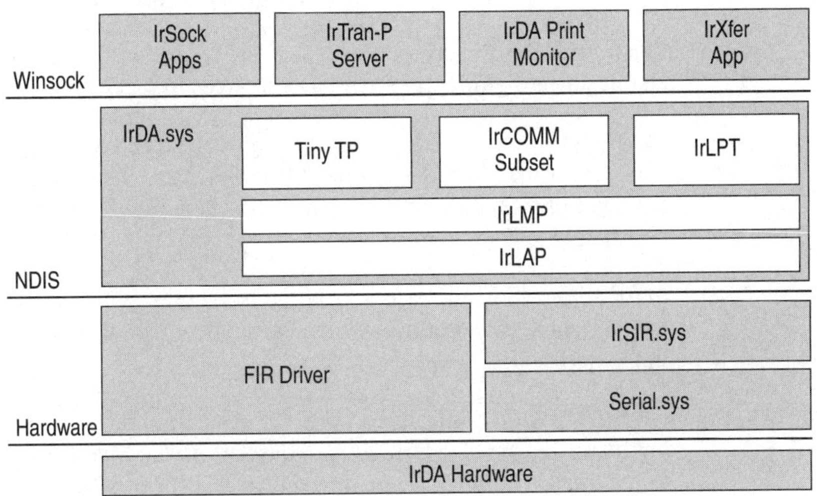

Figure B.10 IrDA Architecture

The components of IrDA are:

Winsock Winsock is an API that allows Windows-based applications to access the transport protocols. The IrDA protocol stack is made available to applications by using Winsock.

IrTran-P IrTran-P is a bidirectional image transfer protocol. Windows 2000 IrTran-P receives data only and is used for cameras with infrared capability. Many cameras have digital ports and can beam infrared data to a receiving computer. That data is then placed in a user-specified (or default) directory.

IrDA Print Monitor IrDA Print Monitor is a software component that interfaces with an IrDA-connected printer to make that printer appear as any other printer to Windows 2000 users.

IrXfer IrXfer is an IrDA file transfer application. Files can be dragged and dropped from the desktop to another computer. The Windows 2000 implementation of IrXfer has bidirectional transfer capabilities.

Tiny TP Tiny TP is a flow control mechanism for IrDA. Tiny TP acts as a regulator to control the rate of data input or output. This prevents an overflow of data from occurring and creating data errors.

IrDA.sys IrDA.sys is the transport protocol stack that supports IrDA. It provides support for applications through Winsock to the NDIS layer.

IrCOMM IrCOMM is a software component that supports IrTran-P. IrCOMM uses Winsock, and is interfaced by default to the IrTran-P server. The IrTran-P server must be disabled if other applications need to use the IrCOMM port.

IrLPT IrLPT is the protocol support that is used by IrDA Print Monitor. IrLPT enables printing directly from IrDA devices to IrDA printers.

IrLMP Infrared Link Management Protocol is used to multiplex various connections over one IrDA link. Multiplexing is the technique of splitting data from various sources into time slices and sending the data slices in sequence to a destination.

IrLAP Infrared Link Access Protocol is a media access control software component that determines which component can access the media during each time slice.

FIR Driver A Fast Infrared driver (FIR) is a miniport driver provided by a hardware vendor to link hardware devices on the lower side of the protocol stack to the transport protocol above, such as TCP/IP or IPX/SPX. FIR devices can exchange data up to 4 megabytes (MB) per second. All FIR devices are also required to support serial transmission using Serial Infrared driver (SIR).

IrSIR.sys Serial Infrared driver is a Microsoft-provided miniport driver. It is an alternate driver to the Fast Infrared driver and can be used only in combination with Serial.sys. The maximum data transfer rate is 115.2 kilobytes per second (Kbps). In combination with Serial.sys, IrSIR.sys provides support for serial ports.

Serial.sys Serial.sys is used to connect infrared devices to the IrSIR.sys driver above in the protocol stack and the hardware device below. It is a software driver that sends and receives data from a hardware device and presents it to the IrSIR.sys driver in a format that conforms to the requirements of IrSIR.sys.

Transport Driver Interface

The Transport Driver Interface (TDI) is a common interface for drivers (such as the Windows 2000 redirector and server) to use to communicate with the various network transport protocols. This allows services to remain independent of transport protocols. Unlike NDIS, there is no driver for TDI, which is a specification for passing messages between two layers in the network architecture.

Microsoft developed TDI to provide greater flexibility and functionality than is provided by existing interfaces (such as Winsock and NetBIOS). All Windows 2000 transport providers directly interface with the Transport Driver Interface. This allows the TDI to provide a consistent interface for the transport protocols. The TDI specification describes the set of functions and call mechanisms by which transport drivers and TDI clients communicate. The specific software requirements on both sides of the interface are provided by adherence to the TDI specification. Some applications, such as NetBEUI, do not directly interface to the TDI layer.

Emulator Modules

Emulator Modules provide a single common interface to all Windows 2000 transport drivers. This simplifies the task of transport driver development since only the interface needs to be coded. The transport drivers provide the Transport Driver Interface. Therefore, they can only be used by applications that can use TDI. Some older applications are written to use older existing interfaces. Windows 2000 includes emulator modules for the most popular existing network interfaces (such as NetBIOS). Emulator modules provide a mapping layer between network interfaces and TDI-compliant protocols.

Network Application Programming Interfaces

An Application Programming Interface (API) is a set of routines that an application program uses to request and carry out lower-level services performed by the operating system. Windows 2000 network APIs include:

- Winsock API
- NetBIOS API
- Telephony API
- Messaging API
- WNet API

Winsock API

Winsock is an API that allows Windows-based applications to access the transport protocols. Winsock in Windows 2000 is a protocol-independent networking API. Winsock is the Windows 2000 implementation of the widely-used Sockets API, the standard for accessing datagram and session services over TCP/IP, NWLink IPX/SPX NetBIOS, and AppleTalk. Applications written to the Winsock interface include File Transfer Protocol (FTP) and Simple Network Management Protocol (SNMP). Winsock performs the following:

- Provides a familiar networking API for programmers using Windows or UNIX.
- Offers binary compatibility between the heterogeneous, Windows-based TCP/IP stack and utility vendors.
- Supports both connection-oriented and connectionless protocols.

Windows 2000 includes Winsock 1.1 support. Winsock 2.0 extends the Winsock 1.1 interface to provide access to networks using protocols other than TCP/IP, such as NetWare and AppleTalk. Winsock 2.0 provides the following enhancements over Winsock 1.1:

- Name registration and resolution.

  Winsock 2.0 provides an interface that applications can use to access many different namespaces, such as Domain Name System (DNS), Novell Directory Services (NDS), and X.500.
- Support for real-time multimedia communications.

  Winsock supports several multimedia enhancements, including Quality of Service (QoS)
- Protocol-independent multipoint and multicast.

  Winsock 2.0 enables applications to take advantage of the multipoint and multicast capabilities of transport stacks.

Winsock Architecture

Winsock 2.0 is a Windows Open Systems Architecture (WOSA)–compliant interface that enables a front-end application and a back-end service to communicate. The Winsock 2.0 interface includes the following components:

- The Winsock 1.1 Application Programming Interface (API)
- The Winsock 2.0 Application Programming Interface (API)
- The Winsock 2.0 Transport Service Providers
- Layered Service Providers

Figure B.11 shows the Winsock 2.0 architecture.

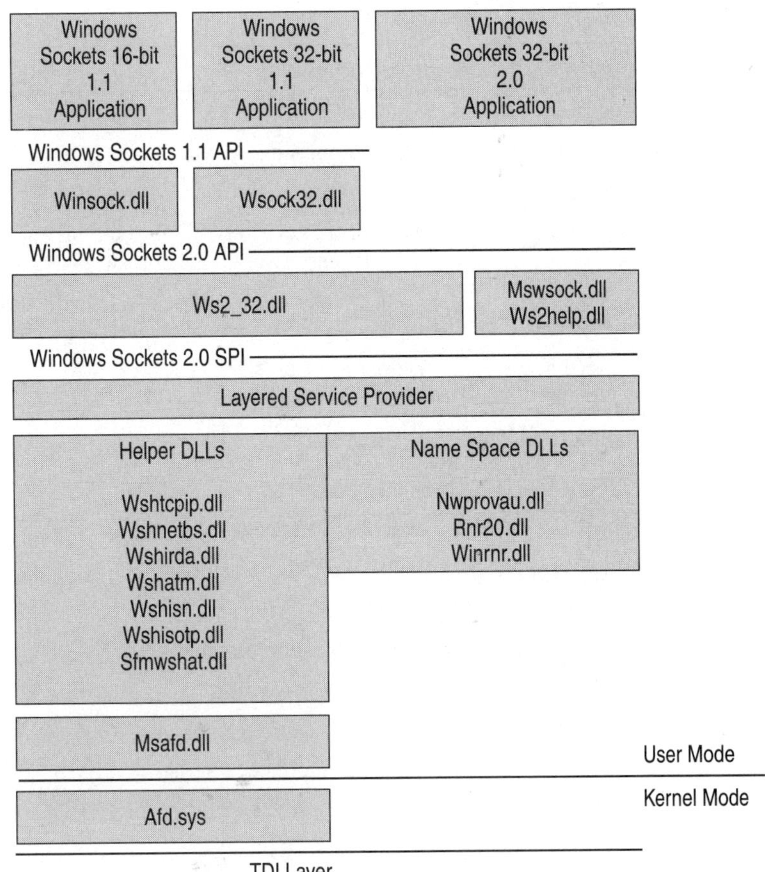

Figure B.11 Winsock 2.0 Architecture

Winsock Files

Table B.1 contains a list of files that Winsock uses to function. The table lists the files in order of the layer that they support and gives a brief description of their function.

Table B.1 Winsock Files

Winsock DLLs	Description
Winsock.dll	16-bit Winsock 1.1
Wsock32.dll	32-bit Winsock 1.1
Ws2_32.dll	Main Winsock 2.0
Mswsock.dll	Microsoft extensions to Winsock. Mswsock.dll is an API that supplies services that are not part of Winsock.
Ws2help.dll	Platform-specific utilities. Ws2help.dll supplies operating system–specific code that is not part of Winsock.
Wshtcpip.dll	Helper for TCP
Wshnetbs.dll	Helper for NetBT
Wshirda.dll	Helper for IrDA
Wshatm.dll	Helper for ATM
Wshisn.dll	Helper for Netware
Wshisotp.dll	Helper for OSI transports
Sfmwshat.dll	Helper for Macintosh
Nwprovau.dll	Name resolution provider for IPX
Rnr20.dll	Main name resolution
Winrnr.dll	LDAP name resolution
Msafd.dll	Winsock interface to kernel
Afd.sys	Winsock kernel interface to TDI transport protocols

Winsock 1.1 API

Winsock 1.1 API is a thunk layer. A thunk layer translates the output from a component into a form another component can use. Winsock 1.1 layer commands are converted to Winsock 2.0 layer commands to allow backward compatibility for legacy applications.

Winsock 2.0 API

Winsock 2.0 API is the interface for Winsock 2.0. For example, it helps Winsock 2.0 to add new APIs (such as Generic Quality of Service). Winsock 2.0 API is located between the Winsock 2.0 dynamic link library (DLL) and a Winsock 2.0 application.

Winsock 2.0 SPI Transport Service Providers

Transport service providers give applications a consistent interface for accessing multiple transport protocols. Located above the transport service provider, the Winsock 2.0 DLL takes requests from applications and sends those requests to the transport service provider. The Winsock 2.0 DLL also provides traffic management. The transport service provider can support one or more transport protocols.

Layered Service Provider Layer

An optional Layered Service Provider layer can be inserted between the Winsock 2.0 DLL and the underlying protocol stack if required by an application. It can extend the underlying protocol stack by providing additional services such as authentication, encryption, or proxy server services.

Winsock Helper DLLs

Winsock helper DLLs provide specific software components to assist Winsock 2.0. Transport protocols such as TCP, ATM, and IrDA have DLLs that supply the necessary program code to support Winsock.

Winsock 2.0 Name Resolution Providers

Name resolution providers enable server and client applications to use a consistent interface for multiple name services. Services register with the Winsock DLL, and client applications send requests for the names of those services to the Winsock DLL. The Winsock DLL manages registration and loading of name resolution providers and sends name resolution operations to the correct provider. Finally, the provider implements an interface with existing name services, such as DNS.

Generic Quality of Service and Resource Reservation Protocol

Connectionless networks (such as Ethernet networks) make only a best effort to deliver packets to their destination. There is no guarantee that packets will arrive, or that they will arrive in the correct order. Instead, protocols such as TCP/IP were developed to ensure retransmission of lost packets and to ensure that out-of-order packets could be reassembled in the correct order. This is sufficient for most applications, such as e-mail. However, for newer applications, such as real-time audio and video, packets must arrive on time and in order or the transmission might be garbled.

Connection-oriented networks enable applications to request certain levels of service, such as bandwidth and reliability, for specific connections. Additionally, they enable computers to set up several different connections with several different qualities of service. For example, on a connection-oriented network, two simultaneous connections can support both a high-delay low-bandwidth connection to send e-mail and a high-bandwidth, low-delay connection for a videoconferencing application.

Windows 2000 makes different service levels possible through its Generic Quality of Service (GQoS) APIs and its support for the Resource Reservation Signaling Protocol (RSVP). Applications can request different network characteristics for a connection. RSVP then handles those requests by attempting to make bandwidth reservations for that connection.

Generic Quality of Service

The GQoS APIs in Winsock 2.0 provide access to most QoS levels of service. The underlying QoS providers make it possible to utilize these levels of service directly from the GQoS APIs. Applications can make calls to GQoS APIs and request attributes such as:

- Peak bandwidth (average or peak bit rate available).
- Latency (the maximum acceptable delay between transmission of a bit and its receipt by the receiver).
- Delay variation (the difference between a packet's minimum and maximum delay).

Figure B.12 shows the architecture of GQoS.

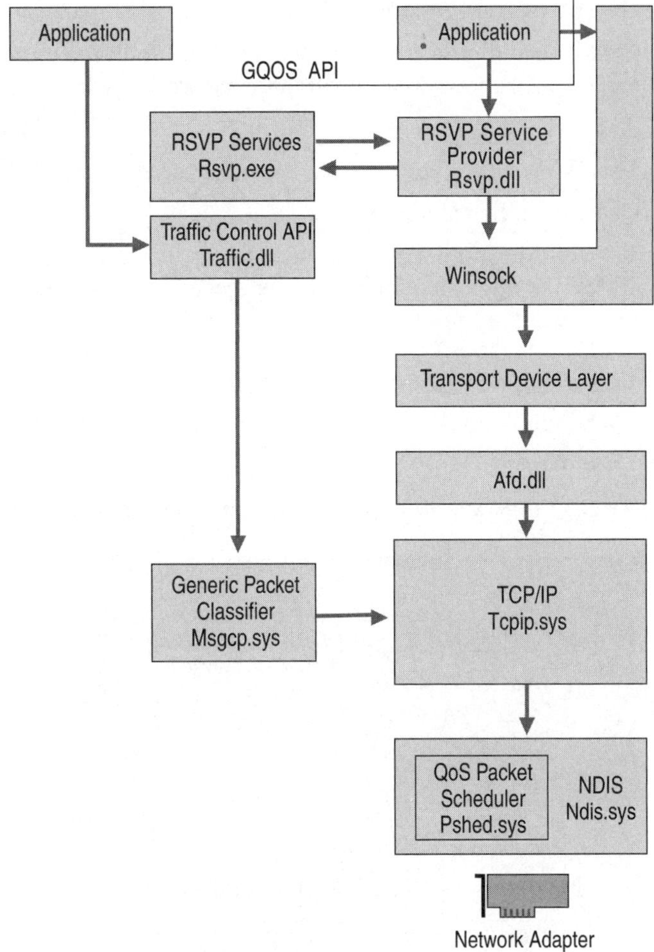

Figure B.12 GQoS Architecture

The GQoS components are:

- RSVP Service Provider

  The QoS component that invokes nearly all QoS functions and services. RSVP Service Provider (rsvpsp.dll and rsvp.exe) starts traffic control and implements, maintains, and handles RSVP signalling for all of Windows 2000 QoS functions.

- Traffic Control API

  A programmatic interface for the traffic control components that regulate network traffic on local hosts. It regulates traffic internally (within the kernel) and on the network. (It also prioritizes and queues packets based on transmission priority.)

- Generic Packet Classifier (GPC)

  Classifies and prioritizes packets, it has the ability to provide lookup tables and classification services within the network stack.
- Afd.sys

  This Winsock Kernel Interface provides access to the TDI transports.
- QoS Packet Scheduler

  This traffic control module regulates how much of the data an application is allowed to transmit at one time, thereby enforcing QoS parameters that are set for a particular flow.

Quality of Service Admission Control Service

The QoS Admission Control Service is responsible for regulating subnet usage for QoS-enabled components.

Figure B.13 illustrates the QoS Admission Control Service architecture.

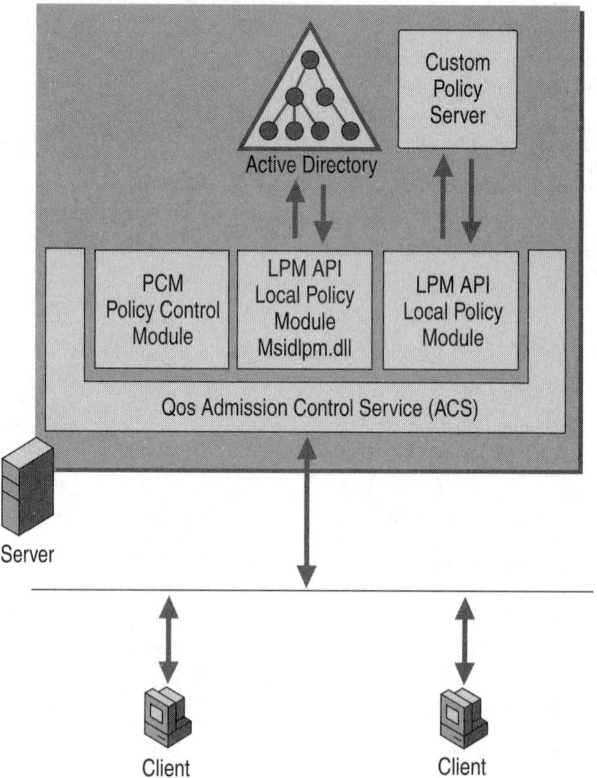

Figure B.13 QoS Admission Control Service

The QoS ACS administers subnet bandwidth resources that are necessary to ensure QoS transmission of data. The QoS ACS operates on a Windows 2000 Server residing on a subnet. On the shared segments, all QoS reservation messages are routed through the QoS ACS, so subnet clients can share their bandwidth and the administration of bandwidth allocation can be centralized. The QoS ACS sends messages, called *beacons*, to let other clients on the network know it is present and ready to receive subnet bandwidth reservation requests. QoS Admission Control Service components govern QoS-enabled applications. The QoS ACS must be installed in a server that does not have QoS components present.

The QoS ACS components are:

- Quality of Service Admission Control Service (QoS ACS)

  A QoS component that regulates subnet usage for QoS-enabled applications. The QoS ACS exerts its control over QoS-aware applications or clients by placing itself within the RSVP message path. The QoS ACS intercepts Resource Reservation Protocol (RSVP) and Reservation (RESV) messages and passes the messages with the user information to Local Policy Modules for authentication. RSVP messages are sent to request transmission characteristics and RESV messages confirm that the transmission characteristics can be granted.

- Policy Control Module (PCM)

  Mediates the interaction between the QoS ACS and LPMs. PCMs send user information to each LPM and gathers all the responses, then performs logical checks on the information. The PCM gathers the information and sends it as one response to QoS ACS.

- Local Policy Module (LPM)

  The API that communicates with the QoS Admission Control Service. The LPM API also specifies how LPMs are registered and initialized within the construct of QoS ACS.

- Active Directory

  Provides a single point of management for Windows-based policies, user accounts, clients, servers, and applications. In QoS, Active Directory stores information about the levels of service that GQoS uses.

- Custom Policy Server

  A third-party component that can be used to store policies for GQoS levels of service.

Applications request QoS levels of service. The RSVP signaling provider negotiates with the network for the requested levels of service. The packet classifier and scheduler determine when to send the packets and with what priority. Finally, the QoS-aware router forwards the packets as requested.

For more information about QoS and RSVP, see "Quality of Service" in this book.

Telephony API

Telephony is a technology that integrates computers with telephone networks. With telephony, people can use their computers to take advantage of a wide range of communications features and services over a telephone line.

The Telephony API (TAPI) allows programmers to develop applications that provide personal telephony to users. TAPI supports both speech and data transmission, and allows for a variety of terminal devices. It supports complex connection types and call-management techniques such as call conferencing, call waiting, and voice mail. TAPI allows all elements of telephone usage, from the simple dial-and-speak call to international e-mail, to be controlled within applications developed for Microsoft® Win32® application programming interfaces.

Many applications can utilize telephony:

- Multicast multimedia IP conferencing.
- Voice calls over the Internet.
- Call center applications capable of tracking multiple agents.
- Basic voice calls on the Public Switched Telephone Network (PSTN).
- Private Branch Exchange (PBX) control.
- Interactive voice response (IVR) systems.
- Voice mail.

Figure B.14 shows the major components of the TAPI architecture.

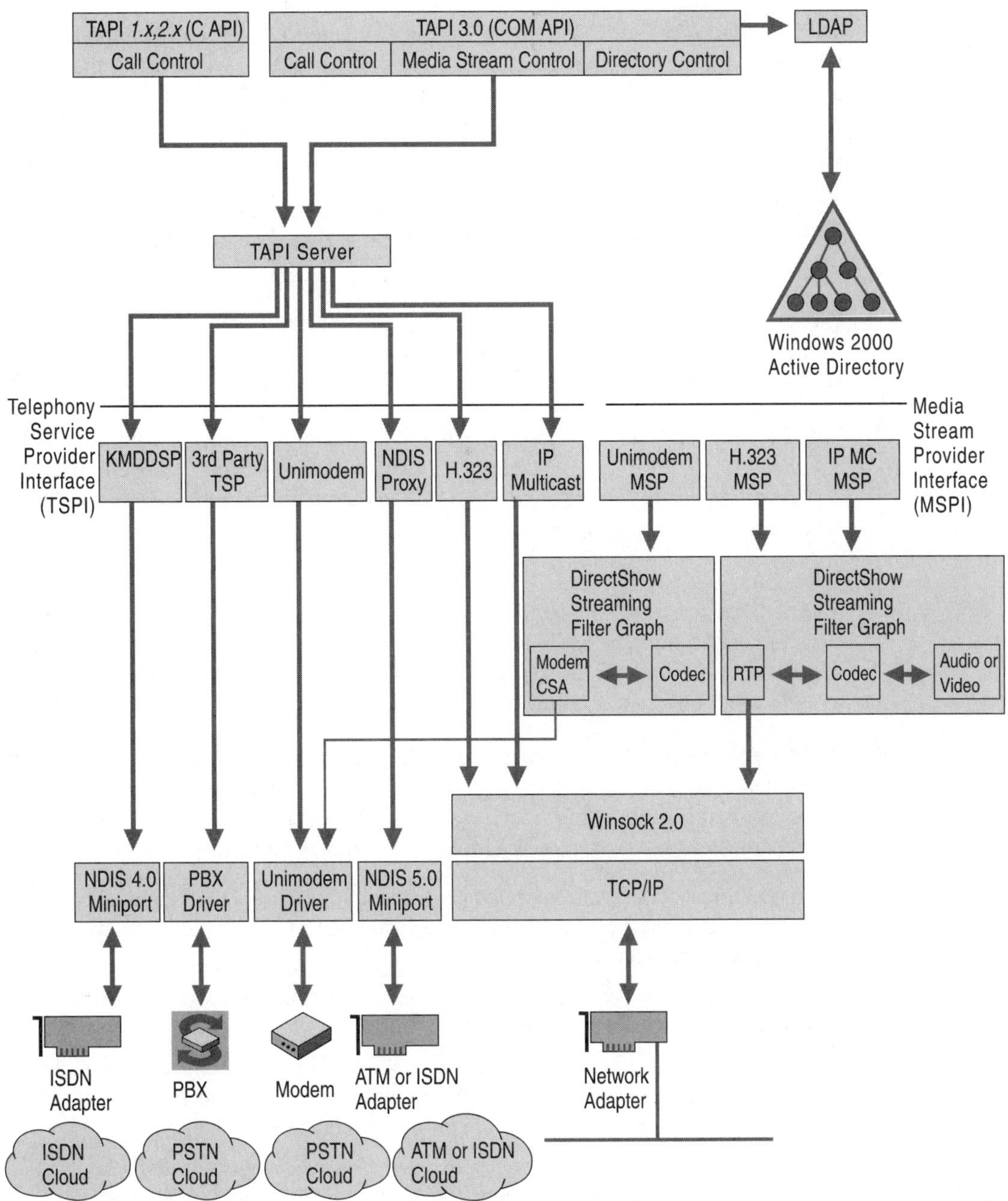

Figure B.14 TAPI Architecture

TAPI 3.0 COM API The TAPI 3.0 API is implemented as a suite of Component Object Model (COM) interfaces. This allows developers to write TAPI-enabled applications in any COM-aware language, such as Java, Microsoft® Visual Basic, or Microsoft® Visual C++®. TAPI 3.0 supports two classes of service providers: telephony and media.

TAPI 2.1 COM API TAPI 2.1 COM API provides compatibility with TAPI 3.0. TAPI 2.1 is a translation layer that maps 16-bit addresses to 32-bit addresses and passes requests along to Tapi32.dll.

Tapi32.dll Tapi32.dll is a thin marshaling layer, that transfers function requests for Tapisrv.exe. When needed, it loads and calls service provider user interface DLLs.

TAPI Server TAPI server is implemented by Tapisrv.exe, the core component of TAPI. TAPI server runs as a separate service process in which all telephony service providers run. API functions communicate with the TAPI server to send service requests to telephony service providers.

Telephony Service Providers Telephony service providers are dynamic-link libraries that carry out low-level and device-specific actions needed to complete telephony tasks through hardware devices such as fax adapters, ISDN adapters, telephones, and modems. Applications link to and call functions in the TAPI dynamic-link library only; they never call the service providers directly.

Media Service Providers The Microsoft H.323 Telephony Service Provider and its associated Media Service Provider (MSP) allow TAPI-enabled applications to engage in multimedia audio/video sessions with any H.323-compliant terminal on a local area network (LAN) or the Internet. Examples include:

- The multicast conference service provider. Uses IP multicast techniques to provide efficient multiparty audio and video conferencing facilities over IP networks, intranets and the Internet.
- The NDIS Proxy Service Provider. Offers a TAPI interface to wide area network (WAN) devices, such as ISDN or ATM.
- TAPI, which has a Remote Service Provider to support client/server telephony. The Remote SP provides TAPISRV telephony service extensions for client access to TAPI devices that reside on networked server machines.
- The TAPI Kernel-Mode Service Provider. Communicates with NDIS components in order to provide a TAPI interface to NDISWAN drivers.
- Unimodem 5. A Telephony Service Provider that provides an abstraction for modem devices so that applications can operate transparently across a wide variety of modems.
- Third-party hardware and software vendors. Can write Telephony Service Providers that are compatible with TAPI for additional applications.

For more information about TAPI, see "Telephony Integration" in the *Windows 2000 Internetworking Guide*.

NetBIOS API

NetBIOS is a standard application programming interface in the personal-computing environment. NetBIOS is used for developing client/server applications. NetBIOS has been used as an interprocess communication (IPC) mechanism since its introduction. It is included with Windows 2000 to support legacy applications.

A NetBIOS client/server application can communicate over various protocols:

- NetBEUI Frame protocol (NBF)

  NetBEUI is a NetBIOS-compatible transport. NBF was designed for small networks of 50 to 200 computers. Since NetBEUI has no networking layer, it is not routable. It is included with Windows 2000 to support legacy networks.

- NetBIOS over TCP/IP (NetBT)

  Since NetBEUI is not routable, alternate means were created to transport it through routers. RFCs 1001 and 1002 defined methods by which NetBEUI can be transported in IP packets. With this technique, NetBEUI networks can be connected.

- NWLink NetBIOS (NWNBLink)

  NetWare NetBIOS Link (NWNBLink) contains Microsoft enhancements to NetBIOS. The NWNBLink component is used to format NetBIOS-level requests and pass them to the NWLink component for transmission on the network.

NetBIOS uses the following components:

- Netapi32.dll. Linked to the NetBIOS emulator to allow communication with TCP/IP, NetBEUI, and NWLink. It shares the address space of the NetBIOS user-mode application.
- NetBIOS emulator. Provides the NetBIOS mapping layer between NetBIOS applications and the TDI-compliant protocols.

The Winsock APIs can also be used to access the NetBIOS protocols.

For more information about NetBIOS, see "NetBEUI" in the *Windows 2000 Internetworking Guide*.

Messaging API

The Messaging Application Programming Interface (MAPI) is an industry standard that enables applications to interact with many different messaging services using a single interface. MAPI is a set of API functions that allow messaging clients, such as Microsoft Exchange, to interact with various message service providers, such as Microsoft Mail, and Fax.

For more information about MAPI, see the Platform Software Development Kit (SDK).

WNet API

WNet APIs provide Windows networking (WNet) functions that allow networking capabilities for applications. Also known as the Win32 APIs, applications that are created by using Wnet APIs function independently from the network on which they operate. By using WNet APIs, applications can be developed that run successfully on all platforms while still able to take advantage of unique features and capabilities of any particular platform.

Network services are one of many categories of services that the Win32 API's can provide. Requests for network services are provided by the Multiple Provider Router. Multi Provider Routing receives WNet commands, determines the appropriate redirector, and passes the command to that redirector. Multi Provider Routing then routes the requests for network service to the appropriate provider for transmission over the network.

For more information about WNet APIs, see the Platform Software Development Kit (SDK).

Other Network APIs

Windows 2000 uses many APIs in addition to the ones that have been covered:

- The firewall API is a low-level API that allows greater and more complex filtering than the Filter Driver API.
- The Dynamic Host Configuration Protocol (DHCP) API allows applications to request DHCP options.
- The Multicast Address Dynamic Client Allocation Protocol (MADCAP) API allows applications to request multicast addresses.
- The DHCP Server Call API allows custom extensions to a DHCP server.
- The IP Helper API (IPHLP API) is a public API that provides TCP/IP information to Win32 applications.

- The Multiple Provider Router API (MPR API) is used to configure and administer routers.
- The Filter Driver API allows configuration of packet filtering for IP traffic.
- The Message Queuing API provides loosely-coupled, reliable communications. Message Queuing can be used for transaction processing to communicate transaction status.

For more information about network APIs, see the Platform Software Development Kit (SDK).

Interprocess Communication

Interprocess communication (IPC) allows bidirectional communication between clients and servers using distributed applications. IPC is a mechanism used by programs and multi-user processes. IPCs allow concurrently running tasks to communicate between themselves on a local computer or between the local computer and a remote computer.

IPC mechanisms are used to support distributed processing. Applications that split processing between networked computers are called distributed applications. The split portions of a distributed application can be located on the same machine or on separate machines. A client/server application uses distributed processing, in which processing is divided between a workstation (the client) and a more powerful server. The client portion is sometimes referred to as the front end and the server portion is referred to as the back end. The client portion of a client/server application can consist of just the user interface to the application. However, the application can be split at various places in the distributed application. It runs on the client workstation and takes a lesser amount of processing power. For example, the client portion might handle only screen graphics, mouse movements, and keystrokes.

Multi-tier applications are an extension of the basic client/server model. This common distributed business model is sometimes called the three-tier model. It is composed of three parts: the client tier, the components tier and the server tier.

For example, your company's payroll department uses an application to print paychecks. When a payroll employee runs a client application, the application starts a business-rules server in the component tier. The component tier is composed of various components such as business rules, transaction management, and other business logic components.

The business rules server organizes the appropriate components for the task. The server application connects to a database server in the database tier and retrieves employee records such as salary information. The business-rules server transforms the payroll information into the final output and returns it to the client.

The application server can then process information that the client computer normally does in the client/server model. The application server handles the business or application logic and communicates with the back-end database, usually with structured query language (SQL). The server or back-end database often utilizes large amounts of data storage, computing power, and specialized hardware. The component parts make it easier to manage, deploy, and update these objects.

The goal of distributed processing is to move the actual application processing from the client to the servers that have the power to run large applications. While running, the client portion formats requests and sends them to the server for processing. Servers run the request and pass the result back to the client.

There are a number of ways to establish this connection. The Windows 2000 operating system provides many different Interprocess Communication (IPC) mechanisms.

Distributed Component Object Model

In addition to supporting component object model (COM) for interprocess communication on a local computer, Windows 2000 supports the distributed component object model (DCOM). DCOM is a system of software objects designed to be reusable and replaceable. Objects are software components that can perform and support applications. The objects support sets of related functions such as sorting, random-number generation, and database searches. Each set of functions is called an interface, and each DCOM object can have multiple interfaces. When applications access an object, they receive an indirect pointer to the interface functions. The pointer has information on the location of an object. After receiving this pointer, the calling application doesn't need to know where the object is or how it does its job since the pointer directs the calling application to it.

DCOM allows processes to be efficiently distributed to multiple computers so that the client and server components of an application can be placed in optimal locations on the network. Processing occurs transparently to the user because DCOM handles this function. Thus, the user can access and share information without needing to know where the application components are located. If the client and server components of an application are located on the same computer, DCOM can be used to transfer information between processes. DCOM is platform independent and supports any 32-bit application that is DCOM-aware.

Advantages of Using DCOM

DCOM is a preferred method for developers to use in writing client/server applications for Windows 2000. With DCOM, interfaces to software objects can be added or upgraded, so applications aren't forced to upgrade each time the software object changes. Objects are software entities that perform specific functions. These functions are implemented as dynamic-link libraries so that changes in the functions, including new interfaces or the way the function works, can be made without rewriting and recompiling the applications that call them.

Windows 2000 supports DCOM by making the implementation of application pointers transparent to the application and the object. Only the operating system needs to know if the function called is handled in the same process or across the network. This frees the application from concerns with local or remote procedure calls. Administrators can choose to run DCOM applications on local or remote computers, and can change the configuration for efficient load balancing.

Your application might support its own set of DCOM features. For more information about configuring your application to use DCOM, see your application's documentation.

DCOM builds upon remote procedure call (RPC) technology by providing an easy-to-use mechanism for integrating distributed applications on a network. A distributed application consists of multiple processes that cooperate to accomplish a single task. Unlike other interprocess communication (IPC) mechanisms, DCOM gives you a high degree of control over security features, such as permissions and domain authentication. It can also be used to start applications on other computers or to integrate Web browser applications that run on the Microsoft® ActiveX® platform.

Remote Procedure Call

Remote Procedure Call (RPC) is an interprocess communication technique to allow client and server software to communicate. The Microsoft RPC facility is compatible with the Open Group's Distributed Computing Environment (DCE) specification for remote procedure calls and is interoperable with other DCE-based RPC systems, such as those for HP-UX and IBM AIX UNIX–based operating systems. The RPC facility is compatible with the Open Group specification.

The Microsoft RPC mechanism is unique in that it uses other IPC mechanisms, such as named pipes, NetBIOS, or Winsock, to establish communications between the client and the server. With the RPC facility, essential program logic and related procedure code can exist on different computers, which is important for distributed applications.

RPC is based on the concepts used for creating structured programs, which can be viewed as having a backbone to which a series of ribs can be attached. The backbone is the mainstream logic of the program that rarely changes. The ribs are the procedures that the backbone calls upon to do work or perform functions. In traditional programs, these ribs are statically linked to the backbone and stored in the same executable file. RPC places the backbone and the ribs on different computers.

Windows 2000 uses dynamic link libraries (DLLs) to provide procedure code and backbone code. This enables the DLLs to be modified or updated without changing or redistributing the backbone portion.

Client applications are developed with specially-compiled stub libraries that are provided by the application program. In reality, these stubs transfer the data and the function to the RPC run-time module.This module is responsible for finding the server that can satisfy the RPC command. Once found, the function and data are sent to the server, where they are picked up by the RPC run-time component on the server. The server builds the appropriate data structure, and calls the function.

The function interprets the call as coming from the client application. The server may impersonate the client. For security, RPC can use NTLM, Kerberos, or Secure Sockets Layer (SSL). When the function is completed, any return values are collected, formatted, and sent back to the client through the RPC run-time module. When the function returns to the client application, it has the appropriate returned data or an indication that the function failed. Figure B.15 illustrates Remote Procedure Calls.

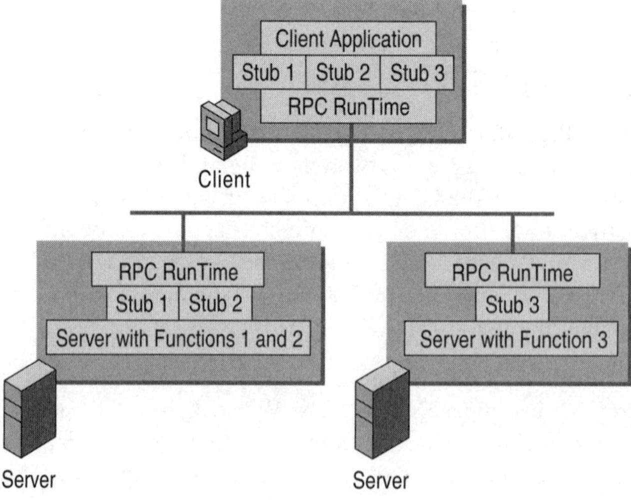

Figure B.15 Remote Procedure Calls

If the client and server portions of the application are on the same computer, local procedure calls (LPCs) can be used to transfer information efficiently between processes. This makes RPC a flexible and portable IPC choice.

Figure B.16 illustrates the software components of RPC.

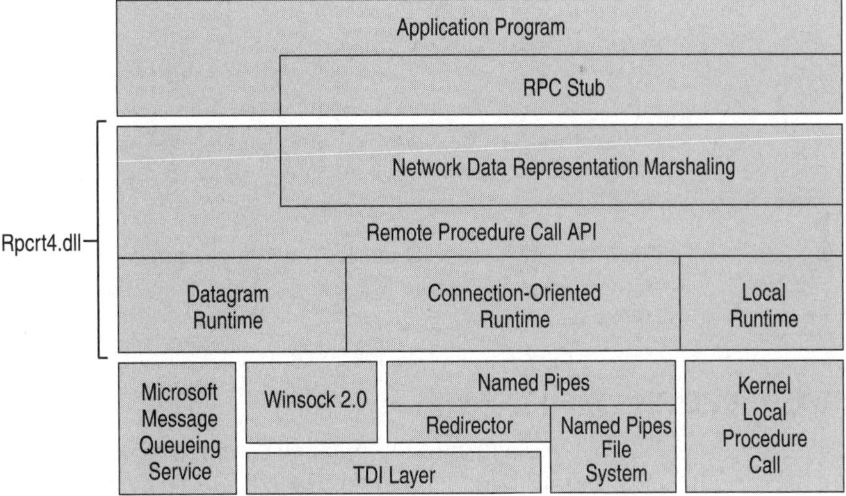

Figure B.16 Windows 2000 RPC Client and Workstation Architecture

The components of RPC are:

RPC Stub Part of an application executable file or a DLL that is generated by the Microsoft Interface Description Language (MIDL) compiler specifically for each interface.

Network Data Representation Marshaling Marshaling is the process of packaging and unpackaging parameters into Network Data Representation (NDR) format for communication over the network.

Remote Procedure Call APIs A series of protocol-independent APIs responsible for establishing connections and security as well as registering servers, naming, and endpoint resolution.

Datagram Runtime A connectionless RPC protocol engine that transmits and receives requests using connectionless protocols, such as UDP.

Connection-Oriented Runtime A connection-oriented RPC protocol engine that transmits and receives requests using connection-oriented protocols, such as TCP.

Local Runtime A local RPC protocol engine that transmits and receives RPC requests between processes on the local computer.

RPC Name Resolution

The function of RPC name resolution is to allow clients to find RPC servers. Servers on a Windows 2000 network send messages to the Active Directory directory service by a locator, which is a software service that runs on RPC servers. The locator exports bindings, interfaces, protocols, and endpoints for servers running on the local computer. This server information is stored in Active Directory in System\RPCServices. When a client wants to find a server, it queries Active Directory. The client receives information, including server names, protocols, and endpoints that were placed in Active Directory by the server. With this information, the client can directly connect to the server. Windows 2000 still supports named pipes, mailslots and broadcast messaging for name resolution by NetBIOS.

For more information about RPC name resolution, see "Service Publication in Active Directory" in the *Microsoft® Windows® 2000 Server Resource Kit Distributed Systems Guide*.

Named Pipes and Mailslots

Named pipes and mailslots are high-level interprocess communication mechanisms used by networked computers. Named pipes and mailslots are written as file system drivers, so implementation of named pipes and mailslots differs from implementation of other IPC mechanisms. Local processes can also use named pipes and mailslots. As with all other file systems, remote access to named pipes and mailslots is accomplished through the Common Internet File System (CIFS) redirector. A redirector intercepts file input/output (I/O) requests and directs them to a drive or resource on another networked computer. The redirector allows a CIFS client to locate, open, read, write, and delete files on another network computer running CIFS.

Named Pipes

Named pipes provide connection-oriented messaging by using pipes. Connection-oriented messaging requires that the communication occur over a virtual circuit and maintain reliable and sequential data transfer. A pipe is a portion of memory that can be used by one process to pass information to another. A pipe connects two processes so that the output of one can be used as input to the other. This technique is used for passing data between client and server. Named pipes are based on OS/2 API calls, which have been ported to the WNet APIs. Additional asynchronous support has been added to named pipes to pass data between client/server applications. Named pipes is included to provide backwards compatibility with Microsoft® LAN Manager and related applications.

The Windows 2000 operating system provides special APIs that increase security for named pipes. Using a feature called impersonation, the server can change its security identity to that of the client at the other end of the message. A server typically has more permissions to access databases on the server than a client requesting services. When the request is delivered to the server through a named pipe, the server changes its security identity to the security identity of the client. This limits the server to only those permissions granted to the client rather than its own permissions, thus increasing the security of named pipes.

Mailslots

Mailslots are a connectionless, high-level interprocess communication mechanism between networked computers, often used to locate and provide notification of services and computers. That is, mailslots are a broadcast service used for message delivery. The delivery of a message is not guaranteed, although the delivery rate on most networks is high.

The Windows 2000 operating system supports only second-class mailslots, not first-class mailslots. First-class mailslots are connection-oriented. Second-class mailslots provide connectionless messaging for broadcast messages.

A mailslot can be created on any networked computer. When a message is sent to a mailslot, the sending application specifies in the mailslot message structure whether the message is a first-class or second-class delivery. Connectionless messaging is most useful for identifying other computers or services on a network, such as the Browser service offered in the Windows 2000 operating system. Mailslots are included to provide backward compatibility with LAN Manager applications.

Common Internet File System

The *Common Internet File System* (CIFS) is the standard way that computer users share files across corporate intranets and the Internet. An enhanced version of the Microsoft open, cross-platform Server Message Block (SMB) protocol, CIFS is a native file-sharing protocol in Windows 2000.

CIFS defines a series of commands used to pass information between networked computers. The redirector packages requests meant for remote computers in a CIFS structure. CIFS can be sent over a network to remote devices. The redirector also uses CIFS to make requests to the protocol stack of the local computer. The CIFS messages can be broadly classified as follows:

- Connection establishment messages consist of commands that start and end a redirector connection to a shared resource at the server.
- Namespace and File Manipulation messages are used by the redirector to gain access to files at the server and to read and write them.

- Printer messages are used by the redirector to send data to a print queue at a server and to get status information about the print queue.
- Miscellaneous messages are used by the redirector to write to mailslots and named pipes.

Some of the platforms that CIFS supports are:

- Microsoft Windows 2000, Microsoft® Windows NT®, Microsoft® Windows® 98, Microsoft® Windows® 95
- Microsoft® OS/2 LAN Manager
- Microsoft® Windows® for Workgroups
- UNIX
- VMS
- Macintosh
- IBM LAN Server
- DEC PATHWORKS
- Microsoft® LAN Manager for UNIX
- 3Com 3+Open
- MS-Net

CIFS complements Hypertext Transfer Protocol (HTTP) while providing more sophisticated file sharing and file transfer than older protocols, such as FTP. CIFS is shown servicing a user request for data from a networked server in Figure B.17.

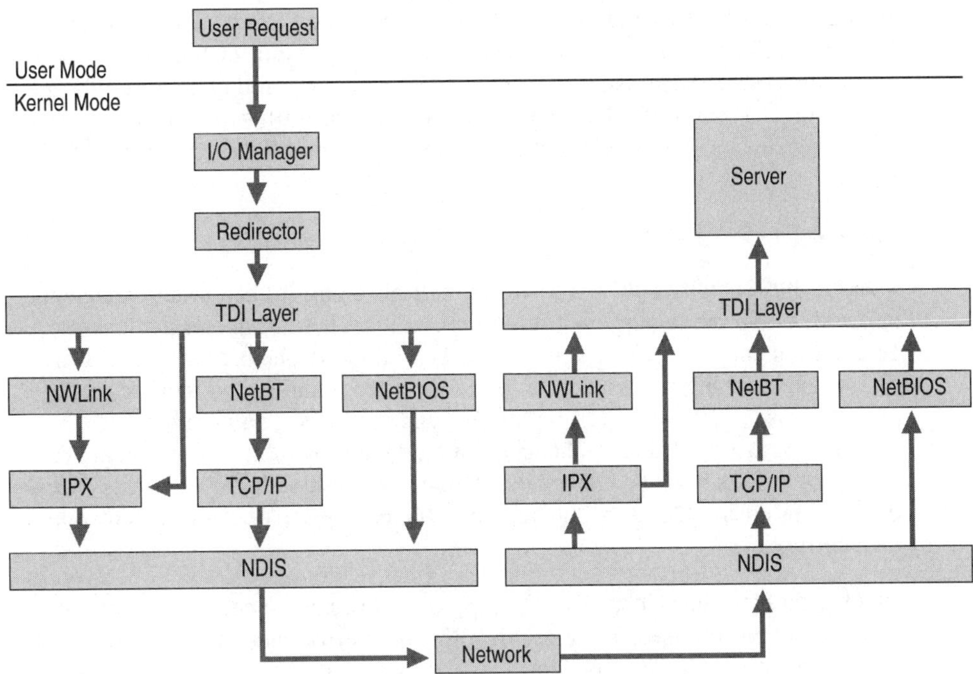

Figure B.17 CIFS Architecture

When there is a request to open a shared file, the I/O calls the redirector, which in turn requests the redirector to choose the appropriate transport protocol. For NetBIOS requests, NetBIOS is encapsulated in the IP protocol and transported over the network to appropriate server. The request is passed up to the server, which sends data back to satisfy the request.

Components in the redirector provide support for CIFS, such as:

- Rdbss.sys

  All kernel-level interactions are encapsulated in this driver. This includes all cache managers, memory managers, and requests for remote file systems so the specified protocol can use the requested server.

- Mrxsmb.sys

  This mini-redirector for CIFS has commands specific to CIFS.

- Mrxnfs.sys

  This mini-redirector for the Network File System (NFS) provides support for NFS. Mrxnfs.sys is included in Services for Unix.

In Windows NT 4.0, Windows Internet Name Service (WINS), and Domain Name System (DNS) name resolution was accomplished by using TCP port 134. Extensions to CIFS and NetBT now allow connections directly over TCP/IP with the use of TCP port 445. Both means of resolution are still available in Windows 2000. It is possible to disable either or both of these services in the registry.

Features that CIFS offers are:

Integrity and Concurrency CIFS allows multiple clients to access and update the same file while preventing conflicts by providing file sharing and file locking. File sharing and file locking is the process of allowing one user to access a file at a time and blocking access to all other users. These sharing and locking mechanisms can be used over the Internet and intranets. They also permit aggressive caching and read-ahead and write-behind without loss of integrity. File caches of buffers must be cleared before the file is usable by other clients. These capabilities ensure that only one copy of a file can be active at a time, preventing data corruption.

Optimization for Slow Links The CIFS protocol has been tuned to run well over slow-speed dial-up lines. The effect is improved performance for users who access the Internet using a modem.

Security CIFS servers support both anonymous transfers and secure, authenticated access to named files. File and directory security policies are easy to administer.

Performance and Scalability CIFS servers are highly integrated with the operating system, and are tuned for maximum system performance.

Unicode File Names File names can be in any character set, not just character sets designed for English or Western European languages.

Global File Names Users do not have to mount remote file systems, but can refer to them directly with globally significant names (names that can be located anywhere on the Internet), instead of ones that have only local significance (on a local computer or LAN). Distributed File Systems (DFS) allows users to construct an enterprise-wide namespace. Uniform Naming Convention (UNC) file names are supported so a drive letter does not need to be created before remote files can be accessed.

Basic Network Services

Network services support application programs and provide the components and APIs necessary to access files on networked computers. Both the server service and the workstation service also assist in accessing I/O requests.

Server Service

The server service is located above the TDI and is implemented as a file system driver. The CIFS server service interacts directly with other file-system drivers to satisfy I/O requests, such as reading or writing to a file. The server service supplies the connections requested by client-side redirectors and provides them with access to the resources they request. Figure B.18 shows the server service receiving a data request.

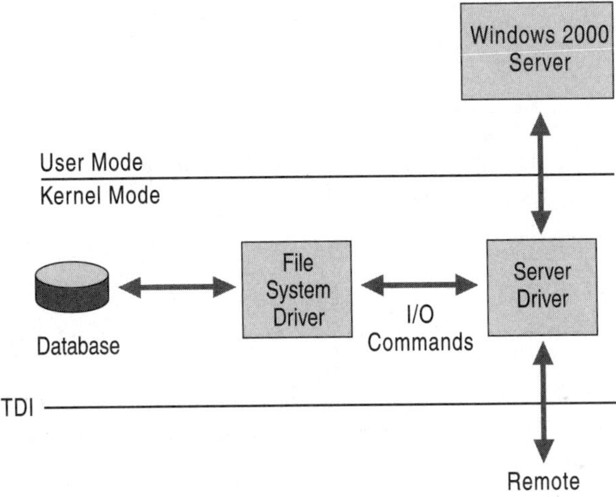

Figure B.18 Server Service

When the server service receives a request from a remote computer asking to read a file that resides on the local hard drive, the following steps occur:

1. The low-level network drivers receive the request and pass it to the server driver.
2. The server service passes the request to the appropriate local file-system driver.
3. The local file-system driver calls lower-level, disk -device drivers to access the file.
4. The data is passed back to the local file-system driver.
5. The local file-system driver passes the data back to the server service.
6. The server service passes the data to the lower-level network drivers for transmission back to the remote computer.

The server service is composed of two parts:

- Server service is a component of Services.exe. Services.exe is the Service Control Manager, where all services start. Unlike the workstation service, the server service is not dependent on the Multiple Uniform Naming Convention Provider (MUP). The MUP selects the appropriate UNC provider to handle the requests.
- Srv.sys is a file system driver that handles the interaction with the lower levels of the protocol stack and directly interacts with various file system devices to satisfy command requests, such as file read and write.

Workstation Service

All user-mode requests from the MUP go through the workstation service. This service consists of two components:

- The user-mode interface, which resides in Services.exe in Windows 2000.
- The redirector (Mrxsmb.sys), is a file-system driver that interacts with the lower-level network drivers by means of the TDI interface.

The workstation service receives the user request, and passes it to the kernel-mode redirector. The workstation service is shown in Figure B.19.

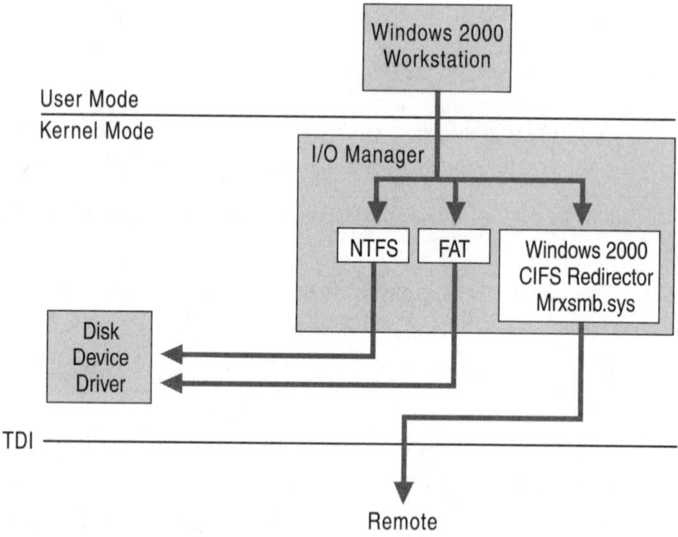

Figure B.19 Workstation Service

Windows 2000 Redirector

The redirector is a component that resides above TDI and through which one computer gains access to another computer. The Windows 2000 operating system redirector allows connection to Windows 98, Windows 95, Windows for Workgroups, LAN Manager, LAN Server, and other CIFS servers. The redirector communicates to the protocols by means of the TDI interface.

The redirector is implemented as a Windows 2000 file system driver. Implementing a redirector as a file system has many benefits:

- Allows applications to call a single API (the Windows 2000 I/O API) to access files on local and remote computers. From the I/O manager perspective, there is no difference between accessing files stored on a remote computer on the network and accessing those stored locally on a hard disk.
- Runs in kernel mode and can directly call other drivers and other kernel-mode components, such as cache manager. This improves the performance of the redirector.
- Can be dynamically loaded and unloaded, like any other file-system driver.
- Can coexist with other redirectors.

Figure B.20 shows the network architecture of the Windows 2000 Redirector.

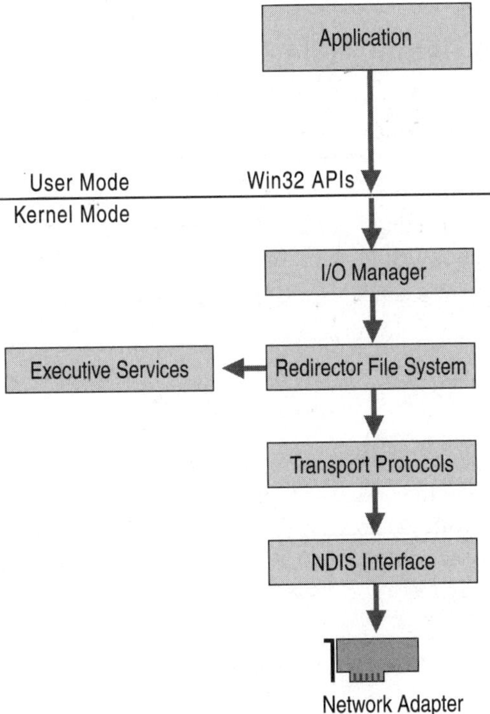

Figure B.20 Windows 2000 Redirector

Interoperating with Other Networks

Besides allowing connections to Windows 98, Windows 95, peer-to-peer networks, LAN Manager, LAN Server, and MS-Net servers, the Windows 2000 redirector can coexist with redirectors for other networks, such as Novell NetWare and UNIX networks.

Providers and the Provider-Interface Layer

For each additional type of network, such as NetWare or UNIX, you must install a component called a provider. The provider is the component that allows a computer running Windows 2000 Server or Windows 2000 Professional to communicate with the network. The Windows 2000 operating system includes several providers: Client Services for NetWare and Gateway Services for NetWare.

Client Services for NetWare is included with Windows 2000 Professional and allows a computer running Windows 2000 Professional to connect as a client to the NetWare network. The Gateway service, included with Windows 2000 Server, allows a computer running Windows 2000 to connect as a client to the NetWare network and provide gateway services between Microsoft network-based clients and Novell NetWare servers. Other provider DLLs are supplied by the appropriate network vendors.

Accessing a Remote File

When a process on a Windows 2000 computer tries to open a file that resides on a remote computer, the following steps occur:

1. The process calls the I/O manager to request that the file be opened.
2. The I/O manager recognizes that the request is for a file on a remote computer, and passes the request to the redirector file-system driver.
3. The redirector passes the request to lower-level network drivers that transmit it to the remote server for processing.

Network Resource Access

Applications reside above the redirector and server services in user mode. Like all other layers in the Windows 2000 networking architecture, there is a unified interface for accessing network resources, which is independent of any redirectors installed on the system. Access to resources is provided through the Multiple Uniform Naming Convention Provider (MUP) and the Multi-Provider Router (MPR).

Multiple Universal Naming Convention Provider

When applications make I/O calls containing Uniform Naming Convention (UNC) names, these requests are passed to the Multiple UNC Provider (MUP). MUP selects the appropriate UNC provider (redirector) to handle the I/O request.

Universal Naming Convention Names

UNC is a naming convention for describing network servers and the share points on those servers. UNC names start with two backslashes followed by the server name. All other fields in the name are separated by a single backslash. A typical UNC name appears as: *server**share**subdirectory**filename*.

Not all of the components of the UNC name need to be present with each command; only the share component is required. For example, the command **dir** *servername**sharename* can be used to obtain a directory listing of the root of the specified share. One of the design goals of the Windows 2000 networking environment is to provide a platform upon which others can build. MUP is a vital part of allowing multiple redirectors to coexist in the computer. MUP frees applications from maintaining their own UNC-provider listings. If there are multiple redirectors present there must be a means of deciding which one to use. MUP's function is to act as an arbitrator to decide the most appropriate redirector to use. Figure B.21 shows the Windows 2000 architecture of MUP.

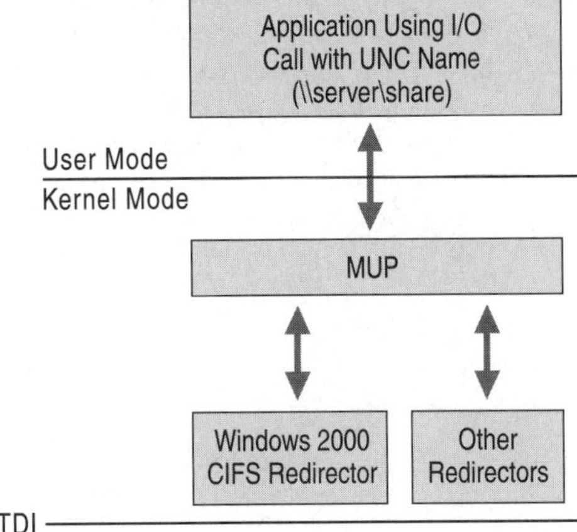

Figure B.21 MUP Architecture

MUP is a driver, unlike the TDI interface, which merely defines the way a component on one layer communicates with a component on another layer. MUP also has defined paths to UNC providers (redirectors).

I/O requests from applications that contain UNC names are received by the I/O manager, which passes the requests to MUP. If MUP has not seen the UNC name during the previous 15 minutes (this is only an approximate time period and is subject to change), MUP sends the name to each of the UNC providers registered with it. MUP is a prerequisite of the workstation service.

When a request containing a UNC name is received by MUP, it checks with each redirector to find out which one can process the request. MUP looks for the redirector with the highest registered-priority response that claims it can establish a connection to the UNC. This connection remains as long as there is activity. If there has been no request for 15 minutes (this is only an approximate time period and is subject to change) on the UNC name, then MUP negotiates to find another appropriate redirector.

Multi-Provider Router

Not all programs use UNC names in their I/O requests. Some applications use WNet APIs, which are the Win32 network APIs. The Multi-Provider Router (MPR) was created to support these applications.

MPR is similar to MUP. MPR receives WNet commands, determines the appropriate redirector, and passes the command to that redirector. Because different network vendors use different interfaces for communicating with their redirector, there is a series of provider DLLs between MPR and the redirectors. The provider DLLs provide a standard interface so that MPR can communicate with them. The appropriate DLLs take the request from MPR and communicate it to their corresponding redirector. Figure B.22 illustrates the Multi-Provider Router architecture.

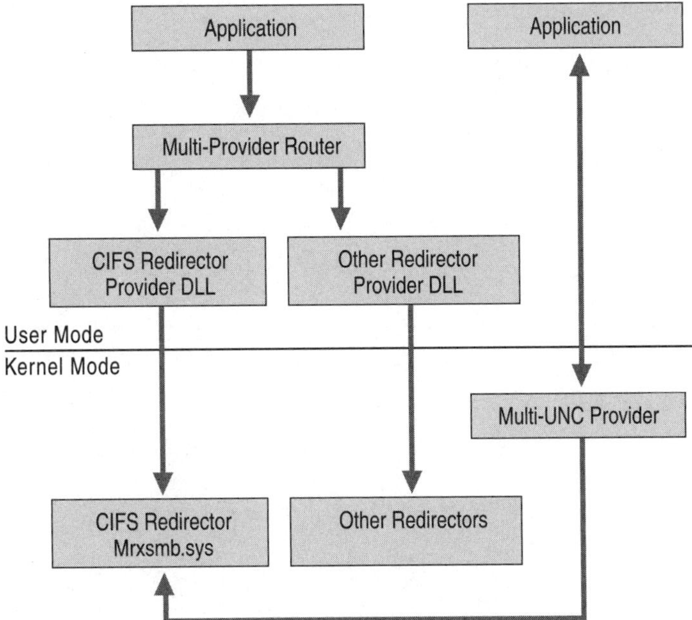

Figure B.22 Multi-Provider Router

The provider DLLs are supplied by the network-redirector vendor and are automatically installed when the redirector is installed.

Note The acronym MPR is also used for the Multi-Protocol Routing, a series of routing components supplied with Windows NT 4. In Windows 2000, Multi-Protocol Routing has become the Routing and Remote Access Service.

Additional Resources

- For more information about Windows 2000 network programming, see the Microsoft Platform Software Development Kit (SDK) link on the Web Resources page at http://windows.microsoft.com/windows2000/reskit/webresources.
- For more information about NDIS device driver development, see the Microsoft Platform Software Development Kit (SDK) link on the Web Resources page at http://windows.microsoft.com/windows2000/reskit/webresources.

APPENDIX C

TCP and UDP Port Assignments

Transport Control Protocol (TCP), User Datagram Protocol (UDP) ports, and Protocol Numbers are important to TCP/IP networking, intranets, and the Internet. Ports and protocol numbers provide access to a host computer. However, they also create a security hazard by allowing uninvited access. Therefore, knowing which port to allow or disable increases a network's security. If the wrong ports or protocol numbers are disabled on a firewall, router, or proxy server as a security measure, essential services might become unavailable.

In This Appendix

Related Information in the Resource Kit

- For a complete listing of Well-Known Ports, Registered ports, and protocol numbers, see the Port Assignments link on the Web Resources page at http://windows.microsoft.com/windows2000/reskit/webresources.

Port Assignments and Protocol Numbers

In TCP/IP networking, a port is a mechanism that allows a computer to simultaneously support multiple communication sessions with computers and programs on the network. A port directs the request to a particular service that can be found at that IP address. The destination of a packet can be further defined by using a unique port number. The port number is determined when the connection is established.

The Internet Assigned Numbers Authority (IANA) defines the unique parameters and protocol values necessary for operation of the Internet and its future development. In the past, these numbers were documented through the RFC document series. Since that time, the assignments have been listed on the IANA Web site, constantly updated and revised when new information is available and new assignments are made. The description of the ports and protocols in this chapter is from the IANA. The Internet Engineering Task Force (IETF) is the protocol engineering and developmental arm of the Internet. Also, the Internet Society (ISOC), a professional organization of Internet experts, comments on policies and practices and oversees a number of other boards and task forces dealing with network policy issues. For more information about port assignments, see the Port Assignments link on the web resources page at http://windows.microsoft.com/windows2000/reskit/webresources.

This appendix describes Microsoft® Windows® 2000 Server and Microsoft® Windows® 2000 Professional default port assignments and IP Protocol Numbers. Protocol Numbers direct a packet to the appropriate protocol, such as UDP or TCP, that is one layer higher in the protocol stack. This appendix contains three tables:

- Table C.1 lists Well-Known Ports.
- Table C.2 lists the Registered Ports.
- Table C.3 lists TCP and UDP ports that support commonly-used Windows 2000 services.
- Table C.4 lists IP Protocol Numbers and the functions they support.

  By definition, Dynamic Ports are randomly assigned and therefore cannot be known until they are assigned. Private Ports are not registered with the IANA but are used by software applications.

Port Assignments for Well-Known Ports

The Well-Known Ports are assigned by the IANA.

Ports are used in TCP or UDP communications to name the ends of logical connections that transfer data. For the purpose of providing services to unknown clients, ports were created. Table C.1 specifies the port used by the server process as its contact port. The contact port is sometimes called a Well-Known Port.

The assigned ports use a small portion of the possible port numbers. For many years the assigned ports were in the range 0-255. The range for assigned ports managed by the IANA has been expanded to the range 0-1023. The list in Table C.1 contains most of the port assignments that are significant to the Windows 2000 operating system.

Table C.1 Well-Known Ports

Port No.	Protocol	Service Name	Aliases	Comment
7	TCP	echo		Echo
7	UDP	echo		Echo
9	TCP	discard	sink null	Discard
9	UDP	discard	sink null	Discard
13	TCP	daytime		Daytime
13	UDP	daytime		Daytime
17	TCP	qotd	quote	Quote of the day
17	UDP	qotd	quote	Quote of the day
19	TCP	chargen	ttytst source	Character generator
19	UDP	chargen	ttytst source	Character generator
20	TCP	ftp-data		File Transfer
21	TCP	ftp		FTP Control
23	TCP	telnet		Telnet
25	TCP	smtp	mail	Simple Mail Transfer
37	TCP	time		Time
37	UDP	time		Time
39	UDP	rlp	resource	Resource Location Protocol
42	TCP	nameserver	name	Host Name Server
42	UDP	nameserver	name	Host Name Server
43	TCP	nicname	whois	Who Is
53	TCP	domain		Domain Name
53	UDP	domain		Domain Name Server
67	UDP	bootps	dhcps	Bootstrap Protocol Server
68	UDP	bootpc	dhcpc	Bootstrap Protocol Client

(continued)

Table C.1 Well-Known Ports *(continued)*

Port No.	Protocol	Service Name	Aliases	Comment
69	UDP	tftp		Trivial File Transfer
70	TCP	gopher		Gopher
79	TCP	finger		Finger
80	TCP	http	www, http	World Wide Web
88	TCP	kerberos	krb5	Kerberos
88	UDP	kerberos	krb5	Kerberos
101	TCP	hostname	hostnames	NIC Host Name Server
102	TCP	iso-tsap		ISO-TSAP Class 0
107	TCP	rtelnet		Remote Telnet Service
109	TCP	pop2	postoffice	Post Office Protocol - Version 2
110	TCP	pop3	postoffice	Post Office Protocol - Version 3
111	TCP	sunrpc	rpcbind portmap	SUN Remote Procedure Call
111	UDP	sunrpc	rpcbind portmap	SUN Remote Procedure Call
113	TCP	auth	ident tap	Authentication Sevice
117	TCP	uucp-path		UUCP Path Service
119	TCP	nntp	usenet	Network News Transfer Protocol
123	UDP	ntp		Network Time Protocol
135	TCP	epmap	loc-srv	DCE endpoint resolution
135	UDP	epmap	loc-srv	DCE endpoint resolution
137	TCP	netbios-ns	nbname	NETBIOS Name Service
137	UDP	netbios-ns	nbname	NETBIOS Name Service
138	UDP	netbios-dgm	nbdatagram	NETBIOS Datagram Service
139	TCP	netbios-ssn	nbsession	NETBIOS Session Service
143	TCP	imap	imap4	Internet Message Access Protocol
158	TCP	pcmail-srv	repository	PC Mail Server
161	UDP	snmp	snmp	SNMP
162	UDP	snmptrap	snmp-trap	SNMP TRAP
170	TCP	print-srv		Network PostScript

(continued)

Table C.1 Well-Known Ports *(continued)*

Port No.	Protocol	Service Name	Aliases	Comment
179	TCP	bgp		Border Gateway Protocol
194	TCP	irc		Internet Relay Chat Protocol
213	UDP	ipx		IPX over IP
389	TCP	ldap		Lightweight Directory Access Protocol
443	TCP	https	MCom	
443	UDP	https	MCom	
445	TCP			Microsoft CIFS
445	UDP			Microsoft CIFS
464	TCP	kpasswd		Kerberos (v5)
464	UDP	kpasswd		Kerberos (v5)
500	UDP	isakmp	ike	Internet Key Exchange (IPSec)
512	TCP	exec		Remote Process Execution
512	UDP	biff	comsat	Notifies users of new mail
513	TCP	login		Remote Login
513	UDP	who	whod	Database of who's logged on, average load
514	TCP	cmd	shell	Automatic Authentication
514	UDP	syslog		
515	TCP	printer	spooler	Listens for incoming connections
517	UDP	talk		Establishes TCP Connection
518	UDP	ntalk		
520	TCP	efs		Extended File Name Server
520	UDP	router	router routed	RIPv.1, RIPv.2
525	UDP	timed	timeserver	Timeserver
526	TCP	tempo	newdate	Newdate
530	TCP,UDP	courier	rpc	RPC
531	TCP	conference	chat	IRC Chat
532	TCP	netnews	readnews	Readnews
533	UDP	netwall		For emergency broadcasts
540	TCP	uucp	uucpd	Uucpd

(continued)

Table C.1 Well-Known Ports *(continued)*

Port No.	Protocol	Service Name	Aliases	Comment
543	TCP	klogin		Kerberos login
544	TCP	kshell	krcmd	Kerberos remote shell
550	UDP	new-rwho	new-who	New-who
556	TCP	remotefs	rfs rfs_server	Rfs Server
560	UDP	rmonitor	rmonitord	Rmonitor
561	UDP	monitor		
636	TCP	ldaps	sldap	LDAP over TLS/SSL
749	TCP	kerberos-adm		Kerberos administration
749	UDP	kerberos-adm		Kerberos administration

Port Assignments for Registered Ports

Registered Ports, ports between 1024 and 49151, are listed by the IANA and on most systems can be used by applications or programs executed by users. Table C.2 specifies the port used by the server process as its contact port. The IANA registers uses of these ports as a convenience to the Internet community. To the extent possible, these same port assignments are used with UDP. The Registered Ports are in the numerical range of 1024-49151. The Registered Ports between 1024 and 5000 are also referred to as the Ephemeral Ports. The list below contains most of the port assignments that are significant to Windows 2000.

Table C.2 Registered Ports

Port No.	Protocol	Service Name	Aliases	Comment
1109	TCP	kpop		Kerberos POP
1167	UDP	phone		Conference calling
1433	TCP	ms-sql-s		Microsoft-SQL-Server
1433	UDP	ms-sql-s		Microsoft-SQL-Server
1434	TCP	ms-sql-m		Microsoft-SQL-Monitor
1434	UDP	ms-sql-m		Microsoft-SQL-Monitor
1512	TCP	wins		Microsoft Windows Internet Name Service
1512	UDP	wins		Microsoft Windows Internet Name Service
1524	TCP	ingreslock	ingres	Ingres
1701	UDP	l2tp		Layer Two Tunneling Protocol

(continued)

Table C.2 Registered Ports *(continued)*

Port No.	Protocol	Service Name	Aliases	Comment
1723	TCP	pptp		Point-to-point tunneling protocol
1812	UDP	radiusauth		RRAS (RADIUS authentication protocol)
1813	UDP	radacct		RRAS (RADIUS accounting protocol)
2049	UDP	nfsd	nfs	Sun NFS server
2053	TCP	knetd		Kerberos de-multiplexer
2504	UDP	nlbs		Network Load Balancing
9535	TCP	man		Remote Man Server

Port Assignments for Commonly-Used Services

There are many services associated with the Windows 2000 operating system. These services might require more than one TCP or UDP port for the service to be functional. Table C.3 shows the default ports that are used by each service mentioned.

Table C.3 Default Port Assignments for Common Services

Service Name	UDP	TCP
Browsing datagram responses of NetBIOS over TCP/IP	138	
Browsing requests of NetBIOS over TCP/IP	137	
Client/Server Communication		135
Common Internet File System (CIFS)	445	139, 445
Content Replication Service		560
Cybercash Administration		8001
Cybercash Coin Gateway		8002
Cybercash Credit Gateway		8000
DCOM (SCM uses udp/tcp to dynamically assign ports for DCOM)	135	135
DHCP client		67
DHCP server		68
DHCP Manager		135
DNS Administration		139
DNS client to server lookup (varies)	53	53

(continued)

Table C.3 Default Port Assignments for Common Services *(continued)*

Service Name	UDP	TCP
Exchange Server 5.0		
Client Server Communication		135
Exchange Administrator		135
IMAP		143
IMAP (SSL)		993
LDAP		389
LDAP (SSL)		636
MTA - X.400 over TCP/IP		102
POP3		110
POP3 (SSL)		995
RPC		135
SMTP		25
NNTP		119
NNTP (SSL)		563
File shares name lookup	137	
File shares session		139
FTP		21
FTP-data		20
HTTP		80
HTTP-Secure Sockets Layer (SSL)		443
Internet Information Services (IIS)		80
IMAP		143
IMAP (SSL)		993
IKE (For more information, see Table C.4)	500	
IPSec Authentication Header (AH) (For more information, see Table C.4)		
IPSec Encapsulation Security Payload (ESP) (For more information, see Table C.4)		
IRC		531
ISPMOD (SBS 2nd tier DNS registration wizard)		1234
Kerberos de-multiplexer		2053
Kerberos klogin		543
Kerberos kpasswd (v5)	464	464
Kerberos krb5	88	88

(continued)

Table C.3 Default Port Assignments for Common Services *(continued*

Service Name	UDP	TCP
Kerberos kshell		544
L2TP	1701	
LDAP		389
LDAP (SSL)		636
Login Sequence	137, 138	139
Macintosh, File Services (AFP/IP)		548
Membership DPA		568
Membership MSN		569
Microsoft Chat client to server		6667
Microsoft Chat server to server		6665
Microsoft Message Queue Server	1801	1801
Microsoft Message Queue Server	3527	135, 2101
Microsoft Message Queue Server		2103, 2105
MTA - X.400 over TCP/IP		102
NetBT datagrams	138	
NetBT name lookups	137	
NetBT service sessions		139
NetLogon	138	
NetMeeting Audio Call Control		1731
NetMeeting H.323 call setup		1720
NetMeeting H.323 streaming RTP over UDP	Dynamic	
NetMeeting Internet Locator Server ILS		389
NetMeeting RTP audio stream	Dynamic	
NetMeeting T.120		1503
NetMeeting User Location Service		522
NetMeeting user location service ULS		522
Network Load Balancing	2504	
NNTP		119
NNTP (SSL)		563
Outlook (see "Exchange" for ports)		
Pass Through Verification	137, 138	139
POP3		110

(continued)

Table C.3 Default Port Assignments for Common Services *(continued*

Service Name	UDP	TCP
POP3 (SSL)		995
PPTP control		1723
PPTP data (see Table C.4)		
Printer sharing name lookup	137	
Printer sharing session		139
Radius accounting (Routing and Remote Access)	1646 or 1813	
Radius authentication (Routing and Remote Access)	1645 or 1812	
Remote Install TFTP		69
RPC client fixed port session queries		1500
RPC client using a fixed port session replication		2500
RPC session ports		Dynamic
RPC user manager, service manager, port mapper		135
SCM used by DCOM	135	135
SMTP		25
SNMP	161	
SNMP Trap	162	
SQL Named Pipes encryption over other protocols name lookup	137	
SQL RPC encryption over other protocols name lookup	137	
SQL session		139
SQL session		1433
SQL session		1024 - 5000
SQL session mapper		135
SQL TCP client name lookup	53	53
Telnet		23
Terminal Server		3389
UNIX Printing		515
WINS Manager		135
WINS NetBios over TCP/IP name service	137	
WINS Proxy	137	
WINS Registration		137
WINS Replication		42
X400		102

Protocol Numbers

In an IP header, the Protocol field identifies the service in the next higher level in the protocol stack to which data is passed. Table C.4 shows these commonly used IP protocol numbers. Protocol numbers are used to configure firewalls, routers and proxies.

Table C.4 Common Protocol Numbers

Service	Protocol Number
Internet Control Message Protocol (ICMP)	1
Transmission Control Protocol (TCP)	6
User Datagram Protocol (UDP)	17
General Routing Encapsulation (PPTP data over GRE)	47
Authentication Header (AH) IPSec	51
Encapsulation Security Payload (ESP) IPSec	50
Exterior Gateway Protocol (EGP)	8
Gateway-Gateway Protocol (GGP)	3
Host Monitoring Protocol (HMP)	20
Internet Group Management Protocol (IGMP)	88
MIT Remote Virtual Disk (RVD)	66
OSPF Open Shortest Path First	89
PARC Universal Packet Protocol (PUP)	12
Reliable Datagram Protocol (RDP)	27
Reservation Protocol (RSVP) QoS	46

Additional Resources

- For a current list of protocol numbers and TCP and UDP ports, see the Internet Assigned Numbers Authority (IANA) links on the Web Resources page at http://windows.microsoft.com/windows2000/reskit/webresources.

APPENDIX D

TCP/IP Remote Utilities

The tools described in this appendix allow a network administrator to manage network computers from a distance. Many are similar to UNIX utilities.

In This Appendix

Note All passwords used by Windows networking services are encrypted. However, the Ftp, and Rexec connectivity tools all rely on cleartext password authentication by the remote computer. Cleartext passwords are not encrypted before being sent over the network. This enables another user equipped with a network analyzer on the same network to steal a user's remote account password. For this reason, choose different passwords from those used for Windows 2000–based computers or domains when connecting to non-Microsoft remote computers with the Ftp, Rexec, or Telnet tools. Note that the protocols themselves prohibit encryption; cleartext passwords are not a standard that Microsoft encourages.

Finger

This connectivity command displays information about a user on a specified host running the Finger service. Output varies based on the configuration of the remote host.

Syntax

finger [–l] [*user*]@*hostname*

Switches

–l

Displays information in long list format; not supported on all remote computers.

Variables

user

Specifies the user you want information about. Omit the user parameter to display information about all users on the specified host.

@*hostname*

Specifies the host name or IP address of the remote computer whose users you want information about.

Ftp

This connectivity tool transfers files to and from a host running an FTP server service (such as Microsoft® Internet Information Services). A service is called a *daemon* in UNIX. The Ftp tool uses the session-oriented File Transfer Protocol. Ftp can be used interactively or by processing ASCII text files.

Syntax

ftp [**–v**] [**–n**] [**–i**] [**–d**] [**–g**] [**–s:** *filename*] [-a] [-A] [-w:*windowsize*] [*hostname*]

Switches

–v

Suppresses display of remote server responses.

–n

Suppresses autologon upon initial connection.

–i

Turns off interactive prompting during multiple file transfers.

–d

Enables debugging, displaying all FTP commands passed between the client and server.

–g

Disables file name globbing, which permits the use of wildcard characters in local file and path names. (Also see the **glob** command in Table D.1.)

–s: [*filename*]

Specifies a text file containing FTP commands; the commands automatically run after Ftp starts. Use this switch instead of redirection (<).

–a

Specifies that any local interface can be used when binding the FTP data connection.

–A

Logs in to the FTP server as anonymous.

–w:*windowsize*

Specifies the size of the transfer buffer. The default windowsize is 4096 bytes.

Variables

Hostname

Specifies the host name or the IP address of the remote host to connect to. The host, if specified, must be the last parameter on the line.

Table D.1 lists the FTP commands. For details about syntax of individual commands, see Windows 2000 Help.

Table D.1 Ftp Commands in Windows 2000

Command	Function
!	Runs the specified command on the local computer.
?	Displays descriptions for Ftp commands. **?** is identical to **help**.
Append	Appends a local file to a file on the remote computer using the current file type setting.
Ascii	Sets the file transfer type to ASCII, which is the default.
Bell	Toggles a bell to ring after each file transfer command is completed. By default, the bell is off.
Binary	Sets the file transfer type to binary.
Bye	Ends the FTP session with the remote host and exits Ftp.
Cd	Changes the working directory on the remote host.
Close	Ends the FTP session with the remote server and returns to the command interpreter.

(continued)

Table D.1 Ftp Commands in Windows 2000 *(continued)*

Command	Function
Debug	Toggles debugging. When debugging is on, each command sent to the remote host is printed, preceded by the string – – – >. By default, debugging is off.
Delete	Deletes files on remote hosts.
Dir	Displays a list of a remote directory's files and subdirectories.
Disconnect	Disconnects from the remote host, retaining the Ftp prompt.
Get	Copies a remote file to the local host using the current file transfer type.
Glob	Toggles file name globbing. Globbing permits use of wildcard characters in local file or path names. By default, globbing is on.
Hash	Toggles number-sign (#) printing for each data block transferred. The size of a data block is 2,048 bytes. By default, number-sign printing is off.
Lcd	Changes the working directory on the local host. By default, the current directory on the local host is used.
Literal	Sends arguments, verbatim, to the remote FTP server. A single FTP reply code is expected in return.
Ls	Displays an abbreviated list of a remote directory's files and subdirectories.
Mdelete	Deletes multiple files on remote hosts.
Mdir	Displays a list of a remote directory's files and subdirectories.
Mget	Copies multiple remote files to the local host using the current file transfer type.
Mkdir	Creates a remote directory.
Mls	Displays an abbreviated list of a remote directory's files and subdirectories.
Mput	Copies multiple local files to the remote host using the current files and subdirectories.
Open	Connects to the specified FTP server.
Prompt	Toggles prompting. Ftp prompts during multiple file transfers to enable you to selectively retrieve or store files; **mget** and **mput** transfer all files if prompting is turned off. By default, prompting is on.
Put	Copies a local file to the remote host using the current file transfer type.
Pwd	Displays the current directory on the remote host.
Quit	Ends the FTP session with the remote host and exits Ftp.
Quote	Same as the **Literal** command.
Recv	Copies a remote file to the local host using the current file transfer type. **Recv** is identical to **get**.

(continued)

Table D.1 Ftp Commands in Windows 2000 *(continued)*

Command	Function
Remotehelp	Displays help for remote commands.
Rename	Renames remote files.
Rmdir	Deletes a remote directory.
Send	Copies a local file to the remote host using the current file transfer type. **Send** is identical to **put**.
Status	Displays the current status of FTP connections and toggles.
Trace	Toggles packet tracing; trace displays the route of each packet when running an Ftp command.
Type	Sets or displays the file transfer type.
User	Specifies a user to the remote host.
Verbose	Toggles verbose mode. If on, all FTP responses are displayed; when a file transfer completes, statistics regarding the efficiency of the transfer are also displayed. By default, verbose is on.

Rcp

This connectivity command copies files between a computer running Microsoft® Windows® 2000 and a computer running Rshd, the remote shell server service or daemon. The **rcp** command can also be used for third-party transfer to copy files between two computers running Rshd when the command is issued from a Windows 2000–based computer. The Rshd server service (daemon) is available on UNIX computers, but not on a Windows 2000–based computer. The computer running Windows 2000 can only participate as the computer from which the commands are issued. The remote computers must also support the Rcp tool in addition to running Rshd.

Syntax

rcp [**–a**] [**–b**] [**–h**] [**–r**] [*source1 source2 sourceN*] [*destination*]

Switches

–a

Specifies ASCII transfer mode. This mode converts the carriage return/linefeed characters to carriage returns on outgoing files, and linefeed characters to carriage return/linefeeds for incoming files. This is the default transfer mode.

–b

Species binary image transfer mode. No carriage return/linefeed conversion is performed.

–h

Transfers source files marked with the hidden attribute on the computer running Windows 2000. Without this option, specifying a hidden file on the **rcp** command line has the same effect as if the file did not exist.

–r

Recursively copies the contents of the all subdirectories of the source to the destination. Both the *source* and the *destination* must be directories.

Variables

source and *destination*

Must be of the form [*host*[**.***user*]**:**]*filename*. If the [*host*[**.***user*]**:**] portion is omitted, the host is assumed to be the local computer. If the *user* portion is omitted, the currently logged-on Windows 2000 user name is used. If a fully qualified host name is used, which contains the period (**.**) separators, then [**.***user*] must be included. Otherwise, the last part of the host name is interpreted as the user name. If multiple source files are specified, *destination* must be a directory.

If the file name does not begin with a forward slash (/) for UNIX computers or a backslash (\) for Windows-based computers, it is assumed to be relative to the current working directory. Under Windows 2000 this is the directory from which the command is issued. On the remote computer, it is the logon directory for the remote user. A period (**.**) means the current directory. Use the escape characters (\, ", or ') in remote paths to use wildcard characters on the remote host.

Remote Privileges

The **rcp** command does not prompt for passwords; the current or specified user name must exist on the remote host and enable remote command execution via Rcp.

Rhosts File

The Rhosts file specifies which remote computer or users can access a local account using **rsh** or **rcp** commands. This file (or a file called hosts.equiv) is required on the remote computer for access to a remote computer using these commands. **Rsh** and **rcp** both transmit the local user name to the remote computer. The remote computer uses this name plus the IP address (usually resolved to a host name) or the requesting computer to determine whether to grant access. There is no provision for specifying a password to access an account using these commands.

If the user is logged on to a Windows 2000 Server domain, the domain controller must be available to resolve the currently logged-on name, because the logged-on name is not cached on the local computer. Because the user name is required as part of the RSH protocol, the command fails if the user name cannot be obtained.

The Rhosts file is a text file where each line is an entry. An entry consists of the local host name, the local user name, and any comments about the entry or a local host name and any comments about the entry. Entries are separated by a tab or space, and comments begin with a number sign (#), for example:

```
Computer5   marie   #This computer is in room 41A.
Computer7           #This computer is in room 42.
```

This Rhosts file must be in the user's home directory on the remote computer.

Additionally, have your host name added to the remote computer's /Etc/Hosts file. (Normally a DNS name server is used instead of the Hosts file.)

For more information about a remote computer's specific implementation of the Rhosts file, see the remote computer's documentation.

Specifying Hosts

Use the *host.user* variables to use a user name other than the current user name. If *host.user* is specified with source, the Rhosts file on the remote host must contain an entry for user.

If a host name is supplied as a full domain name containing periods, a user name must be appended to the host name. This prevents the last element of the domain name from being interpreted as a *user* name. For example:

```
Rcp domain-name1.user:johns domain-name2.user:buddyg
```

Remote Processing

Remote processing is performed by a command run from the user's logon shell on most UNIX computers. The user's profile or Cshrc is executed before parsing file names, and exported shell variables can be used (using the escape characters or quotation marks) in remote file names.

Copying Files

If you try to copy several files to a file rather than to a directory, only the last file is copied. Also, the **rcp** command cannot copy a file onto itself.

Rcp Syntax

These examples demonstrate syntax for the most common uses of **rcp**.

To copy a local file to the logon directory of a remote computer:

```
rcp <file name remote computer>
```

To copy a local file to an existing directory and a new file name on a remote computer:

```
rcp <file name remote computer:/directory/newfile name>
```

To copy multiple local files to a subdirectory of a remote logon directory:

```
rcp <file1 file2 file3 remote computer:subdirectory/filesdirectory>
```

To copy from a remote source to the current directory of the local computer:

```
rcp <remote computer:file name>
```

To copy multiple files from multiple remote sources to a remote destination with different user names:

```
rcp <remote1.user1:file1 remote2.user2:file2
remotedest.destuser:directory>
```

To copy from a remote computer using an IP address to a local computer (where the user name is mandatory because a period is used in the remote host name):

```
rcp <IP address.user:file name file name>
```

Rexec

This connectivity tool runs commands on remote hosts running the Rexecd service. Rexec authenticates the user name on the remote host by using a password, before carrying out the specified command.

Syntax

rexec *host* [**–l** *username*] [**–n**] *command*

Switches

–l [*username*]

Specifies the user name on the remote host.

–n

Redirects the input of Rexec to NUL.

Variables

host

Specifies the remote host on which to run the command.

command

Specifies the command to run.

Using Rexec

Rexec prompts the user for a password and authenticates the password on the remote host. If the authentication succeeds, the command is executed.

Rexec copies standard input to the remote *command*, standard output of the remote *command* to its standard output, and standard error of the remote *command* to its standard error. Interrupt, quit, and terminate signals are propagated to the remote command. Rexec normally terminates when the remote command does.

Using Redirection Symbols

Use quotation marks around redirection symbols to redirect onto the remote host. If quotation marks are not used, redirection occurs on the local computer. For example, the following command appends the remote file *remotefile* to the local file *localfile*:

```
Rexec otherhost cat remotefile >> localfile
```

The following command appends the remote file *remotefile* to the remote file *otherremotefile*:

```
Rexec otherhost cat remotefile ">>" otherremotefile
```

Using Interactive Commands

You cannot run most interactive commands using Rexec. For example, **vi** and **emacs** cannot be run using Rexec. Use telnet to run interactive commands.

Rsh

This connectivity tool runs commands on remote hosts using the Rsh service. For information about the Rhosts file used to enable this tool, see the Rcp tool.

Syntax

rsh *host* [**–l** *username*] [**–n**] *command*

Switches

–l [*username*]

Specifies the user name to be used on the remote host. If this parameter is omitted, the logged-on user's name is used.

–n

Redirects the input of Rsh to NUL.

Variables

host

Specifies the remote host.

command

Specifies the command to run.

Using Rsh

Rsh copies standard input to the remote *command*, standard output of the remote *command* to its standard output, and the standard error of the remote *command* to its standard error. Rsh terminates when the remote command does.

Using Redirection Symbols

Use quotation marks around redirection symbols to redirect onto the remote host. If quotation marks are not used, redirection occurs on the local computer. For example, the following command appends the remote file *remotefile* to the local file *localfile*:

```
Rsh otherhost cat remotefile >> localfile
```

The following command appends the remote file *remotefile* to the remote file *otherremotefile*:

```
Rsh otherhost cat remotefile ">>" otherremotefile
```

Using Rsh on a Windows 2000 Server Domain

If the user is logged on to a Microsoft® Windows® 2000 Server domain, the domain controller must be available to resolve the currently logged-on name, because the logged-on name is not cached on the local computer. Because the user name is required as part of the RSH protocol, the command fails if the user name cannot be obtained.

Rhosts File

The Rhosts file generally permits network access rights on UNIX computers. The Rhosts file lists computer names and associated logon names that have access to remote computers. When issuing **rcp**, **rexec**, or **rsh** commands to a remote computer with a properly configured Rhosts file, you do not need to provide logon and password information for the remote computer.

The Rhosts file is a text file in which each line is an entry. An entry consists of the local computer name, the local user name, and any comments about the entry. Entries are separated by a tab or space, and comments begin with a number sign (#), for example:

```
Computer5   marie   #This computer is in room 41A
```

The Rhosts file must be in the user's home directory on the remote computer. For more information about a remote computer's specific implementation of the Rhosts file, see the remote computer's documentation.

Telnet

This connectivity tool starts terminal emulation with a remote host running a telnet server service. Telnet provides DEC VT 100, DEC VT 52, or ANSI emulation, using the connection-based services of TCP.

To provide terminal emulation from a Windows computer, the remote host must be running TCP/IP and a telnet server service. The Windows-based telnet user must also have a user account on the remote telnet server.

To start the telnet client, type **telnet** at a command prompt. The syntax and usage for starting the telnet client from the command prompt are described in this section.

Note Windows 2000 Server and Microsoft® Windows® 2000 Professional provide the telnet client tool and also provide a telnet server. This service is built in, but the service must be started before it can serve telnet clients.

Syntax

telnet [*host* [*port*]]

Variables

host

Specifies the host name or IP address of the remote host to which you want to connect.

port

Specifies the remote port you want to connect to. If unspecified, the default connection TCP port value is 23.

Tftp

This connectivity tool transfers files to and from a remote computer running the Trivial File Transfer Protocol (TFTP) service. This tool is similar to Ftp, but it does not provide user authentication, although the files require read and write UNIX permissions. Tftp can only be used for unidirectional transfer of files.

Syntax

tftp [**–i**] *host* [**get** | **put**] *source* [*destination*]

Switches

–i

Specifies binary image transfer mode (also called octet). In binary image mode, the file is moved literally byte by byte. Use this mode when transferring binary files.

If **–i** is omitted, the file is transferred in ASCII mode. This is the default transfer mode. This mode converts the end-of-line (EOL) characters to an appropriate format for the given system. Use this mode when transferring text files. If a file transfer is successful, the data transfer rate is displayed.

get

Transfer *destination* on the remote computer to *source* on the local computer.

Because the TFTP protocol does not support user authentication, the user must be logged on, and the files must be writable on the remote computer.

put

Transfers *source* on the local computer to *destination* on the remote computer.

Variables

host

Specifies the local or remote host.

source

Specifies the file to transfer.

destination

Specifies where to transfer the file.

APPENDIX E

DHCP Options

The following topics provide descriptions of all predefined options available for use with the Microsoft® Windows® 2000 DHCP service. These options are defined according to the updated standards reference for DHCP options (RFC 2132, *DHCP Options and BOOTP Vendor Extensions*).

You can use the **Properties** dialog boxes in DHCP Manager to configure each DHCP option for specific values and then enable it for assignment and distribution to DHCP clients based on server, scope, class, or client-specific levels of preference.

In This Appendix

Related Information in the Resource Kit

- For more information about DHCP, see "Dynamic Host Configuration Protocol" in this book.
- For more information about DHCP messages, see "DHCP Message Formats" in this book.

Basic Options (RFC 1497)

The following tables list basic DHCP option types originally defined in RFC 1497, "BOOTP Vendor Information Extensions," for use with DHCP and the BOOTP service. In the BOOTP service, these option types are referred to as *vendor extensions*.

The DHCP service supports configuration and distribution of any of these options that are assigned using DHCP Manager. By default, Microsoft DHCP-enabled clients require and provide storage and interpretation only for options 1, 3, 6, and 15 of the option types listed in this section for default client configuration. Other options are predefined for assignment and distribution by the DHCP service, but are recognized only where clients use third-party DHCP software supporting these other option types.

Pad Option

Code 0

Length Not used.

Value Not used.

Description This option type is a single octet of zero ("00") used for padding. This option differs from most DHCP option types in that it does not use a length or value field. When used, this option causes subsequent DHCP option types as they appear in the DHCP packet to align on word boundaries. This option does not require configuration.

Structure

Code
0

End Option

Code 255

Length Not used.

Value Not used.

Description

This option is a single octet of decimal 255 ("FF") used to indicate the end of a DHCP options area in DHCP message packets. This option differs from most DHCP option types because it does not use a length or value field. Typically, it is used at the end of the options field to indicate that there is no more option data in a DHCP message packet. It can also be used within the message, in connection with the vendor-specific information (option 43), to indicate the end of an encapsulated vendor-specific options subfield. This option does not require configuration.

Structure

Code
255

Subnet Mask

Code

1

Length

Fixed, 4 octets.

Value

Signed 32-bit integer representing the subnet mask for an IP address provided in a DHCP message.

Description

Specifies the subnet mask of the client subnet, as described in RFC 950, "Internet Standard Subnetting Procedure." The value for this option type is taken from the **Subnet Mask** field, as defined in the DHCP scope **Properties** dialog box in DHCP Manager.

Structure

Code	Length	Subnet Mask
1	4	*m1*, *m2*, *m3*, *m4*

Time Offset

Code

2

Length

Fixed, 4 octets

Value

Signed 32-bit used for offset of Universal Coordinated Time (UCT).

Description

Specifies an offset value (in seconds) from the UCT that applies to the client's subnet. This value is configurable as a signed 32-bit integer. Positive offset values indicate a subnet location east of the zero meridian. Negative offset values indicate a subnet location west of the zero meridian.

Structure

Code	Length	Time Offset
2	4	*time*

Router

Code 3

Length Variable; minimum length of 4 octets; octet length increases in multiples of 4 for each router address listed.

Value Signed 32-bit integer representing the IP address of each assigned router

Description Specifies a list of IP addresses for routers on the client's subnet. When more than one router is assigned, the client interprets and uses the addresses in the specified order.

Structure

Code	Length	Address 1	Address 2
3	*n*	*a1, a2, a3, a4*	*a1, a2, ...*

Time Server

Code 4

Length Variable; minimum length of 4 octets; octet length increases in multiples of 4 for each RFC 868 time server address listed.

Value Signed 32-bit integer representing the IP address of each assigned RFC 868 time server.

Description Specifies a list of IP addresses for RFC 868 time servers that are available to the client. When more than one time server is assigned, the client interprets and uses the addresses in the specified order.

Structure

Code	Length	Address 1	Address 2
4	*n*	*a1, a2, a3, a4*	*a1, a2, ...*

IEN Name Server

Code 5

Length Variable; minimum length of 4 octets; octet length increases in multiples of 4 for each IEN name server address listed.

Value Signed 32-bit integer representing the IP address of each assigned IEN name server.

Description Specifies a list of IP addresses for Internet Engineering Note (IEN) name servers available to the client. When more than one server is assigned, the client interprets and uses the addresses in the specified order.

Structure

Code	Length	Address 1	Address 2
5	*n*	*a1, a2, a3, a4*	*a1, a2, ...*

DNS Server

Code 6

Length Variable; minimum length of 4 octets; octet length increases in multiples of 4 for each DNS server address listed.

Value Signed 32-bit integer representing the IP address of each assigned DNS server.

Description Specifies a list of IP addresses for Domain Name System (DNS) name servers available to the client. When more than one server is assigned, the client interprets and uses the addresses in the specified order. DHCP client computers that are multihomed and can obtain multiple DHCP leases can have only one DNS server list per host computer, not per adapter interface, except for Windows 2000 clients.

Structure

Code	Length	Address 1	Address 2
6	*n*	*a1, a2, a3, a4*	*a1, a2, ...*

Log Server

Code 7

Length Variable; minimum length of 4 octets; octet length increases in multiples of 4 for each log server address listed.

Value Signed 32-bit integer representing the IP address of each assigned log server.

Description Specifies a list of IP addresses for MIT-LCS UDP log servers available to the client. When more than one server is assigned, the client interprets and uses the addresses in the specified order.

Structure

Code	Length	Address 1	Address 2
7	*n*	*a1, a2, a3, a4*	*a1, a2, ...*

Cookie Server

Code 8

Length Variable; minimum length of 4 octets; octet length increases in multiples of 4 for each cookie server address listed.

Value Signed 32-bit integer representing the IP address of each assigned cookie server.

Description Specifies a list of IP addresses for RFC 865 cookie servers available to the client. When more than one server is assigned, the client interprets and uses the addresses in the specified order.

Structure

Code	Length	Address 1	Address 2
8	*n*	*a1, a2, a3, a4*	*a1, a2, ...*

LPR Server

Code 9

Length Variable; minimum length of 4 octets; octet length increases in multiples of 4 for each LPR server address listed.

Value Signed 32-bit integer representing the IP address of each assigned LPR server.

Description Specifies a list of IP addresses for RFC 1179 line printer servers available to the client. When more than one server is assigned, the client interprets and uses the addresses in the specified order.

Structure

Code	Length	Address 1	Address 2
9	*n*	*a1, a2, a3, a4*	*a1, a2, ...*

Impress Server

Code 10

Length Variable; minimum length of 4 octets; octet length increases in multiples of 4 for each Impress server address listed.

Value Signed 32-bit integer representing the IP address of each assigned Impress server.

Description Specifies a list of IP addresses for Imagen Impress servers available to the client. When more than one server is assigned, the client interprets and uses the addresses in the specified order.

Structure

Code	Length	Address 1	Address 2
10	*n*	*a1, a2, a3, a4*	*a1, a2, ...*

Resource Location Server

Code 11

Length Variable; minimum length of 4 octets; octet length increases in multiples of 4 for each resource location server address listed.

Value

Signed 32-bit integer representing the IP address of each assigned resource location server.

Description

Specifies a list of IP addresses for RFC 887 resource location servers available to the client. When more than one server is assigned, the client interprets and uses the addresses in the specified order.

Structure

Code	Length	Address 1	Address 2
11	*n*	*a1, a2, a3, a4*	*a1, a2, ...*

Host Name

Code

12

Length

Length varies depending on data in value. Minimum length is 1 octet. Maximum length is limited to 63 characters, or one octet for each character used in the host name configured for use with this option.

Value

ASCII character text.

Description

Specifies a host name for the client of up to 63 characters in length. (See RFC 1035, *Domain Names—Implementation and Specification*, for possible character set restrictions.) In some cases, this name can also be fully qualified by appending the name value provided here with the DNS domain name, as specified in option 15. For Windows clients, this option is not supported for use when configuring the client's host name, which is set in **Computer Name** in the **Network Identification Properties** dialog box on the client computer.

Structure

Code	Length	Host Name
12	*n*	*name*

Boot File Size

Code

13

Length

Fixed, 2 octets.

Value

Unsigned 16-bit integer to indicate the number of 512-octet blocks needed to make up the boot file.

Description

Specifies the size of the default boot image file for the client.

Structure

Code	Length	File Size
13	02	*16-bit integer*

Merit Dump File

Code 14

Length Length varies depending on data in value. Minimum length is 1 octet.

Value ASCII character text

Description Specifies a path name of a file to which the client's core memory image should be dumped in the event the client crashes. For this option type, data used for a value is ASCII character text. The length of the value field depends on the number of characters used in the path specified here. For example, if the path entered has 20 characters, the value field for this option should also be 20 octets in length.

Structure

Code	Length	Dump File Path
14	*n*	*pathname*

DNS Domain Name

Code 15

Length Length varies depending on data in value. Minimum length is 1 octet.

Value ASCII character text

Description Specifies the domain name that the DHCP client should use when resolving host names using the DNS. For this option type, ASCII character text is used for the data value. The length of the value field depends on the number of characters used in the DNS domain name specified here. For example, if the domain name has 20 characters, the value field for this option should also be 20 octets in length.

Structure

Code	Length	Domain Name
15	*n*	*domain name*

Swap Server

Code 16

Length Length is fixed at 4 octets.

Value A single IP address for the client's swap server (unsigned 32-bit integer).

Description Specifies the IP address of the client's swap server.

Structure

Code	Length	Swap Server Address
16	*n*	*a1*, *a2*, *a3*, *a4*

Root Path

Code 17

Length Length varies depending on data in value. Minimum length is 1 octet.

Value ASCII character text.

Description Specifies the path that contains the client's root disk. The path is formatted as ASCII text. For this option type, data used for a value is ASCII character text. The length of the value field depends on the number of characters used in the root path specified here. For example, if the root path entered has 20 characters, the value field for this option should also be 20 octets in length.

Structure

Code	Length	Root Disk Path
17	*n*	*pathname*

Extensions Path

Code 18

Length Length varies depending on data in value. Minimum length is 1 octet.

Value ASCII character text.

Description Specifies a file that can be retrieved using Trivial File Transfer Protocol (TFTP) containing information to be interpreted in the same way as the 64-octet vendor-extension field within a BOOTP response. To allow more than 64 octets of BOOTP vendor extension information, this option can be used. When this option is used, the length of the specified extension path file is not constrained in size and all references in the extensions file to tag 18 (such as instances of the BOOTP Extensions Path field) are ignored.

Structure

Code	Length	Extensions Path
18	*n*	*filename*

Note For all option types provided in "Extensions Path" that use a list of IP addresses as the valued options data, IP addresses are always used in order of preference by the DHCP client, so that the first address in the list is used first.

IP Host Options

The following tables describe the DHCP options that affect operation of the IP layer on a per-host basis.

IP Forwarding Enable/Disable

Code 19

Length Length is fixed at 1 octet.

Value 1 = Enable IP forwarding.
0 = Disable IP forwarding.

Description Used to determine whether the DHCP client enables or disables forwarding of datagrams at the IP layer.

Structure

Code	Length	Value
19	1	0 | 1

Nonlocal Source Routing Enable/Disable

Code 20

Length Length is fixed at 1 octet.

Value 1 = Enable forwarding of datagrams from nonlocal sources.
0 = Disable forwarding of datagrams from nonlocal sources.

Description Used to determines whether the DHCP client enables or disables forwarding of datagrams at the IP layer, based on whether a received datagram is from a local or nonlocal source.

Structure

Code	Length	Value
20	1	0 | 1

Policy Filter

Code 21

Length Variable. Minimum length is 8 octets for a single destination-and-mask pairing. Length increases in multiples of 8 octets for each additional pairing used.

Value Two consecutive, unsigned 32-bit integers indicating a paired value, consisting of an IP address followed by a subnet mask.

Description Specifies policy filters for nonlocal source routing on the client. The filters consist of a list of IP address and mask pairs specifying destination-and-mask pairs for which to filter source routes of any incoming datagrams. The client discards any source routed datagram with a next-hop address that does not match one of the filters. For further information about policy filtering as it applies to this option type, see RFC 1122, "Requirements for Internet Hosts—Communication Layers."

Structure

Code	Length	Address 1	Mask 1
21	*n*	*a1, a2, a3, a4*	*m1, m2, m3, m4*
		Address 2	**Mask 2**
		a1, a2, a3, a4	*m1, m2, m3, m4, ...*

Maximum Datagram Reassembly Size

Code 22

Length Fixed, 2 octets.

Value A 16-bit integer specifying the maximum datagram size for reassembly. The minimum size for a datagram is 576.

Description Specifies the maximum size datagram that the client can reassemble.

Structure

Code	Length	Size
22	2	*16 bit integer*

Default IP Time-To-Live

Code 23

Length Fixed, 1 octet.

Value A number (in seconds) between 1 and 255.

Description Specifies the default Time-To-Live (TTL) that the client uses on outgoing datagrams.

Structure

Code	Length	TTL
23	1	*TTL value in seconds*

Path MTU Aging Time-out

Code 24

Length Fixed, 4 octets.

Value A 32-bit unsigned integer that specifies a time-out value (in seconds).

Description Specifies the time-out for aging Path Maximum Transmission Unit (MTU) values. (Values are discovered by the mechanism defined in RFC 1191, "Path MTU Discovery.")

Structure

Code	Length	Time-out
24	4	*timeout value in seconds*

Path MTU Plateau Table

Code 25

Length Variable; minimum length is 2 octets. When length is more than 2, it increases in multiples of 2.

Value A table formatted as a list of 16-bit unsigned integers, ordered from smallest to largest. The minimum tabled MTU value cannot be smaller than **68**.

Description Specifies a table of MTU sizes to use when performing Path MTU Discovered, as defined in RFC 1191, "Path MTU Discovery."

Structure

Code	Length	Size	Size 2
25	*n*	*s1, s2*	*table of MTU sizes*

IP Interface Options

The following tables describe the DHCP options that affect operation of the IP layer on a per-interface basis.

Interface MTU

Code 26

Length Fixed, 2 octets.

Value A 16-bit unsigned integer specifying the interface MTU. The minimum legal value for the MTU is **68**.

Description Specifies the MTU size that can be used on a specified host adapter interface.

Structure

Code	Length	MTU
26	2	*interface MTU*

All Subnets Are Local

Code 27

Length Fixed, 1 octet.

Value 1 = Clients assume all subnets are local and share the same MTU size.
0 = Clients assume some subnets are not local and that smaller MTU sizes might be in use on remote subnets.

Description Specifies whether the client assumes that all subnets within the client's internetwork use the same MTU size as the local subnet on which the client is connected.

Structure

Code	Length	Value
27	1	0 | 1

Broadcast Address

Code 28

Length Fixed, 4 octets.

Value Typically, the limited broadcast IP address (255.255.255.255), but can be modified using legal values for broadcast addresses, as specified in section 3.2.1.3 of RFC 1122, *Requirements for Internet Hosts—Communication Layers.*

Description Specifies the broadcast address used on the client's subnet.

Structure

Code	Length	Broadcast Address
28	4	*b1*, *b2*, *b3*, *b4*

Perform Mask Discovery

Code 29

Length Fixed, 1 octet.

Value 1 = Client performs subnet mask discovery.
0 = Client does not perform subnet mask discovery.

Description Specifies whether the client uses Internet Control Message Protocol (ICMP) for subnet mask discovery.

Structure

Code	Length	Value
29	1	0 | 1

Mask Supplier

Code 30

Length Fixed, 1 octet.

Value 1 = Client responds to subnet mask requests.
0 = Client does not respond to subnet mask requests.

Description Specifies whether the client responds to subnet mask requests using ICMP.

Structure

Code	Length	Value
30	1	0 | 1

Perform Router Discovery

Code 31

Length Fixed, 1 octet.

Value 1 = Client performs router discovery.
0 = Client does not perform router discovery.

Description Specifies whether the client solicits routers using the router discovery method in RFC 1256, *ICMP Router Discovery Messages*.

Structure

Code	Length	Value
31	1	0 | 1

Router Solicitation Address

Code 32

Length Fixed, 4 octets.

Value An IP address (unsigned 32-bit integer).

Description Specifies the IP address to which the client submits router solicitation requests.

Structure

Code	Length	Address
32	4	*a1*, *a2*, *a3*, *a4*

Static Route

Code 33

Length Variable; minimum length of 8 octets; octet length increases in multiples of 8 for each additional static route provided with this option.

Value A list of IP address pairs. Each 8 octets provides two consecutive IP addresses pairing the destination and router addresses used for each route. The first 4 octets specifies the destination address, and the second 4 octets specifies the router for the destination address.

Description Specifies a list of static routes the client installs in its routing cache. Any multiple routes to the same destination are listed in descending order of priority. The default route of 0.0.0.0 is an illegal destination for a static route.

Structure

Code	Length	Destination 1	Router 1
33	*n*	*d1, d2, d3, d4*	*r1, r2, r3, r4*
		Destination 2	**Router 2**
		d1, d2, d3, d4	*r1, r2, r3, r4, ...*

Link Layer Options

The following tables describe the DHCP options that affect operation of the data link layer on a per-interface basis.

Trailer Encapsulation

Code 34

Length Fixed, 1 octet.

Value 1 = Client attempts to use trailer.
0 = Client does not attempt to use trailers.

Description Specifies whether the client negotiates the use of trailers, as described in RFC 893, *ISO Transport Services on Top of the TCP*, when using the Address Resolution Protocol (ARP).

Structure

Code	Length	Value
34	1	0 | 1

ARP Cache Time-Out

Code 35

Length Fixed, 4 octets.

Value An unsigned 32-bit integer specifying a time-out value, in seconds.

Description Specifies the time-out for ARP cache entries.

Structure

Code	Length	Time
35	4	*timeout value in seconds*

Ethernet Encapsulation

Code 36

Length Fixed, 1 octet.

Value 1 = Client uses RFC 1042 encapsulation.
0 = Client uses RFC 894 encapsulation.

Description Specifies whether the client uses Ethernet v.2 (RFC 894) or IEEE 802.3 (RFC 1042) encapsulation if the interface is Ethernet.

Structure

Code	Length	Value
36	1	0 | 1

TCP Options

The following tables describe the DHCP options that affect operation of the TCP session layer on a per-interface basis.

TCP Default TTL

Code 37

Length Fixed, 1 octet.

Value An unsigned 8-bit integer specifying a Time-To-Live (TTL) value (in seconds). The minimum TTL value is **1**.

Description Specifies the default TTL the client uses when sending TCP segments.

Structure

Code	Length	TTL
37	1	*TTL value in seconds*

TCP Keep-Alive Interval

Code 38

Length Fixed, 4 octets.

Value An unsigned 32-bit integer that specifies a keep-alive interval, in seconds.

Description Specifies the interval the client waits before sending a keep-alive message on a TCP connection. A value of **0** indicates that the client does not send keep-alive messages on connections unless specifically requested by an application.

Structure

Code	Length	Time
38	4	*keepalive interval in seconds*

TCP Keep-Alive Garbage

Code 39

Length Fixed, 1 octet.

Value 1 = Client sends keep-alive garbage octet.
0 = Client does not send keep-alive garbage octet.

Description Specifies whether or not the client sends TCP keep-alive messages with an octet of garbage data for compatibility with older implementations.

Structure

Code	Length	Value
39	1	0 | 1

Application Layer Options

The following tables describe the DHCP options that affect operation of the application layer on a per-interface basis. These are miscellaneous options you can use to configure programs and services.

For these options, you can dynamically configure DHCP clients that have more than one interface on a per-interface basis using additional DHCP leases (one per interface) for any of these option types.

NIS Domain Name

Code 40

Length Length varies depending on data in value. Minimum length is 1 octet.

Value ASCII character text.

Description Specifies the Network Information Service (NIS) domain name as an ASCII string.

Structure

Code	Length	NIS Domain Name
40	*n*	*NIS domain name*

NIS Servers

Code 41

Length Variable; minimum length is 4 octets; octet length increases in multiples of 4 for each server address listed.

Value Signed 32-bit integer representing the IP address of an NIS server.

Description Lists the IP addresses in the order of preference for Network Information Service (NIS) servers available to the client.

Structure

Code	Length	Address 1	Address 2
41	*n*	*a1, a2, a3, a4*	*a1, a2, ...*

NTP Servers

Code 42

Length Variable; minimum length is 4 octets; octet length increases in multiples of 4 for each server address listed.

Value Signed 32-bit integer representing the IP address of an NTP server.

Description Lists the IP addresses in the order of preference for Network Time Protocol (NTP) servers available to the client.

Structure

Code	Length	Address 1	Address 2
42	*n*	*a1, a2, a3, a4*	*a1, a2, ...*

X Window System Font Servers

Code 48

Length Variable; minimum length is 4 octets; octet length increases in multiples of 4 for each server address listed.

Value Signed 32-bit integer representing each server IP address.

Description Lists the IP addresses in the order of preference for X Window System font servers available to the client.

Structure

Code	Length	Address 1	Address 2
48	*n*	*a1, a2, a3, a4*	*a1, a2, ...*

X Window System Display Manager Servers

Code 49

Length Variable; minimum length is 4 octets; octet length increases in multiples of 4 for each server address listed.

Value Signed 32-bit integer representing each server IP address.

Description Lists the IP addresses in the order of preference for X Window System display manager servers available to the client.

Structure

Code	Length	Address 1	Address 2
49	*n*	*a1, a2, a3, a4*	*a1, a2, ...*

NIS+ Domain Name

Code 64

Length Length varies depending on data in value. Minimum length is 1 octet.

Value ASCII character text.

Description Specifies the name of the client's Network Information Service Plus (NIS+) domain name as an ASCII string.

Structure

Code	Length	NIS+ Domain Name
64	*n*	*NIS domain name*

NIS+ Servers

Code 65

Length Variable; minimum length is 4 octets; octet length increases in multiples of 4 for each server address listed.

Value Signed 32-bit integer representing IP address of NTP servers.

Description Lists the IP addresses in the order of preference for Network Information Service Plus (NIS+) servers available to the client.

Structure

Code	Length	Address 1	Address 2
65	*n*	*a1, a2, a3, a4*	*a1, a2, ...*

Mobile IP Home Agents

Code 68

Length Variable; minimum length is 4 octets; octet length increases in multiples of 4 for each mobile IP home agent address listed.

Value Signed 32-bit integer representing IP address of a mobile IP home agent.

Description Lists the IP addresses in the order of preference for mobile IP home agents available to the client.

Structure

Code	Length	Address 1	Address 2
68	*n*	*a1, a2, a3, a4*	*a1, a2, ...*

NetBIOS over TCP/IP Options

The following option types are used for NetBIOS over TCP/IP support. All Microsoft-based DHCP clients and DHCP servers can recognize and support the use of these option types.

NetBIOS Name Server

Code 44

Length Variable; minimum length is 4 octets; length can be increased only by multiples of 4 for each address listed.

Value Each 4 octets in this field contains a listed WINS server IP address, specified as an unsigned 32-bit integer.

Description Lists the IP addresses for Windows Internet Name Service (WINS) servers or NetBIOS name servers (NBNS).

Structure

Code	Length	Address 1	Address 2
44	*n*	*a1*, *a2*, *a3*, *a4*	*b1*, *b2*, *b3*, ,, ...

NetBIOS Datagram Distribution (NBDD) Server

Code 45

Length Variable; minimum length is 4 octets; length can be increased only by multiples of 4.

Value Each 4 octets in this field contains a listed NBDD server IP address, specified as an unsigned 32-bit integer.

Description Lists the IP addresses for NetBIOS datagram distribution (NBDD) servers.

Structure

Code	Length	Address 1	Address 2
45	*n*	*a1*, *a2*, *a3*, *a4*	*b1*, *b2*, *b3*, *b4*, ...

NetBIOS Node Type

Code 46

Length Fixed, 1 octet.

Value 1 = b-node, 2 = p-node, 4 = m-node, and 8 = h-node.

Description Configures the client node type for NetBIOS over TCP/IP (NetBT) clients, as described in RFCs 1001and 1002, *Protocol Standard for a NetBIOS Service on a TCP/UDP Transport: Concepts and Methods* and *Protocol Standard for a NetBIOS Service on a TCP/UDP Transport: Detailed Specifications*, respectively. On multihomed computers, the node type is assigned for the computer, not to individual network adapters.

Structure

Code	Length	Node Type
46	1	See above.

NetBIOS Scope ID

Code 47

Length Variable; octet length is equal to the number of characters used in NetBIOS scope ID.

Value Specifies the NetBIOS over TCP/IP scope identifier used by the client. The format used for these scope IDs is further described in RFCs 1001 and 1002, "Protocol Standard for a NetBIOS Service on a TCP/UDP Transport: Concepts and Methods" and "… Detailed Specifications," respectively. See the RFCs for character-set restrictions.

Description Specifies a string that is the NetBIOS over TCP/IP scope ID for the client, as specified in RFCs 1001 and 1002. On multihomed computers, the node type is assigned for the computer, not to individual network adapters.

Structure

Code	Length	NetBIOS Scope
47	*n*	*scope identifier string*

Vendor-Specific Options

This section describes reserved DHCP option types specified for vendor class use. The vendor-specific option types are specified in RFC 2132. Vendor classes can be used by the DHCP service and DHCP-enabled client computers running under Windows 2000. For other DHCP clients, default classes provided by the DHCP service can be used to group and classify non-identifying clients at the DHCP server.

In addition, DHCP Manager provides a single default vendor class, the DHCP Standard options class, that can be used to group and classify clients that do not identify a vendor class to the DHCP service.

Vendor-Specific Information

Code 43

Length Variable; minimum length is 1 octet.

Value An object of *n* octets (where *n* is equal to the length specified with this option). The definition of values stored for this option type is vendor specific, and values provided here are presumed to be interpreted by vendor-specific code on DHCP clients and the DHCP server.

Description This option is used by clients and servers to exchange vendor-specific information. Servers that are not equipped to interpret the information ignore it. Clients that expect but don't receive the information attempt to operate without it.

In some cases, a vendor uses this option type to send more than one information item; therefore, this option can serve as an encapsulated options subfield for encapsulating vendor-specific options. When encapsulating options, DHCP servers maintain the same syntax (that is, the same code/length/value fields sequence) for each encapsulated option type as it would normally appear in the full standard options field, with the following exceptions for the encapsulated vendor-specific subfield:

"Magic cookies" cannot be used.

All standard option codes—other than the padding option (0) or the end option (255)—can be redefined.

If present, the end option (255) signifies the end of the encapsulated vendor options, but not the end of the encapsulated vendor-specific subfield. If no end option is present, the end for the encapsulated vendor-specific subfield is taken from its stated length.

Structure

Code	Length	Vendor-Specific Information
43 …	*n*	*i1*, *i2*, ...

When this option type uses an encapsulated vendor-specific subfield, the information bytes 1–*n* have the following format:

Code	Length	Data Item	Code	Length	Data Item	Code
T1	*n*	*d1*, *d2*, ...	T2	*n*	*D1*, *D2*, ...	...

Vendor Class Identifier

Code 60

Length Minimum is 1 octet. Length varies according to *n* (the number of octets used as an identifier).

Value A value of *n* octets interpreted by DHCP servers that can support vendor classification of clients.

Description

Can be used by DHCP clients to identify their vendor type and configuration. When using this option, vendors can define their own specific identifier values, such as to convey a particular hardware or operating system configuration or other identifying information.

For Windows 2000, all computers that function either as DHCP servers or DHCP clients can use and support this option type. When vendor classes are used, the DHCP server responds to identifying clients using option code 43 (described earlier), the reserved option type for returning vendor-specific information to the client.

DHCP servers that do not automatically interpret this option are expected to ignore it when it is specified by clients. For earlier Windows-based clients and other clients that do not support this option type, the DHCP service classifies these clients as part of the default vendor class, the DHCP Standard options class, which is predefined for Microsoft-based DHCP servers.

Structure

Code	Length	Vendor Class Identifier
60	*n*	*i1*, *i2*, ...

User Class Options

This section describes reserved DHCP option types specified for user class use. The user class option type is an additional DHCP draft specification currently under proposal as an Internet standard. User classes can be used by the DHCP service and DHCP-enabled client computers running under Windows 2000. For other DHCP clients, default classes provided by the DHCP service can be used to group and classify non-identifying clients at the DHCP server.

User Class Information

Code 77

Length Variable; minimum is 2 octets.

Value ASCII character text.

Description

A DHCP client can use this option to identify the type or category of user or applications it represents. The information contained in this option is an NVT ASCII text object that represents the user class of which the client is a member.

You can use DHCP Manager to define specific user classes. When user classes are created, each class sets an identifying string of information to be used by the DHCP service to classify identifying clients. Also, default user classes can be created for classifying clients that are unable to support a user class ID.

User classes can be helpful for separating client computers that have a shared or common need for similar software configuration or user preferences. For example, an identifier can specify that a particular DHCP client be a member of the class "accounting auditors," who have special service needs, such as a particular database server.

For Microsoft DHCP clients, only computers running Windows 2000 support sending or using this option type. Other legacy DHCP clients do not send a class ID or have the ability to recognize the concept of a user class. Therefore, these clients are assigned as members to the Default User Class, which is a user class predefined for immediate use in DHCP Manager. Other user classes must be manually created.

Structure

Code	Length	User Class Information
77	*n*	*c1*, *c2*, *c3*, *c4*, ...

DHCP Extensions

The following option types are specific to DHCP and are used to implement default protocol interaction and system behavior between servers and clients. Some of these options are implicitly set when you configure server and scope properties using DHCP Manager.

Requested IP Address

Code 50

Length Fixed, 4 octets.

Value Single, signed 32-bit integer indicating a requested IP address.

Description Can be used by clients when sending a DHCPDiscover message to request that a specific IP address be assigned by the server.

Structure

Code	Length	Requested IP Address
50	*n*	*a1*, *a2*, *a3*, *a4*

IP Address Lease Time

Code 51

Length Fixed, 4 octets.

Value Single, signed 32-bit integer representing a client's lease time, in seconds.

Description

This option type is used to negotiate and exchange lease-time information between DHCP clients and servers in two possible ways. First, the option can be used in a DHCPDiscover or DHCPRequest message sent by a client to request a lease time for its IP address. Second, the option can be used in a DHCPOffer message sent by a server to specify a lease time the server can offer to the client.

Structure

Code	Length	Lease Time
51	4	*lease time in seconds*

Option Overload

Code

52

Length

Fixed, 1 octet.

Value

Predefined, accepted values for this option type include:

1 = **File** field is overloaded.

2 = **Sname** field is overloaded.

3 = Both **file** and **sname** fields are overloaded.

Description

Used in messages sent by the DHCP server to indicate that either of the standard message fields in a DHCP packet for *server_host_name* (**sname**) and *boot_file_name* (**file**) are to be overloaded (used to hold options).

When this option is used, it extends the options area in each packet by indicating that unused space for one or both of these two standard fields should be allocated to the area used to carry DHCP options.

Structure

Code	Length	Value
52	1	1 | 2 | 3

TFTP Server Name

Code

66

Length

Length varies depending on data in value. Minimum length is 1 octet.

Value

ASCII character text.

Description

Specifies the host name of the Trivial File Transfer Protocol (TFTP) server when the *server_host_name* (**sname**) field in a DHCP message packet is overloaded and used for carrying additional DHCP options.

Structure

Code	Length	TFTP Server
66	*n*	*TFTP hostname*

Boot File Name

Code 67

Length Length varies depending on data in value. Minimum length is 1 octet.

Value ASCII character text.

Description Specifies the name of a boot image file on the TFTP server when the *boot_file_name* (**file**) field in a DHCP message packet is overloaded and used for carrying additional DHCP options.

Structure

Code	Length	Bootfile Name
67	*n*	*c1*, *c2*, *c3*, ...

DHCP Message Type

Code 53

Length Fixed, 1 octet.

Value Predefined, accepted values for this option type are:

1 = DHCP Discover message (DHCPDiscover).

2 = DHCP Offer message (DHCPOffer).

3 = DHCP Request message (DHCPRequest).

4 = DHCP Decline message (DHCPDecline).

5 = DHCP Acknowledgment message (DHCPAck).

6 = DHCP Negative Acknowledgment message (DHCPNak).

7 = DHCP Release message (DHCPRelease).

8 = DHCP Informational message (DHCPInform).

Description This option is required for use in all DHCP messages to convey the type of message being sent.

Structure

Code	Length	Type
53	1	1–8

Server Identifier

Code 54

Length Fixed, 4 octets.

Value A single, signed 32-bit IP address that identifies the DHCP server.

Description

This option is used in DHCPOffer and DHCPRequest messages and sometimes appears in DHCP Acknowledgment messages (DHCPAck, DHCPNak). The server identifier is the IP address of a selected DHCP server. This option type is used in two possible ways. First, servers include this option type in DHCPOffer messages so that clients can distinguish between multiple lease offers.

Second, clients include this option type in DHCPRequest messages to select a lease and indicate which offer is accepted from multiple lease offers. Also, clients can use the contents of this field for unicast sending of request messages to specific DHCP servers to renew a current lease.

Structure

Code	Length	Address
54	4	*a1, a2, a3, a4*

Parameter Request List

Code

55

Length

Minimum of 1 octet. Length increases by 1 octet for each additional option code included in the request list.

Value

List of 8-bit values, each representing an option type code between 0 and 255.

Description

Used by a DHCP client to request specific option type values from the DHCP server. Each option type is requested and listed by a single octet value containing a valid or recognized DHCP option code for the server.

For clients that use this option type, the list can be ordered by preference, although the DHCP server is not required to return options in the order they are requested. However, the DHCP server attempts to insert the requested options in the order requested by the client.

Structure

Code	Length	Option Codes
55	*n*	*c1, c2, ...*

Optional Message

Code

56

Length

Minimum of 1 octet. Length depends on the length of the sent message.

Value

ASCII character text.

Description

Can be used by both the DHCP server and DHCP clients in the following ways:

A server can use this option type to provide and embed an error message in a DHCP Negative Acknowledgment message (DHCPNak) in the event of a failure.

A client can use this option type in a DHCPDecline message to indicate why it declined offered parameters.

The message consists of a variable-length ASCII text string, which the receiving computer can then either log or display.

Structure

Code	Length	Text
56	*n*	*c1, c2, ...*

Maximum Message Size

Code 57

Length Fixed, 2 octets.

Value A 16-bit integer indicating the maximum size, in bytes/octets, for a DHCP message packet. The maximum legal value for this option type is **576**.

Description Used by client to specify the maximum length for a DHCP message packet that it can accept. A client can include this option type in DHCPDiscover or DHCPRequest messages; however, it does not include this option type in DHCPDecline messages.

Structure

Code	Length	Length
57	2	*maxsize*

Renewal Time Value (T1)

Code 58

Length Fixed, 4 octets.

Value A 32-bit unsigned integer indicating the number of seconds before the client begins to renew its address lease with the DHCP server.

Description This time is a function that is typically 50 percent of the full configured duration (or lease time) for a client's lease. To adjust this time value, change the length of the client lease in the client scope properties or the per user class on the DHCP server. You can also change the value using NetShell (for more information, see the online Help).

Structure

Code	Length	T1 Interval
58	4	*begin renewal interval*

Rebinding Time Value (T2)

Code 59

Length Fixed, 4 octets.

Value A 32-bit unsigned integer indicating the number of seconds before the client enters the rebinding state if it has not renewed its current address lease with the DHCP server.

Description This time is a function (typically, 87.5 percent) of the full configured duration (or lease time) for a client's lease. To adjust this time value, change the length of the client lease in the properties for the client's scope or per user class on the DHCP server. You can also change the value using NetShell (For more information, see the online Help).

Structure

Code	Length	T2 Interval
59	4	*begin rebinding interval*

Client Unique Identifier

Code 61

Length Variable length; minimum length is 2 octets.

Value A series of 2 or more octets that is treated as a variable object by the DHCP server. Servers can interpret and use this value to uniquely identify clients.

Description Used by clients to specify their unique identifier to the server. This option type is most useful for reserved clients. When a reserved client contacts the server, the DHCP service can check and match the client's identifier value to a corresponding identifier used to configure an address reservation in the server's database. When a matching reservation is found, the DHCP server returns the reserved address and its related parameters to the correct client. For this reason, each client's identifier must be unique among all other client identifiers used on the effective DHCP network to which the client is attached (that is, the client's local subnet and any remote subnets reachable using DHCP relay). Vendors and system administrators are responsible for choosing client identifiers that meet this requirement for uniqueness.

One common approach to ensure uniqueness is to configure client reservations at the DHCP server based on the client's media access control address as the client identifier value. Media access control addresses are encoded in the client's network adapter hardware, and are assigned to hardware manufacturers in such as way as to ensure that they are unique for each device.

Structure

Code	Length	Type	Client Identifier
61	*n*	*t1*	*i1, i2, ...*

Options Not Defined

This section describes DHCP option types that are reserved and specified for use in RFC 2132, *DHCP Options and BOOTP Vender Extensions*, but are not predefined for use in DHCP Manager. These option types can be added to support third-party DHCP clients that recognize these options.

Simple Mail Transport Protocol (SMTP) Server

Code 69

Length Variable; minimum length is 4 octets; octet length increases in multiples of 4 for each server IP address listed.

Value Signed 32-bit integers representing IP addresses of servers.

Description Lists the IP addresses in order of preference for SMTP servers available to the client.

Structure

Code	Length	Address 1	Address 2
69	*n*	*a1, a2, a3, a4*	*a1, a2, ...*

Post Office Protocol (POP3) Server

Code 70

Length Variable; minimum length is 4 octets; octet length increases in multiples of 4 for each server IP address listed.

Value Signed 32-bit integers representing IP addresses of servers.

Description Lists the IP addresses in order of preference for POP3 servers available to the client.

Structure

Code	Length	Address 1	Address 2
70	*n*	*a1, a2, a3, a4*	*a1, a2, ...*

Network News Transport Protocol (NNTP) Server

Code 71

Length Variable; minimum length is 4 octets; octet length increases in multiples of 4 for each server IP address listed.

Value Signed 32-bit integers representing IP addresses of servers.

Description Lists the IP addresses in order of preference for NNTP servers available to the client.

Structure

Code	Length	Address 1	Address 2
71	*n*	*a1, a2, a3, a4*	*a1, a2, ...*

Default World Wide Web Server

Code 72

Length Variable; minimum length is 4 octets; octet length increases in multiples of 4 for each server IP address listed.

Value Signed 32-bit integers representing IP addresses of servers.

Description Lists the IP addresses in order of preference for default Web servers available to the client.

Structure

Code	Length	Address 1	Address 2
72	*n*	*a1, a2, a3, a4*	*a1, a2, ...*

Default Finger Server

Code 73

Length Variable; minimum length is 4 octets; octet length increases in multiples of 4 for each server IP address listed.

Value Signed 32-bit integers representing IP addresses of servers.

Description Lists the IP addresses in order of preference for default Finger servers available to the client.

Structure

Code	Length	Address 1	Address 2
73	*n*	*a1, a2, a3, a4*	*a1, a2, ...*

Default Internet Relay Chat Server

Code 74

Length Variable; minimum length is 4 octets; octet length increases in multiples of 4 for each server IP address listed.

Value Signed 32-bit integers representing IP addresses of servers.

Description Lists the IP addresses in order of preference for default IRC servers available to the client.

Structure

Code	Length	Address 1	Address 2
74	*n*	*a1, a2, a3, a4*	*a1, a2, ...*

StreetTalk Server

Code 75

Length Variable; minimum length is 4 octets; octet length increases in multiples of 4 for each server IP address listed.

Value Signed 32-bit integers representing IP addresses of servers.

Description Lists the IP addresses in order of preference for StreetTalk servers available to the client.

Structure

Code	Length	Address 1	Address 2
75	*n*	*a1, a2, a3, a4*	*a1, a2, ...*

StreetTalk Directory Assistance Server

Code 76

Length Variable; minimum length is 4 octets; octet length increases in multiples of 4 for each server IP address listed.

Value Signed 32-bit integers representing IP addresses of servers.

Description Lists the IP addresses in order of preference for STDA servers available to the client.

Structure

Code	Length	Address 1	Address 2
76	*n*	*a1, a2, a3, a4*	*a1, a2, ...*

Microsoft Options

This section describes reserved DHCP option types defined by Microsoft. These options are only available for use with supporting Microsoft DHCP clients, such as computers running Windows 2000.

These options are provided as encapsulated vendor-specific data fields within the vendor-specific information option.

Currently, these options are only assignable in the DHCP console through the following vendor classes: Microsoft options and Microsoft Windows 2000 options.

Disable NetBIOS over TCP/IP (NetBT)

Code 1

Length 4

Value

1= NetBT remains enabled.

2=Disable NetBIOS over TCP/IP (NetBT) for Windows 2000 DHCP clients.

Description

This option can be used to selectively enable or disable NetBT for DHCP-enabled computers running Windows 2000 only. By installation default, if this option is not present Windows 2000 enables the use of NetBT for network connections that are configured to use TCP/IP. Earlier Windows clients require NetBT and do not support this option.

Structure

Code	Length	NetBT
001	*4*	*On/Off*

Release DHCP Lease on Shutdown

Code

2

Length

4B

Value

0=Windows 2000 DHCP clients do not send a DHCPRelease message on proper shutdown.

1=Windows 2000 DHCP clients send a DHCPRelease message on proper shutdown.

Description

This option can be used to control whether DHCP-enabled computers running Windows 2000 send a release for their current DHCP lease to the DHCP server when shutdown occurs. It is actually implemented and interpreted as a bitmasked value by the DHCP client service. In most cases, the default (that is, the functional equivalent to this option value not being used or present in DHCP messages) is that Windows 2000 clients do not send DHCPRelease messages on proper shutdown.

Structure

Code	Length	Release
002	*4*	*On/Off*

Default Router Metric Base

Code

3

Length

4B

Value

This value is a specified router metric base to be used for all default gateway routes used at Windows 2000 DHCP-enabled client computers.

This value can be assigned as an integer cost metric ranging from 1 through 9,999. It is used in calculating the fastest, most reliable, and least expensive routes. If a value is not specified, a default of either one (1) or the currently set interface-specific metric is used.

Description This option can be used to set the default base metric for Windows 2000 DHCP clients. When this option is set, the DHCP client service uses the value configured here as the base metric for its default gateways.

Structure

Code	Length	Route Metric
003	*4*	*router metric base*

Proxy Autodiscovery for Internet Explorer 5 Only

Code 252

Length Variable

Value A URL that points to the configuration file that the client should use for automatic configuration of Internet Explorer 5. The file this URL points to can be a .pac, .jvs, .js, or .ins configuration file created by your system or Web administrator when deploying Internet Explorer 5 on your intranet. It might include settings for other Internet Explorer 5 configurable options, such as which home page to use, or settings for locating and using a proxy server.

Description This option is communicated between Internet Explorer 5 client computers and the DHCP server using the DHCPInform message, which is currently only supported for Windows 2000 DHCP server and clients.

The use of additional DHCP configuration is only supported by Internet Explorer 5, not earlier versions that use different methods for automatic detection and configuration of proxy server settings.

You can also add and configure an alias (CNAME) resource record at the DNS server to support Internet Explorer 5 proxy server autodiscovery and configuration features.

For further details, see the Microsoft® Internet Explorer 5 Resource Kit.

Structure

Code	Length	URL
252	*n*	*url name*

APPENDIX F

DHCP Message Formats

The following tables provide detailed information and descriptions of all DHCP messages in use with the Microsoft® Windows® 2000 DHCP service. These message formats are defined according to the updated standards reference for DHCP, RFC 2131, *Dynamic Host Configuration Protocol*. This information is provided primarily for network administrators while troubleshooting or monitoring DHCP communication.

In This Appendix

Related Information in the Resource Kit

- For more information about DHCP, see "Dynamic Host Configuration Protocol" in this book.
- For more information about DHCP options, see "DHCP Options" in this book.

DHCP Messages

Table F.1 shows the fields in a DHCP message.

Table F.1 DHCP Message Fields

Field Name	Octets	Description
op	1	Message op code/message type. 1 = BOOTREQUEST, 2 = BOOTREPLY
htype	1	Hardware address type.
hlen	1	Hardware address length.
hops	1	Client sets to zero; optionally used by relay agents when booting via a relay agent.
xid	4	Transaction ID, a random number chosen by the client, used by the client and server to associate messages and responses between a client and a server.
secs	2	Filled in by client; seconds elapsed since client began address acquisition or renewal process.
flags	2	Flags. To work around some clients that cannot accept IP unicast datagrams before the TCP/IP software is configured, DHCP uses the **flags** field. The leftmost bit is defined as the BROADCAST (B) flag. The remaining bits of the **flags** field are reserved for future use. They must be set to zero by clients and ignored by servers and relay agents.
ciaddr	4	Client IP address; only filled in if client is in BOUND, RENEW, or REBINDING state and can respond to ARP requests.
yiaddr	4	Client IP address.
siaddr	4	IP address of next server to use in bootstrap; returned in DHCPOffer, DHCPAck by server.
giaddr	4	Relay agent IP address; used in booting via a relay agent.
chaddr	16	Clients hardware address.
sname	64	Optional server host name, null terminated string.
file	128	File name, null terminated string; "generic" name or null in DHCPDiscover, fully qualified path name in DHCPOffer.
options	variable	Optional parameters field. For more information about DHCP options, see "DHCP Options" in this book.

Table F.2 shows the fields and options used by DHCP servers.

Note In Tables F.2 and F.3, "MUST," "MUST NOT," "SHOULD," and "MAY" refer to whether or not that particular information must, must not, should, or may be included in the message.

Table F.2 Message Fields and Options

Field	DHCPOffer	DHCPAck	DHCPNak
op	BOOTREPLY	BOOTREPLY	BOOTREPLY
htype	Dependent on hardware type; see RFC 1700, *Assigned Numbers*, for more information.		
hlen	Hardware address length in octets		
hops	0	0	0
xid	xid from client DHCPDiscover message	xid from client DHCPRequest message	xid from client DHCPRequest message
secs	0	0	0
ciaddr	0	ciaddr from 0 DHCPRequest or 0	0
yiaddr	IP address offered to client	IP address assigned to client	0
siaddr	IP address of next bootstrap server	IP address of next bootstrap server	0
flags	flags from client DHCPDiscover	flags from client DHCPRequest	flags from client DHCPRequest
giaddr	giaddr from client DHCPDiscover	giaddr from client DHCPRequest	giaddr from client DHCPRequest
chaddr	chaddr from client DHCPDiscover	chaddr from client DHCPRequest	chaddr from client DHCPRequest
sname	Server host name or options	Server host name or options	(Unused)
file	Client file or options	Client file or options	(Unused)
options	Options	Options	
Option	DHCPOffer	DHCPAck	DHCPNak

(continued)

Table F.2 Message Fields and Options *(continued)*

Field	DHCPOffer	DHCPAck	DHCPNak
Requested IP address	MUST NOT	MUST NOT	MUST NOT
IP address lease time	MUST	MUST (DHCPRequest) MUST NOT (DHCPInform)	MUST NOT
Use **file** or **sname** field	MAY	MAY	MUST NOT
DHCP message type	DHCPOffer	DHCPAck	DHCPNak
Parameter request list	MUST NOT	MUST NOT	MUST NOT
Message	SHOULD	SHOULD	SHOULD
Client identifier	MUST NOT	MUST NOT	MAY
Vendor class identifier	MAY	MAY	MAY
Server identifier	MUST	MUST	MUST
Maximum message size	MUST NOT	MUST NOT	MUST NOT
All others	MAY	MAY	MUST NOT

Table F.3 shows the fields and options used by DHCP clients.

Table F.3 DHCP Client Message Fields and Options

Field	DHCPDiscover DHCPInform	DHCPRequest	DHCPDecline DHCPRelease
op	BOOTREQUEST	BOOTREQUEST	BOOTREQUEST
htype	Dependent on hardware type; see RFC 1700, *Assigned Numbers*, for more information.	Dependent on hardware type; see RFC 1700, *Assigned Numbers*, for more information.	Dependent on hardware type; see RFC 1700, *Assigned Numbers*, for more information.
hlen	Hardware address length in octets	Hardware address length in octets	Hardware address length in octets
hops	0	0	0
xid	Selected by client	xid from server DHCPOffer message	Selected by client
secs	0 or seconds since DHCP process started	0 or seconds since DHCP process started	0
flags	Set BROADCAST flag if client requires broadcast reply	Set BROADCAST flag if client requires broadcast reply	0
ciaddr	0 (DHCPDiscover) or network address (DHCPInform)	0 or network address (BOUND/RENEW/ REBIND)	0 (DHCPDecline) network address (DHCPRelease)

(continued)

Table F.3 DHCP Client Message Fields and Options *(continued)*

Field	DHCPDiscover DHCPInform	DHCPRequest	DHCPDecline DHCPRelease
yiaddr	0	0	0
siaddr	0	0	0
giaddr	0	0	0
chaddr	hardware address	hardware address	hardware address
sname	Options, if indicated in sname/file option; otherwise unused	Options, if indicated in sname/file option; otherwise unused	(Unused)
file	Options, if indicated in sname/file option; otherwise unused	Options, if indicated in sname/file option; otherwise unused	(Unused)
options	Options	Options	(Unused)
Requested IP address	MAY (DISCOVER) MUST NOT (INFORM)	MUST (in SELECTING or INIT-REBOOT) MUST NOT (in BOUND or RENEWING)	MUST (DHCPDecline) MUST NOT (DHCPRelease)
IP address lease time	MAY (DISCOVER) MUST NOT (INFORM)	MAY	MUST NOT
Use **file** or **sname** field	MAY	MAY	MAY
DHCP message type	DHCPDiscover/ DHCPInform	DHCPRequest	DHCPDecline/ DHCPRelease
Client identifier	MAY	MAY	MAY
Vendor class identifier	MAY	MAY	MUST NOT
Server identifier	MUST NOT	MUST (after SELECTING, MUST NOT (after INIT-REBOOT, BOUND, RENEWING, or REBINDING)	MUST
Parameter request list	MAY	MAY	MUST NOT
Maximum message size	MAY	MAY	MUST NOT
Message	SHOULD NOT	SHOULD NOT	SHOULD
Site-specific	MAY	MAY	MUST NOT
All others	MAY	MAY	MUST NOT

APPENDIX G

MIB Object Types

The Microsoft® Windows® 2000 SNMP Service supports a full range of industry standard, third-party, and Microsoft enterprise Management Information Base (MIB) objects. The following information provides a brief overview of MIB and includes information on its sanctioning body, the IETF, the organization of MIB objects, and a table listing of the MIB objects that ship with Windows 2000 SNMP Service.

In This Appendix

Related Information in the Resource Kit

- For information about SNMP, see "Simple Network Management Protocol Service" in this book.
- For information about securing SNMP messages, see "Internet Protocol Security" in this book.

Management Information Base

A *Management Information Base (MIB)* is a collection of formally described objects, each of which represents a particular type of information. MIB objects can be accessed and managed with the Simple Network Management Protocol (SNMP) through a network management system. This collection of objects contains information required by a management system and the information is stored as a set of MIB variables.

MIB object extensions are defined for each set of related entities that can be managed. They define status records for information such as traffic statistics, error counts, and the current contents of internal data structures such as the computer's IP routing table.

All MIB objects are based on a common definition of management information. This is called the Structure of Management Information (SMI) and includes the model of management information, the allowed data types and the rules for specifying classes of management information.

Object Identifiers

To keep track of all of the information stored in a MIB, each object is labeled with a unique tag called an object identifier. The object identifier is implemented as an internationally accepted, multi-part, hierarchical naming scheme that is governed by the Internet Engineering Task Force (IETF). This naming scheme allows developers and vendors to create new components and resources and to assign a globally unique object identifier for each new component or resource without duplicating any existing namespace.

SNMP management software applications use the object identifier to identify the managed objects on each agent. The management system sends a message that requests information about an object and identifies the object by the object identifier. The agent uses the object identifier to retrieve the appropriate information and sends the response back to the management system.

The object identifier itself is actually a sequence of labels that begins at the top of the hierarchy and ends with the object to which the object identifier is being assigned. As the example in Figure G.1 illustrates, iso.org.dod.internet.private.enterprise.lanmanager is the object name for LAN Manager and the object number is 1.3.6.1.4.1.77.

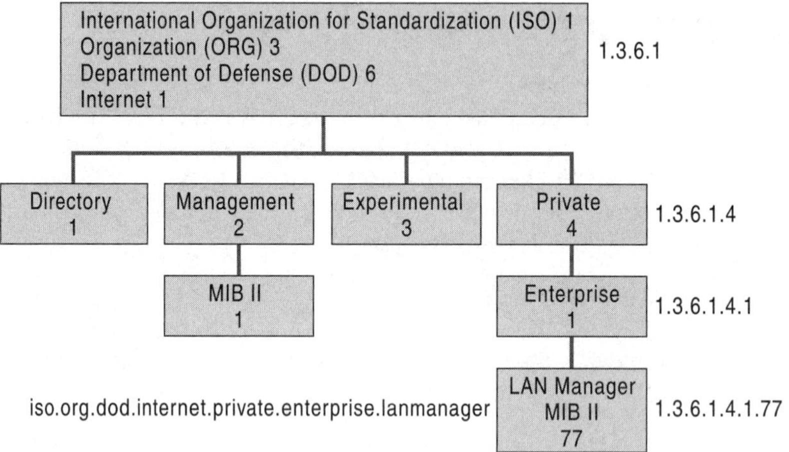

Figure G.1 MIB Namespace Hierarchy

At a specific level in the namespace hierarchy, the IETF grants to individual organizations the authority to create new MIBs under that organization. The private namespace assigned to Microsoft is *1.3.6.1.4.1.311*. Microsoft has the authority to create new MIB objects under this namespace and to assign names to them, such as the MIB object Microsoft IIS Service.

Windows 2000 SNMP Agent

The Windows 2000 SNMP agent has a modular, extensible design that supports multiple MIBs through an agent application programming interface (API). The Windows 2000 SNMP agent is also known as the extensible agent, whereas the supported MIB objects are also known as SNMP subagents or extension-agents. When the SNMP service is started, the SNMP agent loads any SNMP extension-agent dynamic-link libraries (DLLs) that are configured in the registry. This design makes it possible to add new MIBs easily. Microsoft and third-party developers can develop MIBs for new hardware and software components and integrate them easily into an existing SNMP service.

When the SNMP service is started, each agent sends the object identifier for the base object in its MIB to the management system. This allows the management system to identify what managed objects are actually installed on each agent when the manager submits requests for information.

Table G.1 identifies the Windows 2000–based MIBs and the base object from which all other objects in the MIB are derived. The DLLs for MIB-II, LAN Manager MIB-II, and the Host Resources MIBs are installed with the SNMP service. The other MIBs listed in this table are installed when their respective services are installed.

Table G.1 MIBs that Ship with Windows 2000 SNMP Service

MIB and File name	Description	Object Identifier	RFC	Dependency
ACS.MIB acsmib.dll	Microsoft-defined MIB for the Quality of Service Admission Control Service (QoS ACS)	1.3.6.1.4.1.311.1.15	(None)	(None)
ACCSERV.MIB iasperf.dll	RADIUS-ACC-Server-MIB contains object-types for monitoring accounting information between a network access server and a shared accounting server.	1.3.6.1.3.79	2139	Internet Authentication Service
AUTHSERV.MIB iasperf.dll	RADIUS-AUTH-Server-MIB contains object-types for monitoring authentication, authorization, and configuration information of a network access server.	1.3.6.1.3.79	2138	Internet Authentication Service
DHCP.MIB dhcpmib.dll	Microsoft-defined MIB contains object-types for monitoring the network traffic between remote hosts and the DHCP server.	1.3.6.1.4.1.311.1.3	(None)	DHCP service
FTP.MIB ftpmib.dll	Microsoft-defined MIB contains object-types for monitoring the File Transfer Protocol (FTP) service.	1.3.6.1.4.1.311.1.7.2	(None)	IIS Server
HOSTMIB.MIB hostmib.dll	Contains object-types for monitoring and managing host resources.	1.3.6.1.2.1.25	1514	(None)
HTTP.MIB httpmib.dll	Microsoft-defined MIB for the Hypertext Transfer Protocol (HTTP) service	1.3.6.1.4.1.311.1.7.3	(None)	IIS Server
IGMPV2.MIB igmpagnt.dll	Collects information on what groups are joined on the subnet.	1.3.6.1.359	(None)	Routing and Remote Access service
IPFORWD.MIB inetmib1.dll	Defines objects for managing routes on the IP Internet.	1.3.6.1.2.1.2	1354 2096	(None)
LMMIB2.MIB lmmib2.dll	LAN Manager MIB-II covers workstation and server services.	1.3.6.1.4.1.77.1	(None)	(None)

(continued)

Table G.1 MIBs that Ship with Windows 2000 SNMP Service *(continued)*

MIB and File name	Description	Object Identifier	RFC	Dependency
MCASTMIB.MIB mcastmib.dll	MIB module for managing IP Multicast routing	1.3.6.1.3.60.1.1	(Pending)	Routing and Remote Access service
MIB_II.MIB intermib1.dll	Management Information Base (MIB-II) provides a simple, workable architecture and system for managing TCP/IP-based internets.	1.3.6.1.2.1.1 1.3.6.1.2.1.2 1.3.6.1.2.1.4 1.3.6.1.2.1.5 1.3.6.1.2.1.6 1.3.6.1.2.1.7	1213	(None)
MIB_II.MIB snmpmib.dll	Management Information Base (MIB-II) provides a simple, workable architecture and system for managing TCP/IP-based internets.	1.3.6.1.2.1.11	1213	(None)
MIPX.MIB rtipxmib.dll	Microsoft-defined MIB for the Internetwork Packet Exchange (IPX) Protocol	1.3.6.1.4.1.311.1.8	(None)	Routing and Remote Access service
MRIPSAP.MIB rtipxmib.dll	Microsoft-defined MIB for the Routing Information Protocol (RIP)	1.3.6.1.4.1.311.1.9	(None)	Routing and Remote Access service
MSIPBTP.MIB btpagnt.dll	Microsoft-defined MIB for the Boot Protocol (BOOTP) service	1.3.6.1.4.1.311.1.12	(None)	Routing and Remote Access service
MSIPRIP2.MIB ripagnt.dll	Microsoft-defined MIB for the Routing Information Protocol version 2 (RIP2)	1.3.6.1.4.1.311.1.11	(None)	Routing and Remote Access service
NIPX.MIB rtipxmib.dll	Novell-defined MIB for the IPX Protocol	1.3.6.1.4.1.23.2.5	(None)	Routing and Remote Access service
SMI.MIB (No .dll)	Provides the common definitions for the structure and identification of management information for TCP/IP-based internets.	(No object identifier available)	1155 1215 1902 1903 1904	(None)

(continued)

Table G.1 MIBs that Ship with Windows 2000 SNMP Service *(continued)*

MIB and File name	Description	Object Identifier	RFC	Dependency
WFOSPF.MIB ospfagnt.dll	Nortel Networks–defined MIB for the Open Shortest Path First (OSPF) routing	1.3.6.1.4.1.18	(None)	Routing and Remote Access service
WINS.MIB winsmib.dll	Microsoft-defined MIB for the Windows Internet Name Service (WINS)	1.3.6.1.4.1.311.1.2	(None)	WINS

In addition to being configured in the registry of the SNMP agent, new MIB objects must also be registered in the SNMP management software application on the management system. For more information about registering new MIB objects in the manager, see the documentation included with your management software application.

Additional Resources

For more information about MIB and SNMP, see the following books:

- *Internetworking with TCP/IP* by Douglas E. Comer, 1995, Upper Saddle River: Prentice Hall, Inc.
- *Understanding SNMP MIBs* by D. Perkins and E. McGinnis, 1997, Upper Saddle River: Prentice Hall PTR.
- *The Simple Book: An Introduction to Internet Management, Revised Second Edition* by M. T. Rose, 1996, Upper Saddle River: Prentice-Hall PTR.
- *SNMP, SNMPv2,SNMPv3, and RMON 1 and 2 Third Edition* by W. Stallings, 1999, Reading: Addison-Wesley Publishing Company.

APPENDIX H

LMHOSTS File

Microsoft® Windows® 2000 supports several different name resolution services to locate, communicate with, and connect to resources on the network. For example, a command to connect to an application server by using the server name must be resolved to an IP address in TCP/IP networks before the command can be successfully completed. This is referred to as *name resolution*.

If Windows Internet Name Service (WINS) is available on the network, the LMHOSTS file can be used to support the subnets that do not have a WINS server, and to provide a backup name resolution service in case the WINS server is not available. The LMHOSTS file provides a NetBIOS name resolution method that can be used for small networks that do not use a WINS server.

In This Appendix

Using the LMHOSTS File to Find Computers and Services

Windows 2000 and Microsoft® Windows NT® versions 4.0 and 3.5*x* provide name resolution services for both NetBIOS computer names and Domain Name System (DNS) host names on TCP/IP networks. For information about name resolution through WINS, and LMHost files, see "Windows Internet Name Service" in this book. For information about name resolution through DNS, see "Windows 2000 DNS" in this book.

Using the LMHOSTS file is one method of name resolution for NetBIOS names in TCP/IP networks. Depending on the computer's configuration, the following methods might also be used to resolve NetBIOS names on a TCP/IP network:

- NetBIOS name cache
- IP subnet broadcasts
- WINS NetBIOS name server
- DNS name resolution

Note NetBIOS over TCP/IP (NetBT) is defined by Internet Engineering Task Force RFCs 1001 and 1002. These RFCs define the different name resolution modes—broadcast, point-to-point, mixed, and hybrid—that a computer uses to resolve IP addresses from NetBIOS names.

By installation default, a Windows 2000–based computer not configured as a WINS client or WINS server uses broadcast mode for name resolution and is called a *B* node. A B node is a computer that uses IP broadcasts for NetBIOS name resolution.

IP broadcast name resolution can provide dynamic name resolution. However, the disadvantages of broadcast name queries include increased network traffic and ineffectiveness in routed networks. Resources located outside the local subnet do not receive IP broadcast name query requests because, by definition, IP-level broadcasts are not passed to remote subnets by the router (default gateway) on the local subnet.

As an alternate method to IP broadcasts, Windows 2000 enables you to manually map NetBIOS names to IP addresses for remote computers by using the LMHOSTS file. Selected mappings from the LMHOSTS file are maintained in a limited cache of mappings. This memory cache is initialized when a computer is started. When the computer needs to resolve a name, the cache is examined first and, if there is no match in the cache, Windows 2000 uses broadcast mode IP broadcasts to try to find the NetBIOS computer. If the IP broadcast name query fails, the computer parses the complete LMHOSTS file (not just the cache) to find the NetBIOS name and the corresponding IP address. This strategy enables the LMHOSTS file to contain a large number of mappings without requiring a large chunk of static memory to maintain an infrequently used cache. Then, if the computer cannot resolve the name with the LMHOSTS file, the computer uses DNS for name resolution.

The LMHOSTS file can be used to map computer names and IP addresses for computers outside the local subnet (an advantage over the broadcast method). You can use the LMHOSTS file to find remote computers for network file, print, and remote procedure services and for domain services, such as logging on, browsing, and replication.

The Windows 2000–based LMHOSTS method of name resolution is compatible with the TCP/IP LMHOSTS files of Microsoft® LAN Manager 2.*x*.

Locating Remote Computers

Names for computers outside the local broadcast subnet can be resolved if the names of the remote computers and their corresponding IP addresses are specified in the LMHOSTS file. For example, suppose your computer, named ClientA, is configured without the WINS client service, but you want to use TCP/IP to connect to a computer, named ServerB, that is located on another TCP/IP subnet. By default, your computer is a B node that uses NetBIOS cache and IP broadcasts and is enabled for LMHOSTS file lookup using an LMHOSTS file provided by your network administrator.

At system startup, the name cache on ClientA is "preloaded" only with entries from the LMHOSTS file that are designated for preloading with the keyword #PRE. (For more information about LMHOSTS keywords, see "Creating Entries in the LMHOSTS File" later in this appendix.) For this example, ServerB is on a remote subnet outside of your local subnet IP broadcast area and is *not* one of the entries in preloaded cache. A strict B node IP broadcast (as defined in RFCs 1001 and 1002) fails by timing out when no response is received, because ServerB is located on a remote subnet and cannot receive ClientA's broadcast requests.

In this example case, an operation involving name resolution might go through the following steps:

1. A user on ClientA runs a Windows 2000 command, such as a print file command, using the NetBIOS name of ServerB.
2. The NetBIOS name cache on ClientA is checked for the IP address that corresponds to the NetBIOS name of ServerB.
3. Because ServerB's NetBIOS name and IP address were not preloaded, its NetBIOS name is not found in the name cache, and ClientA broadcasts a Name Query Request with the NetBIOS name of ServerB.
4. Because ServerB is on a remote subnet, and IP broadcasts are not routed to remote subnets, ClientA does not receive a reply to its name request broadcast. (If ServerB were on the local network, ClientA would receive a response to its broadcast and the response would contain the IP address of ServerB.)
5. Because the LMHOSTS method of name resolution has been enabled on ClientA, Windows 2000 continues to attempt to resolve the IP address from the NetBIOS. The LMHOSTS file in the directory *%systemroot%*\System32\Drivers\Etc is examined to find the NetBIOS name, ServerB, and its corresponding IP address. If the NetBIOS name is not found in the LMHOSTS file, and no other name resolution method is configured on ClientA, the user receives an error message.

Specifying Domain Controllers

The most common use of the LMHOSTS file is to locate remote servers for file and print services. However, the LMHOSTS file can also be used to find domain controllers providing domain services on routed TCP/IP networks. Examples of such domain controller activities include domain controller pulses (used for account database synchronization), logon authentication, password changes, master browser list synchronization, and other domain management activities.

Windows 2000 primary domain controllers (PDCs) and backup domain controllers (BDCs) maintain the user account security database and manage other network-related services. Because large Microsoft® Windows NT® domains can span multiple IP subnets, it is possible that routers could separate the domain controllers from one another or separate other computers in the domain from the domain controllers. In a network that does not use WINS servers, LMHOSTS name resolution can be used to allow client computers to connect to domain controllers located across routers on different subnets.

Using Centralized LMHOSTS Files

The primary LMHOSTS file on each computer is always located in the directory *%systemroot%*\System32\Drivers\Etc. With Microsoft TCP/IP, you can include other LMHOSTS files from local and remote computers.

Network administrators can manage the LMHOSTS files used by computers on the network by providing one or more global LMHOSTS files on a central server. Windows 2000–based computers on the network can be configured to import the correct and up-to-date computer name–to–IP address mappings.

Users can import the LMHOSTS file from remote computers on the network by using #INCLUDE statements in the LMHOSTS file or by clicking **Import LMHOSTS** in the **Advanced TCP/IP Settings** dialog box.

Alternatively, an administrator can use the replicator service to distribute multiple copies of the global LMHOSTS file to multiple servers.

Note If network clients access a central LMHOSTS file, the computer on which the file is located must include the registry entry **NullSessionShares** for the LMHOSTS location. **NullSessionShares** is in the following registry subkey:

HKEY_LOCAL_MACHINE\SYSTEM\CurrentControlSet\Services
\lanmanserver\parameters

For detailed information on the registry, see Windows 2000 Server Help. For information about registry content, see the Technical Reference to the Windows 2000 Registry (Regentry.chm) on the Windows 2000 Resource Kit CD.

Creating the LMHOSTS File

Before configuring a computer to use the LMHOSTS file, you must create the primary LMHOSTS file on each computer, name the file LMHOSTS, and save the file in the directory *%systemroot%*\System32\Drivers\Etc.

You can create and change the LMHOSTS file by using a text editor—for example, Notepad—because it is a simple text file. (An example LMHOSTS file named LMHOSTS.sam is provided with Windows 2000 in the directory *%systemroot%*\System32\Drivers\Etc. This is only an example file; do not use this file as the primary LMHOSTS file.)

The following sections describe the different types of entries that you can create and edit in the LMHOSTS file.

Creating Entries in the LMHOSTS File

Use the following rules to create and to edit entries in the LMHOSTS file:

- An entry consists of a computer's IP address followed by at least one space or tab and the computer's NetBIOS name.

> **Caution** You cannot add an LMHOSTS entry for a computer that is a DHCP client, because the IP addresses of DHCP clients change dynamically. To avoid problems, make sure that the computers whose names are entered in the LMHOSTS files are configured with static IP addresses.

- Each entry must be on a separate line. The final entry in the file must be terminated by a carriage return.
- NetBIOS names can contain uppercase and lowercase characters and special characters. If a name is placed between double quotation marks, it is used exactly as entered. For example `"AccountingPDC"` is a mixed-case name, and `"HumanRscSr     \0x03"` specifies a name with a special character.
- Every NetBIOS name is 16 bytes long. The user-definable portion of the NetBIOS name is the first 15 characters. The16th character is set by default to identify the network client service that registered the name. The most familiar example of a NetBIOS name is the computer name on any Windows-based computer. When the computer is started, the Microsoft Network Client services are started and register their names, which consist of the computer name plus a unique 16th character. For example, the name <*computer_name*[0x00]> is the Microsoft Workstation service; the name <*computer_name*[0x20]> is the Microsoft Server service. As you can see, the only difference between these two names is the 16th character. The 16th character makes it possible to uniquely identify each of the Network Client services running on the computer.
- Entries in the LMHOSTS file can represent computers running Microsoft® Windows® 2000 Server, Microsoft® Windows® 2000 Professional, Microsoft® Windows NT® Server, Microsoft® Windows NT® Workstation, Microsoft® Windows® 95, Microsoft® LAN Manager, and Microsoft® Windows® for Workgroups 3.11 with Microsoft TCP/IP. There is no need to distinguish between different platforms in the LMHOSTS file.
- The pound sign (#) is usually used to mark the start of a comment. However, it also designates special keywords, as described in Table H.1.

The keywords listed in the following table can be used in the LMHOSTS file for Windows 2000–based computers. (LAN Manager 2.*x*, which also uses LMHOSTS for NetBT name resolution, treats these keywords as comments.)

Table H.1 LMHOSTS Keywords

Keyword	Description
\0x*nn*	Support for nonprinting characters in NetBIOS names. Enclose the NetBIOS name in double quotation marks and use \0x*nn* notation to specify a hexadecimal value for the character. This enables the proper functioning in routed topologies of custom applications that use special names. However, LAN Manager TCP/IP does not recognize the hexadecimal format, and so you cannot use backward compatibility if you use this feature. Note that the hexadecimal notation applies only to one character in the name. The name should be padded with spaces so that the special character (character 16) is last in the string.
#BEGIN_ALTERNATE	Used to group multiple #INCLUDE statements. Any single successful #INCLUDE statement in a group causes the group to succeed.
#END_ALTERNATE	Used to mark the end of a group of #INCLUDE statements.
#DOM:<*domain*>	Part of the NetBIOS name–to–IP address mapping entry that indicates that the IP address is a domain controller in the domain specified by *domain*. This keyword affects how the Browser and Logon services behave in routed TCP/IP environments. To preload a #DOM entry, the #PRE keyword must appear first in the entry. #DOM groups are limited to 25 members.
#INCLUDE <*file name*>	Forces the system to seek the file specified by *file_name* and parse it as if it were part of the LMHOSTS file. Specifying a Universal Naming Convention (UNC) <*file name*> allows you to use a centralized LMHOSTS file on a server. If the server on which <*file name*> exists is outside of the local broadcast subnet, you must add a preloaded entry for the server that precedes the entry in the #INCLUDE section.
#MH	Part of the NetBIOS name–to–IP address mapping entry that designates the entry as a unique name that can have more than one address. The maximum number of addresses that can be assigned to a unique name is 25. The number of entries is equal to the number of network adapters in the computer.

(continued)

Table H.1 LMHOSTS Keywords *(continued)*

Keyword	Description
#PRE	Part of the NetBIOS name–to–IP address mapping entry that causes that entry to be preloaded into the name cache. By default, entries are not preloaded into the name cache but are parsed only after WINS and name query broadcasts fail to resolve a name. The #PRE keyword must be appended to entries that also appear in #INCLUDE statements; otherwise, the entry in the #INCLUDE statement is ignored.
#SG *<name>*	Part of the NetBIOS name–to–IP address mapping entry that associates that entry with a user-defined special (Internet) group specified by *name*. The #SG keyword defines Internet groups by using a NetBIOS name that has 0x20 as the 16th byte. A special group is limited to 25 members.

The following example shows how all of these keywords are used:

```
102.54.94.102   "appname        \0x14"              #special app server
102.54.94.123   printsrv        #PRE                #source server
102.54.94.98    localsrv        #PRE
102.54.94.97    primary         #PRE #DOM:mydomain  #PDC for mydomain
102.54.94.112   machinename      #SG:sg26members
102.54.94.167   multihome26      #MH
102.54.94.168   multihome26      #MH

#BEGIN_ALTERNATE
#INCLUDE \\localsrv\public\lmhosts   #adds LMHOSTS from this server
#INCLUDE \\primary\public\lmhosts        #adds LMHOSTS from this server
#END_ALTERNATE
```

Note the following characteristics of the preceding example:

- The servers named `printsrv`, `localsrv`, and `primary` are designated with the keyword #PRE as entries to be preloaded into the NetBIOS cache at system startup.
- The servers named `localsrv` and `primary` are also identified in the #INCLUDE statements as the location of the centrally maintained LMHOSTS file.
- The server named "`appname        \0x14`" includes spaces in its name and contains a special character after the first 15 characters. Since its name includes spaces, the name and the special character are enclosed in double quotation marks.

The following sections further explain the use of the keywords #PRE, #DOM, #INCLUDE, and #SG.

Adding Remote System Names by Using #PRE

Using #PRE entries improves access to the identified computers because their names and IP addresses are contained in the computer's cache memory. However, by default, Windows 2000 limits the preloaded name cache to 100 entries. (This limit affects only entries marked with the #PRE keyword.)

If you specify more than 100 #PRE entries, only the first 100 #PRE entries are preloaded into the computer's cache. Any additional #PRE entries are ignored at startup and are used only if name resolution by the cache and IP broadcast fails. When neither the cache nor IP broadcasts lead to name resolution, Windows 2000 parses the complete LMHOSTS file, including the #PRE entries that exceeded the cache limit of 100.

You can change the default maximum allowable #PRE entries by adding the entry **MaxPreloadEntries** to the registry. This entry must be added to the following registry subkey:

HKEY_LOCAL_MACHINE\SYSTEM\CurrentControlSet\Services
\Netbt\Parameters

MaxPreloadEntries has a default and minimum value of 1000 entries for Windows 2000 and Windows NT, versions 3.x and 4.0; the maximum value is 2000 entries. For Windows 9x, the default and minimum value is 100 entries, and the maximum value is 500 entries.

Caution Do not use a registry editor to edit the registry directly unless you have no alternative. The registry editors bypass the standard safeguards provided by administrative tools. These safeguards prevent you from entering conflicting settings or settings that are likely to degrade performance or damage your system. Editing the registry directly can have serious, unexpected consequences that can prevent the system from starting and require that you reinstall Windows 2000. To configure or customize Windows 2000, use the programs in Control Panel or Microsoft Management Console (MMC) whenever possible.

For example, the LMHOSTS file could contain the following information:

```
102.54.94.91    accounting                 #accounting server
102.54.94.94    payroll                    #payroll server
102.54.94.97    stockquote        #PRE     #stock quote server
102.54.94.102   printqueue                 #print server in Bldg 7
```

In this example, the server named `stockquote` is preloaded into the name cache, because it is tagged with the #PRE keyword. The servers named `accounting`, `payroll`, and `printqueue` are resolved only after the cache entries failed to match and after broadcast queries failed to locate them. After resolving the names of hosts whose entries in the LMHOSTS file are not designated for preloading, Windows 2000 keeps the NetBIOS name–to–IP address mappings cached for a period of time for reuse.

Adding Domain Controllers by Using #DOM

The #DOM keyword can be used in LMHOSTS files to distinguish a Windows 2000 domain controller from other computers on the network. To use the #DOM tag, follow the NetBIOS name and IP address of the domain controller in the LMHOSTS file with the #DOM keyword, a colon, and the domain in which the domain controller participates. For example:

```
102.54.94.97 primary    #PRE#DOM:mydomain   #The mydomain PDC
```

Using the #DOM keyword to designate domain controllers causes the computer to add entries to a cache of domain names that the computer uses to contact available controllers to process domain requests. When domain controller activity, such as a logon request, occurs, the computer sends requests to the domain group name. On the local subnet, the computer broadcasts the request, and it is picked up by any local domain controllers. However, domain controllers on remote subnets also receive the requests, because Microsoft TCP/IP uses datagrams to forward the request to domain controllers located on remote subnets when you use the #DOM keyword to specify domain controllers in the LMHOSTS file. Adding more domain controllers in the LMHOSTS file will help distribute the domain requests load across all domain controllers.

When mapping important members of the domain by using the #DOM keyword, use the following guidelines:

- #DOM entries should be preloaded in the cache by using the #PRE keyword. Note that the #PRE keyword must precede the #DOM keyword in the LMHOSTS file.
- For each local LMHOSTS file on a Windows 2000 computer that is a member in a domain, there needs to be #DOM entries for all domain controllers in the domain that are located on remote subnets. This ensures that logon authentication, password changes, browsing, and so on, work properly for the local domain.

- Local LMHOSTS files on all servers that can be backup domain controllers needs to contain the primary domain controller's name and IP address, plus mappings for all other backup domain controllers. This ensures that promoting a backup domain controller to primary domain controller does not affect the promoted domain controller's ability to offer all services to members of the domain.
- If trust relationships exist between domains, all domain controllers for all trusted domains must also be listed in the local LMHOSTS file.
- For domains that you want to browse from your local domain, the local LMHOSTS files needs to contain at least the name and IP address for the primary domain controller in the remote domain. Again, backup domain controllers in remote domains must also be included so that promotion to primary domain controller does not impair the ability to browse remote domains.

Names that appear with the #DOM keyword in the LMHOSTS file are placed in a special domain cache for NetBT. When a datagram is sent by NetBT to this domain using the DOMAIN<1C> name, the name is resolved first by using WINS or IP broadcasts. The datagram is then sent to all the addresses contained in the list from LMHOSTS, and a broadcast on the local subnet is also sent.

Adding User-Defined Special Groups by Using #SG

You can group resources, such as printers or computers that belong to groups on an intranet, by using the #SG keyword to define a special group in the LMHOSTS file. Special groups are limited to a total of 25 members.

You specify the special group name just as you would specify a domain name except that the keyword portion of the entry is #SG. The following example creates the special group `mycompany`:

```
102.54.94.99 printsrvsg     #SG:mycompany   #Specialgroup of computers
```

In some cases, you might want to specify only the name of a special group without specifying an IP address. This can be done by not entering the IP address in the otherwise complete entry, as in the following example:

```
printsrvsg      #SG:mycompany   #Specialgroup of computers
```

Adding Multihomed Devices by Using #MH

A multihomed device is a computer with multiple network adapters. A multihomed device can be defined by a single, unique name with which multiple IP addresses are associated.

You can provide multihomed NetBIOS name–to–IP address mappings in the LMHOSTS file by creating entries that are designated as multihomed with the keyword #MH. An #MH entry associates a single, unique NetBIOS computer name with an IP address. You can create multiple entries for the same NetBIOS computer name for each network adapter in the multihomed device, up to a maximum of 25 different IP addresses for the same name.

The format of the LMHOSTS entry that is used to specify NetBIOS name–to–IP address mappings for multihomed devices is the same as the other keyword entries. The following example shows the entries required to map names to IP addresses for a multihomed computer with two network adapters:

```
102.54.94.91 accounting          #MH #accounting server NIC 1
102.54.94.92 accounting          #MH #accounting server NIC 2
```

Defining a Central LMHOST File by Using #INCLUDE

For small- to medium-sized networks with fewer than 20 domains, a single common LMHOSTS file usually satisfies the demands of all workstations and servers on the network. An administrator can use the Windows 2000 Replicator service to maintain synchronized local copies of the global LMHOSTS file, and use centralized LMHOSTS files, as described in this section.

Use the keywords #BEGIN_ALTERNATE and #END_ALTERNATE to provide a list of servers maintaining copies of the same LMHOSTS file. This is known as a *block inclusion*, which allows multiple servers to be searched for a valid copy of a specific file. The following example shows the use of the keyword #INCLUDE to include a local LMHOSTS file (located in the directory C:\Private) and the keyword #_ALTERNATE to include servers maintaining copies of the same LMHOSTS file:

```
102.54.94.97primary       #PRE  #DOM:mydomain     #primary DC
102.54.94.99backupdc      #PRE  #DOM:mydomain     #backup DC
102.54.94.98localsvr      #PRE  #DOM:mydomain

#INCLUDE    c:\private\lmhosts                  #include a local lmhosts

#BEGIN_ALTERNATE
#INCLUDE    \\primary\public\lmhosts            #source for global file
#INCLUDE    \\backupdc\public\lmhosts           #backup source
#INCLUDE    \\localsvr\public\lmhosts           #backup source
#END_ALTERNATE
```

Important This feature should never be used to include a remote file from a redirected drive because the LMHOSTS file is shared between local users who have different profiles and different logon scripts. Even on single-user systems, redirected drive mappings can change between logon sessions.

In the preceding example, the servers `primary` and `backupdc` are located on remote subnets from the computer that owns the file. The local user has decided to include a list of preferred servers in a local LMHOSTS file located in the directory C:\Private. During name resolution, Windows 2000 first includes this private file, then gets the global LMHOSTS file from one of three locations: `primary`, `backupdc`, or `localsvr`. All names of servers in the #INCLUDE statements must have their addresses preloaded using the #PRE keyword; otherwise, the #INCLUDE statements are ignored.

The block inclusion is satisfied if one of the three sources for the global LMHOSTS file is available and none of the other servers is used. If no server is available, or for some reason the LMHOSTS file or path is incorrect, an event is added to the event log to indicate that the block inclusion failed.

Configuring TCP/IP to Use LMHOSTS Name Resolution

By default, Windows 2000 is enabled to use the LMHOSTS file for name resolution when TCP/IP is installed on the computer. You can disable the use of LMHOSTS for name resolution by clearing the **Enable LMHOSTS Lookup** check box on the **WINS** tab of the **Advanced TCP/IP Settings** dialog box. However, disabling the use of LMHOSTS for name resolution is not recommended, because the LMHOSTS file provides a backup name service for WINS servers that are offline or unavailable.

To use an LMHOSTS file from a remote computer or from a different directory on the local computer, click **Import LMHOSTS** on the **WINS** tab of the **Advanced TCP/IP Settings** dialog box.

Maintaining the LMHOSTS File

When you use an LMHOSTS file, be sure to keep it up-to-date and organized. Use the following guidelines:

- Update the LMHOSTS file whenever the NetBIOS name of a computer on the network is changed or removed.
- Because LMHOSTS files are searched one line at a time from the beginning, list remote computers in priority order, with those used most often at the top of the file, followed by remote systems listed in #INCLUDE statements.

- Use #PRE entries to preload into the local computer's name cache frequently accessed workstations and servers listed in the #INCLUDE statements. #PRE keyword entries should be entered at the end of the file, because these are preloaded into the cache at system startup time and are not accessed later. This increases the speed of searches for the entries used most often, because any comment text that you add increases the time required to parse the file.
- Use the **nbtstat** command to remove or correct preloaded entries that might have been typed incorrectly or any names cached by successful broadcast resolution. You can refresh the name cache by running **nbtstat -R**, which purges and reloads the name cache, rereads the LMHOSTS file, and then inserts entries tagged with the #PRE keyword. For more information about **nbtstat**, see Windows 2000 Server Help.

Troubleshooting the LMHOSTS File

When using the LMHOSTS file, problems, like failure to locate a remote computer, can occur due to the presence in the LMHOSTS file of one or more of the following errors:

- Absence of an entry for the remote server.
- Misspelling of a computer's NetBIOS name. (Note that NetBIOS names are automatically converted to uppercase.)
- Invalid IP address for a computer name.
- Missing the required carriage return character at the end of the last entry.

APPENDIX I

Windows 2000 Browser Service

Microsoft® Windows® 2000 Server and Microsoft® Windows® 2000 Professional continue to support the browser service, originally introduced with Microsoft® Windows® for Workgroups version 3.1, to provide for interoperability with domains and computers that are not enabled to use Active Directory™ directory service. On a network of computers running only Windows 2000, clients can find network servers and file sharing resources through the shared folder object in the Active Directory directory service. However, as a practical matter, most organizations will use the browser service for the foreseeable future to service legacy computers that are not Active Directory–capable. The browser service and NetBIOS are enabled by default when Windows 2000 is installed.

In This Appendix

Related Information in the Resource Kit

- For information about Windows 2000 IPX routing services, see "IPX Routing" in *Microsoft® Windows 2000 Server Resource Kit Internetworking Guide.*
- For information about migrating from NetWare to Windows 2000, see "Determining Domain Migration Strategies" in *Microsoft® Windows 2000 Server Resource Kit Deployment Planning Guide.*

Introduction to the Browser Service

Users often need to know what domains and computers are accessible from their local computer. Viewing all the network resources available on a network of computers running Microsoft® Windows® 2000 or Microsoft® Windows NT® is called *browsing*. The Windows browser service maintains a list—called the *browse list*—of all available domains and servers. The browse list can be viewed using Explorer and is provided by a browser in the domain of the local computer.

Note For the purposes of this discussion, the term *server* refers to any computer that can provide resources to the rest of the network. If a computer running Microsoft® Windows® 95, Microsoft® Windows® 98, Microsoft® Windows® for Workgroup version 3.11, Microsoft® Windows NT® Workstation, or Windows 2000 Professional can share file or print resources with other computers on the network, it is considered a server in the context of the browser system. The computer does not need to be actively sharing resources to be considered a server.

This appendix includes descriptions of the following topics:

- Roles of browser computers in the browser system.
- Coordination by browser computers to provide an accurate browse list, even if the master browser fails.
- Election of the master browser.
- Application programming interface (API) calls used to register computers for the browser list and to receive the list from the master browser.
- Browsing across domains.
- Troubleshooting browser problems.

Windows 2000 Browser System Overview

Windows 2000 and Windows NT assign tasks to specific computers on the network to provide browser services. The computers work together to provide a centralized list of shared resources, eliminating the need for all computers to maintain their own lists. This reduces the CPU time and network traffic needed to build and maintain the list.

The Windows 2000 browser system consists of a master browser, backup browsers, and browser clients. The computer that is the master browser maintains the browse list and periodically sends copies to the backup browsers. When a browser client needs information, it obtains the current browse list by remotely sending a **NetServerEnum** API call to either the master browser or a backup browser.

The browser system consists of two components, the browser service and the datagram receiver.

The browser service is the user-mode portion of the browser system and is responsible for maintaining the browse list, sending the API requests, and managing the various browser roles that a computer can have. The browser service actually resides within the Service Control Manager (Services.exe which calls browser.dll).

The datagram receiver is the kernel-mode portion of the browser system and is simply a datagram receiver and mailslot. It receives directed and broadcast datagrams that are of interest to the Windows 2000 Professional and Windows 2000 Server services. The datagram receiver also provides kernel-level support for the **NetServerEnum** API, support for remote mailslot message reception (second-class, datagram-based, mailslot messages), and the request announcement services.

In Microsoft® Windows NT® version 3.5 and later, the datagram receiver is implemented in the Windows NT redirector (Rdr.sys). In Microsoft® Windows NT® version 3.1, there is a separate driver, Browser.sys, for the datagram receiver.

The centralized browser architecture also reduces demands on the client CPU and memory.

Specifying Browser Computers

When you start a computer running Windows 2000, the browser service looks in the registry for the entry **MaintainServerList** to determine whether a computer will become a browser. **MaintainServerList** is found in the following registry subkey:

\HKEY_LOCAL_MACHINE\SYSTEM\CurrentControlSet\Services
\Browser\Parameters

Table I.1 shows the values to which **MaintainServerList** can be set and the meaning for the computer's participation in browser services.

Table I.1 Allowable Values for the MaintainServerList Registry Entry

Value	Meaning
No	This value prevents the computer from participating as a browser.
Yes	This value makes the computer a browser. Upon startup, the computer attempts to contact the master browser to get a current browse list. If the master browser cannot be found, the computer will force a browser election. The computer will either be elected master browser or become a backup browser. This value is the default on a computer running Windows 2000 Server and Windows NT Server.
Auto	This value makes the computer a *potential browser*. It might become a browser, depending on the number of currently active browsers. The master browser notifies this computer whether or not it is to become a backup browser. This value is the default for computers running Windows 2000 Professional and Windows NT Workstation.

On any computer with the value of **MaintainServerList** set to **Yes** or **Auto**, the browser service starts when the computer is booted.

Caution Do not use a registry editor to edit the registry directly unless you have no alternative. The registry editors bypass the standard safeguards provided by administrative tools. These safeguards prevent you from entering conflicting settings or settings that are likely to degrade performance or damage your system. Editing the registry directly can have serious, unexpected consequences that can prevent thc system from starting and require that you reinstall Windows 2000. To configure or customize Windows 2000, use the programs in Microsoft Management Console (MMC) or Control Panel whenever possible.

Another entry in the registry, **IsDomainMaster**, helps determine which servers become master browsers and backup browsers. Setting the value of the **IsDomainMaster** entry to **True** makes the computer a *preferred master browser*. Any computer running Windows 2000 or Windows NT can be configured as a preferred master browser.

When the browser service is started on the preferred master browser, the browser service forces an election. Preferred master browsers are given priority in elections, which means the preferred master browser always wins the election if no other condition prevents it. This gives an administrator the ability to configure a specific computer as the master browser.

To specify a computer as the preferred master browser, set the value of the **IsDomainMaster** entry to **True**. This entry (data type Reg_SZ) appears in the following registry subkey:

\HKEY_LOCAL_MACHINE\SYSTEM\CurrentControlSet\Services \Browser\Parameters

Unless the computer is configured as the preferred master browser, the value of the **IsDomainMaster** entry is always set to **False** or **No**. There is no user interface for making these changes; the registry must be modified using a registry editor (Regedt32.exe or Regedit.exe).

Browser System Roles

Computers running Windows 2000, Windows NT 3.1, Microsoft® Windows NT® Advanced Server version 3.1, Microsoft® Windows NT® Workstation version 3.5 or later, Microsoft® Windows NT® Server version 3.5 or later, Windows for Workgroups 3.11, Windows 95, or Windows 98 can be browsers. There are five types of computers in the browser system:

- Nonbrowsers
- Potential browsers
- Backup browsers
- Master browsers
- Domain master browsers

Figure I.1 Shows a browser and nonbrowser computers in a subnet.

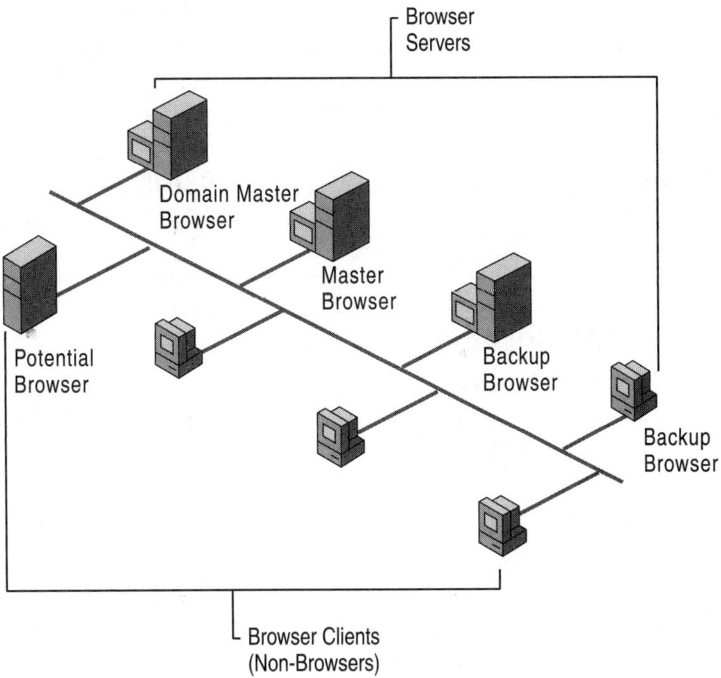

Figure I.1 Browser and Non-Browser Computers

Non-Browser

A *non-browser* is a computer that has been configured not to maintain a network resource or browse list.

Potential Browser

A *potential browser* is a computer that is capable of maintaining a network resource browse list and can be elected as a master browser. The potential browser computer can act as a backup browser if instructed to do so by the master browser.

Backup Browser

The *backup browser* receives a copy of the network resource browse list from the master browser and distributes the list upon request to computers in the domain or workgroup. All Windows 2000 domain controllers are configured as either master or backup browsers.

Computers running Windows 2000 Professional, Windows NT Workstation, Microsoft® Windows® for Workgroups, or Windows 95 can be backup browsers if there are fewer than three Windows 2000 or Windows NT Server computers performing backup browser functions for the domain.

The list of servers is limited in size to 64 kilobyte (KB) on computers running a version of Windows NT earlier than version 4.0, Windows for Workgroups, and Windows 95. This limits the number of computers in a browse list for a single workgroup or domain to between 2,000 and 3,000.

Note Verbose server comments can significantly reduce the numbers of computers allowable in a browse list since the list size is limited to 64 kilobytes (KB).

Master Browser

The *master browser* is responsible for collecting the information necessary to create and maintain the browse list. The browse list includes all servers in the domain or workgroup of the master browser and the list of all domains on the network.

Individual servers announce their presence to the master browser by sending a directed datagram called a *server announcement* to the domain or workgroup master browser. Computers running Windows 2000, Windows NT, Windows for Workgroups, Windows 95, Windows 98, or Microsoft® LAN Manager send server announcements. When the master browser receives a server announcement from a computer, it adds that computer to the browse list.

When a domain spans more than one subnet, the master browser will do the following tasks:

- Maintain the browse list for the portion of the domain on its subnet.
- Provide lists of backup browsers on the local subnet of a TCP/IP-based network to computers running Windows 2000, Windows NT, Windows 95, Windows 98, and Windows for Workgroups.

If a TCP/IP-based subnet is comprised of more than one domain, each domain has its own master browser and backup browsers. On networks using NWLink, the IPX/SPX-compatible network protocol, routers are typically configured to forward packets of type 0x14. Since broadcast packets including elections are propagated in this manner, this insures that there is always only one master browser. In contrast, NetBEUI Frame (NBF), which is not designed for a routed network, requires a separate master browser per subnet.

When a computer starts and the value of the **MaintainServerList** entry in its registry is set to **Auto**, the master browser must tell that computer whether or not to become a backup browser.

Domain Master Browser

The domain master browser is responsible for collecting announcements for the entire domain, lists from master browsers on other subnets, and for providing a list of domain resources to master browsers. The domain master browser is always the primary domain controller (PDC) of a domain.

The PDC of a domain is given priority in browser elections to ensure that it becomes the master browser. The Windows browser service running on a PDC has the special, additional role of being the domain master browser.

For a domain that uses TCP/IP and spans more than one subnet, each subnet functions as an independent browsing entity with its own master browser and backup browsers. NWLink and NBF transports don't use the domain master browser role because those transports have only a single master browser for the entire network. Browsing across an IP router to other subnets requires at least one browser running Windows 2000, Windows NT, or Microsoft® Windows® for Workgroups 3.11b on the domain for each subnet. A PDC typically functions as the domain master browser on its subnet.

When a domain spans multiple subnets, the master browser of each subnet announces itself as the master browser to the domain master browser, using a directed datagram called a MasterBrowserAnnouncement. The domain master browser then sends a remote **NetServerEnum** API call to each master browser, to collect the list of servers from each subnet. The domain master browser merges the server list from each subnet master browser with its own server list, forming the browse list for the domain. This process is repeated every 12 minutes to ensure that the domain master browser has a complete browse list of all the servers in the domain.

Note The Domain Master Browser must be able to resolve the server name of each master browser on a TCP/IP network (using WINS, for example). Each Master Browser must be able to resolve the DOMAIN[1B] name as well as the Primary Domain Controllers machine name.

The master browser on each subnet also sends a remote **NetServerEnum** API call to the domain master browser to obtain the complete browse list for the domain. This browse list is available to browser clients on the subnet.

A single computer can play multiple browser roles. For example, the master browser might also be the domain master browser.

Note Windows workgroups cannot span multiple networks. Any Windows workgroup that spans subnets actually functions as two separate workgroups with identical names.

Browser Elections

Browser elections occur to select a new master browser under the following circumstances:

- When a computer cannot locate a master browser.
- When a preferred master browser comes online.
- When a Windows domain-controller system starts.

A computer initiates an election by sending a special datagram called an *election datagram*. When an election occurs, the browser service on the computer forcing the election logs an event in the system log, indicating that it forced the election. An event is logged for each protocol on which the browser service forces an election.

All browsers can receive election datagrams. When a browser receives an election datagram, it examines the election criteria of that datagram. If the browser has better election criteria than the sender of the election datagram, the browser issues its own election datagram and enters what is called an *election in progress* state. If the browser does not have better election criteria than the sender of the election datagram, the browser attempts to determine which system is the new master browser. Figure I.2 Shows computers performing a browser election.

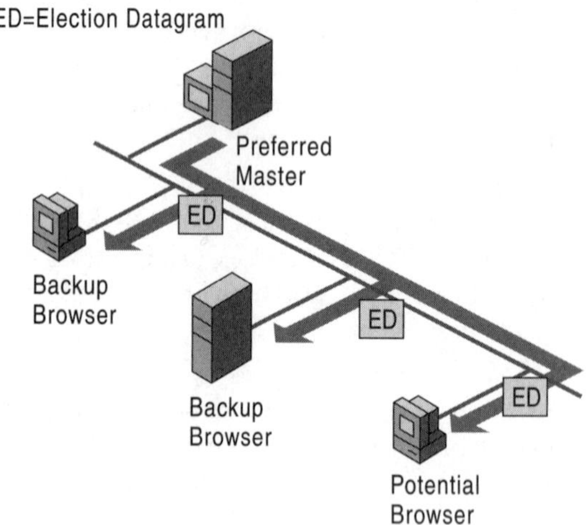

Figure I.2 Browser Election

The election criteria for a browser is based on the current role of the browser in the domain and its current state, using the hierarchy shown in Table I.2.

Table I.2 Hierarchy of Criteria for a Browser Election

Operating System Type	Windows Election field
Windows for Workgroups and Windows 95 and Windows 98	0x01000000
Windows 2000 Professional and Windows NT Workstation	0x10000000
Windows 2000 Server and Windows NT Server	0x20000000
Election Version	0x00FFFF00
Per Version Criteria	0x000000FF
PDC	0x00000080
WINS System	0x00000020
Preferred Master	0x00000008
Running Master	0x00000004
MaintainServerList = Yes	0x00000002
Running backup browser	0x00000001

The browser uses all of the appropriate election criteria to determine the election criteria of the sending computer.

The following criteria determine whether or not a browser has won an election:

- If the election version of the browser is greater than the election version of the sender, the browser wins. If not, the browser uses the next election criterion. The *election version* is a constant value that identifies the version of the browser-election protocol. The election version is the revision of the browser protocol and is not related to the operating-system version.
- If the election criteria of the browser is greater than the election criteria of the sender, the browser wins. If not, the browser uses the next election criterion.
- If the browser has been running longer than the sender, the browser wins. If not, the browser uses the next election criterion.
- If none of the criteria above have determined the election, then the server with the lexically (alphabetically, including numbers and symbols) lowest name wins. For example, a server named "A" will become master browser over a server named "X."

When a browser receives an election datagram indicating that it wins an election, the browser enters the *running election state*. While in this state, the browser sends out an election request after a delay. The delay is based on the current role of the browser in the domain:

- Master browsers and the primary domain controllers delay for 100 microseconds (ms).

- Backup browsers and backup domain controllers randomly delay for 200 ms and 600 ms.
- All other browsers randomly delay between 800 ms and 3000 ms.

This delay is programmed to occur because Windows for Workgroups browsers go "deaf" for several hundred microseconds after sending an election datagram. This delay reduces the number of election datagrams sent, because a browser winning an election might then receive a different election datagram, causing it to lose an election later. By having computers that are less likely to win an election delay their sending of election requests, those computers are less likely to send election datagrams.

The browser sends up to four election datagrams. If no other browser responds with an election datagram that wins the election, the computer is promoted to master browser. If the browser receives an election datagram indicating that another computer wins the election, and the computer is currently the master browser, the computer demotes itself from master browser and becomes a backup browser.

Browser Announcements

The browser service must be notified by a resource when the resource is available for use on the network. When a network computer running Windows 2000, Windows NT, Windows for Workgroups, Windows 95, or Windows 98 starts, it sends an announcement to the browser service to inform the browser of its availability. Figure I.3 shows browser announcements being transmitted.

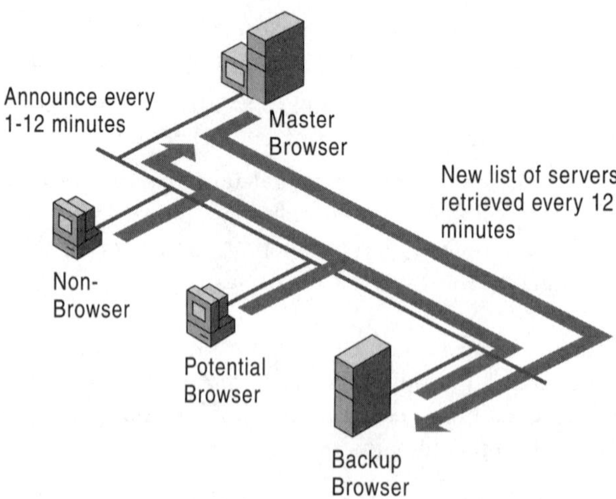

Figure I.3 Browser Announcements

Master browsers are responsible for receiving announcements from and returning lists of backup browsers to computers running any of the following operating systems:

- Windows NT 3.1
- Windows NT Advanced Server 3.1
- Windows for Workgroups
- Windows 95
- Windows 98
- Windows NT Workstation 3.5, or later
- Windows NT Server 3.5, or later
- Windows 2000 Professional
- Windows 2000 Server

When a computer starts and the value of the **MaintainServerList** entry in its registry is set to **Auto**, the master browser is responsible for telling the system whether or not to become a backup browser.

When a computer becomes the master browser by winning an election, and the browse list is empty, the master browser forces all systems to reply with an announcement. The master browser broadcasts a datagram called a RequestAnnouncement. All computers that receive this datagram must answer after a random delay of up to 30 seconds. This 30-second range for response prevents the master browser from becoming overloaded and losing replies, and it protects the network from being flooded with responses. Figure I.4 shows computers browsing for backup lists.

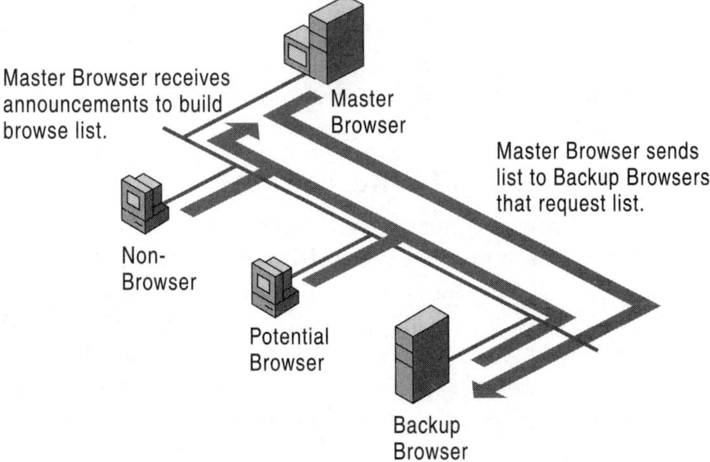

Figure I.4 Browsing for Backup Lists

A master browser cannot be forced to rebuild the browse list for a workgroup or domain. However, shutting down and restarting a computer that is configured as the preferred master browser, or stopping and restarting the browser service, forces the building of a new browse list. When a preferred master browser starts, it forces an election, which it wins. Because there is no browse list, it then forces all members of the domain or workgroup to announce themselves.

If a master browser receives an announcement from another computer that claims to be the master browser, the master browser will demote itself from master browser and force an election. This ensures that there is never more than one master browser in each workgroup or domain.

Non-Browser Announcements

A non-browser computer periodically announces itself to the master browser by sending a directed datagram to the master browser on the network. The computer announces its availability in intervals of 1 minute, 2 minutes, 4 minutes, 8 minutes, and 12 minutes, thereafter announcing itself to the master browser every 12 minutes. If the master browser has not heard from the non-browser for three consecutive announcement periods, the master browser removes the non-browser from the browse list.

Note Therefore it can take up to 36 minutes for the local master browser to remove a stale entry. In addition, the remainder of the domain might require 12 - 24 minutes (twice the master-periodicity) to discover the removal of the stale entry.

Potential-Browser Announcements

Most computers are potential browsers; that is, they are capable of becoming either backup browsers or master browsers. These computers announce themselves in the same manner as non-browsers.

Backup-Browser Announcements

Backup browsers announce themselves in the same manner as non-browsers. However, backup browsers participate in browser elections. Backup browsers connect to the master browser every 12 minutes to obtain updated network-resource browse lists and lists of workgroups and domains. The backup browser caches these lists and returns the browse list to any client that sends out a browse request by making a call, using the **NetServerEnum** API, to the backup browser. If the backup browser cannot find the master browser, it forces an election.

Browser Announcement Time Configuration

To change how often a browser announces itself, add a registry entry called **Announce** with a value that has the REG_DWORD data type. Set the value of the **Announce** entry to the number of seconds that the browser should wait between announcements. Add **Announce** to the following registry subkey:

HKEY_LOCAL_MACHINE\SYSTEM\CurrentControlSet\Services \lanmanserver\parameters

For example, if the value of the **Announce** entry is set to 720 by default, the announcement interval is 12 minutes.

The value of the **Announce** entry must be changed on all computers in the workgroup or domain before the new value can be used by all computers. As you decrease this value, announcement traffic increases. Increasing the value of **Announce** reduces the amount of announcement traffic, but it increases the length of time that an unavailable computer appears on the browse list.

Browser Requests

The purpose of the browser service is to make a list of network resources available to browser clients. To use this resource list, the browser client must know which computer to contact to request a copy of the list.

Figure I.5 shows the flow of browser request.

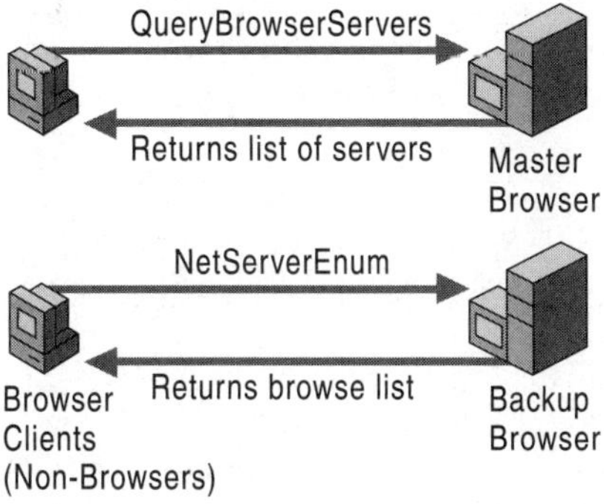

Figure I.5 Flow of the Browser Request

The request issued to obtain the list of available network resources is a **NetServerEnum** API call. This request is sent when **net view** is run at the command prompt and when **Browse** button is selected from the **Map Network Drive** dialog box. The client issues the **NetServerEnum** API call to a backup browser.

Before a client can send a **NetServerEnum** API call for the first time, it must first discover which computers are the backup browsers for its workgroup or domain. The client does this by issuing a datagram called GetBackupList to the master browser.

The master browser receives and processes the GetBackupList datagram. The master browser returns a list of backup browsers active within the workgroup or domain being queried. The client selects the names of three backup browsers from the list and stores these names for future use. The **NetServerEnum** API call is sent to a backup browser randomly chosen from the three saved names.

If the master browser for the workgroup or domain being queried cannot be found after three attempts, the client forces the election of a new master browser in the domain. The client also returns the message ERROR_BAD_NETPATH to the browsing application, indicating that the master browser cannot be found.

Number of Browsers in a Domain or Workgroup

The following rules determine the number of browsers in a domain or workgroup.

If there is currently a PDC in the domain, it is the master browser for the domain.

Every backup domain controller (BDC) in the domain is a backup browser for the domain. The only exception to this is when the BDC is needed as a master browser because the PDC has failed. In that case, the BDC is the master browser for the domain.

Note This can be a problem because the DOMAIN[1B] entry, used to locate the Domain Master Browser, is only updated if the backup domain controller is promoted.

If the registry of a computer has the value of the **MaintainServerList** entry set to **Yes**, the computer is a backup browser for the domain or TCP/IP subnet.

If no backup browsers are selected for the domain based on the preceding rules, the master browser determines the number of backup browsers for the domain. The master browser selects some of those computers with the value of the **MaintainServerList** entry set to **Auto** to act as backup browsers.

Table I.3 shows the number of backup browsers that are selected, based on the number of computers in the domain.

Table I.3 Number of Browsers in a Domain or Workgroup

Number of Computers	Number of Backup Browsers	Number of Master Browsers
1	0	1
2 to 31	1	1
32 to 63	2	1

For each additional 32 computers added to the domain, another backup browser is selected for the domain.

In a TCP/IP network, each subnet independently enforces the preceding rules.

Browser Shutdown or Failure

If a backup browser shuts down properly, it sends an announcement to the master browser that it is shutting down. The backup browser does this by sending an announcement that does not include the browser service in the list of running services.

If a master browser shuts down gracefully, it will send a ForceElection datagram so that a new master browser will be chosen.

If a computer does not shut down properly, or if it fails for any reason, it must be removed from the browse list. The browser service manages browser failures.

Nonbrowser Failure

When a non-browser fails, it stops announcing itself. The configured announcement period is between 1 and 12 minutes. If the non-browser has not announced itself after three announcement periods, the master browser removes the computer from the browse list. Therefore, it can take up to 72 minutes before all browsers know of the failure of a nonbrowser. This potential delay includes up to 36 minutes for the master browser to detect the failure and 12 minutes for all of the backup browsers to retrieve the updated list from the master browser.

Backup-Browser Failure

As with a nonbrowser failure, when a backup browser fails, it might not be removed from the master-browser list for up to 72 minutes. If a browse list cannot be obtained from the missing backup browser, the client selects another backup browser from its cached list of three backups. If all of the client's known backup browsers fail, the client attempts to get a new list of backup browsers from the master browser. If the client is unable to contact the master browser, the client forces an election.

Master-Browser Failure

When a master browser fails, a backup browser detects the failure within 12 minutes and forces an election of a new master browser.

If a client performs its browse request (using the **NetServerEnum** API call) after a master browser fails but before a backup browser detects the failure, the client forces an election. If a master browser fails and there are no backup browsers, browsing in the workgroup or domain does not function correctly.

During the gap between the failure of a master browser and the election of a new master browser, the workgroup or domain can disappear from the lists that are visible to computers in other workgroups and domains.

Domain Master Browser Failures

If the domain master browser fails, the master browser for each network subnet provides a browse list, containing only the servers in the local network subnet. All servers that are not on the local network subnet are eventually removed from the browse list. Even after the servers are removed, users are still able to connect to servers on the other network subnets if they know the name of the server.

Because a domain master browser is also a PDC, an administrator can correct the failure by promoting a BDC to PDC; this causes the DOMAIN[IB] record to be updated in WINS. A BDC can perform most PDC network tasks, such as validating logon requests, but it does not promote itself to PDC and does not become the domain master browser in the event of a PDC failure. Figure I.6 shows events in a Master Browser failure.

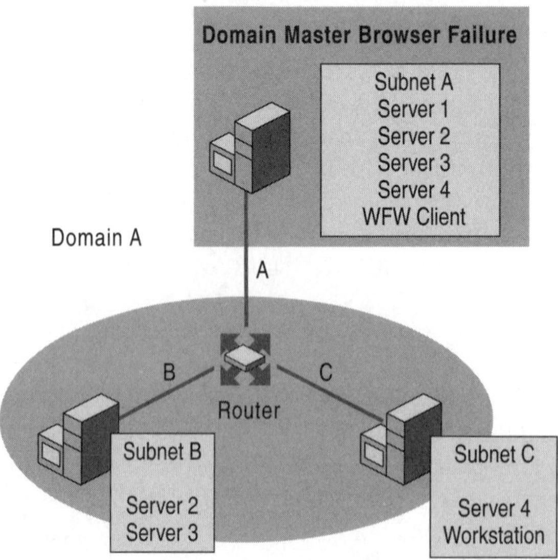

Figure I.6 Master Browser Failure

Browse Service Across Multiple Workgroups and Domains

Users need to browse multiple workgroups and domains to retrieve a list of servers within their workgroup or domain and a list of other workgroups and domains.

Figure I.7 shows Browser Service across multiple workgroups and domains.

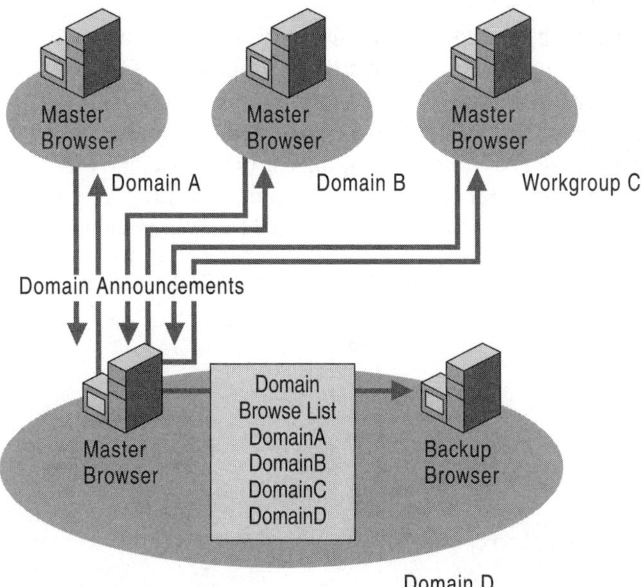

Figure I.7 Browser Service Across Multiple Workgroups and Domains

Upon becoming a master browser, each master browser in each workgroup and domain will broadcast a DomainAnnouncement datagram every minute for the first five minutes. After the first five minutes, the master browser will broadcast a DomainAnnouncement once every 12 minutes. If a workgroup or domain has not announced itself for three announcement periods, the workgroup or domain is removed from the list of workgroups and domains. Therefore, it is possible that a workgroup or domain appears in the browse list 45 minutes after the workgroup or domain has failed or been shut down.

A DomainAnnouncement datagram contains the following information.

- Name of the domain
- Name of a master browser for that domain which may or not be a Primary Domain Controller.
- Version of the operating software

If the browser computer is running Windows 2000 Server or Windows NT Server, the DomainAnnouncement also specifies whether or not the browser computer is the domain PDC.

Browse Service Across an IP Router

When using domains that are split across routers, each TCP/IP network subnet functions as an independent browsing entity with its own master browser and backup browsers. Therefore, browser elections occur within each network subnet.

Domain master browsers are responsible for spanning the network subnets to collect computer name information to maintain a domain-wide browse list of available resources. The domain master browser and cooperating master browsers on each subnet provide browsing of domains that exist across multiple TCP/IP network subnets. The domain master browser is the PDC of a domain. The master browser computers on the subnets can be running Windows 2000, Windows NT, Windows for Workgroups version 3.11b, Windows 95, or Windows 98.

Figure I.8 shows Browser Service across an IP router.

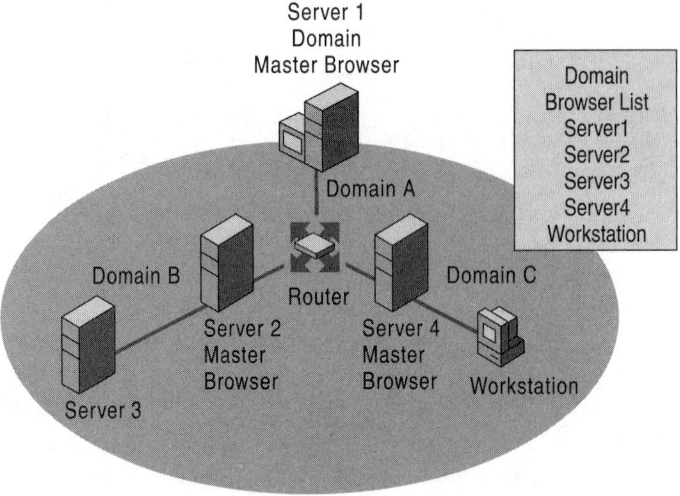

Figure I.8 Browser Service Across an IP Router

When a domain spans multiple network subnets, the master browsers for each network subnet use a directed datagram called a *MasterBrowserAnnouncement* to announce themselves to the domain master browser. The MasterBrowserAnnouncement notifies the domain master browser that the sending computer is a master browser in the same domain and that the domain master browser needs to obtain a copy of the master browser's browse list. When the domain master browser receives a MasterBrowserAnnouncement, it returns a request to the announcing master browser for a list of the servers in the master browser's network subnet. The domain master browser then merges its own server list with the server list from the master browser that issued the announcement.

This process is repeated every 15 minutes and guarantees that the domain master browser has a complete browse list of all the servers in the domain. When a client issues a browse request to a backup browser, the backup browser returns a list of all the servers in the domain, regardless of the network subnet on which they are located.

Name Resolution

Name resolution is critical for distributed browsing to operate properly.

All computers that have the potential to become master browsers on an IP internetwork must be able to resolve the DomainName<1b> entry for the domain master browser. After receiving a positive response to the datagram Query for Primary DC, the master browsers must also be able to resolve the ComputerName<00> of the domain master browser. For the domain master browser to connect with each of the master browsers, it must be able to resolve the names of all servers that have the potential to become master browsers. The domain master browser listens for the directed MasterBrowserAnnouncement datagram sent by the master browsers over UDP port 138. These announcements cause the domain master browser to resolve the ComputerName<00> of the master browser and request from the master browser its locally collected browse list.

It is also important to understand that once a browse list is presented to the client, the client must resolve the ComputerName<20> of any server in the list in order to view its shared resources. Therefore, all clients in the domain must be able to resolve the IP address of any server in the domain. For most networks this means that the distributed WINS or DNS infrastructure must be working properly.

For information about name resolution through WINS, DNS, or LMHOSTS files, see "Windows Internet Name Service" in this book.

Browse Service Across an IP Router with TCP/IP

Currently, browser service communication relies almost entirely on broadcasts. On an IP internetwork, where domains are separated by routers, special broadcast problems can arise because broadcasts, by default, do not pass through routers. There are two issues to consider:

- How browsers separated by a router can perform browser functions
- How local clients can browse remote domains that are not on their local network subnet

The following topics discuss three methods that you can use to set up browsing on an IP internetwork with TCP/IP. They are presented in order of preference.

Domain Name System

Windows 2000 uses DNS as its primary method of name resolution. Every Windows 2000–based domain controller registers two names at startup: a DNS domain name with the DNS service and a NetBIOS name with WINS or another transport service.

If the originating computer and the targeted computer are configured to use IP and DNS, the name is resolved using DNS; otherwise, WINS resolves IP addresses from NetBIOS names so that datagrams can be sent to the targeted computer. Name resolution may not work properly if only DNS is used, due to limitations of resolving NetBIOS names through DNS. It is recommended that you use WINS as well as DNS.

For more information about DNS concepts, see "Introduction to DNS" in this book.

Windows Internet Name Service

The Windows Internet Name Service (WINS) resolves IP addresses from NetBIOS names so that datagrams can be sent to the targeted computer. Implementing WINS eliminates the need to configure the LMHOSTS file or to enable UDP port 137. Using WINS requires the following configuration:

- WINS is configured on a computer running Windows 2000 Server, Windows NT Server 3.5 or later.
- Clients are WINS-enabled.

  WINS clients can be computers running Windows 2000, Windows NT 3.5 or later, Windows 95, Windows 98, Windows for Workgroups 3.11b running TCP/IP-32, Microsoft® LAN Manager 2.2c for MS-DOS, or Microsoft Network Client 3.0 for MS-DOS. The latter two are provided on the installation CDs for Windows NT Server version 3.5 or later.

It is recommended that you implement WINS for name resolution and browsing support. As an alternative, it is possible to have full domain browsing by using only LMHOSTS files on all computers, but this limits browsing to the local domain. Non-WINS clients still need the LMHOSTS file to browse across an IP internetwork, even if WINS has been implemented in the domain.

Note A client will participate in domain browsing only when that client is using a workgroup name that is equivalent to the domain name.

LMHOSTS File

NetBIOS name resolution is typically performed through broadcasts, which will resolve names only on the local network subnet. To resolve names of computers located on another network subnet, the LMHOSTS file (located in the directory *%Systemroot%*\System32\drivers\etc) must be configured. The LMHOSTS file must contain a NetBIOS name–to–IP address mapping for all computers that are not on the local network subnet.

To implement communication between network subnets and the domain master browser, the administrator must configure the LMHOSTS file with the NetBIOS names and IP addresses of all browsers. To ensure that the master browser for each network subnet can access the domain's PDC, the PDC for each domain must have an entry in the LMHOSTS file on each master browser. Also, each entry must have the tag #DOM, which designates the named computer as a domain controller.

The LMHOSTS file on the master browser of each network subnet needs to contain the following information:

- IP address and NetBIOS name of the domain master browser
- Domain name, preceded by the tags #PRE and #DOM, as in the following example:

  ```
  130.20.7.80 <Browser_name> #PRE #DOM:<domain_name>
  ```

To guarantee that the PDC can request the local browse list from the master browser of the network subnet, TCP/IP must cache the IP address of the client.

NetBIOS Name Service Broadcasts

Not all routers block all types of broadcast traffic. Some routers can be configured to forward specific types of broadcasts.

All broadcasts of NetBIOS over TCP/IP (NetBT) are sent to the UDP port number 137, which is defined as the port for NetBT Name Service. Routers normally block the forwarding of these frames because they are sent to the hardware and subnet broadcast addresses. However, some routers allow all broadcast frames sent to this particular UDP port—which is used only by NetBT—to be forwarded. As a result, to the browser it looks as if it is on one big network segment. All domains and workgroups on all network segments are seen by all computers.

Note This can be problematic since latency across the router or other connectivity problems can cause the wrong number of browsers to be elected (none or two or more.) Microsoft Support recommends that customers do not enable the forwarding of UDP port 137 and UDP port 138 broadcast packets.

Computers Running Windows for Workgroups, Windows 95, and Windows 98 as Master Browsers

The files Vserver.386 and Vredir.386 on the installation CDs of Windows NT Server versions 3.51 and 4.0 are different from the files of the same names on the Windows NT Server version 3.5 installation CD.

In Windows 2000, these two files have been modified so that computers running Windows for Workgroups 3.11b, Windows 95, or Windows 98 can be master browsers for a network. This modification enables a computer on a network with computers running one of those three operating systems to browse Windows 2000 and Windows NT domains on other networks.

As the master browser for the network, a computer running Windows for Workgroups 3.11b, Windows 95, or Windows 98 communicates with the PDC of the domain to obtain the browse list for the entire domain.

A master browser on a computer running Windows for Workgroups 3.11b, Windows 95, or Windows 98 functions as if a master browser running Windows 2000 were on the network. It contacts the PDC every 15 minutes to give it the local network's browse list and to obtain the domain-wide browse list.

For a computer running Windows for Workgroups 3.11b, Windows 95, or Windows 98 to be a master browser, the computer and the PDC for the domain must both be WINS clients. The master browser must also meet the following conditions:

- Be using TCP/IP
- Be using WINS for name resolution
- Be in a workgroup that has the same name as the domain

Registration and Propagation

The browser service relies on connectionless server broadcasts for host announcements which, by definition, are unreliable. When a server boots up, it immediately sends a host announcement datagram. Host announcement datagrams are then transmitted again after four and eight minutes. The announcement period then stabilizes, and a datagram is issued by default every 12 minutes.

Allowing for the loss of a few datagrams, it is reasonable to expect the server acting as the master browser to add the new server to its list within 12 minutes of the new server starting up.

Note After the initial broadcast announcements and host announcements, new entries to the browse list of the domain master browser and new entries from the domain master browser to master browsers are transmitted by way of sessions. Sessions are connection-oriented and are, therefore, deterministic and more reliable.

Within another 12 minutes, the master browser connects to the domain master browser to obtain the domain-wide list, and at the same time, the domain master browser connects to the master browser and learns of the new server. Master browsers on remote subnets connect to the domain master browser at 12-minute intervals and soon learn of the new server. Within 12 minutes of the remote master browser learning of the new server, all of the backup browsers connect to their master browser and learn of the new server. Thus, in a multi-subnet environment, the maximum amount of time it takes for all clients within the domain to see the new server is 72 minutes. On a fully functional network where broadcasts and network use are well within safe parameters, this period might be approximately half as long.

Figure I.9 shows host announcement propagation.

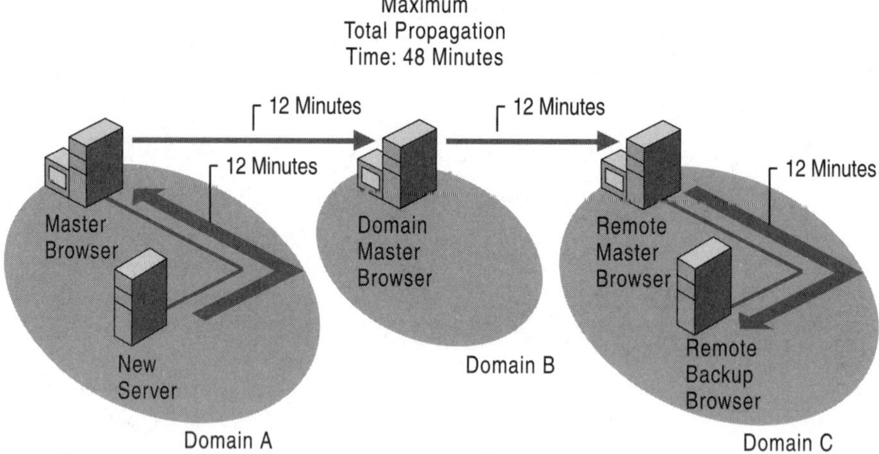

Figure I.9 Host Announcement Propagation

Removing computers from the browse list can take longer. To allow for lost datagrams, the master browser does not remove a server from its list until three announcement periods have passed. If the server is not shut down gracefully, or if network connectivity is lost, the server remains in the master browsers list for up to 36 minutes. After that time, the domain master browser is notified to remove the server name from its list. Within another 12 minutes, a master browser on a remote subnet obtains the domain-wide list from the domain master browser, and within an additional 12 minutes, each backup browser on the remote subnet is notified to remove the server name from its list. Removing a computer from the browse list can take as long as 72 minutes to complete. If the server is shut down gracefully, the browser sends a single HostAnnouncement indicating that it is no longer acting as a server. Upon receipt of this datagram, the master browser immediately removes the server from its local list. On a healthy network, where broadcasts and network use are well within safe parameters, the removal of a server's name can take less than half as long.

A browser's server roles are not statically defined, as they are with WINS or DNS, but are instead dynamically defined with periodic elections. As a result, determining the flow of communication used by the servers to provide the browse list to a specific client can be rather complex. The distributed design of the browser service relies on servers staying active on the network and, thereby, maintaining their browser roles consistently over time.

If a master browser is gracefully shut down, it forces an election and a new master browser is established promptly. The quickest conversion occurs when a backup browser, which already has a fully populated list, wins the election.

If a server, acting as the master browser for a network subnet is not shut down gracefully, or if the ForceElection datagram was lost, there may be a delay of several minutes before browsing is active on that subnet again. If a client cannot find a master browser by issuing the GetBackupListRequest datagram, it forces an election. If a client does not request a browse list, it can take up to 12 minutes before a backup browser discovers that there is no master browser. When it does, it forces an election, and within another 12 minutes, browsing is again enabled.

Testing Techniques

While there is no centralized method to determine if the browse lists of all servers on an IP internetwork are complete, there are testing techniques to determine if the servers on a particular subnet are represented in the browse list on a remote subnet. These tests can be applied to all subnets throughout the internetwork. The results of these tests can change due to servers changing roles when browser elections occur. Only if all the servers in a domain remain completely static for the duration of the tests can the results continue to have meaning.

Important The tests described here rely on the command-line tool Browstat.exe. For more information about Browstat.exe, see Windows 2000 Support Tools Help. For more information about installing and using the Windows 2000 Support Tools and Support Tools Help, see the file Sreadme.doc in directory \Support\Tools on the Windows 2000 operating system CD.

The output in the following examples are for TCP/IP only. As with most network problem diagnoses, in order to troubleshoot the browser service, the Administrator must have full knowledge of the network subnet boundaries and router configurations on the network.

Name resolution between all browsers is critical. Name resolution (using WINS, DNS, or LMHOSTS files) must be working properly throughout the network for browsing to operate correctly. You can waste a significant amount of time trying to track down browser problems that are really caused by faulty name resolution. For information about name resolution using WINS and LMHOSTS files, see “Windows Internet Name Service” in this book. For information about name resolution using DNS, see “Windows 2000 DNS” in this book.

Due to the time sensitivity of the browser service, wait 48 minutes after the server you are testing has booted before performing the following tests.

Monitoring Browsers

You can monitor the master and backup browsers within a workgroup or domain with the command-line tool Browstat.exe. In addition to gathering information on browser functionality, Browstat.exe has the ability to force an election and the ability to force a master browser to stop so that an election occurs. Running **Browstat.exe** displays the option list.

Figure I.10 shows the command options for Browstat.exe.

```
MS-DOS Prompt
8 x 12

C:\>browstat
Usage: BROWSTAT Command [Options | /HELP]
Where <Command> is one of:

 ELECT         ( EL) - Force election on remote domain
 GETBLIST      ( GB) - Get backup list for domain
 GETMASTER     ( GM) - Get remote Master Browser name (using NetBIOS)
 GETPDC        ( GP) - Get PDC name (using NetBIOS)
 LISTWFW       (WFW) - List WFW servers that are actually running browser
 STATS         (STS) - Dump browser statistics
 STATUS        (STA) - Display status about a domain
 TICKLE        (TIC) - Force remote master to stop
 VIEW          ( VW) - Remote NetServerEnum to a server or domain on transport

In server (or domain) list displays, the following flags are used:
     W=Workstation, S=Server, SQL=SQLServer, PDC=PrimaryDomainController,
     BDC=BackupDomainController, TS=TimeSource, AFP=AFPServer, NV=Novell,
     MBC=MemberServer, PQ=PrintServer, DL=DialinServer, XN=Xenix,
     NT=Windows NT, WFW=WindowsForWorkgroups, MFPN=MS Netware,
     SS=StandardServer, PBR=PotentialBrowser, BBR=BackupBrowser,
     MBR=MasterBrowser, DMB=DomainMasterBrowser, OSF=OSFServer, VMS=VMSServer,
     W95=Windows95, DFS=DistributedFileSystem

C:\>_
```

Figure I.10 Browstat.exe Command Option List

Tracing a Problem

The most frequent problem with the browser service is server names not replicating on browse lists across the network. The following example assumes that a client on one subnet cannot see a server located on another subnet in its browse list. By completing the sequence of commands described in the following steps, you can determine at which point a server missing from a browse list has stopped name replication. It is important that you understand the architecture of your network in order to perform a proper analysis.

For best results, run the following test procedures in the direction of propagation, starting from the subnet where the missing server is located and continuing through to the subnet where the client that cannot find the missing server is located.

Note If any of these steps prevent you from proceeding to the next step, verify that none of the browser servers that you have identified have a name conflict error. You can determine whether there is a name conflict by running the following command:

nbtstat –n

If there is a name conflict, Nbtstat lists it in its Status column. If the DomainName <1d> or <1e> is in conflict, stop and restart the browser service on the computer in question.

This command can be run remotely by using the command line option **–a**.

Figures included with the following procedures use placeholders for various parts of the commands you need to use. Table I.4 describes these placeholders.

Table I.4 Placeholder Description for Figures

Placeholders	Description
<Domain Name>	The name of the domain
<Protocol>	Identifies the transmission protocol. Format: netbt_tcpip
<Network Adapter ID>	Unique identifier for the computer's network adapter Format: *nn-nn-nn-nn-nn-nn* where *n* represents a hexadecimal integer
<Master Browser>	The name of the master browser
<Backup Browser>	The name of the backup browser
<DMB>	The name of the domain master browser. Because the domain master browser functionality resides on a PDC, the domain master browser is commonly referred to as "the PDC."
<Missing Server>	The server that is missing from the browse list

Figure I.11 shows the direction of propagation.

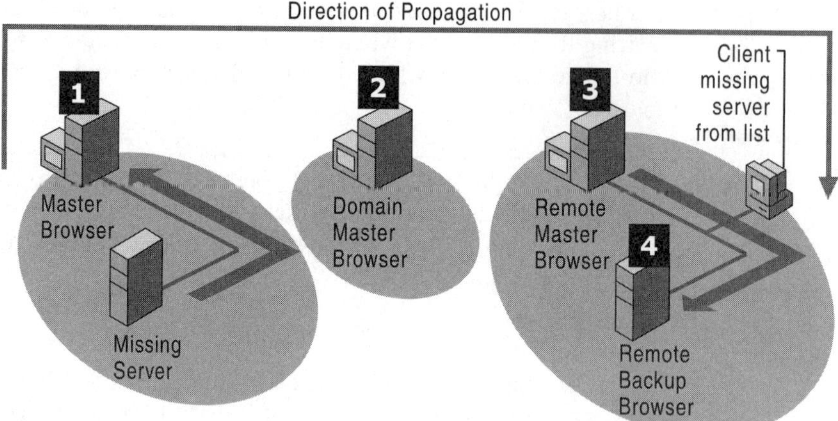

Figure I.11 Direction of Propagation

The following command enables you to determine which server is acting as the master browser on the subnet where the missing server resides.

▶ **To find the master browser on the subnet where the missing server resides**

- At the command prompt, on the subnet where the missing server resides, run the command **browstat status**

Running this command tells you which server is acting as the master browser on the subnet, but if the local master browser is slow to respond, you might receive this information from the domain master browser.

Note The results of this command gives you the address string **\Device**<*Protocol*>_<*Network Adapter ID*> of the interface of the computer where the command is run. This address string can then be used with other Browstat.exe commands.

▶ **To determine which server is acting as the master browser on the subnet**

- At the command prompt, on the subnet where the missing server resides, run **browstat status**.

Browstat.exe returns information similar to the example shown if Figure I.12.

```
Command Prompt
C:\WINNT>browstat status
Status for domain <DomainName> on transport \Device\<Protocol>_<NIC-ID>
  Browsing is active on domain.
  Master browser name is: <MasterBrowser>
       Master Browser is running build 1877
  1 backup servers retrieved from master<MasterBrowser>
       \\<BackupBrowser>
  There are 1132 servers in domain <DomainName> on transport \Device\<Protocol>_<NIC-ID>
1
  There are 8946 domains in domain <DomainName> on transport \Device\<Protocol>_<NIC-ID>
1

C:\WINNT>
```

Figure I.12 Results of Running Browstat.exe

While the command-line switch **status** causes **Browstat.exe** to run both a local DomainName[1D] and a remote DomainName[1B] query for the domain master browser, the switch **getmaster** only issues a DomainName[1D] query and returns the current master browser for that subnet.

▶ To query only the local subnet for a master browser

- At the command prompt, on the subnet where a missing server resides, run the following command:

  browstat getmaster \device<*Protocol*>_<*Network AdapterID*> <*Domain Name*>

Browstat.exe returns information similar to the example shown in Figure I.13.

```
Command Prompt
C:\>browstat getmaster \Device\<Protocol>_<NIC-ID> <DomainName>
Master Browser: <MasterBrowser>

C:\>
```

Figure I.13 Locating the Current Master Browser

Using the **getmaster** switch produces the most accurate results when determining the master browser, since this method only issues the request on the local subnet.

This step can also be performed remotely by using the browser service itself to tell you which computers are acting as the master browser on the subnet, but this requires both that the administrator know the names of all the servers on each of the subnets and that the distributed browser service be working properly.

▶ To remotely determine the list of master browsers on a domain

- At the command prompt, run the following command:

  browstat view \device<*Protocol*>_<*Network Adapter ID*> ****<*DMBname*> **| findstr /i mbr**

Browstat.exe returns information similar to the example shown in Figure I.14.

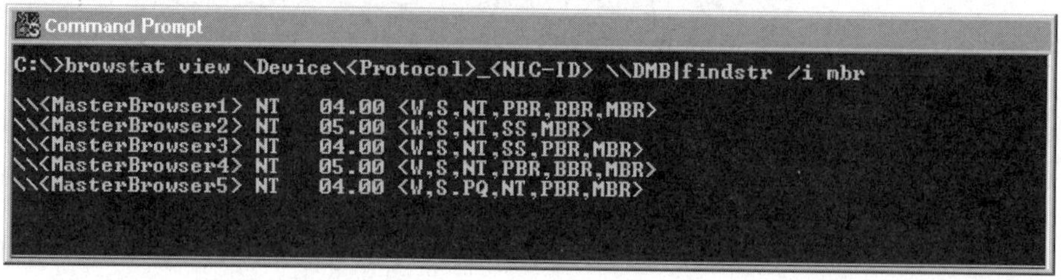

```
Command Prompt
C:\>browstat view \Device\<Protocol>_<NIC-ID> \\DMB|findstr /i mbr
\\<MasterBrowser1> NT   04.00 <W,S,NT,PBR,BBR,MBR>
\\<MasterBrowser2> NT   05.00 <W,S,NT,SS,MBR>
\\<MasterBrowser3> NT   04.00 <W,S,NT,SS,PBR,MBR>
\\<MasterBrowser4> NT   05.00 <W,S,NT,PBR,BBR,MBR>
\\<MasterBrowser5> NT   04.00 <W,S.PQ,NT,PBR,MBR>
```

Figure I.14 Locating Master Browsers on a Domain

The benefit of this method is that you can issue this command remotely. However, the results can be inconsistent, because this is a test that uses the browser service itself to troubleshoot a browser problem. Additionally, even if this piece of the browser does not have a problem, the list returned may be as much as 36 minutes old.

Because this remote method produces a complete master browser list, you need to determine which master browser is on the subnet containing the missing server's name.

If the master browser on the missing server's subnet cannot be found, you can force an election by stopping and starting the browser service on a domain controller or backup browser that is on the server's subnet. In a few minutes, run this test again to see if the missing browser reappears in the list. Alternately, you can force an election on the server's subnet from within the console of a server.

▶ To force election of a master browser from a server console

- At the command prompt, run the following command:

  browstat elect \device<*Protocol*>_<*Network Adapter ID*> <*Domain Name*>

Determine If the Master Browser Has the Missing Server's name In Its List

The master browser on the missing server's subnet is the first server in the communication chain that must contain the names of the servers on its subnet. If the missing server's name is not on its list, you have isolated the point of failure in the propagation sequence.

▶ To determine if the master browser has the missing server in its name list

- At the command prompt, run the following command:

  browstat view \device<*Protocol*>_<*Network Adapter ID*> \\<*Master Browser*> | **findstr /i** <*Missing Server*>

If the master browser has the server in its list, Browstat.exe returns information similar to the example shown in Figure I.15.

```
Command Prompt
C:\>browstat view \Device\<Protocol>_<NIC-ID> \\<MasterBrowser>|findstr /i <MissingServer>
\\<MissingServer> NT   04.00 <W,S,NT>
```

Figure I.15 Determining if a Master Browser has the Missing Server in its List

If the local master browser does not have the server's name, Browstat.exe displays no information, and you are returned to the command prompt. In this event, you can force all hosts on the subnet to announce themselves, and the missing server should reappear on the master browser's list.

▶ To force all hosts on a subnet to announce themselves

- At the command prompt on any computer on the subnet of the missing server, run the following command:

  browstat forceannounce \device<*Protocol*>_<*Network Adapter ID*> <*Domain Name*>

Remember that host announcements are broadcasts, and broadcasts can get lost. The missing server can also be rebooted to force it to send a HostAnnouncement datagram.

It might also be useful to verify that the missing server can map a network drive to the master browser to verify network connectivity.

After 12 minutes, check to see if the master browser has the missing server in its list. If it does, the name should propagate through the rest of the domain and resolve the problem.

▶ Determine if the domain master browser has received the server's name from the master browser.

- Follow the propagation chain from the master browser on the missing server's subnet to the domain master browser, and determine if the domain master browser has received the server's name from the master browser.

▶ **To determine if the domain master browser has the missing server in its name list**

- At the command prompt, run the following command:

  browstat view \device_<Protocol>__<Network Adapter ID>_ ****_<DMB>_ **| findstr /i** _<Missing Server>_

If the domain master browser has the server in its list, Browstat.exe returns information similar to the example shown in Figure I.16.

```
Command Prompt
C:\>browstat view \Device\<Protocol>_<NIC-ID> \\<DMB> |findstr /i <MissingServer>
\\<MissingServer> NT   04.00 <W,S,NT>
```

Figure I.16 Determining if the Domain Master Browser has Received the Server's Name From the Master Browser

If the domain master browser does not have the server's name, Browstat.exe displays no information, and you are returned to the command prompt with no further information.

If the server's name is missing in the domain master browser's list, its absence is most likely due to a problem with name resolution. In order for the domain master browser to obtain the list of servers from the master browser, the server's master browser must be able to resolve the DomainName[1B] name query so it can send the directed MasterAnnouncement datagram using UDP port 138 of the domain master browser. Also, in order for the domain master browser to respond to this announcement and obtain the server's list, it must be able to resolve the master browser's computer name from the master browser's IP address. Being able to resolve both IP addresses from computer names and computer names from IP addresses is critical.

▶ **To verify that the server's master browser can resolve the DomainName<1b> entry in the browse list**

- At the command prompt, run the following command:

  browstat getpdc \device<*Protocol*>_<*Network Adapter ID*> <*Domain Name*>

If the server's master browser can resolve the DomainName<1b> query, Browstat.exe returns information similar to the example shown in Figure I.17.

```
Command Prompt
C:\>browstat getpdc \device\<Protocol>_<NIC-ID> <DomainName>
PDC:<DMB>

C:\>
```

Figure I.17 Verifying That the Server's Master Browser can Resolve the DomainName<1b> entry

To verify that both the domain master browser and the master browser can resolve each other's computer name, map a network drive from the master browser to the domain master browser and from the domain master browser to the master browser. If you cannot map drives in either direction the problem might be a name resolution problem.

Find the Master Browser On the Network Subnet of the Client

This step follows the propagation chain by moving the testing process to the client's network subnet. Use the same procedures as listed in step 1, but run them on the client's network subnet.

Determine If the Master Browser On the Subnet of the Client Has the Name of the Missing Server

The master browser on the missing client's subnet receives its list from the domain master browser in exchange for its own name list. Determine if the client's master browser has the missing server in its name list.

▶ To determine if the master browser on the client's subnet has the missing server's name

- At the command prompt, run the following command:

  browstat view \device<*Protocol*>_<*Network Adapter ID*> \\\\<*Master Browser*> **| findstr /i** <*Missing Server*>

If the master browser has the server in its list, Browstat returns information similar to the example shown in Figure I.18.

```
Command Prompt
C:\>browstat view \Device\<Protocol>_<NIC-ID> \\<MasterBrowser> |findstr /i<MissingServer>
\\<MissingServer> NT    04.00 <W,S,NT,PBR>
C:\>
```

Figure I.18 Determining if a Client's Master Browser has Exchanged Lists with the Domain Master Browser

If the master browser does not have the missing server's name, it is probably due to a name resolution problem. You then need to verify that the master browser on the client's network subnet is able to resolve the DomainName<1b> name.

▶ To determine if the master browser can resolve the DomainName<1b> entry in the name list

- At the command prompt, run the following command:

  browstat getpdc \device<*Protocol*>_<*Network Adapter ID*> <*Domain Name*>

If the client's master browser can resolve the DomainName<1b> entry, Browstat returns information similar to the example shown in Figure I.19.

```
Command Prompt
C:\>browstat getpdc \device\<Protocol>_<NIC-ID> <DomainName>
PDC:<DMB>
C:\>
```

Figure I.19 Verifying That the Master Browser on the Client's Subnet is Able to Resolve the DomainName<1b> Name

Also, the master browser must be able to resolve the computer name of the domain master browser. To verify this, map a network drive from the master browser to the domain master browser, then map a network drive from the domain master browser to the master browser on the client's subnet.

If either of these tests fail, you need to correct the name resolution problems.

Determine the Backup Browsers On the Subnet of the Client

To reduce the processing demands on the master browser of a network subnet, client requests for a browse list are primarily directed to the backup browser.

▶ **To retrieve a list of backup browsers on the client's subnet remotely through the master browser**

- At the command prompt, run the following command:

  browstat view \device<*Protocol*>_<*Network Adapter ID*> \\\\<*MasterBrowser*> **0X40000000 | findstr /i bbr**

If there are backup browsers on the client's subnet, Browstat returns information similar to the example shown in Figure I.20.

```
Command Prompt
C:\>browstat view \device\<Protocol>_<NIC-ID> \\<MasterBrowser> 0x40000000 |findstr /i bbr

\\BackupBrowser1      NT   05.00 <W,S,NT,SS,BBR>
\\BackupBrowser2      NT   05.00 <W,S.NT,SS,BBR,02000000>
\\BackupBrowser3      NT   05.00 <W,S,NT,SS,BBR>
\\BackupBrowser4      NT   05.00 <W,S,NT,SS,BBR>
\\BackupBrowser5      NT   05.00 <W,S,NT,SS,BBR>
C:\>
```

Figure I.20 Retrieving a List of Backup Browsers

The hexadecimal number **0x40000000** is a bit mask that instructs the specified master browser that the list is to be generated from its local domain. These bit masks are defined in the Common Internet File System Browsing Protocol.

Determine If the Backup Browsers Have the Name of the Missing Server

For the clients on this subnet to retrieve a reliable browse list, every backup browser must be checked for the missing server's name.

▶ **To check the name lists of the backup browsers for the missing server's name**

- For each backup browser, at the command prompt, run the following command:

  browstat view \device<*Protocol*>_<*Network Adapter ID*>****<*Backup Browser*>**| findstr /i** <*Missing Server*>

Browstat returns information similar to the example shown in Figure I.21.

```
Command Prompt
C:\>browstat view \device\<Protocol>_<NIC-ID> \\<BackupBrowser> |findstr /i <MissingServer>
\\<MissingServer>       NT    05.00 <W,S,NT,SS,BBR>

C:\>
```

Figure I.21 Checking Backup Browsers for the Missing Server's Name

If a backup browser does not contain the missing server's name, verify that the backup browser can map a network drive to the master browser.

The backup browser role is the most dynamic browser role. Master browsers instruct potential browsers to become backup browsers. The number of backup browsers that are placed into service depends on the number of servers running on the master browser's network subnet.

If there is a browser election in progress, wait 12 minutes or more, and then attempt to find missing servers.

Other Considerations

If you experience continual or intermittent problems with browser functionality, you can choose to dedicate computers to the browsing process on each network subnet to maintain a consistent domain-wide list. If servers are frequently shut down and restarted, consider placing a BDC or a Windows NT member server on each network subnet with the value of the **IsDomainMaster** entry in the computer's registry set to **True**. This entry (data type Reg_SZ) appears in the following registry subkey:

\HKEY_LOCAL_MACHINE\SYSTEM\CurrentControlSet\Services\Browser \Parameters

Setting the value of IsDomainMaster to true gives the server preference during elections in becoming the master browser for the network subnet. For more information on **IsDomainMaster**, see "Specifying Browser Computers" earlier in this chapter.

Caution Do not use a registry editor to edit the registry directly unless you have no alternative. The registry editors bypass the standard safeguards provided by administrative tools. These safeguards prevent you from entering conflicting settings or settings that are likely to degrade performance or damage your system. Editing the registry directly can have serious, unexpected consequences that can prevent the system from starting and require that you reinstall Windows 2000. To configure or customize Windows 2000, use the programs in Microsoft Management Console (MMC) or Control Panel whenever possible.

The browser service is very sensitive to the configuration of routers on an IP internetwork. Since the browser roles are determined by broadcast elections, UDP broadcasts must not be forwarded. Unpredictable behavior can occur if UDP broadcast traffic is forwarded in one direction but not the other. This can cause a continuous cycle of elections.

Another step that can be taken to resolve browser problems is to capture network traffic with a protocol analyzer such as Microsoft Network Monitor. To directly view the communication between browsers, the browser service can be stopped and then restarted. Unfortunately, there is no guarantee that a browser assumes the same role that it had before the browser service is restarted. However, this method can be especially useful to verify the communication process when the master browser requests the domain-wide list from the domain master browser, and immediately following that when the domain master browser requests the local list from the master browser. After the browser service has started on the master browser, within a few minutes the full exchange takes place. Configure the protocol analyzer's capture buffer and frame size settings to allow for this quantity of traffic.

The size of the list of servers returned by the browser service prior to Windows NT 4.0 was limited to 64 kilobytes. When this size is exceeded, the user sees a truncated alphabetical list of servers. To avoid this behavior, all browsers must be running Windows NT version 4.0 or later.

Glossary

3

3DES An encrypting algorithm that processes each data block three times, using a unique key each time. 3DES is much more difficult to break than straight DES. It is the most secure of the DES combinations, and therefore slower in performance.

8

802.1p A protocol that supports the mapping of RSVP signals to Layer 2 signals using 802.1p priority markings to enable the prioritization of traffic across Layer 2 devices, such as switches, on a network segment. IEEE 802 refers to the Layer 2 technology used by LANs including the data-link layer and the media access control layer.

10

10BaseT An 802.3 Ethernet specification that defines how data is carried through category 3, 4, or 5 twisted pair cable.

A

A resource record See address (A) resource record.

access control The security mechanism in Windows NT and Windows 2000 that determines which objects a security principal can use and how the security principal can use them. See also authorization; security principal.

access control list (ACL) A list of security protections that apply to an entire object, a set of the object's properties, or an individual property of an object. There are two types of access control lists: discretionary and system. See also access control entry; discretionary access control list; security descriptor; system access control list.

ACL See access control list.

Active Directory The directory service included with Windows 2000 Server. It stores information about objects on a network and makes this information available to users and network administrators. Active Directory gives network users access to permitted resources anywhere on the network using a single logon process. It provides network administrators with an intuitive hierarchical view of the network and a single point of administration for all network objects. See also directory; directory service.

Active Directory Connector (ADC) A synchronization agent in Windows 2000 Server, Windows 2000 Advanced Server, and Windows 2000 Enterprise Server that provides an automated way of keeping directory information consistent between directories. Without the ADC, you would have to manually enter new data and updates in both directory services.

Active Directory data model A model derived from the LDAP data model. The directory holds objects that represent entities of various sorts, described by attributes. The objects and classes of objects that can be stored in the directory are defined in the schema. For each class of objects, the schema defines what attributes an instance of the class must have, what additional attributes it may have, and what class can be its parent. See also attribute; LDAP; schema.

Active Directory Installation wizard
A Windows 2000 Server tool that allows the following during Setup: installation of Active Directory, creation of trees in a forest, replication of an existing domain, installation of Kerberos authentication software, and promotion of servers to domain controllers.

Active Directory replication Synchronization of directory partition replicas between Windows 2000 domain controllers. Directory partition replicas are writable on each domain controller, except for Global Catalog replicas. Replication automatically copies the changes from a given directory partition replica to all other domain controllers that hold the same directory partition replica. More specifically, a server called the "destination" pulls changes from another server called the "source." See also directory partition; File Replication Service; multimaster replication; replication.

Active Directory Service Interfaces (ADSI)
A set of high-level programming interfaces that provide a single, consistent, open set of interfaces that enables Windows 2000, Windows NT, and Windows 9x client applications to access several network directory services, including Active Directory. ADSI provides the means for client applications of directory services to use one set of interfaces to communicate with any namespace that provides an ADSI implementation (provider)

Active Directory Users and Computers
An administrative tool designed to perform day-to-day Active Directory administration tasks. These tasks include creating, deleting, modifying, moving, and setting permissions on objects stored in the directory. These objects include organizational units, users, contacts, groups, computers, printers, and shared file objects. See also object; permissions.

Active Directory–integrated zone
A primary zone stored in Active Directory. See also zone.

ActiveX A set of technologies that enables software components to interact with one another in a networked environment, regardless of the language in which the components were created.

address (A) resource record A resource record used to map a DNS domain name to a host IP address on the network. See also resource record.

address class See internet address class.

address pool A group of IP addresses in a scope. Pooled addresses are then available for dynamic assignment by a DHCP server to DHCP clients.

Address Resolution Protocol (ARP)
In TCP/IP, a protocol that uses broadcast traffic on the local network to resolve a logically assigned IP address to its physical hardware or media access control layer address. In ATM the ARP protocol is used two different ways. For classical IP over ATM, ARP is used to resolve addresses to ATM hardware addresses. For ATM LAN emulation, ARP is used to resolve Ethernet/802.3 or Token Ring addresses to ATM hardware addresses. See also media access control; Transmission Control Protocol/Internet Protocol.

admission control The service used to administratively control network resources on shared network segments.

agent An application that runs on a Simple Network Management Protocol (SNMP) managed device. The agent application is the object of management activities. A computer running SNMP agent software is also sometimes referred to as an agent.

algorithm A rule or procedure for solving a problem. Internet Protocol security uses cryptographically-based algorithms to encrypt data.

alias An additional name that can be used to access a specific port.

all-ones subnet The subnet for which all the bits in the subnet portion of the subnetted network ID are set to 1.

all-subnets directed broadcast address The broadcast address designed to reach all subnets of a subnetted class-based IP network ID.

all-zeros subnet The subnet for which all the bits in the subnet portion of the subnetted network ID are set to 0.

allocate To mark media for use by an application. Media in the available state may be allocated.

AppleTalk The Apple Computer network architecture and network protocols. A network that has Macintosh clients and a computer running Windows 2000 Server with Services for Macintosh functions as an AppleTalk network.

application layer The layer at which applications access network services. This layer represents the services that directly support applications, such as software for file transfers, database access, and e-mail.

application programming interface (API) A set of routines that an application uses to request and carry out lower-level services performed by a computer's operating system. These routines usually carry out maintenance tasks such as managing files and displaying information.

ARP See Address Resolution Protocol.

ARP cache A table of IP addresses and their corresponding media access control address. There is a separate ARP cache for each interface.

Asynchronous Transfer Mode (ATM) A high-speed connection-oriented protocol used to transport many different types of network traffic.

attribute (object) In Active Directory, an attribute describes characteristics of an object and the type of information an object can hold. For each object class, the schema defines what attributes an instance of the class must have and what additional attributes it might have.

auditing To track the activities of users by recording selected types of events in the security log of a server or a workstation.

authentication The IPSec process that verifies the origin and integrity of a message by assuring the genuine identity of each computer. Without strong authentication, an unknown computer and any data it sends is suspect. IPSec provides multiple methods of authentication to ensure compatibility with earlier systems running earlier versions of Windows, non-Windows-based systems, and shared computers.

authentication In network access, the process by which the system validates the user's logon information. A user's name and password are compared against an authorized list. If the system detects a match, access is granted to the extent specified in the permissions list for that user. When a user logs on to an account on a computer running Windows 2000 Professional, the authentication is performed by the client. When a user logs on to an account on a Windows 2000 Server domain, authentication can be performed by any server of that domain. See also server; trust relationship.

Authentication Header (AH) A header that provides authentication, integrity, and anti-replay for the entire packet (both the IP header and the data payload carried in the packet).

authoritative In the Domain Name System (DNS), the use of zones by DNS servers to register and resolve a DNS domain name. When a DNS server is configured to host a zone, it is authoritative for names within that zone. DNS servers are granted authority based on information stored in the zone. See also zone.

authoritative restore In Backup, a type of restore operation on a Windows 2000 domain controller in which the objects in the restored directory are treated as authoritative, replacing (through replication) all existing copies of those objects. Authoritative restore is applicable only to replicated System State data such as Active Directory data and File Replication service data. The Ntdsutil.exe utility is used to perform an authoritative restore. See also nonauthoritative restore; System State.

Automatic Private IP Addressing (APIPA) A feature of Windows 2000 TCP/IP that automatically configures a unique IP address from the range 169.254.0.1 to 169.254.255.254 and a subnet mask of 255.255.0.0 when the TCP/IP protocol is configured for dynamic addressing and a Dynamic Host Configuration Protocol (DHCP) is not available.

autonomous system (AS) A group of routers exchanging routing information by using a common routing protocol.

availability A measure of the fault tolerance of a computer and its programs. A highly available computer runs 24 hours a day, 7 days a week. See also fault tolerance.

available bit rate (ABR) An ATM service type that supports available-bit-rate traffic, minimum guaranteed transmission rate, and peak data rates. ABR also allows bandwidth allocation depending on availability, and it uses flow control to communicate bandwidth availability to the end node.

available state A state in which media can be allocated for use by applications.

AXFR See full zone transfer.

B

backup domain controller In Windows NT Server 4.0 or earlier, a computer running Windows NT Server that receives a copy of the domain's directory database (which contains all account and security policy information for the domain). The copy synchronizes periodically with the master copy on the primary domain controller. A backup domain controller also authenticates user logon information and can be promoted to function as primary domain controllers as needed. Multiple backup domain controllers can exist in a domain. Windows NT 3.51 and 4.0 backup domain controllers can participate in a Windows 2000 domain when the domain is configured in mixed mode. See also mixed mode; primary domain controller.

bandwidth In analog communications, the difference between the highest and lowest frequencies in a given range. For example, a telephone line accommodates a bandwidth of 3,000 Hz, the difference between the lowest (300 Hz) and highest (3,300 Hz) frequencies it can carry. In digital communications, the rate at which information is sent expressed in bits per second (bps).

basic disk A physical disk that contains primary partitions or extended partitions with logical drives used by Windows 2000 and all versions of Windows NT. Basic disks can also contain volume, striped, mirror, or RAID-5 sets that were created using Windows NT 4.0 or earlier. As long as a compatible file format is used, basic disks can be accessed by MS-DOS, Windows 95, Windows 98, and all versions of Windows NT.

Berkeley Internet Name Domain (BIND) An implementation of the Domain Name System (DNS) written and ported to most available versions of the UNIX operating system. The Internet Software Consortium maintains the BIND software. See also BIND boot file.

binary A base-2 number system in which values are expressed as combinations of two digits, 0 and 1.

BIND See Berkeley Internet Name Domain.

BIND boot file Configuration file used by Domain Name System (DNS) servers running under versions of the Berkeley Internet Name Domain (BIND) software implementation. The BIND boot file is a text file, Named.boot, where individual lines in the file list boot directives used to start a service when the DNS server is started. By default, Microsoft DNS servers use DNS service parameters stored in the Windows 2000 registry, but allow the use of a BIND boot file as an alternative for reading boot configuration settings. See also BIND; registry boot.

bindery A database in Novell NetWare 2.*x* and 3.*x* that contains organizational and security information about users and groups.

binding A process by which software components and layers are linked together. When a network component is installed, the binding relationships and dependencies for the components are established. Binding allows components to communicate with each other.

bit The smallest unit of information handled by a computer. One bit expresses a 1 or a 0 in a binary numeral, or a true or false logical condition. A group of 8 bits makes up a byte, which can represent many types of information, such as a letter of the alphabet, a decimal digit, or other character. Bit is also called binary digit.

bit-wise logical AND A mathematical operation that compares equal numbers of bits using the logical AND comparison. If both bits being compared are 1, the result is 1. Otherwise, the result is 0.

black hole A condition of an internetwork where packets are lost without an indication of the error.

boot To start or reset a computer. When first turned on or reset, the computer executes the software that loads and starts the computer's operating system, which prepares it for use.

bootstrap protocol (BOOTP) A set of rules or standards to enable computers to connect with one another, used primarily on TCP/IP networks to configure workstations without using media disks. RFCs 951 and 1542 define this protocol. DHCP is a boot configuration protocol that uses this protocol.

boundary layer A common interface between two software components that is standardized to allow other components to connect to this interface.

branch A segment of a logical tree structure, representing a folder and any folders that it contains.

broadcast An address that is destined for all hosts on a particular network segment. See also broadcast network.

broadcast datagram An IP datagram sent to all hosts on the subnet. See also datagram.

broadcast message A network message sent from a single computer that is distributed to all other devices on the same segment of the network as the sending computer.

broadcast name resolution A mechanism defined in RFC 1001/1002 that uses broadcasts to resolve names to IP addresses through a process of registration, resolution, and name release. See also broadcast datagram; Request for Comments (RFC).

broadcast network A network that supports more than two attached nodes and has the ability to address a single physical message to all of the attached nodes (broadcast). Ethernet is an example of a broadcast network.

browse list Any list of items that can be browsed, such as a list of servers on a network, or a list of printers displayed in the Add Printer wizard.

browser A client tool for navigating and accessing information on the Internet or an intranet. In the context of Windows networking, "browser" can also mean the Computer Browser service, a service that maintains an up-to-date list of computers on a network or part of a network and provides the list to applications when requested. When a user attempts to connect to a resource in a domain, the domain's browser is contacted to provide a list of available resources.

buffer An area of memory used for intermediate storage of data until it can be used.

C

cache For DNS and WINS, a local information store of resource records for recently resolved names of remote hosts. Typically, the cache is built dynamically as the computer queries and resolves names; it helps optimize the time required to resolve queried names. See also cache file; naming service; resource record.

cache file A file used by the Domain Name System (DNS) server to preload its names cache when service is started. Also known as the "root hints" file because resource records stored in this file are used by the DNS service to help locate root servers that provide referral to authoritative servers for remote names. For Windows DNS servers, the cache file is named Cache.dns and is located in the %SystemRoot%\System32\Dns folder. See also authoritative; cache; systemroot.

cache hints file see cache file.

caching For DNS, the ability of DNS servers to store information about the domain namespace learned during the processing and resolution of name queries. In Windows 2000, caching is also available through the DNS client service (resolver) as a way for DNS clients to keep a cache of name information learned during recent queries. See also caching resolver.

caching resolver For Windows 2000, a client-side Domain Name System (DNS) name resolution service that performs caching of recently learned DNS domain name information. The caching resolver service provides system-wide access to DNS-aware programs for resource records obtained from DNS servers during the processing of name queries. Data placed in the cache is used for a limited period of time and aged according to the active Time To Live (TTL) value. You can set the TTL either individually for each resource record (RR) or default to the minimum TTL set in the start of authority RR for the zone. See also cache; caching; expire interval; minimum TTL; resolver; resource record; Time To Live (TTL).

caching-only server A DNS name server that only performs queries, caches the answers, and returns the results. It is not authoritative for any names and does not contain any zones. It only stores data that it has cached while resolving queries. See also caching; name server; zone.

Call Manager A software component that establishes, maintains and terminates a connection between two computers.

capture buffer The maximum size of the capture file. When the capture file reaches the maximum size, the oldest frames are removed to make room for newer frames (FIFO queue).

Challenge Handshake Authentication Protocol (CHAP)
A challenge-response authentication protocol for PPP connections documented in RFC 1994 that uses the industry-standard Message Digest 5 (MD5) one-way encryption scheme to hash the response to a challenge issued by the remote access server.

child domain For DNS and Active Directory, a domain located in the namespace tree directly beneath another domain name (its parent domain). For example, "example.reskit.com" is a child domain of the parent domain, "reskit.com." Child domain is also called subdomain. See also directory partition; domain; parent domain.

CIDR block A block of IP addresses allocated using Classless Interdomain Routing (CIDR).

cipher The method of forming a hidden message. The cipher is used to transform a readable message called plaintext (also sometimes called cleartext) into an unreadable, scrambled, or hidden message called ciphertext. Only someone with a secret decoding key can convert the ciphertext back into its original plaintext. See also ciphertext; plaintext; cryptography.

cipher block chaining (CBC) A process used to hide patterns of identical blocks of data within a packet. An Initialization Vector (an initial random number) is used as the first random block to encrypt and decrypt a block of data. Different random blocks are used in conjunction with the secret key to encrypt each block.

ciphertext Text that has been encrypted using an encryption key. Ciphertext is meaningless to anyone who does not have the decryption key. See also decryption; encryption; encryption key; plaintext.

Class A IP address A unicast IP address that ranges from 1.0.0.1 to 126.255.255.254. The first octet indicates the network, and the last three octets indicate the host on the network. See also Class B IP address; Class C IP address; IP address.

Class B IP address A unicast IP address that ranges from 128.0.0.1 to 191.255.255.254. The first two octets indicate the network, and the last two octets indicate the host on the network. See also Class A IP address; Class C IP address; IP address.

Class C IP address A unicast IP address that ranges from 192.0.0.1 to 223.255.255.254. The first three octets indicate the network, and the last octet indicates the host on the network. Network Load Balancing provides optional session support for Class C IP addresses (in addition to support for single IP addresses) to accommodate clients that make use of multiple proxy servers at the client site. See also Class A IP address; Class B IP address; IP address.

Class D IP address The Internet address class designed for IP multicast addresses. The value of the first octet for Class D IP addresses and networks varies from 224 to 239.

Class E IP address The Internet address class designed for experimental use only. The value of the first octet for Class E IP addresses and networks starts at 240.

class-based IP addressing or routing that is based on the internet address classes.

classical IP over ATM (CLIP) A proposed Internet standard, described in RFC 2225 and other related RFCs, that allows IP communication directly on the ATM layer. See also Asynchronous Transfer Mode; Internet Protocol.

Classless Interdomain Routing (CIDR) A method of allocating public IP addresses that is not based on the original internet address classes. Classless Interdomain Routing (CIDR) was developed to help prevent the depletion of public IP addresses and minimize the size of Internet routing tables.

cleartext See plaintext.

client Any computer or program connecting to, or requesting services of, another computer or program. See also server.

Client Service for NetWare A service included with Windows 2000 Professional that allows clients to make direct connections to resources on computers running NetWare 2.*x*, 3.*x*, 4.*x*, or 5.*x* server software.

CLIP See Classical IP over ATM.

cluster A group of independent computer systems known as nodes or hosts, that work together as a single system to ensure that mission-critical applications and resources remain available to clients. A server cluster is the type of cluster that the Cluster service implements. Network Load Balancing provides a software solution for clustering multiple computers running Windows 2000 Server that provides networked services over the Internet and private intranets.

Cluster service Clussvc.exe, the primary executable of the Windows Clustering component that creates a server cluster, controls all aspects of its operation, and manages the cluster database. Each node in a server cluster runs one instance of the Cluster service.

CNAME For Active Directory, an object's distinguished name presented with the root first and without the LDAP attribute tags (such as: CN= or DC=). The segments of the name are delimited with forward slashes (/). For example,CN=MyDocuments,OU=MyOU,DC=Microsoft,DC=Com is presented as microsoft.com/MyOU/MyDocuments in canonical form. For DNS, a type of resource record. See also distinguished name; Lightweight Directory Access Protocol (LDAP); canonical name (CNAME) resource record.

Common Internet File System (CIFS) A protocol and a corresponding API used by application programs to request higher level application services. CIFS was formerly known as SMB (Server Message Block).

compaction A process that reclaims space and defragments disks to improve WINS server performance.

Component Object Model (COM) An object-based programming model designed to promote software interoperability; it allows two or more applications or components to easily cooperate with one another, even if they were written by different vendors, at different times, in different programming languages, or if they are running on different computers running different operating systems. COM is the foundation technology upon which broader technologies can be built. Object linking and embedding (OLE) technology and ActiveX are both built on top of COM.

computer name A unique name of up to 15 uppercase characters that identifies a computer to the network. The name cannot be the same as any other computer or domain name in the network.

confidentiality A basic security function of cryptography. Confidentiality provides assurance that only authorized users can read or use confidential or secret information. Without confidentiality, anyone with network access can use readily available tools to eavesdrop on network traffic and intercept valuable proprietary information. For example, an Internet Protocol security service that ensures a message is disclosed only to intended recipients by encrypting the data. See also cryptography; authentication; integrity; nonrepudiation.

connection-oriented A type of network protocol that requires an end-to-end virtual connection between the sender and receiver before communicating across the network.

connection-oriented communication A network transmission service where a physical or logical link is negotiated and established prior to packet transmission.

Connection-Oriented NDIS (Co-NDIS) A Network Driver Interface Specification that supports connection-oriented data transfer.

connection-specific DNS suffix A DNS suffix specific to an adapter, rather than global to the computer. During the name resolution process, it is appended to an incomplete name. An incomplete name might be a single-label name or a multiple-label name that is not dot-terminated and can not be resolved as an fully qualified domain name. Connection-specific DNS suffixes can also be used for registration of the computer's name.

connection-specific domain name A domain name specific to an adapter, rather than global to the computer. See also domain name.

connectionless A network protocol in which a sender broadcasts traffic on the network to an intended receiver without first establishing a connection to the receiver.

constant bit rate (CBR) An ATM service type that supports constant bandwidth allocation. This service type is used for voice and video transmissions that require little or no cell loss and rigorous timing controls during transmission.

container object An object that can logically contain other objects. For example, a folder is a container object. See also noncontainer object; object.

convergence The process of stabilizing a system after changes occur in the network. For routing, if a route becomes unavailable, routers send update messages throughout the internetwork, reestablishing information about preferred routes. For Network Load Balancing, a process by which hosts exchange messages to determine a new, consistent state of the cluster and to elect the host with the highest host priority, known as the default host. During convergence, a new load distribution is determined for hosts that share the handling of network traffic for specific TCP or UDP ports. See also cluster; default host; host; User Datagram Protocol (UDP).

convergence time The time it takes for the internetwork to achieve convergence. See convergence.

CryptoAPI (CAPI) An application programming interface (API) that is provided as part of Windows 2000. CryptoAPI provides a set of functions that allow applications to encrypt or digitally sign data in a flexible manner while providing protection for private keys. Actual cryptographic operations are performed by independent modules known as cryptographic service providers (CSPs). See also cryptographic service provider; private key.

cryptographic key See encryption key.

cryptographic service provider (CSP) An independent software module that performs cryptography operations such as secret key exchange, digital signing of data, and public key authentication. Any Windows 2000 service or application can request cryptography operations from a CSP. See also CryptoAPI.

cryptography The art and science of information security. It provides four basic information security functions: confidentiality, integrity, authentication, and nonrepudiation. See also confidentiality; integrity; authentication; nonrepudiation.

custom subnet mask A subnet mask that is not based on the internet address classes. Custom subnet masks are commonly used when subnetting.

D

DARPA model The four-layer model that is used to describe the TCP/IP protocol suite. The four layers of the DoD (Department of Defense) Advanced Research Projects Agency (DARPA) model are: Application, Transport, Internet, and Network Interface.

Data Encryption Standard (DES) An encryption algorithm that uses a 56-bit key, and maps a 64-bit input block to a 64-bit output block. The key appears to be a 64-bit key, but one bit in each of the 8 bytes is used for odd parity, resulting in 56 bits of usable key.

Data Link Control (DLC) A protocol used primarily for IBM mainframe computers and printer connectivity.

data stream All information transferred over a network at any given time.

data-link layer A layer that packages raw bits from the physical layer into frames (logical, structured packets for data). This layer is responsible for transferring frames from one computer to another, without errors. After sending a frame, the data-link layer waits for an acknowledgment from the receiving computer.

datagram An unacknowledged packet of data sent to another network destination. The destination can be another device directly reachable on the local area network (LAN) or a remote destination reachable using routed delivery through a packet-switched network.

datagram socket A socket using the Windows Sockets API that provides a connectionless, unreliable flow of data.

DCOM See Distributed Component Object Model.

dead gateway detection The practice of the Windows 2000 TCP/IP protocol to change the default gateway to the next default gateway in the list of configured default gateways when a specific number of connections retransmit segments.

decryption The process of making encrypted data readable again by converting ciphertext to plaintext. See also ciphertext; encryption; plaintext.

default gateway A configuration item for the TCP/IP protocol that is the IP address of a directly reachable IP router. Configuring a default gateway creates a default route in the IP routing table.

default route A route that is used when no other routes for the destination are found in the routing table. For example, if a router or end system cannot find a network route or host route for the destination, the default route is used. The default route is used to simplify the configuration of end systems or routers. For IP routing tables, the default route is the route with the network destination of 0.0.0.0 and netmask of 0.0.0.0.

default subnet mask A subnet mask that is used on an Internet Address Class-based network. The subnet mask for Class A is 255.0.0.0. The subnet mask for Class B is 255.255.0.0. The subnet mask for Class C is 255.255.255.0.

default zone The zone to which all Macintosh clients on a network are assigned by default.

delegation The ability to assign responsibility for management and administration of a portion of the namespace to another user, group, or organization. For DNS, a name service record in the parent zone that lists the name server authoritative for the delegated zone. See also inheritance; parenting.

demand-dial connection A connection, typically using a circuit-switched wide area network link, that is initiated when data needs to be forwarded. The demand-dial connection is typically terminated when there is no traffic.

Dfs See Distributed file system.

DHCP See Dynamic Host Configuration Protocol.

DHCP Manager The primary tool used to manage DHCP servers. The DHCP Manager is a Microsoft Management Console (MMC) tool that is added to the Administrative Tools menu when the DHCP service is installed.

DHCP relay agent A routing component that transfers messages between DHCP clients and DHCP service located on separate networks.

DHCP service A service, that enables a computer to function as a DHCP server and configure DHCP-enabled clients on a network. DHCP runs on a server, enabling the automatic, centralized management of IP addresses and other TCP/IP configuration settings for a network's clients.

Diffie-Hellman (DH) algorithm An algorithm that predates Rivest-Shamir-Adleman (RSA) encryption and offers better performance. It is one of the oldest and most secure algorithms used for key exchange. The two parties publicly exchange keying information, which Windows 2000 additionally protects with hash function encryption. Neither party ever exchanges the actual key; however, after their exchange of keying material, each is able to generate the identical shared key. At no time is the actual key ever exchanged.

Diffie-Hellman Groups Groups used to determine the length of the base prime numbers (key material) for the DH exchange. The strength of any key derived from a DH exchange depends in part on the strength of the DH group the primes are based upon.

direct delivery The delivery of an IP packet by an IP node to the final destination on a directly attached network.

direct hosting A feature that allows Windows 2000 computers using Microsoft file and print sharing to communicate over IPX, bypassing the NetBIOS layer.

direct memory access (DMA) Memory access that does not involve the microprocessor. DMA is frequently used for data transfer directly between memory and a peripheral device, such as a disk drive.

directory An information source that contains information about computer files or other objects. In a file system, a directory stores information about files. In a distributed computing environment (such as a Windows 2000 domain), the directory stores information about objects such as printers, applications, databases, and users.

directory service Both the directory information source and the service that make the information available and usable. A directory service enables the user to find an object given any one of its attributes. See also Active Directory; directory.

directory tree A hierarchy of objects and containers in a directory that can be viewed graphically as an upside-down tree, with the root object at the top. Endpoints in the tree are usually single (leaf) objects, and nodes in the tree, or branches, are container objects. A tree shows how objects are connected in terms of the path from one object to another. A simple tree is a single container and its objects. A contiguous subtree is any unbroken path in the tree, including all the members of any container in that path.

discovery A process by which the Windows 2000 Net Logon service attempts to locate a domain controller running Windows 2000 Server in the trusted domain. Once a domain controller has been discovered, it is used for subsequent user account authentication. For SNMP, dynamic discovery is the identification of devices attached to an SNMP network.

discretionary access control list (DACL) The part of an object's security descriptor that grants or denies specific users and groups permission to access the object. Only the owner of an object can change permissions granted or denied in a DACL; thus access to the object is at the owner's discretion. See also access control entry; object; system access control list; security descriptor.

disjoint networks Networks that are separate and unaware of each other.

disk A physical data storage device attached to a computer. See also basic disk; dynamic disk.

distinguished name (DN) A name that uniquely identifies an object by using the relative distinguished name for the object, plus the names of container objects and domains that contain the object. The distinguished name identifies the object as well as its location in a tree. Every object in Active Directory has a distinguished name. An example of a distinguished name is CN=MyName,CN=Users,DC=Reskit,DC=Com.

This distinguished name identifies the "MyName" user object in the reskit.com domain.

Distributed Component Object Model (DCOM) The Microsoft Component Object Model (COM) specification that defines how components communicate over Windows-based networks. Use the DCOM Configuration tool to integrate client/server applications across multiple computers. DCOM can also be used to integrate robust Web browser applications. See also DCOM Configuration tool.

Distributed file system (Dfs) A Windows 2000 service consisting of software residing on network servers and clients that transparently links shared folders located on different file servers into a single namespace for improved load sharing and data availability.

distributed processing A computing environment that contains a client and a server. This structure allows the workload to be divided into parts yet appear as a single process.

DNS Notify A revision to the DNS standard (RFC 1996) that proposes that the master server for a zone notify certain secondary servers for that zone of changes, and the secondary servers can then check to see whether they need to initiate a zone transfer. See also master server; secondary server.

DNS resolver A component of the TCP/IP protocol that sends Domain Name System (DNS) queries to a DNS server.

DNS server A computer that runs DNS server programs containing name-to-IP address mappings, IP address-to-name mappings, information about the domain tree structure, and other information. DNS servers also attempt to resolve client queries.

DNS suffix For DNS, an optional parent domain name that can be appended to the end of a relative domain name that is used in a name query or host lookup. The DNS suffix can be used to complete an alternate fully qualified DNS domain name to be searched when the first attempt to query a name fails.

DNS suffix search list A list of domain names specified on the DNS tab of the Advanced TCP/IP Settings page. During name resolution, the resolver appends these domain names one by one to form a fully qualified domain name.

domain For Windows NT and Windows 2000, a networked set of computers running Windows NT or Windows 2000 that share a Security Accounts Manager (SAM) database and that can be administered as a group. A user with an account in a particular domain can log on to and access his or her account from any computer in the domain. A domain is a single security boundary of a Windows NT computer network. For DNS, a branch under a node in the DNS tree.

domain controller For a Windows NT Server or Windows 2000 Server domain, the server that authenticates domain logons and maintains the security policy and the security accounts master database for a domain. In a Windows 2000 domain, a computer running Windows 2000 Server that manages user access to a network, which includes logging on, authentication, and access to the directory and shared resources.

domain controller locator (Locator) An algorithm that runs in the context of the Netlogon service and that finds domain controllers on a Windows 2000 network. Locator can find domain controllers by using DNS names (for IP/DNS-compatible computers) or by using NetBIOS names (for computers that are running Windows 3.*x*, Windows for Workgroups, Windows NT 3.5 or later, Windows 95, or Windows 98, or it can be used on a network where IP transport is not available).

domain local group A Windows 2000 group only available in native mode domains and can contain members from anywhere in the forest, in trusted forests, or in a trusted pre-Windows 2000 domain. Domain local groups can only grant permissions to resources within the domain in which they exist. Typically, domain local groups are used to gather security principals from across the forest to control access to resources within the domain.

domain name In Windows 2000 and Active Directory, the name given by an administrator to a collection of networked computers that share a common directory. For DNS, domain names are specific node names in the DNS namespace tree. DNS domain names use singular node names, known as "labels," joined together by periods (.) that indicate each node level in the namespace. See also Domain Name System (DNS); namespace.

domain name label Each part of a full DNS domain name that represents a node in the domain namespace tree. Domain names are made up of a sequence of labels, such as the three labels ("noam," "reskit," and "com") that make up the DNS domain name "noam.reskit.com." Each label used in a DNS name must have 63 or fewer characters.

Domain Name System (DNS) A hierarchical naming system used for locating domain names on the Internet and on private TCP/IP networks. DNS provides a service for mapping DNS domain names to IP addresses, and vice versa. This allows users, computers, and applications to query the DNS to specify remote systems by fully qualified domain names rather than by IP addresses. See also domain; Ping.

domain namespace The database structure used by the Domain Name System (DNS). See also Domain Name System (DNS).

domain tree In DNS, the inverted hierarchical tree structure that is used to index domain names. Domain trees are similar in purpose and concept to the directory trees used by computer filing systems for disk storage. See also domain name; namespace.

dotted decimal notation The format of an IP address after it is divided along byte boundaries, converted to decimal (Base 10 numbering system), and separated by periods (.). (Example: 192.168.3.24)

duplex A system capable of transmitting information in both directions over a communications channel. See also full-duplex; half-duplex.

DWORD A data type composed of hexadecimal data with a maximum allotted space of 4 bytes.

Dynamic Host Configuration Protocol (DHCP) A networking protocol that provides safe, reliable, and simple TCP/IP network configuration and offers dynamic configuration of Internet Protocol (IP) addresses for computers. DHCP ensures that address conflicts do not occur and helps conserve the use of IP addresses through centralized management of address allocation.

dynamic ports Ports in the range from 49151 - 65535 that are issued on a randomly numbered basis.

dynamic re-keying A method used by IPSec policy to control how often a new key is generated during the communication. The communication is sent in blocks, and each block of data is secured with a different key. This prevents an attacker who has obtained part of a communication and the corresponding session keys from obtaining the rest of the message.

dynamic router A router with dynamically configured routing tables. Dynamic routing consists of routing tables that are built and maintained automatically through an ongoing communication between routers. This communication is facilitated by a routing protocol. Except for their initial configuration, dynamic routers require little ongoing maintenance, and therefore can scale to larger internetworks.

dynamic routing The use of routing protocols to update routing tables. Dynamic routing responds to changes in the internetwork topology.

dynamic update An updated specification to the Domain Name System (DNS) standard that permits hosts that store name information in DNS to dynamically register and update their records in zones maintained by DNS servers that can accept and process dynamic update messages.

dynamic-link library (DLL) A feature of the Microsoft Windows family of operating systems and the OS/2 operating system. DLLs allow executable routines, generally serving a specific function or set of functions, to be stored separately as files with .dll extensions, and to be loaded only when needed by the program that calls them.

E

election datagram A specific datagram generated by computers on Microsoft networks to initiate elections in the browser system.

emulator modules Software components that allow applications written to NetBIOS and Windows Sockets interfaces to connect to the Transport Driver Interface.

encapsulating security payload (ESP) An IPSec protocol that provides confidentiality, in addition to authentication, integrity, and anti-replay. ESP can be used alone, in combination with AH, or nested with the Layer Two Tunneling Protocol (L2TP). ESP does not normally sign the entire packet unless it is being tunneled—ordinarily, just the data payload is protected, not the IP header.

encapsulation See tunneling.

encryption The process of disguising a message or data in such a way as to hide its substance.

encryption key A bit string that is used in conjunction with an encryption algorithm to encrypt and decrypt data. See also public key; private key; symmetric key.

end system A network device without the ability to forward packets between portions of a network. See also host.

entry The lowest level element in the registry. Entries appear in the right pane of a Registry Editor window. Each entry consists of an entry name, its data type and its value.

They store the actual configuration data that affects the operating system and programs that run on the system. As such, they are different from registry keys and subkeys, which are containers.

ephemeral ports Ports in the range from 1024 - 5000.

error detection A technique for detecting when data is lost during transmission. This allows the software to recover lost data by requesting that the transmitting computer retransmit the data.

event Any significant occurrence in the system or an application that requires users to be notified or an entry to be added to a log.

Event Log The file in which event logging entries are recorded.

event logging The Windows 2000 process of recording an audit entry in the audit trail whenever certain events occur, such as services starting and stopping or users logging on and off and accessing resources. You can use Event Viewer to review Services for Macintosh events as well as Windows 2000 events.

everyone category In the Macintosh environment, one of the user categories to which permissions for a folder are assigned. Permissions granted to everyone apply to all users who use the server, including guests.

expire interval For DNS, the number of seconds that DNS servers operating as secondary masters for a zone use to determine if zone data should be expired when the zone is not refreshed and renewed. See also zone.

export In NFS, to make a file system available by a server to a client for mounting.

external namespace A public namespace that anyone on the Internet can view.

extinction interval A WINS database value that establishes how long entries linger in the released and tombstoned states.

F

fast zone transfer A form of zone transfer in which more than one resource record can be sent in one message.

fault tolerance The assurance of data integrity when hardware failures occur. On the Windows NT and Windows 2000 platforms, fault tolerance is provided by the Ftdisk.sys driver.

Fiber Distributed Data Interface (FDDI) A type of network media designed to be used with fiber-optic cabling. See also LocalTalk; Token Ring.

file server A server that provides organization-wide access to files, programs, and applications.

File Transfer Protocol (FTP) A protocol that defines how to transfer files from one computer to another over the Internet. FTP is also a client/server application that moves files using this protocol.

filter In IPSec, a rule that provides the ability to trigger security negotiations for a communication based on the source, destination, and type of IP traffic.

Filter Actions An IPSec negotiation policy that sets the security requirements for the IPSec SA, or Phase 2 of the communication. These requirements are specified in a list of security methods contained in the filter action, including which algorithms, security protocols, and key properties are to be used.

filters In IP and IPX packet filtering, a series of definitions that indicate to the router the type of traffic allowed or disallowed on each interface.

firewall A combination of hardware and software that provides a security system, usually to prevent unauthorized access from outside to an internal network or intranet. A firewall prevents direct communication between network and external computers by routing communication through a proxy server outside of the network. The proxy server determines whether it is safe to let a file pass through to the network. A firewall is also called a security-edge gateway.

flat namespace A namespace that is unstructured and cannot be partitioned, such as the network basic input/output system (NetBIOS) namespace. In a flat namespace, every object must have a unique name. See also namespace; hierarchical namespace; noncontiguous namespace.

flow A stream of data sent or received by a host. Also called network traffic.

Flowspec A traffic parameter that specifies the type of QoS requested. Flowspec is used to set parameters in the QoS packet scheduler.

forest A collection of one or more Windows 2000 Active Directory trees, organized as peers and connected by two-way transitive trust relationships between the root domains of each tree. All trees in a forest share a common schema, configuration, and Global Catalog. When a forest contains multiple trees, the trees do not form a contiguous namespace.

forward lookup In DNS, a query process in which the friendly DNS domain name of a host computer is searched to find its IP address. In DNS Manager, forward lookup zones are based on DNS domain names and typically hold host address (A) resource records.

forwarder A DNS server designated by other internal DNS servers to be used to forward queries for resolving external or offsite DNS domain names.

forwarding IP address The IP address to which a packet is being forwarded based on the destination IP address and the contents of the IP routing table.

fragment offset A field in the Internet Protocol (IP) header that is used to reconstruct the fragmented IP payload. The fragment offset indicates the position of the fragment relative to the original IP payload.

fragmentation and reassembly The process used by the Internet Protocol (IP) to fragment an IP datagram into smaller packets that are reassembled by the destination host.

frame In synchronous communication, a package of information transmitted as a single unit from one device to another. Frame is a term most often used with Ethernet networks. A frame is similar to the packet used on other networks. See also packet.

full computer name A type of FQDN. The fully qualified domain name is also known as the full computer name. The same computer could be identified by more than one FQDN. However, only the FQDN that is a concatenation of the host name and the primary DNS suffix is a full computer name.

full zone transfer (AXFR) The standard query type supported by all DNS servers to update and synchronize zone data when the zone is changed. When a DNS query is made using AXFR as the specified query type, the entire zone is transferred as the response. See also incremental zone transfer (IXFR); zone; zone transfer.

full-duplex A system capable of simultaneously transmitting information in both directions over a communications channel. See also duplex; half-duplex.

fully qualified domain name (FQDN) A DNS domain name that has been stated unambiguously so as to indicate with absolute certainty its location in the domain namespace tree. For example, client1.reskit.com. The FQDN is also known as a full computer name.

G

gateway A device connected to multiple physical TCP/IP networks, capable of routing or delivering IP packets between them. A gateway translates between different transport protocols or data formats (for example, IPX and IP) and is generally added to a network primarily for its translation ability. See also IP address; IP router.

Gateway Service for NetWare A service that creates a gateway in which Microsoft clients can access NetWare core protocol networks, such as NetWare file and print services, through a Windows 2000 server.

generic Quality of Service A method by which a TCP/IP network can offer Quality of Service guarantees for multimedia applications. Generic Quality of Service allocates different bandwidths for each connection on an as-needed basis.

geographical domain A type of domain named by using the 2-character region/country codes established under (ISO) 3166 of the International Organization of Standardization.

globally unique identifier (GUID) A 16-byte value generated from the unique identifier on a device, the current date and time, and a sequence number. A GUID is used to identify a particular device or component.

glue record A record indicating the IP address of a server when delegating authority for a zone from one name server to another.

gratuitous ARP An ARP Request frame sent by a host for the host's own IP address when the TCP/IP protocol obtains addressing information. Gratuitous ARPs are used to check for duplicate IP addresses on the subnet.

group A collection of users, computers, contacts, and other groups. Groups can be used as security or as e-mail distribution collections. Distribution groups are used only for e-mail. Security groups are used both to grant access to resources and as e-mail distribution lists. In a server cluster, a group is a collection of resources, and the basic unit of failover. See also domain local group; global group; native mode; universal group.

group address An IP multicast address in the Class D range of 224.0.0.0 to 239.255.255.255 as defined by setting the first four high order bits of the IP address to 1110.

group name A unique name identifying a local group or a global group to Windows 2000. A group's name cannot be identical to any other group name or user name in its own domain or computer. See also global group; local group.

Group Policy An administrator's tool for defining and controlling how programs, network resources, and the operating system operate for users and computers in an organization. In an Active Directory environment, Group Policy is applied to users or computers on the basis of their membership in sites, domains, or organizational units.

Group Policy object A collection of Group Policy settings. Group Policy objects are the documents created by the Group Policy snap-in. Group Policy objects are stored at the domain level, and they affect users and computers contained in sites, domains, and organizational units. Each Windows 2000-based computer has exactly one group of settings stored locally, called the local Group Policy object.

H

h-node A NetBIOS node type that uses a hybrid of b-node and p-node to register and resolve NetBIOS names to IP addresses. An h-node computer uses a server query first and reverts to broadcasts only if direct queries fail. Windows 2000-based computers are h-node by default.

half-duplex A system capable of transmitting information in only one direction at a time over a communications channel. See also duplex; full-duplex.

Hardware Compatibility List (HCL)
A list of the devices supported by Windows 2000, available from the Microsoft Web site.

hash See message digest; message digest function.

hash function See message digest; message digest function.

hash message authentication code (HMAC)
A mechanism for ensuring the data integrity of online communications that uses cryptographic message digest functions to provide online integrity checking of data that is transmitted. HMAC can be used with any iterative cryptographic message digest function, for example, MD5, SHA-1, in combination with a secret shared key. The cryptographic strength of HMAC depends on the properties of the underlying message digest function. HMAC is also called Hash-based Message Authentication Code algorithm. See also message digest; message digest function.

hash message authentication code-secure hash algorithm (HMAC-SHA)
An algorithm developed by the National Institute of Standards and Technology as described in FIPS PUB 180-1. The SHA process is closely modeled after MD5. SHA uses 79, 32-bit constants during the computation, which results in a 160-bit key that is used for integrity check.

heartbeat In a server cluster or Network Load Balancing cluster, a periodic message sent between nodes to detect system failure of any node.

hexadecimal A base-16 number system whose numbers are represented by the digits 0 through 9 and the letters A (equivalent to decimal 10) through F (equivalent to decimal 15).

hierarchical namespace A namespace, such as the DNS namespace or Active Directory namespace, that is hierarchically structured and provides rules that allow the namespace to be partitioned. See also namespace; flat namespace; noncontiguous namespace.

high availability The ability to keep an application or service operational and usable by clients most of the time.

hop count The value in the Transport Control field that indicates the number of IPX routers that have processed the IPX packet.

host A Windows 2000 computer that runs a server program or service used by network or remote clients. For Network Load Balancing, a cluster consists of multiple hosts connected over a local area network.

host address See host ID.

host group The set of hosts listening for IP multicast traffic sent to a specific multicast group address.

host ID A number used to identify an interface on a physical network bounded by routers. The host ID should be unique to the network.

host name The name of a computer on a network. In the Windows 2000 Server Resource Kit, host name is used to refer to the first label of a fully qualified domain name. See also Hosts file.

host route A route to a specific internetwork address (network ID and host ID). Instead of making a routing decision based on just the network ID, the routing decision is based on the combination of network ID and host ID. Host routes allow intelligent routing decisions to be made for each internetwork address. Host routes are typically used to create custom routes to control or optimize specific types of internetwork traffic. For IP routing tables, a host route has a netmask of 255.255.255.255.

Hosts See Hosts file.

Hosts file A local text file in the same format as the 4.3 Berkeley Software Distribution (BSD) UNIX/etc/hosts file. This file maps host names to IP addresses. In Windows 2000, this file is stored in the \%SystemRoot%\System32\Drivers\Etc folder. See also systemroot.

HTTP See Hypertext Transfer Protocol.

hub A network-enabled device joining communication lines at a central location, providing a common connection to all devices on the network.

hub-and-spoke A WINS server configuration that uses a central "hub" as a point of contact for many outlying WINS server "spokes" to improve convergence time.

Hypertext Transfer Protocol (HTTP)
The protocol used to transfer information on the World Wide Web. An HTTP address (one kind of Uniform Resource Locator [URL]) takes the form: http://www.microsoft.com.

I

ICMP router discovery See router discovery.

illegal address A duplicate address that conflicts with a public IP address already assigned by the InterNIC to other organizations.

impersonation A circumstance that occurs when Windows NT or Windows 2000 allows one process to take on the security attributes of another.

in-addr.arpa domain A special top-level DNS domain reserved for reverse mapping of IP addresses to DNS host names. See also reverse lookup; top-level domains.

incremental zone transfer (IXFR) An alternate query type that can be used by some DNS servers to update and synchronize zone data when a zone is changed. When incremental zone transfer is supported between DNS servers, servers can keep track of and transfer only those incremental resource record changes between each version of the zone. See also full zone transfer (AXFR); zone; zone transfer.

independent software vendors (ISVs)
A third-party software developer; an individual or an organization that independently creates computer software.

indirect delivery The delivery of an IP packet by an IP node to an intermediate router.

infrared (IR) Light that is beyond red in the color spectrum. While the light is not visible to the human eye, infrared transmitters and receivers can send and receive infrared signals. See also Infrared Data Association; infrared device; infrared port.

Infrared Data Association (IrDA) A networking protocol used to transmit data created by infrared devices. Infrared Data Association is also the name of the industry organization of computer, component, and telecommunications vendors who establish the standards for infrared communication between computers and peripheral devices, such as printers. See also infrared; infrared device; infrared port.

infrared device A computer, or a computer peripheral such as a printer, that can communicate using infrared light. See also infrared.

infrared port An optical port on a computer that enables communication with other computers or devices by using infrared light, without cables. Infrared ports can be found on some portable computers, printers, and cameras. See also infrared device.

input/output (I/O) port A channel through which data is transferred between a device and the microprocessor. The port appears to the microprocessor as one or more memory addresses that it can use to send or receive data.

Integrated Services Digital Network (ISDN) A type of phone line used to enhance WAN speeds. ISDN lines can transmit at speeds of 64 or 128 kilobits per second, as opposed to standard phone lines, which typically transmit at 28.8 kilobits per second. An ISDN line must be installed by the phone company at both the server site and the remote site. See also wide area network (WAN).

Integrated Services over slow links (ISSLOW) A queuing mechanism used to optimize slow (low capacity) network interfaces by reducing latency. In particular, it is designed for interfaces that forward traffic to modem links, ISDN B-channels, and sub-T1 links.

integrity A basic security function of cryptography. Integrity provides verification that the original contents of information have not been altered or corrupted. Without integrity, someone might alter information or the information might become corrupted, but the alteration can go undetected. For example, an Internet Protocol security property that protects data from unauthorized modification in transit, ensuring that the data received is exactly the same as the data sent. Hash functions sign each packet with a cryptographic checksum, which the receiving computer checks before opening the packet. If the packet-and therefore signature-has changed, the packet is discarded. See also cryptography; authentication; confidentiality; nonrepudiation.

intermediate system A network device with the ability to forward packets between portions of a network. Bridges, switches, and routers are examples of intermediate systems.

internet Two or more network segments connected by routers. Another term for internetwork. With TCP/IP, an internet can be created by connecting two or more IP networks to a multihomed computer running either Windows 2000 Server or Windows 2000 Professional. IP forwarding must be enabled to route between attached IP network segments.

Internet A worldwide public TCP/IP internetwork consisting of thousands of networks, connecting research facilities, universities, libraries, and private companies.

Internet address class The original Internet design of dividing the IP address space into defined classes to accommodate different sizes of networks. Address classes are no longer used on the modern Internet. See Class A IP address, Class B IP address, and Class C IP address.

Internet Assigned Numbers Authority (IANA) An organization that delegates IP addresses and their allocation to organizations such as the InterNIC.

Internet Control Message Protocol (ICMP) A required maintenance protocol in the TCP/IP suite that reports errors and allows simple connectivity. ICMP is used by the Ping tool to perform TCP/IP troubleshooting.

Internet Engineering Task Force (IETF)
An open community of network designers, operators, vendors, and researchers concerned with the evolution of Internet architecture and the smooth operation of the Internet. Technical work is performed by working groups organized by topic areas (such as routing, transport, and security) and through mailing lists. Internet standards are developed in IETF Requests for Comments (RFCs), which are a series of notes that discuss many aspects of computing and computer communication, focusing on networking protocols, programs, and concepts.

Internet Group Management Protocol (IGMP)
A protocol in the TCP/IP protocol suite that is responsible for the management of IP multicast group membership.

Internet Information Services (IIS)
Software services that support Web site creation, configuration, and management, along with other Internet functions. Internet Information Services include Network News Transfer Protocol (NNTP), File Transfer Protocol (FTP), and Simple Mail Transfer Protocol (SMTP). See also File Transfer Protocol (FTP); Network News Transfer Protocol (NNTP); Simple Mail Transfer Protocol (SMTP).

internet layer A layer of the TCP/IP DARPA model that is responsible for addressing, packaging, and routing functions.

Internet Protocol (IP) A routable protocol in the TCP/IP protocol suite that is responsible for IP addressing, routing, and the fragmentation and reassembly of IP packets.

Internet Protocol Control Protocol (IPCP)
The Network Control Protocol for IP-based PPP connections. IPCP negotiates IP-based parameters to dynamically configure a TCP/IP-based PPP peer across a point-to-point link. IPCP is documented in RFCs 1332 and 1877.

Internet Protocol security (IPSec)
A set of industry-standard, cryptography-based protection services and protocols. IPSec protects all protocols in the TCP/IP protocol suite and Internet communications using L2TP. See also Layer Two Tunneling Protocol (L2TP).

Internet Protocol security policy Enforces Internet Protocol security by specifying which security services are used to protect data, and for whom Internet Protocol security Management is used to administer Internet Protocol security policies. See also Internet Protocol Security.

internet router A device that connects networks and directs network information to other networks, usually choosing the most efficient route through other routers. See also router.

internetwork At least two network segments connected using routers.

Internetwork Packet Exchange (IPX)
A network protocol native to NetWare that controls addressing and routing of packets within and between LANs. IPX does not guarantee that a message will be complete (no lost packets). See also Internetwork Packet Exchange/Sequenced Packet Exchange (IPX/SPX).

Internetwork Packet Exchange Control Protocol (IPXCP)
The Network Control Protocol for IPX-based PPP connections. IPXCP negotiates IPX-based parameters to dynamically configure an IPX-based PPP peer across a point-to-point link. IPXCP is documented in RFC 1552.

Internetwork Packet Exchange/Sequenced Packet Exchange (IPX/SPX)
Transport protocols used in Novell NetWare and other networks.

interprocess communication (IPC) A series of components used by both the programs and processes of networked computers. IPC allows client and server computers to communicate with other computers.

interrupt request (IRQ) lines Hardware lines over which devices can send signals to get the attention of the processor when the device is ready to accept or send information. Interrupt request (IRQ) lines are numbered from 0 to 15. Each device must have a unique IRQ line.

intranet A network within an organization that uses Internet technologies and protocols, but is available only to certain people, such as employees of a company. An intranet is also called a private network.

IP See Internet Protocol.

IP address A 32-bit address used to identify a node on an IP internetwork. Each node on the IP internetwork must be assigned a unique IP address, which is made up of the network ID, plus a unique host ID. This address is typically represented with the decimal value of each octet separated by a period (for example, 192.168.7.27). In Windows 2000, the IP address can be configured manually or dynamically through DHCP. See also Dynamic Host Configuration Protocol (DHCP); node.

IP Filter List A list of filters. Each describes a particular subset of network traffic to be secured, both for inbound and outbound traffic.

IP multicast group See host group.

IP router A system connected to multiple physical TCP/IP networks that can route or deliver IP packets between the networks. See also packet; router; routing; Transmission Control Protocol/Internet Protocol.

IPSec driver A driver that uses the IP Filter List from the active IPSec policy to watch for outbound IP packets that must be secured and inbound IP packets that need to be verified and decrypted.

IPSec Policy Agent Service A Windows 2000 mechanism that retrieves the IPSec policy information and passes it to the other IPSec mechanisms that require the information in order to perform security services.

iteration A method of resolving a name request from a client. When using iteration, the DNS server might not provide the requested name. If the DNS server is authoritative for the requested name, it returns the name. If not, the server returns a list of the NS and A resource records of servers with names similar to the name requested, but it does not attempt to contact those servers. The client can continue the name search by contacting the recommended servers. The alternative method is recursive resolution.

iterative name query See iterative query.

iterative query A query made to a DNS server in which the requester instructs the server that it expects the best answer the server can provide without seeking further help from other DNS servers to assist in answering the query. Iterative queries are also called non-recursive queries. See also iteration; recursion; referral.

IXFR See incremental zone transfer.

K

Kerberos authentication protocol
An authentication mechanism used to verify user or host identity. The Kerberos v5 authentication protocol is the default authentication service for Windows 2000. Internet Protocol security and the QoS Admission Control Service use the Kerberos protocol for authentication. See also Internet Protocol security (IPSec); NTLM authentication protocol; QoS Admission Control Service.

kernel The core of layered architecture that manages the most basic operations of the operating system and the computer's processor for Windows NT and Windows 2000. The kernel schedules different blocks of executing code, called threads, for the processor to keep it as busy as possible and coordinates multiple processors to optimize performance. The kernel also synchronizes activities among Executive-level subcomponents, such as I/O Manager and Process Manager, and handles hardware exceptions and other hardware-dependent functions. The kernel works closely with the hardware abstraction layer.

kernel mode A highly privileged mode of operation where program code has direct access to all memory, including the address spaces of all user-mode processes and applications, and to hardware. Kernel mode is also known as supervisor mode, protected mode, or Ring 0.

key A secret code or number required to read, modify, or verify secured data. Keys are used in conjunction with algorithms to secure data. Windows 2000 automatically handles key generation. For the registry, a key is an entry in the registry that can contain both subkeys and entries. In the registry structure, keys are analogous to folders, and entries are analogous to files. In the Registry Editor window, a key appears as a file folder in the left pane. In an answer file, keys are character strings that specify parameters from which Setup obtains the needed data for unattended installation of the operating system.

Key Distribution Center (KDC) A network service that supplies session tickets and temporary session keys used in the Kerberos authentication protocol. In Windows 2000, the KDC runs as a privileged process on all domain controllers. The KDC uses Active Directory to manage sensitive account information such as passwords for user accounts. See also Kerberos authentication protocol; session ticket.

key exchange Confidential exchange of secret keys online, which is commonly done with public key cryptography. See also public key cryptography.

key management Secure management of private keys for public key cryptography. Windows 2000 manages private keys and keeps them confidential with CryptoAPI and CSPs. See also private key; CryptoAPI; cryptographic service provider.

kilobit A data unit equal to 1,000 bits.

kilobits per second (Kbps) Data transfer speed, as on a network, measured in multiples of 1,000 bits per second.

L

label See domain name label.

LAN See local area network.

LAN emulation (LANE) A set of protocols that allow existing Ethernet and Token Ring LAN services to overlay an ATM network. LANE allows connectivity among LAN- and ATM-attached stations. See also Asynchronous Transfer Mode (ATM).

large window support In TCP communications, the largest amount of data that can be transferred without acknowledgment. The window has a fixed size. Large window support dynamically recalculates the window size and allows larger amounts of data to be transferred at one time causing greater throughput.

latency See replication latency.

layer 2 switch A switch that operates at the datalink layer of the OSI reference model.

layer 3 switch A switch that operates at the network layer of the OSI reference model.

Layer two Tunneling Protocol (L2TP) A tunneling protocol that encapsulates PPP frames to be sent over IP, X.25, Frame Relay, or ATM networks. L2TP is a combination of the Point-to-Point Tunneling Protocol (PPTP) and Layer 2 Forwarding (L2F), a technology proposed by Cisco Systems, Inc.

LDAP See Lightweight Directory Access Protocol.

Lightweight Directory Access Protocol (LDAP) A directory service protocol that runs directly over TCP/IP and the primary access protocol for Active Directory. LDAP version 3 is defined by a set of Proposed Standard documents in Internet Engineering Task Force (IETF) RFC 2251. See also Lightweight Directory Access Protocol application programming interface (LDAP API).

limited broadcast address The broadcast address of 255.255.255.255.

Line Printer Daemon (LPD) A service on the print server that receives documents (print jobs) from line printer remote (LPR) tools running on client systems. See also Line Printer Remote (LPR).

Line Printer Remote (LPR) A connectivity tool that runs on client systems and is used to print files to a computer running an LPD server. See also Line Printer Daemon (LPD).

link station Hardware and software components within a node that represent a connection to an adjacent node over a specific link.

Lmhosts file A local text file that maps NetBIOS names (commonly used for computer names) to IP addresses for hosts that are not located on the local subnet. In Windows 2000, this file is stored in the SystemRoot\System32\Drivers\Etc folder.

load sharing See round robin.

local area network (LAN) A communications network connecting a group of computers, printers, and other devices located within a relatively limited area (for example, a building). A LAN allows any connected device to interact with any other on the network. See also wide area network (WAN).

local computer A computer that can be accessed directly without using a communications line or a communications device, such as a network adapter or a modem. Similarly, running a local program means running the program on your computer, as opposed to running it from a server.

local policy module A Windows 2000 mechanism that provides the QoS Admission Control Service with a means of retrieving policy information from Active Directory. The QoS Admission Control Service invokes the LPM when a policy object with a Windows 2000 Kerberos ticket is detected. The LPM takes the user name from the policy object and the RSVP message, and looks up the user's admission control policy in Active Directory.

local security authority (LSA) A protected subsystem that authenticates and logs users onto the local system. In addition, the LSA maintains information about all aspects of local security on a system (collectively known as the local security policy), and provides various services for translation between names and identifiers.

LocalTalk The Apple networking hardware built into every Macintosh computer. LocalTalk includes the cables and connector boxes to connect components and network devices that are part of the AppleTalk network system. LocalTalk was formerly known as the AppleTalk Personal Network.

log file A file that stores messages generated by an application, service, or operating system. These messages are used to track the operations performed. For example, Web servers maintain log files listing every request made to the server. Log files are usually ASCII files and often have a .log extension. In Backup, a file that contains a record of the date the tapes were created and the names of files and directories successfully backed up and restored. The Performance Logs and Alerts service also creates log files.

log on To begin using a network by providing a user name and password that identifies a user to the network.

logical IP subnet (LIS) A group of IP hosts/members belonging to the same IP subnet and whose host ATMARP server ATM address is the same.

loopback address The address of the local computer used for routing outgoing packets back to the source computer. This address is used primarily for testing.

LPM See Local Policy Module.

M

m-node A NetBIOS node type that uses a mix of b-node and p-node communications to register and resolve NetBIOS names. M-node first uses broadcast resolution; then, if necessary, it uses a server query.

Magic Packet A packet that contains 16 contiguous copies of the receiving network adapter's Ethernet address. A magic packet is used to awaken a computer from a low power state.

Management Information Base (MIB) A collection of formally described objects, each of which represents a particular type of information, that can be accessed and managed by the Simple Network Management Protocol (SNMP) through a network management system.

master server In a DNS zone transfer, the computer that is the source of the zone. Master servers can vary and are one of two types (either primary or secondary masters), depending on how the server obtains its zone data. See also primary server; secondary server; zone; zone transfer.

maximum segment size The maximum size of a TCP segment that can be sent on a TCP connection.

maximum transmission unit (MTU) The maximum frame size supported by a network technology such as Ethernet or Token Ring.

media access control A sublayer of the IEEE 802 specifications that defines network access methods and framing.

media access control address The address used for communication between network adapters on the same subnet. Each network adapter has an associated media access control address.

member server A computer that runs Windows 2000 Server but is not a domain controller of a Windows 2000 domain. Member servers participate in a domain, but do not store a copy of the directory database.

memory address A portion of computer memory that can be allocated to a device or used by a program or the operating system. Devices are usually allocated a range of memory addresses.

message digest A fixed-size result obtained by applying a one-way mathematical function called a message digest function (sometimes called a "hash function" or "hash algorithm") to an arbitrary amount of data. Given a change in the input data, the resulting value of the message digest will change. Message digest is also called a hash. See message digest function.

message digest function One-way mathematical algorithm used to produce a message digest (also called a hash). See also message digest.

Messaging API (MAPI) See Messaging Application Programming Interface.

metric A number used to indicate the cost of a route in the IP routing table to enable the selection of the best route among possible multiple routes to the same destination.

Microsoft Management Console (MMC) A framework for hosting administrative consoles. A console is defined by the items on its console tree, which might include folders or other containers, World Wide Web pages, and other administrative items. A console has one or more windows that can provide views of the console tree and the administrative properties, services, and events that are acted on by the items in the console tree. The main MMC window provides commands and tools for authoring consoles. The authoring features of MMC and the console tree might be hidden when a console is in User Mode. See also console tree.

migrate The process of moving files or programs from an older file format or protocol to a more current format or protocol. For example, WINS database entries can be migrated from static WINS database entries to dynamically-registered DHCP entries.

minimum TTL A default Time To Live (TTL) value set in seconds for use with all resource records in a zone. This value is set in the start of authority (SOA) resource record for each zone. By default, the DNS server includes this value in query answers to inform recipients how long it can store and use resource records provided in the query answer before they must expire the stored records data. When TTL values are set for individual resource records, those values will override the minimum TTL. See also Time To Live (TTL).

miniport drivers A driver that is connected to an intermediate driver and a hardware device.

mixed mode The default mode setting for domains on Windows 2000 domain controllers. Mixed mode allows Windows 2000 domain controllers and Windows NT backup domain controllers to co-exist in a domain. Mixed mode does not support the universal and nested group enhancements of Windows 2000. You can change the domain mode setting to Windows 2000 native mode after all Windows NT domain controllers are either removed from the domain or upgraded to Windows 2000. See also native mode.

more fragments flag A field in the Internet Protocol (IP) header that indicates that more fragments follow this fragment.

multicast Network traffic destined for a set of hosts that belong to a multicast group. See also multicast group.

multicast address resolution service (MARS) A service for resolving multicast IP addresses to the ATM addresses of the clients that have joined that multicast group. The MARS can work in conjunction with the multicast server MCS and clients to distribute multicast data through point-to-multipoint connections.

multicast DHCP (MDHCP) An extension to the DHCP protocol standard that supports dynamic assignment and configuration of IP multicast addresses on TCP/IP-based networks.

multicast group A group of member TCP/IP hosts configured to listen and receive datagrams sent to a specified destination IP address. The destination address for the group is a shared IP address in the Class D address range (224.0.0.0 to 2239.255.255.255). See also datagram.

multicast routing protocol Protocols such as Distance Vector Multicast Routing Protocol (DVMRP), Multicast Open Shortest Path First (MOSPF), or Protocol Independent Multicast (PIM) used to exchange IP multicast host membership information. Group membership is either communicated explicitly, by exchanging [group address, subnet] information, or implicitly, by informing upstream routers that there either are or are not group members in the downstream direction from the source of the multicast traffic.

multicast scope A range of IP multicast addresses in the range of 239.0.0.0 to 239.254.255.255. Multicast addresses in this range can be prevented from propagating in either direction (send or receive) through the use of scope-based multicast boundaries.

multihomed computer A computer that has multiple network adapters or that has been configured with multiple IP addresses for a single network adapter.

multinetting The practice of using multiple logical subnets on the same physical network.

multiple provider router (MPR) A software component that supports Win32 network API requests for redirectors and passes them to the appropriate redirector.

multiple universal naming convention provider (MUP)
A mechanism that chooses the appropriate redirector when an application attempts to resolve a universal naming convention (UNC) name.

mutual authentication The process when the calling router authenticates itself to the answering router and the answering router authenticates itself to the calling router. Both ends of the connection verify the identity of the other end of the connection. MS-CHAP v2 and EAP-TLS authentication methods provide mutual authentication.

N

name devolution A process by which a DNS resolver appends one or more domain names to an unqualified domain name, making it a fully qualified domain name, and then submits the fully qualified domain name to a DNS server.

name management Registering, querying, and releasing NetBIOS names.

name mapping A Windows 2000 feature that enables file system access by MS-DOS and Windows 3.*x* users to NTFS and FAT volumes, and enables user account assignments for Kerberos users from non-Windows 2000 Kerberos realms or for external (non-enterprise) users with X.509 certificates. For file system access, Windows 2000 allows share names of up to 255 characters, as opposed to MS-DOS and Windows 3.*x*, which are restricted to eight characters followed by a period and an extension of up to three characters. Each file or folder with a name that does not conform to the MS-DOS 8.3 standard is automatically given a second name that does. MS-DOS and Windows 3.*x* users connecting to the file or directory over the network see the name in the 8.3 format; Windows 2000 users see the long name.

name query A query broadcast to a local network or to a NetBIOS name server in order to resolve the IP address when one NetBIOS application wants to communicate with another NetBIOS application.

name registration The process of registering a computer name with a name server, such as a DHCP or WINS server, when a client computer joins a computer network. This process of name registration creates a database entry that other network services use to locate that computer.

name registration request A message sent to a NetBIOS name server when a TCP/IP host begins an attempt to register the domain name.

name release A message sent to a NetBIOS server to indicate that a domain name has been released and is available for use by another server.

name resolution The process of having software translate between names that are easy for users to work with, and numerical IP addresses, which are difficult for users but necessary for TCP/IP communications. Name resolution can be provided by software components such as the Domain Name System (DNS) or the Windows Internet Name Service (WINS). In directory service, the phase of LDAP directory operation processing that involves finding a domain controller that holds the target entry for the operation. See also Domain Name System (DNS); Transmission Control Protocol/Internet Protocol (TCP/IP); Windows Internet Name Service (WINS).

name resolution service A service required by TCP/IP internetworks to convert computer names to IP addresses and IP addresses to computer names. (People use "friendly" names to connect to computers; programs use IP addresses.) See also internetwork; IP address; Transmission Control Protocol/Internet Protocol (TCP/IP).

name server In the DNS client/server model, a server authoritative for a portion of the DNS database. The server makes computer names and other information available to client resolvers that are querying for name resolution across the Internet or an intranet. See also Domain Name System (DNS).

name server (NS) resource record A resource record used in a zone to designate the DNS domain names for authoritative DNS servers for the zone. See also resource record.

Named Pipe A portion of memory that can be used by one process to pass information to another process, so that the output of one process is the input of the other process. The second process can be local (on the same computer as the first) or remote (on a networked computer).

namespace A set of unique names for resources or items used in a shared computing environment. The names in a namespace can be resolved to the objects they represent. For Microsoft Management Console (MMC), the namespace is represented by the console tree, which displays all of the snap-ins and resources that are accessible to a console. For Domain Name System (DNS), namespace is the vertical or hierarchical structure of the domain name tree. For example, each domain label, such as "host1" or "example," used in a fully qualified domain name, such as "host1.example.microsoft.com," indicates a branch in the domain namespace tree. For Active Directory, namespace corresponds to the DNS namespace in structure, but resolves Active Directory object names.

naming service A service, such as that provided by WINS or DNS, that allows friendly names to be resolved to an address or other specially defined resource data that is used to locate network resources of various types and purposes.

native mode The condition in which all domain controllers within a domain are Windows 2000 domain controllers and an administrator has enabled native mode operation (through Active Directory Users and Computers). See also mixed mode.

negative caching A situation in which computers that use and query DNS, cache negative responses to a query for a limited period of time. A negative response is obtained when a DNS server directly answers a name query, indicating that no records of the requested DNS domain name were found to exist. The use of this kind of caching can help speed the response for successive queries from other computers for the same name.

negative name registration response A response to a name registration request from a host or a NetBIOS server indicating that another host or NetBIOS server has already registered the requested name.

negotiation policy A named collection of security methods in a rule, contained in an Internet Protocol security policy used to establish a security association between the two communicating parties. See also Internet Protocol security policy.

NetBEUI See NetBIOS Extended User Interface.

NetBIOS See network basic input/output system.

NetBIOS Extended User Interface (NetBEUI) A network protocol native to Microsoft Networking, that is usually used in local area networks of one to 200 clients. NetBEUI uses Token Ring source routing as its only method of routing. It is the Microsoft implementation of the NetBIOS standard.

NetBIOS name A 16-byte name of a process using NetBIOS. A name recognized by WINS, which maps the name to an IP address.

NetBIOS name query A packet sent to either a NetBIOS name server, such as a WINS server, or as a broadcast to resolve the IP address of a NetBIOS name.

NetBIOS name resolution The process of resolving a NetBIOS name to its IP address.

NetBIOS name server A computer that resolves NetBIOS names to IP addresses. A WINS server is a NetBIOS name server.

NetBIOS Node Type A designation of the exact mechanisms by which NetBIOS names are resolved to IP addresses.

NetBIOS over TCP/IP (NetBT) A feature that provides the NetBIOS programming interface over the TCP/IP protocol. It is used for monitoring routed servers that use NetBIOS name resolution.

NetBT See NetBIOS over TCP/IP.

NetWare Novell's network operating system.

network access server (NAS) The device that accepts PPP connections and places clients on the network that the NAS serves. NAS is also called Terminal server.

network adapter Software or a hardware plug-in board that connects a node or host to a local area network.

network address See network ID.

network address translator An IP router defined in RFC 1631 that can translate IP addresses and TCP/UDP port numbers of packets as they are being forwarded.

network administrator A person responsible for setting up and managing domain controllers or local computers and their user and group accounts, assigning passwords and permissions, and helping users with networking issues. Administrators are members of the Administrators group and have full control over the domain or computer.

network basic input/output system (NetBIOS) An application programming interface (API) that can be used by applications on a local area network or computers running MS-DOS, OS/2, or some version of UNIX. NetBIOS provides a uniform set of commands for requesting lower level network services.

Network Driver Interface Specification (NDIS) A software component that provides Windows 2000 network protocols a common interface for communications with network adapters. NDIS allows more than one transport protocol to be bound and operate simultaneously over a single network adapter card.

network ID A number used to identify the systems that are located on the same physical network bounded by routers. The network ID should be unique to the internetwork.

network interface layer A layer of the TCP/IP DARPA model that is responsible for placing TCP/IP packets on the network medium and receiving TCP/IP packets off the network medium. The network interface layer is also called the network access layer.

network layer A layer that addresses messages and translates logical addresses and names into physical addresses. It also determines the route from the source to the destination computer and manages traffic problems, such as switching, routing, and controlling the congestion of data packets.

network media The type of physical wiring and lower-layer protocols used for transmitting and receiving frames. For example, Ethernet, FDDI, and Token Ring.

Network Monitor A packet capture and analysis tool used to view network traffic. This feature is included with Windows 2000 Server; however, Systems Management Server has a more complete version.

network name In server clusters, the name through which clients access server cluster resources. A network name is similar to a computer name, and when combined in a resource group with an IP address and the applications clients access, presents a virtual server to clients.

Network Plug and Play A combination of hardware and software support that enables a computer system to recognize and adapt to hardware configuration changes with little or no user intervention.

network prefix The number of bits in the IP network ID starting from the high order bit. The network prefix is another way of expressing a subnet mask.

network prefix notation The practice of expressing a subnet mask as a network prefix rather than a dotted decimal notation.

network route A route to a specific network ID in an internetwork.

NNTP See Network News Transfer Protocol.

node In tree structures, a location on the tree that can have links to one or more items below it. In local area networks (LANs), a device that is connected to the network and is capable of communicating with other network devices. In a server cluster, a server that has Cluster service software installed and is a member of the cluster. See also local area network (LAN).

noncontainer object An object that cannot logically contain other objects. A file is a noncontainer object. See also container object; object.

noncontiguous namespace A namespace based on different DNS root domain names, such as that of multiple trees in the same forest. See also namespace; hierarchical namespace; flat namespace.

nonrepudiation A basic security function of cryptography. Nonrepudiation provides assurance that a party in a communication cannot falsely deny that a part of the communication occurred. Without nonrepudiation, someone can communicate and then later deny the communication or claim that the communication occurred at a different time. See also cryptography; authentication; confidentiality; integrity.

notify list A list maintained by the primary server for a zone of other DNS servers that should be notified when zone changes occur. The notify list is made up of IP addresses for DNS servers configured as secondary servers for the zone. The secondary servers can then check to see if they need to initiate a zone transfer. See also DNS Notify.

Novell Directory Services (NDS) On networks running Novell NetWare 4.*x* and NetWare 5.*x*, a distributed database that maintains information about every resource on the network and provides access to these resources.

NS (name server) resource record See name server (NS) resource record.

Nslookup A command-line tool that allows users to make DNS queries for testing and troubleshooting DNS installations.

NWLink An implementation of the Internetwork Packet Exchange (IPX), Sequenced Packet Exchange (SPX), and NetBIOS protocols used in Novell networks. NWLink is a standard network protocol that supports routing and can support NetWare client/server applications, where NetWare-aware Sockets-based applications communicate with IPX/SPX Sockets-based applications. See also Internetwork Packet Exchange (IPX); network basic input/output system (NetBIOS).

O

object An entity, such as a file, folder, shared folder, printer, or Active Directory object, described by a distinct, named set of attributes. For example, the attributes of a File object include its name, location, and size; the attributes of an Active Directory User object might include the user's first name, last name, and e-mail address. For OLE and ActiveX objects, an object can also be any piece of information that can be linked to, or embedded into, another object. See also attribute; container object; noncontainer object; parent object; child object.

octet In programming, an octet refers to eight bits or one byte. IP addresses, for example, are typically represented in dotted-decimal notation; that is, with the decimal value of each octet of the address separated by a period. See also IP address.

offset When defining a pattern match within a filter using Network Monitor, the number of bytes from the beginning of the frame where the pattern occurs in a frame.

OnNow Power Initiative A system-wide approach to power management. All components can be instantly on or off and work in conjunction with hardware and software components to alter their power state as system use requires.

open database connectivity (ODBC) An application programming interface (API) that enables database applications to access data from a variety of existing data sources.

Open Shortest Path First (OSPF) A routing protocol used in medium-sized and large-sized networks. This protocol is more complex than RIP, but allows better control and is more efficient in propagating routing information.

open systems interconnection reference model A networking model introduced by the International Organization for Standardization (ISO) to promote multi-vendor interoperability. Open Systems Interconnection (OSI) is seven-layered conceptual model consisting of the application, presentation, session, transport, network, data-link, and physical layers.

option types Client configuration parameters that a DHCP server can assign when offering an IP address lease to a client. Typically, these option types are enabled and configured for each scope. Most options are predefined through RFC 2132, but DHCP Manager can be used to define and add custom option types if needed.

organizational domain A type of domain signified by a three-character code that indicates the primary function or activity of the organizations contained within the domain, such as .org, .edu, or .gov.

organizational unit (OU) An Active Directory container object used within domains. An organizational unit is a logical container into which users, groups, computers, and other organizational units are placed. It can contain objects only from its parent domain. An organizational unit is the smallest scope to which a Group Policy object can be linked, or over which administrative authority can be delegated.

OSI See Open Systems Interconnection model.

OSPF See Open Shortest Path First.

output filters Filters which define the traffic that is allowed to be sent from that interface.

owner In Windows 2000, the person who controls how permissions are set on objects and can grant permissions to others. In the Macintosh environment, an owner is the user responsible for setting permissions for a folder on a server. A Macintosh user who creates a folder on the server automatically becomes the owner of the folder. The owner can transfer ownership to someone else. Each Macintosh-accessible volume on the server also has an owner.

P

p-node A NetBIOS node type that uses point-to-point communication with a name server to resolve names as IP addresses.

packet A transmission unit of fixed maximum size that consists of binary information. This information represents both data and a header containing an ID number, source and destination addresses, and error-control data.

packet filtering Prevents certain types of network packets from either being sent or received. This can be employed for security reasons (to prevent access from unauthorized users) or to improve performance by disallowing unnecessary packets from going over a slow connection. See also packet.

parent domain For DNS and Active Directory, domains that are located in the namespace tree directly above other derivative domain names (child domains). For example, "reskit.com" would be the parent domain for "eu.reskit.com", a child domain. See also child domain; directory partition; domain.

parent object The object that is the immediate superior of another object in a hierarchy. A parent object can have multiple subordinate, or child, objects. In Active Directory, the schema determines what objects can be parent objects of what other objects. Depending on its class, a parent object can be the child of another object. See also child object; object.

parenting The concept of managing the growth and delegation of a parent domain into further child domains, which are derived and delegated from the parent name. See also child domain; parent domain.

partition A logical division of a hard disk. Partitions make it easier to organize information. Each partition can be formatted for a different file system. A partition must be completely contained on one physical disk, and the partition table in the Master Boot Record for a physical disk can contain up to four entries for partitions.

path A sequence of directory (or folder) names that specifies the location of a directory, file, or folder within the Windows directory tree. Each directory name and file name within the path must be preceded by a backslash (\). For example, to specify the path of a file named Readme.doc located in the Windows directory on drive C, type C:\Windows\Readme.doc.

path maximum transmission unit (PMTU) The maximum packet size that is supported by all of the network technologies in a path between a source and destination host.

path maximum transmission unit discovery The process of discovering the maximum sized IP datagram that can be sent along a path without fragmentation.

permission A rule associated with an object to regulate which users can gain access to the object and in what manner. Permissions are granted or denied by the object's owner. See also object; privilege; user rights.

persistent connection A connection that is always active. For instance, the WINS servers in Windows 2000 use persistent connections to constantly update their WINS databases.

persistent route Routes that are not based on the TCP/IP configuration, that are automatically added to the IP routing table when the TCP/IP protocol is started. Routes added to the IP routing table using the route utility with the "-p" command line option are recorded.

physical layer A software layer that transmits bits from one computer to another and regulates the transmission of a stream of bits over a physical medium. This layer defines how the cable is attached to the network adapter and which transmission technique is used to send data over the cable.

physical media A storage object that data can be written to, such as a disk or magnetic tape. A physical medium is referenced by its physical media ID (PMID).

Ping A tool that verifies connections to one or more remote hosts. The ping command uses the ICMP Echo Request and Echo Reply packets to determine whether a particular IP system on a network is functional. Ping is useful for diagnosing IP network or router failures. See also Internet Control Message Protocol (ICMP).

plaintext Data that is not encrypted. Sometimes also called clear text. See also ciphertext; encryption; decryption.

Plug and Play A set of specifications developed by Intel that allows a computer to automatically detect and configure a device and install the appropriate device drivers.

PMTU See Path Maximum Transmission Unit.

PMTU black hole router A router that silently discards IP datagrams that require fragmentation when the Don't Fragment (DF) flag in the IP header is set to 1.

PMTU Discovery See path maximum transmission unit discovery.

Point-to-Point Protocol (PPP) An industry standard suite of protocols for the use of point-to-point links to transport multiprotocol datagrams. PPP is documented in RFC 1661.

Point-to-Point Tunneling Protocol (PPTP) A tunneling protocol that encapsulates Point-to-Point Protocol (PPP) frames into IP datagrams for transmission over an IP-based internetwork, such as the Internet or a private intranet.

pointer (PTR) resource record A resource record used in a reverse lookup zone created within the in-addr.arpa. domain to designate a reverse mapping of a host IP address to a host DNS domain name. See also resource record.

policy agent An Internet Protocol security mechanism that retrieves the computer's assigned Internet Protocol security policy from the Windows 2000 directory service (or the registry if the computer is not connected to a domain) and passes it to the IKE service to use when establishing secure communications. See also Internet Protocol security policy.

port A mechanism that allows multiple sessions. A refinement to an IP address. In Device Manager, a connection point on a computer where devices that pass data in and out of a computer can be connected. For example, a printer is typically connected to a parallel port (also known as an LPT port), and a modem is typically connected to a serial port (also known as a COM port).

Post Office Protocol A maildrop service that allows a client to retrieve mail that the server is holding for it. The most recent implementation is Version 3, or POP3.

PPP See Point-to-Point Protocol.

pre-shared key An authentication technology used by IPSec. Pre-shared means the parties must agree on a shared, secret key that becomes part of the IPSec policy. Information is encrypted before transmission using the shared key, and decrypted on the receiving end using the same key. If the receiver can decrypt the information, identities are considered authenticated.

presentation layer A network layer that translates data from the application layer into an intermediary format. This layer also manages security issues by providing such services as data encryption, and compresses data so that fewer bits need to be transferred on the network.

primary domain name The name used to indicate the domain in which the computer resides. See also connection-specific domain name.

primary server An authoritative DNS server for a zone that can be used as a point of update for the zone. Only primary masters have the ability to be updated directly to process zone updates, which include adding, removing, or modifying resource records that are stored as zone data. Primary masters are also used as the first sources for replicating the zone to other DNS servers.

primary zone A copy of the zone that is administered locally. See also zone, secondary zone.

print server A computer that is dedicated to managing the printers on a network. The print server can be any computer on the network.

print sharing The ability for a computer running Windows 2000 Professional or Windows 2000 Server to share a printer on the network.

private address space The set of private addresses. The private address space consists of the following three blocks of addresses: 10.0.0.0/8, 172.16.0.0/12, 192.168.0.0/16.

private addresses IP addresses that are designed to be used by organizations for private intranet addressing within one of the following blocks of addresses: 10.0.0.0/8, 172.16.0.0/12, 192.168.0.0/16.

private key The secret half of a cryptographic key pair that is used with a public key algorithm. Private keys are typically used to digitally sign data and to decrypt data that has been encrypted with the corresponding public key. See also public key.

private ports See dynamic ports.

protection against wrapped sequence numbers (PAWS)
The use of TCP timestamps to prevent a TCP receiver from misinterpreting a new sequence number with an old sequence number that it is expecting to receive.

protocol A set of rules and conventions by which two computers pass messages across a network. Networking software usually implements multiple levels of protocols layered one on top of another. Windows NT and Windows 2000 include NetBEUI, TCP/IP, and IPX/SPX-compatible protocols.

protocol number A field in the IP packet which identifies the next level higher in the protocol stack.

PTR (pointer) resource record See pointer (PTR) resource record.

public addresses IP addresses assigned by the Internet Network Information Center (InterNIC) that are guaranteed to be globally unique and reachable on the Internet.

public key The non-secret half of a cryptographic key pair that is used with a public key algorithm. Public keys are typically used to verify digital signatures or decrypt data that has been encrypted with the corresponding private key. See also private key.

public key cryptography A method of cryptography in which two different but complimentary keys are used: a public key and a private key for providing security functions. Public key cryptography is also called asymmetric key cryptography. See also cryptography; public key; private key.

pull partner A Windows Internet Name Service (WINS) feature that pulls in replicas from its push partner by requesting them and then accepting the pushed replicas. See also push partner.

push partner A Windows Internet Name Service (WINS) feature that sends replicas to its pull partner upon receiving a request from the pull partner. See also pull partner.

Q

QoS Admission Control Service A software service that controls bandwidth and network resources on the subnet to which it is assigned. Important applications can be given more bandwidth, less important applications less bandwidth. The QoS Admission Control Service can be installed on any network-enabled computer running Windows 2000.

Quality of Service (QoS) A set of quality assurance standards and mechanisms for data transmission, implemented in Windows 2000.

queue A list of programs or tasks waiting for execution. In Windows 2000 printing terminology, a queue refers to a group of documents waiting to be printed. In NetWare and OS/2 environments, queues are the primary software interface between the application and print device; users submit documents to a queue. In Windows 2000, however, the printer is that interface; the document is sent to a printer, not a queue.

R

recursion One of the three process types for DNS name resolution. In this process, a resolver (a DNS client) requests that a DNS server provide a complete answer to a query that does not include pointers to other DNS servers. When a client makes a query and requests that the server use recursion to answer, it effectively shifts the workload of resolving the query from the client to the DNS server. If the DNS server supports and uses recursion, it will contact other DNS servers as necessary (using iterative queries on behalf of the client) until it obtains a definitive answer to the query. This type of resolution allows the client resolver to be small and simple. See also iteration; iterative query; recursive query.

recursive name query See recursive query.

recursive query A query made to a DNS server in which the requester asks the server to assume the full workload and responsibility for providing a complete answer to the query. The DNS server then uses separate iterative queries to other DNS servers on behalf of the requester to assist in completing an answer for the recursive query. See also iteration; iterative query; recursion.

redirector See Windows 2000 Redirector.

refresh To update displayed information with current data.

refresh interval In DNS, a 32-bit time interval that needs to elapse before the zone data is refreshed. When the refresh interval expires, the secondary server checks with a master server for the zone to see if its zone data is still current or if it needs to be updated by using a zone transfer. This interval is set in the start of authority (SOA) resource record for each zone. See also resource record; secondary server; start of authority (SOA) resource record; zone; zone transfer.

registered ports Ports in the range from 1024 – 49151.

registry In Windows 2000, Windows NT, Windows 98, and Windows 95, a database of information about a computer's configuration. The registry is organized in a hierarchical structure and consists of subtrees and their keys, hives, and entries.

registry boot The default boot option used by most Microsoft DNS servers. When registry boot is used, the DNS service is started by using the DNS Service parameters and their values that are stored in the Windows 2000 registry. A Berkeley Internet Name Domain (BIND) boot file may be used as an alternative to this method of boot configuration for the DNS service. See also BIND boot file.

registry key An identifier for a record or group of records in the registry.

relay agents A small program that relays a certain type of message to others on a network. In TCP/IP networking, routers are used to interconnect hardware and software used on different subnets and forward IP packets between the subnets.

remote access server A Windows 2000 Server–based computer running the Routing and Remote Access service and configured to provide remote access.

Remote Access Service (RAS) A Window NT 4.0 service that provides remote networking for telecommuters, mobile workers, and system administrators who monitor and manage servers at multiple offices.

remote computer A computer that is accessible only by using a communications line or a communications device, such as a network adapter or a modem.

remote procedure call (RPC) A message-passing facility that allows a distributed application to call services that are available on various machines in a network. Used during remote administration of computers.

renewal interval The amount of time available to a client to refresh its name with the WINS server. If the name is not renewed by the end of this period, the name is released. Renewal interval is also known as the name refresh timeout, or the Time To Live (TTL).

replica In Active Directory replication, a copy of a logical Active Directory partition that is synchronized through replication between domain controllers that hold copies of the same directory partition. "Replica" can also refer to the composite set of directory partitions held by any one domain controller. These are specifically called a directory partition replica and server replica, respectively. See also full replica; partial replica.

replication The process of copying data from a data store or file system to multiple computers that store the same data for the purpose of synchronizing the data. In Windows 2000, replication of the directory service occurs through Active Directory replication, and replication of the file system occurs through the file replication service. See also Active Directory replication; File Replication service; Distributed File System.

replication latency In Active Directory replication, the delay between the time an update is applied to a given replica of a directory partition and the time it is applied to some other replica of the same directory partition. A server will receive changes no sooner than either

· It is notified of a change from its neighbor in the same site, or

· Its periodic replication timer expires.

Latency is sometimes referred to as propagation delay. See also multimaster replication.

Request for Comments (RFC) A document that defines a standard. RFCs are published by the Internet Engineering Task Force (IETF) and other working groups.

reservation A specific IP address within a scope permanently reserved for a specific DHCP client. Client reservations are made in the DHCP database using DHCP Manager and based on a unique client device identifier for each reserved entry. In QoS ACS, an allocation of network resources, contained in a Resource Reservation Protocol (RSVP) reservation request administered by the QoS Admission Control Service. See also Dynamic Host Configuration Protocol (DHCP).

resolver DNS client programs used to look up DNS name information. Resolvers can be either a small "stub" (a limited set of programming routines that provide basic query functionality) or larger programs that provide additional lookup DNS client functions, such as caching. See also caching, caching resolver.

resource record (RR) Information in the DNS database that can be used to process client queries. Each DNS server contains the resource records it needs to answer queries for the portion of the DNS namespace for which it is authoritative.

resource record set (RRset) A collection of more than one resource record returned in a query response by a DNS server. Resource record sets (RRsets) are used in responses where more than one record is part of the answer. See also resource record.

Resource Reservation Protocol (RSVP) A signaling protocol that allows the sender and receiver in a communication to set up a reserved highway for data transmission with a specified quality of service.

response time The amount of time required to do work from start to finish. In a client/server environment, this is typically measured on the client side.

reverse domain A special domain, named in-addr.arpa, that is used for IP address-to-name mappings (referred to as reverse lookup).

reverse lookup A query in which the IP address is used to determine the DNS name for the computer.

reverse lookup zone A zone that contains information needed to perform reverse lookups. See also reverse lookup.

RFC See Request for Comments.

RIP See routing information protocol.

rogue DHCP server An unauthorized DHCP server.

root The highest or uppermost level in a hierarchically organized set of information. The root is the point from which further subsets are branched in a logical sequence that moves from a broad or general focus to narrower perspectives.

root DNS server A DNS server authoritative for the root of the Internet. See also DNS server.

root domain The beginning of the Domain Name System (DNS) namespace. In Active Directory, the initial domain in an Active Directory tree. Also the initial domain of a forest.

root hints Local information stored on a DNS server that provides helping resource records to direct the server to its root servers. For the Microsoft DNS service, the root hints are stored in the file Cache.dns, located in the \%SystemRoot%\System32\Dns folder. Root hints are also called cache hints. See also authoritative; namespace; root; root servers; systemroot.

root hints file See root hints.

root servers DNS servers that are authoritative for the root of the namespace. See also authoritative; namespace; root; root hints.

round robin A simple mechanism used by DNS servers to share and distribute loads for network resources. Round robin is used to rotate the order of resource record (RR) data returned in a query answer when multiple RRs exist of the same RR type for a queried DNS domain name.

round trip time estimation (RTTE) The amount of time necessary to complete a round trip from sender to receiver and back.

route determination process The process of selecting an interface and forwarding IP address based on the destination IP address of an IP datagram and the contents of the IP routing table.

router A network device that helps LANs and WANs achieve interoperability and connectivity and that can link LANs that have different network topologies, such as Ethernet and Token Ring.

router discovery The use of Internet Control Message Protocol (ICMP) messages to provide fault tolerance for the configuration of a host's default gateway.

routing The process of forwarding a packet through an internetwork from a source host to a destination host.

Routing Information Protocol (RIP) A suite of networking protocols that provides communications across interconnected networks made up of computers with diverse hardware architectures and various operating systems. TCP/IP includes standards for how computers communicate and conventions for connecting networks and routing traffic. See also protocol; Transmission Control Protocol/Internet Protocol (TCP/IP).

routing loop A path through an internetwork for a network ID that loops back onto itself.

routing protocol A series of periodic or on-demand messages containing routing information that is exchanged between routers to exchange routing information and provide fault tolerance. Except for their initial configuration, dynamic routers require little ongoing maintenance, and therefore can scale to larger internetworks.

routing table A database of routes containing information on network IDs, forwarding addresses, and metrics for reachable network segments on an internetwork.

rules An IPSec policy mechanism that governs how and when an IPSec policy protects communication. A rule provides the ability to trigger and control secure communication based on the source, destination, and type of IP traffic. Each rule contains a list of IP filters and a collection of security actions that take place upon a match with that filter list.

S

SA See Security Association.

scalability A measure of how well a computer, service, or application can expand to meet increasing performance demands. For server clusters, the ability to incrementally add one or more systems to an existing cluster when the overall load of the cluster exceeds its capabilities.

scavenging The process of cleaning and removing extinct or outdated name data from the WINS database.

script A type of program consisting of a set of instructions to an application or utility program. A script usually expresses instructions by using the application's or utility's rules and syntax, combined with simple control structures such as loops and if/then expressions. "Batch program" is often used interchangeably with "script" in the Windows environment.

second-level domain A domain in the Domain Name System (DNS) that is immediately under a top–level domain.

secondary server An authoritative DNS server for a zone that is used as a source for replication of the zone to other servers. Secondary masters only update their zone data by transferring zone data from other DNS servers and do not have the ability to perform zone updates. See also master server; zone transfer.

secondary zone A copy of the zone that must be replicated from a server containing the primary zone.

secret key An encryption key that two parties share with each other and with no one else. See also symmetric key encryption.

secure dynamic update The process by which a secure dynamic update client submits a dynamic update request to a DNS server, and the server attempts the update only if the client can prove its identity and has the proper credentials to make the update. See also dynamic update.

Secure Sockets Layer (SSL) A proposed open standard developed by Netscape Communications for establishing a secure communications channel to prevent the interception of critical information, such as credit card numbers. Primarily, it enables secure electronic financial transactions on the World Wide Web, although it is designed to work on other Internet services as well.

Security Accounts Manager (SAM) A protected subsystem that manages user and group account information. In Windows NT 4.0, both local and domain security principals are stored by SAM in the registry. In Windows 2000, workstation security accounts are stored by SAM in the local computer registry, and domain controller security accounts are stored in Active Directory.

security association (SA) A set of parameters that defines the services and mechanisms necessary to protect Internet Protocol security communications. See also Internet Protocol security (IPSec).

security method A process that determines the Internet Protocol security services, key settings, and algorithms that will be used to protect the data during the communication.

Security Parameters Index (SPI) A unique, identifying value in the SA used to distinguish among multiple security associations existing at the receiving computer.

security principal An account-holder, such as a user, computer, or service. Each security principal within a Windows 2000 domain is identified by a unique security ID (SID). When a security principal logs on to a computer running Windows 2000, the Local Security Authority (LSA) authenticates the security principal's account name and password. If the logon is successful, the system creates an access token. Every process executed on behalf of this security principal will have a copy of its access token. See also access token; security ID; security principal name.

selective acknowledgement (SACK) A Transmission Control Protocol (TCP) option that allows the receiver to re-request only the missing data from the sender.

server A computer that provides shared resources to network users.

Server Announcement A specific datagram generated by computers on Microsoft networks to announce their presence on the network to master browsers.

Server Message Block (SMB) A file-sharing protocol designed to allow networked computers to transparently access files that reside on remote systems over a variety of networks. The SMB protocol defines a series of commands that pass information between computers. SMB uses four message types: session control, file, printer, and message.

Server service A software component that provides RPC (remote procedure call) support and file, print, and Named Pipe sharing. See also Named Pipe; remote procedure call (RPC).

service (SRV) resource record A resource record used in a zone to register and locate well-known TCP/IP services. The SRV resource record is specified in RFC 2052 and is used in Windows 2000 to locate domain controllers for Active Directory service. See also resource record.

service name The name by which a port is known.

session key A key used primarily for encryption and decryption. Session keys are typically used with symmetric encryption algorithms where the same key is used for both encryption and decryption. For this reason, session and symmetric keys usually refer to the same type of key. See also symmetric key encryption.

session layer A network layer that allows two applications on different computers to establish, use, and end a session. This layer establishes dialog control between the two computers in a session, regulating which side transmits, as well as when and how long it transmits.

sessions A logical connection created between two hosts to exchange data. Typically, sessions use sequencing and acknowledgments to send data reliably.

shell The command interpreter that is used to pass commands to the operating system.

silent discard When a packet is discarded and the sending host is not informed as to why the packet was discarded.

silent RIP The capability of a computer to listen for and process Routing Information Protocol (RIP) announcements but without announcing its own routes.

Simple Mail Transfer Protocol (SMTP) A protocol used on the Internet to transfer mail. SMTP is independent of the particular transmission subsystem and requires only a reliable, ordered, data stream channel.

Simple Network Management Protocol (SNMP) A network management protocol installed with TCP/IP and widely used on TCP/IP and Internet Package Exchange (IPX) networks. SNMP transports management information and commands between a management program run by an administrator and the network management agent running on a host. The SNMP agent sends status information to one or more hosts when the host requests it or when a significant event occurs.

site server A computer running Windows NT Server on which Systems Management Server (SMS) site setup has been run. When SMS is installed on a computer, that computer is assigned the site server role. The site server, which hosts SMS components needed to monitor and manage an SMS site, typically performs several additional SMS roles, including component server, client access point, and distribution point.

slave A server that does not attempt to resolve queries on its own. Instead, it sends all queries to forwarders. See also forwarder.

Small Office/Home Office (SOHO) An office with a few computers that can be considered a small business or part of a larger network.

smart card A credit card-sized device that is used with a PIN number to enable certificate-based authentication and single sign-on to the enterprise. Smart cards securely store certificates, public and private keys, passwords, and other types of personal information. A smart card reader attached to the computer reads the smart card. See also authentication; certificate; nonrepudiation.

sniffer An application or device that can read, monitor, and capture network data exchanges and read network packets. If the packets are not encrypted, a sniffer provides a full view of the data inside the packet.

SNMP See Simple Network Management Protocol.

SNMP Management Console The interface through which a manager, either a user or a program, performs management activities.

SOA (start of authority) resource record See start of authority (SOA) resource record.

socket A bidirectional pipe for incoming and outgoing data between networked computers. The Windows Sockets API is a networking API used by programmers to create TCP/IP-based sockets programs.

software router A router that is not dedicated to performing routing but performs routing as one of multiple processes running on the router computer.

source routing The practice of specifying the list of networks or routers in the network layer header to forward a packet along a specific path in an internetwork.

SRV (service) resource record See service (SRV) resource record.

start of authority (SOA) resource record A record that indicates the starting point or original point of authority for information stored in a zone. The SOA resource record (RR) is the first RR created when adding a new zone. It also contains several parameters used by others to determine how long other DNS servers will use information for the zone and how often updates are required. See also authoritative; zone.

static router A router with manually configured routing tables. A network administrator, with knowledge of the internetwork topology, manually builds and updates the routing table, programming all routes in the routing table. Static routers can work well for small internetworks but do not scale well to large or dynamically changing internetworks due to their manual administration.

static routing Routing limited to fixed routing tables, as opposed to dynamically updated routing tables. See also dynamic routing; routing; routing table.

stream socket A socket using the Windows Sockets API that provides a two-way, reliable, sequenced, and unduplicated flow of data.

structured query language (SQL)
A widely accepted standard database sublanguage used in querying, updating, and managing relational databases.

subdomain A DNS domain located directly beneath another domain name (the parent domain) in the namespace tree. For example, "eu.reskit.com" is a subdomain of the domain "reskit.com."

subnet A subdivision of an IP network. Each subnet has its own unique subnetted network ID.

subnet mask A 32-bit value expressed as four decimal numbers from 0 to 255, separated by periods (for example, 255.255.0.0). This number allows TCP/IP to determine the network ID portion of an IP address.

subnetted network ID A network ID for a subnetted network segment that is the result of a subdivision of a TCP/IP network ID.

subnetted reverse lookup zone A reverse lookup zone authoritative for only a portion of a Class C network address. Subnetted reverse lookup zones are not required even if a network is subnetted; they are merely an administrative choice. See also reverse lookup zone.

subnetting The act of subdividing the address space of a TCP/IP network ID into smaller network segments, each with its own subnetted network ID.

supernetting The practice of expressing a range of IP network IDs using a single IP network ID and subnet mask. Supernettting is a route aggregation and summarization technique.

superscope An administrative grouping of scopes that can be used to support multiple, logical IP subnets on the same physical subnet. Superscopes contain a list of member scopes, or child scopes, that can be activated as a collection.

switch A computer or other network-enabled device that controls routing and operation of a signal path. In clustering, a switch is used to connect the cluster hosts to a router or other source of incoming network connections. See also routing.

symmetric key encryption An encryption algorithm that requires the same secret key to be used for both encryption and decryption. This is often called secret key encryption. Because of its speed, symmetric encryption is typically used rather than public key encryption when a message sender needs to encrypt large amounts of data.

systemroot The path and folder name where the Windows 2000 system files are located. Typically, this is C:\Winnt, although a different drive or folder can be designated when Windows 2000 is installed. The value %systemroot% can be used to replace the actual location of the folder that contains the Window 2000 system files. To identify your systemroot folder, click Start, click Run, and then type %systemroot%.

Systems Management Server A part of the Windows BackOffice suite of products. Systems Management Server (SMS) includes inventory collection, deployment, and diagnostic tools. SMS can significantly automate the task of upgrading software, allow remote problem solving, provide asset management information, manage software licenses, and monitor computers and networks.

Systems Network Architecture (SNA) A communications framework developed by IBM to define network functions and establish standards for enabling computers to share and process data.

T

T1 A wide-area carrier that transmits data at 1.544 Mbps. A T1 line is also known as DS-1 line.

T3 A wide-area carrier that transmits data at 44.736 Mbps. A T3 line is also known as a DS-3 line.

Task Offload A process that allows tasks normally performed by the transport layer to be processed by the network adapter. This reduces the overhead required of the system CPU for these tasks, thus increasing the throughput.

TCP Transmission Control Protocol.

TCP connection The logical connection that exists between two processes that are using TCP to exchange data.

TCP segment The quantity consisting of the TCP header and its associated data. TCP segments are exchanged using a TCP connection.

TCP timestamps The TCP option used to record the time a TCP segment was sent and a time the segment was acknowledged by the receiver.

TCP Window Scaling The use of TCP options to create a TCP receive window size greater than 65,535 bytes. The use of TCP window scaling can improve TCP throughput in large bandwidth, high-delay environments.

TCP/IP See Transmission Control Protocol/Internet Protocol.

Telephony API (TAPI) An application programming interface (API) used by communications programs to communicate with telephony and network services. See also Internet Protocol.

Telnet A terminal-emulation protocol that is widely used on the Internet to log on to network computers. Telnet also refers to the application that uses the Telnet protocol for users who log on from remote locations.

terminal A device consisting of a display screen and a keyboard that is used to communicate with a computer.

thread A type of object within a process that runs program instructions. Using multiple threads allows concurrent operations within a process and enables one process to run different parts of its program on different processors simultaneously. A thread has its own set of registers, its own kernel stack, a thread environment block, and a user stack in the address space of its process.

three-way handshake The series of three TCP segments that are exchanged when a TCP connection is established.

throughput For disks, the transfer capacity of the disk system.

Time To Live (TTL) A timer value included in packets sent over TCP/IP-based networks that tells the recipients how long to hold or use the packet or any of its included data before expiring and discarding the packet or data. For DNS, TTL values are used in resource records within a zone to determine how long requesting clients should cache and use this information when it appears in a query response answered by a DNS server for the zone.

Token Ring A type of network media that connects clients in a closed ring and uses token passing to allow clients to use the network. See also Fiber Distributed Data Interface (FDDI).

top-level domains Domain names that are rooted hierarchically at the first tier of the domain namespace, directly beneath the root (.) of the DNS namespace. On the Internet, top-level domain names such as ".com" and ".org" are used to classify and assign second-level domain names (such as "microsoft.com") to individual organizations and businesses according to their organizational purpose. See also second-level domains.

topology In Windows operating systems, the relationships among a set of network components. In the context of Active Directory replication, topology refers to the set of connections that domain controllers use to replicate information among themselves. See also domain controller; replication.

tracing A capability of components of the Windows 2000 Routing and Remote Access service that records internal component variables, function calls, and interactions. You can use tracing to troubleshoot complex network problems.

Traffic Control A Windows 2000 mechanism that creates and regulates data flows with defined QoS parameters. The Traffic Control API (TC API) creates filters to direct selected packets through this flow. Traffic control is invoked by the QoS API and subsequently serviced by the RSVP SP.

Transmission Control Protocol/Internet Protocol (TCP/IP)
A set of software networking protocols widely used on the Internet that provide communications across interconnected networks of computers with diverse hardware architectures and operating systems. TCP/IP includes standards for how computers communicate and conventions for connecting networks and routing traffic.

Transport Driver Interface (TDI) In the Windows NT and Windows 2000 networking model, a common interface for network layer components. The TDI is not a single program, but a protocol specification to which the upper bounds of transport protocol device drivers are written. It allows software components above and below the transport layer to be mixed and matched without reprogramming.

transport layer The network layer that handles error recognition and recovery. When necessary, it repackages long messages into small packets for transmission and, at the receiving end, rebuilds packets into the original message. The receiving transport layer also sends receipt acknowledgments.

transport protocol A protocol that defines how data should be presented to the next receiving layer in the Windows NT and Windows 2000 networking model and packages the data accordingly. The transport protocol passes data to the network adapter driver through the network driver interface specification (NDIS) interface and to the redirector through the Transport Driver Interface (TDI).

trap In Simple Network Management Protocol (SNMP), a message sent by an agent to a management system indicating that an event has occurred on the host running the agent. See also agent; authentication; Internet Protocol; Simple Network Management Protocol (SNMP).

trap destination The management system that receives an SNMP trap message.

Trap message An SNMP alarm message.

trigger For Network Monitor data captures, a set of conditions defined by a user that, when met, initiate an action such as stopping a capture or executing a program or command file.

Trivial File Transfer Protocol (TFTP) A protocol that is used by an IntelliMirror server to download the initial files needed to begin the boot or installation process.

trust relationship A logical relationship established between domains that allows pass-through authentication in which a trusting domain honors the logon authentications of a trusted domain. User accounts and global groups defined in a trusted domain can be given rights and permissions in a trusting domain, even though the user accounts or groups do not exist in the trusting domain's directory. See also authentication; domain; two-way trust relationship.

tunnel The logical path by which the encapsulated packets travel through the transit internetwork.

tunneling A method of using an internetwork infrastructure of one protocol to transfer a payload (the frames or packets) of another protocol.

two-way trust relationship A link between domains in which each domain trusts user accounts in the other domain to use its resources. Users can log on from computers in either domain to the domain that contains their account. See also trust relationship.

U

UDP See User Datagram Protocol.

UNC See Universal Naming Convention.

UNC name A full Windows 2000 name of a resource on a network. It conforms to the \\servername\sharename syntax, where servername is the server's name and sharename is the name of the shared resource. UNC names of directories or files can also include the directory path under the share name, with the following syntax: \\servername\sharename\directory\filename. UNC is also called Universal Naming Convention.

unicast An address that identifies a specific, globally unique host.

universal group A Windows 2000 group only available in native mode that is valid anywhere in the forest. A universal group appears in the Global Catalog but contains primarily global groups from domains in the forest. This is the simplest form of group and can contain other universal groups, global groups, and users from anywhere in the forest. See also domain local group; forest; Global Catalog.

Universal Naming Convention (UNC) A convention for naming files and other resources beginning with two backslashes (\), indicating that the resource exists on a network computer. UNC names conform to the \\SERVERNAME\SHARENAME syntax, where SERVERNAME is the server's name and SHARENAME is the name of the shared resource. The UNC name of a directory or file can also include the directory path after the share name, with the following syntax: \\SERVERNAME\SHARENAME\DIRECTORY\FILENAME.

Universal Serial Bus (USB) A serial bus with a bandwidth of 1.5 megabits per second (Mbps) for connecting peripherals to a microcomputer. USB can connect up to 127 peripherals, such as external CD-ROM drives, printers, modems, mice, and keyboards, to the system through a single, general-purpose port. This is accomplished by daisy chaining peripherals together. USB supports hot plugging and multiple data streams.

UNIX A powerful, multiuser, multitasking operating system initially developed at AT&T Bell Laboratories in 1969 for use on minicomputers. UNIX is considered more portable—that is, less computer-specific—than other operating systems because it is written in C language. Newer versions of UNIX have been developed at the University of California at Berkeley and by AT&T.

user account A record that consists of all the information that defines a user to Windows 2000. This includes the user name and password required for the user to log on, the groups in which the user account has membership, and the rights and permissions the user has for using the computer and network and accessing their resources. For Windows 2000 Professional and member servers, user accounts are managed by using Local Users and Groups. For Windows 2000 Server domain controllers, user accounts are managed by using Microsoft Active Directory Users and Computers. See also domain controller; group; user name.

User Datagram Protocol (UDP) A TCP/IP component that offers a connectionless datagram service that guarantees neither delivery nor correct sequencing of delivered packets.

user name A unique name identifying a user account to Windows 2000. An account's user name must be unique among the other group names and user names within its own domain or workgroup.

V

variable bit rate (VBR) An ATM service type that guarantees service based on average and peak traffic rates. VBR is used for traffic that requires little or no cell loss. It transmits data in spurts, or bursts, rather than in a continuous stream.

variable length subnet masks (VLSM) Subnet masks used to produce subnets of an IP network ID of different sizes.

variable length subnetting The practice of subdividing the address space of an IP network ID into subnets of different sizes.

version ID A counter used to determine which WINS database entries must be updated during replication. See also replication.

Virtual Circuit (VC) A point-to-point connection for the transmission of data. This allows greater control of call attributes, such as bandwidth, latency, delay variation, and sequencing.

virtual private network (VPN) The extension of a private network that encompasses links across shared or public networks, such as the Internet.

volume A portion of a physical disk that functions as though it were a physically separate disk. In My Computer and Windows Explorer, volumes appear as local disks, such as drive C or drive D.

VPN See virtual private network.

VPN connection The portion of the connection in which your data is encrypted.

W

Wake-On-LAN A feature that controls shut down and wake-up based on network events such as lack of network activity or disconnection.

Web server A server that provides the ability to develop COM-based applications and to create large sites for the Internet and corporate intranets.

Well-Known Ports Ports in the range from 0 - 1023.

wide area network (WAN) A communications network connecting geographically separated computers, printers, and other devices. A WAN allows any connected device to interact with any other on the network. See also local area network (LAN).

wildcard In DNS, a character that can be substituted for another character during a query.

Windows 2000 Redirector A software component that intercepts network requests and redirects them to network servers, workstations, printers and directory shares.

Windows Driver Model (WDM) A specification for I/O device drivers that supports both Windows 2000 and Windows 98. WDM is based on a class/miniport driver architecture that is modular and extensible. WDM easier for hardware vendors to support hardware devices.

Windows Internet Name Service (WINS) A software service that dynamically maps IP addresses to computer names (NetBIOS names). This allows users to access resources by name instead of requiring them to use IP addresses that are difficult to recognize and remember. WINS servers support clients running Windows NT 4.0 and earlier versions of Windows operating systems. See also Domain Name System (DNS).

Windows Sockets (Winsock) An industry-standard application programming interface (API) used on the Microsoft Windows operating system that provides a two-way, reliable, sequenced, and unduplicated flow of data.

WINS See Windows Internet Name Service.

WINS database The database used to register and resolve computer names to IP addresses on Windows-based networks. The contents of this database are replicated at regular intervals throughout the network. See also push partner, pull partner, replication.

WINS lookup A process by which a DNS server queries WINS to resolve names it does not find in its authoritative zones.

WINS proxy A computer that listens to name query broadcasts and responds for those names not on the local subnet. The proxy communicates with a WINS server to resolve names and then caches them for a specific time period. See also Windows Internet Name Service (WINS).

WINS referral zone A zone that refers DNS queries to WINS.

Workstation service The system service that provides network connections and communications.

Z

zone In a DNS database, a zone is a contiguous portion of the DNS tree that is administered as a single separate entity by a DNS server. The zone contains resource records for all the names within the zone. In the Macintosh environment, a logical grouping that simplifies browsing the network for resources, such as servers and printers. It is similar to a domain in Windows 2000 Server networking. See also domain; Domain Name System (DNS); DNS server.

zone file A text file on a DNS name server containing resource records for a zone. See also zone.

zone transfer The process by which DNS servers interact to maintain and synchronize authoritative name data. When a DNS server is configured as a secondary server for a zone, it periodically queries the master DNS server configured as its source for the zone. If the version of the zone kept by the master is different than the version on the secondary server, the secondary server will pull zone data from its master DNS server to update zone data. See also full zone transfer (AXFR); incremental zone transfer (IXFR); secondary server; zone.

Index

B

C

D

E

I

J

K

L

M

N

O

Q

R

S

T

U

V

W

X

Y

Z

Proof of Purchase

Use this page as proof of purchase if participating in a promotion or rebate offer on this title. Proof of purchase must be used in conjunction with other proof(s) of payment such as your dated sales receipt—see offer details.

Microsoft® Windows® 2000 Server TCP/IP Core Networking Guide

0-7356-1798-8

____

CUSTOMER NAME

Microsoft Press, PO Box 97017, Redmond, WA 98073-9830

END-USER LICENSE AGREEMENT FOR MICROSOFT SOFTWARE

Microsoft WINDOWS 2000 RESOURCE KIT

IMPORTANT-READ CAREFULLY: This Microsoft End-User License Agreement ("EULA") is a legal agreement between you (either an individual or a single entity) and Microsoft Corporation for the Microsoft software identified above, which includes computer software and may include associated media, printed materials, additional computer software applications, and "online" or electronic documentation ("SOFTWARE"). By downloading, installing, copying, or otherwise using the SOFTWARE, you agree to be bound by the terms of this EULA. If you do not agree to the terms of this EULA, do not install or use the SOFTWARE. This print EULA supercedes any End User License Agreement found on the CD.

SOFTWARE LICENSE

The SOFTWARE is protected by copyright laws and international copyright treaties, as well as other intellectual property laws and treaties. **The SOFTWARE is licensed, not sold.**

1. **GRANT OF LICENSE.** This EULA grants you the following rights:

   a. SOFTWARE. Except as otherwise provided herein, you, as an individual, may install and use copies of the SOFTWARE on an unlimited number of computers, including workstations, terminals or other digital electronic devices ("COMPUTERS"), provided that you are the only individual using the SOFTWARE. If you are an entity, you may designate one individual within your organization to have the right to use the SOFTWARE in the manner provided above. The SOFTWARE is in "use" on a COMPUTER when it is loaded into temporary memory (i.e.. RAM) or installed into permanent memory (e.g., hard disk, CD-ROM, or other storage device) of that COMPUTER.

   b. Client/Server Software. The SOFTWARE may contain one or more components which consist of both of the following types of software: "Server Software" that is installed and provides services on a COMPUTER acting as a server ("Server"); and "Client Software" that allows a COMPUTER to access or utilize the services provided by the Server Software. If the component of the SOFTWARE consists of both Server Software and Client Software which are used together, you may also install and use copies of such Client Software on COMPUTERS within your organization and which are connected to your internal network.

Such COMPUTERS running this Client Software may be used by more than one individual.

2. **DESCRIPTION OF OTHER RIGHTS AND LIMITATIONS.**

   a. Limitations on Reverse Engineering, Decompilation, and Disassembly. You may not reverse engineer, decompile, or disassemble the SOFTWARE, except and only to the extent that such activity is expressly permitted by applicable law notwithstanding this limitation.

   b. Rental. You may not rent, lease, or lend the SOFTWARE.

   c. Support Services. Microsoft does not support the SOFTWARE, however, in the event Microsoft does provide you with support services related to the SOFTWARE ("Support Services"), use of such Support Services is governed by the Microsoft policies and programs described in the user manual, in "online" documentation, and/or in other Microsoft-provided materials. Any supplemental software code provided to you as part of the Support Services shall be considered part of the SOFTWARE and subject to the terms and conditions of this EULA. With respect to technical information you provide to Microsoft as part of the Support Services, Microsoft may use such information for its business purposes, including for product support and development. Microsoft will not utilize such technical information in a form that personally identifies you.

   d. Software Transfer. You may permanently transfer of all of your rights under this EULA, provided you retain no copies, you transfer all of the SOFTWARE (including all component parts, the media and printed materials, any upgrades, this EULA, and, if applicable, the Certificate of Authenticity), **and** the recipient agrees to the terms of this EULA. If the SOFTWARE is an upgrade, any transfer must include all prior versions of the SOFTWARE.

   e. Termination. Without prejudice to any other rights, Microsoft may terminate this EULA if you fail to comply with the terms and conditions of this EULA. In such event, you must destroy all copies of the SOFTWARE and all of its component parts.

3. **UPGRADES**. If the SOFTWARE is labeled as an upgrade , you must be properly licensed to use a product identified by Microsoft as being eligible for the upgrade in order to use the SOFTWARE. SOFTWARE labeled as an upgrade replaces and/or supplements the product that formed the basis for your eligibility for the upgrade. You may use the resulting upgraded product only in accordance with the terms of this EULA. If the SOFTWARE is an upgrade of a component of a package of software programs that you licensed as a single product, the SOFTWARE may be used and transferred only as part of that single product package and may not be separated for use on more than one computer

4. **INTELLECTUAL PROPERTY RIGHTS**. All title and intellectual property rights in and to the SOFTWARE (including but not limited to any images, photographs, animations, video, audio, music, text and "applets" incorporated into the SOFTWARE), and any copies you are permitted to make herein are owned by Microsoft or its suppliers. All title and intellectual property rights in

and to the content which may be accessed through use of the SOFTWARE is the property of the respective content owner and may be protected by applicable copyright or other intellectual property laws and treaties. This EULA grants you no rights to use such content. If this SOFTWARE contains documentation which is provided only in electronic form, you may print one copy of such electronic documentation. You may not copy the printed materials accompanying the SOFTWARE.

5. **U.S. GOVERNMENT LICENSE RIGHTS**. SOFTWARE provided to the U.S. Government pursuant to solicitations issued on or after December 1, 1995 is provided with the commercial license rights and restrictions described elsewhere herein. SOFTWARE provided to the U.S. Government pursuant to solicitations issued prior to December 1, 1995 is provided with "Restricted Rights" as provided for in FAR, 48 CFR 52.227-14 (JUNE 1987) or DFAR, 48 CFR 252.227-7013 (OCT 1988), as applicable.

6. **EXPORT RESTRICTIONS**. You agree that you will not export or re-export the SOFTWARE (or portions thereof) to any country, person or entity subject to U.S. export restrictions. You specifically agree not to export or re-export the SOFTWARE (or portions thereof): (i) to any country subject to a U.S. embargo or trade restriction; (ii) to any person or entity who you know or have reason to know will utilize the SOFTWARE (or portion thereof) in the production of nuclear, chemical or biological weapons; or (iii) to any person or entity who has been denied export privileges by the U.S. government. For additional information see http://www.microsoft.com/exporting/.

7. **DISCLAIMER OF WARRANTIES. To the maximum extent permitted by applicable law, Microsoft and its suppliers provide the SOFTWARE and any (if any) Support Services *AS IS AND WITH ALL FAULTS*, and hereby disclaim all warranties and conditions, either express, implied or statutory, including, but not limited to, any (if any) implied warranties or conditions of merchantability, of fitness for a particular purpose, of lack of viruses, of accuracy or completeness of responses, of results, and of lack of negligence or lack of workmanlike effort, all with regard to the SOFTWARE, and the provision of or failure to provide Support Services. ALSO, THERE IS NO WARRANTY OR CONDITION OF TITLE, QUIET ENJOYMENT, QUIET POSSESSION, CORRESPONDENCE TO DESCRIPTION OR NON-INFRINGEMENT, WITH REGARD TO THE SOFTWARE. THE ENTIRE RISK AS TO THE QUALITY OF OR ARISING OUT OF USE OR PERFORMANCE OF THE SOFTWARE AND SUPPORT SERVICES, IF ANY, REMAINS WITH YOU.**

8. **EXCLUSION OF INCIDENTAL, CONSEQUENTIAL AND CERTAIN OTHER DAMAGES. TO THE MAXIMUM EXTENT PERMITTED BY APPLICABLE LAW, IN NO EVENT SHALL MICROSOFT OR ITS SUPPLIERS BE LIABLE FOR ANY SPECIAL, INCIDENTAL, INDIRECT, OR CONSEQUENTIAL DAMAGES WHATSOEVER (INCLUDING, BUT NOT LIMITED TO, DAMAGES FOR LOSS OF PROFITS OR CONFIDENTIAL OR OTHER INFORMATION, FOR BUSINESS INTERRUPTION, FOR PERSONAL INJURY, FOR LOSS OF PRIVACY, FOR FAILURE TO MEET ANY DUTY INCLUDING OF GOOD FAITH OR OF REASONABLE CARE, FOR NEGLIGENCE, AND FOR ANY OTHER PECUNIARY OR OTHER LOSS WHATSOEVER) ARISING OUT OF OR IN ANY WAY RELATED TO THE USE OF OR INABILITY TO USE THE SOFTWARE, THE PROVISION OF OR FAILURE TO PROVIDE SUPPORT SERVICES, OR OTHERWISE UNDER OR IN CONNECTION WITH ANY PROVISION OF THIS EULA, EVEN IN THE EVENT OF THE FAULT, TORT (INCLUDING NEGLIGENCE), STRICT LIABILITY, BREACH OF CONTRACT OR BREACH OF WARRANTY OF MICROSOFT OR ANY SUPPLIER, AND EVEN IF MICROSOFT OR ANY SUPPLIER HAS BEEN ADVISED OF THE POSSIBILITY OF SUCH DAMAGES.**

9. **LIMITATION OF LIABILITY AND REMEDIES. Notwithstanding any damages that you might incur for any reason whatsoever (including, without limitation, all damages referenced above and all direct or general damages), the entire liability of Microsoft and any of its suppliers under any provision of this EULA and your exclusive remedy for all of the foregoing shall be limited to the greater of the amount actually paid by you for the SOFTWARE or U.S.$5.00. The foregoing limitations, exclusions and disclaimers shall apply to the maximum extent permitted by applicable law, even if any remedy fails its essential purpose.**

10. **NOTE ON JAVA SUPPORT**. THE SOFTWARE MAY CONTAIN SUPPORT FOR PROGRAMS WRITTEN IN JAVA. JAVA TECHNOLOGY IS NOT FAULT TOLERANT AND IS NOT DESIGNED, MANUFACTURED, OR INTENDED FOR USE OR RESALE AS ONLINE CONTROL EQUIPMENT IN HAZARDOUS ENVIRONMENTS REQUIRING FAIL-SAFE PERFORMANCE, SUCH AS IN THE OPERATION OF NUCLEAR FACILITIES, AIRCRAFT NAVIGATION OR COMMUNICATION SYSTEMS, AIR TRAFFIC CONTROL, DIRECT LIFE SUPPORT MACHINES, OR WEAPONS SYSTEMS, IN WHICH THE FAILURE OF JAVA TECHNOLOGY COULD LEAD DIRECTLY TO DEATH, PERSONAL INJURY, OR SEVERE PHYSICAL OR ENVIRONMENTAL DAMAGE. Sun Microsystems, Inc. has contractually obligated Microsoft to make this disclaimer.

11. **APPLICABLE LAW.** If you acquired this SOFTWARE in the United States, this EULA is governed by the laws of the State of Washington. If you acquired this SOFTWARE in Canada, unless expressly prohibited by local law, this EULA is governed by the laws in force in the Province of Ontario, Canada; and, in respect of any dispute which may arise hereunder, you consent to the jurisdiction of the federal and provincial courts sitting in Toronto, Ontario. If this SOFTWARE was acquired outside the United States, then local law may apply.

12. **ENTIRE AGREEMENT. This EULA (including any addendum or amendment to this EULA which is included with the SOFTWARE) is the entire agreement between you and Microsoft relating to the SOFTWARE and the Support Services (if any) and it supersedes all prior or contemporaneous oral or written communications, proposals and representations with respect to the SOFTWARE or any other subject matter covered by this EULA. To the extent the terms of any Microsoft policies or programs for Support Services conflict with the terms of this EULA, the terms of this EULA shall control.**

13. **QUESTIONS?** Should you have any questions concerning this EULA, or if you desire to contact Microsoft for any reason, please contact the Microsoft subsidiary serving your country, or write: Microsoft Sales Information Center/One Microsoft Way/ Redmond, WA 98052-6399.

SI VOUS AVEZ ACQUIS VOTRE PRODUIT MICROSOFT AU CANADA, LA GARANTIE LIMITÉE SUIVANTE VOUS CONCERNE :

RENONCIATION AUX GARANTIES. Dans toute la mesure permise par la législation en vigueur, Microsoft et ses fournisseurs fournissent le PRODUIT LOGICIEL et tous (selon le cas) Services d'assistance TELS QUELS ET AVEC TOUS LEURS DÉFAUTS, et par les présentes excluent toute garantie ou condition, expresse ou implicite, légale ou conventionnelle, écrite ou verbale, y compris, mais sans limitation, toute (selon le cas) garantie ou condition implicite ou légale de qualité marchande, de conformité à un usage particulier, d'absence de virus, d'exactitude et d'intégralité des réponses, de résultats, d'efforts techniques et professionnels et d'absence de négligence, le tout relativement au PRODUIT LOGICIEL et à la prestation ou à la non-prestation des Services d'assistance. DE PLUS, IL N'Y A AUCUNE GARANTIE ET CONDITION DE TITRE, DE JOUISSANCE PAISIBLE, DE POSSESSION PAISIBLE, DE SIMILARITÉ À LA DESCRIPTION ET D'ABSENCE DE CONTREFAÇON RELATIVEMENT AU PRODUIT LOGICIEL. Vous supportez tous les risques découlant de l'utilisation et de la performance du PRODUIT LOGICIEL et ceux découlant des Services d'assistance (s'il y a lieu).

EXCLUSION DES DOMMAGES INDIRECTS, ACCESSOIRES ET AUTRES. Dans toute la mesure permise par la législation en vigueur, Microsoft et ses fournisseurs ne sont en aucun cas responsables de tout dommage spécial, indirect, accessoire, moral ou exemplaire quel qu'il soit (y compris, mais sans limitation, les dommages entraînés par la perte de bénéfices ou la perte d'information confidentielle ou autre, l'interruption des affaires, les préjudices corporels, la perte de confidentialité, le défaut de remplir toute obligation y compris les obligations de bonne foi et de diligence raisonnable, la négligence et toute autre perte pécuniaire ou autre perte de quelque nature que ce soit) découlant de, ou de toute autre manière lié à, l'utilisation ou l'impossibilité d'utiliser le PRODUIT LOGICIEL, la prestation ou la non-prestation des Services d'assistance ou autrement en vertu de ou relativement à toute disposition de cette convention, que ce soit en cas de faute, de délit (y compris la négligence), de responsabilité stricte, de manquement à un contrat ou de manquement à une garantie de Microsoft ou de l'un de ses fournisseurs, et ce, même si Microsoft ou l'un de ses fournisseurs a été avisé de la possibilité de tels dommages.

LIMITATION DE RESPONSABILITÉ ET RECOURS. Malgré tout dommage que vous pourriez encourir pour quelque raison que ce soit (y compris, mais sans limitation, tous les dommages mentionnés ci-dessus et tous les dommages directs et généraux), la seule responsabilité de Microsoft et de ses fournisseurs en vertu de toute disposition de cette convention et votre unique recours en regard de tout ce qui précède sont limités au plus élevé des montants suivants: soit (a) le montant que vous avez payé pour le PRODUIT LOGICIEL, soit (b) un montant équivalant à cinq dollars U.S. (5,00 $ U.S.). Les limitations, exclusions et renonciations ci-dessus s'appliquent dans toute la mesure permise par la législation en vigueur, et ce même si leur application a pour effet de priver un recours de son essence.

LÉGISLATION APPLICABLE.. Sauf lorsqu'expressément prohibé par la législation locale, la présente convention est régie par les lois en vigueur dans la province d'Ontario, Canada. Pour tout différend qui pourrait découler des présentes, vous acceptez la compétence des tribunaux fédéraux et provinciaux siégeant à Toronto, Ontario.

Si vous avez des questions concernant cette convention ou si vous désirez communiquer avec Microsoft pour quelque raison que ce soit, veuillez contacter la succursale Microsoft desservant votre pays, ou écrire à: Microsoft Sales Information Center, One Microsoft Way, Redmond, Washington 98052-6399.